E 6-3 3. Credits to Investment account: $190,000 and $175,000; $228,000 and $221,000

E 6-4 3. Credits to Investment account: $334,000 and 59,000; Debits to Investment account: $42,000 and $39,000

E 6-5 NCI in net income, $140,000;
CI in net income, $1,420,000

E 6-6 1. Stane: NCI in net income, $27,000
CI in net income, $243,000
Steele: NCI in net income, $18,000
CI in net income, $72,000
2. Stane: NCI in net income, $18,000
CI in net income, $162,000

E 6-7 1. NCI in net income, $15,000;
CI in net income, $295,000
2. NCI in net income, $14,000;
CI in net income, $292,000

E 6-8 1. NCI in net income, $42,000;
CI in net income, $926,000
3. $126,000

E 6-9 Goodwill, $50,000;
Investment balance, $240,000 + $(21,000)
NCI in net assets, $160,000 + $(14,000)

E 6-10 Goodwill, $40,000;
Investment balance, $147,000 + $56,000
NCI in net assets, $63,000 + $24,000

E 6-11 1. $110,000
2. Retained earnings column, $60,000

P 6-1 3. Consolidated assets, $2,735,000

P 6-2 3. Consolidated assets, $5,130,000

P 6-3 1. Bargain purchase element, $50,000
2. Total cost at 12/31/X1, $539,000
4. Consolidated net income, $310,000;
Consolidated assets, $4,512,000

P 6-4 2. Investment balance at 12/31/X1, $650,000 + $298,000
5. Consolidated net income, $474,000
Consolidated assets, $9,041,000

P 6-5 1. Total investment cost, $474,000
3. Total investment cost at 12/31/X1, $378,000 + $123,000
5. Consolidated net income, $551,000;
Consolidated assets, $4,521,000

P 6-6 1. Goodwill, $40,000;
3. Consolidated assets, $2,270,000

P 6-7 1. Goodwill at 12/31/X2, $30,000;
Investment balance at 12/31/X2: Equity method, $156,000 + $76,000; Cost method, $240,000
3. NCI in net income, $9,000;
CI in net income, $336,000
Consolidated assets, $2,784,000

P 6-8 1. Long-Term debt, $40,000
3. Consolidated assets, $4,940,000

P 6-9 1. NCI at 12/31/X2, $88,000 + $(7,000);
Investment balance at 12/31/X2: Equity method, $352,000 + $(28,000); Cost method, $320,000
3. NCI in net income, $1,000;
CI in net income, $1,054,000
Consolidated assets, $5,210,000

P 6-10 1. Goodwill at 1/1/X1, $48,000 + $32,000

P 6-10 2. Goodwill at 12/31/X1, $70,000
Investment balance at 12/31/X2, $405,000 + $198,000
5. NCI in net income, $72,000;
CI in net income, $1,308,000
NCI in net assets, $402,000
Consolidated assets, $9,815,000

P 6-11 3. Parent's separate earnings, $172,000
4. Consolidated retained earnings, $377,000

P 6-12 1. Total investment cost, $552,000
3. Investment balance at 12/31/X2, $440,000 + $104,000
5. NCI in net income, $5,000;
CI in net income, $520,000
Consolidated assets, $5,945,000
NCI in net assets, $136,000

P 6-13 1. Investment balance at 12/31/X2, $294,000;
Goodwill at 12/31/X2, $66,667
NCI in net assets, $32,667

P 6-14 1. Investment balance at 4/1/X8, $885,000;
Goodwill at 4/1/X8, $120,000
NCI in net assets at 12/31/X8, $317,000
4. Debit Goodwill $148,000

P 6-1A Cash flow from: Operations, $138,000;
Investing, $(90,000); Financing, $2,000

CHAPTER 7

E 7-21 1. Independence is met—5%
2. Independence is *not* met—15%

E 7-3 1. Independence is *not* met—13%
2. 12:1

E 7-4 1. Independence not met—12%

E 7-5 1. Credit APIC $500,000

E 7-6 1. Credit Retained Earnings $35,000

E 7-7 1. Credit Retained Earnings $34,000

E 7-8 1. Credit APIC $80,000

E 7-9 1. Credit APIC $72,000

E 7-10 1. $45,000
2. c

E 7-11 $1,700,000

E 7-12 d. $127,000

E 7-13 $21,200,000

E 7-14 c.

P 7-1 1. Investment carrying value at pooling date, $128,000

P 7-2 5. Consolidated net income, $80,000;
Consolidated assets, $1,000,000

P 7-3 3. Investment carrying value at 12/31/X2, $144,000
5. Consolidated net income, $77,000;
Consolidated assets, $1,000,000

P 7-4 3. Consolidated net income, $1,620,000;
Consolidated retained earnings, $2,130,000

P 7-5 3. Consolidated net income, $1,600,000;
Consolidated retained earnings, $2,079,000

P 7-6 5. Consolidated net income, $102,000;
Consolidated retained earnings, $156,000

P 7-7 1. $909,000
2. $744,000

Continued on p. 1166

Sixth Edition

ADVANCED ACCOUNTING

Concepts and Practice

Sixth Edition

ADVANCED ACCOUNTING

Concepts and Practice

Arnold J. Pahler
San Jose State University

Joseph E. Mori
San Jose State University

THE DRYDEN PRESS
HARCOURT BRACE COLLEGE PUBLISHERS

FORT WORTH   PHILADELPHIA   SAN DIEGO   NEW YORK   AUSTIN   ORLANDO   SAN ANTONIO
TORONTO   MONTREAL   LONDON   SYDNEY   TOKYO

EXECUTIVE EDITOR
Mike Reynolds

ACQUISITIONS EDITOR
Sara Tenney

DEVELOPMENTAL EDITOR
Van Strength

PROJECT EDITOR
Michele Tomiak

ART DIRECTOR
Linda Wooton

PRODUCTION MANAGER
Carlyn Hauser

PERMISSIONS EDITOR
Annette Coolidge

PRODUCT MANAGER
Craig Johnson

COPY EDITOR
JaNoel Lowe

COMPOSITOR
ETP Harrison

TEXT TYPE
10/12 Palatino

Cover photo © David Sharpe, Inc.

Address for Editorial Correspondence
The Dryden Press, 301 Commerce Street, Suite 3700, Fort Worth, TX 76102

Address for Orders
The Dryden Press, 6277 Sea Harbor Drive, Orlando, FL 32887-6777
1-800-782-4479, or 1-800-433-0001 in Florida

ISBN: 0-03-018612-9

Library of Congress Catalog Card Number: 96-85081

Printed in the United States of America

6 7 8 9 0 1 2 3 4 5 039 9 8 7 6 5 4 3 2 1

The Dryden Press
Harcourt Brace College Publishers

To my son, Brett
Arnold J. Pahler

To my family, Carol Ann, David, and Julie
Joseph E. Mori

THE DRYDEN PRESS SERIES IN ACCOUNTING

PREFACE

The sixth edition of *Advanced Accounting: Concepts and Practice* has been substantially revised in the following ways.

I   NEW PRONOUNCEMENT-RELATED CHANGES

The text reflects the latest FASB, GASB, and AICPA pronouncements and exposure drafts pertinent to the topics covered:

SFAS No. 124, "Accounting for Certain Investments Held by Not-for-Profit Organizations" (November 1995).

SFAS No. 119, "Disclosure About Derivative Financial Instruments and Fair Value of Financial Instruments" (October 1994).

Proposed SFAS, "Consolidated Financial Statements: Policy and Procedures" (October 1995). In May 1996, the FASB revised its position on certain proposals in this document.

Proposed SFAS, "Accounting for Derivative and Similar Financial Instruments and for Hedging Activities" (June 1996).

Proposed SFAS, "Reporting Comprehensive Income" (June 1996).

Proposed SFAS, "Reporting Disaggregated Information about a Business Enterprise" (January 1996).

Proposed SGAS, "Accounting and Financial Reporting for Certain Investments and for External Investment Pools (March 1996).

AICPA Audit and Accounting Guide, "Not-for-Profit Organizations" (June 1996).

AICPA Audit and Accounting Guide, "Health Care Organizations" (June 1996).

PROPOSED NEW STANDARD ON CONSOLIDATION POLICY AND PROCEDURES (CHAPTERS 1, 3, 6, AND 13)

In October 1995, the FASB issued the exposure draft "Consolidated Financial Statements: Consolidation Policy and Procedures." When finalized, this new FASB standard will supersede both (1) *Accounting Research Bulletin No. 51*, "Consolidated Financial Statements" (issued in 1951), and (2) *Statement of Financial Accounting Standard No. 94*, "Consolidation of All Majority-owned Subsidiaries" (a 1987 amendment to *ARB No. 51*). The major changes proposed in this exposure draft would

- Broaden the existing consolidation rules to conform to those of the Securities and Exchange Commission so that consolidation is required whether control exists by *legal means* (owning a majority voting interest) or *nonlegal means* (having financial arrangements that effectively achieve control). (This issue is contained to portions of Chapters 1 and 3 in this text.)

- Require use of the *economic unit concept* rather than the *parent company concept*, an issue that exists only for less than 100%-owned *acquired* subsidiaries. (This issue is contained to portions of Chapters 3, 6, and 13 of this text.)

In May 1996, the FASB slightly modified its position on certain issues in the October 1995 exposure draft in response to concerns raised by respondents and participants at the public hearings held in February 1996. **The only substantive May 1996 change was to require the imputing of goodwill to a noncontrolling interest to prevent possible "gaming" abuses.** (This issue is contained to only a portion of Chapter 6 and all of Chapter 13 of this text.)

Because the FASB could finalize its consolidation policy and procedures rules in early 1997, **the consolidation rules we present and discuss in this text are the ones set forth in the FASB's May 1996 working draft document.** (As this book goes to print, the FASB is deliberating between going to a final statement or a *revised* exposure draft.)

PROPOSED NEW STANDARD ON DERIVATIVE FINANCIAL INSTRUMENTS AND HEDGING (CHAPTER 17)

In June 1996, after ten years of intensive research and study, the FASB published for public comment an exposure draft titled "Accounting for Derivative and Similar Financial Instruments and for Hedging Activities." This proposed statement would (1) **amend** *SFAS No. 52* and *SFAS No. 107* and (2) **supersede** *SFAS No. 80, SFAS No. 105*, and *SFAS No. 119*. (The FASB's timetable is to issue this standard in the second quarter of 1997.)

Because of extensive participation by industry and practitioners prior to the issuance of this exposure draft, the FASB has indicated that it expects this proposed standard to be enacted largely intact. The proposed standard would become effective for fiscal years beginning after December 15, 1997.

Of the three categories of foreign exchange (FX) exposures we discuss in Chapter 17, "Using Derivatives to Manage Foreign Exchange Exposures," substantive rule changes are proposed only for the *hedges of forecasted transactions* category. Accordingly, **our discussion of the treatment of FX gains and losses on** *hedges of forecasted transactions* **is based on this proposed standard.**

REVISED AICPA ACCOUNTING AND AUDIT GUIDES FOR NOT-FOR-PROFIT ORGANIZATIONS AND HEALTH-CARE ORGANIZATIONS (CHAPTERS 26 AND 27)

These new guides were issued in mid-1996, and we discuss them fully in Chapters 26 and 27. Of significance is that the new Health Care Organizations (HCOs) guide (1) applies to both *private* and *public* HCOs and (2) requires that financial reporting for both *private* and *public* HCOs be on an *aggregated basis,* which is consistent with *SFAS No. 117,* "Financial Statements of Not-for-Profit Organizations" (before, reporting could be on an *aggregated* or *disaggregated* basis).

As a result of the issuance of the *SFAS No. 117, 116,* and *124* and these audit guides, we were able to substantially simplify and streamline material in this edition (reducing the number of pages devoted to this material from 120 to 72, a 40% decrease).

II ORGANIZATIONAL AND PEDAGOGICAL CHANGES

EQUAL PROMINENCE GIVEN TO THE COST METHOD (CHAPTERS 2, 3, 6, 9, 10, 11, AND 12)

Because of the continued extensive use in practice of both the *cost method* and the *equity method,* we now give equal prominence to both methods in Chapters 2 and 3 (the relatively simple situations involving *parent-created* subsidiaries), Chapter 6 (the more complex situation involving *acquired* subsidiaries), and Chapters 9–12 (intercompany transactions). Problems requiring consolidation worksheets now present consolidation data in a unique manner that allows students to use either the *cost method* or the *equity method* and readily see how the parent's financial statements differ under each method.

DISCUSSION OF PARTIALLY OWNED *CREATED* SUBSIDIARIES DISCUSSED SEPARATELY FROM *ACQUIRED* SUBSIDIARIES

To introduce major concepts on a full step-by-step basis, we now discuss noncontrolling interest situations first in the relatively simple situation in which the parent *creates* a partially owned subsidiary. Accordingly, Chapter 3 is a newly designed chapter that is a logical extension of Chapters 1 and 2, both of which deal with 100%-owned *created* subsidiaries. Noncontrolling interest situations involving *acquired* subsidiaries are discussed in Chapter 6, thus enabling the emphasis in that chapter to be entirely on the *change in basis of accounting* concept.

Chapter 3 also contains the more involved discussion of controlling a subsidiary by *nonlegal means* (financial arrangements); the simpler situation of control by *legal means* (owning a majority voting interest) is discussed in Chapter 1.

Accounting for *unconsolidated* subsidiaries (formerly in Chapter 2) was moved to Chapter 3 to balance more evenly the technical material in Chapters 2 and 3.

EXPANDED DISCUSSION OF INTRODUCTION TO INTERCOMPANY TRANSACTIONS PLACED IN A SEPARATE CHAPTER

To give students the biggest and broadest possible picture of intercompany transactions before immersing them in detailed intercompany transaction elimination entry procedures, we greatly expanded the material that describes the nature, types, and **operational importance** of these transactions. Formerly the first part of the intercompany inventory transfer chapter, this material is now in a self-contained chapter, Chapter 9.

MOVING THE INCOME TAXES, EARNINGS PER SHARE, AND CASH FLOWS TOPICS INTO APPENDICES

The discussion of these topics (Chapter 13 in the fifth edition) has been substantially simplified and streamlined as well as separated and moved to appendices of the chapters in which the related financial reporting topics are discussed (Chapters 3, 5, 6, 7, 8, and 19).

EXPANDED DISCUSSION OF USING DERIVATIVES TO MANAGE FOREIGN CURRENCY EXPOSURES (CHAPTER 17)

To make the material on translation of foreign currency *transactions* less intimidating to students, we placed the discussion of FX forwards and FX option contracts in a separate chapter, Chapter 17. We also standardized and simplified the account descriptions used to record FX forwards and FX option contracts.

More important, we added a **general discussion of derivative financial instruments** so that students obtain a broader understanding of (1) the unique *characteristics* and *features* of derivatives in general—not just FX forwards and FX options—and (2) the various types of exposures that can exist (*market risk, credit risk,* and *liquidity risk*). We also greatly expanded our discussion of the FASB-mandated disclosures required for FX derivatives.

SIMPLER MANNER OF PRESENTING THE *CURRENT RATE METHOD* AND THE *TEMPORAL METHOD* (CHAPTERS 18 AND 19)

We substantially reorganized this material so that students learn on a step-by-step basis the two translation methods allowed under *SFAS No. 52*. Accordingly, the *current rate method* is discussed entirely in Chapter 18 (along with hedging a *net asset* position). The *temporal method* is discussed entirely in Chapter 19 (along with hedging a *net monetary* position). Tax reporting issues are discussed in an appendix to each chapter.

EXPANDED DISCUSSION OF THE SEC'S ENFORCEMENT POWERS (CHAPTER 22)

To make the rather technical material in Chapter 22 come alive as much as possible, we added an in-depth discussion of the procedures the SEC uses to exercise its enforcement powers (based on our discussions with SEC enforcement office personnel).

EXPANDED DISCUSSION OF GOVERNMENTAL MEASUREMENT FOCUS AND BASIS OF ACCOUNTING (CHAPTER 24)

We extensively revised and expanded our discussion in Chapter 24 of "what to measure" and "how to measure it" to better show that the so-called *operating statement* is *not* really a true operating statement. We also extensively revised this chapter's introductory material and streamlined the discussion of revenues and expenditures.

EXPANDED DISCUSSION OF THE GASB'S MAJOR CURRENT PROJECT INVOLVING A REEXAMINATION OF GOVERNMENTAL FINANCIAL REPORTING (CHAPTER 25)

In Chapter 25's appendix, we greatly expanded our discussion of the GASB's current ongoing efforts to reexamine governmental financial reporting. These efforts involve the following two broad areas:

- The Financial Reporting Model: *Dual*-Perspective Reporting versus *Single*-Perspective Reporting.
- Measurement Focus and Basis of Accounting (*SGAS No. 11*).

FULL DISCUSSION OF LIMITED LIABILITY PARTNERSHIPS (LLPs) ADDED (CHAPTER 28)

In Chapter 28, we have added a full discussion of *limited liability partnerships* in light of so many public accounting partnerships' (including all of the Big Six firms in 1994) changing to this new form of organization that burst on the scene in 1994 (largely as a result of the AICPA's efforts begun in 1992).

III   ACCOUNTING EDUCATION TREND CHANGES

Much of the change in accounting education in the past few years is along the following lines: (1) less emphasis on the traditional lecture and problem-solving mode of instruction in favor of making more use of assignments involving unstructured problem settings; (2) extensive use of group work in light of recent research that documents the value of students learning from one another; (3) a shift in emphasis from memorizing existing GAAP to developing critical-thinking skills; and (4) teaching accounting courses with integrated coverage of related topics in economics, finance, managerial accounting, law, tax, international business, ethics, and interpersonal skills.

Building on changes begun in the fourth edition, we have expanded the number of end-of-chapter assignments that lend themselves to teaching in this manner. These assignments consist of (1) **cases,** (2) **financial analysis problems,** and (3) **personal situations** involving **ethics** or **interpersonal skills.** For convenience they are grouped together at the end of each chapter in a section entitled "Thinking Critically" that follows the regular assignment material.

THE FINANCIAL ANALYSIS PROBLEMS (FAPs)

The financial analysis problems (FAPs) are much longer than the cases and the personal situations. When we first started using the FAPs, we were apprehensive about students becoming frustrated at trying to perform financial analysis without having an explanation or illustration in the chapter for developing "their solution." In using the FAPs the past two editions, however, the one comment we repeatedly received from students is that even though the FAPs pushed them beyond what they thought they were capable of, they were grateful for having a unique accounting course that continually forced them to think on their own and use their creativity and imagination rather than merely receive assignments for which they continually referred to the text to see "how it is done" or how an approach should be developed. Furthermore, instructors have encouraged us to develop more of these types of assignments. Also, some instructors indicated to us that by their use of these types of assignments, their course serves as a highly desirable "capstone" financial accounting course (something we also believe occurs).

A consequence of using a substantial portion of these FAPs is that fewer chapters can be assigned. Thus a trade-off question arises as to the relative value of (1) obtaining a technical understanding of issues and accounting procedures versus (2) developing critical thinking skills. Our experience in using the FAPs leads us to believe that a balanced approach is possible and that students receive far more value from being assigned a fewer number of topics and using the FAPs than by being assigned a greater number of topics and not using the FAPs. Some suggestions are set forth in the *Instructor's Resource Manual* regarding ways to obtain the maximum benefit from the FAPs—certain approaches do *not* achieve the desired consequences.

IV UNIQUE EMPHASIS ON *CREATED* SUBSIDIARIES RELATIVE TO *ACQUIRED* SUBSIDIARIES

Two of the findings of a major Institute of Management/Financial Executive Institute joint research project (completed in late 1994) were that (1) preparing consolidated financial statements is one of the more important of 15 accounting skill and knowledge areas deemed most important for corporate entry-level accountants and (2) accounting for *external expansion* (*purchase* and *pooling*-of-interests accounting) is *not* one of these 15 skills. The 15 skills were deemed "the essence of management."

In discussing the relative importance of these two areas with many corporate controllers in the electronics industry in the "Silicon Valley" region of California, the unanimous consensus was that preparing consolidated financial statements is far more important than accounting for external expansion, which typically is encountered infrequently.

These findings confirmed our belief that our decision in the fifth edition to separate the basic conceptual issues involving consolidated financial statements from the conceptual issues associated with business combinations better reflects practices and serves students.

Accordingly, the basic concept of preparing consolidated statements for *created* subsidiaries is discussed in Chapter 1. Accounting for a parent's investment in a *created* subsidiary is discussed in Chapter 2. Accounting for *created partially owned* subsidiaries is discussed in Chapter 3. Accounting for *acquired* subsidiaries is *not* discussed until Chapter 4. By focusing solely on parent-created subsidiaries for the first three chapters, we separate the basic concept of preparing consolidated statements from the much more involved concept of changing or not changing the basis of accounting for *acquired* subsidiaries. The separation of concepts results in a *step-by-step, building-block approach to the consolidation topic.*

BETTER REFLECTION OF ACTUAL BUSINESS EXPANSION PRACTICES

Aside from the pedagogical advantage, the initial emphasis on *created* subsidiaries better reflects actual business expansion practices. The vast majority of existing subsidiaries were *not acquired* but *created* by their parent companies. (Approximately 600 subsidiaries of U.S. parent companies were created in Ireland alone in the past 25 years.) Consequently, we treat *external expansion* as one facet of preparing consolidated statements—not as an integral part around which the consolidations area is structured.

GREATER INSTRUCTOR FLEXIBILITY IN DECIDING WHAT TO GIVE PRIMARY EMPHASIS

Two recent business trends suggest that this course give more emphasis to international transactions and operations and less emphasis to business combinations. The first trend is the extensive globalization of business that has occurred during the past 15 years. The second trend is the major decline in the 1990s of the number of business combinations relative to the preceding 35 years. An additional consideration is that accounting graduates in their entry-level positions will most likely not be exposed to business combination issues, which are usually handled only at the manager and partner level in public accounting firms.

By discussing *created* subsidiaries (*internal expansion*) separately from *acquired* subsidiaries (*external expansion*), instructors now have the option of either bypassing the business combinations material (Chapters 4–8) until later in the course or omitting it altogether. The advantage to this option is that in a one-semester course, the international topics (Chapters 16–20) can become the centerpiece of the course for those instructors desiring to give greater emphasis to this topic relative to the business combinations topic.

DISCUSSION OF INTERCOMPANY TRANSACTIONS USING *CREATED* SUBSIDIARIES (CHAPTERS 9, 10, 11, AND 12) INSTEAD OF *ACQUIRED* SUBSIDIARIES

Consistent with this emphasis on *created* subsidiaries in Chapters 1–3, the textual material and illustrations in Chapters 9–12 (intercompany transactions) are based on *created* subsidiaries instead of *acquired* subsidiaries. We believe intercompany transaction topics are difficult enough for students to initially learn without being burdened by the carryforward of the change- or no-change-in-basis-of-accounting issue that arises with *external expansion*. Accordingly, the *purchase* versus *pooling* issue is largely contained in Chapters 4–7.

Furthermore, substantially all of the consolidation problems in Chapters 9–12 are based on *created* subsidiaries, enabling these chapters to be taught before the business combinations chapters if an instructor desires to do so. (A few of the problems, however, are labeled as "comprehensive" and involve the additional complexity of either *purchased* or *pooled* subsidiaries so that instructors have the flexibility of integrating these situations into the intercompany transactions topics if they desire.)

V   OTHER FEATURES

CURRENT ARTICLES

We have expanded to 13 the number of current articles from business magazines and newspapers as follows:

Chapter 1   "AT&T Won't Cover Eo's Debts," *San Jose Mercury News*

Chapter 3   "Accountant Metcalf Knew Firsthand Give and Take of Taxes," *The Wall Street Journal*

Chapter 4   "Hostile Takeovers Are Revived, and Some Embrace 'Bear Hug,' " *The Wall Street Journal*

Chapter 7   "AT&T Pools with NCR—$5.7 Billion of Goodwill Avoided," *The Wall Street Journal*

Chapter 9   "The Corporate Shell Game," *Newsweek*

Chapter 16   "Clashing Values," *San Jose Mercury News*

Chapter 16   "All Accountants May Speak the Same Language," *The Wall Street Journal*

Chapter 17   "Derivatives Could Hedge Career Growth," *The Wall Street Journal*

Chapter 22   "Votes Today, Taxes Tomorrow," *Forbes*

Chapter 26   "The Accounting Games Charities Play," *Forbes*

Chapter 26   "Unlikely Hero, a Persistent Accountant Brought New Era's Problems to Light," *The Wall Street Journal*

Chapter 28   "Partnership Structure Is Called in Question as Liability Risk Rises," *The Wall Street Journal*

Chapter 30   "Behind the Fall of Laventhol," *Forbes*

INTEGRATION OF INTERNATIONAL GAAP PERSPECTIVES

More brief capsules of international GAAP have been added for the consolidation and foreign currency topics so that students can place U.S. GAAP in perspective relative to GAAP around the world. The capsules are:

Chapter 1   Foreign Consolidation Practices

Chapter 2   Widespread Use of Parent-Company-Only Statements Overseas

Chapter 3   Manner of Presenting Noncontrolling Interests in Foreign Countries

Chapter 3   Basis of Control for Consolidation

Chapter 4   Foreign Goodwill Accounting Practices

Chapter 7   Pooling of Interests Practice Around the World

Chapter 19   Worldwide Translation Practices

HISTORICAL DEVELOPMENT OF GAAP CAPSULES

The following historical development of GAAP capsules are included:

Chapter 4   Goodwill
Chapter 7   Pooling of Interests

INTEGRATION OF ETHICS

Numerous ethics cases, many of which relate to topics discussed, are included in the "Personal Situations" assignment material at the end of the chapters.

VI STUDENT-ORIENTED FEATURES

The following is a list of sixth edition features designed to heighten students' interest and make the text easy to read and use:

1. A list of **key learning objectives** to accompany the **topic outline** preceding each chapter.

2. A literary, anecdotal, or humorous **chapter-opening quotation** for each chapter.

3. A **chapter overview** introducing each chapter.

4. Inclusion of more **relevant articles** than ever before from *Forbes, Newsweek,* and *The Wall Street Journal* so that students can better relate the material to current events.

5. Use of **roman numerals** to distinguish major chapter sections so that students can more readily find topics.

6. Extensive use of **boldface type for key terms and key concepts.**

7. Convenient **vertical format for consolidation worksheets** that uses a plus-and-minus scheme consistent with Excel® and LOTUS 1-2-3® **spreadsheet software.**

8. Clearly marked **review points** for major illustrations.

9. **End-of-chapter review sections** for each chapter that include: (a) a **summary of key points;** (b) a **glossary of new terms;** (c) **demonstration problems and solutions** in key consolidation chapters (Chapters 5 and 6); and (d) **multiple-choice self-study questions.**

10. **Descriptive overviews** of all exercises, problems, cases, financial analysis problems, and personal situations.

11. Placement of **cases, financial analysis problems,** and **personal situations** in a readily identifiable section called **"Thinking Critically."**

12. Placement of **chapter appendix material** after *all* chapter assignment material.

13. **Checklist of key figures** for both exercises and problems on the inside covers for easy reference.

14. Use of a **marginal icon** to identify problems that can be worked on the computer using the spreadsheet software models provided to adopters.

15. **Display of dates** in the assignment material in a graphic manner (12/31/X1) rather than in a *non*graphic manner (December 31, 19X1) for greater ease of use.

VII ANCILLARIES

The following updated ancillaries, all written and revised by the authors, are available with this edition:

SOLUTIONS MANUAL   To assist instructors in evaluating and selecting assignment materials, the *Solutions Manual* contains a description of each exercise, problem, case, financial analysis problem, and personal situation. The **relative difficulty** and **estimated time for completion** of the assignment materials are also included.

INSTRUCTOR'S RESOURCE MANUAL AND TESTBOOK   The manual is divided into five parts:

- Part I consists of **course coverage considerations.**
- Part II contains a master list of both **teaching transparencies** for lectures and **problem solution transparencies** that accompany the text.
- Part III is an **instructor's introduction to the spreadsheet software models** that are provided free to instructors and students.
- Part IV contains **teaching-related materials for each individual chapter.** The materials consist of (1) teaching suggestions (including additional items of current interest to students), (2) descriptions of assignment material (including level of difficulty and estimated times), (3) a list of selected readings, and (4) a list of transparencies provided.
- Part V is a **test bank** for each chapter of the text. The test bank is highly accessible as a result of grouping items by subtopics and is also available on EXAMaster software, which is easy to install and use.

TRANSPARENCIES OF SELECTED PROBLEM SOLUTIONS   For nearly all problems involving consolidation or foreign currency translation worksheets, a solutions transparency is available of that worksheet. In addition, selected solutions transparencies are provided for certain other chapters.

TRANSPARENCIES FOR TEACHING   Teaching transparencies for use in lecturing on chapter material are available for selected chapters.

WORKING PAPERS   Working papers are provided for selected problems in Chapters 2, 3, 5–7, 9–13, 18, 19, and 28.

STUDY GUIDE   The *Study Guide* contains approximately 65 study items per chapter, grouped into (1) chapter highlights, (2) completion statements, (3) true-or-false statements, (4) *conceptual* multiple-choice questions, (5) *application* multiple-choice questions, and (6) problems (for Chapters 5–7 only).

SPREADSHEET SOFTWARE MODELS   A master diskette is available free to adopting instructors. The models on the diskette are designed for use on IBM® personal computers and compatibles with Excel (version 4.0 or higher) or LOTUS 1-2-3 (version 2.0 or higher) software. **Excel users must instruct Excel to *read all files.*** Approximately 60 problems from the text can be worked on the computer using this software, in 15 class-tested models for 15 chapters. No computer experience is required; each model has its own on-screen instructions that are displayed above the worksheet area. Each problem that can be worked using one of the models is identified with a spreadsheet icon in the margin of the book.

To give students the opportunity to design a template of their own, program some macros for this model, and create logic functions for this model, an assignment containing detailed instructions is provided in Chapter 2 (Problem 2–8). We also have included an assignment in Chapter 10 containing detailed instructions (Problem 10–7) on how to automate the entire consolidation process when intercompany transactions exist.

The Dryden Press may provide complimentary instructional aids and supplements or supplement packages to those adopters qualified under our adoption policy. Please contact your sales representative for more information. If as an adopter or potential user you receive supplements you do not need, please return them to your sales representative or send them to:

Attn: Returns Department
Troy Warehouse
465 South Lincoln Drive
Troy, MO 63379

VIII   ACKNOWLEDGMENTS

We are indebted to the following individuals who gave generously of their time and provided many fine suggestions in reviewing material for the sixth edition before publication:

Orapin Duangploy	University of Houston, Downtown
Francene Feldbrugge	San Jose State University
George J. Haytko	San Jose, California
Stuart S. Karlinsky	San Jose State University
Stanley Martens	DePaul University
Mallory L. McWilliams	San Jose State University
Michael E. Solt	San Jose State University
Frederic M. Stiner	University of Delaware
Charles A. Tritschler	Purdue University
Charles F. Vincent	San Jose State University (Emeritus)
Larry M. Walther	University of Texas, Arlington

We are grateful to Charlie Tritschler of Purdue University, who, in addition to having reviewed many of the substantially revised consolidation and foreign currency chapters, effectively served as a consulting technical editor. He gave us considerable guidance in reorganizing the sequence of the various consolidation and foreign currency topics and in developing new material that discusses derivative financial instruments in a broad context (Chapter 17). We consider ourselves extremely fortunate to have been able to draw and learn from his extensive teaching experience, remarkable insights, and unequalled expertise in foreign currency translation and derivative financial instruments. He spent so many hours with us discussing technical matters and pedagogical approaches that it seems he ran not only an extra lap but an extra race as well. Charlie, you are a true professional in the highest sense of the word and an absolute gem of a person. To the extent that these chapters have been improved, great credit goes to you. We, the authors, of course, assume full responsibility for any shortcomings in these areas.

We express appreciation to the American Institute of Certified Public Accountants, the Financial Accounting Standards Board, the Governmental Accounting Standards Board, and the Government Finance Officers Association for their permission to quote material from their pronouncements and various other publications. We also thank the American Institute of Certified Public Accountants for their permission to use and adapt material from the CPA examinations.

We also express our appreciation to many partners and managers of the Big 6 international accounting firms to whom we made numerous inquiries concerning current accounting issues and practices.

Finally, we express our appreciation to Mike Reynolds, acquisitions editor; Van Strength, our dedicated and conscientious developmental editor; JaNoel Lowe, our in-a-class-by-herself copy editor; Linda Wooton, our talented art and design director; Michele Tomiak, our delightful project editor; Carlyn Hauser, our energetic production manager; and Annette Coolidge, our thorough permissions editor. Their commitment and professionalism were greatly appreciated.

We encourage and welcome all comments from users of the sixth edition.

Arnold J. Pahler

Joseph E. Mori

BRIEF CONTENTS

CONTENTS

PART IV   CONSOLIDATED FINANCIAL STATEMENTS:
           OTHER TOPICS   453

20 Translating Foreign Statements: Evaluating the Validity of the Functional Currency Concept 699

PART VI   **MISCELLANEOUS CORPORATE REPORTING TOPICS**   **725**

21 Interim Reporting 725

22 Securities and Exchange Commission Reporting 745

23 Troubled Debt Restructurings, Bankruptcy Reorganizations, and Liquidations 779

PART VIII   **PARTNERSHIPS AND ESTATES AND TRUSTS**   **1023**

Sixth Edition

ADVANCED ACCOUNTING

Concepts and Practice

WHOLLY OWNED SUBSIDIARIES— AT DATE OF CREATION

LEARNING OBJECTIVES

TO UNDERSTAND

- The business reasons for choosing between the subsidiary and branch forms of organization.
- The way to create (incorporate) a subsidiary.
- The concept and purpose of consolidated financial statements.
- The way to prepare a consolidated balance sheet.
- The major conceptual issues pertaining to consolidated statements.
- The basic reporting standards for consolidated statements.

TOPIC OUTLINE

Nothing is particularly hard if you divide it into small jobs.

HENRY FORD

1

A substantial portion of the subject matter of advanced accounting concerns businesses that expand their operations or diversify into new fields. A business may expand or diversify in one of two ways: **internal expansion** and **external expansion.**

INTERNAL EXPANSION

Internal expansion may be accomplished by constructing or leasing additional facilities, most often for use in the same line of business in which the entity currently operates. Many companies have dramatically increased revenues by expanding in this manner.

CASE IN POINT

Spectacular Growth from Internal Expansion

Walt Disney's revenues increased from $1.5 billion in 1984 to $10 billion in 1996—virtually all of this growth was the result of internal expansion. (IBM, Kmart, and Wal-Mart are also renowned for having dramatically increased revenues by internal expansion.)

Before expanding in this way, management must decide whether to organize the new operation as (1) a **subsidiary** (a separate legal entity)[1] or (2) a **branch** or **division** (an extension of the existing legal entity).

SUBSIDIARY FORM OF ORGANIZATION   When the subsidiary form of organization is used, the relationship between the existing company and the newly created company is called a **parent-subsidiary** relationship. Because a subsidiary is a separate legal entity, it must keep its own records (a "stand-alone" basis). Thus a **decentralized accounting** system is used.

BRANCH OR DIVISION FORM OF ORGANIZATION   When the branch or division form of organization is used, the relationship between the two operations is called a **home office–branch/division** relationship. The record-keeping system for a branch or division can be either (1) **decentralized** accounting (as subsidiaries use) or (2) **centralized accounting** whereby all transactions pertaining to the branch or division are recorded in the home office's general ledger (usually in separate accounts so that separate operating statements can be prepared for each location).

EXTERNAL EXPANSION

External expansion takes place when two existing businesses **combine into a unified larger business.** A significant percentage of business combinations occurs among companies in unrelated fields, enabling the expanding company to diversify its product lines. Much of the growth of ITT and General Electric was due to external expansion.

FOCUSING INITIALLY ON INTERNAL EXPANSION

This chapter and Chapters 2 and 3 deal exclusively with internal expansion. Chapters 4 through 8 deal with external expansion. By discussing internal expansion

---

[1]Creating a subsidiary is not always done in connection with internal expansion. Sometimes subsidiaries are created "on paper only" for legal and related purposes.

first, we address basic financial reporting standards for multilocation operations in the much simpler of the two areas, which results in a step-by-step learning approach. Furthermore, most expansion that occurs is internal expansion (although external expansion is usually more noticeable because it gets far more headlines in the financial press).[2] For instance, more than 600 subsidiaries of U.S. companies were created in Ireland alone in the last 25 years, whereas virtually no U.S. firms expanded externally in Ireland. See the following **Cases in Point** for two specific company examples.

CASES IN POINT

Subsidiaries of Intel Corporation, the World's Largest Computer Chip Manufacturer

	Created	Acquired
Intel Japan	X	
Intel France	X	
Intel United Kingdom	X	
Intel Germany	X	
Intel Hong Kong	X	
Intel Canada	X	

Subsidiaries of Seagate Technology, One of the World's Largest Disk Drive Manufacturers

	Created	Acquired
Seagate Singapore	X	
Seagate Thailand	X	
Seagate Germany	X	
Seagate Cayman Islands	X	
Seagate Scotland	X	
Seagate Japan	X	
Seagate Magnetics		X
Conner Peripherals, Inc.		X

Although we initially compare the subsidiary form of organization with the branch/division form of organization, we then deal solely with the subsidiary form. The branch/division form is discussed in detail in Appendix B to Chapter 2.

When a parent-subsidiary relationship is established, the first financial reporting issue from the parent's perspective is whether to present (1) separate company financial statements for both the parent and the subsidiary or (2) consolidated statements (**as though** one company instead of two exists). Most of this chapter discusses this issue. Additional reporting issues (ranging from simple to complex) are discussed in this and later chapters.

When a parent has one or more subsidiaries, it is common to refer to all of the entities collectively as the **group** or the *consolidated group*. Occasionally, we use these terms.

---

[2]Two of the findings of a major Institute of Management Accountants/Financial Executive Institute research project completed in 1994 were that (1) preparing consolidated financial statements was one of eight accounting and knowledge skill areas deemed most important for corporate entry-level accountants and (2) accounting for external expansion (purchase and pooling of interests accounting) was not. These eight skills were deemed "the essence of management." In discussing the relative importance of these two areas with many corporate controllers in the electronics industry in the "Silicon Valley" region of Northern California, the consensus was that preparing consolidated statements is far more important compared to accounting for external expansion, which often is encountered infrequently.

I   SUBSIDIARY VERSUS BRANCH/DIVISION FORM OF ORGANIZATION

In referring to the new operation established by an extension of the existing legal entity, we use the lone term *branch* rather than the dual terms *branch* and *division*, even though *division* is used in business as frequently as *branch*. Using only the term *branch* also is consistent with the Internal Revenue Code terminology for all such outlying locations.

LIMITING LEGAL LIABILITY EXPOSURE

A major consideration in selecting the form of organization for the new operation is whether to insulate the existing operation from the new (and therefore highly uncertain) operation so that if something adverse happens at the new one, the problem can be contained and not have a spillover effect on the existing operation. **This limits the existing operation's potential loss exposure to the amount it has invested in the new operation.** Accordingly, some businesses have a policy of forming a separate subsidiary—that is, a separate legal entity with limited liability—for each new state or country into which they expand. This strategy is not foolproof, however; sometimes the corporate shield of the parent is pierced.[3]

In the motion picture industry, each newly conceived movie is assigned to either a newly created or dormant subsidiary partly for limiting the investor's exposure. (Recall the unfortunate helicopter crash several years ago during the filming of *Twilight Zone* that resulted in the deaths of several people and subsequent multimillion dollar lawsuits alleging negligence.) When the accounting for a movie has been completed (usually three to five years after filming and showing), that particular subsidiary (which over time becomes dormant) may be used again for a new movie.

SUBSIDIARY CREDITORS BEWARE   Some subsidiaries obtain credit from vendors partly by referring to the parent's strong financial condition and asserting that the parent stands behind its subsidiaries. Often such assertions prove to be hot air, as shown in the Business Perspective on page 5.

CONSIDERING INCOME TAXES

When a company expands into foreign countries, income taxes become an important consideration (discussed more fully in Chapter 18). Foreign tax authorities can examine in great detail the books and records of a branch or subsidiary; however, the subsidiary form of organization greatly limits the foreign taxing authorities' ability to examine data concerning the parent because all aspects of the overseas unit's operations are contained at the subsidiary level—a separate legal entity.

Another consideration is that the Internal Revenue Service **taxes as current income the earnings of overseas branches** but in most situations taxes earnings of foreign subsidiaries **when the parent receives dividends** in the United States—a major concern for companies expanding in foreign countries that grant "tax holidays" (very low income tax rates, if any) to entice foreign investment. Possibly for these reasons, along with the legal insulation consideration, IBM's extensive foreign expansion was the result of creating subsidiaries—not branches. On the other hand, because foreign tax considerations were not an issue, both Kmart and Wal-

---

[3]Perhaps the best example of this is Union Carbide Corporation, which had a plant explosion in Bhopal, India, in 1984 that killed nearly 4,000 people and disabled nearly 20,000 people. Possibly to preserve its image as a good corporate citizen, the parent company paid $470 million to the Indian government to settle claims, far in excess of the assets available at the subsidiary level.

BUSINESS PERSPECTIVE

AT&T Won't Cover Eo's Debts

"Eo Inc. is an AT&T Company."

That proud statement is displayed on the letterhead of Eo, a Santa Clara start-up company that tried and failed to develop a market for wireless portable computers. AT&T Corp., which owns 52 percent of Eo stock, pulled the plug last week, forcing cash-starved Eo to shut down.

Now, Eo is pulling the plug on its suppliers—telling them AT&T will not make good on Eo's debts.

Some of those suppliers said they let Eo slip behind in payments earlier this year only after Eo employees assured them AT&T— one of the nation's largest corporations with sales of $67 billion last year— stood behind Eo.

"Because of AT&T, we felt more confident," said Mike Greenberg, president of Sequent Associates, a temporary staffing firm in San Jose that supplied Eo with contract software engineers.

"Everyone has done business with Eo on the basis that they're an AT&T company," added Brenda Hall, head of Hall Kinion, another San Jose staffing firm. "It's an attempt to pull a fast one."

AT&T promoted its connection with Eo heavily, featuring Eo's pen-based handheld computers in television commercials and selling the device in AT&T Phone Center stores.

Outside analysts estimate AT&T sank $50 million into Eo. But AT&T said it decided earlier this year not to invest any further unless Eo could find other backers to share the burden.

No one came to Eo's rescue, prompting AT&T to announce the July 29 shutdown.

William M. Daniher, Eo's chief financial officer, sent a letter to vendors last week telling them the bad news.

"A small transition team led by myself will be put in place to liquidate the assets and settle claims with vendors, lessors and creditors," the letter said. "Although Eo has over $30 million in secured debt, the transition team is hopeful that a compromise will be reached with these creditors and funds will be made available for unsecured vendors and lessors.

"We believe the approach we have outlined will allow the maximum amount of payment to be made to vendors and thus would appreciate your patience and support," Daniher wrote.

Greenberg, whose firm is owed $20,200, said an Eo official told him earlier this week that Eo is prepared to pay only 20 cents on the dollar.

Hall, owed $15,000, said she and Eo "are discussing daily how much they can pay" and still hopes to recover all or most of the debt.

AT&T, however, didn't appear eager to give ground Friday.

"We've said all along Eo will pay suppliers to the extent that assets permit," said Kevin Compton, an AT&T spokesman in San Jose. "I can't speak for what Eo employees might have told people (about AT&T backing Eo's debts). Eo management was responsible for day-to-day operations and the conduct of Eo employees."

Bob Evans, Eo's chief executive, declined to comment on the situation when contacted by a reporter Friday. Eo had about 100 permanent employees and 25 contract employees when it suspended operations last week.

Shareholders are not legally obligated to pay the debts of a corporation, even if they own a majority of the corporation's stock.

Source: Mike Langberg, "AT&T Won't Cover Eo's Debts," *San Jose Mercury News*, August 6, 1994, p. 10D. Reprinted by permission of *San Jose Mercury News*, August 6, 1994. © *San Jose Mercury News*, 1994.

Mart's extensive domestic expansions resulted from creating branches—not subsidiaries.

CARVING UP AN ENTITY TO SAVE STATE INCOME TAXES   Many existing companies have restructured themselves into a parent and one or more subsidiaries so that they can report more income in low–income tax states rather than in a high–income tax state. Such restructurings, although neither *internal* nor *external* expansion, also show how tax considerations can weigh heavily in determining an entity's organization structure.

RETAINING PATENT AND COPYRIGHT PROTECTION

Many developing foreign countries have virtually no patent or copyright law protection. The transfer of these items to a *foreign subsidiary* results in the total loss of protection. If the *branch* organization form were used, however, the patents and copyrights remain subject to U.S. laws. Accordingly, many domestic companies use the branch form of organization.

To retain patent and copyright protection and to obtain the legal liability advantages associated with the subsidiary organization form, many companies transfer these technology rights to a *domestic subsidiary* created solely for the purpose of establishing a *branch* in the foreign country.

MEETING FOREIGN COUNTRY LOCAL OWNERSHIP REQUIREMENTS

Some foreign countries prohibit foreign investment within them unless local citizens own some portion of the operation. This automatically eliminates the use of the branch organization form. The only way to share ownership is to use the subsidiary organization form, whereby local citizens can own stock (sometimes only 10% but often as high as 51%). For instance, China requires 50% local ownership. Several years ago, IBM closed its subsidiary in India rather than give up a major portion of its ownership as newly enacted local legislation required.

CREATING A PERCEPTION OF SEPARATENESS

Often an entity creates a subsidiary to market a new product or enter a new field. The following are examples:

1. General Motors Corporation's 1982 creation of Saturn Corporation to give the Saturn car a separate identity.
2. Syntex Corporation's 1993 creation of Hamilton Pharmaceuticals Ltd., solely to market its own generic form of naproxen, an anti-inflammatory drug developed by Syntex, whose patent protection expired in 1993. It would have been potentially confusing to consumers if Syntex were selling both the original and the generic brand (which differ considerably in price).
3. Silicon Graphic Corporation's 1994 creation of DreamWorks SKG to enhance its ability to cultivate business from the entertainment industry.

BREAKING UP TO SHAKE THINGS UP AND ACHIEVE BETTER FOCUSING

Sometimes an entity will reorganize itself so that managers can focus more clearly on the areas for which they are responsible. The following are examples:

1. In 1995, IBM Corporation announced it was establishing a separate company to develop, manufacture, distribute, and market personal computers. Previously, these functions were handled by different divisions of IBM. This reorganization is part of IBM's determination to shake up its bureaucratic corporate culture by breaking up (the fourth-largest industrial corporation in the United States) into a confederation of 13 companies. Carried to its conclusion, IBM will end up being a **holding company,** an entity that has no operations of its own but only investments in one or more subsidiaries.
2. In 1995, Pacific Gas & Electric Company (the largest utility in California) announced its intention to reorganize itself as a decentralized group of companies managed by a holding company.

GETTING AROUND IMPORTING RESTRICTIONS

Sometimes a subsidiary can do what a parent cannot. For example, federal trade restrictions imposed by the Carter administration in 1979 made it illegal for U.S.

companies to import oil from Iran. In practice, foreign subsidiaries of U.S. companies purchase nearly 25% of Iran's oil production, most of which is marketed in Europe and Japan.

GETTING AROUND UNION REQUIREMENTS

In the motion picture industry, each of the numerous union guilds (for actors, directors, screenwriters, etc.) has provisions requiring a movie company that hires a guild member (say a director) to use guild directors for all its movies. To get around this limitation, thousands of subsidiaries have been created to cover all possible variations that occur. Thus a subsidiary can be created for use only in situations in which, for example, the director is a guild member but the actors and screenwriter are not. After the subsidiary becomes dormant, it can be used again in this situation.

II CREATING (INCORPORATING) A SUBSIDIARY

The remainder of this chapter deals with accounting for created 100%-owned subsidiaries. Accounting for newly created branches is discussed in Appendix B to Chapter 2.

INCORPORATING THE NEW OPERATION

The creation (formation) of a subsidiary merely involves obtaining a **corporate charter** from the state (or country) in which the subsidiary is being formed, paying incorporation fees, and investing some capital in the newly formed company. Because the subsidiary is a separate legal entity, it must (1) have its own board of directors and officers (often the same individuals serving as officers and directors for the company that formed it) and (2) maintain its own books and records (as mentioned earlier).

CREATING THE PARENT-SUBSIDIARY RELATIONSHIP

Virtually all "created" subsidiaries (as opposed to "acquired" subsidiaries resulting from external expansion) are 100% owned by the parent company. However, a parent-subsidiary relationship can exist with less than 100% ownership, so long as **more than** 50% of the outstanding common stock is owned. Subsidiaries **less than 100% owned** present special reporting problems for the voting interest *not* owned by the parent (called the *noncontrolling interest*); they are introduced in Chapter 3.

RECORDING THE PARENT'S INITIAL CAPITAL INVESTMENT

Assume that on December 31, 19X0, P Company (the parent) invested $60,000 cash in S Company (its newly created subsidiary), with the subsidiary issuing 1,000 shares of its no par value common stock to the parent. The entries to record this transaction follow:

P Company's Books (the parent)

Investment in S Company	60,000	
Cash		60,000

S Company's Books (the subsidiary)

Cash	60,000	
Common Stock (1,000 shares)		60,000

Note that at the creation date, S Company's assets of $60,000 equal P Company's investment in S Company; thus **S Company's assets are the economic resources that underlie P Company's investment in S Company.** In Chapter 2, we discuss a subsidiary with liabilities, in which case its **net assets** (Total Assets – Total Liabilities) underlie the parent's investment in the subsidiary.

CREATING A PARENT COMPANY TO ALLOW FOR EXPANSION

When a company wants to diversify into areas prohibited by its corporate charter, it can transform itself into a subsidiary. Procedurally, a new corporate entity (having different charter provisions) is created to serve as the parent company, and this new entity issues common stock in exchange for the first entity's outstanding common stock. The parent can then expand into the prohibited areas. This has occurred most notably in the banking and the savings and loan industries.

Furthermore, in these industries, the parent is usually a **holding company.** For instance, Citicorp is a holding company that has 24 subsidiaries (almost all having been created instead of acquired), one of which is Citibank, N.A. (the largest U.S. bank).

III CONSOLIDATED STATEMENTS: THE CONCEPT

Consolidated statements, which have been used in the United States for nearly a century, refer to the financial statements that a parent company produces when its financial statements and those of a subsidiary are added together in a manner that portrays the resulting financial statements **as if they represent a single company.**

The idea is to disregard the separate legal entity status of each company and instead portray both as a **single economic entity** in light of one entity controlling the other entity—**regardless of the fact that each entity maintains its own separate records and prepares its own separate financial statements.** Consequently, consolidated statements are **pro forma** or "as-if" statements.

THE PARENT'S POWER TO LIQUIDATE THE SUBSIDIARY INTO A BRANCH

A supporting argument for presenting consolidated statements is that a parent usually has the power to liquidate a subsidiary into a branch at any time using the **statutory merger** provisions in state corporation laws. Thus a subsidiary's legal entity status can be taken away easily (its corporate charter is canceled) with the result that the remaining legal entity, the **parent** (which takes title to the subsidiary's assets and assumes responsibilities for the subsidiary's liabilities), is the economic entity.

Consolidated statements are extremely important because they constitute the **general-purpose financial statements** of companies having one or more subsidiaries—that is, the statements to be furnished to a parent's stockholders when a parent-subsidiary relationship exists.

Before discussing the many conceptual issues and the detailed requirements of the current accounting standards, we briefly illustrate the general idea of consolidated statements. Recall from our earlier example that the parent created a subsidiary on December 31, 19X0, by making a $60,000 cash investment. Let us further assume that S Company's only other transaction on December 31, 19X0, was to purchase a parcel of land costing $12,000 cash. S Company's balance sheet at December 31, 19X0, is shown in Illustration 1–1, along with the P Company's separate balance sheet at that date.

ILLUSTRATION 1–1	**Separate Company Statements**

P Company
Balance Sheet—Unconsolidated
As of December 31, 19X0

Assets		Liabilities and Equity	
Cash	$ 58,000	Accounts payable and	
Accounts receivable	52,000	accruals	$150,000
Inventory	90,000	Long-term debt	250,000
Investment in S Company ..	**60,000**	Total Liabilities	$400,000
Land	220,000		
Buildings and equipment	500,000	Common stock, no par	$200,000
Accumulated depreciation	(280,000)	Retained earnings	100,000
		Total Equity	$300,000
	$700,000		$700,000

S Company
Balance Sheet
As of December 31, 19X0

Assets		Equity	
Cash	$48,000	Common stock	$60,000
Land	12,000		
	$60,000		$60,000

ISSUING UNCONSOLIDATED STATEMENTS

If consolidated statements were *not* required to be furnished (contrary to current practice), P Company would publish its separate "unconsolidated" balance sheet (more commonly referred to as a **parent-company-only statement**) as shown in the top section of Illustration 1–1. In most instances, P Company would also include in its financial statement notes the separate balance sheet of S Company to show what economic resources underlie P Company's investment in S Company.

Later in the chapter and in Chapter 3, we discuss infrequently encountered situations for which it is inappropriate to furnish consolidated statements. In such situations, the parent-company-only statements constitute the general-purpose financial statements.

PRESENTING CONSOLIDATED STATEMENTS:
TWO POSSIBLE REPORTING APPROACHES

If consolidated financial statements were required to be furnished, the consolidated balance sheet could be presented in one of two manners:

1. A **disaggregated,** "layered," reporting **format.**
2. An **aggregated,** "unlayered," reporting **format.**[4]

THE DISAGGREGATED FORMAT   In the disaggregated format, the subsidiary's assets and liabilities are shown separately from the parent's assets and liabilities in a **layered manner** (also referred to as a **tiered, stacked,** or **"pancake"** manner). This reporting format makes sense when a parent has a subsidiary in a different line of

[4]The *aggregated* versus *disaggregated* terminology is used in various FASB publications (for example, see *Reporting Disaggregated Information about a Business Enterprise,* a proposed standard published in 1996 and discussed in Chapter 15).

ILLUSTRATION 1–2	Consolidated Balance Sheet: Disaggregated Format

P Company
Consolidated Balance Sheet—Disaggregated Format
As of December 31, 19X0

Assets		Liabilities and Equity	
Cash	$ 58,000	Accounts payable and	
Accounts receivable	52,000	accruals	$150,000
Inventory	90,000	Long-term debt	250,000
		Total Liabilities	$400,000
Land	220,000		
Buildings and equipment	500,000	Common stock, no par	$200,000
Accumulated depreciation	(280,000)	Retained earnings	100,000
	$640,000	Total Equity	$300,000

Assets of Subsidiary			
Cash	$ 48,000		
Land	12,000		
	$ 60,000		
		Total Liabilities	
Total Assets	$700,000	and Equity	$700,000

Note: If the subsidiary had liabilities, its liabilities would also be shown separately.

business, such as when a manufacturing company has a captive finance subsidiary (as is the case for the Big Three auto companies).[5]

By presenting the assets and liabilities of such subsidiaries in a layered manner, the consolidated balance sheet shows exactly what assets and liabilities exist at the subsidiary level and how much they contribute to the parent. Ford Motor Company uses this manner of reporting, showing an automotive category and a financial services category in both its consolidated balance sheet and its consolidated income statement (see pages 11 and 12).

Note that Ford classifies the automotive category as to current and noncurrent but not the financial services category (the usual case for finance subsidiaries). This disaggregated manner of reporting is shown in Illustration 1–2.

REVIEW POINTS FOR ILLUSTRATION 1–2   Note the following:

1. The effect of presenting consolidated statements is to substitute the subsidiary's assets (Cash of $48,000 and Land of $12,000) for the parent's Investment in S Company account that totals $60,000, as shown in Illustration 1–1.

2. S Company's equity is *not* reported in the consolidated balance sheet because from a consolidated perspective, its issued stock is *not* outstanding—it is held internally. Thus the Investment in S Company is treated as "treasury stock," which must be subtracted from or offset against S Company's equity. (Recall from intermediate accounting that treasury stock purchases are shown as a reduction of equity.)

3. When a subsidiary is in a different line of business than the parent, the disaggregated (layered) format is often used. If they have too many subsidiaries in unrelated lines of business (in relation to the line of business of the parent and its remaining subsidiaries), however, companies shy away from this format. In practice, the aggregated (unlayered) format is much more prevalent than the disaggregated (layered) format.

[5]A captive finance subsidiary is a company whose business purpose is to provide financing solely to its parent's customers.

ILLUSTRATION 1–4	Consolidation Worksheet at Date of Creation (Balance Sheet Only)

P Company and Subsidiary (S Company)
Consolidation Worksheet as of December 31, 19X0

	P Company	S Company	Consolidation Entries Dr.	Consolidation Entries Cr.	Consolidated
Balance Sheet					
Cash	58,000	48,000			106,000
Accounts receivable	52,000				52,000
Inventory	90,000				90,000
Investment in S Company	**60,000**			60,000(1)	–0–
Land	220,000	12,000			232,000
Buildings and equipment	500,000				500,000
Accumulated depreciation	(280,000)				(280,000)
Total Assets	700,000	60,000		60,000	700,000
Payables and accruals	150,000				150,000
Long-term debt	250,000				250,000
P Company:					
Common stock	200,000				200,000
Retained earnings	100,000				100,000
S Company:					
Common stock		**60,000**	60,000(1)		–0–
Total Liabilities & Equity	700,000	60,000	60,000		700,000
Proof of debit and credit postings			60,000	60,000	

Explanation of entry:
(1) To eliminate accounts having reciprocal balances.

REVIEW POINTS FOR ILLUSTRATION 1–4   Note the following:

1. Conceptually, the entry shown in the Debit and Credit columns of the worksheet merely reclassifies the Investment in S Company account—a treasury stock holding from a consolidated perspective—to S Company's equity section. Consequently, it is commonly said that this entry "eliminates" the account balances that are not presented in the consolidated balance sheet—namely the Investment in S Company account on the parent's books and the Common Stock account on the subsidiary's books. Eliminating these accounts achieves the desired substitution of S Company's assets (that underlie the parent's investment) for P Company's Investment account.

2. In practice, such worksheet entries are called *consolidation entries*—as contrasted with *general ledger adjusting entries*. **Because consolidated amounts are *not* maintained in a general ledger, worksheet entries are never posted to a general ledger.** Hereafter, all worksheet entries are so labeled (as shown at the left margin) and are shaded to differentiate them from general ledger entries.

WORKSHEET ENTRY ONLY

3. **For ease of reference only,** we refer to this particular consolidation entry, **which is made in all consolidations,** as **the basic elimination entry.** In later chapters, other types of consolidation entries that relate to various types of transactions that a parent and subsidiary may have with each other (such as inventory sales, lending transactions, and leasing transactions) are encountered—all of which are called *intercompany transactions.*

4. In this example, the $60,000 debit balance in the Investment in S Company account equals the $60,000 credit balance in the subsidiary's Common Stock account. These two accounts have what is called *reciprocal balances.* In practice,

---

ILLUSTRATION 1–3   **Consolidated Balance Sheet: Aggregated Format**

P Company
Consolidated Balance Sheet—Aggregated Format
As of December 31, 19X0

Assets		Liabilities and Equity	
Cash	**$106,000**	Accounts payable and	
Accounts receivable.........	52,000	accruals	$150,000
Inventory	90,000	Long-term debt	250,000
		Total Liabilities	$400,000
Land	**232,000**	Common stock, no par	$200,000
Buildings and equipment	500,000	Retained earnings	100,000
Accumulated depreciation	(280,000)	Total Equity	$300,000
		Total Liabilities	
Total Assets	$700,000	and Equity	$700,000

THE AGGREGATED FORMAT   In aggregated consolidated statements, the individual accounts of the parent and the subsidiary are summed, thus presenting only one amount for each asset, liability, and income statement account. This manner of reporting is shown in Illustration 1–3.

REVIEW POINTS FOR ILLUSTRATION 1–3   Note the following:

1. The substitution effect mentioned for Illustration 1–2 also occurs in Illustration 1–3. Here, however, each company's Cash and Land accounts have been summed together (shown in boldface for emphasis).

2. When a parent and subsidiary are in the *same* line of business, the aggregated format is almost always used because financial statement users have not expressed any significant desire for the disaggregated format in such situations.

SHORTCOMINGS OF THE AGGREGATED REPORTING FORMAT   The aggregated format makes the most sense if the parent and the subsidiary are in the *same* line of business. In these cases, the asset composition and liability structure of the two entities are *not* radically different. However, many situations exist in which (1) the two entities are in totally unrelated industries and (2) the asset composition and liability structures *are* radically different. For example, when a manufacturing parent has a bank, savings and loan, or insurance subsidiary, it is not uncommon for (1) the parent to have roughly a 60–40% debt-to-equity ratio and (2) the subsidiary to have roughly a 95–5% debt-to-equity ratio. Such disparities make it somewhat difficult to analyze or use an aggregated balance sheet. Later in this chapter we discuss the aggregated format of reporting in more detail.

EFFECTING A CONSOLIDATION: THE MECHANICAL PROCEDURES

To prepare consolidated statements, accountants use a working paper called a **consolidation worksheet** because **a general ledger is not kept for the "consolidated reporting entity."** However, the consolidation worksheets are just as much a part of the books and records of the parent company as its general ledger—especially because the consolidated statements derived therefrom are the general-purpose financial statements. Thus the consolidation worksheets are much more important than other types of working papers (such as analyses and schedules).

The worksheet used to accomplish the consolidation of P Company's and S Company's balance sheets at December 31, 19X0, **into the aggregated format shown earlier in Illustration 1–3** is presented in Illustration 1–4 on page 14.

Ford Motor Company and Subsidiaries Consolidated Statement of Income for the Years Ended December 31, 1995, 1994 and 1993 (in millions, except amounts per share)

	1995	1994	1993
AUTOMOTIVE			
Sales	$110,496	$107,137	$91,568
Costs and expenses			
Costs of sales	101,171	95,887	85,280
Selling, administrative, and other expenses	6,044	5,424	4,856
Total costs and expenses	107,215	101,311	90,136
Operating Income	3,281	5,826	1,432
Interest income	800	665	563
Interest expense	622	721	807
Net interest income/(expense)	178	(56)	(244)
Equity in net (loss)/income of affiliated companies	(154)	271	127
Net expense from transactions with Financial Services	(139)	(44)	(24)
Income before income taxes—Automotive	3,166	5,997	1,291
FINANCIAL SERVICES			
Revenues	26,641	21,302	16,953
Costs and expenses			
Interest expense	9,424	7,023	6,482
Depreciation	6,500	4,910	3,064
Operating and other expenses	5,499	4,607	3,196
Provision for credit and insurance losses	1,818	1,539	1,523
Loss on disposition of Granite Savings Bank (formerly First Nationwide Bank)	—	475	—
Total costs and expenses	23,241	18,554	14,265
Net revenue from transactions with Automotive	139	44	24
Income before income taxes—Financial Services	3,539	2,792	2,712
TOTAL COMPANY			
Income before income taxes	6,705	8,789	4,003
Provision for income taxes	2,379	3,329	1,350
Income before minority interests	4,326	5,460	2,653
Minority interests in net income of subsidiaries	187	152	124
Net income	$ 4,139	$ 5,308	$ 2,529
Income attributable to Common and Class B Stock after preferred stock dividends	$ 3,839	$ 5,021	$ 2,241
Average number of shares of Common and Class B Stock outstanding	1,071	1,010	986
AMOUNTS PER SHARE OF COMMON AND CLASS B STOCK			
Income	$ 3.58	$ 4.97	$ 2.27
Income assuming full dilution	$ 3.33	$ 4.44	$ 2.10
Cash dividends	$ 1.23	$ 0.91	$ 0.80

Ford Motor Company and Subsidiaries Consolidated Balance Sheet (in millions)

	December 31, 1995	December 31, 1994
ASSETS		
Automotive		
Cash and cash equivalents	$ 5,750	$ 4,481
Marketable securities	6,656	7,602
Total cash, cash equivalents, and marketable securities	12,406	12,083
Receivables	3,321	2,548
Inventories	7,162	6,487
Deferred income taxes	2,709	3,062
Other current assets	1,483	2,006
Net current receivable from Financial Services	200	677
Total current assets	27,281	26,863
Equity in net assets of affiliated companies	2,248	3,554
Net property	31,273	27,048
Deferred income taxes	4,802	4,414
Other assets	7,168	6,760
Total Automotive assets	72,772	68,639
Financial Services		
Cash and cash equivalents	2,690	1,739
Investments in securities	4,553	6,105
Net receivables and lease investments	149,694	130,356
Other assets	13,574	12,783
Total Financial Services assets	170,511	150,983
Total assets	$243,283	$219,622
LIABILITIES AND STOCKHOLDERS' EQUITY		
Automotive		
Trade payables	$ 11,260	$ 10,777
Other payables	1,976	2,280
Accrued liabilities	13,392	11,943
Income taxes payable	316	316
Debt payable within one year	1,832	155
Total current liabilities	28,776	25,471
Long-term debt	5,475	7,103
Other liabilities	25,677	24,920
Deferred income taxes	1,186	1,216
Total Automotive liabilities	61,114	58,710
Financial Services		
Payables	5,476	2,361
Debt	141,317	123,713
Deferred income taxes	3,831	2,958
Other liabilities and deferred income	6,116	7,669
Net payable to Automotive	200	677
Total Financial Services liabilities	156,940	137,378
Company-obligated mandatorily redeemable preferred securities of a subsidiary trust (aggregate principal amount of $632 million)	682	—
Preferred stockholders' equity in a subsidiary company	—	1,875
Stockholders' equity		
Capital stock		
Preferred Stock, par value $1.00 per share (aggregate liquidation preference of $1 billion and 3.4 billion)	*	*
Common Stock, par value $1.00 per share (1,089 and 952 million shares issued)	1,089	952
Class B Stock, par value ($1.00 per share (71 million shares issued)	71	71
Capital in excess of par value of stock	5,105	5,273
Foreign currency translation adjustments and other	594	189
Earnings retained for use in business	17,688	15,174
Total stockholders' equity	24,547	21,659
Total liabilities and stockholders' equity	$243,283	$219,622

*Less than $1 million.

they are usually referred to as either the **reciprocal accounts** or the **intercompany accounts.** In later chapters, you will see numerous other types of intercompany accounts that arise from intercompany transactions.

5. If the Investment in S Company balance were not eliminated (reclassified to equity) in consolidation, S Company's assets would be double counted because its individual assets are included in the consolidated totals. Thus consolidated assets would be $760,000 instead of $700,000 (the proper amount).

6. By eliminating S Company's Common Stock account, only P Company's equity—the equity of external shareholders to the consolidated entity—is reported in the consolidated column.

7. If S Company had issued par value common stock (instead of no par), the total of its Common Stock and Additional Paid-in Capital accounts would have a reciprocal balance relationship to the parent's Investment in S Company account.

8. As shown in Chapter 2 in consolidation worksheets that include income statements, this reciprocal relationship between the parent's Investment account and the subsidiary's equity accounts may or may not be maintained in future periods, depending on how the parent subsequently accounts for its investment in the subsidiary (discussed in Chapter 2).

IV   CONSOLIDATED STATEMENTS: CONCEPTUAL ISSUES

Many conceptual issues concerning consolidated statements exist. For discussion purposes, we separate these issues into (1) those that can apply to 100%-owned created subsidiaries in which no intercompany transactions take place (other than dividend payments) and (2) all other situations.

CONCEPTUAL ISSUES THAT CAN EXIST FOR 100%-OWNED CREATED SUBSIDIARIES— NO INTERCOMPANY TRANSACTIONS ASSUMED

When the parent-subsidiary relationship results from the parent's creation of a 100%-owned subsidiary and when no intercompany transactions occur between the parent and the subsidiary, only a few major conceptual issues can exist:

1. **Appropriateness of consolidating.** Is it appropriate to present consolidated statements in view of the fact that each company is a separate legal entity? The alternative is to present the separate company financial statements of the parent and the subsidiary, something not very practical for companies having numerous (exceeding 100 in some cases) subsidiaries.

2. **Potential for users to draw misleading inferences.** Does it make sense to show one combined amount for cash when restrictions exist on the transferability of cash within the consolidated group? For example, to protect creditors, federal and state laws restrict the ability of banks, savings and loans, and insurance subsidiaries to transfer cash to a parent or other subsidiaries. Would the parent's bondholders be misled into thinking all of the cash is available for liquidation of the bond indebtedness? Could this problem be eliminated by requiring extensive disclosures in notes to the consolidated statements regarding restrictions on asset transferability?

3. **Appropriateness of consolidating a subsidiary in a different line of business.** Would consolidated financial statements be understandable and meaningful if the subsidiary is in an entirely different industry than the parent, thereby having a radically different (1) asset composition, (2) debt-to-equity structure, and

(3) income statement format? Some claim that the activities of finance subsidiaries (the most controversial area of the unrelated businesses issue) would be submerged if they are consolidated instead of being disclosed in a note to the financial statements if not consolidated. On the other hand, consolidated statements do present the big picture. If consolidation is required, should the disaggregated format be mandatory to clearly set out these different industries? If the aggregated format is allowed, should industry segment information disclosures be required in notes to the consolidated statements?

4. **Appropriateness of consolidating foreign subsidiaries.** Should subsidiaries located in foreign countries be consolidated, even though they are exposed to several unique risks not faced by domestic subsidiaries? Such risks include (1) government seizure or confiscation of assets following political upheaval (as was done in Cuba, Iran, and Peru, for example) and (2) currency exchange restrictions (the subsidiary's inability to pay dividends to the parent).

CASE IN POINT

In 1992, both Ireland and Spain imposed controls on capital flows (payment of dividends to foreign parent companies) to stabilize their currencies, which speculators were driving down in value.

---

5. **Appropriateness of consolidating domestic subsidiaries having "blocked funds."** Should domestic subsidiaries that are prohibited from distributing their earnings to their parents be consolidated? Should guidelines be established for these situations, or should management use its best judgment? Would disclosure of these restrictions in the consolidated statements be sufficient?

The accounting profession's current rules governing consolidated statements in light of these conceptual issues are discussed later. Our purpose here was to merely acquaint you with these basic issues.

MAJOR CONCEPTUAL ISSUES EXISTING FOR OTHER SITUATIONS

Many additional conceptual issues arise when (1) the parent and subsidiary have intercompany transactions in which one party reports a profit or loss on the transaction, (2) the subsidiary is *less than* 100% owned or controlled by means other than common stock ownership, and (3) the subsidiary was *acquired* instead of *created*. These issues are addressed in later chapters.

V CONSOLIDATED STATEMENTS: CURRENT REPORTING STANDARDS

Before discussing the U.S. consolidation rules, it is useful to present a brief list of some consolidation practices that exist internationally to place our U.S. rules in perspective relative to those of other countries. Accordingly, please refer to the International Perspective on page 17.

The U.S. consolidation rules are more demanding than the consolidation rules of the foreign countries listed. The consolidation rules we present and discuss are the ones that the Financial Accounting Standards Board is currently proposing, as discussed in section VII, "The FASB's Current Project on Consolidations and Related Matters," pages 22–24.[6]

---

[6]When finalized, this new FASB standard will supersede both *Statement of Financial Accounting Standard No. 94*, "Consolidation of All Majority-owned Subsidiaries" (issued in 1987 to amend *ARB No. 51*) and *Accounting Research Bulletin No. 51*, "Consolidated Financial Statements" (issued in 1951).

Foreign Consolidation Practices

International Accounting Standards

The London-based International Accounting Standards Committee (formed in 1973) issues international accounting standards. However, compliance with its standards is voluntary. *International Accounting Standard 27*, "Consolidated Financial Statements and Accounting for Investments in Subsidiaries" (issued in 1987), requires all subsidiaries to be consolidated unless (1) control is likely to be temporary or (2) the subsidiary operates under severe long-term restrictions (e.g., foreign government restrictions) that limit its ability to transfer funds to the parent.

In practice, substantial diversity exists around the world concerning consolidated statements. Even in the European Union (EU), where member countries must abide by its Seventh Company Directive that requires consolidated reporting, the member countries have diverse consolidation rules because of the options and elections permitted under the Seventh Directive. Selected examples of this worldwide diversity follow:

Canada. All subsidiaries must be consolidated; consolidation ceases only when control is lost.

France. A subsidiary is excluded from consolidation if it is (1) in a dissimilar line of business from that of the parent and consolidation would be misleading, (2) insignificant, and (3) unable to prepare its statements on a timely basis.

Germany. A subsidiary may be excluded from consolidation if (1) it is immaterial, (2) the parent's right to control subsidiary assets or management are seriously impaired, (3) unreasonable expense or delays would be incurred, and (4) the investment is held solely for resale purposes.

Italy. Only listed companies need prepare consolidated statements. Even so, they are furnished as supplements to the parent company's separate statements.

Japan. A subsidiary may be excluded from consolidation if (1) consolidation would be misleading and (2) it is insignificant (not meeting a 10% size test). Consolidated statements are deemed supplementary information, which need be filed only with the government; accordingly, they are not widely disseminated to stockholders.

United Kingdom. A subsidiary may be excluded from consolidation if (1) it is immaterial, (2) severe long-term restrictions substantially impede the parent's exercise of its rights over management or subsidiary assets, (3) the investment is held exclusively with the intent to resell it (providing it was never previously consolidated), and (4) it is so dissimilar in nature that a true and fair view would not result (this exception is rarely allowed).

THE PURPOSE AND PRESUMPTION OF CONSOLIDATED STATEMENTS

Recall that the result of the consolidation process is to present financial statement information as if the group were a single company with one or more branches. Consequently, a presumption exists that consolidated statements are more meaningful, useful, and necessary for a fair presentation than are separate statements.

THE REQUIREMENT TO CONSOLIDATE ALL CONTROLLED ENTITIES

All controlled entities must be consolidated (with one exception discussed shortly). Thus consolidation is the general rule, not the exception. This rule makes consolidated statements the *general-purpose financial statements* of companies having one or more majority-owned subsidiaries.

Once a subsidiary is consolidated, it must continue to be consolidated until the parent loses control. One event that causes a parent to lose control occurs when a subsidiary files for bankruptcy protection; in such situations, **the bankruptcy court effectively controls the subsidiary.**

THE MEANING OF CONTROL
An entity that has the ability to elect a majority of the board of directors of another entity has control over it. **Control** enables a parent company to do as it pleases with the subsidiary's assets—as the parent can do with its own assets. Thus the parent can (1) direct the subsidiary to expand, contract, or distribute cash to the parent, (2) establish the subsidiary's financing

structure (debt versus equity levels), (3) enforce its will on the subsidiary's management by having the power to hire and fire it, and (4) set compensation levels for the subsidiary's management.

THE TWO TYPES OF CONTROL   One entity can attain either **legal control** (control by *legal* means) or **effective control** (control by *nonlegal* means) over another entity. Ownership of a majority of the subsidiary's outstanding voting shares gives the parent *legal control* because it has the legal right to elect a majority of the board of directors (a right that is enforceable by law). *Effective control* occurs when a majority of the board of directors can be elected by means other than by having legal control. Thus situations exist in which *50% or less* ownership may result in control.

DELAYED DISCUSSION OF EFFECTIVE CONTROL SITUATIONS AND LOSS OF CONTROL SITUATIONS

We delay until Chapter 3 a discussion of situations in which (1) one entity effectively controls another entity even though it owns 50% or less of the outstanding voting shares (such situations are encountered infrequently in U.S. practice) and (2) one entity owns more than 50% of the outstanding voting shares but has lost control (recall the earlier example of a subsidiary that has filed for bankruptcy protection). Thus all consolidation illustrations in Chapters 1 and 2 assume that *legal control* exists.

Our government officials evidently do not fully understand the concept of control, as the following Case in Point reveals.

CASE IN POINT

Does the Government Understand the Concept of Control?

In 1995 the federal government, by an executive order, prohibited all trade by U.S. companies with Iran (this is above and beyond the executive order issued in 1979 mentioned earlier). The executive order also applies to foreign subsidiaries of U.S. companies. Government officials stated, however, that foreign subsidiaries of U.S. companies can continue buying Iranian oil, providing that those subsidiaries are autonomous and not controlled, run, or directed by U.S. companies.

WHAT IF THE PARENT CHOOSES *NOT* TO EXERCISE ITS POWERS?   When a parent has a "hands-off" decentralized operating philosophy, its status as a controlling entity is unchanged. Thus consolidation is still required.

RESTRICTIONS OF CONTROL POWERS

A subsidiary *can* still be consolidated if the parent's control powers are restricted—depending on the severity and expected length of the restriction (a judgment call). Two examples of restrictions are when (1) a foreign government prohibits a foreign-owned subsidiary from paying dividends and (2) regulatory authorities prohibit a domestic bank or savings and loan subsidiary from paying dividends until the subsidiary's financial condition improves.

THE ONE ALLOWABLE EXCEPTION TO CONSOLIDATING A CONTROLLED ENTITY

The only exception to consolidation that is allowed when **control exists is when control is expected to be temporary** (a one-year time frame is used) at the date a subsidiary was *acquired* in a business combination (external expansion). For example, assume that (1) Partex acquires Sartex on January 1, 19X1, (2) Sartex has 12 subsidiaries, (3) the Justice Department has ordered Partex to sell Subsidiary 7 because Partex's ownership results in significantly lessened competition, and (4) Partex wishes to dispose of Subsidiary 11 because it is in an undesired line of business.

Partex *cannot* consolidate Subsidiary 7 if it has been ordered to sell Subsidiary 7 within one year of January 1, 19X1. Partex *cannot* consolidate Subsidiary 11 if management has a plan and a reasonable expectation of disposing of it by December 31, 19X1. Absent these conditions, these two subsidiaries must be consolidated.

THE MOST CONTROVERSIAL ISSUE: WHETHER TO CONSOLIDATE NONHOMOGENEOUS SUBSIDIARIES

Prior to 1987, the consolidation rules permitted a parent *not* to consolidate a subsidiary in a different line of business than the parent (commonly referred to as the *nonhomogeneity exception*). Beginning in the 1960s, many businesses began to be more diverse and complex. For example, many companies previously considered nonfinancial in the scope of their operations diversified into financial services (financing, insurance, leasing, investment banking, and real estate).

The liabilities carried by unconsolidated financial subsidiaries had become enormous, contributing greatly to the growing "off-balance-sheet financing" controversy. Practice had become quite diverse. Some companies consolidated such subsidiaries; others did not.

In 1987 the FASB eliminated the homogeneity exception.[7] The requirement to consolidate these subsidiaries has drastically changed the reported assets, liabilities, and resulting financial analysis ratios of many companies. For example, Ford Motor Company, which did *not* consolidate its financial services subsidiary prior to 1987, reports financial services assets and liabilities of $170 billion and $157 billion, respectively, in its consolidated balance sheet at the end of 1995 (shown on page 11)—compared to automotive assets and liabilities of $73 billion and $61 billion, respectively. Consequently, its debt-to-equity ratio using these statements is approximately 9:1 instead of 5:1 (the difference was fourfold for 1988, the first year under the new rules).

The consolidation of nonhomogeneous subsidiaries is highly controversial. To look at the pros and cons of this issue, we (1) present the major criticisms of the 1987 rule and (2) discuss the shortcomings that existed under the pre-1987 rule. In this chapter, balance sheet issues are examined; income statement issues are examined in Chapter 2.

CRITICISMS OF AND PROBLEMS WITH THE CONSOLIDATION OF SUBSIDIARIES IN DIVERSE LINES OF BUSINESS   The requirement to consolidate subsidiaries in unrelated businesses has *not* been overwhelmingly accepted by financial statement preparers and users. Many believe that this rule should be repealed, and some of their reasons follow:

1. The fundamental nature of the business is *not* clearly evident. For example, General Motors, now fully consolidated, looks like a finance company with a car division instead of a car company with a finance division. When GMAC (GM's finance subsidiary) was reported as an investment as a result of *not* being consolidated, the magnitude of the finance receivables and payables did not swamp the automobile accounts.

[7]This rule change was implemented as a result of the issuance of *Statement of Financial Accounting Standard No. 94*, "Consolidation of All Majority-owned Subsidiaries" (Stamford: Financial Accounting Standards Board, 1987). This pronouncement amended *Accounting Research Bulletin No. 51*, "Consolidated Financial Statements" (issued in 1951), the governing pronouncement at the time.

2. The debt-to-equity ratio on a consolidated basis, which often is far higher than on an unconsolidated basis, usually is not used by (1) lenders because they extend credit on an entity-by-entity basis or (2) the parent's stockholders because they perceive the subsidiary as a service and are concerned with the parent's ratio. The consolidated debt-to-equity ratio becomes even more irrelevant when the subsidiary has substantial debt that is *not* guaranteed by the parent.

3. The financial ratios produced are *not* industry oriented. Thus valid comparisons cannot be made with the financial ratios of competing entities.

4. Financial analysis is now much more difficult for analysts who prefer to evaluate a group on a disaggregated basis. (See Chapter 15 for a discussion of disaggregated reporting, its shortcomings, and its advantages.

CRITICISMS OF AND PROBLEMS WITH THE *NONCONSOLIDATION* OF SUBSIDIARIES IN DIVERSE LINES OF BUSINESS   The pre-1987 practice of allowing the exclusion of unrelated businesses also had its share of criticisms and reporting problems.[8]

1. Critics claimed that it did not portray a comprehensive representation of the economic entity—especially when the subsidiary's operations were functionally related to the parent, such as for a captive finance (credit or leasing) subsidiary that effectively purchased the parent's receivables.

2. The parent's debt-to-equity ratio (a *leverage* ratio) was usually much lower when captive finance subsidiaries were excluded, thus not presenting the true capital structure of the economic entity. Also, *liquidity* ratios were often significantly higher than under consolidated reporting.

3. The business relationship of the subsidiary to the parent was not always disclosed.

4. Condensed balance sheet information required to be disclosed for unconsolidated subsidiaries (pursuant to *APB Opinion No. 18*, "The Equity Method of Accounting") ranged from a complete set of financial statements to one-line disclosures of total assets and total equity, with information on the subsidiary's long-term debt ranging from complete to nonexistent. The subsidiary's intercompany receivable (or payable) was not disclosed in a uniform manner; it was either shown separately or combined with the subsidiary's equity.

5. The parent reported its equity in the subsidiary's net income in diverse manners, such as (1) a component of consolidated revenues, (2) a separate line item in arriving at operating income, (3) a separate line item below operating income (either before tax or net of tax), or (4) netted against the parent's interest expense.

6. Collection costs relating to receivables were effectively shifted to captive subsidiaries formed to buy the parents' receivables, enabling parent companies to report higher operating income.

CONFORMITY OF ACCOUNTING POLICIES

When different accounting methods are permitted for the same type of transactions or events, the subsidiary *need not* use the same method the parent uses. For exam-

---

[8]For a fuller discussion, see Martin L. Gosman and Philip E. Meyer, "*SFAS No. 94*'s Effect on Liquidity Disclosure," *Accounting Horizons*, March 1992, pp. 88–100; James B. Heian and James B. Thies, "Consolidation of Finance Subsidiaries: $230 Billion in Off-Balance-Sheet Financing Comes Home to Roost," *Accounting Horizons*, March 1989, pp. 1–9; and Joseph C. Rue and David E. Tosh, "Should We Consolidate Finance Subsidiaries?" *Management Accounting*, April 1987, pp. 45–50.

ple, the parent could use the first-in, first-out method for inventory costing and the subsidiary could use the last-in, last-out method.

If a foreign subsidiary uses an accounting method *not* allowed under U.S. reporting standards (GAAP), the subsidiary's financial statements must be *restated* to U.S. GAAP before consolidation (and before translation into U.S. dollars, as explained in Chapter 18).

VI DISCLOSURES REQUIRED

FISCAL PERIODS DO NOT CONFORM

A subsidiary's financial statements must cover the same period as the parent's financial statements—unless it is *not* practicable to achieve conformity. If conformity is *not* practicable, disclosure is necessary of (1) that fact, (2) the reasons that it is not practicable, (3) the period covered by the subsidiary's statements, and (4) any material and unrecognized events occurring during the "gap" period.

In the vast majority of instances, conformity occurs because (1) parents and their subsidiaries have the same fiscal year-end and (2) the ability to send financial statements over telephone lines enables subsidiaries to submit financial information on a timely basis. When a parent allows a subsidiary to have a fiscal year-end different than its own, the subsidiary's financial information will be from two different fiscal years to cover the same period as the parent's financial information (a fact that need *not* be disclosed).

CONSOLIDATION PROCEDURES

As we discuss in detail in later chapters, all intercompany transactions between a parent and its subsidiaries are eliminated (undone) in preparing consolidated statements. Thus the consolidated results are as if none of the intercompany transactions had occurred. A disclosure that intercompany transactions have been eliminated must be made. Briefly, intercompany transactions are eliminated because, from a consolidated perspective, they are **internal transactions**—only transactions with third parties outside the consolidated entity can be reported in the consolidated statements.

To illustrate, assume that (1) P Company lent $6,000 to S Company during 19X1 and (2) the $6,000 has *not* been repaid at year-end. In consolidation at year-end, the following consolidation entry is made:

WORKSHEET ENTRY ONLY	Intercompany Payable 6,000	
	Intercompany Receivable	6,000

If the loan were interest bearing, the Intercompany Interest Income and Intercompany Interest Expense accounts also are eliminated in consolidation as follows:

WORKSHEET ENTRY ONLY	Intercompany Interest Income 400	
	Intercompany Interest Expense	400

Neither entry affects the group net income or equity, but the effects on the gross array of accounts can be dramatic in some instances. How to "undo" more complex intercompany transactions for consolidated reporting purposes is discussed in Chapters 9 through 12.

INDUSTRY SEGMENTS AND FOREIGN GEOGRAPHIC AREAS

Because of the limitations of consolidated statements, *Statement of Financial Accounting Standard No. 14*, "Financial Reporting for Segments of a Business Enterprise," was issued in 1976. It requires specified information on industry segments and foreign operations to be presented as *supplementary information* to the consolidated statements.[9] This pronouncement, which is discussed at length in Chapter 15, imposes extensive public reporting requirements on companies with diversified or foreign operations.

RESTRICTIONS ON A SUBSIDIARY'S ABILITY TO TRANSFER FUNDS TO ITS PARENT

A reader of consolidated statements is entitled to presume that cash can be freely transferred within the consolidated group unless he or she is informed otherwise. When a subsidiary *cannot* distribute some or all of its earnings to its parent, the ramification is that it may limit the parent's ability to (1) pay dividends to its stockholders or (2) pay for its corporate expenses.

THE SECURITIES AND EXCHANGE COMMISSION'S (SEC'S) DISCLOSURE RULES CONCERNING RESTRICTIONS When a subsidiary of a publicly owned company is restricted from transferring funds to its parent in the form of cash dividends, loans, or advances (such as the result of borrowing arrangements, regulatory restraints, or foreign government actions), the SEC requires disclosure of (1) the nature of the restriction and (2) the amounts of restricted net assets for consolidated subsidiaries. In general, however, disclosure is required only if the **restricted net assets** of all subsidiaries (including any unconsolidated subsidiaries) **exceed 25% of consolidated net assets.**[10]

Bank subsidiaries, savings and loan subsidiaries, and insurance subsidiaries usually have significant fund transferability restrictions imposed by law or regulatory agencies, thereby usually requiring such disclosures. See the Case in Point on page 23 for an example.

VII THE FASB'S CURRENT PROJECT ON CONSOLIDATIONS AND RELATED MATTERS

THE REASONS FOR THIS PROJECT

The Financial Accounting Standards Board currently has underway an all-encompassing project dealing with the issues associated with consolidated financial statements. The reason for this reexamination of the issues resulted from (1) the increased use of subsidiaries in unrelated industries, (2) the emergence of innovative arrangements apparently designed to circumvent the existing consolidation rules, (3) the need to address areas not covered by existing rules, and (4) the need to take a fresh look at rules issued more than 35 years ago in a different environment.

---

[9]The term *supplementary information* has a precise meaning in accounting and auditing literature. It refers to GAAP–required information to be included with the historical cost basis financial statements.

[10]Rule 4–08 (e) of Article 4 (Rules of General Application) of Regulation S–X.

CASE IN POINT

Disclosure of Fund Transferability Limitations for Citicorp's Banking Subsidiaries

14. Citicorp (Parent Company Only)

The Parent Company is a legal entity separate and distinct from Citibank, N.A. and its other subsidiaries and affiliates. There are various legal limitations on the extent to which Citicorp's banking subsidiaries may extend credit, pay dividends or otherwise supply funds to Citicorp. The approval of the Office of the Comptroller of the Currency is required if total dividends declared by a national bank in any calendar year exceed net profits (as defined) for that year combined with its retained net profits for the preceding two years. In addition, dividends for such a bank may not be paid in excess of the bank's undivided profits. State-chartered bank subsidiaries are subject to dividend limitations imposed by applicable state law.

Citicorp's national and state-chartered bank subsidiaries can declare dividends to their respective parent companies in 1996, without regulatory approval, of approximately $3.9 billion, adjusted by the effect of their net income (loss) for 1996 up to the date of any such dividend declaration. In determining whether and to what extent to pay dividends, each bank subsidiary must also consider the effect of dividend payments on applicable risk-based capital and leverage ratio requirements as well as policy statements of the federal regulatory agencies that indicate that banking organi-

zations should generally pay dividends out of current operating earnings. Consistent with these considerations, Citicorp estimates that its bank subsidiaries can distribute dividends to Citicorp of approximately $3.5 billion of the available $3.9 billion, adjusted by the effect of their net income (loss) up to the date of any such dividend declaration.

Citicorp also receives dividends from its non-bank subsidiaries. These nonbank subsidiaries are generally not subject to regulatory restrictions on their payment of dividends except that the approval of the Office of Thrift Supervision may be required if total dividends declared by a savings association in any calendar year exceed amounts specified in that agency's regulations.

Source: Citicorp's 1995 annual report.
Note: In 1992, the Office of the Comptroller of the Currency and the Federal Reserve Bank of New York imposed strict regulatory controls on Citibank, the nation's largest bank and a subsidiary of Citicorp. One of those controls was the **prohibition of paying any dividends.** In 1994, these controls were lifted because Citibank had recovered financially from its weakened condition, which had resulted from an excessive number of problem loans. **In both 1992 and 1993, Citicorp still consolidated Citibank—a judgment call.**

PROGRESS TO DATE

This project contains five phases; the nature and status of each phase are as follows and provide a preview of subsequent chapters:

1. **Phase 1 [active]: Policies and Procedures** (Exposure draft issued in October 1995). Phase 1 is the most important phase of the FASB's consolidation issues project. This phase will be completed when the exposure draft (entitled "Consolidated Financial Statements: Policy and Procedures") is finalized in a standard. This new standard's major change will be to modify the *ownership-level-based* consolidation rules (*legal control*) to *control-based* consolidation rules, the latter being similar to those of the SEC and the European Union.

   As this book goes to print, the FASB is close to finalizing this new standard. In May 1996, the FASB modified its exposure draft position on certain issues to address concerns raised by respondents and participants at the public hearings held in February 1996.

   Accordingly, the consolidation rules we present and discuss are the ones set forth in the FASB's May 1996 *working draft* document. The FASB expects to finalize its consolidation policy and procedural rules in early 1997.

2. **Phase 2 [active]: Reporting Disaggregated Information** (Exposure draft issued in 1996). This phase is a reexamination of FASB *Statement No. 14*, "Segment Reporting," discussed in Chapter 15.

3. **Phase 3 [inactive]: New Basis of Accounting** (Discussion memorandum issued in 1991). This phase is peculiar to external expansion and special types of ownership changes, which we discuss in Chapter 8.

4. **Phase 4 [inactive]: Accounting for Investments in Unconsolidated Entities.** This phase addresses accounting for investments in *noncontrolled* corporations and partnerships, including joint ventures (50%-ownership situations). No substantive work has begun yet. In Chapter 3, we discuss subsidiaries that are *not* consolidated because control no longer exists.

5. **Phase 5 [inactive]: Similar Matters (in Phases 2, 3, and 4) for Not-for-Profit Entities.** The exposure draft document mentioned in Phase 1 applies to not-for-profit entities as well as to business enterprises.

END-OF-CHAPTER REVIEW

SUMMARY OF KEY POINTS

1. Consolidated statements (which can be in a **disaggregated** or **aggregated** format) constitute the **general-purpose financial statements** for reporting to stockholders.
2. The **purpose of consolidated statements** is to present a single set of financial statements as if the parent and its subsidiaries were a **single company** having one or more divisions; the separate legal entity status of each company within the consolidated group is disregarded.
3. The result of the consolidation process is the **substitution** of the subsidiary's assets and liabilities for the Investment in Subsidiary account on the parent's books.
4. Consolidation entries are **worksheet entries**—never to be posted to the general ledger—because a general ledger is *not* kept for the consolidated entity.
5. U.S. GAAP requires that all subsidiaries be consolidated unless (1) **control** is lacking or (2) if at the date control is obtained over an *acquired* subsidiary, such control is expected to be **temporary.**
6. **Control** over a subsidiary means that the parent can use the subsidiary's assets in the same manner as its own assets.
7. The normal means of control is ownership of *more than* 50% of the outstanding voting shares **(legal control).**
8. Control can exist when *50% or fewer* of the voting shares of an entity are owned **(effective control).** Also, control *may not* exist even though *more than* 50% of the voting shares are owned.
9. All **intercompany receivables and payables** must be eliminated (offset against each other) in consolidation.
10. Significant cash transfer restrictions placed on a subsidiary must be disclosed in notes to the consolidated statements.

GLOSSARY OF NEW TERMS

Aggregated format   A format that does *not* display the subsidiary's financial statement accounts separately in the consolidated statements.

Branch (division)   An extension of an existing legal entity.

Centralized accounting   A system in which the transactions for a branch are recorded in the home office's general ledger.

Consolidation   The process of combining the financial statements of a parent and one or more subsidiaries to present financial position and results of operations as though the separate companies were a single company with one or more divisions or branches.

Consolidation worksheet   A working paper or spreadsheet in which the financial statements of a parent and its subsidiaries are consolidated using elimination entries.

Corporate charter   A document issued by a state or country that grants legal entity status to a business being incorporated.

Decentralized accounting   A system in which a subsidiary or branch maintains its own general ledger.

Disaggregated format   A format that displays the subsidiary's financial statement accounts separately in the consolidated statements in a "layered" manner.

Effective control   The ability to control an entity by means other than majority ownership (legal control).

External expansion   The expansion of a business by combining with another existing business.

General-purpose financial statements   The financial statements used for reporting to stockholders.

Group (consolidated group)   A manner of referring to a parent and its subsidiaries collectively.

Holding company   An entity that has no operations of its own but only investments in one or more subsidiaries.

Home office   The headquarters office of the legal entity that establishes a branch.

Intercompany accounts (reciprocal accounts)   Accounts in different general ledgers for which the debit balance in one account (or set of accounts) equals the credit balance in the other account (or set of accounts). In parent-subsidiary relationships, the Investment in Subsidiary account on the parent's books can be maintained so that its balance equals the sum of the Common Stock, Additional Paid-in Capital, and Retained Earnings accounts on the subsidiary's books.

Internal expansion   The expansion of a business by constructing or leasing additional facilities at an existing or outlying location.

Legal control   The ability to control an entity by ownership of more than 50% of the entity's outstanding voting shares.

Net assets   The difference between an entity's assets and liabilities.

Parent   A company that controls another company (usually achieved by direct or indirect ownership of more than 50% of the voting interest).

Parent-company-only statements   The unconsolidated financial statements of a parent company.

Pro forma   A manner of presenting financial information on an "as-if" basis.

Reciprocal accounts   See *intercompany accounts*.

Statutory merger   A legal term referring to the loss of a subsidiary's corporate legal entity status by canceling its corporate charter. The parent takes title to the subsidiary's assets and assumes responsibility for its liabilities. Thus the subsidiary is transformed into a branch.

Subsidiary   A company controlled by another company (usually resulting from direct or indirect ownership of more than 50% of the voting interest).

SELF-STUDY QUESTIONS

(Answers are at the end of this chapter.)

1. The economic resources that (normally) underlie the parent's investment in a subsidiary are the subsidiary's
   a. Assets.   **b.** Net assets.   **c.** Equity.   **d.** Noncurrent assets.
2. In a *disaggregated* consolidated balance sheet, the subsidiary's assets are
   a. Netted against its liabilities and shown as a net amount.
   b. Not included.
   c. Shown separately.
   d. Summed with the parent's assets.
3. Consolidation entries are
   a. Recorded in the parent's general ledger.
   b. Posted only to the consolidation worksheet.
   c. Recorded in the consolidated entity's general ledger.
   d. Reversed at the beginning of the following year.
4. A parent *cannot* consolidate a subsidiary that
   a. Is in an unrelated line of business.
   b. Is in a foreign country.
   c. Has a different year-end.
   d. Has filed for bankruptcy protection.

5. *Legal control* always exists when a subsidiary is
   a. Wholly owned.
   b. More than 50% owned.
   c. More than 50% owned or wholly owned.
   d. Effectively controlled.

6. A subsidiary is unable to distribute dividends because of restrictions imposed by regulatory authorities. The parent should always
   a. Consolidate the subsidiary anyway.
   b. Not consolidate the subsidiary and present the subsidiary's condensed financial statements in a note.
   c. Not consolidate the subsidiary and explain why.
   d. Use its judgment in determining whether to consolidate the subsidiary.

7. In the absence of other factors, a parent usually does *not* consolidate a subsidiary that
   a. Was created and has been sold under a contract of sale—closing of sale not yet consummated.
   b. Was created and is expected to be sold within one year.
   c. Was acquired but control is expected to be temporary.
   d. Is in a different line of business and is located in a foreign country.
   e. Is reporting such large losses that the subsidiary is no longer viewed as being a going concern.

ASSIGNMENT MATERIAL

REVIEW QUESTIONS

1. What are the advantages of the *subsidiary* organization form?
2. What are the advantages of the *branch/division* organization form?
3. Does establishing a subsidiary always legally insulate the parent's operations from the subsidiary's operations?
4. How can a company expand into an industry prohibited by its corporate charter?
5. What is a *holding company*?
6. What underlies the parent's Investment account?
7. What is the concept of consolidated statements?
8. What does the term *general-purpose financial statements* mean?
9. What two types of consolidated balance sheets can be issued? When does it make most sense to use each type?
10. Is a general ledger maintained for the consolidated reporting entity? Why or why not?
11. How important are *consolidation worksheets* relative to the parent's general ledger?
12. Are *consolidation elimination entries* posted to a general ledger? Why or why not?
13. What is the definition of the term *intercompany transaction*?
14. What does *intercompany accounts* mean?
15. What do *reciprocal balances* and *reciprocal accounts* mean? In a parent-subsidiary relationship, what are the reciprocal accounts?
16. What would be the reporting results if the reciprocal accounts were *not eliminated* in consolidation?
17. What is the formal name for a *consolidation worksheet*?
18. How are many of the limitations of consolidated statements overcome?
19. What is the usual condition for *control* by one entity over another entity?
20. What does having control enable a parent to do?
21. What does the term *nonhomogeneity exception* mean?
22. What are the exceptions to the general rule requiring consolidation of all subsidiaries?
23. What types of disclosures typically accompany consolidated statements?
24. **Computers and Spreadsheets:** The term *booting the computer* is a metaphor. Can you explain this metaphor?

EXERCISES

E 1—1 **Subsidiary or Branch: Choose Wisely** Each item in the left-hand column represents various corporate objectives in connection with establishing a new foreign operation. To the right of these items is a list of possible forms of organization.

Corporate Objectives	Possible Forms of Organization
1. To legally insulate the new operation.	A. U.S. subsidiary.
2. To minimize paying U.S. income taxes on the foreign operation's earnings.	B. Foreign subsidiary.
3. To pay U.S. taxes currently on the foreign operation's earnings.	C. Branch.
4. To restrict the ability of foreign tax authorities to examine the U.S. operation's records.	D. U.S. subsidiary having a foreign branch.
5. To have complete ownership of the foreign operation.	E. Foreign subsidiary having a foreign branch.
6. To share ownership of the foreign operation with local foreign citizens.	
7. To retain patent protection.	
8. To retain patent protection and to legally insulate the new operation.	
9. To retain patent protection and to minimize paying U.S. income taxes on the foreign operation's earnings.	
10. To retain patent protection, to legally insulate the new operation, and to minimize paying U.S. income taxes on the foreign operation's earnings.	

Required   For each corporate objective, which of the possible choices in the right-hand column accomplish that objective? If an objective has more than one possible answer, your first choice should be the one that accomplishes the objective in the simplest manner.

E 1–2   Consolidation Theory

1. Which item does *not* occur as a result of the consolidation process?
   a. The parent's equity is decreased.
   b. The parent's Investment account disappears.
   c. The subsidiary's equity disappears.
   d. The subsidiary's net assets are substituted for the parent's Investment account.
2. Which of the following items is *false* concerning the consolidation process?
   a. The entry made in consolidation is essentially a reclassification entry.
   b. The parent's Investment account is reported as a long-term treasury stock investment in the noncurrent asset section of the consolidation balance sheet.
   c. The entry made in consolidation accomplishes a substitution process.
   d. A double counting of the subsidiary's net assets is avoided.
3. Which of the following items is *true* concerning the consolidation process?
   a. The subsidiary's equity is combined with the parent's equity.
   b. The disaggregated reporting format is automatically achieved.
   c. The entry made in consolidation is posted to the parent's general ledger.
   d. A pro forma presentation is achieved.

E 1–3   Consolidation Rules

1. A parent normally consolidates a *created* subsidiary that
   a. Is a captive finance subsidiary created to furnish financing to the parent's retail customers.
   b. Is expected to be sold in the very near future.
   c. Is in an entirely different line of business.
   d. Is located in a developing country.
   e. Is described by items *a* through *d*.
2. Which of the following is an *acceptable* reason for excluding a subsidiary from consolidation?
   a. The subsidiary's assets equal its liabilities.
   b. Currency transfer restrictions prevent the subsidiary from paying dividends.
   c. The subsidiary has substantial intercompany inventory sales to its parent.
   d. The parent presents the subsidiary's separate financial statements in the parent's annual report.
3. Which of the following statements is *true*?
   a. The *disaggregated* reporting format is *not* allowed.
   b. The parent and subsidiary must have the same year-end to be consolidated.

    c. A subsidiary *need not* be consolidated if the parent requires the subsidiary to reinvest all of its earnings and not pay any dividends.

    d. The *aggregated* reporting format is acceptable for a subsidiary in a completely different line of business than the parent.

E 1–4 **Consolidation Worksheet Entries** The following accounts exist on the separate company financial statements of a parent and its newly created subsidiary at the end of 19X1:

	Parent's Books	Subsidiary's Books
Investment in subsidiary	$400,000	
Intercompany receivable	50,000	
Common stock		$100,000
Additional paid-in capital		300,000
Intercompany payable		50,000

Assume that the subsidiary has not yet commenced operations and therefore has no income statement account activity for 19X1.

Required What are the consolidation elimination entry(ies) at 12/31/X1?

E 1–5 **Consolidation Worksheet Entries** On 4/1/X1, Piltco created Siltco as a 100%-owned subsidiary. Piltco made a cash investment of $500,000 by purchasing 1,000 shares of Siltco's $5 par value common stock. For 19X1, Siltco reported net income of $66,000 and declared no dividends. At 12/31/X1, the carrying amount of Piltco's investment in Siltco was its initial investment of $500,000.

Required 1. What is the required consolidation elimination entry as of 12/31/X1?

    2. Should Siltco's retained earnings at year-end be reported in the consolidated balance sheet? Why or why not? If so, how?

E 1–6 **Intercompany Receivables and Payables** At 12/31/X1, Plethora had the following receivables and payables with its subsidiaries, all of which are consolidated except Sebco:

	Receivables	Payables
Advance (long term) to Sabco	$100,000	
Interest receivable from Sebco	20,000	
Interest payable to Sibco		$ 30,000
Long-term receivable from Sobco	400,000	
Intercompany payable to Subco		55,000
Long-term payable to Subco		600,000

Required 1. In the consolidated balance sheet at 12/31/X1, what net amount should Plethora report as being receivable from its subsidiaries?

    2. Repeat Question 1 for payables instead of receivables.

✳ THINKING CRITICALLY ✳

✳ CASES ✳

C 1–1 **Lending to a Parent: Extra Caution Needed?** Pyne Inc. is the parent of Syne Inc., a 100%-owned subsidiary created many years ago. Pyne is a holding company in the process of issuing debenture bonds to the public through an investment banking firm (the underwriter). The bond proceeds will be lent to Syne under a lending agreement having the same interest rate and repayment terms of the bond offering (this use of proceeds information is disclosed in the bond offering prospectus).

Required 1. What financial statements do you think should be provided to potential bond investors for their review before buying the bonds? Why?

    2. Can you think of any special concerns that potential bond investors should have because of the existence of the *parent-subsidiary* form of organization instead of a *home office–branch* form of organization?

C 1–2 **Lending to a Subsidiary: Extra Caution Needed?** Poma Inc. is the parent of Soma Inc., a 100%-owned subsidiary created many years ago. A bank is considering making a loan to Soma, which is financially strong. Poma will *not* be guaranteeing the loan.

Required 1. Would the *consolidated* financial statements or the *subsidiary's* separate financial statements (or both) be useful to the bank? Why?
2. If the parent were to file for bankruptcy under Chapter 7 of the bankruptcy statutes (the *liquidation* chapter), would the parent's creditors have a legal claim against the subsidiary's assets—either on a parity with the subsidiary's creditors or a higher priority than the subsidiary's creditors—in settling creditor claims? Why or why not?
3. Can you think of two major special restrictions the bank might insist on to protect the loan to Soma because of its subsidiary status?

C 1–3 **Foreign Subsidiary with Currency Transfer Restrictions: Is This Really Any Big Deal?** Pilla has a 100%-owned foreign subsidiary, Silla. The foreign government recently imposed currency transfer restrictions on all local companies owned by foreign corporations. Accordingly, Silla cannot declare any dividends.

Required 1. What reporting issue does this restriction raise?
2. What factors are relevant in deciding how to resolve this issue?
3. What reporting issue is raised for parent-company-only statements that Pilla must issue to its major lender?

C 1–4 **How to Save Taxes and Distribute Foreign Earnings** Pisa Company is forming a foreign subsidiary in a country having a high tax rate (relative to the United States). The foreign country's laws will make it difficult for the subsidiary to pay dividends.

Required How might the parent avoid these problems in setting up the capital structure of the subsidiary?

✳ FINANCIAL ANALYSIS PROBLEMS ✳

FAP 1–1 **The Social Security "Trust" Fund: Real or Imaginary—Will a Consolidated Perspective Reveal the Truth?** Around the year 2010, the "baby-boom" generation (those born shortly after World War II) will begin reaching retirement age. Accordingly, in a single decade (while the overall population increases by only 2%), a 30% increase in the number of citizens eligible for social security retirement benefits will occur. As a result, the ratio of retirees to workers will increase markedly. Consequently, the government must either (1) increase social security taxes significantly between 2010 and 2030 or (2) increase social security taxes prior to 2010 and set aside the additional taxes collected in a trust fund (to be invested until needed).

In 1983, the federal government chose the latter course. Consequently, it abandoned the "pay-as-you-go" system used for nearly a half century. (Under that system, social security taxes collected equaled the benefits that were paid out each year.) The excess FICA taxes collected and put into the trust fund each year are commonly referred to as the *surplus* (approximately $65 billion for 1995). At the end of 1995, the Social Security Trust Fund totaled approximately $500 billion. (This amount is expected eventually to increase to over $2 trillion.) The Social Security Administration has invested the funds in U.S. Treasury bonds.

Required 1. Taking a *consolidated* perspective, what conclusions would you draw?
2. Why would an agency of the federal government purchase Treasury bonds from the U.S. Treasury Department? (*Hint:* You need to know what the Treasury Department does with the money received.)
3. What conclusion would you draw if the $500 billion had been lent to private corporations?

FAP 1–2 **Real Estate Transaction Involving Controlled Entities** Pye Inc. owns Sye Savings and Loan, which in turn owns 100% of Tye Realty. Tye owns several parcels of undeveloped land on the outskirts of Phoenix, Arizona. On 4/1/X1, Tye sold its Hidden Valley parcel to Dymo Development for $16 million. Tye had purchased this parcel two years before for $5 million.

Dymo made a cash down payment of $4 million to Tye and issued a $12 million, 10% promissory note for the balance. Dymo, which is thinly capitalized (at $30,000), borrowed $4 million from Sye Savings and Loan to make the $4 million cash down payment. Under current GAAP, the minimum down payment needed to recognize profit on a real estate sale is 25%. Pye, Sye, and Tye are audited by the same firm of certified public accountants, Lowe, Price, and Sells.

Required   May Pye report this transaction as a sale in its 19X1 consolidated statements?

✳ PERSONAL SITUATIONS: ETHICS AND INTERPERSONAL SKILLS ✳

PS 1–1   **Ethics: Let's Shaft the Subsidiary's Creditors**   Subco is a financially healthy, 100%-owned subsidiary of Pubco, which, in contrast, has serious financial problems (liabilities exceed the fair market value of its assets). On 4/1/X1, Pubco liquidated Subco into a division under allowable provisions of state corporation law. On 8/15/X1, Pubco filed for bankruptcy protection under Chapter 11 of the federal bankruptcy statutes.

Required   1. What are the ramifications of this liquidation to Subco's unsecured creditors? Do these creditors have any legal redress?
2. Why might Pubco have liquidated Subco?
3. Was liquidating Subco into a division ethical in this situation?
4. In retrospect, what precautions should Subco's unsecured creditors have taken in dealing with it?

PS 1–2   **Ethics: Suspicious Upstream Cash Transfers—What's an Auditor to Do?**   You are the outside auditor for a parent and its subsidiary. The subsidiary is a financial institution, which regulatory authorities have prohibited from paying dividends until its financial condition improves. During the audit, you notice several unusually large cash payments from the subsidiary to the parent to pay for management services. You suspect that these payments are dividends in disguise.

Required   1. What audit procedures would you perform to determine whether these cash payments are bona fide?
2. If you conclude that these payments are illegal, should you report them to the appropriate regulatory authorities? If not, what would you do?

PS 1–3   **Interpersonal Skills: Does It Do Any Good to Express Anger?**   As accountants move higher within organizations, they usually assume supervisory responsibilities over certain employees. Occasionally, the performance of these employees will not be to the accountant's satisfaction. Sometimes this occurs when deadlines are tight and everyone is working substantial amounts of overtime—situations in which the likelihood of becoming upset and expressing anger is high.

Required   1. If a supervisor expresses anger, what probably is the intended effect on the employee?
2. What most likely will be the unintended effect on the working relationship?
3. What might be an alternative and better emotion for one to feel and possibly express when things go wrong?
4. What do you think studies have shown as to the long-term effect on individuals who continually become angry when things go wrong?

ANSWERS TO SELF-STUDY QUESTIONS

1. a   **2.** c   **3.** b   **4.** d   **5.** c   **6.** d   **7.** c

WHOLLY OWNED SUBSIDIARIES: POSTCREATION PERIODS

2

TO UNDERSTAND

- The cost method and the equity method of valuing a parent's investment in a subsidiary.
- The way to prepare a full set of consolidated statements at reporting dates subsequent to the creation date of a subsidiary.
- The way to present a parent's separate financial statements in notes to the consolidated statements when required.

TOPIC OUTLINE

One who does not read great books has no advantage over one who cannot read great books.

MARK TWAIN

For periods subsequent to a subsidiary's creation, consolidated statements are prepared at each financial reporting date. The consolidation entries at these future dates depend on how the parent values its investment in the subsidiary after the initial investment.

Any company that makes an investment must decide how to value that investment at future reporting dates. For investments in common stock of 100%-owned subsidiaries, two valuation methods have evolved: the *cost method* and the *equity method*. These valuation methods, which are at the opposite ends of the conceptual spectrum, are explained in this chapter.

Because the carrying value of a parent's investment differs under the cost method and the equity method at postcreation financial reporting dates, the basic elimination entry at these dates will differ slightly under each of the methods as to both (1) amounts and (2) certain accounts. We explain the consolidation procedures peculiar to each valuation method.

THE BIG PICTURE

From a **consolidated reporting perspective,** however, it does *not* matter which method a parent uses to value its investment in a subsidiary because the Investment in Subsidiary account is always eliminated in preparing consolidated statements. **The key point is that all of the consolidated amounts are the same no matter which method a parent uses to account for its investment in a subsidiary.** Thus valuing investments in subsidiaries is usually **an internal reporting issue—** *not* **an external reporting issue.**

Most publicly owned banks and savings and loans must also present the parent company's separate statements (**parent-company-only statements**) in a note to the consolidated statements. We discuss the very detailed disclosures required in this note by the Securities and Exchange Commission (SEC), which has certain regulatory powers over these entities.

I   METHODS FOR VALUING INVESTMENTS IN COMMON STOCK

The current rules for valuing all corporate investments in common stocks can be categorized and **stated generally** as follows:

1. **Control exists by means of stock ownership [the subsidiary must be consolidated].** If the investor **owns more than 50% of the voting shares,** the investor can use either the **cost method** or the **equity method.** These situations are governed by *APBO No. 18*, "The Equity Method of Accounting for Investments in Common Stock" (introduced in intermediate accounting texts). These situations are the subject of this chapter. (Although not evident by its title, *APBO No. 18* also discusses the cost method in detail.)

2. **Control does** *not* **exist but more than 50% of the voting stock is owned [the subsidiary** *cannot* **be consolidated].** Either the **cost method,** the **equity method,** or the **fair value method** may be used, as appropriate. These situations are governed by *APBO No. 18* and *SFAS No. 115*, "Accounting for Certain Investments in Debt and Equity Securities" (also introduced in intermediate accounting texts). These situations are discussed in Chapter 3 in the section dealing with unconsolidated subsidiaries.

3. **Significant influence exists [typical ownership level: 20–50%].** If it exerts significant influence over the investee *and* **does not own more than 50% of the vot-**

ing shares, the investor must use the equity method. These situations are (1) governed by *APBO No. 18* and (2) addressed fully in intermediate accounting texts.

4. *No* Significant Influence Exists [typical ownership level: less than 20%]. If it does *not* exert significant influence over the investee, the investor must use its cost or the fair value, depending on whether the investee's stock has a readily determinable fair value. These situations are (1) governed by *SFAS No. 115* and (2) addressed fully in intermediate accounting texts.

II THE COST METHOD OF VALUING A PARENT'S INVESTMENT

Fundamental to addressing the way to value a parent's investment in a subsidiary is the issue of determining what to report as the parent's income on its investment in the subsidiary. Two choices are possible: it must report (1) the **dividends** received from the subsidiary (the *distributed* earnings) or (2) the subsidiary's **earnings** (includes both *distributed* and *undistributed* earnings).

THE WAY THE COST METHOD WORKS

Under the cost method, the parent's investment income is limited to dividends it receives from the subsidiary. Thus **the parent reports investment income only when the subsidiary declares dividends.** In years in which the subsidiary declares a dividend, the parent credits its *Dividend Income* account—with the offsetting debit being to *Dividends Receivable* (or the Cash account if it is paid the same day). Because the parent reports only the subsidiary's dividends as its investment income, it ignores the subsidiary's earnings and losses. Consequently, the carrying value of the parent's investment remains constant—unless an impairment of value occurs.[1]

IMPAIRMENT OF VALUE If the subsidiary reports losses, these too are ignored—unless they result in reducing the subsidiary's equity to below the carrying value of the parent's investment. In such cases, **if serious doubt exists as to realization of the investment, a permanent write-down** is made. The result of a write-down is the establishment of a **new cost basis**—the investment cannot be written back up to original cost if the subsidiary later reports profits.

DETERMINING THE AMOUNT OF A WRITE-DOWN When an impairment of value has occurred, the amount to which the investment should be written down under the *cost method* is largely a judgment call. Writing down the investment to the book value of the subsidiary's net assets certainly is a justifiable possibility. *SFAS No. 121,* "Accounting for the Impairment of Long-Lived Assets and for Long-Lived Assets to Be Disposed Of" is *not* applicable to investments in common stock. However, the guidance in that pronouncement applied to this situation also justifies a valuation based on using the present value of estimated expected future cash flows.

THE RATIONALE OF THE COST METHOD

The general idea of the cost method is that income on the parent's investment should be recognized only to the extent that it has been realized. Because it ignores the subsidiary's reported earnings results and focuses instead on dividends, the

---

[1]An exception to this general statement occurs in the case of *liquidating dividends*, something that may happen with an *acquired* subsidiary (as opposed to a *created* subsidiary), as discussed in Chapter 6.

cost method produces a **conservative** (although usually unrealistic) **carrying value** for profitable subsidiaries.

CRITIQUE OF THE COST METHOD

The cost method makes sense only when conservatism is warranted. Such conservatism may be appropriate when realization of the subsidiary's undistributed earnings is in doubt. The most common such situation is when a foreign subsidiary is unable to pay cash dividends because of (1) government-imposed currency transfer restrictions (often to support the value of the local currency) or (2) when the foreign country's banks continually have a very limited number of dollars available for the subsidiary to purchase to pay dividends.

A major criticism of the cost method is that the parent (by having control) can manipulate the subsidiary's dividend policy to report income at the parent level as it pleases. For example, a parent could require the subsidiary to pay dividends only in years in which the parent has losses or depressed earnings on its own separate operations. As shown later, however, this is not an issue if the subsidiary's financial statements are consolidated with those of the parent (the typical situation). Thus **the parent can manipulate only its own book net income—not the consolidated net income.**

After discussing the equity method, we present a comparative illustration of the equity method and the cost method (Illustration 2–1 on page 36). You may want to review the cost method portion of that illustration at this point.

III THE EQUITY METHOD OF VALUING A PARENT'S INVESTMENT: BASIC SITUATIONS

HOW THE EQUITY METHOD WORKS

Under the equity method, the parent's investment income is deemed to be the subsidiary's earnings—**whether or not they are distributed.** Procedurally, the parent's interest in a subsidiary's earnings is reflected as an upward adjustment of the Investment in Subsidiary account; the parent effectively has more capital invested in the subsidiary.[2] Increasing the carrying value of the Investment in Subsidiary account is somewhat analogous to updating a bank savings passbook for interest earned that one leaves invested in the bank. The offsetting credit is reported as investment income in the parent's income statement (the account Equity in Net Income of Subsidiary is used).

SUBSIDIARY'S LOSSES If the subsidiary reports **losses,** the carrying value of the parent's investment account is **decreased** and **the parent records an investment loss on its income statement** (the account Equity in Net Loss of Subsidiary is used).

SUBSIDIARY'S DIVIDENDS **Cash dividends** declared by the subsidiary (which can easily be paid the same day in parent-subsidiary relationships) are treated as a **liquidation of the investment**—the parent has less capital invested in the subsidiary than before the dividend declaration. Accordingly, cash dividends are credited to the Investment in Subsidiary account **at the declaration date,** and the offsetting debit is made to the Dividends Receivable account (or the Cash account if paid the same day as declared). Reducing the carrying value of the Investment ac-

---

[2]The result is as if the parent had instructed the subsidiary to pay a cash dividend equal to its net income and the parent had then made an additional cash investment equal to the cash dividend it received.

count for dividends is somewhat analogous to withdrawing a portion of the interest that has been accumulated in a savings account.

THE RATIONALE OF THE EQUITY METHOD

The general idea of the **equity method** is that the earnings generated by the subsidiary "belong" to the parent. Accordingly, those earnings should be "accrued" on the parent's books (an asset)—even though the accrued asset (given an appropriate descriptive name in accordance with its substance) is **unrealized** in nature.

When the subsidiary distributes some or all of its earnings to the parent (as dividends), the parent has **realized** those earnings (Cash goes up and the accrued asset goes down).

CRITIQUE OF THE EQUITY METHOD

Note that as a result of these procedures, the carrying value of the investment always equals the subsidiary's net assets—**the economic resources underlying the parent's investment.** Thus the equity method reflects in the Investment in Subsidiary account the increase or decrease in the subsidiary's net assets based on the economic activity (earnings and distributions) occurring at the subsidiary as determined under the accrual basis. Consequently, the equity method perfectly matches reporting earnings and losses based on the economic transactions and events affecting the subsidiary.

DISTINGUISHING BETWEEN ADJUSTED CARRYING VALUE AND MARKET VALUE

The valuation of the parent's investment in a subsidiary under the equity method is only as good as the accounting practices and estimates the subsidiary uses. Furthermore, the valuation produced under the equity method is *not* necessarily the market value of the subsidiary's common stock—the parent may be able to sell its common stock investment at more or less than the carrying value.[3]

IV COMPARING THE COST METHOD WITH THE EQUITY METHOD

Illustration 2–1 shows how the carrying value of the Investment account for a 100%-owned created subsidiary is adjusted under each method for several years of assumed earnings, losses, and dividends.

REVIEW POINTS FOR ILLUSTRATION 2–1   Note the following:

1. Under the *equity method*, the Investment account's carrying value parallels the subsidiary's reported equity—this *always* occurs when the subsidiary's equity is **positive** (*negative* situations are discussed later).

2. Under the *cost method*, the amount to which the Investment account is written down establishes a **new cost basis,** which may *not* be written back up.

3. Under the *cost method*, no write-down was made at the end of 19X3, even though the $70,000 loss for 19X3 would certainly raise the issue of whether the original

---

[3]The concept of lower of cost or market is generally not applied to subsidiaries. An exception exists for an unconsolidated, partially owned subsidiary in which the common stock shares not owned by the parent are actively traded on a stock exchange (discussed in Chapter 3). For 100%-owned subsidiaries, such trading cannot occur, and, accordingly, no ready market price exists.

ILLUSTRATION 2-1	Comparison of the Cost and Equity Methods

I. General Ledger Accounts

	Investment in Subsidiary				Subsidiary's Equity
	Cost Method		Equity Method		
Initial capital investment	$100,000		$100,000		$100,000
19X1 Net income			35,000		35,000
19X1 Dividends declared				15,000	(15,000)
Balances, 12/31/X1	$100,000		$120,000		$120,000
19X2 Net income			40,000		40,000
19X2 Dividends declared				50,000	(50,000)
Balances, 12/31/X2	$100,000		$110,000		$110,000
19X3 Net loss				70,000	(70,000)
Balances, 12/31/X3	$100,000		$ 40,000		$ 40,000
19X4 Net income		55,000[a]	5,000		5,000
Balances, 12/31/X4	$ 45,000		$ 45,000		$ 45,000

[a]This assumes that the parent concluded that the recoverability of its investment was in substantial doubt, thus warranting a permanent write-down. The write-down could have been any amount; here we assumed that it should be to the net assets of the subsidiary.

II. General Ledger Journal Entries

	Cost Method		Equity Method	

19X1

Investment in Subsidiary			35,000	
Equity in Net Income (of S Co.)......................				35,000
Dividends Receivable....................................	15,000[a]		15,000[a]	
Investment in Subsidiary				15,000
Dividend Income (from S Co.)		15,000		

19X2

Investment in Subsidiary			40,000	
Equity in Net Income (of S Co.)......................				40,000
Dividends Receivable....................................	50,000[a]		50,000[a]	
Investment in Subsidiary				50,000
Dividend Income (from S Co.)		50,000		

19X3

Equity in Net Loss (of S Co.)			70,000	
Investment in Subsidiary				70,000

19X4

Investment in Subsidiary			5,000	
Equity in Net Income (of S Co.)......................				5,000
Loss on Investment (in S Co.)	55,000			
Investment in Subsidiary		55,000		
To write down the investment as a result of concluding that its value has been permanently impaired.				

[a]When the dividend is paid, Cash is debited and Dividends Receivable is credited.

$100,000 investment could be recovered at the end of 19X3. We assumed here that management concluded that the $100,000 was fully recoverable at that date (but that it was *not* fully recoverable one year later).

4. If management believed the subsidiary could be sold at the end of 19X4 for, say, $80,000, then only a $20,000 write-down (instead of $55,000) would have been made under the *cost method*.

ILLUSTRATION 2–2	Summary of the Cost and Equity Methods		
		Cost Method	Equity Method
Subsidiary's Earnings:			
Increases Investment account		No	Yes
Report as investment income		No	Yes
Subsidiary's Losses:			
Decreases Investment account		No[a]	Yes[b]
Report as investment loss		No[a]	Yes
Subsidiary's Dividends Declared:			
Reduces Investment account		No	Yes
Report as dividend income		Yes	No
Investment account may be written back up after a write-down		No	Yes
Investment account's carrying value normally equals the subsidiary's net assets		No	Yes[c]
Event That Impacts the *Parent's* Retained Earnings:			
Earnings and losses		No	Yes
Dividend declarations		Yes	No

[a]Unless the parent concludes that serious doubt exists as to recoverability of the investment.

[b]The Investment in Subsidiary account can (1) be written down to a zero balance or (2) become a negative balance (classified as a liability in the parent's separate statements) when the parent is obligated to invest additional funds into the subsidiary (as discussed later in the section The Equity Method of Valuing a Parent's Investment: Total Investment Loss Situations).

[c]This equality usually does not exist for "acquired" subsidiaries (as shown in Chapters 5 and 6).

5. How the Investment account is carried on the parent's books is irrelevant from a consolidated perspective because the Investment account is *always* eliminated in consolidation.

Illustration 2–2 summarizes the accounting under the equity method and the cost method.

WHETHER TO USE THE COST METHOD OR THE EQUITY METHOD

Both the *cost method* and the *equity method* are widely used in practice.[4] Accordingly, we generally give equal prominence to each method throughout the consolidation chapters.

[4]Both of these methods are used for income tax–reporting purposes. The Internal Revenue Code, however, uses the terms *cash basis* (instead of *cost method*) and *accrual basis* (instead of *equity method*) because it addresses the area from the perspective of the taxable income to be reported on the parent's investment—not the manner of determining the tax basis of the parent's investment (which is the "other side of the coin"). In most cases, the *cash basis* is required, with the *accrual basis* required only for certain types of foreign income characterized as *passive income.* Income tax issues pertaining to consolidated statements are discussed in appendices to Chapter 3 (for domestic subsidiaries) and 19 (for foreign subsidiaries).

ADVANTAGES OF THE COST METHOD

The cost method involves less bookkeeping by the parent than does the equity method because it is *not* necessary to record the subsidiary's earnings on the parent's books under the cost method. Entries are necessary only when the subsidiary declares dividends.

ADVANTAGES OF THE EQUITY METHOD

In addition to more closely reflecting the probable market value of the investment (which could be significantly more or less than the equity method carrying value), the following are other advantages of the equity method:

1. **It provides built-in self-checking features in the consolidation process.** As shown shortly, the equity method provides two useful self-checking features in preparing consolidated statements (the consolidated net income and the consolidated retained earnings amounts always equal the parent's net income and parent's retained earnings amounts, respectively), which can make the consolidation effort easier. Under the *cost method*, no such features exist.

2. **It enables parent-company-only (PCO) statements to articulate with the consolidated statements.** Often PCO statements must be presented either (1) in a condensed manner in a note to the consolidated statements or (2) separately (uncondensed) for reporting to a parent's creditor pursuant to a loan agreement requirement. We discuss the importance of this articulation later.

3. **It enables PCO statements to be used more meaningfully internally.** To the extent that PCO statements are used for internal management purposes, they are usually meaningful only if investments in subsidiaries are accounted for under the equity method. Under the cost method, such statements can become of limited usefulness.

4. **It facilitates financial analysis.** By tracking the amount invested (including the reinvestment of the subsidiary's undistributed earnings), meaningful return-on-investment (ROI) calculations can be made readily. Using the amounts produced by the cost method usually gives artificial and nonmeaningful percentages (recall that the parent controls the subsidiary's dividend policy). Accordingly, if the cost method is used, meaningful ROI percentages can be obtained only by using amounts as if the equity method were being used instead. Illustration 2–3 shows how the ROI percentages can be (1) greatly different for the two methods and (2) arbitrarily determined under the cost method (the amounts used in the illustration are from Illustration 2–1).

5. **It achieves a "one-line consolidation."** When a subsidiary is *not* consolidated and is reported under the *equity method,* the equity method is often viewed as a *one-line consolidation.* This happens because the subsidiary's earnings are reported on one line in the parent's income statement (using the Equity in Net Income of Subsidiary account[5]) instead of the subsidiary's sales, cost of sales, and expenses.

   Likewise in the parent's balance sheet, one account (the Investment in Subsidiary account[6]) is reported instead of the individual assets and liabilities of the subsidiary. Thus the amounts for both net income and retained earnings reported to the parent's stockholders are identical whether the subsidiary is consolidated or not.

---

[5]The analogy is to an income statement that displays only a net income amount and none of the elements it comprises, that is, sales, cost of sales, expenses, gains, and losses.

[6]The analogy is to a balance sheet that shows only the stockholders' equity, not the assets and liabilities, the net of which equals the stockholders' equity.

ILLUSTRATION 2–3	Parent's Annual[a] Return on Investment (AROI) Calculations			
		Cost Method		**Equity Method**

19X1:	$\dfrac{\text{Net Income}}{\text{Beginning Investment}}$	$\dfrac{\$15,000}{\$100,000} = 15\%$	$\dfrac{\$35,000}{\$100,000} = 35\%$
19X2:	$\dfrac{\text{Net Income}}{\text{Beginning Investment}}$	$\dfrac{\$50,000}{\$100,000} = 50\%$	$\dfrac{\$40,000}{\$120,000} = 33\%$
19X3:	$\dfrac{\text{Net Income}}{\text{Beginning Investment}}$	$\dfrac{\$\text{–0–}}{\$100,000} = 0\%$	$\dfrac{\$(70,000)}{\$110,000} = (64)\%$
19X4:	$\dfrac{\text{Net Income}}{\text{Beginning Investment}}$	$\dfrac{\$(55,000)}{\$100,000} = (55)\%$	$\dfrac{\$5,000}{\$40,000} = 12\%$

Source of these dollar amounts: Illustration 2–1.

Average annual return on investment (AROI) (4 years) . 2.5%   4%

Internal rate of return . . . . 1.9%[b]

[a]Some texts call these calculations the *"accounting" return on investment.* We use the more descriptive term *annual.*

[b]Using the following actual and assumed cash flows:

Initial investment	$(100,000)
End of Year 1 (dividends)	15,000
End of Year 2 (dividends)	50,000
End of Year 3	–0–
End of Year 4 (Assumes the subsidiary was sold at this time for an amount equal to the book value of its net assets)	45,000

Note: Some view the internal rate of return (IRR) as the most reliable indicator of an investment's "true" profitability. However, the IRR calculation (which covers four years and cannot tell anything regarding any particular year's profitability) can be compared only to the average of the AROIs—not to the AROI for an individual year. Thus the IRR and the AROI calculations serve entirely different purposes.

Therefore, the only difference between furnishing the parent's stockholders (1) unconsolidated statements reflecting the equity method and (2) consolidated statements is the manner of presenting amounts (gross or net) pertaining to the subsidiary within the income statement and balance sheet furnished to these stockholders.

V CONSOLIDATION WORKSHEETS: THE COST METHOD

In preparing consolidated statements at dates subsequent to the creation date, it is also necessary to prepare a consolidated income statement and a consolidated statement of retained earnings.

THREE-TIER ARTICULATION FORMAT OF THE CONSOLIDATION WORKSHEET

These two additional statements can be readily prepared when the consolidated balance sheet is prepared by having the three statements articulate with one another on the worksheet, having (1) the net income line of the income statement tie into the net income line in the statement of retained earnings and (2) the ending balance line in the statement of retained earnings tie into the retained earnings line in the balance sheet.

This tie-in is accomplished in the Debit and Credit columns by carrying forward their totals from one statement to the next. At this point, you may want to familiarize yourself with the format of such a consolidation worksheet (see page 42).

CONSOLIDATING THE BALANCE SHEETS: THE BASIC ELIMINATION ENTRY

As long as no write-down has been made, the basic elimination entry is always the same as the basic elimination entry used at the date the subsidiary was created. With the initial investment being $60,000, that entry is as follows:

WORKSHEET ENTRY ONLY	Common Stock	60,000	
	Investment in Subsidiary		60,000

Recall from Chapter 1 that the purpose of this entry is to substitute the subsidiary's assets and liabilities for the Investment in Subsidiary account.

CONSOLIDATING THE INCOME STATEMENTS: THE INTERCOMPANY DIVIDEND ELIMINATION ENTRY

On the worksheet, the sales, cost of sales, and expenses of both companies are summed, and the parent's Dividend Income account is "eliminated" (prevented from being reported in the Consolidated column). Eliminating the **Dividend Income account in consolidation** prevents partial double counting of the subsidiary's earnings. Thus the subsidiary's income statement accounts are effectively substituted for the parent's Dividend Income account. This substitution is accomplished using a separate consolidation entry, which we call the *intercompany dividend elimination entry*. Using assumed dividend amounts, that entry at assumed consolidation dates is as follows:

		Consolidation Date	
		December 31, 19X1	**December 31, 19X2**
WORKSHEET ENTRY ONLY	Dividend Income (from S Co.)	4,000	12,000
	Dividends Declared	4,000	12,000

CONSOLIDATING THE STATEMENTS OF RETAINED EARNINGS

To arrive at consolidated retained earnings, the parent's beginning and ending retained earnings—**an amount that includes only those earnings of the subsidiary that *have* been distributed to the parent in the form of dividends**—are added to the subsidiary's beginning and ending retained earnings—**the earnings that have *not* been distributed to the parent.**

ELIMINATING THE SUBSIDIARY'S DIVIDENDS DECLARED   Recall from Chapter 1 that from a consolidated perspective, a subsidiary's outstanding common stock is treated as *not* being outstanding (just as treasury stock is treated). Thus it would be illogical and inconsistent to add a subsidiary's dividends declared to the parent's dividends declared in the statement of retained earnings. Consequently, in preparing the consolidated statement of retained earnings, dividends declared by a subsidiary are eliminated. **Thus a subsidiary's dividends are *not* summed with the parent's dividends on the consolidation worksheet.**

A Subsidiary's Dividend Is an Intercompany Transaction A dividend declared by a 100%-owned subsidiary is *not* a dividend from the consolidated group to the parent's stockholders. It is only one of many types of intercompany transactions. Recall from Chapter 1 that *all* intercompany transactions are eliminated in consolidation because they are **internal transactions** (taking place entirely within the consolidated group)—as contrasted with **external transactions** (taking place entirely with outside unrelated parties). Prior to payment, an intercompany payable and intercompany receivable merely exist. Upon payment, cash is transferred from the subsidiary to the parent—**thus the cash never leaves the consolidated entity.**

The *Nonimpact* of the Intercompany Dividend Elimination Entry on the Consolidated Balance Sheet The intercompany dividend elimination entry does *not* affect the balance sheet because the debit is carried forward from the income statement to the net income line in the statement of retained earnings section of the worksheet. **Thus the entry has a "wash" effect on the ending retained earnings.** Note that the entry serves a twofold purpose: (1) to consolidate the income statement by preventing the dividend income recorded by the parent from appearing in the Consolidated column because this would result in partially double counting the subsidiary's net income and (2) to prevent the subsidiary's dividends from being added to the parent's dividends in arriving at the consolidated dividends declared.

Illustrations 2–4 and 2–5 show the consolidation worksheets as of December 31, 19X1 (the first year subsequent to the creation date) and December 31, 19X2 (the second year subsequent to the creation date), assuming that the parent uses the cost method.

Review Points for Illustrations 2–4 and 2–5 Note the following:

1. P Company's Retained Earnings account under the *cost method* includes **only those earnings that have been distributed through dividends,** whereas P Company's Retained Earnings account under the *equity method* includes *all* of S Company's earnings.

2. S Company's beginning and ending retained earnings were added to P Company's beginning and ending retained earnings, respectively, to obtain the beginning and ending consolidated retained earnings amounts. This *always* occurs for subsidiaries created by the parent. (For *acquired* subsidiaries, which are discussed in Chapter 6, it does *not* hold true.)

VI CONSOLIDATION WORKSHEETS: THE EQUITY METHOD

Recall that the consolidated amounts are *always* identical—regardless of whether the parent uses the *cost method* or the *equity method*. Accordingly, the consolidation entry or entries must be *slightly* different—in both amounts and accounts used—when the parent uses the *equity method* versus the *cost method*.

This difference results because the parent has recorded on its books the subsidiary's *undistributed* earnings (as well as the subsidiary's *distributed* earnings, which are the only earnings recorded under the *cost method*). Consequently, to prevent double counting the subsidiary's undistributed earnings (its entire retained earnings balance), it is necessary to eliminate in consolidation *all* amounts presented in the subsidiary's analysis of retained earnings.

When the parent uses the *equity method*, only the basic elimination entry is needed. It is much more encompassing than the one shown earlier for the cost

ILLUSTRATION 2–4	Cost Method: First Year Subsequent to Date of Creation

P Company and S Company
Consolidation Worksheet as of December 31, 19X1

	P Company	S Company	Consolidation Entries Dr.	Consolidation Entries Cr.	Consolidated
Income Statement (19X1)					
Sales	600,000	234,000			834,000
Cost of sales	(360,000)	(110,000)			(470,000)
Expenses	(190,000)	(100,000)			(290,000)
Dividend income (from S Co.) . . .	4,000		4,000(2)		–0–
Net Income	54,000	24,000	4,000		74,000
Statement of Retained Earnings					
Balances, 1/1/X1	100,000	–0–			100,000
+ Net income	54,000	24,000	4,000		74,000
– Dividends declared	(51,000)	(4,000)		4,000(2)	(51,000)
Balances, 12/31/X1	103,000	20,000	4,000	4,000	123,000
Balance Sheet					
Cash	65,000	11,000			76,000
Accounts receivable	75,000	37,000			112,000
Inventory	110,000	55,000			165,000
Investment in S Company	60,000			60,000(1)	–0–
Land	220,000	30,000			250,000
Buildings and equipment	500,000	150,000			650,000
Accumulated depreciation	(320,000)	(13,000)			(333,000)
Total Assets	710,000	270,000		60,000	920,000
Payables and accruals	157,000	70,000			227,000
Long-term debt	250,000	120,000			370,000
P Company:					
Common stock	200,000				200,000
Retained earnings	103,000				103,000
S Company:					
Common stock		60,000	60,000(1)		–0–
Retained earnings		20,000	4,000	4,000	20,000
Total Liabilities and Equity . .	710,000	270,000	64,000	4,000	920,000
Proof of debit and credit postings			64,000	64,000	

Explanation of entries:
(1) The basic elimination entry.
(2) The intercompany dividend elimination entry.

Recap of Retained Earnings

P Company	$103,000
S Company	20,000
Total	$123,000

method, however—it includes amounts for the subsidiary's current earnings, dividends declared, and beginning retained earnings.

The amounts used in the basic elimination entry at each consolidation date can be readily obtained by updating an analysis of the parent's Investment account. Recall from Chapter 1 that this analysis shows the reciprocal relationship between the parent's Investment account and the subsidiary's equity accounts.

Such an analysis is presented in Illustration 2–6, which shows assumed amounts for earnings and dividends of S Company for two years subsequent to its creation date of December 31, 19X0. Also shown there are the basic elimination entries (as derived from the updated analysis) required in consolidation as of December 31, 19X1 (one year after the subsidiary's creation date), and December 31, 19X2 (two years after the creation date).

ILLUSTRATION 2–5	Cost Method: Second Year Subsequent to Date of Creation

P Company and S Company
Consolidation Worksheet as of December 31, 19X2

	P Company	S Company	Consolidation Entries Dr.	Consolidation Entries Cr.	Consolidated
Income Statement (19X2)					
Sales	710,000	282,000			992,000
Cost of sales	(390,000)	(130,000)			(520,000)
Expenses	(210,000)	(120,000)			(330,000)
Dividend income (from S Co.) . . .	12,000		12,000(2)		–0–
Net Income	122,000	32,000	12,000		142,000
Statement of Retained Earnings					
Balances, 1/1/X2	103,000	20,000			123,000
+ Net income	122,000	32,000	12,000		142,000
– Dividends declared	(85,000)	(12,000)		12,000(2)	(85,000)
Balances, 12/31/X2	140,000	40,000	12,000	12,000	180,000
Balance Sheet					
Cash	66,000	31,000			97,000
Accounts receivable	84,000	43,000			127,000
Inventory	140,000	82,000			222,000
Investment in S Company	60,000			60,000(1)	–0–
Land	220,000	30,000			250,000
Buildings and equipment	500,000	150,000			650,000
Accumulated depreciation	(360,000)	(26,000)			(386,000)
Total Assets	710,000	310,000		60,000	960,000
Payables and accruals	160,000	90,000			250,000
Long-term debt	210,000	120,000			330,000
P Company:					
Common stock	200,000				200,000
Retained earnings	140,000				140,000
S Company:					
Common stock		60,000	60,000(1)		–0–
Retained earnings		40,000	12,000	12,000	40,000
Total Liabilities and Equity . .	710,000	310,000	72,000	12,000	960,000
Proof of debit and credit postings			72,000	72,000	

Explanation of entries:
(1) The basic elimination entry.
(2) The intercompany dividend elimination entry.

Recap of Retained Earnings

P Company	$140,000
S Company	40,000
Total	$180,000

REVIEW POINTS FOR ILLUSTRATION 2–6 Note the following:

1. **The debit to the Equity in Net Income of Subsidiary account.** Summing the sales, cost of sales, and expenses of both entities without eliminating this account double counts the subsidiary's net income in the Consolidated column. (Recall that under the *cost method*, the Dividend Income account was debited.)

2. **The credit to the Dividends Declared account.** This credit posting accomplishes the same result as the identical credit posting used in the intercompany dividend elimination entry for the *cost method* shown earlier.

3. **The manner of eliminating the subsidiary's Retained Earnings account.** Unlike the Common Stock account, which is debited at each date using its *end-of-year*

ILLUSTRATION 2–6 | **Preparing and Updating the Analysis of the Parent's Investment Account**

	Parent's Investment Account	=	Subsidiary's Equity Accounts		
			Common Stock	+	Retained Earnings
Balances, Dec. 31, 19X0	$ 60,000		$60,000		$ –0–
+ Equity in net income	24,000				24,000
– Dividends	(4,000)				(4,000)
Balances, Dec. 31, 19X1	$ 80,000		$60,000		$20,000
+ Equity in net income	32,000				32,000
– Dividends	(12,000)				(12,000)
Balances, Dec. 31, 19X2	$100,000		$60,000		$40,000

The Basic Elimination Entry

		Consolidation Date			
		December 31, 19X1		December 31, 19X2	
WORKSHEET ENTRIES ONLY	Common Stock	60,000		60,000	
	Retained Earnings, 1/1/X1 and 1/1/X2 ..	–0–		20,000	
	Equity in Net Income (of S Co.)	24,000		32,000	
	Dividends Declared		4,000		12,000
	Investment in Subsidiary		80,000		100,000

Note: The analysis is a powerful tool. In later chapters, we show how it can be expanded to readily handle more involved aspects of consolidations.

---

balance, the end-of-year Retained Earnings account is *not* debited using the end-of-year balance. It is necessary to eliminate *all* amounts in the subsidiary's analysis of retained earnings—as well as the ending balance in the balance sheet.

4. **The effect on the subsidiary's statement of retained earnings.** The combination of (1) the direct postings to the analysis of retained earnings (for the beginning balance and dividends declared) and (2) the carryforward from the income statement to the net income line in the analysis of retained earnings result in eliminating *all* of the balances in the subsidiary's statement of retained earnings. Thus the Consolidated column reports only the parent's amounts.

5. **The effect on the balance sheet.** The total of the eliminations in the analysis of retained earnings is then carried forward to the subsidiary's retained earnings line in the balance sheet. This carryforward process results in eliminating the end-of-year balance in this account—as though a debit amount equal to the year-end balance had been directly posted to this **reciprocal account.**

Illustrations 2–7 and 2–8 show the consolidation worksheets as of December 31, 19X1 (one year after the creation date), and December 31, 19X2 (two years after the creation date), using the preceding basic elimination entries.

REVIEW POINTS FOR ILLUSTRATIONS 2–7 AND 2–8 Note the following:

1. The consolidated net income is the same as P Company's net income **(a built-in checking feature).**

2. The consolidated retained earnings is the same as P Company's retained earnings **(another built-in checking feature).**

3. As in Chapter 1, all of the subsidiary's stockholder's equity accounts (the total of which is the reciprocal balance of the parent's Investment account) have been eliminated.

	ILLUSTRATION 2–7		Equity Method: First Year Subsequent to Date of Creation			

P Company and S Company
Consolidation Worksheet as of December 31, 19X1

	P Company	S Company	Consolidation Entries Dr.	Consolidation Entries Cr.	Consolidated
Income Statement (19X1)					
Sales	600,000	234,000			834,000
Cost of sales	(360,000)	(110,000)			(470,000)
Expenses	(190,000)	(100,000)			(290,000)
Equity in net income (of S Co.)	24,000		24,000(1)		–0–
Net Income	74,000	24,000	24,000		74,000
Statement of Retained Earnings					
Balances, 1/1/X1	100,000	–0–			100,000
+ Net income	74,000	24,000	24,000		74,000
– Dividends declared	(51,000)	(4,000)		4,000(1)	(51,000)
Balances, 12/31/X1	123,000	20,000	24,000	4,000	123,000
Balance Sheet					
Cash	65,000	11,000			76,000
Accounts receivable	75,000	37,000			112,000
Inventory	110,000	55,000			165,000
Investment in S Company	80,000			80,000(1)	–0–
Land	220,000	30,000			250,000
Buildings and equipment	500,000	150,000			650,000
Accumulated depreciation	(320,000)	(13,000)			(333,000)
Total Assets	730,000	270,000		80,000	920,000
Payables and accruals	157,000	70,000			227,000
Long-term debt	250,000	120,000			370,000
P Company:					
Common stock	200,000				200,000
Retained earnings	123,000				123,000
S Company:					
Common stock		60,000	60,000(1)		–0–
Retained earnings		20,000	24,000	4,000	–0–
Total Liabilities and Equity	730,000	270,000	84,000	4,000	920,000
Proof of debit and credit postings			84,000	84,000	

Explanation of entry:
(1) The basic elimination entry.

4. The amounts in the P Company column that pertain to the subsidiary differ from the subsidiary-related amounts in Illustrations 2–4 (page 42) and 2–5 (page 43), the comparable consolidation worksheets at these dates when the cost method is used. Yet **the amounts in the Consolidated column are the same.**

VII PRESENTING PARENT-COMPANY-ONLY STATEMENTS IN NOTES TO THE CONSOLIDATED STATEMENTS

In the United States, consolidated statements have primacy relative to parent-company-only statements. PCO statements, when presented, are usually in a

ILLUSTRATION 2–8	Equity Method: Second Year Subsequent to Date of Creation

P Company and S Company
Consolidation Worksheet as of December 31, 19X2

	P Company	S Company	Consolidation Entries Dr.	Consolidation Entries Cr.	Consolidated
Income Statement (19X2)					
Sales	710,000	282,000			992,000
Cost of sales	(390,000)	(130,000)			(520,000)
Expenses	(210,000)	(120,000)			(330,000)
Equity in net income (of S Co.)	32,000		32,000(1)		–0–
Net Income	142,000	32,000	32,000		142,000
Statement of Retained Earnings					
Balances 1/1/X2	123,000	20,000	20,000(1)		123,000
+ Net income	142,000	32,000	32,000		142,000
– Dividends declared	(85,000)	(12,000)		12,000(1)	(85,000)
Balances, 12/31/X2	180,000	40,000	52,000	12,000	180,000
Balance Sheet					
Cash	66,000	31,000			97,000
Accounts receivable	84,000	43,000			127,000
Inventory	140,000	82,000			222,000
Investment in S Company	100,000			100,000(1)	–0–
Land	220,000	30,000			250,000
Buildings and equipment	500,000	150,000			650,000
Accumulated depreciation	(360,000)	(26,000)			(386,000)
Total Assets	750,000	310,000		100,000	960,000
Payables and accruals	160,000	90,000			250,000
Long-term debt	210,000	120,000			330,000
P Company:					
Common stock	200,000				200,000
Retained earnings	180,000				180,000
S Company:					
Common stock		60,000	60,000(1)		–0–
Retained earnings		40,000	52,000	12,000	–0–
Total Liabilities and Equity	750,000	310,000	112,000	12,000	960,000
Proof of debit and credit postings			112,000	112,000	

Explanation of entry:
(1) The basic elimination entry.

condensed form in notes to the consolidated statements; they are usually presented only if required by the Securities and Exchange Commission.

SPECIAL RULES FOR CERTAIN HOLDING COMPANIES

Many U.S. banks and savings and loans are subsidiaries of **holding companies.** A holding company has no operations of its own—only investments in other companies that have operations. Concerning banks, federal law and bank regulations impose certain restrictions on transactions between a bank holding company and a bank subsidiary that is a federally insured depository institution.

The major restriction is that such a bank subsidiary may pay cash dividends to its parent company only if certain capital levels (as determined by the regulatory

---

INTERNATIONAL PERSPECTIVE

Widespread Use of Parent-Company-Only Statements Overseas

In many foreign countries, PCO statements are on a level higher than or equal to the consolidated statements—but not to their exclusion. The practices for selected countries follow:

France. A full set (not condensed) of PCO statements must be published separately (not just in a note to the consolidated statements). These statements are usually included in the annual report containing the consolidated statements.

Italy. PCO statements are the statutory-required statements, whereas the consolidated statements are presented as additional disclosures to the PCO statements.

Japan. PCO statements (uncondensed) are the required statements for reporting to creditors and stockholders. Consolidated statements are supplementary.

Spain. Consolidated statements must be presented separately from the PCO statements. Efforts are underway to make PCO statements subordinate to consolidated statements.

United Kingdom. At a minimum, a parent company's separate balance sheet (uncondensed) must be presented with the consolidated statements.

---

agency) are maintained. Thus a portion of a bank subsidiary's stockholder's equity (net assets) may be restricted. As discussed in Chapter 1, the SEC requires all publicly owned companies (all industries) to disclose such restrictions if the *subsidiary's restricted* net assets exceed 25% of *consolidated* net assets.

THE SEC'S 25% TEST FOR PRESENTING PARENT-COMPANY-ONLY STATEMENTS
When the **restricted net assets** of all subsidiaries of a bank holding company exceed **25% of *consolidated* net assets,** the SEC's rules also require that the notes to the consolidated statements include PCO **condensed financial statements.**[7] These rules also apply to savings and loan holding companies.

THE EXCLUSIVE USE OF THE EQUITY METHOD   In presenting PCO statements in the notes to the consolidated statements, bank holding companies and savings and loan holding companies report their investments in their subsidiaries using the equity method. Consequently, the PCO retained earnings amount and the PCO total stockholder's equity amount agree with consolidated retained earnings and consolidated total stockholders' equity amounts, respectively. Thus the statements articulate with each other.

As the accompanying International Perspective shows, PCO statements are accorded a different stature overseas.

WHY EXCLUSIVE USE OF THE EQUITY METHOD?   The SEC requires the use of the equity method because such articulation is considered essential. The use of the cost method is incongruous with the consolidated statements. Furthermore, state laws regarding dividend distributions clearly provide that they are to be based on the parent's retained earnings—not consolidated retained earnings. Accounting for the investment under the equity method avoids any possible confusion that investors might otherwise experience as to the amount of retained earnings available for dividend distribution.

Virtually all bank holding companies and savings and loan holding companies are publicly owned and thus are subject to the SEC's reporting requirements. Consequently, holding companies of banks and savings and loans use the equity

---

[7]Rule 9-06 of Article 9 ("Bank Holding Companies") of Regulation S–X. Even though the title of Article 9 indicates that it applies only to bank holding companies, the SEC considers it applicable to savings and loan holding companies as well.

method almost exclusively.[8] To put matters in further perspective, these publicly owned holding companies—approximately 800 banks and 250 savings and loans—control the vast majority of bank and savings and loan assets in the United States.

THE SEC'S DIVIDEND INCOME DISCLOSURE RULE   In presenting the PCO condensed income statement, the SEC's rules require separate display of cash dividends received from all subsidiaries. Because the equity method is used in the PCO condensed statements, the parent's equity interest in the **undistributed earnings** of the subsidiaries is shown on a separate line in the PCO condensed income statement. An example of PCO condensed balance sheets and income statements for Citicorp (with consolidated assets and equity of approximately $257 billion and $19.6 billion, respectively, at December 31, 19X5) is shown on page 49 (Note 14 from its 1995 annual report).

REVIEW POINTS FOR THE CITICORP EXAMPLE   Note the following:

1. The dividends received (the *distributed* earnings) from the subsidiaries are shown on the top line of the income statement.

2. The *undistributed* earnings are shown at the bottom of the income statement slightly above the net income line. This amount plus the dividend income constitute the parent company's equity in the earnings of its subsidiaries.

3. The SEC believes that presenting condensed PCO statements in notes to the consolidated statements is useful for bank holding companies (and savings and loan holding companies) having bank subsidiaries with significant asset transferability restrictions. Such statements show that a holding company's ability to service its debt—which is substantial for some bank holding companies (such as Citicorp, which has approximately $14 billion of debt at the parent level)—and to pay its corporate expenses depend highly on its ability to obtain cash from its banking subsidiaries.

VIII   THE EQUITY METHOD OF VALUING A PARENT'S INVESTMENT: TOTAL INVESTMENT LOSS SITUATIONS

If the subsidiary reports losses to the extent that it exhausts its equity and its equity becomes negative (properly called a *stockholder's deficiency*), the parent's Investment account is automatically written down to zero when the subsidiary's stockholder's equity becomes zero.

Unlike individuals who invest in corporate stocks, however, a parent can lose *more than* it has invested, depending on whether it has obligated itself to make additional investments in the subsidiary. Frequently, subsidiaries cannot obtain certain types of credit unless the parent will guarantee that indebtedness. Consequently, the parent often guarantees some or all of the debt of its subsidiaries.

THE PARENT *IS* OBLIGATED TO INVEST ADDITIONAL FUNDS

If the subsidiary has a stockholder's deficiency *and* **the parent is obligated to invest additional funds in the subsidiary** in the event that the subsidiary is unable to pay creditors, the parent must recognize a liability on its books equal to the sub-

---

[8]Inquiries to audit partners of the Big 6 accounting firms that specialize in auditing these institutions uniformly stated that the bank holding companies and the savings and loan holding companies account for these investments in the parent's books using the equity method—they do *not* account for them using the *cost method* and merely convert to the *equity method* for presenting PCO statements in the notes to the consolidated statements.

CITICORP Note 14: Parent-Company-Only Financial Statements (1995 annual report)

Condensed Statement of Income (In Millions of Dollars)

	Citicorp (Parent Company Only)		
	1995	1994	1993
Revenue			
Dividends from Subsidiary Banks...	$1,600	$ 100	$ 120
Dividends from Subsidiaries Other Than Banks............................	730	900	586
Interest from Subsidiaries..	787	579	491
Other Revenue[1]..	72	36	10
	3,189	1,615	1,207
Expense			
Interest on Other Borrowed Funds.......................................	132	102	80
Interest and Fees Paid to Subsidiaries	137	111	173
Interest on Long-Term Debt and Subordinated Capital Notes[2]	947	730	724
Other Expense	14	21	39
	1,230	964	1,016
Income Before Taxes, Cumulative Effect of Accounting Change and Equity in Undistributed Income of Subsidiaries	1,959	651	191
Income Tax Benefit—Current	102	132	614
Cumulative Effect of Accounting Change	—	—	(20)
Equity in Undistributed Income of Subsidiaries, Before Cumulative Effects of Accounting Changes	1,403	2,639	1,564
Income Before Cumulative Effects of Accounting Changes of Subsidiaires	3,464	3,422	1,899
Equity in Cumulative Effects of Accounting Changes of Subsidiaries	—	(56)	320
Net Income	$3,464	$3,366	$2,219

(1) Includes net securities gains (losses) of $1 million, $2 million, and $(9) million in 1995, 1994, and 1993, respectively.

(2) Includes interest on long-term debt of $829 million, $643 million, and $623 million in 1995, 1994, and 1993, respectively.

Condensed Balance Sheet (In Millions of Dollars)

	Citicorp (Parent Company Only)	
	December 31, 1995	December 31, 1994
Assets		
Deposits with Subsidiary Banks, Principally Interest-Bearing	$ 2,424	$ 2,040
Securities—Available for Sale	1,207	759
Investments in and Advances to:		
Citibank, N.A. and Other Subsidiary Banks	23,461	21,074
Subsidiaries Other Than Banks	8,386	9,645
Other Assets	477	546
Total	$35,955	$34,064
Liabilities and Stockholders' Equity		
Purchased Funds and Other Borrowings	$ 1,466	$ 1,626
Advance from Subsidiaries	94	182
Other Liabilities	1,240	1,102
Long-Term Debt and Subordinated Capital Notes (Note 1)	13,574	13,385
Stockholders' Equity	19,581	17,769
Total	$35,955	$34,064

sidiary's stockholder's deficiency. Mechanically, rather than using a separate liability account, the parent's Investment in Subsidiary account can be allowed to become a *negative* amount, which is classified as a *liability* in the parent's separate balance sheet. The offsetting debit is recorded in the parent's income statement (using the Equity in Net Loss of Subsidiary account). **Thus no stoppage occurs in the application of the equity method.**

THE PARENT IS *NOT* OBLIGATED TO INVEST ADDITIONAL FUNDS

If the subsidiary has a stockholder's deficiency and the parent is *not* obligated to invest additional funds, the parent cannot lose more than it has invested. Thus it **stops applying the equity method** when the Investment account balance reaches zero. If the subsidiary subsequently reports profits, the parent **waits until the subsidiary's stockholder's deficiency is eliminated before resuming application of the equity method.**

CASE IN POINT

Disney Suspends Use of the Equity Method of Accounting for Euro Disney[a]

In November 1993, Walt Disney Company stopped recording Euro Disney's losses on its books since its investment in Euro Disney had been written down to zero at that point using the equity method of accounting.	[a]Although Disney is not a parent company of Euro Disney (owning only 49% of the voting shares), the principle involved is the same as when a parent company writes down to zero its investment in a subsidiary.

Illustration 2–9 is a continuation of Illustration 2–1 for three additional years to show total investment loss situations.

IX CONSOLIDATION SOFTWARE AND REPORTING SYSTEMS

Both software development companies and private corporations have developed software programs that enable (1) subsidiaries to submit their financial statements to their parent companies by electronic transmission over telephone lines, (2) foreign currency statements received in the United States to be automatically translated into U.S. dollars, (3) parent companies to readily load such transmitted statements into their consolidation software programs, and (4) companies to modify the display format of the financial statements for managerial purposes.[9]

USING SPREADSHEET SOFTWARE TO SOLVE PROBLEMS As described in the preface, most of the consolidation problems in this book can be solved using consolidation models we have designed using spreadsheet software (EXCEL and LOTUS 1-2-3™). If the problem you are working has an asterisk (and an icon) by its number, you can work that problem using the computer.

SPREADSHEET SOFTWARE PROGRAMMING ASSIGNMENTS Included in this chapter's assignment material are two spreadsheet software programming prob-

---

[9]For example, Micro Control™ for DOS and Hyperion Enterprise™ for Windows by Hyperion Software (a publicly owned software development company) are the leading commercially developed software consolidation programs.

ILLUSTRATION 2–9	Comparison of the Equity and Cost Methods: Continued from Illustration 2–1

Parent *Has* Guaranteed All of the Subsidiary's Debt—*No* Temporary Discontinuance of the Equity Method

	Investment in Subsidiary				Subsidiary's Equity
	Cost Method		Equity Method		
Balances, 12/31/X4 (from Illustration 2–1 on page 36)	$45,000		$45,000		$ 45,000
19X5 Net loss $(75,000)		$45,000[a]		75,000	(75,000)
Balances, 12/31/X5	$ –0–			$30,000[b]	$(30,000)
19X6 Net income—$22,000			22,000		22,000
Balances, 12/31/X6	$ –0–			$ 8,000[b]	$ (8,000)
19X7 Net income—$12,000			12,000		12,000
Balances, 12/31/X7	$ –0–		$ 4,000		$ 4,000

[a]This assumes that the parent concluded that the recoverability of its investment was in substantial doubt, thus warranting a permanent write-down.

[b]This credit balance is classified as a liability in the parent's separate financial statements.

Parent *Has Not* Guaranteed Any of the Subsidiary's Debt—Temporary Discontinuance of the Equity Method

	Investment in Subsidiary				Subsidiary's Equity
	Cost Method		Equity Method		
Balances, 12/31/X4 (from Illustration 2–1 on page 36)	$45,000		$45,000		$ 45,000
19X5 Net loss $(75,000)		$45,000[a]		45,000	(75,000)
Balances, 12/31/X5	$ –0–		$ –0–		$(30,000)
19X6 Net income—$22,000					22,000
Balances, 12/31/X6	$ –0–		$ –0–		$ (8,000)
19X7 Net income—$12,000			4,000[b]		12,000
Balances, 12/31/X7	$ –0–		$ 4,000		$ 4,000

[a]This assumes that the parent concluded that its recoverability of its investment was in substantial doubt, thus warranting a permanent write-down at this time.

[b]This amount is the difference between (1) the 19X5 unrecognized loss of $(30,000) and (2) the sum of the net income reported for 19X6 and 19X7, which totals $34,000 ($22,000 + $12,000).

---

lems designed to give you spreadsheet programming experience in (1) automating the spreadsheet and (2) creating a spreadsheet model (with two stored-instruction macros) from scratch. See Problems 2–7 and 2–8 for details.

END-OF-CHAPTER REVIEW

SUMMARY OF KEY POINTS

1. Parent companies may account for investments in subsidiaries using the **equity method** or the **cost method**—the consolidated amounts are the same regardless of which method is used.
2. Under the **cost method** (which is overly conservative), the carrying value of the investment is *not* adjusted unless the subsidiary **incurs losses** to such an extent that the carrying

value of the investment is permanently **impaired.** Also, the subsidiary's dividends constitute the parent's investment income.

3. Under the **equity method,** the carrying value of the investment is automatically adjusted for the subsidiary's **economic activity** so that the Investment account balance is always in a **reciprocal relationship** with the subsidiary's equity accounts. Also, the subsidiary's **earnings are accrued** on the parent's books and constitute the parent's **investment income.**

4. A subsidiary's dividends are **not** summed with the parent's retained earnings in consolidation—they are eliminated.

5. The subsidiary's **undistributed earnings** account for the difference between the amounts reported under the equity and cost methods for (a) the investment's carrying value and (b) the parent's retained earnings.

6. In presenting PCO statements in notes to the consolidated statements, the use of the equity method results in **articulation with the consolidated statements**—a result *not* achieved using the cost method.

7. In determining the maximum amount of dividends that can **legally be paid** under state laws, parents refer to their *own* retained earnings—which under the *equity method* is the same as the *consolidated* retained earnings.

8. Under the *equity method,* a parent that is **obligated to invest additional funds** in a subsidiary reports a liability to the subsidiary to the extent that the subsidiary has a stockholder's deficiency.

GLOSSARY OF NEW TERMS

Cost method   A method of accounting for certain common stock investments whereby the carrying value of the investment is never changed unless it is believed to be permanently impaired (or *liquidating dividends* occurs, as discussed in Chapter 6). The only income reported on the investment is from dividends declared by the subsidiary.

Equity method   A method of accounting for certain common stock investments whereby the carrying value of the investment is adjusted for the subsidiary's earnings, losses, and dividends.

SELF-STUDY QUESTIONS

(Answers are at the end of this chapter preceding the appendices.)

1. A parent *cannot* consolidate a subsidiary when which of the following is true for the parent?
   a. It uses the equity method of accounting.
   b. It uses the cost method of accounting.
   c. It is unable to do as it pleases with the subsidiary's assets.
   d. It allows the subsidiary to operate freely and independently of the parent.

2. Which account is *not* used under the *equity method*?
   a. Dividends Receivable.
   b. Dividend Income.
   c. Equity in Net Income of Subsidiary.
   d. Investment in Subsidiary.

3. Which account is *not* debited or credited under the *cost method* when the subsidiary reports profits and distributes them?
   a. Dividends Receivable.
   b. Dividend Income.
   c. Investment in Subsidiary.
   d. Cash.

4. On 4/1/X1, Pitco created Sitco by investing $100,000 cash. For 19X1, Sitco reported net income of $17,000 and declared and paid cash dividends of $7,000. What is Pitco's carrying value of its investment in Sitco at 12/31/X1?

	Cost Method	Equity Method
a.	$100,000	$110,000
b.	$110,000	$117,000
c.	$100,000	$117,000
d.	$ 93,000	$117,000

5. Assume the same information as in Question 4, but the dividend was declared on December 31, 19X1, and paid two days later. What is the investment's carrying value?
6. On 5/1/X1, Paxco created Saxco by investing $500,000 cash. Saxco reported a highly unexpected $230,000 loss for 19X1. For 19X2 Saxco reported a $10,000 profit, which was far below expectations. What is or could be an appropriate carrying value of Paxco's investment in Saxco at 12/31/X2?

	Cost Method	Equity Method
a.	$270,000 or $500,000	$270,000
b.	$270,000 or $500,000	$280,000
c.	$280,000 or $500,000	$280,000
d.	$270,000 or $500,000	$510,000

ASSIGNMENT MATERIAL

REVIEW QUESTIONS

1. What are the general rules for valuing all corporate investments in common stocks?
2. What is the *general idea* of the equity method? The cost method?
3. To what is the equity method analogous? The cost method?
4. What *income statement* account is used under the equity method? The cost method?
5. How are *dividends* treated under the equity method? The cost method?
6. Does a subsidiary's *dividend declaration* or *actual dividend payment* impact the carrying value of the investment under the equity method? The cost method?
7. Does a subsidiary's *dividend declaration* or *actual dividend payment* impact the parent's retained earnings under the equity method? The cost method?
8. Why must the consolidated amounts be the *same* regardless of whether the parent uses the equity method or the cost method?
9. Can a parent lose *more* than it has invested in a subsidiary? Explain.
10. Can a parent's investment account be *written back up* after it has been written down?
11. Why are a subsidiary's dividends *not* reported in the consolidated statement of retained earnings?
12. What are the two *built-in checking features* under the equity method?
13. What are the *advantages* of the equity method? The cost method?
14. Would it be a good idea for the Financial Accounting Standards Board to require the use of only the equity method or the cost method (and to eliminate the other method)? Why?
15. Does the IRS use either the equity method or the cost method? Explain.
16. How are PCO *statements* generally presented when required by the SEC?
17. What are some of the *detailed disclosures* the SEC requires in PCO income statements?
18. Legally, is the maximum amount of dividends that a parent can pay determined by referring to the *parent's* retained earnings or the *consolidated* retained earnings?
19. If a parent has *discontinued* applying the equity method because of the subsidiary's losses, when would it start applying the equity method again?
20. How is a *negative balance* in the parent's Investment account reported in the parent's separate balance sheet? Why?
21. **Computers and Spreadsheets:** When a personal computer is turned on, why does it always automatically first search the A disk drive?

EXERCISES

E 2–1   Investment Valuation: Cost and Equity   On 6/1/X1, Pyco created Syco by investing $300,000 cash. Syco reported the following items:

	Net Income (Loss)	Dividends Declared
19X1	$45,000	$15,000
19X2	(60,000)	20,000[a]

[a]Paid in the first quarter of 19X2 (which was profitable).

Required   What is the investment's carrying value at 12/31/X2 under the *cost method*? Under the *equity method*?

E 2–2   Journal Entries: Cost and Equity   A 100%-owned subsidiary reported the following amounts:

	Net Income (Loss)	Dividends Declared
19X1	$140,000	$80,000[a]
19X2	(90,000)	–0–

[a]Of this amount, $60,000 was paid in 19X1 and $20,000 was paid in early 19X2.

Required   What are the general ledger entries for 19X1 and 19X2 under the *cost method*? The *equity method*?

E 2–3   Conceptualizing Consolidated Amounts   For 19X1, a parent and subsidiary reported the following amounts from their own separate operations:

	Parent[a]	Subsidiary
Net income	$200,000	$50,000
Dividends declared	140,000	30,000[b]

[a]Excludes earnings and dividends relating to subsidiary.
[b]Of this amount, $20,000 was paid in 19X1 and $10,000 was paid on 1/2/X2.

Required   1. What is the consolidated net income for 19X1?
2. What amount is reported as dividends in the 19X1 consolidated statement of retained earnings?

E 2–4   Consolidated Dividends   During 19X1, Pixcor declared dividends of $100,000 and its 100%-owned subsidiary, Sixcor, declared dividends of $40,000 ($30,000 was paid in 19X1 and $10,000 was paid on 1/1/X2).

Required   What amount is reported as dividends in the consolidated statement of retained earnings for 19X1? Why?

E 2–5   Consolidation Entries: Cost and Equity   Pelco created Selco, a 100%-owned subsidiary, several years ago. For 19X5, Selco reported net income of $80,000 and declared and paid cash dividends of $50,000. At 12/31/X5, Selco's equity accounts were as follows:

Common stock	$100,000
Additional paid-in capital	400,000
Retained earnings	240,000

Required   1. What entry(ies) was (were) made in consolidation at the end of 19X5 if Pelco uses the *cost method*?
2. Repeat Question 1 but assume the use of the *equity method*.

E 2–6 **Investment Valuation: Cost and Equity—All Debt Guaranteed**   On 4/1/X1, Pote Inc. formed Sote Inc. by investing $600,000 cash. Pote guaranteed all of Sote's debt. Sote reported the following items:

	Net Income (Loss)	Dividends Declared
19X1	$(650,000)	$ –0–
19X2	770,000	40,000ª

ªPaid on 1/3/X3.

At 12/31/X1, Pote doubted that it could recover but $200,000 of its initial investment.

Required   **1.** What is the investment's carrying value at 12/31/X1 and 19X2 under the *cost method*? The *equity method*?
   2. What amount did Pote report in its income statement for each year?

E 2–7 **Investment Valuation: Equity and Cost—No Debt Guaranteed**   Use the information in Exercise 2–6 but assume that Pote has guaranteed *none* of Sote's debt.

E 2–8 **Investment Valuation: Cost and Equity—Some Debt Guaranteed**   On 5/1/X1, Potu Inc. created Sotu Inc. by investing $100,000 cash. Potu has guaranteed $50,000 of Sotu's debt. Sotu subsequently reported the following items:

	Net Income (Loss)	Dividends Declared
19X1	$(160,000)	$ –0–
19X2	290,000	40,000ª

ªOf this amount, $25,000 was paid in 19X2 and $15,000 was paid on 1/2/X3.

At 12/31/X1, Potu seriously doubted that it could recover but $30,000 of its initial investment.

Required   **1.** What is the investment's carrying value at 12/31/X1 and 12/31/X2 under the *cost method*? The *equity method*?
   2. How much did the parent report in its income statement for each year?

E 2–9 **Mini Review: Consolidation (no worksheet): Cost Method**   The following six accounts appear on the *separate company financial statements* (as opposed to a trial balance) of Partex and its 100%-owned subsidiary, Sartex (created in 19X1), at the end of 19X9:

	Partex	Sartex
Dividend income (from Sartex)	$ 40,000	
Investment in subsidiary	200,000	
Common stock	100,000	$ 20,000
Additional paid-in capital	400,000	180,000
Retained earnings	660,000	90,000
Dividends declared	(123,000)	(40,000)
Additional information:		
Retained earnings at 1/1/X9	$610,000	$144,000

Required   **1.** What consolidation entries are required at 12/31/X9?
   2. What is the consolidated retained earnings amount at 12/31/X9?
   3. What amount is reported as dividends in the consolidated statement of retained earnings for 19X9?
   4. What is the subsidiary's net income for 19X9?

E 2–10 **Mini Review: Consolidation (no worksheet): Equity Method**   The following six accounts appear on the *separate company financial statements* (as opposed to a *trial balance*) of a parent and its 100%-owned subsidiary (created in 19X1) at the end of 19X9:

	Paymor	Saymor
Equity in net income (of subsidiary)	$ 33,000	
Investment in subsidiary	480,000	
Common stock	50,000	$ 10,000
Additional paid-in capital	250,000	340,000
Retained earnings	550,000	130,000
Dividends declared	(64,000)	(11,000)
Additional information:		
Retained earnings at 1/1/X9	$494,000	

Required

1. What consolidation entries are required at 12/31/X9?
2. What is the consolidated retained earnings amount at 12/31/X9?
3. What amount is reported as dividends in the consolidated statement of retained earnings for 19X9?
4. What is the consolidated net income for 19X9?

PROBLEMS

P 2–1* **Consolidation Worksheet: Cost Method** The comparative financial statements of Pane Inc. and its 100%-owned subsidiary, Sill Inc. (created six years ago), follow:

	Pane Inc.		Sill Inc.
	Cost Method[a]	Equity Method[b]	
Income Statement (19X6)			
Sales	$400,000	$400,000	$225,000
Cost of sales	(210,000)	(210,000)	(120,000)
Expenses	(140,000)	(140,000)	(80,000)
Dividend income (from Sill)	20,000		
Equity in net income (of Sill)		25,000	
Net Income	$ 70,000	$ 75,000	$ 25,000
Statement of Retained Earnings			
Balances, 1/1/X6	$150,000	$205,000	$ 55,000
+ Net income	70,000	75,000	25,000
– Dividends declared	(40,000)	(40,000)	(20,000)
Balances, 12/31/X6	$180,000	$240,000	$ 60,000
Balance Sheet (as of 12/31/X6)			
Cash	$ 35,000	$ 35,000	$ 30,000
Accounts receivable, net	65,000	65,000	45,000
Intercompany receivable	15,000	15,000	
Inventory	190,000	190,000	70,000
Investment in subsidiary	50,000	110,000	
Property and equipment	370,000	370,000	180,000
Accumulated depreciation	(160,000)	(160,000)	(40,000)
Total Assets	$565,000	$625,000	$285,000
Payables and accruals	$135,000	$135,000	$ 70,000
Intercompany payable			15,000
Long-term debt	150,000	150,000	90,000
Common stock	100,000	100,000	50,000
Retained earnings	180,000	240,000	60,000
Total Liabilities and Equity	$565,000	$625,000	$285,000

[a]Use this column for working the problem under the *cost method,* as called for in this problem.

[b]Use this column for working the problem under the *equity method,* as called for in Problem 2–2.

---

*The financial statement information presented for problems accompanied by asterisks is also provided on Model 2 (filename: MODEL2) of the software file disks that are available with the text, allowing the problem to be worked on the computer.

Required   **1.** Prepare all consolidation entries as of 12/31/X6.
             2. Prepare a consolidation worksheet at 12/31/X6.

P 2–2* **Consolidation Worksheet: Equity Method**   Use the information provided in Problem 2–1 but assume that

             the parent uses the *equity method.*

Required   **1.** Analyze the parent's Investment account for 19X6 (work backward to do so).
             2. Prepare all consolidation entries as of 12/31/X6.
             3. Prepare a consolidation worksheet at 12/31/X6.

P 2–3* **Consolidation Worksheet: Cost Method**   The comparative financial statements of Pylo Inc. and its 100%-
             owned subsidiary, Sylo Inc. (created seven years ago), follow:

	Pylo Inc.		Sylo Inc.
	Cost Method[a]	Equity Method[b]	
Income Statement (19X7)			
Sales	$700,000	$700,000	$250,000
Cost of sales	(430,000)	(430,000)	(130,000)
Expenses	(170,000)	(170,000)	(90,000)
Dividend income (from Sill)	10,000		
Equity in net income (of Sill)		30,000	
Net Income	$110,000	$130,000	$ 30,000
Balance Sheet (as of 12/31/X7)			
Cash	$ 45,000	$ 45,000	$ 40,000
Accounts receivable, net	95,000	95,000	55,000
Inventory	170,000	170,000	75,000
Investment in subsidiary	50,000	130,000	
Property and equipment	280,000	280,000	175,000
Accumulated depreciation	(120,000)	(120,000)	(25,000)
Total Assets	$520,000	$600,000	$320,000
Payables and accruals	$140,000	$140,000	$ 70,000
Long-term debt	300,000	300,000	120,000
Common stock	10,000	10,000	50,000
Retained earnings	70,000	150,000	80,000
Total Liabilities and Equity	$520,000	$600,000	$320,000
Dividends declared in 19X7	$ 90,000	$ 90,000	$ 10,000

[a]Use this column for working the problem under the *cost method*, as called for in this problem.

[b]Use this column for working the problem under the *equity method*, as called for in Problem 2–4.

Required   **1.** Prepare all consolidation entries as of 12/31/X7.
             2. Prepare a consolidation worksheet at 12/31/X7.

P 2–4* **Consolidation Worksheet: Equity Method**   Use the information provided in Problem 2–3 but assume that
             the parent uses the *equity method.*

             1. Analyze the parent's Investment account for 19X7 (work backward to do so).
             2. Prepare all consolidation entries as of 12/31/X7.
             3. Prepare a consolidation worksheet at 12/31/X7.

P 2–5   **Comprehensive Review: Consolidation Entries—Cost and Equity**   The following accounts are as they ap-
             pear on the *separate company financial statements* of Pifo Inc. and its 100%-owned subsidiary, Sifo Inc.
             (created in 19X1), at *the end of 19X5*:

	Pifo Inc.	Sifo Inc.
Dividend income (from Sifo)	$ 14,000	
Dividends receivable	7,000	
Investment in subsidiary	200,000	
Dividends payable	30,000	$ 7,000
Common stock	50,000	30,000
Additional paid-in capital	450,000	170,000
Retained earnings	330,000	51,000
Dividends declared	(120,000)	(14,000)
Additional information:		
Reported net income (loss) for 19X5	$150,000	$(23,000)

Required
1. What consolidation entries, given these data, are required at the end of 19X5?
2. What is the consolidated net income amount?
3. What is the consolidated retained earnings amount?
4. What amount is reported as dividends in the consolidated statement of retained earnings for 19X5?
5. If Pifo used the *equity method* instead of the *cost method,* what would be its retained earnings balance at the end of 19X5?
6. If Pifo used the *equity method* instead of the *cost method,* what consolidation entries would it make at the end of 19X5?

P 2–6 **Comprehensive Review: Consolidation Entries—Equity and Cost** The following accounts are as they appear on the *separate company financial statements* of Pufa Inc. and its 100%-owned subsidiary, Sufa Inc. (created in 19X1), at *the end of 19X6:*

	Pufa Inc.	Sufa Inc.
Equity in net loss of subsidiary	$(49,000)	
Dividends receivable	6,000	
Investment in subsidiary	660,000	
Dividends payable	20,000	$ 6,000
Common stock	300,000	20,000
Additional paid-in capital	100,000	380,000
Retained earnings	500,000	260,000
Dividends declared	(80,000)	(24,000)
Additional information:		
Retained earnings at 1/1/X6	$400,000	

Required
1. What consolidation entries, given these data, are required at the end of 19X6?
2. What is the consolidated net income amount?
3. What did the parent earn from its own separate operations?
4. What is the consolidated retained earnings amount?
5. What amount is reported as dividends in the consolidated statement of retained earnings for 19X6?
6. If Pufa used the *cost method* instead of the *equity method,* what would be its retained earnings balance at the end of 19X6?
7. If the parent used the *cost method* instead of the *equity method,* what consolidation entries would it make at the end of 19X6?

SPREADSHEET INTEGRATION PROBLEMS

P 2–7 **Automating the Spreadsheet Consolidation Model** This assignment is designed to enable you to see how the entire consolidation process can be automated so that no amounts need to be entered manually anywhere in (1) the analysis of the parent's Investment account, (2) the basic elimination entry, or (3) the worksheet's Debit and Credit columns. Thus the entire consolidation worksheet can be performed automatically once the problem data amounts are entered into the spreadsheet's Parent and Subsidiary columns. This automation can be accomplished by inserting formulas wherever you otherwise would manually insert an amount (so that the amount is automatically brought forward from another location in the worksheet). Before trying to automate the spreadsheet model, you should

1. Work Problem 2–2 or 2–4 using MODEL 2 of the software package accompanying the text (so that you have a hard copy solution from which to work).
2. Enter problem data for P 2–2 or P 2–4 in the Parent and Subsidiary columns of the accompanying spreadsheet model for Chapter 2 (using macro B or D, as appropriate).
3. Read an EXCEL or LOTUS 1-2-3™ manual regarding the distinction between **relative addresses** and **absolute (nonrelative) addresses** so that you use the proper address type in working this assignment. A cell formula such as (B24) is an *absolute* (nonrelative) address, whereas a cell formula such as (B24) is a *relative* address.

Required Insert formulas in the spreadsheet model to automate the consolidation process. Your model should be flexible enough so that the insertion of a row between a cell containing one of your formulas and the cell that the formula refers to does not invalidate your formula—this is the reason that it is necessary to differentiate between *absolute* and *relative* addresses.

P 2–8 **Creating a Consolidation Template and Two Keystroke Macros (Stored Instructions)** Employers expect accounting graduates to be able to (1) create accounting models containing macros and (2) use models created by others. Accordingly, this assignment gives you programming experience in (1) creating a model and (2) creating two specific keystroke macros (stored instructions that can be automatically executed instantaneously at the touch of a key). These two macros are highly useful in reviewing a newly created model to detect bugs in programmed formulas.

You should use one of the leading spreadsheet programs such as EXCEL or LOTUS 1-2-3™. Refer to an EXCEL or LOTUS 1-2-3 manual for particulars about creating and naming macros (so that you can execute your macros by pressing a letter of the alphabet after holding down either the Control key or the Alt key, depending on which spreadsheet program you use).

Required 1. Prepare a consolidation model (complete with formulas) for the trial balance consolidation worksheet shown in Appendix A. Use an appropriate format (such as the "Comma" format of EXCEL and LOTUS 1-2-3) with zero decimal places.

   Caution: Avoid using the Range command of LOTUS 1-2-3 to format individual cells, such as a cell for a column total. Macros will *not* execute within a range.

   You may abbreviate account descriptions and omit the *vertical* lines. To code your consolidation entries, program a three-character column immediately to the right of the Debit column; do likewise for the Credit column. (Program formulas in the Income Statement column as well as the Balance Sheet and Retained Earnings columns.)
2. Program a keystroke macro (a stored instruction) to convert your model from your selected format to a format that will display your formulas (Excel: Tools, Options, Formulas; Lotus 1-2-3: /Worksheet Global Format Text). Include in this macro instructions to change column widths as necessary to fully display the formulas you programmed.
3. Program a macro to reverse the macro you programmed in requirement 2 (to go back to your selected format).
4. Program a logic formula (=IF function for EXCEL and @IF function for LOTUS 1-2-3) for (a) the cell containing the $142,000 balancing debit in the Income Statement Debit column and (b) the cell to its immediate right. (Logic formulas will be displayed in the Text format.) Thus your model must be able to accommodate a loss situation (in which you now balance the Credit column instead of the Debit column. (To test this second logic formula, create a loss by decreasing the parent's Sales account by $200,000 to see whether you are now balancing in the Credit column with a $58,000 amount.)
5. Program either a logic function or a formula in the Retained Earnings column so that the $142,000 net income in the income statement is extended to the Retained Earnings column. (This logic function or formula should also be able to accommodate a loss situation—a loss amount must appear in the Retained Earnings column in parentheses.) Accordingly, check out your solution as you did in requirement 4.

❋ THINKING CRITICALLY ❋

❋ CASES ❋

C 2–1 **My Goodness: Not Disclosing an Accounting Method!** The notes to the consolidated statements do *not* disclose the parent's manner of accounting for its investments in its numerous subsidiaries, all of which are consolidated. Contrary to what is stated in Chapter 1 regarding required disclosures, assume that GAAP requires such a disclosure.

Required   Should the company's outside auditors mention this omission in their audit report or qualify their opinion on the consolidated statements?

C 2–2   Assessing Impairment of Value: Time to Bite the Bullet?   Sebco, a 100%-owned created subsidiary of Pebco, has *total* stockholder's equity of $300,000, which is $200,000 below the parent's *initial* capital investment of $500,000. Pebco uses the *cost method* to account for its investment in Sebco.

Required   How would you go about assessing whether an impairment in value has occurred and whether a write-down is appropriate? In the absence of an outright offer from a potential buyer, what analysis would you perform to support an assumption or contention that the subsidiary probably could be sold to a willing buyer for at least $500,000?

C 2–3   Cost Method: Maybe the Parent Can Write Its Investment Back Up!   Ponn Inc. owns 100% of Sonn's outstanding common stock. In 19X1, Ponn, which uses the *cost method*, wrote down to zero its $1,000,000 investment in Sonn because of Sonn's severe going concern problems. In 19X2, Sonn had a remarkable recovery, and its stockholder's equity at the end of 19X2 was $1,500,000. Ponn now wishes to write the investment back up to $1,000,000. It has always issued consolidated statements.

Required   Under what circumstances, if any, could Ponn write the investment back up to its original cost of $1,000,000 and still comply with GAAP?

✳ FINANCIAL ANALYSIS PROBLEMS ✳

FAP 2–1   How Much Can the Parent Legally Pay in Cash Dividends?   Selected account balances at 12/31/X1 for Pitticorp and its 100%-owned banking subsidiary, Sittibank, are as follows:

	Pitticorp	Sittibank	Consolidated
Cash	$300,000	$250,000	$550,000
Investment in Sittibank (under the equity method). . . .	440,000		–0–
Retained earnings	500,000	400,000	500,000

Required   1. How much of a cash dividend could Pitticorp legally declare on its outstanding common stock?
2. Repeat requirement 1 but first revise the amounts given to reflect use of the *cost method* instead of the equity method.
3. Repeat requirement 1 but also assume that federal bank regulators have imposed *upstream* cash transfer restrictions that prevent Sittibank from paying any dividends until its stockholder's equity has become a much higher percentage of total assets.
4. What disclosure should be made in the consolidated statements regarding intercompany upstream cash transfer restrictions by the banking regulators? What purpose would it serve?
5. If the parent had $1,000,000 in cash instead of $300,000, do you think the disclosure in requirement 4 would still be needed? Why or why not?

FAP 2–2   How Much Did the Parent Really Earn on Its Investment?   Presto Inc. created Seco Inc. on 1/1/X1 by investing $1,000,000 cash. Information regarding Seco follows:

	Net Income	Dividends Declared
19X1	$200,000	$ –0–
19X2	300,000	400,000
19X3	330,000	130,000

Seco's earnings occurred evenly throughout each year. Seco's dividends were declared and paid at the *end* of each year.

Required   1. What is the parent's annual return on investment for each year under the *equity method*? Use the *beginning* investment balances for this requirement—*not* the *average* balances.
2. Repeat requirement 1 but use the *cost method*.
3. Which method depicts the parent's true annual return on investment for 19X2? Why?

4. Repeat the calculation for 19X2 under the *equity method* but assume that $200,000 of the dividends was declared and paid on 1/1/X2 and $200,000 was declared and paid on 12/31/X2.

5. Repeat the calculation for 19X2 under the *equity method* but assume that the entire $400,000 of dividends was declared and paid on 6/30/X2.

6. Repeat the calculation for 19X1 under the *equity method* using the average investment balance. Is the correct annual return on investment this percentage or the percentage in requirement 1? Why?

FAP 2–3   **Is the SEC's 25% Test for Disclosing Restrictions Effective?**   Sanko is a 100%-owned banking subsidiary of Panko. In 19X7, bank regulators imposed a prohibition against paying any dividends until Sanko's equity exceeds 5% of its total assets. Sanko has $100 million in assets and $97.5 million of liabilities. In consolidation at the end of 19X7, the following basic elimination entry was made to consolidate only the balance sheets:

Common stock	50,000	
Paid-in capital	650,000	
Retained earnings	1,800,000	
Investment in Sanko		2,500,000

At the end of 19X7, Panko—in its separate balance sheet—reported retained earnings of $2,000,000 and total stockholders' equity of $8,000,000.

Required   1. Is Panko using the *cost method* or the *equity method*?

2. Perform the 25% test the SEC uses to determine whether disclosures are needed in the consolidated statements regarding this restriction.

3. Redo the 25% test but use the consolidated *retained earnings* in the denominator.

4. In your opinion, which test better serves investors?

5. Draft the disclosure that would be made in the consolidated statements regarding the dividend restriction if the result in requirement 2 was more than 25%.

6. Draft the disclosure, if any, that would be made in Sanko's separate statements.

FAP 2–4   **Cost Method: Reporting the Sale of a Subsidiary Can Be Tricky!**   On 4/1/X3, Parba Inc. sold its 100%-owned subsidiary, Sarba Inc., for $700,000 cash. Sarba, which was created on 1/1/X1 with Parba's $1,000,000 equity investment, reported the following results of operations since inception:

		Net Loss
19X1		$ (22,000)
19X2		(78,000)
		$(100,000)
19X3 (1/1 through 3/31):		
Sales	$400,000	
Costs and expenses	(510,000)	(110,000)
		$(210,000)

Parba used the cost method and had never written down in value the cost of its investment. Sarba, which was in the same line of business as Parba, has always been consolidated.

Required   1. What is Parba's entry to record Sarba's sale?

2. What amount should be reported for the loss on the sale of Sarba in Parba's 19X3 financial statements customarily sent to stockholders?

3. Would this loss be reported as a loss on discontinued operations? Why or why not?

4. What consolidation entry, if any, should be made at 12/31/X3 relating to Sarba?

✳ **PERSONAL SITUATIONS: ETHICS AND INTERPERSONAL SKILLS** ✳

PS 2–1   **Ethics: Bankruptcy on the Horizon—Start Draining the Subsidiary**   Poes Inc. owns 100% of the outstanding common stock of Soes Inc. Soes has a growing number of liability suits against it, which could very well force it into financial distress or bankruptcy, in which case the parent would most likely lose its entire investment. Accordingly, during the past three years, Poes had Soes pay huge cash dividends, which has reduced Soes' retained earnings from $280 million to $80 million.

Required   1. Are creditors, existing claimants, and potential claimants being treated fairly?

2. May a subsidiary legally pay dividends to its parent right up to the time it files for bankruptcy?

3. If you were an existing supplier to Soes, would you continue to grant credit? What precautions might you take to put your company in a more secure position relative to existing and potential lawsuit claimants?

PS 2–2   **Interpersonal Skills: *Who* Is Right?**   You are having a dispute with your supervisor, with whom you have a significant personality conflict, as to the proper way to apply the *equity method* of accounting.

Required   In resolving this issue, what is far more important than *who* is right?

ANSWERS TO SELF-STUDY QUESTIONS

1. c   **2.** b   **3.** c   **4.** a   **5.** a   **6.** b

■APPENDIX A

THE TRIAL BALANCE WORKSHEET TECHNIQUE

In practice one occasionally encounters a consolidation worksheet technique different from the three-statement approach shown earlier. This technique (1) begins with the separate trial balances of each company and then (2) proceeds in a horizontal fashion to prepare the three consolidated financial statements. The major disadvantage to this approach is that one does not see the separate statements of each company.

Inquiries to many international companies in the electronics industry have led us to conclude that very few companies use this approach, which is an old-fashioned technique. The reason for its negligible use is that virtually all parent companies require their subsidiaries to submit financial statements—not trial balances.[10]

For the sole purpose of merely acquainting you with this technique, we present it in Illustration 2–10 (using the amounts shown in Illustration 2–8). The basic elimination entry used for Illustration 2–8 is repeated for convenience:

WORKSHEET ENTRY ONLY

Common Stock	60,000	
Retained Earnings, 1/1/X2	20,000	
Equity in Net Income (of S Co.)	32,000	
Dividends Declared		12,000
Investment in Subsidiary		100,000

[10]For many decades, the CPA examination has consistently used the financial statement technique—not the trial balance technique—for consolidation problems.

ILLUSTRATION 2–10 Consolidation Worksheet—Trial Balance Technique

P Company and S Company
Consolidation Worksheet as of December 31, 19X2

	P Company Dr.	P Company Cr.	S Company Dr.	S Company Cr.	Consolidation Entries Dr.	Consolidation Entries Cr.	Consolidated Income Statement Dr.	Consolidated Income Statement Cr.	Consolidated Retained Earnings (Dr.) Cr.	Consolidated Balance Sheet
Cash	66,000		31,000							97,000
Accounts receivable	84,000		43,000							127,000
Inventory	140,000		82,000							222,000
Investment in S Co.	100,000					100,000(1)				–0–
Land	220,000		30,000							250,000
Buildings and equipment	500,000		150,000							650,000
Accumulated depreciation		360,000		26,000						(386,000)
										960,000
Payables and accruals		160,000		90,000						250,000
Long-term debt		210,000		120,000						330,000
P Company:										
Common stock		200,000								200,000
Retained earnings, 1/1/X2		123,000							123,000	
Dividends declared	85,000								(85,000)	
S Company:										
Common stock				60,000	60,000(1)				–0–	
Retained earnings, 1/1/X2				20,000	20,000(1)				–0–	
Dividends declared			12,000			12,000(1)			–0–	
Sales		710,000		282,000				992,000		
Cost of sales	390,000		130,000				520,000			
Expenses	210,000		120,000				330,000			
Equity in net income (of S Co.)		32,000			32,000(1)			–0–		
	1,795,000	1,795,000	598,000	598,000	112,000	112,000	850,000	992,000		
Consolidated net income							142,000		→142,000	
Consolidated retained earnings									180,000	→180,000
							992,000	992,000		960,000

Explanation of entry:
(1) The basic elimination entry.

■APPENDIX B

THE BASICS OF BRANCH/DIVISION ACCOUNTING

As discussed earlier, internal expansion using a branch/division form of organization is merely the extension of the existing legal entity—not the creation of a new legal entity, as when a subsidiary is formed. The headquarters location of the legal entity that establishes the newly formed branch/division is referred to as the **home office.** Hereafter, we use the lone term **branch** rather than the dual term branch/division.

I   ACCOUNTING SYSTEMS

Unlike a subsidiary, which is a separate legal entity that must maintain its own books and records, home offices with branches have the option either to (1) allow the branch to maintain its own books and records in a *decentralized accounting system* or (2) account for the branch on the home office's books in a *centralized accounting system.* The decision is based on what is most practical and economical.

CENTRALIZED ACCOUNTING

Under a **centralized accounting** system, an outlying location does *not* maintain a separate general ledger in which to record its transactions. Instead, it sends source documents on sales, purchases, and payroll to the home office. Outlying locations usually deposit cash receipts in local bank accounts on which only the home office can draw. When the home office receives source documents, it reconciles sales information with bank deposits, reviews and processes invoices for payment, and prepares payroll checks and related payroll records. Inventory and fixed assets at each outlying location also are recorded in the home office general ledger, appropriately coded to signify the location to which they belong. Journal entries pertaining to each outlying location's transactions are then prepared and posted to the home office general ledger. These entries are usually coded so that accountants at the home office can readily prepare operating statements for each outlying location. Centralized accounting systems commonly use computers at the home office to minimize the clerical aspects of keeping records and preparing financial statements. The home office reviews operating statements for each outlying location and provides copies to outlying management. Centralized accounting systems are usually practical when the operations of the outlying location do not involve complex manufacturing operations or extensive retailing or service activities. Grocery, drug, and shoe store chains usually use centralized accounting systems. Because they present no unusual accounting issues, centralized accounting systems are not discussed any further.

DECENTRALIZED ACCOUNTING

Under a **decentralized accounting** system, an outlying location maintains a separate general ledger in which to record its transactions. Thus the outlying location is a separate **accounting entity,** even though it is not a separate legal entity. It prepares its own journal entries and financial statements, submitting the latter to the home office, usually on a monthly basis. Decentralized accounting systems are common for outlying locations that have complex manufacturing operations or extensive retailing operations involving significant credit sales. The following two accounting issues must be resolved in a decentralized accounting system:

1. The manner in which transactions between the home office and the outlying locations are recorded.

2. The procedures by which the revenues, costs, and expenses of the outlying locations are reported for financial and income tax–reporting purposes.

The remainder of this appendix discusses these two issues.

II BRANCH GENERAL LEDGER ACCOUNTS

INTRACOMPANY ACCOUNTS

A branch is established when a home office transfers cash, inventory, or other assets to an outlying location. Because the home office views the assets transferred to the branch as an investment, it makes the following entry:

```
Investment in Branch  . . . . . . . . . . . . . . . . . . . . . . . . . . . . . . . . . .  xxx
     Asset(s)  . . . . . . . . . . . . . . . . . . . . . . . . . . . . . . . . . . . . . .        xxx
```

This Investment in Branch account (sometimes called *Branch Current*) is used to track and maintain control over (1) the assets transferred to the branch and (2) the increase or decrease in the branch's net assets as a result of the branch's operations.

On receipt of the assets from the home office, the branch makes the following entry:

```
Asset(s)  . . . . . . . . . . . . . . . . . . . . . . . . . . . . . . . . . . . . . . . . .  xxx
     Home Office Capital  . . . . . . . . . . . . . . . . . . . . . . . . . . . . .        xxx
```

The Home Office Capital account represents the equity interest of the home office in the branch. The use of such an account allows double-entry bookkeeping procedures to be used at the branch level. (Remember that branches are *not* separate legal entities and do *not* have Common Stock, Additional Paid-in Capital, and Retained Earnings accounts.)

The balance in the Investment in Branch account on the books of the home office always equals the balance in the Home Office Capital account on the books of the branch. In practice, these accounts are referred to as the **intracompany** or **reciprocal accounts.** At the end of each accounting period, the branch closes its income or loss to its Home Office Capital account. Upon receipt of the branch's financial statements, the home office adjusts its Investment in Branch account to reflect the branch's income or loss and makes the offsetting credit or debit to an income statement account called **Branch Income** or **Branch Loss** (the equivalent of applying the *equity method* of accounting for a subsidiary's earnings). As a result of this entry and upon closing the Branch Income or Branch Loss account to the Retained Earnings account, the branch's income or loss is included in the home office's Retained Earnings account.

CENTRALIZATION OF FINANCE/TREASURY ACTIVITIES

Branches are usually financed entirely by the home office and typically do *not* establish relations with local banks, but this is not always the case with subsidiaries. Therefore, branches usually do *not* incur interest expense. Some home offices that borrow money to expand will, however, require such debt to be carried on the branch books and serviced by the branch.

If a branch has cash in excess of its immediate needs, it usually transfers the excess to the home office, which is responsible for investing excess cash on a companywide basis. Thus branches usually do *not* have interest income from investments.

INCOME TAX ACCOUNTS AND REPORTING

Because branches are *not* separate legal entities, they do *not* file their own income tax returns. The home office must include the income or loss from its branches along with its own income or loss from operations for federal income tax–reporting purposes. If the home office has operations in states that impose income taxes, it must file branch income tax returns in those states. Federal and state income taxes are almost always computed at the home office and recorded exclusively in the home office's general ledger. Few companies attempt to allocate or transfer income tax expense from the home office general ledger to branch general ledgers. This not only simplifies the tax-recording procedures but also eliminates the need to make arbitrary allocation assumptions. Furthermore, the potential benefits, if any, from allocating income tax expense to the branches are minimal in most instances.

Because branches do *not* have interest income, interest expense, or income tax expense, the income or loss from their operations is an **operating income** or **loss,** not a *net* income or loss. Hereafter, all references to a branch's income or loss are in this context.

HOME OFFICE ALLOCATIONS

The home office usually arranges and pays for certain expenses that benefit the branches. The most common example is insurance. In theory, some portion of the insurance expense should be allocated to the various branches so that the home office may determine the true operating income or loss of each branch. In practice, however, allocations of home office expenses vary widely. Numerous home offices allocate only those expenses that relate directly to the branch operations, such as insurance and national advertising costs. Some home offices without any revenue-producing operations of their own allocate all of their expenses (including salaries of home office executives, facilities costs, legal fees, audit fees, and interest expense) to the branches. Branch managers are therefore continually aware that branch operations must cover these costs. Some home offices do not allocate any home office expenses to the branches on the theory that because the branches have no control over them, arbitrary allocations serve no useful purpose. The home office records allocations by debiting the Investment in Branch account and crediting the applicable expense accounts. The branch debits the applicable expense accounts and credits its Home Office Capital account. **The result is the same as though the home office had transferred cash to the branch and the branch had arranged for and incurred the expenses.**

FIXED ASSET ACCOUNTS

Some home offices require their branches' fixed assets to be recorded on the home office's books instead of on the branches' books. Such a procedure automatically ensures that uniform depreciation methods and asset lives are used for all branches. The home office usually charges the branch for the depreciation expense of its fixed assets. It does this by crediting Accumulated Depreciation and debiting the Investment in Branch account instead of debiting Depreciation Expense. The branch debits Depreciation Expense and credits the Home Office Capital account instead of crediting Accumulated Depreciation. When fixed assets are recorded on the home office's books, the fixed assets pertaining to the branch must be added to the Investment in Branch account to evaluate the profitability of branch operations in relation to the total assets actually invested in the branch. Branch fixed assets recorded on the home office's books are always coded or recorded in separate accounts so that they may be readily identified.

OTHER GENERAL LEDGER ACCOUNTS

The branch maintains the balance sheet and income statement accounts necessary to record transactions that take place between (1) the home office and the branch and (2) the branch and its customers, creditors, and employees. The extent of the accounts required depends on the scope of the branch's operations.

INTRACOMPANY INVENTORY TRANSFERS   Many home offices and their branches have intracompany inventory transfers. When such transfers are made at a markup, the issue of unrealized intracompany profit arises. The appendix to Chapter 10 discusses how to account for unrealized intracompany inventory profit involving a home office and a branch.

START-UP COSTS

Expenses incurred by a branch *before* it formally opens for business are start-up costs. An operating loss incurred for a period of time after the formal opening is not considered a start-up cost.

Start-up costs may be expensed as incurred, or they may be capitalized for subsequent amortization over a reasonably short period of time (usually no more than a three- to five-year amortization period). Most companies expense start-up costs as incurred.

III   COMBINED STATEMENTS

MONTH-END VERIFICATION OF INTRACOMPANY ACCOUNT BALANCES

Before the *branch* prepares its closing entries and submits financial statements to the home office, it must verify that its Home Office Capital account agrees with the Investment in Branch reciprocal account maintained by the *home office*. If the accounts do not agree, there are two possible explanations:

1. A transaction initiated by one of the accounting entities has been improperly recorded by the other accounting entity. The accounting entity that made the error must make the appropriate adjusting entry.

2. A transaction initiated by one of the accounting entities has been recorded by the initiating entity but not yet by the receiving entity—for example, cash transfers in transit, inventory shipments in transit, and intracompany charges. Normally, the receiving accounting entity prepares the adjusting entry as though it has completed the transaction before the end of the accounting period. (It would be more disruptive to have the initiating accounting entity reverse the transaction.)

These adjusting entries to bring the intracompany accounts into agreement are absolutely necessary for the proper preparation of combined financial statements. After making any necessary adjustments, the branch submits an income statement and a balance sheet to the home office.

THE BASIC ELIMINATION ENTRY

After the home office general ledger is adjusted for the branch's income or loss, it reflects the overall net income earned by the home office and the branch. In reporting to stockholders, however, it is necessary to prepare combined financial statements—just as it was necessary to prepare consolidated financial statements for a parent and subsidiary. The combining process is nearly identical for the consolidation of a parent and subsidiary. The worksheet used is called a *combining worksheet,* however, rather than a consolidation worksheet. The *basic elimination entry* used to effect the combining is substantively the same as the basic elimination shown for the consolidation of a subsidiary. This entry eliminates (1) the Investment in Branch account in the Home Office column (a reciprocal account), (2) the Branch Income account in the Home Office column, and (3) the preclosing balance of the Home Office Capital account (a reciprocal account) in the Branch column of the statement of retained earnings/analysis of home office equity section.

ILLUSTRATION   **A COMBINING WORKSHEET**

A combining worksheet is shown in Illustration 2–11. The amounts used come from Illustration 2–7 (consolidation of a parent and subsidiary) as revised to reflect the branch form of organization. The basic elimination entry is as follows:

WORKSHEET ENTRY ONLY

Branch Income	24,000	
Home Office Capital (preclosing balance)	56,000	
Investment in Branch		80,000

REVIEW POINTS FOR ILLUSTRATION 2–11   Note the following:

1. The combining worksheet is started *after* the home office has made its adjusting entry concerning the branch's income and after it has provided for income taxes on the branch's income.

2. The balance in the Retained Earnings account in the Home Office column includes the branch's income net of applicable income taxes. This retained earnings amount is the combined retained earnings.

3. The net income in the Combined column is the same as the net income in the Home Office column.

4. The amounts in the Combined column are identical to the amounts in the Consolidated column of Illustration 2–7.

GLOSSARY OF NEW TERMS FOR APPENDIX B

Home office   The headquarters location of a legal business entity that establishes a branch.

Centralized accounting   A system whereby the accounting for outlying locations is performed at the home office; the outlying locations do *not* maintain general ledgers.

ILLUSTRATION 2–11	First Year of Branch Operations

Home Office and Branch
Combining Worksheet as of December 31, 19X1

	Home Office	Branch	Combining Entries Dr.	Combining Entries Cr.	Combined
Income Statement					
Sales	600,000	234,000			834,000
Cost of sales	(360,000)	(110,000)			(470,000)
Expenses	(190,000)	(100,000)			(290,000)
Branch income	24,000		24,000(1)		–0–
Net Income	74,000	24,000	24,000		74,000
Statement of Retained Earnings/					
Analysis of Home Office Capital					
Retained earnings, 1/1/X1	100,000	n/a			100,000
Home office capital (preclosing) ..	n/a	56,000ᵃ	56,000(1)		–0–
+ Net income	74,000	24,000	24,000		74,000
– Dividends declared	(51,000)				(51,000)
Balances, 12/31/X1	123,000	80,000	80,000		123,000
Balance Sheet					
Cash	65,000	11,000			76,000
Accounts receivable	75,000	37,000			112,000
Inventory	110,000	55,000			165,000
Investment in branch	80,000			80,000(1)	–0–
Land	220,000	30,000			250,000
Buildings and equipment	500,000	150,000			650,000
Accumulated depreciation	(320,000)	(13,000)			(333,000)
Total Assets	730,000	270,000		80,000	920,000
Payables and accruals	157,000	70,000			227,000
Long-term debt	250,000	120,000			370,000
Common stock	200,000				200,000
Retained earnings	123,000				123,000
Home office capital		80,000	80,000		–0–
Total Liabilities and Equity	730,000	270,000	80,000	80,000	920,000
Proof of debit and credit postings			80,000	80,000	

ᵃThis amount is the balance in the Home Office Capital account excluding the current year earnings ($80,000 ending balance – $24,000 of 19X1 earnings).

Explanation of entry:
(1) The basic elimination entry.

Decentralized accounting A system whereby outlying locations maintain their own general ledgers and submit financial reports periodically to the home office.

SELF-STUDY QUESTIONS FOR APPENDIX B

1. Which of the following accounts is a **reciprocal** account to the Investment in Branch account?
   a. Branch Income.
   b. Capital in Home Office.
   c. Home Office Capital.
   d. Contributed Capital.

2. In preparing combined statements, which of the following accounts are eliminated (brought to a zero balance) in the combining process?

	Branch Income or Loss	**Home Office Capital**
a.	Yes	Yes
b.	No	Yes
c.	No	No
d.	Yes	No

3. Which of the following would account for the Investment in Branch account being *less than* the Home Office Capital account?
   a. A cash transfer to the branch that is in transit.
   b. A cash transfer to the home office that is in transit.
   c. A home office expense allocation to the branch that the branch has not yet recorded.
   d. Payment by a home office customer of its bill at the branch that the branch neglected to report to the home office.
4. A month-end allocation of previously recorded advertising expenses to a branch requires which of the following entries on the **home office books?**

	Debit	**Credit**
a.	Investment in Branch	Advertising Expense
b.	Home Office Capital	Advertising Expense
c.	Branch Income	Home Office Capital
d.	Investment in Branch	Accrued Liabilities

5. A month-end allocation of previously recorded advertising expenses to a branch requires which of the following entries on the **branch books?**

	Debit	**Credit**
a.	Advertising Expense	Accrued Liabilities
b.	Branch Income	Home Office Capital
c.	Advertising Expense	Home Office Capital
d.	Home Office Capital	Accrued Liabilities

6. In the combining worksheet at year-end, the Home Office Capital account has an ending balance of $200,000 as shown in the balance sheet. The branch reported $44,000 of income for the year. What would the basic elimination entry include?
   a. A $200,000 debit to the Home Office Capital account in the analysis of home office capital.
   b. A $156,000 credit to the Home Office Capital account in the analysis of home office capital.
   c. A $156,000 debit to the Home Office Capital account in the balance sheet.
   d. A $44,000 debit to the Home Office Capital account in the balance sheet.
7. Use the information in Question 6. What would the basic elimination entry include?
   a. A $44,000 debit to the Branch Income account.
   b. A $44,000 credit to the Branch Income account.
   c. A $156,000 debit to the Branch Income account.
   d. A $200,000 debit to the Branch Income account.

EXERCISES FOR APPENDIX B

E 2–1 B   **Recording Intracompany Transactions**   The following are intracompany transactions between a home office and its branch:

1. The home office sent $100,000 cash to the branch.
2. The home office shipped inventory costing $200,000 to the branch; the intracompany billing was at cost. Assume that each location uses a perpetual inventory system.

3. The home office allocated to the branch $3,000 of previously recorded advertising expenses totaling $9,000.
4. A branch customer erroneously remitted a $4,000 payment to the home office instead of to the branch. The home office recorded the deposited check and notified the branch.
5. The home office, which carries branch fixed assets on its books, allocated $5,000 of depreciation expense to the branch.
6. The branch remitted $60,000 excess cash to the home office.

Required
1. Prepare the home office and branch journal entries for these transactions.
2. Assuming that the branch reported $22,000 of net income for the period, prepare the home office's entry in recognition of this income.

E 2–2B **Reconciling Intracompany Accounts** On 12/31/X1, the Home Office Capital account on the branch's books has a $44,000 balance, and the Investment in Branch account on the home office's books has an $85,000 balance. In analyzing the activity in each of these accounts for December, you find the following differences:

1. A $10,000 branch remittance to the home office initiated on 12/27/X1 was recorded on the home office books on 1/3/X2.
2. A home office inventory shipment to the branch on 12/28/X1 was recorded by the branch on 1/4/X2: the $20,000 billing was at cost.
3. The home office incurred $12,000 of advertising expenses and allocated $5,000 of this amount to the branch on 12/15/X1. The branch has *not* recorded this transaction.
4. A branch customer erroneously remitted $3,000 to the home office. The home office recorded this cash collection on 12/23/X1. Meanwhile, the branch has made no entry yet.
5. Inventory costing $43,000 was sent to the branch by the home office on 12/10/X1. The billing was at cost, but the branch recorded the transaction at $34,000.

Required Prepare the entries to bring the intracompany accounts into balance as of 12/31/X1. Assume that a *perpetual* inventory system is in use. (Use T accounts.)

E 2–3B **Reconciling Intracompany Accounts** The following entries are reflected in the intracompany accounts of a home office and its lone branch for June 19X2:

Investment in Branch

6/1	Balance	$ 50,000			
6/5	Inventory shipment	30,000	6/2	Remittance	10,000
6/12	Inventory shipment	12,000	6/8	Collection of branch	
6/20	Inventory shipment	17,000		receivable	1,000
6/25	Advertising allocation to branch (50% of $8,000 incurred)	4,000	6/27	Equipment purchase by branch	7,000
6/28	Inventory shipment	14,000			
6/30	Depreciation allocation	2,000			
6/30	Balance	$111,000			

Home Office Capital

			6/1	Balance	$50,000
6/2	Remittance	10,000	6/8	Inventory shipment	30,000
6/24	Purchase of equipment (carried on home office books)	7,000	6/10	Collection of home office receivable	2,000
6/29	Remittance	15,000	6/16	Inventory shipment	12,000
6/30	Inventory returned to home office	1,000	6/24	Inventory shipment	17,000
6/30	Depreciation allocation	2,000	6/28	Advertising allocation	400
			6/30	Balance	$76,400

Required 1. Prepare a schedule to reconcile the intracompany accounts. Assume that (1) inventory shipments to the branch are billed at the home office's cost and (2) a *perpetual* inventory system is used.

2. Prepare the adjusting journal entries to bring the intracompany accounts into balance.

PROBLEM FOR APPENDIX B

P 2–1B* **Combining Worksheet: Inventory Transfers at Cost** The 12/31/X1 financial statements of Kringle Inc. and its 34th Street branch (established in 19X1) are given as follows:

	Home Office	Branch
Income Statement		
Sales	$ 700,000	$200,000
Cost of sales	(390,000)	(135,000)
Selling expenses	(42,000)	(11,000)
Administrative expenses	(28,000)	(4,000)
Interest expense	(40,000)	
Branch income	50,000	
Income before Income Taxes	$ 250,000	$ 50,000
Income tax expense @ 40%	(100,000)	
Net Income	$ 150,000	$ 50,000
Balance Sheet		
Cash	$ 90,000	$ 10,000
Accounts receivable, net	80,000	20,000
Inventory:		
Acquired from vendors	180,000	10,000
Acquired from home office		30,000
Fixed assets, net	770,000	140,000
Investment in branch	170,000	
Total Assets	$1,290,000	$210,000
Payables and accruals	$ 200,000	$ 40,000
Long-term debt	350,000	
Common stock	500,000	
Retained earnings	240,000	
Home office capital		170,000
Total Liabilities and Equity	$1,290,000	$210,000
Dividends declared during 19X1	$ 110,000	

Required Prepare a combining statement worksheet as of 12/31/X1, assuming that inventory transfers to the branch from the home office are at cost.

ANSWERS TO APPENDIX B SELF-STUDY QUESTIONS

1. c   2. a   3. d   4. a   5. c   6. c   7. a

---

*The financial statement information presented for problems accompanied by asterisks is also provided on Model 10B (filename: MODEL10B) of the software file disk that is available for use with the text, allowing the problem to be worked on the computer.

PARTIALLY OWNED SUBSIDIARIES AND UNCONSOLIDATED SUBSIDIARIES

3

TO UNDERSTAND

- The way to handle a noncontrolling interest in preparing consolidated statements.
- The way to control an entity other than by owning a majority voting interest.
- The way to value a parent's Investment account when a wholly owned or partially owned subsidiary is *not* consolidated.
- The way earnings of *domestic* groups are taxed.
- The way tax rules for related entities can affect a parent's decision to increase or decrease its ownership in a subsidiary.

TOPIC OUTLINE

There is only one good and that is knowledge. There is only one evil and that is ignorance.

ARISTOTLE

75

CHAPTER OVERVIEW

In partial ownership situations (which occur less frequently than 100% ownership situations), the voting shares *not* owned by the parent are referred to formally as the **noncontrolling interest.** (In practice, these small owners are usually referred to collectively as the *minority interest*.)

This chapter discusses the basic issues associated with reflecting a noncontrolling interest in a subsidiary in the consolidated statements. Additional, more complex issues arise when one entity "acquires" (in a business combination) a majority voting interest in another entity; we discuss these issues in Chapter 6. For brevity, we hereafter use the abbreviation **NCI** for *noncontrolling interest* in most instances and **CI** for *controlling interest* in limited instances.

Beginning in the early 1980s, a very small number of companies designed novel ways to justify *not* consolidating entities that substantively were subsidiaries. We address (1) the substance versus form aspects of these situations and (2) the ways the Financial Accounting Standards Board (FASB) and the Securities and Exchange Commission (SEC) have responded to this effective versus legal control issue.

Occasionally, consolidating a subsidiary is no longer appropriate, which raises the issue of how to value the parent's Investment account in the statements that it issues to its stockholders (its *general-purpose financial statements*). Such statements could be either (1) parent-company-only statements (when the parent has only one subsidiary) or (2) consolidated statements (when other subsidiaries exist and are consolidated). Accordingly, we discuss when the parent may use the (1) equity method, (2) the cost method, and (3) the fair value (market value) method.

Creating a subsidiary raises an issue as to whether the investment income recorded on the parent's books relating to the subsidiary (the Equity in Net Income account under the *equity method* or the Dividend Income account under the *cost method*) will be taxed at the parent level. The financial statement implications of this tax issue for domestic subsidiaries, which we discuss in this chapter's appendix, represent a relatively simple area. This tax issue for foreign subsidiaries, which we discuss in the Appendix of Chapter 19, is a much more involved area.

The Wall Street Journal infrequently publishes an article that profiles an accountant. We present such an article (in the Practitioner Perspective in the appendix) because of its uniqueness insofar as the extraordinary perseverance that one individual had in becoming a successful tax accountant.

I CONSOLIDATION METHODS FOR PARTIALLY OWNED CREATED SUBSIDIARIES

Many reasons exist as to why a subsidiary is *not* 100% owned. Recall from Chapter 1, for instance, that some foreign countries require local citizens to own a percentage of a foreign company's subsidiary. Another instance is when a parent sells a portion of its common stock holdings in a subsidiary to obtain needed cash.

CASE IN POINT

Sears, Roebuck and Co. had its 100%-owned Allstate Corporation subsidiary complete a primary initial public offering of 19.9% of the Allstate common shares held by Sears. This partial disposal a few years ago raised $2.29 billion of needed cash for Sears. It also increased the Noncontrolling Interest account in Sears' consolidated balance sheet from $300 million to $2.3 billion.

CONCEPTUAL ISSUES

When a subsidiary is partially owned, two basic issues arise:

1. Should the noncontrolling interest (NCI) in the subsidiary's net assets and net income be reported in the consolidated statements? The debate concerns the use of (1) the **full consolidation** method (using 100% of the subsidiary's account balances) or (2) the **proportional consolidation** method (using, say 75%, of the subsidiary's account balances).

2. If the NCI is presented in the consolidated statements (as it does only under *full consolidation*), how should it be classified? Several conceptual treatments exist.

CONCEPTUAL ISSUE 1: PROPORTIONAL OR FULL CONSOLIDATION?

PROPORTIONAL CONSOLIDATION (NOT PERMITTED UNDER GAAP) Under the **proportional consolidation concept,** the parent consolidates only its ownership in each of the items in the subsidiary's financial statements. In other words, for a 75%-owned subsidiary, we multiply the cash, accounts receivable, sales, and so forth by 75% to arrive at the amounts to include in the consolidation. Under this method, accounting for the NCI in the consolidated statements is *not* necessary because it is *not* reported there. The rationale underlying proportional consolidation is summarized as follows:

1. The consolidated statements should be merely an extension of the parent's statements.

2. In substance (although not as a legality), the parent has a percentage interest in each of the subsidiary's assets, liabilities, revenues, costs and expenses, gains, and losses.

In recent years, *proportional consolidation* has become one of several methods to account for investments in real estate partnerships and construction joint ventures. Moreover, it has been advocated increasingly for consolidated statements.[1] However, proportional consolidation has never been permitted in the United States—only *full consolidation* is allowed.

FULL CONSOLIDATION (REQUIRED UNDER GAAP) Under the *full consolidation method*, the parent consolidates the entire amount of each of the subsidiary's individual asset, liability, and income statement accounts with those of the parent company. Because the subsidiary is only partially owned, however, the additional amounts consolidated constitute the NCI. Therefore, the NCI in (1) the subsidiary's net assets (Assets – Liabilities) and (2) the subsidiary's net income is reported as separate items in the consolidated statements. The rationale underlying *full consolidation* is summarized as follows:

1. Legally, the parent does *not* have a separable percentage in each individual asset, liability, and income statement account of the subsidiary. Its ownership interest is a percentage of the net assets and net income *as a whole*.

---

[1]Perhaps the strongest argument in favor of proportional consolidation is proposed by Harold Bierman, Jr., "Proportionate Consolidation and Financial Analysis," *Accounting Horizons*, December 1992, pp. 5–17.

2. The parent controls *all* of the subsidiary even though its ownership is less than 100%.

3. The purpose of consolidated statements is to present financial information as if the parent and the subsidiary were a single company.

CONCEPTUAL ISSUE 2: MANNER OF REPORTING THE NCI UNDER FULL CONSOLIDATION

Two concepts exist for reporting the NCI in the consolidated statements under the full consolidation method: (1) the **parent company concept** and (2) the **economic unit concept.**[2] We now discuss both of these concepts—only one of which is permitted under current GAAP.

THE PARENT COMPANY CONCEPT (*NOT* TO BE PERMITTED UNDER U.S. GAAP)[3]

Under the *parent company concept*, consolidated reporting is merely a different manner of reporting the parent's financial position and results of operations. Accordingly, the reporting format emphasizes the interests of the controlling shareholders (the parent's shareholders).

For the balance sheet, the subsidiary's assets and liabilities are viewed as **merely being substituted** for the parent's Investment in Subsidiary account. Consequently, the stockholders' equity in the *parent-company-only statements* is also the stockholders' equity in the *consolidated statements.* For the income statement, the subsidiary's sales, costs and expenses, gains, and losses are viewed as merely being substituted for the parent's investment income reported in the parent's income statement.

The purpose of these multiline substitutions for the single-line items in the parent's balance sheet and the parent's income statement is to make the parent's financial statements more informative to its stockholders. Therefore, the NCI is presented in the consolidated statements in a somewhat suppressed manner as follows:

1. **In the consolidated balance sheet.** The NCI in the subsidiary's net assets is treated as an outside interest and is shown *outside* the stockholders' equity section—**in the aggregate**—in one of the following two ways:
   a. **Between liabilities and stockholders' equity.** This presentation reflects the unique nature of the NCI. It is an equity interest but not of the parent company, which is the reporting entity.
   b. **Among liabilities.** This presentation has little or no supporting theory. If the NCI is insignificant and a separate classification is unwarranted, however, this classification is used.
2. **In the consolidated income statement.** The NCI in the subsidiary's net income is shown as a *deduction* in the consolidated income statement in arriving at the consolidated net income. For example, assuming that a 75%-owned subsidiary had net income of $32,000 for the year, the NCI deduction is $8,000 (25% of $32,000) and is presented as follows:

---

[2]Prior to 1991, these concepts were referred to in the accounting literature as *theories.* Furthermore, the *economic unit concept* was called the *entity theory.* In this chapter, we use the same terminology used in the applicable FASB documents issued in the 1990s, which is more accurate and descriptive.

[3]The *parent company concept* is acceptable under GAAP until the new FASB rules requiring the *economic unit concept* take effect, as discussed in Chapter 1 on page 23.

	Consolidated Income Statement
Sales	$992,000
Cost of sales	(520,000)
Expenses	(330,000)
NCI in net income	(8,000)
Net Income (consolidated)	$134,000

3. **In the consolidated statement of changes in stockholders' equity.** Because the NCI is presented *outside* the equity section in the consolidated balance sheet, **all amounts in the consolidated statement of changes in stockholders' equity pertain solely to the controlling interests.**

THE ECONOMIC UNIT CONCEPT (TO BE PERMITTED UNDER U.S. GAAP)
Under the *economic unit concept*, consolidated reporting is viewed as providing information about a group of legal entities (the parent and its subsidiaries) under the control of a single management. Therefore, the assets, liabilities, sales, costs and expenses, gains, and losses of the individual legal entities are the assets, liabilities, revenues, costs and expenses, gains, and losses of the consolidated entity. Accordingly, no special emphasis is given to the controlling interest, even though the noncontrolling stockholders' ownership interest relates solely to the ownership in the subsidiary. Because the controlling and noncontrolling interests are viewed as being of the same nature, they are treated the same way in the consolidated statements.

For the balance sheet, the stockholders' equity in the *parent's* statements is *not* the stockholders' equity in the *consolidated* statements because the *consolidated* stockholders' equity includes the NCI. Likewise, the *parent's* net income is *not* the *consolidated* net income. The *consolidated* net income is the combined net incomes of all companies within the group (exclusive of the parent's investment income on investments in subsidiaries).

Consequently, the NCI is presented in the consolidated statements as follows:

1. **In the consolidated balance sheet.** The NCI in the subsidiary's net assets is shown—**in the aggregate**—as a separate category *inside* the stockholders' equity section.

2. **In the consolidated income statement.** The NCI in the subsidiary's net income is shown as an apportionment of the consolidated net income in one of the following ways (assuming that a 75%-owned subsidiary had net income of $32,000 for the year):

	Consolidated Income Statement[a]	
	Dual Emphasis Format	Single Emphasis Format
Sales	$992,000	$992,000
Cost of sales	(520,000)	(520,000)
Expenses	(330,000)	(330,000)
Net Income (consolidated)	$142,000	$142,000
Net income accruing to the NCI	$ 8,000	(8,000)
Net income accruing to the CI	$134,000	$134,000

[a]These formats are displayed in paragraph 107 of the FASB's October 16, 1995, Exposure Draft.

3. **In the consolidated statement of stockholders' equity.** To illustrate the manner of reporting for this statement, we (1) use the preceding $134,000 and $8,000

apportioned income amounts and (2) assume that for the year, the parent declared dividends of $85,000 and the subsidiary declared dividends of $12,000, $3,000 of which was paid to the NCI (25% of $12,000), and (3) the subsidiary had total stockholder's equity of $80,000 at the beginning of the year, $20,000 of which accrues to the NCI (25% of $80,000). The NCI is presented as follows:

Consolidated Statement of Changes in Stockholders' Equity

Subsidiary's Equity[a]		Non-controlling Interest +	Controlling Interest		Total Stockholders' Equity =
			Common Stock +	Retained Earnings =	
$80,000	Balances, 1/1/X1	$20,000	$200,000	$117,000	$337,000
32,000	+ Net income	8,000		134,000	142,000
(12,000)	− Dividends	(3,000)		(85,000)	(88,000)
$100,000	Balances, 12/31/X1	$25,000	$200,000	$166,000	$391,000

[a]Shown for informational purposes only.

The key point here is that the amounts reported in the Retained Earnings column exclude any amounts accruing to the NCI.

WHICH CONCEPT IS CORRECT? Whether the *parent company concept* or the *economic unit concept* is correct depends on whether the reporting entity is considered to have changed as a result of the consolidation process—a purely subjective judgment. The NCI shareholders do *not* influence the parent's operating policies. Thus the consolidated statements are of no benefit whatsoever to these shareholders. This group is entitled only to the financial statements of the partially owned subsidiary. The proposed new FASB rules permit only the use of the **economic unit concept.**[4]

The manner of presenting the NCIs in the balance sheet is mixed in foreign countries as shown in the International Perspective.

CONSOLIDATION WORKSHEET: MANNER OF ESTABLISHING THE NCI IN THE BALANCE SHEET

The existence of an NCI adds an additional slight complexity to the consolidation process. To show worksheet techniques available to reflect the NCI in a subsidiary's net assets in the consolidated balance sheet, assume that S Company is a 75%-owned subsidiary that reported the following balances at December 31, 19X2:

Common stock	$ 60,000
Retained earnings	40,000
	$100,000

The NCI in S Company's net assets is thus $25,000 (25% of $100,000). The $25,000 could be established in the Consolidated column of the worksheet in either of the following two ways:

1. **The residual technique.** Under this technique, only the parent's interest in S Company's common stock and retained earnings is eliminated. The amounts *not* eliminated are extended into the Consolidated column. Consequently, these extended amounts for each of the subsidiary's equity accounts must be summed

---

[4]Regardless of the fact that the proposed new FASB rules permit the use of only the *economic unit method*, the format of the consolidation worksheet and the consolidation entries are the same as used in the *parent company concept*.

INTERNATIONAL PERSPECTIVE

Manner of Presenting the Noncontrolling Interest in the Balance Sheet in Foreign Countries

Presented *Outside* Stockholders' Equity	Presented *Inside* Stockholders' Equity	Not Specified
Canada	Australia	France
Italy	Germany	Japan
The Netherlands (below equity)	United States	United Kingdom
Spain (below equity)		

International Accounting Standard 27, "Consolidated Financial Statements and Accounting for Investments in Subsidiaries" (1987):

Minority [noncontrolling] interests should be presented in the consolidated balance sheet separately from liabilities and the parent shareholders' equity.

Note: When the manner of classifying the NCI is prescribed, *full consolidation,* not *proportional consolidation,* is being used. A review of international accounting materials relating to these countries revealed that none of them allows *proportional consolidation.*

---

to obtain the amount to report for the NCI in the net assets. This technique is as shown here:

	P Company	S Company	Consolidation Entries Dr.	Consolidation Entries Cr.	Consolidated
Investment in S Co.	75,000			75,000(1)	–0–
S Company:					
Common stock		60,000	45,000(1)		15,000 NCI
Retained earnings		40,000	30,000(1)		10,000 NCI

2. **The nonresidual technique.** Under this technique, 100% of each of S Company's equity accounts is eliminated. Consequently, a single amount is established for the NCI in the subsidiary's net assets. This technique is as shown here:

	P Company	S Company	Consolidation Entries Dr.	Consolidation Entries Cr.	Consolidated
Investment in S Co.	75,000			75,000(1)	–0–
NCI in net assets				25,000(1)	25,000
S Company:					
Common stock		60,000	60,000(1)		–0–
Retained earnings		40,000	40,000(1)		–0–

In illustrating the preparation of consolidation worksheets under both the *cost method* and the *equity method,* we use the *nonresidual* technique.

CONSOLIDATION WORKSHEET: THE COST METHOD

When the parent uses the *cost method* of accounting, a third consolidation entry (in addition to the basic elimination entry and the intercompany dividend elimination entry that were explained in Chapter 2) is needed. This additional entry establishes the proper amounts in the Consolidated column for the NCI; it also prevents dividends paid to the NCI from being summed with the parent's dividends in the statement of retained earnings.

To illustrate, we assume that (1) S Company was created on December 31, 19X0, (2) the parent invested $45,000 cash for a 75% equity interest, (3) outside investors invested $15,000 cash for a 25% equity interest, and (4) S Company issued no par common stock (thus the Additional Paid-in Capital account is *not* needed). We also assume that S Company subsequently reported the following items for 19X1 and 19X2:

	Net Income	Dividends Declared
19X1	$24,000	$ 4,000
19X2	32,000	12,000

The three entries required in consolidation at December 31, 19X1, and December 31, 19X2 (under the *cost method*), follow:

1. The basic elimination entry:

		Consolidation Date			
		Dec. 31, 19X1		Dec. 31, 19X2	
WORKSHEET ENTRY ONLY	Common Stock	45,000		45,000	
	Investment in Subsidiary		45,000		45,000

2. The intercompany dividend elimination entry:

		Consolidation Date			
		Dec. 31, 19X1		Dec. 31, 19X2	
WORKSHEET ENTRY ONLY	Dividend income (from subsidiary). . .	3,000		9,000	
	Dividends Declared		3,000		9,000

3. The NCI entry (all amounts are at 25% of S Company's accounts):

		Consolidation Date			
		Dec. 31, 19X1		Dec. 31, 19X2	
WORKSHEET ENTRY ONLY	Common Stock	15,000		15,000	
	Retained Earnings,				
	1/1/X1 and 1/1X2	–0–		5,000	
	NCI in Net Income	6,000		8,000	
	Dividends Declared.		1,000		3,000
	NCI in Net Assets		20,000		25,000

Illustration 3–1 shows a consolidation worksheet at December 31, 19X2, using the related three consolidation entries at this date.

REVIEW POINTS FOR ILLUSTRATION 3–1   Note the following:

1. The $25,000 reported for NCI in S Company's net assets at year-end can be proven by multiplying S Company's total stockholders' equity of $100,000 by the NCI ownership percentage ($100,000 × 25% = $25,000).

| ILLUSTRATION 3–1 | The Cost Method: Second Year Subsequent to Date of Creation |

P Company and S Company
Consolidation Worksheet as of December 31, 19X2

	P Company	75%-owned S Company	Consolidation Entries Dr.	Consolidation Entries Cr.	Consolidated
Income Statement (19X2)					
Sales	710,000	282,000			992,000
Cost of Sales	(390,000)	(130,000)			(520,000)
Expenses	(210,000)	(120,000)			(330,000)
Dividend income (from S Co.) . . .	9,000		9,000(2)		–0–
Net income	119,000	32,000	9,000		142,000[a]
NCI in net income			8,000(3)		(8,000)
CI in Net Income			17,000		134,000
Statement of Retained Earnings[b]					
Balances, 1/1/X2	102,000	20,000	5,000(3)		117,000
+ Net income	119,000	32,000	17,000		134,000
				3,000(3)	
– Dividends declared	(85,000)	(12,000)		9,000(2)	(85,000)
Balances, 12/31/X2	136,000	40,000	22,000	12,000	166,000
Balance Sheet					
Cash	77,000	31,000			108,000
Accounts receivable	84,000	43,000			127,000
Inventory	140,000	82,000			222,000
Investment in S Co.	45,000			45,000(1)	–0–
Land	220,000	30,000			250,000
Buildings and equipment	500,000	150,000			650,000
Accumulated depreciation	(360,000)	(26,000)			(386,000)
Total Assets	706,000	310,000		45,000	971,000
Liabilities	370,000	210,000			580,000
NCI in net assets				25,000(3)	25,000
P Company:					
Common stock	200,000				200,000
Retained earnings	136,000				136,000
S Company:					
Common stock		60,000	45,000(1) 15,000(3)		–0–
Retained earnings		40,000	22,000	12,000	30,000
Total Liabilities and Equity . .	706,000	310,000	82,000	37,000	971,000

Proof of debit and credit postings   82,000   82,000

[a]Recall that the consolidated net income is $142,000 under the *economic unit concept*.
[b]Recall that the consolidated statement of retained earnings includes only amounts that accrue to the controlling interest.

Explanation of entries:
  (1) The basic elimination entry.
  (2) The intercompany dividend elimination entry.
  (3) The NCI entry.

Recap of Retained Earnings
P Company $136,000
S Company   30,000
      Total $166,000

2. If P Company were required to furnish a consolidated statement of changes in stockholders' equity (a GAAP requirement for publicly owned entities), it would appear as follows:

Consolidated Statement of Changes in Stockholders' Equity

	Non-controlling Interest	+	Controlling Interest Common Stock	+	Controlling Interest Retained Earnings	=	Total Stockholders' Equity
Balances, 1/1/X2	$20,000		$200,000		$117,000		$337,000
+ Net income	8,000				134,000		142,000
– Dividends	(3,000)				(85,000)		(88,000)
Balances, 12/31/X2	$25,000		$200,000		$166,000		$391,000

3. The $3,000 of dividends paid to the NCI was eliminated in consolidation so that it would *not* be summed with dividends paid by the parent—just as dividends paid by a subsidiary to its parent are also *not* reported as dividends in the consolidated statement of retained earnings (as illustrated in Chapter 2). (Note that this $3,000 of dividends is reported in the noncontrolling interest column in the statement in Review Point 2—not in the retained earnings column.)

CONSOLIDATION WORKSHEET: THE EQUITY METHOD

When the parent uses the equity method of accounting, the additional complexity of an NCI can be easily handled by slightly modifying the parent's analysis of its Investment account to include the NCI. Even in later chapters when more complexities are introduced, the inclusion of the NCI in the analysis of the Investment account minimizes the consolidation effort.

MODIFYING THE ANALYSIS OF THE INVESTMENT ACCOUNT   Illustration 3–2 shows the way that the analysis of the Investment account can be expanded at the date of a subsidiary's creation to accommodate the NCI. In this illustration, we assume that (1) S Company was created on December 31, 19X0, (2) the parent invested $45,000 cash for a 75% equity interest, (3) outside investors invested $15,000 cash for a 25% equity interest, and (4) S Company issued no par common stock (thus the Additional Paid-in Capital account is not needed).

Illustration 3–2 also shows the basic elimination entry made to consolidate S Company at December 31, 19X0. Because of the simplicity of this situation, we do not show a consolidation worksheet at this date of creation. We do so shortly at December 31, 19X2 (two years later).

ILLUSTRATION 3–2	**Modifying the Analysis of the Investment Account to Include the Noncontrolling Interest**					
	Noncontrolling Interest (25%)	+	Parent's Investment Account	=	Subsidiary's Equity Accounts Common Stock	+ Retained Earnings
Balances, 12/31/X0	$15,000		$45,000		$60,000	$–0–

The Basic Elimination Entry at December 31, 19X0
(using the amounts in the above analysis)

WORKSHEET ENTRY ONLY	Common Stock 60,000		
	Investment in Subsidiary		45,000
	NCI in Net Assets		15,000

ILLUSTRATION 3–3	**Updating the Analysis of the Investment Account**				
		Noncontrolling Interest (25%) +	Parent's Investment Account =	Subsidiary's Equity Accounts	
				Common Stock +	Retained Earnings
Balances, 12/31/X0		$15,000	$45,000	$60,000	
+ Equity in net income:					
To parent (75%)			18,000		$18,000
To NCI (25%)		6,000			6,000
– Dividends:					
To parent (75%)			(3,000)		(3,000)
To NCI (25%)		(1,000)			(1,000)
Balances, 12/31/X1		$20,000	$60,000	$60,000	$20,000
+ Equity in net income:					
To parent (75%)			24,000		24,000
To NCI (25%)		8,000			8,000
– Dividends:					
To parent (75%)			(9,000)		(9,000)
To NCI (25%)		(3,000)			(3,000)
Balances, 12/31/X2		$25,000	$75,000	$60,000	$40,000

The Basic Elimination Entry
(using the amounts in the above analysis)

		Consolidation Date	
		Dec. 31, 19X1	Dec. 31, 19X2
WORKSHEET ENTRY ONLY	Common Stock	60,000	60,000
	Retained Earnings, 1/1/X1 and 1/1/X2 ...	–0–	20,000
	Equity in Net Income	18,000	24,000
	NCI in Net Income	6,000	8,000
	Dividend Declared	4,000	12,000
	Investment in Subsidiary ..../..	60,000	75,000
	NCI in Net Assets	20,000	25,000

UPDATING THE EXPANDED ANALYSIS OF THE INVESTMENT ACCOUNT Assume that S Company subsequently reported the following items for 19X1 and 19X2:

	Net Income	Dividends Declared
19X1	$24,000	$ 4,000
19X2	32,000	12,000

Under the *equity method* of accounting, the parent records its share of these amounts. The expanded analysis of the Investment account is updated as shown in Illustration 3–3. This illustration also shows the basic elimination entry used in consolidation at each year-end; the amounts were readily obtained from the updated analysis.

Illustration 3–4 shows a consolidation worksheet as of December 31, 19X2, using the related basic elimination entry shown in Illustration 3–3.

REVIEW POINTS FOR ILLUSTRATION 3–4 Note the following:

1. The same equalities and control features that existed for 100%-owned subsidiaries exist for partially owned subsidiaries. That is, the net income and retained earnings amounts in the Consolidated column are the same as the comparable items in the P Company column.
2. The consolidated amounts are the same as in Illustration 3–1 (the cost method).

| ILLUSTRATION 3–4 | The Equity Method: Second Year Subsequent to Date of Creation |

P Company and S Company
Consolidation Worksheet as of December 31, 19X2

	P Company	75%-owned S Company	Consolidation Entries Dr.	Consolidation Entries Cr.	Consolidated
Income Statement (19X2)					
Sales	710,000	282,000			992,000
Cost of sales	(390,000)	(130,000)			(520,000)
Expenses	(210,000)	(120,000)			(330,000)
Equity in net income (of S Co.)	24,000		24,000(1)		–0–
Net income	134,000	32,000	24,000		142,000[a]
NCI in net income			8,000(1)		(8,000)
CI in Net Income			32,000		134,000
Statement of Retained Earnings[b]					
Balances, 1/1/X2	117,000	20,000	20,000(1)		117,000
+ Net income	134,000	32,000	32,000		134,000
– Dividends declared	(85,000)	(12,000)		12,000(1)	(85,000)
Balances, 12/31/X2	166,000	40,000	52,000	12,000	166,000
Balance Sheet					
Cash	77,000	31,000			108,000
Accounts receivable	84,000	43,000			127,000
Inventory	140,000	82,000			222,000
Investment in S Co.	75,000			75,000(1)	–0–
Land	220,000	30,000			250,000
Buildings and equipment	500,000	150,000			650,000
Accumulated depreciation	(360,000)	(26,000)			(386,000)
Total Assets	736,000	310,000		75,000	971,000
Liabilities	370,000	210,000			580,000
NCI in net assets				25,000(1)	25,000
P Company:					
Common stock	200,000				200,000
Retained earnings	166,000				166,000
S Company:					
Common stock		60,000(1)	60,000(1)		–0–
Retained earnings		40,000	52,000	12,000	–0–
Total Liabilities and Equity	736,000	310,000	112,000	37,000	971,000
Proof of debit and credit postings			112,000	112,000	

[a]Recall that the consolidated net income is $142,000 under the *economic unit concept.*
[b]Recall that the consolidated statement of retained earnings includes only amounts that accrue to the controlling interest.

Explanation of entry:
 (1) The basic elimination entry.

II CONTROL OTHER THAN BY OWNING A MAJORITY VOTING INTEREST

In the early 1980s, a few entities (mostly publicly owned) began "sponsoring" the creation of new entities in which the sponsoring entity did *not* purchase a majority voting interest. The sponsoring entity typically lent money to the new entity, however, to fund its start-up costs (often research and development or marketing related).

Furthermore, the financial arrangements usually had terms such that the sponsoring entity *effectively controlled* the new entity, **thus achieving the same result as if it held a majority voting interest instead.** (Recall from Chapter 1 that *control* enables an entity to elect or appoint a majority of the board of directors.) Such arrangements raised "substance" versus "form" issues as to consolidating the new entity. Such new entities were often branded as *nonsubsidiary subsidiaries* or *orphan subsidiaries*.

The Securities and Exchange Commission investigated some of these financial arrangements and concluded that they were shams designed merely to avoid consolidating the newly created entities.[5] By not consolidating these entities, the sponsoring entities did *not* report expenses and losses it otherwise would report for consolidated subsidiaries. The SEC characterized the reporting results of these arrangements, in general, as "cute accounting."[6]

How Control Can Exist without Majority Ownership

Some of the many ways that control can effectively exist without a majority ownership are as follows:

1. The sponsor's loan agreement has terms that allow it to approve the appointment of board members by the new entity's common stockholders.

2. The sponsor's loan is convertible *at will* into the new entity's common stock, and such conversion gives the sponsor a majority voting interest.

3. The new entity's charter prohibits it from buying or selling merchandise to any company other than the sponsor without the sponsor's written approval.

4. An entity owns 45% of the common stock and is able to appoint a majority of the board members because the remaining shares are widely held (no single party holds more than 3%).

The International Perspective shows that the concept of **control by any means** is widely used and has replaced the concept of **legal control** (control by having a majority ownership interest).

The FASB Acts to Require Use of *Effective Control*

As mentioned in Chapter 1, the FASB in late 1995 issued an Exposure Draft, "Consolidated Financial Statements: Policy and Procedures" in connection with its current consolidations project. The consolidation rules set forth in this pronouncement are patterned after the SEC's *effective control*–based rules (which can be characterized as *judgment driven*). When the FASB's new rules become effective, both *ARB No. 51* and *SFAS No. 94* (which are based on legal control and can be characterized as *rule driven* (merely seeing if the ownership level is over 50%) will be superseded.

The Impact of the Proposed New FASB Rule on Practice

The vast majority of entities that must address whether consolidation of an entity is required fall into the category of having legal control because they own a majority

---

[5]In 1984, the SEC changed its consolidation rules (which at the time coincided with the consolidation rules of the private sector) so that *effective control* instead of *legal control* became the criteria for consolidation. In doing so, the SEC emphasized that *substance* must take precedence over *form.*

[6]The SEC also let its displeasure be known to CPA firms that had gone along with these arrangements and thus did *not* require consolidation even though it was appropriate when these transactions were evaluated from a *substance* versus *form* standpoint.

INTERNATIONAL PERSPECTIVE

Basis of Control for Consolidation

Legal Control (by ownership of more than 50% of the voting interest)	Control by Any Means (by either ownership of more than 50% of the voting interest or a financial arrangement)
Japan	Australia
France (40%)	Canada
Italy	Germany
	The Netherlands
	Spain
	United Kingdom
	United States

---

voting interest (usually 100%). Thus even with broadened consolidation rules, practice will change for only a small percentage of entities.

For these entities, however, expert professional judgment will usually be needed (as has been the case since 1984 for entities subject to the SEC's reporting rules). In current practice, some of these "financial arrangement" situations are often quite challenging to assess, usually requiring evaluation at high levels within both companies and their outside auditing firms.

III UNCONSOLIDATED SUBSIDIARIES

Recall from Chapter 1 that the only reasons for *not* consolidating a subsidiary[7] are (1) lack of control or (2) expectations of temporary control when it is *acquired* in a business combination.

Lack (loss) of control situations occur, for example, when (1) a subsidiary has filed for bankruptcy protection (the bankruptcy judge then controls the subsidiary) and (2) a subsidiary is placed under severe operating restrictions. Examples of severe operating restrictions are (1) a foreign government–imposed prohibition on paying dividends whereby the foreign government effectively owns the subsidiary and (2) a foreign government's involvement in the day-to-day operations of the foreign subsidiary.

When a subsidiary is justifiably *not* consolidated, the parent must determine how to value its Investment account because this account (instead of being eliminated in consolidation) is now reported in the financial statements the parent issues to its stockholders (those financial statements being the parent's *general-purpose financial statements*). These financial statements could be either (1) the parent's statements *alone* or (2) consolidated statements if the parent has other subsidiaries that are consolidated.

The factors that determine how to value the parent's Investment account in these statements are (1) whether the parent can exert *significant influence* (a condi-

---

[7]Technically, when control is lacking, it may be incorrect to refer to the relationship between the two companies as being a *parent-subsidiary relationship,* a term that conjures up images of control of the one entity by the other. *Investor-investee* may be more appropriate. In practice and the accounting literature, however, *parent* and *subsidiary* are used as a matter of convenience in these situations.

tion for using the *equity method*) and (2) whether unowned shares in partial ownership situations are *publicly traded*.[8]

INVESTMENT VALUATION METHODS

Depending on the circumstances, the parent uses the *cost method,* the *equity method,* or the *fair value method.* When a parent has the option to use only the *equity method* (allowed only if the parent *can* exert significant influence) or the cost method, the parent usually focuses on the particular circumstances that resulted in nonconsolidation and decides accordingly.

WHOLLY OWNED SUBSIDIARY JUSTIFIABLY *NOT* CONSOLIDATED: COST AND EQUITY METHODS ALLOWED
In these situations, the *cost method* can always be used. In contrast, the *equity method* is permitted *only* if the parent is able to exert *significant influence,* which is the rationale underlying its required use if an investor has significant influence but not control (typically 20–50% ownership situations).

PARTIALLY OWNED AND *NON*PUBLICLY TRADED SUBSIDIARY JUSTIFIABLY *NOT* CONSOLIDATED: COST AND EQUITY METHODS ALLOWED
In these situations, the rules are the same as when the unconsolidated subsidiary is 100% owned as explained above.

PARTIALLY OWNED AND PUBLICLY TRADED SUBSIDIARY JUSTIFIABLY *NOT* CONSOLIDATED: EQUITY AND FAIR VALUE METHODS ALLOWED
In these situations, the *cost method* is *not* permitted. Instead, the *equity method* or the *fair value method* must be used. However, the fair value method, which is allowed pursuant to *SFAS No. 115,* "Accounting for Certain Investments in Debt and Equity Securities," can be used **only if the fair value is readily determinable** (using a quoted market price).

When the *fair value method* is used, keep in mind that an equity investment in a subsidiary is usually intended as a long-term investment. Thus an equity investment in an unconsolidated subsidiary that is accounted for at fair value is classified in the *available-for-sale* category described in *SFAS No. 115*— not the *trading* category. Unrealized gains and losses on *available-for-sale securities* are excluded from earnings and reported in a separate component of shareholders' equity until realization occurs.

LOSS OF CONTROL SITUATIONS
In these situations, the *cost method* is the predominant method used because realization of the subsidiary's future earnings usually is the critical issue. Accordingly, the conservatism of the cost method (report no investment income until dividends have been received) is usually more appropriate.

WHEN CONTROL IS EXPECTED TO BE TEMPORARY AT THE DATE A SUBSIDIARY IS ACQUIRED
In these situations, the realization of the subsidiary's future earnings is usually *not* a critical issue. The parent can generally expect to realize those earnings either by (1) directing the subsidiary to pay dividends up to the disposal date or (2) negotiating a higher sales price if the earnings are *not* distributed. Consequently, the *equity method* is generally used in these situations.

For all other subsidiaries for which control is expected to be temporary—such as when a parent takes steps to sell either (1) a created subsidiary or (2) an acquired subsidiary that it has owned for several years—the subsidiary must be consolidated.

Illustration 3–5 summarizes the methods allowed for the various types of nonconsolidation situations.

---

[8]These rules concerning how to value the parent's Investment account in *non*consolidation situations also apply to situations in which the parent issues *parent-company-only statements* **in addition to consolidated statements.**

ILLUSTRATION 3–5	Summary of the Use of Cost and Equity Methods When a Subsidiary Is *Not* Consolidated		
Reason for ***Not* Consolidating**	**Significant Influence Exists**	**Wholly Owned** ***or* Partially Owned & *Not* Publicly Traded**	**Partially Owned & Publicly Traded**
Loss of control	Yes	Cost[a] or equity	Fair value or equity
Loss of control	No	Cost[a]	Fair value
Control expected to be temporary[b]	Yes	Cost[a] or equity	Fair value or equity
Control expected to be temporary[b]	No	Cost[a]	Fair value

[a]The carrying value under the *cost method* must be adjusted downward if the fair value of the investment is below the *cost method* carrying value. Thus the *cost method* is effectively a lower-of-cost-or-market method.

[b]This reason for nonconsolidation can be used only for subsidiaries acquired in business combination and then only if control is expected to be temporary at the business combination date.

END-OF-CHAPTER REVIEW

SUMMARY OF KEY POINTS

1. Under the **proportionate consolidation method,** no amounts relating to the NCI are presented in the consolidated statements.
2. Under current GAAP, partially owned subsidiaries must be **fully consolidated**—not *proportionally* consolidated.
3. Under the **parent company concept,** (a) the NCI in the subsidiary's net income is shown **as a deduction** in arriving at consolidated net income and (b) the NCI in the subsidiary's net assets is presented **outside** the consolidated stockholders' equity section.
4. Under the **economic unit concept,** (a) the NCI in the subsidiary's net income is shown as **an apportionment** of the combined earnings of both companies (the consolidated net income) and (b) the NCI in the subsidiary's net assets is presented **inside** the consolidated stockholders' equity section.
5. The proposed new FASB rules **permit only the economic unit concept.**
6. **Dividends paid to NCI shareholders** are never reported in the consolidated statement of retained earnings as declared dividends.
7. The consolidated statement of retained earnings includes **only amounts accruing to the controlling interest.** (Thus the parent company concept applies under the umbrella of the economic unit concept in this statement.)
8. The proposed new FASB consolidation rules are substantively the same as the SEC's consolidation rules that are based on **control by any means** rather than **legal control** (control is having the ability to elect or appoint a majority of the board of directors).
9. If a subsidiary is *not* consolidated, a parent may value its Investment account using either (1) the **equity method** (only if significant influence exists), (2) the **cost method** (but not if unowned shares are publicly traded), or (3) the **fair market value (required whenever the unowned shares are publicly traded and the parent does *not* use the *equity method*).**

GLOSSARY OF NEW TERMS

Controlling interest (CI)   The interest of the shareholders of a parent company of a partially owned subsidiary in the combined earnings of the parent and the subsidiary.

Economic unit concept   The GAAP concept pertaining to how the assets and liabilities of a partially owned subsidiary and the related NCI in the subsidiary's earnings and net assets should be valued and reported in consolidated statements. A new reporting entity is deemed to exist as a result of the consolidation process. The NCI therefore *is* treated as an equity interest of the consolidated reporting entity. (The need to address this valuation and reporting issue is more frequently encountered in *external expansion* [acquisitions] than in *internal expansion* in which a subsidiary is created.)

Effective control   Refer to the glossary in Chapter 1.

Legal control   Refer to the glossary in Chapter 1.

Noncontrolling interest (NCI)   The interest of the shareholders of a partially owned subsidiary, other than the parent, in the subsidiary's earnings, losses, and net assets.

Parent company concept   A concept concerning the valuation and reporting of the assets and liabilities of a partially owned subsidiary and the related noncontrolling shareholders' interest in the subsidiary's earnings and net assets in consolidated statements. The parent company is deemed the consolidated reporting entity. The NCI therefore is *not* treated as an equity interest of the consolidated reporting entity.

Proportional consolidation concept   A concept concerning the valuation and reporting of a partially owned subsidiary's assets and liabilities and the related NCI in its earnings and net assets in consolidated statements. Only the parent's proportionate interest in each of the subsidiary's assets, liabilities, revenues, and costs and expenses are reported in consolidation. Thus no amounts are reported for the NCI in the consolidated statements.

SELF-STUDY QUESTIONS

(Answers are at the end of this chapter preceding the appendix.)

1. An amount for NCI in net assets of subsidiary is reported under which concept?

	Economic Unit	Parent Company	Proportionate
a.	Yes	Yes	Yes
b.	No	Yes	Yes
c.	No	No	Yes
d.	No	Yes	No
e.	Yes	Yes	No

2. How are dividends paid to NCI shareholders reported in the consolidated statements?
   a. They reduce the amount reported as NCI in the subsidiary's net income in the consolidated income statement.
   b. They reduce the amount reported as NCI in the subsidiary's net assets in the consolidated balance sheet.
   c. They are included in dividends declared in the consolidated statement of retained earnings.
   d. They are combined with expenses in the consolidated income statement.

3. Puntex is currently taking steps to sell its 100%-owned *created* subsidiary. Which of the following should most likely be used to value the investment in Puntex's unconsolidated statements?
   a. The net realizable value.
   b. The cost method or the equity method, as most appropriate.
   c. Only the equity method.
   d. Only the cost method.
   e. The fair value method.
   f. The subsidiary must be consolidated.

4. A foreign government has forcibly taken over Potter's 100%-owned overseas subsidiary. Which of the following should most likely be used in valuing the investment in Potter's unconsolidated statements?
   a. The cost method.
   b. The equity method.
   c. The equity method or net realizable value.
   d. The cost method or net realizable value.
   e. The lower of the cost method or net realizable value.
   f. The net realizable value.

ASSIGNMENT MATERIAL

REVIEW QUESTIONS

1. What is the *proportional consolidation* method?
2. What are the arguments for *full* consolidation?
3. Which concepts fit under *full consolidation*?
4. What are the three theoretical ways to classify the NCI in the balance sheet?
5. How is *consolidated net income* defined under the *parent company* concept? Under the *economic unit* concept?
6. How are dividends paid to a subsidiary's NCI shareholders treated for consolidated reporting purposes?
7. What does *legal control* mean?
8. What does *effective control* mean?
9. Are the SEC's consolidation rules based on *legal control* or *effective control*?
10. What are three ways an entity could have *effective control* over another entity without having a majority ownership interest?
11. When a subsidiary is *not* consolidated, what factors are relevant in deciding between the equity and cost methods?
12. When is the *equity method not* allowed in reporting an investment in an unconsolidated subsidiary?
13. When is the *cost method not* allowed in reporting an investment in an unconsolidated subsidiary?
14. When is the *fair market value* used to value an investment in a subsidiary?

EXERCISES

E 3–1   **Partially Owned Subsidiaries: Consolidated Net Income**   Pila Inc. owns 80% of Sila Inc. For 19X1, Sila reported net income of $55,000 and declared dividends of $15,000. Pila reported $100,000 from its own separate operations exclusive of its investment income from Sila.

Required
1. What is the consolidated net income under the *parent company* concept?
2. What is the consolidated net income under the *economic unit* concept?
3. What is Pila's investment income under the *equity method*? The *cost method*?

E 3–2   **Partially Owned Subsidiaries: Consolidation Entries—Equity Method**   Information for a 70%-owned created subsidiary for 19X1 follows:

Common stock (year-end)	$20,000
Retained earnings, 1/1/X1	80,000
Net income	40,000
Dividends declared	30,000

Required
1. Prepare an analysis of the parent's investment for 19X1, assuming that the parent uses the *equity* method.
2. Prepare the consolidation entry(ies) required at 12/31/X1.

E 3–3   **Partially Owned Subsidiaries: Consolidation Entries—Cost Method**   Use the information in Exercise 3–2 but assume that the parent uses the *cost method*.

Required   Prepare the consolidation entries required at 12/31/X1.

E 3–4   **Partially Owned Subsidiaries: Concepts**   The following items were obtained from the financial statements of a 75%-owned created subsidiary at the end of 19X1:

Dividends declared	$ 40,000
Net income	84,000
Common stock	200,000
Additional paid-in capital	100,000
Retained earnings, 1/1/X1	144,000

In addition, the parent declared and paid dividends of $90,000 in 19X1.

Required   What is the amount for each of the following items?

     a. The parent's year-end investment balance under the *equity method.*
     b. The parent's year-end investment balance under the *cost method.*
     c. The amount reported in the consolidated statements for the NCI in the subsidiary's net assets.
     d. The amount reported in the consolidated statements for the NCI in the subsidiary's net income.
     e. The amount reported for dividends declared in the 19X1 consolidated statement of retained earnings.

E 3–5   **Partially Owned Subsidiaries: Consolidation Entries**   Use the information in the preceding exercise.

Required   **1.** Prepare all consolidation entries at year-end if the parent uses the *equity* method.
     2. Prepare all consolidation entries at year-end if the parent uses the *cost* method.

E 3–6   **Partially Owned Subsidiaries: Working in Reverse**   A parent company of a 60%-owned subsidiary uses the *cost* method. At the end of 19X1, the parent made the following consolidation entry, among others:

     The NCI entry:

Common Stock	4,000	
Additional Paid-in Capital	200,000	
Retained Earnings, 1/1/X1	30,000	
NCI in Net Income	22,000	
Dividends Declared		16,000
NCI in Net Assets		240,000

The parent also declared and paid dividends of $800,000 in 19X1.

Required   What is the amount for each of the following items?

     a. The subsidiary's retained earnings balance at 12/31/X1.
     b. The subsidiary's total equity at 12/31/X4.
     c. The parent's year-end investment balance under the *cost method.*
     d. The parent's year-end investment balance under the *equity method.*
     e. The dividends declared by the subsidiary in 19X1.
     f. The amount reported for dividends declared in the 19X1 consolidated statement of retained earnings.

E 3–7   **Unconsolidated Subsidiaries: Intended Disposal**   Pynco is currently taking steps to sell Synco, its subsidiary for which it has, as a minimum, significant influence. Use the following choices to answer the questions.

     a. Unconsolidated—the cost method.
     b. Unconsolidated—the equity method.
     c. Unconsolidated—the fair value method.
     d. Unconsolidated—the cost method or the equity method, as most appropriate.
     e. Unconsolidated—the equity method or the fair value method.
     f. Unconsolidated—the cost method or the fair value method.
     g. The subsidiary must be consolidated.

Required   How should Synco be reported in Pynco's general-purpose financial statements that it issues to its stockholders if Synco is

     1. A wholly owned *created* subsidiary.
     2. A partially owned *created* subsidiary—the unowned shares *are* publicly traded.
     3. A partially owned *created* subsidiary—the unowned shares are *not* publicly traded.
     4. A wholly owned subsidiary *acquired* four years ago.
     5. A wholly owned subsidiary *acquired* today.
     6. A partially owned subsidiary *acquired* four years ago—the unowned shares *are* publicly traded.
     7. A partially owned subsidiary *acquired* four years ago—the unowned shares are *not* publicly traded.
     8. A partially owned subsidiary *acquired* today—the unowned shares *are* publicly traded.
     9. A partially owned subsidiary *acquired* today—the unowned shares are *not* publicly traded.

E 3–8   **Unconsolidated Subsidiaries: Currency Restrictions**   A foreign government has imposed severe dividend payment restrictions on Prell's 100%-owned foreign subsidiary. Consequently, consolidation is *no longer* appropriate.

Required

1. How should the investment be valued in Prell's unconsolidated statements if it *can* exercise significant influence?
   a. The cost method.
   b. The equity method.
   c. The cost method or the equity method, as most appropriate.
   d. The equity method or the fair value method.
   e. The cost method or the fair value method.
2. Use the information in Question 1 but assume that Prell *cannot* exercise significant influence.
3. Use the information in Question 1 but assume that (a) Prell *can* exercise significant influence, (b) it owns 80% of the voting shares, and (c) the unowned shares are *not* publicly traded.
4. Use the information in Question 1 but assume that (a) Prell *can* exercise significant influence, (b) it owns 80% of the voting shares, and (c) the unowned shares *are* publicly traded.

PROBLEMS

P 3–1* **Consolidation Worksheet: Cost Method** The comparative financial statements of Pane Inc. and its 60%-owned subsidiary, Sill Inc. (created six years ago), follow:

	Pane Inc.		Sill Inc.
	Cost Method[a]	Equity Method[b]	
Income Statement (19X6)			
Sales	$400,000	$400,000	$225,000
Cost of sales	(210,000)	(210,000)	(120,000)
Expenses	(140,000)	(140,000)	(80,000)
Dividend income (from Sill)	12,000		
Equity in net income (of Sill)		15,000	
Net Income	$ 62,000	$ 65,000	$ 25,000
Statement of Retained Earnings			
Balances, 1/1/X6	$150,000	$183,000	$ 55,000
+ Net income	62,000	65,000	25,000
– Dividends declared	(40,000)	(40,000)	(20,000)
Balances, 12/31/X6	$172,000	$208,000	$ 60,000
Balance Sheet (as of 12/31/X6)			
Cash	$ 47,000	$ 47,000	$ 30,000
Accounts receivable, net	65,000	65,000	45,000
Intercompany receivable	15,000	15,000	
Inventory	190,000	190,000	70,000
Investment in subsidiary	30,000	66,000	
Property and equipment	370,000	370,000	180,000
Accumulated depreciation	(160,000)	(160,000)	(40,000)
Total Assets	$557,000	$593,000	$285,000
Payables and accruals	$135,000	$135,000	$ 70,000
Intercompany payable			15,000
Long-term debt	150,000	150,000	90,000
Common stock	100,000	100,000	50,000
Retained earnings	172,000	208,000	60,000
Total Liabilities and Equity	$557,000	$593,000	$285,000

[a]Use this column to work the problem under the *cost method*, which is called for in this problem.

[b]Use this column to work the problem under the *equity method*, which is called for in Problem 3–2.

---

*The financial statement information presented for problems accompanied by asterisks is also provided on Model 3 (filename: MODEL3) of the software file disks that are available with the text, allowing the problem to be worked on the computer.

Assume that the parent uses the *cost method*.

Required 1. Prepare all consolidation entries as of 12/31/X6.
2. Prepare a consolidation worksheet at 12/31/X6.

P 3–2* **Consolidation Worksheet: Equity Method** Use the information in Problem 3–1 but assume that the parent uses the *equity method*.

Required 1. Prepare an analysis of the Investment account for 19X6.
2. Prepare all consolidation entries as of 12/31/X6.
3. Prepare a consolidation worksheet at 12/31/X6.

P 3–3* **Consolidation Worksheet: Cost Method** The comparative financial statements of Pylo Inc. and its 90%-owned subsidiary, Sylo Inc. (created seven years ago), follow:

	Pylo Inc.		Sylo Inc.
	Cost Method[a]	Equity Method[b]	
Income Statement (19X7)			
Sales	$700,000	$700,000	$250,000
Cost of sales	(430,000)	(430,000)	(130,000)
Expenses	(170,000)	(170,000)	(90,000)
Dividend income (from Sylo)	9,000		
Equity in net income (of Sylo)		27,000	
Net Income	$119,000	$127,000	$ 30,000
Balance Sheet (as of 12/31/X7)			
Cash	$ 49,000	$ 49,000	$ 40,000
Accounts receivable, net	95,000	95,000	55,000
Inventory	170,000	170,000	75,000
Investment in subsidiary	45,000	117,000	
Property and equipment	280,000	280,000	175,000
Accumulated depreciation	(120,000)	(120,000)	(25,000)
Total Assets	$519,000	$591,000	$320,000
Payables and accruals	$140,000	$140,000	$ 70,000
Long-term debt	300,000	300,000	120,000
Common stock	10,000	10,000	50,000
Retained earnings	69,000	141,000	80,000
Total Liabilities and Equity	$519,000	$591,000	$320,000

[a]Use this column to work the problem under the *cost method*, as called for in this problem.

[b]Use this column to work the problem under the *equity method*, as called for in Problem 3–4.

Assume that the parent (1) uses the *cost method* of accounting and (2) declared $90,000 of dividends in 19X7.

Required 1. Prepare all consolidation entries as of 12/31/X7.
2. Prepare a consolidation worksheet at 12/31/X7.

P 3–4* **Consolidation Worksheet: Equity Method** Use the information in Problem 3–3 but assume that the parent uses the *equity method*.

Required 1. Prepare an analysis of the Investment account for 19X7.
2. Prepare all consolidation entries as of 12/31/X7.
3. Prepare a consolidation worksheet at 12/31/X7.

P 3–5 **Partially Owned Subsidiaries: Equity and Cost—Other Objective Format Used on the CPA Examination** The following (1) eight account balances and (2) statements of retained earnings were obtained from the *separate company statements* of Pya Inc. and its 90%-owned created subsidiary, Sya Inc. (Pya's only subsidiary), at the end of 19X5:

				Answers	
Item		Pya Inc.	Sya Inc.	Equity Method	Cost Method
	Accounts				
1	Equity in net income (of Sya)	$ 36,000		_____	_____
2	Dividend income (from Sya)			_____	_____
3	Cash	77,000	$ 11,000	_____	_____
4	Intercompany receivable.	18,000		_____	_____
5	Investment in subsidiary	225,000		_____	_____
6	Dividends payable.	20,000	10,000	_____	_____
7	Common stock	1,000	5,000	_____	_____
8	Additional paid-in capital	299,000	95,000	_____	_____
	Statements of Retained Earnings				
9	Retained earnings, 1/1/X5	$395,000	$120,000	_____	_____
10	+ Net income	115,000	40,000	_____	_____
11	– Dividends declared	(80,000)	(10,000)	_____	_____
12	Retained earnings, 12/31/X5	$430,000	$150,000	_____	_____
	Additional Items (to be calculated)				
13	Pya's investment income from Sya—if the **cost method** were used instead of the **equity method**	_____		_____	_____
14	Noncontrolling interest in net income			_____	
15	Noncontrolling interest in net assets			_____	
16	Consolidated net income—**Parent company concept**			_____	
17	Consolidated net income—**Economic unit concept**			_____	

When Sya was created (in 19X1), 10% of the common shares it issued were sold to other private investors. For 19X5, Pya had $79,000 of net income from its own separate operations—excluding its investment income relating to Sya.

(AICPA examination format adapted)

Required 1. How is each of the preceding 13 items reported in Pya's 19X5 consolidated statements? Use the following list of possible answer codes in the answer columns:
  a. Report at the amount shown in Pya's separate statements.
  b. Report at the amount shown in Sya's separate statements.
  c. Report at the **sum of** the amounts shown in Pya's and Sya's separate statements.
  d. Report at **less than** the sum of the amounts shown in Pya's and Sya's separate statements.
  e. Do **not** report this item in the consolidated statements.
  f. Create this item in the consolidation process.
  g. Do **not** report this item in the consolidated statements or in either Pya's or Sya's separate statements.
  2. For items 14 through 17, calculate the amount that would appear in the 19X5 consolidated statements.

✳ THINKING CRITICALLY ✳

✳ CASES ✳

C 3–1 **Partially Owned Subsidiaries: "If I Made the Rules"** Pax Inc. owns 51% of the outstanding common stock of Sax Inc. Rax Inc. owns the other 49% of Sax. The separate company income statements for 19X1, excluding any income recorded under the equity or cost methods, follow (in thousands):

	Pax Inc.	Rax Inc.	Sax Inc.
Revenues	$ 2,000	$ 2,000	$ 300
Costs and expenses	(1,800)	(1,800)	(200)
Net Income	$ 200	$ 200	$ 100

Required   1. Show the four possible manners of reporting that Pax could use to present its 19X1 income statement to its shareholders.
2. Repeat requirement 1 for Rax.
3. If you were one of the seven FASB members, for which manner of reporting would you vote? Why?

C 3–2   Rules or Judgment: Which Is Better?   The accounting standards setters continually face the issue of whether to include detailed rules in their standards or to allow companies and their outside auditors to use judgment. Such is the case in the issue of whether an entity should be consolidated.

Required   1. What are the arguments for allowing judgment?
2. What are the arguments for having detailed rules?
3. What has been the direction of the standards setters in this respect since the FASB's establishment in 1973? Why do you think this is so?

C 3–3   FASB versus SEC Rules: How to Live with a Double Standard   You are a CPA who audits both Privex, a privately owned parent company, and Publex, a publicly owned parent company. Assume that the SEC's consolidation rules are slightly more stringent than the FASB's consolidation rules as to (1) when consolidation is required and (2) what detailed disclosures are required.

Required   1. If Privex follows only the FASB consolidation rules, would you still be able to give an unqualified "clean" opinion on Privex's financial statements?
2. If your answer was yes, how comfortable do you feel giving unqualified opinions using two different reporting standards?
3. What do you think CPAs commonly do in such situations?

C 3–4   Walks, Talks, and Looks Like a Duck: Is It One?   Platt Inc. and Dee Ziner, Platt's head of research and development, formed Secrex Inc., which will perform research and development. Secrex issued 5,000 shares of common stock to Ziner, who is now Secrex's president. (Ziner is no longer employed by Platt.) Platt lent $400,000 to Secrex for initial working capital in return for a note receivable that can be converted at will into 95,000 shares of Secrex's common stock. Platt also granted Secrex a line of credit of $1,000,000.

Required   1. Is consolidation appropriate?
2. What would Platt accomplish with this arrangement?
3. For this question only, assume that consolidating Secrex is *not* appropriate. What serious reporting issue exists regarding Platt's separate financial statements?

✳ PERSONAL SITUATIONS: ETHICS AND INTERPERSONAL SKILLS ✳

PS 3–1   Ethics: Does Company Loyalty Include Filing a False Corporate Tax Return?   Your employer has asked you to file a false corporate income tax return.

Required   1. If you comply and the IRS discovers the filing of a false return, what could be the consequences to you? (The instructor's solution manual describes what happened to Georgia Pacific Corporation and its employees who were responsible for filing such a return.)
2. If you do *not* comply and are fired for not cooperating, what legal recourse might you have? (The instructor's solution manual describes what happened to one such accountant.)

PS 3–2   Interpersonal Skills: Leadership—Is Vision Enough?   You recently became an officer in your college accounting club. You have some good ideas as to how the club could be run more effectively and be more fun.

Required   What else usually must accompany vision for leadership to be effective?

ANSWERS TO SELF-STUDY QUESTIONS

1. e   **2.** b   **3.** f   **4.** e

■APPENDIX

CONSOLIDATED U.S. INCOME TAXES: DOMESTIC SUBSIDIARIES ONLY

When a domestic parent-subsidiary relationship exists, knowledge of certain tax rules and elections peculiar to such situations is needed to determine how the domestic group is taxed. Furthermore, because various ownership levels are taxed differently, these tax rules are a factor to consider when a parent decides to change its ownership level in a subsidiary.

In this appendix, we discuss the issue of taxation of a subsidiary's earnings at the parent level as well as taxation at the subsidiary level. This area cannot be meaningfully discussed without also briefly describing (1) the nature of **consolidated income tax returns,** (2) the conditions to be met for filing such a return, and (3) the advantages and disadvantages of filing such a return. We first present a Practitioner Perspective of a tax accountant.

MANNER OF TAXING SUBSIDIARIES VERSUS BRANCHES

When a subsidiary distributes its earnings to its parent, the parent has **dividend income** for tax-reporting purposes. Thus an element of "double **corporate** taxation"[9] appears to exist when an entity has a subsidiary instead of a *branch.* Recall from Chapter 1 that a branch's earnings are included with its home office's earnings for tax reporting. Thus branch earnings are taxed only once—when the earnings occur—not a second time when branch earnings are remitted to the home office.

THE INTENT OF CONGRESS   The intent of Congress, however, is to tax a subsidiary's earnings only once (in the United States) at the **corporate level.** Accordingly, if a subsidiary has paid U.S. income taxes at the **subsidiary level (as only *domestic subsidiaries* do),** its earnings (net of the taxes paid) will *not* be taxed again in the form of dividend income at the parent level. Special provisions in the tax code (discussed shortly) exist so that such dividend income is not taxed at the **parent level.** However, 20% of the dividend income from less than 80%-owned subsidiaries is taxed at the parent level.

DOMESTIC VERSUS FOREIGN SUBSIDIARIES   As stated, only a **domestic subsidiary** can pay U.S. income taxes at the subsidiary level. In contrast, a **foreign subsidiary** pays income taxes to the foreign government. Because a foreign subsidiary pays no U.S. income taxes at the subsidiary level, a parent's dividend income from a foreign subsidiary **is** assessed a **parent-level tax** in the United States. The manner of calculating the U.S. income taxes on this foreign income (which requires a pro forma tax calculation to which allowable foreign tax credits can be applied) is discussed in the Appendix of Chapter 19.

THE RESULT OF THIS MANNER OF TAXATION   The result of this manner of taxation is that subsidiaries and branches are taxed the same—only once **in the United States.** Accordingly, whether the subsidiary or branch form of organization is used for an outlying location does not matter insofar as U.S. income taxes are concerned (except for the timing factor of reporting the income as earned versus when distributed).

---

[9]*Double corporate taxation* differs from the more commonly familiar term *double taxation,* which refers to the fact that income is taxed both at the corporate level and at the individual level when that income is distributed as dividends.

PRACTITIONER PERSPECTIVE

Perseverance: Accountant Metcalf Knows Firsthand Give and Take of Taxes

Robert Metcalf was a teenage showoff. So when he and his friends went to the reservoir for a swim, he made a spectacular dive to impress the girls.

He hit a rock. He awoke a quadriplegic.

That was 42 years ago. Today, Mr. Metcalf is a CPA with 550 tax clients, practicing law and selling securities on the side. Each spring he works furiously, making enough money to spend the rest of the year indulging his passions for travel, wine making and ancient languages.

Though inspiring in its own right, his story is a parable for the evolving values of the business world. Affirmative action is under attack; no one seems to know the difference between a moral workplace and a politically correct one. At a time like this, it's comforting to find proof that the entrepreneurial economy can create a profitable opportunity for someone with a sharp mind, an iron constitution, a little marketing savvy and the right help early in the effort.

Bob Metcalf was born in a workaday world, riding with his father in the cab of a truck hauling Packards from Detroit to Chicago. His mother was a hairdresser. He liked boxing.

The accident, when he was 18, threw him not only into bed but into a deep depression. But it was 1953, in the midst of the polio scourge, and rehabilitation was in its ascendancy. A specialist gave the former pugilist the pep talk of a lifetime. Mr. Metcalf entered a publicly subsidized rehab institution, where he remained until past his 20th birthday.

Soon he was in City College of San Francisco (with a wheelchair and tuition paid for by his family, the Easter Seals and, once again, the U.S. Treasury). As a freshman he took Spanish II, organic chemistry and political science; those were the courses offered in ground-floor classrooms.

Ultimately he landed at Golden Gate College to study accounting, a field in which he had precisely no personal interest. "What's to like?" he says. "I had to make a living."

He put out his shingle as a tax man in 1961, recruiting 10 clients in his first year. His biggest problem, alas, was numbers—writing them down and tallying them up. Clumsily clutching a pencil, he could scrawl on a scratch pad or peck an adding machine, but his legibility and accuracy were low. He compensated with fanatical rechecking and by reading his notes into a tape recorder when the client had left.

Still, he lacked the temperament for accounting creativity. To him the Tax Code was a system of rules; the rules were complex because taxes were progressive, which swelled the U.S. Treasury with money to be spent in the public interest.

His by-the-book mindset became a virtue. Believe it or not, a huge segment of the working populace doesn't view the Tax Code as mainly an obstacle to wealth. Mr. Metcalf found that many clients engaged a tax professional simply for the assurance that they were paying neither too much nor too little tax.

"He doesn't try to cut corners to get us a tax break," says one long-time client, Jean M.F. Dubois, a property appraiser in Los Gatos. "I never have to worry that I'll get stuck with an audit."

But he was still a quadriplegic accountant, so he spent years in night school for a law degree—his way of trying to overcome the disadvantages he faced in the marketplace.

"I've got to be better than the average accountant," he told himself. Whether it's a disability or anything else that hinders you in the business or professional world, "you've got to be head and shoulders above the average," he says, "because you're starting out with a disadvantage." As a lawyer he could offer estate planning to his tax clients (eventually adding a sideline in mutual funds).

In the early 1970s, as his practice grew, Mr. Metcalf hired Mindy Meyers, one of his part-time tape transcribers, as his full-time assistant. While interviewing clients he and Ms. Meyers carried on a banter calculated to display their familiarity with the intricacies of the code—and their commitment to operating within the rules.

Transcribing gave way in 1980 to his first desktop computer, an ungainly $15,000 contraption. Soon track balls and drag-down menus supplanted the unrelenting keystroke demands of the DOS world. He installed a signal splitter between two monitors, allowing clients to watch the process unfold on a screen facing them from above his desk—another small marketing touch. He supplemented his arsenal with speed-dialers, speaker phones and the availability of instant tax research through a Triple Check Income Tax Service franchise.

He quotes the law in Hebrew and Greek. He reels off aphorisms from Churchill, Santayana, "Richard II" and Henny Youngman. He looks arrestingly youthful for 60 years (perhaps from his organic diet and love of wine). The guy should be a state court judge, or a talking head on a Sunday morning news show.

His politics, however, are all wrong for 1995. Though a case study in the meritocracy of the market economy, Bob Metcalf is a tainted hero by today's standards because he overcame adversity with help from taxpayer money.

"I'm very grateful for what the taxpayers and the Congress have done for me," he says. But for the country, the investment was profitable. "For many years I've been a net contributor to the national Treasury. I don't resent that at all."

THE SPECIAL PROVISIONS IN THE U.S. TAX LAW REGARDING A PARENT'S DIVIDEND INCOME

The special provisions of the Internal Revenue Code that allow dividend income from **domestic subsidiaries** *not* to be taxed at the **parent level** pertain to (1) the **election to file a consolidated income tax return** and (2) the **dividend received deduction,** which is a factor only when a parent and its domestic subsidiary file **separate income tax returns.** We now discuss each of these provisions.

SPECIAL PROVISION 1: FILING A CONSOLIDATED INCOME TAX RETURN

A parent company and its subsidiaries may file a consolidated federal income tax return—as opposed to the parent and the subsidiaries each filing **separate income tax returns**—if the parent owns **directly or indirectly at least 80%** of both (1) the **voting power of all classes of stock** and (2) the **value of all classes of stock** included in the consolidated return. (The 80% requirement must be satisfied by direct ownership for at least one subsidiary included in the consolidated return.[10]

THE NATURE OF A CONSOLIDATED RETURN A consolidated income tax return is the tax equivalent of a consolidated income statement for financial reporting purposes. Thus all **intercompany transactions**—including intercompany dividends—are eliminated for income tax–reporting purposes. A consolidated income tax return can be prepared in two ways. The easier way is to start with the consolidated income statement for financial reporting purposes and merely make necessary adjustments on a worksheet to obtain consolidated taxable income. The second way is to make tax adjustments for each separate company to arrive at separate company taxable income amounts and then prepare a consolidating tax worksheet/spreadsheet.

THE MAJOR RESTRICTION ON FILING A CONSOLIDATED RETURN The restriction of major significance is that consolidated income tax returns may be filed **only with domestic subsidiaries,** and then only if certain ownership conditions are met. **Foreign subsidiaries are automatically excluded** because they must always file separate income tax returns in the foreign country in which they are incorporated.

OTHER ADVANTAGES OF FILING A CONSOLIDATED RETURN Filing a consolidated return has several other distinct advantages, beyond the freedom from paying income taxes on dividends received from a subsidiary. These other advantages are as follows:

1. **Offsetting operating losses against operating profits.** Operating losses of companies within the consolidated group that do not generate profits can offset operating profits of the other members of the consolidated group.

2. **Offsetting capital losses against capital gains.** Capital losses of one company can offset capital gains of other members of the consolidated group.

3. **Deferring profits on intercompany transactions. Intercompany profits** recorded on the sale of assets between entities are deferred until such assets are sold (for inventory transfers) or depreciation occurs (for depreciable asset transfers).

4. **Avoiding Section 482 problems.** As noted previously, Section 482 of the Internal Revenue Code (discussed more fully in Chapter 9) requires supportable fair

---

[10]The detailed requirements are set forth in the U.S. Internal Revenue Code of 1954, Sec. 1504(a).

transfer pricing between affiliated entities. Section 482 permits the IRS to allocate income and deductions among affiliated entities. Because all intercompany transactions are undone in preparing a consolidated return, there is never any Section 482 problem. Thus the Section 482 problem primarily affects parents and their *foreign subsidiaries.*

5. **Using certain tax credits.** If a foreign branch of a domestic subsidiary has "excess foreign tax credits" (discussed in the Appendix of Chapter 19), the group may be able to use it.

DISADVANTAGES OF FILING A CONSOLIDATED RETURN   The following are some of the disadvantages of consolidated returns:

1. **Losses** on intercompany transactions must be deferred.
2. The IRS rules for determining consolidated income are quite complex.

The complexity of the IRS rules pertaining to (1) consolidated tax returns, (2) transfer pricing, and (3) excess foreign tax credits cannot be overstated. The Economic Perspective by Milton Friedman, who was awarded the Nobel Prize in economics a few years ago, offers his view as to why such enormous complexity exists in the corporate (and personal) tax system.

ALLOCATING CONSOLIDATED INCOME TAX EXPENSE: A FINANCIAL REPORTING ISSUE   When a company files a consolidated income tax return, a financial reporting issue arises if either the parent or the subsidiary issues separate financial statements (possibly for loan covenant agreements). In such cases, the total consolidated income tax expense must be **allocated** among the companies included in the consolidated income tax return. We discuss possible manners of making this allocation in Chapter 9. Even in consolidated statements, companies often disclose how the allocation is made.

CASE IN POINT

Chevron Corporation's Tax Allocation Disclosure (1995 annual report)

It is the company's policy for subsidiaries included in the U.S. consolidated tax return to record income tax expense as though they filed separately, with the par- ent recording the adjustment to income tax expense for the effects of consolidation.

IMPACT OF FILING A CONSOLIDATED TAX RETURN ON THE PARENT'S TAX BASIS OF ITS INVESTMENT   When a consolidated tax return is filed, the parent's tax basis of its investment in the subsidiary (1) increases for the subsidiary's earnings and (2) decreases for (a) the subsidiary's losses and (b) dividends paid. Essentially, this treatment is the same as if the *equity method* of accounting were applied for tax-reporting purposes.

SPECIAL PROVISION 2: USING THE DIVIDEND RECEIVED DEDUCTION (SEPARATE TAX RETURNS FILED)

80%- OR MORE OWNED DOMESTIC SUBSIDIARIES   When both a parent and an 80%- or more owned *domestic* subsidiary file *separate* income tax returns, the Internal Revenue Code permits a "dividend received deduction" of 100% of the dividend received from the *domestic subsidiary.* Thus *none* of the intercompany dividend is taxed on the parent's *separate* tax return. Without such a provision, triple

The Complexity of the Income Tax System

"Former IRS commissioner Shirley Petersen says one multinational corporation recently filed a tax return of 21,000 pages in 30 volumes. 'They had to use a truck to deliver it to the IRS.'"

Source: *Forbes* magazine, August 14, 1995, p. 28.

Why a Flat Tax Is Not Politically Feasible

The following two seemingly contradictory propositions are, I believe, both correct.

1. Almost all informed persons, including members of Congress, agree that a flat-rate tax of 19%, a la Robert Hall and Alvin Rabushka (and Dick Armey), on personal income or consumption in excess of a generous exemption would be both more equitable and more efficient, in terms of dead weight cost per dollar of tax, than our present obscenely complex personal and corporate income taxes, while at the same time raising at least the same revenue.

2. There is next to no chance that Congress will adopt such a tax to replace our present personal and corporate income taxes.

How to reconcile this apparent contradiction?

The answer hinges on recognizing that there is a widespread misconception about the function of income taxes. It is generally simply taken for granted that their major function is to raise revenue to finance government spending. They do indeed serve that function, but that is not their most important political function. As already noted, a flat-rate tax would perform the function of raising revenue far better.

The political function of the income taxes, which is served by their being complex, is to provide a means whereby the members of Congress who have anything whatsoever to do with taxation can raise campaign funds. That is what supports the army of lobbyists in Washington who are seeking to produce changes in the income tax, to introduce special privileges or exemptions for their clients, or to have what they regard as special burdens on their clients removed. A strict flat-rate tax would offer nothing that any lobbyist could hope to achieve since the structure of the tax is so simple and straightforward.

To illustrate the importance of the political factor, ask yourself why it is that we have a new tax law every year or so (six in the past 10 years). However good or bad the tax, it would be a great convenience for everyone if it stayed the same for a lengthy period. Instead, every year or so a new tax law complicates everybody's life, requiring new forms and embodying new provisions.

Why? The answer is obvious: only when there are new tax laws do the members of Congress have something to sell. Only then is there something that lobbyists can buy to earn their incomes. Since members of the House need to get election funds every two years, and since a third of the members of the Senate need to get election funds every two years, there is a continual supply of purveyors of special privileges.

It is hard to see any easy way to overcome this obstacle to the enactment of a flat-rate tax. The only way I can see to overcoming it is along the lines of what has been happening with respect to term limits. Term limits are overwhelmingly popular, yet I believe there is not a chance in the world that the members of Congress will adopt a term-limit measure on their own. It is too much against their own separate personal interest, just as replacing the complex income tax with a simple flat-rate tax would be.

Individual states are passing term-limit laws. They may be declared constitutional or unconstitutional. If declared unconstitutional, the alternative will be for the states to use the procedure provided in Article V of the Constitution—to call for a constitutional convention to enact a term-limit amendment. When the number of states that have supported such a convention is within one or two of the constitutionally required number, Congress will itself introduce the amendment.

The same thing goes for the flat-rate tax. The only way we are ever likely to get it is if there is a drive for a constitutional convention to repeal the 16th Amendment (which gives Congress the power to tax income) and replace it with one mandating a flat-rate tax.

However, I regret that that is not an immediate prospect.

Source: Milton Friedman, "Why a Flat Tax Is Not Politically Feasible," *The Wall Street Journal*, March 30, 1995, p. A16, Copyright © 1995 by *The Wall Street Journal*. Reprinted by permission.

taxation of a subsidiary's earnings results (first at the subsidiary level, second at the parent level, and third at the individual level when dividends are paid).

Consequently, because the dividend received deduction is *not* allowed for dividends received from foreign subsidiaries and because foreign subsidiaries *cannot* be consolidated for income tax–reporting purposes, the taxation of subsidiary dividends at the parent level is usually a problem almost exclusively for foreign subsidiaries (the taxation of which is discussed in the Appendix of Chapter 19). It is also a problem for less than 80%-owned *domestic* subsidiaries, as discussed below.

Note that this 80%-ownership level is the same percentage required for filing a consolidated tax return. Thus *no* parent-level tax is recorded for all 80%- or more owned domestic subsidiaries—regardless of whether they file separate tax returns or are included in a consolidated tax return.

LESS THAN 80%-OWNED DOMESTIC SUBSIDIARIES If a *domestic* subsidiary is less than 80% owned, the dividend received deduction allowed is only 80% of the dividend received.[11] Thus a parent-level tax *is* incurred. To avoid incurring any parent-level tax, companies must carefully control their ownership levels in partially owned subsidiaries.

CASE IN POINT

Note from the earlier case in point that when Sears, Roebuck and Company had a partial disposal of its Allstate Insurance subsidiary, the percentage of shares sold was *not* more than 20% to avoid the parent-level tax.

WHEN TO RECORD THE PARENT-LEVEL TAX Under *APB Opinion No. 23,* "Accounting for Income Taxes— Special Areas," this parent-level tax must be recorded for financial reporting purposes in the year in which the *domestic* subsidiary reports the income—not when it pays dividends. Furthermore, for *undistributed* earnings that arise in fiscal years beginning after December 15, 1992, *SFAS No. 109,* "Accounting for Income Taxes," requires recording the parent-level income taxes on those undistributed earnings—**regardless of whether the intent is to reinvest them for the indefinite future.** For undistributed earnings that arose in fiscal years prior to December 15, 1992, the parent-level tax is recorded only if those undistributed earnings are *not* being reinvested indefinitely.

SUMMARY OF APPENDIX KEY POINTS

1. For 80%- or more owned *domestic* **subsidiaries,** no parent-level tax exists because of the use of (1) **consolidated tax returns** or (2) the **dividend received deduction** allowed for dividends received from domestic subsidiaries.
2. **Consolidated tax returns** have several advantages over **separate company tax returns,** such as the ability to offset losses of one entity against the profits of another entity. Another big advantage is the elimination of Section 482 transfer pricing problems.
3. A subsidiary's earnings may be taxed at the **parent level** if the subsidiary is (1) a foreign subsidiary or (2) a less than 80%-owned domestic subsidiary.
4. For less than 80%-owned domestic subsidiaries, parent-level taxes (for financial reporting purposes) on **undistributed earnings** are recorded in the year the subsidiary earns the income—not when the dividends are paid. No "indefinite investment" exemption is available (as exists for foreign subsidiaries).

GLOSSARY OF NEW TERMS FOR APPENDIX

Consolidated tax return   A tax return in which the combined income of a parent and one or more of its domestic subsidiaries that meet certain ownership conditions are reported.

---

[11]This 80% dividend received deduction for intercorporate investments extends down to the 20% ownership level. For less than 20% intercorporate investments, the dividend received deduction is only 70%.

Dividend received deduction The deduction the IRS allows to parent companies reporting as income the dividends received from their domestic subsidiaries (80–100%, depending on parent's ownership level).

Parent-level tax Income tax that a parent company records based on a subsidiary's earnings.

SELF-STUDY QUESTIONS FOR APPENDIX

(Answers are at the end of this appendix.)

1. Which of the following is *not* an advantage unique to filing a consolidated tax return?
   a. The *non*taxability of intercompany dividends.
   b. The deferral of intercompany profits on the intercompany transactions.
   c. The offsetting of loss operations against profitable operations.
   d. The avoidance of Section 482 problems.

2. The parent-level tax *is* essentially an issue for which of the following?
   a. All *domestic* subsidiaries.
   b. 100%-owned *domestic* subsidiaries.
   c. Less than 100%-owned *domestic* subsidiaries.
   d. Less than 80%-owned *domestic* subsidiaries.

3. Sax is a 75%-owned *domestic* subsidiary of Pax. For 19X1, Sax had $500,000 of pretax income and $300,000 of net income. At the end of 19X1, Sax paid a $160,000 dividend. The remaining $140,000 of net income is expected to be invested indefinitely. The tax rate is 40%. What parent-level tax does Pax record for 19X1?
   a. $ –0–
   b. $9,600
   c. $18,000
   d. $24,000

REVIEW QUESTIONS FOR APPENDIX

1. When does a parent report on its tax return the earnings of its subsidiary?
2. What is the purpose of the *parent-level tax* on a subsidiary's earnings?
3. What are two ways to avoid the parent-level tax when *domestic* subsidiaries exist?
4. What is the nature of a *consolidated income tax return*?
5. Which subsidiaries can be included in a *consolidated return*?
6. What are four *advantages* of a consolidated return? Two *disadvantages*?
7. What *financial reporting issue* exists when a consolidated income tax return is filed?
8. When is the *dividend received deduction* allowed?
9. Is the *dividend received deduction* used in preparing a consolidated return?
10. *When* and *to what extent* does *APBO No. 23* require recording the parent-level taxes on a *domestic* subsidiary's earnings?

EXERCISES FOR APPENDIX

E 3–1A **Income Taxes: Parent Level** Sunco is a 60%-owned *domestic* subsidiary of Punco. For 19X1, Sunco had $500,000 of pretax income and $300,000 of net income. At the end of 19X1, Sunco paid a $160,000 dividend. The remaining $140,000 of net income is expected to be invested indefinitely. The tax rate is 40%.

Required 1. What parent-level tax does Punco record for 19X1?
2. Repeat requirement 1, assuming that Sunco is 80% owned.

E 3–2A **Income Taxes: Parent Level** Sorr is a 70%-owned *domestic* subsidiary of Porr. For 19X1, Sorr had $333,333 of pretax income and $200,000 of net income. At the end of 19X1, Sorr paid an $80,000 dividend. The remaining $120,000 of net income is expected to be invested indefinitely. The tax rate is 40%.

Required 1. What parent-level tax does Porr record for 19X1?
2. Repeat requirement 1, assuming that Sorr is 80% owned.

✳ FINANCIAL ANALYSIS PROBLEM FOR APPENDIX ✳

FAP 3–1A **The Time Value of Money: Why 28% Is Not 28%!**   You are preparing your employer's consolidated tax return in which the parent's $500,000 capital gain on land that it had held for 20 years fully offsets the subsidiary's capital loss of $100,000. Your supervisor, Kelly Ganes, mentions to you that (1) the effective tax rate on capital gains is lower than the statutory tax rate because of the time value of money factor and (2) the longer the capital asset is held, the lower the effective capital gain tax rate.

You are perplexed and ask for further explanation. Kelly asks you to suppose that (1) you invest $1,000 and earn a 10% pretax dividend each year (taxable at ordinary rates), (2) the ordinary income tax rate is 28%, and (3) the after-tax income is reinvested at the same 10% rate of return. Using a pocket calculator, Kelly shows that you would accumulate $4,017 after 20 years.

If instead you had invested in a common stock that paid no dividend but had increased in value each year by 10%, the common stock would be worth $6,728 after 20 years. If you then sold the stock, you would report a realized capital gain of $5,728 ($6,728 – $1,000). If the capital gain tax rate were 28%, you would pay taxes of $1,604 ($5,718 × 28%), leaving you with $5,124 ($6,728 – $1,604). This $5,124 amount is $1,107 more ($5,124 – $4,017) than the annual dividend situation.

To have accumulated this additional $1,107, the effective tax rate had to be 15%—not 28%. In other words, if you had paid taxes at 15% each year on the 10% increase in value (and then reinvested the remaining 85% each year), you would have accumulated $5,124. Therefore, the effective capital gain tax rate was 15%—not 28%.

Required   What is the effective tax rate if the common stock investment were held for only 10 years?

ANSWERS TO SELF-STUDY QUESTIONS FOR APPENDIX B

1. a   **2.** d   **3.** c

INTRODUCTION TO BUSINESS COMBINATIONS

LEARNING OBJECTIVES

TO UNDERSTAND

- The legal and business environment in which business combinations occur.
- The change versus no-change in the basis of accounting issue.
- The nature and controversy surrounding goodwill.
- The business reasons for acquiring assets versus common stock.
- The organizational forms that can be used for the acquired business *after* the combination.
- The basic tax considerations in business combinations.
- The built-in conflicts of interest that exist.

TOPIC OUTLINE

The crown of all faculties is common sense. It is not enough to do the right thing, it must be done at the right time and place. Talent knows what to do; tact knows when and how to do it.

W. MATHEWS

CHAPTER OVERVIEW

This chapter deals with *external expansion,* whereby one company expands by combining with another existing company. Bringing together two separate businesses under common ownership is known as a *business combination.* Most of the problems of *internal expansion* are *not* encountered in external expansion; only the assessment of the prospects of an existing business is involved: If the assessment is favorable, efforts to combine the businesses can be made. Most business combinations are completed in far less time than it would take to develop a new product, build manufacturing facilities to produce it, and then successfully market it. Often the newly acquired business produces a profit from the start. The management of the newly acquired business may be retained, and no new competitor is introduced into the field.

I   THE DESIRE TO MERGE

TERMINOLOGY

In the business community, business combinations are referred to as *mergers* and *acquisitions.* The company whose business is being sought is often called the **target company.** The company attempting to acquire the target company's business is referred to as the **acquiring company.** The legal agreement that specifies the terms and provisions of the business combination is known as the *acquisition, purchase,* or *merger agreement.* For simplicity, we refer to this legal agreement as the **acquisition agreement.** The process of trying to acquire a target company's business is often called a **takeover attempt.** Business combinations can be categorized as vertical, horizontal, or conglomerate. **Vertical combinations** take place between companies involved in the same industry but at different levels—for example, a tire manufacturer and a tire distributor. **Horizontal combinations** take place between companies that are competitors at the same level in a given industry—two tire manufacturers, for example. **Conglomerate combinations** involve companies in totally unrelated industries—such as a tire manufacturer and an insurance company. These categories of business combination have no bearing on how the combination is recorded for financial reporting purposes.

LEGAL RESTRICTIONS ON BUSINESS COMBINATIONS

Before discussing business combinations any further, we should note that certain combinations are prohibited. Section 7 of the Clayton Act (1914) prohibits any business combination in which "the effect of such acquisition may be substantially to lessen competition or tend to create a monopoly." The Justice Department and the Federal Trade Commission, the two federal agencies with antitrust jurisdiction, enforce this law.

CASE IN POINT

U.S. Justice Department Prevails over Microsoft's Plan to Acquire Intuit for $2.1 Billion

In 1995, Microsoft Corp. abandoned its effort to acquire Intuit Inc. (which dominates the personal-finance software market with its highly popular QUICKEN program) after the U.S. Justice Department filed an antitrust suit seeking an injunction to block the planned combination. The Justice Department claimed that the merger would give Microsoft total dominance over the burgeoning market for personal-finance software.

Even when the government does *not* challenge a proposed business combination before it is consummated, it can later issue a *divestiture order* requiring the acquiring company to dispose of its acquired business. If the acquiring company appeals the order, the courts may or may not uphold it.

Although the Clayton Act apparently applies only to horizontal and vertical combinations, the regulatory agencies have challenged certain conglomerate combinations too. For the most part, these challenges have not been successful, and companies expanding externally into unrelated fields generally have no problem complying with the Clayton Act. Many companies obtain a legal opinion on the application of this law to each contemplated business combination before taking steps that lead to consummation.

ARE LARGE MERGERS BAD BY DEFINITION? Many observers believe that certain mergers should be prohibited simply because of their size, even though they would not reduce competition or create a monopoly. Their concern is that huge combinations concentrate economic power in fewer hands, which is deemed undesirable. The courts and the governmental agencies have taken the position in recent years, however, that mergers are not bad merely because they are large. As a result, virtually all of the 25 largest business combinations in U.S. history have occurred in the last 15 years.

WHICH PARTY IS IN POWER? The political party in the White House greatly influences the zeal with which governmental agencies interpret and enforce antitrust laws. In general, fewer combinations between competing companies are challenged under Republican administrations than under Democratic administrations because of differing philosophies.

THE PREVALENCE OF BUSINESS COMBINATIONS

External expansion is a major vehicle for corporate growth. The number of business combinations occurring in a given year is largely a function of the state of the economy: Merger activity is usually low during recessionary periods and high during boom periods when companies tend to accumulate healthy amounts of cash. Excess cash not used for dividends must be reinvested. (Of course, the alternative is to distribute the excess cash as dividends and allow the *stockholders* to diversify individually.) Stock market prices tend to rise during a boom, which enables acquiring companies that use stock (instead of cash) as consideration to issue fewer shares of its stock to acquire another company.

In the 1990s, approximately 3,000 business combinations have occurred each year. In the mid-1990s, the banking industry experienced consolidation—nearly 600 *horizontal* bank combinations occurred in 1995 alone (the largest being the merger of Chemical Banking Corporation and Chase Manhattan Corporation, a $10 billion deal that was one of the 25 largest business combinations ever consummated). Although many business combinations involve two large companies, most combinations involve a large company combining with a small company. Often such combinations enable a small company to expand more rapidly than would be possible with its existing resources.

THE IMPETUS FOR BUSINESS COMBINATIONS

Much of the impetus for business combinations comes from the belief that the results will be (1) substantial cost savings through economies of scale (the reason given for the high number of recent bank mergers) or (2) synergies so that the combined entity will be more of a force than the two entities are on a stand-alone basis.

Much of the impetus also comes, however, from the belief that high asset returns and growth rates exist in other businesses—what could be called the *greener pastures syndrome.* As a result, capital is redeployed; the less desirable companies are sold and the presumed emerging "stars" are bought.

MANY COMBINATIONS FALL FLAT

Bringing together two companies through a business combination is not without risks. As high as 40% of all acquired businesses do *not* achieve their projected sales and profit growth (in retrospect, buyers find that they paid far too much). In many instances, the merger destroys much value. When managements attempt to diversify, they often find that they cannot manage a new business that they know nothing about any better than they could manage businesses with which they are familiar.

CASE IN POINT

Sony Corporation's Costly Foray into Hollywood

In 1994, Sony Corporation took a staggering $2.7 billion write-off on its $5 billion 1989 acquisition of Columbia Pictures, one of the largest losses ever recognized on an attempt to diversify. Analysts attributed the loss to mismanagement.

THE NEW BUREAUCRACY   Often the target company's top management and key employees become both frustrated at having to work within the acquiring company's newly imposed operating procedures and resentful of the unwanted involvement in daily operations. Many of them simply leave the firm rather than continue under the new management—draining the company of leadership and talent needed to remain competitive. Often major operating losses result. (This is most notable in the electronics industry.)

DIVERSIFICATION THAT RESULTED IN RETRENCHMENT   When the major U.S. oil companies became flush with cash in the 1970s as a result of rising oil prices, many of them feared the day when the world's oil reserves would run out and began diversifying heavily into other industries. Within a few years, they sold or shut down most of the acquired operations.

Because their vast operations simply became unmanageable, conglomerates created in the 1960s and 1970s began in the 1980s to dispose of many of the companies they had so eagerly acquired (General Electric Co. alone disposed of more than 200 subsidiaries during the 1980s). In the 1990s, more and more diversified companies have decided to shed units so that they can concentrate on their core businesses. Thus the days of the conglomerate or highly diversified company may be passing.

CASE IN POINT

Sears, Roebuck and Co. Returns to Its Merchandising Roots

In the 1980s, Sears, Roebuck and Co. tried to build a financial services empire on the shoulders of its huge retailing business by acquiring a savings and loan, the Coldwell Banker real estate brokerage, and the Dean Witter stockbrokerage. It also introduced the Discover credit card. From 1990 to 1995, however, Sears discarded all of these units, as well as its Allstate Insurance subsidiary. As a result, Sears now manages only its retailing business.

Some firms try to diversify within their own industry by filling out a product line. Although such endeavors would seem to be much less risky than diversifying into totally unrelated fields, they often have the same unfortunate consequences.

CASE IN POINT

Novell Corporation Sells WordPerfect and Quattro Pro

In late 1995, Novell Corporation announced that it would sell its WordPerfect and Quattro Pro programs, acquired in 1994, in an attempt to go head to head with Microsoft in the sale of application "suites." In doing so, Novell stated that it will concentrate instead on the networking programs that are its foundation. The problem with WordPerfect was that it rapidly lost most of its market share to Microsoft by fall 1995 as a result of fierce competition. Thus it virtually imploded. In early 1996, Novell sold WordPerfect for $124 million, roughly one-eleventh of Novell's $1.4 billion purchase price.

SPLIT-UPS: BUSINESS COMBINATION REVERSALS

Rather than selling certain units to focus on the core business, some entities split the business into distinct independent companies. Doing so acknowledges that the vision of *synergy*—the term used for decades to justify all manner of mergers and most recently to explain the wave of big media industry deals—was not achieved.

CASE IN POINT

AT&T to Split into Three Companies

In a move to allow it to focus on long-distance communications and aggressive competition from the Baby Bells, AT&T announced in 1995 that it will split into three independent publicly traded companies: a communication services company (a highly profitable operation that prior to the planned split-up provided 80% of AT&T's annual sales and 60% of its profits), a communication equipment company, and a computing company. Thus AT&T will jettison its ailing computing operation, the bulk of which it acquired from NCR Corporation for $7.48 billion in 1990 (an acquisition that has been a huge disappointment in light of NCR's subsequent performance).

Note: In 1995, IT&T Corporation split itself into three independent publicly traded companies.

Many of the takeover attempts began when a bidder recognized that a company's stock was selling at a depressed level (in relation to the value of the business) precisely because of management's inability to effectively oversee diversified operations. In this common scenario, discussed in the next section, one segment of the company begins to experience operating losses, which leads to a significant drop in the price of the stock as investors begin to lose confidence in the entire company. This situation makes the company a potential takeover candidate. After buying the company's stock at a fraction of its value, thus gaining management control, the acquirer can then sell off the various divisions at a substantial profit (called a *breakup*).

II THE ATTEMPTED TAKEOVER

PREVENTING A TAKEOVER ATTEMPT

Because business combinations are so prevalent, managements fearing a potential takeover have in the last few years taken defensive steps (colloquially known as *shark repellant*) to make it more difficult for an acquiring company to effect a takeover. Some of the more routine steps involve requesting stockholders to approve such articles of incorporation, charter, and bylaw provisions as the following:

1. **Elimination of cumulative voting.** Under cumulative voting, each stockholder has as many votes as the number of shares owned multiplied by the number of directors to be elected. Thus a potential acquiring company with a relatively small holding of common stock could obtain representation on the board of directors. Many companies have reincorporated in Delaware, which does *not* require cumulative voting.

2. **Use of staggered terms for directors.** If directors have staggered terms, changes in the composition of the board of directors occur more slowly, making it impossible for a successful suitor to gain control of the board upon either consummation of the business combination or winning a proxy contest.

3. **Adoption of supermajority provisions.** For votes on *statutory mergers* and acquisitions of assets (specific types of business combinations that are discussed in detail later in the chapter), imposing a stipulated percentage in excess of a simple majority (80% is commonly used) makes a takeover by either of these types of business combinations more difficult.

4. **Authorization of blank-check preferred stock.** Such authorization enables management to place the preferred stock privately in friendly hands. Typically, the owners of the preferred stock have either (1) the right to approve any proposed merger or sale of assets or (2) multiple voting rights (such as three votes for each vote of common stock).

STEPS LEADING TO A BUSINESS COMBINATION

Few business activities match the excitement that can be generated by an attempt to acquire a target company's business. Often an acquiring company must operate in strict secrecy until the last possible moment to avoid attracting the attention of other companies that might be interested in acquiring the business. Such secrecy minimizes the possibility of a bidding war. (Some companies, as a matter of policy, immediately cease their takeover efforts if a bidding war starts; the presumption here is that the successful bidder would probably wind up paying too much.) The acquiring company may start purchasing the common stock of the target company slowly, over a period of time, until it owns just under 5% of the target company's common stock (5% ownership requires public disclosure). Such secrecy also affects the target company: If it opposes the takeover, its management has less time in which to take defensive actions.

THE FRIENDLY APPROACH   In theory, a business combination should involve only the acquiring company and the stockholders of the target company. In its simplest terms, the target company's stockholders must decide whether to accept the acquiring company's offer. In evaluating the offer, the stockholders consider the recommendation of their directors and management. Because of this, most acquiring companies attempt to obtain a favorable recommendation from the directors and management of the target company before they present the offer to its stockholders. The usual procedure for this involves negotiating an acquisition agreement with the target company's management. If successful, and if the target company's directors also approve the agreement, the offer is then submitted to the target company's stockholders for their approval or rejection. This sequence of events is characterized as a "friendly" takeover attempt.

This approach of first making a proposal to management is also referred to as the *bear-hug* tactic because the threat of making an offer directly to the shareholders looms in the background.

THE REFUSAL TO BE FRIENDLY Less friendly situations occur when (1) the acquiring company does *not* seek the approval of the target company's directors and its management, (2) the target company's directors and management refuse to negotiate an acquisition agreement, and (3) negotiations do not result in an offer that the target company's directors and management believe is in the best interests of the target company's stockholders. The acquiring company must then present its offer directly to the stockholders of the target company without the approval of its directors and management. These cases are characterized as "unfriendly" takeover attempts. Some companies have a policy of pursuing a target company only if the takeover can be done on a friendly basis.

RESORTING TO THE TENDER OFFER An offer made by an acquiring company directly to the target company's stockholders is known as a **tender offer,** commonly known as a *takeover bid*. Under a tender offer, the acquiring company requests the target company's stockholders to give up their shares in exchange for cash or securities. The usual features of a tender offer are the following:

1. It is made in newspapers.
2. The offering price substantially exceeds the current market price of the target company's common stock.
3. The offer must be accepted by a certain specified date, usually in the near future (such as 30 days).
4. The acquiring company reserves the right to withdraw the offer if a specified number of shares are not tendered. (If more than the specified number of shares are tendered, the acquiring company reserves the right to reject such excess shares.)

Because the stockholders send their shares to a financial institution, which holds the shares in a fiduciary capacity until the expiration date of the offer, the shares are said to have been *tendered*—not sold. At the expiration date and provided that the minimum number of shares have been tendered, the acquiring company then pays for the tendered shares.

The accompanying Business Perspective discusses the merits of the friendly approach versus the tender offer.

STATUTES GOVERNING TENDER OFFERS

FEDERAL STATUTES In 1968, in response to that decade's wave of takeovers, Congress passed the Williams Act, which provides for federal regulation of tender offers. The avowed purpose of the law, which the Securities and Exchange Commission (SEC) enforces, is to protect the target company's shareholders by requiring the bidder to furnish detailed disclosures to the target company and its stockholders. Some believe that the Williams Act should be abolished entirely, allowing a return to the pre-1968 open-market takeover environment. Others believe that the act should be tougher.

STATE STATUTES Since 1968, almost all states have passed legislation ostensibly to provide further protection to stockholders of the target company. For the most part, these statutes require more detailed disclosures than the federal statutes. Furthermore, most of them do not permit a tender offer to be made until 20 days after the initial public disclosure, whereas the federal requirement is only 5 days. A great controversy has developed over whether these state laws are really essential to protect the stockholders or whether they merely favor the in-state targets over out-of-state bidders because the additional disclosures and waiting period give the target company extra time to thwart the takeover bid if it desires. The constitutionality of

---

BUSINESS PERSPECTIVE

Hostile Takeovers Are Revived, and Some Embrace "Bear Hug"

The revival of hostile takeovers is also bringing back a related tactic—the "bear hug."

Instead of trying to take over a company by making an immediate unsolicited offer to buy up its shares, this gambit involves writing a letter to the target and proposing to buy the stock. The idea is to force the target to embrace the offer whether it wants to or not.

Sometimes the letter is all it takes to strike a deal. But if the target refuses, the suitor can take the bear hug a step further by taking its proposal public. Then the suitor sits back and waits for shareholders to pressure the target company into agreeing to a friendly combination. Only then does the suitor make a firm offer to buy up the shares.

That is the approach General Electric Co. took in its aborted $2.4 billion raid on Kemper Corp. Now American General Corp. is taking the same route in its $2.6 billion attempt to take over Unitrin Inc.

It is no coincidence that both deals involve insurance companies. Surprise offers to buy a company's shares are seen as fruitless in regulated industries, where state agencies get involved and can raise all sorts of pesky, time-consuming, and often-fatal objections. With politically complex transactions such as these, it is better to coax the company into a friendly combination, dealmakers believe.

Hostile buyers of banks and utilities also find advantages in the bear-hug approach. In those cases "a tender offer doesn't do you any good," said Dennis Block, an attorney with Weil, Gotschal & Manges. Mr. Block advised General Electric on the Kemper bid. "You are going to have to negotiate with the board of directors anyway."

Advantages of Bear Hug

The bear hug offers several advantages. First, it saves money. Tender offers, or cash bids to buy shares, require costly disclosures with the Securities and Exchange Commission. That money is wasted if the target company doesn't agree to a deal. But a bear hug costs no more than the price of a stamp. That's for the letter informing the target company of the takeover proposal.

Second, a bear hug keeps the door open for doing a friendly deal. This appeals to corporations, which have replaced corporate raiders as the leading acquirers in the current market. The reason: Corporate buyers are reluctant to enter a deal unless they have first inspected a target company's books, and that's all but impossible in a hostile situation. "Strategic buyers want to know more about the business before buying it," Mr. Block said.

Bearing Down on Holders

What's more, in public bear hugs—such as the ones pursued by G.E. and American General—the target company's shareholders do much of the work. When G.E. made its proposal for Kemper in March, it offered to pay 37% more for Kemper's shares than their quoted price just prior to the offer. The generous premium obligated mutual funds, including T. Rowe Price and Templeton Funds, to lobby Kemper into accepting a bid.

Bear hugs also allow strategic buyers to preserve the accounting benefits of a friendly deal. In a famous bear hug of the 1980s takeover wave, May Department Stores Co. proposed to buy Associated Dry Goods Corp. in a stock swap. By using a stock swap, May could book the acquisition in a way that wouldn't damage its earnings. Because cash is used in tender offers, such acquisitions can force accounting adjustments that eat into profit.

In the May-Associated case, the bear hug failed to produce the desired stock deal, but it compelled Associated to the bargaining table. After Associated rebuffed the stock swap idea, May was able to force it to accept a cash offer.

---

these laws may be questioned on the grounds that they interfere with interstate commerce and that federal statutes preempt state statutes. Until 1987, the courts generally declined to enforce these laws for these reasons. As a result, bidding companies routinely filed suits (at the public announcement of their takeover bids) seeking injunctions against the enforcement of these laws. In 1987, the United States Supreme Court for the first time upheld a state law (Indiana) regulating corporate takeovers. Since that decision, more than 30 states have modified their takeover statutes, primarily by adopting provisions similar to those in the Indiana statute.

DEFENSIVE TACTICS DURING TAKEOVER ATTEMPTS

The board of directors of a target company may authorize management to take aggressive action to try to prevent a takeover. A common defensive action is to file

Friend or Foe

"May wasn't sure how Associated would react to a takeover proposal," said Gilbert Harrison, an investment banker at Financo Inc. who worked on the deal. "The bear hug kept the options open to go either friendly or hostile."

Allen Finkelson, a takeover attorney with Cravath, Swaine & Moore, notes the latest wave of bear hugs coincides with the diminished power of surprise tender offers, the favorite tactic of 1980s corporate raiders. That strategy became less effective because of the rise of the "poison pill" takeover defense, which makes such unfriendly attempts prohibitively expensive. By 1988, poison pills had worked their way into bylaws across corporate America.

Before poison pills, a buyer could launch a tender offer and, twenty days later when the offer expired, own enough of the company's shares to take it over. But given the power of poison pills, the only way to buy a company nowadays is to persuade a target company to drop its takeover defense, usually by making an offer too good to refuse. "The pill eliminated the time element of a tender offer," Mr. Finkelson said.

Preferred by Corporations

In the current environment, bear hugs have more clout than ever, since corporations rather than raiders are leading the buyout wave. That is a change from the 1980s, when this tactic carried a lot less weight, Mr. Block said. In those days, with corporate raiders making hostile takeover proposals rather than firm offers, bear hugs were often dismissed as naive attempts to put a company in play.

"In the 1980s, a tender offer was a way of declaring that you were financially capable," Mr. Block said. For instance, in 1985, when then-unknown Ronald Perelman put an offer on the table for giant Revlon Inc., the company had to take him seriously. "But with large companies, financing isn't an issue."

Bear hugs can come in different forms. Earlier this year, **LDDS Communications** Inc., a long-distance phone company, used a variation of the bear hug to coax **Williams** Cos. into selling its WilTel communications unit. After offering $2 billion for the unit, Williams's stock price shot up, stirring debate about whether Williams, a natural-gas company, should rebuff the offer and stay in the communications business. LDDS, which had no use for a hostile cash offer because it had no interest in buying the entire company, eventually got Williams to agree to sell the communications unit for $2.5 billion.

Following the lead of LDDS, **Nine West Group** Inc., a shoe company, is now using a bear hug to incite shareholders of **U.S. Shoe** Corp. to persuade the company to sell its footwear division. Nine West has offered $425 million for the unit, and a number of shareholders are agreeing that the price is right.

Tender Offer Sets Mechanism

But tender offers are still the way to go in many cases, argues Robert Kindler, a Cravath takeover lawyer in New York. Tender offers, despite their diminished power, at least establish a formal mechanism to take over a company, so the target can't forever drag its feet in responding. "With a bear hug, there's no time pressure," he said.

American Home Products Corp. apparently came to the same conclusion in making its $9 billion bid for **American Cyanamid** Co. American Home started with a bear hug proposal. But after its own board had the chance to consider the idea this week, it then launched a tender offer. Unlike banks, insurance companies, and utilities, drug companies enjoy relatively little regulation. Cash offers, rather than bear hugs, tend to get the best results.

Source: Greg Steinmetz, "Hostile Takeovers Are Revived, and Some Embrace 'Bear Hug,'" *The Wall Street Journal*, August 12, 1994, p. C–1.

lawsuits against the acquiring company on various grounds relating to probable violation of antitrust laws, violation of state takeover laws, and violation of securities laws pertaining to public disclosures. Even if a lawsuit by itself is not successful, it entangles the acquiring company in legal proceedings and usually gives management more time to fight the takeover attempt.

Prior to the 1980s, these **legalistic defenses** were reasonably successful and were often referred to as *showstoppers* (a defense that stops a bidder dead in its tracks). Beginning in the 1980s, however, legalistic defenses lost much of their effectiveness as courts began taking the position that the stockholders must decide on such attempts. As a result, other types of defensive tactics emerged, most of which are considered **financial defenses.** The following list summarizes the major financial defenses, along with selected examples of their use in certain large takeover attempts of the past 15 years involving widely known companies. (Some of these attempts became titanic struggles between the bidder and the target company.)

1. **Seeking a "white knight."** When the bidder is unlikely to need the target company's management after the takeover, management may seek a bidder (the "white knight") that *will* need it. For example, after Mobil Corp. sought to acquire Marathon Oil Co. in 1984 for $5.1 billion, Marathon attracted U.S. Steel Corp., which won the bidding war with a $6.4 billion offer. This tactic is also used when the bidder's management is not to the liking of the target company's management, even though management is likely to be retained.

2. **The "scorched earth" (or "selling the crown jewels") defense.** When a bidder's primary interest in a target company is one or more prized segments, management may sell those segments to make itself less attractive as a target. For example, after GAF Corp. sought to acquire Union Carbide Corp. in 1986 for $4.1 billion, Union Carbide sold its cherished consumer products lines (which included Eveready batteries and Glad plastic bags) to other companies, causing GAF to abandon its takeover efforts. A variation of this tactic is the *lock-up option*, whereby a friendly company is granted the option to acquire the prized segment in the event the takeover succeeds.

3. **Adding a fair price amendment to the corporate charter.** Some tender offers are two-tiered offers, whereby cash—for example, $100 per share—is offered for just over 50% of the target company's outstanding common stock, but a lower amount—for example, $80 per share—is offered for the remaining shares. Individuals who tender their shares early receive an extra premium of $20 per share. Fair price amendments are designed to ensure that all stockholders receive an equivalent price for their shares. Sometimes the second tier of the offer consists of noncash consideration, such as common or preferred stock and notes, making the first tier of the offer even more attractive.

    Critics of two-tiered offers claim that such offers are coercive and place enormous pressure on stockholders to tender their shares promptly to avoid a lower price on the second tier.

4. **Making a self-tender offer.** When the bidder's offer is deemed unfairly low, the target company may make a higher tender offer to a large percentage of its shareholders, called a *self-tender offer*. This tactic is usually paired with the "selling the crown jewels" defense, which raises money from which to pay for the shares acquired in the self-tender offer.

    Many self-tender offers are two-tiered tender offers, thus having the same supposed coercive effect as hostile tender offers that are two tiered. (Of course, fair price amendments are worded so that they do not apply to two-tiered self-tender offers.)

5. **The recapitalization defense.** When an increased debt load is likely to make the acquisition unattractive to the acquiring company, the target company may try to boost its debt and use the proceeds to pay a huge one-time dividend to its shareholders, thereby shrinking its equity drastically. (This tactic has the same effect on the debt-to-equity ratio as the self-tender offer.)

6. **The Pac-Man defense.** When the target company is fairly large relative to the acquiring company, it may attempt to acquire the acquiring company. For example, when Bendix Corp. sought to acquire Martin-Marietta Corp. in 1982 for $1.5 billion, Martin-Marietta then sought to acquire Bendix. Considered the most bizarre and spectacular takeover attempt to date, the two companies exhausted their liquid assets trying to gain control of each other and be the first to oust the other's management and directors. As it became evident that the two companies would end up owning each other and the result would be a unified but financially ailing enterprise, Bendix sought refuge by being acquired

by Allied Chemical Corp. Martin-Marietta thus successfully resisted the takeover attempt.

7. **The mudslinging defense.** When the acquiring company offers stock instead of cash, the target company's management may try to convince the stockholders that the stock would be a bad investment. In some takeover attempts, the fierce attacks on the integrity and ability of the acquiring company's management (in light of certain past transactions and recent performance) put the acquiring company on the defensive to such a degree that it abandoned its takeover attempts. Many target companies hire private investigators to discover embarrassing information that would discredit the management of the hostile bidder. For example, immediately after receiving a $2.1 billion offer from Amway Corp. in 1989, Avon Products Inc. hired the well-known New York private detective firm of Kroll Associates Inc., which shortly thereafter unearthed allegations about Amway's chief operating officer that threatened to embarrass the company. Shortly after making Amway aware that it had this information, Amway dropped its offer (which had been made only eight days earlier).[1]

8. **The defensive acquisition tactic.** When a major reason for an attempted takeover is the target company's favorable cash position, the target company may try to rid itself of this excess cash by attempting a takeover of its own. Such action may also result in a combined business that the initial acquiring company is not interested in acquiring. For example, acquiring a competitor of the initial acquiring company creates antitrust issues that would probably derail the takeover attempt with prospective litigation.

9. **The leveraged buyout defense.** When management desires to own the business, it may arrange to buy out the stockholders using the company's assets to finance the deal. (This increasingly common tactic is discussed later in the chapter and in Chapter 8.)

10. **Adopting a "poison pill" provision.** Although many variations exist, the common procedure is to grant the company's stockholders—excluding shares owned by the acquiring company—the right to purchase additional common shares of the company (or of an acquiring company) at bargain prices (typically at 50% of the market price of the stock). The rights usually become exercisable (or *triggered*) when an "unfriendly" acquiring company acquires 20% of the common stock or makes a bid to acquire 30% of the common stock. The purpose of the provision is to make the acquisition prohibitively expensive to the unfriendly company (or make it suffer unwanted dilution of its own shares if the rights pertain to its own common stock). The provision customarily enables the company to redeem the rights if it chooses to complete a friendly merger. A 1985 Delaware Supreme Court decision upheld the right of managements to use the "poison pill" defenses without shareholder approval. Since then, this tactic has become widely used (both during takeover attempts and to prevent future takeover attempts). Approximately 200 of the Fortune 500 companies have adopted poison pill provisions.

11. **Paying "greenmail."** When a bidder acquires perhaps 10–20% of the target company's stock, the company may agree to purchase these stockholdings at a premium, allowing the bidder (most commonly called a *corporate raider*) to walk away with a hefty profit (on the condition that it not buy any stock in the future). For example, Walt Disney Productions paid a $60 million premium in

---

[1]"Did Avon's Digging for Amway Skeletons Scuttle Takeover Bid?" *The Wall Street Journal*, May 25, 1989, p. 1.

1984 to a bidder that had acquired 11% of Disney's stock (a total buyback of $325 million). (Over 20 antigreenmail stockholder lawsuits were subsequently filed against Disney alleging mismanagement, breach of fiduciary duty, and waste of corporate assets.)

DEFENSIVE TACTICS: WHOSE INTEREST IS SERVED?

Sometimes turning down an offer or even refusing to negotiate results in the acquiring company's making a higher offer. This is clearly in the best interest of the target company's stockholders. In some cases, however, such management actions are self-serving; managers oppose the takeover because they want to remain top executives of an independent company rather than become top executives of a small part of a much larger company—or they fear the loss of their jobs. In some instances, management's actions in defending against takeover attempts are irresponsible, especially when their stockholders are overwhelmingly tendering their shares and thereby accepting the offer.

The preceding examples make evident that more and more stockholders of target companies file lawsuits against their managers and directors alleging one of two things: (1) misuse of corporate resources in resisting takeover attempts (in a great number of instances, millions have been spent fighting the takeover attempt) or (2) violation of their fiduciary duty to stockholders by refusing to negotiate for the highest price possible. For the most part, the courts have been reluctant to find managements and directors guilty of these charges. Some companies attempt to protect their directors from such potential actions by dissatisfied stockholders by having the stockholders require the board of directors (through an amendment to the articles of incorporation) to consider factors other than the value and type of consideration offered when determining whether to accept an offer. Such factors might include the economic effects the takeover would have on employees and communities in which the target company operates.

In the late 1980s, financial circles and congressional committees extensively debated whether these widespread defensive tactics are (1) really necessary to protect stockholders (presumably from voluntarily selling their stock at a higher price) or (2) nothing more than self-serving management entrenchment devices that should be legally banned or at least voted on annually by the stockholders because of the changing composition of the stockholders from year to year. Congress, however, has enacted no federal legislation.

PROXY CONTESTS

In recent years, several factors (poison pills, increased state antitakeover legislation, and the decreased availability of financing since the 1987 stock market crash) have weakened the case for making tender offers. As a result, many acquiring companies have turned to **proxy contests** (often called *proxy wars*) to obtain control instead of making a direct purchase. In a proxy contest, both management and the acquirer solicit votes from the target company's stockholders for their respective proposed slates of directors.

In theory, the proxy system appears to be a superior way to obtain control of a target company because the insurgents can have their people (who will approve a proposed merger) placed on the board without having to buy more than 50% of the company to obtain control. In practice, however, the proxy system is extremely inefficient and gives management several built-in advantages over challengers. For example, management has full access to the corporate treasury to pay for its proxy solicitation effort (which can cost up to $10 million), but the acquirer must use its own funds. Obtaining lists of shareholders, although easy for management, is quite difficult for challengers (who often have to go through the courts). Tracking down stockholders is often impossible when brokers hold the stock in a street name. In most cases, managements win these proxy contests. The most famous recent proxy contest was in 1988 when Carl Icahn (once referred to as the most feared corporate raider in America) sought control of Texaco Inc., but incumbent management narrowly won.

THE DEBATE OVER TAKEOVERS

During the period 1982 through 1989, mergers and acquisitions, divestitures, breakups, leveraged buyouts, buybacks, and recapitalizations (collectively called *restructurings*) reached a record high in terms of the value of the transactions (mergers and acquisitions alone approached $200 billion per year). The sheer magnitude of the restructurings during this period raised questions as to whether all this restructuring is good or bad for the country.

Some observers contend that restructuring results in (1) many companies becoming overleveraged; (2) substantial disruption of the job market, with a consequent major adverse social impact on the communities affected; and (3) inordinate enrichment of the investment bankers and lawyers who are paid seemingly huge sums for their services ($100 million on a $2 billion deal is not uncommon) and who therefore are highly motivated to continually "put companies into play."

Others contend that restructuring is revitalizing our industry in response to fierce foreign competition by simplifying or "streamlining" corporations that have become too large and too complicated to be efficient, enabling managers to be in closer touch with production workers, customers, and stockholders.

THE DEBATE FROM A HISTORICAL PERSPECTIVE Four distinct periods of financial restructurings have occurred in the last 100 years: (1) the *horizontal* combinations near the turn of the century, (2) the *vertical* combinations of the 1920s, (3) the *conglomerate* combinations of the 1960s, and (4) most recently in the 1980s when *leveraged reorganizations* undid many of the conglomerate combinations of the 1960s. Why do financial restructurings occur so frequently? Many contend that periodic waves of restructurings are necessary in an economy based on capitalism to force the business sector to adapt to economic and technological change (the invisible hand of Adam Smith at work that makes for a more productive and competitive economy).

LEVERAGED BUYOUTS

A different kind of takeover of an existing business is a **leveraged buyout (LBO).** The typical LBO involves a group of investors that buys out an existing ownership using an extremely high percentage of debt to pay for the acquisition. The target company's assets are used as collateral to secure the loans. Such buyouts—in which the buyer is a group of investors rather than an existing business—are not combinations of two existing businesses. The new basis of accounting issue (discussed next) pertains, however, to LBOs as well as to combinations. We discuss LBOs in Chapter 8.

III ACCOUNTING METHODS: WHETHER TO CHANGE THE BASIS OF ACCOUNTING

The two basic methods of accounting for business combinations are the **pooling of interests method** and the **purchase method.** They are discussed in detail in *APB*

Opinion No. 16, "Accounting for Business Combinations," which became effective in November 1970. When the acquiring company gives consideration above or below the book value of the target company's net assets, these two methods produce dramatically different reporting of results of operations and financial position. Acquiring companies are fully aware of these consequences and often attempt to use the method that maximizes future earnings and earnings per share amounts. A major result of this pronouncement, however, has been to eliminate the considerable latitude that previously existed in the use of either the purchase method or the pooling of interests method. If one of these methods is desired, the terms and provisions of the acquisition agreement must be structured accordingly. This is a key point because **for a given set of terms and provisions, only one accounting method applies.** The methods used in a given set of circumstances are no longer elective.

In this respect, company accountants must be thoroughly familiar with *APBO No. 16* so they can properly advise top management during the negotiations. Many corporate controllers routinely obtain an opinion from their certified public accountants concerning whether a proposed set of terms and conditions allows the use of the desired accounting method. This is practically essential, considering the complexity of the pronouncement. The objective of this practice is to prevent a situation in which a combination is completed under the assumption that it will be accounted for under a desired method only to have the certified public accountants later uncover something in the acquisition agreement that disallows its use.

THE POOLING OF INTERESTS METHOD

THE UNDERLYING CONCEPT   The concept underlying pooling of interests accounting is that **a sale and purchase of a business have *not* occurred.** Two companies have simply pooled their financial resources and managerial talents in such a manner that the owners of each separate business are now the owners of an enlarged business. This **fusion of equity interests** is the foundation of the pooling of interests concept, and **it occurs only if the target company's shareholders receive common stock of the other company as consideration for their business.**

THE REQUIREMENT TO SATISFY 12 CONDITIONS   Twelve conditions must be met if pooling of interests accounting is to be allowed. These conditions involve (1) the attributes of the combining companies (three conditions), (2) the mechanics of the exchange (six conditions [one of which is that common stock be issued as consideration]), and (3) transactions that are prohibited in periods subsequent to the exchange (three conditions). **If any one of these 12 conditions is *not* met, the pooling of interests method *cannot* be used. If all 12 conditions are complied with, the pooling of interests method *must* be used.** These 12 conditions are discussed in Chapter 7, which discusses and illustrates the application of this method in detail.

THE ACCOUNTING RESULT: NO CHANGE IN BASIS OF ACCOUNTING OCCURS AND GOODWILL IS *NEVER* REPORTED   When a combination qualifies for pooling of interests treatment, **the recorded assets and liabilities of the separate companies are carried forward to the combined corporation at their historically recorded amounts.** Consequently, the **old basis of accounting** is maintained.

Often of equal or greater significance is the fact that **goodwill is never created.** Consequently, future income statements of the combined, enlarged business never include goodwill amortization expense.

Furthermore, if *precombination period* income statements are presented with *postcombination period* income statements for comparative purposes, the *separate in-*

come statements of each constituent company are combined, restated, and then reported as income of the combined corporation. (The annual reporting rules of the
SEC require two prior years of comparative income statements for publicly owned
companies.)

THE PURCHASE METHOD

THE UNDERLYING CONCEPT   The underlying concept of the purchase method is
that **one company has acquired the business of another company and a sale has
occurred.** Unlike the pooling of interests method, any type of consideration—
namely, cash, bonds, preferred stock, and common stock—may be given for purchase accounting treatment.

AUTOMATIC USE IF THE 12 CONDITIONS FOR POOLING OF INTERESTS ARE *NOT*
MET   If the transaction does *not* qualify for *pooling of interests* treatment, the **purchase method** *must* **be used.**

THE ACCOUNTING RESULT: A CHANGE IN BASIS OF ACCOUNTING OCCURS AND
GOODWILL IS REPORTED   When a combination is reported as a purchase, the acquiring company's cost (the value of the consideration given for the acquired business) must be allocated to the individual assets acquired. The result is to revalue
the acquired business's assets to their current values. Consequently, a **new basis of
accounting** is established.

In an economy experiencing inflation, the acquiring company usually pays an
amount in excess of the book value of the net assets of the acquired business. If this
excess relates to assets other than land (a nondepreciable asset), future income
statements reflect higher depreciation and amortization charges than had the *pooling of interests* method been used. Accordingly, future earnings are lower under the
purchase method.

To the extent that the acquiring entity's cost exceeds the current value of the acquired entity's identifiable net assets, **goodwill** arises and must be amortized to income over a period not to exceed 40 years.

The usual upward revaluation of the acquired business's assets and the creation
of goodwill are the major disadvantages of the *purchase method* compared with the
pooling of interests method from the viewpoint of future earnings and earnings per
share.

ILLUSTRATION   **POOLING OF INTERESTS VERSUS PURCHASE METHOD**

To illustrate the different reporting results under each method, assume the following information:

1. On December 31, 19X1, P Company issued 5,000 shares of its no-par value com-
    mon stock having a fair market value of $20 per share ($100,000 total fair value)
    in exchange for all of the outstanding common stock of S Company.

2. S Company's net assets of $60,000 at book value have a current value of $88,000.
    The $28,000 undervaluation (which is relevant only under the purchase method)
    pertains to the following accounts:

Inventory	$ 4,000
Land	8,000
Equipment	16,000
	$28,000

3. Under the purchase method, $12,000 of goodwill was paid for ($100,000 Fair Market Value of Common Stock Issued −$88,000 Current Value of S Company's Net Assets).

Each company's financial statements *immediately before* the combination and the combined ones that P Company would issue for the year ended December 31, 19X1, are shown in Illustration 4–1, with asset account reporting differences boldfaced.

CRITICISM OF *APB OPINION NO. 16*

APBO No. 16 received barely the required two-thirds majority vote. Since its issuance, it has been widely criticized for not being a sound or logical solution to the issues associated with business combinations. The main criticism is that the results produced under the pooling of interests method often do not accurately portray the underlying economics of the business combination. For example, a company that has sales and assets of $100,000 could "pool" its resources and management with a company having sales and assets of $100 million. Many accountants believe that to treat such a combination as a pooling is just not sensible. In this situation, the substance of the combination is obviously the acquisition of the small business by the large business—a reality that the pooling of interests method ignores.

Most accountants agree with the fundamental concept of the purchase method, except for the treatment of goodwill. Many accountants and corporate executives believe that goodwill should *not* be shown as an asset of the acquiring company

ILLUSTRATION 4–1	Comparison of Reporting Results: Pooling of Interests versus Purchase Method				
			S Company		Combined
	P Company	Book Amounts	Current Values	Pooling of Interests Method (old basis)	Purchase Method (new basis)
Income Statement (19X1)					
Sales	$500,000	$210,000		$710,000	$ 500,000
Cost of sales	(330,000)	(140,000)		(470,000)	(330,000)
Expenses	(120,000)	(60,000)		(180,000)	(120,000)
Net Income	$ 50,000	$ 10,000		$ 60,000	$ 50,000
Balance Sheet (as of 12/31/X1)					
Cash	$118,000	$ 15,000	$ 15,000	$133,000	$ 133,000
Accounts receivable	52,000	23,000	23,000	75,000	75,000
Inventory	90,000	42,000	46,000	**132,000**	**136,000**
Land	220,000	30,000	38,000	**250,000**	**258,000**
Buildings and equipment, net	220,000	150,000	166,000	**370,000**	**386,000**
Goodwill			12,000		**12,000**
	$700,000	$260,000	$300,000	$960,000	$1,000,000
Liabilities	$400,000	$200,000	$200,000	$600,000	$ 600,000
Common stock	200,000	40,000 ⎱ 100,000		240,000[a]	300,000[b]
Retained earnings	100,000	20,000 ⎰		120,000	100,000
	$700,000	$260,000	$300,000	$960,000	$1,000,000

Note: Asset account reporting differences in the Combined columns are in boldface.
[a]$200,000 + $40,000 = $240,000.
[b]$200,000 + $100,000 (5,000 shares × $20 fair market value) = $300,000.

but should be charged to the equity section of the acquiring company at the acquisition. Their reasoning is that the acquiring entity has, in substance, given up some of its equity with the hope of recouping it in subsequent years through the acquired company's superior earnings (which may or may not materialize). Also criticized are the arbitrary rules relating to the amortization of goodwill, as set forth in *APB Opinion No. 17*, "Intangible Assets." Goodwill created before November 1, 1970, does not have to be amortized at all, whereas goodwill created after October 31, 1970, must be amortized over a period no longer than 40 years.

IV THE GOODWILL CONTROVERSY

Goodwill is perhaps the most unique of all intangibles because, unlike other types of intangibles (and tangibles), it is not separable from the business and thus cannot be sold apart from the business as a whole. In general, goodwill represents an existing or perceived future capability to achieve superior earnings. Goodwill has been a controversial issue for more than a century, and the controversy has heated up in the last few years because goodwill is becoming a larger percentage of business combination purchase prices and consequently of assets and equity than ever before (in many cases exceeding equity).[2]

The magnitude of the goodwill issue may best be exemplified by the savings and loan industry, in which billions of dollars of nonexistent goodwill (using the superior earnings concept) was created in the 1980s by merging near-bankrupt savings and loans with healthier ones at virtually no out-of-pocket costs to the healthy institution. If goodwill were eliminated from the balance sheet of thrifts in this industry, the industry's nearly $40 billion of equity would be reduced to $10 billion. Even Congress recognized that goodwill is a dubious asset for this industry when it passed legislation in 1990 phasing out the inclusion of goodwill as an asset for regulatory purposes (used to assess whether an institution has insufficient capital that may trigger seizure and closure by the federal regulators). The Financial Accounting Standards Board's response to all of this has been largely to ignore the problem.

CONCEPTUAL ISSUES   The conceptual issues for goodwill are as follows:

1. **Should goodwill—either purchased or internally generated—be reported as an asset?** The accounting alternatives are (1) capitalizing it or (2) charging it to equity (either directly or through the income statement).

2. **If goodwill is reported as an asset, how should its valuation be determined subsequent to the date it is recorded as an asset?** The accounting alternatives are to (1) treat goodwill as a permanent asset, (2) amortize it systematically, or (3) write it down when its value has been impaired.

A capsule history of accounting for goodwill in the United States appears on pages 124–126 of this chapter. This history allows you to see the many approaches that have been used in accounting for goodwill during the last century. What makes goodwill such a difficult issue is that, if properly maintained, it can last forever. For example, many—but certainly not all—leading name brands of the 1920s (Steinway pianos, Gold Medal flour, Colgate toothpaste) are still the leading name

---

[2]One recent study comparing the Standard & Poor's 500 from 1969 to 1989 showed intangibles as a percentage of total assets nearly doubling from 5.1% to 9.7% and intangibles as a percentage of equity nearly tripling from 10.9% to 29.8%. See Michael Davis, "Goodwill Accounting: Time for an Overhaul," *Journal of Accountancy*, June 1992, pp. 75–83.

HISTORICAL PERSPECTIVE

A Capsule History of Accounting for Goodwill

Accounting for goodwill has been studied and debated since about 1880. Through the years, it has evolved from a state of "anything goes" to the restrictive, arbitrary, and uniform accounting requirements of *APB Opinion Nos. 16* and *17*, issued in 1970. No accounting topic has inspired more diversely held views (and fiercely strong ones) than goodwill. Consequently, students must not simply memorize the rules of the current pronouncements; they must also understand how and why we have arrived at the present rules from what was tried in the past and rejected. And as their predecessors have done, they must continually question the logic and practicality of these rules and their current application.

Prior to 1917 The entire cost of an acquisition in excess of book value is treated as goodwill. Accountants favor charging goodwill to stockholders' equity at the acquisition date. There is no support for charging goodwill to income, either through amortization or in a lump sum.

1917 The American Institute of Accountants, the predecessor to the AICPA, "recommends" that goodwill be shown as a reduction to stockholders' equity (if it is not already charged to capital).

1918–1929 Companies begin capitalizing internally generated goodwill. (Amounts range from advertising costs to arbitrary estimates of the value of the goodwill.) Many abuses result.

1930–1944 Recording as goodwill only purchased goodwill becomes the prevalent thinking. Permanent retention of goodwill as an asset and periodically amortizing it to income, retained earnings, or additional paid-in capital become acceptable practice (in addition to immediately charging these to capital). Accounting writers begin advocating the analysis of the cost in excess of book value.

1944 *Accounting Research Bulletin No. 24* is issued. It states that only historical cost should be used to value goodwill. Arbitrary write-ups and capitalization of start-up costs as goodwill are thus banned. The door is left open for companies to capitalize advertising costs as goodwill.

1945 The Securities and Exchange Commission (SEC) begins encouraging companies to amortize goodwill if they have been using the permanent retention treatment.

1953 *Accounting Research Bulletin No. 43* is issued. It prohibits charging goodwill to

stockholders' equity immediately after acquisition. The discretionary write-downs of goodwill are banned—a loss of value must take place for a write-down or write-off.

1968 *Accounting Research Study No. 5*, "Accounting for Goodwill" (written by two senior partners of Arthur Andersen and Co.) is issued. The study concludes that goodwill is *not* an asset and should be charged to stockholders' equity at the time of the acquisition.

1968–1970 A fierce and heated debate takes place within the accounting profession concerning accounting for business combinations and the related issue of goodwill.

1970 *APBO Nos. 16* and *17* are issued, the first by a vote of 12 to 6 and the second by a vote of 13 to 5. As a result, (1) goodwill can arise only from a business combination; (2) the cost in excess of book value must be analyzed; (3) goodwill existing as of October 31, 1970, *need not* be amortized to income; (4) goodwill arising after that date must be amortized to income over no more than 40 years; and (5) if goodwill loses its value, it must be written off to income as an extraordinary charge. (The positions of the various opposing factions of the APB are so strongly held that, with a two-thirds majority required for passage, many members cannot talk to one another for three months after the vote. One of the largest CPA firms seriously considers not supporting these pronouncements in its practice but decides to continue to work within the profession to bring about needed changes.)

1971 The APB's handling of the business combinations and goodwill issues (in which strong positions were taken only to be withdrawn because of pressure from client companies) ultimately leads to the demise of the APB and the establishment of the FASB in 1973.

1971–1980 Goodwill becomes a dead issue.

1981 A crisis develops in the savings and loan (S&L) industry because of high interest rates. More than a thousand S&L associations become financially distressed—many actually exhausting their net worths and thus facing bankruptcy—and are forced to merge with stronger ones. Seeking ways to report higher earnings, the acquiring firms take advantage of a quirk in *APBO No. 16* and account for these arranged, regulatory mergers as purchases (rather than as poolings of interests, the usual practice for such mergers). Consequently, billions of dollars of goodwill are reported as being amortized over 30 to 40 years. (The offsetting loan discount is credited to income over 10 to 12 years.)

Undaunted by the peculiarity (some would say absurdity) that companies facing bankruptcy could possibly possess goodwill, auditors of these acquiring companies allow this reporting of artificial income without exception. Form prevails over substance.

1983   In response to public criticism of the reporting of artificial income in the S&L industry, the FASB amends *APBO No. 17* in FASB *Statement No. 72,* "Accounting for Certain Acquisitions of Banking or Thrift Institutions." It requires much shorter lives for goodwill (10 to 12 years)—but only for that portion of goodwill attributable to the acquired financial institution having an excess of liabilities over assets on a fair value basis.

Some S&Ls rush through their mergers to beat the effective date of the pronouncement, which is retroactive only to September 30, 1982. The auditors of these firms give unqualified ("clean") opinions on the financial statements presented under the old rules as well as those presented under the new rules—deeming all the statements to "present fairly."

Analyzing and understanding the financial statements of such S&Ls become quite difficult. (Perplexed investors ask their stockbrokers, "What are the 'real' earnings?")

1983–1985   Scores of companies that went on acquisition binges in the 1970s begin disposing of hundreds of previously acquired companies due to their operating problems and unprofitability. Billions of dollars of unamortized goodwill (most companies were choosing a 40-year life) must be written off.

1985   The staff of the SEC issues *Staff Accounting Bulletin No. 42A,* which states that the maximum amortization life for goodwill that it will accept for financial institutions is 25 years.

1985–1986   A congressional committee headed by Rep. John Dingell holds hearings on the conduct of the accounting profession because of the rising number of collapses, corporate failures and abuses, and alleged auditing failures among large financial institutions.

1986–1987   The accounting profession explores ways to enhance public confidence in itself.

1989   The S&L industry, which reported a $12.1 billion loss for 1988, continues to report approximately $38 billion of goodwill (about 75% of its net worth at book value).

Congress passes the most expensive taxpayer bailout in U.S. history by approving a $306 billion rescue bill for the S&L industry. The bill requires them to maintain "real capital" equal to at least 3% of total assets—with goodwill to be excluded from capital after 1994. (Goodwill may be considered part of capital up to 1.5% until then.) Prior to the bill's passage, the S&L industry attempted to have goodwill counted as part of capital to its fullest extent.

1991   The SEC confirms that it is reducing its allowable life for goodwill in acquisitions involving high-technology companies because the technology may become quickly outmoded. In many cases, the SEC allows only three years.

1992   Since 1970, goodwill has become a much higher percentage of total assets and equity. Many believe that the FASB should reexamine this issue.

In late 1992, the FASB added accounting for the impairment of goodwill to its project on impairment of long-lived assets and intangibles.

1994   The Financial Accounting Policy Committee of the Association for Investment Management and Research (AIMR), the professional association of financial analysts, issues the report "Financial Reporting in the 1990s and Beyond." It recommends that purchased goodwill be written off at the date it is acquired because (1) it depicts value only at a particular date and (2) its presence on the balance sheet is of no significant use in estimating an entity's future cash flows or gauging the entity's value. (The FASB acknowledges that this document is an important summary of how financial analysts use financial

continued

statements and how they would like to see financial reporting evolve.)

1995 The FASB completes its impairment project with the issuance of *SFAS No. 121*. Unfortunately, the impairment of goodwill is addressed only for limited situations in which related long-lived assets are impaired (as discussed in Chapter 5).

Source: A major portion of the capsule history prior to 1970 is based on Research Monograph No. 80, *Goodwill in Accounting: A History of the Issues and Problems,* by Hugh P. Hughes (Atlanta: Georgia State University, 1982).

brands 70 years later.[3] On the other hand, poor management can result in a loss of value over time or even overnight. For example, Perrier had a virtual stranglehold over the U.S. imported bottled water market until it had to issue a recall in 1990 when traces of benzene, a suspected carcinogen, were found in some bottles after a worker forgot to change a filter. Nearly a year after the recall, Perrier's sales were still down 40% from pre-recall levels. (Consumers had a chance to try other brands, many of which were less expensive, and found no essential difference.)

A BALANCE SHEET PHRASE MORE DESCRIPTIVE THAN GOODWILL Possibly a more descriptive and useful phrase than *goodwill* is as follows:

> Amount paid in a business combination for the estimated future superior earnings that management hopes will materialize in the belief that it can run the acquired business as well as or better than the previous owners and their management for the next (1–40) years.

ACCOUNTING FOR GOODWILL IN THE UNITED STATES

As stated earlier, U.S. GAAP requires goodwill to be capitalized and amortized over no more than 40 years.

WHY 40 YEARS? For many years prior to 1970, goodwill had to be written off only if there were evidence that its value had diminished—a rule that many would like to see restored. One problem with the old rule was that managements often overpaid for goodwill as a result of a bidding war. Another problem was that in many cases, managements refused to recognize that the value of goodwill (including the brand name element that is generally lumped in with goodwill) had eroded or had been overpaid. Finally, the accounting rule-making bodies did *not* set forth either (1) a commonsense return-on-investment test (using either average versus superior earnings) or (2) an expected versus actual results as a benchmark in assessing whether value had diminished. So amortization over no more than 40 years—a length of time that minimizes the impact on earnings— became the compromise between those who wanted the old rule left intact and those who thought goodwill should be amortized over a relatively short period, such as 3–10 years.

ECONOMIC CONSEQUENCES OF THE MANDATORY AMORTIZATION RULE

Amortizing goodwill reduces earnings and earnings per share, and a drop in these two measures may cause the price of a stock to fall. Because executive compensation plans are almost always tied to earnings—instead of cash flows—manage-

---

[3]David N. Martin, "Romancing the Brand," *Amacon* (New York: 1989), p. 19.

ments are usually reluctant to enter into a business combination in which a substantial amount of goodwill will be reported. The following are statements from an investment banker and a vice-president of finance and operations of a billion-dollar company:

> Twenty acquisitions he personally worked on in the last two years fell through because goodwill amortization would have reduced reported earnings, a risk the acquiring companies' managers were "loath to take." [Investment Banker] Goodwill doesn't always kill the deal, but it sure does weigh heavily. Generally, investors are still looking for earnings per share [Vice-President of Finance and Operations].[4]

This concern is greater for some industries than others. For instance, in capital-intensive businesses such as steel or automobiles, the bulk of the purchase price can be attributed to physical assets, but for consumer products and media businesses, the bulk of the purchase price may be goodwill. For instance, $11 billion (80%) of the $14 billion purchase price that Time Inc. paid to acquire Warner Communications in 1989 was for goodwill. Annual goodwill amortization charges using a 40-year amortization period are $275 million—this caused Time-Warner to report a $217 million loss for 1990, with losses expected to occur for several years. One consequence of the Time-Warner merger is that many investment bankers have switched their emphasis to cash flows as a sign of a company's strength (as the leveraged buyout enthusiasts do) rather than earnings. One of the alleged advantages of taking a company private in a leveraged buyout is that the company can later pursue other firms without worrying about the effects of goodwill amortization on the price of its stock.

CONCERN FOR U.S. FIRMS BECAUSE OF FOREIGN COMPETITION

Some investment bankers and analysts believe that in acquisitions and mergers, U.S. firms are at a disadvantage relative to foreign bidders domiciled in countries that either can immediately charge goodwill to stockholders' equity or do not have to amortize goodwill. In our opinion, this is not a valid assertion because the way that goodwill is treated does not affect the cash flows of an acquisition. Accordingly, investors should be able to reinterpret correctly accounting reports in terms of economic information. To the extent that foreign bidders can deduct goodwill for income tax–reporting purposes over a significantly shorter life than allowed under U.S. tax laws, however, they *do* have an advantage over U.S. firms.

The International Perspective on page 128 describes the way certain foreign countries deal with goodwill.

U.S. TAX RULES CONCERNING THE DEDUCTIBILITY OF GOODWILL

Historically, goodwill has *not* been tax deductible. In 1991, the General Accounting Office (GAO) recommended to Congress, however, that the tax code be amended to allow goodwill (as well as other purchased intangible assets) to be deducted to eliminate the continuous, costly, and counterproductive legal warfare between the Internal Revenue Service and corporate taxpayers on this issue. Consequently, in a historic shift of position, Congress changed the tax rules (in the Revenue Reconciliation Act of 1993) so that goodwill and other purchased intangibles are now deductible over 15 years. (Goodwill purchased in a business combination prior to this legislation, however, is *not* tax deductible.)

---

[4]"A Peculiar Beauty Contest," *Forbes*, July 10, 1989, p. 44. This article discusses the then-proposed Time-Warner combination, consummated later in 1989.

INTERNATIONAL PERSPECTIVE

Foreign Goodwill Accounting Practices

Substantial diversity exists among foreign countries as to the treatment of goodwill for both financial and tax-reporting purposes, as evidenced by the practices of the following countries:

United Kingdom. Goodwill is immediately charged to stockholders' equity, thus bypassing the income statement. To avoid the drastic reduction or elimination of equity that can occur under this practice, a recent trend is to separate "brand names" from goodwill and report brand names as an asset. No tax deduction is allowed for goodwill.

Japan. Goodwill is capitalized and amortized to income over no more than 5 years. Goodwill is tax deductible over 5 years.

Germany. Capitalizing goodwill is an option; if capitalized, it must be amortized over 4 years unless it is systematically amortized over the benefiting years. Goodwill is tax deductible over 15 years.

The Netherlands. Goodwill is usually charged to stockholders' equity at the acquisition date, thereby bypassing the income statement. An acceptable alternative practice is to allow amortization over 5–10 years. Goodwill is tax deductible over 5 years.

Canada. Goodwill is capitalized and amortized to income over no more than 40 years. 75% of goodwill is tax deductible.

The International Accounting Standards Committee (IASC). The IASC, a London-based organization attempting to develop world GAAP, currently has outstanding an exposure draft on intangible assets (E 50), which would require goodwill to be capitalized and amortized within 20 years. If passed, this proposal will eliminate the IASC's currently allowed alternative of immediately charging goodwill to stockholders' equity. (The IASC is discussed in more detail in Chapter 18.)

V   ACQUIRING ASSETS VERSUS COMMON STOCK

The purchase versus pooling of interests treatment issue is often the focal point in negotiating the terms of a proposed business combination. Also usually of major importance to the acquiring company, however, is the type of property it will receive in exchange for the type of consideration it gives to the target company or its shareholders. In practice, some classic blunders have been made (one of which we describe shortly) as a result of receiving the wrong type of property.

TYPES OF PROPERTY THAT MAY BE RECEIVED IN EXCHANGE FOR THE CONSIDERATION GIVEN

A business may be acquired in one of two ways, by acquiring the target company's (1) assets or (2) outstanding common stock from the stockholders.

1. **Acquiring assets.** Assume that the agreed-upon value of the target company's assets is $7 million and that the current value of the target company's liabilities is $5 million. When it acquires the target company's assets, the acquiring company has the option to either give consideration of (1) $7 million or (2) give $2 million and to assume responsibility for paying the target company's $5 million of liabilities. (The latter option is most common.) If the pooling of interests treatment is desired, 100% of the assets must be acquired; no such requirement exists for the purchase method.

2. **Acquiring common stock.** The acquiring company must purchase *more than* 50% of the target company's outstanding common stock to be considered a business combination. With an ownership interest of more than 50%, the acquiring company can control the target company. If the pooling of interests treatment is desired, at least 90% of the common stock must be acquired; no such requirement exists for the purchase method.

REASONS FOR ACQUIRING ASSETS VERSUS COMMON STOCK

Many circumstances and factors affect the determination of whether to obtain the target company's assets or common stock in exchange for the consideration given. Here are some of the more common items:

1. **Unrecorded liabilities.** A major concern of a buyer contemplating acquiring common stock is whether the target company has unrecorded liabilities, such as accounts payable omissions and inadequate or unrecognized accruals. **If common stock is obtained for the consideration given, the buyer inherits responsibility for the unrecorded liabilities.** By acquiring assets, however, the acquiring company can best insulate itself from responsibility for these contingencies, inasmuch as a well-drafted acquisition agreement pertaining to the acquisition of assets can clearly specify those liabilities for which the acquiring company assumes responsibility. One of the major pitfalls for acquiring companies in the 1980s was unrecorded other postretirement benefits (primarily the obligations to pay for retirees' medical costs not covered by Medicare), which were being accounted for on the "pay-as-you-go" (cash) basis and were estimated to be between $300 billion and $1 trillion for all U.S. corporations as of 1990. (*SFAS No. 106,* "Employers' Accounting for Postretirement Benefits Other Than Pensions" eliminated this grossly deficient reporting practice by requiring companies to convert to the accrual basis.)

CASE IN POINT

A $600 Million Oversight

Probably the most unfortunate omission of an unrecognized liability in an acquisition was the 1987 acquisition of Uniroyal for $1 billion, which stuck the buyer with unrecorded benefits estimated to be as high as $600 million.

---

2. **Contingent liabilities.** When the acquisition of common stock is contemplated, a full understanding of contingent liabilities is often of far more importance than the risk posed by unrecorded liabilities. Some of the types of contingent liabilities that are usually of major concern and thus investigated are as follows:

    Litigation in process and unasserted claims. Inquiring of the seller's legal counsel about litigation in process and potential unasserted claims is customary.

    Open years for income taxes. Assessing the likelihood of possible IRS tax and penalty assessments for years prior to the business combination date that the IRS has not yet examined is also customary.

3. **Nontransferability of contracts.** If the target company's contracts, leases, franchises, or operating rights *cannot* be transferred through the sale of assets, common stock must be acquired.

4. **Ease of transfer.** Transferring stock certificates is easier than transferring assets. The transfer of assets may require the preparation of separate bills of sale for each asset or class of asset; also, state laws concerning bulk sales must be observed.

5. **Unwanted facilities or segments.** If the acquiring company does not wish to acquire all of the target company's assets, the acquisition of assets allows the acquiring company to obtain only those assets it desires. (To arrange for the acquisition of its common stock, the target company could dispose of the unwanted assets, but it may not always be feasible to do so in the time specified in the acquisition agreement.)

6. **Access to the target company's cash.** If the acquiring company offers cash as consideration and the target company has substantial cash and short-term investment assets, the acquisition of assets makes the target company's cash and short-term investment assets available to the acquiring company to either help replenish its cash or repay loans obtained to finance the acquisition. In effect, the acquisition can be partially paid for using the funds of the target company. If common stock were acquired, the target company's cash and short-term investment assets would not be available to the acquiring company, except to the extent that the target company (as a subsidiary and a separate legal entity) could pay dividends to the acquiring company (as the parent).

7. **Eliminating the target company's labor union.** If the target company has a labor unit that the acquiring company does *not* want to inherit, it can avoid the union only by acquiring assets and then hiring all new employees to run the newly acquired operation.

8. **Tax factors.** Sometimes tax factors play an important role in whether to acquire assets or common stock. For example, goodwill is effectively tax deductible only if assets are acquired (as explained more fully in the Appendix to Chapter 8). We discuss some of the other tax ramifications later in the chapter.

Sometimes a potential problem cannot be avoided merely by acquiring assets instead of common stock. For example, a buyer would inherit liabilities for toxic waste cleanup (estimated to be $500 billion for the 10,000 toxic waste sites identified by the Environmental Protection Agency)—regardless of whether it acquires assets or common stock. As a result of the growing awareness of the contingent liabilities associated with toxic waste sites (General Motors, for instance, has 140 toxic waste sites designated by the EPA as requiring urgent attention), environmental attorneys are now routinely hired to comb company records and inspect waste sites before consummation of a proposed deal. Consequently, many proposed deals are either (1) abandoned because of the magnitude of the potential problems found or (2) revised to have a drastically reduced offering price. (One prominent New York City-based law firm that specializes in takeover work now employs more than 20 environmental attorneys.)

VI THE RESULTING ORGANIZATION FORM OF THE ACQUIRED BUSINESS

Accounting for business combinations focuses on **how the acquiring company initially records the transaction that brings about the combination.** The detailed accounting entries for the acquiring company require substantial explanation under both the purchase method and the pooling of interests method; these are discussed and illustrated in detail in Chapters 5 and 7, respectively. The entries made by the target company, on the other hand, are quite simple. The following discussion is general in nature so that an overall understanding of the organizational effects of business combinations can be grasped.

ACQUISITION OF ASSETS

When the target company's assets are acquired, these assets (and any liabilities assumed) are recorded in the acquiring company's general ledger. The newly acquired operation is usually referred to as a *division*. For example, Punn Company acquired all of the assets and assumed all of the liabilities of Sunn Company by giving cash as the consideration. Each company makes the following entries (in condensed format):

Punn Company (the acquiring company)			Sunn Company (the target company)	
Assets	xxx[a]	← Assets		xxx
Liabilities	xxx[a]	← Liabilities	xxx	
Cash	xxx	→ Cash	xxx	
		Gain (*if cash exceeds book value of net assets*)		xxx
		Loss (*if cash is less than book value of net assets*)	xxx	

[a]Because cash is the consideration given, the transaction must be accounted for as a purchase. Accordingly, the assets acquired and liabilities assumed are recorded at their current values based on the purchase price. (This is discussed further in Chapter 5.)

CREATING A SUBSIDIARY TO ACQUIRE THE ASSETS   In some cases, the acquiring company creates a subsidiary to effect the acquisition of the target company's assets. This occurs in situations in which it is not possible, practicable, or desirable to acquire the target company's common stock, but it is desirable to operate the acquired business as a separate legal entity insulated from the existing operations of the acquiring company.

REMOVAL OF RECORDS   The target company must pack its records (including its general ledger) and remove them from the location of the business that was sold.

SUBSEQUENT COURSES OF ACTION FOR THE TARGET COMPANY   If all of its assets are disposed of and all of its liabilities are assumed, the target company's remaining assets consist solely of the consideration received from the acquiring company. At this point, the target company (still a separate legal entity) is referred to as a **nonoperating company** because it has no operating business—but only passive assets. The target company then has three courses of action:

1. Continue as a nonoperating company.
2. Use the assets to enter a new line of business.
3. Distribute the assets to its shareholders. (This option is the one most commonly selected.)

If it chooses option 3, the target company becomes a **shell company** because it has no operating business and no assets. It still is a separate legal entity, however, until steps are taken to have its charter withdrawn (which is usually done).

ACQUIRING RIGHTS TO THE TARGET COMPANY'S NAME   The acquiring company usually specifies in the acquisition agreement that in addition to assets it is acquiring the exclusive right to the target company's corporate name. Accordingly, if the target company intends to remain in business (either as a nonoperating company or as an operating company in a new line of business), it must make a corporate name change. This avoids any future confusion that might arise between, as in the earlier example, the acquirer's Sunn Division and the target Sunn Company.

TAX TREATMENT ON ANY GAIN BY THE TARGET COMPANY   The target company is taxed on any gain resulting from the sale of its assets only if the transaction is a taxable combination. (Taxable versus nontaxable combinations are discussed later in the chapter.)

ACQUISITION OF COMMON STOCK

As discussed in Chapter 1, a company owning more than 50% of the outstanding common stock of another company is referred to as the *parent* of that company. Conversely, a company whose outstanding common stock is more than 50% owned by another company is referred to as a *subsidiary* of that company. A subsidiary (as opposed to a division) is a separate legal entity that must maintain its own general ledger. Accordingly, the subsidiary's operations must be accounted for on a decentralized basis. The acquisition of the outstanding common stock of the acquired company is a personal transaction involving the acquiring company and the acquired company's shareholders. For the target company, the only change is that the company's ownership is concentrated in the hands of significantly fewer stockholders, or even one stockholder if 100% of the outstanding common stock has been acquired. Consequently, only the acquiring company (the parent) must make an entry relating to the business combination.

Assuming that Punn Company acquired more than 50% of the outstanding common stock of Sunn Company, the relationship is depicted as follows:

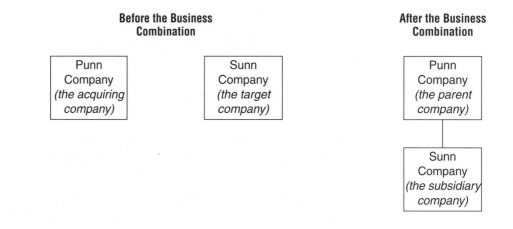

CASH-FOR-STOCK EXCHANGE   If the acquiring company gives cash as consideration for the target company's outstanding common stock (such a cash-for-stock exchange automatically disqualifies the transaction for pooling of interests treatment), it makes the following entry:

Investment in Subsidiary   xxx
      Cash   xxx

STOCK-FOR-STOCK EXCHANGE   If the acquiring company gives common stock as consideration (a necessary consideration for pooling of interests treatment) for the target company's outstanding common stock, it is necessary to understand what is known as the *exchange ratio*. The **exchange ratio** is the number of common shares to be issued by the acquiring company for each outstanding common share of the target company to be surrendered. Say that the acquiring company will issue 30,000 shares and the target company has 10,000 shares outstanding, all of which are to be exchanged. This produces a 3:1 exchange ratio. Note that the number of shares to be issued by the acquiring company first has to be calculated by dividing the price the acquiring company is willing to pay for the target company (say, $1,200,000) by the market price per share of the acquiring company's common stock (say, $40 per share), producing the number of shares to be issued (30,000). The exchange ratio is usually set forth in the acquisition agreement.

If the acquiring company issues 30,000 shares of common stock to effect the business combination, the acquiring company makes the following entry:

Investment in Subsidiary   xxx
        Common Stock (30,000 × Par Value)   xxx
        Additional Paid-in Capital   xxx

This entry is slightly more involved if pooling of interests treatment applies (more about this in Chapter 7).

STATUTORY MERGERS

A third common way to effect a business combination is the **statutory merger,** in which the target company's equity securities are retired and its corporate existence is terminated. This can be depicted as follows:

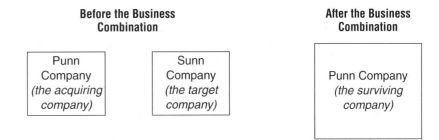

The target company's assets and liabilities are transferred to the acquiring company. Because the acquiring company is the only surviving legal entity, the target company is said to have been "merged" into the acquiring company. Because these combinations take place pursuant to state laws, they are called *statutory mergers.* The state statutory merger laws have two primary requirements:

1. The board of directors of each company must approve the plan of proposed merger before the plan can be submitted to the shareholders of each company.

2. The required percentage (usually a simple majority to 80%) of the voting power of each company must approve the plan of proposed merger.

The result of a statutory merger is as though the acquiring company had acquired directly the target company's assets and the target company had then ceased its legal existence. The reasons for using this roundabout manner to acquire a target company's assets are explained in the following paragraphs.

FORCING OUT DISSENTING SHAREHOLDERS   In most cases in which the acquiring company acquires common stock, it desires 100% of the target company's outstanding common stock. In some of these situations, this outcome may be unlikely because some of the target company's shareholders object to the business combination and refuse to sell their shares. If the acquiring company acquires the required percentage of outstanding shares to approve a statutory merger, however, it can force out the dissenting shareholders by taking the necessary steps to liquidate the target company. In some tender offers, the acquiring company clearly specifies that once it obtains the required ownership percentage, it intends to effect a statutory merger with the target company if all of the target company's shareholders do *not* accept the offer. This message means "tender your shares now or be forced out later."

In these cases, the business combination technically occurs when the acquiring company acquires more than 50% of the target company's outstanding common stock, which creates a parent-subsidiary relationship. Thus the statutory merger takes place after the business combination date, a process that normally can be completed within 30 to 60 days after approval of the plan of merger.

When the statutory merger subsequently becomes effective, entries are made (1) to transfer the target company's assets and liabilities to the acquiring company and (2) to close out the equity accounts in the target company's general ledger. In addition, it is necessary to make a settlement with the target company's dissenting stockholders (who did not tender their shares). State laws pertaining to statutory mergers generally provide that dissenting shareholders have the right to receive (in cash) the fair value of their shares as of the day before shareholder approval of the merger. Such value may have to be established through a judicial determination as provided under state law if the dissenting shareholders and the acquiring company cannot agree on the value of these shares.

FORCING OUT SHAREHOLDERS WHO CANNOT BE LOCATED   The company acquiring common stock in a takeover cannot always locate all of the target company's shareholders; in most publicly held companies, a small number of shareholders simply cannot be found. When the acquiring company desires 100% ownership notwithstanding, it may take the statutory merger route to liquidate these interests in the target company.

ACQUIRING ASSETS INDIRECTLY   In unfriendly takeover attempts, the acquiring company is prevented from acquiring the assets directly from the target company because the directors' refusal of the offer prevents the target company's shareholders from voting on it. The acquiring company must then make a tender offer to the shareholders. If the acquiring company acquires the required percentage of outstanding shares through the tender offer and does not wish to maintain a parent-subsidiary relationship, it can then take the necessary steps to liquidate the target company via a statutory merger.

HOLDING COMPANIES

Infrequently, two companies (generally of comparable size) combine in such a manner that **a new corporate entity is established that controls the operations of both combining companies.** This occurs when (1) the existing name of each corporation would not indicate the scope of operations of the combined business or (2) it is desired to have the top-level corporation operate as a **holding company.** A holding company has no revenue-producing operations of its own, only investments in subsidiaries. To illustrate, assume that Punn Company and Sunn Company wish to combine. They form Integrated Technology Company, which issues its stock for the stock of Punn Company and Sunn Company. Punn and Sunn are now subsidiaries of Integrated Technology Company. This is depicted as follows:

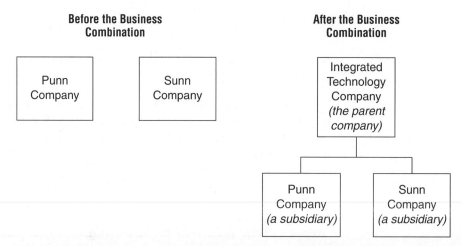

STATUTORY CONSOLIDATION

More infrequent than forming a holding company is the formation of a **statutory consolidation,** in which a new legal entity takes over the assets and assumes the liabilities of each of the combining companies. **The combining companies simultaneously cease their separate corporate existences.** Because the new entity is the only surviving legal entity, the combining companies are said to have been "consolidated" into the new corporation. Because these combinations take place pursuant to state laws, they are called *statutory consolidations.* The primary requirements of the state statutory consolidation laws are the same as for statutory mergers.

For example, assume that Punn Company and Sunn Company agree to combine using a statutory consolidation. The surviving company is Integrated Technology Company. This is depicted as follows:

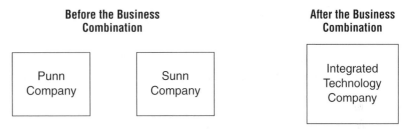

Before the Business Combination		After the Business Combination
Punn Company	Sunn Company	Integrated Technology Company

SUMMARY COMPARISON OF BUSINESS COMBINATIONS   Illustration 4–2 presents the interrelationships of the various topics discussed to this point.

ILLUSTRATION 4–2	Summary Comparison of Business Combination Accounting Methods			
	Purchase Method		**Pooling of Interests Method**[a]	
Consideration given may be	Cash, bonds, preferred stock or common stock		Common stock only	
Property received in exchange for the consideration given	Common stock held by target company's shareholders	Assets of target company	Common stock held by target company's shareholders	Assets of target company
Asset account(s) used to record the property received	Investment in Subsidiary	Various assets	Investment in Subsidiary	Various assets
Change in basis of accounting occurs for the property received	Yes	Yes	No	No
Resulting organizational form of business acquired or pooled	Subsidiary	Branch/ Division	Subsidiary	Branch/ Division

[a]The discussion in this chapter focuses on the general concept of a pooling of interest. Chapter 7 discusses in detail this method's finer points.

Note: Regardless of the diametrically opposite accounting treatments that exist for the entity that gives the consideration, these manners of accounting have no bearing on how the target company or its shareholders account for their side of the transaction. When assets are received for the consideration given, the target company reports a gain or loss on the disposition of those assets. When common stock is received for the consideration given, the shareholders surrendering their stock have a gain or loss.

VII TAX CONSIDERATIONS

The income tax rules for business combinations are quite complex and thus more properly the topic of an advanced income tax course. It is important at this point, however, to understand the relationship and similarities between the accounting rules and the income tax rules—an understanding that does not always result when advanced tax courses deal solely with the tax rules. Accordingly, the following discussion is limited, general in nature, and designed to accomplish this purpose.

For financial reporting purposes, the terms and provisions in the acquisition agreement (along with other factors discussed in Chapter 7) determine whether the *purchase method* or the *pooling of interests* method is used to record the combination. For income tax–reporting purposes, the same terms and provisions in the acquisition agreement determine whether the combination is treated as a *taxable combination* or a *nontaxable combination*. The latter is commonly referred to as (1) a **tax-free combination** (a term that is slightly inaccurate because income taxes avoided at this point in time may have to be paid at a later date), (2) a **tax-deferrable combination** (totally accurate), or (3) a **tax-free reorganization** (the terminology used in the Internal Revenue Code).

TAXABLE COMBINATIONS

THE UNDERLYING CONCEPT: *A SALE HAS OCCURRED* The underlying concept of *purchase accounting*—that one company has acquired the business of another company—is essentially the same as that embodied in the Internal Revenue Code with respect to taxable combinations. For income tax-reporting purposes, **a taxable combination is a completed and closed transaction in that a sale is deemed to have occurred.** Accordingly, an acquired business or its shareholders report a gain or loss in the year of the transaction. The fair value of the consideration that the acquired business or its shareholders receives is compared with the tax basis of the assets sold to the acquiring business to compute the taxable gain or tax-deductible loss.

THE RESULTING CHANGE IN BASIS The acquiring company's tax basis for the acquired property (whether assets or common stock) is the purchase price paid. If assets are acquired for more than their carrying value as of the acquisition date, the acquired assets are stepped up in basis for tax depreciation and amortization purposes. If common stock is acquired, the assets of the acquired business can be stepped up in basis only if the acquiring company elects to treat the acquisition of the target company's common stock as an asset purchase (called a *Section 338 election*). Accordingly, if it elects to do so, the basis of the common stock is effectively transferred to the assets of the acquired business. (A more detailed discussion of this election is contained in the Appendix to Chapter 8.) This allows the acquirer to be in the same position as it would be had assets rather than common stock been acquired.

ACCOUNTING AND TAX RULES COMPARED Although the underlying concept of the *purchase method* for financial reporting purposes is the same as that embodied in the Internal Revenue Code for *taxable combinations*, it is important to recognize that the specific rules of *APBO No. 16* regarding the purchase method differ from those of the Internal Revenue Code regarding taxable combinations. In other words, each set of rules is independent; the treatment for financial reporting purposes does not determine the treatment for tax-reporting purposes and vice versa. Accordingly, some combinations accounted for under the *purchase method* for financial reporting purposes are treated as *taxable combinations* for income tax–reporting purposes, whereas other combinations accounted for under the *purchase method* for financial reporting purposes are treated as *nontaxable combinations* for income tax–reporting purposes. Because of this similarity of the concepts but the difference in their specific rules, the only generalization that can be made is that **combinations accounted for under the** *purchase method* **for financial reporting purposes are more likely to be** *taxable combinations* **than** *nontaxable combinations.*

NONTAXABLE COMBINATIONS

THE UNDERLYING CONCEPT: *NO SALE HAS OCCURRED* The underlying concept of *pooling of interests* accounting—that the two equity interests of the combining companies pool together in such a manner that there is a continuity of interest in the new, enlarged business—is essentially the same concept as that embodied in the Internal Revenue Code with respect to *nontaxable combinations.* **For income tax–reporting purposes, a** *tax-free reorganization* **is not a completed or closed transaction in that a sale is** *not* **deemed to have occurred.** Accordingly for tax–reporting purposes, the acquired business (or its shareholders) *does not* report a gain or loss in the year of the transaction. Only the form of the investment has changed; the investment in the business itself is maintained even though such business is now part of a larger one. (This is the same principle used in "like-kind" real estate exchanges, which also are *not* taxable because the owners are continuing their investment in real estate.) At some later time, when the property that was received in the combination (typically the acquiring company's common stock) is disposed of in a completed taxable transaction, a gain or loss is reportable for income tax–reporting purposes. Accordingly, in a tax-free reorganization, income taxes are merely deferred or postponed until a later date.

NO RESULTING CHANGE IN BASIS With respect to the continuing enlarged business, the basis of the property acquired is *not* changed for income tax–reporting purposes, regardless of whether assets or common stock is received in the exchange. The tax rules relating to *tax-free reorganizations* can accommodate acquisitions of assets and acquisitions of common stock. Section 368a of the Internal Revenue Code describes the various procedures by which tax-free combinations may be attained. Three specific procedures for accomplishing this are set forth in subsections a1A, a1B, and a1C. In practice, these are referred to as "A," "B," and "C" reorganizations. *Type A reorganizations* pertain to statutory mergers and statutory consolidations that occur under a specific state statute. *Type B reorganizations* pertain to stock-for-stock exchanges. *Type C reorganizations* pertain to an exchange of stock for assets. If the combining companies agree on a tax-free reorganization, the terms and provisions of the acquisition agreement must be structured carefully around one of these three specific procedures. The requirements of the Internal Revenue Code must be fully complied with before the tax-free treatment is allowed. The safest course of action is to secure a specific ruling in advance from the Internal Revenue Service. Because this is a highly specialized area of tax practice, competent tax advice should be obtained.

In 1994, congressional tax committees in search of additional tax revenues considered proposals to make many "like-kind" real estate exchanges taxable. This raised a larger question of whether Congress would make changes to stock-for-stock exchanges, inasmuch as (1) the provisions are identical in purpose to "like-kind" exchanges and (2) substantial tax revenues could be raised by limiting the use of nontaxable stock for stock exchanges. So far, nothing has been enacted along these lines.

ACCOUNTING AND TAX RULES COMPARED The underlying concept of the *pooling of interests* method for financial reporting purposes is the same as that embodied in the Internal Revenue Code with respect to *tax-free reorganizations.* The same independent relationship exists between the *pooling of interests* method (for financial reporting) and *tax-free reorganizations* (for income tax reporting) as was explained for *purchase accounting* (for financial reporting) in relation to *taxable combinations* (for income tax reporting). The *pooling of interests* requirements, however, are much more stringent than the *tax-free reorganization* rules. Accordingly, **combinations accounted for under the *pooling of interests* method for financial reporting purposes almost always qualify for *tax-free reorganization* treatment.**

DISINCENTIVE FOR ACQUIRING A COMPANY FOR ITS NET OPERATING LOSS CARRYFORWARD

In spite of enacted limitations prior to 1986, a major consideration in many business combinations was the possibility of using the target company's net operating loss carryforward that might otherwise expire. The strict provisions of the 1986 Tax Reform Act have neutralized the impact of net operating loss carryforwards as a factor in planning acquisitions.

TERMINOLOGY DIFFERENCES BETWEEN FINANCIAL AND TAX REPORTING

Note that the terminology for financial and tax reporting differs, even though the generic issue of change or no change in basis exists for both. The terminology differences are shown in Illustration 4–3.

VIII NEGOTIATING POSITIONS AND CONFLICTING INTERESTS

FACTORS DETERMINING THE POSITIONS OF THE PARTIES

It is useful at this point to look at the factors that shape the negotiating or posturing positions of each of the parties in an acquisition. Structuring the transaction entails the financial reporting treatment, the tax-reporting treatment, and the use of specific types of consideration. We may then discuss conflicts that can arise between the parties.

ILLUSTRATION 4–3	**Terminology and Reporting Consistency Differences between Financial and Tax Reporting**	
	Financial Reporting	**Tax Reporting**
Terminology used	Purchase versus pooling of interests	Taxable versus nontaxable
Focus of Terminology	Acquirer/Issuer's basis of accounting (change or no change in basis)	Seller's tax treatment
Reporting symmetry *always* occurs between parties	No—Accounting treatment by either party has no bearing on other party's accounting treatment. **In practice, however, symmetry usually *does* occur for *purchases*.**[a]	Yes—Seller's tax treatment determines buyer's basis of accounting.

[a]Thus in situations in which the company that *gives* the consideration uses *purchase accounting*, the party that *receives* consideration almost always reports a gain or loss for financial reporting purposes. In situations in which the company that *gives* the consideration uses *pooling of interests accounting*, however, the party that *receives* the consideration sometimes reports a gain or loss for financial reporting purposes (even though the symmetrical treatment would be to report no gain or loss).

THE PERSPECTIVE OF THE TARGET COMPANY'S OWNERS   Income tax considerations usually shape the position of the owners of the business for sale. Sometimes tax considerations are of primary importance. In such cases, the owners do not insist on a specific type of consideration for nontax reasons (such as desiring cash because of financial need or desiring common stock to have a continuing equity participation in the combined businesses). The owners do insist, however, on a specific type of consideration to be able to minimize taxes and maximize their wealth. Sometimes this manifests itself in a preference for receiving stock or notes so that income taxes that otherwise would be paid in a cash deal can be deferred to a later date (using a nontaxable exchange if stock is received and using the installment basis for reporting the gain if notes are received).[5] This is particularly useful for an elderly owner whose death before either the sale of the stock or the collection of the installment notes would totally eliminate the reporting of the untaxed gain because the estate is entitled to a step-up in tax basis. Sometimes tax considerations motivate the target's owners to prefer cash, such as when they expect future income tax rates to be significantly higher,[6] or when they have capital losses that they would like to offset with capital gains from the purchaser's cash.[7]

At other times, tax considerations are of secondary importance, as when the owners insist on receiving cash (either out of financial need or from an unwillingness to assume the risk of owning notes or stock in the acquiring company). But even in cash deals, the owners can wind up with much higher after-tax proceeds by selling stock to the purchaser instead of assets (as explained in detail later).

In summary, the target company's owners are very motivated by tax consequences and the specific type of consideration. How the transaction is reported for financial reporting purposes by the target company (if it relinquishes its assets) or by the owners individually (if they relinquish their stock) is of no importance to the owners in negotiations.

THE PERSPECTIVE OF THE ACQUIRING COMPANY   The acquiring company's position may or may not be shaped by tax considerations, depending on the focus of its management. Some managements focus solely on *maximizing net income:* For them, financial reporting considerations prevail and tax considerations are secondary. (Financial reporting considerations include whether to structure the transaction as a purchase or a pooling of interests to minimize any future depreciation and amortization charges.) At the other extreme are managements that focus solely on *minimizing cash outflows.* In these cases, tax considerations prevail and financial reporting considerations are secondary. Such tax considerations include whether to structure the transaction as taxable or nontaxable to obtain the highest possible basis in the target company's assets for depreciation purposes and thus minimize cash outflows for income taxes.

FINANCIAL REPORTING CONFLICTS

The most common financial reporting conflict occurs when the acquiring company desires to use *pooling of interests* accounting (which requires that it issue common stock to the target company or to its shareholders), whereas the owners of the target company want cash or other nonstock consideration. (Recall that a pooling of interests avoids reporting goodwill and the related amortization charges to future income statements.) Because of the enormous importance that many acquiring

---

[5]The installment basis is available only when the target company is a nonpublic company.

[6]This occurred in 1986 when the individual capital gains tax of 20% was eliminated, with future rates on capital gains to be 28% or 33%.

[7]The October 19, 1987, stock market crash caused many corporate and private investors to incur capital losses.

companies place on obtaining pooling of interests treatment for financial reporting, we consider this a financial reporting conflict even though the target company (or its shareholders) has only one financial reporting method available. Technically from the target's perspective, the issue is merely which type of consideration should be used—not a financial reporting conflict.

TAX-REPORTING CONFLICTS

The tax-reporting conflicts center around two issues: (1) whether the acquiring company desires to change the tax basis of the property it received in the combination (assets or common stock) to its current value based on the consideration given by the acquiring company and (2) whether the acquired company or its shareholders want a nontaxable treatment. The position of each party usually depends on whether the value of the consideration is above or below the tax basis of the target company's property, as discussed more fully below.

THE VALUE OF CONSIDERATION EXCEEDS THE TAX BASIS   In an economy experiencing inflation, the acquiring company usually gives consideration that is higher in value than the tax basis of the property it is to receive. The acquiring company prefers a *taxable treatment* so that it can step up the basis of the property it is to receive. Thus it will have higher depreciation and amortization deductions for income tax–reporting purposes (or a higher basis in the acquired company's stock if a parent-subsidiary relationship is to be maintained). The acquired company or its shareholders, however, may prefer a *nontaxable treatment* to defer or postpone the recognition of a gain for income tax–reporting purposes.

THE VALUE OF CONSIDERATION IS BELOW THE TAX BASIS   The roles are usually reversed when the acquiring company gives consideration that is lower in value than the tax basis of the property it is to receive. In such situations, the acquiring company prefers a *nontaxable treatment* so that the higher basis of the property it is to receive will carry over. Thus it will have greater depreciation and amortization deductions for income tax–reporting purposes (or a higher basis in the acquired company's stock if a parent-subsidiary relationship is to be maintained). The acquired company or its shareholders, however, may prefer a *taxable treatment* to immediately recognize a loss for income tax–reporting purposes.

CONFLICTS ARISING FROM DOUBLE TAXATION   When a corporation sells its assets in a *taxable transaction*, it must pay taxes at the corporate level on any gain resulting from the sale (that is, when the value of the consideration exceeds the tax basis). Assuming that the corporation then distributes the net proceeds (the sales price less taxes) to its stockholders, the stockholders themselves then must pay taxes on any gain they realize. From the perspective of these stockholders, they are incurring a double tax—once *before* distribution and once *after* distribution. One way for the stockholders to avoid taxes at the corporate level is for the seller to stipulate that the purchaser must acquire *common stock* instead of *assets*. This merely shifts the burden of paying the corporate-level tax from the seller to the buyer, however, because the buyer has now inherited (some might say "is stuck with") the low carryover-adjusted basis of the underlying property. The buyer pays this tax under either of the following two options:

1. **Make a Section 338 election.** By making a Section 338 election, the basis of the common stock is effectively transferred to the underlying assets of the acquired business. The acquired business (now a subsidiary) would have to report a taxable gain, however, to achieve a step-up in basis. In most cases, this option makes no sense because the subsidiary pays taxes now merely to have higher tax deductions in future years (through higher depreciation charges, inventory costs, and so on).

2. **Do not make a Section 338 election.** By not making a Section 338 election, no taxes are payable at the corporate level at the acquisition date. As the underlying assets are either disposed of or used and depreciated, however, the acquired business (now a subsidiary) will pay higher taxes. Thus the corporate-level tax is deferred and paid in future periods.

As we have seen, a *taxable transaction* has a built-in conflict of interest over whether it should be structured as a purchase of *assets* or of *common stock,* with the real issue being which party should pay the corporate-level tax. With the problem of the corporate-level tax looming in a taxable transaction, clearly the tax-deferred treatment becomes doubly attractive because it allows taxes at the corporate level (as well as at the individual stockholder level) to be deferred. Taxable stock purchases without a Section 338 election also are more attractive because the corporate-level tax is deferred.

CONCLUDING COMMENTS ON CONFLICTING INTERESTS

The ultimate resolution of the conflicting financial reporting interests (pooling of interests versus purchase) and of the conflicting tax interests (taxable versus nontaxable, and which party should be responsible for taxes at the corporate level in a taxable transaction) depends on the relative bargaining strengths and positions of each party.

END-OF-CHAPTER REVIEW

SUMMARY OF KEY POINTS

1. The acquiring company may structure a business combination to be either a **purchase** or a **pooling of interests.**
2. The purchase method treats the combination as a purchase of the target company's business, whereby the target company's assets are to be **reported at the acquiring company's cost,** which is based essentially on the **fair value of the consideration given.**
3. In contrast, the pooling of interests method treats the combination as a **fusion of equity interests,** whereby the target company's assets are to be **reported at historical book values** as of the acquisition date.
4. This fusion of equity interests is accomplished by issuing the acquiring company's **common stock** as consideration.
5. If the **12 conditions for a pooling of interests** are *not* met, the combination must be accounted for as a purchase.
6. Many important factors must be considered in deciding whether to acquire the target company's **assets** or its outstanding **common stock.**
7. Whether assets or common stock shares are acquired has no bearing on the accounting treatment: Only the resulting organizational form of the acquired business differs.
8. Business combinations are treated as either **taxable** or **nontaxable transactions.**
9. In a **taxable** transaction, the acquiring company establishes a **new tax basis** for the acquired assets.
10. In a **nontaxable transaction,** the tax basis of the target company's assets as of the combination date **carries over** to the acquiring company.
11. The desired **financial reporting treatment** for the acquirer, the **type of consideration to be used,** and **tax considerations** are important issues that often lead to conflicts between the parties in negotiating the terms of the acquisition agreement.

GLOSSARY OF NEW TERMS

Acquiring company   A company attempting to acquire the business of another company.

Acquisition agreement   The legal agreement that specifies the terms and provisions of a business combination.

Conglomerate combination A business combination that takes place between companies in unrelated industries.

Exchange ratio The number of common shares issued by the acquiring company in exchange for each outstanding common share of the target company.

Goodwill In a purchase business combination, the acquiring company's cost in excess of the current value of the target company's net assets.

Holding company A company that has no revenue-producing operations of its own, only investments in subsidiaries.

Horizontal combination A business combination that occurs between companies involved as competitors at the same level in a given industry.

Leveraged buyout (LBO) Investors and management buy a controlling interest in a company, financing the purchase by borrowing from a financial institution and using the company's own assets as collateral.

Nonoperating company A company that has no operations of its own—only passive assets.

Pooling of interests method A method of accounting for a business combination whereby the assets of the acquired business are carried forward to the combined corporation at their historically recorded amounts. A fusion of equity interests is deemed to have occurred as opposed to a sale.

Proxy contest A system whereby both management and an opposing group solicit votes from the stockholders concerning proposed slates of directors or another issue such as a proposed change to the company's charter.

Purchase method A method of accounting for a business combination whereby the assets and liabilities of the acquired business are valued at their current values based on the consideration given by the acquiring company. A sale is deemed to have occurred.

Shell company A corporation that has no assets or liabilities.

Statutory consolidation A legal term referring to a specific type of business combination in which a new corporation is formed to carry on the businesses of two predecessor corporations that are liquidated.

Statutory merger A legal term referring to a specific type of business combination in which a newly acquired target company is liquidated into a division at the time of the business combination.

Takeover attempt The process of trying to acquire the business of a target company.

Target company The company whose business a company is seeking to acquire.

Tax-free combination A specific type of business combination in which the acquired business or its shareholders do not report a gain or loss at the time of the business combination for income tax–reporting purposes.

Tax-deferrable combination See tax-free combination.

Tax-free reorganization See tax-free combination.

Tender offer An offer made by an acquiring company directly to the stockholders of the target company, whereby the target company's stockholders are requested to give up their common shares in exchange for the consideration offered by the acquiring company.

Vertical combination A business combination that takes place between companies involved at different levels in a given industry.

SELF-STUDY QUESTIONS

(Answers are at the end of this chapter.)

The nine choices listed A through I pertain to how a business combination is structured. From these choices, select the appropriate answer for questions 1–15 that follow the choices.

a. Acquisition of assets
b. Acquisition of common stock
c. Statutory merger
d. Statutory consolidation
e. Purchase accounting

    f. Pooling of interests accounting
    g. Taxable transaction
    h. Nontaxable (tax-deferred) transaction
    i. None of the above

More than one choice may be appropriate for some of the questions.

1. The acquiring company does *not* want to report any goodwill.
2. The acquiring company does *not* want to be responsible for the target company's unrecorded postretirement benefit obligations.
3. The acquiring company does *not* want to be responsible for the target company's potential unrecorded liabilities pertaining to toxic waste site cleanups.
4. The target company's contracts and leases are *not* transferable.
5. The legal existence of the target company is to be terminated.
6. The legal existence of the acquiring company and the target company is to be terminated.
7. The target company desires to continue in business as a nonoperating company.
8. The target company's directors have turned down the acquiring company's offer.
9. The acquiring company will have to force out a small minority of dissenting stockholders of the target company.
10. A holding company is to be formed.
11. The acquiring company desires to issue preferred stock as consideration.
12. The acquiring company does not want to change the basis of accounting for the target company's assets.
13. The target company's stockholders desire a cash deal that maximizes the after-tax dollars they will receive.
14. The acquiring company does *not* want to be responsible for taxes at the corporate level.
15. The value of the consideration exceeds the tax basis of the target company's underlying property.

ASSIGNMENT MATERIAL

REVIEW QUESTIONS

1. What is the difference between horizontal, vertical, and conglomerate combinations?
2. How does the purchase method contrast with the pooling of interests method of accounting?
3. Why is the acquisition agreement so important in determining the ultimate accounting method used in recording a business combination?
4. On what grounds has *APBO No. 16* been criticized?
5. What types of consideration can be given under purchase accounting and under pooling of interests accounting?
6. What types of assets can the acquiring company obtain in business combinations?
7. What various organization forms can result from a business combination?
8. What is the difference between centralized and decentralized accounting systems?
9. How is the selling entity's gain or loss computed on the disposition of its assets?
10. What is the relationship between *APBO No. 16* and the income tax rules relating to business combinations?
11. What does *tax-free combination* mean?
12. Why does a conflict often exist between the acquiring company and the target company or its stockholders with respect to whether the combination should be treated in a taxable or nontaxable manner?
13. For the acquiring company, what is "the best of both worlds" from the standpoint of financial reporting and tax reporting?
14. Does a target company that sells its assets have to pay taxes if there is a gain?

TECHNICAL RESEARCH QUESTION

Answers to technical research questions that appear here and elsewhere in the book may be found by consulting the pronouncements of the Financial Accounting Standards Board, the Accounting Principles Board, and the Securities and Exchange Commission.

Pickens Company acquired 15% of the outstanding common stock of Selno Company. In a defensive move to prevent being taken over, Selno entered into an agreement with Pickens to purchase the stock acquired by Pickens at a 20% premium above market value. As part of this agreement, Pickens agrees not to acquire any more of Selno's common stock for the next 10 years. How should the premium be accounted for and classified?

EXERCISES

E 4–1 **Terminology**   Indicate the appropriate term or terms for each of the following:

1. The expansion of a business by constructing a manufacturing facility.
2. A business combination in which a company acquires one of its suppliers.
3. A business combination in which a company acquires one of its competitors.
4. A business combination in which a company acquires businesses to diversify its product lines.
5. The broad terms used to refer to business combinations.
6. A business combination in which the target company's corporate existence is terminated in conjunction with the transfer of its assets and liabilities to the acquiring company.
7. A business combination in which a new corporation is formed to acquire the businesses of two existing corporations.
8. The two methods of accounting for business combinations as set forth in *APBO No. 16*.
9. The two types of assets that can be acquired in a business combination.
10. The expansion of a business by acquiring an existing business.
11. An acquired business that maintains its separate legal existence.
12. An acquiring business that acquires common stock of the acquired business, the latter maintaining its separate legal existence.
13. An acquired business that ceases to be a separate legal entity but continues to use a separate general ledger.
14. The primary type of consideration given in a business combination that is accounted for as a *pooling of interests*.
15. The allowable types of consideration that can be given in a business combination accounted for as a *purchase*.

E 4–2 **Pooling of Interests Method: Acquisition of Assets**   Patco acquired all of Satco's assets in a business combination that qualified for pooling of interests treatment. The current value of the common stock issued by Patco exceeded the book value of Satco's net assets by $300,000.

Required   Explain the general accounting procedures that Patco must follow in recording the acquisition of the assets.

E 4–3 **Purchase Method: Acquisition of Assets**   Pertex acquired all of Sertex's assets in a business combination that did *not* qualify for pooling of interests treatment. Pertex paid $800,000 cash. The book value of Sertex's net assets is $600,000, and their current value is $750,000.

Required   Explain the general accounting procedures that Pertex must follow in recording the acquisition of the assets.

E 4–4 **Divestiture Accounting: Sale of Common Stock**   Phaco acquired all of Shaco's outstanding common stock from its shareholders by issuing common stock.

Required   Explain in general how Shaco should account for this change in ownership of its outstanding common stock.

E 4–5 **Divestiture Accounting: Sale of Assets**   Panco acquired all of Sanco's assets by issuing common stock (and assuming Sanco's liabilities).

Required   Explain in general how Sanco should account for this transaction.

E 4–6 **Statutory Merger and Statutory Consolidation**   Parco is considering a merger or consolidation with Sarco. Both methods of acquisition are being considered under applicable corporate statutory law. Parco is the larger of the two corporations and is in reality acquiring Sarco.

Required   Discuss the meaning of the terms *merger* and *consolidation* as used in corporate law with particular emphasis on the legal difference between the two.

(AICPA adapted)

E 4–7   **Basic Understanding of the Nature of Goodwill**   Shelley and Brett are children who live one street apart. Shelley has saved $100 and Brett has saved $250. Each child desires to open a lemonade stand on his or her own front lawn. Each invests $100 in the business, using $80 to buy a table, a chair, a pitcher, and a stirrer. Each uses the remaining $20 to purchase supplies (lemons, sugar, paper cups). Shelley lives on a street with many other children; Brett does not. After one year in business, Shelley made a profit of $45, but Brett made a profit of only $15. Each withdraws from the business the profits made and spends the money on personal items. On the first day of the second year of business, the two children meet for lunch and discuss business. Shelley indicates that she is willing to sell her business if the price is right. Brett wants to make more money than his business now generates; he knows that Shelley's lemonade stand sells much more lemonade than his does. Brett offers to buy Shelley's business; she knows that she has a far better business location than Brett does.

Brett and Shelley agree on a purchase price of $130, with $100 for the purchase of equipment and supplies. Brett pays the remaining $30 in anticipation of being able to make substantial profits in the future above and beyond what would be considered average (goodwill).

Required   **1.** How much capital was invested in each separate business just before Brett acquired Shelley's business?

2. How much capital is invested in each separate business location just after Brett acquired Shelley's business?

3. How much money does each child have after Brett acquired Shelley's business?

4. Considering that the children had a combined capital of $350 just prior to the commencement of their businesses and distributed and spent their profits for year 1, how can they now have more capital than they started with? (Combine the answers to Questions 2 and 3 to arrive at their total capital.)

PROBLEMS

P 4–1   **COMPREHENSIVE: Acquisition of Assets for Cash**   PBX Company acquired all of the assets of Sprint Company by assuming responsibility for all of its liabilities and paying $1,500,000 cash. Information with respect to Sprint at the date of combination follows:

	Book Value	Current Value
Cash	$ 10,000	$ 10,000
Accounts receivable, net (including $30,000 due from PBX Company)	90,000	90,000
Inventory	200,000	200,000
Land	400,000	500,000
Building and equipment	2,500,000	1,600,000
Accumulated depreciation	(1,200,000)	
Total Assets	$2,000,000	$2,400,000
Accounts payable and accruals	$ 300,000	$ 300,000
Long-term debt	800,000	800,000
Total Liabilities	$1,100,000	$1,100,000
Common stock, $1 par value	$ 100,000	
Additional paid-in capital	500,000	
Retained earnings	300,000	
Total Stockholders' Equity	$ 900,000	$1,300,000
Total Liabilities and Stockholders' Equity	$2,000,000	$2,400,000

Required   **1.** Does the acquisition appear to be a horizontal, vertical, or conglomerate type of combination?

2. Would the transaction be accounted for as a purchase or a pooling of interests?

3. Is PBX Company the parent company of Sprint Company? Why or why not?

4. Is Sprint Company a subsidiary? Why or why not?

5. Is Sprint Company a legal entity after the transaction has been consummated?
6. How should the newly acquired operation be referred to?
7. Prepare the journal entry that Sprint Company makes on the date of the combination. Assume a 40% income tax rate.
8. Prepare a balance sheet for Sprint Company after recording the entry in requirement 7.
9. What options are available to Sprint Company after the business combination?
10. What is Sprint's book value in total and per share after the business combination?
11. What is the most likely market price of Sprint Company's common stock immediately after the transaction? (How would your answer change if Sprint planned to liquidate and distribute cash to its stockholders one year from now?)
12. Prepare the entry—in condensed form—that PBX would make, assuming that it uses centralized accounting.
13. Why did PBX pay $1,500,000 for a company whose net assets are worth only $1,300,000?
14. How could PBX have determined the current value of Sprint's assets and liabilities?
15. Tax questions (optional):
   a. What is the treatment for income tax–reporting purposes?
   b. From your answer in requirement 15a, what is PBX's tax basis of the land, buildings, and equipment it obtained?

P 4–2 **COMPREHENSIVE: Acquisition of Assets for Common Stock** Assume the same information as in Problem 4–1 except that PBX Company gave as consideration 50,000 shares of its $10 par value common stock (of which 950,000 shares are already outstanding) having a market value of $30 per share. Assume that all conditions for pooling of interests are met.

Required Respond to requirements 2–11 in Problem 4–1. Then continue with the following requirements:

12. At what amount does PBX record the assets acquired from Sprint? (Do not prepare PBX's entry to record the combination; doing so requires an understanding of material in Chapter 7.)
13. Reevaluate your answer to requirement 7 in light of your answer to requirement 12. (*Hint:* Does PBX's accounting treatment affect Sprint's accounting treatment—that is, is symmetry required?)
14. How will Sprint account for its 5% interest in PBX?
15. Tax questions (optional):
   a. What is the probable treatment for income tax–reporting purposes?
   b. From your answer in requirement 15a, what is PBX's tax basis of the land, buildings, and equipment it obtained?
   c. What is Sprint's tax basis in the PBX common stock it received?

P 4–3 **COMPREHENSIVE: Acquisition of Common Stock for Cash** Assume the same information as in Problem 4–1 except that PBX Company acquired all of the outstanding common stock of Sprint Company rather than acquiring all of Sprint's assets and assuming all of its liabilities.

Required Respond to requirements 2–10 in Problem 4–1. Then continue with the following requirements:

11. Prepare the entry that PBX makes to record the combination.
12. Where is the goodwill that PBX paid for recorded?
13. Tax questions (optional):
   a. What is the treatment for income tax–reporting purposes?
   b. If the combination is taxable, who is taxed?
   c. Do the selling shareholders have a taxable gain or a taxable loss?
   d. Assuming the selling shareholders were all initial founders of Sprint, calculate their taxable gain or loss in total.
   e. In what asset does PBX have a tax basis?
   f. How much is its tax basis in this asset?
   g. Does the tax basis of Sprint's land, buildings, and equipment change?

P 4–4 **COMPREHENSIVE: Acquisition of Common Stock for Common Stock** Assume the same information as provided in Problem 4–1 except that PBX Company gave as consideration 50,000 shares of its $10 par value common stock (of which 950,000 shares are already outstanding) having a market value of $30 per share for all of the outstanding common stock of Sprint Company. Assume that all conditions for *pooling of interests* are met.

Required   Respond to requirements 2–10 in Problem 4–1. Then continue with the following requirements:

11. At what amount does PBX record the Sprint common stock it obtained? (Do not prepare PBX's entry to record the combination; doing so requires an understanding of material in Chapter 7.)
12. What is the exchange ratio used in the transaction?
13. Tax questions (optional):
    a. What is the probable tax treatment?
    b. In what asset does PBX have a tax basis?
    c. How much is its tax basis in this asset?
    d. Nick Tymer acquired 3,000 shares of Sprint's common stock for $34,000 (shortly before the announcement of the business combination). What is his tax basis of the PBX shares he received in the exchange?
    e. Did Tymer gain from his investment?

P 4–5   **COMPREHENSIVE: Acquisition of Common Stock for Common Stock**   Assume the same information as provided in Problem 4–1 except that PBX Company gave as consideration 50,000 shares of its $10 par value common stock (of which 950,000 shares are already outstanding) having a market value of $30 per share for all of the outstanding common stock of Sprint Company. Also, one of the remaining 11 conditions for *pooling of interests* was *not* met.

Required   Respond to requirements 2–10 in Problem 4–1. Then continue with the following requirements:

11. Prepare the entry that PBX makes to record the combination.
12. What is the exchange ratio used in the transaction?
13. Tax questions (optional):
    a. What is the probable treatment for income tax–reporting purposes?
    b. In what asset does PBX Company have a tax basis?
    c. How much is its tax basis in this asset?
    d. Nick Tymer acquired 3,000 shares of Sprint's common stock for $34,000 (shortly before the announcement of the business combination). What is his tax basis of the PBX shares he received in the exchange?
    e. Did Tymer gain from his investment?

P 4–6   **Comparing Reporting Results of Pooling of Interests Method versus Purchase Method**   Supresso Company's assets consist of undervalued land holdings acquired many years ago for $4,000,000. The fair value of these holdings at various dates follows:

	Fair Value
January 1, 19X1	$7,000,000
January 1, 19X4	8,000,000
January 1, 19X7	9,000,000

On 1/1/X1, Pal Company acquired all of Supresso's assets by issuing common stock having a market value of $7,000,000. (None of Supresso's liabilities were assumed.) On 1/1/X4, Penn Company acquired all of Pal Company's assets by issuing common stock having a market value of $20,000,000. Of this amount, assume that $8,000,000 was for Pal's real estate holdings acquired from Supresso in 19X1. On 1/1/X7, Penn sold for $9,000,000 cash all of the real estate holdings initially owned by Supresso.

Required   1. Determine the gain to be reported by Supresso, Pal, and Penn upon the disposal of the land assuming that the 19X1 and 19X4 business combinations are recorded under *purchase accounting*. (Assume that the proceeds received in these transactions are properly recordable at their current value.) Add up the total reportable gain by the three companies and compare them to the difference between Supresso's cost of the land and Penn's proceeds. Evaluate the soundness of these reporting results.
2. Repeat requirement 1, but assume that the 19X1 and 19X4 business combinations qualified for *pooling of interests* accounting treatment.

✳ THINKING CRITICALLY ✳

✳ CASES ✳

C 4–1   **Purchase versus Pooling of Interests**   On 7/1/X1, Plodco acquired all of the outstanding common stock of Shodco by issuing 80,000 shares of common stock as consideration (valued at $4,000,000). Plodco's controller informed you of the business combination in August 19X1 and indicated that management has not yet decided whether to use the purchase method or the pooling of interests method to account for this business combination. The controller has asked you to assist in evaluating the alternative accounting treatments between now and 12/31/X1, Plodco's year-end.

Required   How would you advise the controller?

C 4–2   **Limiting Legal Liability and Consistency**   Pentex is having merger discussions with Sentex. All of Pentex's business acquisitions to date have been acquisitions of common stock resulting in parent-subsidiary relationships. Pentex prefers to legally insulate each of its acquired businesses from all other operations. Sentex has been and still is involved as a defendant in several lawsuits. As a result, Pentex plans to acquire Sentex's assets to insulate itself from any current or potential legal entanglements.

Further, the controller indicates to you that if the merger is consummated in this manner, the company will *not* be accounting for its acquisitions consistently, which will violate a fundamental accounting principle. All businesses acquired to date have been consistently recorded as *pooling of interests;* the acquisition of Sentex will *not* qualify for pooling of interests treatment, which means that an additional inconsistency will be created.

Required   1. How could Pentex achieve the objective of insulating the business of Sentex?
2. Is the consistency principle violated as a result of acquiring assets? Why or why not?
3. Is the consistency principle violated because the combination does not qualify for pooling of interests treatment? Why or why not?

C 4–3   **How Much to Pay for an Accounting Practice**   The practitioner of an accounting sole proprietorship is retiring and plans to sell the practice, which grosses $100,000 per year and nets $60,000.

Required   How much would you be willing to pay to acquire this practice?

C 4–4   **Accounting versus Tax Treatment**   Pineco plans to embark on a business acquisition program to diversify its product lines. The controller is unclear about whether the tax treatment determines the accounting treatment or whether the accounting treatment determines the tax treatment.

Required   How would you advise the controller?

✳ FINANCIAL ANALYSIS PROBLEMS ✳

FAP 4–1   **Determining Financial Reporting Impact of a Merger under Pooling of Interests versus Purchase Method (Debt Ratios and Returns on Investment)**   PDQ Inc. is contemplating a business combination with Sprint Inc. on 1/1/X1. Selected information follows:

1. PDQ will issue 10,000 shares of its $1 par value common stock to Sprint in exchange for 100% of Sprint's assets.
2. PDQ will assume all of Sprint's liabilities.
3. PDQ will account for Sprint's operations as a decentralized division to be evaluated as a profit center.
4. Other financial information:

	PDQ	Sprint
Book Values		
Assets	$3,000,000	$1,300,000
Liabilities	2,000,000	1,000,000
Current Values		
Assets	4,000,000	1,700,000
Liabilities	2,000,000	1,000,000
Current market price of common stock	$80	$35
Common stock shares outstanding	40,000	20,000

5. The terms of the combination are being negotiated. Accordingly, it is *not* known whether all conditions for *pooling of interests* accounting treatment will be satisfied. The expected future annual net income of the acquired business is

Under pooling of interests accounting	$90,000
Under purchase accounting	80,000

6. For 19X0, PDQ reported $150,000 of net income, all of which was distributed as dividends at the end of 19X0.

Required

1. Calculate the issuing company's debt-to-equity ratio:
   a. Before the combination.
   b. After the combination on a consolidated basis, assuming *pooling of interests* treatment.
   c. After the combination on a consolidated basis, assuming *purchase method* treatment.
2. Calculate PDQ's return on equity (ROE) for 19X0.
3. Calculate the issuing company's expected annual return on its investment (AROI) in Sprint for 19X1, assuming that the combination qualifies for *pooling of interests* treatment.
4. Calculate the issuing company's expected AROI in Sprint for 19X1, assuming that the combination does *not* qualify for *pooling of interests* treatment.
5. Comment on the impact of each alternative. Which method reflects economic reality?
6. Calculate PDQ's expected ROE for 19X1 under both accounting methods (combined earnings of both operations) assuming that PDQ expects to earn $150,000 for 19X1 from its own separate operations.

FAP 4–2 **Analyzing Financial Statements** In a classic acquisition in late 1983, Financial Corporation of America (FCA) acquired all of American Savings and Loan. FCA paid cash of $290,000,000 and issued common and preferred stock valued at $625,000,000. At the acquisition date, American had a book value net worth of $600,000,000. In valuing American's loans at their current values (using current interest rates, which were higher than contractual rates), the current value was found to be $793,000,000 lower than the book value.

The consolidated balance sheet and certain income statement data for the two years ended 12/31/84 and 12/31/87 follow in condensed form:

	1987	1984
	(in millions)	
Assets		
Cash and security investments	$20,962	$ 7,249
Loans receivable	10,326	18,020
Property acquired through foreclosure	417	733
Real estate investments	714	934
Intangible assets arising from acquisition	995	1,105
Premises and equipment, net	229	258
Deferred charges and other assets	221	219
Total Assets	$33,864	$28,518
Liabilities		
Deposits	$16,683	$20,308
All other liabilities	17,344	8,017
Total Liabilities	$34,027	$28,325
Stockholders' Equity		
Common stock and paid-in capital	$ 635	$ 634
Accumulated deficit	(798)	(441)
Total Stockholders' Equity	(163)	193
Total Liabilities and Equity	$33,864	$28,518
Income Statement Data		
Net loss	$(468)	$(590)
Amortization of intangibles	(62)	(55)

Required
1. Calculate the goodwill paid for by FCA.
2. As a potential depositor of FCA, evaluate its financial soundness. (Ignore the fact of deposit insurance.) *Hint:* Do you notice anything that does *not* make sense?

FAP 4–3   **Applying Finance Concepts to Evaluate Profitability: Accounting for Goodwill**   Cork City Batters is a major league baseball team formed 11 years ago. Operations quickly reached expected levels. In each of Years 8, 9, and 10, the team reported net income of approximately $1,000,000. (For simplicity, ignore income taxes.)

At the end of Year 10, the team was sold to a partnership formed with capital of $5,000,000. The purchase price was $4,000,000. The remaining $1,000,000 is needed for working capital purposes. For simplicity, assume that (1) the initial capital of the team, when formed, was $1; (2) all earnings for the 10 years had been distributed to the owners by the end of the 10th year; (3) assets therefore equaled liabilities at the time of sale; and (4) none of the recorded assets or liabilities are over- or undervalued.

As the partnership's accountant, you assigned the $4,000,000 to goodwill having a four-year life, inasmuch as the partnership's plans were to own the team for four to six years. (The partners believed that the goodwill should be recovered over the minimum period.) The income statement for Year 11 follows:

Revenues	$8,600,000
Expenses (excluding goodwill)	(7,000,000)
Subtotal	$1,600,000
Goodwill amortization	(1,000,000)
Net Income	$ 600,000

The players' union and management are currently negotiating a new contract for Year 12. Management and the players' union are in wide disagreement as to the team's true profitability. At issue is the validity of the goodwill amortization. Management contends that the 12% return on investment for Year 11 ($600,000 ÷ $5,000,000) is not excessive, and, therefore, no pay raises are appropriate.

Additional Information and Assumptions
1. The decision to form the partnership and acquire the baseball team was based on the high rate of return calculated using the internal rate of return method. The calculation produced an estimated annual return on capital exceeding 30% for the six years that the partnership expected to exist. (The calculation included an estimate that the team would be sold for a minimum of $4,000,000 at the end of Year 16.)
2. Revenues and income from operations are expected to remain constant through Year 16.
3. Cash is to be distributed to partners at the end of each year equal to net income.
4. At the end of each year, 11 through 14, an additional $1,000,000 cash is to be distributed to partners as a return *of* capital.
5. The partnership sells the team at the end of Year 16 for $4,000,000. (At the end of Years 11, 12, 13, and 14, a group of outside investors had offered to buy the team for $4,500,000.)
6. All cash on hand at the end of Year 16 was distributed to the partners, and the partnership was dissolved.

Required
1. Before completing requirements 2 through 7, assess whether management's position is reasonable.
2. Using the reported or assumed net income for Years 12 through 16, calculate the partners' annual return on investment (AROI). (For simplicity, ignore the impact of each year's earnings in determining the capital balances to be used in the denominator. In other words, use the beginning capital balances for the denominator for each year rather than an average capital balance.)
3. Assuming that revenues and income from operations occurred as expected through the end of Year 16 when the team was sold for $4,000,000, how accurately did the AROI calculations in requirement 2 portray the economics of what transpired? Why?

Guidance Questions
As the partnership's accountant, you should be able to explain the following to the partners:
  a. The reason that the AROI for Year 11 (and almost every year thereafter) is so greatly different from the more than 30% initial projected return on capital.
  b. Whether the partners really earned twice as much on their capital in Year 14, in terms of return on investment, as in Year 12.

4. Calculate the internal rate of return (IRR) from the perspective of the partners from the time the partnership was formed until it was dissolved. (Use $5,000,000 as the initial cash outflow.)

Integration Spreadsheet Note: You may readily obtain this answer using the IRR function available in the EXCEL or LOTUS® 1–2–3® spreadsheet programs. You merely need to set up a cash flow table *and then* program the IRR function with the cell cursor located in the cell in which you want your answer to appear. For EXCEL, the IRR function is located under the *financial* function category of the "Function Wizard" (the f_x icon on the first of the two tool-bar lines); merely follow the prompts once you have selected the IRR function. For older versions of LOTUS 1–2–3, you will get an ERR message if the cell in which you want your answer to appear has *not* been formatted for some decimal places.

5. Why does the IRR answer in requirement 4 differ from the AROI answers in requirement 2? (*Hint:* The fact that the IRR considers the time value of money is *not* the reason.) Which result portrays the economic reality of what transpired during these six years?
6. How does the methodology of the IRR differ from the methodology used in lease accounting in which the implicit interest rate (IIR) is encountered?
7. Given that none of the team's recorded assets or liabilities were under- or overvalued at the acquisition date, to what else might the $4,000,000 (or some portion of it) be assigned? (*Hint:* Refer to paragraph 88 of *APBO No. 16*, which discusses assigning cost in excess of book value.)

FAP 4–4 **Financial Analysis Problem 4–3 with Changed Assumption** Use the information in Financial Analysis Problem 4–3 except assume that the team's value is zero at the end of Year 16; that is, the team is disbanded, cash on hand is distributed to the partners, and the partnership is dissolved. This happened because the city closed its ballpark at the end of Year 16 to make room for a new freeway. The closing was voted on and passed in Year 15. Through the end of Year 14, the team could have been sold at any time for the partnership's purchase price of $4,000,000. Once the decision to build the new freeway was made, no other investors were interested in buying the team.

Required 1. Repeat requirement 4 of Financial Analysis Problem 4–3 under the new assumption. (Round your IRR answer to the nearest number with no decimal places; for example, 18.92% becomes 19%. Lump your dollar, rounding differences into Year 16.)
2. Starting with both the IRR percentage calculated in requirement 1 and the $5,000,000 beginning capital balance of the partners, determine for Year 11 how much of the $1,600,000 cash distribution to the partners is assumed to be
   a. Net income under the IRR method (a return *on* capital).
   b. Return of the initial capital investment of $5,000,000 (a recovery *of* capital). Repeat for Years 12 through 16 using (1) the same IRR percentage and (2) the beginning-of-year capital balance, as reduced by the prior year's return *of* capital. (Round all amounts to the nearest thousand and include any rounding error in Year 16.) Use the following format (omit 000s):

Year	Internal Rate of Return	Beginning (unrecovered) Capital Balance	Cash Flow Returned to Partners	**Cash Flow Deemed to Be**	
				A Return *on* Investment (net income)	A Return *of* Investment (recovery of capital)
11		$5,000	$1,600		

Spreadsheet Integration Note: You can simplify the preceding calculations by putting the format on an electronic spreadsheet, programming three simple formulas, and duplicating these formulas for subsequent years.

3. Using the net income amounts calculated in requirement 2 (and the cash distributions to the partners), prepare a T-account analysis of the partners' capital account by year from inception through dissolution of the partnership. (Omit 000s.)
4. Supply the missing amounts for the following tables:
   a. As reported by the partnership's accountant:

	Year					
	11	**12**	**13**	**14**	**15**	**16**
Operating income before goodwill expense	$1,600					
Goodwill expense	(1,000)					
Net Income	$ 600					
Beginning capital	$5,000					
Annual return on investment	12%					

b. As assumed in the internal rate of return method:

	Year					
	11	**12**	**13**	**14**	**15**	**16**
Operating income before goodwill expense	$1,600					
Goodwill expense						
Net Income						
Beginning capital	$5,000					
Annual return on investment						

5. Why does the IRR answer in requirement 1 differ from the AROI percentages calculated in requirement 4a?
6. Does the IRR method assume amortization of goodwill? How can you determine this?
7. Which section in requirement 4 reflects the economic reality of what transpired in these six years? Explain the reasoning behind your answer.
8. If no accounting rules existed concerning goodwill, how would you account for goodwill looking into the future?

FAP 4–5 **Calculating the Amount to Be Paid for Goodwill**   On 1/1/X5, Pointer Inc. entered into negotiations with the management of Setter Inc. to acquire Setter. Information concerning Setter follows:

	Book Value	Current Value
Total assets	$2,600,000[a]	$3,000,000
Stockholders' equity	600,000	1,000,000
Net income for 19X4	250,000	
Average net income for 19X4, 19X3, and 19X2	250,000	

[a]Land is undervalued by $300,000 and equipment having a 10-year life is undervalued by $100,000.

The average return on equity for this industry is 15%. Pointer's management is confident that Setter will be able to continue to earn $250,000 per year indefinitely.

Required   1. Calculate the goodwill that Setter possesses.
2. How much should Pointer pay for goodwill?
3. Should the amount of goodwill calculated for Setter be discounted to its present value? Why? If so, what discount rate should be used?
4. Considering the amount you calculated that Setter should pay for goodwill, what is Pointer's expected annual return on investment for 19X5?
5. What life should be assigned to the goodwill?

✳ **PERSONAL SITUATIONS: ETHICS AND INTERPERSONAL SKILLS** ✳

PS 4–1 **Ethics: Yes, You Can—No, You Can't After All** In the 1980s, the savings and loan (S&L) regulatory agencies encouraged strong S&Ls to acquire financially failing S&Ls. The regulators allowed the acquirers to treat goodwill as an asset for regulatory purposes. In 1990, Congress passed S&L bailout legislation, which contained provisions that prohibited counting goodwill as an asset after 1994 for regulatory purposes.

As a result of massive subsequent write-offs of goodwill for regulatory purposes, many S&Ls did *not* have sufficient capital for regulatory purposes. Consequently, the S&L regulators forced the closure of these S&Ls, and stockholders lost their entire investment.

Required
1. Did the federal government act ethically?
2. Do you think that the stockholders of these closed S&Ls would be able to recover damages from the federal government?

ANSWERS TO SELF-STUDY QUESTIONS

1. f   **2.** a   **3.** i   **4.** b   **5.** c   **6.** d   **7.** a   **8.** b   **9.** c   **10.** i   **11.** e   **12.** f, h   **13.** e, b, g

14. a, g   **15.** g (from buyer's perspective), h (from seller's perspective)

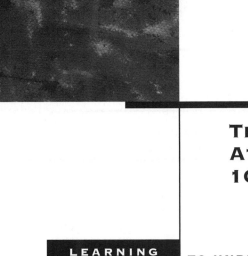

THE PURCHASE METHOD: AT DATE OF ACQUISITION— 100% OWNERSHIP

5

The quality of a person's life is in direct proportion to his or her commitment to excellence.

VINCE LOMBARDI

CHAPTER OVERVIEW

Chapter 4 introduced the purchase method and the pooling of interests method of accounting for business combinations. Because these two methods are conceptual opposites, they are best discussed and illustrated separately. Consequently, this chapter and Chapter 6 cover the purchase method; Chapter 7 focuses on the pooling of interests method.

The purchase method, like the pooling of interests method, can be applied to either form of business combination, the *acquisition of assets* and the *acquisition of common stock;* with either, the results of reporting operations and the financial position of the combined businesses are the same. To make this point, we discuss and illustrate each form of business combination. In the illustrations, we must compare a situation in which *all* of the assets are acquired with one in which *all* of the common stock is acquired; otherwise, a comparison is not possible. Acquisition of less than 100% of the common stock requires some additional considerations that are not relevant in situations in which all of the common stock is acquired. Discussion of these more involved situations is delayed until Chapter 6.

Regardless of whether the acquisition is achieved by acquiring common stock or assets (the *form* of the acquisition), the consolidated financial statement amounts are always the same—both at the date of acquisition and for dates and periods subsequent to it. This chapter deals only with achieving purchase accounting results at the acquisition date. In Chapter 6, we discuss achieving purchase accounting results for dates and periods subsequent to the acquisition date.

I THE ESSENCE OF THE PURCHASE METHOD

The underlying concept of the purchase method is that one entity has purchased the business of another entity—that is, a sale has been consummated. The acquiring entity records at its cost the assets or common stock acquired. The cost is based essentially on **the value of the consideration given.**

GOODWILL SITUATIONS

If the acquirer's cost is *above* the current value of the target company's net assets, goodwill exists and must be amortized over a period not to exceed 40 years. Thus **goodwill is determined in a residual manner.** The target company's current value is determined by valuing its tangible assets, identifiable intangible assets, and liabilities at their current values, which may involve qualified appraisers.

BARGAIN PURCHASE ELEMENT ("NEGATIVE GOODWILL") SITUATIONS

In the far less frequent circumstances in which the acquiring company's cost is *below* the current value of the target company's net assets, a bargain purchase element exists and must be allocated against the current value of certain noncurrent assets. If the bargain purchase element is so great that it reduces the applicable noncurrent assets to zero, the remaining amount is recorded as a **deferred credit** and amortized over a period not to exceed 40 years.

The purchase method parallels accounting for the acquisition of individual assets—that is, historical cost is used. Consequently, some assets and liabilities of the enlarged business are recorded at their historical cost (the assets and liabilities of the *acquiring* company), whereas some assets and liabilities of the enlarged business (the assets and liabilities of the *acquired* business) are reported at their current values as of the acquisition date. These current values become the acquiring company's historical cost. From the date of acquisition, the income of the acquired business is combined with the income of the acquiring company. **The acquired business's preacquisition earnings are never combined with the preacquisition earnings of the acquiring company.**

The purchase method can be neatly addressed by two questions:

1. What is the cost of the acquired business to the acquiring business?
2. What specifically is acquired for the cost incurred?

The rest of the chapter discusses the procedures for answering these questions, in addition to the procedures for presenting the financial statements of the enlarged business.

II DETERMINING THE COST OF THE ACQUIRED BUSINESS

The cost of the acquired business equals the sum of the following:

1. The **fair value of the consideration given.**
2. The **direct costs** incurred in connection with the acquisition, excluding costs of registering with the Securities and Exchange Commission (SEC) any securities given as consideration by the acquiring company.
3. The **fair value of any contingent consideration** given subsequent to the acquisition date.

Each of these areas is discussed in the three following sections.

THE FAIR VALUE OF THE CONSIDERATION GIVEN

The following three types of consideration may be given in any business combination:

1. **Cash or other assets.** Cost is the amount of cash or the fair value of other assets given.
2. **Debt.** Cost is the present value of the debt issued, determined by applying the provisions of *APB Opinion No. 21*, "Interest on Receivables and Payables."
3. **Equity securities.** Cost is the fair value of the equity securities issued. If the fair value of the property acquired is more clearly evident than the fair value of the equity securities issued, however, the fair value of the property acquired is used to determine cost.

As a practical matter, when equity securities issued are identical to the acquiring company's outstanding publicly traded securities, the fair value of the equity securities given is readily determinable and is almost always used to determine cost. (An example of an exception is a common stock that is thinly traded.) If the acquiring company's equity securities are *not* publicly traded or a new class of stock is issued, obtaining an appraisal of either (1) the fair value of the equity securities issued (usually obtainable from an investment banker) or (2) the property acquired is usually necessary, the second alternative being preferable.

DIRECT COSTS

Costs and expenses incurred that are *directly traceable* to the acquisition may be capitalized as part of the cost of the acquisition. Examples of capitalizable and noncapitalizable items follow:

	Capitalizable	Noncapitalizable
Legal fees	X	
Investment banker advising fees	X	
Accounting fees (such as for a purchase investigation)	X	
Finders' fees	X	
Travel costs	X	
General expenses (pro rata)		X
Salary and overhead of an internal acquisitions department		X

Costs and fees pertaining to the issuance
    or registration of debt or equity securities
    (including investment banker underwriting fees) . . . .
		X[a]

[a]If an equity security, additional paid-in capital is charged; if a debt security, debt issuance costs are charged (to be amortized over the life of the debt).

CONTINGENT CONSIDERATION

Contingent consideration is often used as a compromise when the buyer and seller disagree on the purchase price or the form of consideration to be given, or both. Contingent consideration may be divided into two mutually exclusive categories: contingencies (1) whose outcomes *are* currently determinable and (2) whose outcomes are *not* currently determinable.

CONTINGENCIES WHOSE OUTCOMES *ARE* CURRENTLY DETERMINABLE   If it can be determined beyond a reasonable doubt at the acquisition date that the outcome of the contingency will be such that the contingent consideration will have to be paid, the fair value of the additional consideration should be recorded at that time as part of the cost of the acquired business. Relatively few contingencies fall into this category.

CONTINGENCIES WHOSE OUTCOMES ARE *NOT* CURRENTLY DETERMINABLE   If it cannot be determined beyond a reasonable doubt at the acquisition date that the contingent consideration will have to be paid, it should be disclosed but not recorded as a liability or shown as outstanding securities until it is determinable beyond a reasonable doubt. This **"determinable beyond a reasonable doubt"** criterion of *APB Opinion No. 16*, "Accounting for Business Combinations," is more demanding than the "probable" criterion set forth in FASB *Statement No. 5*, "Accounting for Contingencies," which applies only to loss and gain contingencies, as shown below.

Contingencies that are *not* currently determinable can be divided into two categories:

1. **Contingencies based on other than security prices.** This type of contingency is often based on sales or earnings goals for the acquired business. It is commonly used when the target company or its shareholders want to protect themselves from selling out too cheaply in the event that the acquired business later realizes the potential they believe it possesses and the buyer wants to protect itself from paying too much in the event that the acquired business does *not* realize such potential. Contingent consideration is the compromise whereby an additional amount of consideration is given to the seller(s) at a later date if the acquired business achieves certain agreed-upon sales or earnings levels within a specified period of time. Later, when the contingency is resolved and any additional con-

sideration is distributable, **the current value of the additional consideration is added to the acquiring company's cost of the acquired business.** (Usually this increases the amount of goodwill.)

2. **Contingencies based on security prices.** This type of contingency is common when the target company or its shareholders receive as consideration the acquiring company's equity securities, which must be held for a certain period of time. In this situation, the target company or its shareholders want protection in the event the market price of the securities at the expiration of the holding period is below their market price at the acquisition date. The acquiring company must issue an additional number of securities if the market price at the end of the holding period is below the market price that existed on the acquisition date. The result brings the total value of the holdings of the target company or its shareholders at that time up to the total value existing on the acquisition date. If additional securities are later issued, the current value of the additional consideration is added to the acquiring company's cost of the acquired business. The amount previously recorded for securities issued at the date of acquisition should simultaneously be reduced, however, to the lower current value of those securities. **The net effect of this procedure is not to increase the cost of the acquired business above what was recorded at the acquisition date.** The rationale is that the initial recorded cost represents the amount that would have been paid for the business in a straight cash transaction. Illustration 5–1 gives an example of the accounting entries for this type of contingency.

ILLUSTRATION 5–1	**An Example of Contingent Consideration Based on Security Prices**

Pine Inc. acquires the business of Spruce Inc. (Whether it acquires assets or common stock is irrelevant.) The total consideration Pine pays is $1,000,000 worth of its $5 par value common stock. The market price of Pine's common stock on the acquisition date is $50 per share; thus 20,000 shares are issued at that time. A condition of the purchase is that the common stock issued be held by the seller for two years. If, at the end of two years, the market price of the common stock is below $50 per share, an appropriate additional number of shares must be issued so that the total value of the issued shares equals $1,000,000. Two years later, the market price of Pine's common stock is $40 per share. Thus, $1,000,000 divided by $40 per share equals 25,000 shares. Because 20,000 shares have already been issued, an additional 5,000 shares are issued at that time.

Entry at the acquisition date:

Cost of Acquired Business[a] (20,000 shares × $50 market price)	1,000,000	
Common Stock (20,000 shares × $5 par)		100,000
Additional Paid-in Capital		900,000
To record the issuance of 20,000 shares of $5 par value common stock.		

Entries required two years later:

Cost of Acquired Business[a] (5,000 shares × $40 market price)	200,000	
Common Stock (5,000 shares × $5 par)		25,000
Additional Paid-in Capital		175,000
To record the issuance of 5,000 shares of $5 par value common stock as additional consideration.		

Additional Paid-in Capital	200,000	
Cost of Acquired Business[a]		200,000
To reflect the reduction in value of the previously issued shares from $50 per share to $40 per share.		

    Note that the effect of the entries recorded two years after acquisition is to debit Additional Paid-in Capital for $25,000 and credit Common Stock for $25,000. Thus there is no effect on the cost of the acquired business as initially recorded on the acquisition date.

[a]Later in the chapter, more descriptive account titles are used: "Investment in Subsidiary" when common stock is acquired and "Investment in Division" when assets are acquired.

III THE RELATIONSHIP OF COST TO THE CURRENT VALUE OF THE ACQUIRED BUSINESS'S NET ASSETS

Once the cost of the acquired business is determined, the next step in purchase accounting is to determine the current value of its assets and liabilities. Assume that the assets have a current value of $288,000 and the liabilities have a current value of $200,000. The $88,000 difference between the two is the current value of the net assets. This current value is then multiplied by the acquiring company's ownership interest in the acquired business (always 100% when assets are acquired or when all of the outstanding common stock is acquired) to obtain the acquiring company's ownership interest in the current value of the net assets. This amount is then compared to the cost of the acquisition to determine whether goodwill exists (the most common situation) or a bargain purchase element is present. This process can be expressed in a formula applicable to all combinations, as well as the preceding example, as shown in Illustration 5–2.

REVIEW POINTS FOR ILLUSTRATION 5–2   Note the following:

1. Both goodwill and bargain purchase elements are determined in a residual manner.

2. When a bargain purchase element is present, its amount must be allocated to certain noncurrent assets (reducing their current values) to the extent possible. The adjusted amounts then become the current values for financial reporting purposes.

ACCOUNTING FOR GOODWILL

When the acquiring company's cost is *higher than* its ownership interest in the current value of the acquired business's net assets, the excess amount is considered **goodwill.** Note that goodwill is a residually determined amount. It is reported in the financial statements as an asset of the enlarged, combined business. It must be amortized over **no more than 40 years,** and its value and remaining life must be reassessed in each subsequent period.

GOODWILL VERSUS COVENANTS NOT TO COMPETE   Prior to August 1993, goodwill was *not* deductible for income tax–reporting purposes. Accordingly, acquiring companies often tried to include in the acquisition agreement a tax-deductible feature known as a *covenant not to compete.* Covenants not to compete are intangible assets similar to goodwill. Such covenants prevent the target company or certain of its key shareholders or employees from reentering the same line of business for

ILLUSTRATION 5–2	Relationship of Total Cost to the Current Value of the Acquired Business's Net Assets				
		Cost	–	Acquiring Company's Ownership Interest in *Current Value* of Net Assets	=	Goodwill (Bargain Purchase) Element
Goodwill situation		$100,000	–	$88,000[a]	= $12,000
Bargain purchase element situation		$83,000	–	$88,000[a]	= $(5,000)

[a]Assume that assets have a current value of $288,000, liabilities have a current value of $200,000, and either assets or all of the outstanding common stock was acquired.

a specified period of time. Because goodwill is now tax deductible, this built-in incentive favoring the assignment of part of the purchase price to covenants not to compete instead of goodwill no longer exists. Furthermore, both goodwill and covenants not to compete are tax deductible over 15 years. Thus no incentive exists to assign part of the purchase price to one versus the other as might otherwise exist if each had a different life for tax-reporting purposes.

TAX RULES FOR DETERMINING GOODWILL   In allocating the purchase price of a business between depreciable and nondepreciable assets for tax-reporting purposes, the amount allocated to goodwill must be calculated in a residual manner (termed the *residual method of allocation*). Thus goodwill is determined in the same manner for both financial reporting and tax reporting.

ACCOUNTING FOR BARGAIN PURCHASE ELEMENTS

When the acquiring company's cost is *below* its ownership interest in the current value of the acquired business's net assets, a **bargain purchase element** exists. Bargain purchase elements are treated arbitrarily under the provisions of *APBO No. 16*. First, the bargain purchase element must be treated as a reduction of the current values assigned to any noncurrent assets acquired other than long-term investments in marketable securities. If the bargain purchase element is so large that the applicable noncurrent assets are reduced to zero (which rarely, if ever, happens), any remaining credit is recorded as a deferred credit and amortized to income over a period of not more than 40 years.

The rationale for attempting to eliminate the bargain purchase element is that the values assigned to the net assets as a whole should not exceed the purchase price paid. Under historical cost-based accounting, the purchase price constitutes cost. Were it not for this requirement, managements would have the opportunity to seek or use the highest possible appraisals for the assets to obtain the highest possible bargain purchase element. The high (artificial) bargain purchase element could then be amortized to income over a relatively short period of time in comparison with time periods assigned to the noncurrent assets. Thus, substantial opportunity for manipulating income would exist.

Because bargain purchase elements arise most frequently when the acquired business has recently experienced operating losses, this treatment results in a conservative valuation of the noncurrent assets other than long-term investments in marketable securities. This makes sense; such noncurrent assets acquired from a company experiencing operating losses are subject to greater realization risks than if the target company had not experienced operating losses.

To illustrate the manner of allocating a bargain purchase to the appropriate assets, assume a $5,000 bargain purchase element. Assume further that the only noncurrent assets of the acquired business are land and buildings and equipment. The $5,000 bargain purchase element is allocated to these accounts based on their relative current values as follows:

Appropriate Noncurrent Assets	Current Value	Percentage to Total (Rounded)		Bargain Purchase Element		Percentage Times Bargain Purchase Element	Adjusted Current Value
Land	$ 38,000	20%	×	$5,000	=	$1,000	$ 37,000
Buildings and equipment. . . .	166,000	80	×	5,000	=	4,000	162,000
	$204,000	100%				$5,000	$199,000

KEY REVIEW POINT   The presence of a bargain purchase element clearly suggests that the assets are worth more individually than as part of a going business. If this were true, the previous owners of the acquired business would have been better off to liquidate the company by selling its individual assets than by selling the business as a whole. Because they did *not* do this, the initially determined current values must be overstated to the extent of the bargain purchase element.

"NEGATIVE GOODWILL"   As noted in paragraph 87 of *APBO No. 16,* some accountants refer to an excess of current value over cost as *negative goodwill* rather than as a bargain purchase element. We point this term out only because you may encounter it in practice.

IV THE IRRELEVANCE OF THE ACQUIRED BUSINESS'S BOOK VALUES FOR CONSOLIDATED REPORTING PURPOSES

For future reporting purposes, the book values of the acquired business's various assets and liabilities as of the combination date become irrelevant to the acquiring company, inasmuch as a *new basis of accounting* occurs under the purchase method. By comparing the current value of the net assets to their book value, however, we determine by how much the net assets are under- or overvalued. For example, assume that the acquiring company's cost is $100,000 and the net assets of the acquired business have a current value of $88,000 and a book value of $60,000. The formula shown in Illustration 5–2 can be modified slightly to display this information by separating the acquiring company's ownership interest in the current value of the net assets into its interest in (1) the book value of the net assets and (2) the amount of the under- or overvaluation of the net assets:

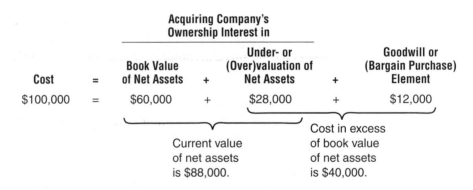

This additional information concerning the amount by which the net assets are under- or overvalued is not necessary to record the combination, regardless of whether it takes the form of acquiring assets or common stock. When common stock is acquired, however, we must have this additional information to prepare consolidated financial statements. The remainder of this chapter deals with recording business combinations and preparing combined and consolidated statements as of the date of the business combination and at subsequent dates. In an economy that has experienced inflation over many years, the net assets of an acquired business are usually undervalued. Accordingly, we will continue under this assumption.

ACQUISITION OF ASSETS

When assets are acquired, the procedures to record the business combination and to prepare financial statements reflecting the enlarged, combined operations are not complicated. This is because **the assets acquired and liabilities assumed are recorded directly by the acquiring company in its own general ledger** (or in the general ledger of a newly established division) **at their current values.**

ACQUISITION OF COMMON STOCK

When common stock is acquired, the procedures used to record the business combination are also relatively simple. The procedures to prepare financial statements reflecting the enlarged, combined operations *are* somewhat involved, however, because **the acquired subsidiary continues to account for its assets and liabilities using its recorded book values.** Stated differently, the parent does *not* directly record the acquired business's assets and liabilities in its own general ledger. The only account in which the parent records the cost of the acquired business is called *Investment in Subsidiary.* As a result, the parent must deal with the **amount of the under- or overvaluation in preparing financial statements that reflect the enlarged, combined operations.**

V ACQUIRING ASSETS

The acquisition of assets is merely the purchase of the target company's assets. Part of the purchase price takes the form of assuming responsibility for the target company's existing liabilities. Before the acquiring company can record the acquisition of assets, it must determine whether the acquired business's operations will be accounted for on a centralized or decentralized basis. This decision is based on what is most practical and economical.

CENTRALIZED ACCOUNTING

Under a centralized accounting system, the acquiring company records the assets acquired and liabilities assumed at their current values directly in the general ledger maintained at its own headquarters. Thus the combined businesses are accounted for entirely in one general ledger, eliminating the need to combine financial statements produced from multiple general ledgers (as is necessary in decentralized accounting). In practice, centralized accounting is used infrequently.

DECENTRALIZED ACCOUNTING

Under a decentralized accounting system, the individual assets acquired and liabilities assumed are recorded at their current values in a new general ledger maintained at the acquired business's location. This location is usually referred to as a *division* of the acquiring company. The acquiring company, referred to as the *home office*, charges the cost of the acquired business to an account called *Investment in Division.*

| ILLUSTRATIONS | MOST COMMONLY ENCOUNTERED SITUATION |

Acquisition of Assets When
- Assets Are Undervalued
- Goodwill Exists

To illustrate recording the acquisition and preparing combined financial statements as of the acquisition date, we assume in this basic example that the acquired business's net assets are undervalued and the purchase price includes an amount for goodwill (the most commonly encountered situation).

Assume that P Company acquired all of S Company's assets on January 1, 19X1, by assuming responsibility for all of its liabilities and paying $100,000 cash. The balance sheets for each company as of January 1, 19X1—**immediately** *prior* **to the business combination**—are as follows:

	P Company	S Company
Assets		
Cash	$118,000	$ 15,000
Accounts receivable, net	52,000	23,000
Inventory	90,000	42,000
Land	220,000	30,000
Buildings and equipment	500,000	200,000
Accumulated depreciation	(280,000)	(50,000)
	$700,000	$260,000
Liabilities and Stockholders' Equity		
Liabilities	$400,000	$200,000
Common stock	200,000	10,000
Retained earnings	100,000	50,000
	$700,000	$260,000

Additional assumed information is stated in items 2 and 4:

1. Cost (given above) $100,000
2. Current value of net assets .... $ 88,000
3. Book value of net assets ($260,000 – $200,000) .... $ 60,000
4. The current values of S Company's assets and liabilities are assumed to equal their book values, except for the following assets:

	Book Value	Current Value	Undervaluation
Inventory	$ 42,000	$ 46,000	$ 4,000
Land	30,000	38,000	8,000
Buildings and equipment	150,000[a]	166,000	16,000[b]
			$28,000

[a]Net of $50,000 accumulated depreciation.

[b]For simplicity, we have combined buildings and equipment. (Also for simplicity, we will later assume that the entire $16,000 pertains to equipment.)

Accordingly, $28,000 of the cost in excess of the book value of the net assets is attributable to these assets. The remaining $12,000 of cost in excess of the book value of the net assets represents goodwill.

CENTRALIZED ACCOUNTING   The entries to record the combination using centralized accounting follow:

Accounts Receivable	23,000	
Inventory	46,000	
Land	38,000	
Buildings and Equipment	166,000	
Goodwill	12,000	
Liabilities		200,000
Cash ($100,000 – $15,000)		85,000

Thus the balance sheet of the combined business **immediately** *after* **the acquisition** contains amounts obtained solely from P Company's general ledger. That balance sheet is as follows:

P Company
As of January 1, 19X1
(immediately *after* the acquisition)

Assets

Cash.	$ 33,000
Accounts receivable, net	75,000
Inventory	136,000
Land.	258,000
Buildings and equipment	666,000
Accumulated depreciation	(280,000)
Goodwill.	12,000
Total Assets	$900,000

Liabilities and Stockholders' Equity

Liabilities	$600,000
Common stock.	200,000
Retained earnings	100,000
Total Liabilities and Equity	$900,000

DECENTRALIZED ACCOUNTING The entries to record the combination using decentralized accounting follow:

Home Office's Books

Investment in S Division	100,000	
Cash		100,000

Division's Books

Cash.	15,000	
Accounts Receivable	23,000	
Inventory	46,000	
Land.	38,000	
Buildings and Equipment	166,000	
Goodwill	12,000	
Liabilities		200,000
Home Office Capital		100,000

REVIEW POINTS FOR THE PRECEDING ENTRIES Note the following:

1. Each asset and each liability is recorded at its current value.

2. The accumulated depreciation accounts relating to the fixed assets recorded on S Company's books **do not carry over to the acquiring company.** The current values of these assets are the new cost basis for P Company.

3. After S Company records the receipt of the cash and the sale of its assets, its sole asset is $100,000 cash, which most likely will be distributed to its stockholders. S Company will then end its legal existence.

4. The Investment in S Division account and the Home Office Capital account are reciprocal accounts (the same concept was discussed in Chapter 1).

COMBINED FINANCIAL STATEMENTS For financial reporting purposes, the financial statements of the home office and the division must be combined. This is

ILLUSTRATION 5–3   **The Acquisition of Assets When They Are Undervalued and Goodwill Exists**

P Company
Combining Statement Worksheet as of January 1, 19X1

	Home Office	S Division	Combining Entry Dr.	Combining Entry Cr.	Combined
Balance Sheet					
Cash.......................	18,000	15,000			33,000
Accounts receivable, net........	52,000	23,000			75,000
Inventory....................	90,000	46,000			136,000
Investment in S Division........	100,000			100,000(1)	–0–
Land......................	220,000	38,000			258,000
Buildings and equipment	500,000	166,000			666,000
Accumulated depreciation	(280,000)	–0–			(280,000)
Goodwill		12,000			12,000
Total Assets...............	700,000	300,000		100,000	900,000
Liabilities...................	400,000	200,000			600,000
Home office capital...........		100,000	100,000(1)		–0–
Common stock	200,000				200,000
Retained earnings	100,000				100,000
Total Liabilities and Equity.....	700,000	300,000	100,000		900,000
Proof of debit and credit postings			100,000	100,000	

Explanation of entry:
(1) The basic elimination entry.

done outside the general ledger on a worksheet. The worksheet entry to combine the two balance sheets as of the acquisition date is as follows:

WORKSHEET ENTRY ONLY	Home Office Capital 100,000	
	Investment in S Division	100,000

Illustration 5–3 shows a combining statement worksheet, which combines the balance sheets of the home office and the newly established division as of the acquisition date. Note that the combined amounts are the same as those in the balance sheet shown earlier for *centralized* accounting.

VI   ACQUIRING COMMON STOCK (100%-OWNED SUBSIDIARY)

When common stock is acquired, the acquiring company charges its cost to an account called *Investment in Subsidiary*. Assuming that the value of the consideration given by the acquiring company (hereafter referred to as the *parent company*) is $90,000 and direct costs incurred are $10,000 (that may be properly added to the cost of the acquisition), the entry to record the acquisition is as follows, assuming that $90,000 cash is the consideration given:

Investment in Subsidiary 100,000
      Cash 100,000

The following entry assumes that 1,000 shares of $1 par value common stock (having a market value of $90,000) are the consideration given:

Investment in Subsidiary	100,000	
Common Stock (1,000 shares × $1 par)		1,000
Additional Paid-in Capital		89,000
Cash		10,000

Note that if the common stock issued is registered with the SEC, the following additional entry is made for the additional direct costs incurred to register the common stock:

Additional Paid-in Capital	xxx	
Cash		xxx

ADDITIONAL ISSUES FOR ACQUIRED SUBSIDIARIES

When *common stock* is acquired and the purchase method of accounting is used, two issues that do not exist for *created* subsidiaries do exist concerning *acquired* subsidiaries:

1. **Manner of revaluing the assets and liabilities of a subsidiary acquired in a purchase transaction.** An internal issue, solely concerning the mechanics of preparing consolidated statements, is whether the assets and liabilities of a subsidiary acquired in a purchase transaction should be revalued to their current values in (a) the subsidiary's general ledger or (b) the consolidation process (on the consolidation worksheet).

2. **Manner of presenting subsidiary's separate financial statements.** If a subsidiary acquired in a purchase transaction issues separate financial statements (perhaps because of a loan agreement requirement), on what basis should its assets and liabilities be reported—its historical cost or current values based on the parent's cost?

PUSH-DOWN ACCOUNTING In 1983, the SEC staff issued *Staff Accounting Bulletin No. 54*. This bulletin requires that **when a subsidiary acquired in a purchase transaction issues separate financial statements, such statements shall reflect the new basis of accounting.** In other words, the assets and liabilities must be revalued to their current values. Thus the new basis of accounting is "pushed down" to the subsidiary. **This pronouncement applies only to publicly owned companies.** The manner of implementing the **push-down basis of accounting** is shown briefly on page 176 and discussed in detail in Chapter 8.

VII CONSOLIDATION WORKSHEET: AT DATE OF ACQUISITION

THE CONSOLIDATION WORKSHEET

Unless the business combination occurs on the last day of the parent's reporting year (which rarely happens), preparing consolidated financial statements as of the acquisition date is not necessary. They are illustrated in the worksheets in this chapter for instructional purposes only.

The balance sheet is the only financial statement of the subsidiary that can be consolidated with the parent's financial statement as of the acquisition date. This follows from a fundamental concept of the purchase method: **The parent company can report to its stockholders only the operations of the subsidiary that occur subsequent to the acquisition date.** Combining the future income statements of a parent and a subsidiary is discussed in Chapter 6.

THE NON-PUSH-DOWN BASIS OF ACCOUNTING: THE SUBSIDIARY RETAINS THE HISTORICAL COST BASIS OF ITS ASSETS AND LIABILITIES

The **non-push-down basis of accounting** holds that the subsidiary *cannot* revalue its assets and liabilities to their current values merely because its outstanding common stock has changed hands and has become concentrated in the hands of significantly fewer stockholders or even a single one.

The obvious question, then, is this: How are the subsidiary's assets and liabilities revalued to their current values as required under the purchase method of accounting? The answer requires an understanding of the major conceptual elements of the parent's cost of the investment as reflected in its Investment in Subsidiary account.

THE MAJOR CONCEPTUAL ELEMENTS OF INVESTMENT COST

The cost of the investment as recorded on the parent's books must be separated into its major conceptual elements. We do this by analyzing the relationship among the cost, the current value of the subsidiary's net assets, and the book value of the subsidiary's net assets as shown earlier in the chapter. For clarity, we repeat the information and data as in the discussion on page 164 involving the acquisition of assets, except that we assume that common stock was acquired instead of assets. All of the assumed information is as follows:

1. P Company acquired 100% of S Company's outstanding common stock on January 1, 19X1, by paying $100,000 cash.

2. Cost $100,000

3. Current value of net assets . . . . $ 88,000

4. Book value of net assets ($260,000 – $200,000) . . . . $ 60,000

5. The current values of S Company's assets and liabilities are assumed to equal their book values, except for the following assets:

	Book Value	Current Value	Undervaluation
Inventory	$ 42,000	$ 46,000	$ 4,000
Land	30,000	38,000	8,000
Buildings and equipment	150,000[a]	166,000	16,000
			$28,000

[a]Net of $50,000 accumulated depreciation.

Accordingly, $28,000 of the cost in excess of the book value of the net assets is attributable to these assets. The remaining $12,000 of cost in excess of the book value represents goodwill.

Thus the cost of the investment may be considered to comprise three major elements:

1. **The book value element.** The parent's ownership interest in the subsidiary's recorded net assets at their book value (100% of $60,000) . . . . $ 60,000

2. **The under- or (over)valuation of net assets element.** The parent's ownership interest in the subsidiary's excess of the current value of its net assets over their book value (100% of $28,000)   28,000

3. **The goodwill element.** The parent's cost in excess of the current value of the subsidiary's net assets ($100,000 – $88,000)   12,000

  Cost of the Investment $100,000

The $28,000 difference between the current value of the subsidiary's net assets and their book value is included in the parent's Investment account. When the subsidiary's financial statements are consolidated with those of its parent, this $28,000 difference is reclassified from the Investment account to the specific assets with which it has been identified. (In this situation, $4,000 is identified with undervalued inventories, $8,000 with undervalued land, and $16,000 with undervalued equipment.) The parent accounts for the individual items that make up this difference in the same manner that the subsidiary accounts for the specific undervalued assets. Specifically, the following occurs:

1. The subsidiary continues to depreciate its assets at their historical cost as though the business combination had never occurred.

2. The parent amortizes to its future income that portion of its cost in excess of book value that is attributable to depreciable or amortizable assets (in this example, $4,000 pertaining to the inventory and $16,000 pertaining to the equipment). The $4,000 amount relating to inventory is amortized to income as the subsidiary sells its inventory. The $16,000 amount relating to the equipment is amortized to income using the same remaining life that the subsidiary uses to depreciate its historical cost.

3. The parent also amortizes that portion of its Investment account that represents goodwill ($12,000 in this example).

In other words, depreciation and amortization of the subsidiary's assets take place on *two* sets of books instead of just *one* set, as when assets are acquired. These amortization procedures on the parent company's books are necessary to charge the combined operations with the current value of the assets acquired because the assets were *not* revalued on the subsidiary's books. In substance, the net effect on the enlarged business as a whole is the same as though the subsidiary had revalued its assets to their current values (push-down accounting).

ILLUSTRATION | **SEPARATING THE COST OF THE INVESTMENT INTO ITS MAJOR CONCEPTUAL ELEMENTS**

Separating the cost of the investment into its major conceptual elements is possible for all common stock investments, regardless of the price the parent paid, the current value of the net assets, or the book value of the net assets. Many possible relationship combinations between these three items can be shown. To show how the cost is separated into its major conceptual elements for various possible relationship combinations, Illustration 5–4 shows four selected situations.

REVIEW POINTS FOR ILLUSTRATION 5–4   Note the following:

1. In situation A, only one major conceptual element exists because cost equals current value and current value equals book value.

2. In situation B, all three major conceptual elements exist. If the cost of the investment had been $12,000 less, no goodwill element and only two major conceptual elements would have existed.

3. In situation C, all three major conceptual elements exist, but the parent has a negative balance instead of a positive balance for its under- or (over)valuation of net assets element. This negative balance is identified with depreciable assets and is amortized in future periods to the parent's income statement, as are the positive balances in situations B and D, which are identified with depreciable assets.

ILLUSTRATION 5-4	The Major Conceptual Elements of the Cost of the Investment

	Net Assets of Subsidiary			Separation of Cost into Its Major Conceptual Elements						
Situation	Current Value (1) (Given)	Book Value (2) (Given)	Under- or (Over)valuation (3) (1)-(2)	Cost (4) (Given)	=	Book Value Element (5) (2)	+	Under- or (Over)valuation of Net Assets Element (6) (3)	+	Goodwill (Bargain Purchase) Element (7) (Residual)
A	$60,000	$60,000		$ 60,000	=	$60,000				
B	88,000	60,000	$28,000	100,000	=	60,000	+	$28,000	+	$12,000
C	50,000	60,000	(10,000)	55,000	=	60,000	+	(10,000)	+	5,000
D	80,000	60,000	20,000	75,000	=	60,000	+	20,000	+	(5,000)[a]

[a]This bargain purchase element must be allocated to the extent possible to noncurrent assets other than long-term investments. If all of it is allocated thus, the amounts in the column to the left decrease by $5,000, and no deferred credit remains. (See Illustration 5–5, in which all of it is allocated to the appropriate noncurrent assets.)

DISPLAYING THE MAJOR CONCEPTUAL ELEMENTS BY THEIR COMPONENTS

The analysis of the parent's cost by its major conceptual elements can be expanded to display the *components* of (1) the book value element and (2) the under- or (over)valuation of net assets element. This expanded analysis can be used as the source of two entries that consolidate the parent's financial statements with those of the subsidiary. The preparation of consolidated financial statements has always been an involved process. The use of this expanded analysis of the cost of the investment, which displays the components of the major conceptual elements, however, substantially simplifies the consolidation procedures. The procedures for expanding the analysis are explained below using situation B of Illustration 5–4, in which cost is above current value and current value is above book value.

SEPARATING THE BOOK VALUE ELEMENT   The book value element is easily separated into its components by multiplying the parent's ownership interest by the balance in each of the subsidiary's individual capital accounts—Common Stock, Additional Paid-in Capital, and Retained Earnings—as of the acquisition date. S Company's capital accounts as of the acquisition date are as follows:

Common stock	$10,000
Retained earnings.	50,000
Total Stockholders' Equity	$60,000

Because we assume that P Company acquires 100% of S Company's outstanding common stock, the $60,000 book value element comprises these two components.

SEPARATING THE UNDER- OR (OVER)VALUATION OF NET ASSETS ELEMENT   As stated previously, the parent accounts for the components of the under- or (over)valuation element—not for the total difference as a lump sum. Thus, the under- or (over)valuation of net assets element can be thought of as comprising the following three components:

Inventory	$ 4,000
Land	8,000
Equipment.	16,000
Total Undervaluation of Net Assets	$28,000

THE GOODWILL ELEMENT AND THE BARGAIN PURCHASE ELEMENT   No separation is needed for goodwill, which is a residual amount accounted for as a lump sum. When a bargain purchase element exists, the initial credit must be allocated as much as possible to noncurrent assets other than long-term investments in marketable securities. Any remaining bargain purchase element is amortized to income in future periods.

RECAPPING THE CONCEPTUAL ELEMENTS   The analysis of the investment cost in situation B of Illustration 5–4 is shown below by the major conceptual elements and their components:

	Analysis of Investment Cost	
	By the Major Conceptual Elements	By the Components of the Major Conceptual Elements
Book value element:		
Common stock		$ 10,000
Retained earnings		50,000
Total	$ 60,000	$ 60,000
Under- or (over)valuation of net assets element:		
Inventory.		$ 4,000
Land		8,000
Equipment		16,000
Total	28,000	$ 28,000
Goodwill element	12,000	$ 12,000
Cost	$100,000	$100,000

Illustration 5–5 displays the major conceptual elements for the situations in Illustration 5–4 by their components.

REVIEW POINTS FOR ILLUSTRATION 5–5   Note the following:

1. In situation A, in which only the book value element exists, the parent has completed accounting for its investment under the purchase method of accounting. No additional accounting procedures are necessary because no other major conceptual elements exist.

2. In situations B and D, in which the current value of the net assets exceeds their book value and the parent pays more than the book value of the net assets, the

ILLUSTRATION 5–5	The Major Conceptual Elements and Their Components													
			BOOK VALUE ELEMENT			+	**UNDER- OR (OVER)VALUATION OF NET ASSETS ELEMENT**					+	**GOODWILL (BARGAIN PURCHASE) ELEMENT**
Situation From Illustration 5–4	Cost	=	Common Stock	+	Retained Earnings	+	Inventory	+	Land	+	Equipment	+	
A	$ 60,000	=	$10,000	+	$50,000								
B	100,000	=	10,000	+	50,000	+	$4,000	+	$ 8,000	+	$16,000	+	$12,000
C	55,000	=	10,000	+	50,000					+	(10,000)	+	5,000
D	$ 75,000	=	$10,000	+	$50,000	+	$2,000	+	$12,000	+	$ 6,000	+	$ (5,000)
									(1,000)[a]		(4,000)[a]		5,000[a]
	$ 75,000	=	$10,000	+	$50,000	+	$2,000	+	$11,000	+	$ 2,000	+	$ –0–

[a]This allocation is the same as that illustrated on page 161.

amount applicable to the equipment is amortized to the parent's future income over the remaining life of these assets, using the same remaining life that the subsidiary uses to depreciate these items. The amount determined for inventory is amortized in the following year, assuming the subsidiary sells its inventory. The amount determined for the land is not amortized because land is never depreciated. When the land is sold, the amount determined for it is charged to income at that time; thereby reducing the gain or increasing the loss that otherwise would be reported. In summary, the parent accounts for each individual component in a manner consistent with the way the subsidiary accounts for its historical cost. Goodwill is amortized over its expected life, up to 40 years.

3. In situation C, in which the current value of the net assets is below their book value, the parent has credit amounts instead of debit amounts to amortize to its subsequent income statements. Otherwise, the procedures are the same as in point 2 above. The amortization partially offsets the depreciation expense recorded on the subsidiary's books from the viewpoint of combined operations.

SPLITTING THE COST OF THE INVESTMENT TO SIMPLIFY THE CONSOLIDATION PROCESS   Once the cost of the parent's investment has been broken down as shown in Illustration 5–5, the future consolidation procedures can be simplified by splitting the cost into the book value element and cost in excess of book value elements. For situation B of Illustration 5–5, the split is as follows:

Investment in S Company:
Book value element. $60,000
Excess cost elements   40,000

The individual components within each category will be tracked outside the general ledger in supporting schedules and used in preparing consolidation entries. For this situation, the supporting schedules at the acquisition date are as follows:

I. Book Value Element:

Total	=	Common Stock	+	Retained Earnings
$60,000	=	$10,000	+	$50,000

II. Excess Cost Elements:

Total	=	UNDERVALUATION OF NET ASSETS ELEMENT					+	GOODWILL ELEMENT
		Inventory	+	Land	+	Equipment		
$40,000	=	$4,000	+	$8,000	+	$16,000	+	$12,000

ILLUSTRATION   **MOST COMMONLY ENCOUNTERED SITUATION**

Acquisition of Common Stock When

- Assets Are Undervalued
- Goodwill Exists

Using the preceding information, the following consolidation entries are used to (1) eliminate the Investment account balance, (2) eliminate the subsidiary's equity accounts (which have a reciprocal relationship to the parent's book value element), (3) revalue the subsidiary's undervalued assets to their current values, and (4) report goodwill as a separate account:

(handwritten: Book Value Elimination)

The Basic Elimination Entry

WORKSHEET ENTRY ONLY

Common Stock	10,000	
Retained Earnings	50,000	
Investment in Subsidiary		60,000

The Excess Cost Entry

WORKSHEET ENTRY ONLY

Inventory	4,000	
Land	8,000	
Equipment	16,000	
Goodwill	12,000	
Investment in Subsidiary		40,000

Illustration 5–6 shows the consolidation worksheet as of the acquisition date using the preceding entries. In addition, the following accumulated depreciation entry is needed to recognize that a **new cost basis has been established for the subsidiary's fixed assets** for consolidated reporting purposes:

(handwritten: Sub's Book)

WORKSHEET ENTRY ONLY

(handwritten: Remove Acc Depn)

Accumulation Depreciation	50,000	
Buildings and Equipment		50,000

REVIEW POINTS FOR ILLUSTRATION 5–6   Note the following:

1. The parent's investment cost in excess of the book value of the subsidiary's net assets becomes clear in the consolidation process. The excess is effectively reclassified to the balance sheet accounts with which it has been identified.

2. The amounts in the Consolidated column are composed of (a) the parent's items based on book values and (b) the subsidiary's items based on the current value of those items as of the acquisition date.

3. The amounts shown in the Consolidated column are the same as those in the Combined column of Illustration 5–3 on page 166—in which assets were acquired.

4. The investment in Subsidiary account and the subsidiary's equity accounts are eliminated in consolidation and have a zero balance in the consolidated column.

UNDER- OR OVERVALUED LIABILITIES

For simplicity, the previous discussions and illustrations dealt only with certain under- and overvalued assets. The current values of accounts payable and accrued liabilities (using present value procedures) are usually so close to their book values—because of the relatively short period until payment of the obligation—that the difference is often ignored in the interest of practicality. The current value of borrowings that have a floating interest rate always equals the book value. If the borrowings have a *fixed* interest rate that differs from the interest rate existing at the acquisition date, however, the present value of the debt does *not* equal its book value. Thus the difference must be reflected as one of the components of the under- or (over)valuation of net assets element in the conceptual analysis of the Investment in Subsidiary account. For liabilities, however, note that an *undervalued* liability means that the net assets are *overvalued* and that an *overvalued* liability means that the net assets are *undervalued*. For example, assume that a subsidiary has 8% bonds payable outstanding at the acquisition date. If the current rate is 12%, the

	ILLUSTRATION 5–6	The Acquisition of Common Stock (Non-Push-Down Accounting Used by Subsidiary)

P Company and S Company
Consolidation Worksheet as of January 1, 19X1

	P Company	S Company[a]	Consolidation Entries Dr.	Consolidation Entries Cr.	Consolidated
Balance Sheet					
Cash	18,000	15,000			33,000
Accounts receivable, net	52,000	23,000			75,000
Inventory	90,000	42,000	4,000(2)		136,000
Investment in subsidiary:					
Book value element	60,000			60,000(1)	–0–
Excess cost elements	40,000			40,000(2)	–0–
Land	220,000	30,000	8,000(2)		258,000
Buildings and equipment	500,000	200,000	16,000(2)	50,000(3)	666,000
Accumulated depreciation	(280,000)	(50,000)	50,000(3)		(280,000)
Goodwill			12,000(2)		12,000
Total Assets	700,000	260,000	90,000	150,000	900,000
Liabilities	400,000	200,000			600,000
P Company:					
Common stock	200,000				200,000
Retained earnings	100,000				100,000
S Company:					
Common stock		10,000	10,000(1)		–0–
Retained earnings		50,000	50,000(1)		–0–
Total Liabilities and Equity . . .	700,000	260,000	60,000		900,000
Proof of debit and credit postings			150,000	150,000	

[a]The amounts in this column reflect the historical cost basis that applied to the previous owners.
Explanation of entry:
  (1) The basic elimination entry.
  (2) The excess cost entry.
  (3) The accumulated depreciation entry.

present value of the debt is below its book value, meaning that net assets are undervalued. (The low fixed interest rate of 8% in relation to the current interest rate of 12% means that the debt appears larger than it really is.)

REPORTING THE DEBT AT ITS PRESENT VALUE   To illustrate, assume that on the acquisition date of January 1, 19X1, the subsidiary has 8% bonds outstanding having a face amount of $100,000 and a maturity date of December 31, 19X2 (two years from now). If the current interest rate is 12%, the present value of the bonds is calculated as follows:

Present value of $100,000 principal payment due 12/31/X2	
($100,000 × 0.79719)	$79,719
Present value of two $8,000 interest payments due at the end of 19X1	
and 19X2 ($8,000 × 1.69005)	13,520
Total	$93,239

Accordingly, the $6,761 difference between the bonds' book value ($100,000) and their present value ($93,239) is reflected as an individual component of the under- or overvaluation of the net assets element. If consolidated statements were prepared as of the acquisition date, the bonds are reported in the Consolidated column at their present value of $93,239 because the $6,761 amount is debited to the Bonds Payable account in consolidation:

	P Company	S Company	Consolidation Entries Dr.	Consolidation Entries Cr.	Consolidated
Bonds payable		100,000	6,761		93,239

SUBSEQUENT TREATMENT OF THE DIFFERENCE The $6,761 amount is **analogous to a discount** and is **amortized to interest expense** over the next two years using the interest method of amortization. Over the next two years, interest expense is reported at 12% of the debt's carrying value (rather than at 8% of the book value of $100,000). For 19X1, interest expense of $11,190 is reported (12% × $93,239), and the $3,190 difference between the $11,190 and the $8,000 cash payment is amortized out of the Investment account. At December 31, 19X1, this component of the Investment account has an unamortized balance of $3,571, which results in a $96,429 carrying value of the debt in consolidation at that date. For 19X2, interest expense of $11,571 would be reported (12% × $96,429), which is made up of the $8,000 cash payment and $3,571 amortized out of the Investment account. In Chapter 6, we show in detail how to amortize amounts out of the Investment account.

UNDER- OR OVERVALUED RECEIVABLES

For practical reasons, only long-term receivables usually need be evaluated as over- or undervalued. Conceptually, under- or overvalued receivables are treated in the same manner as under- or overvalued liabilities, except that (1) the effect of subsequent amortizations on the income statement is the opposite because we are now on the other side of the balance sheet and (2) the income statement account affected for subsequent amortizations is *Interest Income*—not Interest Expense.

Thus an *overvalued* receivable causes a *credit* to be posted to its account in consolidation. This credit is analogous to a discount and its subsequent amortization to income *increases* interest income so that interest income is reported in subsequent periods based on the current interest rate (at the acquisition date) instead of the contractual interest rate. Likewise, an *undervalued* receivable causes a *debit* to be posted to its account in consolidation. This debit's subsequent amortization to income *reduces* interest income.

"OLD GOODWILL"

Sometimes an acquired business has unamortized goodwill on its books at the acquisition date. In determining the current value of the net assets, this "old goodwill" is assumed to always have a zero value under the requirements of *APBO No. 16.* In the conceptual analysis of the Investment account, old goodwill is treated as an *overvalued* asset in the under- or (over)valuation of net assets element. This allows the goodwill that the parent was willing to pay for to be properly shown as a single amount for which **a single amortization period will be used.** Otherwise, goodwill is considered to comprise two amounts, each with a different life. Assuming that old goodwill of $3,000 exists at the acquisition date and new goodwill is calculated to be $10,000, the consolidation worksheet section pertaining to these accounts appears as follows:

	P Company	S Company	Consolidation Entries Dr.	Consolidation Entries Cr.	Consolidated
Goodwill (old)		3,000		3,000 (2)	–0–
Goodwill (new)			10,000 (2)		10,000

THE PUSH-DOWN BASIS OF ACCOUNTING: A BRIEF LOOK

As stated earlier, the push-down basis of accounting is discussed in detail in Chapter 8.[1] Obviously, accounting for the target company's assets and liabilities on only one set of books is much simpler than the two sets of books involved in the non-push-down basis of accounting. Push-down accounting is simple to apply. It merely requires **adjusting the subsidiary's assets and liabilities to their current values at the acquisition date.** Goodwill paid for is also recorded on the subsidiary's books. For the example used in this chapter, which had $40,000 of cost in excess of the subsidiary's book value of $60,000, the general ledger entries on the subsidiary's books are as follows:

Inventory	4,000	
Land	8,000	
Buildings and Equipment	16,000	
Revaluation Capital[a]		28,000
To adjust assets to current values.		
Goodwill	12,000	
Revaluation Capital[a]		12,000
To reflect goodwill.		

[a]Recall from intermediate accounting that capital is always shown by source.

Consequently, push-down accounting achieves the same results as if the target company's assets had been acquired as shown earlier. The only difference is that the acquired business is accounted for as a **subsidiary**—which has the Common Stock, Retained Earnings, and Revaluation Capital equity accounts—instead of as a **division**—which has the lone Home Office Capital account. Note also that the subsidiary's equity accounts now total $100,000 and in total have a **reciprocal balance** to the parent's Investment in Subsidiary account, which has a $100,000 balance at the acquisition date. Subsequently, the reciprocal balance relationship is maintained under the equity method but not under the cost method.

ASSESSING THE RECOVERABILITY OF GOODWILL

Two professional pronouncements, each of which deals with a specific category of goodwill, address the recoverability of goodwill. Their main elements are summarized here:

1. *SFAS No. 121*, **"Accounting for the Impairment of Long-Lived Assets to Be Disposed Of."** It requires that goodwill associated with assets being tested for recoverability (assets acquired in a *purchase* business combination in which goodwill arose) be included as part of the asset grouping in determining recoverability. (Proration of goodwill is required if only one or some of the purchased assets are being evaluated for impairment.) If such an asset is impaired, the carrying amount of the identified goodwill is eliminated *before* reducing the carrying amounts of (1) the impaired long-lived asset and (2) identifiable intangibles. Because impairments of long-lived assets are discussed in intermediate accounting texts, we do not discuss this category further.

2. *Accounting Principles Board Opinion No. 17*, **"Intangible Assets."** This pronouncement pertains to goodwill *not* associated with an asset being tested for recoverability. For such goodwill, *APBO No. 17* requires that a continual assess-

---

[1]In May 1992, the CPA examination had a theory question on push-down accounting for the first time.

ment be made to determine whether subsequent events and circumstances warrant either (1) **a change in the estimated remaining life** (it can never exceed 40 years in total) or (2) **a write-down or write-off of the unamortized balance** (which would never be treated as an extraordinary item). This is one of the most judgmental areas in all of accounting.

TAKING A MAJOR WRITE-DOWN OR WRITE-OFF

A major problem in practice is how to value goodwill when a business begins experiencing operating or financial difficulties. *APBO No. 17* suggests that if the business has a loss for one year or possibly a few consecutive years, serious consideration should be given to lowering the carrying value of goodwill. This guidance focuses entirely on recoverability.

RECOVERABILITY VERSUS LOSS OF VALUE   When a company is reporting losses, the goodwill obviously is *not* being recovered—that is, it is not being converted back into cash. Thus as long as the business is profitable or breaking even, the goodwill is being recovered. Unfortunately, by focusing solely on recoverability, accountants lose sight of the real issue, which is **whether the value of the goodwill has diminished.** A company does not have to incur losses for goodwill to have diminished in value. It can lose its value when a company becomes marginally profitable, operates at a break-even point, or operates at a level far below that anticipated when the business was acquired.

Far too often, goodwill is carried on the books long after its value has diminished as a result of poor (but still profitable) operating results. Perhaps the most glaring example of all time of reporting goodwill as an asset long after it should have been cleared off the balance sheet is given in the accompanying Case in Point.

CASE IN POINT

Goodwill Recoverability: Denial or Misrepresentation?

Financial Corporation of America (FCA) was the parent of American Savings and Loan (American), the largest savings and loan (S&L) in the country in the 1980s. FCA acquired American in 1983, paying $1.1 billion for goodwill, which it chose to amortize over 30 years. In 1984, American incurred a loss of $600 million, wiping out 75% of its stockholders' equity. American was so financially distressed that the federal regulators imposed stringent operating restrictions (a common procedure when the equity of a federal S&L drops below the minimum 3% of total assets). American was barely profitable in 1985 and 1986. In 1987, it reported another huge loss ($470 million), which lowered stockholders' equity to a negative $170 million.

From 1984 through 1988, American (with more than $30 billion in assets) was the number one problem institution of the federal regulators. After numerous attempts to sell it failed, American was finally sold at the end of 1988, with federal agencies agreeing to provide aid of $1.7 billion. During these five years of troubled times, American's supposedly independent auditors did not insist on, nor did management make, a write-down or write-off of goodwill. At the time of the disposal, $950 million of unamortized goodwill was written off—none of it having been recovered from the sales proceeds.

X   STEP ACQUISITIONS RESULTING IN 100% OWNERSHIP

Earlier we discussed only situations in which one entity acquired 100% of another entity's outstanding common stock in a single transaction. In many cases, however, an entity acquires blocks of another entity's common stock in a series of steps over time until achieving control as a result of having acquired the last block of stock (for example, acquiring 25%, then 5%, and then 70%). Such acquisitions are called **step acquisitions.**

VALUING THE INVESTMENT IN THE INVESTEE PRIOR TO ACHIEVING CONTROL

Until control is achieved, the *investor* (not a *parent* yet) accounts for its investment in the *investee* as follows:

1. **When Significant Influence Does *Not* Exist (typically less than 20% ownership):** Use either (1) cost (when the investee's common stock is *not* publicly traded) or (2) the fair value, as prescribed by *SFAS No. 115*, "Accounting for Certain Investments in Debt and Equity Securities" (when the investee's common stock *is* publicly traded).

2. **When Significant Influence *Does* Exist (typically 20–50% ownership situations).** Use the equity method of accounting as prescribed in *APB Opinion No. 18*, "The Equity Method of Accounting for Investments in Common Stock."

POSSIBLE SEQUENCES TO ACHIEVING CONTROL

An investor could follow three possible sequences of step transactions that would eventually result in control:

Sequence 1: **From *never* having had significant influence to obtaining control** (for example, 10% + 90% = 100%), thus bypassing the 20–50% ownership range.

Sequence 2: **From having significant influence to obtaining control** (for example, 30% + 70% = 100%), thus bypassing the *less than* 20% ownership range.

Sequence 3: **From *not* having significant influence, to having significant influence, to obtaining control** (for example, 10% + 30% + 60% = 100%), thus *not* bypassing the earlier two ownership ranges.

DETERMINING THE PURCHASE PRICE (COST OF ACQUISITION)

Under *all* three sequences, the parent's purchase price (the cost of the acquisition) is determined by summing (1) the *carrying value* of the Investment account *immediately prior* to acquiring the block of stock that results in control and (2) the cost of the block of stock that results in control.

Furthermore, **under *all* three sequences,** the purchase price is then analyzed in the same manner as when 100% of an entity's common stock is acquired in a single transaction as explained earlier in the chapter. Thus the purchase price is analyzed **using the fair values of the acquired entity's identifiable assets and liabilities at the date on which control is achieved.**

UNIQUE ASPECTS ASSOCIATED WITH EACH POSSIBLE SEQUENCE

Each of the three possible sequences used to achieve control has a unique accounting aspect that we now discuss.

SEQUENCE 1: FROM *NEVER* HAVING HAD SIGNIFICANT INFLUENCE TO OBTAINING CONTROL (10% + 90% = 100%)

In this situation, when the earlier investment (1) is carried at fair value (pursuant to the requirements of *SFAS No. 115*), (2) is classified as an "available-for-sale" security pursuant to *SFAS No. 115*, and (3) has an unrealized holding gain or loss (which is reported in equity pursuant to *SFAS No. 115*), such unrealized gains and losses are to be reversed.

SEQUENCE 2: FROM HAVING SIGNIFICANT INFLUENCE TO OBTAINING CONTROL (30% + 70% = 100%)

In this situation, the investor has had to account for its earlier investment using the *equity method* of accounting. In doing so, the investor will have (1) analyzed the cost of this earlier investment and determined individual components thereof (one component that usually exists is goodwill) and (2) amortized a portion of its investment cost to income, if appropriate.

Thus *immediately prior* to acquiring the block of stock that results in control, the analysis of the parent's earlier investment may show that a "layer" exists as to goodwill and other under- or overvalued assets of the investee. If one or more additional blocks of stock are acquired and control does *not* result, additional layers will also exist. Layers that exist for goodwill and these other components *immediately prior* to the date on which control is obtained **are *not* carried forward and used in any way.** They are purged. Thus goodwill and other components are recalculated on a "fresh" basis at the date of control using the fair values at that date. We demonstrate this situation shortly.

SEQUENCE 3: FROM *NOT* HAVING SIGNIFICANT INFLUENCE, TO HAVING SIGNIFICANT INFLUENCE, TO OBTAINING CONTROL (10% + 30% + 60% = 100%)

The only difference between this situation and Sequence 2 is that the investor has to deal with changing accounting principles to the *equity method* when it achieves significant influence and thus establish a layer at that time. We do not demonstrate how to do this because it would repeat a topic discussed in intermediate accounting.

ILLUSTRATION	ANALYZING THE INVESTMENT ACCOUNT FOR A STEP ACQUISITION—SIGNIFICANT INFLUENCE PERIOD EXISTED

Assume the following block acquisition information:

			Information Relating to Investee		
			BOOK VALUE ELEMENT		UNDER- OR (OVER)VALUATION OF NET ASSETS ELEMENT
Ownership Percentage Acquired	Date Block Was Acquired	Investor's Cost	Common Stock	Retained Earnings	Land[a]
30%	January 1, 19X1	$ 52,000	$10,000	$ 60,000	$50,000
	+ 19X1 net income.			40,000	
	− 19X1 dividends declared.			(10,000)	
10%	January 1, 19X2	$ 23,000	$10,000	$ 90,000	$70,000
	+ 19X2 net income (6 mo.).			20,000	
	− 19X2 dividends declared			−0−	
60%	July 1, 19X2	$155,000	$10,000	$110,000	$75,000
100%					

[a]For simplicity, we assume that the entire undervaluation of net assets relates to a parcel of land held by the investee.

In Illustration 5–7, we use the above information to show the analysis of the Investment account through the date that control was obtained.

ILLUSTRATION 5–7	Analysis of Investment Account—Step Acquisition

Ownership Percentage Acquired		Investor's Cost =	BOOK VALUE ELEMENT			UNDER- OR (OVER)VALUATION OF NET ASSETS ELEMENT		GOODWILL ELEMENT[d]
			Common Stock +	Retained Earnings +		Land +		
	Assigned Life					Indefinite		4 Yrs.
30%	**Block Purchase—1/1/X1**	$ 52,000	$ 3,000[a]	$ 18,000[b]		$15,000[c]		$16,000
	+ Equity in net income							
	(30% of $40,000).	12,000		12,000				
	– Dividends (30% of $10,000) . . .	(3,000)		(3,000)				
	– Amortization ($16,000/4)	(4,000)						(4,000)
30%	Balances, 12/31/X1.	$ 57,000	$ 3,000	$ 27,000		$15,000		$12,000
10%	**+ Block purchase—1/1/X2**	23,000	1,000	9,000		7,000[e]		6,000
	Balances, 1/1/X2.	$ 80,000	$ 4,000	$ 36,000		$22,000		$18,000
	+ Equity in net income for 6 mo.							
	(40% of $20,000).	8,000		8,000				
	– Dividends (40%).	–0–		–0–				
	– Amortization:							
	Block 1 ($16,000/4 × 1/2 yr.) . . .	(2,000)						(2,000)
	Block 2 ($6,000/3 × 1/2 yr.)	(1,000)						(1,000)
40%	Balances, 6/30/X2.	$ 85,000	$ 4,000	$ 44,000		$22,000		$15,000
60%	**+ Block purchase—7/1/X2**	155,000	6,000	66,000				
100%	Balances, 7/1/X2.	$240,000	$10,000	$110,000		$75,000[f]		$45,000[g]

[a]Calculated at 30% of $10,000. (Subsequent additions to this column are based on ownership percentages and book values.)

[b]Calculated at 30% of $60,000. (Subsequent additions to this column are based on ownership percentages and book values.)

[c]Calculated at 30% of $50,000 of undervaluation at this date.

[d]A remaining life of four years from the initial acquisition date is used to amortize goodwill. Thus the $6,000 of goodwill from the second block purchase has a 3-year life. All additions to this column are determined residually.

[e]Calculated at 10% of the $70,000 of undervaluation at this date.

[f]Calculated at 100% of the $75,000 of undervaluation at this date.

[g]Determined residually using fair values at this date.

END-OF-CHAPTER REVIEW

SUMMARY OF KEY POINTS

1. The total cost of an acquisition is the sum of (1) the **fair value** of the consideration given, (2) any **direct costs** clearly **traceable** to the acquisition, and (3) the fair value of any **contingent consideration.**

2. The acquisition of either assets or common stock results in a **revaluation** of the assets and liabilities of the acquired business to their **current values.**

3. When **assets are acquired,** the acquired assets and assumed liabilities are recorded at their current values **directly in the books of the acquiring company** (which may require the creation of a new general ledger at the division level if **decentralized accounting** is used).

4. When **common stock is acquired,** the revaluation to current values is done by making adjustments to the subsidiary's book values **in the consolidation process (non-push-**

down accounting). The alternative is to have the subsidiary **adjust its general ledger accounts (push-down accounting).**

5. Under the **non-push-down basis of accounting,** the amounts reported by the subsidiary are wholly irrelevant from the perspective of the parent.
6. In a **step acquisition,** the parent's **cost of the acquisition** is the sum of (1) the **carrying value of the earlier investments** at date on which control is obtained and (2) the cost of the block of stock that resulted in control.
7. In a **step acquisition,** the amounts assigned to over- or undervalued assets are based on the **fair values on the date on which control is obtained.** At this date, balances identified with the earlier investments are discarded. Thus no "layering" occurs.

GLOSSARY OF NEW TERMS

Bargain purchase element   The amount by which the cost of the investment is *below* the current value of an acquired business's net assets.

Contingent consideration   Consideration that must be paid if certain future conditions are satisfied.

Goodwill   The amount by which the cost of the investment is *above* the current value of an acquired business's net assets.

Non-push-down basis of accounting   The subsidiary retains its historical cost basis in accounting for its assets and liabilities. (Adjustments to current values are made in the consolidation process.)

Push-down basis of accounting   The subsidiary's assets and liabilities are adjusted to their current values in the general ledger based on the parent's cost.

Step acquisition   An acquisition in which blocks of an investee company's outstanding common stock are acquired over time until the ownership level results in control over the investee.

SELF-STUDY QUESTIONS

(Answers are at the end of this chapter, preceding the appendix.)

1. A business combination is accounted for appropriately as a purchase. Which of the following should be deducted in determining the combined corporation's net income for the current period?

	Direct Costs of Acquisition	General Expenses Related to Acquisition
a.	Yes	No
b.	Yes	Yes
c.	No	Yes
d.	No	No

2. Pitt Inc. acquired all of Seed Inc.'s assets by (1) giving cash of $200,000, (2) issuing 3,000 shares of common stock that had a market value of $100 per share, and (3) assuming responsibility for all of Seed's liabilities totaling $400,000 (at book value and current value). Seed's assets have a book value of $800,000 and a current appraised value of $1,100,000. For financial reporting purposes, each company has or reports

	Pitt	Seed
a.	Goodwill.	Negative goodwill.
b.	Gain on acquisition.	Loss on disposal.
c.	Negative goodwill.	Bargain purchase element.
d.	Bargain purchase element.	Gain on disposal.
e.	None of the above.	

3. Assume the information in Question 2. In recording the acquisition, each company would

	Pitt	Seed
a.	Debit Investment in Seed Inc.	Debit Common Stock.
b.	Credit Common Stock.	Debit Investment in Pitt Inc.
c.	Credit Common Stock.	Make no entry.
d.	Credit Bargain Purchase Element.	Debit Investment in Pitt Inc.
e.	Do none of the above.	

4. Pax Inc. acquired 100% of the outstanding common stock of Sax Inc. in exchange for cash. The acquisition price exceeds the fair value of the net assets. How should Pax determine the amounts to be reported for Sax's inventories and long-term debt in its consolidated statements?

	Inventories	Long-Term Debt
a.	Fair value	Sax's carrying amount
b.	Fair value	Fair value
c.	Sax's carrying amount	Fair value
d.	Sax's carrying amount	Sax's carrying amount

5. On 4/1/X6, Place Inc. paid $400,000 for 100% of the issued and outstanding common stock of Show Inc. in a transaction properly accounted for as a purchase. Show's assets and liabilities on 4/1/X6 are as follows:

Cash	$ 40,000
Inventory	120,000
Property and equipment (net of accumulated depreciation of $160,000)	240,000
Liabilities	(90,000)

On 4/1/X6, the current value of Show's inventory was $95,000, and its property and equipment (net) had a current value of $280,000. What is the amount of goodwill as a result of the business combination?

a. $–0–   **b.** $25,000   **c.** $75,000   **d.** $90,000

6. Page Inc. acquired 100% of Sage Inc.'s outstanding common stock at a total cost of $100,000. Sage's net assets have a book value of $60,000 and a current value of $90,000. In the parent's general ledger, how much would be shown in the Goodwill account?

a. $–0–   **b.** $10,000   **c.** $30,000   **d.** $40,000

7. Patro Inc. acquired 100% of the outstanding common stock of Satro Inc. at a total cost of $200,000. Satro's net assets have a book value of $160,000 and a current value of $210,000. In the consolidated financial statements, which of the following would be reported?

a. Goodwill of $10,000.   **c.** Goodwill of $40,000.
b. A deferred credit of $10,000.   **d.** None of the above.

(AICPA adapted, Nos. 2, 4, 5)

DEMONSTRATION PROBLEM 1: ACQUISITION OF COMMON STOCK

On 6/30/X3, Pane Inc. acquired 100% of Sill Inc.'s outstanding common stock by issuing 20,000 shares of its $1 par value common stock (having a market price of $30 per share). Pane incurred legal and accounting fees of $75,000, of which $25,000 pertained to registering the shares issued with the SEC. If Sill's sales for the two years ended 6/30/X5 exceed $8 million, then Pane must issue an additional 4,000 shares of common stock to Sill's former owners. The balances in the capital accounts of the subsidiary as of the acquisition date are as follows:

Common Stock	$ 40,000
Retained Earnings	360,000
	$400,000

All of Seed's assets and liabilities had a current value equal to their book value, except the following:

	Book Value	Current Value
Land	$150,000	$270,000
Long-term debt, 8%	200,000	230,000

Sill had $20,000 of goodwill on its books as of the acquisition date that Sill's management believes is fully realizable. Of the $75,000 incurred for legal and accounting fees, $33,000 was paid by 6/30/X3, and charged to a Deferred Charges account pending consummation of the acquisition. The remaining $42,000 has not been paid or accrued.

Required
1. Prepare the entry to record the acquisition.
2. Prepare an expanded analysis of the investment account.
3. Prepare the consolidation entries at 6/30/X3.

SOLUTION TO DEMONSTRATION PROBLEM 1

1. Investment in Sill Inc.

(20,000 shares × $30 market price)	600,000	
Common Stock (20,000 shares × $1 par)		20,000
Additional Paid-in Capital		580,000
To record issuance of common stock.		

Investment in Sill Inc.	50,000	
Additional Paid-in Capital	25,000	
Deferred Charges		33,000
Accrued Liabilities		42,000
To record direct acquisition costs of $50,000 and		
$25,000 cost of registering common stock.		

No entry would be made pertaining to the contingent consideration at this time. Disclosure would be made in the notes to the financial statements.

2.

	Parent's Investment Account— Book Value	BOOK VALUE ELEMENT	
		Subsidiary's Equity Accounts	
	=	Common Stock +	Retained Earnings
Balances, 6/30/X3	$400,000	$40,000	$360,000

	Parent's Investment Account— Excess Cost	UNDER- OR (OVER)VALUATION OF NET ASSETS ELEMENT			GOODWILL
	= +	Land +	Old Goodwill +	L-T Debt +	ELEMENT
Balances, 6/30/X3 ...	$250,000	$120,000	$(20,000)	$(30,000)	$180,000

3. The basic elimination entry:

Common Stock	40,000	
Retained Earnings	360,000	
Investment in Subsidiary		400,000

4. The excess cost entry:

Land	120,000	
Goodwill (new)	180,000	

Goodwill (old)	20,000
Long-Term Debt	30,000
Investment in Subsidiary	250,000

DEMONSTRATION PROBLEM 2: ACQUISITION OF ASSETS

Pitt Inc. acquired 100% of Seed Inc.'s assets by (1) giving cash of $100,000; (2) issuing 2,000 shares of its $5 par value common stock that had a market value of $150 per share; and (3) assuming responsibility for *all* of Seed's liabilities having a book value and current value of $500,000. Seed's assets have a book value of $840,000 and a current value of $950,000. Assume *centralized* accounting is to be used by Pitt.

Required   Prepare the entries to be recorded by *both* companies as a result of this business combination.

SOLUTION TO DEMONSTRATION PROBLEM 2

Pitt Inc.

Assets (net of $50,000 bargain purchase element)	900,000	
Cash		100,000
Common Stock (2,000 shares × $5 par)		10,000
Additional Paid-in Capital		290,000
Liabilities		500,000
To record acquisition of Seed Inc.'s assets.		

Seed Inc.

Cash	100,000	
Liabilities	500,000	
Investment in Pitt Inc. (2,000 shares @ $150/share)	300,000	
Assets		840,000
Gain on Sale of Assets		60,000
To record sale of assets.		

ASSIGNMENT MATERIAL

REVIEW QUESTIONS

1. What is the essence of the *purchase method* of accounting?
2. What two basic questions must be answered with respect to the purchase method of accounting?
3. What types of consideration can the acquiring entity give in a business combination?
4. When is it preferable in recording a business combination to use the *fair value* of the *equity securities* issued instead of the *current value* of the *net assets* of the acquired business?
5. How should *direct costs* incurred in a business combination be treated?
6. What is contingent consideration and how should it be accounted for?
7. What are the three major conceptual elements into which the cost of an investment could possibly be separated?
8. In which situations would only one major conceptual element exist? In which situation would only two major conceptual elements exist?
9. What is the purpose of separating the cost of the investment into the individual components of the major conceptual elements?
10. Why is there no separate account for goodwill on the parent company's books (under *non-push-down accounting*)?
11. If the acquiring entity's cost equals or is more than the target company's net assets at book value, can it be said that the acquirer purchased the target's retained earnings?
12. Under non-push-down accounting, why are the subsidiary's reported amounts deemed not relevant?
13. In *step acquisitions* in which the investor has never had significant influence, what unique aspect must be dealt with at the date control is obtained?

14. In *step acquisitions*, does "layering" of goodwill occur in the consolidated balance sheet?
15. In *step acquisitions*, how are the excess cost components of an investor's Investment account as determined for the *earlier acquisitions* dealt with when control is achieved?

TECHNICAL RESEARCH QUESTIONS

Here and elsewhere in the book, answers to technical research questions may be found by consulting the pronouncements of the FASB, the APB, and the SEC.

1. Pert Products purchases Sprig & Sons and immediately incurs costs to close Sprig's duplicate facilities. Should those costs be added to the cost of the acquisition?
2. Should the costs that Pert incurs in Question 1 be added to the cost of the acquisition if it closes its own duplicate facilities instead?

EXERCISES

E 5–1 **Recording Acquisition of Assets for Cash** Pom Inc. acquired 100% of the assets (except cash of $30,000) and assumed all of the liabilities of Som Inc. for $1,100,000 cash. The acquired business is to be accounted for as a division with a *decentralized* accounting system. Som's assets and liabilities as of the acquisition date are as follows:

	Book Value	Current Value
Cash	$ 30,000	$ 30,000
Accounts receivable, net	80,000	80,000
Inventory	90,000	70,000
Land	100,000	160,000
Buildings and equipment	1,200,000	870,000
Accumulated depreciation	(500,000)	
Total Assets	$1,000,000	$1,210,000
Payables and accruals	$ 100,000	$ 100,000
Long-term debt	200,000	200,000
Total Liabilities	$ 300,000	$ 300,000
Total Stockholders' Equity	$ 700,000	910,000
Total Liabilities and Equity	$1,000,000	$1,210,000

Required 1. Prepare the entry to record the acquisition on the books of both the home office and the newly formed division.
2. How would the entries differ if the accounting for the acquired business were *centralized*?

E 5–2 **Recording Acquisition of Assets for Stock** Assume the same information as in Exercise 5–1, except that Pom issued 10,000 shares of its common stock ($5 par value), which was selling for $110 per share at the acquisition date, instead of giving cash to effect the business combination.

Required 1. Prepare the entry to record the acquisition on the books of both the home office and the newly formed division.
2. How would the entries differ if the accounting for the acquired business were *centralized*?

E 5–3 **Recording Acquisition of Common Stock for Cash and Stock** Purl Inc. acquired 100% of the outstanding common stock of Surl Inc. for $2,300,000 cash and 10,000 shares of its common stock ($2 par value), which was traded at $40 per share at the acquisition date.

Required Prepare the entry to record the business combination.

E 5–4 **Recording Direct Costs** Assume the same information provided in Exercise 5–3. In addition, assume that Purl incurred the following direct costs:

Legal fees for preparing the acquisition agreement	$ 47,000
Accounting fees for the purchase investigation	17,000
Travel expenses for meetings held with Surl management	8,000
Legal fees for registering the common stock issued with the SEC	32,000

Accounting fees for the review of unaudited financial statements and other data included in the registration statement	16,000
SEC filing fees	4,000
	$124,000

Prior to the consummation date, $103,000 had been paid and charged to a Deferred Charges suspense account pending consummation of the acquisition. The remaining $21,000 has *not* been paid or accrued.

Required   Prepare the journal entry to record the business combination and the direct costs.

E 5–5   **Contingent Consideration: Future Sales**   Poly Inc. acquired 100% of the outstanding common stock of Soly Inc. for $1,000,000 cash. If Soly's cumulative sales for the three years subsequent to the acquisition date exceed $10,000,000, the additional cash of $200,000 is to be paid to Soly's former shareholders.

Required   Prepare the entry to record the business combination. Explain the accounting treatment of the contingent consideration. What is the entry if Soly's cumulative sales exceed $10,000,000?

E 5–6   **Contingent Consideration: *Existing* Security Price to Be Maintained**   Palco Inc. acquired 100% of Salco Inc.'s outstanding common stock by issuing 80,000 shares of its common stock ($10 par value), which had a market value of $40 per share at the acquisition date. If the market value of Palco's common stock below $40 per share two years after the acquisition date, Palco must issue additional shares at that time to Salco's former shareholders so that the total value of the shares issued equals $3,200,000.

Required   *Note:* You may want to review paragraphs 81 and 82 of *APBO No. 16* before solving.

1. Prepare the entry to record the business combination. Explain the accounting treatment of the contingent consideration.
2. Assume that the market value of Palco's common stock is $32 per share two years later. Prepare the entry to record the additional shares issued.

E 5–7   **Contingent Consideration: *Higher* Security Price to Be Attained**   Phota Inc. acquired 100% of Sota Inc.'s outstanding common stock by issuing 60,000 shares of its common stock ($5 par value), which had a market value of $50 per share as of the acquisition date. If the market value of Phota's common stock is not at least $70 per share two years after the acquisition date, additional shares must be issued to Sota's former shareholders so that the total value of the shares issued equals $4,200,000.

Required   *Note:* Review paragraphs 81 and 82 of *APBO No. 16* before solving.

1. Prepare the entry to record the business combination. Explain the accounting treatment of the contingent consideration.
2. Assume that the market value of Phota's common stock is $60 per share two years later. Prepare the entry to record the additional shares issued.

E 5–8   **Separating Cost into Major Conceptual Elements**   Potasha Inc. acquired 100% of Sulpha Inc.'s outstanding common stock at a cost of $1,000,000. Sulpha's net assets have a book value of $600,000 and a current value of $880,000 as of the acquisition date.

Required   Separate the cost of the investment into its major conceptual elements as of the acquisition date.

E 5–9   **Separating Cost into Major Conceptual Elements**   Pomona Inc. acquired 100% of the outstanding common stock of Sonora Inc., a manufacturing company with extensive manufacturing facilities, at a cost of $2,000,000. Sonora's net assets have a book value of $1,800,000 and a current value of $2,100,000 as of the acquisition date.

Required   Separate the cost of the investment into its major conceptual elements as of the acquisition date.

E 5–10   **Separating Cost into Components of the Major Conceptual Elements**   Penn Inc. acquired all of Senn Inc.'s outstanding common stock for $800,000 cash. (Assume that there were no direct costs or contingent consideration.) Information about Senn as of the acquisition date is as follows:

	Book Value	Current Value
Cash	$ 50,000	$ 50,000
Accounts receivable, net	100,000	100,000
Inventory	200,000	210,000
Land	300,000	420,000
Buildings and equipment	670,000	680,000
Accumulated depreciation	(120,000)	
Total Assets	$1,200,000	$1,460,000
Payables and accruals	$ 100,000	$ 100,000
Long-term debt	600,000	625,000
Total Liabilities	$ 700,000	$ 725,000
Common stock	$ 50,000	
Additional paid-in capital	300,000	
Retained earnings	150,000	
Total Stockholders' Equity	$ 500,000	735,000
Total Liabilities and Equity	$1,200,000	$1,460,000

Required **1.** Separate the cost of the investment into the individual components of the major conceptual elements as of the acquisition date.

2. Explain why the current value of the long-term debt is higher than its book value.

PROBLEMS

P 5–1   Analyzing Cost   Perusal Inc. acquired 100% of Scanner Inc.'s outstanding stock for $1,500,000 cash. Information with respect to Scanner as of the acquisition date is as follows:

	Book Value	Current Value
Cash	$ 55,000	$ 55,000
Accounts receivable, net	180,000	180,000
Notes receivable	100,000	60,000
Inventory	300,000	330,000
Land	500,000	600,000
Buildings and equipment	600,000[a]	750,000
Patent	45,000	105,000
Goodwill, net of amortization to date	120,000	See note.
Total Assets	$1,900,000	
Payables and accruals	$ 300,000	$ 300,000
Long-term debt (10% bonds)	700,000	650,000
Total Liabilities	$1,000,000	
Common stock	$ 100,000	
Additional paid-in capital	500,000	
Retained earnings	300,000	
Total Stockholders' Equity	$ 900,000	
Total Liabilities and Equity	$1,900,000	

[a]Net of accumulated depreciation of $123,000.

Note   The $120,000 of unamortized goodwill arose from Scanner's acquisition two years ago of the assets of a local competitor. The goodwill is being amortized over 10 years. During the negotiations with Perusal, Scanner's management indicated that these acquired operations have produced superior earnings since acquisition, which are expected to continue for at least another eight years.

Required **1.** For other than existing goodwill, what procedures and guidelines are used to determine current values of assets acquired and liabilities assumed? (Refer to paragraphs 87 and 88 of *APBO No. 16*.)

2. As to the 10% bonds payable, is the current rate of interest more or less than 10%? Will future interest expense be at a rate more or less than 10%?

3. Separate the investment cost into the individual components of the major conceptual elements.

4. Prepare all consolidation entries as of the acquisition date.

P 5–2 **Analyzing Cost** Pladd Inc. acquired 100% of Stripes Inc.'s outstanding common stock for $310,000 cash. Information about Stripes as of the acquisition date is as follows:

	Book Value	Current Value
Cash	$ 20,000	$ 20,000
Accounts receivable, net	40,000	40,000
Inventory	200,000	140,000
Land	90,000	300,000
Buildings, net	130,000[a]	180,000
Equipment, net	100,000[b]	120,000
Total Assets	$580,000	$800,000
Payables and accruals	$100,000	$100,000
Long-term debt	280,000	280,000
Total Liabilities	$380,000	$380,000
Common stock	$ 30,000	
Additional paid-in capital	270,000	
Accumulated deficit	(100,000)	
Total Stockholders' Equity	$200,000	420,000
Total Liabilities and Equity	$580,000	$800,000

[a]Net of accumulated depreciation of $55,000.
[b]Net of accumulated depreciation of $44,000.

Required
1. Separate the investment cost into the components of the major conceptual elements.
2. Prepare all consolidation entries as of the acquisition date.

P 5–3 **Analyzing Cost** Plugg Inc. acquired 100% of Sparks Inc.'s outstanding common stock for $150,000 cash. Information about Sparks, which leases its manufacturing facilities and is in poor financial condition as of the acquisition date, is as follows:

	Book Value	Current Value
Cash	$ 20,000	$ 20,000
Accounts receivable, net	380,000	380,000
Inventory	300,000	270,000
Equipment, net	100,000[a]	60,000
Total Assets	$800,000	$730,000
Payables and accruals	$450,000	$450,000
Long-term debt	50,000	50,000
Total Liabilities	$500,000	$500,000
Common stock	$210,000	
Additional paid-in capital	340,000	
Accumulated deficit	(250,000)	
Total Stockholders' Equity	$300,000	230,000
Total Liabilities and Equity	$800,000	$730,000

[a]Net of accumulated depreciation of $77,000.

Required
1. Separate the investment cost into the components of the major conceptual elements.
2. Prepare all consolidation entries as of the acquisition date.

P 5–4* **Consolidation Worksheet** Pya Inc., which is a calendar-year–reporting company, acquired 100% of Sya Inc.'s outstanding common stock at a cost of $300,000 on 12/31/X1. The analysis of Pya's investment account by the individual components of the major conceptual elements as of the acquisition date is as follows:

Book value element:
Common stock	$100,000
Retained earnings	90,000

Under- or (over)valuation of net assets element:
Inventory	5,000
Land	30,000
Equipment	50,000
Patent	(15,000)
Goodwill element	40,000
Cost	$300,000

Each company's financial statements for the year ended 12/31/X1 immediately *after* the acquisition are as follows:

	Pya Inc.	Sya Inc.
Income Statement (19X1)		
Sales	$2,500,000	$500,000
Cost of sales	(1,400,000)	(250,000)
Expenses	(860,000)	(202,000)
Net Income	$ 240,000	$ 48,000
Balance Sheet (as of 12/31/X1)		
Cash	$ 100,000	$ 20,000
Accounts receivable, net	200,000	55,000
Inventory	350,000	80,000
Investment in Sya (total cost)	300,000	
Land	400,000	70,000
Buildings and equipment	800,000	203,000
Accumulated depreciation	(150,000)	(43,000)
Patent		15,000
Total Assets	$2,000,000	$400,000
Payables and accruals	$ 250,000	$ 60,000
Long-term debt	1,000,000	150,000
Common stock	300,000	100,000
Retained earnings	450,000	90,000
Total Liabilities and Equity	$2,000,000	$400,000
Dividends declared in 19X1	$ 80,000	$ 10,000

Required

1. Prepare all consolidation entries as of 12/31/X1. (First split the Investment account into the book value element and the excess cost elements.)
2. Prepare a consolidation worksheet as of 12/31/X1.

P 5–5* **Consolidation Worksheet** Poz Inc., which is a calendar-year–reporting company, acquired 100% of Soz Inc.'s outstanding common stock at a cost of $400,000 on 12/31/X1. The analysis of Poz's Investment account by the individual components of the major conceptual elements as of the acquisition date is as follows:

Book value element:
Common stock	$ 50,000
Additional paid-in capital	200,000
Retained earnings	250,000

Under- or (over)valuation of net assets element:
Inventory	(70,000)
Land	30,000
Building	(100,000)
Long-term debt	40,000
Cost	$400,000

Each company's financial statements for the year ended 12/31/X1 immediately after the acquisition are as follows:

	Poz	Soz
Income Statement (19X1)		
Sales	$6,000,000	$800,000
Cost of sales	(3,300,000)	(600,000)
Expenses	(1,500,000)	(250,000)
Net Income	$1,200,000	$ (50,000)
Balance Sheet (as of 12/31/X1)		
Cash	$ 240,000	$ 30,000
Accounts receivable, net	360,000	50,000
Inventory	800,000	220,000
Investment in Soz (total cost)	400,000	
Land	500,000	100,000
Buildings and equipment	2,600,000	553,000
Accumulated depreciation	(400,000)	(53,000)
Total Assets	$4,500,000	$900,000
Payables and accruals	$ 800,000	$100,000
Long-term debt	2,100,000	300,000
Common stock	20,000	50,000
Additional paid-in capital	480,000	200,000
Retained earnings	1,100,000	250,000
Total Liabilities and Equity	$4,500,000	$900,000
Dividends declared during 19X1	$ 700,000	–0–

Required   **1.** Prepare all consolidation entries as of 12/31/X1. (First split the Investment account into the book value element and the excess cost elements.)
   2. Prepare a consolidation worksheet as of 12/31/X1.

P 5–6* **Analyzing Cost and Consolidation Worksheet**   Pud Inc. acquired 100% of Sud Inc.'s outstanding common stock for $900,000 cash on 1/1/X1. Pud also incurred $55,000 of costs in connection with the acquisition. Of this amount, $15,000 was a finder's fee, $12,000 an allocation of overhead from the mergers and acquisition department, and $8,000 an allocated portion of the president's salary (the president had devoted approximately 20% of her time during 19X0 to the merger). The remaining $20,000 was for legal and accounting fees and travel costs.

Financial data for each company immediately *before* the acquisition are as follows:

	Pud Inc. Book Value	Sud Inc. Book Value	Sud Inc. Current Value
Cash	$1,345,000	$ 100,000	$ 100,000
Accounts receivable, net	900,000	140,000	140,000
Notes receivable		80,000	60,000
Inventory	1,100,000	310,000	340,000
Land	500,000	250,000	410,000
Buildings and equipment	4,500,000	800,000	620,000
Accumulated depreciation	(1,400,000)	(300,000)	
Patent, net	200,000	40,000	100,000
Goodwill, net of amortization		80,000	
Deferred acquisition costs	55,000		
Total Assets	$7,200,000	$1,500,000	$1,770,000
Payables and accruals	$1,800,000	$ 250,000	$ 250,000
Long-term debt	4,000,000	600,000	670,000
Common stock	600,000	150,000	
Retained earnings	800,000	500,000	
Total Liabilities and Equity	$7,200,000	$1,500,000	

If Sud's sales for 19X2 exceed $850,000, Pud must pay an additional $60,000 cash to Sud's stock-holders. Management is optimistic that this sales level can be attained.

Required 1. Analyze the investment account by the components of the major conceptual elements as of 1/1/X1.
2. Prepare the consolidation entries as of 1/1/X1.
3. Prepare a consolidation worksheet as of 1/1/X1.

P 5–7* **Acquisition of Assets** Use the same information provided in Problem 5–6, except that (1) all of the assets were acquired instead of all of the common stock and (2) Pud assumed all of Sud's liabilities.

Required 1. Prepare Pud's entries to record the acquisition, assuming a decentralized accounting system is used.
2. Prepare the combining entry as of 1/1/X1.
3. Prepare a combining statement worksheet as of 1/1/X1.

P 5–8 **Step Acquisition: No Significant Influence** Penco acquired two blocks of Senco, a family-owned company. Related information is as follows:

| | | | Information Relating to Investee | | |
Percentage Acquired	Date Block Was Acquired	Penco's Cost	Common Stock	Retained Earnings	Undervaluation of Net Assets
10%	1/1/X4	$ 100,000	$400,000	$300,000	$ 80,000
90%	12/31/X6	1,200,000	400,000	640,000	110,000
100%					

Additional information:

1. Senco's only under- or (over)valued asset or liability at 1/1/X4 and 12/31/X6 was land.
2. Senco declared cash dividends on its common stock of $90,000 in 19X4, 19X5, and 19X6.
3. Penco was *not* able to exert significant influence after acquiring the first block of stock.
4. No impairment of value adjustment was made to Penco's Investment account in 19X4, 19X5, or 19X6.

Required 1. Prepare a conceptual analysis of the Investment account through the date control was achieved.
2. Prepare all consolidation entries at 12/31/X2.

P 5–9 **Step Acquisition: Significant Influence** Pomco acquired blocks of Somco's outstanding common stock over a two-year period. Related information is as follows:

| | | | Information Relating to Investee | | |
Percentage Acquired	Date Block Was Acquired	Pomco's Cost	Common Stock	Retained Earnings	Undervaluation of Net Assets
20%	1/1/X1	$ 35,000	$100,000	$ 25,000	not obtainable
20%	1/1/X2	56,000	100,000	55,000	not obtainable
60%	12/31/X2	216,000	100,000	120,000	$40,000
100%					

Additional information:

1. Somco's only under- or (over)valued asset or liability at 12/31/X2 was land.
2. Somco declared cash dividends on common stock of $15,000 in both 19X1 and 19X2.
3. Pomco uses a 5-year life for any purchased goodwill identified at any particular block acquisition date.
4. Pomco *was* able to exert significant influence after acquiring the first block of stock.

Required 1. Prepare a conceptual analysis of the Investment account through the date control was achieved.
2. Prepare all consolidation entries at 12/31/X2.

✴ THINKING CRITICALLY ✴

✴ CASES ✴

C 5–1   **Manner of Reporting "Cost in Excess of Net Assets"**   Hyde Company's 12/31/X1 consolidated balance sheet has the following described asset:

Excess of cost over related net assets of businesses acquired $75,000,000

The related footnote reads as follows:

The excess of cost over related net assets applicable to businesses acquired prior to November 1, 1970, amounts to $11,000,000 and is not amortized because it is believed to have continuing value; the balance applicable to businesses acquired after October 31, 1970, is being amortized on a straight-line basis over 40 years.

Required   1. Is the title of the asset informative?
2. What does the asset represent?
3. What is the theoretical justification for amortizing only part of this amount?

C 5–2   **Assigning Excess of Cost over Book Value**   Ponda Inc., a highly diversified company, acquired 100% of the outstanding common stock of three companies during the current year. In each case, Ponda's cost was $500,000 in excess of the $4,000,000 book value of the net assets. The reason it paid more than the book value of the net assets of each company is stated below:

1. **Acquisition of Ironex Inc.** Ironex mines iron ore from land it owns. Ponda acquired Ironex to ensure a continual supply of iron ore for its steel-making operation.
2. **Acquisition of Memco Inc.** Memco manufactures high-quality memory chips for computers. Few companies can manufacture high-quality chips of this type. Ponda acquired Memco to ensure a continual supply of high-quality memory chips for its computer manufacturing operation.
3. **Acquisition of Farmco Inc.** Farmco manufactures farm machinery and earns a return on investment that is average for its industry. On this basis, Farmco was *not* worth acquiring. Ponda believes, however, that it can bring about substantial efficiencies by integrating Farmco's operations with those of another subsidiary, which also manufactures farm machinery. The combined results are expected to increase substantially the overall return on investment of each previously separate operation.

Required   For each of these acquisitions, determine how you would classify Ponda's cost in excess of book value and how you would account for it in future period consolidated statements.

C 5–3   **Theory: Bargain Purchase Element**   Pinkle Inc. recently acquired 100% of Sinkle Inc.'s assets at an amount *below* their current value. The controller has listed the following ways to account for the bargain purchase element:

1. Credit it to income in the year of the acquisition, possibly classified as an extraordinary item.
2. Amortize it to income over the two-year period needed to turn the acquired operation into a profit-making operation.
3. Allocate it to the acquired assets based on relative current values, thereby lowering the recorded values of these items.
4. Credit it to contributed capital.

Required   Evaluate the theoretical soundness of each alternative regardless of the requirements of *APBO No. 16.*

C 5–4   **Acquiring R&D in Process**   Plado Inc. recently acquired Slado Inc. in a purchase business combination. The acquisition's cost was allocated based on an independent appraisal. Of the $50 million acquisition cost, $18 million was allocated to Research & Development in Process.

Required   How would you report the $18 million in the consolidated balance sheet at the acquisition date? In subsequent period consolidated statements?

C 5–5   **Recording a Liability Before Its Time?**   Palto Inc. and Salto Inc. recently combined in a purchase business combination. Goodwill of $10,000,000 was initially calculated residually (to be amortized over

10 years). To integrate the two operations, certain facilities of both entities will be closed. Consequently, some of the employees will be terminated. The controller has proposed that the estimated severance pay of $4,000,000 ($1,000,000 pertaining to Palto's employees and $3,000,000 pertaining to Salto's employees) be reflected as an undervalued liability of Salto in assigning Palto's cost to Salto's assets and liabilities.

Required 1. How will treating the $4,000,000 as an undervalued liability at the acquisition date impact goodwill?
2. Does a financial reporting benefit result from this proposal?
3. Is this proposed treatment theoretically correct?

C 5–6 **Valuing "Cost in Excess of Net Assets" in Subsequent Years**   Payto Inc. acquired the business of Sayto Inc. on 1/1/X1 at a cost of $800,000 in excess of the current value of Sayto's net assets. Sayto's operations had been unprofitable for the two years preceding the business combination and thus did not possess superior earning power. Payto paid the $800,000 so that it could readily establish itself in this high-risk industry. Payto expects Sayto's operations to report profits within three years. The cost in excess of current value is being amortized over 10 years.

Required 1. Assume that at 12/31/X4, Sayto's operations are still unprofitable. Management is uncertain whether Sayto's operations will ever be profitable. What are the implications of this situation?
2. What if Sayto was only marginally profitable for 19X4 (Payto earning only 6% return on its investment) a situation expected to continue?

※ FINANCIAL ANALYSIS PROBLEMS ※

FAP 5–1 **Evaluating Future Results under the Purchase Method in a Business Combination with a Troubled Savings and Loan**   You are the auditor for Pyramid Savings and Loan Association, which recently acquired 100% of the outstanding common stock of Sham Savings and Loan Association. The combination was structured so that the transaction did *not* qualify for pooling of interests treatment. Sham had incurred losses for approximately two years prior to the combination as a result of paying a higher interest rate to its depositors than it was earning on its loans. Federal regulators arranged the combination to prevent Sham's liquidation because it had exhausted its net worth. Selected data for Sham as of the combination date are as follows:

	Book Value	Current Value
Assets	$300,000,000[a]	$250,000,000
Liabilities	300,000,000	300,000,000
Common stock	12,000,000	
Accumulated deficit	(12,000,000)	

[a]Includes real estate of $270 million.

The current value of the assets is lower than the book value because the current lending rate on home mortgages is 15%, whereas the yield on its loans (which have an average remaining life of 10 years) is only 10%. Accordingly, a $50 million *over*valuation component exists and will be amortized to interest income to report a 15% yield on the loan portfolio's $220 million current value instead of reporting a 10% yield on its $270 million book value. Pyramid did not have to pay any consideration; it merely took title to all of Sham's outstanding common stock. Management intends to amortize goodwill over 40 years.

Required 1. Analyze the Investment account at the acquisition date.
2. Prepare all consolidation entries as of the acquisition date. (Assume that *non-push-down accounting* was used.)
3. For Years 1–10 (in total) and for Years 11–40 (in total), show in T accounts the effect on income of amortizations made from the parent's Investment account.
4. Evaluate the soundness of the results that are reported under the *purchase method* at the acquisition date and for future periods.
5. What, if anything, should be done differently to better reflect the economics of the situation?

FAP 5–2 **Time to Write Down Goodwill: Pick a Number**   On 1/1/X1, Pong Inc. acquired 100% of Spinner Inc.'s outstanding common stock. Spinner's net assets (excluding goodwill) had a current value of $4,000,000.

Pong estimated that Spinner would have $700,000 of average annual earnings for the foreseeable future, which is a 17.5% return on the $4,000,000 of its net assets at current value. For this industry, a 15% return on equity was considered normal. Accordingly, the expected superior earnings were $100,000 (2.5% × $4,000,000). Pong agreed to pay for five years of expected superior earnings, discounted to its present value. In choosing a discount rate, a minimum of 10% was established, inasmuch as this was deemed appropriate for a relatively risk-free investment. Pong added to the 10% minimum an extra 10% for the additional risk associated with this industry. Thus, a 20% discount rate was used in arriving at the present value of the goodwill to be paid for, the calculation of which follows:

Expected superior earnings	$100,000
Present value factor for an annuity of 5 years at 20%	2.9906
Goodwill calculated	$299,060

Accordingly, the purchase price was $4,300,000. This is $4,000,000 for the current value of the net assets and $300,000 (rounded) for the goodwill.

For 19X1 and 19X2, Spinner reported annual earnings of approximately $650,000 (approximately $50,000 below initial expectations). The shortfall was attributable partly to overly optimistic projections and partly to new product innovations introduced by competitors. Management does *not* expect Spinner's future annual earnings to increase beyond $650,000. Pong is amortizing the goodwill over a five-year life.

Required   How much should the unamortized goodwill be written down to at 12/31/X2 (two years later)?

FAP 5–3   **Time to Sell the Family-Owned Business and Retire: Seller Beware!**   Ponzi Equities is a publicly owned company with approximately 5 million common shares outstanding, which are traded (thinly) on the over-the-counter market. During its 15 years of existence, Ponzi issued common stock to acquire all of the outstanding common stock of approximately 20 companies, all of which were small, financially strong, family-owned businesses in which the owner(s) was(were) planning to retire. All of the combinations were structured to obtain purchase accounting.

Required   1. What major item must be addressed in applying the provisions of *APBO No. 16* to purchase business combinations in which common stock is given as consideration?
2. If you were the owner of such a company, what would you do differently if Ponzi offered you common stock as consideration instead of cash?

✳ PERSONAL SITUATIONS: ETHICS AND INTERPERSONAL SKILLS ✳

PS 5–1   **Ethics: Gambling—A Surefire Way to Become an Embezzler?**   The authors know of two former CPA employees of a Big Six accounting firm (both very bright and talented individuals) who (1) went to work for separate companies in industry at controllership positions, (2) were making very respectable salaries (along with stock options), (3) began gambling (evidently because life was not exciting enough for them), and (4) embezzled money to feed their gambling addiction. Each eventually stole nearly $1,500,000, was caught, and was sentenced to a federal penitentiary for eight years. In both cases, their spouses (who became sole providers for the children) divorced them, and their employers recovered one-half of the family's remaining personal assets (the spouses retaining the other half). Thus each professional had largely achieved the good ("yuppie") life.

Required   Would you be willing to throw it all away merely for some extra excitement in your life?

ANSWERS TO SELF-STUDY QUESTIONS

1. c   **2.** d   **3.** b   **4.** b   **5.** c   **6.** a[a]   **7.** d[b]

---

[a]The $10,000 of goodwill is in the parent's Investment account.
[b]The $10,000 bargain purchase element normally would be extinguished.

■APPENDIX

RECORDING DEFERRED TAXES AT THE ACQUISITION DATE

Some business combinations are **purchases** for financial reporting purposes (as distinct from **pooling of interests** business combinations) but are **nontaxable/tax deferred** for income tax-reporting purposes (as distinct from **taxable** combinations). For such asymmetrical combinations, the issue is whether deferred income taxes should be recorded at the combination date for differences between the acquired business's **assigned values** of assets and liabilities (the **new basis of accounting** for financial reporting purposes) and the **tax basis** of those assets and liabilities (based on the **old basis of accounting**). These differences will result in **taxable or tax-deductible amounts** when the asset or liability in the financial statements is later **recovered or settled at its reported amount.** *SFAS 109,* "Accounting for Income Taxes," amended paragraphs 87–89 of *APB Opinion No. 16,* "Business Combinations," so that deferred income taxes must be recorded for these differences. **Goodwill** (because its amortization is nondeductible for tax purposes in this situation) **and unextinguished bargain purchase elements** are excluded from this requirement.

I TAXABLE VERSUS NONTAXABLE PURCHASE COMBINATIONS

Recall from Chapter 4 that most purchase business combinations are taxable combinations for tax-reporting purposes; only a minor percentage are nontaxable (tax deferred). Differences between the assigned values of assets and liabilities and the tax bases of those assets and liabilities nearly **always exist in nontaxable purchase business combinations. For taxable purchase business combinations, however, such differences are the exception rather than the rule.** This occurs because the acquiring entity assigns its purchase price to the target company's assets and liabilities for both financial reporting and tax-reporting purposes. For this assignment to be done for tax purposes when common stock is acquired, the parent would have to make an election under Section 338 of the Internal Revenue Code (discussed in Chapter 8) to step up the bases of the subsidiary's assets based on the purchase price. The following section shows how to recognize deferred taxes in nontaxable purchase business combinations.

II NONTAXABLE PURCHASE COMBINATIONS: THE ACQUIRED BUSINESS HAS *NO* DEFERRED TAX ACCOUNTS AT THE COMBINATION DATE

Assume that P Company and S Company's stockholders entered into a nontaxable purchase business combination on January 1, 19X1. Other assumptions follow:

1. P Company issued 1,000 shares of its $1 par value common stock, which has a market value of $90,000.
2. The book value of S Company's assets is $260,000, and the book value of its liabilities is $200,000. Thus the book value of the net assets is $60,000.
3. The book values of S Company's assets and liabilities equal their tax bases. Thus no deferred tax liability or asset accounts exist on S Company's books at the combination date.
4. S Company's assets have a current value of $20,000 in excess of their book values.
5. The enacted income tax rate for future years is 40%.

ILLUSTRATION 5–8	**Nontaxable Purchase Business Combination: The Acquired Business Has No Deferred Tax Accounts at the Combination Date**

1. Acquisition of Assets

Assets ($260,000 + $20,000)	280,000	
Goodwill (residual amount)	18,000	
Liabilities		200,000
Deferred Tax Liability		8,000
Common Stock (1,000 shares × $1 par)		1,000
Additional Paid-in Capital		89,000

2. Acquisition of Common Stock

Investment in Subsidiary	90,000	
Common Stock (1,000 shares × $1 par)		1,000
Additional Paid-in Capital		89,000

Conceptual Analysis of Investment Account by Major Conceptual Elements

				UNDERVALUATION OF NET ASSETS ELEMENT				
Cost	=	BOOK VALUE ELEMENT	+	Various Assets	+	Deferred Tax Liability	+	GOODWILL ELEMENT
$90,000		$60,000		$20,000		$(8,000)		$18,000

Because of the temporary difference of $20,000 between the assigned values of the assets and their tax bases, a deferred tax liability of $8,000 ($20,000 × 40%) must be recognized in recording the business combination. Illustration 5–8 presents the entries that would be made assuming that the assets are acquired (part 1) and the common stock is acquired (part 2). The analysis of the investment by its major conceptual elements is also shown for the latter situation.

III   NONTAXABLE PURCHASE COMBINATIONS: THE ACQUIRED BUSINESS *HAS* A DEFERRED TAX LIABILITY AT THE COMBINATION DATE

Based on the facts in Illustration 5–8, let us assume that the acquired business (1) has used accelerated depreciation for income tax–reporting purposes and (2) has a $4,000 deferred tax liability on its books at the combination date as a result of having deducted $10,000 more depreciation expense for tax purposes than for financial reporting purposes. Accordingly, a $30,000 difference exists between the assigned values and the tax bases of the assets. Thus a $12,000 deferred tax liability needs to be recognized at the combination date ($30,000 × 40%). Because of the deferred tax situation, however, the target company would have $4,000 of additional assets in addition to the deferred tax liability of $4,000. (S Company retained $4,000 cash that otherwise would have been remitted to the government.) If assets are acquired, P Company records the entry:

Assets ($264,000 + $20,000)	284,000	
Goodwill (residual amount)	18,000	
Liabilities		200,000
Deferred Tax Liability		12,000
Common Stock (1,000 shares × $1 par)		1,000
Additional Paid-in Capital		89,000

If common stock is acquired, the entry is the same as shown in Illustration 5–8 because S Company has a $4,000 deferred tax liability recorded on its books.

EXERCISES FOR APPENDIX

E 5–1A **Recognizing Deferred Taxes at the Acquisition Date**   Pirl Inc. acquired Swirl Inc.'s business in a *nontaxable* purchase business combination on 7/1/X5. Other information follows:

1. Pirl issued 5,000 shares of its $1 par value common stock, which had a fair market value of $40 per share.
2. The book value of Swirl's net assets is $160,000.
3. The book value of Swirl's assets and liabilities equals their tax bases just prior to the combination.
4. Swirl's fixed assets have a current value of $330,000 and a book value of $355,000.
5. Swirl's liabilities of $500,000 equal their current value.
6. The enacted income tax rate for current and future years is 40%.

Required   1. Prepare the entry to record the acquisition, assuming that the *assets* are acquired.
2. Prepare the entry to record the acquisition, assuming that 100% of the common stock is acquired. Also prepare a conceptual analysis of the Investment account.

E 5–2A **Recognizing Deferred Taxes at the Acquisition Date**   Parr Inc. entered into an agreement with Sarr Inc.'s stockholders providing for a nontaxable purchase business combination. Other information as of the acquisition date follows:

1. Parr issued 10,000 shares of its $5 par value common stock, which had a fair market value of $70 per share on the combination date.
2. Sarr's net assets have a book value of $600,000.
3. Sarr has a deferred tax liability of $24,000 as a result of using accelerated depreciation for tax-reporting purposes.
4. Sarr's fixed assets have a current value of $490,000 and a book value of $410,000.
5. Sarr's long-term debt has a current value of $500,000 and a book value of $450,000.
6. The enacted income tax rate for current and future years is 40%.

Required   1. Prepare the entry to record the acquisition, assuming that the assets are acquired.
2. Prepare the entry to record the acquisition, assuming that all the common stock is acquired. Also prepare a conceptual analysis of the Investment account.

THE PURCHASE METHOD: POSTACQUISITION PERIODS AND PARTIAL OWNERSHIPS

6

LEARNING OBJECTIVES

TO UNDERSTAND

- The way to apply the purchase method for partially owned subsidiaries at the acquisition date.
- The way to achieve purchase accounting results for postacquisition periods—100% ownership and partial ownership situations.

"The best thing for being sad," replied Merlin, beginning to puff and blow, "is to learn something. That is the only thing that never fails. . . . There is only one thing for it then—to learn. Learn why the world wags and what wags it. That is the only thing which the mind can never exhaust, never alienate, never be tortured by, never fear or distrust, and never dream of regretting. Learning is the thing for you. Look at what a lot of things there are to learn."

THEODORE WHITE,
THE ONCE AND
FUTURE KING

The first part of this chapter continues the discussion that we began in Chapter 5 by examining the application of the purchase methods for periods after the acquisition date for 100%-owned subsidiaries.

We then discuss applying the purchase method to situations in which only partial ownership of the target company is obtained. We address an additional conceptual issue unique to partial ownership situations.

For both of these topics, we show the preparation of consolidated statements. For postacquisition periods, we present illustrations for both the equity method and the cost method.

I CONSOLIDATION WORKSHEETS: 100% OWNERSHIP—POSTACQUISITION PERIODS

THE EQUITY METHOD

ACCOUNTING FOR THE BOOK VALUE ELEMENT Recall that the procedures for applying the equity method to a *created* subsidiary were discussed in Chapter 2. The identical procedures are used for an *acquired* subsidiary to account for the *book value element* of the parent's cost (the various elements of the parent's cost having been discussed in Chapter 5).

We now continue with the purchase acquisition example discussed on pages 168–173 in Chapter 5. We further assume that S Company reported (1) earnings of $24,000 for 19X1 and $32,000 for 19X2 and (2) dividends declared of $4,000 for 19X1 and $12,000 for 19X2. Under the equity method, P Company makes the following *general ledger* entries:

	19X1		19X2	
Investment in Subsidiary	24,000		32,000	
Equity in Net Income (of S Company)		24,000		32,000
Dividend Receivable	4,000		12,000	
Investment in Subsidiary		4,000		4,000

The analysis of the book value element of the parent's cost is updated as shown in Illustration 6–1.

ILLUSTRATION 6–1	Updating the Book Value Element of the Conceptual Analysis		
		BOOK VALUE ELEMENT	
	Parent's Investment Account—	Subsidiary's Equity Accounts	
	Book Value =	Common Stock +	Retained Earnings
Balances, 1/1/X1	$ 60,000	$10,000	$50,000
+ Equity in net income	24,000		24,000
− Dividends declared	(4,000)		(4,000)
Balances, 12/31/X1	$ 80,000	$10,000	$70,000
+ Equity in net income	32,000		32,000
− Dividends declared	(12,000)		(12,000)
Balances, 12/31/X2	$100,000	$10,000	$90,000

REVIEW POINTS FOR ILLUSTRATION 6–1   Note the following:

1. **Procedures.** No special procedures were needed merely because P Company acquired rather than created the subsidiary.

2. **The basic elimination entry.** The basic elimination entry at each year-end will be obtained from this analysis—the same analysis used for a *created* subsidiary.

3. **Liquidating dividends.** In this example, the *postacquisition dividends* (totaling $16,000) did *not* exceed the *postacquisition earnings* (totaling $56,000). If the postacquisition dividends had exceeded the postacquisition earnings, the subsidiary would be paying dividends out of the $50,000 of retained earnings existing at the acquisition date and thus liquidating part of the parent's initial investment cost. Such dividends are called **liquidating dividends. Under the equity method, liquidating dividends are treated the same as nonliquidating dividends.**

ACCOUNTING FOR THE EXCESS COST ELEMENTS   Under the *equity method*, the parent's cost in excess of book value is accounted for as though these were separate general ledger accounts. Accordingly, amounts pertaining to land are *not* amortized to income, but amounts pertaining to depreciable or amortizable assets *are* amortized to income. This amortization can be recorded in the parent's general ledger under the equity method. Continuing with the Chapter 5 acquisition example shown in Illustration 5–6 (on page 174), the cost in excess of book value elements would be updated for 19X1 and 19X2 as shown in Illustration 6–2.

The parent's *general ledger* amortization entries for 19X1 and 19X2 (based on the amounts calculated in Illustration 6–2) are as follows:

	19X1		19X2	
Equity in Net Income				
(of S Company)	8,000		4,000	
Investment in S Company ...		8,000		4,000

The advantages to recording this amortization in the general ledger are as follows:

1. **Provides a better means to keep records.** The alternative is to make these entries on the worksheet (as under the cost method, which is illustrated later).[1] General ledger entries provide a more efficient means to keep records than do consolidation worksheet entries.

ILLUSTRATION 6–2	**Updating the Cost in Excess of Book Value Elements of the Conceptual Analysis**						
	Parent's Investment Account— Excess Cost	=	UNDER- OR (OVER)VALUATION OF NET ASSETS ELEMENT			+	GOODWILL ELEMENT
			Inventory	+ Land	+ Equipment		
Remaining life			*(3 months)*	*(Indefinite)*	*(8 years)*		*(6 years)*
Balances, 1/1/X1	$40,000		$4,000	$8,000	$16,000		$12,000
– Amortization—19X1	(8,000)		(4,000)		(2,000)		(2,000)
Balances, 12/31/X1	$32,000		$ –0–	$8,000	$14,000		$10,000
– Amortization—19X2	(4,000)				(2,000)		(2,000)
Balances, 12/31/X2	$28,000		$ –0–	$8,000	$12,000		$ 8,000

[1]This alternative is called the "simplified" equity method.

2. **Retains the built-in checking feature.** The built-in checking features discussed in Chapter 2 (consolidated net income and retained earnings equaling the parent's net income and retained earnings) are retained.

CHARGING THE AMORTIZATION TO THE EQUITY IN NET INCOME ACCOUNT   Note that under the equity method, the parent's amortization of cost in excess of book value is charged directly to the Equity in Net Income of Subsidiary account—**it is improper to charge the parent's expense accounts because the amortization relates solely to the parent's investment in the subsidiary, not to any of the parent's separate operations.** Charging this amortization to the Equity in Net Income of Subsidiary account reveals the true earnings of the subsidiary—**using the** *new basis of accounting* **that results from the purchase transaction.** This may be depicted as follows for the example we have been using:

	Equity in Net Income (of Subsidiary)			
	19X1		**19X2**	
Subsidiary's **reported earnings** using basis applicable to *previous* owners		$24,000		$32,000
Parent's amortization of cost in excess of book value	8,000		4,000	
Subsidiary's **true earnings** using new basis applicable to *new* owner (the parent)		$16,000		$28,000

Under the non-push-down basis of accounting, no revaluation to current values is made in the subsidiary's general ledger. Accordingly, the financial statement amounts reported by the subsidiary reflect the *old basis* **of accounting. From the parent's perspective, such amounts are wholly irrelevant.** Under the push-down basis of accounting (discussed briefly in Chapter 5 and in detail in Chapter 8), adjustments are made in the subsidiary's general ledger to revalue its assets and liabilities to their current values as of the acquisition date. If S Company had applied push-down accounting, the amortization relating to the undervalued assets and goodwill ($8,000 for 19X1 and $4,000 for 19X2) would have been recorded on S Company's books. As a result, its reported net income for 19X1 and 19X2 would have been $16,000 and $28,000, respectively.

RECLASSIFYING THE AMORTIZATION IN CONSOLIDATION   Charging the amortization recorded by the parent to the Equity in Net Income of Subsidiary account adds a minor extra step to the consolidation effort. An additional entry must be made to *reclassify* this amortization to the appropriate income statement accounts it would have been charged to had S Company (1) adjusted its assets and liabilities to their current values and (2) used the new basis of accounting in computing depreciation and amortization.

Because the Equity in Net Income of Subsidiary account was debited on P Company's books for the amortization, the reclassification is effected by (1) crediting the Equity in Net Income of Subsidiary account and (2) debiting the various appropriate expense accounts. This entry does *not* affect consolidated net income because it takes place entirely within the income statement section of the worksheet.[2]

---

[2]Recall from intermediate accounting that (1) in an *adjusting* entry, both the income statement and the balance sheet are adjusted and (2) in a *reclassification* entry, the debit and credit are both posted to the same financial statement.

The following table shows the accounts to which various amortizations would be reclassified:

Amortization Pertaining to	Appropriate Income Statement Account
Inventory	Cost of Sales
Buildings and equipment	Cost of Sales, Marketing Expenses, and Administration Expenses (as appropriate)[a]
Patents	Cost of Sales
Long-term debt	Interest Expense
Notes receivable	Interest Income
Goodwill	Cost of Sales or Administrative Expenses

[a]Amortization pertaining to manufacturing assets would be charged solely to Cost of Sales.

For ease of reference, we call the entry made to effect this reclassification the *Amortization of Excess Cost Entry.* An example of this entry for a parent having $30,000 of amortization relating to (1) an *under*valued building, (2) goodwill, (3) an *over*valued note payable, (4) an *over*valued patent, and (5) an *over*valued note receivable is as follows:

WORKSHEET ENTRIES ONLY	Cost of Sales (for the **undervalued** building) 22,000	
	Expenses (for the goodwill) 7,000	
	Interest Expense (for the **overvalued** note payable) 8,000	
	Cost of Sales (for the **overvalued** patent)	3,000
	Interest Income (for the **overvalued** note receivable).	4,000
	Equity in Net Income (of subsidiary)	30,000

Note that **the debits and credits depend on whether an item is under- or overvalued.** In this case, a $30,000 debit amount was reclassified, which is the usual case when goodwill exists and an economy has been inflationary. Situations could exist, however, in which a credit amount is reclassified.

We now continue with the example we have been using. The consolidation entries at the end of 19X1 and 19X2 are as follows:

1. The basic elimination entry (amounts are from Illustration 6–1):

		Consolidation Date			
		December 31, 19X1		December 31, 19X2	
WORKSHEET ENTRIES ONLY	Common Stock	10,000		10,000	
	Retained Earnings, 1/1/X1 and 1/1/X2	50,000		70,000	
	Equity in Net Income (of S Company)	24,000		32,000	
	Dividends Declared		4,000		12,000
	Investment in Subsidiary		80,000		100,000

2. The excess cost entry (amounts are from Illustration 6–2):

		Consolidation Date			
		December 31, 19X1		December 31, 19X2	
WORKSHEET ENTRIES ONLY	Land........................	8,000		8,000	
	Equipment	16,000		16,000	
	Goodwill	10,000		8,000	
	Accumulated Depreciation ...		2,000		4,000
	Investment in Subsidiary		32,000		28,000

3. **The amortization of excess cost entry** (amounts are from Illustration 6–2):

		Consolidation Date	
		December 31, 19X1	December 31, 19X2
WORKSHEET ENTRIES ONLY	Cost of sales	8,000	4,000
	Equity in Net Income		
	(of S Company)	8,000	4,000

Note: For simplicity, we arbitrarily assumed that all of the equipment amortization and goodwill amortization should be classified as part of Cost of Sales. The amortization relating to the inventory obviously belongs in Cost of Sales.

4. **The accumulated depreciation entry** (same amounts as used in Illustration 5–6 [on page 174] at the acquisition date):

		Consolidation Date	
		December 31, 19X1	December 31, 19X2
WORKSHEET ENTRIES ONLY	Accumulated Depreciation	50,000	50,000
	Buildings and Equipment	50,000	50,000

These consolidation entries are used in preparing the consolidation worksheets shown in Illustrations 6–3 and 6–4.

MID-YEAR ACQUISITIONS

The preceding examples used an acquisition date as of the beginning of the parent's reporting year (January 1, 19X1). Most business combinations occur at various times during a year. **Regardless of the acquisition date, only the postacquisition income statement of the subsidiary is consolidated.** For example, assume that the acquisition date is April 1, 19X1, and that S Company had the following income statement amounts for 19X1:

	Jan. 1–Mar. 31	April 1–Dec. 31	Total
Revenues	$64,000	$170,000	$234,000
Cost of sales	(23,000)	(87,000)	(110,000)
Expenses	(34,000)	(66,000)	(100,000)
Net Income	$ 7,000	$ 17,000	$ 24,000
Relevance of above amounts:	**Disregard**	**Use**	**Disregard**

Accordingly, the parent would apply the equity method of accounting to the $17,000 of earnings occurring *after* the acquisition date, and only the income statement amounts for this period would be consolidated. As a practical matter, however, it is also acceptable to (1) consolidate the entire year and (2) report an artificial debit in the income statement called **preacquisition earnings** to negate the nonreportable net income earned prior to the acquisition date.

THE COST METHOD

When the parent accounts for its investment under the cost method, it prepares the consolidated statements as follows:

1. The portion of the parent's cost identified with the book value element and any dividends declared by the subsidiary are handled in the same manner as shown in Chapter 2 for a created subsidiary.

ILLUSTRATION 6–3	*Equity* Method: *First* Year Subsequent to the Acquisition Date—100% Ownership

P Company and S Company
Consolidation Worksheet as of December 31, 19X1

	P Company	S Company	Consolidation Entries Dr.	Consolidation Entries Cr.	Consolidated
Income Statement (19X1)					
Sales	600,000	234,000			834,000
Cost of sales	(360,000)	(110,000)	8,000(3)		(478,000)
Expenses	(190,000)	(100,000)			(290,000)
Equity in net income (of S Co.) ..	16,000[a]		24,000(1)	8,000(3)	–0–
Net Income	66,000	24,000	32,000(1)	8,000	66,000
Statement of Retained Earnings					
Balances, 1/1/X1	100,000	50,000	50,000(1)		100,000
+ Net income	66,000	24,000	32,000	8,000	66,000
– Dividends declared	(51,000)	(4,000)		4,000(1)	(51,000)
Balances, 12/31/X1	115,000	70,000	82,000	12,000	115,000
Balance Sheet					
Cash	25,000	11,000			36,000
Accounts receivable, net	75,000	37,000			112,000
Inventory	110,000	55,000			165,000
Investment in S Company:					
Book value element	80,000			80,000(1)	–0–
Excess cost elements	32,000			32,000(2)	–0–
Land	220,000	30,000	8,000(2)		258,000
Buildings and equipment	500,000	200,000	16,000(2)	50,000(4)	666,000
Accumulated depreciation	(320,000)	(63,000)	50,000(4)	2,000(2)	(335,000)
Goodwill			10,000(2)		10,000
Total Assets	722,000	270,000	84,000	164,000	912,000
Liabilities	407,000	190,000			597,000
P Company:					
Common stock	200,000				200,000
Retained earnings	115,000				115,000
S Company:					
Common stock		10,000	10,000(1)		–0–
Retained earnings		70,000.	82,000	12,000	–0–
Total Liabilities and Equity ..	722,000	270,000	92,000	12,000	912,000
Proof of debit and credit postings			176,000	176,000	

Explanation of entries:
(1) The basic elimination entry.
(2) The excess cost entry.
(3) The amortization of excess cost entry.
(4) The accumulated depreciation entry.
[a]S Company's $24,000 of reported net income less $8,000 of amortization of cost in excess of book value.

2. The portion of the parent's cost in excess of book value is *not* amortized in the parent's general ledger (as it is under the equity method). Consequently, **the amortization of cost in excess of book value is instead accomplished in the consolidation worksheet elimination columns.**

We now assume that P Company is using the *cost method*. To be able to make ready comparisons between the cost and equity method illustrations, we use the same facts used in the equity method discussion concerning (1) the acquisition cost,

ILLUSTRATION 6–4	**Equity Method: Second Year Subsequent to the Acquisition Date—100% Ownership**

P Company and S Company
Consolidation Worksheet as of December 31, 19X2

	P Company	S Company	Consolidation Entries Dr.	Consolidation Entries Cr.	Consolidated
Income Statement (19X2)					
Sales	710,000	282,000			992,000
Cost of sales	(390,000)	(130,000)	4,000(3)		(524,000)
Expenses	(210,000)	(120,000)			(330,000)
Equity in net income (of S Co.) . .	28,000ᵃ		32,000(1)	4,000(3)	–0–
Net income	138,000	32,000	36,000	4,000	138,000
Statement of Retained Earnings					
Balances, 1/1/X2	115,000	70,000	70,000(1)		115,000
+ Net income	138,000	32,000	36,000	4,000	138,000
– Dividends declared	(85,000)	(12,000)		12,000(1)	(85,000)
Balances, 12/31/X2	168,000	90,000	106,000	16,000	168,000
Balance Sheet					
Cash	26,000	31,000			57,000
Accounts receivable, net	84,000	43,000			127,000
Inventory	140,000	82,000			222,000
Investment in S Company:					
Book value element	100,000			100,000(1)	–0–
Excess cost elements	28,000			28,000(2)	–0–
Land	220,000	30,000	8,000(2)		258,000
Buildings and equipment	500,000	200,000	16,000(2)	50,000(4)	666,000
Accumulated depreciation	(360,000)	(76,000)	50,000(4)	4,000(2)	(390,000)
Goodwill			8,000(2)		8,000
Total Assets	738,000	310,000	82,000	182,000	948,000
Liabilities	370,000	210,000			580,000
P Company:					
Common stock	200,000				200,000
Retained earnings	168,000				168,000
S Company:					
Common stock		10,000	10,000(1)		–0–
Retained earnings		90,000	106,000	16,000	–0–
Total Liabilities and Equity . .	738,000	310,000	116,000	16,000	948,000
Proof of debit and credit postings			198,000	198,000	

Explanation of entries:
(1) The basic elimination entry.
(2) The excess cost entry.
(3) The amortization of excess cost entry.
(4) The accumulated depreciation entry.
ᵃ$32,000 of income recorded under the equity method, net of $4,000 of amortization of cost in excess of book value.

(2) the asset lives, and (3) S Company's earnings and dividends for the two years following the acquisition date.

Under the cost method, the only *general ledger* entries that P Company makes subsequent to the acquisition date pertain to the intercompany dividends. (Recall from Chapter 2 that under the cost method, the parent's investment income is re-ported using a Dividend Income account instead of an Equity in Net Income account used under the equity method.) Accordingly, P Company's general ledger entries are limited to the following two entries:

	19X1	19X2
Dividends Receivable	4,000	12,000
Dividend Income	4,000	12,000

Note that P Company does *not* record any amortization of cost in excess of book value in its general ledger—thus it must record it in consolidation, as shown shortly.

The consolidation entries under the cost method at the end of 19X1 and 19X2 are as follows:

1. **The basic elimination entry** (amounts are frozen):

		Consolidation Date			
		December 31, 19X1		December 31, 19X2	
WORKSHEET ENTRIES ONLY	Common Stock	10,000		10,000	
	Retained Earnings (at date of acquisition)	50,000		50,000	
	Investment in Subsidiary		60,000		60,000

2. **The excess cost entry** (amounts are frozen):

		Consolidation Date			
		December 31, 19X1		December 31, 19X2	
WORKSHEET ENTRIES ONLY	Inventory.	4,000		4,000	
	Land	8,000		8,000	
	Equipment	16,000		16,000	
	Goodwill	12,000		12,000	
	Investment in Subsidiary		40,000		40,000

3. **The amortization of excess cost entry** (for balance sheet accounts, the amounts after the first year become **cumulative**):

		Consolidation Date			
		December 31, 19X1		December 31, 19X2	
WORKSHEET ENTRIES ONLY	Cost of Sales	8,000		4,000	
	Retained Earnings, 1/1/X2			8,000[a]	
	Inventory		4,000		4,000[a]
	Accumulated Depreciation . . .		2,000		4,000[a]
	Goodwill		2,000		4,000[a]
	[a]A cumulative amount.				

4. **The intercompany dividend elimination entry** (same as shown in Chapter 2):

		Consolidation Date			
		December 31, 19X1		December 31, 19X2	
WORKSHEET ENTRIES ONLY	Dividend Income	4,000		12,000	
	Dividends Declared		4,000		12,000

These four entries along with the accumulated depreciation entry for $50,000 shown earlier under the equity method are used to prepare the consolidation worksheets shown in Illustrations 6–5 and 6–6.

LIQUIDATING DIVIDENDS As noted previously, when an acquired subsidiary declares dividends in excess of *postacquisition earnings,* the excess is a *liquidating dividend.* Accordingly, the parent must credit the Investment in Subsidiary account—not the Dividend Income account.

"CONVERSION TO EQUITY METHOD" TO PERFORM THE CONSOLIDATION A slightly different way to prepare the consolidation worksheet when the parent uses the cost method is to make (1) a worksheet entry to convert to the equity method of accounting and (2) the consolidation entries that would have been made under the equity method. The conversion entries follow:

ILLUSTRATION 6–5	*Cost* Method: *First* Year Subsequent to the Acquisition Date—100% Ownership				

P Company and S Company
Consolidation Worksheet as of December 31, 19X1

	P Company	S Company	Consolidation Entries Dr.	Consolidation Entries Cr.	Consolidated
Income Statement (19X1)					
Sales	600,000	234,000			834,000
Cost of sales	(360,000)	(110,000)	8,000(3)		(478,000)
Expenses	(190,000)	(100,000)			(290,000)
Dividend income	4,000			4,000(4)	–0–
Net income	54,000	24,000	12,000		66,000
Statement of Retained Earnings					
Balances, 1/1/X1	100,000	50,000	50,000(1)		100,000
+ Net income	54,000	24,000	12,000		66,000
– Dividends declared	(51,000)	(4,000)		4,000(4)	(51,000)
Balances, 12/31/X1	103,000	70,000	62,000	4,000	115,000
Balance Sheet					
Cash	25,000	11,000			36,000
Accounts receivable, net	75,000	37,000			112,000
Inventory	110,000	55,000	4,000(2)	4,000(3)	165,000
Investment in S Company:					
Book value element	60,000			60,000(1)	–0–
Excess cost elements	40,000			40,000(2)	–0–
Land	220,000	30,000	8,000(2)		258,000
Buildings and equipment	500,000	200,000	16,000(2)	50,000(5)	666,000
Accumulated depreciation	(320,000)	(63,000)	50,000(5)	2,000(3)	(335,000)
Goodwill			12,000(2)	2,000(3)	10,000
Total Assets	710,000	270,000	90,000	158,000	912,000
Liabilities	407,000	190,000			597,000
P Company:					
Common stock	200,000				200,000
Retained earnings	103,000				103,000
S Company:					
Common stock		10,000	10,000(1)		–0–
Retained earnings		70,000	62,000	4,000	12,000
Total Liabilities and Equity	710,000	270,000	72,000	4,000	912,000

Proof of debit and credit postings 162,000   162,000

Explanation of entries:
(1) The basic elimination entry.
(2) The excess cost entry.
(3) The amortization of excess cost entry.
(4) The intercompany dividend entry.
(5) The accumulated depreciation entry.

Recap of Retained Earnings

P Company	$103,000
S Company	12,000
Total	$115,000

		Consolidation Date	
		December 31, 19X1	December 31, 19X2
WORKSHEET ENTRIES ONLY	Dividend Income	4,000	12,000
	Investment in Subsidiary	12,000	28,000
	Equity in Net Income	16,000[a]	28,000[b]
	Retained Earnings, 1/1/X2 ...		12,000

[a]$24,000 of S Company's reported net income − $8,000 of amortization.
[b]$32,000 of S Company's reported net income − $4,000 of amortization.

ILLUSTRATION 6–6   *Cost* Method: *Second* Year Subsequent to the Acquisition Date—100% Ownership

P Company and S Company
Consolidation Worksheet as of December 31, 19X2

	P Company	S Company	Consolidation Entries Dr.	Consolidation Entries Cr.	Consolidated
Income Statement (19X2)					
Sales	710,000	282,000			992,000
Cost of sales	(390,000)	(130,000)	4,000(3)		(524,000)
Expenses	(210,000)	(120,000)			(330,000)
Dividend income	12,000		12,000(4)		–0–
Net Income	122,000	32,000	⌐ 16,000		138,000
Statement of Retained Earnings			8,000(3)		
Balances, 1/1/X2	103,000	70,000	50,000(1)	⎫	115,000
+ Net income	122,000	32,000	↳16,000	⎬	138,000
− Dividends declared	(85,000)	(12,000)		12,000(4)	(85,000)
Balances, 12/31/X2	140,000	90,000	⌐ 74,000	⌐ 12,000	168,000
Balance Sheet					
Cash	26,000	31,000			57,000
Accounts receivable	84,000	43,000			127,000
Inventory	140,000	82,000	4,000(2)	4,000(3)	222,000
Investment in S Company:					
Book value element	60,000			60,000(1)	–0–
Excess cost elements	40,000			40,000(2)	–0–
Land	220,000	30,000	8,000(2)		258,000
Buildings and equipment	500,000	200,000	16,000(2)	50,000(5)	666,000
Accumulated depreciation	(360,000)	(76,000)	50,000(5)	4,000(3)	(390,000)
Goodwill			12,000(2)	4,000(3)	8,000
Total Assets	710,000	310,000	90,000	162,000	948,000
Liabilities	370,000	210,000			580,000
P Company:					
Common stock	200,000				200,000
Retained earnings	140,000				140,000⌐
S Company:					
Common stock		10,000	10,000(1)		–0–
Retained earnings		90,000	↳74,000	↳12,000	28,000⌐
Total Liabilities and Equity ..	710,000	310,000	84,000	12,000	948,000

Proof of debit and credit postings 174,000   174,000

Explanation of entries:
(1) The basic elimination entry.
(2) The excess cost entry.
(3) The amortization of excess cost entry.
(4) The intercompany dividend entry.
(5) The accumulated depreciation entry.

Recap of Retained Earnings

P Company	$140,000
S Company	28,000
Total	$168,000

II   THE PURCHASE METHOD: PARTIAL OWNERSHIP—CONCEPTUAL ISSUES

PARTIAL OR FULL REVALUATION OF THE SUBSIDIARY'S ASSETS AND LIABILITIES

When a partially owned subsidiary has under- or overvalued assets or liabilities at the acquisition date, to what extent should these items be revalued to their current values? Two schools of thought exist: partial revaluation and full revaluation.

PARTIAL REVALUATION (NOT PERMITTED UNDER EXPECTED GAAP)   Under *partial revaluation,* undervalued items are revalued only to the extent of the parent's ownership interest. For example, assets that are undervalued by $28,000 are revalued upward by only $21,000 if the parent's ownership percentage was 75%. Partial revaluation occurs under the *parent company concept* (discussed in Chapter 3). This reporting result also occurs under *proportionate consolidation* (also discussed in Chapter 3).

Partial revaluation is *not* permitted, however, under the FASB rules set forth in the FASB's exposure draft *Consolidated Financial Statements: Policy and Procedures* issued in late 1995 and mentioned in Chapters 1 and 3. (The rules existing prior to this document permitted partial revaluation.) Accordingly, we do *not* demonstrate this manner of revaluation.

FULL REVALUATION (PERMITTED UNDER EXPECTED GAAP)   Under *full revaluation,* undervalued items are revalued to 100% of current values. In comparison to the *partial revaluation* method example in which assets undervalued by $28,000 are revalued upward by only $21,000, an additional $7,000 of valuation is reported in the asset section of the consolidated balance sheet. On the other side of the balance sheet, an additional $7,000 is reflected for the noncontrolling interest.

The $7,000 of additional valuation results in additional amortization charges in future consolidated income statements. A corresponding reduction in the amount of consolidated net income is allocated, however, to the noncontrolling interest shareholders. Thus the amount of consolidated net income allocated to the controlling interest (the parent's shareholders) is *not* affected.

Full revaluation occurs under the *economic unit concept* (discussed in Chapter 3), and we demonstrate this manner of valuation. The FASB rules in its exposure draft permit only this method of revaluation. As in Chapter 5 and the first section of Chapter 6 in which 100% ownership situations are discussed, we demonstrate this establishment of a new basis of accounting using the *non-push-down* basis of accounting.

DETERMINING THE AMOUNT TO REPORT FOR GOODWILL

When part of the parent's purchase price includes an amount for goodwill, the issue arises as to whether goodwill should be reported at (1) this cost-based amount or (2) its amount *implicit* in the transaction.

THE CONCEPT OF IMPLICIT GOODWILL   To illustrate the concept of implicit goodwill, assume that an acquiring company was willing to pay $12,000 for goodwill in acquiring 100% of the common stock. If the acquiring company acquired only a 75% ownership interest, however, it should have been willing to pay only $9,000 for goodwill (75% of $12,000). Accordingly, if the acquiring company paid $9,000 for goodwill in acquiring a 75% ownership interest, the goodwill implicit in the transaction must be $12,000. Thus $3,000 of additional goodwill is presumed to exist.

THE PURCHASED GOODWILL METHOD VERSUS THE FULL GOODWILL METHOD
Under the *parent company concept,* only $9,000 of goodwill is reported. Under a

"pure" view of the *economic unit concept,* an additional $3,000 of goodwill is reported in the consolidated balance sheet. Accordingly, an additional $3,000 is also reported on the other side of the balance sheet for the noncontrolling interest. As in the case of undervalued assets, this additional goodwill results in additional amortization expense in future consolidated income statements. A corresponding reduction in the amount of consolidated net income is allocated, however, to the noncontrolling shareholders. Therefore, the amount of consolidated net income allocated to the controlling interest (the parent's shareholders) is *not* affected.

EXPECTED GAAP REPORTING: ONLY THE FULL GOODWILL METHOD PERMITTED
Under the rules set forth in the FASB's exposure draft, goodwill is reported only to the extent that the parent bought and paid for it, $9,000 in our example. Thus no amount is imputed to the noncontrolling interest for the incremental goodwill implicit in the transaction. In May 1996, however, the FASB reversed its position because certain potential "gaming" abuses were brought to its attention. Accordingly, its revised proposal standard allows only the *full goodwill* method.

Thus the FASB theoretically considers the *economic unit concept* to have two alternative valuation methods for goodwill, only one of which is allowed. We demonstrate the use of only the allowed alternative—the *full goodwill* method.

III THE PURCHASE METHOD: PARTIAL OWNERSHIP—ANALYZING COST

SEPARATING THE PARENT'S COST INTO THE MAJOR CONCEPTUAL ELEMENTS

Knowing the factors that enter into how much the acquiring company is willing to pay in partial ownership situations, we separate the parent's cost into its major conceptual elements using the following procedures:

1. **The book value element.** Multiply the book value of the subsidiary's stockholders' equity by the parent's ownership percentage.
2. **The undervaluation of net assets element.** Multiply the total amount of the undervaluation of the subsidiary's net assets times the parent's ownership percentage.
3. **The goodwill element.** Add the amounts determined in procedures 1 and 2 to arrive at the parent's interest in the current value of the subsidiary's net assets. Subtract this total from the parent's cost to obtain goodwill (a residually determined amount).

Once these procedures are completed, we can include the noncontrolling interest in the conceptual analysis. In the illustrations in Chapter 5, we assumed that P Company acquired 100% of the outstanding common stock of S Company at a cost of $100,000, which was $40,000 in excess of the book value of the subsidiary's net assets. The $40,000 excess payment was identified as undervalued assets ($28,000) and goodwill ($12,000). Assume instead that P Company purchased only 75% of the outstanding common stock for $75,000 (75% of $100,000). The separation of the parent's cost into its major conceptual elements and the inclusion of amounts for the noncontrolling interest are shown as follows:

Noncontrolling Interest (25%)	+	Parent's Cost	=	Book Value Element (100% of $60,000)	+	Undervaluation of Net Assets Element (100% of $28,000)	+	Goodwill Element (Residual)
		$75,000		$45,000 (75%)		$21,000 (75%)		$ 9,000
$25,000				15,000 (25%)		7,000 (25%)		3,000
$25,000		$75,000		$60,000		$28,000		$12,000

As was done in Chapter 5, once the cost of the parent's investment has been broken down in this manner, the future consolidation procedures can be simplified by splitting the parent's cost into the parent's share of the book value element and the parent's excess cost elements:

Investment in S Company:
Book value element $45,000
Excess cost elements ($21,000 + $9,000)   30,000

SEPARATING THE UNDERVALUATION OF NET ASSETS ELEMENT INTO ITS COMPONENTS

We separate the undervaluation of net assets element into its components by multiplying the appropriate ownership percentages by the amount that each asset is undervalued. In Illustration 5–5, the $28,000 undervaluation was attributed to Inventory, Land, and Equipment accounts. This $28,000 is separated into its components as follows:

Asset	Undervaluation	Parent's Interest in Undervaluation (75%)	Noncontrolling Interest in Undervaluation (25%)
Inventory	$ 4,000	$ 3,000	$1,000
Land	8,000	6,000	2,000
Building	16,000	12,000	4,000
	$28,000	$21,000	$7,000

As shown in Chapter 5, the individual components within each category will be tracked outside the general ledger in supporting schedules, which are used to prepare consolidation entries. For the preceding situation, the supporting schedules at the acquisition date are as follows:

			BOOK VALUE ELEMENT	
Noncontrolling Interest (25%)	+	Parent's Investment Account— Book Value	Subsidiary's Equity Accounts	
			Common Stock	+	Retained Earnings
		=			
$15,000		$45,000	$10,000		$50,000

Noncontrolling Interest (25%)	+	Parent's Investment Account— Excess Cost	=	UNDERVALUATION OF NET ASSETS ELEMENT				GOODWILL ELEMENT
				Inventory	+	Land	+	Equipment	+	
		$30,000		$3,000		$6,000		$12,000		$ 9,000
$10,000				1,000		2,000		4,000		3,000
$10,000		$30,000		$4,000		$8,000		$16,000		$12,000

The excess cost entry obtained with this procedure (which would be used only if *non*-push-down accounting were used) revalues the subsidiary's assets to 100% of their current values and reports Goodwill in the consolidated statements at the amount of goodwill implicit in the transaction.

IV   CONSOLIDATION WORKSHEET: PARTIAL OWNERSHIP—AT THE ACQUISITION DATE

For this example, the consolidation entries as of the acquisition date, taken from these supporting schedules to the parent's Investment account, are as follows:

1. The Basic Elimination Entry:

WORKSHEET ENTRY ONLY	Common Stock	10,000	
	Retained Earnings	50,000	
	Investment in Subsidiary		45,000
	NCI in Net Assets		15,000

2. The Excess Cost Entry:

WORKSHEET ENTRY ONLY	Inventory	4,000	
	Land	8,000	
	Equipment	16,000	
	Goodwill	12,000	
	Investment in Subsidiary		30,000
	NCI in Net Assets		10,000

3. The Accumulated Depreciation Entry: *IN FULL*

WORKSHEET ENTRY ONLY	Accumulated Depreciation	50,000	
	Equipment		50,000

Even though only 75% of the common stock was acquired, the entire $50,000 balance in the Accumulated Depreciation account at the acquisition date is eliminated because doing so is consistent with the full revaluation method used.

These consolidation entries are used in Illustration 6–7 to prepare a consolidation worksheet as of January 1, 19X1 (the acquisition date), for P Company and S Company.

V CONSOLIDATION WORKSHEET: PARTIAL OWNERSHIP—POSTACQUISITION PERIODS

THE EQUITY METHOD

UPDATING THE SUPPORTING SCHEDULES TO THE INVESTMENT ACCOUNT   Assume that S Company had the following earnings and dividends for the two years subsequent to the acquisition date:

	19X1	19X2
Net income	$24,000	$32,000
Dividends	4,000	12,000

Also assume the following amortizations pertaining to the undervalued assets and goodwill:

	19X1	19X2
Excess cost amortizations	6,000	3,000
Amortizations attributable to the NCI	2,000	1,000

ILLUSTRATION 6–7	At the Acquisition Date					

P Company and S Company
Consolidation Worksheet as of January 1, 19X1

	P Company	75%-owned S Company	Consolidation Entries Dr.	Consolidation Entries Cr.	Consolidated
Balance Sheet					
Cash	43,000	15,000			58,000
Accounts receivable	52,000	23,000			75,000
Inventory	90,000	42,000	4,000(2)		136,000
Investment in S Company:					
Book value element	45,000			45,000(1)	–0–
Excess cost elements	30,000			30,000(2)	–0–
Land	220,000	30,000	8,000(2)		258,000
Buildings and equipment	500,000	200,000	16,000(2)	50,000(3)	666,000
Accumulated depreciation	(280,000)	(50,000)	50,000(3)		(280,000)
Goodwill			12,000(2)		12,000
Total Assets	700,000	260,000	90,000	125,000	925,000
Liabilities	400,000	200,000			600,000
NCI in net assets				15,000(1)	25,000
P Company:				10,000(2)	
Common stock	200,000				200,000
Retained earnings	100,000				100,000
S Company:					
Common stock		10,000	10,000(1)		
Retained earnings		50,000	50,000(1)		–0–
Total Liabilities and Equity ..	700,000	260,000	60,000	22,000	925,000
Proof of debit and credit postings			150,000	150,000	

Explanation of entries:
(1) The basic elimination entry.
(2) The excess cost entry.
(3) The accumulated depreciation entry.

Under the *equity method,* P Company makes the following *general ledger* entries (the amounts in the first two entries are at 75% of S Company's reported amounts):

	19X1		19X2	
Investment in Subsidiary	18,000		24,000	
Equity in Net Income				
(of S Company)		18,000		24,000
Dividend Receivable	3,000		9,000	
Investment in Subsidiary		3,000		9,000
Equity in Net Income				
(of S Company)	6,000		3,000	
Investment in Subsidiary		6,000		3,000

Illustrations 6–8 and 6–9 show the updated supporting schedules to the Investment account for the two years following the acquisition date, using the preceding information. These illustrations also show the related consolidation entries required at the end of 19X1 and 19X2.

Illustrations 6–10 and 6–11 show the related consolidation worksheets at the end of 19X1 and 19X2.

| ILLUSTRATION 6-8 | Updating the Book Value Element of the Investment Account—75%-Owned |

	Noncontrolling Interest (25%)	+	Parent's Investment Account	=	Common Stock	+	Retained Earnings
					BOOK VALUE ELEMENT		
					Subsidiary's Equity Accounts		
Balances, 1/1/X1	$15,000		$45,000		$10,000		$50,000
+ Equity in net income:							
To parent (75%)			18,000				18,000
To NCI (25%)	6,000						6,000
− Dividends:							
To parent (75%)			(3,000)				(3,000)
To NCI (25%)	(1,000)						(1,000)
Balances, 12/31/X1	$20,000		$60,000		$10,000		$70,000
+ Equity in net income:							
To parent (75%)			24,000				24,000
To NCI (25%)	8,000						8,000
− Dividends:							
To parent (75%)			(9,000)				(9,000)
To NCI (25%)	(3,000)						(3,000)
Balances, 12/31/X2	$25,000		$75,000		$10,000		$90,000

The Basic Elimination Entry
(using the amounts in the preceding analysis)

		Consolidation Date	
WORKSHEET ENTRY ONLY		**December 31, 19X1**	**December 31, 19X2**
	Common Stock	10,000	10,000
	Retained Earnings, 1/1/X1 and 1/1/X2 ..	50,000	70,000
	Equity in Net Income	18,000	24,000
	NCI in Net Income	6,000	8,000
	Dividends Declared	4,000	12,000
	Investment in Subsidiary	60,000	75,000
	NCI in Net Assets	20,000	25,000

REVIEW POINTS FOR ILLUSTRATIONS 6–10 AND 6–11   Note the following:

1. The basic elimination entry was obtained from the updated analysis of the book value element as is usually done.

2. Entry (4) in Illustrations 6–10 and 6–11 is new and is necessary because of the additional values attributable to the noncontrolling interest. These entries have no effect on the parent's net income or the consolidated net income because the additional amounts reported for Cost of Sales ($2,000 for 19X1 and $1,000 for 19X2) are exactly offset by the lower amounts reported for the noncontrolling interest in S Company's net income.

3. Illustration 6–10 shows that $4,000 of the consolidated net income accrues to the noncontrolling interest for 19X1. The proof of this amount follows:

	19X1
S Company's reported net income (**old basis**)	$24,000
Less—Amortization of undervalued assets and goodwill	
P Company's portion	(6,000)
Noncontrolling interest portion	(2,000)
S Company's Adjusted Net Income (**new basis**)	$16,000
Noncontrolling interest ownership percentage	25%
Noncontrolling Interest in Net Income	$ 4,000

| ILLUSTRATION 6–9 | Updating the Excess Cost Elements of the Investment Account: 75%-Owned Subsidiary |

	Noncontrolling Interest (25%) +	Parent's Investment Account— Excess Cost =	UNDERVALUATION OF NET ASSETS ELEMENT				
			Inventory +	Land +	Equipment		GOODWILL ELEMENT
					Cost +	Accum. Depr. +	
Remaining Life			*(3 mo.)*	*n/a*	*(8 yrs.)*		*(6 yrs.)*
Balances, 1/1/X1:							
Parent's amounts		$30,000	$3,000	$6,000	$12,000		$ 9,000
NCI amounts........	$10,000		1,000	2,000	4,000		3,000
Subtotal	$10,000	$30,000	$4,000	$8,000	$16,000		$12,000
Amortizations:.......							
Parent's share		(6,000)	(3,000)			$(1,500)	(1,500)
NCI share	(2,000)[a]		(1,000)			(500)	(500)
Balances, 12/31/X1	$ 8,000	$24,000	$ –0–	$8,000	$16,000	$(2,000)	$10,000
Amortizations:.......							
Parent's share		(3,000)				(1,500)	(1,500)
NCI share	(1,000)[a]					(500)	(500)
Balances, 12/31/X2	$ 7,000	$21,000	$ –0–	$8,000	$16,000	$(4,000)	$ 8,000

[a]No general ledger entry concerning the amortization relating to the noncontrolling interest is ever made in the parent's books. A consolidation entry (following), however, is made to reflect this amortization in the consolidated income statement.

Consolidation Entries (using the amounts in the preceding analysis)

		Consolidation Date	
		December 31, 19X1	December 31, 19X2
	The Excess Cost Entry		
WORKSHEET ENTRY ONLY	Land	8,000	8,000
	Equipment	16,000	16,000
	Goodwill	10,000	8,000
	Accumulated Depreciation	2,000	4,000
	Investment in Subsidiary	24,000	21,000
	NCI in Net Assets	8,000	7,000
	The Amortization of Excess Cost Entry		
WORKSHEET ENTRY ONLY	Cost of Sales	6,000	3,000
	Equity in Net Income (of S Co.)	6,000	3,000
	The NCI Additional Amortization Entry		
WORKSHEET ENTRY ONLY	Cost of Sales	2,000	1,000
	NCI in Net Income	2,000	1,000

4. From P Company's perspective—but not from that of the noncontrolling interest shareholders—**the amounts reported in S Company's financial statements are wholly irrelevant amounts.** Under the non-push-down basis of accounting, such amounts do *not* reflect the *new basis of accounting* that occurs as a result of accounting for the acquisition as a *purchase* (as opposed to a *pooling of interest*). Accordingly, when P Company records its 75% share of S Company's reported net income, it has recorded income based on the *old basis of accounting*. By also recording amortization of cost in excess of book value, P Company's investment income is adjusted from the *old basis of accounting* to the *new basis of accounting*.

ILLUSTRATION 6–10	The *Equity* Method: *First* Year Subsequent to the Acquisition Date—75% Ownership

P Company and S Company
Consolidation Worksheet as of December 31, 19X1

	P Company	75%-owned S Company	Consolidation Entries Dr.	Consolidation Entries Cr.	Consolidated
Income Statement (19X1)					
Sales	600,000	234,000			834,000
Cost of sales	(360,000)	(110,000)	6,000(3) 2,000(4)		(378,000)
Expenses	(190,000)	(100,000)			(290,000)
Equity in net income (of S Co.) . .	12,000ᵃ		18,000(1)	6,000(3)	–0–
Net Income	62,000	24,000	26,000	6,000	66,000
NCI in net income			6,000(1)	2,000(4)	(4,000)
CI in net income			32,000	8,000	62,000
Statement of Retained Earnings					
Balances, 1/1/X1	100,000	50,000	50,000(1)		100,000
+ Net income	62,000	24,000	32,000	8,000	62,000
– Dividends declared	(51,000)	(4,000)		4,000(1)	(51,000)
Balances, 12/31/X1	111,000	70,000	82,000	12,000	111,000
Balance Sheet					
Cash	49,000	11,000			60,000
Accounts receivable	75,000	37,000			112,000
Inventory	110,000	55,000			165,000
Investment in S Company:					
Book value element	60,000			60,000(1)	–0–
Excess cost elements	24,000			24,000(2)	–0–
Land	220,000	30,000	8,000(2)		258,000
Buildings and equipment	500,000	200,000	16,000(2)	50,000(5)	666,000
Accumulated depreciation	(320,000)	(63,000)	50,000(5)	2,000(2)	(335,000)
Goodwill			10,000(2)		10,000
Total Assets	718,000	270,000	84,000	136,000	936,000
Liabilities	407,000	190,000			597,000
NCI in net assets				20,000(1) 8,000(2)	28,000
P Company:					
Common stock	200,000				200,000
Retained earnings	111,000				111,000
S Company:					
Common stock		10,000	10,000(1)		–0–
Retained earnings		70,000	82,000	12,000	–0–
Total Liabilities and Equity . .	718,000	270,000	92,000	40,000	936,000
Proof of debit and credit postings			176,000	176,000	

Explanation of entries:
(1) The basic elimination entry.
(2) The excess cost entry.
(3) The amortization of excess cost entry.
(4) The NCI additional amortization entry.
(5) The accumulated depreciation entry.

ᵃ$18,000 share of S Company's reported net income, net of $6,000 of excess cost amortization = $12,000.

ILLUSTRATION 6–11	The *Equity* Method: *Second* Year Subsequent to the Acquisition Date—75% Ownership

P Company and S Company
Consolidation Worksheet as of December 31, 19X2

	P Company	75%-owned S Company	Consolidation Entries Dr.	Consolidation Entries Cr.	Consolidated
Income Statement (19X2)					
Sales	710,000	282,000			992,000
Cost of sales	(390,000)	(130,000)	3,000(3) 1,000(4)		(524,000)
Expenses	(210,000)	(120,000)			(330,000)
Equity in net income (of S Co.)	21,000ª		24,000(1)	3,000(3)	–0–
Net Income	131,000	32,000	28,000	3,000	138,000
NCI in net income			8,000(1)	1,000(4)	(7,000)
CI in net income			36,000	4,000	131,000
Statement of Retained Earnings					
Balances, 1/1/X2	111,000	70,000	70,000(1)		111,000
+ Net income	131,000	32,000	36,000	4,000	131,000
– Dividends declared	(85,000)	(12,000)		12,000(1)	(85,000)
Balances, 12/31/X2	157,000	90,000	106,000	16,000	157,000
Balance Sheet					
Cash	47,000	31,000			78,000
Accounts receivable	84,000	43,000			127,000
Inventory	140,000	82,000			222,000
Investment in S Company:					
Book value element	75,000			75,000(1)	–0–
Excess cost elements	21,000			21,000(2)	–0–
Land	220,000	30,000	8,000(2)		258,000
Buildings and equipment	500,000	200,000	16,000(2)	50,000(5)	666,000
Accumulated depreciation	(360,000)	(76,000)	50,000(5)	4,000(2)	(390,000)
Goodwill			8,000(2)		8,000
Total Assets	727,000	310,000	82,000	150,000	969,000
Liabilities	370,000	210,000			580,000
NCI in net assets				25,000(1) 7,000(2)	32,000
P Company:					
Common stock	200,000				200,000
Retained earnings	157,000				157,000
S Company:					
Common stock		10,000	10,000(1)		–0–
Retained earnings		90,000	106,000	16,000	–0–
Total Liabilities and Equity	727,000	310,000	116,000	48,000	969,000
Proof of debit and credit postings			198,000	198,000	

Explanation of entries:
(1) The basic elimination entry.
(2) The excess cost entry.
(3) The amortization of excess cost entry.
(4) The NCI additional amortization entry.
(5) The accumulated depreciation entry.

ª$24,000 share of S Company's reported net income, net of $3,000 of excess cost amortization = $21,000.

END-OF-CHAPTER REVIEW

SUMMARY OF KEY POINTS

1. **Only postacquisition** income statements can be consolidated.
2. **Amortization** of the parent's **cost in excess of book value** is recorded (a) in the **general ledger** under the **equity method** and (b) in the **consolidation worksheet** under the **cost method**.
3. When **non-push-down accounting** is used, the subsidiary's reported amounts are **irrelevant** because they are based on its **old basis of accounting**—not the parent's **new basis of accounting.**
4. Under the **parent company concept,** a partially owned subsidiary's assets and liabilities are revalued to their current values **only to the extent that the undervaluation is bought and paid for** (likewise for goodwill).
5. Under the **economic unit concept,** a partially owned subsidiary's assets and liabilities are **revalued to their full current values.** Goodwill can be reported either at its full value or at the parent's purchased amount. (The FASB chose the former.)

GLOSSARY OF NEW TERMS

Liquidating dividend   Dividends declared by a subsidiary that are in excess of its earnings subsequent to the acquisition date.

Postacquisition earnings   Earnings of a subsidiary that occur subsequent to the acquisition date.

SELF-STUDY QUESTIONS

(Answers are at the end of this chapter, preceding the appendices.)

1. On 4/1/X1, Pax Inc. acquired 100% of Sax Inc.'s outstanding common stock for cash of $500,000. For 19X1, Sax had net income of $20,000 each quarter. Also for 19X1, Sax declared and paid cash dividends of $12,000 for each of the first three quarters and $40,000 for the fourth quarter. Amortization of cost in excess of book value for 19X1 is $10,000. What is the carrying value of Pax's investment in Sax at 12/31/X1 under the *equity method*?
   a. $486,000   **b.** $494,000   **c.** $496,000   **d.** $504,000   **e.** $546,000
2. Assume the same information as in Question 1. What is the carrying value of the investment in Sax at 12/31/X1 under the *cost* method?
   a. $486,000   **b.** $494,000   **c.** $496,000   **d.** $500,000   **e.** $504,000
3. Assume the same information as in Question 1. What amount appears in Pax's 19X1 income statement if it accounts for its investment in Sax under the *equity* method?
   a. $(6,000)   **b.** $4,000   **c.** $46,000   **d.** $50,000   **e.** $70,000
4. Assume the same information as in Question 1. What amount appears in Pax's 19X1 income statement if it accounts for its investment in Sax under the *cost* method?
   a. $50,000   **b.** $54,000   **c.** $60,000   **d.** $64,000   **e.** $76,000
5. Which of the following choices is an *incorrect* completion of the sentence? Consolidated financial statement amounts are always the same regardless of whether
   a. The acquisition is of common stock or assets.
   b. The equity method or the cost method is used.
   c. The *non*-push-down basis of accounting or the push-down basis of accounting is used.
   d. The "purchase" acquisition occurs at the beginning of the parent's reporting year or later in the year.
6. How are dividends paid to noncontrolling shareholders reported in the consolidated statements?
   a. They reduce the amount reported as "noncontrolling interest in net income of subsidiary" in the consolidated income statement.
   b. They reduce the amount reported as "noncontrolling interest in net assets of subsidiary" in the consolidated balance sheet.

    c. They are included in the dividends declared line in the consolidated statement of retained earnings.

    d. They are combined with expenses in the consolidated income statement.

    e. None of the above.

7. Pantu Inc. acquired 60% of Santu Inc.'s outstanding common stock for $156,000 cash. The book value of Santu's net assets is $200,000. Santu's only over- or undervalued asset or liability is land that has a book value of $100,000 and a current value of $150,000. Under the *parent company concept,* at what amounts are the land, the noncontrolling interest, and goodwill reported in the consolidated balance sheet?

Land	Goodwill	Noncontrolling Interest
a. $130,000	$ 6,000	$ 80,000
b. $130,000	$10,000	$100,000
c. $130,000	$44,000	$104,000
d. $150,000	$ 6,000	$ 80,000
e. $150,000	$10,000	$100,000
f. $150,000	$44,000	$104,000
g. $150,000	$ 6,000	$100,000
h. $150,000	$ 6,000	$104,000
i. $150,000	$10,000	$104,000

8. Repeat Question 7 but use the *economic unit concept.*

9. Plumex Inc. acquired 75% of Soarex Inc.'s outstanding common stock on 4/1/X1. For 19X1, Soarex reported $80,000 of net income, all of which it earned evenly throughout the year. In 19X1, Plumex recorded $3,000 of amortization of cost in excess of book value. Plumex's share of Soarex's true earnings (from Plumex's perspective) are

    a. $60,000.   **b.** $56,000.   **c.** $45,000.   **d.** $42,000.   **e.** $41,000.

DEMONSTRATION PROBLEM 1: *100%-OWNED SUBSIDIARY*

On 4/1/X4, Poda Inc. acquired 100% of Soda Inc.'s outstanding common stock at a cost of $540,000 cash. Soda's capital accounts at the acquisition date follow:

Common stock	$ 90,000
Retained earnings.	310,000

    Soda's only assets and liabilities that were over- or undervalued at the acquisition date were (1) patents (overvalued by $40,000 [10-year remaining life]) and (2) land (undervalued by $120,000). Goodwill was assigned a five-year life. For 19X4, Soda had the following earnings and dividends:

	First Quarter	Remainder of Year	Total[a]
Net Income	$30,000	$70,000	$100,000
Dividends declared	20,000	60,000	80,000

[a]All dividends were paid in the same quarter in which they were declared.

Required   **1.** Prepare the entry to record the acquisition.

    2. Prepare the entries Poda would make for the year ended 12/31/X4 under the *equity method.*

    3. Prepare an analysis of the Investment account as of the acquisition date, and update it through 12/31/X4.

    4. Prepare all consolidation entries at 12/31/X4.

SOLUTION TO DEMONSTRATION PROBLEM 1

1. Investment in Subsidiary 540,000
       Cash 540,000
       To record the acquisition.

2. Investment in Subsidiary 70,000
       Equity in Net Income (of subsidiary) 70,000
       To record share of subsidiary's earnings
       from 4/1/X4 to 12/31/X4.

      Dividends Receivable 60,000
       Investment in Subsidiary 60,000
       To record dividends from subsidiary for
       period 4/1/X4 to 12/31/X4.

      Equity in Net Income (of subsidiary) 6,000
       Investment in Subsidiary 6,000
       To amortize cost in excess of book value.

3. Conceptual analysis of Investment account:

	Parent's Investment Account— Book Value	BOOK VALUE ELEMENT Subsidiary's Equity Accounts	
	=	Common Stock +	Retained Earnings
Balances, 4/1/X4.	$400,000	$90,000	$310,000
+ Net income	70,000		70,000
– Dividends.	(60,000)		(60,000)
Balances, 12/31/X4.	$410,000	$90,000	$320,000

	Parent's Investment Account— Excess Cost =	UNDER- OR (OVER)VALUATION OF NET ASSETS ELEMENT		GOODWILL ELEMENT
		+ Land	+ Patent +	
Balances, 4/1/X4	$140,000	$120,000	$(40,000)	$60,000
– Amortization	(6,000)		3,000[a]	(9,000)[b]
Balances, 12/31/X4	$134,000	$120,000	$(37,000)	$51,000

Investment carrying
value at 12/31/X4
(in total) $544,000

[a]$40,000 \times 1/10 \times 3/4$ yr. = $3,000.
[b]$60,000 \times 1/5 \times 3/4$ yr. = $9,000.

4. The basic elimination entry:

   Common Stock 90,000
   Retained Earnings, 4/1/X4 310,000
   Equity in Net Income (of subsidiary) 70,000
       Dividends Declared 60,000
       Investment in Subsidiary 410,000

   The excess cost entry:

   Land 120,000
   Goodwill 51,000
       Patent....................................... 37,000
       Investment in Subsidiary 134,000

   The amortization of excess cost entry:

   Cost of Sales 6,000
       Equity in Net Income (of subsidiary) 6,000

DEMONSTRATION PROBLEM 2: *PARTIALLY OWNED* SUBSIDIARY

On 5/1/X5, Parr Inc. acquired 60% of Subb Inc.'s outstanding common stock at a cash cost of $273,000. Subb's capital accounts at the acquisition date were

Common stock	$ 10,000
Retained earnings.	240,000

All of Subb's assets and liabilities had current values equal to book values as of the acquisition date, except copyrights, which had a current value of $90,000 and a book value of $20,000. The copyrights had a remaining life of 14 years. Goodwill was assigned a 9-year life. For 19X5, Subb had the following earnings and dividends:

	Jan. 1– April 30, 19X5	May 1– Dec. 31, 19X5	Total[a]
Net income	$25,000	$55,000	$80,000
Dividends declared	15,000	60,000	75,000

[a]All dividends were paid in the same quarter in which they were declared.

Required   1. Prepare the entry to record the acquisition.
2. Prepare the entries Parr would make for the year ended 12/31/X5 under the *equity method*.
3. Prepare an analysis of the Investment account as of the acquisition date and update it through 12/31/X5.
4. Prepare all consolidation entries at 12/31/X5.

SOLUTION TO DEMONSTRATION PROBLEM 2

1. Investment in Subsidiary	273,000	
Cash		273,000
2. Investment in Subsidiary	33,000	
Equity in Net Income		33,000
To record share of earnings of subsidiary		
from 5/1/X5 to 12/31/X5 ($55,000 × 60%).		
Dividends Receivable	36,000	
Investment in Subsidiary		36,000
To record dividends from subsidiary		
from 5/1/X5 to 12/31/X5 ($60,000 × 60%).		
Equity in Net Income	8,000	
Investment in Subsidiary		8,000
To amortize cost in excess of book value ($2,000		
for copyrights and $6,000 for goodwill).		

3. Conceptual analysis of Investment account:

			BOOK VALUE ELEMENT		
				Subsidiary's Equity Accounts	
	Noncontrolling Interest (40%)	+	Parent's Investment Account— Book Value =	Common Stock +	Retained Earnings
Balances, 5/1/X5.			$150,000	$ 6,000	$144,000
+ NCI amounts	$100,000			4,000	96,000
Balances, 5/1/X5.	$100,000		$150,000	$10,000	$240,000
+ Net income:					
To Parr (60%)			33,000		33,000
To NCI (40%).	22,000				22,000
– Dividends:					
To Parr (60%)			(36,000)		(36,000)
To NCI (40%).	(24,000)				(24,000)
Balances, 12/31/X5.	$ 98,000		$147,000	$10,000	$235,000

	Noncontrolling Interest (40%)	+	Parent's Investment Account— Excess Cost =	UNDER- OR (OVER)VALUATION OF NET ASSETS ELEMENT + Copyrights	+	GOODWILL ELEMENT
Balances, 5/1/X5						
Parent's amounts			$123,000	$42,000		$ 81,000
+ NCI amounts	$82,000			28,000		54,000
Subtotal	$82,000		$123,000	$70,000		$135,000
– Amortizations:						
Parent's share.			(8,000)	(2,000)[a]		(6,000)[b]
NCI share	(5,333)			(1,333)[c]		(4,000)[d]
Balances, 12/31/X5	$76,667		$115,000	$66,667		$125,000

Investment carrying
value at 12/31/X5 (in total). $262,000

[a]$42,000 × 1/14 × 2/3 yr. = $2,000.
[b]$81,000 × 1/9 × 2/3 yr. = $6,000.
[c]$28,000 × 1/14 × 2/3 yr. = $1,333.
[d]$54,000 × 1/9 × 2/3 yr. = $4,000.

4. The basic elimination entry:

Common Stock	10,000	
Retained Earnings, 5/1/X5	240,000	
Equity in Net Income	33,000	
NCI in Net Income	22,000	
Dividends Declared		60,000
NCI in Net Assets		98,000
Investment in Subsidiary		147,000

The excess cost entry:

Copyrights	66,667	
Goodwill	125,000	
Investment in Subsidiary		115,000
NCI in Net Assets		76,667

The amortization of excess cost entry:

Cost of Sales	8,000	
Equity in Net Income		8,000

5. The NCI additional amortization entry:

Cost of Sales	5,333	
NCI in Net Income		5,333

ASSIGNMENT MATERIAL

REVIEW QUESTIONS

1. How are an acquired business's *preacquisition* earnings treated under the purchase method?

2. What is a *liquidating dividend*?

3. How are *liquidating dividends* treated under the *equity* method? Under the *cost* method?

4. How is amortization of cost in excess of book value treated under the *equity* method? Under the *cost* method?

5. Under what circumstances are an *acquired* subsidiary's financial statements relevant amounts from the *parent's* perspective?

6. To what extent are a partially owned *acquired* subsidiary's assets and liabilities revalued to current values under the *parent company concept*? Under the *economic unit concept*?
7. How is goodwill determined under the *parent company concept*? Under the *economic unit concept*?
8. In an acquisition of less than 100% of the voting shares, how is goodwill calculated?
9. In a *step acquisition* in which a noncontrolling interest exists, to what extent are the subsidiary's assets and liabilities reported at their current values in the consolidated statement prepared at the date control was obtained?

EXERCISES FOR *100%-OWNED* SUBSIDIARIES

E 6–1 **Recording Parent's Entries Under the Equity and Cost Methods** For 19X1, a 100%-owned subsidiary reported net income of $90,000 and declared dividends of $40,000. Amortization of cost in excess of book value, as calculated by the parent, was $12,000.

Required 1. Prepare the parent's general ledger entries under the *equity method.*
2. Repeat requirement 1 using the *cost method.*

E 6–2 **Calculating Consolidated and Parent Company Amounts** On 9/30/X5, Port Inc. acquired all of Shipp Inc.'s outstanding common stock for cash. Both companies have calendar year-ends. Data for each company pertaining to its *own separate operations* follows:

	Port	Shipp
Net Income:		
9 months ended 9/30/X5	$700,000	$280,000
3 months ended 12/31/X5	200,000[a]	120,000
	$900,000	$400,000
Dividends Declared:		
9 months ended 9/30/X5	$150,000	$ 75,000
3 months ended 12/31/X5	50,000	25,000
	$200,000	$100,000
Amortization of cost in excess of book value	$ 8,000	

[a]Excludes any amounts relating to Shipp.

Required 1. Determine the consolidated net income for 19X5.
2. Determine the consolidated dividends declared for 19X5.
3. Determine the investment income recorded in the parent's separate income statement for 19X5 under the *equity method.*
4. Repeat requirement 3 using the *cost method.*

E 6–3 **Applying the Equity Method: Consolidation Entries** On 1/1/X1, Pele Inc. acquired 100% of Soccerex Inc.'s outstanding common stock at a cost of $400,000. The analysis of Pele's investment in Soccerex by the individual components of the major conceptual elements as of the acquisition date follows:

		Remaining Life
Book value element:		
Common stock	$100,000	
Retained earnings	60,000	
Under- or (over)valuation of net assets element:		
Inventory	5,000	3 months
Land	105,000	Indefinite
Building	90,000	15 years
Goodwill element	40,000	40 years
Cost	$400,000	

Soccerex declared the following net income (loss) and dividends for 19X1 and 19X2:

	Net Income (Loss)	Dividends Declared (and Paid)
19X1	$35,000	$5,000
19X2	(10,000)	5,000

Required
1. Assuming that the parent company uses the *equity method* of accounting, prepare the journal entries it would make for 19X1 and 19X2 for its investment in the subsidiary.
2. Prepare an analysis of the Investment account by the components of the major conceptual elements as of the acquisition date, and update it for the entries developed in requirement 1.
3. Prepare all consolidation entries as of 12/31/X1 and 12/31/X2.

E 6–4 **Applying the Equity Method: Consolidation Entries** Pitt Inc. acquired 100% of Sitters Inc.'s outstanding common stock at a cost of $310,000 on 1/1/X1. The analysis of the investment by the components of the major conceptual elements as of the acquisition date (after appropriate allocation of the bargain purchase element) follows:

		Remaining Life
Book value element:		
Common stock	$250,000	
Retained earnings	100,000	
Under- or (over)valuation of net assets element:		
Inventory	5,000	3 months
Land	30,000	Indefinite
Building	(75,000)	25 years
Cost	$310,000	

Sitters declared the following net income (loss) and dividends for 19X1 and 19X2:

	Net Income (Loss)	Dividends Declared (and Paid)
19X1	$(15,000)	$1,000
19X2	30,000	5,000

Required
1. Assuming that Pitt uses the *equity method* of accounting, prepare the journal entries it would make for 19X1 and 19X2 with respect to its investment in the subsidiary.
2. Prepare an analysis of the Investment account by the individual components of the major conceptual elements as of the acquisition date and update it for the entries developed in situation 1.
3. Prepare all consolidation entries as of 12/31/X1 and 12/31/X2.

EXERCISES FOR *PARTIALLY OWNED* SUBSIDIARIES

E 6–5 **Calculating Consolidated Net Income** Pushco Inc. owns 75% of Shovex Inc.'s outstanding common stock. Each company's 19X1 net income from its own separate operations, exclusive of earnings and amortization recorded under the *equity method*, follows:

Pushco	$1,000,000
Shovex	600,000

During 19X1, Pushco amortized from its Investment account $30,000 of cost in excess of book value.

Required
1. Determine the amount of consolidated net income accruing to the controlling interest.
2. Determine the amount of consolidated net income accruing to the noncontrolling interest.

E 6–6 **Calculating Consolidated Net Income** Potter Inc. owns 90% of Stane Inc.'s outstanding common stock and 80% of Steele Inc.'s outstanding common stock. Each company's 19X1 net income from its *own* *separate operations*, exclusive of earnings recorded under the *equity method* and amortization of cost over book value of net assets, follows:

Potter	$1,000,000
Stane	300,000
Steele.	100,000

Amortization of cost over book value of net assets on a full-year basis is $27,000 and $8,000 for Stane and Steele, respectively.

Required   **1.** Calculate (a) the noncontrolling interest in each subsidiary's net income and (b) the controlling interest in the consolidated net income for 19X1, assuming that the subsidiaries were owned during the *entire* year.

2. Calculate (a) the noncontrolling interest in each subsidiary's net income and (b) the controlling interest in the consolidated net income for 19X1, assuming that Stane was acquired on 5/1/X1 and Steele was acquired on 7/1/X1. (Assume that earnings occurred evenly throughout the year.)

E 6–7   **Calculating Consolidated Net Income**   On 1/1/X1, Palmer Inc. acquired 75% of Snead Inc.'s outstanding common stock at an amount equal to 75% of Snead's net assets at carrying value. Each company's 19X1 income statement, exclusive of earnings recorded under the *equity method*, follows:

	Palmer	Snead
Sales	$800,000	$200,000
Cost of sales	(400,000)	(100,000)
Expenses	(150,000)	(40,000)
Net Income	$250,000	$ 60,000

Balance sheet amounts for each company at 12/31/X1 are purposely not furnished; therefore, a formal consolidation worksheet cannot be prepared. The consolidated amounts still can be determined, however, if you understand the main concept of the chapter.

Required   **1.** Determine the consolidated income statement amounts.

2. Determine the consolidated income statement amounts assuming that Palmer amortized from its Investment account $3,000 of cost in excess of book value of net assets that pertains to goodwill.

E 6–8   **Calculating Consolidated and Parent Company Amounts**   On 4/30/X3, Pal Inc. acquired 75% of Salle Inc.'s outstanding common stock for cash. Both companies have calendar year-ends. Data for each company pertaining to its *own separate operations* follow:

	Pal	Salle
Net Income:		
4 months ended 4/30/X3	$350,000	$100,000
8 months ended 12/31/X3	450,000[a]	200,000
	$800,000	$300,000
Dividends Declared:		
4 months ended 4/30/X3	$140,000	$ 40,000
8 months ended 12/31/X3	280,000	80,000
	$420,000	$120,000
Amortization of cost in excess of book value recorded by Pal for 19X3 (all for goodwill)	$ 24,000	

[a]Excludes any amounts relating to Salle.

Required   **1.** Determine the consolidated net income for 19X3 that accrues to the controlling interest.

2. Determine the consolidated dividends declared for 19X3.

3. Determine the investment income recorded in the parent's separate income statement for 19X3 under the *equity method*.

E 6−9 **Separating Parent's Cost into Components** On 5/1/X1, Pana Inc. acquired 60% of Sonic Inc.'s outstanding common stock at a cost of $219,000. Sonic's capital account balances at that date are as follows:

Common stock	$ 50,000
Additional paid-in capital.	550,000
Accumulated deficit.	(200,000)

Each of Sonic's assets and liabilities has a current value equal to its book value, except for the following items:

	Book Value	Current Value
Leasehold improvements	$ 95,000	$ 60,000
Deferred charges	40,000	–0–
Note receivable	75,000	85,000
12% bonds payable	100,000	120,000

Required Analyze the Investment account as of the acquisition date. Include the noncontrolling interest.

E 6−10 **Separating Parent's Cost into Components** On 1/1/X6, Prima Inc. acquired 70% of Seconde Inc.'s outstanding common stock at a cost of $203,000. Seconde's capital account balances at 12/31/X5 are as follows:

Common stock	$100,000
Additional paid-in capital	50,000
Retained earnings	60,000
	$210,000

Each of Seconde's assets and liabilities has a current value equal to its book value, except for the following items:

	Book Value	Current Value
Land.	$170,000	$240,000
Goodwill.	50,000	–0–
10% Bonds payable	160,000	140,000

Required Analyze the Investment account as of the acquisition date. Include the noncontrolling interest.

E 6−11 **Determining Subsidiary's Equity from Consolidated Data** Popp Inc. acquired 70% of Soda Inc.'s outstanding common stock. Popp's separate balance sheet immediately *after the acquisition* and the consolidated balance sheet follow:

	Popp	Consolidated
Current assets.	$101,000	$160,000
Investment in Soda (cost)	105,000	—
Goodwill	—	10,000
Fixed assets (net)	270,000	370,000
Total Assets	$476,000	$540,000
Current liabilities	$ 15,000	$ 34,000
Noncontrolling interest.	—	45,000
Capital stock	350,000	350,000
Retained earnings	111,000	111,000
Total Liabilities and Equity	$476,000	$540,000

Of the excess payment for the investment in Soda, $21,000 was attributed to undervaluation of its fixed assets; the balance was attributed to goodwill. Soda's no par Common Stock account had a $50,000 balance at the acquisition date.

Required
1. Calculate the total stockholders' equity of the subsidiary when it was acquired.
2. Prepare a conceptual analysis of the Investment account at the acquisition date.

PROBLEMS FOR *100%-OWNED* SUBSIDIARIES

P 6–1*

Consolidation Worksheet (Continuation of Problem 5–4) Pya Inc., a calendar-year reporting company, acquired 100% of Sya Inc.'s outstanding common stock at a cost of $300,000 on 12/31/X1. The analysis of the parent's Investment account as of the acquisition date follows:

		Remaining Life
Book value element:		
Common stock....................................	$100,000	
Retained earnings	90,000	
Under- or (over)valuation of net assets element:		
Inventory	5,000	2 months
Land	30,000	Indefinite
Equipment	50,000	10 years
Patent	(15,000)	3 years
Goodwill element..................................	40,000	4 years
Cost	$300,000	

Each company's financial statements for the year ended 12/31/X2 follow:

	Pya		Sya
	Cost Method[a]	**Equity Method[b]**	**Sya**
Income Statement (19X2)			
Sales	$2,800,000	$2,800,000	$600,000
Cost of sales	(1,500,000)	(1,500,000)	(300,000)
Expenses......................	(1,000,000)	(1,000,000)	(240,000)
Equity in net income (of Sya).............		45,000	
Dividend income	55,000		
Net Income........................	$ 355,000	$ 345,000	$ 60,000
Balance Sheet (as of 12/31/X2)			
Cash	$ 120,000	$ 120,000	$ 25,000
Accounts receivable, net	300,000	300,000	50,000
Inventory	500,000	500,000	120,000
Investment in Sya......................	300,000	290,000	
Land........................	400,000	400,000	70,000
Buildings and equipment.................	1,100,000	1,100,000	223,000
Accumulated depreciation	(210,000)	(210,000)	(68,000)
Patent.......................			10,000
Total Assets	$2,510,000	$2,500,000	$430,000
Payables and accruals...................	$ 320,000	$ 320,000	$ 85,000
Long-term debt	1,300,000	1,300,000	150,000
Common stock........................	300,000	300,000	100,000
Retained earnings	590,000	580,000	95,000
Total Liabilities and Equity	$2,510,000	$2,500,000	$430,000
Dividends declared during 19X2	$ 215,000	$ 215,000	$ 55,000

[a]Use this column if working the problem under the cost method.
[b]Use this column if working the problem under the equity method.

*The financial statement information presented for problems accompanied by asterisks is also provided on Model 6 (filename: MODEL6) of the software file disk that is available for use with the text, allowing the problem to be worked on the computer.

Required 1. Equity method only: Update the analyses of the Investment account through 12/31/X2.
2. Prepare all consolidation entries as of 12/31/X2.
3. Prepare a consolidation worksheet at 12/31/X2. (The parent's retained earnings as of 1/1/X2 was $450,000.)

P 6–2* **Consolidation Worksheet (Continuation of Problem 5–5)** Poz Inc., a calendar-year reporting company, acquired 100% of Soz Inc.'s outstanding common stock at a cost of $400,000 on 12/31/X1. The analysis of Poz's Investment account as of the acquisition date follows:

		Remaining Life
Book value element:		
Common stock.	$ 50,000	
Additional paid-in capital	200,000	
Retained earnings	250,000	
Under- or (over)valuation of net assets element:		
Inventory	(70,000)	6 months
Land.	30,000	Indefinite
Building	(100,000)	20 years
Long-term debt	40,000	4 years
Cost	$400,000	

Each company's financial statements for the year ended 12/31/X2 follow:

	Poz		Soz
	Cost Method[a]	Equity Method[b]	
Income Statement (19X2)			
Sales	$7,000,000	$7,000,000	$850,000
Cost of sales	(3,800,000)	(3,800,000)	(600,000)
Expenses.	(1,700,000)	(1,700,000)	(310,000)
Equity in net income (of Soz)		5,000	
Net Income (Loss)	$1,500,000	$1,505,000	$ (60,000)
Balance Sheet (as of 12/31/X2)			
Cash	$ 295,000	$ 295,000	$ 20,000
Accounts receivable, net	400,000	400,000	80,000
Inventory	700,000	700,000	130,000
Investment in Soz	400,000	405,000	
Land	500,000	500,000	100,000
Buildings and equipment.	3,100,000	3,100,000	553,000
Accumulated depreciation.	(600,000)	(600,000)	(83,000)
Total Assets	$4,795,000	$4,800,000	$800,000
Payables and accruals.	$ 495,000	$ 495,000	$ 60,000
Long-term debt	2,000,000	2,000,000	300,000
Common stock.	20,000	20,000	50,000
Additional paid-in capital	480,000	480,000	200,000
Retained earnings	1,800,000	1,805,000	190,000
Total Liabilities and Equity	$4,795,000	$4,800,000	$800,000
Dividends declared during 19X2.	$ 800,000	$ 800,000	$ –0–

[a]Use this column if working under the *cost method*.
[b]Use this column if working under the *equity method*.

Required 1. Equity method only: Update the analyses of the Investment account through 12/31/X2.
2. Prepare all consolidation entries as of 12/31/X2.
3. Prepare a consolidation worksheet at 12/31/X2. (The parent's retained earnings as of 1/1/X2 was $1,100,000.)

P 6–3*   **COMPREHENSIVE: Recording the Acquisition; Analyzing the Investment Account; Applying the Equity Method; Consolidation Worksheet**   On 1/1/X1, Pina Inc. acquired 100% of Sina Inc.'s outstanding common stock by issuing 7,000 shares of $10 par value common stock (which was trading at $60 per share on that date). In addition, Pina incurred direct costs of $95,000 relating to the acquisition, $25,000 of which was for registering the shares issued with the SEC. (All these direct costs were charged to the Investment account.) The balances in the subsidiary's capital accounts as of the acquisition date follow:

Common stock.	$100,000
Retained earnings	402,000
	$502,000

All of the subsidiary's assets and liabilities have a current value equal to their book value, except for the following:

	Book Value	Current Value	Remaining Life
Land held for development	$600,000	$710,000	Indefinite
Deferred charges	42,000	–0–	3 years
Long-term debt, 10%	200,000	230,000	6 years

Additional Information

1. Sina is a real estate development company that owns several parcels of land. None of the land owned was developed during 19X1. One parcel acquired eight years ago was sold, however, in its undeveloped stage. This was the only sale for 19X1.
2. Pina is privately owned and chose to use *non*-push-down accounting.
3. Pina's accounting policy is to amortize goodwill over 10 years.
4. The only entry Pina made in its books relating to the subsidiary was at the acquisition date.
5. The combination did *not* qualify for pooling of interests treatment.
6. Sina's buildings and equipment were fully depreciated at the acquisition date.

Each company's financial statements for the year ended 12/31/X1 follow:

	Pina	Sina
Income Statement (19X1)		
Sales	$ 950,000	$330,000
Cost of sales	(520,000)	(200,000)
Expenses	(204,000)	(45,000)
Net Income	$ 226,000	$ 85,000
Balance Sheet (as of 12/31/X1)		
Cash	$ 200,000	$ 22,000
Accounts receivable, net	300,000	
Notes receivable		350,000
Inventory	600,000	
Investment in Sina	515,000	
Land	500,000	
Buildings and equipment	2,700,000	5,000
Accumulated depreciation	(600,000)	(5,000)
Land held for development		400,000
Deferred charges		28,000
Total Assets	$4,215,000	$800,000
Payables and accruals	$ 160,000	$ 13,000
Dividends payable		35,000
Long-term debt	1,600,000	200,000
Common stock	700,000	100,000
Additional paid-in capital	1,015,000	
Retained earnings	740,000	452,000
Total Liabilities and Equity	$4,215,000	$800,000
Dividends declared during 19X1	$ 100,000	$ 35,000

Required
1. Analyze the Investment account by the components of the major conceptual elements as of the acquisition date. Make any appropriate adjusting entries.
2. Update the analysis of the Investment account to reflect activity under the *equity method* through 12/31/X1.
3. Prepare the consolidation entries as of 12/31/X1.
4. Adjust Pina's financial statements as shown above to reflect the *equity method* and then prepare a consolidation worksheet at 12/31/X1.

P 6–4* **COMPREHENSIVE CHALLENGER: Converting to the Equity Method from the Cost Method Two Years After the Acquisition Date; Consolidation Worksheet**   Pali Inc. acquired all of Sali Inc.'s outstanding common stock for $820,000 cash on 1/1/X1. Pali also incurred $47,000 of direct costs in connection with the acquisition. Selected information on Sali as of the acquisition date follows:

	Book Value	Current Value	Remaining Life
Inventory	$ 303,000	$ 310,000	4 months
Buildings and equipment	1,400,000[a]	1,490,000	15 years
Patent	20,000	60,000	5 years
Goodwill	60,000	–0–	6 years
10% bonds payable	1,200,000	1,000,000	10 years

[a]Net of $300,000 of accumulated depreciation.

Additional Information
1. Pali is privately owned and chose to use *non*-push-down accounting.
2. Pali has used the *cost method* since the acquisition date and has decided to change to the *equity method* to account for its investment in the subsidiary.
3. Assume a 40-year life for any goodwill paid in the transaction.

Each company's financial statements for the year ended 12/31/X2 (two years after the acquisition date) follow:

	Pali	Sali
Income Statement (19X2)		
Sales	$8,500,000	$ 980,000
Cost of sales	(4,500,000)	(530,000)
Expenses	(3,640,000)	(310,000)
Dividend income	50,000	
Net Income	$ 410,000	$ 140,000
Balance Sheet (as of 12/31/X2)		
Cash	$ 458,000	$ 118,000
Accounts receivable, net	750,000	190,000
Inventory	820,000	380,000
Investment in Sali	867,000	
Land	760,000	240,000
Buildings and equipment	6,260,000	1,720,000
Accumulated depreciation	(2,465,000)	(480,000)
Patent	100,000	12,000
Goodwill		40,000
Total Assets	$7,550,000	$2,220,000
Payables and accruals	$1,600,000	$ 370,000
Long-term debt	3,000,000	1,200,000
Common stock	2,000,000	250,000
Retained earnings	950,000	400,000
Total Liabilities and Equity	$7,550,000	$2,220,000
Dividends declared during 19X2	$ 100,000	$ 50,000
Dividends declared during 19X1	80,000	40,000
Reported net income for 19X1	200,000	90,000

Required   1. Analyze the Investment account by the components of the major conceptual elements as of the acquisition date.
2. Update the analysis of the Investment account to reflect activity under the *equity method* of accounting through 12/31/X2 (a two-year period).
3. Prepare the journal entry(s) to convert to the *equity method* from the *cost method*.
4. Prepare the consolidation entries as of 12/31/X2.
5. Adjust the parent's financial statements to reflect the *equity method,* and then prepare a consolidation worksheet at 12/31/X2.
6. Would the parent's outside auditors have to mention the change to the *equity method* in their audit report?

P 6–5*   **COMPREHENSIVE: Recording the Acquisition and Selecting Relevant Data; Consolidation Worksheet**   On 7/1/X1, in a business combination that did not qualify as a pooling of interests, PBM Inc. acquired 100% of SOS Inc.'s outstanding common stock by issuing 6,000 shares of its $10 par value common stock (which was trading at $70 per share on that date). In addition, PBM incurred direct costs of $90,000 relating to the acquisition, $40,000 of which was to register the shares issued with the SEC. Selected relevant data follow:

| | June 30, 19X1 | | |
	Book Value	Current Value	Remaining Life
SOS			
Inventory	$ 66,000	$ 70,000	3 months
Buildings and equipment	310,000[a]	382,000	12 years
Goodwill	20,000	–0–	5 years
Long-term debt	400,000	384,000	8 years
Common stock	200,000		
Retained earnings	138,000		
PBM			
Common stock	100,000		
Additional paid-in capital	500,000		
Retained earnings	800,000		

[a]Net of $140,000 accumulated depreciation.

Additional Information   1. Assume that any goodwill arising from the combination has a 10-year life from the acquisition date of 7/1/X1.
2. The *non*-push-down basis of accounting was selected.
3. The *equity* method of accounting is to be used.
4. For 19X1, SOS had the following earnings and dividends:

	Jan. 1– June 30, 19X1	July 1– Dec. 31, 19X1	Total
Sales	$400,000	$500,000	$900,000
Cost of sales	(220,000)	(260,000)	(480,000)
Expenses	(130,000)	(180,000)	(310,000)
Net Income	$ 50,000	$ 60,000	$110,000
Dividends declared and paid	$ 15,000	$ 20,000	$ 35,000

5. During 19X1, PBM declared and paid $75,000 of dividends each quarter. Also, PBM reported a net income of $200,000 for the six months ended 6/30/X1.

Required   1. Prepare the entry to record the business combination on 7/1/X1.
2. Complete PBM's and SOS's financial statements that follow:

	PBM	SOS
Income Statement (19X1)		
Sales	$2,600,000	
Cost of sales	(1,300,000)	
Expenses	(800,000)	
Net Income		
Statement of Retained Earnings		
Balances, beginning	$ 750,000	
+ Net income		
− Dividends declared	(300,000)	
Balances, 12/31/X1		
Balance Sheet (as of 12/31/X1)		
Current assets	$ 700,000	$400,000
Land	943,000	202,000
Buildings and equipment	2,200,000	450,000
Accumulated depreciation	(330,000)	(170,000)
Investment in SOS		
Goodwill		18,000
Total Assets		$900,000
Payables and accruals	$ 433,000	$122,000
Long-term debt	1,600,000	400,000
PBM:		
Common stock		
Additional paid-in capital		
Retained earnings		
SOS:		
Common stock		200,000
Retained earnings		178,000
Total Liabilities and Equity		$900,000

3. Prepare an analysis of the Investment account updated through 12/31/X1.
4. Prepare the consolidation entries.
5. Prepare a consolidation worksheet.

PROBLEMS FOR *PARTIALLY OWNED* SUBSIDIARIES

P 6–6* **Consolidation Worksheet as of the Acquisition Date**   On 12/31/X1, Pya Inc., a calendar-year reporting company, acquired 80% of Sya Inc.'s outstanding common stock at a cost of $240,000. Selected information on Sya as of the acquisition date follows:

	Book Value	Current Value	Remaining Life
Inventory	$80,000	$ 85,000	2 months
Land	70,000	100,000	Indefinite
Equipment	40,000	90,000	10 years
Patent	15,000	–0–	3 years

Assume a 4-year life for any goodwill paid in the transaction.

Each company's financial statements for the year ended 12/31/X1, *immediately after* the acquisition date, follow:

	Pya	Sya
Income Statement (19X1)		
Sales	$2,500,000	$500,000
Cost of sales	(1,400,000)	(250,000)
Expenses	(860,000)	(202,000)
Net Income	$ 240,000	$ 48,000
Balance Sheet (as of 12/31/X1)		
Cash	$ 160,000	$ 20,000
Accounts receivable, net	200,000	55,000
Inventory	350,000	80,000
Investment in Sya	240,000	
Land	400,000	70,000
Buildings and equipment	800,000	203,000
Accumulated depreciation	(150,000)	(43,000)
Patent		15,000
Total Assets	$2,000,000	$400,000
Payables and accruals	$ 250,000	$ 60,000
Long-term debt	1,000,000	150,000
Common stock	300,000	100,000
Retained earnings	450,000	90,000
Total Liabilities and Equity	$2,000,000	$400,000
Dividends declared during 19X1	$ 80,000	$ 10,000

Required   **1.** Prepare an analysis of the Investment account by the components of the major conceptual elements as of 12/31/X1. (First separate the Investment account into the book value element and the excess cost elements.)
2. Prepare the consolidation entries required as of 12/31/X1.
3. Prepare a consolidation worksheet at 12/31/X1.
4. What amount of income does Pya report to its stockholders for the year 19X1?

P 6–7*   **Consolidation Worksheet Subsequent to the Acquisition Date (Continuation of Problem 6–6)**   As described in Problem 6–6, Pya Inc. acquired 80% of Sya Inc. for $240,000 on 12/31/X1. The financial statements as of 12/31/X2, one year after the acquisition date, follow:

	Pya		Sya
	Cost Method	Equity Method	Sya
Income Statement (19X2)			
Sales	$2,800,000	$2,800,000	$600,000
Cost of sales	(1,500,000)	(1,500,000)	(300,000)
Expenses	(1,000,000)	(1,000,000)	(240,000)
Equity in net income		36,000	
Dividend income	44,000		
Net Income	$ 344,000	$ 336,000	$ 60,000
Balance Sheet (as of 12/31/X2)			
Cash	$ 169,000	$ 169,000	$ 25,000
Accounts receivable, net	300,000	300,000	50,000
Inventory	500,000	500,000	120,000
Investment in Sya	240,000	232,000	
Land	400,000	400,000	70,000
Buildings and equipment	1,100,000	1,100,000	223,000
Accumulated depreciation	(210,000)	(210,000)	(68,000)
Patent			10,000
	$2,499,000	$2,491,000	$430,000

Payables and accruals	$ 320,000	$ 320,000	$ 85,000
Long-term debt	1,300,000	1,300,000	150,000
Common stock	300,000	300,000	100,000
Retained earnings	579,000	571,000	95,000
	$2,499,000	$2,491,000	$430,000
Dividends declared during 19X2	$ 215,000	$ 215,000	$ 55,000

Required   **1.** Update the expanded analysis of the Investment account through 12/31/X2 using the *equity method*.

2. Prepare the consolidation entries at 12/31/X2.

3. Prepare a consolidation worksheet at 12/31/X2. (The parent's retained earnings at 12/31/X2 were $450,000.)

P 6–8*   **Consolidation Worksheet as of the Acquisition Date**   Poz Inc., a calendar-year reporting company, acquired 80% of Soz Inc.'s outstanding common stock at a cost of $320,000 on 12/31/X1. Selected information on Soz as of the acquisition date follows:

	Book Value	Current Value	Remaining Life
Inventory	$220,000	$150,000	6 months
Land	100,000	130,000	Indefinite
Building	410,000	310,000	20 years
Long-term debt	300,000	260,000	4 years

Each company's financial statements for the year ended 12/31/X1, immediately *after* the acquisition date, follow:

	Poz	Soz
Income Statement (19X1)		
Sales..	$6,000,000	$800,000
Cost of sales	(3,300,000)	(600,000)
Expenses	(1,500,000)	(250,000)
Net Income (Loss)	$1,200,000	$ (50,000)
Balance Sheet (as of 12/31/X1)		
Cash	$ 320,000	$ 30,000
Accounts receivable, net	360,000	50,000
Inventory......................................	800,000	220,000
Investment in Soz	320,000	
Land	500,000	100,000
Buildings and equipment	2,600,000	553,000
Accumulated depreciation	(400,000)	(53,000)
Total Assets	$4,500,000	$900,000
Payables and accruals	$ 800,000	$100,000
Long-term debt...............................	2,100,000	300,000
Common stock	20,000	50,000
Additional paid-in capital	480,000	200,000
Retained earnings	1,100,000	250,000
Total Liabilities and Equity	$4,500,000	$900,000
Dividends declared during 19X1	$ 700,000	$ –0–

Required   **1.** Prepare an analysis of the Investment account by the components of the major conceptual elements as of 12/31/X1. (First separate the Investment account into the book value element and the excess cost elements.)

2. Prepare the consolidation entries at 12/31/X1.

3. Prepare a consolidation worksheet at 12/31/X1.

4. What amount of income does the parent company report to its stockholders for 19X1?

P 6–9*   **Consolidation Worksheet Subsequent to the Acquisition Date (Continuation of Problem 6–8)**   As described in Problem 6–8, Poz acquired 80% of Soz for $320,000 on 12/31/X1. The financial statements as of 12/31/X2, one year after the acquisition date, follow:

	Poz		Soz
	Cost Method	Equity Method	Soz
Income Statement (19X2)			
Sales	$7,000,000	$7,000,000	$ 850,000
Cost of sales	(3,800,000)	(3,800,000)	(600,000)
Expenses	(1,700,000)	(1,700,000)	(310,000)
Equity in net income (of Soz)		4,000	
Dividend income			
Net Income (Loss)	$1,500,000	$1,504,000	$ (60,000)
Balance Sheet (as of 12/31/X2)			
Cash	$ 375,000	$ 375,000	$ 20,000
Accounts receivable, net	400,000	400,000	80,000
Inventory	700,000	700,000	130,000
Investment in Soz	320,000	324,000	
Land	500,000	500,000	100,000
Buildings and equipment	3,100,000	3,100,000	553,000
Accumulated depreciation	(600,000)	(600,000)	(83,000)
Total Assets	$4,795,000	$4,799,000	$ 800,000
Payables and accruals	$ 495,000	$ 495,000	$ 60,000
Long-term debt	2,000,000	2,000,000	300,000
Common stock	20,000	20,000	50,000
Additional paid-in capital	480,000	480,000	200,000
Retained earnings	1,800,000	1,804,000	190,000
Total Liabilities and Equity	$4,795,000	$4,799,000	$ 800,000
Dividends declared during 19X2	$ 800,000	$ 800,000	$ –0–

Required   **1.** Update the expanded analysis of the Investment account through 12/31/X2 under the *equity method*.
2. Prepare the consolidation entries at 12/31/X2.
3. Prepare a consolidation worksheet at 12/31/X2. (Poz's retained earnings at 12/31/X2 was $1,100,000.)

P 6–10*   **COMPREHENSIVE: Analyzing the Investment; Applying the Equity Method; Consolidation Worksheet**   PDQ Inc. acquired 60% of SAS Inc.'s outstanding common stock for cash of $503,000 on 1/1/X1. PDQ also incurred $25,000 of direct out-of-pocket costs in connection with the acquisition. Information with respect to SAS as of the acquisition date follows:

	Book Value	Current Value	Remaining Life
Cash	$ 74,000	$ 74,000	
Accounts receivable, net	266,000	266,000	
Inventory	280,000	260,000	6 months
Land	780,000	780,000	Indefinite
Buildings and equipment	900,000	675,000	15 years
Accumulated depreciation	(300,000)		
Patent	40,000	165,000	5 years
Goodwill	60,000		2 years
Total Assets	$2,100,000	$2,220,000	
Payables and accruals	$ 380,000	$ 380,000	
Long-term debt	1,200,000	1,040,000	4 years
Common stock	200,000	800,000	
Retained earnings	320,000		
Total Liabilities and Equity	$2,100,000	$2,220,000	

PDQ intends to use the *equity method* to account for its investment. The only entry it has made to the Investment account since the acquisition date, however, is to reflect the receipt of its share of $55,000 of dividends that SAS declared and paid during 19X1. PDQ assigned an 8-year life to goodwill that it paid for.

Each company's financial statements for the year ended 12/31/X1, one year after the acquisition date, follow:

	PDQ	SAS
Income Statement (19X1)		
Sales	$9,000,000	$ 870,000
Cost of sales	(5,000,000)	(470,000)
Expenses	(2,800,000)	(190,000)
Net Income	$1,200,000	$ 210,000
Balance Sheet (as of 12/31/X1)		
Cash	$ 665,000	$ 168,000
Accounts receivable, net	840,000	270,000
Inventory	1,200,000	560,000
Investment in SAS	495,000	
Land	1,000,000	780,000
Buildings and equipment	4,800,000	1,050,000
Accumulated depreciation	(1,700,000)	(390,000)
Patent	300,000	32,000
Goodwill		30,000
Total Assets	$7,600,000	$2,500,000
Payables and accruals	$1,100,000	$ 625,000
Long-term debt	2,600,000	1,200,000
Common stock	2,000,000	200,000
Retained earnings	1,900,000	475,000
Total Liabilities and Equity	$7,600,000	$2,500,000
Dividends declared during 19X1	$ 900,000	$ 55,000

Required   1. Analyze the Investment account as of the acquisition date.
2. Update the analyses of the Investment account to reflect activity under the *equity method* through 12/31/X1.
3. Adjust the parent's statements as of 12/31/X1 to reflect the equity method of accounting.
4. Prepare the consolidation entries at 12/31/X1.
5. Prepare a consolidation worksheet at 12/31/X1.

P 6–11   **REVIEW (Chapters 5 and 6): Analyzing the Investment; Applying the Equity Method; Computing Noncontrolling Interest and Consolidated Retained Earnings**   On 1/1/X1, Puttnam Inc. made the following investments:

1. It acquired 75% of Shaft Inc.'s outstanding common stock for $14 cash per share. Shaft's stockholders' equity on 1/1/X1 consisted of the following:

   Common stock, $10 par value...................................... $100,000
   Retained earnings 20,000

2. It acquired 60% of Tee Inc.'s outstanding common stock for $40 cash per share. Tee's stockholders' equity on 1/1/X1 consisted of the following:

   Common stock, $20 par value $60,000
   Paid-in capital in excess of par value 10,000
   Retained earnings 50,000

The current values of each subsidiary's net assets equal their book values except for a parcel of land Shaft owned that has a current value of $40,000 *less* than its book value. At the time of these acquisitions, Puttnam expected both companies to have superior earnings for the next 15 years.

Puttnam has accounted for these investments using the *cost method*. An analysis of each company's retained earnings for 19X1 follows:

	Puttnam	Shaft	Tee
Balances, 1/1/X1	$300,000	$20,000	$50,000
+ Net income (loss)	193,000	36,000	(15,000)
– Cash dividends declared and paid	(110,000)	(28,000)	(10,000)
Balances, 12/31/X1	$383,000	$28,000	$25,000

Required   1. Under the *equity* method, what entries should have been made on the parent's books during 19X1 to record the following:
   a. Investments in subsidiaries.
   b. Parent's share of subsidiary income or loss.
   c. Subsidiary dividends received.
   d. Amortization of cost in excess of (under) book value, if any.
2. Compute the amount of the noncontrolling interest in each subsidiary's stockholders' equity at 12/31/X1 using each's *book values*. What additional amounts must be imputed?
3. What were the parent's earnings from *its own operations* for 19X1, excluding accounts relating to its ownership in these subsidiaries?
4. What amount should be reported as consolidated retained earnings as of 12/31/X1?

(AICPA adapted)

P 6–12*   **COMPREHENSIVE: Recording the Acquisition; Selecting Relevant Data; Consolidation Worksheet**   On 7/1/X2, in a business combination that did *not* qualify as a pooling of interests, Pepsi Inc. acquired 80% of Sprite Inc.'s outstanding common stock by issuing 8,000 shares of its $5 par value common stock (which was trading at $65 per share on that date). In addition, Pepsi incurred *direct costs* of $92,000 relating to the acquisition, $60,000 of which was for registering the shares issued with the SEC. Selected relevant data follow:

	June 30, 19X2		
	Book Value	Current Value	Remaining Life
Sprite			
Inventory	$110,000	$120,000	2 months
Buildings and equipment	700,000[a]	770,000	14 years
Patents	90,000	60,000	3 years
Long-term debt	500,000	475,000	1 year
Common stock	300,000		
Retained earnings	225,000		
Pepsi			
Common stock	$500,000		
Additional paid-in capital	500,000		
Retained earnings	400,000		

[a]Net of $200,000 of accumulated depreciation.

Additional   1. Assume that any goodwill arising from the combination has a 5-year life.
Information   2. The *equity* method of accounting is to be used.
3. For 19X2, Sprite had the following earnings and dividends:

	Jan. 1–June 30, 19X2	July 1–Dec. 31, 19X2	Total
Sales	$600,000	$800,000	$1,400,000
Cost of sales	(320,000)	(430,000)	(750,000)
Expenses	(240,000)	(310,000)	(550,000)
Net Income	$ 40,000	$ 60,000	$ 100,000
Dividends declared	$ 25,000	$ 35,000[a]	$ 70,000
Dividends paid	25,000	–0–	25,000

[a]This dividend was paid 1/5/X3.

4. During 19X2, Pepsi declared and paid $80,000 of dividends each quarter. Also, Pepsi reported a net income of $200,000 for the six months ended 6/30/X2.

Required 1. Prepare the entry to record the business combination on 7/1/X2.

2. Complete Pepsi's and Sprite's financial statements that follow for consolidation purposes:

	Pepsi	Sprite
Income Statement (19X2)		
Sales	$2,200,000	
Cost of sales	(1,100,000)	
Expenses	(600,000)	
Net Income		
Statement of Retained Earnings		
Balances, beginning		
+ Net income		
− Dividends declared		
Balances, 12/31/X2		
Balance Sheet (as of 12/31/X2)		
Current assets	$1,356,000	$ 475,000
Investment in Sprite		
Land	700,000	200,000
Buildings and equipment	3,000,000	900,000
Accumulated depreciation	(600,000)	(250,000)
Patents	–0–	75,000
Total Assets		$1,400,000
Accounts payable	$ 913,000	$ 350,000
Long-term debt	2,100,000	500,000
Common stock		300,000
Additional paid-in capital		
Retained earnings		250,000
Total Liabilities and Equity		$1,400,000

3. Prepare an analysis of the Investment account updated through 12/31/X2.
4. Prepare the consolidation entries at 12/31/X2.
5. Prepare a consolidation worksheet at 12/31/X2.

P 6–13 **Step Acquisition: Significant Influence; 90% Ownership Obtained** Use the information in Problem 5–9 but assume that on 12/31/X2 Pomco acquired only 50% of Somco's outstanding common stock for $180,000 (instead of 60% for $216,000), thus obtaining a 90% ownership interest (instead of a 100% ownership interest).

Required 1. Analyze the Investment account through the date control was achieved. Be sure to include the noncontrolling interest.

2. Prepare all consolidation entries at 12/31/X2.

P 6–14 **Step Acquisition: Significant Influence; 75% Ownership Obtained; Mid-Year Acquisition—Postacquisition Period** On 1/1/X8, Plazco Inc. acquired 30% of Slazco Inc.'s outstanding common stock at a cost of $380,000. At that time, Slazco's capital accounts were as follows:

Common stock	$ 600,000
Retained earnings	400,000
	$1,000,000

On 4/1/X8, Plazco acquired 45% of Slazco's outstanding common stock at a cost of $501,000. Earnings and dividend information for Slazco for 19X8 are as follows:

	First Quarter	Remaining Quarters	Full Year
Net income	$70,000	$240,000	$310,000
Dividends declared	50,000	140,000	190,000

Plazco uses a 10-year life for goodwill residually determined at each stock purchase date. Assume also that *none* of Slazco's assets or liabilities is over- or undervalued at either block acquisition date.

Required

1. Analyze the Investment account through the date control was achieved (4/1/X8). Include the noncontrolling interest.
2. Prepare all consolidation entries at 4/1/X8.
3. Update the conceptual analysis through 12/31/X8.
4. Prepare all consolidation entries at 12/31/X8.
5. If Plazco chose to consolidate Slazco's income statement for *all* of 19X8—instead of only the nine-month period from 4/1/X8 through 12/31/X8—what two acceptable manners of presentation could it use?

✳ THINKING CRITICALLY ✳

✳ CASE ✳

CASE 6–1 **Actual Practice Case: Subsequently Found Unrecorded Liability**   On 6/30/X1, Primex Inc. acquired 100% of Sumex Inc.'s outstanding common stock for consideration of $300 million. Of this purchase price, $50 million was assigned to undervalued assets and $70 million to goodwill. In September 19X1, Primex discovered that Sumex's liabilities at the acquisition date were understated by $40 million.

Required

1. Does Primex have legal recourse to Sumex's previous owners? Why or why not?
2. How should the $40 million be accounted for if Primex does *not* have recourse to Sumex's previous owners?

✳ FINANCIAL ANALYSIS PROBLEMS ✳

FAP 6–1 **Calculating Parent's Annual Return on Investment: 100% Ownership**   On 1/1/X1, Pynco Inc. acquired 100% of Synco Inc.'s outstanding common stock for $1,000,000 cash. For 19X1, Synco reported net income of $150,000. On 12/31/X1, Synco declared and paid a $100,000 cash dividend to Pynco. During 19X1, Pynco (which uses the *equity method*) amortized $30,000 of cost in excess of book value.

Required

1. Calculate Pynco's annual return on investment (AROI) for 19X1.
2. Calculate Pynco's AROI for 19X1 assuming that the dividend was declared and paid on 1/3/X1—not 12/31/X1.

FAP 6–2 **Calculating Parent's Annual Return on Investment: 75% Ownership**   Certain accounts of PBM Inc. and its 75%-owned subsidiary SOS Inc. (acquired in a purchase business combination in 19X1) for the year ended 12/31/X2 follow:

	PBM	SOS
Sales	$900,000	$150,000
Costs and expenses	(500,000)	(70,000)
Net Income	$400,000	$ 80,000
Dividends Declared in 19X2:		
Declared and paid on 1/2/X2		$100,000
Declared and paid on 12/30/X2		100,000
Investment in SOS Inc., balance at 1/1/X2		325,000

PBM uses the *equity method* but has *not* made any entries on its books in 19X2 pertaining to the subsidiary's 19X2 earnings. SOS reported $20,000 of net income for each quarter of 19X2. For 19X2, amortization of cost in excess of book value has not yet been recorded in PBM's general ledger; the unrecorded amount is $10,000. Thus PBM is using *non*-push-down accounting.

Required   Calculate PBM's annual return on its investment (AROI) in SOS for 19X2.

FAP 6–3   **Evaluating the Profitability of the Parent's Investment**   PTA Inc. acquired 80% of Scoole Inc.'s outstanding common stock on 1/1/X1 for $400,000 cash. Selected financial information follows:

	PTA	Scoole	
Year	Amortization of Cost in Excess of Book Value	Reported Net Income (Loss)	Dividends Declared
19X1	$20,000	$150,000	
19X2	20,000	275,000	$125,000
19X3	20,000	100,000	200,000
19X4	10,000	(75,000)	–0–

Additional Information

1. The decision to acquire Scoole was based on cash flow projections, which showed an estimated *internal rate of return* of approximately 30%.
2. Of the $400,000 purchase price, $150,000 was assigned to goodwill having a 15-year life, $20,000 to land, and $30,000 to depreciable assets having a remaining life of 3 years. (Scoole had a book value of $250,000 on 1/1/X1.)
3. PTA chose to use (a) *non*-push-down accounting and (b) the *equity method*.
4. Scoole's reported net income or loss amounts occurred evenly throughout the year.
5. Scoole declared and paid its dividends on December 20 of each year.
6. In early 19X4, Scoole's major competitor announced a startling patented improvement to its main product, placing Scoole at a major competitive disadvantage.
7. On 12/31/X4, PTA (in light of its assessment that Scoole would be only marginally profitable in the future because of the competitor's improvement) sold its entire interest in Scoole for $288,640 cash. Just prior to this sale, the market price of Scoole's common stock was approximately 7% below the book value of its common stock.
8. PTA had net income of $500,000 in 19X4 from its own separate operations, excluding any amounts relating to Scoole's operations.

Required

1. Prepare a T-account analysis of the Investment in Subsidiary account over the life of the investment.
2. Prepare PTA's entry to record the sale of Scoole.
3. What amounts should be reported in PTA's 19X4 income statement relating to Scoole?
4. Calculate PTA's annual return on its investment (AROI) for each year.
5. Is it correct to use the *beginning-of-year* investment balance or the *average* investment balance for the year in the denominator in requirement 4? Why?
6. Repeat requirement 4 for 19X2 under each of the following changed assumptions concerning the $125,000 of dividends declared in 19X2:

Assumption	Date Declared and Paid
A	1/1/X2
B	7/1/X2

7. Calculate the internal rate of return (IRR) over the life of the investment. State your answer to the nearest whole percent, for example, 15%.

   Spreadsheet Integration: You may easily obtain this answer using the IRR function available in EXCEL or LOTUS 1–2–3. You merely need to set up a cash flow table and *then* program the IRR function.

8. Repeat requirement 7 under each of the following changed assumptions concerning the $125,000 of dividends declared in 19X2:

Assumption	Date Declared	Date Paid
A	12/20/X2	1/3/X3
B	1/1/X2	1/5/X2
C	6/25/X2	1/1/X2

9. Prepare a T-account analysis of the Investment account by year over the life of the investment using (a) the dividend information provided and (b) the net income amounts assumed under the IRR method. (Use the percentage you calculated in requirement 7 to calculate each year's assumed net income.)

10. Compare the AROI calculations in requirement 4 with the IRR calculation in requirement 7. Which is best suited for evaluating the profitability on this investment? Why?

11. If Scoole had been sold on 1/3/X5 (instead of 12/31/X4), would PTA's AROI for 19X4 be any different? Why or why not?

ANSWERS TO SELF-STUDY QUESTIONS

1. a   **2.** c[a]   **3.** d   **4.** c[b]   **5.** d   **6.** b   **7.** a   **8.** i   **9.** d

[a]A $4,000 *liquidating dividend* was paid.
[b]$12,000 + $12,000 + $36,000 [$40,000 − $4,000 liquidating dividend] = $60,000.

■ APPENDIX
CONSOLIDATED STATEMENT OF CASH FLOWS

When a consolidated balance sheet and income statements are presented, a consolidated statement of cash flows also must be presented.

I THE TWO POSSIBLE WORKSHEET APPROACHES

Two worksheet approaches can be used to prepare a consolidated statement of cash flows: (1) analyzing the changes in the consolidated balance sheets and (2) combining the separate company cash flow statements. Regardless of which approach they take, parent companies usually require each subsidiary to submit a statement of cash flows to facilitate the preparation of the consolidated statement. Thus information is provided for each company within the consolidated group as to property additions, retirements, depreciation expense, borrowings, and repayments—items commonly presented separately in a statement of cash flows.

APPROACH 1: ANALYZING THE CHANGES IN THE CONSOLIDATED BALANCE

A parent can use its consolidated balance sheets for the beginning and end of the year to prepare a statement of cash flows. The change in each individual account balance for the year is analyzed in terms of sources and uses of cash (the approach illustrated in intermediate accounting texts). When transactions for intercompany inventory, fixed assets, or bonds have occurred, this method is much quicker because these intercompany transactions have been eliminated in preparing the consolidated balance sheet and income statement. Thus these intercompany transactions are not dealt with again in preparing the consolidated statement of cash flows, as they must be under the approach of combining the separate statements.

APPROACH 2: COMBINING THE SEPARATE STATEMENTS

A multicolumn worksheet can be used to consolidate the separate company statements of cash flows. The columnar headings for the worksheet follow:

		Eliminations		
P Company	S Company	Dr.	Cr.	Consolidated

This approach is practical when no intercompany inventory, fixed asset, or bond transactions have occurred. Consolidation entries are needed only to (1) eliminate the parent's Equity in Net Income account (to prevent double counting), (2) eliminate intercompany dividends, and (3) reflect the noncontrolling interest in the subsidiary's net income as an item that did not require the use of cash. Dividends paid to the noncontrolling interest shareholders constitute a use of cash and are shown as such in the consolidated statement of cash flows, along with dividends paid to the parent's stockholders.

ILLUSTRATION | CONSOLIDATING STATEMENT OF CASH FLOWS

Illustration 6–12 shows a consolidating statement of cash flows worksheet using the approach of combining the separate statements for a 75%-owned subsidiary.

ILLUSTRATION 6–12	Consolidating Statement of Cash Flows Worksheet: Created Subsidiary—75% Owned

P Company and S Company
Consolidating Statement of Cash Flows
For the Year Ended December 31, 19X2

	P Company	S Company	Consolidation Entries Dr.	Consolidation Entries Cr.	Consolidated
Cash Flows from Operating Activities:					
Net income	134,000	32,000	24,000(1) 8,000(3)		134,000
Charges (credits) *not* affecting cash:					
Depreciation expense	40,000	13,000			53,000
Equity in reported net income of subsidiary	(24,000)			24,000(1)	–0–
Net change in receivables, inventory, and payables	(36,000)	(13,000)			(49,000)
NCI in net income of S Company				8,000(3)	8,000
Net Cash Flow from Operating Activities	114,000	32,000	32,000(1)	32,000	146,000
Cash Flows from Investing Activities:					
Dividends received from S Company	9,000		9,000(2)		–0–
Net Cash Flow from Investing Activities	9,000		9,000		–0–
Cash Flows from Financing Activities:					
Decrease in long-term debt	(40,000)				(40,000)
Dividends paid	(85,000)	(12,000)		9,000(2)	(88,000)
Net Cash Flow from Financing Activities	(125,000)	(12,000)		9,000	(128,000)
Net Increase (Decrease) in Cash	(2,000)	20,000	41,000	41,000	18,000

Explanation of entries:
 (1) To eliminate parent's Equity in Net Income of Subsidiary account.
 (2) To eliminate the intercompany dividend.
 (3) To eliminate the NCI share of S Company's net income and show the NCI deduction (that is present in the consolidated income statement) as a charge that did *not* require the use of cash.

Source: The amounts were either obtained or developed from Illustrations 2–7 and 2–8, as revised to reflect only a 75% ownership interest instead of 100%.

Illustration 6–12 is relatively straightforward. Additional complexities arise when (1) the subsidiary was acquired (instead of created) and accounted for using the purchase method of accounting (discussed in Chapters 4–6), (2) the subsidiary has preferred stock outstanding, and (3) the parent's ownership percentage changes during the year. These additional complexities are beyond our purpose here, which is to merely acquaint you with the basics of this statement.

PROBLEM FOR APPENDIX

P 6–1A **Consolidated Statement of Cash Flows** The 19X1 separate-company statements of cash flows for Pac Inc. and its 90%-owned *created* subsidiary, Sac Inc., follow:

	Statement of Cash Flows (19X1)	
	Pac	Sac
Cash Flows from Operating Activities:		
Net income	$127,000	$ 30,000
Charges (credits) not affecting cash		
Depreciation expense	14,000	6,000
Patent amortization	4,000	
Equity in reported net income of subsidiary	(27,000)	
Net increase in receivables, inventory, and payables	(11,000)	(5,000)
Net Cash Flow from Operating Activities	$107,000	$ 31,000
Cash Flows from Investing Activities:		
Purchase of equipment	$ (71,000)	$(19,000)
Dividends received from Sac	9,000	
Net Cash Flow from Investing Activities	$ (62,000)	$(19,000)
Cash Flows from Financing Activities:		
Sale of common stock	$ 50,000	
Sale of preferred stock	40,000	
Sale of bonds at par		$ 20,000
Retirement of debt	(30,000)	(15,000)
Dividends on common stock	(60,000)	(10,000)
Dividends on preferred stock	(2,000)	
Net Cash Flow from Financing Activities	$ (2,000)	$ (5,000)
Net Increase (Decrease) in Cash	$ 43,000	$ 7,000

Required Prepare a consolidated statement of cash flows using the approach of combining the separate statements.

THE POOLING OF INTERESTS METHOD

7

One who does not read great books has no advantage over one who cannot read great books.

MARK TWAIN

CHAPTER OVERVIEW

In this chapter, the pooling of interests method of accounting for a business combination is discussed, illustrated, and contrasted with the purchase method. Recall from Chapter 4 that the terms of the combination agreement and certain other
conditions determine whether the purchase method or the pooling of interests
method is used to record a business combination. The terms and provisions that
qualify a business combination as a pooling of interests are reviewed in general and
then in detail.

Paragraphs 27–65 of *APB Opinion No. 16* cover the pooling of interests method.
Throughout these paragraphs, the terms *acquiring company* and *acquired company*
are purposely not used because the word *acquiring* describes the purchase method
of accounting in paragraphs 66 to 96. Instead, the discussion uses the terms **combining company, combined company,** and **company issuing stock to effect the
combination.**[1] This language is consistent with the underlying concept of pooling
of interests accounting, which is that a combining, or pooling, of the equity interests rather than an *acquisition* occurs. The latter term refers to a situation in which
one company acquires the business of another company, for which purchase accounting is appropriate.

It is more convenient in some instances, however, to refer to a company that
gives up its assets (or whose stockholders give up their common stock) as the
target company (which is how that company is commonly referred to by the parties
involved).

I THE CONCEPT OF NO CHANGE IN BASIS OF ACCOUNTING

THE ESSENCE OF A POOLING OF INTERESTS

Under the pooling of interests method, **each company's stockholders are presumed to have combined or fused their ownership interests in such a manner
that each group becomes an owner of the combined, enlarged business.** To accomplish this fusing of ownership interests, the target company or its stockholders
must receive common stock as consideration from the other company.

THE RELEVANCE OF THE NEGOTIATED VALUE   Of course, the number of common shares to be issued to consummate the transaction is based on the negotiated
agreed-upon value of the target company, regardless of either the book value or
current value of the target company's net assets. For example, if the target company's net assets have a book value of $60,000, a current value of $88,000, but an
agreed-upon value of $90,000, the other combining company issues common
shares having a market value of $90,000. Assuming that the market price of the
other combining company's common stock is $30 per share, it issues 3,000 shares
of its common stock ($90,000 ÷ $30 per share). If the target company has 5,000
shares outstanding, for instance, and all of these shares are exchanged for the 3,000
shares being issued by the other combining company (a stock-for-stock exchange),
the exchange ratio (discussed in Chapter 4) is 3:5.

THE RELEVANCE OF THE BOOK VALUE   Because a fusing of the ownership interests is deemed to occur in a pooling of interests (as opposed to a buyout of one
business by the other business, the concept in purchase accounting), the fair value

---

[1]*Opinions of the Accounting Principles Board, No. 16,* "Accounting for Business Combinations" (New York: American Institute of Certified Public Accountants, 1970).

of the consideration given ($90,000 in the preceding example) and the current value of the target company's net assets ($88,000 in the preceding example) are completely irrelevant. Instead, the book value of the target company's net assets ($60,000 in the preceding example) is used as the basis for recording the "cost" of the investment to the company issuing common stock. As a result, the assets and liabilities of the target company are reported at their historical costs in the consolidated financial statements. Furthermore, **goodwill is never created.** In an economy in which inflation has occurred over many years, the assets of companies are usually undervalued. Thus the pooling of interests method is popular because the acquired company's assets do not have to be reflected at their current values, along with any goodwill, in the future financial statements. Future charges to income are thereby avoided. The disadvantage—an understatement of the consolidated stockholders' equity—is almost always of secondary importance compared with the advantages that result in the income statement. This manner of accounting—**in which there is no change in the basis of accounting for financial reporting purposes**—is completely the opposite of that under the *purchase method.*

PRESENTING PRECOMBINATION EARNINGS AND DIVIDENDS When financial statements are presented for periods prior to the combination date, **the earnings and dividends of each company are combined as though the combination had occurred at the beginning of the earliest period presented, but only to the extent of the ownership interest combined.** This is the opposite of the *purchase method,* which disallows presenting the operations results and dividend information of the two companies together for preacquisition periods. This may be depicted as follows:

Precombination Periods Combined	Combination Date	Postcombination Periods Combined
←——— Pooling of Interests ———————	| ——————— ———————	Purchase Accounting ——→ Pooling of Interests ——→

II THE GROWTH OF POOLING OF INTERESTS

When the pooling of interests concept emerged in the early 1940s, its implementation was limited to businesses of comparable size. The following are simple examples of such poolings, one for similarly sized professional businesses and one for equally matched corporations:

1. Two CPAs practice as sole proprietorships. One CPA specializes in taxes, the other in auditing. Each realizes that by joining together as a partnership, both can achieve certain advantages, among them (a) economics related to overhead, (b) better servicing of clients, and (c) greater attractiveness to prospective clients. Because each CPA continues as an owner in the partnership, it is obvious that no buyout of the other has occurred. The combination is one of association, not of acquisition.

2. Two companies of approximately the same size are in the same industry. One company has an excellent research and development department; the other company has excellent manufacturing and marketing organizations. The owners of each company realize that each firm, on its own, will have a difficult time becoming a major force in the industry. By combining the strengths of the two companies, however, the unified firm could have a better chance of success. Accordingly, one of the combining companies issues common stock to the stockholders of the other company. Each owner in the formerly separate businesses

is now a fellow owner in the same company, sharing the risks and rewards of common ownership with the others. None of the owners sells his or her stock as a result of the combination. Thus neither group has bought out the other group.

Because of the favorable effects on the income statement that often result in a pooling of interests compared to a purchase transaction, companies have tried over the years to broaden (and thereby alter) the original concept of a pooling of interests so that many other types of business combinations can be classified as poolings of interests and thereby obtain the more desirable accounting treatment. (Examples are industrial giants combining with start-up companies and companies combining from unrelated industries.) These efforts have been so successful that pooling of interests is no longer considered in the abstract by businesspeople (and probably by most accountants as well) but as simply an accounting method.

In fact, because most business combinations that are accounted for under the pooling of interests method involve companies of disproportionate sizes, the parties involved view them as acquisitions in the sense that one entity acquires the business of another entity, and the acquiring entity is completely dominant. In other words, the transaction is viewed as an acquisition (from other than an accounting viewpoint) that is merely recorded as a pooling of interests.

CONCEPTUAL ISSUES

Although accounting authorities agree that a pooling of interests cannot take place without the equity interests of the two companies joining together, they differ widely and vehemently over the relevance of several other factors, among them (1) the relative size of the combining interests, (2) the ready negotiability of each interest's common stock, (3) the similarity or complementary nature of the two lines of business, (4) the possible lack of continuity of interests, and (5) the interests in one or the other company that dissent from the combination.

1. **Relative size:** *Should the equity interests be approximately the same size for a pooling of interests to take place?* For example, could an 8-partner partnership have a pooling of interests with one having 2 partners? What about 48 partners and 2? Could a combination between IBM Corporation, which has revenues approaching $70 billion, and an electronics company having revenues of only $100 million—a 700:1 ratio—be considered a pooling of interests? Or should this be considered a buyout? Should a line be drawn? If so, where?

2. **Ready negotiability of common stock:** Assume that each group of former owners now holds common stock that is negotiable and readily exchangeable into cash. Does this mean that there is no real significance to the fact that common stock instead of cash was given to one of the equity interests? In other words, *does a true pooling of interests occur just because common stock is given?*

3. **Similar or complementary lines of business:** *Should there be a compelling economic relationship (similar or complementary lines of business) between the combining companies to have a pooling of interests?* For example, in 1986 Burroughs Corp., which had the third largest revenues in its industry, and Sperry Corp., with the seventh largest revenues, combined to create Unisys Corp., the world's second largest computer company. The reason these firms gave for their combination was to be able to compete aggressively with IBM, the world's largest computer company, in the computer mainframe market. Could a business combination between Burroughs and Ford Motor Co., for example, be considered a pooling of interests?

4. **Continuity of interests:** Suppose that some or all of one of the former businesses sell their newly received common stock holdings shortly after the combination, effectively "cashing out" rather than continuing as owners in the combined business. *Should there be continuity of interests for a reasonable period after the consummation date? If so, for how long?*

5. **Dissenting interests:** Suppose that some members of one of the equity interests choose not to be a party to the combination. For example, two partnerships of 10 partners each contemplate combining, but 2 of the 10 from one firm choose to withdraw their capital from the partnership and not be parties to the combination. *Should dissenting interests in one firm prevent the remaining partners from having a pooling of interests with the other partnership?*

GROUNDS FOR DIFFERENCE

At one end of the spectrum are accountants who would disregard all five of these factors. For them, as long as a fusion of equity interests occurs (through the issuance of common stock by one of the combining companies in exchange for the assets or common stock of the other combining company), a pooling of interests occurs. In general, *APBO No. 16* takes this approach.

Critics of *APBO No. 16* contend that for most combinations treated as poolings of interests, the fusion of the equity interests is irrelevant. They maintain that what is relevant is whether one company has acquired or obtained *control* over the business of another company. If this control is the substance of the transaction, then purchase accounting is appropriate—regardless of the type of consideration given. This is the primary conclusion of *Accounting Research Study No. 5*, "A Critical Study of Accounting for Business Combinations," by Arthur R. Wyatt, which the American Institute of Certified Public Accountants (AICPA) published in 1963. (Research studies do *not* constitute the official position of the AICPA; they are for discussion purposes only.) This group would allow poolings of interests only when the companies involved are of comparable size and it is evident that a buyout is not occurring. Because most transactions accounted for as poolings of interests involve companies of significantly disproportionate sizes, few business combinations would be treated as poolings of interests with this approach.

In summary, each group views the economic substance of a business combination involving the issuance of common stock differently.

The use of the pooling of interests method overseas is discussed in the International Perspective.

INTERNATIONAL PERSPECTIVE

Foreign Pooling of Interests Practices

Pooling of interests accounting is virtually unused outside the United States. Of the major industrial countries, only Canada and Great Britain allow something similar to a pooling of interests. Canada allows pooling of interests only when an acquirer *cannot* be identified. Great Britain severely restricts the use of poolings of interests largely because of a size test rule that says neither combining party can be 50% larger than the other combining party (this translates to a relative size ratio of 3:2).

The pronouncement of the International Accounting Standards Committee (IASC) on business combinations, *IASC No. 22* (issued December 1993) allows poolings. The exposure draft that preceded *IASC No. 22* proposed to eliminate the practice in most circumstances, but this proposal was abandoned, evidently to accommodate the U.S. standard.

WILL THE FASB EVER REEXAMINE *APBO No. 16*?

As mentioned in Chapter 4, *APBO No. 16* is a controversial pronouncement that received substantial criticism for many years after its inception (though not much in recent years). In the 1970s, the Financial Accounting Standards Board (FASB) began a project to reexamine it. This project was dropped in the mid-1980s, however, ostensibly because of its low priority relative to other pressing accounting issues.

In our opinion, managements so strongly desire pooling of interests accounting treatment that the FASB undoubtedly would face fierce opposition if it tried to either eliminate or curtail this practice. *APBO No. 16* involved a real dogfight, and it may be that the FASB does not desire to awaken that sleeping dog. Consequently, pooling of interests treatment apparently has achieved "sacred cow" status (last-in, first-out inventory valuation being another untouchable).[2]

IV CRITERIA FOR POOLING OF INTERESTS: A BRIEF OVERVIEW

Before *APBO No. 16* was issued, only general guidelines determined when a business combination should be treated as a pooling of interests. Because the guidelines could not be logically supported for the most part, in practice they were often ignored or broadly interpreted. The relative looseness of accounting principles in this area resulted in substantial criticism of the accounting profession, which led to the issuance of a pronouncement that contained specific pooling of interests criteria. In addition, *APBO No. 16* eliminated management's ability to choose between accounting alternatives for a given set of terms and conditions:

1. It specifically defines the criteria under which a business combination is treated as a pooling of interests.

2. It requires all business combinations meeting each of these specific criteria to be accounted for as a pooling of interests.

3. It requires all business combinations failing to meet any one of the specific criteria to be accounted for using purchase accounting.

APBO No. 16 outlines 12 specific conditions that the combining firms must meet before pooling of interests accounting is permitted. In many respects, the conditions are arbitrary and not totally clear or comprehensive. As a result, the AICPA and the FASB have issued numerous interpretations. With the possible exception of accounting for leases, more interpretations have been issued for this pronouncement than for any other professional pronouncement. In practice, it has been one of the most difficult professional pronouncements with which to work. Many large public accounting firms have prepared lengthy booklets for internal use that explain how certain areas of the pronouncement are to be interpreted for uniform application within their firms.

The 12 conditions generally allow pooling of interests treatment only when a combination of independent equity interests occurs rather than a buyout of one of the common shareholder equity interests. As a result, *APBO No. 16* places most emphasis on the form and manner of accomplishing the combination so that the two stockholder groups fuse their ownership interests. Most of the conditions pertain

---

[2]In 1989 the International Accounting Standards Committee issued a comprehensive exposure draft (*ED No. 32*), which, among other things, proposed to eliminate both pooling of interests accounting and the last-in, first-out inventory valuation method. These proposals were unsuccessful.

to the manner of effecting the combination. The more salient points of the criteria are as follows:

1. Common stock must be the sole consideration given for the pooled interest.
   a. **Common stock exchanged for assets:** In this type of transaction, the target company must transfer **100% of its assets** to the issuing company solely for common stock of the issuing company.
   b. **Common stock exchanged for common stock:** In this type of transaction, **at least 90% of the outstanding common stock** of the target company must be exchanged solely for common stock of the issuing company. (Cash or other consideration may be given to dissenting stockholders of the target company so long as this group does not hold more than 10% of the target company's outstanding common stock.)
2. The common stock issued **must have the same rights and privileges** as the already issued and outstanding common stock of the issuing company. In other words, the issuing company's new stockholders must be full-fledged stockholders of the enlarged business.
3. **Neither combining company may alter its own equity interest or the equity interest of the other combining company in contemplation of a pooling of interests.**
4. There can be **no arrangements to reacquire the common stock issued** as consideration for the assets or common stock exchanged.

Interestingly, the stockholders receiving common stock from the issuing company can sell the stock immediately after the combination is consummated if they do not want to continue as owners in the combined business. No continuity of ownership interest is required whereby the new stockholders must remain shareholders of the combined business for any specified period of time. Thus, the "fusion" of equity interests may take place for only an instant.

V   SPECIFIC CONDITIONS FOR POOLING OF INTERESTS

The 12 conditions for the pooling of interests method in *APBO No. 16* fit into three broad categories:

1. The attributes of the combining companies (2 conditions).
2. The manner of combining equity interests (7 conditions).
3. The absence of planned transactions (3 conditions).

Each condition is quoted under the appropriate category and discussed in detail in the following sections. Because all the conditions are found in *APBO No. 16*, only paragraph references to that pronouncement are given. (The letter that precedes each quotation corresponds to the letter used in *APBO No. 16*.) Note that many of the conditions are designed to prevent companies from circumventing the basic concept of having to combine substantially all common shareholder equity interests.

1. ATTRIBUTES OF THE COMBINING COMPANIES

Two conditions pertain to the necessary attributes of the combining companies:

A. **Each of the combining companies is autonomous and has not been a subsidiary or division of another corporation within two years before the plan of combination is initiated.** [Paragraph 46a]

This condition presumes that the pooling of interests concept applies only to independent companies. For the most part, this condition is sound; most divestitures of subsidiaries or divisions are intended disposals of interests as opposed to intended poolings of equity interests.

A subsidiary that is spun off pursuant to a governmental divestiture order or a new company that acquires assets it must dispose of is an arbitrary exception to this condition and is deemed an "autonomous company." This exception does not appear to be based on logic, and its inclusion is apparently an accommodation to the disposing company for purposes of facilitating the disposal.

When a portion of a business is spun off to certain stockholders in exchange for some or all of their stock, the stockholders of the newly established corporation may wish to combine their equity interests with another company in the true sense of the pooling of interests concept. Such a combining of equity interests could not be accounted for as a pooling of interests unless two years had elapsed from the spin-off date. Thus a portion of a business cannot be spun off in this manner and then pooled with another company shortly thereafter. This is so because the spinning off and subsequent combination are viewed as mere steps of a single transaction, the substance of which is a disposal of an interest.

> **B. Each of the combining companies is independent of the other combining companies.** [Paragraph 46b]

This condition means that at the initiation date and until the business combination is consummated, the combining companies cannot hold more than 10% of the outstanding voting common stock of any combining company. Voting common stock that is acquired during this time interval in exchange for voting common stock issued in connection with the terms of the business combination agreement is excluded in the percentage computation.

This condition is intended to prevent a combining company from altering the equity interests of the other combining company. (Paragraph 47c, which is discussed later in the chapter, prohibits each combining company from altering the equity interest of its own voting common stock in contemplation of a pooling.) If this condition were not imposed, a combining company could circumvent the intended purpose of paragraph 47c by buying out a large group of dissenting shareholders of the other combining company and then effecting a pooling of interests with its remaining shareholders.

INDEPENDENCE BASED ON EQUITY INVESTED   Usually, each combining company is independent of the other if neither company owns more than 10% of the outstanding voting common stock of the other. Occasionally, however, neither company owns more than 10% of the outstanding common stock of the other and independence still does not exist. This can occur when the smaller company has a significant investment—**in terms of its own equity**—in the larger company. For example, assume that Mini-Computer Company (the target company) owns 6% of IBMM Company's outstanding common stock. If this investment constitutes more than 10% of Mini-Computer's equity, then the companies are not independent. The calculation to determine whether the 10% figure is exceeded uses the following facts:

1. IBMM has 600,000 common shares outstanding.

2. Mini-Computer has 100,000 common shares outstanding.

3. IBMM will issue two shares of its common stock for each share of Mini-Computer's outstanding common stock—in other words, a 2-for-1 exchange ratio. Recall that before this 2:1 exchange ratio could have been calculated, it first would have been necessary to calculate the number of shares IBMM Company would issue (200,000 shares in this example) by dividing the negotiated agreed-upon value of Mini-Computer Company (say, $10 million) by the market price of IBMM's common stock (say, $50 per share).

4. Mini-Computer owns 24,000 IBMM common shares, which is 4% of IBMM's outstanding common shares.

Because Mini-Computer's shareholders will receive 200,000 shares of IBMM common stock, Mini-Computer's equity can be considered the equivalent of 200,000 shares of IBMM common stock. The following calculation is then made:

$$\frac{\text{Shares of IBMM Common Stock Held by Mini-Computer}}{\substack{\text{Shares of IBMM Common Stock to Be Issued} \\ (100{,}000 \text{ Shares of Mini-Computer} \times 2)}} = \frac{24{,}000}{200{,}000} = 12\%$$

In an alternate approach, the 24,000 shares of IBMM owned by Mini-Computer are considered the equivalent of 12,000 shares of Mini-Computer common stock. The following calculation is then made:

$$\frac{\substack{\text{Equivalent Number of Mini-Computer's} \\ \text{Shares Invested in IBMM } (24{,}000 \div 2)}}{\text{Shares of Mini-Computer Common Stock Outstanding}} = \frac{12{,}000}{100{,}000} = 12\%$$

In this example, the companies are *not* independent because the 10% level has been exceeded.

Accordingly, independence is evaluated not only from the perspective of how much of the other combining company's outstanding common stock is owned but also from the perspective of how much of a company's own equity is invested in the other combining company.

SMALLER COMPANY ISSUES THE COMMON STOCK In the preceding situation, the larger of the two companies issued common stock to bring about the combination (the typical case). In a stock-for-stock exchange, the relative holdings of each group of stockholders can be the same regardless of which company issues the common stock to effect the pooling of interests. In that situation, the relative holdings of each group of stockholders was 3:1 (IBMM's shareholders owning 600,000 shares and Mini-Computer's shareholders receiving 200,000 shares of IBMM common stock). Let us change the facts of the situation to make Mini-Computer the issuing company. The same relative holdings of each group of stockholders are maintained if Mini-Computer issues one share for each two shares of IBMM outstanding common stock (a 1-for-2 exchange ratio). This still gives IBMM's shareholders three times as many shares (300,000 shares) in Mini-Computer as those held by Mini-Computer's stockholder group just prior to the combination (100,000 shares). In this case, the issuing company has the intercorporate investment. The companies are still *not* independent, however, for the reasons discussed in the preceding paragraph. The smaller of the two companies issues the common stock (and thereby becomes the parent company) when it is more desirable to use the smaller company's name than the larger company's name. For example, the larger company may have an unfavorable public image, or the smaller company may have a wider investor following.

DUAL INTERCORPORATE INVESTMENTS The 10% independence test must be performed in a cumulative manner when each company has an investment in the other. To illustrate, assume the following facts:

1. IBMM Company has 600,000 common shares outstanding.

2. Mini-Computer Company has 100,000 common shares outstanding.

3. IBMM will issue two shares of its common stock for each share of Mini-Computer's outstanding common shares—a 2-for-1 exchange ratio.

4. Mini-Computer owns 18,000 IBMM outstanding common shares, which is 3% of IBMM's outstanding common shares.

5. IBMM owns 2,000 shares of Mini-Computer's outstanding common shares, which is 2% of Mini-Computer's outstanding common shares.

Although neither company owns more than 10% of the other company's outstanding common stock and neither company has more than 10% of its own net worth invested in the other company, the *combination* of intercorporate investments exceeds the 10% level, as the following calculation shows:

Percent of Mini-Computer's common stock owned by IBMM	2%
Percent of Mini-Computer's net worth invested in IBMM	
[18,000 Shares ÷ 200,000 Common Shares to Be Received in the	
Exchange, or 9,000 Shares (Adjusted for the 2-for-1 Exchange	
Ratio) ÷ 100,000 Outstanding Shares]	9%
	11%

The manner of dealing with an investment in the company issuing the common stock is explained in connection with paragraph 47b of *APBO No. 16*. The approach treats shares owned in the issuing company (adjusted for the exchange ratio) as a reduction of the target company's outstanding shares to determine whether 90% of the target company's outstanding common stock has been acquired in exchange for the issuing company's common stock:

Mini-Computer's outstanding common shares	100,000
Less: Shares owned by IBMM	(2,000)
Equivalent number of shares invested in IBMM by	
Mini-Computer (18,000 ÷ 2)	(9,000)
	89,000
Shares needed to reach the 90% level	90,000

Thus the 90% level has not been reached. This analysis is difficult to understand. Because the issue is *independence,* we presented the discussion of dealing with investments in the issuing company from paragraph 46b rather than paragraph 47b.

2. MANNER OF COMBINING EQUITY INTERESTS

Seven conditions pertain to the manner of effecting the combination, as follows:

A. The combination is effected in a single transaction or is completed in accordance with a specific plan within the year after the plan is initiated. [Paragraph 47a]

Evidently, the APB believed that the transaction should be consummated within a reasonable period of time—one year.

B. A corporation offers and issues only common stock with rights identical to those of its outstanding voting common stock in exchange for substantially all of the voting common stock interest of another company at the date the plan of combination is consummated. [Paragraph 47b]

This condition is the fundamental requirement for effecting a pooling of interests. It means that the company issuing common stock must acquire at least 90% of the other combining company's outstanding common stock **subsequent to the initiation date** in exchange for its own common stock. **Thus shares acquired prior to the initiation date—no matter how acquired—*cannot* be used to determine whether the 90% requirement has been met.** To illustrate how the 90% rule is applied, assume the following facts:

1. P is the company issuing common stock.
2. S has 102,000 common shares issued, of which 2,000 shares are held in treasury. Thus, S has 100,000 common shares outstanding.

company's equity interests results, which was deemed contrary to a pure combining of the equity interests.

This also means that the 20% shareholder *cannot* pool part of his or her holdings and be a dissenter, or a minority, for the remaining shares. **Thus an individual shareholder cannot at the same time be both an assenter and a dissenter.**

> F. **The voting rights to which the common stock ownership interests in the resulting combined corporation are entitled are exercisable by the stockholders; the stockholders are neither deprived of nor restricted in exercising those rights for a period.** [Paragraph 47f]

Any limitations on voting rights are obviously inconsistent with the pooling of interests concept.

> G. **The combination is resolved at the date the plan is consummated and no provisions of the plan relating to the issue of securities or other considerations are pending.** [Paragraph 47g]

This condition is intended primarily to prohibit poolings of interests when contingent consideration is issuable based on future sales, earnings, or market prices. Such contingencies are incompatible with the mutual sharing of risks and rewards, which underlies the pooling of interests concept. An interpretation says the following:

> The only contingent arrangement permitted under paragraph 47g is for settlement of a contingency pending at consummation, such as the later settlement of a lawsuit. A contingent arrangement would also be permitted for an additional income tax liability resulting from the examination of "open" income tax returns.[4]

3. Absence of Planned Transactions

Three conditions pertain to certain types of postcombination transactions that cannot be included either explicitly or implicitly in either the negotiations or the terms of the combination agreement. The conditions are as follows:

> A. **The combining corporation does not agree directly or indirectly to retire or reacquire all or part of the common stock issued to effect the combination.** [Paragraph 48a]

This condition prevents an issuing company from circumventing the intended purpose of paragraph 47b. Obviously, issuing common shares to effect a combination and subsequently repurchasing the shares issued is not, in substance, a combining of equity interests.

APBO No. 16 does not prohibit an issuing company from reacquiring shares issued in a pooling of interests (or an equivalent number of shares issued). It prohibits the company only from making an agreement to repurchase the shares issued. In this area, the Securities and Exchange Commission (SEC) has taken the following position:

> In specific fact situations, subsequent reacquisitions may be so closely related to the prior combination that they should be considered part of the combination plan. Thus, significant reacquisitions closely following a plan of combination which otherwise qualified as a pooling of interests may invalidate the applicability of that method. . . .[5]

---

[4] *Accounting Interpretation No. 14 to APB Opinion No. 16,* "Accounting for Business Combinations" (New York: American Institute for Certified Public Accountants, 1971).

[5] *Accounting Series Release No. 146,* "Effect of Treasury Stock Transactions on Accounting for Business Combinations" (Washington, D.C.: Securities and Exchange Commission, 1973), par. 10. This release is now part of *Financial Reporting Release No. 1* (Section 201.02), which was issued in 1982 and is a codification of all accounting-related releases in effect at that time. Treasury stock acquisitions are also addressed by the SEC in *Staff Accounting Bulletin No. 96* (issued in 1996).

The Commission does not intend to establish an additional criterion for determining the accounting treatment of a business combination. Rather it intended simply to caution registrants and auditors that the substance of reacquisitions closely following consummation of a combination should not be ignored. . . .[6]

B. The combined corporation does not enter into other financial arrangements for the benefit of the former stockholders of a combining company, such as a guaranty of loans secured by stock issued in the combination, which in effect negates the exchange of securities. [Paragraph 48b]

Arrangements of this nature are considered "bailouts" of former stockholders of the target company. Such provisions are inconsistent with the pooling of interests concept.

C. The combined corporation does not intend or plan to dispose of a significant part of the assets of the combining companies within two years after the combination other than disposals in the ordinary course of business of the formerly separate companies and to eliminate duplicate facilities or excess capacity. [Paragraph 48c]

The apparent purpose of this condition is to prohibit companies from effecting pooling of interests with companies having substantially undervalued assets when the intent is to sell the undervalued assets shortly after consummation and thereby report immediate profits from the sale. (Such widely criticized practices existed before *APBO No. 16* was issued.)

If a significant portion of the assets of either combining company is **disposed of within two years** after the combination is consummated, any material profit or loss is to be classified as an **extraordinary item.**

VI VIEWS OF DISSENTING MEMBERS OF THE ACCOUNTING PRINCIPLES BOARD

Six of the 18 members of the Accounting Principles Board dissented to the issuance of *APBO No. 16*. The following is a summary of their views:

1. *APBO No. 16* will curtail some abuses in pooling of interests accounting; however, the real abuse is pooling of interests itself. Instead of creating 12 complex criteria, simply prohibit pooling of interests.

2. The form of the consideration (cash or common stock) is irrelevant; the value of the consideration is what is relevant. Substance should prevail over form.

3. The value of the consideration is determined in a bargained exchange. To ignore this value (the buyer's true cost) and record the combination based on the wholly irrelevant amount of the seller's financial reporting cost basis (the seller's cost) is an aberration from historical cost reporting that should be abolished.

4. The abuse of acquiring other companies having substantially undervalued assets and then reporting profits on the subsequent sale of those assets (allowing the same gain to be reported by both corporations) continues, even though the second company did not actually earn anything and should not report a profit on such subsequent sale (except to the extent that assets appreciated in value after the combination date).

---

[6]*Accounting Series Release No. 146-A*, "Statement of Policy and Interpretations in Regard to *Accounting Series Release No. 146*" (Washington, D.C.: Securities and Exchange Commission, 1974), par. 3. (Section 201.02 of *Financial Reporting Release No. 1*.)

BUSINESS PERSPECTIVE

AT&T Pools with NCR—$5.7 Billion of Goodwill Avoided

In May 1991, one of the largest recent mergers accounted for as a pooling of interests occurred between American Telephone & Telegraph Co. and NCR Corp. During the five-month takeover battle, NCR bought back millions of shares of its common stock as a defensive move to alter its equity interest for the purpose of preventing AT&T from using the pooling of interests accounting treatment, a treatment that AT&T considered necessary to consummate the deal. AT&T agreed to sell all of these shares to obtain the pooling treatment, which avoided the creation of $5.7 billion of goodwill that would have been reported under purchase accounting. A comparison of the two companies, which are of disproportionate size, using 1990 data follows:

	(Dollar Amounts in Millions)	
	AT&T	NCR
Revenues	$ 37,285	$ 6,285
Net income	$ 2,735	$ 369
Total assets	$ 43,775	$ 4,547
Employees	273,700	55,000

Source: John R. Wilke and John J. Keller, "NCR Agrees to AT&T Takeover for $110 a Share, or $7.48 Billion," *The Wall Street Journal*, May 7, 1991, pp. A–3.

---

5. Pooling of interests should not be kept alive because some fear its demise would discourage mergers (which occurred for many decades before pooling was concocted). The purpose of accounting is to account for transactions fairly, not to aid or discourage certain types of transactions (here, mergers).

VII   RECORDING A POOLING OF INTERESTS: TYPICAL SITUATION—CREDIT NEEDED TO BALANCE

Assume the following information:

1. P Company and S Company have agreed to combine under terms that provide for P Company to issue common stock (in exchange for either the assets or all of the outstanding common stock of S Company).

2. Information with respect to each company as of the combination date (January 1, 19X1) is as follows:

	P Company	S Company
Common stock, $1 par value (3,000 shares outstanding)	$ 3,000	
Common stock, $2 par value (5,000 shares outstanding)		$ 10,000
Additional paid-in capital	197,000	
Retained earnings	100,000	50,000
Total Stockholders' Equity	$300,000	$ 60,000
Book value of assets	Irrelevant	$260,000
Book value of liabilities	Irrelevant	$200,000
Current value of net assets	Irrelevant	$ 88,000[a]
Market price of stock on combination date	$90[a]	Irrelevant

[a]This amount is relevant only under the purchase method.

3. All conditions for pooling of interests have been met.

4. P Company issues 1,000 shares of its common stock (a 1:5 exchange ratio).

The next two sections show the entries to record the pooling of interests, assuming, first, that the assets are exchanged and, second, that the common stock is exchanged.

COMMON STOCK EXCHANGED FOR ASSETS

When assets are exchanged, the issuing company records these assets and the liabilities assumed at their book values as shown on the target business's books as follows:

Assets (record at book value)[a]	260,000	
Liabilities (record at book value)		200,000
Common Stock (1,000 shares issued × $1 par value)		1,000
Retained Earnings (100% of the		
target company's retained earnings)		50,000
Additional Paid-in Capital (residual amount		
to balance)		9,000

[a]Recall that 100% of the assets must be exchanged.

The preceding entry is also made if the combination were made pursuant to a **statutory merger,** in which the target company's legal existence is terminated (discussed in Chapter 4).

COMMON STOCK EXCHANGED FOR COMMON STOCK

The entry when common stock is exchanged is nearly the same as when assets are exchanged. The only difference is that rather than recording assets and liabilities at their book values, the Investment in Subsidiary account is debited an amount equal to the book value of the net assets ($60,000 in the preceding example) as shown:

Investment in Subsidiary		
(record at book value of net assets)	60,000	
Common Stock (1,000 shares issued × $1 par value)		1,000
Retained Earnings (100% of the target		
company's retained earnings)		50,000
Additional Paid-in Capital (residual amount		
to balance)		9,000

The residual balancing amount in the preceding example is a $9,000 credit. Credits are typical because low par value amounts, which most companies use, generally require credits to balance the entry. Later we modify the parent's capital account balances and increase the par value from $1 to $20 to show how to balance the entry when a debit is needed.

TREATMENT OF DIRECT COSTS AND REGISTRATION EXPENSES

FINANCIAL ACCOUNTING TREATMENT   Under the purchase method of accounting, direct costs relating to the acquisition of the common stock or the assets are included in the cost of the investment. In contrast, **under the pooling of interests method, direct costs are charged to income in the period in which they are incurred. In addition, the costs of registering equity shares issued by the issuing company are charged to income as incurred** instead of being charged to Additional Paid-in Capital as under the purchase method. The rationale is that no new capital is raised—only a "pooling" of the existing capital occurs. In practice, these costs and expenses are customarily deferred until the combination is consummated so that the costs and expenses are charged against the first period in which income from the newly combined business is included in net income.

Assuming that P Company incurred $10,000 of direct costs related to the pooling, it makes the following entry:

Pooling of Interests Expenses	10,000	
Cash		10,000

INCOME TAX ACCOUNTING TREATMENT Recall from Chapter 4 that a combination that qualifies for pooling of interests treatment for financial reporting purposes is almost always treated as a tax-free reorganization for income tax–reporting purposes. In almost all instances, direct costs are not currently deductible for income tax–reporting purposes. The obtaining of assets is treated as a capital expenditure that results in the creation of a capital asset with an indeterminable useful life. This asset remains intact until it is totally worthless or is disposed of, at which time a tax deduction may be obtained. When common stock is obtained, direct costs are treated as an upward adjustment to the basis of the common stock received by the acquiring company. If the subsidiary is ever sold, these costs are effectively deducted against the proceeds from the sale.

VIII RECORDING A POOLING OF INTERESTS: *NONTYPICAL* SITUATION—DEBIT NEEDED TO BALANCE

In rare instances, a debit is needed to balance the entry to record the pooling, which occurs when the parent has negligible additional paid-in capital and a high par value for its common stock. Illustration 7–1 shows how to balance the entry in such situations.

ILLUSTRATION 7–1 Recording a Pooling of Interests When a Debit Is Needed to Balance—P Company's Par Value and Capital Account Balances Modified to Require a Debit

	P Company's Modified Capital Account Balances ($20 Par Value instead of $1 and lower APIC)	
	Sufficient Additional Paid-in Capital	**Insufficient** Additional Paid-in Capital
Common stock ($20 par)	$ 80,000	$ 80,000
Additional paid-in capital	12,000	7,000
Retained earnings	208,000	213,000
	$300,000	$300,000

P Company's entries to record pooling of interests (shown in the **sequential order in which each entry would be developed**):

Investment in Subsidiary (100% of $60,000 book value)	60,000		60,000	
Common Stock (1,000 shares issued × $20 par)		20,000		20,000
Retained Earnings (100% of $50,000 book value)		50,000		50,000
Additional Paid-in Capital (residual amount to balance)	10,000[a]		7,000[a]	
Retained Earnings (residual amount to balance)			3,000[b]	

[a]A debit plug cannot be greater than the Additional Paid-in Capital account balance on the parent's books. Any additional debit needed is charged to Retained Earnings, which is the last resort.

[b]A net credit of $47,000 ($50,000 – $3,000) is posted to the Retained Earnings account in the general ledger.

IX   CONSOLIDATION WORKSHEETS: 100% OWNERSHIP

ILLUSTRATION	COMBINATION DATE AND FIRST YEAR SUBSEQUENT: WHOLLY OWNED SUBSIDIARY

Assume that for 19X1 S Company had net income of $24,000 and declared dividends of $4,000. Using the information given earlier as to S Company's capital account balances as of the combination date (page 261), we analyze P Company's Investment account by the individual components of the book value element as of the combination date (January 1, 19X1) and then update the analysis for the subsequent year's activity (under the equity method) as follows:

	Parent's Investment Account— Book Value	=	BOOK VALUE ELEMENT	
			Subsidiary's Equity Accounts	
			Common Stock +	Retained Earnings
Balances, Jan. 1, 19X1	$60,000[a]		$10,000	$50,000
+ Equity in net income	24,000			24,000
– Dividends	(4,000)			(4,000)
Balances, Dec. 31, 19X1	$80,000		$10,000	$70,000

[a]This amount equals the book value of S Company's net assets on this date.

Note that this analysis would be the same regardless of the number of shares that P Company issues.

The basic elimination entries as of January 1, 19X1 (the combination date), and December 31, 19X1 (one year subsequent to the combination date), are as follows:

		Consolidation Date	
		January 1, 19X1	December 31, 19X1
WORKSHEET ENTRY ONLY	Common Stock	10,000	10,000
	Retained Earnings, 1/1/X1	50,000	50,000
	Equity in Net Income (of subsidiary)		24,000
	Dividends Declared		4,000
	Investment in S Company . . .	60,000	80,000

Because the book value element is the only major element under pooling of interests accounting, there is no cost over or under book value to amortize, and thus no excess cost amortization elimination entry is necessary.

Illustrations 7–2 and 7–3 show consolidation worksheets as of the above dates.

REVIEW POINTS FOR ILLUSTRATIONS 7–2 AND 7–3   Note the following:

1. The basic elimination entry is developed in exactly the same way as in purchase accounting except that updating the analysis of the Investment account is simpler because it involves only the book value element.

2. The amounts in the Consolidated column are composed of (a) the parent's items based on book values and (b) the subsidiary's items based on book values. No revaluation to current values has been made.

3. The use of the equity method to account subsequently for the parent's investment maintains the Investment account balance equal to the subsidiary's net assets at book value, which simplifies the consolidation process.

| ILLUSTRATION 7-2 | At Date of Combination |

P Company and S Company
Consolidation Worksheet as of January 1, 19X1

	P Company	S Company	Consolidation Entries Dr.	Consolidation Entries Cr.	Consolidated
Balance Sheet					
Cash	108,000	15,000			123,000
Accounts receivable, net	52,000	23,000			75,000
Inventory	90,000	42,000			132,000
Investment in S Company	60,000			60,000(1)	–0–
Land	220,000	30,000			250,000
Buildings and equipment	500,000	200,000			700,000
Accumulated depreciation	(280,000)	(50,000)			(330,000)
Total Assets	750,000	260,000		60,000	950,000
Liabilities	400,000	200,000			600,000
P Company:					
Common stock	4,000				4,000
Additional paid-in capital	206,000				206,000
Retained earnings	140,000				140,000
S Company:					
Common stock		10,000	10,000(1)		–0–
Retained earnings		50,000	50,000(1)		–0–
Total Liabilities and Equity ..	750,000	260,000	60,000		950,000
Proof of debit and credit postings			60,000	60,000	

Explanation of entry:
(1) The basic elimination entry.

Note that the journal entries recorded by the parent for the pooling (which effect is included in the P Company column) are as follows:

Investment in S Company (100% of $60,000)	60,000	
Common Stock (1,000 shares × $1)		1,000
Retained Earnings (100% of $50,000)		50,000
Additional Paid-in Capital (residual amount)		9,000
Pooling of Interests Expenses	10,000[a]	
Cash		10,000

[a]Shown as a reduction of retained earnings above.
Note: Prior to the combination, the parent's Additional Paid-in Capital account had a balance of $197,000.

4. When ownership of the subsidiary is less than 100% (it must be at least 90% to qualify for pooling of interests treatment), the necessary noncontrolling interest deduction is determined and derived in the same manner as shown in the preceding chapter for situations in which *purchase accounting* is used.

5. The formal consolidated statement of retained earnings is presented as follows:

Balance, December 31, 19X0, as previously reported	$100,000
+ Effect of pooling of interests with S Company	50,000
Balance, December 31, 19X0, as restated	$150,000
+ Net income for the year	64,000
Subtotal	$214,000
– Dividends	(51,000)
Balance, December 31, 19X1	$163,000

| ILLUSTRATION 7–3 | First Year Subsequent to Combination Date | | | | |

P Company and S Company
Consolidation Worksheet as of December 31, 19X1

	P Company	S Company	Consolidation Entries		Consolidated
			Dr.	Cr.	
Income Statement (19X1)					
Sales	600,000	234,000			834,000
Cost of sales	(360,000)	(110,000)			(470,000)
Expenses	(190,000)	(100,000)			(290,000)
Pooling expenses	(10,000)				10,000
Equity in net income (of S Co.) ..	24,000		24,000(1)		–0–
Net Income	64,000	24,000	24,000		64,000
Statement of Retained Earnings					
Balances, 1/1/X1	100,000	50,000	50,000(1)		100,000
+ Effect of Pooling	50,000				50,000
+ Net income	64,000	24,000	24,000		64,000
– Dividends declared	(51,000)	(4,000)		4,000(1)	(51,000)
Balances, 12/31/X1	163,000	70,000	74,000	4,000	163,000
Balance Sheet					
Cash	115,000	11,000			126,000
Accounts receivable, net	75,000	37,000			112,000
Inventory	110,000	55,000			165,000
Investment in S Company	80,000			80,000(1)	–0–
Land	220,000	30,000			250,000
Buildings and equipment	500,000	200,000			700,000
Accumulated depreciation	(320,000)	(63,000)			(383,000)
Total Assets	780,000	270,000		80,000	970,000
Liabilities	407,000	190,000			597,000
P Company:					
Common stock	4,000				4,000
Additional paid-in capital	206,000				206,000
Retained earnings	163,000				163,000
S Company:					
Common stock		10,000	10,000(1)		–0–
Retained earnings		70,000	74,000	4,000	–0–
Total Liabilities and Equity ..	780,000	270,000	84,000	4,000	970,000
Proof of debit and credit postings			84,000	84,000	

Explanation of entry:
(1) The basic elimination entry.

KEY POINTS

a. **Effect of pooling:** The retained earnings of S Company on January 1, 19X1, when multiplied by the parent's ownership percentage ($50,000 × 100% in this case), always equals the "effect of pooling" amount, regardless of the actual business combination date.

b. **Earnings:** The rationale for the preceding statement stems from the fact that in a pooling of interests the subsidiary's earnings for the entire year are combined with those of the parent, no matter when during the year the combination occurs.

c. **Dividends:** Dividends declared by the subsidiary prior to the combination date—none in this case—that went to those stockholders who pooled (thus excluding dividends to noncontrolling shareholders) are combined with the parent's dividends in this statement. Accordingly, the amount shown for dividends declared in the Consolidated column always includes dividends paid to persons who no longer own the pooled subsidiary.

Illustration 7–3 assumed that the parent company used the *equity method* to account for its investment in the subsidiary. The parent may, however, account for its investment in the subsidiary using the *cost method*. The *cost method* is not illustrated, because the procedures are the same as those shown in Chapter 2.

MID-YEAR POOLING OF INTERESTS

For poolings of interests that occur other than at the beginning of the year, the simplest manner to both record the pooling of interests and prepare the consolidation worksheet is to (1) record the pooling of interests as though it had been consummated at the beginning of the year (using the book value of the net assets at that date) and (2) apply the equity method of accounting for the full year (using the parent's ownership percentage). One slight variation from normal equity procedures must be made, however: **For dividends declared by the subsidiary** *prior* **to the consummation date (dividends paid to S Company's former shareholders), debit the Dividends Declared account instead of Dividends Receivable or Cash.** This allows dividends paid to shareholders who pooled their equity interest to be combined with dividends declared by the parent, the combined amount of which must be reported in the consolidated statement of retained earnings.

Let us change the consummation date from January 1, 19X1 (the beginning of the year), to April 1, 19X1. Assume further that S Company's earnings and dividends for 19X1 were as follows:

	Jan. 1–Mar. 31	April 1–Dec. 31	Total
Net income	$5,000	$19,000	$24,000
Dividends	1,000	3,000	4,000

Accordingly, the entries under the equity method of accounting for 19X1 are as follows:

Investment in Subsidiary	24,000	
Equity in Net Income		24,000
To record equity in net income.		
Dividends Declared	1,000[a]	
Investment in Subsidiary		1,000
To reflect dividends declared *prior* to the consummation date as dividends to be reported in consolidation along with the parent's dividends.		
Dividends Receivable	3,000	
Investment in Subsidiary		3,000
To record dividends declared *after* the consummation date of April 1, 19X1.		

[a]This account serves only to simplify the preparation of the consolidated statements. If P Company were to issue parent-company-only statements for 19X1, it reports this $1,000 amount (as well as the $5,000 of S Company's first quarter earnings that P Company has recorded in its Equity in Net Income account) as part of the credit made to P Company's Retained Earnings account to record the combination.

Illustration 7–4 shows the retained earnings section of the consolidation worksheet, assuming that the pooling of interests was consummated on April 1, 19X1

ILLUSTRATION 7–4 | **Combination Occurs in Mid-Year**

P Company and Subsidiary (S Company)
Consolidation Worksheet (Retained Earnings Section Only)
For the Year Ended December 31, 19X1

	P Company	S Company	Consolidation Entries Dr.	Consolidation Entries Cr.	Consolidated
Statement of Retained Earnings					
Balances, 1/1/X1	100,000	50,000	50,000(1)		100,000
+ Effect of pooling	50,000				50,000
+ Net income	64,000	24,000	24,000		64,000
– Dividends declared	(52,000)	(4,000)		4,000(1)	(52,000)
Balances, 12/31/X1	162,000	70,000	74,000	4,000	162,000

and that the preceding entries had been made. Comparing this illustration to Il-lustration 7–3 (consummation at the beginning of the year), note that here divi-dends declared are $1,000 higher in both the parent's column and the Consolidated column. The income statement is not presented because it is identical to the one in Illustration 7–3. The balance sheet is not presented either because it is also identi-cal to the one in Illustration 7–3 except that both cash and retained earnings in both the parent's column and the Consolidated column are $1,000 less.

X   DISSENTING SHAREHOLDERS

Occasionally, some shareholders of the target company refuse to either (1) be a party to the business combination regardless of the consideration offered or (2) take common stock as consideration. We call these shareholders the **dissenting share-holders. So long as holders of at least 90% of the outstanding shares of the tar-get company agree to exchange their shares for common stock of the issuing company, the pooling of interests treatment is allowed.**

DISSENTING SHAREHOLDERS *NOT* BOUGHT OUT

If P Company had pooled with only 90% of S Company's outstanding shares by is-suing 900 shares of its common stock in exchange for 4,500 shares outstanding of S Company and had not acquired any shares from the dissenting shareholders, it would have made the following entry:

Investment in Subsidiary (90% of $60,000 book value)	54,000	
Common Stock (900 Shares × $1 Par)		900
Retained Earnings (90% of $50,000 book value)		45,000
Additional Paid-in Capital		
(residual amount to balance)		8,100

DISSENTING STOCKHOLDERS BOUGHT OUT WITH CASH

Sometimes the dissenting shareholders merely refuse to take common stock of the issuing company as consideration, preferring cash or other means. If these shares are acquired for cash or other types of noncommon stock consideration, logic sug-gests that *purchase accounting* be used for the acquisition of these shares because these shareholders did *not* fuse their ownership interest and become shareholders of the combined businesses. This would result, however, in recording the combination as part pooling and part purchase. As a practical matter, *APBO No. 16* requires that **a single method be used to account for the combination—providing that the dissenting shares are acquired at the same time the business combination is consummated.** Accordingly, the pooling of interests method is used to account for all of the shares surrendered to the issuing company. Thus, **the combination *cannot* be recorded as part pooling and part purchase.** Continuing with the example used earlier, let us assume that holders of 10% of S Company's outstanding common stock were given cash of $9,000 for their shares at the combination date.

If one tried to apply pooling of interests accounting to the acquisition of these shares alone, the following entry would be made (shown in the **sequential order in which the entry would be developed**):

Investment in Subsidiary (10% of $60,000 book value)	6,000	
Cash		9,000
Retained Earnings (10% of book value of $50,000)		5,000
Additional Paid-in Capital		
(residual amount to balance)	8,000	

In practice, the following single entry is made to account for the entire combination, which is the unification of the previous two entries shown (shown in the **sequential development order**):

Investment in Subsidiary (100% of $60,000 book value)	60,000	
Common Stock (900 shares × $1 par)		900
Cash		9,000
Retained Earnings (100% of book value of $50,000)		50,000
Additional Paid-in Capital		
(residual amount to balance)		100

HISTORICAL PERSPECTIVE

A Capsule History of Pooling of Interests Accounting

Early 1940s The term *pooling of interests* emerges. In rate-base cases brought before it involving business combinations, the Federal Power Commission (FPC) prohibits companies from revaluing their assets upward to their current values when the separate parties have merely pooled their interests. This policy is applied to both related parties and unrelated parties. For revaluation to be allowed, the FPC requires that a sale must occur—one party must dispose of an interest and the other party must acquire that interest.

1945 The Committee on Accounting Procedure of the American Institute for Certified Public Accountants (AICPA) begins to address poolings of interests. Internal memos show that only combinations of two or more interests of comparable size are considered to be poolings of interests.

1950 *ARB No. 40,* "Business Combinations," is issued. It lists four factors to be considered in determining whether the transaction is a purchase or pooling of interests: (1) The **continuity of the former ownership:** Eliminating one of the ownerships or altering the equity interests of either interest immediately before or after the combination indicates a purchase transaction. (2) The **relative size:** One party that is "quite minor" in size compared to the other suggests a purchase transaction. (3) **Continuity of management:** If the management of one of the interests is eliminated or has little influence after the combination, a purchase transaction is indicated. (4) **Similar or complementary**

(continued)

lines of business: If the businesses are in similar or complementary lines of business, a presumption of a pooling of interests is strengthened.

No single factor is the deciding one; the presence or absence of each of the factors is to be considered cumulatively.

OBSERVATION: After *ARB No. 40* was issued, it was possible in most cases to have the assets reported at the same values regardless of whether purchase accounting or pooling of interests accounting were used. This occurred because it was acceptable practice to immediately charge to retained earnings the cost in excess of book value that arose under the purchase method. As a result, there was no major controversy at this time.

1953 *ARB No. 43*, a restatement and revision of *ARB Nos. 1 to 42*, is issued. No substantive changes are made concerning business combinations. Of great importance, however, is the prohibition of immediately charging intangibles arising from acquisition to retained earnings (or to additional paid-in capital). Capitalization as an asset is required and amortization to income is encouraged.

OBSERVATIONS: The effect of *ARB No. 43* was to make pooling of interests much more desirable because the cost in excess of book value can be eliminated from accountability only under pooling of interests. Thus the stage was set for the explosive shift to the pooling of interests method that would occur during the 1950s and 1960s.

At this time, the accounting profession did not have detailed rules concerning pooling of interests—only factors to be evaluated. The burden of determining whether pooling of interests should be applied was placed squarely on the auditors' judgment and integrity.

1950– 1956 Because of the manner in which *ARB Nos. 40* and *43* are written—no single factor determines the need for pooling of interests—companies and their auditors interpret them loosely. The result in most cases is that companies have almost complete discretion to account for a combination as a purchase or as a pooling of interests.

1957 *ARB No. 48*, "Business Combinations," is issued, superseding the business combinations section of *ARB No. 43*. The "similar or complementary" lines of business factor is dropped.

Concerning the relative size of the combining interests, the wording "quite minor" is replaced by a range of percentages: If one of the combining interests ends up with 90–95% of the stock, *purchase accounting* is indicated.

OBSERVATIONS: The fast-growing trend toward diversification most likely played a role in the deletion of the similar or complementary business factor. Thus one of the major reasons that companies might want to pool their interests was deemed nonessential. It was now considered perfectly reasonable for the shareholders of a medical equipment manufacturer and a toy manufacturer to pool their interests.

The insertion of the 90–95% wording removed the intent of *ARB No. 40* that the combining companies be of comparable size. Now companies of greatly disproportionate size could have a pooling of interests.

1958– 1962 The relative size factor having been already weakened, it becomes virtually ignored in practice. Companies begin to use preferred stock to maintain the "continuity of ownership." An abuse known as *retroactive poolings* becomes widespread and is severely criticized.[a]

1963 *Accounting Research Study No. 5*, "A Critical Study of Accounting for Business Combinations," by Arthur R. Wyatt and sponsored by the American Institute of Certified Public Accountants, is issued.[b] It recommends the following: (a) The pooling of interests accounting treatment should be abolished unless the parties are related. (b) When the parties are unrelated and approximately the same size, a fresh start (termed *fair value pooling of interests*) should be made by revaluing the assets of both companies to their current values.

1965 The Accounting Principles Board issues *APB Opinion No. 6*, "Status of Accounting Research Bulletins." Commenting on *ARB No. 48*, it states that the factors set forth therein are guidelines rather than literal requirements.

1966– 1968 New abuses crop up, such as the part-purchase, part-pooling method. Finding a company with undervalued assets, recording a combination with it as a pooling of interests, and then later selling off the undervalued assets to report phenomenal gains becomes a popular practice. Many companies call on their auditors to teach them the intricacies of pooling of interests accounting.

The profession comes under mounting criticism for not having adequate standards by which to judge pooling of interests, especially in light of the largest wave of business combinations in history. One of the most scathing articles during this period is "Dirty Pooling" by Abraham J. Briloff of Baruch College.[c] Briloff subsequently becomes one of the leading critics of the accounting profession and is often referred to as its conscience.

Feb. 1969 The chairman of the Securities and Exchange Commission, testifying before a congressional committee, states that unless the accounting profession takes prompt action to resolve the business combinations controversy, the SEC would establish rules in this area.

June 1969 The AICPA holds a symposium on accounting for business combinations.

Sept. 1969 The AICPA's executive vice-president, Leonard Savoie, states in an address that a forthcoming exposure draft will propose abolishing the pooling of interests method. He also states: "Anything less than this solution will mean simply a 'repositioning' of the abuses which have become so rampant in recent years."[d]

Nov. 1969 The Accounting Principles Board tentatively decides to abolish pooling of interests accounting. A Federal Trade Commission study (authorized by a Senate antitrust committee) released about the same time recommends that the SEC eliminate pooling of interests accounting when stock is given as consideration.

Dec. 1969 The APB reverses itself and tentatively decides pooling of interests accounting should be allowed but not as an alternative that can be freely chosen if desired. For a given set of circumstances and conditions, only one method will apply.

Feb. 1970 The APB issues an exposure draft. The detailed conditions set forth to be met for a pooling of interests will severely limit its use. A three-to-one comparable size test is included. Lawsuits are subsequently threatened over this condition.

June 1970 The APB reduces the size test to nine to one (about what it was under *ARB No. 48*).

Aug 1970 *APB Opinion No. 16* is issued; it barely passes on a 12-to-6 vote. The requirement that the combining companies effect a continuity of interests becomes the cornerstone for pooling of interests treatment; the size test is dropped entirely, and there are no requirements for continuity of management or similar or complementary lines of business. The combining interests must meet 12 detailed conditions to effect a pooling of interests. If they do not meet any one of the 12 conditions, they must use *purchase accounting* in their combination.

> OBSERVATION: The fact that the conditions for pooling of interests treatment are spelled out in such detail clearly shows that setting guidelines requiring the use of professional judgment and integrity does not work very well. This may be because the judgment of so many is either questionable or compromised as a result of concern over loss of clients to other CPAs who are more willing to liberally interpret the guidelines.

1970–1973 *APB Opinion No. 16* proves to be difficult to apply. Because of its complexity and to close loopholes, the AICPA issues 30 interpretations and the SEC issues four Accounting Series Releases. (Later, from 1974 to 1987, the FASB will issue three interpretations and three technical bulletins.)

1973 The FASB replaces the APB and immediately requests views on previous APB pronouncements. The responses show that *APB Opinion Nos. 16* and *17* are of greatest concerns.

1974 The FASB decides to reevaluate the 12 conditions for pooling of interests in *APB Opinion No. 16.*

1975 The FASB expands the scope of the project to encompass all issues associated with business combinations and goodwill.

1976 The FASB issues a discussion memorandum on the topic, "Accounting for Business Combinations and Purchased Intangibles."

1981 The FASB removes the project from its active agenda because of its "low priority in relation to other existing and potential projects."

1996 Business combinations and purchased intangibles continue to be low in priority for the FASB, even though 24 years have passed since

(continued)

HISTORICAL PERSPECTIVE

respondents indicated that they were most concerned with these issues.

[a]Retroactive poolings is a technique in which poolings of interests consummated after the year-end but before the issuance of the year-end annual report are given effect in the current year's financial statements rather than in the year of the combination.

[b]Wyatt was then a professor of accountancy at the University of Illinois. A short time later, he became a senior partner in the home office of Arthur Andersen & Co. and subsequently became one of the most respected accountants in the profession. In 1985 he became a member of the Financial Accounting Standards Board. He resigned in 1988 over philosophical differences and returned to Arthur Andersen & Co. (retiring in 1992).

[c]*The Accounting Review* (July 1967), p. 489.

[d]"The Accounting Profession at the Hump of the Decades." By Abraham J. Briloff, *Financial Analysts Journal* (May–June 1970), p. 61.

Sources: A good portion of the history prior to 1971 was based on information contained in:

Arthur R. Wyatt, *A Critical Study of Accounting for Business Combinations* (New York: American Institute of Certified Public Accountants, 1963).

Hugh P. Hughes, *Goodwill in Accounting: A History of the Issues and Problems.* Research Monograph No. 80 (Atlanta: Georgia State University, 1982). Because of the close relationship of the goodwill issue with pooling of interests accounting, this publication devotes considerable attention to the pooling of interests issue.

END-OF-CHAPTER REVIEW

SUMMARY OF KEY POINTS

1. A pooling of interests is a **fusing** together **of ownership interests.**
2. This fusion occurs only when one of the combining companies **issues voting common stock** in exchange for either (a) 100% of the target company's assets or (b) at least 90% of the outstanding common stock of the target company.
3. In addition, numerous other conditions grouped into **three broad areas** (attributes of the combining companies, the manner of combining, and the absence of planned transactions) must be met.
4. If **any one of the 12 conditions** is *not* met, purchase accounting must be used.
5. The **basis of accounting** for the target company's assets and liabilities is **not changed** in a pooling of interests, nor is goodwill ever reported.
6. **Precombination earnings and dividends** of the target company are always combined with those of the issuing company—but only to the extent of the ownership interest exchanged—whenever periods prior to the combination date are presented.

GLOSSARY OF NEW TERMS

Dissenting shareholders Target company shareholders who refuse to exchange their common shares for only common stock of the acquiring company.

Spin-off A divestiture of a portion of a business whereby certain assets, liabilities, or common stock holdings of a subsidiary are given to certain stockholders of a company in exchange for some or all of their outstanding common stock holdings in the company.

SELF-STUDY QUESTIONS

(Answers are at the end of this chapter.)

1. Which of the following is a condition or requirement for pooling of interests treatment?
   a. A common-stock-for-common-stock exchange must take place.
   b. The companies must be in similar or complementary lines of business.
   c. The target company cannot own any stock of the company issuing common stock between the *initiation* date and the *consummation* date.
   d. The common stock issued must be voting common stock.

2. Which of the following is a condition or requirement for pooling of interests treatment?
   a. Holders of at least 90% of the target company's common stock agree not to sell the shares they receive from the issuing company for two years.
   b. Dissenting shareholders may not receive cash for their interest.
   c. The issuing company cannot agree to buy back (as a purchase of treasury stock) any of the shares issued to effect the combination.
   d. The smaller of the two combining companies cannot be the company that issues common stock to effect the pooling of interests.

3. Which of the following is a condition or requirement for pooling of interests treatment?
   a. Neither combining company can be a subsidiary.
   b. Treasury stock, no matter why or when acquired, cannot be used to effect a pooling of interests.
   c. Shares of the target company acquired prior to the *consummation* date—no matter whether acquired for cash or common stock—are disregarded in calculating whether the 90% test has been satisfied.
   d. The companies must be of comparable size.

4. Which of the following is a condition or requirement for pooling of interests treatment?
   a. Shares of the target company acquired prior to the *initiation* date—no matter whether acquired for cash or common stock—are disregarded in calculating whether the 90% test has been satisfied.
   b. The 90% group of shareholders cannot receive any cash whatsoever from the issuing company.
   c. Neither combining company can have been involved in a business combination accounted for as a pooling of interests within the preceding two years.
   d. No more than 10% of the common stock issued to effect the pooling of interests can be required to be purchased back for cash.

5. Which of the following is a condition or requirement for a pooling of interests?
   a. Treasury stock may be used by the issuing company to effect a pooling of interests so long as the specific shares used were acquired at least two years prior to the *initiation* date.
   b. Restrictions must be placed on the negotiability of the common stock issued.
   c. Continuity of management must be expected.
   d. The stock issued cannot be voting preferred stock that is convertible into common stock.

6. Which of the following is a condition or requirement for a pooling of interests?
   a. If each combining company has an ownership interest in the other combining company, the cumulative ownership percentage cannot be more than 20%.
   b. Neither combining company has been a subsidiary or division of another corporation for two years prior to the *initiation* date.
   c. Purchases of treasury stock are *not* deemed to be alterations of the equity interests, even when made within two years before the *initiation* date.
   d. Financial arrangements made for the benefit of former stockholders of a combining company cannot extend beyond two years after the *consummation* date.

7. A supporting argument for the pooling of interests method for a business combination is that
   a. One company is clearly the dominant and continuing entity.
   b. Goodwill is generally a part of any acquisition.
   c. It was developed within the boundaries of the historical cost system and is compatible with it.
   d. A portion of the total cost is assigned to individual assets acquired on the basis of their current value.

8. When a parent-subsidiary relationship is established as a result of a business combination, which of the following items should be reported in the consolidated statements at the same amount under both the purchase method and the pooling of interests method?
   a. Noncontrolling interest.
   b. Goodwill.
   c. Retained earnings.
   d. Capital stock accounts (in total).

9. Perkins incurred a $20,000 finder's and consultation fee and $7,000 of SEC registration costs in acquiring Sayco. Of these costs, how much should be reported in the income statement as business combination expenses in the year of the acquisition under each of the following methods?
   a. Pooling of interests.
   b. Purchase method.
10. Using the information in the preceding question, how much would be capitalized as part of the acquisition cost?
    a. Under pooling of interests.
    b. Under the purchase method.
11. A business combination between Plata and Silva occurs 9/30/X1. During 19X1 Plata declares dividends of $25,000 per quarter except for the fourth quarter when it declares $30,000. Silva declares dividends of $10,000 each quarter. Assume that Silva is 100% owned (10% of Silva's shareholders dissented and were bought out with cash). From the choices available, what amount would appear in the consolidated statement of retained earnings as dividends declared for the year ended 12/31/X1 under (a) the pooling of interests method and (b) the purchase method?
    a. $105,000   b. $114,000   c. $132,000   d. $135,000   e. $145,000
12. Using the information in Question 11, but assuming that Silva is only 90% owned, answer the same questions.

DEMONSTRATION PROBLEM

On 10/1/X6, Pak Inc. combined with Shipp Inc. Pak issued 19,000 shares of its common stock in exchange for 45,000 outstanding shares of Shipp. Pak paid $50,000 cash for the remaining 5,000 outstanding shares of Shipp. Pak's common stock had a market price of $40 at the combination date. The capital accounts of each company on 9/30/X6 follow:

	Pak	Shipp
Common stock, $5 par value	$150,000	
Common stock, $2 par value		$100,000
Additional paid-in capital	20,000	15,000
Retained earnings	720,000	485,000

For 19X6, each company—on a stand-alone basis—had the following earnings and dividends:

	Jan. 1– Sept. 30, 19X6	Oct. 1– Dec. 31, 19X6	Total
Pak Inc.			
Net income	$120,000	$50,000	$170,000
Dividends declared	90,000	49,000	139,000
Shipp Inc.			
Net income	$ 70,000	$20,000	$ 90,000
Dividends declared	30,000	10,000	40,000

Pak incurred $35,000 of costs *directly related* to the combination and $25,000 of costs in registering the shares issued with the SEC. These costs are *not* included in the preceding amounts.

Required
1. Prepare the entries required at the combination date.
2. Prepare the entries required under the *equity method* for 19X6.
3. Prepare an analysis of the Investment account as updated through 12/31/X6.
4. Prepare the basic elimination entry for consolidation at 12/31/X6.
5. Prepare a consolidated statement of retained earnings for 19X6.

SOLUTION TO DEMONSTRATION PROBLEM

1. Entry to record the combination as if it occurred as of the beginning of the year:

Investment in Shipp (100% of Shipp's total stockholders' equity at 1/1/X6	560,000	
Common Stock (19,000 shares × $5 par value)		95,000
Cash (to dissenting shareholders)		50,000
Retained Earnings (100% of Shipp's 12/31/X5 retained earnings balance)		445,000

At this point a $30,000 debit is needed to balance the entry:

Additional Paid-in Capital (a $20,000 debit brings this account to a zero balance)	20,000	
Retained Earnings (residual)	10,000	

Note: The effect of the pooling is $435,000 ($445,000 – $10,000), the amount reported in the consolidated statement of retained earnings for the year 19X6.

Entry to account for costs incurred:

Pooling of Interests Expenses	60,000	
Accrued Liabilities		60,000

2.

Investment in Shipp	90,000	
Equity in Net Income		90,000
To record equity in 19X6 earnings (100% of $90,000).		
Dividends Declared	30,000	
Investment in Shipp		30,000
To reflect dividends paid *prior* to the combination date (to Shipp shareholders who surrendered their stock) as dividends to be reported in the consolidated statement of retained earnings.		
Dividends Receivable	10,000	
Investment in Shipp		10,000
To record dividends declared *after* the combination date.		

3.

	Parent's Investment Account— Assigned Value	Subsidiary's Equity Accounts		
	=	Common Stock +	Additional Paid-in Capital +	Retained Earnings
Balances, 1/1/X6	$560,000	$100,000	$15,000	$445,000
+ Net income	90,000			90,000
– Dividends, precombination ..	(30,000)			(30,000)
– Dividends, postcombination..	(10,000)			(10,000)
Balances, 12/31/X6..........	$610,000	$100,000	$15,000	$495,000

4. The basic elimination entry:

Common Stock	100,000	
Additional Paid-in Capital	15,000	
Retained Earnings, 1/1/X6	445,000	
Equity in Net Income	90,000	
Dividends Declared		40,000
Investment in Shipp		610,000

5.

Pak Inc.
Statement of Retained Earnings
For the Year Ended December 31, 19X6

Balance, 12/31/X5, as previously reported	$ 690,000
+ Effect of pooling of interests with Shipp	435,000
Balance, 12/31/X5, as restated	$1,125,000
+ Net Income for the Year	200,000[a]
Subtotal	$1,325,000
− Dividends declared	(169,000)[b]
Balance, 12/31/X6	$1,156,000

[a]Composed of $170,000 from Pak, $90,000 from Shipp, and less $60,000 of expenses incurred.

[b]Composed of $139,000 for Pak plus $30,000 for Shipp that was paid to Shipp's shareholders prior to the combination date. (The entire $30,000 is reported even though 5% of Shipp's shareholders dissented—Pak obtained a 100% interest in Shipp.)

ASSIGNMENT MATERIAL

REVIEW QUESTIONS

1. Why is the term *acquired business* not used in the discussion of pooling of interests accounting in *APB Opinion No. 16?*
2. What is the essence of a pooling of interests?
3. What accounts for the popularity of the pooling of interests method?
4. How has the original concept of a pooling of interests changed over the years?
5. What is the difference between a joining together of the equity interests and a continuity of ownership of the separate equity interests?
6. What are the major conceptual issues pertaining to pooling of interests?
7. What criteria determine whether a business combination is treated as a pooling of interests?
8. What is the major criticism of the pooling of interests criteria in *APB Opinion No. 16?*
9. How is the value of the consideration given by the acquiring company accounted for in a business combination that qualifies as a pooling of interests?
10. Can cash be given to the shareholders of the target company in a business combination that is accounted for as a pooling of interests?
11. How are preacquisition earnings of the target business treated in income statements for periods before the combination date when the combination has been accounted for as a pooling of interests?
12. Why might pooling of interests be considered "the lesser of two evils" by some accountants?

TECHNICAL RESEARCH QUESTIONS

1. Immediately after a business combination, a third party buys all or a portion of the common stock issued to effect the combination. Does such an arrangement disqualify the use of the pooling of interests method?
2. Is the accounting for a business combination affected if the consummation is contingent on the purchase by a third party or parties of all or part of the common stock issued in the combination?
3. Can the common stock issued in a business combination to be accounted for as a pooling of interests be designated as a class of stock different from the majority class (for example, Class A if the majority class has no designation)?
4. A company issues some maximum number of shares to stockholders of the target company under an agreement that part of the shares are to be returned if future earnings are below a certain amount or the future market price of the stock is above a stipulated price. Would this invalidate pooling of interests treatment?
5. Would the granting of an employment contract or a deferred compensation plan by the combined enterprise to former stockholders of the combining company invalidate pooling of interests treatment?

EXERCISES

E 7–1 **Review of Conditions for Pooling of Interests**   Indicate whether each of the following conditions or terms disqualifies the pooling of interests accounting treatment:

1. Issuing common stock in exchange for 90% of the target company's assets. N
2. Issuing common stock in exchange for 90% of the target company's outstanding shares. Y
3. Distribution of common stock and cash—on a pro rata basis—to the target company's share-holders.
4. Additional common stock to be issued by the issuing company if its common stock has a fair market value below $50 per share two years after the combination date.
5. After a common-stock-for-common-stock exchange, the subsidiary is to be liquidated into a division. (No sell-off of assets will take place.)
6. The issuing company plans to use treasury shares it acquired three years ago rather than issue new shares of common stock.
7. The only dissenting shareholder of the target company (a 15% owner holding 15,000 shares) agrees to (a) exchange 10,000 of the shares for common stock of the issuing company using the same exchange ratio that other shareholders have agreed to and (b) exchange the remaining 5,000 shares for cash.   N 10%
8. The common stock issued to the target company's shareholders has certain limited voting restrictions.
9. Additional common shares are to be issued by the issuing company, depending on the subsequent sales level of the target business for three years after the combination date.
10. The issuing company agrees to purchase for cash less than 10% of the shares issued within three years of the combination date. N can be no agreement

E 7–2 **Testing for Independence**   Plix Inc. and Slix Inc. are contemplating a business combination structured to qualify as a pooling of interests. Common stock information is as follows:

	Plix	Slix
Outstanding common shares	300,000	100,000
Plix common stock owned by Slix		15,000
Market price of stock	$20	

Required 1. Determine whether the companies are independent. Assume that Plix will issue three shares for every one outstanding share of Slix.
2. Determine whether the companies are independent, but assume that Plix will issue one share for every one outstanding share of Slix.
3. Explain why the answers in requirements 1 and 2 are different.

E 7–3 **Testing for Independence: Dual Intercorporate Investments**   Peca Inc. and Seca Inc. are contemplating a business combination structured to qualify as a pooling of interests. Common stock information is as follows:

	Peca	Seca
Outstanding common shares	600,000	100,000
Seca common stock owned by Peca	5,000	
Peca common stock owned by Seca		4,000
Market price of stock	$25	

Peca will issue one common share for each two outstanding common shares of Seca.

Required 1. Determine whether the companies are independent.
2. If Seca were the company issuing the common stock, what exchange ratio would it use to maintain the relative holdings between the two stockholder groups?

E 7–4 **CHALLENGER   Testing for Independence: Dual Intercorporate Investments**   Piga Inc. and Siga Inc. are contemplating a business combination structured to qualify as a pooling of interests. Common stock information is as follows:

	Piga	Siga
Outstanding common stock	900,000	200,000
Piga common stock owned by Siga		9,000
Siga common stock owned by Piga	18,000	
Market price of stock	$10	

Piga will issue three common shares for every two common shares of Siga.

Required 1. Determine whether the companies are independent.
2. Determine whether the companies are independent, but assume that Siga will be the issuing company and will issue 600,000 shares to Piga's stockholders. (These shares maintain the same relationship as when Piga was the issuing company.)
3. Explain why the answers in requirements 1 and 2 are different even though the relative holdings between the two stockholder groups were held constant. Which answer must be used to determine independence?

E 7–5 **Recording a Pooling of Interests (100% Ownership)** On 1/1/X1 Pida Inc. obtained 100% of the outstanding common stock of Sida Inc. by issuing 20,000 shares of its $5 par value common stock. Selected information as of the combination date is as follows:

	Pida	Sida
Common stock, $5 par value	$1,000,000	
Common stock, $1 par value		$200,000
Additional paid-in capital	3,000,000	400,000
Retained earnings	2,000,000	250,000
	$6,000,000	$850,000
Fair market value per share	$50	$25
Net assets at current value	$7,000,000	$900,000

Assume that the business combination qualifies for pooling of interests treatment.

Required 1. Prepare the entry to record the business combination.
2. Prepare an analysis of the Investment account as of the combination date.
3. Prepare the basic elimination entry at 1/1/X1.
4. What amount should be reported as the consolidated retained earnings at the combination date?

E 7–6 **Recording a Pooling of Interests (100% Ownership)** On 1/1/X1 Pina Inc. obtained 100% of Sina Inc.'s outstanding common stock by issuing shares of its common stock. Each company's equity accounts immediately *before the combination* are as follows:

	Pina	Sina
Common stock, $10 par value	$1,000,000	
Common stock, $5 par value		$ 80,000
Additional paid-in capital	25,000	20,000
Retained earnings	200,000	50,000
	$1,225,000	$150,000

Assume that the business combination qualifies for pooling of interests accounting.

Required 1. Prepare the entry to record the business combination, assuming that Pina issued
  a. 8,000 shares.
  b. 10,000 shares.
  c. 12,000 shares.
  d. 14,000 shares.
2. Prepare the basic elimination entry as of the combination date for each situation in requirement 1.
3. What amount should be reported as the consolidated retained earnings at the combination date?

E 7–7 **Recording a Pooling of Interests (90% Ownership)** Assume the information provided in Exercise 7–6 except that Pina obtained only 90% of Sina's outstanding common stock.

Required 1. Prepare the entry to record the business combination, assuming that Pina issued
   a. 7,200 shares.
   b. 9,000 shares.
   c. 10,800 shares.
   d. 12,600 shares.
2. Prepare the basic elimination entry as of the combination date for each situation in requirement 1.
3. What amount should be reported as the consolidated retained earnings at the combination date?

E 7–8 **Recording a Pooling of Interests (100% Ownership): Consolidation Entry One Year Later** On 1/1/X1, Pula Inc. obtained 100% of Sula Inc.'s outstanding common stock by issuing 20,000 shares of its common stock. Each company's equity accounts immediately *before the combination* are as follows:

	Pula	Sula
Common stock, $1 par value	$ 100,000	
Common stock, $5 par value		$ 5,000
Additional paid-in capital	900,000	95,000
Retained earnings	500,000	60,000
	$1,500,000	$160,000

For the year ended 12/31/X1, Sula had net income of $40,000 and declared cash dividends of $10,000. Assume that the business combination qualifies for pooling of interests accounting.

Required 1. Prepare the entry to record the business combination.
2. Prepare the basic elimination entry as of the combination date.
3. Prepare the entries for 19X1 required under the *equity method.*
4. Update the analysis of the Investment account for 19X1, and prepare the basic elimination entry as of 12/31/X1.

E 7–9 **Recording a Pooling of Interests (90% Ownership): Consolidation Entry One Year Later** Assume the information provided in Exercise 7–8 except that Pula obtained only 90% of Sula's outstanding common stock on 1/1/X1 by issuing 18,000 shares of its common stock.

Required The requirements are the same as those in Exercise 7–8.

E 7–10 **Determining Consolidated Retained Earnings and Consolidated Net Income in Year of Combination** On 6/30/X5, Plif Inc. merged with Slif Inc. in a business combination properly accounted for as a pooling of interests. Plif exchanged six of its shares of common stock for each share of Slif's outstanding common stock. June 30 was the fiscal year-end for both companies. No intercompany transactions occurred during the year. The balance sheets immediately *before the combination* are as follows:

	Plif Inc. Book Value	Slif Inc. Book Value	Slif Inc. Fair Value
Current assets	$ 40,000	$ 30,000	$ 45,000
Equipment (net)	150,000	120,000	140,000
Land	30,000		
	$220,000	$150,000	$185,000
Current liabilities	$ 35,000	$ 15,000	$ 15,000
Notes payable	40,000		
Bonds payable		100,000	100,000
Common stock ($1 par value)	75,000		
Common stock ($5 par value)		50,000	
Retained earnings	70,000	(15,000)	
	$220,000	$150,000	

Required 1. What was the Retained Earnings account balance on the combined balance sheet at 6/30/X5?
   a. $45,000   **b.** $55,000   **c.** $70,000   **d.** $80,000

2. How should the combined net income for the year be computed?
   a. Use only Plif's income because the combination occurred on the last day of the fiscal year.
   b. Use only Slif's income because the combination occurred on the last day of the fiscal year.
   c. Add together both companies' incomes even though the combination occurred on the last day of the fiscal year.
   d. Add together both companies' incomes and subtract the annual amortization of goodwill.

   (AICPA adapted)

E 7–11   **Determining Consolidated Net Income in Acquisition Year**   On 1/1/X7, Peta Inc. issued 100,000 additional shares of $10 par value voting common stock in exchange for all of Seta Inc.'s voting common stock in a business combination appropriately accounted for as a pooling of interests. Net income for the year ended 12/31/X7 was $400,000 for Seta and $1,300,000 for Peta, exclusive of any consideration of Seta. During 19X7 Peta paid $900,000 in dividends to its stockholders, and Seta paid $250,000 in dividends to Peta.

Required   Determine the consolidated net income for the year ended 12/31/X1.

   (AICPA adapted)

E 7–12   **Determining the Effect of Pooling on Parent's Stockholders' Equity**   Plev Inc. issued voting common stock with a $90,000 stated value in exchange for all of Slev Inc.'s outstanding common stock. The combination was properly accounted for as a pooling of interests.
The stockholders' equity section in Slev's balance sheet at the combination date was as follows:

Common stock	$ 70,000
Capital contributed in excess of stated value	7,000
Retained earnings	50,000
	$127,000

Required   What should be the increase in Plev's stockholders' equity at the acquisition date as a result of this business combination?

   1. $–0–   **2.** $37,000   **3.** $90,000   **4.** $127,000

   (AICPA adapted)

E 7–13   **Determining Consolidated Stockholders' Equity**   On 1/1/X1, Platt Inc. issued 200,000 shares of $5 par value common stock in exchange for all of Slatt Inc.'s common stock in a business combination that qualified as a pooling of interests. Immediately *before the combination,* Platt's total stockholders' equity was $16,000,000 and Slatt's was $4,000,000. Other data for 19X1 are as follows:

	Platt	Slatt
Net income (excluding income recorded under the *equity method* or the *cost method*)	$1,500,000	$450,000
Dividends declared	750,000	200,000

Required   What is the consolidated stockholders' equity at 12/31/X1?

   (AICPA adapted)

E 7–14   **Determining the Effect of Pooling of Interests on Parent's Equity**   In a business combination accounted for as a pooling of interests, the combined corporation's retained earnings amount usually equals the sum of the retained earnings amount of the individual combining corporations.

Required   Assuming that there is no contributed capital other than capital stock at par value on each company's books, which of the following describes a situation in which the combined retained earnings must be increased or decreased?

   1. *Increased* if the par value dollar amount of the outstanding shares of the combined corporation *exceeds* the total capital stock of the separate combining companies.
   2. *Increased* if the par value dollar amount of the outstanding shares of the combined corporation is *less than* the total capital stock of the separate combining companies.

3. *Decreased* if the par value dollar amount of the outstanding shares of the combined corporation *exceeds* the total capital stock of the separate combining companies.

4. *Decreased* if the par value dollar amount of the outstanding shares of the combined corporation is *less than* the total capital stock of the separate combining companies. (AICPA adapted)

E 7–15 **Review of the Conditions for Pooling of Interests** The boards of directors of Paterno Corporation, Sata Corporation, Seta Company, and Sita Company are meeting to discuss plans for a business combination. Each company has one class of common stock outstanding; Sata also has one class of preferred stock outstanding. Although terms have not been settled, Paterno will be the acquiring or issuing corporation.

Required For Question 1, determine which position is correct. For the remaining questions, determine how these facts affect the accounting method to be used. (Consider each question independently of the others.)

1. Some of the directors believe that the terms of the combination should be settled immediately and that the method of accounting to be used (whether pooling of interests, purchase, or a mixture) may be chosen at some later date. Others believe that the terms of the combination and the accounting method are closely related.
2. Paterno and Sata are comparable in size; Seta and Sita are much smaller.
3. Seta was formerly a subsidiary of Spinner Corporation, which is not related to any of the four companies discussing combination. Eighteen months ago, Spinner voluntarily spun off Seta.
4. Don Dissento, who holds 5% of Sita's common stock, will almost certainly object to the combination. Assume that Paterno can acquire only 95% (rather than 100%) of Sita's stock, issuing Paterno common stock in exchange. (If Paterno can acquire the remaining 5% at some future time—in five years, for instance—in exchange for its own common stock, which accounting method will be applicable to this second acquisition?)
5. Because the directors believe that one of Sita's major divisions will not be compatible with the combined company's operations, they expect to sell it as soon as possible after the combination is consummated. They expect to have no trouble finding a buyer.
6. Twenty months ago, Sata acquired 12% of its common stock because the price of the stock was attractively low. Fourteen months ago, Sata retired this treasury stock.
7. Sata is in the same industry as Paterno, Seta is in a complementary industry, and Sita is in a totally unrelated industry. (AICPA adapted)

PROBLEMS

P 7–1* **Recording a Beginning-of-Year Pooling of Interests (100% Ownership): Consolidation Worksheet at Year-End** On 1/1/X4 Poca Inc. issued 4,000 shares of its common stock in exchange for 100% of Soca Inc.'s outstanding common stock. The financial statements of each company for the year ended 12/31/X4 are as follows:

	Poca	Soca
Income Statement (19X4)		
Sales	$800,000	$100,000
Cost of sales	(500,000)	(50,000)
Expenses	(270,000)	(44,000)
Equity in net income (of subsidiary)	6,000	
Net Income	$ 36,000	$ 6,000

(continued)

*The financial statement information presented for problems accompanied by asterisks is also provided on Model 7 (filename: MODEL7) of the software file disk that is available for use with the text, allowing the problem to be worked on the computer.

	Poca	Soca
Balance Sheet (as of 12/31/X4)		
Cash	$ 60,000	$ 10,000
Accounts receivable, net	90,000	20,000
Inventory	150,000	60,000
Investment in subsidiary	133,000	
Fixed assets, net	567,000	110,000
	$1,000,000	$ 200,000
Payables and accruals	$ 76,000	$ 17,000
Long-term debt	300,000	50,000
Common stock, $10 par value	100,000	
Common stock, $1 par value		20,000
Additional paid-in capital	400,000	80,000
Retained earnings	124,000	33,000
	$1,000,000	$ 200,000
Dividends declared in 19X4	$ 10,000	$ 1,000

Assume that the business combination qualifies for pooling of interests accounting.

Required   **1.** Prepare an updated analysis of the Investment account for 19X4 using the *equity method.*
2. Determine the entry made on 1/1/X4 to record the business combination.
3. Prepare the basic elimination entry at 12/31/X4.
4. Prepare a consolidation worksheet at 12/31/X4.
5. Prepare a formal consolidated statement of retained earnings for 19X4.

P 7–2*   **Recording a Year-End Pooling of Interests (100% Ownership): Consolidation Worksheet**   On 12/31/X2, Patt Inc. issued 1,000 shares of its common stock in exchange for 100% of Satt Inc.'s outstanding common stock. The financial statements of each company for the year ended 12/31/X2 *before the business combination* are as follows:

	Patt	Satt
Income Statement (19X2)		
Sales	$400,000	$140,000
Cost of sales	(200,000)	(70,000)
Expenses	(150,000)	(40,000)
Net Income	$ 50,000	$ 30,000
Balance Sheet (as of 12/31/X2)		
Cash	$ 50,000	$ 33,000
Accounts receivable, net	60,000	20,000
Inventory	80,000	27,000
Fixed assets, net	610,000	120,000
	$800,000	$200,000
Payables and accruals	$ 90,000	$ 25,000
Long-term debt	260,000	15,000
Common stock, $10 par value	200,000	
Common stock, $2 par value		100,000
Additional paid-in capital	130,000	
Retained earnings	120,000	60,000
	$800,000	$200,000
Dividends declared in 19X2	$ 20,000	$ 10,000

Assume that the business combination qualifies for pooling of interests treatment.

Required   **1.** Prepare the entry to record the business combination.
2. Prepare the entries that would be recorded under the *equity method* for 19X2.
3. Prepare and update the analysis of the Investment account through 12/31/X2.

4. Prepare the basic elimination entry at 12/31/X2.
5. Adjust the parent company's financial statements as shown above to reflect the *equity method*, and then prepare a consolidation worksheet at 12/31/X2.
6. Prepare a formal consolidated statement of retained earnings for 19X2.

P 7–3*   **Recording a Year-End Pooling of Interests (90% Ownership): Consolidation Worksheet**   Assume the information provided in Problem 7–2, except that Patt Inc. issued 900 shares of its common stock in exchange for 90% of Satt Inc.'s outstanding common stock on 12/31/X2.

Required   The requirements are the same as for Problem 7–2.

P 7–4*   **COMPREHENSIVE**   **Recording a Mid-Year Pooling of Interests (100% Ownership: Dissenting Shareholders Bought Out for Cash): Consolidation Worksheet at Year-End**   On 9/30/X2, Pace Inc. issued 270,000 shares of its common stock to holders of 18,000 shares of Sace Inc. common stock and gave $140,000 cash to dissenting holders of 2,000 shares of Sace's common stock. Direct costs incurred in connection with the business combination were $20,000. An additional $60,000 cost was incurred in registering the common stock issued with the SEC. Each company's financial statements for the year ended 12/31/X2 are as follows:

	Pace	Sace
Income Statement (19X2)		
Sales	$9,000,000	$ 900,000
Cost of sales	(5,000,000)	(400,000)
Marketing expenses	(2,500,000)	(300,000)
Net Income	$1,500,000	$ 200,000
Balance Sheet (as of 12/31/X2)		
Cash	$ 410,000	$ 100,000
Accounts receivable, net	900,000	200,000
Inventory	2,000,000	300,000
Investment in subsidiary	110,000	
Fixed assets, net	3,500,000	1,400,000
Deferred charges	80,000	
	$7,000,000	$2,000,000
Payables and accruals	$1,800,000	$ 280,000
Long-term debt	2,000,000	800,000
Common stock, $2 par value	700,000	
Common stock, $5 par value		100,000
Additional paid-in capital	800,000	340,000
Retained earnings	1,700,000	480,000
	$7,000,000	$2,000,000
Dividends declared and paid in 19X2 ..	$ 800,000	$ 120,000

Additional Information
1. Sace's income was earned evenly throughout the year.
2. Sace declared and paid dividends of $30,000 in the middle of each quarter.
3. The $80,000 of out-of-pocket costs were paid and charged to a Deferred Charges suspense account.
4. No entry has been made to record the combination (which qualifies as a pooling of interests) other than for the amount paid to the dissenting shareholders. (The parent desires to use the equity method.)

Required
1. Prepare the entry to record the business combination and any necessary year-end adjusting entries.
2. Prepare the basic elimination entry at 12/31/X2. (*Hint:* Prepare an updated analysis of the Investment account.)
3. Prepare a consolidation worksheet at 12/31/X2.
4. Prepare a formal consolidated statement of retained earnings for 19X2.

P 7–5*   **COMPREHENSIVE**   **Recording a Mid-Year Pooling of Interests (90% Ownership): Consolidation Worksheet at Year-End**   Assume the same information provided in Problem 7–4 except that Pace Inc. issued 270,000 shares of its common stock for 90% of Sace Inc.'s outstanding common stock. Pace did *not* acquire the shares of the dissenting shareholders for $140,000 cash. Accordingly, change certain of Pace's balance sheet amounts as follows:

1. Increase the Cash account by $137,000 ($140,000 – $3,000 of dividends received by Pace in the last quarter that Sace instead would have paid to the noncontrolling interests).
2. Reduce the Investment in Subsidiary account by $137,000.

Required　The requirements are the same as those for Problem 7–4.

P 7–6*　 **COMPREHENSIVE**　**Recording a Mid-Year Pooling of Interests (100% Ownership): Analytical Development of Key Amounts; Consolidation Worksheet at Year-End**　On 9/30/X4, Pana Inc. obtained a 100% interest in Sana Inc. through an exchange of its common stock for Sana common stock on a 1-for-4 basis. Pana's common stock was selling on the market for $8 per share at the time, and the investment was recorded on this basis using the following journal entry:

Investment in Sana	80,000	
Common Stock		50,000
Additional Paid-in Capital		30,000

The transaction qualified for pooling of interests treatment.

No market price was available for Sana's common stock when Pana acquired it. Its book value was $1.60 per share at the combination date. Pana's board of directors justified the premium paid for the Sana stock on the grounds that the fixed assets and inventory were undervalued.

Each company's financial statements for the year ended 12/31/X4 are as follows:

	Pana	Sana
Income Statement (19X4)		
Sales	$450,000	$200,000
Cost of sales	(250,000)	(110,000)
Expenses	(130,000)	(58,000)
Net Income	$ 70,000	$ 32,000
Balance Sheet (as of 12/31/X4)		
Cash	$ 50,000	$ 12,000
Accounts receivable, net	110,000	68,000
Inventory	177,000	22,000
Investment in subsidiary	80,000	
Fixed assets, net	318,000	180,000
	$735,000	$282,000
Payables and accruals	$117,000	$ 98,000
Long-term debt	140,000	106,000
Common stock, $5 par value	200,000	
Common stock, $1 par value		40,000
Additional paid-in capital	160,000	
Retained earnings	118,000	38,000
	$735,000	$282,000
Dividends declared in 19X4	$ 55,000	$ –0–

Required　1. Prepare the entry that should have been made to record the combination as a pooling of interests. Then make the appropriate correcting entry.
2. Prepare the entries resulting from the application of the *equity method* through 12/31/X4.
3. Prepare an expanded analysis of the Investment account, and update it through 12/31/X4.
4. Prepare the basic elimination entry at 12/31/X4.
5. Prepare a consolidation worksheet for 19X4 (after adjusting the financial statements for entries in requirements 1 and 2).
6. Prepare a formal consolidated statement of retained earnings for 19X4.　　(AICPA adapted)

PROBLEMS COMPARING THE POOLING OF INTERESTS METHOD WITH THE PURCHASE METHOD

P 7–7 **Calculation of Consolidated Net Income: Pooling of Interests Method Versus Purchase Method**   Plex Inc. acquired several businesses during 19X1. Information relating to each business is as follows:

Company	Combination Date	Ownership Percentage	Net Income (Loss) for 19X1
Able Company	1/1/X1	100	$100,000
Baker Company	4/1/X1	90	200,000
Charley Company	7/1/X1	100	60,000
Delta Company	11/1/X1	95	120,000
Echo Company	12/31/X1	90	(50,000)

Assume that all earnings and losses occurred evenly throughout the year. Assume that Plex had net income of $500,000 from its own separate operations, exclusive of earnings or losses recorded under the equity method of accounting.

Required   1. Determine the amount of consolidated net income for 19X1, assuming that all business combinations qualified for pooling of interests accounting.
   2. Determine the amount of consolidated net income for 19X1, assuming that none of the business combinations qualified for pooling of interests accounting. Assume that Plex amortized $40,000 cost in excess of book value, which is not reflected in the $500,000 amount given above.

P 7–8 **COMPREHENSIVE** **Comparing the Purchase Method with the Pooling of Interests Method: Consolidation Worksheet**   Sali Inc. merged into Pali Inc. on 6/30/X3 and Sali ceased to exist. Both companies report on a calendar year-end basis.

Additional Information   As of the date of the merger:
   1. The fair value of each corporation's assets and liabilities on 6/30/X3 was as follows:

	Pali	Sali
Current assets	$ 4,900,000	$ 3,400,000
Land	3,000,000	1,000,000
Buildings and equipment	19,000,000	13,000,000
Patents	700,000	400,000
Total Assets	$27,600,000	$17,800,000
Liabilities	(2,500,000)	(2,100,000)
Net Assets	$25,100,000	$15,700,000

   2. Pali has charged $70,000 of direct out-of-pocket costs relating to the merger and $30,000 of internally generated general expenses of the acquisitions department to the Prepaid Expenses account (part of current assets) pending the recording of the combination.
   3. Revaluing Pali's and Sali's assets to their current values results in additional amortization and depreciation of $240,000 and $80,000 for the six months ended 12/31/X3.
   4. Dividends declared and paid for 19X3 were the following:

	Pali	Sali
First six months	$800,000	$400,000
Last six months	900,000	

The balance sheets *immediately before* the merger data and net income data for all of 19X3 are as follows:

	Pali	**Sali**
Balance Sheet (as of 6/30/X3)		
Current assets	$ 4,200,000	$ 3,000,000
Land	2,000,000	1,000,000
Building and equipment	20,500,000	12,300,000
Accumulated depreciation	(4,000,000)	(2,000,000)
Patents	600,000	200,000
	$23,300,000	$14,500,000
Liabilities	$ 2,500,000	$ 2,000,000
Common stock, $10 par value	12,000,000	
Common stock, $5 par value		3,800,000
Paid-in capital in excess of par value	4,200,000	3,200,000
Retained earnings	6,000,000	5,500,000
	$24,700,000	$14,500,000
Less treasury stock, at cost 100,000 shares . . .	(1,400,000)	
	$23,300,000	$14,500,000
Net Income		
1/1/X3 to 6/30/X3	$ 2,200,000	$ 1,500,000
7/1/X3 to 12/31/X3 (excluding amounts that would be		
recorded as a result of the merger)	2,400,000	1,800,000
	$ 4,600,000	$ 3,300,000

Required   Do the following for each of the independent situations given below: (a) prepare a combined balance sheet as of 6/30/X3; (b) determine the combined net income to be reported for 19X3 (12 months); and (c) prepare a formal combined statement of retained earnings for 19X3 (12 months).

1. Pali exchanged 400,000 shares of previously unissued common stock and 100,000 shares of treasury stock for all of Sali's assets and liabilities (which were assumed). All the conditions for pooling of interests accounting were met.
2. Pali purchased the assets and assumed Sali's liabilities by paying cash of $3,100,000 and issuing debentures of $16,900,000 at face value.

(AICPA adapted)

✳ THINKING CRITICALLY ✳

✳ CASES ✳

C 7–1   **What If We Ignore *APBO No. 16* and Do What We Think Is Right?**   Pargo Inc. recently had a business combination that qualified for pooling of interests accounting. You were able to convince top management to use *purchase accounting* because pooling of interests accounting would be misleading.

Required   Can Pargo's financial statements still be in compliance with GAAP if Pargo ignores *APBO No. 16* and uses *purchase accounting?*

C 7–2   **We Followed the Rules**   You are the controller for Parr Inc., which effected a *horizontal* business combination in May 19X1 with Sarr Inc., which had substantially undervalued assets. A major portion of these assets were sold in July 19X3 at a substantial gain, which enabled Parr to show continued earnings growth. The combination was accounted for as a pooling of interests.

   In 19X4 some of its stockholders sued Parr for allegedly issuing false and misleading financial statements as a result of substantially overstating its true earnings for 19X3, which plaintiffs contend can be determined only under purchase accounting.

Required   1. Does Parr have an adequate defense that it used generally accepted accounting principles? In other words, would the judge instruct the jury to determine whether GAAP had been properly followed?
   2. What else might be a critical issue?

C 7–3 **Case Study from Actual Practice Pooling of Interests: A Question of Intent** **Case 10 from** *The Trueblood Professors' Seminar* **The Touche Ross Foundation and American Accounting Association, Copyright © 1988, reprinted by special permission.** Your client is Mega, Inc., a New York Stock Exchange company that has acquired several profitable businesses in recent years. It has subsidiaries in lines such as home computers, seismographic operations, agricultural chemicals, and solar energy. Its earnings have shown steady growth, and the stock market has valued the company with a high price-earnings ratio.

One month ago, you and Mega's treasurer discussed the proposed acquisition of Sellum, Inc., a southwestern real estate brokerage operation with subsidiaries that own and operate apartment houses. Because of the region's depressed real estate market and flat earnings, the stock of Sellum was trading at less than book value. The acquisition was to be made by a straightforward exchange of common stock for common stock using market prices. After reviewing the criteria for business combinations, you and the treasurer agreed that the accounting would follow the pooling of interests method.

But now the treasurer has suggested a complication. She tells you, "It looks like the deal for Sellum will go through. As I see it, if we intend to sell off some of the apartment house subsidiaries, or any of our other assets, we have to use the purchase method of accounting. Then we'll have a minimum of $20,000,000 negative goodwill to take into income over the next three years. We can discuss whether three is the right number of years later, but I just wanted to check and be sure that purchase accounting is OK before we close the deal." You say, "Yes, that's what the accounting standards say, provided it's a significant part of the assets and not a disposal in the ordinary course of business." The treasurer responds, "That's great; you can tell us later what is significant and that's the amount we intend to sell."

Your hesitation centers around the thought that Mega may be able to "manipulate" $20,000,000 or more into its future earnings stream by expressing an intention to sell off some properties. Six months earlier you were confronted with a similar situation. Another client had acquired a ladies' apparel manufacturing complex in a pooling of interests transaction with no intention (represented in writing) of selling off any assets. But 16 months after the acquisition, it had sold off a significant, unprofitable manufacturing subsidiary.

Required 1. Discuss how the auditor can determine a client's intent.
2. Consider the form versus substance of a pooling of interests versus purchase transaction.
3. Was Mega given the right answer?
4. What should you tell the treasurer is a "significant part of the assets"?
5. If the purchase method of accounting is followed, what should be done if Mega does not sell off a significant amount of assets?

C 7–4 **Case Study from Actual Practice: Pooling of Interests—A Question of Substance** Plotter Company recently issued common stock in exchange for all of Sleeper Company's assets in a transaction structured to qualify as a pooling of interests. Sleeper has been in various stages of the timber business since the company's inception 60 years ago. Sleeper had approximately 100 shareholders at the combination date. Many years ago, its sawmills had been closed. Since that time, its only revenues had been contract sales of timber. In recent years, a lack of mature trees has resulted in significantly reduced cutting operations, and income from operations had been nominal. Virtually all of its forest land holdings are now in a regrowth stage. The fair value of the common stock issued by Plotter is $25,000,000. The book value of Sleeper's assets is $3,000,000. The current value of Sleeper's land holdings is $25,000,000. The common stock issued was treasury stock that was acquired in a block purchase six years ago when the price of the company's stock was at a very depressed level.

Required Using only the information provided, assess whether the transaction should be recorded as a pooling of interests. Explain your reasoning.

☀ FINANCIAL ANALYSIS PROBLEMS ☀

FAP 7–1 **Debt Ratios and Returns on Investment: Pooling of Interests Versus Purchase Method** If FAP 4–1 was not assigned in covering Chapter 4, it can be assigned in this chapter instead.

FAP 7–2 **Earnings per Share: Pooling of Interests Versus Purchase Methods** *(Read the first paragraph of the appendix before working this problem.)* Pridex Inc. and Stridex Inc. combined on 4/1/X1. Pridex issued 160,000 shares of its common stock in exchange for 100% of Stridex's outstanding common stock. Selected information follows:

	Pridex	Stridex
Net Income		
Actual—First quarter of 19X1	$ 400,000	$ 75,000
Estimated—Remainder of 19X1		
Old basis of accounting	1,200,000	225,000
New basis of accounting		174,000
Average Common Shares Outstanding during 19X1[a]		
Prior to the combination	840,000	100,000
After the combination	1,000,000	100,000

[a]During 19X1 neither company had any securities outstanding that could dilute earnings per share.

Required 1. Calculate the 19X1 consolidated earnings per share under the pooling of interests method.
2. Repeat requirement 1 under the purchase method.
3. Repeat requirement 1 under the purchase method, assuming that the combination had occurred on 1/1/X1; this is a GAAP required *pro forma* calculation. (When a business combination accounted for under the purchase method occurs at other than the beginning of the year, both the pro forma EPS amount and the pro forma net income for the entire year must be presented in a note to the consolidated statements; thus you must first determine the pro forma net income for 19X1.)

✳ PERSONAL SITUATIONS: ETHICS AND INTERPERSONAL SKILLS ✳

PS 7–1   **Intellectual Honesty: To Go Along or *Not* to Go Along?**   Poolem Inc. recently effected a business combination that qualified for pooling of interests accounting. In college, you thoroughly studied pooling of interests accounting and concluded that it was a deceptive and misleading practice.

Required 1. If you were either Poolem's corporate controller or outside auditor, would you insist that the *purchase method* be used even though all 12 conditions for pooling of interests were satisfied? Why or why not?
2. Assuming that you acquiesce to top management's position of using pooling of interests accounting, how would you feel about continuing to work for an organization that uses a deceptive and misleading accounting practice or enables an entity to use it?

ANSWERS TO SELF-STUDY QUESTIONS

1. d   2. c   3. a   4. a   5. d   6. b   7. c   8. a

9. **a.** $27,000   10. **a.** $–0–   11. **a.** d   12. **a.** c
   b. $–0–   **b.** $20,000   **b.** a   **b.** a

■APPENDIX

CONSOLIDATED EARNINGS PER SHARE

Fundamentally, consolidated earnings per share (EPS) is simply consolidated net income (income accruing to the benefit of the parent's shareholders) divided by the average number of the **parent's** common shares outstanding (adjusted for the parent's common equivalent shares and its other potentially dilutive securities, if any). In the example that follows, we use a single EPS calculation, thus ignoring for now that *APB Opinion No. 15,* "Earnings per Share," requires both a primary EPS calculation and a fully diluted EPS calculation.

I SUBSIDIARY HAS NO POTENTIALLY DILUTIVE SECURITIES OUTSTANDING

Most subsidiaries do not have outstanding potentially dilutive securities such as stock options, warrants, convertible bonds, and convertible preferred stocks. Consequently, making the parent's EPS calculation on a consolidated basis is simple.

The *consolidated* net income, say $700,000, is merely divided by the denominator, say 1,000,000 shares, that the parent would use in computing EPS for its separate parent-company-only statements. Consolidated EPS in this example therefore is $.70 ($700,000/1,000,000 shares). (The subsidiary's outstanding shares are completely ignored in making this calculation because they are deemed not to be outstanding from a consolidated perspective.)

II SUBSIDIARY HAS POTENTIALLY DILUTIVE SECURITIES OUTSTANDING

If a subsidiary has dilutive securities outstanding, however, the consolidated net income amount ($700,000 in our example) cannot be used as the numerator in the EPS calculation. Instead, the consolidated net income amount first must be reduced to the extent that the parent's ownership interest in the subsidiary's net income is potentially dilutive. This reduction is made only for computing consolidated EPS—**no reduction is made to the consolidated net income amount** ($700,000 in our example) reported in the consolidated income statement. Continuing with our example, assume that S Company

1. Is a 100%-owned subsidiary of P Company.
2. Reported $200,000 of net income for 19X1 (which is included in determining the consolidated net income amount, $700,000 in our example).
3. Had 20,000 shares of common stock outstanding during all of 19X1 (all owned by P Company).
4. Has granted stock options to its employees and, as a result, 5,000 additional shares (determined by using the treasury stock method) would be used in S Company's denominator in its separate company EPS calculation. Thus 25,000 shares would be used in S Company's EPS denominator—not 20,000 shares.

Because of the potential dilution of P Company's ownership interest, P Company cannot use all $200,000 of S Company's net income in making the consolidated EPS calculation. Instead, only $160,000 of S Company's net income (20,000/25,000 × $200,000) can be included in the numerator in computing consolidated EPS for 19X1. Thus consolidated net income—for EPS purposes only—is only $660,000 ($700,000 – $40,000 of earnings that accrues to the stock option holders). Consolidated EPS therefore is $.66, not $.70.

A RATIO FOR ALL POTENTIAL DILUTION SITUATIONS

The ratio that was used to determine how much of S Company's earnings effectively accrues to the parent and can be included in the numerator for consolidated EPS purposes (20,000/25,000) can be expressed generically as follows:

$$\frac{\text{Number of Shares in Subsidiary's EPS Denominator}}{\text{That Are Owned by or Accrue to the Parent}}{\text{Total Number of Shares in Subsidiary's EPS Denominator}}$$

This ratio approach for determining the parent's numerator in the calculation of consolidated EPS can be used for both primary EPS and fully diluted EPS (the percentages obtained from each of the ratios usually differ slightly). Furthermore, this ratio approach can be used for all types of a subsidiary's potentially dilutive securities.

EXERCISES FOR APPENDIX A

E 7–1A **75%-Owned Subsidiary with Warrants** Powe Inc. owns 75% of Sowe Inc.'s outstanding common stock. Income and securities data for each company for 19X1 follow:

	Powe Inc.	Sowe Inc.
Income from own operations	$500,000	$100,000
Average number of common shares outstanding	200,000	20,000
Common equivalent shares:		
Warrants—		
Average number of warrants outstanding during 19X1		15,000
Shares assumed repurchased under		
the treasury stock method		10,000

Required
1. What is the consolidated primary EPS?
2. Repeat Question 1, assuming that the parent owns 20% of the warrants.
3. What is the consolidated net income?

E 7–2A **100%-Owned Subsidiary with Convertible Preferred Stock** Pram Inc. owns 100% of Stam Inc.'s outstanding common stock. Income and securities data for each company for 19X1 follow:

	Pram Inc.	Stam Inc.
Income from own operations	$1,000,000	$500,000
Average number of common shares outstanding	100,000	75,000
Common equivalent shares:		
Convertible preferred stock—		
Shares outstanding during 19X1		5,000
Dividends per share (cumulative)		$10
Number of common shares obtainable on conversion		25,000

Required
1. What is the consolidated primary earnings per share?
2. Repeat Question 1, assuming that the parent owns 40% of the preferred stock.
3. What is the consolidated net income?

NEW BASIS OF ACCOUNTING

8

New opinions are always suspected, and usually opposed, without any reason but because they are not already common.

JOHN LOCKE, 1690

Recall from Chapter 1 that phase 3 of the FASB's current project on consolida- tions and related matters addresses the subject of when, if ever, an entity should recognize a "new basis of accounting (or accountability)." In other words, which transactions or other events should cause a change to be made in the basis of accounting of all or most of a company's assets and liabilities from historical cost to current fair value?[1]

The FASB's 1991 *Discussion Memorandum*, "New Basis Accounting," identified four general areas in which a new basis of accounting might be appropriate. Even though we deal with only one of these areas in this chapter, we now list all four areas so that you can appreciate the many areas in which new basis accounting is an issue:

1. **Stock purchase transactions involving a change in majority ownership.** For business combinations in which common stock is acquired, this is the push- down accounting issue discussed briefly in Chapter 5, which we discuss in de- tail in this chapter. This issue also applies to leveraged buyouts, which we also discuss in this chapter.

2. **Significant borrowing transactions not involving a change in majority own- ership.** This is a situation in which a lender lends a company amounts that are far greater than the company's recorded book values justify. In other words, the carrying values of the company's assets and liabilities have lost their practical significance to financial statement users.

3. **Reorganizations in bankruptcy, quasi-reorganizations, unleveraged recapi- talizations, and spin-off of a subsidiary.** In Chapter 23, we discuss reorganiza- tions in bankruptcy, when a company is given a fresh start in business. Similar to category 1, a change in majority ownership usually occurs in a bankruptcy re- organization because the creditors usually become the owners of the company as a result of being issued substantial quantities of common stock in exchange for forgiveness of debt granted.

4. **Formation of and sales of interests in corporate joint ventures.** The issue here is whether the assets and liabilities contributed to a joint venture should be val- ued using the existing basis or a new basis reflecting the negotiated values agreed to by the joint venturers.

I

RECOGNIZING A NEW BASIS OF ACCOUNTING FOR STOCK PURCHASE TRANSACTIONS RESULTING IN THE PURCHASE OF A MAJORITY RESIDUAL INTEREST

Many different kinds of stock purchase transactions resulting in the purchase of a majority residual interest in an entity can occur. The new basis of accounting issue can be raised in all of them. Some examples follow. For ease of reference, we refer to the target company as Entity T:

1. **Cash purchase of 100% of Entity T's outstanding common stock by a corporate entity.** This is the easiest area of all to address. To date, the FASB has tentatively decided to require a new basis of accounting when **another entity** purchases the

---

[1]For convenience, the current accounting model is commonly described as the *historical cost* model, even though it uses at least five measurement bases (historical cost/historical pro- ceeds, current cost, current market value, net realizable (settlement) value, and present (or discounted) value of future cash flows.

voting stock for cash.[2] Accordingly, if Entity T (now a subsidiary) were to issue its separate financial statements to users other than its parent (such as lenders), the financial statements would be on the new basis of accounting.

2. **Cash purchase of 51% of Entity T's outstanding common stock by a corporate entity.** This situation raises the question of **whether a 100% change in ownership** (or a high percentage) should be required to reflect a new basis of accounting in Entity T's financial statements furnished to users other than its parent. Without such a requirement, a new basis of accounting could be implemented only partially, such as to the extent of 51% of the difference between book values and current values.

3. **Purchase of 100% of Entity T's outstanding common stock by a corporate entity using nonmonetary consideration.** This situation raises the question of **whether the type of consideration** is a relevant factor in determining whether a new basis of accounting is appropriate.

4. **Cash purchase of 100% of Entity T's outstanding common stock by a single individual.** This situation raises the question of **whether the "corporate veil" can be pierced** to establish a new basis of accounting. If not, the single individual would first have to create a legal entity to be used as a vehicle for acquiring the common stock of Entity T. By doing so, this barrier to using a new basis of accounting would be removed. Entity T could subsequently be liquidated into the newly created legal entity, however, achieving the same result as if the new legal entity had never been created. Is form needed to create substance?[3]

5. **Cash purchase of 100% of Entity T's common stock by many individual stockholders in market trading activity.** This situation differs from the previous situation in that the trading activity **did not produce a majority owner** of Entity T. To date, the FASB has tentatively decided that a new basis of accounting should be prohibited in these situations.[4]

Many more situations are possible. We listed only some of the more common situations to give an idea of the various factors that can arise. In the discussion that follows concerning the push-down basis of accounting, we deal only with situations 1 and 2.

II THE PUSH-DOWN BASIS OF ACCOUNTING

Under the push-down basis of accounting, the subsidiary does the following as of the acquisition date:

1. Adjusts its assets and liabilities to their current values and records goodwill, if there is any. This makes its adjusted net assets equal the parent company's Investment in Subsidiary account.

2. Eliminates the balance(s) in its Accumulated Depreciation account(s). This recognizes that a new basis of accounting has been established for its fixed assets.

3. Closes its Retained Earnings account balance to Additional Paid-in Capital.

4. Uses this new basis of accounting in its separate financial statements. Retained earnings should be dated.

---

[2]*Financial Accounting Series*, Status Report No. 238, December 31, 1992, p. 3.

[3]Later we discuss leveraged buyouts. In those situations, the FASB's Emerging Issues Task Force required that a new legal entity be created to effect the acquisition so that a new basis of accounting could be implemented.

[4]*Financial Accounting Series*, Status Report No. 238, p. 3.

THE RATIONALE FOR USING THE PUSH-DOWN BASIS OF ACCOUNTING

The rationale for having the subsidiary adjust its assets and liabilities to their current values as of the acquisition date rests on an argument of substance over form. Advocates of push-down accounting contend that **the relevant factor is the acquisition itself, not the form of consummating the acquisition.** In their view, whether the parent company acquires assets or common stock is irrelevant. Recall that when assets are acquired, the individual assets and liabilities are revalued to their current values when they are recorded in the acquiring company's general ledger (or in the division's general ledger if decentralized accounting is used). Because the acquisition itself is the relevant factor, a new basis of accounting has been established for the assets and liabilities. Merely because common stock is acquired instead of assets should not prevent this new basis of accounting from being reflected at the subsidiary level. Furthermore, in most cases **the parent controls the form of the ownership.** That is, **it has the legal power to liquidate the subsidiary into a division.** The fact that the parent chooses to maintain the acquired business as a separate legal entity should not have a bearing on whether a new cost basis should be established at the subsidiary level.

THE SEC LEADS THE WAY

Push-down accounting did not gain significant acceptance or use until 1983 when the Securities and Exchange Commission (SEC) issued *Staff Accounting Bulletin No. 54.* **This bulletin requires push-down accounting in the separate financial statements of a subsidiary acquired in a purchase transaction.** (Exceptions to this policy are discussed later.)

The SEC was convinced about the soundness of its position and concerned by the potentially misleading results from the many subsidiaries that had recently issued common stock based on historical cost-based financial statements using non-push-down accounting. The result of this practice was that these subsidiaries did not report their true cost of doing business and thus overstated their earnings. The SEC concluded that the time for substance over form had come.

GENERAL MOTORS TESTS THE WATERS Perhaps to test the SEC's conviction, General Motors Corp. argued before the commission that it should not have to apply push-down accounting to its $5 billion acquisition of all of Hughes Aircraft Co. in 1985 (in which there was $4 billion of cost in excess of book value). The SEC stood its ground.

ILLUSTRATIONS | **MOST COMMONLY ENCOUNTERED SITUATION**

Acquisition of Common Stock Where

- Assets Are Undervalued
- Goodwill Exists

To illustrate the entries that are made under the push-down basis of accounting and the elimination entry made in preparing consolidated statements as of the acquisition date, we use the same information from Chapter 5 to illustrate the non-push-down basis of accounting (page 168), in which the assets of the acquired business were undervalued and the purchase price includes an amount for goodwill (the most commonly encountered situation). Recall that P Company acquired all of the outstanding common stock of S Company on January 1, 19X1, by paying $100,000 cash. For convenience, we repeat the rest of the assumed information used earlier:

1. Total cost $100,000
2. Current value of net assets 88,000
3. Book value of net assets 60,000
4. The current values of S Company's assets and liabilities are assumed to equal their book values, except for the following assets:

	Book Value	Current Value	Undervaluation
Inventory	$ 42,000	$ 46,000	$ 4,000
Land	30,000	38,000	8,000
Buildings and equipment...........	150,000[a]	166,000	16,000
....			$28,000

[a]Net of $50,000 accumulated depreciation.

5. Goodwill of $12,000 ($100,000 – $88,000) exists.

Additionally, S Company's retained earnings balance at acquisition date is $50,000.

The subsidiary makes the following entries as of the acquisition date.

1. To adjust assets to their current values and record goodwill:

Inventory	4,000	
Land	8,000	
Equipment	16,000	
Goodwill	12,000	
Revaluation Capital		40,000

2. To eliminate the balance in the Accumulated Depreciation account:

| Accumulated Depreciation .... | 50,000 | |
| Buildings and Equipment .... | | 50,000 |

3. To close out the balance in the Retained Earnings account:

| Retained Earnings .... | 50,000 | |
| Additional Paid-in Capital .... | | 50,000 |

Illustration 8–1 is a worksheet that shows the effect of these entries at the acquisition date.

REVIEW POINTS FOR ILLUSTRATION 8–1   Note the following:

1. The equity accounts of the subsidiary, which totaled $60,000 before adjustment to the new basis of accounting, now total $100,000, the amount that equals the parent's cost.

2. A conceptual analysis of the parent's Investment in Subsidiary account shows that only the book value element exists:

		Book Value Element		
Total Cost =	Common Stock +	Additional Paid-in Capital +	Retained Earnings +	Revaluation Capital
$100,000	$10,000	$50,000	$–0–	$40,000

3. The consolidated amounts will be identical regardless of whether the push-down basis of accounting or the non-push-down basis of accounting is used.

ILLUSTRATION 8–1	Worksheet to Reflect the Push-Down Basis of Accounting			

S Company
Worksheet as of January 1, 19X1

	Old Basis	Adjusting Entries		New Basis
		Dr.	Cr.	
Balance Sheet				
Cash	15,000			15,000
Accounts receivable	23,000			23,000
Inventory	42,000	4,000(1)		46,000
Land	30,000	8,000(1)		38,000
Buildings and equipment	200,000	16,000(1)	50,000(2)	166,000
Accumulated depreciation	(50,000)	50,000(2)		–0–
Goodwill		12,000(1)		12,000
	260,000	90,000	50,000	300,000
Liabilities	200,000			200,000
Common stock	10,000			10,000
Additional paid-in capital			50,000(3)	50,000
Retained earnings	50,000	50,000(3)		–0–
Revaluation capital			40,000(1)	40,000
	260,000	50,000	90,000	300,000
Proof of debit and credit postings		140,000	140,000	

Explanation of entries:
(1) To adjust assets to their current fair values and record goodwill paid for by the parent.
(2) To eliminate the balance in the Accumulated Depreciation account.
(3) To eliminate the balance in the Retained Earnings account.

Note: It is logical to expect these adjustments to be recorded in S Company's general ledger. However, this is not absolutely necessary. S Company has the alternative not to adjust its general ledger but to prepare a worksheet such as this one at each date that it prepares financial statements to issue to its external financial statement users other than its parent.

4. The only difference between the push-down basis and the *non*-push-down basis is that the push-down basis accomplishes in the subsidiary's general ledger what the *non*-push-down basis accomplishes on the consolidation worksheet.

5. The push-down basis of accounting is the more logical method because it makes little sense to account for a given asset on two sets of books.

6. The push-down versus non-push-down accounting issue is a debate between relevancy and historical cost.

CONSOLIDATION WORKSHEET AT DATE OF ACQUISITION   Illustration 8–2 shows a consolidation worksheet at the date of acquisition—**after the subsidiary has applied push-down accounting.**

REVIEW POINTS FOR ILLUSTRATION 8–2   Note the following:

1. The consolidation effort is minimal relative to the effort involved for the comparable consolidation worksheet under non-push-down accounting shown in Illustration 5–6 (page 174).

2. The consolidation entry is identical to that for a created subsidiary (except for the added Revaluation Capital account).

CONSOLIDATION WORKSHEET SUBSEQUENT TO DATE OF ACQUISITION   The minimal consolidation effort shown in Illustration 8–2 carries through to consolidations performed at all later dates. **Again, the entries are nearly identical to those**

ILLUSTRATION 8–2	Consolidation Worksheet at Date of Acquisition *After* the Subsidiary Has Applied Push-Down Accounting

P Company and S Company
Consolidation Worksheet as of January 1, 19X1

	P Company	S Company	Consolidation Entries Dr.	Consolidation Entries Cr.	Consolidated
Balance Sheet					
Cash	18,000	15,000			33,000
Accounts receivable, net	52,000	23,000			75,000
Inventory	90,000	46,000			136,000
Investment in S Company	100,000			100,000(1)	–0–
Land	220,000	38,000			258,000
Buildings and equipment	500,000	166,000			666,000
Accumulated depreciation	(280,000)	–0–			(280,000)
Goodwill		12,000			12,000
Total Assets	700,000	300,000		100,000	900,000
Liabilities	400,000	200,000			600,000
P Company					
Common stock	200,000				200,000
Retained earnings	100,000				100,000
S Company					
Common stock		10,000	10,000(1)		–0–
Additional paid-in capital		50,000	50,000(1)		–0–
Revaluation capital		40,000	40,000(1)		–0–
Retained earnings		–0–			–0–
Total Liabilities and Equity ..	700,000	300,000	100,000		900,000
Proof of debit and credit postings			100,000	100,000	

Explanation of entry:
(1) The basic elimination entry.

---

for created subsidiaries. For example, the consolidation entries at the end of 19X1 are as follows (using assumed earnings and dividend amounts):

		December 31, 19X1 Equity Method	Cost Method
(1) The basic elimination entry:			
WORKSHEET ENTRIES ONLY	Common Stock	10,000	10,000
	Additional Paid-in Capital	50,000	50,000
	Revaluation Capital	40,000	40,000
	Equity in Net Income (of subsidiary)	33,000	
	Retained Earnings, 1/1/X1	–0–	
	Dividends Declared	8,000	
	Investment in Subsidiary	125,000	100,000
(2) The intercompany dividend elimination entry:			
WORKSHEET ENTRIES ONLY	Dividend Income (from subsidiary)		8,000
	Dividends Declared		8,000

ALLOWABLE EXCEPTIONS TO PUSH-DOWN ACCOUNTING

Despite its hard line on the matter, the SEC does not require the use of push-down accounting when the parent does not control the form of ownership in its subsidiary. When a subsidiary has preferred stock outstanding, public debt outstanding, or a substantial minority interest (the parent owns less than 100% of the subsidiary's outstanding common stock), the parent is presumed to be unable to control the form of its ownership in the acquired business. In other words, it probably could not legally liquidate the subsidiary into a division if it desired. In such cases, *SEC Staff Accounting Bulletin No. 54* does not require the push-down basis of accounting to be used.

In the absence of preferred stock or public debt outstanding, the SEC staff uses the following guidelines to determine when a firm should use push-down accounting:

Parent's Ownership Percentage	Guidelines
90% or more	Substantially owned. Push-down accounting is required.
80–89%	Push-down accounting is encouraged but not required.
Below 80%	Push-down accounting may not be appropriate.

When a subsidiary is partially owned and push-down accounting is applied, it is done in the same manner illustrated earlier.

PUSHING DOWN CERTAIN PARENT COMPANY DEBT

In *Staff Accounting Bulletin No. 73* (issued in 1987), the SEC staff imposed the pushing down of certain debt of the parent company (including related interest expense and debt issuance costs) to the separate financial statements of a subsidiary when the subsidiary's financial statements are included in a registration statement for (1) a public offering of its stock or debt under the Securities Act of 1933 or (2) trading under the Securities and Exchange Act of 1934. (For a discussion of these acts, see Chapter 22.) The parent company debt to be pushed down is that debt incurred in connection with or otherwise related to the acquisition of the common stock of a company in a purchase transaction. The debt should be "pushed down" to the separate financial statements of the subsidiary if (1) the subsidiary is to assume the debt of the parent, either presently or in a planned transaction in the future; (2) the proceeds of a debt or equity offering of the subsidiary will be used to retire all or a part of the parent's debt; or (3) the subsidiary guarantees or pledges its assets as collateral for the parent's debt.

III LEVERAGED BUYOUTS

A **leveraged buyout (LBO)** is the acquisition of a target company's assets or common stock in which the acquirer uses an extremely high percentage of debt and thus a very low percentage of equity—typically 10%, but sometimes as low as 1% of the purchase price—to pay for the acquisition. The acquirer uses the target company's assets as collateral to secure the loans. Thus the target company's debt structure is refinanced simultaneously with the acquisition, **making an LBO nothing more than a combination of an acquisition and a refinancing.**

HISTORICAL DEVELOPMENT

Pioneered in the 1960s, LBOs became immensely popular and widespread in the early 1980s when large conglomerates began their drive to divest marginal subsidiaries. Because of the recession and resultant depressed stock market from 1980 to 1982, numerous subsidiaries were purchased at bargain prices. As the technique grew in popularity, it also began to be used widely in acquiring privately and publicly owned companies.

In the early days of LBOs, the ideal LBO candidate was in a recession-resistant industry and had abundant hard assets. Currently, however, investors place substantial emphasis on projected cash flows.

Since 1981, more than 1,600 companies have gone private in LBO transactions (the approximate number of companies listed on the New York Stock Exchange), including RJR Nabisco in 1988, the tenth largest company in the country based on stock market valuation. The LBO phenomenon of the 1980s restructured companies, reshaped management's way of thinking, and challenged the status quo of the professionally managed public corporation. LBOs continue to be used in the 1990s but at a level lower than that of the 1980s.

THE MOTIVATION BEHIND LEVERAGED BUYOUTS

The phenomenal surge in the use of LBOs resulted primarily from recognizing and eliminating the inherent conflicts of interest that exist between stockholders and management in publicly owned companies. In a public company, management typically must devote an enormous amount of time to managing the market price of its stock. Recall that if the price of the stock falls to a depressed level in relation to the value of the firm, the company can quickly become a takeover candidate. If the company becomes the object of a takeover attempt, management is forced to spend still less time running the business while it concentrates on fighting the takeover attempt. Accordingly, a short-term focus on quarterly profits takes hold. When given a choice between acting in the best interest of the business and doing what will look good to the public, management all too often chooses the latter. Underlying all of this is the natural conflict of interest between the stockholders (whose desire is wealth maximization) and managements (who wish to keep their jobs). These divergent interests become more pronounced when managements have very little of their own personal wealth invested in the companies they run. A contributing factor is the corporate culture, which fosters incentives to build empires. Managements of mature companies that generate more than sufficient cash flow from operations are reluctant to distribute excess cash to stockholders. Instead, in far too many instances, they use cash to expand the company (often by diversification) beyond the size that maximizes shareholders' wealth. (The oil industry is the prime example of this; according to *Fortune* magazine, it made seven of the worst large acquisitions of the 1970s.) Thus managements go through the motions of acting as though their own money were at stake. Being accountable to a largely anonymous group of stockholders, management is accountable more in theory than in practice and ends up doing what it pleases with the corporation's assets.

THE LBO'S SOLUTION: ALIGNING THE INTERESTS   In the typical LBO transaction, the buyer is a group of investors including management of the target company. In most cases, this investment group forms a corporation that acquires the target company's assets or common stock. Because management is included in the investment group, LBOs are sometimes referred to as *management buyouts*. Participating managers are required to invest a substantial portion of their own money, which results in their having as much as a 50% equity position. Thus these managers are given an enormous incentive to manage effectively. And because they answer to only a handful of co-owners—who want exactly what the managers want—nearly perfect alignment of interests is formed, which makes a tremendous difference that is hard to overstate.

LBO–GENERATED DEBT AS DISCIPLINARIAN By saddling the acquired business with a mountain of debt, management's early fear of disaster focuses its attention and forces it to be more aggressive in making tough decisions. In most cases, virtually all of the cash flow from operations is needed to service the debt. Consequently, a discipline is imposed on management that denies it the opportunity to overexpand the existing business or diversify into new businesses by acquiring other companies. With a rededicated management, the expectation is that (1) the business's operations will substantially improve, (2) the huge debt load will be paid down reasonably fast, and (3) the business (which may have been acquired at 4–10 times earnings) may be taken public in a few years at 20–30 times earnings or sold to another company.

Nevertheless, LBOs are often criticized on the grounds that (1) financial institutions make excessively risky loans to companies effecting takeovers and (2) the large cash flow required to service the debt may deprive a company of cash needed to stay competitive (such as for research and development or reinvestment in fixed assets). Later we discuss some LBOs that encountered financial difficulty.

OTHER CHANGES THAT AFFECT CASH FLOWS The annual direct costs of public ownership generally range between $75,000 and $300,000, depending on the size of the company (excluding management time). Taking the company private eliminates this cost. Because the purchase of the target company is a taxable transaction, the target company's assets are revalued to their current values (based on the purchase price). This allows greater depreciation charges for tax-reporting purposes. The combination of increased depreciation expense and increased interest expense often results in the target company not having to pay income taxes for several years.

SOME SPECTACULAR RESULTS OF LBOS For most leveraged buyouts, the yearly returns on equity have been in the 50–120% range. The most spectacular LBO success story of all is the $1 million equity investment made in 1981 in Gibson Greetings, Inc. (owners of the Garfield the Cat cartoon character). The investors, who were leveraged to the amount of $79 million, later sold their equity interest for $290 million, a phenomenal return on their investment. However, a few LBOs have gone into bankruptcy or troubled debt restructurings. LBOs leave little room for error, but the rewards for managements—if they are successful—are sensational.

LEVERAGED BUYOUT TRANSACTIONS ARE NOT BUSINESS COMBINATIONS

Recall that business combinations occur only when two existing companies—**both of which have operations**—combine. In the typical LBO transaction, however, only the target company has an operating business. Accordingly, LBO transactions are not business combinations. Thus, *APBO No. 16*, "Business Combinations," does not apply.

FORMING A NEW CORPORATION TO EFFECT THE LBO TRANSACTION In most LBO transactions, however, the new ownership group forms a new corporation (which we call Newco for ease of reference) to acquire the outstanding common stock of the target company (which we call Oldco). Even though Newco's acquisition of Oldco's outstanding common shares is a stock acquisition as in a business combination, such acquisitions are still *not* the combining of **two existing operat-**

ing businesses to be accounted for under *APBO No. 16*. Nonetheless, the issue of whether or not a **buyout** has occurred—which is at the heart of accounting for business combinations—is also the key issue for LBOs. Only if a buyout has occurred can a new basis of accounting be established for Oldco's assets and liabilities. Of course, a buyout cannot occur without a change in control. Before discussing the buyout/change-in-control issue in more detail, the rationale for forming Newco to acquire Oldco's outstanding common stock is explained.

THE RATIONALE FOR FORMING NEWCO After the LBO transaction is consummated, the two companies are usually merged; thus Oldco ceases its corporate existence. The reason for forming Newco to acquire Oldco's outstanding common stock pertains to the general practice of **not allowing personal transactions to pierce the corporate veil.** In other words, a new basis of accounting is not allowed on a corporation's books as a result of personal transactions between the corporation's stockholders. For example, the purchase of Oldco's outstanding common shares directly from Oldco's shareholders by an investor or by Oldco's management is a personal transaction. By forming Newco for the purpose of effecting the acquisition of Oldco's outstanding common shares, this objection is overcome. However, creating and using Newco solely for this purpose is mere form over substance. A more valid reason for forming Newco is that **it facilitates the process of effecting the transaction.** For example, if Oldco's management and the new outside investor each are to have a 50% ownership interest, this result usually can be more easily accomplished using a new entity rather than having each party buy a specific number of outstanding Oldco shares from the existing Oldco shareholders.

THE KEY ISSUE: HAS A CHANGE IN CONTROL OCCURRED?

Recall that for business combinations, we did not consider the transaction to be a business combination until a change in control of the target company's outstanding common shares had occurred. Then we dealt with whether to use (1) the **purchase method** (used when a buyout occurs, resulting in a new basis of accounting being established in the consolidated statements for the target company's assets and liabilities) or (2) the **pooling of interests method** (used when a buyout does **not** occur, resulting in carrying forward the old basis of accounting in the consolidated statements for the target company's assets and liabilities).

Accordingly, a change in control was necessary before the purchase method—and the resulting new basis of accounting—could be used. Likewise in LBOs, a change in control must occur before a new basis of accounting can be used.

USING A NEW BASIS PARTIALLY AND THE OLD BASIS PARTIALLY Recall further that a business combination is never recorded partially as a purchase (establishing a new basis of accounting) and partially as a pooling of interests (carryforward of the old basis of accounting); *APBO No. 16* specifically prohibits this. In contrast, however, LBO transactions can be recorded partially using the new basis of accounting and partially using the old basis of accounting. (Compared with business combinations, this is substantively the equivalent of using a part purchase/part pooling of interests method.) Later we explain the rationale and procedures for this manner of accounting.

THE ADDITIONAL COMPLEXITY OF DETERMINING WHETHER A CHANGE IN CONTROL HAS OCCURRED IN A LEVERAGED BUYOUT

Unlike most business combinations, in which determining whether a change in control has occurred is quite simple, determining whether an LBO transaction results in a change in control can be more involved, depending on the terms of the LBO.

The additional complexity usually occurs when some or all of Oldco's shareholders become partial owners of Newco, whose ownership interest is usually called the **continuing ownership interest.** In such cases, it can be difficult sometimes to assess the extent of control that the new controlling shareholder group (collectively referred to as the **control group**) will have after the consummation—even if it has a majority voting interest in Newco at the consummation date. For example, dilutive or convertible securities issued to the continuing ownership interest could allow the former Oldco shareholders to regain control. Likewise, if the terms of nonvoting securities substantially limit the new voting shareholder group's ability to implement major operating and financial policies (such as acquiring and selling assets and refinancing debt), a change in control has not occurred.

The key point is that **the change in control must be genuine, substantive, and nontemporary.** Only if such a change in ownership has occurred can the new basis of accounting be used—either fully or partially. Accordingly, items **other than a change in the voting equity** must be evaluated. In the absence of these other factors, we now indicate the events that constitute a change in control of the voting equity.

WHAT CONSTITUTES A CHANGE IN CONTROL OF THE VOTING EQUITY?

The rules for leveraged buyouts are set forth in *Issue No. 88-16,* "Basis in Leveraged Buyout Transactions" issued by the FASB's Emerging Issues Task Force. (The role of the task force is discussed in more detail in Chapter 22.) *EITF 88-16* stipulates that any one of the following events constitutes a change in control of the voting equity:

1. **New investors.** A single investor (or a group of investors) having no equity interest in Oldco obtains unilateral control of more than 50% of Newco's voting equity. For instance, an independent investor having no equity interest in Oldco obtains a 51% voting interest in Newco.

2. **Oldco's management.** A single member of Oldco's management (or management as a group) having no control of Oldco obtains unilateral control of more than 50% of Newco's voting equity. For example, management owning 5% of Oldco obtains a 51% voting interest in Newco.

3. **Certain Oldco nonmanagement shareholders.** A single nonmanagement shareholder of Oldco having no control of Oldco obtains unilateral control of more than 50% of Newco's voting equity interest. For example, an Oldco nonmanagement shareholder owning 10% of Oldco obtains a 51% equity ownership in Newco.

4. **Combinations of 1, 2, and 3.** Combinations of the three preceding events also constitute a change in the voting equity interest. For example, a new investor having no control over Oldco could obtain a 40% voting interest in Newco, and Oldco management, having no control over Oldco, could increase its ownership interest from 5% in Oldco to 40% in Newco. The new investor and management together now have control.

WHAT IF NO CHANGE IN CONTROL OCCURS? If no genuine, substantive and nontemporary change in control occurs, the cash given to Oldco's shareholders that exceeds the book value of Oldco's equity is accounted for as a charge to Newco's equity—a **recapitalization**—rather than a transaction that qualifies for a new basis of accounting. In such cases, Newco usually has a negative stockholders' equity at the consummation date and for many years thereafter. This often is considered undesirable for reporting to lenders.

USING A NEW BASIS OF ACCOUNTING PREVENTS REPORTING NEGATIVE STOCK-HOLDERS' EQUITY   In LBOs, the new owners usually desire to have the assets of the acquired business revalued upward to reflect the new higher basis of accounting. Using the new basis of accounting usually prevents reporting a negative stockholders' equity at the consummation date. Accordingly, structuring the transaction to achieve the new basis of accounting to the maximum extent possible is usually of major importance.

ACCOUNTING FOR A CHANGE IN CONTROL

We now discuss how to account for a change in control, first for the simplest situation, in which none of Oldco's shareholders become owners of Newco, an then for the more involved situations, in which they do become its owners.

NO CONTINUING OWNERSHIP SITUATIONS   When none of Oldco's shareholders (including management shareholders) continue as owners of Newco, the assets and liabilities of Oldco are adjusted to their current values based on the value of the consideration given (usually cash) to the Oldco shareholders. Thus the new basis of accounting is used entirely. The procedures to assign the investment cost to the individual assets and liabilities parallel the procedures discussed in Chapter 5 for purchase accounting for business combinations. Note that if Oldco had been a publicly owned company, it has now become a privately owned company (owned 100% by Newco).

CONTINUING OWNERSHIP SITUATIONS   When some of Oldco's shareholders (some of which may be management) become owners of Newco, the issue is determining Newco's cost basis of the Oldco shares acquired in exchange for Newco shares. The amount assigned impacts whether Oldco's assets and liabilities are valued fully at the new basis of accounting or only partially at the new basis of accounting. When the basis of the Oldco common stock (the book value of these shares) is assigned as the cost of the Oldco shares acquired in exchange for the Newco shares, it is said that there is **carryover of predecessor basis.** This results in Oldco's assets and liabilities being partially valued on the new basis of accounting and partially on the old basis of accounting. On the other hand, if the amount assigned to the cost of the Oldco shares acquired in exchange for Newco shares is based on the value of the Newco shares issued (as determined by referring to the cash consideration given to acquire the remaining shares of Oldco), the new basis of accounting is used in its entirety.

Continuing ownership situations are best discussed as to whether the continuing ownership percentage **increases** or **decreases,** inasmuch as the *EITF 88-16* rules differ for each situation.

THE BULLS AND THE BEARS   In practice, Oldco shareholders whose continuing ownership percentage **increases** are called **bulls.** Thus these individuals are **buying out some or all of the remaining ownership interest.** Oldco shareholders whose continuing ownership percentage **decreases** are called **bears.** Thus these individuals are **selling out to a large extent** but still maintain a small ownership in the business. For both bears and bulls, the issue is whether Newco should maintain book value for the ownership interest they keep or use a new basis of accounting.

THE CONTINUING OWNERSHIP PERCENTAGE *INCREASES*   This result usually occurs only for Oldco's management that owns a low percentage of Oldco common stock. For example, Oldco's management owning 10% of Oldco's common stock could become a 50% owner in Newco.

ILLUSTRATION   **THE CONTINUING OWNERSHIP PERCENTAGE *INCREASES***

Assume the following information:

1. Management having 10% ownership in Oldco exchanges these shares for a 50% ownership interest in Newco.

2. A new investor makes a $100,000 cash investment in Newco in exchange for a 50% ownership interest in Newco.

3. Management's basis in Oldco is assumed to be equal to its 10% share of Oldco's book value of $500,000.

4. Oldco's net assets have a current value of $800,000.

5. Newco borrowed $800,000 from a financial institution, a loan that is secured by Oldco's assets.

6. Newco paid $900,000 cash to the nonmanagement shareholders of Oldco, who own 90% of Oldco.

The amount by which Oldco's net assets can be revalued upward to reflect a new basis of accounting is $270,000 as calculated in Illustration 8–3. As a practical matter, *EITF 88-16* does *not* allow carryover of predecessor basis treatment if the continuing ownership percentage in Newco does *not* exceed 5%—this results in only the use of the new basis of accounting.

To illustrate how the amounts in Illustration 8–3 are used in presenting a consolidated balance sheet at the buyout date, assume the following information:

1. Both Oldco and Newco have no par common stock.

2. Oldco has the following equity account balances at the buyout date:

Common stock . . . . $ 75,000
Retained earnings 425,000

3. For simplicity, the entire $300,000 undervaluation of Oldco's net assets is attributable solely to land.

A consolidation worksheet at the buyout date is shown in Illustration 8–4.

REVIEW POINTS FOR ILLUSTRATION 8–4   Note the following:

1. The amount of consolidated retained earnings is zero. Thus the clock has been reset to zero for retained earnings. This holds true even if Oldco is dissolved and merged into Newco.

ILLUSTRATION 8–3   **Leveraged Buyout: The Continuing Ownership Percentage *Increases***

Percent of Oldco Acquired	Cost	=	Book Value Element	+	Undervaluation of Net Assets Element	+	Goodwill Element
90%	$900,000		$450,000		$270,000[a]		$180,000
10%	50,000[b]		50,000				
100%	$950,000		$500,000		$270,000		$180,000

Note: The alternative to using the old basis for the 10% interest acquired by Newco is to impute a value for the shares issued to management in exchange for their 10% interest in Oldco. The imputed amount is $100,000 using the following logic: If cash of $900,000 is paid to acquire 90% of the Oldco shares, cash of $1,000,000 is needed to acquire 100% of the Oldco shares. Accordingly, $100,000 must be the value of the Newco shares issued to acquire the 10% interest in Oldco.

[a]90% of $300,000 of undervaluation equals $270,000.

[b]10% of Oldco's $500,000 book value equals $50,000. This is the "carryover of predecessor basis."

2. The land has been revalued upward only 90% of its total undervaluation of $300,000.

3. Goodwill is reported only to the extent that it has been bought and paid for. No amounts are imputed for goodwill for the continuing ownership percentage.

4. If the new basis of accounting were used entirely, an additional $50,000 is assigned to the cost of acquiring the 10% ownership interest in Oldco ($100,000 instead of $50,000). Consequently, an additional $30,000 is reported for land (10% of $300,000 of undervaluation)—an imputed amount. Also an additional $20,000 is reported for goodwill—an imputed amount.

CONTINUING OWNERSHIP SITUATIONS—THE CONTINUING OWNERSHIP PERCENTAGE *DECREASES* In many LBOs, Oldco's existing nonmanagement owners do not sell their entire interest in Oldco for cash (as was assumed in Illustration 8–3). Instead, they receive as consideration both cash and Newco common stock. For example, a sole owner of Oldco could receive $1,600,000 cash and a 20% equity interest in Newco in exchange for 100% of Oldco's outstanding common stock. In such situations, logic dictates that the same approach shown in Illustration 8–3 be used. Using such an approach results in revaluing Oldco's net assets to the extent that they would be revalued if Newco had merely acquired 80% of Oldco's outstanding common stock for cash (leaving a 20% noncontrolling interest). This is the general approach of *EITF 88-16*.

ILLUSTRATION 8–4	Consolidation Worksheet at Date of Buyout: The Continuing Ownership Percentage Increases

Newco and Subsidiary (Oldco)
Consolidation Worksheet (Balance Sheet only) at Date of Buyout

	Newco	Oldco	Consolidation Entries Dr.	Consolidation Entries Cr.	Consolidated
Balance Sheet					
Cash		90,000			90,000
Accounts receivable		310,000			310,000
Inventory		470,000			470,000
Investment in Oldco					
Book value element	500,000			500,000(1)	–0–
Excess cost element	450,000			450,000(2)	–0–
Land		120,000	270,000(2)		390,000
Buildings and equipment		980,000		330,000(3)	650,000
Accumulated depreciation		(330,000)	330,000(3)		–0–
Goodwill			180,000(2)		180,000
	950,000	1,640,000	780,000	1,280,000	2,090,000
Payables and accruals		440,000			440,000
Long-term debt	800,000	700,000			1,500,000
Newco					
Common stock, no par	150,000				150,000
Retained earnings	–0–				
Oldco					–0–
Common stock, no par		75,000	75,000(1)		–0–
Retained earnings		425,000	425,000(1)		–0–
	950,000	1,640,000	500,000		2,090,000
Proof of debit and credit postings			1,280,000	1,280,000	

Explanation of entries:
(1) The basic elimination entry.
(2) The excess cost entry.
(3) The accumulated depreciation entry.

As a practical matter, however, *EITF 88-16* does not require carryover of the predecessor basis if the nonmanagement Oldco shareholders' continuing ownership interest in Newco is below 20% and certain similar tests (a 20% capital-at-risk test and a 20% residual-interest test), which are complex and beyond the scope of this chapter, are satisfied. Accordingly, the new basis of accounting is used in its entirety even though a 100% cash buyout has not occurred. The rationale here is that with such a low level of continuing ownership/investment, the former owners would not have any control and possibly not any significant influence. Therefore, it is best to account for the entire transaction using a single basis of accounting.

END-OF-CHAPTER REVIEW

SUMMARY OF KEY POINTS

1. The **new basis of accounting** issue is only one of five phases of the FASB's project on **consolidations and related matters.**
2. The **new basis of accounting** issue arises in four general areas, one of which is **stock purchase transactions involving a change in ownership.**
3. In applying the **push-down basis of accounting,** the subsidiary adjusts the general ledger carrying values of its assets and liabilities to their **current values.** This is required only for reporting to financial statement users other than the parent.
4. In applying the **push-down basis of accounting,** the subsidiary's Retained Earnings account is brought to a zero balance.
5. After applying the **push-down basis of accounting,** the net assets of a 100% owned subsidiary, as adjusted, equal the balance in the parent's Investment in Subsidiary account.
6. A **leveraged buyout** is a combination of an **acquisition** and a **refinancing.**
7. The primary attraction of a **leveraged buyout** is the **alignment of interest** of management and owners.
8. To establish a **new basis of accounting** for the target company's assets and liabilities in a leveraged buyout, there must be (1) a **genuine, substantive, and nontemporary change in ownership** and (2) a **buyout** (cash or debt securities given as consideration).
9. In an LBO, that portion of the ownership interest in the target company that is acquired **in exchange for common stock** of the new company formed to acquire the common stock of the target company is valued at the basis (usually the book value) of the shares surrendered.
10. **Carryover of predecessor basis** is not required if the continuing ownership interest is (1) below 5% for **bulls** and (2) less than 20% for **bears** (providing two additional tests are satisfied).

GLOSSARY OF NEW TERMS

Bears Shareholders of the target company of a leveraged buyout whose continuing ownership has decreased (the group being mostly bought out).

Bulls Shareholders of the target company of a leveraged buyout whose continuing ownership has increased (usually the case for the target company's management).

Carryover of predecessor basis In leveraged buyouts, the use of the basis of accounting that exists for the target company's common stock in valuing any common stock issued to the target company's shareholders in exchange for some of their common stock holdings.

Continuing ownership interest In leveraged buyouts, that portion of the target company's ownership that is *not* bought out for cash (or debt securities) but is exchanged for common stock of the acquiring company.

Control group A group of shareholders who have obtained control over an entity (can include prior owners who did not previously have control).

SELF-STUDY QUESTIONS

(Answers are at the end of this chapter, preceding the appendix.)

1. The rationale for the push-down basis of accounting is
   a. The parent effectively acquires assets instead of common stock.
   b. The consolidated statements are the same whether assets or common stock is acquired.
   c. The parent controls the form of the organization of the acquired business.
   d. It is easier to account for assets on one set of books than on two sets of books.

2. In applying the push-down basis of accounting, which of the following accounts is *not* brought to a zero balance?
   a. Additional Paid-in Capital.
   b. Retained Earnings.
   c. Accumulated Depreciation.
   d. Revaluation Capital.

3. In applying the push-down basis of accounting, which of the following accounts is used when reflecting the increase in valuation of undervalued fixed assets?
   a. Accumulated Depreciation.
   b. Additional Paid-in Capital.
   c. Retained Earnings.
   d. Revaluation Capital.

4. In a leveraged buyout transaction in which the continuing ownership by the nonmanagement shareholders of Oldco in Newco is 30%, what is the rationale for carrying forward the predecessor basis of accounting for the 30% interest?
   a. A change of control has not occurred.
   b. A buyout has not occurred.
   c. The continuing ownership interest is not part of management.
   d. Control by the 70% group is likely to be temporary.
   e. None of the above.

5. Oldco has 10,000 common shares outstanding and total stockholders' equity of $500,000. Joe and Betty Munee, who founded Oldco six years ago with a cash investment of $50,000, own all shares. The Munees surrendered all 10,000 shares in exchange for $420,000 cash and 30,000 shares of Newco common stock. Newco was formed by a new investor to acquire the Oldco common stock outstanding. The new investor invested $100,000 in Newco in exchange for 70,000 shares of Newco common stock. What amount should be assigned to the Investment in Oldco account on Newco's books for the 10,000 shares of Oldco common stock acquired?
   a. $420,000 b. $500,000 c. $570,000 d. $600,000

ASSIGNMENT MATERIAL

REVIEW QUESTIONS

1. What are the four general areas to which a new basis of accounting could be applied?
2. What does the *push-down basis of accounting* mean?
3. What is the rationale for using the push-down basis of accounting?
4. Which new account is created in implementing the push-down basis of accounting when the target company's assets are undervalued?
5. Which general ledger accounts are brought to a zero balance in implementing the push-down basis of accounting?
6. To which entities does *Staff Accounting Bulletin No. 54* apply?
7. What are the two major differences between a purchase business combination and a leveraged buyout?

8. In leveraged buyouts, what two things occur *simultaneously*?
9. How do leveraged buyouts solve the conflict of interest that exists between stockholders and management?
10. Are leveraged buyouts business combinations? Why or why not?
11. What is the difference between a change in control and a buyout?
12. What reasons exist for forming a *new* corporation to effect a leveraged buyout?
13. Even though more than 50% of a target company's common stock may be acquired in an LBO, what additional factors must be considered to determine whether a change in control is genuine, substantive, and nontemporary?
14. What are four ways in which a change of control could occur in a leveraged buyout?
15. How is a leveraged buyout transaction accounted for if no change in control occurs?
16. In an LBO, when can the new basis of accounting be used in its entirety even though a 100% cash buyout has not occurred?

EXERCISES

E 8–1   **Push-Down Applied to Exercise 5–10**   Use the information provided in Exercise 5–10 (page 186).

Required   1. Prepare the entries the subsidiary makes under the push-down basis of accounting.
2. Prepare the basic elimination entry as of the acquisition date.

PROBLEMS

P 8–1 TO   **Push-Down Applied to Problems 5–1 to 5–6**   Use the following requirements to implement push-down
P 8–6   accounting for Problems 5–1 to 5–6 (pages 187–191).

Required Under   1. Prepare the general ledger entries the subsidiary makes under the push-down basis of ac-
Push-down   counting.
Accounting   2. Prepare the basic elimination entry as of the acquisition date.
3. For Problems 5–4, 5–5, and 5–6, also prepare a consolidation worksheet after having applied push-down accounting.

P 8–7   **Push-Down Applied to Problem 6–1: One Year After the Acquisition Date**   Use the following requirements
for working Problem 6–1 (page 228) under push-down accounting.

Required   1. Adjust the parent and subsidiary column amounts to reflect (1) the push-down accounting adjustments you determined for Problem 8–4 and (2) the related amortization for 19X2.
2. Prepare all consolidation entries as of 12/31/X2.
3. Prepare a consolidation worksheet at 12/31/X2.

P 8–8   **LBO: Continuing Ownership Increases**   Oldco is a publicly owned company having 10,000 shares of common stock outstanding. In November 19X1, Oldco's upper management, which owns 500 common shares (5%) of Oldco, approached an independent investment firm concerning a leveraged buyout of Oldco. The investment company has strong relationships with lending institutions. In December 19X1, a new corporation (Newco) was formed as a holding company to acquire all of Oldco's outstanding common stock. Newco issued 200 shares of common stock as follows:

1. 100 shares to the investment firm for $25,000 cash.
2. 100 shares to Oldco's upper management in exchange for the 500 shares of Oldco common stock it held.

In December 19X1, Newco borrowed $450,000 from a lending institution, a loan secured by Oldco's assets. On 12/31/X1, Newco acquired Oldco's remaining 9,500 outstanding common shares by paying cash of $475,000 ($50 per share). Information concerning Oldco at 12/31/X1 follows:

	Book Value	Current Value
Assets	$600,000	$850,000
Liabilities	$400,000	$400,000
Stockholders' equity	200,000	450,000
	$600,000	$850,000

Assume that management's basis (collectively as individuals) totals $7,000. In solving this problem, it may be helpful to use the following format:

$$\text{Cost} = \text{Book Value of Net Assets} + \text{Undervaluation of Net Assets} + \text{Goodwill}$$

Required **1.** At what amount should the 100 shares of Newco common stock issued to upper management be recorded?
  a. At their personal basis of $7,000.
  b. At 5% of the book value of $200,000.
  c. At the imputed fair market value of their 5% interest ($475,000 = 95%; thus 5% = $25,000).
2. Determine the extent to which Oldco's assets are revalued upward.
3. Determine the amount of goodwill to be reported.
4. Would your answers to requirements 2 and 3 be different if the transaction had been structured as follows: Oldco (a) borrowed $450,000 from the lending institution, (b) issued 500 shares of its common stock to the investment firm for $25,000 cash, and (c) acquired the 9,500 shares of its outstanding common stock held by the outside investors for $475,000 cash through a self-tender offer?

P 8–9 **LBO: Continuing Ownership Decreases** Oldco is a privately owned company having 1,000 shares of common stock outstanding, 100% of which is owned by Ralph and Ruth Richy, the founders of the company. The Richys retired several years ago and are no longer active in the management of the business. In November 19X1, upper management proposed a leveraged buyout to the Richys. The Richys agreed to this, and management approached an independent investment firm that has strong relationships with lending institutions. In December 19X1, a new corporation (Newco) was formed as a holding company to acquire all of the outstanding common stock of Oldco. Newco borrowed $350,000 from a lending institution, a loan secured by Oldco's assets. On 12/31/X1, Newco issued 1,000 shares of common stock as follows:

1. 350 shares to the investment firm for $35,000 cash.
2. 350 shares to upper management for $35,000 cash.
3. 300 shares to the Richys for $30,000 cash.

Also on that date, Newco paid the Richys $450,000 cash for the entire 1,000 shares of Oldco common stock they held.
Information concerning Oldco at 12/31/X1 follows:

	Book Value	Current Value
Assets	$500,000	$800,000
Liabilities	$300,000	$300,000
Stockholders' equity	200,000	500,000
	$500,000	$800,000

Required **1.** Prepare a conceptual analysis of the Investment in Oldco account by the major conceptual elements (showing the extent to which Oldco's assets would be revalued upward in consolidation and the amount to be reported for goodwill in consolidation).
2. Would your answer to requirement 1 be different if the transaction had been structured as follows: (a) Oldco borrowed $350,000 from the financial institution, (b) Oldco paid the Richys a special dividend of $350,000 cash, (c) the investment firm acquired 350 shares of Oldco common stock directly from the Richys for $35,000 cash, and (d) upper management acquired 350 shares of Oldco common stock directly from the Richys for $35,000 cash?
3. Would your answer to requirement 1 be different if the Richys had been issued only 100 shares of Newco common stock (with the remaining 900 shares having been issued to upper management and the investment firm for $90,000 in cash)?

✳ THINKING CRITICALLY ✳

✳ CASE ✳

C 8–1 **Push-Down: Evaluation of Applicability** Press Inc. acquired 100% of the outstanding common stock of Serch Inc. by issuing a new class of common stock (Class B) valued at $700 million. The terms of the issuance call for dividends to be based on Serch's audited net income using its historical cost basis. Serch remains a separate legal entity under the terms of the acquisition and continues to use its own auditors.

For the year following the acquisition, assume that Serch expected the following:

1. To have net income of $100 million.
2. To pay cash dividends of $80 million to the Class B stockholders.
3. To have net income of only $60 million if push-down accounting is used.

Required
1. Evaluate whether the push-down basis of accounting makes sense in this situation.
2. If push-down accounting were used, could the dividends still be based on the earnings excluding the additional depreciation and amortization of $40 million resulting from push-down accounting?

✳ FINANCIAL ANALYSIS PROBLEMS ✳

FAP 8–1   **Push-Down: To Whom Does It Really Matter?**   Pert, Inc.'s 100%-owned subsidiary, Savy, Inc., is considering raising capital from the public by issuing bonds, preferred stock, or common stock. Pert acquired Savy (a 20-year-old company) one year ago at a cost of $500 million. At that time, Savy's net assets had a book value of $300 million and a current value of $460 million.

Required
1. What purpose would be served by furnishing to prospective providers of capital financial statements on the push-down basis instead of on the nonpush-down basis?
2. Would any particular category of capital provider be more interested than the others in having financial statements on the push-down basis? Why or why not?
3. If at the acquisition date, Savy had $50 million of bonds payable (maturing in 5 years), would financial statements on the push-down basis be useful to the bondholders? Why or why not?
4. Assume that (1) Savy defaults on its minimum debt to capital ratio requirement of the bond issue described in requirement 3 (using the *non*push-down basis) and (2) Savy's financial statements on the push-down basis of accounting do *not* result in a violation. Is Savy no longer in violation legally?

FAP 8–2   **LBO: Evaluating a Change in Ownership**   An outside investor formed Newco Inc. as a vehicle for acquiring all of the outstanding common stock of Oldco Inc. The new investor invested $50,000 cash in Newco in exchange for 7,000 shares of Newco common stock. Newco issued 3,000 shares of its common stock in exchange for all of the outstanding common stock of Oldco.

Required
1. Has a change in ownership occurred?
2. Has a buyout occurred?
3. What is the substance of this transaction?

FAP 8–3   **LBO: Evaluating a Change in Ownership**   A new investor and the management of Oldco Inc. form Newco Inc. as a vehicle for acquiring all of the outstanding common stock of Oldco Inc., which is owned solely by the Moola family. The new investor and Oldco's management each invested $50,000 cash in exchange for 450 shares of Newco common stock. Newco borrowed $1,500,000 from a financial institution. The Moola family was given $1,600,000 cash and 100 shares of Newco common stock in exchange for all of its Oldco common stock holdings.

Required
1. How does this transaction differ from the acquisition of 90% of Oldco's common stock by an established operating company that pays $1,600,000 cash?
2. How is the preceding transaction accounted for differently from the transaction described in requirement 1?
3. What rationale exists for the different accounting treatment?

ANSWERS TO SELF-STUDY QUESTIONS

1. c   2. a   3. d   4. e   5. c ($420,000 + $150,000)

■ APPENDIX
PUSH-DOWN ACCOUNTING FOR INCOME TAX–REPORTING PURPOSES

Recall from Chapter 5 the brief discussion of the issue of push-down accounting for **purchase business combinations** in which common stock is acquired (a **parent-subsidiary** relationship having been created). Push-down accounting is also an option for income tax–reporting purposes. Only if push-down accounting is used for income tax–reporting purposes does the parent's **cost** *in excess of* **book value** become deductible. Likewise, when a parent's cost is *below* book value, the amortization (which is a credit to income in these situations) is *not* taxable. We now focus solely on the typical situation when a parent's cost is *above* book value.

THE SECTION 338 (PUSH-DOWN ACCOUNTING) ELECTION WHEN THE PARENT'S COST IS *ABOVE* BOOK VALUE

Under Section 338 of the Internal Revenue Code, an acquiring company in a **taxable transaction** may treat the acquisition of a target company's common stock as an asset purchase. If it does, the tax basis of the target company's assets is "stepped up" based on the purchase cost of the common stock of the target company, **as though the assets instead of common stock had been acquired.** Thus a **new basis of accounting** is established for the subsidiary's assets for tax purposes. As a result, the **subsidiary** will have higher depreciation and amortization deductions for tax purposes than if it had not elected to do so. These deductions include deductions for goodwill, which is deductible over 15 years using the straight-line method.[5]

WHY NOT ACQUIRE ASSETS IN THE FIRST PLACE?

Obviously, it is simpler for the acquiring company to acquire the target company's assets rather than to (1) acquire the target company's common stock and (2) make a Section 338 election. Recall from Chapter 4, however, that certain **nontax reasons** may exist for not doing so.

HOW ATTRACTIVE IS SECTION 338?

The Section 338 election is **usually quite** *unattractive* because the subsidiary must pay taxes currently on the amount of the step-up in basis. Thus a second gain must be reported (the selling shareholders report the first gain). Few companies, if any, would pay taxes *now* to obtain greater tax deductions at *later* dates.

IS SECTION 338 EVER ADVANTAGEOUS?

The Section 338 election (two types are available) is quite advantageous in certain situations such as when (1) the target company has tax loss carryforwards that can be used to offset the reportable gain on the step-up in basis, (2) the target is a domestic subsidiary whose parent has tax loss carryforwards that may otherwise expire unused, and (3) the target company is a foreign entity that will *not* report the

---

[5]Only goodwill arising from taxable combinations occurring after August 10, 1993, is deductible.

ILLUSTRATION 8–5	Portrayal of Section 338 Elections			

	Type of Section 338 Election			
	Regular			(h)(10)
	Stand-alone Corporation	Domestic Subsidiary	Foreign Subsidiary	Domestic Subsidiary
Entity responsible for				
Reporting gain on step-up in basis	Target	Target	N/A	Old parent
Paying tax on gain	Target	Target	N/A	Old parent
Is basis of target's assets increased				
for taxes paid on step-up in basis?	Yes	Yes	Yes[a]	No[b]
Is a gain reported on sale of target's				
stock (using owner's outside basis)?	Yes	Yes	Yes[c]	No
Number of gains reportable	2	2	1[d]	1
Unused loss carryforwards that can be used to offset				
the gain on the step-up in basis				
Target's	Yes	Yes	N/A	Yes
Old parent's	N/A	No	N/A	Yes
Number of gains reported (net) if unused				
loss carryforwards are used to offset the				
gain from the step-up in basis)	1	1	1	–0–

[a]Only in the eyes of the IRS, not of the foreign taxing authority.

[b]The taxes paid do *not* increase the basis of any asset—inclusive of the cost basis of either the old parent's investment or the new parent's investment. (Because the subsidiary is being sold, basis is no longer an issue to the old parent.)

[c]This applies only if the foreign country taxes capital gains; some countries do not, in which case the answer is no.

[d]The answer is none if the foreign country does *not* tax capital gains.

Specific Requirements of Section 338: To use Section 338, the following requirements, among others, must be met:

1. The subsidiary must be 80% owned in a taxable purchase.
2. The 80%-ownership level must have been obtained within a 12-month period.
3. The election must be made within 9½ months after obtaining 80% ownership of the target company's common stock.

step-up in basis for local tax-reporting purposes (asymmetry thus exists between U.S. tax laws and the foreign country tax laws). When the Section 338 election is used, any taxes paid to obtain the step-up in basis increase the tax basis of the target's assets (including goodwill). Illustration 8–5 displays more detailed information regarding Section 338 elections.

INTRODUCTION TO INTERCOMPANY TRANSACTIONS

9

Nothing in the world can take the place of persistence. Talent will not. Education will not. Genius will not. Persistence and determination alone are omnipotent.

PRESIDENT
CALVIN COOLIDGE

Recall from Chapter 1 that when a parent and a subsidiary have transactions with each other, such transactions are (1) called **intercompany transactions,**[1] (2) viewed as **internal transactions** from a consolidated perspective, and (3) eliminated (undone on a worksheet) in preparing consolidated statements. Recall also that the consolidated statements can reflect only transactions between the consolidated entity and outside parties—the **external transactions.** As a result, the consolidated statements are presented as though the intercompany transactions had never occurred.

This chapter discusses intercompany transactions as to (1) their importance operationally, (2) the many different types that can occur, (3) the importance of using supportable (fair) transfer prices, (4) the distinction between (a) no unrealized intercompany profit situations (no significant conceptual reporting issues exist) and (b) unrealized intercompany profit situations (significant conceptual reporting issues do exist), and (5) the general process of eliminating them (along with any related unrealized intercompany profit).

USING ONLY *100%-OWNED* SUBSIDIARIES

In discussing the concept of unrealized intercompany profit, we address only the most basic conceptual issues by assuming that the subsidiary is 100% owned. Additional issues that arise when a subsidiary is *not* 100% owned are discussed in Chapters 10 through 12, which deal with types of intercompany transactions that are more difficult to undo in consolidation.

The same conceptual issues that exist for intercompany transactions (parent-subsidiary relationships) also exist for **intracompany transactions** (home office-branch relationships). We discuss the intricacies of handling intracompany transactions for home office-branch relationships in the Appendix to Chapter 10.

USING ONLY *CREATED* SUBSIDIARIES

All intercompany transaction examples in this chapter (and in Chapters 10 through 12) **assume that the parent created (incorporated) the subsidiary rather than acquired it in a business combination.** This assumption follows the typical situation found in practice. Accordingly, the additional complexity of dealing with cost in excess of book value is avoided, enabling the sole focus to be on how to undo the intercompany transaction in consolidation.

I | OPERATIONAL IMPORTANCE OF INTERCOMPANY TRANSACTIONS

Intercompany transactions between a parent company and its subsidiaries are often critical to the mission of these entities.

HIGH VOLUME OF INTERNATIONAL INTERCOMPANY TRANSACTIONS

Internationally, nearly 40% of world trade constitutes intercompany and intracompany transactions. Accordingly, a high percentage of companies has high volumes of such transactions that must be undone for consolidated reporting purposes.

---

[1] When a home office and branch have transactions with each other, such transactions are called **intracompany transactions.**

PROPER ASSESSMENT OF A SUBSIDIARY'S PERFORMANCE

It is often not possible to meaningfully evaluate a subsidiary's operating performance using financial analysis unless certain types of intercompany transactions are made. This fact is so important that when a subsidiary of a publicly owned parent company issues separate financial statements for capital-raising purposes, the Securities and Exchange Commission (SEC) mandates that expenses incurred at the parent level that benefit a subsidiary be "pushed down" and reported in the subsidiary's financial statements to give potential investors a fairer picture of the subsidiary's profitability.[2] Thus certain types of intercompany transactions must be recorded—even if the parent prefers *not* to record them.

We now discuss the nature and variety of intercompany transactions that can occur.

II   NATURE AND VARIETY OF INTERCOMPANY TRANSACTIONS

First we discuss the unique nature of intercompany transactions.

ALL INTERCOMPANY TRANSACTIONS ARE RELATED-PARTY TRANSACTIONS

Related-party transactions are transactions an entity has with its (1) management and nonmanagement employees, (2) directors, (3) stockholders, and (4) affiliates. An **affiliate** is an entity that, directly or indirectly, through one or more intermediate entities (1) **controls another entity,** (2) **is controlled by another entity,** or (3) **is one of two or more entities under common control** (for instance, Lynn Inc. and Barr Inc. are both owned 100% by Lynn Barr, an individual). Thus not all related-party transactions are intercompany transactions, but all intercompany transactions are related-party transactions.

Intercompany transactions are eliminated in consolidation **because they are internal transactions from a consolidated perspective**—not because they are related-party transactions. The other types of related-party transactions (for example, the purchase or sale of land from or to company officers, directors, and stockholders) are *not* eliminated in reporting to stockholders but merely require disclosure.

We now discuss the various types of intercompany transactions that can occur.

---

[2] Likewise, the SEC requires certain debt of the parent company to be pushed down and reported in the subsidiary's balance sheet (for example, debt that is secured by the subsidiary's assets).

TYPE 1—DIVIDEND PAYMENTS

For many parent companies, the importance of regularly obtaining cash from their subsidiaries via dividends cannot be overstated, especially for parent companies that are **holding companies** (which are quite prevalent in both the banking and savings and loan industries). Recall that a holding company has no operations of its own but only the investments in its subsidiaries. Such parent companies often reduce or suspend their own dividend payouts if they cannot obtain dividends from their subsidiaries. And for some holding companies, the parent's ability to meet its operating expenses depends almost entirely on regularly receiving dividends from the subsidiary.

Not being able to have access to a subsidiary's cash for paying (1) dividends to the parent and (2) liabilities owed the parent (such as for royalties, inventory purchases, and overhead charges) is commonly referred to as having a **blocked funds** problem.

STRATEGIES TO GET AROUND THE BLOCKED FUNDS PROBLEM FOR FOREIGN SUBSIDIARIES Many foreign governments impose cash transfer restrictions on foreign-owned local subsidiaries. Accordingly, many parent companies that have such a blocked fund problem often find it necessary to enter into creative contractual agreements (involving loans, asset swaps, or the sale of the local currency of the subsidiary [often at a discount]) with other companies that need to acquire currency of that foreign country. The result is that the parent companies are effectively able to either (1) repatriate a subsidiary's earnings (and thus minimize the investment at risk) or (2) receive payment for monies legally owed them.[3]

ATTEMPTS TO GET AROUND THE BLOCKED FUNDS PROBLEM FOR FINANCIAL INSTITUTION SUBSIDIARIES During the savings and loan crisis of the 1980s, some parent companies created novel accounting schemes (the courts found some to be illegal) to get around regulatory dividend restrictions. As a result, financial institution regulators now closely monitor all transactions between parents and subsidiaries to determine whether any cash transfers from a subsidiary to a parent (such as for intercompany management fee charges) are either (1) dividend payments in disguise (for subsidiaries having retained earnings) or (2) improper transfers (for subsidiaries not having any retained earnings).

Furthermore, these regulators now not only impose dividend restrictions when necessary but also simultaneously prohibit all intercompany transactions unless prior regulatory approval has been obtained.

Recall from Chapter 2 the way that dividends are negated in consolidation in (1) the basic elimination entry when the parent uses the *equity method* and (2) the intercompany dividend elimination entry when the parent uses the *cost method*. Accordingly, we do not show these procedures again here.

TYPE 2—LOANS

Subsidiaries often do not have local banking relationships because treasury functions are usually centralized at the parent's headquarters for efficiency and economic reasons. This practice also allows the parent to monitor closely the cash positions of

---

[3]Perhaps the most widely known example of a company's having a foreign subsidiary with a blocked funds problem was that of Disney, when it was operating in Japan after World War II. Disney began amassing royalty receivables from showing Mickey Mouse and Donald Duck films in Japan. Disney arranged for U.S. companies that wanted to invest in Japan (which companies needed to purchase yen to do so) to buy Disney's blocked royalty receivables. (The money became known as "Disney yen.")

its subsidiaries, which obtain needed cash from the parent in the form of loans. Practice varies widely as to charging interest on loans to subsidiaries (manipulating income is a motive sometimes).

TYPE 3—REIMBURSEMENTS FOR DIRECTLY TRACEABLE COSTS

Often a parent arranges and pays for a specific external service that is to be performed for a subsidiary. For example, a parent's outside legal counsel may handle a matter relating to the subsidiary's operations, such as a lawsuit. In paying for such services, the parent debits its Intercompany Receivable account and credits Cash. The parent then requests reimbursement from the subsidiary, which debits its Legal Expenses account and credits its Intercompany Payable account (and eventually cash).

Under the SEC's *Staff Accounting Bulletin No. 55* (hereafter *SAB*), "Corporate-level Expenses That Benefit Subsidiaries" (applicable when a subsidiary issues separate financial statements), expenses incurred at the parent level that clearly pertain to a subsidiary must be reported in the subsidiary's income statement.

Note that reimbursements pertain to costs that are **directly traceable** to a subsidiary. Such costs are quite different from **allocations,** which by definition are (1) *not* directly traceable, (2) always transferred at cost without a market price component, and (3) discussed next.

TYPE 4—CORPORATE HEADQUARTERS SERVICES AND EXPENSE ALLOCATIONS

Parents usually charge their subsidiaries for general corporate services and expenses that benefit the subsidiaries, such as centralized research and development services, central computer services, legal and accounting services, and advertising expenses. Procedurally, such charges can be handled in two ways, usually depending on whether the service is from a *profit center* or a *cost center:*

1. **A billing arrangement from a** *profit center.* The parent bills the subsidiary using an invoice. As a result, the parent (1) debits its Intercompany Receivable account and (2) credits a descriptive revenue account. The subsidiary (1) debits a descriptive expense account and (2) credits its Intercompany Payable account.

2. **An allocation arrangement from a** *cost center.* The parent allocates amounts to the subsidiary. The parent (1) debits its Intercompany Receivable account and (2) credits the Overhead Allocation to Subsidiary account (a contra account to its general and administrative expenses). The subsidiary (1) debits the Overhead Allocation from Parent account (part of its general and administrative expenses) and (2) credits its Intercompany Payable account.

ALLOCATION METHODS   Corporate-level *common expenses* can be allocated to a subsidiary on either (1) an incremental basis or (2) a proportional basis (such as sales, number of employees, payroll costs, or some other arbitrary manner). Dramatically different results usually occur between the two methods. The SEC's *SAB No. 55* requires (1) allocation of common expenses to subsidiaries, (2) disclosure in a subsidiary's financial statement notes of the method of allocation, and (3) an assertion by management that the allocation method used is reasonable.

Allocations can have far-reaching consequences as shown in the following Case in Point.

A thorough understanding of intercompany charges and allocations is necessary in analyzing the profitability of a subsidiary and its relative contribution (as you will more fully appreciate after working FAP 9–1).

CASE IN POINT

Recall from Chapter 1 that in the movie industry, a separate subsidiary is used for each movie. Many authors and movie stars, being naive about accounting practices, once negotiated to receive a percentage of a movie's net income. In practice, after corporate allocations had been made for distribution, advertising, and overhead, many of these individuals were often dismayed at being told that the movie's net income was minuscule or a loss, even though the movie did quite well at the box office. Frequently, lawsuits resulted (often successful) in which claims were made that the manner of allocation (1) was inappropriate (because the allocated amounts did not closely reflect the actual expenses) and (2) served only to deprive claimants of profits otherwise due them. (Among the big-name recent movies that lost money under this accounting system are the huge box-office hits "Forrest Gump" and "Batman.")

Consequently, a major shift has occurred in recent years by such individuals to negotiate instead for a percentage of the *gross revenues*—an amount that *cannot* be reduced by arbitrary allocations.

ALLOCATIONS FOR INCOME TAX REPORTING   Under **Section 482** of the Internal Revenue Code, the Internal Revenue Service may adjust the deductions of related companies if necessary to reflect an "arm's-length" price on transactions between them. Thus U.S. parent companies are required to allocate a portion of their development and administration costs to foreign subsidiaries that benefit from those costs. The effect of such allocations is to report to the IRS more taxable income on the parent's tax return.

CASE IN POINT

In 1994, the Internal Revenue Service assessed Seagate Technology (the world's largest independent maker of disk drives) $68 million for taxes, interest, and penalties for underpaying taxes for 1988 through 1990. The IRS contended that Seagate held down its U.S. profits—and U.S. taxes—by incurring development and administrative costs here that actually benefited its subsidiary in Singapore (which has no corporate income tax). Similar deduction disallowances are expected for subsequent years.

TYPE 5—INCOME TAX EXPENSE ALLOCATIONS

When a parent company and a subsidiary file a consolidated federal income tax return (discussed in Chapter 3), it is common practice to have an income tax–sharing agreement, whereby a portion of the consolidated tax expense is allocated to the subsidiary. Such allocations serve two purposes:

1. To justify cash transfers from the subsidiary to the parent so that the parent has sufficient cash to make the required tax payment for the consolidated group.

2. To have each entity within the consolidated group bear a reasonable portion of the companywide income tax expense.

The second objective is particularly important when one of the entities within the consolidated group issues its own separate financial statements, such as to a lender who can look only to the assets of that subsidiary for repayment or for operating performance evaluation.

A reporting issue—from the subsidiary's perspective—is whether the allocated income tax expense should be determined using (1) **a formula-driven allocation method** or (2) **a pro forma separate return method** (as though the subsidiary had filed a separate return on a "stand-alone basis"). Both methods are found in practice.

REQUIREMENTS OF *SFAS NO. 109*   *Statement of Financial Accounting Standard No. 109,* "Accounting for Income Taxes," requires (1) the use of an allocation method consistent with the broad principles of *SFAS No. 109* (the pro forma separate return method complies) and (2) the following disclosures by the consolidated entity:

    a. The aggregate amount of current and deferred tax expense for each statement of earnings presented and the amount of any tax-related balances due to or from affiliates as of the date of each statement of financial position presented.

    b. The principal provisions of the method by which the consolidated amount of current and deferred tax expenses is allocated to members of the group and the nature and effect of any changes in that method (and in determining related balances to or from affiliates) during the years for which the disclosures in (a) above are presented.[4]

REQUIREMENTS OF THE SEC In *SAB No. 55,* the SEC staff expresses a preference for the pro forma separate return method. The SEC staff requires companies that do *not* comply with this "preference" to include in the notes a pro forma income statement reflecting tax expense calculated on a separate return basis.

REQUIREMENTS OF FEDERAL FINANCIAL INSTITUTION REGULATORS These regulators require the use of the pro forma separate return method in both (1) the monthly "call" reports submitted to the regulators and (2) any separate financial statements issued.

TYPE 6—INTANGIBLES

Parent companies often transfer to subsidiaries patents, trademarks, the use of expertise, or other intangibles. For financial reporting purposes, the transfer prices charged can be (1) set (imposed) by the parent or (2) negotiated between the two entities. Transferring the "rights to" an item is a *sale;* transferring the "right to use" an item is *granting a license.* License income can be either (1) a one-time payment or (2) royalty payments over time based on subsequent use or sales.

TYPE 7—INVENTORY TRANSFERS

Sales of inventory are most common in vertically integrated operations in which a customer-supplier relationship exists. Because the selling and buying entities are legally separate, the transfer prices usually approximate outside market prices (a necessary condition for meaningful performance evaluation). Consequently, the selling entity usually reports a gross profit on the sale.

    Intercompany inventory sales are classified as (1) **downstream sales** (parent sells to subsidiary), (2) **upstream sales** (subsidiary sells to parent), and (3) **lateral sales** (subsidiary sells to a sister subsidiary). Inventory transfers at other than cost are discussed in Chapter 10.

TYPE 8—FIXED ASSET TRANSFERS

Far less common than inventory transfers are transfers of land, buildings, and equipment. Such transfers occur most often when one entity has surplus fixed assets or one entity is an equipment manufacturer. Fixed asset transfers are discussed in Chapter 11.

TYPE 9—INVESTMENT IN A SUBSIDIARY'S BONDS

Infrequently, an entity within a consolidated group purchases bonds of another entity within the group. Intercompany bond holdings are discussed in Chapter 12.

---

[4]*SFAS No. 109,* "Accounting for Income Taxes" (Norwalk: Financial Accounting Standards Board, 1992), par. 49.

INCREASED INHERENT RISK FOR COVERING UP FRAUD

When a parent-subsidiary relationship exists, the potential to cover up losses by shifting one entity's losses to the other entity is possible; thus an element of inherent risk exists. Several spectacular frauds have been perpetrated over many years by shifting account balances from one entity to another using intercompany transactions.

CASE IN POINT

United American Bank

With its eight subsidiaries, United American, the largest bank in Tennesee at the time, was able to shift tens of millions of dollars of illegal loans from one entity to another entity, always one step ahead of the federal examiners who followed the practice of never examining all nine entities simultaneously. The fraud was uncovered as a result of an anonymous phone call to the regulators, who then descended on all nine entities at once with more than 150 examiners (at which time the bank's outside auditors were completing their examination).

Very shortly thereafter, the outside auditors (one of the so-called Big 8 accounting firms at that time) issued an unqualified "clean" audit report on the bank's consolidated statements. Three weeks later, the federal examiners declared the bank and its subsidiaries insolvent and proceeded to liquidate them.

ESM Government Securities, Inc.

This 100%-owned subsidiary of ESM Group, Inc. was able to shift massive securities' trading losses ($10 million initially and $200 million eventually) and embezzlement losses by employees ($100 million) to another unaudited sister subsidiary over several years by using thousands of intercompany transactions.

ESM's eventual collapse shook the international financial markets and triggered a banking crisis in Ohio. (The governor imposed a "banking holiday," the first in the United States since the Great Depression.) Banks and municipalities, ESM's major customers, lost hundreds of millions of dollars.

III IMPORTANCE OF USING SUPPORTABLE (FAIR) TRANSFER PRICES

In this section, we discuss, in general, the pricing of transfer transactions between a parent and a subsidiary that result in one of the entities recording revenues, namely (1) sales of inventory (intercompany sales), (2) sales of fixed assets (intercompany gain on fixed asset sale), (3) billings for services (intercompany services income), (4) licensing arrangements (intercompany license fee income, a one-time revenue, or royalty income, revenue reported over time as the buying entity manufactures or sells a unit made using the licensed technology), (5) leases (intercompany lease income), and (6) loans (intercompany interest income). Thus this section does *not* apply to allocations of costs.

The prices used in these transactions (called *transfer prices*) are either (1) set by the parent company or (2) negotiated between the entities. Determining transfer prices to achieve goal congruence is a topic usually addressed in a separate chapter of cost accounting textbooks. In this text, we are concerned only with consolidated financial reporting implications that may arise.

TRANSFER PRICES AFFECT LEGAL ENTITY-LEVEL PROFITABILITY— *NOT* CONSOLIDATED BEFORE TAX PROFITABILITY UNDER GAAP

When an asset is sold within a consolidated group of entities at other than its carrying value, the transfer price becomes the new basis of accounting for the item transferred. For example, if a parent's inventory costing $6,000 is sold to a subsidiary for $10,000, the subsidiary's inventory accounting basis is $10,000, not $6,000. Accordingly, the more the selling entity charges, the lower the gross profit that the buying entity will eventually report when it resells the inventory. (Likewise, this holds true for prices charged for services, licenses, royalties, leases, and interest.)

Thus the transfer prices directly impact the profitability of each entity. Consequently, the potential exists to manipulate the profit reported by each entity if it would serve a useful purpose (as it often does for tax planning). Illustration 9–1 shows how the gross profit of each entity is affected by different transfer prices.

In reviewing Illustration 9–1, note that it is *not* possible to manipulate the total profit from a consolidated perspective, regardless of the intercompany transfer price used in an *internal* transaction.

Because all intercompany transactions are eliminated in consolidation (as if they had never occurred), the transfer prices used appear, at first glance, to be irrelevant from a consolidated perspective. This is not always true. To understand why, we first need to address the importance of fair transfer pricing for income tax–reporting purposes—something that is of enormous concern to the taxing authorities in a global economy.

TAX CONSEQUENCES OF *UNSUPPORTABLE* TRANSFER PRICES

The intercompany transfer prices used are extremely important for income tax–reporting purposes because they determine the amount of income taxes paid domestically versus overseas. Thus national governments may be pitted against each other in efforts to collect taxes. (For transfers within the United States, state governments are pitted against each other.)

THE ARM'S-LENGTH RULE　Transactions between a parent and its child are *not* "arm's-length" transactions in a family. Likewise, transactions between a parent company and its subsidiaries are not arm's-length transactions —even if the transfer prices equal prices charged to third parties. Under Section 482 of the Internal

---

ILLUSTRATION 9–1　**Showing the Impact of Different Transfer Prices**

Intercompany Inventory Transfer Price of $10,000

	U.S. Parent	Foreign Subsidiary	Total
Sales Price	$10,000	$14,000	
Cost (the entity's cost basis)	(6,000)	(10,000)	
Gross Profit Reported	$ 4,000　+	$ 4,000　=	$8,000

Intercompany Inventory Transfer Price of $13,000

	U.S. Parent	Foreign Subsidiary	Total
Sales Price	$13,000	$14,000	
Cost (the entity's cost basis)	(6,000)	(13,000)	
Gross Profit Reported	$ 7,000　+	$ 1,000　=	$8,000

Calculation of Consolidated Gross Profit

Sales Price to outside third party—as reported on the **foreign subsidiary's books**	$14,000
Cost to the consolidated entity—as reported on the **parent's books**	(6,000)
Consolidated Gross Profit	$ 8,000

BUSINESS PERSPECTIVE

Transfer Pricing: The Corporate Shell Game

For taxpayers battling their 1040 forms and legislators peering into the black hole of the federal budget deficit, there's good news: the Internal Revenue Service, armed with fresh troops and new legal tools, is setting out to mine a mother lode of $25 billion in unpaid taxes. But there's also a catch: nobody expects much more than a trickle of new revenue to come from it.

The mother lode is unpaid business taxes, largely from foreign corporations doing business in the United States. In effect, like street-corner artists hiding peas under walnut shells, such companies play games with their profits. By manipulating the prices charged among their own subsidiaries, the multinationals can concentrate profits in countries with low corporate rates and thus get away with a smaller total tax bite. The bottom line is that most foreign corporations operating in the United States pay little or no tax to Washington.

Tax Loss

All told, the Treasury's loss is enormous. At hearings last summer before the House Oversight Subcommittee, chairman J. J. Pickle of Texas said he had heard estimates ranging up to $30 billion. IRS Commissioner Fred T. Goldberg, Jr., said that was "on the high side," but conceded that the agency should be doing better. Michigan tax experts James Wheeler and Richard Weber calculate that foreign-based multinationals dodge $20 billion in U.S. taxes every year. And that's not considering U.S.–based companies, many of which also find ways to tuck away profits in tax havens. They usually do it on a smaller scale, since it's harder for them to dodge the IRS.

The corporate shell game has been going on for at least 30 years, ever since multinational operations became a significant factor in the corporate world, and there have been periodic attempts to crack down. The latest was prompted last summer, when the IRS published a table showing that foreign-based companies sold $543 billion worth of goods and services in the United States in 1986, but claimed to have net losses of $1.5 billion on that trade. That year was an aberration; before and since, overseas companies in the United States have actually reported net profits, albeit tiny ones.

But the 1986 "loss" was riveting. "That tore it," says Ronald Pearlman, former chief of staff of the congressional Joint Tax Committee, now practicing law at Covington & Burling. Congress voted a stiff new 20% fine and gave the IRS broader power to subpoena records from parent companies overseas. The tax agency also got to expand its overworked international staff and dangle a small salary premium to recruit talent.

Abuses in pricing across borders—"transfer pricing," in corporate jargon—are illegal, if they can be proved. Corporations dealing with their own subsidiaries are required to set prices at "arm's length," just as they would for unrelated customers. And there's no question that abuses can be enormous. In its biggest known victory, the IRS made its case that Japan's Toyota had been systematically overcharging its U.S. subsidiary for years on most of the cars, trucks and parts sold in the United States. What would have been profits from the United States had wafted back to Japan. Toyota denied improprieties but agreed to a reported $1 billion settlement, paid in part with tax rebates from the government of Japan.

But such triumphs are rare, and the hurdles are mountainous. For one thing, small armies of accountants are needed to sift through corporate records in several countries, even if access is granted—by no means a sure thing. In one case, an agent who requested a specific document was sent 40 boxes of papers, without an index. Trained economists must rule in each case whether costs were realistically allocated. And since real-world cases are usually far more subtle than simple illustrative anecdotes, there is room for years of legal maneuvering over disputed facts, accounting practices, and business judgments.

Some abuses are blatant. One foreign manufacturer, for instance, sold TV sets to its U.S. subsidiary for $250 each, but charged an unrelated company just $150. Most cases are nowhere near as clear. What if the set sold outside has a slight change in the casing? Which subsidiary gets charged for shipping and insurance? In one current case, the IRS says Japan's Yamaha forced Yamaha Motor Corp., U.S.A., to overstock motorcycles and all-terrain vehicles in the early '80s, and then made

Revenue Code, the pricing for related-party transactions must be at **arm's-length,** which means that **a company must charge a related party the same price it would charge an unrelated party.** The arm's-length standard applies to all intercompany inventory transfers including (1) inventory transfers from domestic parent companies to foreign subsidiaries or branches (**"outbound" transfers**) and (2) inventory transfers from foreign companies to their U.S. subsidiaries or branches (**"inbound"**

the subsidiary pay for discounts and promotions to un-load the excess inventory. The result, says the tax agency, was that Yamaha Motor U.S.A. paid only $5,272 in corporate tax to Washington over four years. Proper accounting would have shown a profit of $500 million and taxes of $127 million, the agency says. But Yamaha argues that the IRS case ignores the colossal reality of the 1982 recession, which caught the company just as unprepared as its U.S. competitors. The U.S. Tax Court is mulling the case.

American-based multinationals have also been ac-cused of squirreling profits away. Tax agents find it eas-ier to monitor their books, since they're all in this coun-try and follow SEC standards; as Wheeler explains it, "It's the difference between examining the head and several arms of an octopus, rather than just one tenta-cle." Even so, he thinks the U.S. multinationals could easily account for an additional $5 billion in lost taxes on profits dubiously allocated to tax havens. Wheeler and Richard Weber say they've found one case that is suggestive: Westinghouse Electric managed to book 27% of its 1986 domestic profit in Puerto Rico, where its final sales are tiny. To spur the Puerto Rican economy, Washington has set the corporate-tax rate there at zero. (Westinghouse says the accounting is proper, since its "highest-profit products are made in Puerto Rico.")

The IRS professes to be delighted with its new pow-ers and loaded for bear. "We've been outmanned and outgunned in the past," says Steven Lainoff, chief IRS lawyer for international enforcement. "Now we've got the tools and people to really attack the problem." But that is at least questionable. The new fine, for instance, stipulates a 20% penalty for any company whose trans-fer pricing results in underpayment of $10 million or more in taxes. Experts call that a crude weapon that may well fail to stand up in court; even the IRS initially objected to it. And in testing their new subpoena pow-ers in foreign countries, IRS agents will be under the scrutiny of tax people there, who stand to lose any taxes that Uncle Sam succeeds in claiming. The prospects for litigation are wearying.

When it comes to litigation, the IRS may also find lit-tle comfort in its expanded international staff (to 700

from 550) or its big-city salary premiums of 8% over government standards. The agency is now eight years behind in merely auditing multinationals; corporate of-ficials who make a decision may well be dead or trans-ferred when the tax people finally show up to question it. And in competing for legal and accounting talent, the IRS is still severely outmatched. Senior partners in private tax practice routinely get $500,000 to $1 million a year. Goldberg recalls ruefully that when he took of-fice as IRS commissioner in 1989, his new salary of $80,000 was just what his former firm was paying newly fledged lawyers fresh out of school.

Bad Record

All told, it's not surprising that when the IRS does bring a case, it frequently loses. Thomas Field of Tax Analysts says the agency typically settles for just 10 cents on the dollar of its initial claims against foreign-ers, and the IRS doesn't dispute that. At one major multinational firm, the head of taxes says he tries to do the right thing. "But there's no way the IRS is going to find chinks in our armor," he says. "We're just too smart and way too well prepared."

If the new reforms don't bear fruit, Pickle and Senate Finance Committee chairman Lloyd Bentsen say they are ready to propose something else. Ideally, that might be a whole new approach to international taxes, one that ignores the details of transactions and focuses on allocating shares of the total profit. Most U.S. states have similar laws, essentially basing cor-porate taxes on what percentage of a company's em-ployees, sales and assets are located in the state. In the long run, reforming international taxes along those lines may be inevitable. But any such attempt would be formidably complicated; few major foreign coun-tries would welcome an overhaul of the entire struc-ture, which in effect would require unanimous con-sent. For the foreseeable future, the corporate shell game goes on.

Source: Larry Martz with Rich Thomas in Washington, "The Corporate Shell Game," *Newsweek,* April 19, 1991, 48–49. Reprinted by permission of *Newsweek* magazine, April 15, 1991, ©Newsweek Inc., 1991.

transfers). **The arm's-length standard also applies to (1) services provided, (2) fixed asset sales, (3) transfers of technology, patents, trademarks, and other in-tangible assets, and (4) interest rates on loans.**

The huge growth of international trade in the last 45 years, especially in the last 15 years, has made transfer pricing a hot topic for taxing authorities and the U.S. Congress, as discussed in the Business Perspective on transfer pricing.

RECENT IRS EFFORTS TO PREVENT TRANSFER PRICING ABUSES For years, the IRS was frustrated by the lack of cooperation by foreign companies having transactions with subsidiaries or branches in the United States. Armed with reports of widespread use of artificially high inbound transfer prices by foreign firms to evade U.S. income taxes, the Internal Revenue Service in 1990 was able to get Congress to grant it broad new enforcement powers to deal with the transfer pricing issue:

1. A new **20% nondeductible penalty** may be imposed if transfer pricing adjustments during a year exceed the lesser of (1) $5 million or (b) 10% of the taxpayer's gross receipts. This penalty increases to 40% if the IRS adjustments exceed $20 million.

2. U.S. subsidiaries and branches of foreign firms engaged in transactions with related companies outside the U.S. **must be able to produce detailed records of the transactions with their foreign parents/home offices that document the basis for their transfer prices.** The transfer pricing records must be kept in the U.S. offices or, if located abroad, produced within 60 days of an IRS request.

3. Failure to comply triggers a **"doomsday"** penalty, whereby **the IRS can make its own determination of what the proper transfer prices should be.**

CASE IN POINT

Just How Aggressive Are Foreign Companies in Setting Transfer Prices with Their U.S. Units?

In 1995 congressional investigators reported that large foreign-owned corporations are becoming more successful at avoiding taxes on their U.S. operations. Of the foreign-owned U.S. subsidiaries that had $100 million or more in total assets in 1991, 73% (715 of 980 firms) paid no U.S. income taxes despite having sales of $359 billion (an amount that continually increases each year). In comparison, 62% (297 of 479 firms) of such firms paid no U.S. federal taxes for 1987.

The Multistate Tax Commission, an organization of state tax authorities, estimated that transfer pricing abuse costs the federal government $10–$15 billion a year.

HOW PREVALENT ARE TAX DISPUTES INVOLVING TRANSFER PRICING? Tax disputes concerning transfer pricing are becoming quite prevalent.

CASE IN POINT

Survey of Prevalence of Transfer Pricing Disputes

In a 1995 survey of 210 U.S. multinational companies concerning transfer pricing for tax-reporting purposes, Ernst & Young found the following:

Firms that have had a transfer
pricing dispute with the tax
authorities 83%

Firms that are currently engaged in
a transfer pricing dispute 49%

Transfer pricing disputes that
involve management and
administrative fees charged
to subsidiaries 93%

Note: The contested areas involving the most money by far are royalties and transfers of finished goods.

CALIFORNIA'S WORLDWIDE COMBINED REPORTING METHOD Most countries use the arm's-length method of taxation and support its use through various treaties between the United States and other countries. In contrast, California uses a *worldwide combined reporting method* (also referred to as the *unitary tax method*) that considers affiliated corporations that share common management and support services **as one single corporate unit.** (Six other states also use this approach, but California is the most aggressive.) It then applies a three-factor [employees, revenues, and properties] apportionment percentage to the worldwide income of all affiliated corporations within the unit and subjects the resulting portion to state tax. Thus if 20% of the unit's employees are in California, 22% of the unit's revenues occur in California, and 33% of the unit's properties are located in California, 25% (20% + 22% + 33% = 75%; 75%/3 = 25%) of the unit's total income is taxed in California. Under this method, transfer prices are irrelevant.

Both domestic and foreign-based multinationals are required to use this method. In 1994, the United States Supreme Court, in a suit brought by Barclays Bank Ltd. of the United Kingdom, upheld the constitutionality of this method of taxation, ending two decades of controversy.[5]

CONSOLIDATION CONSEQUENCES OF UNSUPPORTABLE TRANSFER PRICES UNDER NON-UNITARY TAXATION SYSTEMS

Even though all intercompany transactions are eliminated in consolidation, the use of unsupportable transfer prices may have important consequences on the consolidated financial statements. If taxing authorities find that the transfer prices are *not* supportable and the courts uphold their claims, consolidated income taxes payable will have been understated and consolidated net income and consolidated retained earnings both will have been overstated. Furthermore, the company exposes itself to potential lawsuits from investors who relied on such financial statements and suffered losses (the investors could assert that the company issued false and misleading financial statements).

IV | THE BASIC CONCEPTUAL ISSUE: SHOULD INTERCOMPANY TRANSACTIONS BE ELIMINATED?

Although five major conceptual issues exist regarding intercompany transactions, none of them are highly controversial (as was the case for goodwill and pooling of interests). In this chapter, we discuss only the first and most basic conceptual issue of all: Should intercompany transactions be eliminated?

If intercompany transactions are *not* eliminated, management has virtually unlimited opportunity to influence or manipulate the consolidated sales and earnings, which violates the criterion of reliability in the Financial Accounting Standards Board's *Statement of Financial Accounting Concepts No. 2*, "Qualitative Characteristics of Accounting Information." Thus the consolidated statements would include transactions and balances outstanding that are of no value to users of the statements. The criterion of relevance, as discussed in *SFAC No. 2*, is also not met.

GAAP REQUIREMENTS

The existing accounting consolidation rules require the elimination of (1) *all* intercompany transactions and balances and (2) *all* profits and losses on transactions

---

[5]California's tax method was formulated decades ago to prevent movie companies from shifting profits to another state or country with a *lower* tax rate.

between affiliates of a consolidated group. The concept applied for this purpose is *gross profit or loss.*

The potential for profit and revenue manipulation alone is a sound reason for eliminating intercompany transactions in consolidation. Even if the internal transactions were made at prices equaling or closely approximating what an outside party would charge, however, the intercompany transactions must still be eliminated (nullified for consolidated reporting purposes) because they are internal transactions. Ultimately, **the reason for elimination is that the intercompany transactions are *not* external transactions**—*not* just because sometimes reported profit could be manipulated by management in setting transfer prices. **Intercompany transactions are considered bona fide and reportable only from a separate legal company perspective;** even then, adjustments may be needed to the separate company statements to defer the reporting of unrealized intercompany profit.

Intercompany transfers conveniently fall into two broad categories: those that *do* and *do not* involve *unrealized intercompany profit.* Before addressing each of these categories, we show some basic procedures for minimizing the effort involved in preparing consolidated statements.

V   MINIMIZING THE CONSOLIDATION EFFORT: BASIC PROCEDURES

The use of several procedures can greatly simplify the consolidation effort.

USING SEPARATE INTERCOMPANY ACCOUNTS

Intercompany transactions are normally recorded in separate general ledger accounts to make the consolidation process easier. The income statements usually have several intercompany accounts, as shown shortly in Illustration 9–2. For the balance sheets, however, most intercompany transactions can be dealt with using only one account on each entity's books, Intercompany Receivable/Payable, the balance of which can change back and forth between debit or credit positions.

RECONCILING ALL INTERCOMPANY ACCOUNTS

Before the consolidation process begins, all intercompany accounts that are to have reciprocal balances (both in the income statement and the balance sheet) must be reconciled and adjusted, if necessary, to bring them into agreement. Only by being in agreement will they completely eliminate (offset) each other in consolidation. (Recall that *no* consolidation elimination entry is ever posted to the general ledger.)

Illustration 9–2 summarizes accounts for which reciprocal balances do or do not exist.

ELIMINATION BY REARRANGEMENT

Companies often minimize the number of elimination entries required in consolidation by arranging the individual intercompany accounts on the consolidation worksheet so that elimination entries do not have to be made there. It is necessary only to show in parentheses the intercompany accounts of one of the entities in the corresponding section of the worksheet. For example, by putting the subsidiary's Intercompany Loan Payable amount in parentheses on the same line as the parent's Intercompany Loan Receivable in the asset section of the balance sheet, the bal-

ILLUSTRATION 9–2	**Summary of Accounts for Which Reciprocal Balances Do or Do Not Exist**

Accounts for Which Reciprocal Balances Exist on the Other Entity's Books

Debit Balance	Credit Balance
Income Statement	
Intercompany interest expense	Intercompany interest income
Intercompany management fee expense	Intercompany management fee income
Intercompany lease expense	Intercompany lease revenue
Intercompany royalty fee expense	Intercompany royalty fee income
Balance Sheet	
Intercompany receivable	Intercompany payable
Intercompany note receivable	Intercompany note payable
Investment in a subsidiary that was **created** by the parent	Common stock, additional-paid in capital, and retained earnings—**in total**

Accounts for Which Reciprocal Balances Do *Not* Exist on the Other Entity's Books

Intercompany sales[a]
Intercompany cost of sales
Intercompany gain on equipment transfer
Intercompany dividend income[b]

[a]This assumes that the buying entity uses a **perpetual inventory system** in which the inventory account is debited at the time of purchase. Under a **periodic inventory system**, however, the buying entity uses the Intercompany Purchases account, which has a reciprocal balance to the Intercompany Sales account.

[b]This account is used only when the *cost method* is used to account for the parent's investment. Although a 100%-owned subsidiary will have a debit balance in its Dividends Declared account equal to the credit balance in the parent's Dividend Income account, these accounts are normally not viewed as being reciprocal accounts because they do not exist in the same financial statement.

ances add across to zero in the Consolidated column, as shown:

			Consolidation Entries		
	P Company	S Company	Dr.	Cr.	Consolidated
Intercompany interest income (expense)	1,000	(1,000)			–0–
Intercompany receivable (payable)	10,000	(10,000)			–0–

INTERCOMPANY TRANSFERS *NOT* INVOLVING UNREALIZED INTERCOMPANY PROFIT

This category of intercompany transfers has no substantive, conceptual, consolidated reporting issues because the consolidated net income always equals the sum of the parent's and subsidiary's net incomes from their own separate operations (in 100% ownership situations). Even if the consolidation entries for this category of internal transfers were omitted, the consolidated net income would be the same. The only impact would be overreporting both consolidated revenues and consolidated expenses by the identical amount.

In this category of transfers, an intercompany revenue and an intercompany cost/expense are *simultaneously* reported—**for the identical amount in the same**

accounting period. Some examples are (1) corporate services and management charges, (2) interest on loans, (3) operating leases, (4) royalty payments based on units sold, and (5) intercompany inventory transfers at cost.

To show how the consolidated reporting results would include meaningless amounts if intercompany revenues/expenses and intercompany receivable/payable accounts were *not* eliminated, we use an intercompany loan transaction as an example. Assume that on January 1, 19X1, P Company made a $100,000 three-year loan bearing interest at 8% to its subsidiary, S Company. If no elimination entries are made in consolidation at December 31, 19X1 (the assumed reporting year-end), the following amounts are reported in the consolidated statements:

	Consolidated— If Intercompany Transactions Were *Not* Eliminated
Income Statement	
Intercompany interest income	$ 8,000
Intercompany interest expense	(8,000)
Balance Sheet	
Intercompany note receivable	$100,000
Intercompany note payable	(100,000)

Reporting these offsetting amounts clearly serves no useful purpose to users of consolidated statements.

The intercompany revenue and expense accounts used in this category are easily eliminated in consolidation as shown in the following four examples for the first four items listed above— situations in which the revenue is reported on the *transferor's* books and the expense is recorded on the *transferee's* books:

Intercompany Management Charges

WORKSHEET ENTRY ONLY	Intercompany Management Fee Income	xxx	
	Intercompany Management Fee Expense		xxx

Intercompany Loans

WORKSHEET ENTRY ONLY	Intercompany Interest Income	xxx	
	Intercompany Interest Expense		xxx

Intercompany Operating Leases

WORKSHEET ENTRY ONLY	Intercompany Lease Income	xxx	
	Intercompany Lease Expense		xxx

Intercompany Royalties

WORKSHEET ENTRY ONLY	Intercompany Royalty Income	xxx	
	Intercompany Royalty Expense		xxx

Such intercompany accounts readily lend themselves to be even more easily dealt with in consolidation using the elimination by rearrangement technique discussed earlier.

INTERCOMPANY INVENTORY TRANSFERS AT COST

For inventory transfers at cost, the offsetting Intercompany Revenue and Intercompany Cost of Sales accounts are reported on the *same* set of books (of the selling entity). Regardless, the consolidation effort is as simple as shown in the preceding examples. (Elimination by rearrangement is not possible, however, when the revenue and expense are recorded on the same set of books.) The consolidation entry is as follows:

Intercompany Inventory Transfer at Cost

WORKSHEET ENTRY ONLY	Intercompany Sales XXX	
	Intercompany Cost of Sales	XXX

IMPORTANCE OF FULLY UNDERSTANDING TRANSFERS AT COST Inventory transfers at cost deserve special attention here so that you are well prepared for dealing with transfers *at other than cost,* which are discussed in Chapter 10. Accordingly, assume that P Company sold inventory costing $40,000 to its 100%-owned subsidiary, S Company, in 19X1 for $40,000 (no intercompany markup). Assume also that by year-end S Company had resold all of this inventory for $90,000. If no elimination entry is made in consolidation at December 31, 19X1, the following amounts are reported in the 19X1 consolidated income statement:

	Consolidated— If Intercompany Transactions Were *Not* Eliminated
Sales	$90,000
Cost of sales	(40,000)
Intercompany sales	40,000
Intercompany cost of sales	(40,000)
Gross Profit	$50,000

From a consolidated perspective, the only useful amounts are the $90,000 of sales to outside third parties and the related consolidated entity's $40,000 cost of sales pertaining to that sale. The fact that the inventory had been transferred between companies within the consolidated group prior to the sale to the third party is irrelevant. Reporting total sales of $130,000 and total cost of sales of $80,000 would be misleading; clearly, double counting is taking place. Note also that if intercompany sales were *not* eliminated in consolidation, management would be able to influence the amounts reported for total sales and total cost of sales by merely transferring inventory repetitively between the entities within the consolidated group.

VII INTERCOMPANY TRANSFERS INVOLVING UNREALIZED INTERCOMPANY PROFIT

When a perfect offsetting of intercompany revenues and intercompany costs/expenses does *not* occur in the income statement in the *same* accounting period, the transferee entity has reported some or all of the initially recorded debit amount as an asset. Consequently, profit would be reported in consolidation if the transaction were *not* eliminated. For example, assume the following:

1. P Company sold a parcel of land to its 100%-owned subsidiary, S Company, in 19X1.

2. P Company's cost was $50,000.

3. The intercompany transfer price was $60,000, which was fully paid by the end of 19X1.

Showing only the amounts created as a result of this intercompany transaction, the financial statements of each entity at the end of 19X1 are as follows:

	P Company	S Company
Income Statement		
Intercompany gain on land sale	$10,000	
Balance Sheet		
Land		$60,000
Retained earnings	10,000	

If no consolidation entry is made to undo this intercompany transaction, consolidated net income is $10,000. The consolidated entity cannot report profit as a result of an internal transaction. Thus this $10,000 is viewed as being an *unrealized intercompany gain* from a consolidated perspective. The consolidation entry to undo the intercompany transaction is as follows:

		December 31, 19X1	
WORKSHEET ENTRY ONLY	Intercompany Gain on Land Sale	10,000	
	Land		10,000

Upon posting, the worksheet appears as shown in Illustration 9–3 (we show only the amounts that resulted from this intercompany transaction).

REVIEW POINTS FOR ILLUSTRATION 9–3   Note the following:

1. Either the *cost method* or the *equity method* can be assumed because we do not show either a Dividend Income account or an Equity in Net Income account.

ILLUSTRATION 9–3	Unrealized Intercompany Gain Deferred at the End of 19X1

P Company and S Company
Partial Consolidation Worksheet as of December 31, 19X1

	P Company	100% owned S Company	Consolidation Entries Dr.	Consolidation Entries Cr.	Consolidated
Income Statement (19X1)					
Intercompany gain on land sale . .	10,000		10,000(1)		–0–
Net Income	10,000		⌐ 10,000		–0–
Statement of Retained Earnings					
Balances, 1/1/X1					
+ Net income	10,000		► 10,000		–0–
– Dividends declared					
Balances, 12/31/X1	10,000		⌐ 10,000		–0–
Balance Sheet					
Land		60,000		10,000	50,000
Retained earnings	10,000		► 10,000		–0–

2. Regardless of which method is used, the parent's net income will be $10,000 higher than the consolidated net income. In Chapter 10, we show how an adjustment can be made to the parent's books under the *equity method* of accounting so that the parent's net income and the consolidated net income are the same, which preserves the self-checking feature discussed in Chapter 2 for the *equity method*.

ISSUING PARENT-COMPANY-ONLY STATEMENTS   If P Company were to issue its own separate statements in addition to consolidated statements, it would *not* make sense for it to report a higher profit in its unconsolidated income statement than it could in its consolidated income statement. Accordingly, P Company makes an adjusting entry so that its net income equals the consolidated net income. The exact entry depends on whether the *equity method* or *cost method* is used. As a challenge, we leave you to see whether you can create these entries using the information in Case 9–3.

CONSOLIDATION ENTRIES IN LATER PERIODS

If S Company still owned the land at the end of 19X2, the following consolidation entry would be made:

		December 31, 19X2	
WORKSHEET ENTRY ONLY	Retained Earnings	10,000	
	Land		10,000

If S Company sold the land in 19X3, however, the previously deferred intercompany gain of $10,000 would be realized and reportable in the 19X3 consolidated income statement. The following consolidation entry would be made:

		December 31, 19X3	
WORKSHEET ENTRY ONLY	Retained Earnings	10,000	
	Gain on Land Sale		10,000

These entries are explained more fully in later chapters. Our purpose here is to introduce you to the general idea of *holding back* the reporting of intercompany profit until realization occurs at a later date as a result of a transaction with an outside third party.

END-OF-CHAPTER REVIEW

SUMMARY OF KEY POINTS

1. **Intercompany transactions** can be extremely important operationally.
2. All intercompany transactions are **related-party** transactions; none are arm's-length transactions even if the transfer prices are equal to the prices charged to third parties.
3. A wide variety of intercompany transactions can occur.

4. Intercompany transfer prices must be **supportable to the taxing authorities.** If not supportable, the income tax amounts reported in the consolidated statements may be understated.

5. Intercompany accounts that are to have a **reciprocal balance** must be in agreement prior to consolidation.

6. **All** intercompany transactions are **undone in consolidation** as if they had never occurred because they are **internal transactions** from a consolidated perspective, regardless of whether unrealized intercompany profit exists.

7. All unrealized intercompany profit must be eliminated in consolidation.

GLOSSARY OF NEW TERMS

Affiliate   An entity that, directly or indirectly, through one or more intermediate entities (1) controls another entity, (2) is controlled by another entity, or (3) is one of two or more entities under common control.

Arm's-length transaction   Transactions that take place between completely independent parties.

Blocked funds   The inability of a parent to obtain cash from its subsidiary to pay (1) dividends or (2) liabilities owed the parent.

Downstream sale   The sale of an asset from a parent to one of its subsidiaries.

Inbound transfer   The sale of an asset by a foreign unit to a domestic unit.

Lateral sale   The sale of an asset by a subsidiary to another subsidiary of a common parent.

Outbound transfer   The sale of an asset by a domestic unit to a foreign unit.

Related-party transactions   Transactions an entity has with its (1) management and non-management employees, (2) directors, (3) stockholders, and (4) affiliates.

Section 482   An important section of the Internal Revenue Code that deals with (1) setting transfer prices between related entities and (2) IRS penalties if transfer prices are found to be unsupportable.

Upstream sale   The sale of an asset from a subsidiary to its parent.

SELF-STUDY QUESTIONS

(Answers are at the end of this chapter.)

1. Which of the following is the correct reason for eliminating intercompany transactions in consolidation?
   a. Intercompany transactions are related-party transactions.
   b. Consolidated statements are based on the assumption that they represent the financial position and operating results of a single business enterprise.
   c. It is often impractical and in many cases impossible to determine whether the transfer prices approximate prices that could have been obtained with outside independent parties.
   d. The parent company could manipulate the intercompany transfer prices in a manner that is not equitable to the subsidiary.

2. Which of the following accounts would *not* require reconciliation or adjustment to a reciprocal balance *prior* to beginning the consolidation process?
   a. Intercompany Long-Term Debt.
   b. Intercompany Interest Expense.
   c. Intercompany Sales.
   d. Intercompany Management Fee Expense.

3. Which of the following accounts require reconciliation or adjustment to a reciprocal balance *prior* to beginning the consolidation process?
   a. Long-Term Intercompany Receivables.
   b. Intercompany Sales.
   c. Intercompany Cost of Sales.
   d. Intercompany Dividend Income—when the parent uses the cost method.

4. In consolidation, which of the following intercompany transactions need *not* be undone?
   a. Long-term intercompany borrowings.
   b. Intercompany royalty income and expense.
   c. Intercompany dividend income (when the parent uses the cost method).
   d. Intercompany land transfers involving a gain or loss.
   e. None of the above.
5. Elimination by rearrangement is *not* possible for
   a. Intercompany interest charges.
   b. Intercompany receivables and payables.
   c. Intercompany inventory transfers.
   d. Intercompany management charges.
6. Which of the following is *true?*
   a. Elimination by rearrangement is mandatory under GAAP.
   b. Intercompany inventory transfers *at cost* need *not* be eliminated.
   c. The concept of unrealized intercompany profit applies only to transfers of tangible assets.
   d. Downstream intercompany inventory transfers *at cost* must be eliminated, even if the subsidiary has resold the inventory in the same year.
7. Which of the following is *true?*
   a. The IRS transfer pricing rules apply only to outbound transfers (exports), not to inbound transfers (imports).
   b. A company trying to minimize consolidated income taxes is inclined to set artificially *low* transfer prices for inventory transfers to countries having a *higher* income tax rate than that of the United States.
   c. Other things not considered, the IRS is *more* inclined to audit intercompany transfers *from* a foreign country having a *higher* income tax rate than the U.S. income tax rate versus the opposite situation.
   d. The IRS can assess a nondeductible 40% penalty for transfer pricing adjustments that exceed $10 million for a taxable year.
   e. None of the above.

ASSIGNMENT MATERIAL

REVIEW QUESTIONS

1. What accounts for *intercompany transactions* constituting such a high volume of domestic and international transactions?
2. How do *intercompany* transactions differ from *intracompany* transactions?
3. What are 10 examples of possible *intercompany transactions*?
4. How do *upstream* transfers and *downstream* transfers differ?
5. What benefit results from recording intercompany transactions in *separately identifiable accounts*?
6. Are intercompany transactions eliminated in consolidation because they are *related-party transactions* or because they are *internal transactions,* or both?
7. How must transfer prices for *related-party transactions* be set for U.S. income tax–reporting purposes.
8. How do *inbound* and *outbound* transactions differ?
9. Why is *transfer pricing* a hot topic for taxing authorities?
10. What is Section 482?
11. What are the *IRS penalties* for transfer pricing adjustments?
12. What are the consequences to the consolidated financial statements of using *unsupportable transfer prices*?
13. What is the *primary justification* for eliminating intercompany transactions under current GAAP?
14. What is *elimination by rearrangement*? Is it required or optional?
15. Would a downstream inventory transfer at cost have to be eliminated if the subsidiary sold the inventory in the year of the transfer? Why or why not?

EXERCISES

E 9–1   **Consolidation Entries: Intercompany Loan & Interest**   Ply Inc. owns 100% of Stry Inc.'s common stock. On 11/1/X1, Ply lent $100,000 to Stry. The loan is to be repaid on 1/30/X2 along with $3,000 of interest. All aspects of the intercompany transaction were properly recorded by each company in its separate books.

Required   1. What amounts should be reported in each company's separate 19X1 income statement and 12/31/X1 balance sheet (asset and liability sections only)? Use the following format:

			Consolidation Entries		
Account	Ply Inc.	Stry Inc.	Dr.	Cr.	Consolidated

2. Prepare and post to your format the consolidation entries as of 12/31/X1, relating only to these accounts.

E 9–2   **Consolidation Entries: Intercompany Computer Charges**   Plo Inc. owns 100% of Stro Inc.'s common stock. Plo billed Stro $6,000 per quarter for computer services. The fourth quarter billing was unpaid at year-end. All aspects of the intercompany transaction were properly recorded by each company in its separate books.

Required   1. What amounts should be reported in each company's separate 19X1 income statement and 12/31/X1 balance sheet (asset and liability sections only)? Use the following format:

			Consolidation Entries		
Account	Plo Inc.	Stro Inc.	Dr.	Cr.	Consolidated

2. Prepare and post to your format the consolidation entries as of 12/31/X1, relating only to these accounts.

E 9–3   **Consolidation Entries: Intercompany Operating Lease**   Prin Inc. owns 100% of Strin Inc.'s common stock. On 1/1/X1, Strin leased manufacturing equipment from Prin under an operating lease requiring payments of $3,000 per month. Cash payments of $30,000 were made in 19X1. All aspects of the intercompany transactions were properly recorded by each company in its separate books.

Required   1. Determine the amounts that should be reported in each company's separate 19X1 income statement and 12/31/X1 balance sheet (asset and liability sections only).
2. Prepare the consolidation entries as of 12/31/X1, relating only to these accounts. Use the following format in working both requirements:

			Consolidation Entries		
Account	Prin Inc.	Strin Inc.	Dr.	Cr.	Consolidated

E 9–4   **Consolidation Entries: Inventory Transfer at Cost**   In 19X1, Parma Inc. sold inventory costing $40,000 to its 100%-owned subsidiary, Sarma Inc. for $40,000.

Required   Prepare the consolidation entry at the end of 19X1, 19X2, and 19X3 relating to this intercompany inventory transfer under each of the following assumptions:

1. Sarma resold all of the inventory in 19X3 for $60,000.
2. Sarma resold all of the inventory in 19X1 for $60,000.
3. In 19X1 Sarma sold 75% of the inventory for $45,000 and the remaining 25% in 19X3 for $15,000.

E 9–5   **Reconciling Intercompany Accounts**   The following entries are reflected in the intercompany accounts of a parent and its subsidiary for June 19X1:

Parent's
Intercompany Receivable/Payable

6/1	Balance	$50,000				
			10,000	6/3	Remittance	
6/4	Inventory sale	17,000				
			2,000	6/7	Collection of subsidiary's customer receivable	
6/15	Advertising allocation at 40% of $15,000 incurred	6,000				
6/29	Inventory sale	14,000				
6/30	G & A allocation	7,000				
6/30	Balance	$82,000				

Subsidiary's
Intercompany Receivable/Payable

			$50,000	6/1	Balance
6/2	Remittance	10,000			
			17,000	6/9	Inventory purchase
			600	6/17	Advertising allocation
6/28	Return of defective inventory	5,000			
			$52,600	6/30	Balance

The parent's cost of inventory sold to the subsidiary is always 60% of the transfer price.

Required
1. Prepare a schedule to reconcile the intercompany accounts.
2. Prepare the adjusting entries to bring the accounts into balance.

E 9–6 **Tax Effects of Different Transfer Prices**   During 19X1, Perling Inc. sold inventory costing $100,000 to its 100%-owned British subsidiary, Sterling Inc., for $200,000. Sterling resold all of this inventory locally in 19X1 for 300,000 pounds. For simplicity, assume that during 19X1 one pound equalled one U.S. dollar.

Required
1. Calculate worldwide income tax in dollars. Assume a U.S. income tax rate of 40% and a British income tax rate of 50%.
2. Repeat requirement 1 using a transfer price of $250,000.

PROBLEMS

P 9–1 **Recording a Variety of Intercompany Transactions**   During 19X1, Parr Inc. had the following transactions with Subb Inc., its 100%-owned subsidiary:

1. Parr lent Subb $50,000 on a noninterest-bearing basis.
2. Parr charged Subb management fees of $36,000.
3. On 5/1/X1, Subb shipped to Parr inventory costing $128,000 at a billing price of $160,000. Of this inventory, Parr resold $145,000 worth (for $220,000) by the end of 19X1.
4. Subb declared dividends of $25,000.
5. Subb paid cash dividends of $20,000. The remaining $5,000 was paid on 1/4/X2.
6. Parr charged Subb $15,000 for legal expenses incurred solely on behalf of Subb (a directly traceable cost).
7. On 12/10/X1, Subb shipped to Parr inventory costing $24,000 at a billing price of $30,000. Parr received this inventory on 1/2/X2.
8. On 12/31/X1, Parr allocated 10% of its 19X1 general and administrative expenses of $440,000 to Subb.

Required
1. Prepare T-account analyses of the intercompany receivable and payable accounts for 19X1.
2. Determine the amounts for the following accounts pertaining to the intercompany inventory transactions:

Account	Parr Inc.	Subb Inc.
Income Statement (19X1):		
Sales		
Cost of sales		
Intercompany sales		
Intercompany cost of sales		
Balance Sheet (as of 12/31/X1):		
Intercompany acquired inventory		

3. For the 5/1/X1 intercompany inventory shipment, how much intercompany profit exists at year-end on the $15,000 portion that Parr still has on hand?

P 9–2 Consolidation Entries: Intercompany Patent License Fee   Pota Inc. owns 100% of Sota Inc.'s common stock. In 19X1 Pota licensed to Sota the right to use a manufacturing patent developed by Pota, the costs of which were expensed as research and development costs on Pota's books.

For each inventory item that Sota *manufactures,* Sota pays a $10 royalty fee to Pota. During 19X1, Sota manufactured 12,000 units (reporting this number to Pota) using the patented process, of which 10,000 units had been *sold* by the end of 19X1. On Sota's books, the royalty fee is properly reportable as an inventoriable cost. In 19X1, Sota made cash royalty payments of $77,000 to Pota.

Required 1. How much of the royalty fee charges remain in Sota's inventory at 12/31/X1?

2. What amounts would be reported in each company's separate 19X1 income statement and 12/31/X1 balance sheet (asset and liability sections only)? Use the following format:

			Consolidation Entries		
Account	Pota Inc.	Sota Inc.	Dr.	Cr.	Consolidated

3. Prepare and post to your format the consolidation entries as of 12/31/X1, relating only to these accounts.

P 9–3* Consolidation Worksheet: Intercompany Software Use Charges   Comparative financial statements for Puda Inc. and its 100%-owned subsidiary, Suda Inc., are as follows:

	Puda Inc.		
	Cost Method[a]	Equity Method[b]	Suda Inc.
Income Statement (19X1)			
Sales	$400,000	$400,000	$225,000
Cost of sales	(220,000)	(220,000)	(120,000)
Expenses	(140,000)	(140,000)	(80,000)
Dividend income (from Suda)	20,000		
Equity in net income (of Suda)		25,000	
Intercompany license fee income	10,000	10,000	
Net Income	$ 70,000	$ 75,000	$ 25,000
Statement of Retained Earnings			
Balances, 1/1/X1	$ 75,000	$130,000	$ 55,000
+ Net income	70,000	75,000	25,000
– Dividends declared	(40,000)	(40,000)	(20,000)
Balances, 12/31/X1	$105,000	$165,000	$ 60,000

(continued)

Balance Sheet (as of 12/31/X1)

Cash	$ 45,000	$ 45,000	$ 11,000
Accounts receivable	80,000	80,000	64,000
Inventory	90,000	90,000	85,000
Investment in subsidiary	65,000	125,000	
Property and equipment	370,000	370,000	180,000
Accumulated depreciation	(160,000)	(160,000)	(40,000)
	$490,000	$550,000	$300,000
Payables and accruals	$135,000	$135,000	$ 85,000
Long-term debt	150,000	150,000	90,000
Common stock	100,000	100,000	65,000
Retained earnings	105,000	165,000	60,000
	$490,000	$550,000	$300,000

[a]Use this column for working under the *cost method*.
[b]Use this column for working under the *equity method*.

Additional Information

1. On 1/2/X1, Puda acquired a manufacturing software package costing $100,000, which cost it capitalized into a fixed asset account for amortization (over five years) to a manufacturing overhead account. Thus the amortization expense is an inventoriable cost on Puda's books.
2. On 1/3/X1, Puda made this software available to Suda for use in its manufacturing process at an annual fee of $10,000. On this date, Suda paid $10,000 to Puda and charged the Deferred Charges account. By year-end, the $10,000 had been written off to a manufacturing overhead account. Thus the intercompany software charge is an inventoriable cost on Suda's books.
3. During 19X1, Puda manufactured 500 units and sold 400 units; Suda manufactured 300 units and sold 210 units.
4. In applying the equity method of accounting, the accountant recorded 100% of the subsidiary's reported net income of $25,000.

Required
Equity Method

1. How much of the royalty fee charges remains in Suda's inventory at 12/31/X1?
2. Prepare all consolidation entries as of 12/31/X1.
3. Prepare a consolidation worksheet at 12/31/X1.

Cost Method

4. Prepare all consolidation entries as of 12/31/X1.
5. Prepare a consolidation worksheet at 12/31/X1.

✳ THINKING CRITICALLY ✳

✳ CASES ✳

C 9–1 **Auditing a Subsidiary's Intercompany Receivable**   You are the audit senior (in charge of the field work) for a parent's 100%-owned subsidiary that is a financial institution and issues its separate financial statements to regulatory authorities. The subsidiary has a very large intercompany receivable (30% of total assets and 500% of stockholders' equity) from its parent company. The balance in this account increased from $10 million to $300 million in the past three years. The parent is audited by a different auditing firm.

Required
1. What specific audit procedures would you perform in auditing this receivable?
2. If you believe that substantially more audit work is necessary than the audit partner does, how would you resolve such an impasse?

C 9–2 **Suspicious Upstream Cash Transfers**   You are the outside (and presumably independent) auditor for a parent and its subsidiary. The parent is a publicly owned holding company that historically has paid for its executive payroll and other expenses using cash dividends received from the subsidiary. The subsidiary is a financial institution, which regulatory authorities prohibited at the beginning of the year from paying dividends until it becomes stronger financially. During the audit, you came across several cash payments from the subsidiary to the parent for management services. You suspect that these payments are dividends in disguise.

Required   If all intercompany transactions are eliminated in consolidation as if they had never occurred for consolidation reporting, should these payments concern you as you issue your audit report on the consolidated statements? If so, why?

C 9-3   **Making Parent-Company-Only Statements Articulate**   During 19X1, Pero Inc. recorded $10,000 of intercompany royalty income. As of 12/31/X1, its 100%-owned subsidiary, Sero Inc., which treats the intercompany royalty charge as an inventoriable cost, had charged $9,000 of the royalty cost to cost of sales. The remaining $1,000 remains in inventory.

Additional
Information
1. The parent created Sero on 1/1/X1, making a $400,000 cash investment.
2. During 19X1, Sero reported net income of $80,000 and declared (and paid) $30,000 in cash dividends.
3. Pero issues both consolidated statements and parent-company-only statements.

Required
1. If Pero uses the *equity method,* what adjusting entry does it record to present its parent-company-only statements?
2. Repeat requirement 1, assuming that Pero uses the *cost method.*

✳ FINANCIAL ANALYSIS PROBLEMS ✳

FAP 9-1   **Assessing a Newly Created Subsidiary's Performance (including a library assignment)**   Data for Pola Inc., which operates a large retail store, for the *year* ended 12/31/X0 (its tenth year of business) follow:

Operating income	$ 160,000
Interest expense	(60,000)
Income before Income Taxes	100,000
Income tax expense @ 40%	(40,000)
Net Income	$ 60,000
Current liabilities (average balance)	$ 250,000
Long-term debt, 10% (average balance)	600,000
Stockholders' equity (average balance)	400,000[a]
Total Liabilities and Equity	$1,250,000
Revenues	$1,600,000

[a]At the end of 19X0, Pola declared and paid dividends equal to its net income for 19X0. Pola had no other capital transactions in 19X0.

During 19X0, Pola took steps to open a new store, which opened for business on 1/1/X1. Data for the new store's *quarter* ended 3/31/X1 follow:

Liabilities (average balance, per the store's records)	$200,000
Revenues	400,000
Income for the quarter, as reported to Pola	48,000

Additional
Information
1. **Financing.** To finance the new store, on 1/1/X1, Pola (a) issued 10,000 shares of its common stock, which raised $200,000 and (b) borrowed $800,000 at 12% interest, due in five years. This debt is recorded on Pola's books.
2. **Form of organization.** To legally insulate the new store, Pola (a) created a 100%-owned subsidiary, Sola Inc., and (b) invested the $1,000,000 of capital in Sola.
3. **Use of proceeds.** Sola used the $1,000,000 to acquire fixed assets ($700,000), acquire inventory ($250,000), and provide working capital ($50,000) for the new store. Sola's fixed assets are pledged as collateral on the $800,000, 12% loan.
4. **Inventory purchases.** Pola's purchasing department buys inventory for Sola. All inventory shipments to Sola were billed to Sola at Pola's cost.
5. **Fixed assets.** Sola's store has the same square footage of retail space as Pola. For each location, the land and building are owned.
6. **Annual audit cost.** For 19X0, the annual audit by the company's outside auditors cost $20,000. For 19X1, the cost of the audit will be approximately $24,000. The $4,000 increase is entirely attributable to having the new location. Pola's interim reporting policy is to spread its audit cost

over the four quarters. Accordingly, Pola expensed $6,000 on its books for the first quarter of 19X1, of which $1,000 was allocated to Sola.

7. **Corporate charges.** The only other expenses recorded on Pola's books that were charged or allocated to Sola were for insurance and advertising. The insurance expense (an incremental cost) was directly traceable to Sola. The advertising allocation was a proration based on square footage of retailing space for the two locations.

8. **Sola's expenses.** Expenses incurred directly at the subsidiary level, such as employee salaries, payroll taxes, and utilities, were expensed on Sola's books.

9. **Depreciation.** Both entities use the double- declining-balance method.

10. **Income taxes.** All income taxes are recorded on Pola's books. Pola and Sola will file a *consolidated* income tax return.

Required

1. **ROE and BEP for Pola.** Make a return on equity (ROE) calculation and a basic earning power (BEP) calculation (operating income/total assets) for Pola for 19X0 to be used as a standard in evaluating Sola's profitability. For the ROE calculation, use the beginning-of-year balance in the denominator for simplicity (rather than an average balance).

2. **ROE and BEP for Sola.** Make the same two calculations for Sola for the first quarter of 19X1. *One* of the objectives here is to enable Pola to evaluate its investment in Sola from the perspective of an investor in the same manner that stockholders evaluate a company's performance from their unique perspective. (From Pola's perspective, the ROE calculation for Sola is the same as the annual return on investment [AROI] calculation discussed in Chapter 2.)

3. **ROTC—Library assignment.** In annually evaluating the profitability of companies, both *Forbes* and *Business Week* use a return on "total" capital calculation in addition to the ROE calculation. In your library, find the particular issues of these magazines (usually a January issue for *Forbes* and an April issue for *Business Week*) that explain how they define capital. How does this calculation compare to the ROE calculation?

4. **ROA.** Make a return on asset (ROA) calculation for both entities. Is this calculation of any value? Why or why not?

5. **Manner of handling the new debt.** Can you think of two other ways in which the $800,000 bank borrowing and cash transfer to Sola could have been recorded or handled? Does it matter whether the debt is recorded on the parent's or the subsidiary's books?

6. **Evaluation.** Using the percentages calculated for requirements 1 and 2, evaluate the new store relative to the old store. Can you think of other items that should be considered in making this comparison? Was opening the new store worthwhile?

7. **Separate statements.** If Sola were to issue separate financial statements for whatever reason, what reporting issues would arise? What special disclosures would be needed?

FAP 9–2 **Analyzing a Tax-Sharing Agreement**   Pane Inc. has a 100%-owned subsidiary, Sill Inc., which represents approximately 95% of the consolidated assets. Pane, which is publicly owned, has no operations of its own inasmuch as it is basically a holding company having only an executive payroll of approximately $15 million per year.

Effective 10/1/X6, Sill is prohibited from paying dividends to Pane as a result of regulatory actions taken by an agency of the federal government. Sill's audited annual financial statements must be filed with that federal regulatory agency.

Pane and Sill have always filed a consolidated income tax return. As of 12/31/X5, a $50 million net operating loss (NOL) carryforward existed for income tax–reporting purposes as a result of losses Sill incurred for 19X5. For 19X6, Sill reported pretax income of $20 million. Thus 40% of the $50 million NOL carryforward can be used in 19X6. (Assume that no temporary differences between book income and tax income existed for 19X5 or 19X6.)

In December 19X6, Sill began transferring money to Pane under its tax-sharing agreement. For 19X6 in total, Sill transferred $7,000,000 to Pane (the 35% statutory tax rate multiplied by Sill's pretax income of $20,000,000 for 19X6). Sill made the following tax related entries in 19X6:

Income Tax Expense—Current	7,000,000	
Income Taxes Currently Payable		7,000,000
To record income tax expense (35% × $20,000,000).		
Income Taxes Currently Payable	7,000,000	
Cash		7,000,000
To transfer cash to Pane Company under the		
tax-sharing agreement.		

Required   1. Evaluate the appropriateness of making cash transfers under this tax-sharing agreement.

2. **Instructor Optional:** What amounts should appear in Sill's 19X6 financial statements relating to income taxes, assuming that *no* income tax benefit was recognized prior to 19X6 relating to the NOL carryforward because realization was *not* deemed to be "more likely than not" (the recognition criterion under *SFAS No. 109*, "Accounting for Income Taxes"). Thus the amount established in the Valuation Allowance account was $17,500,000 (35% × $50,000,000).

3. **Instructor Optional:** Repeat requirement 2 but instead assume that a *full* income tax benefit of $17.5 million was recognized prior to 19X6 relating to the $50 million NOL carryforward (35% × $50,000,000) because realization *was* deemed to be "more likely than not." Thus no amount was ever established in the Valuation Allowance account.

✳ PERSONAL SITUATIONS: ETHICS AND INTERPERSONAL SKILLS ✳

PS 9–1   **Ethics: Corporate Loyalty—Does It Require Questionable Practices?**   Your boss, the president of a parent company, has asked you, the company controller, to devise a tax-sharing arrangement that would effectively get around the dividend restriction imposed on your financial institution subsidiary. (The solutions manual discusses the role of such an accountant in a real-world case.)

Required   1. What would you do?
2. Should you seek approval of this arrangement from the financial regulators?
3. What might be the consequences to you if you implement this arrangement without the regulators' knowledge?

PS 9–2   **Ethics: Relatives on the Payroll—A Family Matter?**   You are the outside (and presumably independent) auditor for a parent and its subsidiary. The parent is a publicly owned holding company that is thinly traded on one of the major stock exchanges. The subsidiary is a financial institution that submits its audited financial statements to the federal financial regulators.

The parent's president has numerous relatives on the parent's payroll, all at seemingly excessive salaries. For instance, the president's son became a real estate vice-president at an annual salary of $1,000,000 at the beginning of the current year; his prior real estate experience consisted solely of being a residential real estate salesperson for six months. As you best can determine, these relatives are employees in name only because they often are absent from work.

Required   1. What appears to be the substance of this situation? What is the most likely reason that these salaries are on the parent books instead of the subsidiary's books?
2. What should you do, if anything?

ANSWERS TO SELF-STUDY QUESTIONS

1. b   2. c   3. a   4. e   5. c   6. d   7. e

INTERCOMPANY INVENTORY TRANSFERS

10

Some see things as they are and say why. I dream things that never were and say why not.

ROBERT F. KENNEDY

CHAPTER OVERVIEW

Inventory transfers at other than cost, fixed asset transfers at other than cost (Chapter 11), and bond investments (Chapter 12) require procedures that are more involved than those shown in Chapter 9. This chapter discusses the added complexity that results from the intercompany profit or loss reported by the selling entity on inventory transfers—something that changes the basis of accounting for the inventory at the individual entity level. This chapter shows how to change in consolidation from the **buying entity's new basis** of accounting back to the **selling entity's old basis** of accounting.

Three equally acceptable detailed deferral procedures can be used to achieve the desired consolidated reporting results of not reporting this intercompany profit or loss. The first procedure is shown in Module 1 (The Complete Equity Method). The second procedure is shown in both Module 2 (The Partial Equity Method) and Module 3 (The Cost Method). The third procedure is a slight variation of the deferral procedure used for inventory transfers between a home office and a branch, which is shown in the appendix to this chapter.

We present three self-contained independent modules; each stands on its own when read in conjunction with the nonmodule textual matter. When time does *not* permit, only one of the modules may be assigned. As might be expected, each of the deferral procedures presented has its own merits. The order in which the three modules are presented is arbitrary and completely irrelevant. The three modules are as follows:

Module 1: The Complete Equity Method (deferral occurs in the general ledger)

Module 2: The Partial Equity Method (deferral occurs on the consolidation worksheet)

Module 3: The Cost Method (deferral occurs on the consolidation worksheet)

When a subsidiary is only partially owned, conceptual issues arise as to whether any unrealized intercompany profit deferred in consolidation should be shared with the noncontrolling interests. We discuss these and other conceptual issues.

I CONCEPTUAL ISSUES

CONCEPTUAL ISSUE 1: SHOULD INTERCOMPANY TRANSACTIONS BE ELIMINATED?

Recall that we addressed this issue in Chapter 9. We do so here as well in discussing inventory transfers at other than cost.

Accordingly, assume that P Company sold inventory costing $40,000 to its 100%-owned subsidiary, S Company, in 19X1 for $70,000 (a $30,000 intercompany markup). Also assume that by year-end, S Company had resold all of the inventory for $90,000. Thus P Company has $30,000 of gross profit, and S Company has $20,000. If no elimination entry is made in consolidation at December 31, 19X1, the following amounts are reported in the consolidated income statement:

	Consolidated If Intercompany Transactions Were *Not* Eliminated
Sales	$90,000
Cost of sales **(new basis)**	(70,000)
Intercompany sales	70,000
Intercompany cost of sales **(old basis)**	(40,000)
Gross Profit	$50,000

The only useful reported amounts are the $90,000 of sales to outside third parties and the related consolidated entity's $40,000 cost of sales pertaining to those sales. To achieve this meaningful reporting result, the two intercompany accounts must be eliminated and a downward adjustment of $30,000 to the Cost of Sales account must be made.

Note that as long as the entire intercompany-acquired inventory is resold in the same accounting period in which the intercompany transfer occurs, the reportable gross profit for consolidated reporting is always $50,000—regardless of whether the intercompany transfer price is more or less than $70,000.

An even more compelling reason for eliminating intercompany inventory transfers at other than cost can be seen if the intercompany-acquired inventory is still on hand at year-end. In this case, the following amounts are reported in the consolidated statement if no elimination entry is made:

	Consolidated If Intercompany Transactions Were *Not* Eliminated
Income Statement	
Intercompany sales	$70,000
Intercompany cost of sales **(old basis)**	(40,000)
Gross Profit	$30,000
Balance Sheet	
Inventory	$70,000
Retained earnings	30,000

In this case, management is able to report profits merely by transferring inventory within the consolidated group. This is clearly an **artificial profit from a consolidated perspective,** and the intercompany profit must be deferred and not recognized until the subsidiary resells the inventory. Accordingly, the $30,000 of intercompany profit is unrealized, and realization does not occur until sale to an outside third party. At that time, the entire gross profit—some of which belongs to the parent and some to the subsidiary—is reported.

Thus **from a consolidated perspective,** (1) the sale of inventory among entities within a consolidated group is considered merely the physical movement of inventory from one location to another (similar to the movement of inventory from one branch to another branch) and (2) a bona fide transaction does *not* occur—regardless of the reasonableness of the transfer price. Only **from a separate company perspective** is the transaction considered bona fide.

THE CHANGING BACK TO THE OLD BASIS OF ACCOUNTING OBJECTIVE As is evident from the preceding two scenarios, undoing an intercompany inventory transfer in consolidation has two results. **The first result** is eliminating the Intercompany Sales and Intercompany Cost of Sales accounts in the income statement. **The second result**—which is peculiar to transfers at other than cost—is changing two account balances **from the buying entity's new basis back to the selling entity's old basis.** These two accounts are (1) Inventory (the remaining portion on hand) and (2) Cost of Sales (the portion that the buying entity has resold). Later we show how to calculate the amounts needed to make these adjustments.

CONCEPTUAL ISSUE 2: SHOULD INTERCOMPANY GROSS PROFIT, OPERATING PROFIT, OR PROFIT BEFORE INCOME TAXES BE ELIMINATED?

Recall from Chapter 9 that when inventory and fixed assets are transferred from one entity to another within a consolidated group, the amount of profit to be eliminated in consolidation is the **selling entity's gross profit.** In selecting gross profit as the amount to be eliminated, other measures of profit—such as operating profit and profit before income taxes—were rejected *to prevent the effect of capitalizing the selling entity's marketing, administrative, and borrowing expenses.* Such expenses are period costs on a separate company basis, and there is no justification for treating them otherwise on a consolidated basis.

CONCEPTUAL ISSUE 3: SHOULD INCOME TAXES PROVIDED ON GROSS PROFIT ELIMINATED IN CONSOLIDATION ALSO BE ELIMINATED?

The accounting rules for preparing consolidated statements require elimination of any income taxes that have been provided **on gross profit deferred in consolidation.** For simplicity, however, we assume in our illustrations for Chapters 10–12 that this year-end elimination entry has already been recorded in the parent's or the subsidiary's general ledger. Thus a separate entry dealing with the tax effects of gross profit deferred in consolidation is not required on the consolidation worksheet.

CONCEPTUAL ISSUE 4: SHOULD INTERCOMPANY PROFIT ON DOWNSTREAM SALES TO PARTIALLY OWNED SUBSIDIARIES BE CONSIDERED REALIZED TO THE EXTENT OF THE NONCONTROLLING INTEREST?

Assume that a parent company has **downstream** inventory sales to its 70%-owned subsidiary and that the subsidiary has on hand at year-end $60,000 of intercompany acquired inventory, which cost the parent company $40,000. Thus the total intercompany gross profit is $20,000. Two schools of thought exist regarding the amount of gross profit to be deferred in consolidation.

1. **Complete elimination.** Under this approach, all of the $20,000 of intercompany is considered unrealized and is deferred.

2. **Fractional elimination.** By following this approach, $6,000 ($20,000 × 30%) is considered realized due to the 30% noncontrolling interest ownership in the subsidiary. Accordingly, only $14,000 is deferred in consolidation.

GAAP REQUIREMENTS   The accounting rules for preparing consolidated statements require the first alternative, complete elimination, because it is consistent with the underlying assumption that the consolidated statements represent the financial position and operating results of a single economic unit.

CONCEPTUAL ISSUE 5: WHEN A PARTIALLY OWNED SUBSIDIARY HAS *UPSTREAM* SALES, SHOULD THE INTERCOMPANY PROFIT ACCRUING TO THE NONCONTROLLING INTEREST BE DEFERRED IN CONSOLIDATION?

Assume that an 80%-owned subsidiary has **upstream** inventory sales to its parent company and the parent has on hand at year-end $15,000 of intercompany acquired inventory, which cost the subsidiary $10,000. Thus the total intercompany gross profit is $5,000, of which $4,000 accrues to the parent company and $1,000 accrues to the noncontrolling interest. Again, two schools of thought exist regarding the amount of gross profit to be deferred in consolidation.

1. **Complete elimination.** This approach eliminates the entire $5,000 of gross profit on the grounds that to do otherwise would be inconsistent with the underlying purpose of consolidated statements, which is to report activities as though a single entity exists. As a result, the consolidated net income that accrues to the con-

trolling interest is reduced by $4,000, and the noncontrolling interest is reduced by $1,000.

2. **Fractional elimination.** This approach eliminates only the portion of the gross profit that accrues to the parent. It does *not* eliminate the portion of the gross profit that accrues to the noncontrolling interest on the grounds that profit has been realized from the viewpoint of the noncontrolling interest shareholders. To whom the subsidiary sells as far as the subsidiary's noncontrolling shareholders are concerned is irrelevant. As a result, the consolidated net income that accrues to the controlling interest is reduced by $4,000. The noncontrolling interest is *not* reduced by $1,000.

GAAP REQUIREMENTS   The accounting rules for preparing consolidated statements require the first alternative, complete elimination. Thus the entire $5,000 is deferred. Furthermore, the elimination of the intercompany profit or loss is to be allocated proportionately between the controlling interest and the noncontrolling interests.

When the noncontrolling interest ownership percentage is quite low and the dollar amounts are immaterial, in practice, reducing the consolidated net income that accrues to the controlling interest by the full amount of the gross profit being deferred in consolidation is usually more expedient, rather than taking the additional step of allocating a portion to the noncontrolling interest.

II PROCEDURES FOR CALCULATING UNREALIZED INTERCOMPANY PROFIT

The first step for inventory transfers at above the selling entity's cost is to determine how much of the intercompany-acquired inventory remains on hand at the consolidation date. The amount of the markup pertaining to this inventory is then calculated. This profit is then deferred until the acquiring entity resells the inventory to a third-party customer.

RECORDING THE INTERCOMPANY SALE AND PARTIAL RESALE

Assume that in 19X1 P Company sold inventory costing $60,000 to S Company for $100,000 and that S Company reports $20,000 of this inventory in its balance sheet at December 31, 19X1. Thus S Company has charged to Cost of Sales $80,000 of the $100,000 of inventory acquired from P Company. Each company records the following **general ledger entries:**

	Parent's Books	Subsidiary's Books
P Company		
Intercompany Receivables	100,000	
Intercompany Sales		100,000
Intercompany Cost of Sales	60,000	
Inventory		60,000
S Company		
Inventory		100,000
Intercompany Payable		100,000

Note: This transfer establishes a new basis of accounting for the inventory from S Company's perspective—but not from a consolidated perspective.

Cost of Sales		80,000
Inventory		80,000

Accordingly, the financial statements of each company at December 31, 19X1, appear as follows:

	P Company	S Company
Income Statement		
Cost of sales **(new basis)**		$(80,000)
Intercompany sales	$100,000	
Intercompany cost of sales **(old basis)**	(60,000)	
Balance Sheet		
Inventory—intercompany acquired **(new basis)**		20,000

It is now necessary to calculate how much intercompany profit is associated with the $20,000 of ending inventory, the unrealized portion of P Company's $40,000 of gross profit.

CALCULATING THE UNREALIZED INTERCOMPANY PROFIT USING A MATRIX ANALYSIS

Usually a formal analysis, such as the following one, is prepared to show how much of the total intercompany gross profit is associated with the (1) inventory on hand at year-end (remains within the consolidated group) and (2) inventory that has been resold to an outside third party (has left the consolidated group).

	Total (given)	**Resold**	**On Hand**
Intercompany sales **(new basis)** . . .	**$100,000**	$80,000	**$20,000** (given)
Intercompany cost of			
sales @ 60% **(old basis)**	**(60,000)**	(48,000)	(12,000)
Gross Profit	$ 40,000	$32,000	$ 8,000
		(Realized)	(Unrealized)

The first line of the analysis, intercompany sales, shows what portion of S Company's total intercompany purchases for the year (1) have been charged to its Cost of Sales account and (2) reside in its Inventory account at year-end. This separation is made by subtracting the $20,000 of intercompany inventory purchases on hand at year-end (determined by using either a physical count or perpetual records) from the $100,000 of total intercompany sales for the year to arrive at the $80,000 charged to the Cost of Sales account.

The second line of the analysis, intercompany cost of sales, shows the amounts that would have been reported (pro forma in nature) for the buying entity's (1) Cost of Sales account and (2) Inventory account (at year-end) had the intercompany transfer been at the selling entity's cost (no change in basis situation). The percentage of inventory resold (80%) and the percentage of inventory still on hand (20%), determined by using the amounts on the first line, are applied to the total intercompany cost of sales ($60,000) to determine the amounts in the Resold and On Hand columns.

Gross profit, the difference between the first and second lines, is the amount by which the Cost of Sales account and the Inventory account are overstated as to the consolidated entity because the inventory transfer was made above cost. Following the preceding analysis, this elimination entry is prepared:

WORKSHEET ENTRY ONLY	Intercompany Sales	100,000		
	Intercompany Cost of Sales			60,000
	Cost of Sales			32,000
	Intercompany Profit Deferral (for Module 1)			8,000
or				
	Inventory (for Modules 2 and 3)			8,000

The postings for the first two lines undo the reporting of the intercompany sale. The $32,000 credit posting to the Cost of Sales account results in changing this account balance from the new basis of accounting back to the old basis of accounting. Under Modules 2 and 3, the $8,000 credit posting to the Inventory account also changes this account balance from the new basis of accounting (as reflected in the buying entity's books) back to the old basis of accounting (as previously reflected in the selling entity's books). Under Module 1, the necessary $8,000 credit posting to the Inventory account is made in the basic elimination entry, as explained in Module 1. Under Module 1, the $8,000 credit posting to the Intercompany Profit Deferral account eliminates the balance in this account, which previously would have been established in the parent's general ledger in connection with reducing the carrying value of the parent's Investment account (something done only in Module 1).

This example, involving $100,000 of intercompany sales, is used in each of the three following modules.

III   PROCEDURES FOR DEFERRING UNREALIZED INTERCOMPANY PROFIT

MODULE 1 OVERVIEW

In a complete application of the equity method of accounting in 100% ownership situations, a general ledger adjusting entry is made for the unrealized intercompany profit so that the parent's net income and its retained earnings are the same as consolidated net income and consolidated retained earnings, respectively. Consequently, this highly desirable built-in checking feature of the equity method (discussed in Chapters 2 and 6) is not lost.

For downstream sales, the general ledger adjustment is made directly to the parent's Investment account and the parent's income statement. For upstream sales, the adjustment is made directly to the subsidiary's books—this results in recording lower income on the parent's books when it applies the equity method of accounting and thus a lower carrying value for the parent's Investment account. Because the deferral is recorded in one of the general ledgers, no deferral effect need take place in consolidation.

HARMONY OF *APB OPINION NO. 18* AND THE CONSOLIDATION RULES

When a parent company uses the equity method of accounting in its parent-company-only (PCO) statements, the requirements of *APB Opinion No. 18*, "The Equity Method of Accounting for Investments in Common Stock," must be met. For parent-subsidiary relationships, *APBO No. 18* requires that all unrealized intercompany profit be deferred until realized in a transaction with a third party (even when a noncontrolling interest exists). The accounting rules for preparing consolidated statements require the same treatment.

MODULE 1

THE COMPLETE EQUITY METHOD

SECTION 1: DOWNSTREAM TRANSFERS ABOVE COST

PARENT'S GENERAL LEDGER ENTRY
TO DEFER UNREALIZED PROFIT

To convey the rationale for making a general ledger adjustment on the parent's books for downstream sales, we use the following assumed information:

1. P Company created S Company on December 31, 19X1, with a $100,000 cash investment.
2. S Company's only transaction during 19X1 was to purchase $100,000 of inventory from P Company on December 31, 19X1, with full payment made on this date.
3. P Company's cost was $60,000.
4. S Company did not resell any of the $100,000 of inventory. Thus S Company's only asset at year-end is $100,000 of inventory.

If P Company were to issue PCO statements, it could not report there the $40,000 of intercompany profit on the inventory transfer but would have to defer that amount. Accordingly, assume that P Company makes the following **general ledger adjusting entry** to defer recognizing the $40,000 of intercompany profit for PCO reporting purposes:

```
Intercompany Profit Deferral
    (an income statement account) ....................   40,000
        Investment in Subsidiary .....................             40,000
```

After posting this general ledger entry, the financial statements of the two entities at December 31, 19X1, appear as follows:

	P Company	S Company
Income Statement		
Intercompany sales	$100,000	
Intercompany cost of sales **(old basis)**	(60,000)	
Intercompany profit deferral	(40,000)	
Net Income	$ –0–	
Balance Sheet		
Cash	$100,000	$ –0–
Inventory—intercompany acquired **(new basis)** ..		100,000
Investment in subsidiary	60,000	
Common stock		100,000
Retained earnings	–0–	–0–

CREDITING THE INVESTMENT ACCOUNT From P Company's perspective, it truly has not invested $100,000 in S Company. P Company truly has invested only $60,000, its cost basis in the inventory it transferred to S Company (S Company's only asset). A different way to look at it is that P Company is in the same position as it would have been if instead it had (1) initially invested only $60,000 in S Company and (2) immediately sold the inventory to S Company for $60,000 (a transfer at cost). In such a scenario, P Company thus would have a $60,000 balance in its Investment account and S Company would have total equity of $60,000 (rather than $100,000).

DEBITING THE INTERCOMPANY PROFIT DEFERRAL ACCOUNT By debiting this account, which generically is a *contra* profit account, the parent reports none of the intercompany profit in its PCO statements, which is appropriate. It *can* report (1) the intercompany sale of $100,000 and (2) the intercompany cost of sale of $60,000—these are valid transactions from a PCO perspective. However, P Company cannot merely report the $40,000 of intercompany profit. By using the Intercompany Profit Deferral account, the parent's income statement clearly portrays (1) the intercompany transaction itself and (2) the fact that no profit is being reported on this intercompany transaction because it is intercompany generated (negating the need for any discussion in the notes to the PCO statements). In consolidation, the Intercompany Profit Deferral account is eliminated by a credit posting that originates from the basic elimination entry (explained shortly).

A POSSIBLE ALTERNATIVE ACCOUNT TO DEBIT   An alternative to debiting the Intercompany Profit Deferral account is to debit the Equity in Net Income of Subsidiary account for $40,000. This debit accomplishes the same result as not allowing P Company to report any of the $40,000 of intercompany profit. The rationale for this alternative is that (1) the $40,000 of intercompany profit arises because of the relationship that exists between the two entities and (2) things that relate to this relationship should be reported as part of the parent's investment income. We find this alternative to be less appealing than the earlier approach because the PCO income statement portrayal is not as self-explanatory as when the Intercompany Profit Deferral account is used. Besides, it can be confusing to report a loss for its investment income when S Company did *not* report a $40,000 net loss for 19X1—it had only the two transactions with P Company.

PARENT'S GENERAL LEDGER ENTRY TO SUBSEQUENTLY RECOGNIZE THE PREVIOUSLY DEFERRED UNREALIZED PROFIT

If S Company eventually sells the $100,000 of intercompany-acquired inventory in 19X2, P Company no longer need defer the $40,000 of previously deferred intercompany profit. Accordingly, P Company makes the following **general ledger adjusting entry:**

Investment in Subsidiary	40,000	
Intercompany Profit Recognized		
(an income statement account)		40,000

At this point, P Company's Investment account equals the sum of S Company's equity accounts.

ILLUSTRATIONS | **PREPARING CONSOLIDATED STATEMENTS**

- The Complete Equity Method
- Downstream Transfers Above Cost

We now use the example discussed on pages 345–347 in which (1) P Company sold inventory costing $60,000 to S Company (100% owned) for $100,000 in 19X1, (2) S Company reports $20,000 of the $100,000 of intercompany acquired inventory on its balance sheet at December 31, 19X1, and (3) the results of the analysis of the total intercompany profit of $40,000 are that $32,000 relates to inventory S Company has resold and $8,000 relates to inventory on hand at year-end. To defer recognition of the $8,000 of unrealized intercompany profit, P Company makes the following **year-end general ledger adjusting entry:**

Intercompany Profit Deferral (income statement)	8,000	
Investment in Subsidiary		8,000

As a result of this entry, an inequality now exists between (1) the debit balance in P Company's Investment account and (2) the sum of the credit balances of S Company's equity accounts. To deal with this inequality in consolidation, a column is added to the parent's conceptual analysis of its Investment account.

Illustration 10–1 shows how P Company's analysis of its Investment account is updated for 19X1 and 19X2 using assumed net income and dividend declared

ILLUSTRATION 10–1	THE COMPLETE EQUITY METHOD Downstream Transfers Above Cost: 100% Ownership— Updated Analysis of the Investment Account and Consolidation Entries for Deferral Year and Recognition Year

					Subsidiary's Equity Accounts		
	Unrealized Profit	+	Parent's Investment Account	=	Common Stock	+	Retained Earnings
Balances, 1/1/X1	$ –0–		$ 60,000		$60,000		$ –0–
+ Equity in net income			24,000				24,000
– Dividends			(4,000)				(4,000)
– IC[a] profit deferral	8,000		(8,000)				
Balance, 12/31/X1	$8,000		$ 72,000		$60,000		$20,000
+ Equity in net income			32,000				32,000
– Dividends			(12,000)				(12,000)
+ IC[a] profit recognition	(8,000)		8,000				
Balances, 12/31/X2	$ –0–		$100,000		$60,000		$40,000

[a]IC is the abbreviation for *intercompany*.

The Basic Elimination Entry
(obtained from the amounts in the above analysis)

		Consolidation Date	
		December 31, 19X1	December 31, 19X2
WORKSHEET ENTRIES ONLY	Common Stock	60,000	60,000
	Retained Earnings, 1/1/X1 and 1/1/X2 ..	–0–	20,000
	Equity in Net Income (of S Co.). . .	24,000	32,000
	Dividends Declared	4,000	12,000
	Inventory (intercompany acquired)	8,000	–0–
	Investment in Subsidiary	72,000	100,000

The COS Change in Basis Elimination Entry

		Consolidation Date	
		December 31, 19X1	December 31, 19X2
WORKSHEET ENTRY ONLY	Intercompany Sales	100,000	
	Intercompany Cost of Sales	60,000	
	Cost of Sales	32,000	
	Intercompany Profit Deferral	8,000	

The COS Change in Basis Elimination Entry—Prior Year Intercompany Sales

		Consolidation Date	
		December 31, 19X1	December 31, 19X2
WORKSHEET ENTRY ONLY	Intercompany Profit Recognized		8,000
	Cost of Sales		8,000

Note: This last entry, although considered an elimination entry, serves merely to reclassify the credit balance in the Intercompany Profit Recognized account to Cost of Sales, thereby adjusting that account's balance downward from the new basis of accounting to the old basis of accounting.

amounts. For simplicity, we assume that (1) S Company resold the $20,000 of intercompany-acquired inventory on hand at December 31, 19X1, in 19X2 and (2) no downstream inventory transfers occurred in 19X2. For brevity, we use the abbreviation IC to stand for the word *intercompany*. Illustration 10–1 also shows the elimination entries made in consolidation at December 31, 19X1 and 19X2.

Illustrations 10–2 and 10–3 show consolidation worksheets for the years ended December 31, 19X1 and 19X2.

ILLUSTRATION 10–2	THE COMPLETE EQUITY METHOD — Downstream Transfers Above Cost: 100% Ownership—Year of Deferral

P Company and S Company
Consolidation Worksheet as of December 31, 19X1

	P Company	100%-owned S Company	Consolidation Entries Dr.	Consolidation Entries Cr.	Consolidated
Income Statement (19X1)					
Sales	500,000	234,000			734,000
Cost of sales	(300,000)	(110,000)		32,000(2)	(378,000)
Expenses	(190,000)	(100,000)			(290,000)
Intercompany Accounts					
Equity in net income (of S Co.)	24,000		24,000(1)		–0–
Intercompany sales	100,000		100,000(2)		–0–
Intercompany cost of sales	(60,000)			60,000(2)	–0–
Intercompany profit deferral	(8,000)			8,000(2)	–0–
Net Income	66,000	24,000	124,000	100,000	66,000
Statement of Retained Earnings					
Balances, 1/1/X1	100,000	–0–			100,000
+ Net income	66,000	24,000	124,000	100,000	66,000
– Dividends declared	(51,000)	(4,000)		4,000(1)	(51,000)
Balances, 12/31/X1	115,000	20,000	124,000	104,000	115,000
Balance Sheet					
Cash	65,000	11,000			76,000
Accounts receivable, net	75,000	37,000			112,000
Inventory:					
From vendors	110,000	35,000			145,000
Intercompany		20,000		8,000(1)	12,000
Investment in subsidiary	72,000			72,000(1)	–0–
Land	220,000	30,000			250,000
Buildings and equipment	500,000	150,000			650,000
Accumulated depreciation	(320,000)	(13,000)			(333,000)
Total Assets	722,000	270,000		80,000	912,000
Liabilities	407,000	190,000			597,000
Common stock	200,000	60,000	60,000(1)		200,000
Retained earnings	115,000	20,000	124,000	104,000	115,000
Total Liabilities and Equity	722,000	270,000	184,000	104,000	912,000
Proof of debit and credit postings			184,000	184,000	

Explanation of entries:
(1) The basic elimination entry.
(2) The COS change in basis elimination entry.

THE COMPLETE EQUITY METHOD

ILLUSTRATION 10-3	THE COMPLETE EQUITY METHOD Downstream Transfers Above Cost: 100% Ownership—Year of Recognition

P Company and S Company
Consolidation Worksheet as of December 31, 19X2

	P Company	100%-owned S Company	Consolidation Entries Dr.	Consolidation Entries Cr.	Consolidated
Income Statement (19X2)					
Sales	710,000	282,000			992,000
Cost of sales	(390,000)	(130,000)		8,000(2)	(512,000)
Expenses	(210,000)	(120,000)			(330,000)
Intercompany Accounts					
Equity in net income (of S Co.) ..	32,000		32,000(1)		–0–
Intercompany profit recognized ..	8,000		8,000(2)		–0–
Net Income	150,000	32,000	40,000	8,000	150,000
Statement of Retained Earnings					
Balances, 1/1/X2	115,000	20,000	20,000(1)		115,000
+ Net income	150,000	32,000	40,000	8,000	150,000
– Dividends declared	(85,000)	(12,000)		12,000(1)	(85,000)
Balances, 12/31/X2	180,000	40,000	60,000	20,000	180,000
Balance Sheet					
Cash	66,000	31,000			97,000
Accounts receivable, net	84,000	43,000			127,000
Inventory:					
From vendors	140,000	82,000			222,000
Intercompany		–0–			–0–
Investment in subsidiary	100,000			100,000(1)	–0–
Land	220,000	30,000			250,000
Buildings and equipment	500,000	150,000			650,000
Accumulated depreciation	(360,000)	(26,000)			(386,000)
Total Assets	750,000	310,000		100,000	960,000
Liabilities	370,000	210,000			580,000
Common stock	200,000	60,000	60,000(1)		200,000
Retained earnings	180,000	40,000	60,000	20,000	180,000
Total Liabilities and Equity ..	750,000	310,000	120,000	20,000	960,000
Proof of debit and credit postings			120,000	120,000	

Explanation of entries:
(1) The basic elimination entry.
(2) The COS change in basis elimination entry—prior year intercompany sales.

DEALING WITH MULTIPLE YEAR TRANSFERS

Transfers usually occur each year for a typical consolidation involving intercompany inventory transfers. Accordingly, consolidation entries are required both (1) to reclassify to cost of sales the recognized profit on the beginning intercompany- acquired inventory and (2) to eliminate the current year intercompany transfers. In this regard, keeping these two entries separate is far simpler than attempting to handle them as a single, combined consolidation entry.

Some of the beginning inventory may be physically part of the ending inventory. The consolidation effort is simplified, however, if we assume that (1) the beginning inventory has been resold and (2) all of the ending inventory came from the current year intercompany inventory transfers. So long as the gross profit rates are the same (or very similar) from year to year, the assumption is a safe one.

SECTION 2: UPSTREAM TRANSFERS ABOVE COST

When an intercompany inventory transfer is upstream from a partially owned subsidiary, recall that *all* of the intercompany profit associated with inventory is still on hand but that the deferral **is shared with the noncontrolling interests.**

SUBSIDIARY'S GENERAL LEDGER ENTRY TO DEFER UNREALIZED PROFIT

The simplest way to readily develop the entries for consolidation when unrealized intercompany profit exists as a result of an upstream transfer is to have S Company record a general ledger adjusting entry to defer the *total* unrealized profit. By doing so, the total unrealized intercompany profit is automatically shared between the controlling interest and the noncontrolling interest. (Thus if S Company is 75% owned, P Company records $6,000 [75% × $8,000] less income under the equity method of accounting.) Accordingly, to defer recognition of the $8,000 of unrealized intercompany profit, S Company makes the following year-end **general ledger adjusting entry:**

Intercompany Profit Deferral (income statement)	8,000	
Deferred Profit (a balance sheet account)		8,000

Both of these intercompany-transaction-related accounts are eliminated in consolidation. The Intercompany Profit Deferral entry is eliminated using the same elimination entry shown for the downstream sale situation. The Deferred Profit account is eliminated by a separate consolidation entry that reclassifies the credit balance in this account to the intercompany-acquired inventory line in the balance sheet. The result is to reduce the $20,000 carrying value of the intercompany-acquired inventory from $20,000 to $12,000, thereby changing the basis of accounting from P Company's new basis back to S Company's old basis.

Recall that when P Company made its general ledger adjusting entry for unrealized profit in the downstream sale situation, its Investment account—*not* the Deferred Profit account—was credited. In this situation, the Deferred Profit account allows the consolidation process to be performed as efficiently as possible and equally as well.

SUBSIDIARY'S GENERAL LEDGER ENTRY TO SUBSEQUENTLY RECOGNIZE THE PREVIOUSLY DEFERRED UNREALIZED PROFIT

If S Company resells the $20,000 of intercompany-acquired inventory in 19X2, it no longer need defer the $8,000 of intercompany profit. Accordingly, S Company makes the following **general ledger adjusting entry:**

Deferred Profit	8,000	
Intercompany Profit Recognized (income statement)		8,000

In consolidation, the Intercompany Profit Recognized account is eliminated using the same entry shown previously in the downstream transfer situation, where the $8,000 credit balance is reclassified to Cost of Sales to achieve the old basis of accounting.

SUBSIDIARY'S REPORTING TO ITS NONCONTROLLING INTEREST SHAREHOLD-ERS   Under current reporting standards, S Company need not defer any of its intercompany profit in reporting to the noncontrolling interest. As for the noncontrolling interest, such intercompany profit has been realized. Accordingly, to report to the noncontrolling interest, S Company makes a "financial statement adjusting entry" (on a worksheet) to reverse the intercompany profit deferral entry.

The consolidation effort is greatly simplified if S Company maintains its general ledger for reporting to P Company rather than to the noncontrolling interest. If S Company's general ledger were kept the opposite way, P Company must make a financial statement adjusting entry to S Company's financial statements prior to the start of the consolidation process. Some companies have hundreds of subsidiaries and large numbers of intercompany inventory transfers. Making such an entry for each subsidiary puts a substantial burden on the parent's accounting department. Thus it is far more efficient to have subsidiaries maintain their general ledgers for reporting to the parent.

ALTERNATIVE MANNER OF RECORDING THE DEFERRAL IN THE GENERAL LEDGER   An alternative manner of effecting the deferral is to have P Company record $6,000 less income than it otherwise would record in applying the equity method of accounting. We find this alternative less appealing because it is more involved procedurally in dealing with partially owned subsidiaries. Accordingly, we do not present it.

ILLUSTRATIONS	**PREPARING CONSOLIDATED STATEMENTS**

- The Complete Equity Method
- Upstream Transfers above Cost from 75%-Owned Subsidiary

We now use the example presented in the downstream transfer except that we have converted the situation into an upstream transfer. For convenience, we repeat S Company's general ledger adjusting entry at December 31, 19X1, to defer recognition of the $8,000 of unrealized intercompany profit:

Intercompany Profit Deferral (income statement)	8,000	
Deferred Profit (balance sheet)		8,000

Illustration 10–4 shows how P Company's analysis of its Investment account is updated for 19X1 and 19X2. Illustration 10–4 also shows the entries made in consolidation at December 31, 19X1 and 19X2. For brevity, we use the abbreviation NCI for noncontrolling interest in (1) the analysis, (2) the basic elimination entry, and (3) the consolidation worksheets.

Illustrations 10–5 and 10–6 show consolidation worksheets for the years ended December 31, 19X1 and 19X2.

| **ILLUSTRATION 10–4** | THE COMPLETE EQUITY METHOD　Upstream Transfers Above Cost: 75% Ownership—Updated Analysis of the Investment Account and Entries for Deferral Year and Recognition Year |

	Noncontrolling Interest (25%)	+	Parent's Investment Account	=	Subsidiary's Equity Accounts Common Stock	+	Retained Earnings
Balances, 1/1/X1	$15,000		$45,000		$60,000		$ –0–
+ Equity in net income:							
To parent (75%)			12,000				12,000
To NCI[a] (25%)	4,000						4,000
– Dividends:							
To parent (75%)			(3,000)				(3,000)
To NCI (25%)	(1,000)						(1,000)
Balances, 12/31/X1	$18,000		$54,000		$60,000		$12,000
+ Equity in net income:							
To parent (75%)			30,000				30,000
To NCI (25%)	10,000						10,000
– Dividends:							
To parent (75%)			(9,000)				(9,000)
To NCI (25%)	(3,000)						(3,000)
Balances, 12/31/X2	$25,000		$75,000		$60,000		$40,000

[a]NCI is the abbreviation for *noncontrolling interest*.

The Basic Elimination Entry
(obtained from the amounts in the above analysis)

		Consolidation Date	
		December 31, 19X1	**December 31, 19X2**
WORKSHEET ENTRIES ONLY	Common Stock	60,000	60,000
	Retained Earnings, 1/1/X1 and 1/1/X2 ..	–0–	12,000
	Equity in Net Income (of S Co.)	12,000	30,000
	NCI in Net Income	4,000	10,000
	Dividends Declared	4,000	12,000
	Investment in Subsidiary	54,000	75,000
	NCI in Net Assets	18,000	25,000

The COS Change in Basis Elimination Entry

		Consolidation Date	
		December 31, 19X1	**December 31, 19X2**
WORKSHEET ENTRY ONLY	Intercompany Sales	100,000	
	Intercompany Cost of Sales	60,000	
	Cost of Sales	32,000	
	Intercompany Profit Deferral	8,000	

The Inventory Change in Basis Elimination Entry

		Consolidation Date	
		December 31, 19X1	**December 31, 19X2**
WORKSHEET ENTRY ONLY	Deferred Profit	8,000	
	Inventory (intercompany acquired)	8,000	

The COS Change in Basis Elimination Entry—Prior Year Intercompany Sales

		Consolidation Date	
		December 31, 19X1	**December 31, 19X2**
WORKSHEET ENTRY ONLY	Intercompany Profit Recognized		8,000
	Cost of Sales		8,000

MODULE 1

THE COMPLETE EQUITY METHOD

ILLUSTRATION 10–5	THE COMPLETE EQUITY METHOD Upstream Transfers Above Cost: 75% Ownership—Year of Deferral

P Company and S Company
Consolidation Worksheet as of December 31, 19X1

	P Company	75%-owned S 3Company	Consolidation Entries Dr.	Consolidation Entries Cr.	Consolidated
Income Statement (19X1)					
Sales	600,000	134,000			734,000
Cost of sales	(360,000)	(50,000)		32,000(2)	(378,000)
Expenses	(190,000)	(100,000)			(290,000)
Intercompany Accounts					
Equity in net income (of S Co.) ..	12,000ª		12,000(1)		–0–
Intercompany sales		100,000	100,000(2)		–0–
Intercompany cost of sales		(60,000)		60,000(2)	–0–
Intercompany profit deferral		(8,000)		8,000(2)	–0–
Net Income	62,000	16,000	112,000	100,000	66,000
NCI in net income			4,000(1)		(4,000)
CI in net income			116,000	100,000	62,000
Statement of Retained Earnings					
Balances, 1/1/X1	100,000	–0–			100,000
+ Net income	62,000	16,000	116,000	100,000	62,000
– Dividends declared	(51,000)	(4,000)		4,000(1)	(51,000)
Balances, 12/31/X1	111,000	12,000	116,000	104,000	111,000
Balance Sheet					
Cash	79,000	11,000			90,000
Accounts receivable, net	75,000	37,000			112,000
Inventory:					
From vendors	90,000	55,000			145,000
Intercompany	20,000			8,000(3)	12,000
Deferred profit		(8,000)	8,000(3)		–0–
Investment in subsidiary	54,000			54,000(1)	–0–
Land	220,000	30,000			250,000
Buildings and equipment	500,000	150,000			650,000
Accumulated depreciation	(320,000)	(13,000)			(333,000)
Total Assets	718,000	262,000	8,000	62,000	926,000
Liabilities	407,000	190,000			597,000
NCI in net assets				18,000(1)	18,000
Common stock	200,000	60,000	60,000(1)		200,000
Retained earnings	111,000	12,000	116,000	104,000	111,000
Total Liabilities and Equity ..	718,000	262,000	176,000	122,000	926,000
Proof of debit and credit postings			184,000	184,000	

Explanation of entries:
(1) The basic elimination entry.
(2) The COS change in basis elimination entry.
(3) The inventory change in basis elimination entry.
ª75% of S Company's reported net income of $16,000.

ILLUSTRATION 10–6	THE COMPLETE EQUITY METHOD Upstream Transfers Above Cost: 75% Ownership—Year of Recognition

P Company and S Company
Consolidation Worksheet as of December 31, 19X2

	P Company	75%-owned S Company	Consolidation Entries Dr.	Consolidation Entries Cr.	Consolidated
Income Statement (19X2)					
Sales	710,000	282,000			992,000
Cost of sales	(390,000)	(130,000)		8,000(2)	(512,000)
Expenses	(210,000)	(120,000)			(330,000)
Intercompany Accounts					
Equity in net income (of S Co.) . .	30,000[a]		30,000(1)		–0–
Intercompany profit recognized . .		8,000	8,000(2)		–0–
Net Income	140,000	40,000	38,000	8,000	150,000
NCI in net income			10,000(1)		(10,000)
CI in net income			48,000	8,000	140,000
Statement of Retained Earnings					
Balances, 1/1/X2	111,000	12,000	12,000(1)		111,000
+ Net income	140,000	40,000	48,000	8,000	140,000
– Dividends declared	(85,000)	(12,000)		12,000(1)	(85,000)
Balances, 12/31/X2	166,000	40,000	60,000	20,000	166,000
Balance Sheet					
Cash	77,000	31,000			108,000
Accounts receivable	84,000	43,000			127,000
Inventory:					
From vendors	140,000	82,000			222,000
Intercompany	–0–	–0–			–0–
Investment in S Co.	75,000			75,000(1)	–0–
Land	220,000	30,000			250,000
Buildings and equipment	500,000	150,000			650,000
Accumulated depreciation	(360,000)	(26,000)			(386,000)
Total Assets	736,000	310,000		75,000	971,000
Liabilities	370,000	210,000			580,000
NCI in net assets				25,000(1)	25,000
Common stock	200,000	60,000	60,000(1)		200,000
Retained earnings	166,000	40,000	60,000	20,000	166,000
Total Liabilities and Equity . .	736,000	310,000	120,000	45,000	971,000
Proof of debit and credit postings			120,000	120,000	

Explanation of entries:
(1) The basic elimination entry.
(2) The COS change in basis elimination entry—prior year intercompany sales.
[a]75% of S Company's reported net income of $40,000.

END

MODULE 2 OVERVIEW

Under the partial equity method, the deferral of unrealized intercompany profit is accomplished entirely on the consolidation worksheet. Accordingly, in 100% ownership situations the parent's net income and retained earnings do *not* agree with the consolidated net income and consolidated retained earnings, respectively. Thus the built-in checking feature characteristic of the equity method in going from the parent column to the Consolidated column discussed in Chapters 2 and 3 no longer exists.

SECTION 1: DOWNSTREAM TRANSFERS ABOVE COST

ILLUSTRATIONS	PREPARING CONSOLIDATED STATEMENTS

- The Partial Equity Method
- Downstream Transfers Above Cost

We now use the example discussed on pages 345–347 in which (1) P Company sold inventory costing $60,000 to S Company (100% owned) for $100,000 in 19X1, (2) S Company reports $20,000 of the $100,000 of intercompany acquired inventory on its balance sheet at December 31, 19X1, and (3) the results of the analysis of the total intercompany profit of $40,000 are that $32,000 relates to inventory S Company has resold and $8,000 relates to inventory on hand at year-end.

Illustration 10–7 shows how P Company's conceptual analysis of its Investment account is updated for 19X1 and 19X2 using assumed net income and dividend declared amounts. For simplicity, we assume that (1) S Company resold the $20,000 of intercompany-acquired inventory on hand at December 31, 19X1, during 19X2 and (2) no downstream inventory transfers occurred during 19X2. For brevity, we use the abbreviation IC to stand for the word *intercompany.* Illustration 10–7 also shows entries made in consolidation at December 31, 19X1 and 19X2.

Illustrations 10–8 and 10–9 show consolidation worksheets for the years ended December 31, 19X1 and 19X2.

REVIEW POINTS FOR ILLUSTRATIONS 10–8 AND 10–9   Note the following:

1. In Illustration 10–8, consolidated net income and consolidated retained earnings are both $8,000 lower than the comparable amounts in the Parent's column.

2. In Illustration 10–9, consolidated net income is $8,000 higher than the parent's net income. Consolidated retained earnings is identical to the parent's retained earnings, however, because at the end of 19X2, no unrealized intercompany profit exists to be deferred.

3. If P Company were to issue PCO statements in addition to consolidated statements in 19X1, its net income of $74,000 first would have to be adjusted downward by $8,000. It would not make sense for a parent company that has intercompany transactions to report a higher profit by not consolidating a subsidiary. Accordingly, P Company makes the following "financial statement adjusting entry" (as opposed to a general ledger adjusting entry) to its PCO statements:

Intercompany Profit Deferral (an income statement account) . . .   8,000
    Deferred Profit (a balance sheet account)   8,000
  To defer the recognition of unrealized intercompany profit.

DEALING WITH MULTIPLE YEAR TRANSFERS

Transfers usually occur each year for a typical consolidation involving intercompany inventory transfers. Accordingly, consolidation entries are required both (1) to recognize the profit on the beginning intercompany-acquired inventory and (2) to eliminate the current year intercompany transfers. In this regard, keeping

ILLUSTRATION 10–7	THE PARTIAL EQUITY METHOD Downstream Transfers Above Cost: 100% Ownership— Updated Analysis of the Investment Account and Elimination Entries for Deferral Year and Recognition Year

	Parent's Investment Account	=	Subsidiary's Equity Accounts		
			Common Stock	+	Retained Earnings
Balances, 1/1/X1	$ 60,000		$60,000		$ –0–
+ Equity in net income	24,000				24,000
– Dividends	(4,000)				(4,000)
Balances, 12/31/X1	$ 80,000		$60,000		$20,000
+ Equity in net income	32,000				32,000
– Dividends	(12,000)				(12,000)
Balances, 12/31/X2	$100,000		$60,000		$40,000

The Basic Elimination Entry
(obtained from the amounts in the preceding analysis)

		Consolidation Date			
		December 31, 19X1		December 31, 19X2	
WORKSHEET ENTRIES ONLY	Common Stock	60,000		60,000	
	Retained Earnings, 1/1/X1 and 1/1/X2 ..	–0–		20,000	
	Equity in Net Income (of S Co.)...	24,000		32,000	
	Dividends Declared		4,000		12,000
	Investment in Subsidiary		80,000		100,000

The Inventory/COS Change in Basis Elimination Entry

		Consolidation Date			
		December 31, 19X1		December 31, 19X2	
WORKSHEET ENTRY ONLY	Intercompany Sales	100,000			
	Intercompany Cost of Sales		60,000		32,000
	Cost of Sales				32,000
	Inventory		8,000		

The COS Change in Basis Elimination Entry—Prior Year Intercompany Sales

		Consolidation Date	
		December 31, 19X1	December 31, 19X2
WORKSHEET ENTRY ONLY	Retained Earnings, 1/1/X2		8,000
	Cost of Sales		8,000[a]

[a]If instead the inventory were still on hand at this date, the Inventory account, not Cost of Sales, is credited.

these two entries separate is far simpler than attempting to handle them as a single, combined consolidation entry.

Some of the beginning inventory may be physically part of the ending inventory. The consolidation effort is simplified, however, if we assume that (1) the beginning inventory has been sold and (2) all of the ending inventory came from the current year intercompany inventory transfers. So long as the gross profit rates are the same (or very similar) from year to year, the assumption is a safe one.

SECTION 2: UPSTREAM TRANSFERS ABOVE COST

In discussing *upstream* transfers, we use the same example discussed in the previous section regarding *downstream* transfers, in which $8,000 of unrealized

THE PARTIAL EQUITY METHOD

(MODULE 2 — side tab)

ILLUSTRATION 10–8	THE PARTIAL EQUITY METHOD Downstream Transfers Above Cost: 100% Ownership—Year of Deferral

P Company and S Company
Consolidation Worksheet as of December 31, 19X1

	P Company	100%-owned S Company	Consolidation Entries Dr.	Consolidation Entries Cr.	Consolidated
Income Statement (19X1)					
Sales	500,000	234,000			734,000
Cost of sales	(300,000)	(110,000)		32,000(2)	(378,000)
Expenses	(190,000)	(100,000)			(290,000)
Intercompany Accounts					
Equity in net income (of S Co.) . .	24,000		24,000(1)		–0–
Intercompany sales	100,000		100,000(2)		–0–
Intercompany cost of sales	(60,000)			60,000(2)	–0–
Net Income	74,000	24,000	124,000	92,000	66,000
Statement of Retained Earnings					
Balances, 1/1/X1	100,000	–0–			100,000
+ Net income	74,000	24,000	124,000	92,000	66,000
– Dividends declared	(51,000)	(4,000)		4,000(1)	(51,000)
Balances, 12/31/X1	123,000	20,000	124,000	96,000	115,000
Balance Sheet					
Cash	65,000	11,000			76,000
Accounts receivable, net	75,000	37,000			112,000
Inventory:					
From vendors	110,000	35,000			145,000
Intercompany		20,000		8,000(2)	12,000
Investment in subsidiary	80,000			80,000(1)	–0–
Land	220,000	30,000			250,000
Buildings and equipment	500,000	150,000			650,000
Accumulated depreciation	(320,000)	(13,000)			(333,000)
Total Assets	730,000	270,000		88,000	912,000
Liabilities	407,000	190,000			597,000
Common stock	200,000	60,000	60,000(1)		200,000
Retained earnings	123,000	20,000	124,000	96,000	115,000
Total Liabilities and Equity . .	730,000	270,000	184,000	96,000	912,000
Proof of debit and credit postings			184,000	184,000	

Explanation of entries:
(1) The basic elimination entry.
(2) The inventory/COS change in basis elimination entry.

intercompany profit existed at the end of 19X1. We assume here, however, that the $100,000 of intercompany sales for 19X1 is upstream from S Company, a 75%-owned subsidiary of P Company.

ILLUSTRATIONS	**PREPARING CONSOLIDATED STATEMENTS**

- The Partial Equity Method
- Upstream Transfers Above Cost

Illustration 10–10 shows how P Company's conceptual analysis of its Investment account is updated for 19X1 and 19X2. Illustration 10–10 also shows the entries made in consolidation at December 31, 19X1 and 19X2.

ILLUSTRATION 10–9   THE PARTIAL EQUITY METHOD   Downstream Transfers Above Cost: 100% Ownership—Year of Recognition

P Company and S Company
Consolidation Worksheet as of December 31, 19X2

	P Company	100%-owned S Company	Consolidation Entries Dr.	Consolidation Entries Cr.	Consolidated
Income Statement (19X2)					
Sales	710,000	282,000			992,000
Cost of sales	(390,000)	(130,000)		8,000(2)	(512,000)
Expenses	(210,000)	(120,000)			(330,000)
Intercompany Accounts					
Equity in net income (of S Co.)	32,000		32,000(2)		–0–
Net Income	142,000	32,000	32,000	8,000	150,000
Statement of Retained Earnings			8,000(2)		
Balances, 1/1/X2	123,000	20,000	20,000(1)		115,000
+ Net income	142,000	32,000	32,000	8,000	150,000
– Dividends declared	(85,000)	(12,000)		12,000(1)	(85,000)
Balances, 12/31/X2	180,000	40,000	60,000	20,000	180,000
Balance Sheet					
Cash	66,000	31,000			97,000
Accounts receivable	84,000	43,000			127,000
Inventory:					
From vendors	140,000	82,000			222,000
Intercompany		–0–			–0–
Investment in subsidiary	100,000			100,000(1)	–0–
Land	220,000	30,000			250,000
Buildings and equipment	500,000	150,000			650,000
Accumulated depreciation	(360,000)	(26,000)			(386,000)
Total Assets	750,000	310,000		100,000	960,000
Liabilities	370,000	210,000			580,000
Common stock		60,000	60,000(1)		200,000
Retained earnings		40,000	60,000	20,000	180,000
Total Liabilities and Equity	750,000	310,000	120,000	20,000	960,000
Proof of debit and credit postings			120,000	120,000	

Explanation of entries:
(1) The basic elimination entry.
(2) The COS change in basis elimination entry—prior year intercompany sales.

Illustrations 10–11 and 10–12 show consolidation worksheets for the years ended December 31, 19X1 and 19X2.

REVIEW POINTS FOR ILLUSTRATIONS 10–11 AND 10–12   Note the following:

1. In Illustration 10–11, the $62,000 of consolidated net income that accrues to the controlling interest is $6,000 (75% × $8,000) lower than the $68,000 of net income reported by the parent.

2. In Illustration 10–12, the $140,000 of consolidated net income that accrues to the controlling interest is $6,000 higher than the parent's $134,000 of net income. Consolidated retained earnings is identical, however, to the parent's retained earnings because at the end of 19X2, no unrealized intercompany profit exists to be deferred.

ILLUSTRATION 10–10	THE PARTIAL EQUITY METHOD Upstream Transfers Above Cost: 75% Ownership—Updated Analysis of the Investment Account and Elimination Entries for Deferral Year and Recognition Year

	Noncontrolling Interest (25%)	+	Parent's Investment Account	=	Common Stock	+	Retained Earnings
					Subsidiary's Equity Accounts		
Balances, 12/31/X0	$15,000		$45,000		$60,000		$ –0–
+ Equity in net income:							
To parent (75%)			18,000				18,000
To NCIa (25%)	6,000						6,000
– Dividends:							
To parent (75%)			(3,000)				(3,000)
To NCI (25%)	(1,000)						(1,000)
Balances, 12/31/X1	$20,000		$60,000		$60,000		$20,000
+ Equity in net income:							
To parent (75%)			24,000				24,000
To NCI (25%)	8,000						8,000
– Dividends:							
To parent (75%)			(9,000)				(9,000)
To NCI (25%)	(3,000)						(3,000)
Balances, 12/31/X2	$25,000		$75,000		$60,000		$40,000

aNCI is the abbreviation for *noncontrolling interest.*

The Basic Elimination Entry
(obtained from the amounts in the above analysis)

		Consolidation Date	
		December 31, 19X1	December 31, 19X2
WORKSHEET ENTRIES ONLY	Common Stock	60,000	60,000
	Retained Earnings, 1/1/X1 and 1/1/X2 ..	–0–	20,000
	Equity in Net Income (of S Co.)	18,000	24,000
	NCI in Net Income	6,000	8,000
	Dividends Declared	4,000	12,000
	Investment in Subsidiary	60,000	75,000
	NCI in Net Assets	20,000	25,000

The Inventory/COS Change in Basis Elimination Entry

		Consolidation Date	
		December 31, 19X1	December 31, 19X2
WORKSHEET ENTRY ONLY	Intercompany Sales	100,000	
	Intercompany Cost of Sales	60,000	
	Cost of Sales	32,000	
	Inventory	8,000	

The Sharing of Deferred Profit Elimination Entry
(25% of $8,000 of unrealized profit)

		Consolidation Date	
		December 31, 19X1	December 31, 19X2
WORKSHEET ENTRY ONLY	NCI in Net Assets	2,000	
	NCI in Net Income	2,000	

The COS Change in Basis Elimination Entry—Prior Year Intercompany Sales

		Consolidation Date	
		December 31, 19X1	December 31, 19X2
WORKSHEET ENTRY ONLY	NCI in Net Income (25% of $8,000)		2,000
	Retained Earnings, 1/1/X2 (75% of $8,000)		6,000
	Cost of Sales		8,000b

bIf instead the inventory were still on hand at this date, the Inventory account—*not* Cost of Sales—would be credited.

ILLUSTRATION 10–11 THE PARTIAL EQUITY METHOD   Upstream Transfer Above Cost:
75% Ownership—Year of Deferral

P Company and S Company
Consolidation Worksheet as of December 31, 19X1

	P Company	*75%-owned* S Company	Consolidation Entries Dr.	Consolidation Entries Cr.	Consolidated
Income Statement (19X1)					
Sales	600,000	134,000			734,000
Cost of sales	(360,000)	(50,000)		32,000(2)	(378,000)
Expenses	(190,000)	(100,000)			(290,000)
Intercompany Accounts					
Equity in net income (of S Co.) . .	18,000[a]		18,000(1)		–0–
Intercompany sales		100,000	100,000(2)		–0–
Intercompany cost of sales		(60,000)		60,000(2)	–0–
Net Income	68,000	24,000	118,000	92,000	66,000
NCI in net income			6,000(1)	2,000(3)	(4,000)[b]
CI in net income			124,000	94,000	62,000
Statement of Retained Earnings					
Balances, 1/1/X1	100,000	–0–			100,000
+ Net income	68,000	24,000	124,000	94,000	62,000
– Dividends declared	(51,000)	(4,000)		4,000(1)	(51,000)
Balances, 12/31/X1	117,000	20,000	124,000	98,000	111,000
Balance Sheet					
Cash	79,000	11,000			90,000
Accounts receivable, net	75,000	37,000			112,000
Inventory:					
From vendors	90,000	55,000			145,000
Intercompany	20,000			8,000(2)	12,000
Investment in subsidiary	60,000			60,000(1)	–0–
Land	220,000	30,000			250,000
Buildings and equipment	500,000	150,000			650,000
Accumulated depreciation	(320,000)	(13,000)			(333,000)
Total Assets	724,000	270,000		68,000	926,000
Liabilities	407,000	190,000			597,000
NCI in net assets			2,000(3)	20,000(1)	18,000
Common stock	200,000	60,000	60,000(1)		200,000
Retained earnings	117,000	20,000	124,000	98,000	111,000
Total Liabilities and Equity . .	724,000	270,000	186,000	118,000	926,000
Proof of debit and credit postings			186,000	186,000	

Explanation of entries:
(1) The basic elimination entry.
(2) The inventory/COS change in basis elimination entry.
(3) The sharing of deferred profit elimination entry.

[a]75% share of subsidiary's reported net income of $24,000.

[b]Proof: S Company's reported net income of $24,000 – $8,000 of unrealized profit at 12/31/X1 = $16,000; $16,000 × 25% = $4,000.

ILLUSTRATION 10–12	THE PARTIAL EQUITY METHOD Upstream Transfers Above Cost: 75% Ownership—Year of Recognition

P Company and S Company
Consolidation Worksheet as of December 31, 19X2

	P Company	75%-owned S Company	Consolidation Entries Dr.	Consolidation Entries Cr.	Consolidated
Income Statement (19X2)					
Sales	710,000	282,000			992,000
Cost of sales	(390,000)	(130,000)		8,000(2)	(512,000)
Expenses	(210,000)	(120,000)			(330,000)
Intercompany Accounts					
Equity in net income (of S Co.) ..	24,000[a]		24,000(1)		–0–
Net Income	134,000	32,000	24,000	8,000	150,000
NCI in net income			2,000(2) 8,000(1)		(10,000)[b]
CI in net income			34,000	8,000	140,000
Statement of Retained Earnings					
Balances, 1/1/X2	117,000	20,000	6,000(2) 20,000(1)		111,000
+ Net income	134,000	32,000	34,000	8,000	140,000
– Dividends declared	(85,000)	(12,000)		12,000(1)	(85,000)
Balances, 12/31/X2	166,000	40,000	60,000	20,000	166,000
Balance Sheet					
Cash	77,000	31,000			108,000
Accounts receivable	84,000	43,000			127,000
Inventory:					
From vendors	140,000	82,000			222,000
Intercompany	–0–				–0–
Investment in S Co.	75,000			75,000(1)	–0–
Land	220,000	30,000			250,000
Buildings and equipment	500,000	150,000			650,000
Accumulated depreciation	(360,000)	(26,000)			(386,000)
Total Assets	736,000	310,000		75,000	971,000
Liabilities	370,000	210,000			580,000
NCI in net assets				25,000(1)	25,000
Common stock	200,000	60,000	60,000(1)		200,000
Retained earnings	166,000	40,000	60,000	20,000	166,000
Total Liabilities and Equity ..	736,000	310,000	120,000	45,000	971,000
Proof of debit and credit postings			120,000	120,000	

Explanation of entries:
(1) The basic elimination entry.
(2) The COS change in basis elimination entry—prior year intercompany sales.

[a]75% of S Company's reported net income of $32,000.

[b]Proof: S Company's reported net income of $32,000 + $8,000 of profit realized in 19X2 = $40,000; $40,000 × 25% = $10,000.

END

ILLUSTRATION 10–14   **THE COST METHOD**   Downstream Transfers Above Cost: 100% Ownership—Year of Deferral

P Company and S Company
Consolidation Worksheet as of December 31, 19X1

	P Company	100%-owned S Company	Consolidation Entries Dr.	Consolidation Entries Cr.	Consolidated
Income Statement (19X1)					
Sales	500,000	234,000			734,000
Cost of sales	(300,000)	(110,000)		32,000(3)	(378,000)
Expenses	(190,000)	(100,000)			(290,000)
Intercompany Accounts					
Intercompany sales	100,000		100,000(3)		–0–
Intercompany cost of sales	(60,000)			60,000(3)	–0–
Dividend income (from S Co.) . . .	4,000		4,000(2)		–0–
Net Income	54,000	24,000	104,000	92,000	66,000
Statement of Retained Earnings					
Balances, 1/1/X1	100,000	–0–			100,000
+ Net income	54,000	24,000	104,000	92,000	66,000
– Dividends declared	(51,000)	(4,000)		4,000(2)	(51,000)
Balances, 12/31/X1	103,000	20,000	104,000	96,000	115,000
Balance Sheet					
Cash	65,000	11,000			76,000
Accounts receivable	75,000	37,000			112,000
Inventory:					
From vendors	110,000	35,000			145,000
Intercompany		20,000		8,000(3)	12,000
Investment in S Co.	60,000			60,000(1)	–0–
Land	220,000	30,000			250,000
Buildings and equipment	500,000	150,000			650,000
Accumulated depreciation	(320,000)	(13,000)			(333,000)
Total Assets	710,000	270,000		68,000	912,000
Liabilities	407,000	190,000			597,000
Common stock	200,000	60,000	60,000(1)		200,000
Retained earnings	103,000	20,000	104,000	96,000	115,000
Total Liabilities and Equity . .	710,000	270,000	164,000	96,000	912,000
Proof of debit and credit postings			164,000	164,000	

Explanation of entries:
(1) The basic elimination entry.
(2) The intercompany dividend elimination entry.
(3) The inventory/COS change in basis elimination entry.

ILLUSTRATIONS   **PREPARING CONSOLIDATED STATEMENTS**

- The Cost Method
- Upstream Transfers Above Cost

Illustration 10–15 shows the elimination entries made in consolidation at December 31, 19X1 and 19X2.

Illustrations 10–16 and 10–17 show consolidation worksheets for the years ended December 31, 19X1 and 19X2.

| ILLUSTRATION 10–15 | THE COST METHOD | Downstream Transfers Above Cost: 100% Ownership—Year of Recognition |

P Company and S Company
Consolidation Worksheet as of December 31, 19X2

	P Company	100%-owned S Company	Consolidation Entries Dr.	Consolidation Entries Cr.	Consolidated
Income Statement (19X2)					
Sales	710,000	282,000			992,000
Cost of sales	(390,000)	(130,000)		8,000(3)	(512,000)
Expenses	(210,000)	(120,000)			(330,000)
Intercompany Accounts					
Dividend income (from S Co.) ...	12,000		12,000(2)		–0–
Net Income	122,000	32,000	12,000	8,000	150,000
Statement of Retained Earnings					
Balances, 1/1/X2	103,000	20,000	8,000(3)		115,000
+ Net income	122,000	32,000	12,000	8,000	150,000
– Dividends declared	(85,000)	(12,000)		12,000(2)	(85,000)
Balances, 12/31/X2	140,000	40,000	20,000	20,000	180,000
Balance Sheet					
Cash	66,000	31,000			97,000
Accounts receivable	84,000	43,000			127,000
Inventory:					
From vendors	140,000	82,000			222,000
Intercompany		–0–			–0–
Investment in subsidiary	60,000			60,000(1)	–0–
Land	220,000	30,000			250,000
Buildings and equipment	500,000	150,000			650,000
Accumulated depreciation	(360,000)	(26,000)			(386,000)
Total Assets	710,000	310,000		60,000	960,000
Liabilities	370,000	210,000			580,000
Common stock	200,000	60,000	60,000(1)		200,000
Retained earnings	140,000	40,000	20,000	20,000	180,000
Total Liabilities and Equity ..	710,000	310,000	80,000	20,000	960,000
Proof of debit and credit postings			80,000	80,000	

Explanation of entries:
  (1) The basic elimination entry.
  (2) The intercompany dividend elimination entry.
  (3) The COS change in basis elimination entry—prior year intercompany sales.

ILLUSTRATION 10–16	THE COST METHOD Upstream Transfers Above Cost: 75% Ownership— Elimination Entries for Deferral Year and Recognition Year

The Basic Elimination Entry

		Consolidation Date	
		December 31, 19X1	December 31, 19X2
WORKSHEET ENTRIES ONLY	Common Stock	45,000	45,000
	Investment in Subsidiary	45,000	45,000

The Intercompany Dividend Elimination Entry

		Consolidation Date	
		December 31, 19X1	December 31, 19X2
WORKSHEET ENTRIES ONLY	Dividend Income (from S Co.)	3,000	9,000
	Dividends Declared	3,000	9,000

The Noncontrolling Interest Elimination Entry
(all amounts are at 25% of subsidiary's reported amounts)

		Consolidation Date	
		December 31, 19X1	December 31, 19X2
WORKSHEET ENTRIES ONLY	Common Stock (25% of $60,000)	15,000	15,000
	Retained Earnings, 1/1/X1 and 1/1/X2 (25% of $ –0– and $20,000)	–0–	5,000
	NCI in Net Income (25% of $24,000 and $32,000)	6,000	8,000
	Dividends Declared (25% of $4,000 and $12,000)	1,000	3,000
	NCI in Net Assets (25% of $80,000 and $100,000)	20,000	25,000

The Inventory/COS Change in Basis Elimination Entry

		Consolidation Date	
		December 31, 19X1	December 31, 19X2
WORKSHEET ENTRY ONLY	Intercompany Sales	100,000	
	Intercompany Cost of Sales	60,000	
	Cost of Sales	32,000	
	Inventory	8,000	

The Sharing of Deferred Profit Elimination Entry
(at 25% of $8,000 of unrealized profit)

		Consolidation Date	
		December 31, 19X1	December 31, 19X2
WORKSHEET ENTRY ONLY	NCI in Net Assets	2,000	
	NCI in Net Income	2,000	

The COS Change in Basis Elimination Entry—Prior Year Intercompany Sales

		Consolidation Date	
		December 31, 19X1	December 31, 19X2
WORKSHEET ENTRY ONLY	NCI in Net Income (25% of $8,000)		2,000
	Retained Earnings, 1/1/X2 (75% of $8,000)		6,000
	Cost of Sales		8,000

MODULE 3

THE COST METHOD

| ILLUSTRATION 10–17 | THE COST METHOD | Upstream Transfers Above Cost: 75% Ownership—Year of Deferral |

P Company and S Company
Consolidation Worksheet as of December 31, 19X1

	P Company	75%-owned S Company	Consolidation Entries Dr.	Consolidation Entries Cr.	Consolidated
Income Statement (19X1)					
Sales	600,000	134,000			734,000
Cost of sales	(360,000)	(50,000)		32,000(4)	(378,000)
Expenses	(190,000)	(100,000)			(290,000)
Intercompany Accounts					
Intercompany sales		100,000	100,000(4)		–0–
Intercompany cost of sales		(60,000)		60,000(4)	–0–
Dividend income (from S Co.) . . .	3,000[a]		3,000(2)		–0–
Net Income	53,000	24,000	103,000	92,000	66,000
NCI in net income			6,000(3)	2,000(5)	(4,000)[b]
CI in net income			109,000	94,000	62,000
Statement of Retained Earnings					
Balances, 1/1/X1	100,000	–0–			100,000
+ Net income	53,000	24,000	109,000	94,000	62,000
				1,000(3)	
– Dividends declared	(51,000)	(4,000)		3,000(2)	(51,000)
Balances, 12/31/X1	102,000	20,000	109,000	98,000	111,000
Balance Sheet					
Cash	79,000	11,000			90,000
Accounts receivable	75,000	37,000			112,000
Inventory:					
From vendors	90,000	55,000			145,000
Intercompany	20,000			8,000(4)	12,000
Investment in S Co.	45,000			45,000(1)	–0–
Land	220,000	30,000			250,000
Buildings and equipment	500,000	150,000			650,000
Accumulated depreciation	(320,000)	(13,000)			(333,000)
Total Assets	709,000	270,000		53,000	926,000
Liabilities	407,000	190,000			597,000
NCI in net assets			2,000(5)	20,000(3)	18,000
			15,000(3)		
Common stock	200,000	60,000	45,000(1)		200,000
Retained earnings	102,000	20,000	109,000(2)	98,000	111,000
Total Liabilities and Equity . .	709,000	270,000	171,000	118,000	926,000
Proof of debit and credit postings			171,000	171,000	

Explanation of entries:
  (1) The basic elimination entry.
  (2) The intercompany dividend elimination entry.
  (3) The NCI elimination entry.
  (4) The inventory/COS change in basis elimination entry.
  (5) The sharing of the deferred profit elimination entry.

[a]75% of S Company's $4,000 dividends declared.

[b]Proof: S Company's reported net income of $24,000 – $8,000 of unrealized profit at 12/31/X1 = $16,000; $16,000 × 25% = $4,000.

ILLUSTRATION 10–18	**THE COST METHOD** Upstream Transfers Above Cost: 75% Ownership—Year of Recognition

P Company and S Company
Consolidation Worksheet as of December 31, 19X2

	P Company	75%-owned S Company	Consolidation Entries Dr.	Consolidation Entries Cr.	Consolidated
Income Statement (19X2)					
Sales	710,000	282,000			992,000
Cost of sales	(390,000)	(130,000)		8,000(4)	(512,000)
Expenses	(210,000)	(120,000)			(330,000)
Intercompany Accounts					
Dividend income (from S Co.) ...	9,000		9,000(2)		–0–
Net Income	119,000	32,000	9,000	8,000	150,000
			2,000(4)		
NCI in net income			8,000(3)		(10,000)ᵃ
CI in net income			19,000	8,000	140,000
Statement of Retained Earnings			6,000(4)		
Balances, 1/1/X2	102,000	20,000	5,000(3)		111,000
+ Net income	119,000	32,000	19,000	8,000	140,000
				3,000(3)	
– Dividends declared	(85,000)	(12,000)		9,000(2)	(85,000)
Balances, 12/31/X2	136,000	40,000	30,000	20,000	166,000
Balance Sheet					
Cash	77,000	31,000			108,000
Accounts receivable	84,000	43,000			127,000
Inventory:					
From vendors	140,000	82,000			222,000
Intercompany	–0–				–0–
Investment in S Co.	45,000			45,000(1)	–0–
Land	220,000	30,000			250,000
Buildings and equipment	500,000	150,000			650,000
Accumulated depreciation	(360,000)	(26,000)			(386,000)
Total Assets	706,000	310,000		45,000	971,000
Liabilities	370,000	210,000			580,000
NCI in net assets				25,000(3)	25,000
			15,000(3)		
Common stock	200,000	60,000	45,000(1)		200,000
Retained earnings	136,000	40,000	30,000	20,000	166,000
Total Liabilities and Equity ..	706,000	310,000	90,000	45,000	971,000
Proof of debit and credit postings			90,000	90,000	

Explanation of entries:
(1) The basic elimination entry.
(2) The intercompany dividend elimination entry.
(3) The NCI elimination entry.
(4) The COS change in basis elimination entry—prior year intercompany sales.

ᵃProof: S Company's reported net income of $32,000 + $8,000 of profit realized in 19X2 = $40,000; $40,000 × 25% = $10,000.

END

IV MISCELLANEOUS AREAS

TRANSPORTATION COSTS

Probably because of their immateriality, the accounting consolidation rules do not specifically address the consolidation treatment of transportation costs incurred in moving inventory among entities of a consolidated group. Because normal transportation costs are inventoriable costs, there is no sound reason to treat them otherwise in consolidated statements.

When the buying entity incurs the transportation costs and treats them as inventoriable costs, the elimination of all of the selling entity's gross profit makes the transportation costs part of inventory on a consolidated basis. (Thus no special procedures or elimination entries relating to these costs are needed in consolidation.) When the selling entity incurs the transportation costs—which it records as marketing costs—the elimination of gross profit results, however, in expensing these costs on a consolidated basis. Accordingly, in consolidation, an additional entry must be made in these latter cases to (1) eliminate the transportation costs reported as marketing expenses and (2) charge these costs to inventory.

For the sake of simplicity, the illustrations pertaining to inventory transfers assumed that the transportation costs were insignificant. Such costs are therefore treated as period costs for a separate company and on a consolidated basis.

LOWER-OF-COST-OR-MARKET ADJUSTMENTS

Occasionally, the buying entity makes a market write-down on intercompany-acquired inventory (using its own cost basis when comparing to market). For consolidated reporting, the appropriate valuation is the lower of the selling entity's cost (the old basis) or the market value—*not* the buying entity's cost basis (the new basis).

TRANSFERS AT BELOW COST

When transfers occur at below cost, the procedures are symmetrically the reverse so long as the unsold year-end inventory's market value equals or exceeds the selling entity's cost. If this is not the case, however, the inventory is reported in the consolidated statements at market value—an amount *lower* than the selling entity's cost.

END-OF-CHAPTER REVIEW

SUMMARY OF KEY POINTS

1. In deferring unrealized intercompany profit, **gross profit** is the concept of profit used. (**Income taxes** provided on such gross profit must also be deferred for consolidated reported purposes.)
2. The existence of a **noncontrolling interest** does *not* affect the amount of gross profit to be deferred.
3. For **upstream intercompany sales** from a partially owned subsidiary, the gross profit being deferred is **shared with the noncontrolling interest.**
4. Unrealized intercompany profit *cannot* be reported in parent-company-only statements.

GLOSSARY OF NEW TERMS

Complete elimination   Eliminating all of the intercompany profit associated with an asset regardless of the existence of a noncontrolling interest.

Fractional elimination   Eliminating less than 100% of the intercompany profit associated with an asset because of the existence of a noncontrolling interest.

SELF-STUDY QUESTIONS

(Answers are at the end of this chapter, preceding the appendix.)

1. When consolidating, elimination entries are needed for all
   a. Intercompany inventory sales.
   b. Intercompany inventory sales at other than cost.
   c. Intercompany inventory sales at cost.
   d. Intercompany inventory sales unless the inventory has been resold to an outside third party.

2. Under current GAAP, unrealized intercompany profit is eliminated to the extent
   a. Of 100% regardless of the parent's ownership interest.
   b. Of the parent's ownership interest in the subsidiary.
   c. Of the noncontrolling interest in the subsidiary.
   d. That the inventory has been resold to a third party.

3. Which of the following statements is *false?*
   a. Elimination by rearrangement is *not* mandatory under current GAAP.
   b. Intercompany inventory transfers *at cost* must be eliminated.
   c. If an intercompany inventory sale is made in late 19X1 but the inventory is not resold to a third party until 19X2, the intercompany inventory sale need *not* be eliminated in 19X2.
   d. Downstream inventory sales are not eliminated if the subsidiary has resold the inventory in the same year.

4. In 19X1, Pak Inc. sold inventory costing $240,000 to its 100%-owned subsidiary, Sak Inc., for $360,000. In consolidation at 12/31/X1, the Inventory account was credited for $15,000. In Sak's balance sheet at 12/31/X1, what is the reported amount of intercompany-acquired inventory?
   a. $15,000   b. $30,000   c. $45,000   d. $90,000

5. In 19X1, Pyle Inc. sold inventory costing $90,000 to its 100%-owned subsidiary for $150,000. At 12/31/X1, the subsidiary reported $30,000 of intercompany-acquired inventory in its balance sheet. The unrealized profit at 12/31/X1 is
   a. $12,000   b. $18,000   c. $30,000   d. $60,000

6. Use the information in Question 5. Consolidation at 12/31/X1 requires which of the following postings?
   a. Debit Intercompany Cost of Sales.
   b. Credit Cost of Sales.
   c. Credit Intercompany Sales.
   d. Debit Sales.
   e. Credit Sales.

7. Answer Question 6 for 19X2—not 19X1— assuming that the inventory was resold in 19X2.

8. In 19X2, Pell Inc. resold for $70,000 inventory that it had acquired from its 100%-owned subsidiary in 19X1 for $50,000. The subsidiary's costs was $36,000. Consolidation at 12/31/X2 requires which of the following postings?
   a. Credit Intercompany Cost of Sales.
   b. Debit Intercompany Sales.
   c. Debit Cost of Sales.
   d. Credit Inventory.
   e. Credit Cost of Sales.

9. At the end of 19X2, Pexa Inc. reports in its balance sheet $80,000 for inventory acquired in 19X1 from its 100%-owned subsidiary. The subsidiary's cost was $60,000. Consolidation at 12/31/X2 requires which of the following postings?
   a. Credit Cost of Sales.
   b. Debit Intercompany Sales.
   c. Credit Retained Earnings.
   d. Credit Inventory.

10. **Modules 1 and 2 only.** In 19X1, Syne Inc., a 100%-owned subsidiary of Pyne Inc., sold Pyne inventory costing $98,000 for $140,000. At 12/31/X1 Pyne reported $30,000 of this inventory on its balance sheet. For 19X1, Syne reported net income of $100,000. Under

the procedures shown in the chapter, what is the balance in Pyne's Equity in Net Income of Subsidiary account for 19X1?

    a. $60,000   **b.** $70,000   **c.** $79,000   **d.** $91,000   **e.** $100,000

11. During 19X1, Pya Inc. sold inventory costing $500,000 to Sya Inc., its 100%-owned subsidiary, on the same terms as sales to third parties. As of 12/31/X1, Sya had resold 80% of this inventory. Information regarding *total sales* for both entities follows:

	Pya Inc.	Sya Inc.
Sales	$2,000,000	$1,400,000
Cost of sales	(1,250,000)	(700,000)
Gross Profit	$ 750,000	$ 700,000

What is the reportable consolidated sales for 19X1?

    a. $2,320,000   **b.** $2,600,000   **c.** $2,900,000   **d.** $3,400,000

12. Use the information in Question 11. What is the reportable consolidated cost of sales for 19X1?

    a. $1,210,000   **b.** $1,300,000   **c.** $1,710,000   **d.** $1,950,000

ASSIGNMENT MATERIAL

REVIEW QUESTIONS

1. For intercompany transfers *at a markup,* what concept of profit is used for consolidation elimination purposes?
2. What does current GAAP require as to *income taxes provided on intercompany profits?*
3. Under current GAAP, can intercompany profit on downstream sales to a partially owned subsidiary be realized *to the extent of the noncontrolling interest?*
4. How does *complete elimination* differ from *fractional elimination?*
5. When can *intercompany profit* on intercompany inventory transfers be reported for *consolidated* reporting purposes?
6. Why are intercompany inventory transfers usually recorded at amounts *in excess of cost?*
7. Does the GAAP requirement to defer 100% of the intercompany profit associated with intercompany-acquired inventory fit under the *economic unit concept* or the *parent company concept?*

EXERCISES

E 10–1 **Unrealized Profit Determination** A parent and its subsidiary had intercompany inventory transactions in 19X1 as follows:

	Total	Resold	On Hand
Intercompany sales	$240,000		$36,000
Intercompany cost of sales	(180,000)		
Gross Profit	$ 60,000		

R.quired 1. Complete the analysis.
2. Prepare the inventory transfer elimination entry required in consolidation at the end of 19X1.

E 10–2 **Unrealized Profit Determination** In 19X1, a parent and its 100%-owned subsidiary had intercompany inventory transactions. The following account balances pertain to this inventory:

Account	Plax Inc.	Strax Inc.
Income Statement (19X1)		
Sales	$650,000	
Cost of sales	(300,000)	
Intercompany sales		$500,000
Intercompany cost of sales		(350,000)
Balance Sheet (12/31/X1)		
Intercompany-acquired inventory	$200,000	

Required 1. What is the unrealized intercompany profit at year-end?
2. What amounts should be reported in the Consolidated column?

E 10–3 **Reverse Analysis—Matrix** In consolidation at the end of 19X1, the Cost of Sales account was credited for $60,000 as a result of a posting from the inventory transfer elimination entry. During 19X1 the subsidiary sold 60% of the inventory it had acquired from the parent in 19X1. The parent's markup was 25% of its cost.

Required Prepare a matrix analysis of intercompany transfers for 19X1 (use the format shown in the chapter).

E 10–4 **Reverse Analysis—Matrix** In consolidation at the end of 19X1, the Intercompany-Acquired Inventory account was credited for $25,000 to change from the new basis of accounting to the old basis of accounting. During 19X1, the subsidiary charged its Cost of Sales $400,000 as a result of having sold intercompany-acquired inventory. The parent's markup was 20% of the transfer price.

Required Prepare a matrix analysis of intercompany transfers for 19X1 (use the format shown in the chapter).

E 10–5 **Realized Profit Calculation—Two Years of Downstream Transfers** In 19X2, Soxa Inc., a 100%-owned subsidiary of Poxa Inc., resold for $90,000 inventory it had purchased in 19X1 for $70,000 from Poxa. Poxa's cost was $40,000. Also in 19X2, Poxa sold inventory costing $250,000 to Soxa for $400,000. At the end of 19X2, Soxa reported $72,000 of this 19X2 intercompany-acquired inventory in its balance sheet, the remaining 19X2 intercompany-acquired inventory having been resold for $500,000.

Required 1. How much intercompany profit was realized in 19X2?
2. For Module 1 only: Prepare the general ledger adjusting entry(ies) pertaining to unrealized intercompany profit at the end of 19X2.

E 10–6 **Realized Profit Calculation—Two Years of Upstream Transfers** In 19X2, Perl Inc. resold for $85,000 inventory it had purchased in 19X1 for $60,000 from Serl Inc., its 60%-owned subsidiary. Serl's cost was $40,000. Also in 19X2, Perl purchased for $600,000 inventory costing Serl $450,000. At the end of 19X2, Perl reported $100,000 of this 19X2 intercompany-acquired inventory in its balance sheet, the remaining 19X2 intercompany-acquired inventory having been resold for $475,000.

Required 1. How much intercompany profit was realized in 19X2?
2. For Module 1 only: Prepare the general ledger adjusting entry(ies) pertaining to unrealized intercompany profit at the end of 19X2.

E 10–7 **Calculating Consolidated Cost of Sales** During 19X1, Pyra Inc. sold inventory costing $150,000 to Syra Inc., its 100%-owned subsidiary, on the same terms as sales to third parties. As of 12/31/X1, Syra had resold 90% of this inventory. Information regarding *total sales* for both entities follows:

	Pyra Inc.	Syra Inc.
Sales	$1,200,000	$900,000
Cost of sales	(720,000)	(600,000)
Gross Profit	$ 480,000	$300,000

Required 1. What is the reportable consolidated sales for 19X1?
2. What is the reportable consolidated cost of sales for 19X1?

E 10–8 **Calculating Consolidated Cost of Sales** During 19X1, Sora Inc., an 80%-owned subsidiary, sold inventory costing $420,000 to Pora Inc., its parent, on the same terms as sales to third parties. As of 12/31/X1, Pora reported $90,000 of this inventory in its balance sheet. Information regarding *total sales* for both entities follows:

	Pora Inc.	Sora Inc.
Sales	$4,000,000	$1,100,000
Cost of sales	(1,400,000)	(770,000)
Gross Profit	$2,600,000	$ 330,000

Required 1. What is the reportable consolidated sales for 19X1?
2. What is the reportable consolidated cost of sales for 19X1?

E 10–9   **Multiple Year Elimination Entries—Downstream Sales**   In 19X1, Pobe Inc. sold inventory costing $50,000 to its 75%-owned subsidiary, Sobe Inc., for $70,000. Sobe resold a portion of this inventory for $65,000 in 19X1. At the end of 19X1, Sobe's balance sheet showed $21,000 of intercompany-acquired inventory on hand. Sobe resold this remaining inventory in 19X3 for $28,000.

Required   1. Prepare the general ledger adjusting entry required for 19X1, 19X2, and 19X3, if necessary, under the complete equity method. **Omit this requirement if you are using Modules 2 or 3.**
　　　2. Prepare the consolidation elimination entry(ies) at the end of 19X1, 19X2, and 19X3 relating to this intercompany inventory sales.
　　　3. At what amount is the inventory reported in the consolidated statements at the end of 19X1 and 19X2?

E 10–10   **Calculating the NCI Deduction—Downstream Transfers**   In 19X1, Pebb Inc. sold inventory costing $200,000 to its 90%-owned subsidiary, Sebb Inc., for $250,000. At the end of 19X1, Sebb reported $30,000 of this inventory in its balance sheet. Sebb also reported net income of $100,000 for 19X1.

Required   Calculate the noncontrolling interest deduction to be reported in the 19X1 consolidated income statement.

E 10–11   **Calculating the NCI Deduction—Upstream Transfers**   In 19X1, Sote Inc., an 80%-owned subsidiary of Pote Inc., sold inventory costing $300,000 to Pote for $400,000. Pote resold $340,000 of this inventory in 19X1 for $510,000. Sote also reported net income of $200,000 for 19X1, disregarding any unrealized intercompany profit at the end of 19X1.

Required   Calculate the noncontrolling interest deduction to be reported in the 19X1 consolidated income statement.

E 10–12   **Multiple Year Elimination Entries—Upstream Sales**   In 19X1, Pota Inc. acquired inventory from Sota Inc., its 75%-owned subsidiary, for $100,000. Sota's cost was $80,000. At 12/31/X1, Pota's balance sheet showed $40,000 of intercompany-acquired inventory on hand. A portion of this inventory was resold during 19X1 for $90,000. Pota resold this remaining inventory in 19X3 for $52,000.

Required   1. Prepare the general ledger adjusting entry(ies) required for 19X1, 19X2, and 19X3, if necessary, under the complete equity method. **Omit this requirement if you are using Modules 2 or 3.**
　　　2. Prepare the consolidation elimination entry(ies) at the end of 19X1, 19X2, and 19X3 relating to this intercompany inventory sales.
　　　3. At what amount is the inventory reported in the consolidated statements at the end of 19X1 and 19X2?

E 10–13   **Issuing PCO Statements**   Selected items from the financial statements of Poly Inc. and Soly Inc., a 70%-owned subsidiary, at 12/31/X1, are as follows:

	P Company	S Company
Income Statement		
Sales		$280,000
Cost of sales		(125,000)
Intercompany sales	$150,000	
Intercompany cost of sales	(90,000)	
Net income		100,000
Statement of Retained Earnings		
Dividends declared		–0–
Balance Sheet		
Inventory—intercompany acquired		25,000
Investment in subsidiary, 1/1/X1	500,000	

Required   1. Calculate the unrealized intercompany profit at the end of 19X1.
　　　2. If the parent issued PCO statements in addition to consolidated statements, what amounts would appear in the PCO statements as a result of (1) the intercompany inventory transfers, (2) Soly's operations, and (3) Poly's investment in Soly?
　　　3. Repeat requirement 2 but assume that the transfers are upstream.

E 10–14 **Lower-of-Cost-or-Market Adjustment** In 19X1, Pondo Inc. sold inventory costing $60,000 to its subsidiary for $70,000. At the end of 19X1, the subsidiary recorded a lower-of-cost-or-market adjustment relating to this inventory, 60% of which had been sold during 19X1.

Required Determine the amount at which the inventory should be reported in consolidation, assuming that the adjustment was

1. $3,000.   **2.** $6,000.

PROBLEMS

P 10–1* **Consolidation Worksheet: Downstream Transfers—100% Ownership** In 19X1, Peta Inc. created a 100-owned subsidiary, Seta Inc. In 19X5, intercompany inventory transfers occurred for the first time. Comparative financial statements are as follows:

	Peta Inc.		Seta Inc.
	Cost Method[a]	Equity Method[b]	
Income Statement (19X5)			
Sales	$200,000	$200,000	$125,000
Cost of sales	(114,000)	(114,000)	(56,000)
Expenses	(84,000)	(84,000)	(53,000)
Intercompany Accounts			
Dividend income	11,000		
Equity in net income		16,000	
Intercompany sales	70,000	70,000	
Intercompany cost of sales	(40,000)	(40,000)	
Net Income	$ 43,000	$ 48,000	$ 16,000
Balance Sheet (as of 12/31/X5)			
Inventory:			
From vendors	$ 55,000	$ 55,000	
Intercompany			$ 14,000
Investment in subsidiary	10,000	100,000	
Other assets	345,000	345,000	286,000
Total Assets	$410,000	$500,000	$300,000
Liabilities	$170,000	$170,000	$200,000
Common stock	130,000	130,000	10,000
Retained earnings	110,000	200,000	90,000
Total Liabilities and Equity	$410,000	$500,000	$300,000
Dividends declared—19X5	$ 23,000	$ 23,000	$ 11,000

[a]Use this column if you are using Module 3.
[b]Use this column if you are using Modules 1 or 2.

Required **1.** Determine the unrealized profit at year-end by preparing a matrix analysis. (For Module 1 only: Also make the necessary year-end adjusting entry [for unrealized profit] required for this module. Adjust the statements accordingly.)
2. Prepare all consolidation entries as of 12/31/X5.
3. Prepare a consolidation worksheet at 12/31/X5.

*The financial statement information presented for problems accompanied by asterisks is also provided on Model 10 (filename: MODEL10) of the software file disk that is available with the text, allowing the problem to be worked on the computer. **To the right of the conceptual analysis of the investment account, prepare and present (1) a matrix analysis and (2) your elimination entries other than the basic elimination entry** in the space provided.

P 10-2* **Consolidation Worksheet: Upstream Transfers—90% Ownership** In 19X2, Pino Inc. created a 90%-owned subsidiary, Sino Inc. In 19X5, intercompany inventory transfers occurred for the first time. Comparative financial statements are as follows:

	Pino Inc.		Sino Inc.
	Cost Method[a]	Equity Method[b]	
Income Statement (19X5)			
Sales	$630,000	$630,000	$ 90,000
Cost of sales	(475,000)	(475,000)	(25,000)
Expenses	(95,000)	(95,000)	(45,000)
Intercompany Accounts			
Dividend income	27,000		
Equity in net income		63,000	
Intercompany sales			250,000
Intercompany cost of sales			(200,000)
Net Income	$ 87,000	$123,000	$ 70,000
Balance Sheet (as of 12/31/X5)			
Inventory:			
From vendors	$ 65,000	$ 65,000	$ 90,000
Intercompany	50,000	50,000	
Investment in subsidiary	108,000	198,000	
Other assets	487,000	487,000	310,000
Total Assets	$710,000	$800,000	$400,000
Liabilities	$255,000	$255,000	$180,000
Common stock	300,000	300,000	120,000
Retained earnings	155,000	245,000	100,000
Total Liabilities and Equity	$710,000	$800,000	$400,000
Dividends declared—19X5	$ 80,000	$ 80,000	$ 30,000

[a]Use this column if you are using Module 3.
[b]Use this column if you are using Modules 1 or 2.

Required **1.** Determine the unrealized profit at year-end by preparing a matrix analysis. (For Module 1 only: Also make the necessary year-end adjusting entry(ies) [for unrealized profit] required for this module. Adjust both sets of statements accordingly.)
2. Prepare all consolidation entries as of 12/31/X5.
3. Prepare a consolidation worksheet at 12/31/X5.

P 10-3 **Consolidation Entries: 100% Ownership—Downstream Transfers; Other Intercompany Transactions** On 1/1/X1, Pom Inc. created a 100%-owned subsidiary, Som Inc., with a $25,000 common stock investment.

Additional Information **1.** During 19X1, Pom sold inventory to Som at a profit. The markup percentage was 40% of the transfer price. At 12/31/X1, Som had on hand intercompany-acquired inventory that had cost Pom $18,000. Downstream sales for 19X1 totaled $160,000. Of this amount, Som had paid Pom $130,000 by year-end.
2. On 12/30/X1, Pom allocated $4,000 of previously recorded advertising expense to Som, which received the allocation notice on 1/4/X2.
3. During 19X1, Pom charged Som $5,000 for management services, of which $3,000 had been paid by year-end.
4. On 12/29/X1, Som declared a cash dividend of $10,000. The dividend was paid on 1/3/X2.
5. Som reported retained earnings of $22,000 in its 12/31/X1 balance sheet.
6. No other intercompany transactions occurred during 19X1.

Required Prepare all consolidation entries at the end of 19X1.

P 10-4* **Consolidation Worksheet: Downstream Multiple Year Transfers— 100% Ownership** Comparative financial statements of Puma Inc. and its 100%-owned subsidiary, Suma Inc. (created five years ago), are as follows:

	Puma Inc.		
	Cost Method[a]	Equity Method[b]	Suma Inc.
Income Statement (19X5)			
Sales	$500,000	$500,000	$200,000
Cost of sales	(290,000)	(290,000)	(110,000)
Expenses	(205,000)	(205,000)	(60,000)
Intercompany Accounts			
Dividend income	10,000		
Equity in net income		30,000	
Intercompany sales	100,000	100,000	
Intercompany cost of sales	(60,000)	(60,000)	
Net Income	$ 55,000	$ 75,000	$ 30,000
Statement of Retained Earnings (19X5)			
Balances, 1/1/X5	$150,000	$190,000	$ 40,000
+ Net income	55,000	75,000	30,000
– Dividends declared	(25,000)	(25,000)	(10,000)
Balances, as of 12/31/X5	$180,000	$240,000	$ 60,000
Balance Sheet (as of 12/31/X5)			
Inventory:			
From vendors	$200,000	$200,000	$ 67,500
Intercompany			12,500
Investment in subsidiary	80,000	140,000	
Other assets	500,000	500,000	160,000
Total Assets	$780,000	$840,000	$240,000
Liabilities	$300,000	$300,000	$100,000
Common stock	300,000	300,000	80,000
Retained earnings	180,000	240,000	60,000
Total Liabilities and Equity	$780,000	$840,000	$240,000

[a]Use this column if you are using Module 3.
[b]Use this column if you are using Modules 1 or 2.

Additional Information
1. At 12/31/X4 (the preceding year-end), Suma had on hand inventory it had acquired in 19X4 from Puma at a cost of $24,000. Puma's cost was $20,000. Suma resold all of this inventory in 19X5 for $35,000.
2. No general ledger entries were made at the end of 19X4 or 19X5 to defer unrealized intercompany profit.

Required
1. Determine the unrealized profit at year-end by preparing a matrix analysis. (For Module 1 only: Also make the necessary (1) beginning-of-year correcting entry and (2) end-of-year adjusting entry to reflect the deferral of profit on Pebb's books. Adjust the statements accordingly.)
2. Prepare all consolidation entries as of 12/31/X5.
3. Prepare a consolidation worksheet at 12/31/X5.

P 10–5* **Consolidation Worksheet: Upstream Multiple Year Transfers—80% Ownership** Comparative financial statements of Pebb Inc. and its 80%-owned subsidiary, Sebb Inc. (created five years ago), are as follows:

	Pebb Inc.		
	Cost Method[a]	Equity Method[b]	Sebb Inc.
Income Statement (19X5)			
Sales	$600,000	$600,000	$ 85,000
Cost of sales	(350,000)	(350,000)	(50,000)
Expenses	(150,000)	(150,000)	(40,000)
Intercompany Accounts			
Dividend income	8,000		
Equity in net income		20,000	
Intercompany sales			90,000
Intercompany cost of sales			(60,000)
Net Income	$108,000	$120,000	$ 25,000

continued

	Pebb Inc.		Sebb Inc.
	Cost Method[a]	Equity Method[b]	
Statement of Retained Earnings (19X5)			
Balances, 1/1/X5	$106,000	$150,000	$ 55,000
+ Net income	108,000	120,000	25,000
− Dividends declared	(50,000)	(50,000)	(10,000)
Balances, 12/31/X5	$164,000	$220,000	$ 70,000
Balance Sheet (12/31/X5)			
Inventory			
From vendors	$150,000	$150,000	$ 50,000
Intercompany	15,000	15,000	
Investment in subsidiary	84,000	140,000	
Other assets	363,000	363,000	180,000
Total Assets	$612,000	$668,000	$230,000
Liabilities	$298,000	$298,000	$ 55,000
Common stock	150,000	150,000	105,000
Retained earnings	164,000	220,000	70,000
Total Liabilities and Equity	$612,000	$668,000	$230,000

[a]Use this column if you are using Module 3.
[b]Use this column if you are using Modules 1 or 2.

Additional Information

1. At 12/31/X4 (the preceding year-end), Pebb had on hand inventory it had acquired in 19X4 from Sebb at a cost of $25,000. Sebb's cost was $10,000. Pebb resold all of this inventory in 19X5 for $44,000.
2. No general ledger entries were made at the end of 19X4 or 19X5 to defer unrealized intercompany profit.

Required

1. Determine the unrealized profit at year-end by preparing a matrix analysis. (For Module 1 only: Also make the necessary (1) beginning-of-year correcting entry and (2) end-of-year adjusting entry to reflect the deferral of profit on Sebb's books. Adjust both sets of statements accordingly.)
2. Prepare all consolidation entries as of 12/31/X5.
3. Prepare a consolidation worksheet at 12/31/X5.

P 10–6 **Consolidation Entries: 100% Ownership—Two Years of Downstream Transfers; Other Intercompany Transactions; LCM Adjustment** On 1/1/X1, Pano Inc. created a 100%-owned subsidiary, Sano Inc., with a $40,000 common stock investment.

Additional Information

1. During 19X1, Pano sold inventory costing $63,000 to Sano at a transfer price of $90,000; Sano fully paid Pano in 19X1 for this purchase. At 12/31/X1 Sano reported intercompany-acquired inventory of $20,000 in its balance sheet. In 19X2, all of this inventory was resold for $15,000.
2. During 19X2, Pano sold inventory to Sano for $200,000, of which Sano had paid Pano $170,000 by year-end. The markup percentage was 33 1/3% of Pano's cost. At 12/31/X2, Sano had on hand intercompany-acquired inventory that had cost Pano $24,000. Sano made a $3,000 lower-of-cost-or-market adjustment at the end of 19X2 on this inventory.
3. On 12/31/X2, Pano allocated $12,000 of previously recorded insurance expenses to Sano, which received the allocation notice on 1/1/X3.
4. During 19X2, Pano charged Sano $33,000 for technical services relating to research and development work, of which Sano paid $22,000 by year-end.
5. On 12/31/X2, Sano declared a cash dividend of $20,000; it was paid on 1/4/X3. In 19X1, Sano declared and paid cash dividends of $15,000 (60% of its 19X1 net income).
6. Sano reported retained earnings of $44,000 in its 12/31/X2 balance sheet.
7. No other intercompany transactions occurred during 19X2 or 19X1.

Required

1. Prepare a T-account analysis of Sano's retained earnings account for 19X1 and 19X2.
2. Prepare a matrix analysis for the inventory transfers for 19X1 and 19X2.
3. Prepare all consolidation entries at the end of 19X2.

P 10–7 **Spreadsheet Automation of the Matrix Analysis and the Inventory Transfer Elimination Entry** Before working this assignment, you should first have worked Problems 10–1, 10–2, 10–4, or 10–5 using MODEL10 of the software package that accompanies the text. Second, read an EXCEL or LOTUS 1–2–3 manual regarding the distinction between **relative addresses** and **absolute (nonrelative) addresses** so that you use the proper address type in working this assignment. (The formula (D54), for instance, is an absolute address, whereas deleting the dollar signs changes the formula to a relative address.) Next perform the following steps for automating the inventory transfer elimination entry on the spreadsheet.

Required 1. To the right of the spreadsheet area that displays the posting of the basic elimination entry, program the matrix analysis format (including account descriptions) shown on page 346 of the text.
2. In the matrix analysis you programmed in requirement 1, insert formulas to automatically insert from either the P Company column or the S Company column of the worksheet amounts for (a) intercompany sales, (b) intercompany cost of sales, and (c) intercompany inventory on hand. To allow this matrix analysis to accommodate the possibility of intercompany inventory transfers being either downstream or upstream, you must program a logic formula (using the =IF function of EXCEL or the @IF function of LOTUS 1–2–3) for inserting amounts from either (1) the parent's column or (2) the subsidiary's column, as appropriate.
3. In the matrix analysis, program formulas to automatically insert the remaining five missing amounts.
4. Below the matrix analysis, program the required elimination entry that is derived from this analysis. Insert formulas to bring the appropriate amounts from the matrix analysis.
5. In the Debit and Credit columns of the consolidation worksheet, program formulas to bring forward the amounts that are in the elimination entry you prepared in the preceding instruction.

✳ THINKING CRITICALLY ✳

✳ CASES ✳

C 10–1 **If Better Off Economically, Why Not Report It?** In late 19X1, Pia Inc. sold inventory costing $60,000 to its 60%-owned subsidiary, Sia Inc., for $100,000 with payment being made on delivery. As of 12/31/X1, Sia had not resold any of this inventory.

Required 1. Does the fact that Pia was paid in full have any significance as to whether $40,000 or only $24,000 (60% of $40,000) should be deferred for consolidated reporting purposes? Why or why not?
2. Have Pia's stockholders benefited economically to the extent of $16,000 (40% × $40,000)? Why or why not?
3. If the FASB were to change GAAP so that this $16,000 could be recognized in 19X1 for reporting to Pia's stockholders, can you think of any accompanying provisions that should be stipulated to maintain financial reporting integrity?

C 10–2 ***Sole* Versus *Shared* Control: Does It Really Matter? (Including a Library Assignment)** Alpha Inc. and Beta Inc. are co-owners (50% owners) of a joint venture, Ventura Inc., created in early 19X1 to build and market a newly conceived product. Neither company has control of the joint venture; all important decisions require the agreement of *both* investor entities.

Alpha sells a key inventory component to the joint venture at a markup, the transfer price having been negotiated with and approved by Beta. During 19X1, Ventura (with Beta's formal approval) purchased $1,000,000 of this component from Alpha. Alpha's cost was $600,000. As of 12/31/X1, Ventura had not shipped any of its newly conceived product.

Required 1. Because this is a *shared control* situation instead of a *sole control* situation, can Alpha report 50% of the intercompany profit for 19X1?
2. In your library, or using the FASB's financial accounting research system (FARS) if available in your school's computer center (normally stored on a file-server computer), find the AICPA's *Accounting Interpretations of APB Opinion No. 18*, "The Equity Method of Accounting for Investments in Common Stock," issued in February 1972. Does it allow any profit recognition in this situation?

✳ PERSONAL SITUATIONS: ETHICS AND INTERPERSONAL SKILLS ✳

PS 10–1   **Ethics: Let's Try a Squeeze Play!**   Your client owns 90% of the outstanding common stock of a company to which it sells inventory at a markup. From the date the subsidiary was acquired four years ago, the noncontrolling interest shareholders have stubbornly refused to sell their shares to the parent. During the current year audit, you noticed that the intercompany transfer prices increased by 25% from previous years, which greatly decreased the profitability of the subsidiary. The controller's explanation was that the transfer prices are negotiated and are what they are. Also during the current year, the parent ordered the subsidiary to stop paying dividends, which in the past approximated its net income.

Required   Is it ethical to increase the transfer prices and change the dividend policy to pressure the non-controlling interest shareholders to sell their shares to the parent?

PS 10–2   **Interpersonal Skills: Looking Back?**   Work environments vary greatly.

Required   No matter where you will have worked in life, which one thing—usually above all other things—will (1) you always remember about where you worked and (2) your co-workers always remember about you?

ANSWERS TO SELF-STUDY QUESTIONS

1. a   **2.** a   **3.** d   **4.** c   **5.** a   **6.** b   **7.** b   **8.** e   **9.** d   **10.** e   **11.** b

12. a ($1,250,000 – $500,000 = $750,000; $750,000 + $700,000 – $240,000 markup = $1,210,000)

■APPENDIX

INVENTORY TRANSFERS FOR BRANCHES

RECORDING INVENTORY TRANSFERS TO BRANCHES

Many home offices, most notably in the retail industry, transfer inventory to their branches. Some home offices transfer inventory to their branches at cost; others at above cost. When transfers are made at above the home office's cost, the unrealized intracompany profit issue discussed in Chapter 10 arises. In recording inventory transfers to branches, two accounting procedures are possible (both of which are widely used): **sales treatment** and **nonsales treatment.**

SALES TREATMENT

Some home offices record these transfers as sales—using the Intracompany Sales account—as if the transfers were between a parent and a subsidiary. In such cases, the procedures to (1) prevent reporting these internal sales for combined reporting purposes and (2) defer any unrealized intracompany profit at the combined reporting date are identical to those shown in each of the modules in Chapter 10 for intercompany sales involving subsidiaries. Accordingly, we need not illustrate these procedures here.

NONSALES TREATMENT

If sales treatment is not used, the home office's intracompany markup is recorded in the **Deferred Profit** account at the transfer date—**pending sale of the inventory by the branch to an outside third party.** Upon sale by the branch, the home office adjusts the Deferred Profit account downward, with the offsetting credit being to the Branch Income account—thereby reporting as income the previously deferred profit.

INVOICING THE BRANCH

Regardless of which procedure is used and regardless of whether a markup exists, an **intracompany billing** is prepared so that the inventory can be removed from the home office books and **recorded on the branch books at the invoiced amount.** Otherwise, the branch would have sales but not cost of sales, making it impossible to meaningfully evaluate branch profitability. The remainder of this appendix discusses nonsales treatment.

GENERAL LEDGER JOURNAL ENTRIES BY EACH ACCOUNTING ENTITY

Assume the following information pertaining to a home office intracompany inventory transfer at above cost to a branch:

1. During 19X1, a home office transferred inventory costing $60,000 to its branch at a transfer price of $100,000. The $40,000 markup is 40% of the transfer price.

2. At December 31, 19X1, the branch reported $20,000 of this intracompany-acquired inventory in its balance sheet. Because the markup is 40% of the $20,000 transfer price, $8,000 of intracompany profit must be deferred at the end of 19X1. Consequently, $32,000 of the intracompany profit (40% of $80,000) has been realized from a combined reporting perspective as the result of branch inventory sales to outside parties.

3. The branch reported net income of $24,000 for 19X1.

Illustration 10–19 shows the **general ledger journal entries** made by each accounting entity to record the inventory transfer. Also shown are the **home office's year-end adjustments** to (1) reduce the Deferred Profit account by $32,000 to obtain the proper year-end balance of $8,000 and (2) increase the carrying value of the home office's Investment in Branch account for the branch's $24,000 of reported net income. For simplicity, we assume that each entity uses a **perpetual inventory system.**

REVIEW POINTS FOR ILLUSTRATION 10–19 Note the following:

1. If instead the inventory had been transferred at the home office's cost, the branch would have reported an additional $32,000 of net income or $56,000.

2. As a result of the home office's two year-end adjusting entries, the Branch Income account has a $56,000 balance—the same balance that would have existed if the inventory had been transferred at the home office's cost in the first place.

ENTRIES REQUIRED IN CONSOLIDATION

In consolidation at December 31, 19X1, the following entry is made to reduce the branch's reported cost of sales to the amount it would have been had the inventory been transferred at the home office's cost:

WORKSHEET ENTRY ONLY	Branch Income	32,000	
	Cost of Sales		32,000

In addition, it is necessary to reclassify the $8,000 adjusted balance in the Deferred Profit account—an account for internal reporting purposes only—against the branch's $20,000 of intracompany-acquired inventory as reported in the branch's year-end balance sheet. This entry results in reporting the inventory at the home office's cost of $12,000—the only valid amount for combined reporting purposes. This entry follows:

WORKSHEET ENTRY ONLY	Deferred Profit	8,000	
	Inventory		8,000

ILLUSTRATION 10–19	General Ledger Journal Entries for Intracompany Transfers Above Cost to Branch—Perpetual Inventory System

Home Office Books				Branch Books			
Investment in Branch	100,000			Inventory	100,000		
Inventory		60,000		Home Office Capital		100,000	
Deferred Profit		40,000		To record inventory			
To record inventory transferred to branch.				acquired from home office.			
Deferred Profit	32,000						
Branch Income		32,000					
To adjust the deferred profit account to $8,000.							
Investment in Branch	24,000						
Branch Income		24,000					
To record branch's reported earnings.							

In addition, **the basic elimination entry** is needed. Assuming that the Home Office Equity account had a preclosing balance of $60,000 at December 31, 19X1, that entry is as follows:

WORKSHEET ENTRY ONLY	Branch Income 24,000	
	Home Office Capital (preclosing balance) 60,000	
	Investment in Branch	84,000

The preceding three worksheet entries are posted to the combining worksheet in Illustration 10–20.

PERIODIC INVENTORY SYSTEM

When each accounting entity uses a periodic inventory system, the **general ledger journal entries** made to record the inventory transfer are as follows:

Home Office Books		**Branch Books**	
Investment in		Purchases from	
Branch 100,000		Home Office 100,000	
Purchases Sent		Home Office	
to Branch	60,000	Capital......	100,000
Deferred Profit..	40,000		

The Purchases Sent to Branch account—**a contra Purchases account**—and the Purchases from Home Office account are both closed at year-end when each accounting entity prepares its adjusting entry to record cost of sales and adjust its inventory balance to reflect the physical quantities on hand.

EXERCISES FOR APPENDIX

E 10–1A **Account Analysis** A home office shipped inventory to its branch during 19X1. The following information has been obtained from the records of the home office and the branch at the end of 19X1:

	Total	Resold	On Hand
Purchases from home office	$90,000		$18,000
Purchases sent to branch	75,000	____	____
Markup	$15,000		

Required
1. Complete the analysis.
2. Prepare the branch's entry to record cost of sales, assuming that the branch purchased all of its inventory from the home office and reported a beginning inventory of $24,000, all of which had been sold by the end of the current year. (Assume the same markup percentage for 19X0 as for 19X1.)
3. Prepare an analysis of the Deferred Profit account for the year.

E 10–2A **Deferred Profit Adjustment** A home office ships inventory to its branch at 125% of cost. The Deferred Profit account balance at the beginning of the year was $4,000. During the year, the home office billed the branch $70,000 for inventory transfers from the home office. At year-end, the branch's balance sheet shows $16,000 of inventory on hand acquired from the home office.

Required
1. Determine the amount of the branch's beginning inventory (as shown in its prior year-end financial statements).
2. Prepare the branch's entry to record cost of sales.
3. Calculate the year-end adjustment to the Deferred Profit account and show the adjusting journal entry.

ILLUSTRATION 10–20	Intracompany Inventory Transfers Above Cost to Branch

Home Office and Branch
Combining Worksheet as of December 31, 19X1

	Home Office	Branch	Combining Entries Dr.	Combining Entries Cr.	Combined
Income Statement (19X1)					
Sales	500,000	234,000			734,000
Cost of sales	(300,000)	(110,000)		32,000(2)	(378,000)
Expenses	(190,000)	(100,000)			(290,000)
Branch income	56,000		24,000(1)		–0–
			32,000(2)		
Net Income	66,000	24,000	56,000	32,000	66,000
Statement of Retained Earnings/					
Analysis of Home Office Capital					
Retained Earnings, 1/1/X1	100,000	n/a			100,000
Home office equity **(preclosing)**	n/a	60,000[a]	60,000(1)		–0–
+ Net income	66,000	24,000	56,000	32,000	66,000
– Dividends declared	(51,000)				(51,000)
Balances, 12/31/X1	115,000	84,000	116,000	32,000	115,000
Balance Sheet					
Cash	61,000	15,000			76,000
Accounts receivable	75,000	37,000			112,000
Inventory:					
Vendor acquired	110,000	35,000			145,000
Intercompany acquired		20,000		8,000(3)	12,000
Deferred profit	(8,000)		8,000(3)		–0–
Investment branch	84,000			84,000(1)	–0–
Land	220,000	30,000			250,000
Buildings and equipment	500,000	150,000			650,000
Accumulated depreciation	(320,000)	(13,000)			(333,000)
Total Assets	722,000	274,000	8,000	92,000	912,000
Liabilities	407,000	190,000			597,000
Common stock	200,000				200,000
Retained earnings	115,000				115,000
Home office capital		84,000	116,000	32,000	–0–
Total Liabilities and Equity ..	722,000	274,000	116,000	32,000	912,000
Proof of debit and credit postings			124,000	124,000	

Explanation of entries:
(1) The basic elimination entry.
(2) The recognized profit elimination entry.
(3) The deferred profit elimination entry.
[a] This amount is the balance in the home office capital account excluding the current year earnings ($84,000 ending balance − $24,000 of 19X1 earnings).

E 10–3A **Entries and Adjustments** During 19X1, a home office shipped inventory costing $55,000 to the branch at a transfer price of $66,000. At 12/31/X1 the branch reported $18,000 of this inventory in its balance sheet. At the end of 19X0, the branch reported $6,000 of intracompany-acquired inventory— all of which was sold in 19X1. For 19X1, the branch reported $25,000 of net income in its financial statements.

Required 1. Prepare the home office and branch journal entries to record the inventory transfer, assuming that a perpetual inventory system is used.

2. Prepare the branch's entry to record cost of sales for 19X1.

3. Prepare the home office's year-end adjusting entries relating to the Deferred Profit account and the branch's reported income.

4. Prepare the entry required in consolidation to report the proper amount for the branch's cost of sales.

E 10–4A **Reverse Analysis** A home office transfers inventory to its branch at a 20% markup. During 19X1, it transferred inventory costing $80,000 to the branch. At year-end, the home office adjusted its Deferred Profit account downward by $18,200. The branch's year-end balance sheet shows $4,800 of inventory acquired from the home office.

Required Calculate the home office's cost of the branch's beginning inventory.

PROBLEMS FOR APPENDIX

P 10–1A* **Combining Worksheet** The 12/31/X1 financial statements of Hom Inc. and its branch are as follows:

	Home Office	Branch
Income Statement (19X1)		
Sales	$ 700,000	$200,000
Cost of sales	(390,000)	(149,000)
Selling expenses	(42,000)	(11,000)
Administrative expenses	(28,000)	(4,000)
Interest expense	(40,000)	
Branch income	50,000	
Income before Income Taxes	$ 250,000	$ 36,000
Income tax expense @ 40%	(100,000)	
Net Income	$ 150,000	$ 36,000
Balance Sheet		
Cash	$ 90,000	$ 10,000
Accounts receivable, net	80,000	20,000
Inventory:		
Acquired from vendors	180,000	10,000
Acquired from home office		36,000
Deferred profit	(6,000)	
Fixed assets, net	770,000	140,000
Investment in branch	176,000	
Total Assets	$1,290,000	$216,000
Payables and accruals	$ 200,000	$ 40,000
Long-term debt	350,000	
Common stock	500,000	
Retained earnings	240,000	
Home office capital		176,000
Total Liabilities and Equity	$1,290,000	$216,000
Dividends declared during 19X1	$ 110,000	

Required 1. Prepare a combining statement worksheet as of 12/31/X1.

*The financial statement information presented for appendix problems accompanied by asterisks is also provided on Model 10B (filename: MODEL10B) of the software file disk that is available for use with the text, allowing the problem to be worked on the computer.

2. Complete the following analysis of the branch's inventory:

	Transfers above Cost	Transfers at Cost	Markup
Purchases (from vendors)	$75,000	$75,000	$ –0–
Purchases from home office			
Total Inventory Available for Sale			
Less—Ending Inventory:			
Acquired from vendors			
Acquired from home office			
Cost of Sales	$_____	$_____	$_____

3. Prepare the entry that the branch made to record cost of sales.
4. Calculate the markup percentage.

P 10–2A   **COMPREHENSIVE Combining Worksheet: Sales**   The preclosing trial balances of Homex Inc. and its branch for the year ended 12/31/X3, prior to adjusting and closing entries, are as follows:

	Home Office Dr.	Home Office Cr.	Branch Dr.	Branch Cr.
Cash	$ 35,000		$ 10,000	
Accounts receivable, net	80,000		50,000	
Inventory, 1/1/X3				
Acquired from vendors	230,000		50,000	
Acquired from home office			20,000	
Deferred profit		$ 25,000		
Fixed assets, net	870,000		90,000	
Investment in branch	155,000			
Payables and accruals		221,000		$ 45,000
Long-term debt		400,000		
Common stock		300,000		
Retained earnings, 1/1/X3		350,000		
Home office capital				115,000
Sales		960,000		320,000
Purchases	800,000		120,000	
Purchases from home office			90,000	
Purchases sent to branch		84,000		
Selling expenses	81,000		34,000	
Administrative expenses	54,000		16,000	
Interest expense	35,000			
	$2,340,000	$2,340,000	$480,000	$480,000
Inventory per physical count on 12/31/X3:				
Acquired from vendors	$180,000		$20,000	
Acquired from home office			30,000	

Additional Information
1. Inventory transferred to the branch from the home office is billed at 125% of cost.
2. The home office billed the branch $15,000 for inventory it shipped to the branch on 12/28/X3; the branch received and recorded this shipment on 1/2/X4.
3. The branch remitted $25,000 cash to the home office on 12/31/X3; the home office received and recorded this remittance on 1/4/X4.
4. The Deferred Profit account is normally adjusted at the end of the year.
5. Income taxes are to be recorded at 40%.
6. No dividends were declared during the year.

Required   **1.** Prepare the year-end adjusting entries to
   a. Bring the intracompany accounts into agreement. (Be sure to adjust the other accounts in the trial balance as appropriate.)

b. Adjust the inventory accounts and record cost of sales.
2. Complete the following analysis of the branch's inventory:

	Transfers above Cost	Transfers at Cost	Markup
Beginning inventory	$	$	$
Acquired from vendors			
Acquired from home office			
+ Purchases (from vendors)			
+ Purchases from home office	_____	_____	_____
Total Inventory Available for Sale			
Less—Ending inventory:			
Acquired from vendors			
Acquired from home office	_____	_____	_____
Cost of Sales	_____	_____	_____

3. Prepare the following year-end adjusting entries to
   a. Record the branch's income on the home office's books.
   b. Adjust the Deferred Profit account to the proper balance.
   c. Provide for income taxes.
4. Prepare the year-end closing entries for the home office and the branch.
5. Prepare a combining statement worksheet as of 12/31/X3 after completing requirements 1–4.

INTERCOMPANY FIXED ASSET TRANSFERS

11

LEARNING OBJECTIVES

TO UNDERSTAND

- The concept of changing, in consolidation, from the new basis of accounting to the old basis of accounting.
- The additional complexities associated with intercompany fixed asset transfers in relation to intercompany inventory transfers.
- The procedures to defer recognition of unrealized intercompany gains or losses on fixed asset transfers.

It's easy to have principles when you're rich. The important thing is to have principles when you're poor.

RAY KROC (FOUNDER OF MCDONALD'S)

This chapter discusses how to change from the new to the old basis of accounting when fixed assets have been transferred at a gain or loss among entities of a consolidated group. By changing the basis of accounting in consolidation, the intercompany gain or loss[1] is eliminated for consolidated reporting purposes—as intercompany profit or loss on inventory transfers is eliminated (see Chapter 10).

FREQUENCY AND TYPES OF DEPRECIABLE FIXED ASSET TRANSFERS

In practice, intercompany fixed asset transfers occur much less frequently than intercompany inventory transfers. Furthermore, intercompany transfers of **nondepreciable** fixed assets occur much less frequently than intercompany transfers of **depreciable** fixed assets.

In the typical depreciable fixed asset transfer, the selling entity transfers a partially depreciated fixed asset that it has been using in its operations (occurs usually in horizontally integrated companies). Less frequently encountered are hybrid inventory/fixed asset transfers whereby the selling entity transfers inventory to the buying entity, which then capitalizes the equipment as a fixed asset (occurs usually in conglomerates). Sometimes one entity also leases equipment to another entity with the **lessor** using **sales-type** treatment and the **lessee** using **capital lease** treatment. We discuss only the first mentioned typical depreciable fixed asset transfer because the principles involved can be applied readily to these other situations.

DETAILED DEFERRAL PROCEDURES SHOWN IN MODULES

As was the case with inventory transfers in Chapter 10, detailed deferral procedures are presented in separate modules with each module being a self-contained independent module standing on its own when read in conjunction with the general material that precedes Module 1. The following are the three modules presented:

> **Module 1: The Complete Equity Method** (deferral occurs in the general ledger)
>
> **Module 2: The Partial Equity Method** (deferral occurs on the worksheet)
>
> **Module 3: The Cost Method** (deferral occurs on the worksheet)

I. SUMMARY OF GAAP REGARDING INTERCOMPANY TRANSACTIONS (DISCUSSED IN CHAPTERS 9 AND 10)

Recall from Chapters 9 and 10 the following GAAP requirements for preparing consolidated financial statements:

1. **All intercompany transactions** must be eliminated in consolidation to present the financial position and results of operations **as if the two separate legal entities were a single legal entity having a branch.**

2. For intercompany profit or gain associated with assets on hand at a reporting date, **the entire intercompany profit or gain must be eliminated.**

---

[1]*Historical Note:* During the Great Depression, many parent companies had entities within the consolidated group sell assets to one another to report profits in an attempt to maintain or increase the price of the parent's common stock. At that time, such intercompany gains were *not* required to be deferred for consolidated reporting purposes.

3. The concept of intercompany profit or gain to be eliminated is **gross profit.** For fixed assets, this means the selling entity's **gain (or loss)** on the intercompany sale of a fixed asset (transfer price – carrying value at the transfer date).

4. Any **income taxes (benefit)** recorded on such profits or gains (or losses) must also be deferred in consolidation. As in Chapter 10, we assume in our illustrations for simplicity that the elimination of the tax effects has already been recorded in the parent's or subsidiary's general ledger.

5. For **upstream transfers from partially owned subsidiaries,** the deferral of unrealized intercompany profit or gain **is shared with the noncontrolling interest.** Accordingly, intercompany gains or losses on fixed asset transfers require the same type of elimination treatment as for intercompany profits or losses on inventory transfers.

II CHANGING FROM THE *NEW BASIS* OF ACCOUNTING TO THE *OLD BASIS* OF ACCOUNTING IN CONSOLIDATION

Recall from Chapter 10 that when inventory was transferred within a consolidated entity at a transfer price above or below the selling entity's carrying value, the selling (transfer) price became the buying entity's cost, which became **a new basis of accounting** for the inventory on the buying entity's books. Also recall that for intercompany-acquired inventory still on hand at a consolidated reporting date, the intercompany profit elimination treatment resulted in reporting the inventory in consolidation at the selling entity's carrying value (usually acquisition cost) at the transfer date—**the old basis of accounting.**

Thus this elimination treatment achieved consolidated reporting results *as though* the transfer instead had been made at the selling entity's carrying value of the inventory rather than at a higher (or lower) amount. These same consolidated reporting results must be achieved for intercompany fixed asset transfers.

MAJOR POINT: ALL INTERCOMPANY TRANSFERS   The carrying value for any asset—**whether it be inventory, fixed assets, patents, copyrights, capitalized software, or some other asset**—of any company within a consolidated group cannot change for consolidated reporting purposes merely because the asset has been moved to a different location within the consolidated group.

DETERMINING AMOUNTS BASED ON THE OLD BASIS VERSUS AMOUNTS BASED ON THE NEW BASIS

HAVING A GAIN OR LOSS ON THE SALE CHANGES THE BASIS OF ACCOUNTING
The selling entity's intercompany gain or loss is calculated in the same manner as the sale of a fixed asset to an outside third party by comparing (1) the **sales price** (the proceeds) with (2) the **carrying value** of the asset (**acquisition cost** minus any **accumulated depreciation**) at the transfer date. For example, used equipment costing $40,000 and having accumulated depreciation of $25,000 at the transfer date has a **carrying value** of $15,000. If the intercompany sales price is $18,000, the selling entity reports a $3,000 intercompany gain ($18,000 – $15,000). The $18,000 amount becomes **the new cost basis** to the buying entity, which it uses for calculating depreciation on its books. Accordingly, selling the fixed asset at $3,000 more than the $15,000 carrying value increases the asset's basis of accounting by $3,000, allowing the buying entity to have $3,000 of **incremental cost basis** that will be depreciated in future periods.

CHANGING TO THE OLD BASIS OF ACCOUNTING IN THE BALANCE SHEET   The objective in consolidation is to report amounts based on **the old cost basis.** Thus the historical cost of the equipment must be reported at $40,000, not $18,000. Likewise, accumulated depreciation must be reported at the sum of (1) the $25,000 of accumulated depreciation at the transfer date and (2) any depreciation recorded after the transfer date based on the $15,000 carrying value at the transfer date—not on the $18,000 new cost basis.

CHANGING TO THE OLD BASIS OF ACCOUNTING IN THE INCOME STATEMENT
Depreciation expense reported on consolidated income statements for periods after the transfer date must be based on the $15,000 carrying value at the transfer date—not on the $18,000 new cost basis. Thus if the buying entity were to use a three-year life and record $6,000 of annual depreciation expense ($18,000 ÷ 3 years), a $1,000 adjustment is needed in consolidation to report annual depreciation expense of only $5,000 ($15,000 ÷ 3 years). Note that the **incremental depreciation expense** on the buying entity's books is solely attributable to the equipment's sale at a $3,000 gain.

USING AN INTERCOMPANY GAIN OR LOSS ACCOUNT INSTEAD OF INTERCOMPANY SALES AND INTERCOMPANY COST OF SALES ACCOUNTS

Another difference between intercompany inventory transfers and intercompany fixed asset transfers involves the income statement accounts used to record the transfers. Instead of using an Intercompany Sales account and a related Intercompany Cost of Sales account as it does for inventory transfers, the selling entity uses the lone Intercompany Gain (or Loss) account when it transfers fixed assets. This actually constitutes a slight simplification: only one income statement account instead of two need be eliminated in the year of the transfer.

III THE ADDITIONAL COMPLEXITIES OF FIXED ASSET TRANSFERS IN RELATION TO INVENTORY TRANSFERS

In comparison to the consolidation procedures for intercompany inventory transfers, the consolidation procedures pertaining to intercompany transfers of **nondepreciable** fixed assets are substantively the same, but the consolidation procedures pertaining to **depreciable** fixed assets are more involved.

NONDEPRECIABLE FIXED ASSET TRANSFERS

Because land is not depreciated, the entire unrealized intercompany gain or loss from a consolidated perspective is always associated with the cost of land as reported on the buying entity's books. Accordingly, the consolidation procedures merely result in adjusting the Land account upward or downward to reflect the old basis of accounting—as was done for intercompany-acquired inventory still on hand.

SUBSEQUENT DISPOSAL OF THE LAND From a consolidated perspective, the subsequent sale of the land to an outside third party is no different than reselling intercompany-acquired inventory to an outside third party. For intercompany inventory transfers at a profit, recall that (1) the buying entity's subsequent sale of that inventory to an outside third party caused the buying entity's Cost of Sales account to be overstated from a consolidated perspective and (2) the overstatement was eliminated in consolidation. Likewise, for the sale of intercompany-acquired land to an outside third party **at more than the buying entity's cost basis,** (1) the buying entity's **reported Gain on Sale of Land** account is also understated from a consolidated perspective to the extent that the selling entity records an **intercom-**

pany gain when the intercompany transfer occurred at an earlier date[2] and (2) this understatement must also be eliminated in consolidation.

For a sale of intercompany-acquired land to an outside third party **at less than the buying entity's cost,** (1) the buying entity's reported Loss on Sale of Land account is overstated from a consolidated perspective to the extent of an intercompany gain on the earlier transfer and (2) this overstatement must be eliminated in consolidation.

CONCLUDING POINT   Thus whether a nondepreciable asset continues to be held or is subsequently sold to an outside third party, the consolidation procedures for dealing with intercompany transfers of nondepreciable fixed assets are virtually identical to those used for intercompany inventory transfers.

DEPRECIABLE FIXED ASSET TRANSFERS

Because intercompany-acquired depreciable fixed assets are depreciated, any initially recorded **unrealized** intercompany gain (or loss) becomes lower and lower as time goes by—**from a consolidated perspective**—eventually becoming zero when the asset becomes fully depreciated. This occurs for depreciable fixed assets because (1) such assets are used to generate sales to outside third parties and (2) as long as such sales occur, a portion of them is effectively a recovery of the cost of depreciable fixed assets. In other words, a portion of the depreciable fixed asset—equal to the annual depreciation charge—is converted into cash each year. Thus **partial realization** of the buying entity's cost of the intercompany-acquired fixed asset occurs each year **as though a portion of the intercompany-acquired fixed assets were sold directly to outside third parties each year.**

This gradual reduction of the unrealized intercompany gain or loss over time slightly complicates the consolidation procedures because of the additional steps involved in comparing (1) the new basis of accounting amounts and (2) the old basis of accounting amounts. The difference in the amounts for the two bases reveals the amounts needed at each consolidation date to change to the old basis of accounting.

A DIFFERENT WAY TO VISUALIZE THE RESULT OF THE CONSOLIDATION PROCEDURES   The consolidation procedures for **intercompany gain** situations achieve the same result as though the intercompany gain had been deferred and then amortized to income in a manner that exactly **offsets (cancels out) the future incremental depreciation expense** that occurs each year because **the buying entity's new cost basis exceeded the selling entity's carrying value** at the transfer date. For **intercompany loss** situations, the consolidation procedures achieve the same result as though the intercompany loss had been deferred and then amortized to income in a manner that exactly **makes up the future depreciation expense shortage** that occurs each year because **the buying entity's new cost basis is below the selling entity's carrying value** at the transfer date.

---

[2]The terms *buying entity* and *selling entity* are used in the context of the intercompany transaction—not in the context of the transaction with the outside third party.

IV PROCEDURES FOR DEFERRING UNREALIZED INTERCOMPANY GAIN OR LOSS

MODULE 1 OVERVIEW

Recall from Chapter 10 that under the complete equity method, the parent defers its share of any unrealized intercompany profit (gain in this chapter) in its general ledger by adjusting its Investment in Subsidiary account, an adjustment reversed later when realization—from a consolidated perspective—occurs. In this chapter, the reversal occurs either (1) in a single year for nondepreciable fixed assets (as was the case for reselling inventory to an outside third party) or (2) in increments for depreciable fixed assets over the **new assigned remaining life** (the original remaining life becomes irrelevant).

As for recording general ledger adjusting entries for unrealized intercompany profit or gains, recall that (1) for **downstream transfers** the parent adjusts its Investment in Subsidiary account and (2) for **upstream transfers** the subsidiary adjusts the Deferred Profit account (a balance sheet account).

SECTION 1: TRANSFERS OF NONDEPRECIABLE ASSETS

DOWNSTREAM LAND TRANSFERS: GAIN SITUATIONS

For the following example, assume that P Company sells land costing $20,000 to its 100%-owned subsidiary, S Company, for $30,000 on January 1, 19X1.

CONSOLIDATION AT JANUARY 1, 19X1 If consolidation occurs as of January 1, 19X1—the transfer date—P Company makes the following **general ledger adjusting entry:**

Intercompany Gain Deferral	10,000	
Investment in Subsidiary		10,000

As discussed in Chapter 10, an additional column (Unrealized Gain in this chapter) is added to the conceptual analysis of the Investment account to track the unrealized gain. The balance in this column at any consolidation date is credited to the Land account in consolidation; the posting originates from the basic elimination entry.

Accordingly, in consolidation at the transfer date, the following two entries are made:

WORKSHEET ENTRIES ONLY	Intercompany Gain	10,000	
	Intercompany Gain *Deferral*		10,000
	Credit posting made from the basic elimination entry:		
	Land		10,000

The preceding worksheet entries are made at any other consolidation date in 19X1, assuming that S Company still owns the land at that (those) consolidation date(s).

SUBSEQUENT YEAR TREATMENT OF UNREALIZED GAIN

LAND *NOT* RESOLD AT THE END OF 19X2 If S Company still owns the land at December 31, 19X2, the only entry needed in consolidation is to post a credit to the

Land account for $10,000 (to bring S Company's $30,000 carrying value down to P Company's $20,000 cost, as was done in 19X1). As in 19X1, this $10,000 credit posting originates from the basic elimination entry.

LAND RESOLD BY THE END OF 19X3 If S Company sells the land in 19X3 for $32,000, it then reports a $2,000 gain ($32,000 – $30,000). The previously deferred intercompany gain of $10,000 has now been realized, however, making the reportable gain for consolidated reporting purposes $12,000 ($32,000 – $20,000). P Company makes the following **general ledger adjusting entry:**

Investment in Subsidiary	10,000	
Intercompany Gain Recognized		10,000

As a result of this entry, the $10,000 balance in the Unrealized Gain column in the conceptual analysis of the Investment account is extinguished. Consequently, only one entry is made in consolidation, as follows:

WORKSHEET ENTRIES ONLY

Intercompany Gain Recognized	10,000	
Gain on Sale of Land		10,000
To report the gain based on the old basis of accounting ($32,000–$20,000) instead of the new basis of accounting ($32,000–$30,000).		

DOWNSTREAM LAND TRANSFERS: LOSS SITUATIONS

When an entity transfers land **at below its carrying value,** it must defer the intercompany loss. The principle is the same as that for a transfer above its carrying value, but the debits and credits are reversed.

UPSTREAM LAND TRANSFERS

The procedures for an **upstream** land transfer parallel those shown in Chapter 10 for upstream inventory transfers. Recall that in those situations, the subsidiary deferred the intercompany gain (or loss) in its general ledger using a Deferred Profit (or Loss) account. Upstream transfers are discussed in the last half of Section 2 that follows.

SECTION 2: TRANSFERS OF DEPRECIABLE ASSETS

DOWNSTREAM EQUIPMENT TRANSFERS: GAIN SITUATIONS

Assume that the following downstream equipment transfer occurred between P Company and S Company, its 100%-owned subsidiary created several years ago:

	P Company	S Company
Sales price of equipment sold to S Company on January 1, 19X1		$18,000
Carrying value on P Company's books:		
Cost	$40,000	
Accumulated depreciation	(25,000)	15,000
Gain recorded by P Company		$ 3,000
New remaining life assigned		3 years

Note: For simplicity, we later assume that an administrative department of S Company uses the equipment. Thus the acquiring entity's depreciation expense on this equipment is included in its administrative expenses—not its cost of sales.

| ILLUSTRATION 11–1 | Conceptual Analysis of the Investment Account |

	Unrealized Gain	+	Parent's Investment Account	=	Subsidiary's Equity Accounts Common Stock	+	Retained Earnings
Balances, 1/1/X1	$ –0–		$100,000		$60,000		$ 40,000
+ Equity in net income			24,000				24,000
– Dividends			(4,000)				(4,000)
– IC[a] gain deferral	2,000		(2,000)				
Balances, 12/31/X1	$ 2,000		$118,000		$60,000		$ 60,000
+ Equity in net income			32,000				32,000
– Dividends			(12,000)				(12,000)
+ IC[a] gain recognized	(1,000)		1,000				
Balances, 12/31/X2	$ 1,000		$139,000		$60,000		$ 80,000
+ Equity in net income			25,000				25,000
– Dividends			(15,000)				(15,000)
+ IC[a] gain recognized	(1,000)		1,000				
Balances, 12/31/X3	$ –0–		$150,000		$60,000		$ 90,000

[a]IC is the abbreviation for *intercompany.*

GENERAL LEDGER ADJUSTING ENTRIES P Company makes the following **general ledger adjusting entries** as a result of transferring the asset at a $3,000 gain (which results in S Company's recording $1,000 of incremental depreciation expense each year):

December 31, 19X1 (the year of the transfer):

Intercompany Gain Deferral	2,000	
Investment in Subsidiary		2,000
To defer the intercompany gain unrealized at year-end (total gain of $3,000 – $1,000 realized in 19X1).		

December 31, 19X2, and December 31, 19X3:

Investment in Subsidiary	1,000	
Intercompany Gain Recognized		1,000
To recognize that portion of the intercompany gain realized during the year.		

Illustration 11–1 shows a conceptual analysis of P Company's Investment in Subsidiary account using assumed amounts for S Company's earnings, dividends, and equity account balances.

The consolidation entries to change to the old basis of accounting at any consolidation date are obtained by comparing (1) the existing account balances in each entity's books at that particular consolidation date—**new basis amounts**—with (2) the balances **(pro forma)** that should be reported in consolidation—**old basis amounts.** Illustration 11–2 shows such a comparison.

Illustration 11–3 shows a consolidation worksheet at December 31, 19X1.

UPSTREAM EQUIPMENT TRANSFERS: GAIN SITUATIONS

We now use the facts in the previous example except that we assume that (1) S Company is a 75%-owned created subsidiary and (2) the equipment transfer is upstream.

GENERAL LEDGER ADJUSTING ENTRIES S Company makes the following **general ledger adjusting entries** for 19X1, 19X2, and 19X3 in connection with the intercompany gain:

ILLUSTRATION 11–2	Basis of Accounting Analysis: Downstream Equipment Transfer: Gain Situation (100% ownership)

Analysis at the End of 19X1

	Actual Balances (new basis)		Reportable Balances (old basis)	Differences (to be posted as a Dr. [Cr.])
	P Company	S Company		
Income Statement (19X1)				
Depreciation expense		$ (6,000)	$ (5,000)	$ (1,000)
Intercompany gain	$3,000		–0–	3,000
Intercompany gain deferral	(2,000)		–0–	(2,000)
Balance Sheet (as of 12/31/X1)				
Cost		$18,000	$ 40,000	$ 22,000
Accumulated depreciation		(6,000)	(30,000)[a]	(24,000)

[a]Accumulated depreciation of $25,000 at the transfer date plus $5,000 of depreciation ($15,000 ÷ 3 years) for 19X1.

Consolidation Entries at December 31, 19X1

(1) The equipment change in basis elimination entry—P/L:

Intercompany Gain	3,000	
Intercompany Gain Deferral		2,000
Depreciation Expense		1,000

(2) The equipment change in basis elimination entry—B/S:

Equipment	22,000	
Accumulated Depreciation		22,000
Accumulated Depreciation **(this credit posting originates from the basic elimination entry)**		2,000

Analysis at the End of 19X2

	Actual Balances (new basis)		Reportable Balances (old basis)	Differences (to be posted as a Dr. [Cr.])
	P Company	S Company		
Income Statement (19X2)				
Depreciation expense		$ (6,000)	$ (5,000)	$ (1,000)
Intercompany gain recognized	$1,000		–0–	1,000
Balance Sheet (as of 12/31/X2)				
Cost		$ 18,000	$ 40,000	$ 22,000
Accumulated depreciation		(12,000)	(35,000)[a]	(23,000)

[a]Accumulated depreciation of $25,000 at the transfer date plus $5,000 of depreciation ($15,000 ÷ 3 years) for 19X1 and $5,000 for 19X2.

Consolidation Entries at December 31, 19X2

(1) The equipment change in basis elimination entry—P/L:

Intercompany Gain Recognized	1,000	
Depreciation Expense		1,000

(2) The equipment change in basis elimination entry—B/S:

Equipment	22,000	
Accumulated Depreciation		22,000
Accumulated Depreciation **(this credit posting originates from the basic elimination entry)**		1,000

December 31, 19X1 (the year of the transfer):

Intercompany Gain Deferral	2,000	
Deferred Gain (a balance sheet account)		2,000
To defer the intercompany gain unrealized at year-end (total gain of $3,000 − $1,000 realized in 19X1).		

MODULE 1

THE COMPLETE EQUITY METHOD

| ILLUSTRATION 11–3 | THE COMPLETE EQUITY METHOD Downstream Equipment Transfer: Gain Situation (100% ownership); Year of Transfer |

P Company and S Company
Consolidation Worksheet as of December 31, 19X1

	P Company	100%-owned S Company	Consolidation Entries Dr.	Consolidation Entries Cr.	Consolidated
Income Statement (19X1)					
Sales	597,000	234,000			831,000
Cost of sales	(360,000)	(110,000)			(470,000)
Expenses	(190,000)	(100,000)		1,000(2)	(289,000)
Intercompany Accounts					
Equity in net income (of S Co.) ..	24,000		24,000(1)		–0–
Intercompany gain	3,000		3,000(2)		–0–
Intercompany gain deferral	(2,000)			2,000(2)	–0–
Net Income	72,000	24,000	27,000	3,000	72,000
Statement of Retained Earnings					
Balances, 1/1/X1	140,000	40,000	40,000(1)		140,000
+ Net income	72,000	24,000	27,000	3,000	72,000
– Dividends declared	(51,000)	(4,000)		4,000(2)	(51,000)
Balances, 12/31/X1	161,000	60,000	67,000	7,000	161,000
Balance Sheet					
Cash	65,000	51,000			116,000
Accounts receivable	75,000	37,000			112,000
Inventory	110,000	55,000			165,000
Investment in S Co.	118,000			118,000(1)	–0–
Land	220,000	30,000			250,000
Buildings and equipment	500,000	150,000	22,000(3)		672,000
				2,000(1)	–0–
				22,000(3)	
Accumulated depreciation	(320,000)	(13,000)			(357,000)
Total Assets	768,000	310,000	22,000	142,000	958,000
Payables and accruals	157,000	70,000			227,000
Long-term debt	250,000	120,000			370,000
Common stock	200,000	60,000	60,000(1)		200,000
Retained earnings	161,000	60,000	67,000	7,000	161,000
Total Liabilities and Equity	768,000	310,000	127,000	7,000	958,000
Proof of debit and credit postings			149,000	149,000	

Explanation of entries:
(1) The basic elimination entry.
(2) The equipment change in basis elimination entry—P/L.
(3) The equipment change in basis elimination entry—B/S.

December 31, 19X2, and December 31, 19X3:

Deferred Gain	1,000	
Intercompany Gain Recognized		1,000
To recognize that portion of the intercompany gain realized during the year.		

Illustration 11–4 shows (1) the consolidation entries required at the end of 19X1 and 19X2 and (2) the basis of accounting analyses for these dates. (No special adjustments are required to the noncontrolling interest because the amounts are properly established in the basic elimination entry.) Because of the similarities of the consolidation entries for upstream and downstream transfers, we do not present a consolidation worksheet for either 19X1 or 19X2.

ILLUSTRATION 11–4	Basis of Accounting Analysis: Upstream Equipment Transfer: Gain Situation (75% ownership)

Analysis at the End of 19X1

	Actual Balances (new basis)		Reportable Balances (old basis)	Differences (to be posted as a Dr. [Cr.])
	P Company	S Company		
Income Statement (19X1)				
Depreciation expense	$ (6,000)		$ (5,000)	$ (1,000)
Intercompany gain		$ 3,000	–0–	3,000
Intercompany gain deferral		(2,000)	–0–	(2,000)
Balance Sheet (as of 12/31/X1)				
Cost	$18,000		$ 40,000	$ 22,000
Accumulated depreciation	(6,000)		(30,000)[a]	(24,000)
Deferred gain		$(2,000)	–0–	2,000

[a]Accumulated depreciation of $25,000 at the transfer date plus $5,000 of depreciation ($15,000 ÷ 3 years) for 19X1.

Consolidation Entries at December 31, 19X1

(1) The equipment change in basis elimination entry—P/L:

Intercompany Gain	3,000	
Intercompany Gain Deferral		2,000
Depreciation Expense		1,000

(2) The equipment change in basis elimination entry—B/S:

Equipment	22,000	
Deferred Gain (a balance sheet account)	2,000	
Accumulated Depreciation		24,000

Analysis at the End of 19X2

	Actual Balances (new basis)		Reportable Balances (old basis)	Differences (to be posted as a Dr. [Cr.])
	P Company	S Company		
Income Statement (19X2)				
Depreciation expense	$ (6,000)		$ (5,000)	$ (1,000)
Intercompany gain recognized		$ 1,000	–0–	1,000
Balance Sheet (12/31/X2)				
Cost	$ 18,000		$ 40,000	$ 22,000
Accumulated depreciation	(12,000)		(35,000)[a]	(23,000)
Deferred gain		$(1,000)	–0–	1,000

[a]Accumulated depreciation of $25,000 at the transfer date plus $5,000 of depreciation ($15,000 ÷ 3 years) for 19X1 and $5,000 for 19X2.

Consolidation Entries at December 31, 19X2

(1) The equipment change in basis elimination entry—P/L:

Intercompany Gain Recognized	1,000	
Depreciation Expense		1,000

(2) The equipment change in basis elimination entry—B/S:

Equipment	22,000	
Deferred Gain (a balance sheet account)	1,000	
Accumulated Depreciation		23,000

END

MODULE 1

THE COMPLETE EQUITY METHOD

MODULE 2 OVERVIEW

Recall from Chapter 10 that under the partial equity method, the deferral of any unrealized intercompany profit (gain in this chapter) is accomplished entirely on the consolidation worksheet. As a result, in 100% ownership situations the consolidated net income and consolidated retained earnings are less than the parent's net income and retained earnings, respectively.

SECTION 1: TRANSFERS OF NONDEPRECIABLE ASSETS

DOWNSTREAM LAND TRANSFERS: GAIN SITUATIONS

When land is transferred at above its carrying value, the selling entity records a gain. In preparing consolidated statements, the gain is not reportable and must be deferred until the acquiring entity resells the land. For example, assume that P Company sold land costing $20,000 to its 100%-owned subsidiary, S Company, for $30,000 on January 1, 19X1.

CONSOLIDATION AT JANUARY 1, 19X1   If consolidation occurs as of January 1, 19X1—the transfer date—the following **entry is made in consolidation:**

WORKSHEET ENTRY ONLY	Intercompany Gain 10,000	
	Land	10,000
	To change to the old basis of accounting.	

The preceding worksheet entry is made at any other consolidation date in 19X1, assuming that S Company still owns the land at that (these) consolidation date(s).

Note that if P Company were to issue **parent-company-only statements,** it first would make the following "financial statement adjusting entry" (as opposed to a general ledger adjusting entry) to its PCO statements:

Intercompany Gain 10,000
     Deferred Gain (a balance sheet account) 10,000

SUBSEQUENT YEAR TREATMENT OF UNREALIZED GAIN

LAND NOT RESOLD AT THE END OF 19X2   If S Company still owns the land at December 31, 19X2, the following entry is made in consolidation at that date:

WORKSHEET ENTRY ONLY	Retained Earnings, 1/1/X2 10,000	
	Land	10,000
	To change to the old basis of accounting.	

LAND RESOLD BY THE END OF 19X3   If S Company subsequently sells the land in 19X3 for $32,000, it then reports a $2,000 gain ($32,000 – $30,000). The reportable gain in the consolidated income statement is $12,000 ($32,000 – $20,000), however, because the previously deferred $10,000 intercompany gain has now been realized. Accordingly, the following entry is required in consolidation at the end of 19X3:

WORKSHEET ENTRY ONLY	Retained Earnings, 1/1/X3 10,000	
	Gain on Sale of Land	10,000
	To report the gain based on the old basis of accounting	
	($32,000 – $20,000) instead of the new basis of	
	accounting ($32,000 – $30,000).	

DOWNSTREAM LAND TRANSFERS: LOSS SITUATIONS

When land is transferred **at below its carrying value,** the intercompany loss must be deferred. The principle is the same as that for a transfer above its carrying value, but the debits and credits are reversed.

UPSTREAM LAND TRANSFERS

When the land transfer is **upstream,** the procedures parallel those shown in Chapter 10 for upstream inventory transfers. Upstream transfers are discussed and illustrated in the last half of Section 2 that follows.

SECTION 2: TRANSFERS OF DEPRECIABLE ASSETS

DOWNSTREAM EQUIPMENT TRANSFERS: GAIN SITUATIONS

Assume that the following downstream equipment transfer occurred between P Company and S Company, its 100%-owned subsidiary created several years ago:

	P Company	S Company
Sales price of equipment sold to S Company		
on January 1, 19X1		$18,000
Carrying value on P Company's books		
Cost	$40,000	
Accumulated depreciation	(25,000)	15,000
Gain recorded by P Company		$ 3,000
New remaining life assigned		3 years

Note: For simplicity, we later assume that an administrative department of S Company uses the equipment. Thus the acquiring entity's depreciation expense on this equipment is included in its administrative expenses—not its cost of sales.

The consolidation entry to change to the old basis of accounting at any consolidation date can be obtained by comparing (1) the existing account balances in each entity's books at that particular consolidation date—**new basis amounts**—with (2) the balances **(pro forma)** that should be reported in consolidation—**old basis amounts.** Illustration 11–5 shows such a comparison using the preceding facts as well as the required entry to change to the old basis of accounting in consolidation at December 31, 19X1 and 19X2.

Illustration 11–6 shows a consolidation worksheet at December 31, 19X1 (the transfer year).

MODULE 2

THE PARTIAL EQUITY METHOD

ILLUSTRATION 11–5	Basis of Accounting Analysis: Downstream Equipment Transfer: Gain Situation (100% ownership)

Analysis at the End of 19X1

	Actual Balances (new basis)		Reportable Balances (old basis)	Differences (to be posted as a Dr. [Cr.])
	P Company	S Company		
Income Statement (19X1)				
Depreciation expense		$ (6,000)	$ (5,000)	$ (1,000)
Intercompany gain	$3,000		–0–	3,000
Balance Sheet (12/31/X1)				
Cost		$18,000	$40,000	$22,000
Accumulated depreciation		(6,000)	(30,000)[a]	(24,000)

[a]Accumulated depreciation of $25,000 at the transfer date plus $5,000 of depreciation ($15,000 ÷ 3 years) for 19X1.

Consolidation Entry at December 31, 19X1

(1) The equipment change in basis elimination entry:

Intercompany Gain	3,000	
Equipment	22,000	
Depreciation Expense		1,000
Accumulated Depreciation		24,000

Note: The desired effect on retained earnings at 12/31/X1 occurs as a result of carrying forward amounts from the net income line in the income statement.

Analysis at the End of 19X2

	Actual Balances (new basis)		Reportable Balances (old basis)	Differences (to be posted as a Dr. [Cr.])
	P Company	S Company		
Income Statement (19X2)				
Depreciation expense		$ (6,000)	$ (5,000)	$ (1,000)
Balance Sheet (as of 12/31/X2)				
Cost		$18,000	$40,000	$22,000
Accumulated depreciation		(12,000)	(35,000)[a]	(23,000)
Retained earnings, 1/1/X2	$2,000[b]		–0–	2,000

[a]Accumulated depreciation of $25,000 at the transfer date plus $5,000 of depreciation ($15,000 ÷ 3 years) for 19X1 and $5,000 for 19X2.

[b]Intercompany gain of $3,000 – $1,000 of incremental depreciation expense recorded on S Company's books in 19X1 that flows through to P Company's books as a result of applying the equity method of accounting.

Consolidation Entry at December 31, 19X2

(1) The equipment change in basis elimination entry:

Retained earnings, 1/1/X2	2,000	
Equipment	22,000	
Depreciation Expense		1,000
Accumulated Depreciation		23,000

ILLUSTRATION 11–6	THE PARTIAL EQUITY METHOD Downstream Equipment Transfer: Gain Situation (100% ownership); Year of Transfer

P Company and S Company
Consolidation Worksheet as of December 31, 19X1

	P Company	100%-owned S Company	Consolidation Entries Dr.	Consolidation Entries Cr.	Consolidated
Income Statement (19X1)					
Sales	597,000	234,000			831,000
Cost of sales	(360,000)	(110,000)			(470,000)
Expenses	(190,000)	(100,000)		1,000(2)	(289,000)
Intercompany Accounts					
Equity in net income (of S Co.) . .	24,000		24,000(1)		–0–
Intercompany gain	3,000		3,000(2)		–0–
Net Income	74,000	24,000	27,000	1,000	72,000
Statement of Retained Earnings					
Balances, 1/1/X1	140,000	40,000	40,000(1)		140,000
+ Net income	74,000	24,000	27,000	1,000	72,000
– Dividends declared	(51,000)	(4,000)		4,000(1)	(51,000)
Balances, 12/31/X1	163,000	60,000	67,000	5,000	161,000
Balance Sheet					
Cash	65,000	51,000			116,000
Accounts receivable	75,000	37,000			112,000
Inventory	110,000	55,000			165,000
Investment in S Co.	120,000			120,000(1)	–0–
Land	220,000	30,000			250,000
Buildings and equipment	500,000	150,000	22,000(2)		672,000
Accumulated depreciation	(320,000)	(13,000)		24,000(2)	(357,000)
Total Assets	770,000	310,000	22,000	144,000	958,000
Payables and accruals	157,000	70,000			227,000
Long-term debt	250,000	120,000			370,000
Common stock	200,000	60,000	60,000(1)		200,000
Retained earnings	163,000	60,000	67,000	5,000	161,000
Total Liabilities and Equity	770,000	310,000	127,000	5,000	958,000
Proof of debit and credit postings			149,000	149,000	

Explanation of entries:
(1) The basic elimination entry.
(2) The equipment change in basis elimination entry.

UPSTREAM EQUIPMENT TRANSFERS: GAIN SITUATIONS

When a depreciable asset transfer is upstream, the consolidation entries are the same as those previously shown for a downstream transfer. When the subsidiary is partially owned, however, an additional entry is needed to share the deferral of the unrealized gain with the noncontrolling interest.

We now use the facts for the previous example except that we assume that (1) S Company is a 75%-owned subsidiary and (2) the equipment transfer is upstream. Illustrations 11–7 and 11–8 show (1) the consolidation entries required at the end of 19X1 and 19X2, respectively (including the adjustments required to the noncontrolling interest to share the deferral), and (2) the basis of accounting analyses for these dates that were used to develop the entry to change to the old basis of accounting.

Illustration 11–9 shows a consolidation worksheet for 19X1.

| **ILLUSTRATION 11-7** | **Basis of Accounting Analysis: Upstream Equipment Transfer—Gain Situation (75% ownership); Year of Transfer** |

	Analysis at the End of 19X1			
	Actual Balances (new basis)		**Reportable Balances (old basis)**	**Differences (to be posted as a Dr. [Cr.])**
	P Company	**S Company**		
Income Statement (19X1)				
Depreciation expense	$ (6,000)		$ (5,000)	$ (1,000)
Intercompany gain		$3,000	–0–	3,000
Balance Sheet (12/31/X1)				
Cost	$18,000		$40,000	$22,000
Accumulated depreciation	(6,000)		(30,000)[a]	(24,000)

[a]Accumulated depreciation of $25,000 at the transfer date plus $5,000 of depreciation ($15,000 ÷ 3 years) for 19X1.

Consolidation Entries at December 31, 19X1

(1) The equipment change in basis elimination entry:

Intercompany Gain	3,000	
Equipment	22,000	
Depreciation Expense		1,000
Accumulated Depreciation		24,000

(2) The sharing of the deferral elimination entry:

NCI in Net Assets	500	
NCI in Net Income		500
(25% of $2,000 of unrealized intercompany gain at 12/31/X1)		

Note: The desired effect on retained earnings at 12/31/X1 occurs as a result of carrying forward amounts from the net income line in the income statement.

| **ILLUSTRATION 11-8** | **Basis of Accounting Analysis: Upstream Equipment Transfer—Gain Situation (75% ownership); Year After Year of Transfer** |

	Analysis at the End of 19X2			
	Actual Balances (new basis)		**Reportable Balances (old basis)**	**Differences (to be posted as a Dr. [Cr.])**
	P Company	**S Company**		
Income Statement (19X2)				
Depreciation expense	$ (6,000)		$ (5,000)	$ (1,000)
Balance Sheet (12/31/X2)				
Cost	$18,000		$40,000	$22,000
Accumulated depreciation	(12,000)		(35,000)[a]	(23,000)
Retained Earnings, 1/1/X2	2,000[b]		–0–	2,000

[a]Accumulated depreciation of $25,000 at the transfer date plus $5,000 of depreciation ($15,000 ÷ 3 years) for 19X1 and $5,000 for 19X2.

[b]Intercompany gain of $3,000 – $1,000 of incremental depreciation expense in 19X1— the $3,000 gain flows through to P Company's books as a result of applying the equity method of accounting.

Consolidation Entries at December 31, 19X2

(1) The equipment change in basis elimination entry:

Retained Earnings, 1/1/X2	2,000	
Equipment	22,000	
Depreciation Expense		1,000
Accumulated Depreciation		23,000

(2) The sharing of the deferral elimination entry:

NCI in Net Income (25% of $1,000 intercompany gain realized in 19X2)	250	
NCI in Net Assets (25% of $1,000 intercompany gain unrealized at 12/31/X2) . . .	250	
Retained Earnings, 1/1/X2 (25% of $2,000 intercompany gain unrealized at 1/1/X2)		500

ILLUSTRATION 11–9 | **THE PARTIAL EQUITY METHOD** Upstream Equipment Transfer: Gain Situation (75% ownership); Year of Transfer

P Company and S Company
Consolidation Worksheet as of December 31, 19X1

	P Company	75%-owned S Company	Consolidation Entries Dr.	Consolidation Entries Cr.	Consolidated
Income Statement (19X1)					
Sales	600,000	231,000			831,000
Cost of sales	(360,000)	(110,000)			(470,000)
Expenses	(190,000)	(100,000)		1,000(2)	(289,000)
Intercompany Accounts					
Equity in net income	18,000		18,000(1)		–0–
Intercompany gain		3,000	3,000(2)		–0–
Net Income	68,000	24,000	21,000	1,000	72,000
NCI in net income			6,000(1)	500(3)	(5,500)[a]
CI in net income			27,000	1,500	66,500
Statement of Retained Earnings					
Balances, 1/1/X1	130,000	40,000	40,000(1)		130,000
+ Net income	68,000	24,000	27,000	1,500	66,500
– Dividends declared	(51,000)	(4,000)		4,000(1)	(51,000)
Balances, 12/31/X1	147,000	60,000	67,000	5,500	145,500
Balance Sheet					
Cash	79,000	51,000			130,000
Accounts receivable	75,000	37,000			112,000
Inventory	110,000	55,000			165,000
Investment in S Co.	90,000			90,000(1)	–0–
Land	220,000	30,000			250,000
Buildings and equipment	500,000	150,000	22,000(2)		672,000
Accumulated depreciation	(320,000)	(13,000)		24,000(2)	(357,000)
Total Assets	754,000	310,000	22,000	114,000	972,000
Payables and accruals	157,000	70,000			227,000
Long-term debt	250,000	120,000			370,000
NCI in net assets			500(3)	30,000(1)	29,500
Common stock	200,000	60,000	60,000(1)		200,000
Retained earnings	147,000	60,000	67,000	5,500	145,500
Total Liabilities and Equity	754,000	310,000	127,500	35,500	972,000
Proof of debit and credit postings			149,500	149,500	

[a]Proof: Subsidiary's reported net income of $24,000 − $2,000 of unrealized gain at 12/31/X1 = $22,000; $22,000 × 25% = $5,500.

Explanation of entries:

(1) The basic elimination entry.
(2) The equipment change in basis elimination entry.
(3) The sharing of the unrealized gain elimination entry.

MODULE 2

THE PARTIAL EQUITY METHOD

END

MODULE 3 OVERVIEW

Recall from Chapter 10 that under the cost method, the deferral of any unrealized intercompany profit (gain in this chapter) is accomplished entirely on the consolidation worksheet. As a result, in 100% ownership situations the consolidated net income and consolidated retained earnings are *less* than the parent's net income and retained earnings, respectively.

SECTION 1: TRANSFERS OF NONDEPRECIABLE ASSETS

DOWNSTREAM LAND TRANSFERS: GAIN SITUATIONS

When land is transferred at above its carrying value, the selling entity records a gain. In preparing consolidated statements, the gain is not reportable and must be deferred until the acquiring entity resells the land. For example, assume that P Company sold land costing $20,000 to its 100%-owned subsidiary, S Company, for $30,000 on January 1, 19X1.

CONSOLIDATION AT JANUARY 1, 19X1   If a consolidation occurs as of January 1, 19X1—the transfer date—the following **entry is made in consolidation:**

WORKSHEET ENTRY ONLY	Intercompany Gain	10,000	
	Land		10,000
	To change to the old basis of accounting.		

The preceding worksheet entry is made at any other consolidation date in 19X1, assuming that S Company still owns the land at that (these) consolidation date(s).

Note that if P Company were to issue **parent-company-only statements,** it first would make the following "financial statement adjusting entry" (as opposed to a general ledger adjusting entry) to its PCO statements:

Intercompany Gain	10,000	
Deferred Gain (a balance sheet account).		10,000

SUBSEQUENT YEAR TREATMENT OF UNREALIZED GAIN

LAND *NOT* RESOLD AT THE END OF 19X2   If S Company still owns the land at December 31, 19X2, it makes the following entry in consolidation at that date:

WORKSHEET ENTRY ONLY	Retained Earnings, 1/1/X2	10,000	
	Land		10,000
	To change to the old basis of accounting.		

LAND RESOLD BY THE END OF 19X3   If S Company subsequently sells the land in 19X3 for $32,000, it then reports a $2,000 gain ($32,000 – $30,000). The reportable gain in the consolidated income statement is $12,000 ($32,000 – $20,000), however, because the previously deferred $10,000 intercompany gain has now been realized. Accordingly, the following entry is required in consolidation at the end of 19X3:

WORKSHEET ENTRY ONLY	Retained Earnings, 1/1/X3	10,000	
	Gain on Sale of Land		10,000
	To report the gain based on the old basis of accounting ($32,000 – $20,000) instead of the new basis of accounting ($32,000 – $30,000).		

DOWNSTREAM LAND TRANSFERS: LOSS SITUATIONS

When land is transferred **at below its carrying value,** the intercompany loss must be deferred. The principle is the same as that for a transfer above its carrying value, but the debits and credits are reversed.

UPSTREAM LAND TRANSFERS

When a land transfer is **upstream,** the procedures parallel those shown in Chapter 10 for upstream inventory transfers. Upstream transfers are discussed and illustrated in the last half of Section 2 that follows.

SECTION 2: TRANSFERS OF DEPRECIABLE ASSETS

DOWNSTREAM EQUIPMENT TRANSFERS: GAIN SITUATIONS

Assume that the following downstream equipment transfer occurred between P Company and S Company, its 100%-owned subsidiary created several years ago:

	P Company	S Company
Sales price of equipment sold to S Company on January 1, 19X1		$18,000
Carrying value on P Company's books		
Cost	$40,000	
Accumulated depreciation	(25,000)	15,000
Gain recorded by P Company		$ 3,000
New remaining life assigned		3 years

Note: For simplicity, we later assume that an administrative department of S Company uses the equipment. Thus the acquiring entity's depreciation expense on this equipment is included in its administrative expenses—not its cost of sales.

The consolidation entry to change to the old basis of accounting at any consolidation date can be obtained by comparing (1) the existing account balances in each entity's books at that particular consolidation date—**new basis amounts**—with (2) the balances **(pro forma)** that should be reported in consolidation—**old basis amounts.** Illustration 11–10 shows such a comparison using the preceding facts as well as the required entry to change to the old basis of accounting in consolidation at December 31, 19X1 and 19X2.

Illustration 11–11 shows a consolidation worksheet at December 31, 19X1 (the transfer year).

ILLUSTRATION 11–10	Basis of Accounting Analysis: Downstream Equipment Transfer—Gain Situation (100% ownership)

Analysis at the End of 19X1

	Actual Balances (new basis)		Reportable Balances (old basis)	Differences (to be posted as a Dr. [Cr.])
	P Company	S Company		
Income Statement (19X1)				
Depreciation expense		$ (6,000)	$ (5,000)	$ (1,000)
Intercompany gain	$3,000		–0–	3,000
Balance Sheet (12/31/X1)				
Cost		$18,000	$40,000	$22,000
Accumulated depreciation		(6,000)	(30,000)[a]	(24,000)

[a]Accumulated depreciation of $25,000 at the transfer date plus $5,000 of depreciation ($15,000 ÷ 3 years) for 19X1.

Consolidation Entry at December 31, 19X1

Intercompany Gain	3,000	
Equipment	22,000	
Depreciation Expense		1,000
Accumulated Depreciation		24,000

Note: The desired effect on retained earnings at 12/31/X1 occurs as a result of carrying forward amounts from the net income line in the income statement.

Analysis at the End of 19X2

	Actual Balances (new basis)		Reportable Balances (old basis)	Differences (to be posted as a Dr. [Cr.])
	P Company	S Company		
Income Statement (19X2)				
Depreciation expense		$ (6,000)	$ (5,000)	$ (1,000)
Balance Sheet (12/31/X2)				
Cost		$18,000	$40,000	$22,000
Accumulated depreciation		(12,000)	(35,000)[a]	(23,000)
Retained earnings, 1/1/X2	2,000[b]		–0–	2,000

[a]Accumulated depreciation of $25,000 at the transfer date plus $5,000 of depreciation ($15,000 ÷ 3 years) for 19X1 and $5,000 for 19X2.

[b]Intercompany gain of $3,000 − $1,000 of incremental depreciation expense recorded on S Company's books in 19X1 that flows through to P Company's books as a result of applying the equity method of accounting.

Consolidation Entry at December 31, 19X2

Retained Earnings, 1/1/X2	2,000	
Equipment	22,000	
Depreciation Expense		1,000
Accumulated Depreciation		23,000

ILLUSTRATION 11–11	THE COST METHOD Downstream Equipment Transfer: Gain Situation (100% ownership); Year of Transfer

P Company and S Company
Consolidation Worksheet as of December 31, 19X1

	P Company	100%-owned S Company	Consolidation Entries Dr.	Consolidation Entries Cr.	Consolidated
Income Statement (19X1)					
Sales	597,000	234,000			831,000
Cost of sales	(360,000)	(110,000)			(470,000)
Expenses	(190,000)	(100,000)		1,000(3)	(289,000)
Intercompany Accounts					
Dividend income (from S Co.) . . .	4,000		4,000(2)		–0–
Intercompany gain	3,000		3,000(3)		–0–
Net Income	54,000	24,000	7,000	1,000	72,000
Statement of Retained Earnings					
Balances, 1/1/X1	100,000	40,000			140,000
+ Net income	54,000	24,000	7,000	1,000	72,000
– Dividends declared	(51,000)	(4,000)		4,000(2)	(51,000)
Balances, 12/31/X1	103,000	60,000	7,000	5,000	161,000
Balance Sheet					
Cash	65,000	51,000			116,000
Accounts receivable	75,000	37,000			112,000
Inventory	110,000	55,000			165,000
Investment in S Co.	60,000			60,000(1)	–0–
Land	220,000	30,000			250,000
Buildings and equipment	500,000	150,000	22,000(3)		672,000
Accumulated depreciation	(320,000)	(13,000)		24,000(3)	(357,000)
Total Assets	710,000	310,000	22,000	84,000	958,000
Payables and accruals	157,000	70,000			227,000
Long-term debt	250,000	120,000			370,000
Common stock	200,000	60,000	60,000(1)		200,000
Retained earnings	103,000	60,000	7,000	5,000	161,000
Total Liabilities and Equity	710,000	310,000	67,000	5,000	958,000
Proof of debit and credit postings			89,000	89,000	

Explanation of entries:
(1) The basic elimination entry.
(2) The intercompany dividend elimination entry.
(3) The equipment change in basis elimination entry.

MODULE 3

THE COST METHOD

UPSTREAM EQUIPMENT TRANSFERS: GAIN SITUATIONS

When a depreciable asset transfer is upstream, the consolidation entries are the same as those previously shown for a downstream transfer. When a subsidiary is partially owned, however, an additional entry is needed to share the deferral of the unrealized gain with the noncontrolling interest.

We now use the facts for the previous example except that we assume that (1) S Company is a 75%-owned subsidiary and (2) the equipment transfer is upstream.

Illustrations 11–12 and 11–13 show (1) the consolidation entries required at the end of 19X1 and 19X2 (including the adjustments required to the noncontrolling interest to share the deferral) and (2) the basis of accounting analyses for these dates that are used to change to the old basis of accounting at the end of 19X1 and 19X2.

Illustration 11–14 shows a consolidation worksheet for 19X1 (the transfer year).

ILLUSTRATION 11–12 **Basis of Accounting Analysis: Upstream Equipment Transfer— Gain Situation (75% ownership); Year of Transfer**

| | Analysis at the End of 19X1 | | | |
| | Actual Balances (new basis) | | Reportable Balances (old basis) | Differences (to be posted as a Dr. [Cr.]) |
	P Company	S Company		
Income Statement (19X1)				
Depreciation expense	$ (6,000)		$ (5,000)	$ (1,000)
Intercompany gain		$3,000	–0–	3,000
Balance Sheet (12/31/X1)				
Cost	$18,000		$40,000	$22,000
Accumulated depreciation	(6,000)		(30,000)[a]	(24,000)

[a]Accumulated depreciation of $25,000 at the transfer date plus $5,000 of depreciation ($15,000 ÷ 3 years) for 19X1.

Consolidation Entries at December 31, 19X1

(1) The equipment change in basis elimination entry:

Intercompany Gain	3,000	
Equipment	22,000	
Depreciation Expense		1,000
Accumulated Depreciation		24,000

(2) The sharing of the deferral elimination entry:

NCI in Net Assets	500	
NCI in Net Income		500

(25% of $2,000 of unrealized intercompany gain at 12/31/X1)

Note: The desired effect on retained earnings at 12/31/X1 occurs as a result of carrying forward amounts from the net income line of the income statement.

ILLUSTRATION 11–13 **Basis of Accounting Analysis: Upstream Equipment Transfer— Gain Situation (75% ownership); Year After Year of Transfer**

| | Analysis at the End of 19X2 | | | |
| | Actual Balances (new basis) | | Reportable Balances (old basis) | Differences (to be posted as a Dr. [Cr.]) |
	P Company	S Company		
Income Statement (19X2)				
Depreciation expense	$ (6,000)		$ (5,000)	$ (1,000)
Balance Sheet (12/31/X2)				
Cost	$18,000		$40,000	$22,000
Accumulated depreciation	(12,000)		(35,000)[a]	(23,000)
Retained Earnings	2,000[b]		–0–	2,000

[a]Accumulated depreciation of $25,000 at the transfer date plus $5,000 of depreciation ($15,000 ÷ 3 years) for 19X1 and $5,000 for 19X2.

[b]Intercompany gain of $3,000 − $1,000 of incremental depreciation expense in 19X1—the $3,000 gain flows through to P Company's books as a result of applying the equity method of accounting.

Consolidation Entries at December 31, 19X2

(1) The equipment change in basis elimination entry:

Retained Earnings, 1/1/X2	2,000	
Equipment	22,000	
Depreciation Expense		1,000
Accumulated Depreciation		23,000

(2) The sharing of the deferral elimination entry:

NCI in Net Income (25% of $1,000 intercompany gain realized in 19X2)	250	
NCI in Net Assets (25% of $1,000 intercompany gain unrealized at 12/31/X2) . . .	250	
Retained Earnings, 1/1/X2 (25% of $2,000 intercompany gain unrealized at 1/1/X2)		500

ILLUSTRATION 11–14   **THE COST METHOD**   Upstream Equipment Transfer: Gain Situation (75% ownership); Year of Transfer

P Company and S Company
Consolidation Worksheet as of December 31, 19X1

	P Company	75%-owned S Company	Consolidation Entries Dr.	Consolidation Entries Cr.	Consolidated
Income Statement (19X1)					
Sales	600,000	231,000			831,000
Cost of sales	(360,000)	(110,000)			(470,000)
Expenses	(190,000)	(100,000)		1,000(4)	(289,000)
Intercompany Accounts					
Dividend income (from S Co.) ...	3,000		3,000(2)		–0–
Intercompany gain		3,000	3,000(4)		–0–
Net Income	53,000	24,000	6,000	1,000	72,000
NCI in net income			6,000(3)	500(5)	(5,500)[a]
CI in net income	53,000	24,000	12,000	1,500	66,500
Statement of Retained Earnings					
Balances, 1/1/X1	100,000	40,000	10,000(3)		130,000
+ Net income	53,000	24,000	12,000	1,500	66,500
				1,000(3)	
– Dividends declared	(51,000)	(4,000)		3,000(2)	(51,000)
Balances, 12/31/X1	102,000	60,000	22,000	5,500	145,500
Balance Sheet					
Cash	79,000	51,000			130,000
Accounts receivable	75,000	37,000			112,000
Inventory	110,000	55,000			165,000
Investment in S Co.	45,000			45,000(1)	–0–
Land	220,000	30,000			250,000
Buildings and equipment	500,000	150,000	22,000(4)		672,000
Accumulated depreciation	(320,000)	(13,000)		24,000(4)	(357,000)
Total Assets	709,000	310,000	22,000	69,000	972,000
Payables and accruals	157,000	70,000			227,000
Long-term debt	250,000	120,000			370,000
NCI in net assets			500(5)	30,000(3)	29,500
			15,000(3)		
Common stock	200,000	60,000	45,000(1)		200,000
Retained earnings	102,000	60,000	22,000	5,500	145,500
Total Liabilities and Equity	709,000	310,000	82,500	35,500	972,000
Proof of debit and credit postings			104,500	104,500	

[a]Proof: Subsidiary's reported net income of $24,000 − $2,000 of unrealized gain at 12/31/X1 = $22,000; $22,000 × 25% = $5,500.

Explanation of entries:
(1) The basic elimination entry.
(2) The intercompany dividend elimination entry.
(3) The NCI elimination entry.
(4) The equipment change in basis elimination entry.
(5) The sharing of the unrealized gain elimination entry.

END

END-OF-CHAPTER REVIEW

SUMMARY OF KEY POINTS

1. The transfer of any asset within a consolidated group **never** changes the **basis of accounting** for the asset **from a consolidated perspective.**
2. The result of consolidation entries pertaining to intercompany fixed asset transfers is to change from **the new basis of accounting** to **the old basis of accounting.**
3. In making calculations for changing to the new basis of accounting in consolidation for intercompany depreciable fixed asset transfers, the **new remaining life** assigned to the asset must be used.
4. Regarding intercompany depreciable fixed asset transfers at a gain or loss, the asset's subsequent depreciation effectively results in **realization** of the intercompany gain or loss as time goes by.

GLOSSARY OF NEW TERMS

Carrying value   Historical cost minus any accumulated depreciation.

Pro forma   A presentation on an "as-if" basis.

SELF-STUDY QUESTIONS

(Answers are at the end of this chapter.)

1. On 4/1/X1, Pole Inc. sold equipment costing $105,000 and 20% depreciated (straight line and a five-year life) to its 80%-owned subsidiary, Sole Inc., for $96,000. Sole assigned a remaining life of six years (straight line). What are the cost and accumulated depreciation, respectively, of this equipment in the 12/31/X2 (*not* X1) consolidated balance sheet?
   a. $96,000 and $28,000
   b. $96,000 and $42,000
   c. $105,000 and $45,500
   d. $105,000 and $49,000
   e. $105,000 and $57,750
2. Assume the same information in Question 1. What is the intercompany gain or loss to defer at 12/31/X2 (*not* X1)?
   a. $12,000   b. $8,500   c. $8,400   d. $6,800   e. $6,750
3. On 1/1/X1, Soot Inc., a 60%-owned subsidiary of Poot Inc., sold equipment having a cost of $500,000 and accumulated depreciation of $200,000 to Poot for $240,000. Soot had been using a five-year life. Poot estimated that the equipment would last four years. Each entity uses straight-line depreciation. On 1/4/X2, Poot sold the equipment to an outside third party for $250,000. What is the gain or loss to be reported in the 19X2 consolidated income statement?
   a. $10,000   b. $15,000   c. $25,000   d. $70,000   e. $(35,000)

ASSIGNMENT MATERIAL

REVIEW QUESTIONS

1. For which assets transferred within a consolidated group can an intercompany gain or loss be recognized for *consolidated reporting purposes* at the transfer date?
2. Do intercompany fixed asset transfers fall under the IRS *transfer pricing rules*?
3. What causes the *basis of accounting* for a fixed asset to change in an intercompany sale?
4. What is the effect of the *consolidation entries* relating to intercompany fixed asset transfers?
5. What is the distinction between the *historical cost*, the *book value*, and the *carrying value* of a depreciable fixed asset?
6. How is an *intercompany gain or loss* calculated for a depreciable fixed asset transfer?

7. For intercompany transfers of depreciable fixed assets at a gain or loss, how and when does *realization* of intercompany gains and losses occur?
8. Regarding an intercompany depreciable fixed asset transfer, must the buying entity continue to use the selling entity's *remaining depreciable life* of the asset at the transfer date? Why or why not?
9. What is the relevance of the *old remaining life* to intercompany depreciable fixed asset transfers from a consolidated perspective? Of the new assigned life?
10. Is it necessary for intercompany depreciable fixed asset transfers to use the selling entity's *remaining life* of the asset to reflect the *old basis of accounting* in consolidation?
11. What does a *debit* to depreciation expense in a consolidation entry signify?
12. If the selling entity has a loss on an intercompany depreciable fixed asset transfer, will there be *incremental depreciation* or a *depreciation shortage* to handle in consolidation?

EXERCISES

E 11–1   **Consolidation Entries: Land Transfer—Downstream**   On 3/31/X1, Pasto Inc. sold land costing $40,000 to its 100%-owned subsidiary, Sasto Inc., for $100,000.

Required   1. Prepare the consolidation entry(ies) as of 12/31/X1 and X2. (For Module 1 only: First prepare any necessary general ledger adjusting entry at these dates.)
2. Prepare the consolidation entry at 12/31/X3, assuming that Sasto sold the land in 19X3 for $120,000. (For Module 1 only: First prepare the general ledger adjusting entry at this date.)

E 11–2   **Consolidation Entries: Land Transfer—Upstream**   On 6/30/X1, Pilt Inc. purchased land from Silt Inc., its 80%-owned subsidiary, for $80,000. Silt's cost was $50,000.

Required   1. Prepare the consolidation entry(ies) as of 12/31/X1 and X2. (For Module 1 only: First prepare any necessary general ledger adjusting entry at these dates.)
2. Prepare the consolidation entry(ies) at 12/31/X3, assuming that Pilt sold the land in 19X3 for $85,000. (For Module 1 only: First prepare the general ledger adjusting entry at this date.)

E 11–3   **Calculating Consolidated Amounts: Land and Building Transfer—Upstream**   Sya Inc., a 100%-owned subsidiary of Pya Inc., manufactures and installs air conditioning systems. Sya's sales are normally to third parties, but during 19X0, Pya contracted with Sya to install an air conditioning system in its new corporate headquarters. Sya charged Pya $750,000 for the system and a $125,000 installation fee. Sya's manufacturing cost was $500,000, and its installation costs were $75,000. Installation was completed on 1/2/X1, at which time the billings were rendered. Pya assigned a 25-year life to the system.

Required   1. What amounts pertaining to the air conditioning system should be reported in the consolidated statements at 12/31/X1? Insert your amounts in Pya's column in the following table.
2. Without making formal consolidation or other entries, what debit and credit postings should be made to the following accounts in consolidation at 12/31/X1?

	Pya Inc.	Sya Inc.
Income Statement		
Intercompany sales		$750,000
Intercompany cost of sales		(500,000)
Intercompany installation fee income		125,000
Intercompany installation fee expense		(75,000)
Depreciation expense	$	
Balance Sheet		
Building	$	
Accumulated depreciation		

E 11–4   **Calculating Consolidated Amounts: Equipment Transfer—Downstream**   On 1/1/X1 Pacto Inc. sold equipment to its 100%-owned subsidiary, Sacto Inc., for $800,000. The equipment cost Pacto $1,000,000; accumulated depreciation at the time of the sale was $400,000. Pacto has depreciated the equipment over 10 years using the straight-line method and no salvage value.

Required   Determine the amounts at which the cost and accumulated depreciation should be reported in the consolidated balance sheet at 12/31/X1 under each of the following assumptions:

1. Sacto does not revise the estimated remaining life.
2. Sacto assigns an estimated remaining life of eight years.

E 11–5   **Reverse Analysis: Equipment Transfer—Downstream**   In preparing consolidated statements for the year ended 12/31/X1, an entry debited Depreciation Expense for $2,000. This entry was necessary because of a downstream equipment transfer made on 7/3/X1 between Pyna Inc. and its 100%-owned subsidiary, Syna Inc. This $2,000 entry was an adjustment to the $5,500 of depreciation expense on this equipment that Syna reported for 19X1. On 7/3/X1 the equipment was 62.5% depreciated and had a three-year remaining life. Syna estimated that the equipment would last five years.

Required   1. Calculate the intercompany gain or loss on the transfer.
2. Calculate Pyna's historical cost and carrying value at the transfer date.

E 11–6   **Reverse Analysis: Equipment Transfer—Downstream**   In preparing consolidated statements for the year ended 12/31/X1, an entry credited Depreciation Expense for $3,000. This entry was necessary because of a downstream equipment transfer made on 4/1/X1 between Pyre Inc. and its 100%-owned subsidiary, Syre Inc. This $3,000 entry was an adjustment to the $18,000 of depreciation expense that Syre reported on this equipment for 19X1. On 4/1/X1 the equipment was 20% depreciated and had an eight-year remaining life. Syre estimated that the equipment would last only four years.

Required   1. Calculate the intercompany gain or loss on the transfer.
2. Calculate Pyre's historical cost and carrying value at the transfer date.

E 11–7   **Consolidation Entry: Land and Building Transfer—Upstream (100% ownership)**   On 7/1/X1, Sill Inc., a 100%-owned subsidiary, sold a warehouse facility for $129,000 cash to Pane Inc., its parent, recording a $30,000 gain on the sale. Sill's historical cost for the land and building were $33,000 and $176,000, respectively.

Pane, which allocated $43,000 of the purchase price to the land and $86,000 to the building, uses straight-line depreciation and assigned a five-year remaining life to the building.

Required   Prepare the consolidation entry required at 12/31/X1 relating to this sale. (For Module 1 only: First make the necessary general ledger adjusting entry at this date.)

E 11–8   **Consolidation Entry: Continuation of Exercise 11–7**   Assume the information provided in Exercise 11–7.

Required   Prepare the consolidation entry required at 12/31/X2 (one year later) relating to this sale. (For Module 1 only: First make the necessary general ledger adjusting entry at this date.)

PROBLEMS

P 11–1   **Reverse Analysis and Consolidation Entry: Equipment Transfer— Upstream (100% ownership)**   On 1/1/X1 Sax Inc., a 100%-owned subsidiary of Pax Inc., sold it office equipment to which Pax assigned a six-year life. If Sax had *not* sold the equipment, it would have reported this equipment in its 12/31/X1 balance sheet at $70,000 for cost and $44,000 for accumulated depreciation. Also if Sax had *not* sold this equipment, it would have reported depreciation expense of $4,000 on it for all of 19X1. The equipment's carrying value on Pax's books at 12/31/X1 was $60,000.

Required   1. Calculate the intercompany transfer price.
2. Calculate the intercompany gain or loss on the transfer.
3. Calculate Pax's depreciation expense on this equipment for 19X1.
4. Prepare the consolidation entry at the end of 19X1 relating to this transfer.

P 11–2*   **Consolidation Worksheet: Year of Equipment Transfer—Downstream (100% ownership)**   On 1/2/X1, Pato Inc. sold equipment to its 100%-owned subsidiary, Sato Inc. Information relating to the sale follows:

*The financial statement information presented for problems accompanied by asterisks is also provided on Model 11 (filename: MODEL11) of the software file disk that is available with the text, allowing the problem to be worked on the computer. **Prepare and present (1) your calculation of the unrealized intercompany gain and (2) your elimination entries other than the basic elimination entry in the space provided to the right of the conceptual analysis of the Investment account.**

Sales price	$35,000
Cost $50,000	
Less—Accumulated depreciation . . . . (30,000)	20,000
Gain	$15,000
Original life used by parent	10 years
Remaining life assigned by subsidiary	5 years

Comparative condensed financial statements follow:

	Pato Inc.		
	Cost Method[a]	Equity Method[b]	Sato Inc.
Income Statement (19X1)			
Sales	$440,000	$440,000	$150,000
Cost of sales	(230,000)	(230,000)	(80,000)
Expenses	(75,000)	(75,000)	(40,000)
Intercompany Accounts			
Dividend income (from Sato)	20,000		
Equity in net income (of Sato)		30,000	
Intercompany gain	15,000	15,000	
Net Income	$170,000	$180,000	$ 30,000
Balance Sheet (as of 12/31/X1)			
Investment in subsidiary	$ 45,000	$ 80,000	
Buildings and equipment	250,000	250,000	$ 75,000
Accumulated depreciation	(100,000)	(100,000)	(24,000)
Other assets	620,000	620,000	59,000
Total Assets	$815,000	$850,000	$110,000
Liabilities	$110,000	$110,000	$ 30,000
Common stock	300,000	300,000	45,000
Retained earnings	405,000	440,000	35,000
Total Liabilities and Equity	$815,000	$850,000	$110,000
Dividends declared	$ 80,000	$ 80,000	$ 20,000

[a]Use this column if you are using Module 3.
[b]Use this column if you are using Modules 1 or 2.

Required   **1.** Determine the unrealized gain at year-end. (For Module 1 only: Also make the necessary year-end adjusting entry for the unrealized gain required for this module; adjust the statements accordingly. For Modules 1 and 2 only: Prepare a conceptual analysis of the Investment account for 19X1.)
2. Prepare all consolidation entries as of 12/31/X1.
3. Prepare a consolidation worksheet at 12/31/X1.

P 11–3*   **Consolidation Worksheet: Year of Equipment Transfer—Upstream (75% ownership)**   Several years ago, Pak Inc. created a 75%-owned subsidiary, Shipp Inc. The public acquired the remaining 25% ownership interest on the creation date. On 1/3/X1, Shipp sold equipment to Pak. Information related to the sale follows:

Sales price	$22,000
Cost $25,000	
Less—Accumulated depreciation . . . . (15,000)	10,000
Loss	$12,000
Original life used by subsidiary	5 years
Remaining life assigned by parent	3 years

Comparative condensed financial statements follow:

	Pak Inc.		
	Cost Method[a]	Equity Method[b]	Shipp Inc.
Income Statement (19X1)			
Sales	$520,000	$520,000	$168,000
Cost of sales	(210,000)	(210,000)	(80,000)
Expenses	(93,000)	(93,000)	(40,000)
Intercompany Accounts			
Dividend income (from Shipp)	15,000		
Equity in net income (of Shipp)		45,000	
Intercompany gain			12,000
Net Income	$232,000	$262,000	$ 60,000
Balance Sheet (as of 12/31/X1)			
Investment in subsidiary	$ 75,000	$135,000	
Buildings and equipment	130,000	130,000	$ 44,000
Accumulated depreciation	(40,000)	(40,000)	(14,000)
Other assets	275,000	275,000	165,000
Total Assets	$440,000	$500,000	$195,000
Liabilities	$ 75,000	$ 75,000	$ 15,000
Common stock	200,000	200,000	100,000
Retained earnings	165,000	225,000	80,000
Total Liabilities and Equity	$440,000	$500,000	$195,000
Dividends declared	$135,000	$135,000	$ 20,000

[a]Use this column if you are using Module 3.
[b]Use this column if you are using Modules 1 or 2.

Required   **1.** Determine the unrealized gain at year-end. (For Module 1 only: Also make the necessary year-end adjusting entry for the unrealized gain required for this module; adjust the statements accordingly. For Modules 1 and 2 only: Prepare a conceptual analysis of the Investment account for 19X1.)
2. Prepare all consolidation entries as of 12/31/X1.
3. Prepare a consolidation worksheet at 12/31/X1.

P 11-4   **Reverse Analysis and Consolidation Entries (two years): Equipment Transfer—Downstream (100% ownership)**   On 6/30/X1, Pine Inc. sold its minicomputer to Syne Inc., its 100%-owned subsidiary, which assigned it a three-year life. If it had not sold the computer, Pine would have reported it in its 12/31/X1 balance sheet at $720,000 for cost and $480,000 for accumulated depreciation. If Pine had not sold the computer, it also would have reported depreciation expense of $60,000 for all of 19X1 on the computer. The computer's carrying value on Syne's books at 12/31/X1 was $125,000.

Required   **1.** Calculate the intercompany transfer price.
2. Calculate the intercompany gain or loss on the transfer.
3. Calculate Syne's depreciation expense on this equipment for 19X1.
4. Prepare the consolidation entries at the end of 19X1 and 19X2 relating to this transfer.

P 11-5*   **Consolidation Worksheet: Year After Year of Equipment Transfer—Upstream (75% ownership)**   Comparative condensed financial statements of Pert Inc. and its 75%-owned subsidiary, Savy Inc., follow:

	Pert Inc.		
	Cost Method[a]	Equity Method[b]	Savy Inc.
Income Statement (19X2)			
Sales	$240,000	$240,000	$156,000
Cost of sales	(120,000)	(120,000)	(80,000)
Expenses	(70,000)	(70,000)	(40,000)

(continued)

	Pert Inc.		Savy Inc.
	Cost Method[a]	Equity Method[b]	
Intercompany Accounts			
Dividend income (from Savy)	12,000		
Equity in net income (of Savy)		27,000	
Net Income	$ 62,000	$ 77,000	$ 36,000
Statement of Retained Earnings (19X2)			
Beginning of year	$ 67,000	$100,000	$ 44,000
+ Net income	62,000	77,000	36,000
– Dividends declared	(45,000)	(45,000)	(16,000)
End of year	$ 84,000	$132,000	$ 64,000
Balance Sheet (as of 12/31/X2)			
Investment in subsidiary	$ 75,000	$123,000	
Buildings and equipment	300,000	300,000	$140,000
Accumulated depreciation	(90,000)	(90,000)	(50,000)
Other assets	290,000	290,000	210,000
Total Assets	$575,000	$623,000	$300,000
Liabilities	$291,000	$291,000	$136,000
Common stock	200,000	200,000	100,000
Retained earnings	84,000	132,000	64,000
Total Liabilities and Equity	$575,000	$623,000	$300,000

[a]Use this column if you are using Module 3.
[b]Use this column if you are using Modules 1 or 2.

On 1/4/X1 (the previous year), Savy sold equipment to Pert. Information related to this sale follows:

Sales price		$31,000
Cost	$25,000	
Less—Accumulated depreciation	(10,000)	15,000
Gain		$16,000
Original life used by subsidiary		5 years
Remaining life assigned by parent		4 years

Neither entity made any general ledger adjustment for unrealized intercompany gain at the end of 19X1 or 19X2. (Pert created Savy five years ago, at which time 25% of the ownership was sold to the public.)

Required   **1.** Calculate the unrealized intercompany gain at the end of 19X2. (For Module 1 only: Make the necessary year-end adjusting entry for the unrealized gain required for this module; adjust the statements accordingly. For Modules 1 and 2 only: Prepare a conceptual analysis of the Investment account for 19X1.)
   2. Prepare all consolidation entries as of 12/31/X2.
   3. Prepare a consolidation worksheet at 12/31/X2.

P 11–6* **MINI-COMPREHENSIVE—PURCHASED SUBSIDIARY Consolidation Worksheet: Year of Equipment Transfer—Upstream (80% ownership)**   On 1/1/X1, Puta Inc. purchased 80% of Suta Inc.'s outstanding common stock for $184,000 cash. At that date, Suta had (1) a book value of $175,000 ($100,000 common stock + $75,000 retained earnings) and (2) land that was undervalued by $10,000. Goodwill in the transaction was assigned a 3-year life. On 1/3/X1, Suta sold equipment to Puta. Information related to the sale follows:

Sales price		$ 18,000
Cost	$98,000	
Less—Accumulated depreciation	(56,000)	42,000
Loss		$(24,000)
Original life used by subsidiary		7 years
Remaining life assigned by parent		6 years

Comparative condensed financial statements follow:

	Puta Inc.		
	Cost Method[a]	Equity Method[b]	Suta Inc.
Income Statement (19X1)			
Sales	$625,000	$625,000	$299,000
Cost of sales	(210,000)	(210,000)	(140,000)
Expenses	(180,000)	(180,000)	(70,000)
Intercompany Accounts			
Dividend income (from Suta)	36,000		
Equity in net income (of Suta)		40,000	
Intercompany loss			(24,000)
Net Income	$271,000	$275,000	$ 65,000
Balance Sheet (as of 12/31/X1)			
Investment in subsidiary	$184,000	$188,000	
Buildings and equipment	390,000	390,000	$180,000
Accumulated depreciation	(80,000)	(80,000)	(120,000)[c]
Other assets	202,000	202,000	215,000
Total Assets	$696,000	$700,000	$275,000
Liabilities	$280,000	$280,000	$ 80,000
Common stock	200,000	200,000	100,000
Retained earnings	216,000	220,000	95,000
Total Liabilities and Equity	$631,000	$700,000	$275,000
Dividends declared	$150,000	$150,000	$ 45,000

[a]Use this column if you are using Module 3.
[b]Use this column if you are using Modules 1 or 2.
[c]The balance was $110,000 at the acquisition date.

Neither entity made any general ledger adjustment for unrealized intercompany loss at the end of 19X1.

Required   **1.** Determine the unrealized loss at the end of 19X1. (For Module 1 only: Also make the necessary year-end adjusting entry for the unrealized loss required for this module; adjust the statements accordingly. For Modules 1 and 2 only: Prepare a conceptual analysis of the Investment account for 19X1.)

2. Prepare all consolidation entries as of 12/31/X1.

3. Prepare a consolidation worksheet at 12/31/X1.

P 11–7* **COMPREHENSIVE—ACQUIRED SUBSIDIARY Consolidation Worksheet: Year After Year of Equipment Transfer—Upstream (60% ownership); Multiple Year Inventory Transfers—Downstream** On 1/1/X1, Park Inc. acquired 60% of the outstanding common stock of Stall Inc. for $153,000 cash. Park incurred an additional $12,000 of direct costs. At the time, Stall's common stock had a book value of $34 per share. Stall's land was undervalued by $50,000, and its 5% long-term debt (due 12/31/X4) had a current value of $40,000 less than its book value. Park assigned a 3-year life to goodwill.

On 1/3/X2, Stall sold office equipment to Park. Information related to this sale follows:

Sales price		$27,000
Cost	$44,000	
Less—Accumulated depreciation	(32,000)	12,000
Loss		$15,000
Original life used by subsidiary		4 years
Remaining life assigned by parent		3 years

Comparative financial statements are as follows:

| | Park Inc. | | |
	Cost Method[a]	Equity Method[b]	Stall Inc.
Income Statement (19X2)			
Sales	$600,000	$600,000	$395,000
Cost of sales	(360,000)	(360,000)	(200,000)
Expenses	(226,000)	(226,000)	(119,000)
Intercompany Accounts			
Dividend income (from Stall)	21,000		
Equity in net income (of Stall)		24,000	
Intercompany sales	50,000	50,000	
Intercompany cost of sales	(30,000)	(30,000)	
Intercompany mgt. fee income	36,000	36,000	
Intercompany mgt. fee expense			(36,000)
Intercompany gain			15,000
Net Income	$ 91,000	$ 94,000	$ 55,000
Balance Sheet (as of 12/31/X2)			
Inventory:			
From vendors	$214,000	$214,000	$ 85,000
Intercompany			5,000
Investment in subsidiary	165,000	168,000	
Land	126,000	126,000	45,000
Buildings and equipment	255,000	255,000	140,000
Accumulated depreciation	(150,000)	(150,000)	(55,000)[c]
Other assets	207,000	207,000	90,000
Total Assets	$817,000	$820,000	$310,000
Current liabilities	$103,000	$103,000	$ 63,500
Long-term debt	220,000	220,000	62,000
Common stock, $10 par value	250,000	250,000	
Common stock, $20 par value			100,000
Retained earnings	244,000	247,000	105,000
Less—Treasury stock (at cost) (500 shares)			(20,500)[d]
Total Liabilities and Equity	$817,000	$820,000	$310,000
Dividends declared:[e]			
19X1	$ 30,000	$ 30,000	$ 10,000
19X2	41,000	41,000	35,000

[a]Use this column if you are using Module 3.
[b]Use this column if you are using Modules 1 or 2.
[c]The balance was $40,000 at the acquisition date.
[d]The treasury stock was purchased at a very favorable price on 12/31/X2.
[e]Assume that all dividends were declared on 12/10 and paid 10 days later.

Additional Information

1. Stall's 12/31/X1 inventory included $17,000 of inventory acquired from Park in 19X1. Park's cost was $14,000. Stall resold this inventory for $23,000 in 19X2.
2. Neither entity made any general ledger adjustment for unrealized intercompany gain and profit at the end of 19X1 and 19X2.
3. For Modules 1 and 2 only: In applying the *equity method* of accounting for 19X2, Park recorded $33,000 (60% of $55,000).
4. Because of an overpayment, Park owed Stall $11,000 at the end of 19X2.

Required

1. Calculate the unrealized gain on the equipment transfer at the end of 19X2 and prepare a matrix analysis to determine the unrealized profit on the current year inventory transfers. (For Module 1 only: Also make the necessary year-end adjusting entry(ies) for the unrealized gain

and profit; adjust the statements accordingly. For Modules 1 and 2 only: Prepare an updated conceptual analysis of the Investment account from inception through the end of 19X2.)

2. Prepare all consolidation entries as of 12/31/X2.
3. Prepare a consolidation worksheet at 12/31/X2.

❋ THINKING CRITICALLY ❋

❋ CASES ❋

C 11–1   **Maybe It Is and Maybe It Isn't**   Kelly says that depreciation is part of the *accrual basis* of accounting. Lynn says it is not.

Required
1. Prepare a written solution that need be no more than one page long.
2. Is a fixed asset expensed when a company uses the *cash basis* of accounting? What about for tax purposes?

ANSWERS TO SELF-STUDY QUESTIONS

1. c ($21,000 + $14,000 + $10,500 [3/4 yr.] = $45,500)

2. b, gain ($12,000 – $2,000 – $1,500 [3/4 yr.] = $8,500)

3. c, gain ($250,000 – $225,000 = $25,000)

INTERCOMPANY BOND HOLDINGS

LEARNING OBJECTIVES

TO UNDERSTAND

- Why gains and losses occur as a result of intercompany bond purchases.
- The way to calculate such gains and losses.
- The way to report such gains and losses in the consolidated statements.
- The adjustments required in consolidation in subsequent years to prevent reporting these gains and losses twice.
- The necessary subsequent year adjustment procedures.

TOPIC OUTLINE

People who work hard and play hard, I treat them special. I try to be very consistent in that I don't treat everyone the same.

JIMMY JOHNSON

Recall from Chapter 9 that preparing consolidated statements involves (1) eliminating all amounts reported as a result of intercompany transactions (unsettled balances, intercompany revenues/gains, and intercompany expenses/losses) in consolidation and (2) not reporting any intercompany profit, gain, or loss until it has been realized as a result of transactions with outside third parties. These rules also apply to intercompany bond purchases. The situation is that of recognizing an immediate gain or loss in consolidation, however, not of deferring a gain or loss until a later year(s).

Intercompany bond holdings can arise in two ways:

1. **Direct transactions with another member of the consolidated group.** For example, a subsidiary issuing bonds could sell some or all of the bond issue directly to its parent.

2. **Indirect transactions with another member of the consolidated group.** For example, a parent could acquire in the open market some or all of a subsidiary's already issued and outstanding bonds. The result (in this example) is as if either (1) the parent acquired the bonds directly from the subsidiary or (2) the subsidiary reacquired its bonds in the open market and then sold them directly to the parent.

WHY DO INDIRECT BOND TRANSACTIONS OCCUR?

Recall from intermediate accounting that companies often extinguish bond indebtedness before the maturity date when (1) interest rates have declined significantly since the issuance date and new bonds can be issued at a lower interest rate or (2) excess cash has accumulated beyond foreseeable needs.

More opportunity to extinguish debt exists for a consolidated group of companies than for a single company. The entity within the consolidated group that issued the bonds—**the issuing entity**—may not have the cash available to retire the bonds, or issuing new bonds to retire the old ones may be impractical. However, another entity within the consolidated group that has available cash or the ability to issue debt—**the acquiring entity**—can purchase some or all of the outstanding bonds in the open market. Although it is not unusual for a parent to purchase a subsidiary's bonds, a subsidiary purchases a parent's bonds only if its parent directs it to do so.

NO NEED TO DISTINGUISH BETWEEN DIRECT AND INDIRECT TRANSACTIONS

Because the result of an **indirect** bond transaction is the same as having had a **direct** bond transaction, no distinction need be made between the two in preparing consolidated statements. In consolidation, both types of transactions require elimination of amounts reported resulting from the intercompany bond purchase. Specifically, the Investment in Bonds account on the acquiring entity's books must be offset (on the consolidation worksheet) against the Bonds Payable account on the issuing entity's books—**substantively, this is the same as eliminating an intercompany receivable and an intercompany payable in consolidation.** From the intercompany bond purchase date until the bonds are legally retired by the issuing company, the Intercompany Interest Income account reported by the acquiring entity must be offset (on the worksheet) against the Intercompany Interest Expense account reported by the issuing entity.

THE COMPLICATING FACTOR: PREMIUMS AND DISCOUNTS

If all bonds were issued at face value and all intercompany bond purchases were at face value, this chapter would end here. Under such a scenario, the consolidation entries described above would be readily determinable because the reported amount for each account would have the same absolute dollar balance as its off-setting account on the other entity's books. Furthermore, no gain or loss on extinguishment of debt would ever be reported.

If bond premiums and discounts exist, however, the consolidation process is somewhat involved because these items result in a gain or loss on extinguishment of debt to be reported from a consolidated perspective—**as though the issuing entity had redeemed and retired the bonds.** In later periods, steps are needed to undo the reporting of the amortizations of these premiums and discounts, which are amortized to income in each company's general ledger. Otherwise, income or loss is double reported, once as a gain or loss on extinguishment of debt and once as adjustments to intercompany interest income and intercompany interest expense.

DETAILED RECOGNITION PROCEDURES SHOWN IN MODULES   As presented in Chapters 10 and 11, we present detailed procedures in separate modules, with each module being self-contained and independent, standing on its own when read in conjunction with the general material that precedes Module 1. The three modules presented are

> **Module 1: The Complete Equity Method** (recognition occurs in the general ledgers)
>
> **Module 2: The Partial Equity Method** (recognition occurs on the worksheet)
>
> **Module 3: The Cost Method** (recognition occurs on the worksheet)

Preceding Module 1, we show a simpler approach (relative to the procedures in each of the modules) that eliminates premiums and discounts in the general ledgers at the bond purchase date. This simpler approach can be beneficial in understanding the consolidated reporting objective achieved in each of the modules.

I THE CONSTRUCTIVE RETIREMENT OF THE BONDS

The result of an intercompany bond purchase is that no amounts are owed to any party outside the consolidated group of entities with respect to those bonds. Therefore, the purchase by one entity within the consolidated group of any or all of the outstanding bonds of another group member constitutes the **constructive retirement** of the bonds purchased. Thus from a consolidated perspective, the bonds have been **extinguished**—even though the bonds are still legally outstanding from the issuing entity's perspective.

Recall from intermediate accounting that when an entity extinguishes its debt, it has a reportable gain or loss (an **extraordinary item** if material) whenever the **amount paid to extinguish the debt** differs from the debt's **carrying value** (the face amount plus any unamortized premium or minus any unamortized discount).[1]

For constructive retirement of debt occurring among an affiliated group of companies, a gain or loss—often referred to as an **imputed** *gain or loss*—also occurs when the **acquiring entity's purchase price** differs from the **issuing entity's**

---

[1]These requirements are set forth in *APB Opinion No. 26*, "Early Extinguishment of Debt" and *SFAS No. 4*, "Reporting Gains and Losses from Extinguishment of Debt."

carrying value. This imputed gain or loss must be reported in the consolidated income statement (as an extraordinary item if material) when the intercompany bond purchase occurs.

II   CALCULATING THE GAIN OR LOSS ON DEBT EXTINGUISHMENT

The procedure for calculating the gain or loss on the extinguishment of debt is the same regardless of which particular module is used. The amount of the *imputed* gain or loss on the extinguishment of debt reported in the period in which the affiliate's bonds are purchased is determined by comparing the acquisition **cost to the applicable percentage of the carrying value of the bonds payable as of the bond purchase date.**

For example, assume that (1) P Company acquired in the open market 40% of the $500,000 of outstanding 10% bonds of its 100%-owned subsidiary, S Company, for $195,500 on January 1, 19X4, (2) the assumed maturity date of the bonds is December 31, 19X6 (three years later), and (3) interest is payable on July 1 and January 1 (thus none of the purchase cost relates to interest). The gain or loss is calculated at that date as follows:

		Unamortized		
	Face Amount	Premium (S Co.)	Discount (P Co.)	Carrying Value
Bonds payable	$500,000 +	$30,000		= $530,000
Percent acquired	40%	40%		40%
Amount deemed retired	$200,000 +	$12,000		= $212,000
Investment in bonds	200,000		+ $(4,500)	= 195,500
Unrecorded Gain on Debt Extinguishment		$12,000 +	$ 4,500	= $ 16,500

The gain is attributable to both (1) the applicable percentage (40%) of the **unamortized premium** on S Company's books and (2) all of the **discount** on P Company's books. At the bond purchase date, S Company makes the following **general ledger reclassification entry** to reflect the fact that P Company now holds a portion of the bonds:

Bonds Payable	200,000	
Bond Premium	12,000	
Intercompany Bonds Payable		200,000
Intercompany Bond Premium		12,000

PREMIUMS AND DISCOUNTS: A GAIN OR LOSS?   If the issuing entity has a premium and the acquiring entity has a discount (as in the preceding example), a gain on debt extinguishment always results. If the issuing entity has a discount and the acquiring entity has a premium, a loss on debt extinguishment always results. When each entity has a discount or a premium, the net effect is a gain or a loss, depending on which entity has the greater discount or premium. In all of these situations, the correct procedures for preparing consolidated statements can be determined through careful application of the principles discussed and illustrated in this chapter.

PURCHASE BETWEEN INTEREST PAYMENT DATES

In the preceding example, we assumed for simplicity that the bond purchase occurred on an interest payment date. When an affiliate's bonds are acquired between interest dates, the only other item to account for is the additional amount paid by the acquiring entity for interest from the last interest payment date to the purchase date. This additional amount is charged to interest receivable at the purchase date. The procedures to determine and account for the gains and losses do *not* change.

REISSUANCE OF INTERCOMPANY BOND HOLDINGS

Infrequently, an acquiring entity sells some or all of the intercompany bonds to an outside party instead of holding them until their maturity date. In these cases, the bonds that the acquiring entity sells are considered to be reissued from a consolidated viewpoint. Any difference between the face value of the bonds and the proceeds (excluding amounts for interest) is treated in consolidation in the same manner as a premium or discount on the issuance of bonds.

DETERMINING THE NONCONTROLLING INTEREST SHARE OF THE GAIN OR LOSS

When the subsidiary is partially owned and has a discount or premium, a minor conceptual issue arises as to how much of the gain or loss to allocate to the noncontrolling interest in the consolidated statements. Three possibilities exist:

1. **The parent company method.** Under this approach, no portion of the subsidiary's premium or discount is allocated to the noncontrolling interest. The rationale is that the gain or loss is entirely a result of the parent's decision to purchase the bonds.

2. **The issuing company method.** Under this approach, the entire gain or loss is assumed to be that of the issuing entity inasmuch as the acquiring entity is deemed to be merely the issuing entity's agent. Accordingly, amounts are allocated to the noncontrolling interest only if the subsidiary is the issuing entity. In such cases, the noncontrolling interest also shares in that portion of the gain resulting from the parent's discount or premium.

3. **The face value method.** Under this approach, the noncontrolling interest is allocated only its share of the gain or loss resulting from the subsidiary's premium or discount.

WHICH METHOD IS CORRECT?   In our opinion, only the face value method is valid. Only this method reflects the reality of the legal boundary lines that exist between the parent and the subsidiary. The proof would be in a liquidation of the subsidiary. After selling its assets and paying off creditors, the amount distributed to the noncontrolling interest shareholders would be their share of the book equity—which would exclude amounts relating to the gain or loss resulting from the parent's discount or premium. In dealing with noncontrolling interest situations in each of the modules, we use only the face value approach.

III   *SIMPLIFIED* PROCEDURES: PREMIUMS AND DISCOUNTS ELIMINATED IN THE GENERAL LEDGERS AT THE BOND PURCHASE DATE

The simplest manner of dealing with premiums and discounts is to eliminate those that give rise to the imputed gain or loss. Using the preceding example, the following **general ledger adjusting entries** are made on the bond acquisition date:

	P Company	S Company
Subsidiary's Entry		
Intercompany Bond Premium.		12,000
Gain on Debt Extinguishment. .		12,000
Parent's Entry		
Investment in Subsidiary's Bonds . . .	4,500	
Gain on Debt Extinguishment		
(of Subsidiary's Bonds)		4,500

Under the *equity method* of accounting, P Company records $12,000 in its Equity in Net Income (of Subsidiary) account. Accordingly, P Company's separate income statement reports $16,500 of income, which equals the gain on debt extinguishment reported in consolidation.

THE RATIONALE FOR MAKING THE GENERAL LEDGER ENTRIES   The rationale for eliminating the discount on P Company's books and the intercompany premium on S Company's books is that the accounting treatment should be no different than had P Company formally exchanged $200,000 checks with S Company. That is, P Company advances $200,000 to S Company with the stipulation that S Company retire the $200,000 face value of bonds that P Company holds. Using this procedure, P Company records a $4,500 gain on the debt extinguishment, and S Company records a $12,000 gain. **The accounting should reflect the substance of the result—not the form of the particular alternative selected to achieve that result.**

ENTRIES REQUIRED IN CONSOLIDATION

After recording the general ledger entries to eliminate the intercompany premium and discount (shown earlier), P Company's Investment in Bonds of S Company has a $200,000 balance. Likewise, S Company's Intercompany Bond Payable account has a $200,000 balance. As a result, neither entity needs to show amortization in its general ledger in subsequent periods. At each future year-end consolidation date (preceding the actual retirement of the bonds), the following two entries are made in consolidation:

WORKSHEET ENTRY ONLY	Intercompany Bonds Payable	200,000	
	Investment in Bonds of Subsidiary		200,000
WORKSHEET ENTRY ONLY	Intercompany Interest Income	20,000	
	Investment Interest Expense		20,000

ILLUSTRATIONS	**PREPARING CONSOLIDATED STATEMENTS**

- **SIMPLIFIED REPORTING: PREMIUM AND DISCOUNT ELIMINATED IN GENERAL LEDGERS**
- **AT END OF BOND ACQUISITION YEAR: 100%-OWNED SUBSIDIARY**

Illustration 12–1 presents a consolidation worksheet as of December 31, 19X4.

PARTIALLY OWNED SUBSIDIARIES   Even when a subsidiary is partially owned, the procedures are the same as those for 100%-owned subsidiaries.

ILLUSTRATION 12–1	SIMPLIFIED PROCEDURES Premium and Discount Eliminated in General Ledgers: Consolidation at End of Bond Acquisition Year—100%-Owned Subsidiary

P Company and S Company
Consolidation Worksheet as of December 31, 19X4

	P Company	100%-owned S Company	Consolidation Entries Dr.	Consolidation Entries Cr.	Consolidated
Income Statement (19X4)					
Sales	680,000	280,000			960,000
Cost of sales	(380,000)	(120,000)			(500,000)
Expenses	(265,500)	(114,000)			(379,500)
Gain on debt extinguishment	4,500	12,000			16,500
Intercompany Accounts					
Equity in net income (of S Co.) . .	38,000		38,000(1)		–0–
Intercompany interest income . . .	20,000		20,000(2)		–0–
Intercompany interest expense . .		(20,000)		20,000(2)	–0–
Net Income	97,000	38,000	58,000	20,000	97,000
Statement of Retained Earnings					
Balances, 1/1/X4	156,000	76,000	76,000(1)		156,000
+ Net income	97,000	38,000	58,000	20,000	97,000
– Dividends declared	(51,000)	(24,000)		24,000(1)	(51,000)
Balances, 12/31/X4	202,000	90,000	134,000	44,000	202,000
Balance Sheet					
Intercompany interest receivable/payable	10,000	(10,000)			–0–
Investment in S Co.:					
Common stock	150,000			150,000(1)	–0–
Bonds	200,000			200,000(3)	–0–
Other assets	199,000	710,000			909,000
Total Assets	559,000	700,000		350,000	909,000
Payables and accruals	107,000	38,000			145,000
Bonds payable		300,000			300,000
Bond premium		12,000			12,000
Intercompany bond payable		200,000	200,000(3)		–0–
Common stock	250,000	60,000	60,000(1)		250,000
Retained earnings	202,000	90,000	134,000	44,000	202,000
Total Liabilities and Equity	559,000	700,000	394,000	44,000	909,000
Proof of debit and credit postings			394,000	394,000	

Explanation of entries:
(1) The basic elimination entry.
(2) The intercompany bond interest elimination entry.
(3) The intercompany bond holding elimination entry.

THE WAY THE SUBSIDIARY REPORTS TO THE NONCONTROLLING INTEREST SHAREHOLDERS   If the subsidiary is partially owned, the income or loss it records as a result of eliminating its intercompany premium or discount is *not* realized insofar as the noncontrolling interest shareholders are concerned. Accordingly, in reporting to them, the subsidiary makes a "financial statement adjusting entry" (as opposed to a general ledger adjusting entry) to reflect the intercompany premium or discount in its balance sheet—as though it had not been eliminated in the general ledger. Although keeping the general ledger for reporting to the parent (rather than to the noncontrolling interest shareholders) slightly complicates the subsidiary's process of reporting to the noncontrolling interest, the consolidation process is streamlined—a much greater benefit.

IV CUSTOMARY PROCEDURES: PREMIUMS AND DISCOUNTS *NOT* ELIMINATED IN THE GENERAL LEDGERS AT THE BOND PURCHASE DATE

Although eliminating the premiums and discounts in the general ledgers at the bond purchase date is theoretically sound and efficient, the customary procedure is *not* to do so. Accordingly, each entity instead amortizes any premium or discount to income over the remaining life of the bond issue.

THE EFFECT OF AMORTIZATION ON THE BOND ISSUER

Recall from intermediate accounting that for **bonds issued at a premium,** the income statement effect **decreases interest expense** based on the stated or coupon interest rate so that interest expense is reported based on the market interest rate at the bond issuance date. For **bonds issued at a discount,** the amortization process results in **increasing interest expense** from the stated or coupon rate to the market rate.

THE EFFECT OF AMORTIZATION ON THE BOND PURCHASER

Also recall from intermediate accounting that for **bonds purchased at a premium,** the amortization **decreases interest income.** For **bonds purchased at a discount,** the amortization **increases interest income.** The earlier example in which the issuer has a premium and the acquirer has a discount is used in each of the following modules.

MODULE 1 OVERVIEW

Recall from Chapter 10 that under the complete equity method, the consolidated net income that accrues to the controlling interest *equals* the parent's net income. Recall also that (1) this equality was achieved by making a general ledger adjusting entry at the consolidation date for any unrealized intercompany profit, gain, or loss and (2) the general ledger adjusting entry changed the carrying value of the parent's Investment in Subsidiary account (*directly* when the parent made the general ledger adjusting entry and *indirectly* when the subsidiary made the general ledger adjusting entry [the entry thus impacted the amount of income the parent recorded under the *equity method* of accounting]).

The following discussion uses the example given on page 426 in which a $16,500 gain on debt extinguishment resulted ($12,000 from S Company's intercompany bond premium and $4,500 from P Company's discount).

SECTION 1: 100%-OWNED SUBSIDIARIES

CONSOLIDATION AT THE BOND ACQUISITION DATE

The procedures discussed and illustrated earlier for intercompany bond holdings in the section Simplified Procedures: Premiums and Discounts Eliminated in the General Ledgers at the Bond Purchase Date automatically achieve the equality results under the complete equity method. Accordingly, those procedures are perfectly acceptable under the complete equity method. An alternative procedure is to adjust the parent's (1) Investment in Common Stock of Subsidiary account and (2) Equity in Net Income of Subsidiary account. This is by far a much more involved procedure, however, and for this reason, we do not illustrate it.[2]

---

[2]No studies exist as to which procedure is more widely used in practice. We doubt that practicing accountants would choose a somewhat involved method when a much simpler one is available.

CONSOLIDATION AT THE BOND ACQUISITION YEAR-END

If the intercompany bond premium and discount are *not* eliminated in the general ledgers at the bond acquisition date (the customary procedure), it is necessary to make general ledger adjusting entries at the bond acquisition's year-end for the gain or loss on debt extinguishment that has not yet been recognized in the general ledgers.

As was the case for consolidation at the bond purchase date, the simplest procedure is to (1) eliminate the remaining unamortized intercompany premium and discount in the general ledgers at the bond acquisition year-end and (2) reflect the recognition of the eliminated intercompany premium and discount in Gain on Debt Extinguishment accounts. We illustrate this procedure. Using our example, the following **general ledger adjusting entries** are made at the end of 19X4 to eliminate the unamortized intercompany premium and discount:

	P Company	S Company
Subsidiary's Entry		
Intercompany Bond Premium		8,000
Gain on Debt Extinguishment . . .		8,000
($12,000 − $4,000 of 19X4 amortization).		
Parent's Entry		
Investment in Subsidiary's Bonds	3,000	
Gain on Debt Extinguishment		
(of Subsidiary's Bonds)	3,000	
($4,500 − $1,500 of 19X4 amortization).		

Under the *equity method* of accounting, P Company also records $8,000 of additional income in its Equity in Net Income (of Subsidiary) account. Accordingly, P Company's separate income statement reports $16,500 of income, which equals the gain on debt extinguishment reported in consolidation.

ILLUSTRATIONS | **PREPARING CONSOLIDATED FINANCIAL STATEMENTS**

- **THE COMPLETE EQUITY METHOD**
- **AT END OF BOND ACQUISITION YEAR: 100%-OWNED SUBSIDIARY**

P Company makes the following consolidation entries at December 31, 19X4 (one year after the bond acquisition date):

1. The basic elimination entry (using assumed amounts):

WORKSHEET ENTRY ONLY			
Common Stock		60,000	
Retained Earnings, 1/1/X4		76,000	
Equity in Net Income (of Subsidiary)		38,000	
Dividends Declared			24,000
Investment in Subsidiary			150,000

2. The intercompany bond interest elimination entry:

WORKSHEET ENTRY ONLY			
Intercompany Interest Income		21,500	
Intercompany Interest Expense			16,000
Gain on Debt Extinguishment			5,500

MODULE 1

THE COMPLETE EQUITY METHOD

3. The intercompany bond holding elimination entry:

WORKSHEET
ENTRY ONLY

Intercompany Bonds Payable	200,000	
Investment in Bonds of Subsidiary		200,000

These entries are posted to the December 31, 19X4 consolidation worksheet in Illustration 12–2.

CONSOLIDATION IN LATER YEARS

In later years, the intercompany bond-related consolidation entries are as follows:

1. The intercompany bond interest elimination entry:

WORKSHEET
ENTRY ONLY

Intercompany Interest Income	20,000	
Intercompany Interest Expense		20,000

2. The intercompany bond holding elimination entry:

WORKSHEET
ENTRY ONLY

Intercompany Bonds Payable	200,000	
Investment in Bonds of Subsidiary		200,000

SECTION 2: PARTIALLY OWNED SUBSIDIARIES

NONCONTROLLING INTEREST SITUATIONS

When a partially owned subsidiary has adjusted its general ledger to eliminate its intercompany premium or discount, the amounts to be reported in consolidation for the noncontrolling interest are readily obtained from the analysis of the Investment account (which is updated based on the subsidiary's reported amounts). Accordingly, this procedure also keeps simple the determination of reportable amounts pertaining to the noncontrolling interest.

ILLUSTRATION 12–2	THE COMPLETE EQUITY METHOD Consolidation at Bond Acquisition Year-End: 100%-Owned Subsidiary

P Company and S Company
Consolidation Worksheet as of December 31, 19X4

	P Company	100%-owned S Company	Consolidation Entries Dr.	Consolidation Entries Cr.	Consolidated
Income Statement (19X4)					
Sales	680,000	280,000			960,000
Cost of sales	(380,000)	(120,000)			(500,000)
Expenses	(265,500)	(114,000)			(379,500)
Gain on debt extinguishment	3,000	8,000		5,500(2)	16,500
Intercompany Accounts					
Equity in net income (of S Co.) . .	38,000		38,000(1)		–0–
Intercompany interest income . . .	21,500		21,500(2)		–0–
Intercompany interest expense . .		(16,000)		16,000(2)	–0–
Net Income	97,000	38,000	59,500	21,500	97,000
Statement of Retained Earnings					
Balances, 1/1/X4	156,000	76,000	76,000(1)		156,000
+ Net income	97,000	38,000	59,500	21,500	97,000
– Dividends declared	(51,000)	(24,000)		24,000(1)	(51,000)
Balances, 12/31/X4	202,000	90,000	135,500	45,500	202,000
Balance Sheet					
Intercompany interest receivable/payable	10,000	(10,000)			–0–
Investment in S Co.:					
Common stock	150,000			150,000(1)	–0–
Bonds	200,000			200,000(3)	–0–
Other assets	199,000	710,000			909,000
Total Assets	559,000	700,000		350,000	909,000
Payables and accruals	107,000	38,000			145,000
Bonds payable		300,000			300,000
Bond premium		12,000			12,000
Intercompany bond payable		200,000	200,000(3)		–0–
Common stock	250,000	60,000	60,000(1)		250,000
Retained earnings	202,000	90,000	135,500	45,500	202,000
Total Liabilities and Equity	559,000	700,000	395,500	45,500	909,000
Proof of debit and credit postings			395,500	395,500	

Explanation of entries:
(1) The basic elimination entry.
(2) The intercompany bond interest elimination entry.
(3) The intercompany bond holding elimination entry.

END

MODULE 2 OVERVIEW

Recall from Chapter 10 that under the partial equity method, the consolidated net income and retained earnings do *not* equal the parent's net income and retained earnings, respectively. When intercompany bond holdings exist, this inequality also occurs because the gain or loss on debt extinguishment is reported only in consolidation—not in the general ledgers as well.

The following discussion uses the example given on page 426 in which a $16,500 gain on extinguishment resulted ($12,000 from S Company's intercompany bond premium and $4,500 from P Company's discount).

SECTION 1: 100%-OWNED SUBSIDIARIES

CONSOLIDATION AT THE BOND ACQUISITION DATE

If consolidated statements are prepared on January 1, 19X4 (the bond acquisition date), the following consolidation entry is required to (1) reflect this deemed retirement of the bonds and (2) report the gain on debt extinguishment:

WORKSHEET **ENTRY ONLY**	Intercompany Bonds Payable 200,000	
	Intercompany Bond Premium 12,000	
	Investment in Bonds of Subsidiary	195,500
	Gain on Debt Extinguishment	16,500

This entry produces the same results as though S Company had acquired and retired its own bonds.

SUBSEQUENT AMORTIZATION OF BOND PREMIUM AND DISCOUNT

In the preceding example, the substance of the deemed bond retirement is to accelerate reporting the $12,000 intercompany bond premium and the $4,500 bond discount. In other words, S Company does not report its $12,000 intercompany bond premium as income over the remaining life of the bonds (as a reduction of interest expense through the amortization process) but instead as income in consolidation at the bond acquisition date. Likewise, P Company does not report its $4,500 bond discount as income over the remaining life of the bonds (as additional interest income through the amortization process) but instead as income in consolidation at the bond acquisition date.

Because the $12,000 intercompany bond premium and the $4,500 bond discount are reported as income in consolidation at the bond acquisition date, the consolidated Retained Earnings account balance is $16,500 higher than the books show. Only after the complete amortization of the $12,000 intercompany bond premium and the $4,500 bond discount (that takes place in the general ledgers over the three-year remaining life of the bonds) will the consolidated retained earnings balance equal the retained earnings shown in the books.

If nothing is done in consolidation at the end of 19X4, 19X5, and 19X6 concerning this amortization, the $16,500 will have been reported as income twice:

1. First as a $16,500 gain on debt extinguishment in 19X4 as a result of the consolidation entry to eliminate the Bond Investment and the related Intercompany Bond Payable and Premium accounts.

2. Second as additional interest income ($4,500) and lower interest expense ($12,000) from January 1, 19X4, to December 31, 19X6, as a result of amortizing the $4,500 discount and the $12,000 intercompany bond premium to income in the general ledgers.

Obviously, the $16,500 can be reported as income only once. Thus in periods subsequent to the bond acquisition date, entries are needed in consolidation to undo the reporting of this income resulting from the amortization process. This, of course, is consistent with the consolidated viewpoint that the bonds are deemed retired at the bond acquisition date. Consequently, future period consolidated income statements cannot report any interest income or expense with respect to these intercompany-held bonds.

GENERAL LEDGER ENTRIES SUBSEQUENT TO THE BOND ACQUISITION DATE

Assume that P Company and S Company use the straight-line method to amortize bond premium and discount (the results from the straight-line method do not differ materially from results under the interest method). The entries that would be recorded in **each company's general ledger** during 19X4, 19X5, and 19X6 relating to the entire bond issue are as follows:

	P Company		S Company	
Interest Expense (60%).			30,000	
Intercompany Interest				
Expense (40%)			20,000	
Interest Payable (60%)				30,000
Intercompany Interest				
Payable (40%)				20,000
To record interest expense				
(10% of $500,000 = $50,000).				
Intercompany Interest Receivable	20,000			
Intercompany Interest Income . .		20,000		
To record interest income				
(10% of $200,000).				
Bond Premium (60%)			6,000	
Intercompany Bond Premium (40%) . .			4,000	
Interest Expense (60%)				6,000
Intercompany Interest				
Expense (40%)				4,000
To amortize the total bond premium				
at 1/1/X4 of $30,000 over				
three years.				
Investment in Bonds (of Subsidiary) . .	1,500			
Intercompany Interest Income . .		1,500		
To amortize the $4,500 bond discount				
at 1/1/X4 over three years.				

At the end of each of these years, the balances in the Intercompany Interest Expense and Intercompany Interest Income accounts are as follows:

P Company Intercompany Interest Income		S Company Intercompany Interest Expense	
	$20,000	$20,000	
	1,500		$4,000
	$21,500	$16,000	

The difference between the two accounts is a net credit of $5,500, which results from the amortization of the $4,000 intercompany bond premium and the $1,500 bond discount. As shown shortly, these accounts are eliminated in consolidation.

THE PARTIAL EQUITY METHOD — MODULE 2

| ILLUSTRATIONS | PREPARING CONSOLIDATED FINANCIAL STATEMENTS |

- **THE PARTIAL EQUITY METHOD**
- **AT END OF BOND ACQUISITION YEAR: 100%-OWNED SUBSIDIARY**

P Company makes the following consolidation entries at December 31, 19X4 (one year after the bond acquisition date):

1. **The basic elimination (using assumed amounts):**

WORKSHEET ENTRY ONLY

Common Stock	60,000	
Retained Earnings, 1/1/X4	76,000	
Equity in Net Income (of Subsidiary)	30,000	
Dividends Declared		24,000
Investment in Subsidiary		142,000

2. **The intercompany bond interest elimination entry:**

WORKSHEET ENTRY ONLY

Intercompany Interest Income	21,500	
Intercompany Interest Expense		16,000
Gain on Debt Extinguishment		5,500

3. **The intercompany bond holding elimination entry:**

WORKSHEET ENTRY ONLY

Intercompany Bonds Payable	200,000	
Intercompany Bond Premium ($12,000 − $4,000)	8,000	
Investment in Bonds of Subsidiary		
($195,500 + $1,500 19X4 amortization)		197,000
Gain on Debt Extinguishment		11,000

The combination of entries 2 and 3 results in a $16,500 credit to the Gain on Debt Extinguishment account, which was the amount of gain determined on January 1, 19X4 (the date the intercompany bond investment was made). Because of the actual $5,500 amortization recorded in the general ledgers during 19X4, only $11,000 of premium and discount remain "locked into" the balance sheets at the end of 19X4.

These entries are posted to the December 31, 19X4 consolidation worksheet in Illustration 12–3.

REVIEW POINTS FOR ILLUSTRATION 12–3 Note the following:

1. Both consolidated net income and consolidated retained earnings are $11,000 higher than the corresponding account balances in the parent's column. The difference is attributable to (1) P Company's unamortized discount of $3,000 at December 31, 19X4, and (2) S Company's unamortized intercompany bond premium of $8,000 at December 31, 19X4.

2. The $16,500 gain on debt extinguishment in the Consolidated column is more than 10% of net income. Accordingly, it most likely would be reported as an extraordinary item.

BOND CONSOLIDATION ENTRIES FOR SUBSEQUENT YEARS

For periods subsequent to the bond acquisition year, the bond-related consolidation entries are nearly identical to the two bond consolidation entries shown for Illustration 12–3. The differences are as follows:

1. The bond holding elimination entry contains updated amounts because of the amortization recorded in the general ledgers during the year.
2. The Retained Earnings account (beginning-of-year balance in the analysis of retained earnings) rather than the Gain on Debt Extinguishment account is credited in each of these entries. The credits to the Retained Earnings account merely reestablish on the worksheet the portion of the gain on debt extinguishment not yet recorded in the general Retained Earnings accounts (through the amortization process) at the beginning of the year.

ILLUSTRATION 12-3	THE PARTIAL EQUITY METHOD Consolidation at Bond Acquisition Year-End: 100%-Owned Subsidiary

P Company and S Company
Consolidation Worksheet as of December 31, 19X4

	P Company	100%-owned S Company	Consolidation Entries Dr.	Consolidation Entries Cr.	Consolidated
Income Statement (19X4)					
Sales	680,000	280,000			960,000
Cost of sales	(380,000)	(120,000)			(500,000)
Expenses	(265,500)	(114,000)			(379,500)
Gain on debt extinguishment				5,500(2) 11,000(3)	16,500
Intercompany Accounts					
Equity in net income (of S Co.)	30,000		30,000(1)		–0–
Intercompany interest income	21,500		21,500(2)		–0–
Intercompany interest expense		(16,000)		16,000(2)	–0–
Net Income	86,000	30,000	51,500	32,500	97,000
Statement of Retained Earnings					
Balances, 1/1/X4	156,000	76,000	76,000(1)		156,000
+ Net income	86,000	30,000	51,500	32,500	97,000
– Dividends declared	(51,000)	(24,000)		24,000(1)	(51,000)
Balances, 12/31/X4	191,000	82,000	127,500	56,500	202,000
Balance Sheet					
Intercompany interest receivable/payable	10,000	(10,000)			–0–
Investment in S Co.:					
Common stock	142,000			142,000(1)	–0–
Bonds	197,000			197,000(3)	–0–
Other assets	199,000	710,000			909,000
Total Assets	548,000	700,000		339,000	909,000
Payables and accruals	107,000	38,000			145,000
Bonds payable		300,000			300,000
Bond premium		12,000			12,000
Intercompany bond payable		200,000	200,000(3)		–0–
Intercompany bond premium		8,000	8,000(3)		–0–
Common stock	250,000	60,000	60,000(1)		250,000
Retained earnings	191,000	82,000	127,500	56,500	202,000
Total Liabilities and Equity	548,000	700,000	395,500	56,500	909,000
Proof of debit and credit postings			395,500	395,500	

Explanation of entries:
(1) The basic elimination entry.
(2) The intercompany bond interest elimination entry.
(3) The intercompany bond holding elimination entry.

The bond-related consolidation entries at the end of 19X5 and 19X6 are as follows:

		Consolidation Date	
		Dec. 31, 19X5	Dec. 31, 19X6
WORKSHEET ENTRIES ONLY	Intercompany Interest Income ...	21,500	21,500
	Intercompany Interest Expense	16,000	16,000
	Retained Earnings, 1/1/X5 and 1/1/X6	5,500	5,500
WORKSHEET ENTRIES ONLY	Intercompany Bonds Payable	200,000	200,000
	Intercompany Bond Premium	4,000	–0–
	Investment in Bonds	198,500	200,000
	Retained Earnings, 1/1/X5 and 1/1/X6	5,500	–0–

SECTION 2: PARTIALLY OWNED SUBSIDIARY

When a subsidiary is partially owned, the bond-related consolidation entries also require an adjustment to the noncontrolling interest if part of the gain or loss on debt extinguishment is attributable to the subsidiary's unamortized premium or discount. No adjustment is necessary if the subsidiary issued or acquired the bonds at their face amount.

Let us change our example to reflect 75% ownership in S Company. Of the $16,500 gain on debt extinguishment, we know that $12,000 is a result of the premium on S Company's books. Only 75%, or $9,000, of this $12,000 accrues to P Company. The remaining $3,000 accrues to the noncontrolling interest. In consolidation, this $3,000 is reflected as additional noncontrolling interest in S Company's net income and net assets.

CONSOLIDATION AT THE BOND ACQUISITION DATE

If consolidated statements are prepared at January 1, 19X4, an additional consolidation entry is required to adjust the noncontrolling interest. This worksheet entry is as follows:

WORKSHEET ENTRY ONLY	NCI in Net Income	3,000	
	NCI in Net Assets		3,000

As a result of the noncontrolling interest in S Company, the consolidated net income that accrues to the controlling interest is higher by only $13,500 ($9,000 + $4,500 discount) rather than $16,500 ($12,000 + $4,500 discount).

CONSOLIDATION AT THE BOND ACQUISITION YEAR-END

The noncontrolling interest deduction posted in the basic elimination entry made at December 31, 19X4 (one year after the purchase of the bonds by P Company), is based on S Company's $30,000 reported net income for 19X4. This $30,000 includes $4,000 of 19X4 intercompany bond premium amortization. The amortization of the remaining intercompany bond premium of $8,000 must be accelerated, however, for consolidated reporting purposes. Consequently, the deduction of an additional $2,000 (25% of $8,000) noncontrolling interest must be made in consolidation at December 31, 19X4, as follows:

WORKSHEET ENTRY ONLY	NCI in Net Income	2,000	
	NCI in Net Assets		2,000

ILLUSTRATIONS **PREPARING CONSOLIDATED FINANCIAL STATEMENTS**

- **THE PARTIAL EQUITY METHOD**
- **AT BOND ACQUISITION YEAR-END: 75%-OWNED SUBSIDIARY**

Illustration 12–4 revises Illustration 12–3 to reflect 75% ownership of S Company. The preceding noncontrolling interest entry is used along with the following basic elimination entry:

WORKSHEET ENTRY ONLY	Common Stock	60,000	
	Retained Earnings, 1/1/X4	76,000	
	Equity in Net Income (of subsidiary)	22,500	
	NCI in Net Income (25% of $30,000)	7,500	
	Dividends Declared		24,000
	Investment in Subsidiary's Common Stock		106,500
	NCI in Net Assets (25% of $142,000)		35,500

BOND CONSOLIDATION ENTRIES FOR LATER YEARS

For later years, the bond-related consolidation entries for a partially owned subsidiary are as follows:

		Consolidation Date			
		Dec. 31, 19X5		**Dec. 31, 19X6**	
WORKSHEET ENTRIES ONLY	Intercompany Interest Income ...	21,500		21,500	
	Intercompany Interest Expense		16,000		16,000
	Retained Earnings, 1/1/X5 and 1/1/X6		4,500		4,500
	NCI in Net Income (25% of the $4,000 intercompany bond premium amortized in 19X5 and 19X6)		1,000		1,000
WORKSHEET ENTRIES ONLY	Intercompany Bonds Payable	200,000		200,000	
	Intercompany Bond Premium	4,000		–0–	
	Investment in Bonds		198,500		200,000
	Retained Earnings, 1/1/X5 and 1/1/X6		4,500		–0–
	NCI in Net Assets (25% of $4,000 unamortized inter-company bond premium at 12/31/X5) ...		1,000		–0–

These entries assume that the noncontrolling interest deduction in the income statement—based on S Company's reported net income—has already been established from the posting made from the basic elimination entry. The credit to the NCI in Net Assets account in the second entry merely reestablishes on the worksheet the

ILLUSTRATION 12–4 | **THE PARTIAL EQUITY METHOD** Consolidation at Bond Acquisition Year-End: 75%-Owned Subsidiary

P Company and S Company
Consolidation Worksheet as of December 31, 19X4

	P Company	75%-owned S Company	Consolidation Entries Dr.	Consolidation Entries Cr.	Consolidated
Income Statement (19X4)					
Sales	680,000	280,000			960,000
Cost of sales	(380,000)	(120,000)			(500,000)
Expenses	(265,500)	(114,000)			(379,500)
Gain on debt extinguishment				5,500(2)	16,500
				11,000(3)	
Intercompany Accounts					
Equity in net income (of S Co.) . .	22,500		22,500(1)		–0–
Intercompany interest income . . .	21,500		21,500(2)		–0–
Intercompany interest expense . .		(16,000)		16,000(2)	–0–
Net Income	78,500	30,000	44,000	32,500	97,000
			2,000(4)		
NCI in net income			7,500(1)		(9,500)[a]
CI in net income	78,500	30,000	53,500	32,500	87,500
Statement of Retained Earnings					
Balances, 1/1/X4	137,000	76,000	76,000(1)		137,000
+ Net income	78,500	30,000	53,500	32,500	87,500
− Dividends declared	(51,000)	(24,000)		24,000(1)	(51,000)
Balances, 12/31/X4	164,500	82,000	129,500	56,500	173,500
Balance Sheet					
Intercompany interest receivable/payable	10,000	(10,000)			–0–
Investment in S Co.:					
Common stock	106,500			106,500(1)	–0–
Bonds	197,000			197,000(3)	–0–
Other assets	208,000	710,000			918,000
Total Assets	521,500	700,000		303,500	918,000
Payables and accruals	107,000	38,000			145,000
Bonds payable		300,000			300,000
Bond premium		12,000			12,000
Intercompany bond payable		200,000	200,000(3)		–0–
Intercompany bond premium		8,000	8,000(3)		–0–
				2,000(4)	
NCI in net assets				35,500(1)	37,500
Common stock	250,000	60,000	60,000(1)		250,000
Retained earnings	164,500	82,000	129,500	56,500	173,500
Total Liabilities and Equity	521,500	700,000	397,500	94,000	918,000
Proof of debit and credit postings			397,500	397,500	

[a]Proof: S Company's reported net income of $30,000 + $8,000 of unamortized intercompany premium at 12/31/X4 = $38,000; $38,000 × 25% = $9,500.

Explanation of entries:
(1) The basic elimination entry.
(2) The intercompany bond interest elimination entry.
(3) The intercompany bond holding elimination entry.
(4) The sharing of the gain with the noncontrolling interest.

portion of the gain that accrues to the noncontrolling interest but that has not yet been recorded in S Company's Retained Earnings account (through the amortization process) at this consolidation date.

The credits to retained earnings in both entries merely reestablish on the worksheet the portion of the gain that accrues to P Company and has not been recorded yet in the books (through the amortization process) at the beginning of the year.

END

MODULE 3 OVERVIEW

When the parent uses the cost method, the gain or loss on debt extinguishment is reported only in consolidation—not in the general ledgers as well. The procedures for dealing with intercompany bond holdings in consolidation in this Module 3 are identical to those shown in Module 2. Accordingly, to save unnecessary publication of the same textual matter, to use this Module 3, we ask you to (1) read Sections 1 and 2 of Module 2, (2) substitute the consolidation entries shown in each section of this Module 3 for the consolidation entries shown in each section of Module 2, and (3) substitute the consolidation worksheets shown in this Module 3 for those shown in Module 2.

SECTION 1: 100%-OWNED SUBSIDIARIES

CONSOLIDATION AT THE BOND ACQUISITION YEAR-END

Substitute the following consolidation entries for the consolidation entries on page 426.

1. The basic elimination (using an assumed amount):

WORKSHEET ENTRY ONLY			
Common Stock	60,000	
Investment in Subsidiary		60,000

2. The intercompany dividend elimination entry (using an assumed amount):

WORKSHEET ENTRY ONLY			
Dividends Income	24,000	
Dividends Declared		24,000

3. The intercompany bond interest elimination entry (same entry as shown in Module 2 but repeated here for convenience):

WORKSHEET ENTRY ONLY			
Intercompany Interest Income	21,500	
Intercompany Interest Expense		16,000
Gain on Debt Extinguishment		5,500

4. The intercompany bond holding elimination entry (same entry as shown in Module 2 but repeated here for convenience):

WORKSHEET ENTRY ONLY			
Intercompany Bonds Payable	200,000	
Intercompany Bond Premium ($12,000 – $4,000)	8,000	
Investment in Bonds of Subsidiary		
($195,500 + $1,500 19X4 amortization)		197,000
Gain on Debt Extinguishment		11,000

MODULE 3

THE COST METHOD

Substitute Illustration 12–5 (shown below) for Illustration 12–3 on page 437.

ILLUSTRATION 12–5	**THE COST METHOD** Consolidation at Bond Acquisition Year-End: 100%-Owned Subsidiary

P Company and S Company
Consolidation Worksheet as of December 31, 19X4

	P Company	100%-owned S Company	Consolidation Entries Dr.	Consolidation Entries Cr.	Consolidated
Income Statement (19X4)					
Sales	680,000	280,000			960,000
Cost of sales	(380,000)	(120,000)			(500,000)
Expenses	(265,500)	(114,000)			(379,500)
Gain on debt extinguishment				5,500(3)	16,500
				11,000(4)	
Intercompany Accounts					
Dividend income (from S Co.) ...	24,000		24,000(2)		–0–
Intercompany interest income ...	21,500		21,500(3)		–0–
Intercompany interest expense ..		(16,000)		16,000(3)	–0–
Net Income	80,000	30,000	45,500	32,500	97,000
Statement of Retained Earnings					
Balances, 1/1/X4	80,000	76,000			156,000
+ Net income	80,000	30,000	45,500	32,500	97,000
– Dividends declared	(51,000)	(24,000)		24,000(2)	(51,000)
Balances, 12/31/X4	109,000	82,000	45,500	56,500	202,000
Balance Sheet					
Intercompany interest receivable/payable	10,000	(10,000)			–0–
Investment in S Co.:					
Common stock	60,000			60,000(1)	–0–
Bonds	197,000			197,000(4)	–0–
Other assets	199,000	710,000			909,000
Total Assets	466,000	700,000		257,000	909,000
Payables and accruals	107,000	38,000			145,000
Bonds payable		300,000			300,000
Bond premium		12,000			12,000
Intercompany bond payable		200,000	200,000(4)		–0–
Intercompany bond premium		8,000	8,000(4)		–0–
Common stock	250,000	60,000	60,000(1)		250,000
Retained earnings	109,000	82,000	45,500	56,500	202,000
Total Liabilities and Equity	466,000	700,000	313,500	56,500	909,000
Proof of debit and credit postings			313,500	313,500	

Explanation of entries:
(1) The basic elimination entry.
(2) The intercompany dividend elimination entry.
(3) The intercompany bond interest elimination entry.
(4) The intercompany bond holding elimination entry.

SECTION 2: PARTIALLY OWNED SUBSIDIARIES

CONSOLIDATION AT THE BOND ACQUISITION YEAR-END

Substitute the following consolidation entries for the consolidation entries on page 439.

1. **The basic elimination entry:**

WORKSHEET ENTRY ONLY			
Common Stock (75% of $60,000)	45,000	
Investment in Subsidiary		45,000

2. **The intercompany dividend elimination entry:**

WORKSHEET ENTRY ONLY			
Dividend Income (75% of $24,000)	18,000	
Dividends Declared		18,000

3. **The NCI elimination entry** (all amounts are at 25% of subsidiary's reported amounts):

WORKSHEET ENTRY ONLY			
Common Stock (25% of $60,000)	15,000	
Retained Earnings, 1/1/X4 (25% of $76,000)	19,000	
NCI in Net Income (25% of $30,000)	7,500	
Dividends Declared (25% of $24,000)		6,000
NCI in Net Assets (25% of $142,000)		35,500

4. **The intercompany bond interest elimination entry** (same entry as shown in Module 2):

WORKSHEET ENTRY ONLY			
Intercompany Interest Income	21,500	
Intercompany Interest Expense		16,000
Gain on Debt Extinguishment		5,500

5. **The intercompany bond holding elimination entry** (same entry as shown in Module 2):

WORKSHEET ENTRY ONLY			
Intercompany Bonds Payable	200,000	
Intercompany Bond Premium ($12,000 – $4,000)	8,000	
Investment in Bonds of Subsidiary		
($195,500 + $1,500 19X4 amortization)		197,000
Gain on Debt Extinguishment		11,000

6. **The sharing of the gain on debt extinguishment elimination entry** (same entry as shown in Module 2):

WORKSHEET ENTRY ONLY			
NCI in Net Income (25% of $8,000 unamortized		
intercompany bond premium at 12/31/X4)	2,000	
NCI in Net Assets		2,000

Substitute Illustration 12–6 for Illustration 12–4 on page 440.

MODULE 3

THE COST METHOD

M O D U L E 3

THE COST METHOD

ILLUSTRATION 12-6	THE COST METHOD Consolidation at Bond Acquisition Year-End: 75%-Owned Subsidiary

P Company and S Company
Consolidation Worksheet as of December 31, 19X4

	P Company	75%-owned S Company	Consolidation Entries Dr.	Consolidation Entries Cr.	Consolidated
Income Statement (19X4)					
Sales	680,000	280,000			960,000
Cost of sales	(380,000)	(120,000)			(500,000)
Expenses	(265,500)	(114,000)			(379,500)
Gain on debt extinguishment				5,500(4) 11,000(5)	16,500
Intercompany Accounts					
Dividend income (from S Co.)	18,000		18,000(2)		–0–
Intercompany interest income	21,500		21,500(4)		–0–
Intercompany interest expense		(16,000)		16,000(4)	–0–
Net Income	74,000	30,000	39,500	32,500	97,000
NCI in net income			2,000(6) 7,500(3)		(9,500)[a]
CI in net income			49,000	32,500	87,500
Statement of Retained Earnings					
Balances, 1/1/X4	80,000	76,000	19,000(3)		137,000
+ Net income	74,000	30,000	49,000	32,500	87,500
– Dividends declared	(51,000)	(24,000)		6,000(3) 18,000(2)	(51,000)
Balances, 12/31/X4	103,000	82,000	68,000	56,500	173,500
Balance Sheet					
Intercompany interest receivable/payable	10,000	(10,000)			–0–
Investment in S Co.:					
Common stock	45,000			45,000(1)	–0–
Bonds	197,000			197,000(5)	–0–
Other assets	208,000	710,000			918,000
Total Assets	460,000	700,000		242,000	918,000
Payables and accruals	107,000	38,000			145,000
Bonds payable		300,000			300,000
Bond premium		12,000			12,000
Intercompany bond payable		200,000	200,000(5)		–0–
Intercompany bond premium		8,000	8,000(5)		–0–
NCI in net assets				2,000(6) 35,500(3)	37,500
Common stock	250,000	60,000	15,000(3) 45,000(1)		250,000
Retained earnings	103,000	82,000	68,000	56,500	173,500
Total Liabilities and Equity	460,000	700,000	336,000	94,000	918,000
Proof of debit and credit postings			336,000	336,000	

[a]Proof: S Company's reported net income of $30,000 + $8,000 of unamortized intercompany premium at 12/31/X4 = $38,000; $38,000 × 25% = $9,500.

Explanation of entries:
(1) The basic elimination entry.
(2) The intercompany dividend elimination entry.
(3) The NCI elimination entry.
(4) The intercompany bond interest elimination entry.
(5) The intercompany bond holding elimination entry.
(6) The sharing of the gain with the NCI entry.

END

END-OF-CHAPTER REVIEW

SUMMARY OF KEY POINTS

1. The acquisition of an affiliated entity's outstanding bonds is accounted for in consolidation as a retirement of those bonds, even though they are not actually retired.
2. A gain or loss on early extinguishment of debt is reported in the period in which the affiliate's bonds are acquired—but only to the extent of the intercompany portion acquired.
3. The gain or loss is the difference between the acquisition cost (excluding amounts paid for interest) and the carrying value of the bonds.

GLOSSARY OF NEW TERMS

Constructive retirement   Substantive retirement of a bond issue rather than legal retirement.

SELF-STUDY QUESTIONS

(Answers are at the end of this chapter.)

1. When both the parent and the subsidiary have premiums, what result is reported in consolidation in the year of an intercompany bond purchase?
   a. Always a gain.
   b. Always a loss.
   c. A loss only if the applicable share of the unamortized premium exceeds the acquirer's premium.
   d. A gain only if the applicable share of the unamortized premium exceeds the acquirer's premium.
2. A parent acquired in the open market 30% of its 100%-owned subsidiary's outstanding 10% bonds for $310,000. The bonds have a face value of $1,000,000 and a carrying value of $1,020,000 on the acquisition date. What is the gain or loss to be reported in the consolidated statements in the bond acquisition year?
   a. A gain of $4,000.   c. A loss of $10,000.
   b. A loss of $4,000.   d. A gain of $6,000.

Questions 3 through 7 are based on the following information:
On 4/1/X1, Plow Inc. acquired in the open market 40% of the outstanding 10% bonds of Seed Inc., its 80%-owned subsidiary, for $408,000. The bonds have a face value of $1,000,000, a carrying value of $940,000 on 4/1/X1, and a maturity date of 3/31/X3. For 19X1, Plow reported $100,000 of income—excluding any interest income or loss pertaining to its bond investment and excluding any of Seed's earnings. Also for 19X1, Seed reported net income of $50,000—after reported interest expense of $130,000 on the bond issue. Each entity uses straight-line amortization.

3. What is the reportable gain or loss on debt extinguishment?
   a. A loss of $32,000   c. A loss of $8,000
   b. A loss of $16,000   d. A gain of $16,000
4. What is Plow's intercompany interest income in its separate income statement for 19X1?
   a. $40,000   c. $27,000
   b. $30,000   d. $22,000
5. What is Seed's intercompany interest expense for 19X1?
   a. $42,000   c. $30,000
   b. $39,000   d. $21,000
6. What is the consolidated net income for 19X1?
   a. $170,000   c. $150,000
   b. $158,000   d. $128,000
7. What is the reportable amount for NCI in Net Income for 19X1?
   a. $5,200   c. $8,200
   b. $7,000   d. $10,000

ASSIGNMENT MATERIAL

REVIEW QUESTIONS

1. From a consolidated viewpoint, what is the substance of an intercompany bond purchase?
2. How is the gain or loss on debt extinguishment determined?
3. Are gains and losses on debt extinguishment extraordinary items?
4. Does a gain or loss result when (a) each entity has a premium, (b) each entity has a discount, and (c) one entity has a discount and the other a premium?
5. To which entity should the gain or loss on debt extinguishment be assigned?

EXERCISES

E 12–1 **Gain/Loss Calculation** Parr Inc. owns 100% of the outstanding common stock of Subb Inc. On 4/1/X1, Parr acquired in the open market 25% of Subb's outstanding 10%, 10-year debentures ($4,000,000 face amount) at a cost of $1,015,000. The bonds were issued at a premium of $320,000. They mature on 6/30/X5 and pay interest semiannually on 6/30 and 12/31. Each entity uses straight-line amortization.

Required What is the gain or loss on debt extinguishment to be reported in consolidation for 19X1?

E 12–2 **Gain/Loss Calculation; Bond Consolidation Entry** Pell Inc. owns 100% of the outstanding common stock of Sull Inc. On 1/1/X2, Pell acquired in the open market 40% of Sull's outstanding 10% bonds at a cost of $430,000. On 1/1/X2, the carrying value of all of the bonds ($1,000,000 face amount) was $1,040,000. Their maturity date is 12/31/X5.

Required 1. What is the gain or loss on debt extinguishment to be reported in consolidation for 19X2?
2. Prepare the bond-related consolidation entry at 1/1/X2.

E 12–3 **Gain/Loss Calculation; Bond Consolidation Entry (75% ownership)** Pidd Inc. owns 75% of the outstanding common stock of Sidd Inc. On 1/1/X3, Pidd acquired in the open market 20% of Sidd's outstanding 10% bonds at a cost of $160,000. On 1/1/X3, the carrying value of all of the bonds ($1,000,000 face amount) was $1,020,000. Their maturity date is 12/31/X6.

Required 1. What is the gain or loss on debt extinguishment to be reported in consolidation for 19X3?
2. Prepare the bond-related consolidation entry at 1/1/X3.

E 12–4 **Gain/Loss Calculation; Bond Consolidation Entries at Year-End** Poll Inc. owns 100% of the outstanding common stock of Soll Inc. On 1/1/X4, Poll acquired in the open market 30% of Soll's outstanding 10% bonds at a cost of $340,000. On 1/1/X4, the carrying value of all of the bonds ($1,000,000 face amount) was $1,035,000. Their maturity date is 12/31/X8. Each entity uses straight-line amortization.

Required 1. What is the gain or loss on debt extinguishment to be reported in consolidation for 19X4?
2. Prepare the bond-related consolidation entries at 12/31/X4. (For Module 1, first prepare the appropriate *general ledger* adjusting entries at 12/31/X4.)

E 12–5 **Gain/Loss Calculation; Bond Consolidation Entries at Year-End (80% ownership)** Pudd Inc. owns 80% of the outstanding common stock of Sudd Inc. On 1/1/X5, Pudd acquired in the open market 60% of Sudd's outstanding 10% bonds at a cost of $620,000. On 1/1/X5, the carrying value of all of the bonds ($1,000,000 face amount) was $950,000. Their maturity date is 12/31/X9. Each entity uses straight-line amortization.

Required 1. What is the gain or loss on debt extinguishment to be reported in consolidation for 19X5?
2. Prepare the bond-related consolidation entries at 12/31/X5. (For Module 1, first prepare the appropriate *general ledger* adjusting entries at 12/31/X5.)

PROBLEMS

P 12–1 **Bond-Related Consolidation Entries** The partially completed income statements of Place Inc. and its 100%-owned created subsidiary, Show Inc., for the year ended 12/31/X6 are as follows:

	19X6	
	Place Inc.	**Show Inc.**
Sales	$7,000,000	$3,000,000
Cost of sales	(4,000,000)	(1,600,000)
Expenses (noninterest)	(1,500,000)	(1,000,000)
Interest expense	–0–	
Gain on debt extinguishment		
Intercompany Accounts		
Equity in net income (of Show)		
Dividend income (from Show)		
Intercompany interest income		
Intercompany interest expense		
Net Income	$	$

Additional Information

1. On 1/1/X6, Place acquired 40% of Show's outstanding 10% bonds ($1,000,000 face amount) at 90. Show had initially issued these 10-year bonds on 1/1/X4 at 105.
2. Neither entity had any other investments or indebtedness that would give rise to interest income or interest expense.
3. Each entity uses straight-line amortization.
4. Show declared cash dividends of $200,000 in 19X6.

Required

1. Fill in the blanks in the preceding income statements.
2. Prepare the bond-related consolidation entries at 12/31/X6. (For Module 1, first prepare the appropriate *general ledger* adjusting entries at 12/31/X6.)

P 12–2 **Bond-Related Consolidation Entries: Multiple Years** Stak Inc. is a 100%-owned created subsidiary of Ptak Inc. On 1/1/X3, Stak issued $10,000,000 of five-year, 10% bonds at 98 (maturity date is 1/1/X8). On 1/1/X5 (two years later), Ptak acquired in the open market 30% of these bonds at 102. Each entity uses straight-line amortization.

Required

1. Calculate the gain or loss on debt extinguishment to be reported for 19X5.
2. Prepare the bond-related consolidation entries at 12/31/X5, X6, and X7. (For Module 1, first prepare the appropriate *general ledger* adjusting entries for 12/31/X5.)

P 12–3 **Bond-Related Consolidation Entries: Multiple Years (90% ownership)** Sala Inc. is a 90%-owned created subsidiary of Pala Inc. On 1/1/X1, Sala issued $10,000,000 of five-year, 10% bonds at 95 (maturity date is 1/1/X6). On 1/1/X3 (two years later), Pala acquired in the open market 30% of these bonds at 101. Each entity uses straight-line amortization.

Required

1. Calculate the gain or loss on debt extinguishment to be reported for 19X3.
2. Prepare the bond-related consolidation entries at 12/31/X3, X4, and X5. (For Module 1, first prepare the appropriate *general ledger* adjusting entries for 12/31/X3.)

P 12–4* **Consolidation Worksheet** Sita Inc. is a 100%-owned created subsidiary of Pita Inc. On 3/31/X6, Pita acquired in the open market 25% of Sita's outstanding 12%, 10-year bonds for a total cash payment (including interest) of $106,500. Information regarding Sita's bonds as of the bond acquisition date is as follows:

Total face amount	$400,000
Unamortized bond premium	$56,000
Maturity date	12/31/X7
Interest payment dates	July 1 and January 1
Amortization method	Straight line

*The financial statement information presented for problems accompanied by asterisks is also provided on Model 12 (filename: MODEL12) of the software file disk that is available with the text, allowing the problem to be worked on the computer.

Comparative financial statements of each entity are as follows:

	Pita Inc.		
	Cost Method[a]	Equity Method[b]	Sita Inc.
Income Statement (19X6)			
Sales	$550,000	$550,000	$410,000
Cost of sales	(230,000)	(230,000)	(210,000)
Expenses	(220,000)	(220,000)	(141,000)
Intercompany Accounts			
Dividend income (from Sita)	20,000		
Equity in net income (of Sita)		50,000	
Intercompany interest income	9,000	9,000	
Intercompany interest expense			(9,000)
Net Income	$129,000	$159,000	$ 50,000
Balance Sheet (as of 12/31/X6)			
Investment in subsidiary:			
Common stock	$ 50,000	$150,000	
Bonds	106,500	106,500	
Other assets	344,000	344,000	628,000
Total Assets	$500,500	$600,500	$628,000
Payables and accruals	$ 70,500	$ 70,500	$ 22,000
Bonds payable			400,000
Bond premium			56,000
Common stock	300,000	300,000	50,000
Retained earnings	130,000	230,000	100,000
Total Liabilities and Equity	$500,500	$600,500	$628,000
Dividends declared	$ 51,000	$ 51,000	$ 20,000

[a]Use this column if you are using Module 3.

[b]Use this column if you are using Modules 1 or 2.

Additional Information

1. *Neither* entity has recorded any bond premium or discount amortization since 3/31/X6.
2. Because of a cash shortage, Sita did not make any bond interest payments to Pita during 19X6.

Required

1. Prepare an analysis that shows the calculation of the gain or loss on debt extinguishment.
2. Prepare all general ledger adjusting entries required at 12/31/X6. Then adjust the financial statements accordingly.
3. Prepare all consolidation entries as of 12/31/X6.
4. Prepare a consolidation worksheet at 12/31/X6.

P 12–5* **Consolidation Worksheet (75% ownership)** Senn Inc. is a 75%-owned created subsidiary of Penn Inc. On 10/1/X4, Penn acquired in the open market 40% of Senn's outstanding 10%, 10-year bonds for a total cash payment (including interest) of $128,000. Information regarding Senn's bonds as of the bond acquisition date is as follows:

Total face amount	$300,000
Unamortized bond discount	$37,500
Maturity date	12/31/X5
Interest payment dates	June 30 and December 31[a]
Amortization method	Straight line

[a]The 12/31/X4 bond interest payment was made on 12/31/X4.

Comparative financial statements of each entity are as follows:

	Penn Inc.		
	Cost Method[a]	Equity Method[b]	Senn Inc.
Income Statement (19X4)			
Sales	$600,000	$600,000	$350,000
Cost of sales	(200,000)	(200,000)	(190,000)
Expenses	(250,000)	(250,000)	(94,000)
Intercompany Accounts			
Dividend income (from Senn)	21,000		
Equity in net income (of Senn)		45,000	
Intercompany interest income	2,000	2,000	
Intercompany interest expense			(6,000)
Net Income	$173,000	$197,000	$ 60,000
Balance Sheet (as of 12/31/X4)			
Investment in subsidiary:			
Common stock	$ 30,000	$135,000	
Bonds	124,000	124,000	
Other assets	461,000	461,000	$520,000
Total Assets	$615,000	$720,000	$520,000
Payables and accruals	$ 80,000	$ 80,000	$ 70,000
Bonds payable			300,000
Bond premium			(30,000)
Common stock	200,000	200,000	40,000
Retained earnings	335,000	440,000	140,000
Total Liabilities & Equity	$615,000	$720,000	$520,000
Dividends declared	$ 50,000	$ 50,000	$ 28,000

[a]Use this column if you are using Module 3.
[b]Use this column if you are using Modules 1 or 2.

Required
1. Prepare an analysis that shows the calculation of the gain or loss on debt extinguishment.
2. Prepare all general ledger adjusting entries required at 12/31/X4. Then adjust the financial statements accordingly.
3. Prepare all consolidation entries as of 12/31/X4.
4. Prepare a consolidation worksheet at 12/31/X4.

P 12–6* **COMPREHENSIVE: PURCHASED SUBSIDIARY Year of Bond Acquisition (80% ownership); Upstream Inventory Sales** On 1/1/X1, Pye Inc. acquired 80% of the outstanding common stock of Slye Inc. for $210,000 cash. In addition, $22,000 of direct costs were incurred. At that date, Slye's only asset or liability that had a current value different from book value was the following:

	Book Value	Current Value	Remaining Life
Patent	$ 55,000	$185,000	4 years

The difference between the parent's cost and the current value of the net assets was properly allocated to the Land account because the appraisal report indicated that this was the least firm of the appraisal amounts. On 1/1/X3, Pye paid $72,000 cash to the former owners because Slye's earnings of $110,000 for the two years ended 12/31/X2 ($45,000 in 19X1 and $65,000 in 19X2) exceeded $80,000. At that date, it was determined that the land was actually undervalued by $30,000. (In retrospect, the appraiser's conservatism and caution were unjustified.)

On 12/31/X3, Pye acquired in the open market 40% of Slye's 12% bonds for a total cash payment of $189,000.

Additional
Information

1. Goodwill was assigned a six-year life.
2. The interest payment dates for Slye's bonds are 6/30 and 12/31. The 12/31/X3 interest payment was made on 12/30/X3.
3. At 12/31/X2, Pye held inventory it had acquired from Slye in 19X2 at a cost of $27,000. (Slye's cost was $22,000.)
4. Neither entity has ever made any general ledger entries relating to unrealized intercompany profits, gains, or losses.

Comparative financial statements for each entity are as follows:

| | Pye Inc. | | |
	Cost Method[a]	Equity Method[b]	Slye Inc.
Income Statement (19X3)			
Sales	$590,000	$590,000	$405,000
Cost of sales	(400,000)	(400,000)	(255,000)
Expenses	(113,000)	(113,000)	(123,000)
Intercompany Accounts			
Dividend income (from Slye)	28,000		
Equity in net income (of Slye)		20,000	
Intercompany sales			80,000
Intercompany cost of sales			(32,000)
Net Income	$105,000	$ 97,000	$ 75,000
Balance Sheet (as of 12/31/X3)			
Inventory			
From vendors	$115,000	$115,000	$ 90,000
Intercompany	25,000	25,000	
Investment in subsidiary			
Common stock	304,000	328,000	
Bonds	189,000	189,000	
Other assets	101,000	101,000	810,000
Total Assets	$734,000	$758,000	$900,000
Payables and accruals	$196,000	$196,000	$ 30,000
Bonds payable			300,000
Bond premium			12,000
Intercompany bond payable			200,000
Intercompany bond premium			8,000
Common stock	400,000	400,000	120,000
Retained earnings	138,000	162,000	230,000
Total Liabilities and Equity	$734,000	$758,000	$900,000
Dividends declared	$ 70,000	$ 70,000	$ 35,000

[a]Use this column if you are using Module 3.
[b]Use this column if you are using Modules 1 or 2.

Required

1. Prepare an analysis that shows the calculation of the gain or loss on debt extinguishment.
2. Prepare all general ledger adjusting entries required at 12/31/X3. Then adjust the financial statements accordingly.
3. For Modules 1 and 2 only: Prepare a conceptual analysis of the Investment in Common Stock account from 1/1/X1 through 12/31/X3. For Module 3 only: Prepare an analysis of the excess cost element.
4. Prepare all consolidation entries as of 12/31/X3.
5. Prepare a consolidation worksheet at 12/31/X3.

P 12-7 **Reverse Analysis: Reconstructing Data from a Consolidation Entry** Pull Inc. created Strapp Inc. as a 100%-owned subsidiary on 4/1/X1 by making a $500,000 cash investment in Strapp's no par common stock. On 7/1/X6, Pull instructed Strapp to acquire 40% of Pull's outstanding 10% bonds. Pull's bonds were issued on 1/1/X1 and mature on 12/31/X9. Each company uses straight-line amortization for interest. In consolidation at 12/31/X7 (not X6), the following entry was made:

Intercompany Bonds Payable	400,000	
Intercompany Bond Premium	8,000	
Investment in Bonds		390,000

Required
1. Calculate the gain or loss on debt extinguishment to be reported in consolidation in 19X6.
2. Calculate the parent's issuance price of the bonds.
3. Calculate the consolidated interest expense for 19X6 (the year of the intercompany bond purchase—not 19X7).
4. Prepare the intercompany bond interest elimination entry at 12/31/X7 (not X6). (If you are using Module 1, you must assume that neither entity has adjusted its general ledger to eliminate its intercompany premium or discount, thus departing from the procedures shown in the text for Module 1.)

P 12–8 **Reissuance of Intercompany-Held Bonds** Sitt Inc. is a 100%-owned subsidiary of Pitt Inc. On 7/1/X6, Pitt paid $1,030,000 cash (total amount paid) to acquire 25% of Sitt's $4,000,000 of face value 10% bonds. The bonds pay interest annually on 12/31. The bonds were issued on 1/1/X1 at a premium of $160,000 and mature on 12/31/X8. On 12/31/X6, Pitt sold the bonds in the open market for $1,009,000. For 19X6, Sitt reported $700,000 of net income. Each company uses straight-line amortization for interest.

Required
1. Calculate the gain or loss on debt extinguishment to be reported in consolidation in 19X6.
2. Calculate the parent's reported gain or loss on its sale of the bonds in 19X6.
3. Calculate the *consolidated* interest expense for 19X6.
4. Prepare the intercompany bond interest elimination entry at 12/31/X6.
5. What other bond-related consolidation entries are needed at 12/31/X6?

✳ THINKING CRITICALLY ✳

✳ CASES ✳

C 12–1 **Purchasing Bonds Merely to Report a Gain?** For the first nine months of 19X1, Purdy Company is experiencing lower earnings than forecasted. Management is searching for ways to increase earnings during the remainder of the year. The controller has suggested that Purdy issue $1,000,000 of bonds and use the proceeds to acquire it's subsidiary's outstanding 15-year 10% bonds ($1,000,000 face value), which are currently selling at 90. Those bonds were issued at a premium of $75,000 five years ago, thus a $150,000 gain can be reported in 19X1. Purdy's borrowing rate would be 12%.

Required Evaluate the validity and merits of the controller's idea.

ANSWERS TO SELF-STUDY QUESTIONS

1. d   2. b   3. a   4. c   5. b   6. c   7. b

CHANGES IN A PARENT'S OWNERSHIP INTEREST

TO UNDERSTAND

- The three ways in which the parent's ownership level in a subsidiary can change.
- The reasons a parent may gain or lose economically when its ownership level changes.
- The way to calculate a parent's *deemed economic* gain or loss upon a change in ownership.
- The way to initially report these *deemed economic* gains and losses.
- The subsequent reporting treatment for these *deemed economic* gains and losses if and when the parent's control is lost.
- The rationale for reporting a subsidiary's preferred stock as part of the noncontrolling interest.

TOPIC OUTLINE

Without ideals, without effort, without scholarship, without philosophical continuity, there is no such thing as education.

ABRAHAM FLEXNER

For brevity, we hereafter often use the abbreviation "NCI" for *noncontrolling interest.*

WAYS IN WHICH A PARENT'S OWNERSHIP INTEREST CAN CHANGE

A parent's ownership interest in a subsidiary can change as a result of (1) a parent's or a subsidiary's acquisition of some or all of the NCI, (2) a parent's sale of a portion of its investment (thereby *increasing* the NCI), and (3) a subsidiary's issuance of additional common stock to outside parties (thereby *increasing* the NCI).

This chapter discusses the way to (1) calculate the appropriate change to be made to the parent's Investment account for these ownership changes and (2) calculate and report the parent's resulting deemed economic gain or loss that occurs in virtually all ownership changes.

For simplicity, we assume in all illustrations that (1) the parent uses the *equity method* of accounting for its investment in the subsidiary and that (2) the Investment account has been properly applied (updated) under the *equity method* of accounting to the change in the ownership date. This procedure is necessary so that the proper adjustment can be made to the Investment account for the ownership change.

THE FASB'S LATEST PROPOSED CONSOLIDATION RULES

Recall from Chapter 1 that the Financial Accounting Stantards Board (FASB) (1) issued an Exposure Draft "Consolidated Financial Statements: Policy and Procedures" in October 1995 and (2) modified its exposure draft position on certain issues in May 1996 to address concerns raised by respondents and participants at the public hearings held in February 1996, and (3) opened in May 1996 the possibility of preparing a revised exposure draft for public comment (could be issued by the end of 1996). Accordingly, we focus our discussion in this chapter on the FASB's May 1996 position, which may appear in the revised exposure draft.

Recall from Chapter 3 that the FASB's latest proposed consolidation standards require the use of the *economic unit concept* when a noncontrolling interest exists (the *parent company concept* will no longer be allowed). Recall from Chapter 6 that when a noncontrolling interest exists in an *acquired* subsidiary, these proposed consolidation rules require that amounts be *imputed* to the NCI at the acquisition date (based on the parent's purchase price) for (1) under- and overvalued assets and liabilities and (2) goodwill (imputing amounts to the NCI is not done under the *parent company concept*).

Thus the manner of accounting for changes in a parent's ownership level are substantially different under the FASB's latest proposed consolidation standards compared with the standards they will replace.

I | THE ACQUISITION OF A NONCONTROLLING INTEREST

When some or all of the NCI is acquired at *above* or *below* the *book value* of the NCI shares, the following economic result **is deemed to occur** under the *economic unit concept:*

1. The parent economically *loses* or *gains*.

2. The NCI economically *gains* or *loses,* respectively, by the exact opposite amount.

Under the economic unit concept, the acquisition of any or all of the NCI is viewed as a *capital transaction* between (1) the *controlling* interest **(an additional investment in the subsidiary occurs)** and (2) the NCI **(a *liquidation* of some or all**

of its investment in the subsidiary occurs). Recall from intermediate accounting that capital transactions are *not* reported in the income statement.

Consequently, the parent's deemed *economic* loss or gain is initially reported as a *decrease* or *increase,* respectively, to its Additional Paid-in Capital account. This charge or credit is *not* eliminated in consolidation. These procedures hold true regardless of whether the *parent* or the *subsidiary* acquires *some* or *all* of the NCI. For a *created* subsidiary, the parent's deemed *economic* loss or gain is determined by comparing (1) the *book value* of the NCI shares acquired and (2) the *purchase price* paid to acquire the NCI shares.

PARENT ACQUIRES THE NONCONTROLLING INTEREST

When the parent acquires the NCI, only the parent makes a **general ledger** entry.

ILLUSTRATION	PARENT ACQUIRES 100% OF THE NONCONTROLLING INTEREST AT *ABOVE* BOOK VALUE (75%-OWNED *CREATED* SUBSIDIARY)

Assume the following information, in which the parent acquired *all* of the NCI at *more* than the book value per share:

	Percent	Shares
Parent's ownership in a *created* subsidiary:		
Before the acquisition of the NCI	75	7,500
After the acquisition of the NCI	100	10,000
Subsidiary's equity accounts immediately *before* the acquisition of the NCI:		
Common stock	$ 60,000	
Retained Earnings	$140,000	
Book value per share ($200,000/10,000 shares)	$ 20	
Purchase price the parent paid to acquire *all* 2,500 outstanding shares held by the NCI.	$ 80,000	

The parent makes the following **general ledger** adjusting entry:

Investment in Subsidiary (2,500 shares × $20 per share book value)	50,000	
Additional Paid-in Capital (this amount is the parent's *deemed economic* loss)	30,000	
Cash		80,000

The parent's analysis of its Investment account is adjusted as follows:

			BOOK VALUE ELEMENT	
	Noncontrolling Interest (Decreases from 25% to 0%)	Parent's Investment Account— + Book Value =	Subsidiary's Equity Accounts Common Stock +	Retained Earnings
Balances immediately *before* acquiring the NCI	$50,000	$150,000	$60,000	$140,000
+ Acquisition of *all* of the NCI	(50,000)	50,000		
Balances immediately *after* acquiring the NCI	$ –0–	$200,000	$60,000	$140,000

SUBSIDIARY ACQUIRES THE NONCONTROLLING INTEREST

When the subsidiary acquires some or all of the NCI shares, *both* the *parent* and the *subsidiary* make general ledger entries. We now assume that S Company paid $80,000 to acquire *all* 2,500 shares held by the NCI.

ILLUSTRATION	SUBSIDIARY ACQUIRES 100% OF THE NONCONTROLLING INTEREST AT *ABOVE* BOOK VALUE (75%-OWNED *CREATED* SUBSIDIARY)

SUBSIDIARY'S GENERAL LEDGER ENTRY   The subsidiary's general ledger entry is the same as that made by any entity that acquires **and retires** its outstanding shares; that is, debit the capital accounts and credit the Cash account. We assume that S Company's appropriate *general ledger* entry is as follows:

Common Stock (25% of $60,000)	15,000	
Retained Earnings ($80,000 − $15,000)	65,000	
Cash		80,000

In this situation, S Company's equity contracts by $80,000 (from $200,000 to $120,000).

PARENT'S GENERAL LEDGER ENTRY   The parent's *general ledger* adjusting entry to record its *deemed economic* loss is as follows:

Additional Paid-in Capital	30,000	
Investment in Subsidiary		30,000

Section I of Illustration 13–1 shows the manner of calculating this $30,000 *deemed economic* loss. Section II of Illustration 13–1 shows the required changes to the parent's analysis of its Investment account.

SUBSIDIARY ACQUIRES *PART* OF THE NONCONTROLLING INTEREST

When the subsidiary acquires only a portion of the NCI at *more* or *less* than book value per share, both the parent's **and the *remaining* NCI shareholders'** total dollar interests in the subsidiary's net assets at book value *decrease* or *increase*, respectively. Only the parent's decrease or increase results in a decrease or increase, respectively, to its Additional Paid-in Capital account.

To illustrate, assume that S Company acquired only 1,000 of the NCI shares for $32,000 cash (instead of acquiring *all* of the 2,500 NCI shares for $80,000 cash); the excess payment would be $12,000 (instead of $30,000). (The $32,000 payment minus $20,000 of book value accruing to these 1,000 shares equals $12,000.) In this case, the remaining shareholders (7,500 shares being held by the parent and 1,500 shares being held by the remaining NCI shareholders) share the $12,000 of dilution in relation to their respective holdings (a 5:1 ratio), as follows:

	Remaining Ownership		Dollar Share
	Shares	Percentage	of Dilution
Parent's holdings	7,500	83.33%	$(10,000)
Remaining NCI holdings	1,500	16.67	(2,000)
Total	9,000	100.00	$(12,000)

Consequently, the parent makes the following **general ledger** adjusting entry:

Additional Paid-in Capital	10,000	
Investment in Subsidiary		10,000

ILLUSTRATION 13–1	**Subsidiary's Acquisition of 100% of the Noncontrolling Interest at Amount in Excess of Book Value (75%-Owned *Created* Subsidiary)**

I. Calculation of *Decrease* in Parent's Interest in Subsidiary's Net Assets

	Subsidiary's Equity Accounts	Book Value per Share	Parent's Interest Percent	Parent's Interest Amount	Noncontrolling Interest Percent	Noncontrolling Interest Amount
Before acquisition of *all* of the NCI:						
Common stock	$ 60,000		75	$ 45,000	25	$ 15,000
Retained earnings	140,000		75	105,000	25	35,000
	$200,000	$20		$150,000		$ 50,000
After acquisition of *all* the NCI:						
Common stock	$ 45,000		100	$ 45,000		
Retained earnings	75,000	$16	100	75,000		
	$120,000			$120,000		
Decrease in equity	$ (80,000)			$ (30,000)		$(50,000)

Note: The parent's new ownership percentage is derived by dividing the shares owned by the parent (7,500 shares) by S Company's outstanding shares (7,500 shares). In other words, the parent's holdings remain constant—only S Company's outstanding shares (the denominator used in calculating the parent's ownership percentage) *decrease*.

II. Parent's Adjustment to Its Investment Account

	Noncontrolling Interest (*Decreases* from 25% to 0%)	+	Parent's Investment Account— Book Value	=	BOOK VALUE ELEMENT Common Stock	+	BOOK VALUE ELEMENT Retained Earnings
Balances immediately *before* acquiring the NCI	$50,000		$150,000		$60,000		$140,000
− Acquisition of *all* of the NCI	(50,000)		(30,000)		(15,000)		(65,000)
Balances immediately *after* acquiring the NCI	$ –0–		$120,000		$45,000		$ 75,000

The parent's analysis of its Investment account is adjusted as follows:

	Noncontrolling Interest (*Decreases* from 25% to 16.67%)	+	Parent's Investment Account— Book Value	=	BOOK VALUE ELEMENT Common Stock	+	BOOK VALUE ELEMENT Retained Earnings
Balances immediately *before* acquiring the NCI . .	$50,000		$150,000		$60,000		$140,000
+ Acquisition of 40% (1,000/2,500) of the NCI . .	(22,000)[a]		(10,000)		(6,000)		(26,000)
Balances immediately *after* acquiring the NCI . . .	$28,000[b]		$140,000		$54,000		$114,000

[a]This is composed of $20,000 (10% of $200,000) plus $2,000 of dilution suffered by the remaining NCI shareholders.

[b]The NCI ownership percentage is now 16.67% (1,500 shares/9,000 shares)—not 25% (2,500 shares/10,000 shares). Note also that this $28,000 is 16.67% (1/6) of $168,000 (the book value *after* the acquisition of the 1,000 NCI shares).

POSSIBLE SUBSEQUENT INCOME STATEMENT RECOGNITION OF THE PARENT'S *DEEMED ECONOMIC* GAIN OR LOSS

If a parent loses control of a subsidiary (such as by sale of *some* or *all* of its shares), all *deemed economic* losses and gains previously charged or credited, respectively, to its Additional Paid-in Capital account are (1) removed from this account and (2) recognized in the income statement. These recognized gains and losses are *not* eliminated in consolidation.

ACQUIRED SUBSIDIARIES: COST IN EXCESS OF BOOK VALUE

When a subsidiary is an *acquired* subsidiary, the parent may have unamortized cost in excess of book value at the date the NCI shares are acquired. In such cases, the NCI in these items is considered in calculating the parent's deemed economic loss or gain. We now use the facts on page 455 in which *all* of the 2,500 NCI shares were acquired for $80,000; however, we also assume that (1) S Company is an *acquired* subsidiary and that (2) $44,000 of cost in excess of book value exists at the NCI acquisition date (the $44,000 includes $11,000 that was imputed to the NCI at the date S Company was acquired). The parent's **general ledger** adjusting entry is as follows:

Investment in Subsidiary—Book Value Element		
(2,500 shares × $20 per share book value)	50,000	
Investment in Subsidiary—Excess Cost Elements		
(25% of $44,000 of unamortized excess cost)	11,000[a]	
Additional Paid-in Capital (this amount is the parent's		
deemed *economic* loss)	19,000	
Cash		80,000

[a]For pedagogical purposes only, we show a separate posting for the excess cost portion.

The parent's analysis of its excess cost elements portion of its Investment account is adjusted as follows:

	Noncontrolling Interest (Decreases from 25% to 0%)	+	Parent's Investment Account— Excess Cost	=	UNDERVALUATION OF NET ASSETS ELEMENT Land	+	GOODWILL ELEMENT
Balances immediately *before* acquiring the NCI	$11,000		$33,000		$30,000		$14,000
+ Acquisition of *all* of the NCI	(11,000)		11,000				
Balances immediately *after* acquiring the NCI	$ –0–		$44,000		$30,000		$14,000

Note: Because *all* of the NCI was acquired, none of the *subsequent* goodwill amortization need be shared as is done for amortization occurring *before* the acquisition of the NCI.

IS THE *DEEMED* ECONOMIC LOSS OR GAIN A *TRUE* ECONOMIC LOSS OR GAIN?

A parent's *deemed* economic loss or gain may or may not be a *true* economic loss or gain. The critical factors are whether (1) the subsidiary's net assets are under- or overvalued and (2) a portion of the purchase price is for previously unrecognized goodwill. Certainly, the acquisition of the NCI at *below* book value when a *created* subsidiary's net assets at book value are *not* overvalued *is* a *true* economic gain. Likewise, the acquisition of the NCI at *above* book value when a *created* subsidiary's net assets at book value are *not* undervalued *is* a *true* economic loss. If a *created* subsidiary's net assets *are* undervalued, however, some or all of a deemed economic loss is *not* a *true* economic loss.

▐▐ PARENT'S PARTIAL DISPOSAL OF ITS INVESTMENT

A parent's partial disposal of its common stock investment in a subsidiary is also treated as a capital transaction between the two shareholder interests (the controlling interests and the noncontrolling interests) under the *economic unit concept*. Accordingly, the procedures are identical to those shown earlier for *acquisitions* of some or all of the NCI.

PARTIAL DISPOSAL INVOLVING A *CREATED* SUBSIDIARY

ILLUSTRATION	**PARTIAL DISPOSAL OF PARENT'S INVESTMENT AT *ABOVE* BOOK VALUE (100%-OWNED *CREATED* SUBSIDIARY)**

Assume the following information:

	Percent	Shares
Parent's ownership in a *created* subsidiary:		
Before the partial disposal	100	10,000
After the partial disposal	75	7,500
Subsidiary's equity accounts immediately *before* the partial disposal:		
Common stock		$ 60,000
Retained Earnings		$140,000
Book value per share ($200,000/10,000 shares)		$ 20
Proceeds from sale of the 2,500 shares		$ 80,000

The parent makes the following **general ledger** entry:

Cash...	80,000	
Investment in Subsidiary (2,500 shares × $20 per share book value)		50,000
Additional Paid-in Capital (this amount is the parent's *deemed economic* gain)		30,000

The credit to the Additional Paid-in Capital account is *not* eliminated in consolidation. Illustration 13–2 shows how the parent's analysis of its Investment account is adjusted at an amount equal to the **change in its proportionate interest in the subsidiary's net assets.**

PARTIAL DISPOSAL INVOLVING AN *ACQUIRED* SUBSIDIARY

We now use the information provided in the preceding illustration but assume that (1) the subsidiary was *acquired* and that (2) $44,000 of cost in excess of book value

ILLUSTRATION 13–2	**Parent's Partial Disposal of Its Investment at Amount in Excess of Book Value (100%-Owned *Created* Subsidiary)**

	Noncontrolling Interest (*Increases* from 0% to 25%)	+	Parent's Investment Account— Book Value	=	Common Stock	+	Retained Earnings
					BOOK VALUE ELEMENT		
					Subsidiary's Equity Accounts		
Balances immediately *before* disposal	$ –0–		$200,000		$60,000		$140,000
– Disposal of 25% of S Company shares held	50,000		(50,000)				
Balances immediately *after* disposal	$50,000		$150,000		$60,000		$140,000

exists at the partial disposal date. The parent makes the following **general ledger** entry:

Cash	80,000	
Investment in Subsidiary (2,500 shares × $20 per		
share book value)		50,000
Investment in Subsidiary (25% × $44,000 of		
unamortized excess cost)		11,000
Additional Paid-in Capital (this amount is the		
parent's deemed *economic* gain)		19,000

The parent's analysis of its excess cost elements portion of its Investment account is adjusted as follows:

	Noncontrolling Interest (Increases from 0% to 25%)	+	Parent's Investment Account— Excess Cost	=	UNDERVALUATION OF NET ASSETS ELEMENT Land	+	GOODWILL ELEMENT
Balances immediately *before* disposal	$ –0–		$44,000		$8,000		$36,000
– Disposal of 25% of S Company shares held	11,000		(11,000)				
Balances immediately *after* disposal ...	$11,000		$33,000		$8,000		$36,000

WHAT IF THE PARENT'S SHARES HAD BEEN ACQUIRED IN BLOCK ACQUISI-TIONS? Even if the parent had acquired the subsidiary's shares in block acquisitions, the required adjustment to the Investment account is always made by determining the change in the parent's proportionate ownership interest. Thus the specific identification method and the first-in, first-out method (the only methods allowed for federal income tax-reporting purposes) *cannot* be used.

POSSIBLE SUBSEQUENT INCOME STATEMENT RECOGNITION OF THE PARENT'S *DEEMED ECONOMIC* GAIN OR LOSS

As was the case for the *acquisition* of some or all of the NCI, a parent that loses control of a subsidiary must currently recognize in income all deemed economic losses and gains previously charged or credited, respectively, to its Additional Paid-in Capital account as a result of partial disposals.

III SUBSIDIARY'S ISSUANCE OF ADDITIONAL COMMON STOCK

Rather than disposing of a portion of its stock holdings in a subsidiary to raise funds for the consolidated group, a parent may direct the subsidiary to issue additional common stock to the public.

If the shares issued to the public are sold *below* the current book value per share of the subsidiary's common stock as of the issuance date, the parent's total dollar interest in the subsidiary's net assets at book value is diluted and thus *decreases*. On the other hand, when the subsidiary issues shares *above* the existing book value of its common stock as of the issuance date, the parent's total dollar interest in the subsidiary's net assets at book value *increases*. This may be understood best by realizing that if the subsidiary were liquidated at no gain or loss in the liquidation process, the parent would receive either more or less than it would receive if the subsidiary had *not* issued the additional shares.

ISSUANCE OF ADDITIONAL SHARES BY A *CREATED* SUBSIDIARY

ILLUSTRATION	SUBSIDIARY'S ISSUANCE OF ADDITIONAL SHARES AT *BELOW* BOOK VALUE (75%-OWNED *CREATED* SUBSIDIARY)

Assume the following information:

	Percent	Shares
Parent's ownership in subsidiary:		
Before subsidiary issues additional shares	75	7,500
After subsidiary issues additional shares	60	7,500
Noncontrolling ownership interest in subsidiary:		
Before subsidiary issues additional shares	25	2,500
After subsidiary issues additional shares	40	5,000
Proceeds from issuance of 2,500 additional shares of the		
subsidiary's no-par common stock at $18 per share		$45,000

This information is used in Section I of Illustration 13–3 to calculate the deemed economic loss to the parent. (The procedure is the same when there is a deemed economic gain.) The following entry records the economic loss on the parent's books:

| Additional Paid-in Capital . . . . | 3,000 | |
| Investment in Subsidiary . . . . | | 3,000 |

This charge to the Additional Paid-in Capital account is *not* eliminated in consolidation. The analysis of the Investment account is adjusted as shown in Section II of Illustration 13–3.

ISSUANCE OF ADDITIONAL SHARES BY AN *ACQUIRED* SUBSIDIARY

We now use the information provided in the preceding illustration but assume that (1) the subsidiary was *acquired* and (2) $44,000 of cost in excess of book value exists at the common stock issuance date (the $44,000 includes $11,000 imputed to the NCI). The parent makes the following **general ledger** adjusting entry:

Additional Paid-in Capital	9,600	
Investment in Subsidiary—Book Value		
Element (per Illustration 13–3)		3,000
Investment in Subsidiary—Excess cost		
Elements (see following analysis)		6,600

The parent's analysis of its excess cost elements portion of its Investment account is adjusted as follows:

	Noncontrolling Interest (*Increases* from 25% to 40%)	+	Parent's Investment Account— Excess Cost	=	UNDERVALUATION OF NET ASSETS ELEMENT Land	+	GOODWILL ELEMENT
Balances immediately							
before issuance	$11,000		$33,000 (75%)		$8,000		$36,000
Adjustment to reflect S Company's							
issuance of 2,500 shares.	6,600		(6,600)[a]				
Balances immediately *after* issuance . . .	$17,600		$26,400 (60%)		$8,000		$36,000

[a]Because the parent's ownership level decreased by 20% (from 75% to 60%), the required adjustment is 20% of $33,000.

ILLUSTRATION 13-3 **Subsidiary's Issuance of Additional Common Stock at Below Book Value**

I. Calculation of Parent's Dilution of Equity in Net Assets of Subsidiary

	Subsidiary's Equity Accounts	Book Value per Share	Parent's Interest		Noncontrolling Interest	
			Percent	Amount	Percent	Amount
Before issuance of additional shares:						
Common stock	$ 60,000		75	$ 45,000	25	$15,000
Retained earnings	140,000		75	105,000	25	35,000
	$200,000	$20.00		$150,000		$50,000
After issuance of additional shares:						
Common stock	$105,000[a]		60	$ 63,000	40	$42,000
Retained earnings	140,000		60	84,000	40	56,000
	$245,000	$19.60		$147,000		$98,000
Difference	$ 45,000	$ .40		$ (3,000)		$48,000
Proceeds from issuance	(45,000)	$18.00				(45,000)
Parent's dilution/NCI accretion[b]	$ –0–	[$.40 × 7,500 shares]		$ (3,000)		$ 3,000

[a]For simplicity, we assume that the subsidiary's common stock is no par. Thus the $45,000 of proceeds has been credited to the Common Stock account.

[b]The dilution suffered by the parent is offset by the accretion to the noncontrolling interest.

II. Parent's Adjustment to Its Conceptual Analysis of Its Investment Account

				BOOK VALUE ELEMENT	
				Subsidiary's Equity Accounts	
	Noncontrolling Interest	+	Parent's Investment Account	= Common Stock	+ Retained Earnings
Balances before issuance of additional shares	$50,000		$150,000	$ 60,000	$140,000
+ Issuance of additional shares	45,000			45,000	
Subtotal	$95,000		$150,000	$105,000	$140,000
− Adjustment for parent's dilution/noncontrolling interest accretion	3,000		(3,000)		
Balances after issuance of additional shares	$98,000		$147,000	$105,000	$140,000

POSSIBLE SUBSEQUENT INCOME STATEMENT RECOGNITION OF THE PARENT'S *DEEMED ECONOMIC* GAIN OR LOSS

As was the case for other types of ownership changes (discussed in Sections I and II), a parent that loses control of a subsidiary must currently recognize in income all deemed economic losses and gains previously charged or credited, respectively, to its Additional Paid-in Capital account as a result of a subsidiary's issuing additional common stock.

IV OTHER CHANGES IN THE SUBSIDIARY'S CAPITAL ACCOUNTS

STOCK DIVIDENDS

A subsidiary's stock dividend has no effect on the parent's books or in consolidation. The subsidiary has merely reshuffled amounts within its equity accounts by reducing the Retained Earnings account and increasing the Common Stock and

Additional Paid-in Capital accounts in accordance with procedures discussed in intermediate accounting texts. Although no entry is required to adjust the carrying value of the Investment in Subsidiary account, the parent must adjust these accounts because they exist within the expanded analysis of their Investment account by components. Assume the following information:

	Subsidiary's Books	
	Common Stock	Retained Earnings
Balances immediately *before* stock dividend	$60,000	$140,000
Capitalization of retained earnings as a result of stock dividend	30,000	(30,000)
Balances immediately *after* stock dividend	$90,000	$110,000

The balances in the expanded analysis of the Investment account by individual components are adjusted accordingly.

The reclassification within the parent's expanded analysis of the Investment account by components is necessary so that the posting of the basic elimination entry used to prepare consolidated financial statements properly eliminates the subsidiary's equity accounts.

If the capitalization of retained earnings exceeds the total retained earnings as of the acquisition date, an interesting problem results. Under the equity method of accounting, the parent has included amounts in its Retained Earnings account that it cannot obtain from the subsidiary as a result of the capitalization. If this restriction on dividend availability is material, it should be disclosed in the consolidated statements.

STOCK SPLITS

As with stock dividends, when a stock split occurs, the parent is not required to make an entry on its books to adjust the carrying value of its investment in the subsidiary. The parent does not make any reclassifications within the analysis of the Investment account by individual components, however, because no changes were made to the subsidiary's capital accounts at the time of the stock split. The parent company makes only a memorandum notation of the stock split.

CHANGES FROM PAR VALUE TO NO-PAR AND VICE VERSA

When a subsidiary changes the par value of its common stock to no-par or vice versa, it makes changes on its books in the Common Stock and Additional Paid-in Capital accounts. As a result, the parent makes an adjustment within the expanded analysis of the Investment account. The carrying value of the investment itself does not change.

APPROPRIATION OF RETAINED EARNINGS

Inasmuch as the amount of an *acquired* subsidiary's retained earnings existing as of the acquisition date is eliminated in consolidation, any appropriation of retained earnings by the subsidiary that does not exceed the total amount of retained earnings existing as of the acquisition date (including any amount that accrues to the noncontrolling interests) has no effect on the parent's books or the consolidated statements. When appropriations of retained earnings exceed this amount, however, the restriction on dividend availability must be disclosed in the consolidated statements if it is material.

V ## HISTORICAL DEVELOPMENT OF GAAP

The consolidation standards that will be superseded by the new FASB consolidation standards (1) are based largely on the *parent company concept* (discussed in Chapter 3) and (2) require the following treatment for changes in a parent's ownership:

1. **The Acquisition of a Noncontrolling Interest.** Account for the acquisition as part of the *purchase method* of accounting pursuant to the requirements of *Accounting Principles Board Opinion No. 16*, "Business Combinations." Amounts paid in excess of book value increase the parent's excess cost elements portion of its Investment account. (This treatment is possible only because amounts relating to excess cost are *not* imputed to the NCI under the *parent company concept* when the subsidiary was *acquired*.)

2. **Parent's Partial Disposal of Its Investment in a Subsidiary.** Recognize any gain or loss currently in the consolidated income statement. In determining the cost amount to relieve from the Investment account, it is acceptable to use (a) the **specific identification method,** (b) the **first-in, first-out method,** or (c) the **average cost method** (the soundest of the three methods).

3. **Subsidiary's Issuance of Additional Common Stock.** Recognize gains and losses either currently in the income statement (*parent company concept*) or as a capital transaction (the *economic unit concept*).

Historically, the treatment of gains and losses upon the issuance of additional common stock by a subsidiary has been the most controversial area. For this type of ownership change, we discuss (1) the rationale for the income statement treatment under the *parent company concept,* (2) the role of the American Institute of Certified Public Accountants (AICPA) in developing standards in this area, and (3) the position of the Securities and Exchange Commission.

RATIONALE FOR THE INCOME STATEMENT TREATMENT Under the *parent company concept,* **the parent is viewed as either gaining or losing** as a result of a subsidiary's issuing additional common stock above or below the book value of its existing outstanding common stock. Gains and losses are reported in the income statement. Accordingly, this type of gain or loss also is reflected in the income statement. In regard to the requirements of *APB Opinion No. 9*, "Reporting the Results of Operations" (paragraph 28), that gains or losses from transactions in a company's own stock are to be excluded from the income statement, the argument can be made that this is not a transaction in one's own stock but a transaction involving the investment in the subsidiary's stock; thus *APBO No. 9* is not applicable. The advocates of this approach also contend that the sale of a subsidiary's shares by the parent (pursuant to a partial disposal)—whereby a gain or loss is recorded in the income statement—is substantively no different from the issuance of additional common shares by a subsidiary.

THE AICPA'S POSITION In 1980 the Accounting Standards Executive Committee of the American Institute for Certified Public Accountants (AICPA) prepared an issues paper, "Accounting in Consolidation for Issuances of a Subsidiary's Stock." This paper's advisory conclusions are that such gains or losses should be reflected in the consolidated income statement. The position taken here seems to be that such transactions are not "transactions in one's own stock." Thus *APBO No. 9* is not applicable.

THE POSITION OF THE SECURITIES AND EXCHANGE COMMISSION In 1983 the staff of the Securities and Exchange Commission (SEC) issued *Staff Accounting Bulletin No. 51*, "Accounting for Sales of Stock by a Subsidiary," which expresses its views concerning the subsidiary's issuance of additional common stock. According to the SEC staff, companies **may** (an optional reporting treatment) recognize gains or losses resulting from these transactions when the subsidiary's sale of shares is not a part of a corporate reorganization contemplated or planned by the parent company. (The staff had previously required, without benefit of any ruling or publication, that these transactions be accounted for in consolidated financial statements as capital transactions.) This change in position resulted from the SEC's acceptance of the advisory conclusions in the AICPA's 1980 issues paper. The SEC staff considers this paper to be appropriate interim guidance in the matter until the Financial Accounting Standards Board (FASB) addresses this issue as a part of its project Accounting for the Reporting Entity, Including Consolidations, the Equity Method, and Related Matters. Under *SAB No. 51,* companies electing income statement treatment must report the gain or loss as a separate item in the consolidated income statement regardless of size. Furthermore, the gain or loss must be clearly **designated as nonoperating.** Companies also should include an appropriate description of the transaction in the notes to the financial statements.[1]

In 1989 the staff of the SEC expanded its views on this subject in *Staff Accounting Bulletin No. 84.* In this bulletin, the SEC staff takes the position that no gain should be recognized in consolidation when subsequent capital transactions are contemplated that raise concerns about the likelihood of realization of the gain. Examples of subsequent capital transactions follow:

1. A subsequent spin-off of the subsidiary to shareholders is contemplated at the time of issuance.

2. A reacquisition of the shares issued by the subsidiary is contemplated at the time of issuance. (A contemplation is deemed to have existed at the issuance date if the shares are repurchased within one year of issuance.)

Furthermore, the bulletin holds that no gain should be recognized if the subsidiary is a newly formed *nonoperating* entity, a *research and development start-up* or a *development-stage* company, or an entity whose ability to continue in existence is in question or when other similar circumstances exist.

END-OF-CHAPTER REVIEW

SUMMARY OF KEY POINTS

1. Under the *economic unit concept,* **all changes in a parent's ownership are deemed to be capital transactions.** Consequently, any *deemed economic gains and losses* of the parent are credited and charged, respectively, to the Additional Paid-in Capital account.
2. Under the *economic unit concept,* the parent's Investment account is adjusted for **the change in the parent's *proportionate interest* in the subsidiary's net assets** for *all* types of ownership changes.
3. Under the *economic unit concept,* all deemed economic gains and losses that were credited and charged, respectively, to the Additional Paid-in Capital account as a result of a parent's ownership changes in a subsidiary are **recognized currently in earnings when the parent loses control** of the subsidiary.
4. Under the *parent company concept,* gains and losses that result from partial disposals and subsidiary issuances of common stock are recognized currently in earnings. The FASB's proposed consolidation rules require use of only the *economic unit concept.*

---

[1]*Staff Accounting Bulletin No. 51,* "Accounting by the Parent in Consolidation for Sale of Stock by Subsidiary" (Washington, D.C.: Securities and Exchange Commission, 1983).

SELF-STUDY QUESTIONS

(Answers are at the end of this chapter, preceding the appendix.)

1. When a parent acquires some or all of the noncontrolling interest in a subsidiary, it must use which of the following?
   a. Economic unit concept.
   b. Parent company concept.
   c. Purchase method.
   d. Cost method.
2. When a subsidiary acquires the noncontrolling interest at *less than* the book value of the noncontrolling interest, which of the following does *not* take place?
   a. A currently reportable gain under the parent company concept.
   b. A change in the carrying value of the Investment in Subsidiary account.
   c. An adjustment to the Additional Paid-in Capital account under the economic unit concept.
   d. Accretion to the parent's ownership interest in the net assets of the subsidiary at book value.
3. On 5/1/X1 Saxco, a 60%-owned *created* subsidiary of Paxco, acquired 25,000 shares of its 100,000 outstanding common shares at a cost of $300,000. Prior to this purchase, Saxco's net assets had a total book value of $1,500,000. As a result of this purchase, Paxco's deemed economic gain or loss is which of the following?
   a. –0–
   b. Gain of $60,000.
   c. Loss of $60,000.
   d. Gain of $75,000.
   e. Loss of $75,000.
4. When a parent sells a portion of its common stock holdings in a subsidiary, which of the following could be applied at the date of the disposal in relieving the Investment account?
   a. The specific identification method.
   b. The parent company concept.
   c. The economic unit concept.
   d. SEC Staff Acct. B No. 51.
5. On 6/1/X3 Satco, a 90%-owned created subsidiary of Patco, issued 20,000 shares of its $1 par value common stock to the public for $200,000. Satco had 100,000 outstanding shares with a total book value of $1,300,000 just prior to this issuance. Which amount does Patco report as a deemed economic gain or loss?
   a. –0–
   b. Loss of $45,000.
   c. Gain of $45,000.
   d. Loss of $50,000.
   e. Gain of $50,000.

ASSIGNMENT MATERIAL

REVIEW QUESTIONS

1. When some or all of a noncontrolling interest is acquired, is the purchase method or the pooling of interests method of accounting used?
2. Does the accounting method for the acquisition of some or all of a noncontrolling interest depend on whether the parent or the subsidiary acquires the noncontrolling interest?
3. When a subsidiary has acquired some or all of its outstanding noncontrolling interest at an amount *in excess of* book value, has the parent's interest in the subsidiary's net assets increased or decreased?
4. When a parent's interest in a subsidiary was acquired in blocks and a portion of such holdings is sold, what method is used to reduce the Investment account?
5. Concerning Question 4, which methods are acceptable for federal income tax–reporting purposes?
6. When a parent disposes of a portion of its common stock holdings in a subsidiary, why must the *equity method* of accounting be applied up to the date of sale?
7. In which situations does a parent "lose" when a subsidiary issues additional common shares to the public?
8. Does a parent make a general ledger entry when a subsidiary declares a stock dividend?
9. Does a parent make a general ledger entry when a subsidiary effects a stock split?

EXERCISES

E 13–1 **Parent's Acquisition of NCI** Prost Inc. owns 80% of the outstanding common stock of Skol Inc. A *combined* analysis of the parent's Investment account by components of the major conceptual elements at 1/1/X6 follows:

Book value element:
Common stocks, $10 par value. $100,000
Retained earnings. 120,000
Undervaluation of net assets element:
Land 10,000
Goodwill element . . . . <u>70,000</u>
$300,000

Total cost. $240,000
Noncontrolling interest . . . . <u>60,000</u>
$300,000

On 1/2/X6, Prost acquired 15% of Skol's outstanding common stock from its noncontrolling interest shareholders for $66,000 cash. All of Skol's assets and liabilities have a current value equal to their book value at 1/2/X6 except land, which is worth $60,000 in excess of its book value.

Required   Prepare and update separate analyses of the parent's Investment account to reflect this acquisition. Prepare the parent's adjusting entry.

E 13–2   Subsidiary's Acquisition of NCI   Pyn Inc. owns 75% of the outstanding common stock of Syn Inc. (a *created* subsidiary). On 1/1/X6, Syn acquired 10% of its stock from its noncontrolling interest shareholders for $220,000 cash. These shares were immediately retired (the Common Stock account was charged $10,000, the Additional Paid-in Capital account was charged $90,000, and the Retained Earnings account was charged $120,000). The subsidiary's capital accounts immediately *before* the acquisition are as follows:

Common stock, $1 par value . . . . $ 100,000
Additional paid-in capital. 900,000
Retained earnings . . . . <u>600,000</u>
$1,600,000

Required   **1.** Prepare and update an analysis of the Investment account.
2. Prepare the parent's adjusting entry.

E 13–3   Stock Dividend by Subsidiary   On 4/1/X7, Sem Inc., Pem Inc.'s 75%-owned subsidiary, declared a 10% common stock dividend on its 10,000 outstanding shares of $20 par value common stock. Sem recorded the following entry:

Retained Earnings 160,000
Common Stock   20,000
Additional Paid-in Capital   140,000

Required   Determine the appropriate changes that the parent company should make to its conceptual analysis of the Investment account by individual components.

E 13–4   Stock Split by Subsidiary   On 1/1/X3, Sila Inc., Pila Inc.'s 60%-owned subsidiary, split its $10 par value common stock 4 for 1. At the time of the stock split, Sila's capital accounts were as follows:

Common stock . . . . $ 100,000
Additional paid-in capital. 900,000
Retained earnings . . . . <u>400,000</u>
$1,400,000

Required   Determine the appropriate changes that the parent company should make to its conceptual analysis of the Investment account by components.

PROBLEMS

P 13–1   Parent's Acquisition of NCI Interest   On 1/1/X3, Pree Inc. acquired all of the noncontrolling interest shares of its 90%-owned subsidiary, Spree Inc., by issuing 10,000 shares of its $5 par value common stock. Pree's common stock had a fair market value of $17 per share on 1/1/X3. The business combination with Spree was recorded as a pooling of interests at the time of the combination. Spree's capital accounts on 12/31/X3 were as follows:

Common stock	$1,000,000
Retained earnings	400,000
	$1,400,000

All of Spree's assets and liabilities have a current value equal to their book value at 1/1/X3 except for its building, which is worth $70,000 in excess of book value.

Required Prepare the parent's entry to record this acquisition and update the analysis of the Investment account.

P 13–2 **Subsidiary's Acquisition of NCI** Pebit Inc. owns 60% of the outstanding common stock of Scredit Inc. On 1/1/X6 Scredit acquired 20% of its outstanding common stock from its noncontrolling interest shareholders for $360,000 cash. (These shares were immediately retired by debiting the Common Stock account for $20,000, Additional Paid-in Capital account for $80,000, and Retained Earnings account for $260,000.) A combined analysis of Pebit's Investment account at 12/31/X5 follows:

Book value element:	
Common stock, $10 par value	$ 100,000
Additional paid-in capital	400,000
Retained earnings	700,000
Undervaluation of net assets element:	
Land	100,000
Goodwill element	80,000
	$1,380,000
Total cost	$ 828,000
Noncontrolling interest	552,000
	$1,380,000

The current value of all of Scredit's assets and liabilities is equal to their book value on 1/1/X6, except for land, which has a current value $100,000 over its book value.

Required
1. Calculate the decrease in the parent's interest in the subsidiary's net assets.
2. Prepare and update *separate* analyses of the Investment account.
3. Prepare the parent's adjusting entry.

P 13–3 **Parent's Acquisition of NCI (Problem 13–2 Revised)** Assume the information provided in Problem 13–2 except that the parent acquired 20% of the subsidiary's outstanding common stock from the noncontrolling interest shareholders for $360,000 cash.

Required
1. Prepare and update *separate* analyses of the Investment account.
2. Prepare the parent's adjusting entry.
3. Explain why the parent's loss is higher in this case than in Problem 13–2.

P 13–4 **Parent's Partial Disposal of Its Investment** On 10/1/X4, Pyre Inc. sold 25% of its common stock holdings in its 80%-owned subsidiary Syre Inc. for $500,000 cash. All of Syre's shares were acquired on 1/1/X1 in a business combination accounted for as a *purchase*. A combined analysis of the Investment account as of 10/1/X4 follows:

Book value element:	
Common stock	$ 300,000
Retained earnings	500,000

(continued)

Undervaluation of net assets element:

Land	200,000
Patent	30,000
Goodwill element	10,000
	$1,040,000
Total cost	$ 832,000
Noncontrolling interest	208,000
	$1,040,000

Required   **1.** Prepare and update the parent's *separate* analyses of the Investment account.
            2. Prepare the entry to record the partial disposal by the parent.

P 13–5   **Parent's Partial Disposal of Its Investment**   On 7/1/X7 Proe Inc. sold 3,000 of the 9,000 Soe Inc.'s common shares it held for $170,000 cash. The 9,000 common shares, a 90% interest, were acquired on 1/1/X3 in a business combination accounted for as a *purchase*. A *combined* analysis of the Investment account by components as of 7/1/X7 follows:

Book value element:	
Common stock	$100,000
Retained earnings	150,000
Undervaluation of net assets element:	
Land	75,000
Bonds Payable	55,000
Goodwill element.	50,000
	$430,000
Total cost	$387,000
Noncontrolling interest	43,000
	$430,000

Required   **1.** Prepare and update the parent's *separate* analyses of the Investment account.
            2. Prepare the entry to record the parent's sale of the 3,000 shares.

P 13–6   **Subsidiary's Issuance of Additional Common Shares**   On 7/1/X5, Saver Inc., a 90%-owned subsidiary of Paver Inc., issued 20,000 shares of its common stock to the public for $1,200,000. The balances in Saver's equity accounts immediately prior to the issuance follow:

Common stock, $10 par value	$1,000,000
Additional paid-in capital.	4,000,000
Retained earnings	2,500,000
	$7,500,000

Required   **1.** Determine the economic gain or loss that the parent incurs as a result of the issuance.
            2. How should the economic gain or loss be reported?

P 13–7   **Subsidiary's Issuance of Additional Common Shares**   On 4/1/X8, Sweep Inc., an 80%-owned subsidiary of Prush Inc., issued 10,000 shares of its common stock to the public for $360,000. The balances in Sweep's equity accounts *immediately prior* to the issuance follow:

Common stock, $1 par value	$ 50,000
Additional paid-in capital.	250,000
Retained earnings	1,200,000
	$1,500,000

Required   **1.** Determine the economic gain or loss that the parent incurs as a result of the issuance.
            2. How should the economic gain or loss be reported?

P 13-8* **COMPREHENSIVE** **Purchase Business Combination and Consolidation Worksheet: Parent's Partial Disposal and Inventory Transfers—Equity Method** On 1/1/X3, Penn Inc. acquired 80% of Scribe Inc.'s outstanding common stock by paying $400,000 cash to William Braun, the company's sole stockholder. In addition, Penn acquired a patent from Braun for $40,000 cash. Penn charged the entire $440,000 to the Investment in Scribe Inc. Common Stock account.

Additional Information

1. The book value of Scribe's common stock on the acquisition date was $500,000. The book values of the individual assets and liabilities equaled their current values.
2. The patent had a remaining legal life of 4 years as of 1/3/X3. No amortization has been recorded since the acquisition date.
3. During 19X4, Scribe sold Penn for $130,000 merchandise that included a markup of 50% over Scribe's cost. At 12/31/X4, $45,000 of this merchandise remained in Penn's inventory. In February 19X5 Penn sold this merchandise at an $8,000 profit.
4. On 7/1/X5, Penn reduced its investment in Scribe to 75% of Scribe's outstanding common stock by selling shares to an unaffiliated company for $60,000, a profit of $16,000. Penn credited the proceeds to its Investment account.
5. In November 19X5, Penn sold merchandise to Scribe for the first time. Penn's cost for this merchandise was $80,000, and it made the sale at 120% of its cost. Scribe's 12/31/X5 inventory contained $24,000 of the merchandise that it purchased from Penn.
6. On 12/31/X5, Scribe's $40,000 payment was in transit to Penn. Accounts receivable and accounts payable include intercompany receivables and payables. (Scribe still owes Penn $25,000.)
7. In December 19X5, Scribe declared and paid cash dividends of $100,000 to its stockholders.
8. Scribe had $140,000 of net income for the six months ended 6/30/X5 and $160,000 of net income for the six months ended 12/31/X5.
9. At no time in 19X3–19X5 did Penn make any adjustment to its Investment account or its financial statements for any unrealized intercompany profit.
10. The financial statements of each company for the year ended 12/31/X5 follow:

	Penn Inc.	Scribe Inc.
Income Statement (19X5)		
Sales.	$4,000,000	$1,700,000
Cost of sales.	(3,000,000)	(1,000,000)
Expenses	(382,000)	(400,000)
Intercompany Accounts		
Equity in net income of subsidiary	232,000	
Dividend income.	75,000	
Net Income	$ 925,000	$ 300,000
Balance Sheet (12/31/X5)		
Cash	$ 306,000	$ 80,000
Accounts receivable, net.	170,000	255,000
Inventory.	179,000	355,000
Fixed assets, net.	830,000	290,000
Investment in Scribe Inc.	804,000	
Total Assets.	$2,289,000	$ 980,000
Liabilities.	$ 384,000	$ 40,000
Common stock	1,200,000	300,000
Retained earnings	705,000	640,000
Total Liabilities & Equity	$2,289,000	$ 980,000
Dividends declared.	$ 170,000	$ 100,000

Required

1. Prepare a conceptual analysis of the Investment account from 1/3/X1 to 12/31/X5 as it should have been maintained. (Pay particular attention to the requirements of the specific module from Chapter 10 that you are using to work this problem.)

*The financial statement information presented for problems accompanied by asterisks is also provided on Model 12 (filename: MODEL12) of the software disk that is available for use with the text, allowing the problem to be worked on the computer.

2. Prepare the appropriate adjusting entries required at 12/31/X5.
3. Adjust the financial statements for the entries developed in requirement 2. Modify the financial statements to reflect the use of intercompany accounts.
4. Prepare the consolidation entries at 12/31/X5.
5. Prepare a consolidation worksheet at 12/31/X5. (Parent and subsidiary columns should reflect the adjustments in requirement 3.) (AICPA adapted)

✳ THINKING CRITICALLY ✳

✳ CASES ✳

C 13–1 **Statutory Merger: Rights of NCI** Several years ago, Paso Inc. acquired 80% of Sol Inc.'s outstanding common stock. Paso now decides to merge with Sol. Under state law, the merger requires approval of only two-thirds of Sol's shareholders. Paso votes its 80% of Sol's stock in favor of the merger, which provides that each of Sol's noncontrolling interest stockholders receive one share of Paso's stock in exchange for three shares of Sol's. Your examination of Paso's financial statements after the merger reveals that some of these stockholders voted against it. You are concerned that Paso properly disclose in its financial statements the liability, if any, to these stockholders.

Required 1. What are the rights of Sol's stockholders who opposed the merger?
2. What steps must noncontrolling interest stockholders ordinarily take to protect their rights in these circumstances? (AICPA adapted)

C 13–2 **Theory: Parent's Partial Disposal of Its Investment** Polex Inc. sold a portion of its common stock holdings in one of its subsidiaries at a gain of $80,000. The controller is considering the following options:

1. Crediting this gain to the Investment account to reduce the remaining $240,000 of unamortized goodwill.
2. Reporting the gain as an extraordinary item because this is the first such disposal.
3. Reporting the gain as a partial disposal of a segment under the special reporting provisions of *APBO No. 30* for disposals of segments because neither the parent nor its other subsidiaries are in the same line of business.

Required Evaluate the theoretical merits of these three options.

C 13–3 **Theory: Subsidiary's Issuance of Additional Common Stock** Sona Inc. is a partially owned subsidiary of Pona Inc. In 19X8 Sona issued additional shares of its common stock to the public at an amount below book value. Pona is considering the following options in consolidation:

1. Computing the noncontrolling interest of these new shareholders based on the amounts they paid for their interest plus their share of earnings minus their share of dividends since the date the additional shares were issued.
2. Computing total noncontrolling interest by multiplying the total noncontrolling interest ownership percentage by the subsidiary's net assets at book value.
3. Treating the dollar effect of the parent's decrease in interest in the subsidiary's net assets as additional cost in excess of book value.
4. Treating the dollar effect of the parent's decrease in interest in the subsidiary's net assets as a loss in the current period.

Required Evaluate the theoretical merits of each option.

✳ FINANCIAL ANALYSIS PROBLEM ✳

FAP 13–1 **Whether to Sell Some of Parent's Holdings or Have Subsidiary Issue Additional Shares** Pewter Inc. owns 8,000 common shares of Silverado Inc.'s outstanding common stock. Silverado has 10,000 common shares outstanding on 6/30/X5, the book value of which is $50 per share. On this date, the carrying value of Pewter's investment in Silverado is $400,000. At this time, Pewter's management realizes that its earnings for calendar 19X5 will be below budgeted amounts. To report higher profits for 19X5, management is considering either (1) selling 2,000 shares of its holdings in Silverado at $70 per share or (2) having the subsidiary sell 2,000 additional shares to the public at $70 per share. Pewter is also experiencing a slight cash flow problem. Assume that it *is* acceptable practice to recognize such gains in the *current income statement*.

Required
1. Calculate the gain that Pewter would report under both alternatives.
2. What are the advantages and disadvantages of each alternative?

ANSWERS TO SELF-STUDY QUESTIONS

1. a   **2.** a   **3.** b   **4.** c   **5.** b

■APPENDIX

SUBSIDIARY WITH PREFERRED STOCK OUTSTANDING

In the consolidated balance sheet, a subsidiary's preferred stock is treated as part of the noncontrolling interest in the subsidiary's net assets. Likewise, the subsidiary's earnings that accrue to the preferred stockholders are treated in the consolidated income statement as part of the noncontrolling interest in the subsidiary's net income. Any preferred stock dividends declared reduce the noncontrolling interest in the subsidiary's net assets in the same manner that a portion of common stock dividends reduces this item. Thus parallel procedures exist for the preferred stock interest and the common stock noncontrolling interest.

The conceptual analysis of the parent's Investment account can be modified further to accommodate tracking the preferred stockholders' interest. For example, assume that when P Company created S Company on December 31, 19X0, S Company issued $100,000 of 6% cumulative, preferred stock (in addition to issuing $60,000 of common stock, of which 25% was sold to outside investors). Illustration 13–4 shows how to track the preferred stock interest for one year after the creation date. That illustration also shows the basic elimination entry at December 31, 19X1.

Additional complexities occur when (1) the parent acquires some or all of a subsidiary's outstanding preferred stock or (2) the parent-subsidiary relationship results from a business combination. These situations are beyond our purpose here, which is merely to acquaint you with (1) the fundamental nature of a preferred stock interest and (2) a simple tracking approach.

ILLUSTRATION 13–4 **Tracking the Preferred Stock Interest Within the Conceptual Analysis**

	Noncontrolling Interest	+	Parent's Investment Account	=	Preferred Stock	+	Common Stock	+	Retained Earnings
					Subsidiary's Equity Accounts				
Issuance of common	$ 15,000		$45,000				$60,000		$ –0–
Issuance of preferred	100,000				$100,000				
Balances, 12/31/X0	$115,000		$45,000		$100,000		$60,000		$ –0–
+ Net income ($24,000):									
To preferred	6,000								6,000
To parent (75%)			13,500						13,500
To NCI (25%)	4,500								4,500
– Dividends declared ($10,000):									
To preferred	(6,000)								(6,000)
To parent (75%)			(3,000)						(3,000)
To NCI (25%)	(1,000)								(1,000)
Balances, 12/31/X1	$118,500		$55,500		$100,000		$60,000		$14,000

The Basic Elimination Entry at December 31, 19X1

Preferred Stock	100,000	
Common Stock	60,000	
Retained Earnings, 1/1/X1	–0–	
Equity in Net Income (of subsidiary)	13,500	
NCI in Net Income ($6,000 + $4,500)	10,500	
Dividends Declared		10,000
Investment in Subsidiary		55,500
NCI in Net Assets		118,500

REVIEW POINTS FOR ILLUSTRATION 13–4   Note the following:

1. The first $6,000 of the $24,000 of 19X1 net income is allocated to the preferred stock interest because the preferred stock is cumulative. The remaining $18,000 accrues to the common stockholders.

2. If the preferred stock had additional features such as call premiums or participating dividends, more than $6,000 of the $24,000 of 19X1 earnings would have been allocated to the preferred stock interest (resulting in a lower residual amount that accrues to the common stockholders).

3. In general, the preferred stock interest is the amount that the preferred stockholders legally are entitled to receive in an assumed liquidation of the subsidiary.

TECHNICAL RESEARCH QUESTIONS FOR APPENDIX

1. Under *APBO No. 18*, does a *voting* preferred stock holding enter into the determination of whether or not *significant influence* exists?
2. Does it make sense to apply the *equity method* of accounting to a preferred stock holding when dividends are *cumulative?* Why or why not? What is the position of *APBO No. 18?*

PROBLEMS FOR APPENDIX

P 13–1A   **Consolidation Entries**   On 1/1/X1 Pixx Inc. created Sixx Inc., which issued stock on that date as follows:

5% Preferred stock, cumulative, callable at 103.	$100,000
Common stock, no par:	
To Pixx Inc., 3,000 shares.	60,000
To private investors, 1,000 shares.	20,000

Sixx reported the following items for its first two years:

	Net Income	Dividends Declared
19X1.	$32,000	$ –0–
19X2.	49,000	26,000[a]

[a]$10,000 was paid to preferred stockholders.

Required   1. Prepare and update a conceptual analysis of the parent's Investment account through 12/31/X2.
2. Prepare the basic elimination entry at 12/31/X1 and X2.

P 13–2A   On 12/31/X5, Pata Inc.'s 75%-owned subsidiary, Sata Inc. (which was created in 19X1), issued preferred stock. Information concerning this preferred stock follows:

Number of shares issued	2,000
Par value.	$100
Cumulative	Yes
Dividend rate.	4%
Callable at 103 plus any dividends in arrears	

Sata's equity accounts at 12/31/X5 were as follows:

Common stock	$ 50,000
Additional paid-in capital.	450,000
Retained earnings (accumulated deficit)	(18,000)

Sata reported the following items for 19X6 and 19X7:

	Net Income (Loss)	Dividends Declared
19X6.	$(32,000)	$ –0–
19X7.	80,000	4,000[a]

[a]This $4,000 was paid to the preferred stockholders. On 1/8/X8, Pata called (retired) Sata's preferred stock, making the appropriate cash payment at that time.

Required

1. Prepare a conceptual analysis of the parent's Investment account as of 12/31/X5.
2. Prepare the parent's appropriate *general ledger* entry to adjust its Investment account at 12/31/X5 (use the *economic unit concept*).
3. Update the parent's analysis of its Investment account from 1/1/X6 through 12/31/X7, assuming that the parent uses the *equity method* of accounting.
4. Prepare the basic elimination entry at 12/31/X5, X6, and X7.
5. Prepare the parent's *general ledger* entry to retire the preferred stock on 1/1/X8.

INDIRECT AND RECIPROCAL HOLDINGS

14

*Our characters are the
result of our conduct.*

ARISTOTLE

The most common intercompany relationship is the parent company's direct investment in a subsidiary's common stock. Other types of relationships encountered less frequently can be categorized as follows:

1. Indirect vertical holdings.
2. Indirect horizontal holdings.
3. Reciprocal (mutual) holdings.

These various relationships are shown in Illustration 14–1. The first two categories merely involve applying the equity method of accounting in the proper sequential order. For reciprocal holdings, it is necessary to explore further the parent company concept and the economic unit concept (entity theory) discussed in Chapter 6.

Although this chapter discusses each category independently of the others, the categories are not mutually exclusive; any combination of relationships may occur. Accounting for special corporate relationships involving combinations of indirect vertical holdings, indirect horizontal holdings, and reciprocal holdings can be developed from a careful application of the principles discussed in this chapter.

I INDIRECT VERTICAL HOLDINGS

An **indirect vertical holding** occurs when P Company, for example, owns more than 50% of S Company, and S Company owns more than 50% of T Company. In

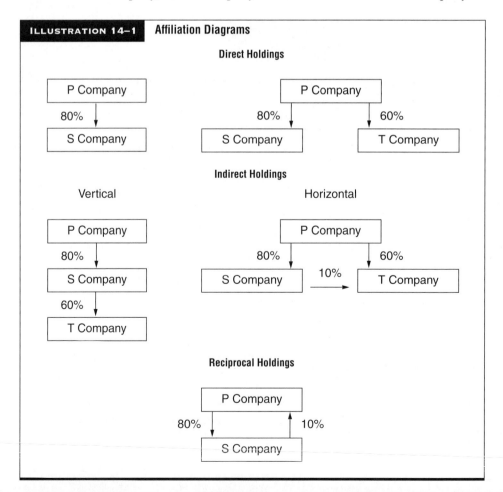

ILLUSTRATION 14–1 **Affiliation Diagrams**

such relationships, commonly referred to as **chains,** S Company, although a subsidiary of P Company, is a parent with respect to T Company.

The procedures used to consolidate the financial statements of the three companies follow:

1. T Company is consolidated into S Company.

2. S Company, now consolidated with T Company, is consolidated into P Company.

When noncontrolling interests exist at each level, the noncontrolling interest deduction in the income statement section and the noncontrolling interest in the balance sheet section of the consolidation worksheet increase at each higher level of consolidation.

Net income for P Company (the top-level parent) can be determined without consolidation by successive application of the equity method of accounting, starting with the lowest-level parent within the chain. For example, assume the following information for 19X1:

1. P Company owns 80% of S Company, and S Company owns 60% of T Company. The affiliation can be diagrammed as follows:

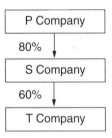

2. Net income from each company's operations, excluding equity in net income of subsidiary and amortization of cost in excess of book value, is as follows:

P Company	$1,000,000
S Company	100,000
T Company	10,000

3. All of P Company's $10,000 cost in excess of book value was allocable to land. All of S Company's $6,000 cost in excess of book value was allocable to goodwill; $1,000 was amortized during 19X1.

The successive application of the equity method of accounting is as follows:

S Company's income from its own operations	$ 100,000
S Company's equity in T Company's net income (60% of $10,000)	6,000
Less—Amortization of cost in excess of book value	(1,000)
Net Income of S Company	$ 105,000
P Company's income from its own operations	$1,000,000
P Company's equity in S Company's net income (80% of $105,000)	84,000
Net Income of P Company	$1,084,000

Note that only 48% of T Company's $10,000 net income is reflected in P Company's net income under the *equity method* of accounting (80% [60% × $10,000]). Of the $1,000 amortization of cost in excess of book value expense S Company records, 80%, or $800, accrues to P Company. Thus the net amount accruing to P Company is $4,000 ($4,800 − $800). Even though a majority of T Company's net income does not accrue to the consolidated group, successive consolidation is still appropriate because P Company indirectly controls T Company through S Company.

We do not illustrate the preparation of consolidated statements for indirect vertical holdings because the process involves no new substantive complexities—an additional intermediate consolidation worksheet is merely prepared. For indirect horizontal holdings (discussed next), however, some additional complexities do exist in the consolidation process, and we illustrate them.

II INDIRECT HORIZONTAL HOLDINGS

Indirect horizontal holdings occur when one subsidiary holds an investment in another subsidiary of a common parent; for example, P Company owns more than 50% of companies S and T, and S Company has an investment in T Company, which obviously must be less than 50%.

Consolidating the financial statements of the three companies is accomplished as follows:

1. S Company (an investor) applies the equity method of accounting with respect to the earnings of T Company (an investee).

2. P Company applies the equity method of accounting to each of its subsidiaries and then consolidates S Company.

3. P Company then consolidates T Company.

When the three companies are consolidated in this sequence, the individual investments in T Company by P and S are added together when the latter are consolidated. This combined investment in T is then eliminated in a single step when T Company is consolidated with P Company, which is already consolidated with S Company. When eliminating the combined investment in T Company, the individual components of P Company's Investment account must be combined with the individual components of S Company's Investment account.

Regardless of one subsidiary's ownership percentage in another subsidiary, the investor subsidiary should use the equity method of accounting (even if the percentage is less than 20%) because the parent exercises significant influence over the investee subsidiary.

P Company's net income can be determined without consolidation by successive application of the equity method of accounting, starting with the lowest-level investor. Assume the following information for 19X1:

1. P Company owns 80% of S Company and 60% of T Company, and S Company owns 10% of T Company. The affiliations are diagrammed as follows:

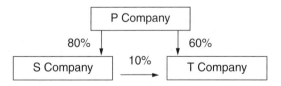

2. Income from each company's operations, excluding the equity in net income of any subsidiary or investee, follows:

P Company.	$1,000,000
S Company.	100,000
T Company.	10,000

3. For simplicity, we assume that all cost in excess of book value was allocable to land. Thus there is no amortization of cost in excess of book value.

The successive application of the equity method of accounting is as follows:

S Company's income from its own operations..................	$ 100,000
S Company's equity in T Company's net income (10% of $10,000) ..	1,000
Total Net Income of S Company.........................	$ 101,000
P Company's income from its own operations..................	$1,000,000
P Company's equity in S Company's net income (80% of $101,000) .	80,800
P Company's equity in T Company's net income (60% of $10,000) ..	6,000
Total Net Income of P Company.........................	$1,086,800

ILLUSTRATION | **PREPARING CONSOLIDATED STATEMENTS FOR INDIRECT HORIZONTAL HOLDINGS**

From the ownership and income information in the preceding example, P and S are consolidated as of December 31, 19X1 (Illustration 14–2), and P Company (now consolidated with S Company) is consolidated with T Company as of December 31, 19X1 (Illustration 14–3). (We assume that no intercompany transactions occurred requiring elimination.) The entries for these illustrations follow:

1. The basic elimination entries:

		Consolidation of	
		Companies P and S	**Companies P and T**
			(See below for source of these amounts)
WORKSHEET ENTRIES ONLY	Common Stock	300,000	40,000
	Retained Earnings, 1/1/X1	100,000	20,000
	Equity in Net Income (of subsidiary)..	80,800	7,000
	NCI in Net Income	20,200	3,000
	Dividends Declared	35,000	5,000
	Investment in Subsidiary	372,800	45,500
	NCI in Net Assets	93,200	19,500

2. The excess cost entries:

WORKSHEET ENTRIES ONLY	Land	40,000	9,500
	Investment in Subsidiary	40,000	9,500

We obtain the basic elimination entry to consolidate companies P and T by combining the individual components of the major conceptual elements of P Company's investment in T Company and S Company's investment in T Company, as follows:

	P Company's Investment in T Company	S Company's Investment in T Company	Total
Book value elements:			
Common stock	$36,000[a]	$ 4,000	$40,000
Retained earnings:			
Balances, 1/1/X1	18,000[a]	2,000	20,000
+ Earnings accruing to P & S	6,000	1,000	7,000
+ Earnings accruing to NCI in T Co. ...	3,000		3,000
– Dividends	(4,500)	(500)	(5,000)

(continued)

Excess cost element:

Land[b]	6,000	3,500	9,500
	$64,500	$10,000	$74,500
Total cost	$45,000	$10,000	$55,000
NCI in net assets of T Company	19,500		19,500
	$64,500	$10,000	$74,500

[a]Because of the 10% horizontal investment, this amount is only 90% of the book
value rather than 100%.
[b]Also for simplicity, we do *not* impute any amounts to the NCI.

ILLUSTRATION 14–2	Indirect Horizontal Holdings: Consolidation 1

P Company and S Company
Consolidation Worksheet as of December 31, 19X1

	P Company	80%-owned S Company	Consolidation Entries Dr.	Consolidation Entries Cr.	P + S Consolidated
Income Statement (19X1)					
Sales	7,500,000	790,000			8,290,000
Cost of sales	(4,000,000)	(360,000)			(4,360,000)
Expenses	(2,500,000)	(330,000)			(2,830,000)
Equity in net income—S Co.	80,800		80,800(1)		–0–
Equity in net income—T Co.	6,000	1,000			7,000
Net Income	1,086,800	101,000	80,800		1,107,000
NCI in net income			20,200(1)		(20,200)
CI in net income			101,000		1,086,800
Statement of Retained Earnings					
Balances, 1/1/X1	1,700,000	100,000	100,000(1)		1,700,000
+ Net income	1,086,800	101,000	101,000		1,086,800
– Dividends declared	(700,000)	(35,000)		35,000(1)	(700,000)
Balances, 12/31/X1	2,086,800	166,000	201,000	35,000	2,086,800
Balance Sheet					
Current assets	2,029,000	368,000			2,397,000
Investment in S Company:					
Book value element	372,800			372,800(1)	–0–
Excess cost element	40,000			40,000(2)	–0–
Investment in T Company:					
Book value element	39,000	6,500			45,500
Excess cost element	6,000	3,500			9,500
Fixed assets, net	2,600,000	350,000	40,000(2)		2,990,000
Total Assets	5,086,800	728,000	40,000	412,800	5,442,000
Liabilities	1,000,000	262,000			1,262,000
NCI in net assets				93,200(1)	93,200
P Company:					
Common stock	2,000,000				2,000,000
Retained earnings	2,086,800				2,086,800
S Company:					
Common stock		300,000	300,000(1)		–0–
Retained earnings		166,000	201,000	35,000	–0–
Total Liabilities and Equity ..	5,086,800	728,000	501,000	128,200	5,442,000
Proof of debit and credit postings			541,000	541,000	

Explanation of entries:
(1) The basic elimination entry.
(2) The excess cost entry.

REVIEW POINTS FOR ILLUSTRATIONS 14–2 AND 14–3 Note the following:

1. For the percentage investment held in T Company, S Company's cost in excess of book value was higher than that of P Company. We assumed that (a) S Company made its investment in T Company after P Company made its investment in T Company and (b) the land appreciated in value during that interval.

2. The consolidation can also be performed using one consolidation worksheet in which companies S and T are simultaneously consolidated with P Company. This is the common procedure in practice; separate consolidations of each company are used here for instructional purposes.

ILLUSTRATION 14–3	Indirect Horizontal Holdings: Consolidation 2

P and S Companies (Consolidated) and Subsidiary (T Company)
Consolidation Worksheet as of December 31, 19X1

	P and S Consolidated[a]	70%-owned T Company	Consolidation Entries Dr.	Consolidation Entries Cr.	P + S + T Consolidated
Income Statement (19X1)					
Sales	8,290,000	200,000			8,490,000
Cost of sales	4,360,000	(120,000)			(4,480,000)
Expenses	(2,830,000)	(70,000)			(2,900,000)
Equity in net income—T Co.	7,000		7,000(1)		–0–
Net Income	1,107,000	10,000	7,000		1,110,000
NCI in net income	(20,200)		3,000(1)		(23,200)
CI in net income	1,086,800	10,000	10,000		1,086,800
Statement of Retained Earnings					
Balances, 1/1/X1	1,700,000	20,000	20,000(1)		1,700,000
+ Net income	1,086,800	10,000	10,000		1,086,800
– Dividends declared	(700,000)	(5,000)		5,000(1)	(700,000)
Balances, 12/31/X1	2,086,800	25,000	30,000	5,000	2,086,800
Balance Sheet					
Current assets	2,397,000	115,000			2,512,000
Investment in T Company:					
Book value element	45,500			45,500(1)	–0–
Excess cost element	9,500			9,500(2)	–0–
Fixed assets, net	2,990,000	155,000	9,500(2)		3,154,500
Total Assets	5,442,000	270,000	9,500	55,000	5,666,500
Liabilities	1,262,000	205,000			1,467,000
NCI in net assets	93,200			19,500(1)	112,700
P Company:					
Common stock	2,000,000				2,000,000
Retained earnings	2,086,800				2,086,800
T Company:					
Common stock		40,000	40,000(1)		–0–
Retained earnings		25,000	30,000	5,000	–0–
Total Liabilities and Equity	5,442,000	270,000	70,000	24,500	5,666,500
Proof of debit and credit postings			79,500	79,500	

Explanation of entries:
(1) The basic elimination entry.
(2) The excess cost entry.
[a]From Illustration 14–2.

III RECIPROCAL HOLDINGS

Reciprocal holdings occur when a subsidiary invests in its parent company's common stock. Such holdings raise two accounting questions:

1. How should the subsidiary account for the investment in the parent company?
2. How should the investment in the parent company be accounted for in consolidation?

ACCOUNTING BY THE SUBSIDIARY

An investment by a subsidiary in its parent's common stock must be considered a long-term investment. Because such investments rarely, if ever, reach the 20% level, ownership in the parent's common stock is usually less than 20%. In this situation, the subsidiary must account for the investment at *cost* or *fair value* (depending on whether the parent's stock is publicly traded), as prescribed by FASB *Statement No. 115*, "Accounting for Certain Investments in Debt and Equity Securities."

Remember that a subsidiary, as a separate legal entity, must follow generally accepted accounting principles without regard to the fact that it is a subsidiary. Many subsidiaries must issue separate financial statements pursuant to loan indenture agreements. When contingent consideration based on the subsidiary's postcombination sales or earnings amounts is a provision of the business combination agreement, separate audited financial statements are often required.

ACCOUNTING IN CONSOLIDATION

Under current GAAP, shares of the parent held by a subsidiary are treated as *not* outstanding stock in the consolidated balance sheet. This requirement means, therefore, that **in consolidation the cost of the investment in the parent's common stock is treated as a cost of treasury shares.** Accordingly, a *reclassification* must be made in the balance sheet section of the consolidation worksheet as follows:

WORKSHEET ENTRY ONLY	Cost of Treasury Stock xxx	
	Investment in Parent Company's Common Stock	xxx

If the parent had acquired its own shares, the cost would be treated as a **cost of treasury shares.** But the parent directed the subsidiary to acquire the shares, which is usually the way such investments are made. If the subsidiary is 100%-owned, this treatment makes sense. If the subsidiary is partially owned, however, the requirement to treat all of the shares it owns as *not* being outstanding ignores the reality that the subsidiary's noncontrolling interest shareholders are *indirectly* shareholders of the parent. The requirement can cause a misleading earnings per share amount to be reported, as we demonstrate later in the chapter.

When a subsidiary has lowered the carrying value of its investment in its parent through a valuation allowance, the offsetting charge to its stockholders' equity section (required for equity investments categorized as *available-for-sale securities* under *SFAS No. 115*) must be reclassified in consolidation as part of the total cost of the treasury shares. Until the subsidiary disposes of some or all of its investment in its parent, the balance of the cost of the treasury shares, as reported in the consolidated statements, remains unchanged.

When a subsidiary is 100%-owned, consolidated net income is the sum of (1) the parent's earnings from its own operations, exclusive of earnings on its investment in the subsidiary, and (2) the subsidiary's earnings from its own operations, exclusive of earnings on its investment in the parent. These situations present no accounting issues in preparing consolidated statements.

The accounting issue for a partially owned subsidiary, however, is how to report the combined earnings for financial reporting purposes **in view of the fact that the subsidiary's noncontrolling interest shareholders are** *indirectly* **the parent's shareholders.** The GAAP consolidation rules do **not** specify the procedures for these situations. Two schools of thought explain how the combined earnings should be reported—one advocating the **treasury stock method** and the other advocating the **traditional allocation method.** Each of these methods is best discussed using an example. Assume the following information:

	P Company	S Company
Number of common shares outstanding	100,000	20,000
Ownership interest in the other:		
Percentage	70%	10%
Number of shares	14,000	10,000
Net income for the year (from own separate operations,		
exclusive of earnings on the investment in the other)	$1,000,000	$500,000

The affiliation diagram is as follows:

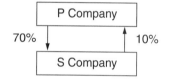

THE TREASURY STOCK METHOD

The **treasury stock method** comes under the *parent company concept* discussed in Chapter 6. Recall that under this concept, the parent is the reporting entity. The consolidation process merely substitutes the subsidiary's assets and liabilities for the parent's Investment in Subsidiary account. From this perspective, consolidated net income should be the sum of (1) the parent's earnings from its own separate operations and (2) the parent's share of the subsidiary's earnings from its own separate operations.

From this information, **consolidated net income under this method is $1,350,000** ($1,000,000 + [70% × $500,000]). Thus the noncontrolling interest deduction is based solely on the percentage of noncontrolling interest ownership in the subsidiary's earnings from its own separate operations, exclusive of earnings on its investment in the parent. Thus the noncontrolling interest deduction is $150,000 (30% of $500,000).

The consolidated net income, therefore, is the amount by which the parent's retained earnings increase if the subsidiary distributed as dividends all of its earnings from its own separate operations, exclusive of its earnings on its investment in the parent. Calculating the amount of this increase ignores dividend distributions to the parent's stockholders. Whether the parent uses the *equity method* or the *cost method* to account for its investment in the subsidiary is irrelevant.

When the parent accounts for its investment in the subsidiary under the *equity method,* it merely applies its ownership percentage in the subsidiary to the subsidiary's earnings from its own separate operations, not including the subsidiary's earnings on its investment in the parent. In the example, this is $350,000 (70% of $500,000). As a result, the parent's $1,350,000 recorded net income equals the $1,350,000 consolidated net income.

EARNINGS PER SHARE: IS IT MEANINGFUL?   The amount of earnings per share on a consolidated basis (assuming no other dilutive securities) is computed by dividing the consolidated net income of $1,350,000 by the 90,000 shares deemed outstanding (100,000 shares issued—10,000 shares held by the subsidiary treated as *not* being outstanding). This computation gives $15 per share. Treating all 10,000 shares of the parent's stock held by the subsidiary as *not* being outstanding results, however, in a meaningless earnings per share amount. If the parent distributed as dividends all of its $1,350,000 consolidated net income, this amount would not be distributed solely to the holders of the 90,000 shares. Because 10,000 shares of the parent's stock are held by the subsidiary and the parent's ownership of the subsidiary is only 70%, the subsidiary's noncontrolling interest shareholders are effectively *indirect* shareholders of the parent to the extent of 3,000 shares (30% of 10,000). Assume that the subsidiary was liquidated immediately after it distributed as dividends its net income from its own separate operations. The 10,000 shares held as an investment in the parent are distributed to the subsidiary's shareholders: 7,000 to the parent and 3,000 to the noncontrolling interest shareholders. Thus the parent's consolidated net income of $1,350,000 is distributed to holders of 93,000 shares, not 90,000 shares. Dividing $1,350,000 by 93,000 gives $14.52 per share. In terms of dollars, the holders of the 90,000 shares receive $1,306,452 (90,000 ÷ 93,000) of the consolidated net income of $1,350,000. The noncontrolling interest shareholders receive $43,548 (3,000 ÷ 93,000) of the $1,350,000 consolidated net income. The $14.52 earnings per share amount is therefore more meaningful.

THE TRADITIONAL ALLOCATION METHOD

The **traditional allocation method** comes under the *economic unit concept* discussed in Chapter 6. Recall that under the concept, a *new reporting entity* is deemed to exist as a result of consolidation. This new reporting entity has two classes of shareholders:

1. The controlling interests (in the example, holders of 90,000 shares of the parent's outstanding common stock).
2. The subsidiary's noncontrolling interest shareholders (who indirectly own 3,000 shares of the parent's outstanding common stock in the example).

From this perspective, parent's and subsidiary's combined earnings should appear in the consolidated income statement to show the amount that accrues to each class of shareholders. As demonstrated in the earnings per share discussion of the *treasury stock method,* the holders of the 90,000 shares are entitled to $1,306,452 of the combined earnings of $1,500,000 ($1,000,000 + $500,000), and the noncontrolling interest shareholders can be thought of as comprising two amounts, as follows:

1. The noncontrolling shareholders' interest in the subsidiary's earnings from its own separate operations, exclusive of earnings from its investment in the parent (30% of $500,000)	$150,000
2. The noncontrolling shareholders' interest in	
a. The parent's earnings from its separate operations	$1,000,000
b. The parent's share of the subsidiary's earnings of $500,000 from its own separate operations (70% of $500,000)	350,000
	$1,350,000

As shown in the discussion of the treasury stock
method, the noncontrolling interest in these amounts
is in the ratio of 3,000 shares to 93,000 shares
$(3,000 \div 93,000) \times \$1,350,000 = $ 43,548

Portion of combined earnings that accrues to the
noncontrolling shareholders $193,548

Recall from Chapter 6 that under the *economic unit concept*, the combined earnings of the parent and the subsidiary are presented in the consolidated income statement as follows:

Consolidated net income $1,500,000
Noncontrolling interest in net income .... (193,548)
Controlling interest in net income $1,306,452

Reporting the combined earnings using this manner of presentation is obviously inconsistent with the *equity method* and the amount reported as consolidated net income. In a strict application of the *equity method*, the parent records $350,000 as its share of the subsidiary's earnings (70% of $500,000). Thus the parent's net income under the *equity method* is $1,350,000, which is *not* reported using the method of presenting the combined earnings discussed here.

EARNINGS PER SHARE: ON THE MARK!   The amount of earnings per share on a consolidated basis (assuming no other dilutive securities) is computed by dividing the $1,306,452 earnings that accrue to the controlling interests by 90,000 shares deemed outstanding (100,000 shares issued – 10,000 shares held by the subsidiary treated as not being outstanding). This computation gives $14.52 per share, a meaningful amount to the holders of the 90,000 shares. (The same earnings per share amount was calculated under the treasury stock approach using 93,000 as the denominator.)

USING SIMULTANEOUS EQUATIONS   Mathematically, the amount of the combined earnings that accrues to each class of shareholders is usually determined under this approach using simultaneous equations. In Illustration 14–4, the data from the example in this section are used with simultaneous equations to arrive at these amounts.

WHICH METHOD IS CORRECT?

Whether to use the *treasury stock method* or the *traditional allocation method* depends on whether the *parent company concept* or the *economic entity concept* produces the more meaningful form of reported combined earnings. This purely subjective evaluation is based on whether the consolidation process transforms the reporting entity into a new reporting entity. The treasury stock method is widely practiced, whereas the traditional allocation method is not, partly because of the treasury stock method's simplicity and management's reluctance to treat part of the parent's earnings as accruing to the noncontrolling interest shareholders.

IV   INTERCOMPANY PROFIT ON ASSET TRANSFERS

Regardless of the degree of complexity of the relationship among the entities within the consolidated group, any unrealized profit on intercompany asset transfers cannot be reported in the consolidated statements. When the *complete equity method* (explained in Chapters 10 and 11) is used, any unrealized intercompany

---

| **ILLUSTRATION 14–4** | **Application of Simultaneous Equations to Traditional Allocation Method** |

Let P equal P Company's net income from its own separate operations plus its share of S Company's net income that would accrue to it on S Company's liquidation. Let S equal S Company's net income from its own separate operations plus its share of P Company's net income that would accrue to it on P Company's liquidation. Thus

$$P = \$1{,}000{,}000 + (.70 \times S)$$
$$S = \$500{,}000 + (.10 \times P)$$

Substituting for P:

$$S = \$500{,}000 + .10(\$1{,}000{,}000 + .70 \times S)$$
$$S = \$500{,}000 + \$100{,}000 + .07S)$$
$$.93S = \$600{,}000$$
$$S = \$645{,}161$$

S Company's noncontrolling shareholders are entitled to $193,548 (30% of $645,161). Subtracting $193,548 from the combined earnings of $1,500,000 gives earnings of $1,306,452, an amount that accrues to the controlling interests.

Alternatively, the earnings that accrue to the controlling interests can be computed by solving the equation for P by substituting for S as follows:

$$P = \$1{,}000{,}000 + .70(\$500{,}000 + .10 \times P)$$
$$P = \$1{,}000{,}000 + \$350{,}000 + .07P$$
$$.93P = \$1{,}350{,}000$$
$$P = \$1{,}451{,}613$$

Because P Company's exisiting shareholders (other than S Company) own 90% of its outstanding common stock, they are entitled to $1,306,452 (90% of $1,451,613) in the event of a double liquidation.

---

profit is deferred in the general ledger or ledgers. Consequently, no special procedures are needed in consolidation merely because of the added complexity of the relationship among the entities within the consolidated group. When the *partial equity method* or the *cost method* (also explained in Chapters 10 and 11) is used, however, a careful analysis must be made to determine how much of the total unrealized intercompany profit (being deferred *in the consolidation process*) is allocable to the noncontrolling interest.

END-OF-CHAPTER REVIEW

SUMMARY OF KEY POINTS

1. For **indirect vertical holdings:** In applying the **equity method** of accounting, the lowest-level parent must apply the equity method before the next highest level in the chain applies it. The consolidation process starts at the **lowest parent-subsidiary level** and then works upward.
2. For **indirect horizontal holdings:** In applying the **equity method** of accounting, the investor-subsidiary must apply it to the investee's earnings *before* the parent applies it to the investor-subsidiary's earnings (even if the horizontal holding is less than 20%).
3. For **reciprocal holdings:** Under the **treasury stock method,** the noncontrolling interest deduction is based solely on the subsidiary's earnings from its own separate operations, excluding earnings on its investment in the parent. Under the **traditional allocation**

method, the portion of the combined earnings that accrues to the noncontrolling interest shareholders includes a portion of the parent's earnings from its own separate operations.

GLOSSARY OF NEW TERMS

Indirect horizontal holdings   An intercorporate relationship in which a subsidiary has a common stock investment in another subsidiary of their common parent.

Indirect vertical holdings   An intercorporate relationship in which a subsidiary has a controlling common stock interest in another company.

Reciprocal holdings   An intercorporate relationship in which two entities of an affiliated group of companies have common stock investments in each other.

Treasury stock method   A procedure by which the combined earnings of companies having reciprocal holdings (the controlled company being partially owned) are presented in a manner that portrays the parent as the reporting entity in consolidation (the *parent company concept*). Under this method, the fact that the subsidiary's noncontrolling interest shareholders are indirectly shareholders of the parent is considered irrelevant.

Traditional allocation method   A procedure by which the combined earnings of companies having reciprocal holdings (the controlled company being partially owned) are presented in a manner that implies the existence of a new reporting entity from the consolidation process (the *economic unit concept*). Under this method, the combined earnings are divided between amounts that accrue to the controlling interests and those accruing to the noncontrolling interests, based on their respective interests in the new reporting entity.

SELF-STUDY QUESTIONS

(Answers are at the end of this chapter.)

1. In indirect *vertical* holdings, which of the following is true?
   a. A third-tier subsidiary can still be consolidated if less than 50% of its earnings accrue to the top-level parent.
   b. A subsidiary has an investment in the parent.
   c. The sequence of consolidation starts at the highest parent-subsidiary level and then works downward.
   d. Either the *treasury stock method* or the *traditional allocation method* can be used.
2. In indirect *horizontal* holdings, which of the following is true?
   a. Investments of less than 20% can be accounted for under the *equity method.*
   b. The parent must consolidate the subsidiary having the investment in the other subsidiary before it consolidates the other subsidiary.
   c. A subsidiary is also a parent.
   d. A portion of the parent's own separate earnings are excluded from consolidated net income.
3. In *reciprocal* holdings, which of the following is true?
   a. The traditional allocation method fits under the *parent company concept.*
   b. The noncontrolling interest is shown as a deduction in arriving at the consolidated net income under the *traditional allocation method.*
   c. The cost of the investment in the parent's common stock is treated as a cost of treasury shares in consolidation under both the *treasury stock method* and the *traditional allocation method.*
   d. The *equity method* can be used under the *traditional allocation method* to calculate the amount of consolidated net income that accrues to the controlling interest.
4. Paxe owns 60% of the stock of Saxe, which owns 70% of the stock of Taxe. For 19X1, each company had $100,000 of earnings from its own separate operations, exclusive of earnings on its investment in affiliates and amortization of cost in excess of book value. For 19X1, Paxe and Saxe had amortization of cost in excess of book value (all goodwill) of $20,000 and $10,000, respectively. What is the consolidated net income for 19X1 under the *parent company concept*?
   a. $172,000   c. $182,000   e. $270,000
   b. $176,000   d. $185,800   f. $300,000

5. Repeat Question 4 using the *economic unit concept*.
6. Poxe owns 80% of the common stock of Soxe and 80% of the common stock of Toxe. Soxe owns 10% of the common stock of Toxe. For 19X1 each company had $500,000 of earnings from its own separate operations, exclusive of earnings on investments in affiliates and amortization of cost in excess of book value. For 19X1, Poxe had amortization of cost in excess of book value (all goodwill) of $40,000 relating to Soxe and $50,000 relating to Toxe. What is the consolidated net income for 19X1 under the *parent company concept*?

   a. $1,210,000   **c.** $1,260,000   **e.** $1,410,000
   b. $1,250,000   **d.** $1,350,000   **f.** $1,500,000

7. Repeat Question 6 using the *economic unit concept*.
8. Puta owns 80% of the common stock of Suta, which owns 20% of the common stock of Puta. For 19X1, each company had net income of $500,000 from its own separate operations, exclusive of earnings on its investment in the other. Under a proper presentation of the *traditional allocation method*, what is the consolidated net income for 19X1 that accrues to the controlling interest?

   a. $857,143   **b.** $900,000   **c.** $940,000   **d.** $1,000,000

9. Use the information in Question 8. What is the consolidated net income under the *parent company concept*?
10. Use the information in Question 8. What is the consolidated net income under the *economic unit concept*?

ASSIGNMENT MATERIAL

REVIEW QUESTIONS

1. What is the difference between an indirect vertical holding and an indirect horizontal holding?
2. What are the two methods of accounting for reciprocal holdings?
3. Can a group of affiliated companies simultaneously have indirect *vertical* holdings, indirect horizontal holdings, and reciprocal holdings?
4. What is the sequence of the consolidation process when indirect *vertical* holdings exist?
5. What is the sequence of the consolidation process when indirect *horizontal* holdings exist?
6. How should a subsidiary account for an investment in its parent company?
7. From a consolidated viewpoint, are shares of a parent company that a subsidiary holds considered issued stock or outstanding stock?
8. How is the cost of a subsidiary's investment in its parent's stock treated in consolidated financial statements?
9. Under the *traditional allocation method*, is the parent viewed as the reporting entity in consolidation? Why or why not?
10. Under the *treasury stock method*, why is it misleading to treat all of the parent's common shares that a partially owned subsidiary holds as not being outstanding when computing consolidated earnings per share?

EXERCISES

E 14–1   **Indirect Vertical Holdings**   Pargo Inc. owns 90% of Sargo Inc.'s outstanding common stock, and Sargo owns 80% of the outstanding common stock of Targo Inc. Each company earned $100,000 during 19X1 from its own operations, exclusive of earnings on its investment in its subsidiary. (Assume that there was no cost in excess of or below book value to amortize.)

Required   1. Determine Pargo's 19X1 net income through successive application of the *equity method*.
2. Determine the noncontrolling interest deduction in Pargo's 19X1 consolidated income statement.
3. Indicate the sequence of the consolidation process.

E 14–2   **Indirect Vertical Holdings**   On 1/1/X1 Syte Inc. acquired 80% of the outstanding common stock of Tyte Inc. On 1/1/X2, Tyte Inc. acquired 80% of the outstanding common stock of Vyte Inc. On 1/1/X3 Pyte Inc. acquired 75% of the outstanding common stock of Syte Inc. Each company's 19X3 earnings (exclusive of earnings on investments in affiliates) are as follows:

Pyte Inc.	$400,000
Syte Inc.	300,000
Tyte Inc.	200,000
Vyte Inc.	100,000

Each company declared cash dividends on its common stock of $10,000 during 19X1, 19X2, and 19X3. (Assume that there was no cost in excess of or below book value to amortize.)

Required   1. Determine the 19X3 net income of Pyte through successive application of the *equity method.*
2. Determine the total 19X3 noncontrolling interest deduction in Pyte's consolidated income statement.
3. Indicate the sequence of the consolidation process.

E 14–3   **Indirect Horizontal Holdings**   On 1/1/X1 Pello Inc. acquired 80% of Sello Inc.'s outstanding common stock and 70% of Tello Inc.'s outstanding common stock. On 7/1/X1 Sello acquired 10% of Tello's outstanding common stock. (Assume that all investments were made at a cost equal to the applicable share of net assets at book value.) For 19X2 the following amounts were reported:

	Income from Own Operations (exclusive of earnings on investments in affiliates)	Dividends Declared
Pello Inc.	$300,000	$50,000
Sello Inc.	100,000	20,000
Tello Inc.	50,000	10,000

Required   1. Determine the 19X2 net income of Pello through successive application of the *equity method.*
2. Determine the total 19X2 noncontrolling interest deduction in Pello's consolidated income statement.
3. Indicate the sequence of the consolidation process.

E 14–4   **Several Indirect Horizontal Holdings**   Pelco, a nonoperating holding company, is a parent of the following subsidiaries with the indicated ownership percentages:

Subsidiary Company	Ownership Percentage
Belco	90
Celco	80
Delco	70
Elco	60

In addition, Belco owns 10% of the outstanding common stock of Celco, Delco, and Elco; Delco owns 20% of the outstanding common stock of Elco. (Assume that all investments were made at a cost equal to the applicable share of net assets at book value.)

Each company's 19X1 net income from its own operations (exclusive of earnings on investments in affiliates) follows:

Pelco	$ –0–
Belco	10,000,000
Celco	1,000,000
Delco	100,000
Elco	10,000

Required   1. Determine Pelco's 19X1 net income through successive application of the *equity method.*
2. Determine Pelco's total noncontrolling interest deduction in its 19X1 consolidated income statement.
3. Indicate the sequence of the consolidated process.

E 14–5   **Reciprocal Holdings**   Pann Inc. owns 80% of the outstanding common stock of Sann Inc., which in turn owns 10% of the outstanding common stock of Pann. During 19X1, Pann earned $500,000 from its own operations, exclusive of earnings on its investment in Sann. (Assume that the cost of the parent company's investment equals its share of the net assets at book value.) Sann earned $100,000 from its own separate operations in 19X1. Neither company declared dividends during 19X1.

Required   1. Compute the consolidated net income and the noncontrolling interest deduction for 19X1 under the *treasury stock method*.
2. Compute the amount of the combined earnings that accrues to the controlling interests and the noncontrolling interests for 19X1 under the traditional allocation method.

PROBLEMS

P 14–1   **Indirect Vertical Holdings: Cost Exceeds Book Value of Net Assets**   On 1/1/X1 Pylo Inc. acquired 80% of Sylo Inc.'s outstanding common stock at a cost of $40,000 in excess of its share of net assets at book value. Assume that this excess is allocable to goodwill, which has a 10-year life.

On 1/1/X2, Sylo acquired 60% of Tylo Inc.'s outstanding common stock at a cost of $20,000 in excess of its share of net assets at book value. Assume that this excess is allocable to goodwill, which has a 10-year life. For simplicity, do *not* impute any goodwill amortization to the NCI.

For 19X2 the companies report the following:

	Income from Own Operations (exclusive of earnings and amortization on investments in affiliates)	Dividends Declared
Pylo Inc.	$500,000	$100,000
Sylo Inc.	100,000	50,000
Tylo Inc.	20,000	10,000

Required   1. Determine the 19X2 net income of Pylo through successive application of the *equity method*.
2. Determine the total noncontrolling interest deduction in Pylo's consolidated income statement.
3. Indicate the sequence of the consolidation process.

P 14–2   **Indirect Horizontal Holdings: Cost Exceeds Book Value of Net Assets**   On 1/1/X1 Pakk Inc. acquired 80% of Sakk Inc.'s outstanding common stock at a cost of $100,000 in excess of its share of net assets at book value. Assume that this excess is allocable to goodwill, which has an estimated 20-year life.

On 1/1/X2 Pakk acquired 65% of Takk Inc.'s outstanding common stock at a cost of $20,000 in excess of its share of net assets at book value. Assume that this excess is allocable to goodwill, which has an estimated 10-year life.

On 1/1/X3, Sakk acquired 20% of Takk's outstanding common stock at a cost of $5,000 in excess of its share of net assets at book value. Assume that this excess is allocable to goodwill, which has an estimated 10-year life.

Each company reported the following amounts during 19X3:

	Income from Own Operations (exclusive of earnings and amortization on investments in affiliates)	Dividends Declared
Pakk Inc.	$1,000,000	$500,000
Sakk Inc.	100,000	50,000
Takk Inc.	10,000	5,000

For simplicity, do *not* impute any goodwill amortization to the NCI.

Required   1. Determine the 19X3 net income for Pakk through successive application of the *equity method*.
2. Determine the 19X3 total noncontrolling interest deduction in Pakk's consolidated income statement.
3. Indicate the sequence of the consolidation process.

P 14–3   **Indirect Horizontal Holdings: Cost Exceeds Book Value of Net Assets**   On 1/1/X1 Parr Inc. acquired 80% of the outstanding common stock of Sarr Inc. and 70% of the outstanding common stock of Tarr Inc.

On 1/2/X1 Sarr acquired 20% of Tarr's outstanding common stock. The analysis of the Investment accounts by the components of the major conceptual elements for each acquisition at the acquisition date is as follows:

	Parr's Investment[a]		Sarr's Investment
	Sarr Inc.	Tarr Inc.	Tarr Inc.
Book value element:			
Common stock	$ 16,000	$ 7,000	$ 2,000
Additional paid-in capital	144,000	63,000	18,000
Retained earnings	40,000	21,000	6,000
Undervaluation of net assets element:			
Land	20,000	7,000	4,000
Goodwill element	40,000	10,000	5,000
Total Cost	$260,000	$108,000	$35,000

[a]Note that the conceptual analysis has *not* been modified to include the noncontrolling interest.

Assume that goodwill has a five-year life from the purchase date. For simplicity, do *not* impute any goodwill amortization to the NCI. Data for 19X1 for each company are as follows:

	Income from Own Operations (exclusive of earnings and amortization on investments in affiliates)	Quarterly Dividends Declared
Parr	$600,000	$100,000
Sarr	80,000	30,000
Tarr	40,000	10,000

Assume that earnings for each company occurred evenly during the year.

Required 1. Calculate Parr's 19X1 net income through successive application of the *equity method.*
2. Determine the noncontrolling interest deduction in Parr's 19X1 consolidated income statement.
3. Indicate the sequence of the consolidation process.

P 14–4 **Reciprocal Holdings: Parent's Cost Exceeds Book Value of Net Assets** Pola Inc. owns 90% of Sola Inc.'s outstanding common stock. In turn, Sola owns 10% of Pola's outstanding common stock. Data for each company for 19X1 are as follows:

	Income from Own Operations (exclusive of earnings and amortization on investments in affiliates)	Dividends Declared
Pola	$800,000	$200,000
Sola	100,000	30,000

In addition, Pola had $12,000 amortization of cost in excess of book value (all for goodwill) during 19X1, which is *not* reflected in its separate earnings of $800,000. For simplicity, do *not* impute any goodwill amortization to the NCI.

Required 1. Calculate the 19X1 consolidated net income and noncontrolling interest deduction using the *treasury stock method* that fits under the *parent company concept.*
2. Calculate the amount of combined earnings that accrues to the controlling interests and the noncontrolling interests under the *traditional allocation method* that fits under the *economic unit concept.*

P 14–5 **CHALLENGER: Reciprocal Holdings: Parent's Cost Exceeds Book Value; Preparing Consolidated Statement of Retained Earnings in Year Subsequent to Acquisition** Pyla Inc. acquired 60% of Syla Inc.'s outstanding common stock on 1/1/X1. On 1/2/X1, Syla acquired 10% of Pyla's outstanding common stock. Data for each company for 19X1 are as follows:

	Pyla Inc.	Syla Inc.
Retained earnings 1/1/X1	$900,000	$300,000
Income from own operations for 19X1, exclusive of earnings on investments in affiliates and amortization of cost in excess of book value	400,000	100,000
Amortization of cost in excess of book value (goodwill)	10,000	
Dividends declared in 19X1	150,000	30,000
Common shares outstanding	100,000	20,000

For simplicity, do *not* impute any goodwill amortization to the NCI.

Required 1. Calculate the 19X1 consolidated net income and noncontrolling interest deduction under the *treasury stock method* and the *parent company concept*.
2. Prepare a 19X1 consolidated statement of retained earnings assuming that the parent uses the *treasury stock method* and the *parent company concept*.
3. Calculate the amount of combined earnings that accrues to the controlling interests and the noncontrolling interests for 19X1 under the *traditional allocation method* and the *economic unit concept*.
4. Prepare a 19X1 consolidated statement of retained earnings assuming that the parent uses the *traditional allocation method* and the *economic unit concept*. To the right of this statement, show in a column the changes to the noncontrolling interest for 19X1.

P 14–6 **Indirect Vertical Holdings: Intercompany Inventory Profit in Ending Inventory from Upstream Sale** Polt Inc. acquired 75% of Solt Inc.'s outstanding common stock on 1/1/X1, and Solt acquired 80% of Tolt Inc.'s outstanding common stock on 1/1/X2. The cost of these acquisitions was at the applicable percentage of net assets at book value.

During 19X2 each company reported $100,000 of income (after income taxes) from its own operations, exclusive of earnings on investments in affiliates. At 12/31/X2, Solt's ending inventory included merchandise it had acquired from Tolt at a cost of $50,000. Tolt's cost was $30,000.

Required 1. Determine the 19X2 net income that Solt reports to Polt through application of the *equity method*.
2. Determine the 19X2 net income that Polt reports to its stockholders through successive application of the *equity method*.
3. Determine the total noncontrolling interest deduction for 19X2 in Polt's consolidated income statement.

✳ THINKING CRITICALLY ✳

✳ CASES ✳

C 14–1 **Reciprocal Holdings: Selection of Accounting Method** During 19X1 Piper Inc. acquired 80% of Siper Inc.'s outstanding common stock and Siper acquired 10% of Piper's outstanding common stock. Piper's top management has indicated to its controller that Siper's noncontrolling interest shareholders will probably not share in Piper's earnings for many years to come because Piper does not expect to pay any dividends on its common stock because it intends to retain earnings for growth.

Required Decide whether to use the *treasury stock method* or the *traditional allocation method*. How does this dividend policy influence your decision?

C 14–2 **Reciprocal Holdings: Determining Consolidated Dividends—Treasury Stock Method** Perk Inc. has an 80%-owned subsidiary that in turn owns 10% of Perk's outstanding common stock. Perk uses the treasury stock method to determine consolidated net income. It declared and paid cash dividends of $100,000 on its outstanding common stock during 19X1, $10,000 of which went to its subsidiary. Perk's controller is uncertain whether the 19X1 consolidated statement of retained earnings should show dividends declared of $100,000, $90,000, or $92,000.

Required How would you advise the controller?

C 14–3   **Reciprocal Holdings: Ramifications of Dual Intercorporate Control** Pax Inc. owns 100% of Sax Inc.'s outstanding common stock. Sax owns 100% of Pax's outstanding common stock.

Required   What are the ramifications of such intercorporate holdings?

SOLUTIONS TO SELF-STUDY QUESTIONS

1. a   **2.** a   **3.** c   **4.** b   **5.** e   **6.** b   **7.** e   **8.** a   **9.** b   **10.** d

REPORTING DISAGGREGATED INFORMATION

15

Better know nothing than half-know many things.

FRIEDRICH NIETZSCHE

CHAPTER OVERVIEW

The preceding chapters focus on preparing consolidated financial statements, which are important to investors and lenders in evaluating the overall performance and condition of an enterprise. Historically, investors and lenders have also used financial statements to prepare trends and ratios that are useful in assessing the future prospects of an enterprise. For companies that have expanded into **different industries** or **geographic areas,** this task is usually more complicated because of different opportunities for growth, degrees and types of risk, and returns on investments among the various segments. As is discussed in Chapter 16, significant additional risks arise in conducting operations in foreign countries. Even when a company has only domestic operations, substantial differences in future prospects may exist among the industry segments.

Because of two major events, accountants believe that lenders and investors would be better served if combined or consolidated statements were **supplemented with information concerning the industries and geographic areas in which an enterprise operates.** The first event was the substantial foreign investment that occurred after World War II. The second was the extensive diversification of products carried out by scores of companies beginning in the 1960s. In 1976, the Financial Accounting Standards Board (FASB) issued *Statement No. 14,* "Financial Reporting for Segments of a Business Enterprise," in response to these events. This pronouncement requires the disclosure of information in addition to the basic financial statements. This information fits into three broad categories:

1. Operations in different industries.

2. Foreign operations and export sales.

3. Major customers.

If a complete set of the basic financial statements is presented for more than one year (for comparative purposes), the information to be disclosed under *SFAS No. 14* must be presented for each such year.

The reporting requirements of this pronouncement are substantial for companies obliged to comply (certain companies are exempted from this pronouncement's reporting requirements). Before *SFAS No. 14* was issued, the Securities and Exchange Commission (SEC) had imposed line-of-business reporting requirements on publicly owned companies. The current SEC reporting requirements in *Regulation S-K,* an integrated disclosure regulation adopted in 1977, are closely patterned after *SFAS No. 14.* (*Regulation S-K* is discussed in detail in Chapter 22.)

SFAS No. 14 is a *nonjudgmental standard* for the most part because arbitrary amounts are used in its various tests. It has been fairly successful because no groundswell of uniform disapproval has occurred. Many financial statement users desire quarterly disaggregated information, however, in addition to the required annual disaggregated information. A major complaint of many corporate executives is that *SFAS No. 14* places U.S. companies at a competitive disadvantage to many foreign companies, which are *not* required to disclose disaggregated information to the extent required by *SFAS No. 14.* These executives would favor allowing omission of disclosures that management deems competitively harmful. See the International Perspective for disclosure practices abroad.

THE PRINCIPLES USED TO PRESENT SEGMENT INFORMATION

Recall that a basic principle in preparing consolidated statements is that all *intercompany transactions* (and intracompany transactions when divisions are used) are completely eliminated as though the transactions had never occurred. This princi-

---

INTERNATIONAL PERSPECTIVE

Foreign Segment Reporting Practices

International Accounting Standard 14, "Reporting Financial Information by Segment" (issued in 1983 by the London-based International Accounting Standards Committee), has requirements that are essentially the same as those of *SFAS No. 14* issued by the FASB. The following table summarizes whether selected foreign countries comply with *IAS 14:*

Substantially Comply	Do *Not* Substantially Comply[a]
Canada	France
Japan (except that segment assets and the basis of intersegment transfer prices are not required to be disclosed)	Germany
	Italy
	Netherlands
United Kingdom	

[a]A major reason for noncompliance is that companies do not wish to disclose information that competing companies from other countries can use.

---

ple is also used in preparing industry segment information, with the modification that any **intersegment sales should be separately disclosed but then also eliminated in reconciling to the consolidated revenues**—and this disclosure and elimination must be shown together. Any *intrasegment* sales (such as those within a vertically integrated operation) need not be disclosed.

With respect to reporting information by **geographic areas,** the modified basic principle requires **separate disclosure of transfers between geographic areas with the elimination of these transfers in reconciling to consolidated revenues;** this disclosure and elimination also are shown together. *Transfer* means shipments of inventory, whether or not accounted for as a sale by the shipping organization. *SFAS No. 14* **ignores the organization structure of companies**—that is, whether divided into branches, divisions, or subsidiaries.

A comprehensive illustration of the type of disclosure that *SFAS No.14* requires is provided at the end of the chapter. Before proceeding, lightly review this illustration to obtain a general understanding of the disclosure required under this pronouncement. Specific sections of the illustration are referred to later in the chapter as the material is discussed.

I   APPLICABILITY OF FASB *STATEMENT NO. 14*

PUBLIC ENTERPRISES ONLY

When it was issued, *SFAS No. 14* applied to all enterprises. Later, however, it was evident that (1) the reporting requirements of this pronouncement burdened small, closely held enterprises and (2) its benefit to nonmanagement investors and creditors was too limited. Consequently, FASB *Statement No. 21,* "Suspension of the Reporting of Earnings per Share and Segment Information by Nonpublic Enterprises," was issued, suspending the requirements of *SFAS No. 14* for nonpublic enterprises. *SFAS No. 21* defines a nonpublic enterprise as follows:

> For purposes of this Statement, a nonpublic enterprise is an enterprise other than one (a) whose debt or equity securities trade in a public market on a foreign or domestic stock exchange or in the over-the-counter market (including securities quoted only locally or regionally) or (b) that is required to file financial statements with the Securities and Exchange Commission. An enterprise is no longer considered a nonpublic enterprise when

its financial statements are issued in preparation for the sale of any class of securities in a public market.[1]

INTERIM FINANCIAL STATEMENTS

SFAS No. 14 required that segment information be included in interim financial reports that constituted a complete set of financial statements in conformity with generally accepted accounting principles. FASB *Statement No. 18,* "Financial Reporting for Segments of a Business Enterprise—Interim Financial Statements," later rescinded this requirement, however.

FINANCIAL STATEMENTS PRESENTED IN ANOTHER ENTERPRISE'S FINANCIAL REPORT

Many situations arise in which a complete set of an entity's financial statements is presented in another enterprise's financial report. The three most common such situations are the following:

1. "Parent-company-only" statements are presented in addition to the consolidated financial statements.
2. The financial statements of an unconsolidated subsidiary are presented in the notes to the parent's financial statements (which may be consolidated with the financial statements of other subsidiaries).
3. The financial statements of a 50%- or less owned investee are presented in the notes to the investor's financial statements.

In a literal interpretation of paragraph 7 of *SFAS No. 14,* the separate "additional" set of statements described in these three situations must include the information required by *SFAS No. 14.* FASB *Statement No. 24,* "Reporting Segment Information in Financial Statements That Are Presented in Another Enterprise's Financial Report," later amended this paragraph to delete this reporting requirement in certain situations. For these three situations, the *SFAS No. 24* provisions are as follows:

1. The disclosure requirements of *SFAS No. 14* do not apply to "parent-company-only" financial statements (because such statements are included in the consolidated statements).
2. The disclosure requirements of *SFAS No. 14* apply to the financial statements of unconsolidated subsidiaries if that information is significant in relation to the financial statements of the primary reporting entity in that financial report.
3. The disclosure requirements of *SFAS No. 14* in these situations depend on whether the 50%-or less owned investee is a domestic or foreign entity.
   a. **Domestic Entity.** The requirements of *SFAS No. 14* apply to a domestic entity's financial statements if that information is significant in relation to the financial statements of the primary reporting entity in that financial report.
   b. **Foreign Entity.** The requirements of *SFAS No. 14* do not apply to a foreign entity's financial statements unless that foreign entity's *separately issued* financial statements disclose the information required by *SFAS No. 14.*

---

[1] *Statement of Financial Accounting Standards No. 21*, "Suspension of the Reporting of Earnings per Share and Segment Information by Nonpublic Enterprises" (Stamford: Financial Accounting Standards Board, 1978), par. 13.

In summary, the disclosure requirements of *SFAS No. 14* currently pertain to *annual* financial statements of *publicly held* companies. When the financial reports of these companies also include a complete set of financial statements of an unconsolidated subsidiary or a 50%- or less owned entity, the requirements of *SFAS No. 14* may also apply to the investee's financial statements (as included in the financial report of the investor), depending on the individual circumstances.

II INFORMATION ABOUT DIFFERENT INDUSTRIES

SFAS No. 14 specifies detailed mathematical tests for determining the components of a business that must disclose certain information regarding its operations. Components that meet these tests are *reportable industry segments*. Before discussing these mathematical tests, we present the information that must be disclosed for each reportable industry segment and the manner of reporting it.

INFORMATION PRESENTED FOR REPORTABLE INDUSTRY SEGMENTS

The following information must be presented for each reportable industry segment and in total for all nonreportable industry segments:

1. *Revenue.* Sales to unaffiliated customers and sales or transfers to other industry segments. . . .
2. *Profitability.* Operating profit or loss . . . [along with an explanation of] the nature and amount of any unusual or infrequently occurring items . . . that have been added or deducted in computing the operating profit or loss. . . .
3. *Identifiable assets.* The aggregate carrying amount of identifiable assets. . . .
4. *Other related disclosures:*
   a. The aggregate amount of depreciation, depletion, and amortization expense. . . .
   b. The amount of . . . capital expenditures, i.e., additions to its property, plant, and equipment. . . .
   c. The . . . equity in the net income from and investment in the net assets of unconsolidated subsidiaries and other equity method investees whose operations are vertically integrated with the operations of that segment. . . .
   d. The effect . . . on the operating profit [of a change in accounting principle].[2]

The pronouncement defines items 1, 2, and 3 as follows:

> **Revenue.** The revenue of an industry segment includes revenue both from sales to unaffiliated customers (i.e., revenue from customers outside the enterprise as reported in the enterprise's income statement) and from intersegment sales or transfers, if any, of products and services similar to those sold to unaffiliated customers. . . .
>
> **Operating Profit or Loss.** The operating profit or loss of an industry segment is its revenue as defined . . . minus all operating expenses. As used herein, operating expenses include expenses that relate to both revenue from sales to unaffiliated customers and revenue from intersegment sales or transfers. . . .
>
> **Identifiable Assets.** The identifiable assets of an industry segment are those tangible and intangible enterprise assets that are used by the industry segment, including

---

[2]*Statement of Financial Accounting Standards No. 14*, "Financial Reporting for Segments of a Business Enterprise" (Stamford: Financial Accounting Standards Board, 1976), pars. 22–27.

(1) assets that are used exclusively by that industry segment and (2) an allocated portion of assets used jointly by two or more industry segments. . . .[3]

The identifiable assets of segments that were acquired in a business combination accounted for as a purchase include the amount of the parent's cost of an investment in excess of its interest in a subsidiary's net assets. This is necessary so that the amount of a segment's identifiable net assets is the same whether assets or common stock was acquired.

METHODS OF PRESENTING INFORMATION ON REPORTABLE SEGMENTS

The required information pertaining to reportable segments must be included in the statements in one of the following ways:

1. Within the body of the financial statements, with appropriate explanatory disclosures in the footnotes to the financial statements.
2. Entirely in the footnotes to the financial statements.
3. In a separate schedule that is included as an integral part of the financial statements.[4]

MANDATORY RECONCILIATION TO THE CONSOLIDATED STATEMENTS The information that must be presented for individual reportable industry segments and in the aggregate for industry segments not deemed reportable must be reconciled to the consolidated statements as follows:

1. Revenue shall be reconciled to revenue reported in the consolidated income statement. . . .
2. Operating profit or loss shall be reconciled to pretax income from continuing operations (before gain or loss on discontinued operations, extraordinary items, and cumulative effect of a change in accounting principle) in the consolidated income statement. . . .
3. Identifiable assets shall be reconciled to consolidated total assets, with assets maintained for general corporate purposes separately identified in the reconciliation.[5]

Reconciling items 2 and 3 to consolidated amounts requires the use of procedures discussed and illustrated in Chapters 8 and 9 for the recognition and deferral of gross profit or gain on intercompany asset transfers.

TRANSFER PRICING

The definition of revenue includes revenues from **intersegment sales and transfers,** if any, of products and services similar to those sold to unaffiliated customers. Accordingly, the reported profitability of each segment is directly affected by the sales or transfer prices used. Because such sales or transfers are *not* determined on an "arm's-length" basis from a consolidated viewpoint, substantial latitude exists for top management to shift profits between the selling and buying segments.

It would be impractical for the FASB to try to establish a basis to set prices for sales or transfers between segments. Instead, the board requires companies to use the same transfer prices (for reporting purposes under the pronouncement) as those used internally to price the intersegment sales or transfers. Because transfer pricing has been associated in the past with vertically integrated operations (which

---

[3]*SFAS No. 14*, par. 10.
[4]*SFAS No. 14*, par. 28.
[5]*SFAS No. 14*, par. 30.

need *not* be disaggregated), the potential for shifting profits is of less apparent concern.

Furthermore, when sales or transfers take place between segments, most often the organization structures of the segments are similar to those of profit centers. This organization structure is a substantial motivating factor for each segment to sell or transfer at no more or no less than independent market prices, as the case may be. The basis of accounting for sales or transfers between industry segments and between geographic areas must be disclosed. If the basis is changed, the nature and effect of the change must be disclosed in the period of change.

ALLOWABLE AND UNALLOWABLE ALLOCATIONS IN DETERMINING EACH INDUSTRY SEGMENT'S OPERATING PROFIT OR LOSS

When determining an industry segment's operating profit or loss, the operating expenses subtracted from revenue (as defined in the pronouncement) include expenses related to both revenue from sales to unaffiliated customers and revenue from intersegment sales or transfers. Operating expenses *not* **directly traceable to an industry segment** are **allocated** on a reasonable basis among those industry segments for whose benefit the expenses were incurred.

The methods used to allocate such operating expenses among industry segments must be consistently applied from period to period. If the methods are changed, however, the nature of the change and the effect on the operating profit or loss of reportable segments must be disclosed in the period of change.

Because many items would have to be allocated on an arbitrary basis, *SFAS No. 14* specifies that the following items are neither added nor deducted, as the case may be, in computing an industry segment's operating profit or loss:

1. Revenue earned at the corporate level and not derived from the operations of any industry segment.
2. General corporate expenses.
3. Interest expense.
4. Domestic and foreign income taxes.
5. Equity in income or loss from unconsolidated subsidiaries and other unconsolidated investees.
6. Gain or loss on discontinued operations.
7. Extraordinary items.
8. Noncontrolling interest.
9. The cumulative effect of a change in accounting principle.

Note that items 3 to 9 appear **below the operating income or loss line** as that term is customarily used in income statements. Thus the meaning of operating profit or loss for a segment is consistent with the customary definition of those terms.

In the Comprehensive Illustration at the end of this chapter, Exhibits A and B and the note to Exhibit B contain the industry segment information discussed to this point.

DETERMINATION OF INDUSTRY SEGMENTS

An **industry segment** is defined as follows:

> A component of an enterprise engaged in providing a product or service or a group of related products and services primarily to unaffiliated customers (i.e., customers outside the enterprise) for a profit. By defining an industry segment in terms of products and

services that are sold primarily to unaffiliated customers, the Statement does not require the disaggregation of the vertically integrated operations of an enterprise.[6]

The products and services that are sold to outside customers must be **grouped by industry lines** to arrive at industry segments. Because the available classification systems are not entirely suitable, the grouping of products and services into appropriate industry segments is left to management's judgment, with the following considerations:

1. The nature of the product.
2. The nature of the production process.
3. Markets and marketing methods.

> Broad categories such as *manufacturing, wholesaling, retailing,* and *consumer* products are not per se indicative of the industries in which an enterprise operates, and those terms should not be used without identification of a product or service to describe an enterprise's industry segments.[7]

The underlying philosophy is to disaggregate the total business into segments with distinct markets and thus different profitability, growth potential, and/or risk patterns. The enterprise's internal data by organizational, divisional, or parent subsidiary lines *may* be used, but only if consistent with this philosophy.

DETERMINATION OF REPORTABLE INDUSTRY SEGMENTS

A **reportable industry segment** is

> an industry segment (or, in certain cases, a group of two or more closely related industry segments . . .) for which information is required to be reported by this Statement.[8]

An industry segment is "reportable" simply if it is big enough. Any industry segment that satisfies **any one** of the following criteria is considered a reportable segment for which specific information should be disclosed:

1. Its revenue (including both sales to unaffiliated customers and intersegment sales or transfers) is 10% or more of the combined revenue (sales to unaffiliated customers and intersegment sales or transfers) of all of the enterprise's industry segments.
2. The absolute amount of its operating profit or operating loss is 10% or more of the greater, in absolute amount, of:
   a. The combined operating profit of all industry segments that did not incur an operating loss, or
   b. The combined operating loss of all industry segments that did incur an operating loss.
3. Its identifiable assets are 10% or more of the combined identifiable assets of all industry segments.[9]

AN ILLUSTRATION OF THE REVENUES TEST   To illustrate application of this test, assume that a company has three industry segments, which have revenues as shown in Illustration 15–1.

---

[6] *SFAS No. 14*, par. 10.
[7] *SFAS No. 14*, par. 101.
[8] *SFAS No. 14*, par. 10.
[9] *SFAS No. 14*, par. 15.

| **ILLUSTRATION 15–1** | **Illustration of the Revenues Test for Determining Reportable Industry Segments (000s omitted)** |

	Aluminum Coil and Can Production	Retail Consumer Goods	Consumer Financing	Total Revenues
Sales of aluminum coils				
To unaffiliated customers	$4,400			$ 4,400
To aluminum can manufacturing division				
(an **intra**segment transfer)	1,200[a]			1,200
Sales of aluminum cans				
To unaffiliated customers	3,400			3,400
Sales of merchandise		$5,700		5,700
Interest income from consumers			$900	900
Intersegment interest income	600			600
Intrasegment interest income	300			300
Subtotal	$9,900	$5,700	$900	$16,500
Less—**Intra**segment sales	(1,200)			(1,200)
Less—**Intra**segment interest income	(300)			(300)
Total Revenues, as defined for the revenues test				
(sales to unaffiliated customers and intersegment				
revenues)	$8,400	$5,700	$900	$15,000
Designated percentage				10%
Qualifying Amount				$ 1,500
Reportable industry segments	Yes	Yes	No	

Note: Because the company has only three industry segments and two of the segments qualify as reportable industry segments, the consumer finance segment must also be shown separately. It need not be identified, however—it can be labeled as an *other segment*. If a fourth nonqualifying segment had existed, it could have been lumped with the consumer finance segment, and those two segments could have been labeled as *all other segments*.

[a]A reasonable argument can be made that the can-manufacturing division is an industry segment separate from the aluminum coil manufacturing segment. In this example, we assumed that both operations combined constituted a single industry segment.

AN ILLUSTRATION OF THE OPERATING PROFIT OR OPERATING LOSS TEST   To illustrate the application of the second test, assume that a company has eight industry segments, which are grouped as follows:

Industry Segment	Operating Profit	Operating Loss
A	$ 80,000	
B	300,000	
C	400,000	
D	220,000	
E	500,000	
F		$160,000
G		90,000
H		250,000
	$1,500,000	$500,000

The total of the operating profits is higher than the total of the operating losses. Applying the 10% test to the total of the operating profits gives $150,000. Any segment that has an operating profit or loss equal to or above $150,000 satisfies the test and is a reportable segment. In this situation, only segments A and G do *not* pass the test. Segments that do *not* satisfy the tests of a reportable segment are shown as a combined group of segments, appropriately described.

THE JUDGMENT FACTOR   After applying the three 10% tests, an enterprise must exercise judgment in evaluating the results of the tests. In this respect, it may be appropriate to

1. Exclude a segment that satisfies one or more of the tests if the result is a freak occurrence, such as an abnormally high revenue or operating profit or loss for the segment.

2. Include a segment that does not meet any of the tests if the result is a freak occurrence, such as an abnormally low revenue or operating profit or loss.

This latitude was granted so that interperiod comparability could be maintained. When a "reportable" segment is excluded or a "nonreportable" segment is included, appropriate disclosure of such circumstances is required.

THE 75% TEST   Enough individual segments must be shown so that at least 75% of the combined revenues (from sales to unaffiliated customers of all industry segments) is shown by reportable segments. To illustrate how the 75% test is applied, assume that a company with eight industry segments has the following revenues:

Industry Segment	Sales to Unaffiliated Customers	Intersegment Sales	Total
A	$ 100,000		$ 100,000
B	200,000		200,000
C	310,000	$ 40,000	350,000
D	340,000		340,000
E	550,000		550,000
F	600,000	60,000	660,000
G	700,000		700,000
H	800,000	300,000	1,100,000
	$3,600,000[a]	$400,000	$4,000,000
	75%		
	$2,700,000		

[a]Note that this amount is consolidated sales.

Assume that the operating profit or loss test and the identifiable assets test do not result in any reportable segments other than those determined below in the 10% of total revenues test.

Industry Segment	Sales to Unaffiliated Customers
E	$ 550,000
F	600,000
G	700,000
H	800,000
	$2,650,000

An additional segment must be selected so that at least $2,700,000 of sales to unaffiliated customers is shown by individual segments. This 75% requirement is determined after the three tests pertaining to revenues, operating profit or loss, and identifiable assets have been performed.

THE "TEN IS ENOUGH" GUIDELINE   There may be situations in which a substantial number of segments must be presented to comply with the 75% test. No specific limit is imposed on the number of segments for which information is reported. For practical reasons, however, the FASB has indicated that if **more than 10** industry segments are reportable segments, a company may combine the most closely related industry segments into broader reportable segments.[10]

THE DOMINANT OR SINGLE INDUSTRY TEST When a company has a dominant segment or only a single segment, the dominant or single industry must be identified. A company has a dominant industry segment when one industry segment has more than 90% of the revenues, identifiable assets, and operating profit or operating loss (all as defined earlier) of all the industry segments. Thus no other segment has 10% or more of revenues, identifiable assets, or operating profit or loss of all the industry segments.

III INFORMATION ABOUT FOREIGN OPERATIONS AND EXPORT SALES

FOREIGN OPERATIONS DEFINED

Foreign operations are revenue-producing operations (except for unconsolidated subsidiaries and other unconsolidated investees) that

> (a) are located outside of the enterprise's home country (the United States for U.S. enterprises) and (b) are generating revenue either from sales to unaffiliated customers or from intraenterprise sales or transfers between geographic areas.[11]

DETERMINATION OF REPORTABLE FOREIGN OPERATIONS

Information about foreign operations must be presented if either of the following criteria is met:

1. Revenue generated by the enterprise's foreign operations from sales to unaffiliated customers is 10% or more of consolidated revenue as reported in the enterprise's income statement.
2. Identifiable assets of the enterprise's foreign operations are 10% or more of consolidated total assets as reported in the enterprise's balance sheet.[12]

These two tests are based on the consolidated amounts, whereas the revenue and identifiable assets tests used to determine reportable industry segments are based on total industry segment amounts. Note that the 10% operating profit or loss test used for industry segments is not used for geographic segments. This test was apparently excluded because potential misinterpretations could occur as a result of significant differences in tax structures among geographic areas.

DETERMINATION OF GEOGRAPHIC AREAS

Disclosures required for foreign operations are presented in total or by geographic area. The grouping of foreign countries into geographic areas is left to the judgment of management, which should consider the following factors: "proximity, economic affinity, similarities in business environment, and the nature, scale, and degree of interrelationship of the various countries."[13] These factors could create different patterns of risk, profitability, and growth.

---

[10]*SFAS No. 14*, par. 19.
[11]*SFAS No. 14*, par. 31.
[12]*SFAS No. 14*, par. 32.
[13]*SFAS No. 14*, par. 34.

DETERMINATION OF REPORTABLE GEOGRAPHIC AREAS

When foreign operations are conducted in more than one geographic area, information must be presented for any geographic area meeting one of the following conditions:

1. Its revenues from sales to unaffiliated customers are 10% or more of consolidated revenues.

2. Its identifiable assets are 10% or more of consolidated total assets.

INFORMATION PRESENTED ABOUT FOREIGN OPERATIONS

The following information must be presented in total (when only one foreign geographic area exists) or for each reportable geographic area, and in the aggregate for all other foreign geographic areas that individually are not reportable as geographic areas:

1. Revenue . . . with sales to unaffiliated customers and sales or transfers between geographic areas shown separately. . . .

2. Operating profit or loss . . . or net income, or some other measure of profitability between operating profit or loss and net income. . . .

3. Identifiable assets. . . .[14]

With respect to item 2, a wide range of profitability can be used in lieu of operating profit and loss (as required for industry segment reporting). The apparent reason for allowing this flexibility is that when there are significant differences among the tax structures of foreign countries and the United States, misleading conclusions could result if the operating income or loss level alone were imposed.

A multinational company that has diversified operations may have to disclose both industry segment information *and* information about its foreign operations.

INFORMATION PRESENTED ABOUT EXPORT SALES

When sales to unaffiliated foreign customers by a domestic company (export sales) are 10% or more of total revenue from sales to unaffiliated customers as reported in the consolidated income statement, the total export sales must be separately reported, in total and by geographic area.

METHODS OF PRESENTING FOREIGN OPERATIONS AND EXPORT SALES INFORMATION

Foreign operations and export sales information may be presented in any of the ways shown previously for presenting industry segment information. The information for foreign operations, however, must be presented with the same information for domestic operations. The information for domestic operations and for foreign operations must then be reconciled to the related amounts in the consolidated statements in a manner similar to that described for industry segment information.

Information regarding export sales may have to be presented even though segment data need not be disclosed. In these cases, the information is normally presented in a simple narrative note rather than as part of a more complex schedule dealing with segment data.

[14]*SFAS No. 14*, par. 35.

At the end of this chapter, Exhibit C and the section on the note to Exhibit C illustrate the type of disclosure required with respect to foreign operations and export sales.

IV | INFORMATION ABOUT MAJOR CUSTOMERS

Some enterprises rely heavily on major customers. *SFAS No. 14*, as amended by FASB *Statement No. 30*, "Disclosure of Information About Major Customers," requires enterprises having revenues from any single customer in excess of 10% of total revenues to disclose the following information:

1. The fact that the enterprise has revenues from one or more single customers in excess of 10% of total revenues.
2. The amount of revenues from each such customer but not the identity of each such customer.
3. The industry segment making the sales to each such customer.

Each of the following is considered a single customer: the federal government (including its agencies), a state government, a local government unit (such as a county or a municipality), a foreign government, and a group of entities under common control. As in the case of export sales, information about major customers may have to be presented even though segment data need not be disclosed. A simple narrative footnote usually suffices in these cases.

V | SUMMARY OF VARIOUS TESTS USED TO DETERMINE THE EXTENT OF DISCLOSURE OF DISAGGREGATED INFORMATION

A summary of the various tests used to determine the extent of disclosure of disaggregated information is presented in Illustration 15–2.

VI | ON THE HORIZON

A FRESH LOOK

As mentioned in Chapter 1, the FASB is in the process of taking a fresh look at the disclosure of disaggregated information in connection with its major project on consolidations, which has five phases currently in process (the second phase being reporting disaggregated information). Much of the impetus for reexamining this issue is the contention by many financial analysts that *SFAS No. 14* (1) lacks specific guidelines for determining industry segments, (2) allows too much latitude by management, and (3) allows the grouping of products and services into overly broad categories so that the usefulness of the disclosed information is severely limited.

In February 1993, the FASB issued a comprehensive research report, "Reporting Disaggregated Information," prepared by Professor Paul Pacter of the University of Connecticut. This research report lists 27 issues to be addressed in taking a fresh look at disclosing disaggregated information, only a few of which we mentioned in the chapter overview. In January 1996, the FASB issued an exposure draft of a proposed standard that would supersede *SFAS No. 14*.

TENTATIVE CONCLUSION: SCRAP *SFAS NO. 14*

Under the exposure draft, disclosures would be made about *operating segments*, which would correspond with the entity's internal organizational structure

ILLUSTRATION 15–2	**Summary of Tests Required by _SFAS No. 14_ for Determining Disaggregated Disclosures to Be Made**	
	Used in Determining Reportable	
	Industry Segments	**Geographic Areas**
Revenues Tests:		
10% or more of revenues to unaffiliated customers and intersegment revenues of all industry segments	Yes	
10% or more of consolidated revenues (includes only revenues with unaffiliated customers)		Yes
Identifiable Assets Tests:		
10% or more of identifiable assets of all industry segments	Yes	
10% or more of consolidated total assets		Yes
Operating Profit or Loss Test:		
10% or more of the higher of the total operating profits or the total operating losses of all industry segments	Yes	
Overall Test (performed only after preceding three tests are performed):		
75% of consolidated sales	Yes	
Dominant or Single Industry Segment Disclosure Test:		
More than 90% of revenues, identifiable assets, and operating profit/loss (as defined) of all industry segments	The dominant or single industry must be identified.	
Export Sales Disclosure Test:		
10% or more of total revenue from sales to unaffiliated customers as reported in the consolidated income statement	The export sales amount must be disclosed.	
Major Customers Disclosure Test:		
10% or more of revenue to any single customer	The amount of revenue from each major customer must be disclosed.	

(subsidiaries, divisions, departments, or other internal units that the chief operating decision maker evaluates in reviewing an entity's performance). Consequently, neither industry nor geographic segment information would be specifically required "by the way the business is managed approach."

Such a change would require many companies that operate in a single industry (IBM and Intel, for instance) to make disclosures not previously made under _SFAS No. 14_.

Companies now making disclosures required by _SFAS No. 14_ also would probably have to make much more detailed disclosures than required by _SFAS No. 14_.

HOW WILL INDUSTRY REACT?   In our opinion, industry will vigorously oppose proposed changes to _SFAS No. 14_ along these lines because of concerns about providing too much financial information that their competitors could use. Thus a gigantic battle over this issue may occur between the FASB and industry in the near future.

VII   REPORTING THE DISPOSAL OF A BUSINESS SEGMENT

A SHORT HISTORY

THE PROFESSIONAL MANAGEMENT APPROACH   In the 1960s and 1970s, a professional management approach became exceedingly popular. Under this approach, it was thought that acquired businesses could be managed by professional managers whose skills could be applied successfully to almost any acquired business. Managing a diverse group of acquired businesses was likened to managing a portfolio of investments. This thinking contributed to the rapid rise in the number of conglomerates during this period (discussed in Chapter 4).

THE REVERSAL OF THE PROFESSIONAL MANAGEMENT APPROACH AND THE DECONGLOMERATION TREND   By the early 1980s, the professional management approach evidently had not been very successful. After an acquisitions binge, many companies found that they had bitten off more than they could chew. Many companies had bought into the wrong industry, or they simply did not have the managerial talent to manage a diverse group of industries effectively. In fact, of the 14 companies identified as having supremely excellent management by Peters and Waterman in their 1982 best-selling book *In Search of Excellence: Lessons from America's Best-Run Companies*, not one was a conglomerate.

In recent years, scores of top managements have undone much of the external expansion of their predecessors because the acquired businesses had lower than expected rates of return or continuous operating losses. Such undoings are referred to as *divestiture programs* rather than *selling your losers*. In the last 15 years, the number of disposals of unwanted businesses per year has increased dramatically (approaching a thousand for several of the recent years). Clearly, there is a trend away from "making deals" and toward operating businesses that managements know best.

RESULTS OF DIVESTITURES   Companies are leaner and healthier after divesting unwanted units. New management may run the divested units more effectively. If existing management buys the business, it may be entrepreneurially oriented and able to make decisions faster than allowed in a major corporations's rigid and stifling reporting structure.

MANNER OF DIVESTING   Companies commonly employ investment advisers (at substantial fees) to assist them in their divestitures. Divestitures can take the following forms: (1) selling segments to other companies (a business combination for the acquiring company); (2) selling segments to managers, employees, or investors in a *leveraged buyout* (increasingly common in recent years); (3) spinning off segments as separate companies (distributing the common stock of the subsidiary to the parent company's shareholders); and, when all else fails, (4) liquidating the business.

ACCOUNTING ISSUES

The following accounting issues are associated with the disposal of a business segment:

1. How should a gain or loss on the disposal of a segment be measured and classified in the income statement?

2. How should the results of operations of the discontinued operation be reported in the income statement?

The reporting and accounting for the disposal of a business segment are governed by *APB Opinion No. 30*, "Reporting the Results of Operations." This pronouncement introduced the idea that the results of operations of a discontinued segment and any gain or loss on the disposal should be reported separately from continuing operations. Before *APBO No. 30* was issued, losses on the disposals of segments were commonly reported as extraordinary items, whereas gains were not commonly shown as extraordinary items; the results of operations of the discontinued segments were not separated from the continuing operations.

MANNER OF REPORTING THE DISPOSAL OF A SEGMENT

APBO No. 30 specifies the manner of reporting the disposal of a segment as follows:

> For purposes of this Opinion, the term "discontinued operations" refers to the operations of a segment of a business . . . that has been sold, abandoned, spun off, or otherwise disposed of or, although still operating, is the subject of a formal plan for disposal.
>
> The Board concludes that the results of continuing operations should be reported separately from discontinued operations and that any gain or loss from disposal of a segment of a business . . . should be reported in conjunction with the related results of discontinued operations and not as an extraordinary item. Accordingly, operations of a segment that has been or will be discontinued should be reported separately as a component of income before extraordinary items and the cumulative effect of accounting changes (if applicable) in the following manner:

Income from continuing operations before income taxes.	$xxxx	
Provision for income taxes.	xxx	
Income from continuing operations		$xxxx
Discontinued operations (Note _____):		
Income (loss) from operations of discontinued Division X		
(less applicable income taxes of $ _____).	$xxxx	
Loss on disposal of Division X, including provision of		
$ _____ for operating losses during phase-out period		
(less applicable income taxes of $ _____).	xxxx	xxxx
Net Income		$xxxx

> Amounts of income taxes applicable to the results of discontinued operations and the gain or loss from disposal of the segment should be disclosed on the face of the income statement or in related notes. Revenues applicable to the discontinued operations should be separately disclosed in the related notes.[15]

---

[15]*Opinions of the Accounting Principles Board, No. 30*, "Reporting the Results of Operations" (New York: American Institute of Certified Public Accountants, 1973), par. 8.

If prior period income statements are presented for comparative purposes, such statements are *restated* to report the results of operations of the segment being disposed of as a separate component of income before extraordinary items, net of taxes.

DEFINITION OF A SEGMENT OF A BUSINESS

The precise definition of a *segment of a business* in *APBO No. 30,* which is different from the definition in *SFAS No. 14,* is as follows:

> For purposes of this Opinion, the term "segment of a business" refers to a component of an entity whose activities represent a separate major line of business or class of customer. A segment may be in the form of a subsidiary, a division, or a department, and in some cases a joint venture or other nonsubsidiary investee, provided that its assets, results of operations, and activities can be clearly distinguished, physically and operationally and for financial reporting purposes, from the other assets, results of operations, and activities of the entity. . . . The fact that the results of operations of the segment being sold or abandoned cannot be separately identified strongly suggests that the transaction should not be classified as the disposal of a segment of the business. The disposal of a segment of a business should be distinguished from other disposals of assets incident to the evolution of the entity's business, such as the disposal of part of a line of business, the shifting of production or marketing activities for a particular line of business from one location to another, the phasing out of a product line or class of service, and other changes occasioned by technological improvements.[16]

This definition is apparently narrower than the one used in *SFAS No. 14* in that the disposal of a discrete operation within a vertically integrated operation would be considered the disposal of a segment. (Actually, this would be the disposal of a portion of a segment as that term is used in *SFAS No. 14.*) This interpretation is consistent with the intent of *SFAS No. 14* because an appendix to the statement illustrates the disposal of a portion of a segment (as that term is defined in *SFAS No. 14*), which is reported in accordance with the procedures set forth in *APBO No. 30.*

DEFINITION OF MEASUREMENT AND DISPOSAL DATES

APBO No. 30 distinguishes between the operations of a segment that occur before a decision to dispose of that segment and operations that occur after that time. The particular point in time, referred to as the **measurement date,** is defined as follows:

> The "measurement date" of a disposal is the date on which management, having authority to approve the action, commits itself to a formal plan to dispose of a segment of the business, whether by sale or abandonment. The disposal should include, as a minimum, identification of the major assets to be disposed of, the expected method of disposal, the period expected to be required for completion of the disposal, an active program to find a buyer if disposal is by sale, the estimated results of operations of the segment from the measurement date to the disposal date, and the estimated proceeds or salvage to be realized by disposal.[17]

The **disposal date** as used in the preceding definition is defined as follows:

> The "disposal date" is the date of closing the sale if the disposal is by sale or the date that operations cease if the disposal is by abandonment.[18]

The format for reporting the discontinued operations of a business includes two categories. The *first* category, the income or loss from operations of a discontinued

---

[16]*APBO No. 30*, par. 13.
[17]*APBO No. 30*, par. 14.
[18]*APBO No. 30*, par. 14.

segment of a business, includes all operations up to the measurement date. The *second* category, the gain or loss on disposal of a segment of a business, includes the following:

1. The income or loss from operations **during the phase-out period** (from the measurement date to the disposal date).
2. The gain or loss on the sale or abandonment of the segment.

The amount reported in the second category **as of the measurement date** depends on the relative amounts determined for items 1 and 2, and whether the amounts are positive or negative. The pronouncement requires companies to recognize losses currently and to recognize income and gains only when realized, but some offsetting is also required. Thus an anticipated loss on the sale or abandonment of the segment is recognized as of the measurement date, whereas an anticipated gain is recognized when realized. Estimated losses from operations during the phase-out period are included, however, in this calculation. Estimated income from operations during the phase-out period is included only to the extent of the estimated loss on the sale or abandonment of the segment (with any remaining amount to be recognized when realized).

To illustrate, assume that on October 1, 19X1, a company with a calendar year-end decides to dispose of a segment of its business. The expected sales date is March 31, 19X2. Illustration 15–3 shows the amounts reported for 19X1 and 19X2 under various assumptions.

GUIDELINES FOR DETERMINING GAIN OR LOSS ON DISPOSAL

APBO No. 30 specifies the following guidelines to determine the amount of gain or loss on disposal:

> Estimated amounts of income or loss from operations of a segment between measurement date and disposal date included in the determination of loss on disposal should be limited to those amounts that can be projected with reasonable accuracy. In the usual circumstance, it would be expected that the plan of disposal would be carried out within a

ILLUSTRATION 15–3	**Determining the Amount Reported for Category 2: Loss or Gain on Disposal (thousands of dollars)**					
	Estimated Income (Loss) from Operations During the Phase-Out Period (October 1, 19X1, to March 31, 19X2)			**Estimated Gain (Loss) on Sale of Segment March 31, 19X2**	**Category 2 Gain (Loss) to Be Reported**	
	19X1	**19X2**	**Total**		**19X1**	**19X2**
A.	$(30)	$(70)	$(100)	$(140)	$(240)[a]	
B.	(30)	(70)	(100)	80	(20)[a]	
C.	(30)	(70)	(100)	130		$ 30[b]
D.	30	70	100	(140)	(40)[a]	
E.	30	70	100	(90)		10[b]
F.	30	70	100	160	30[b]	230[b]

Note: For simplicity, income tax effects were not considered.
[a]Reported as of the measurement date (10/1/X1).
[b]Reported when realized.

period of one year from the measurement date and that such projections of operating income or loss would not cover a period exceeding approximately one year.

Gain or loss from the disposal of a segment of a business should not include adjustments, costs, and expenses associated with normal business activities that should have been recognized on a going-concern basis up to the measurement date, such as adjustments of accruals on long-term contracts or write-down or write-off of receivables, inventories, property, plant, and equipment used in the business, equipment leased to others . . . or other intangible assets. However, such adjustments, costs, and expenses which (a) are clearly a "direct" result of the decision to dispose of the segment and (b) are clearly not the adjustments of carrying amounts or costs, or expenses that should not have been recognized on a going-concern basis prior to the measurement date should be included in determining the gain or loss on disposal. Results of operations before the measurement date should not be included in the gain or loss on disposal.

Costs and expenses "directly" associated with the decision to dispose include items such as severance pay, additional pension costs, employee relocation expenses, and future rentals on long-term leases to the extent they are not offset by sublease rentals.[19]

DISCLOSURE

In addition to the manner of reporting in the income statement gains or losses on the disposal of a segment, the notes to the financial statements for the period encompassing the measurement date should disclose the following:

1. The identity of the business segment that has or will be discontinued.
2. The expected disposal date, if known.
3. The expected manner of disposal.
4. A description of the remaining assets and liabilities of the segment at the balance sheet date, and
5. The income or loss from operations and any proceeds from disposal of the segment during the period from the measurement date to the date of the balance sheet.[20]

VIII COMPREHENSIVE ILLUSTRATION

This comprehensive illustration contains illustrations of the type of information required by *SFAS No. 14*, as follows:

Exhibit A   Consolidated income statement of a hypothetical company for the year ended December 31, 19X1.

Exhibit B   Information about operations in different industries and sales to major customers.

Exhibit C   Information about operations in different geographic areas and export sales.

The consolidated income statement in Exhibit A is *not* required pursuant to *SFAS No. 14;* it is included so that amounts in Exhibits B and C can be identified in the consolidated income statement.

Exhibits A, B, and C, and the notes to B and C in the text were adapted from FASB *Statement No. 14*, "Financial Reporting for Segments of a Business Enterprise."[21] Amounts in the notes are in thousands.

---

[19]*APBO No. 30*, pars. 15–17.
[20]*APBO No. 30*, par. 18.
[21]*SFAS No. 14*, Appendix F.

Exhibit A

X Company
Consolidated Income Statement
For the Year Ended December 31, 19X1
(thousands of dollars)

Sales		$4,700
Cost of sales	$3,000	
Selling, general, and administrative expense	700	
Interest expense	200	(3,900)
		$ 800
Equity in net income of Z Company (25% owned)		100
Income from continuing operations before income taxes		$ 900
Income taxes		(400)
Income from continuing operations		$ 500
Discontinued operations		
Loss from operations of discontinued farm machinery		
manufacturing business (net of $50 income tax effect)	$ 70	
Loss on disposal of farm machinery manufacturing		
business (net of $100 income tax effect)	130	(200)
Income before extraordinary gain and before cumulative effect		
of change in accounting principle		$ 300
Extraordinary gain (net of $80 income tax effect)		90
Cumulative effect on prior years of change from straight-line		
to accelerated depreciation (net of $60 income tax effect) . . .		(60)
Net Income		$ 330

NOTE TO EXHIBIT B

X Company operates principally in three industries: computers, food processing, and can manufacturing. Operations in the computer industry include the design, development, manufacture, and marketing of large computers. Operations in the food-processing industry include the cleaning, cooking, canning, and marketing of vegetables. Operations in the can-manufacturing industry include the production and sale of aluminum and steel cans for the canning industry. Total revenue by industry includes both sales to unaffiliated customers, as reported in the company's consolidated income statement, and intersegment sales, which are accounted for at negotiated prices between the segments. The company believes that these negotiated prices approximate outside market prices.

Operating profit is total revenue less operating expenses. In computing operating profit, none of the following items has been added or deducted: general corporate expenses, interest expense, income taxes, equity in income from unconsolidated investee, loss from discontinued operations of the farm machinery manufacturing business (which was a separate industry), extraordinary gain (which relates to the company's operations in the computer industry, and the cumulative effect of the change from straight-line to accelerated depreciation, of which $30 relates to the company's operations in the computer industry, $10 to the food-processing industry, and $20 to the can-manufacturing industry). Depreciation for each of these three industries was $80, $100, and $150, respectively. Capital expenditures for each were $100, $200, and $400, respectively.

Changing from straight-line to accelerated depreciation reduced the 19X1 operating profit of the computer industry, the food-processing industry, and the can-manufacturing industry by $40, $30, and $20, respectively.

Identifiable assets by industry are assets used in the company's operations in each industry. Corporate assets are principally cash and marketable securities.

Exhibit B

X Company
Information About the Company's Operations
in Different Industries
(thousands of dollars)

	Computers	Food Processing	Can Manufacturing	Other Industries	Adjustments and Eliminations	Consolidated
Sales to unaffiliated customers	$1,200	$2,000	$1,300	$ 200		$ 4,700
Intersegment sales.			700		$(700)	
Total Revenue	$1,200	$2,000	$2,000	$ 200	$(700)	$ 4,700
Operating Profit.	$ 200	$ 290	$ 600	$ 50	$ (40)[a]	$ 1,100
Equity in net income of Z Company						100
General corporate expenses						(100)
Interest expense.						(200)
Income From Continuing Operations Before Income Taxes						$ 900
Identifiable Assets at 12/31/X1 . .	$2,000	$4,050	$6,000	$1,000	$ (50)[b]	$13,000
Investment in net assets of Z Company						400
Corporate assets						1,600
Total Assets at 12/31/X1						$15,000

See accompanying note in text.

[a]$10,000 of intersegment operating profit in beginning inventory, net of $50,000 of intersegment operating profit in ending inventory.

[b]$50,000 of intersegment operating profit in ending inventory.

Exhibit C

X Company
Information About the Company's Operations
in Different Geographic Areas
For the Year Ended December 31, 19X1
(thousands of dollars)

	United States	Western Europe	South America	Adjustments and Eliminations	Consolidated
Sales to unaffiliated customers	$3,000	$1,000	$ 700		$ 4,700
Transfers between geographic areas	1,000			$(1,000)	
Total Revenue	$4,000	$1,000	$ 700	$(1,000)	$ 4,700
Operating Profit	$ 800	$ 400	$ 100	$ (200)	$ 1,100
Equity in net income of Z Company					100
General corporate expenses.					(100)
Interest expense					(200)
Income From Continuing Operations Before Income Taxes					$ 900
Identifiable Assets at 12/31/X1	$7,300	$3,400	$2,450	$ (150)	$13,000
Investment in net assets of Z Company					400
Corporate assets.					1,600
Total Assets at 12/31/X1					$15,000

See accompanying note in text.

The company has a 25% interest in Z Company, whose operations are in the United States and are vertically integrated with the company's operations in the computer industry. The equity in Z Company's net income was $100; the investment in Z Company's net assets was $400.

To reconcile industry information with the consolidated amounts, the following eliminations have been made: $700 of intersegment sales, $40 from the net change in intersegment operating profit in beginning and ending inventories, and $50 intersegment operating profit in inventory at December 31, 19X1.

Contracts with a U.S. government agency account for $1,000 of the sales to unaffiliated customers of the food-processing industry.

NOTE TO EXHIBIT C

Transfers between geographic areas are accounted for at prices negotiated between the buying and selling units. The company believes that such prices approximate outside market prices. Operating profit is total revenue less operating expenses. In computing operating profit, none of the following items has been added or deducted: general corporate expenses, interest expense, income taxes, equity in income from unconsolidated investee, loss from discontinued operations of the farm machinery manufacturing business (which was part of the company's domestic operations), extraordinary gain (which relates to the company's operations in Western Europe), and the cumulative effect of the change from straight-line to accelerated depreciation (which relates entirely to the company's operations in the United States).

The company's identifiable assets are identified with the operations in each geographic area. Corporate assets are principally cash and marketable securities.

Of the $3,000 U.S. sales to unaffiliated customers, $1,200 were export sales, principally to South America.

END-OF-CHAPTER REVIEW

SUMMARY OF KEY POINTS

1. Because of the limitations of consolidated statements, **supplemental data** on **industry segments and foreign operations** are considered necessary to assist users of financial statements to assess future prospects.

2. The process of supplying information **by industry** involves (1) **identifying** the various industry segments in which the enterprise operates; (2) **applying** three tests to each industry segment to determine whether it is considered a **reportable** industry segment; and (3) **presenting** financial information for each reportable industry segment and all other industry segments combined in such a manner that the amounts shown **tie into the consolidated statements.**

3. The basic criterion for determining whether a component of a business is an industry segment is whether that component sells products or provides services **primarily to unaffiliated customers for a profit.**

4. The **three major disclosures** for a **reportable industry segment** pertain to **revenues, operating profit or loss, and identifiable assets** used by the segment. In addition, a fourth category of miscellaneous disclosures relates primarily to capital investments, depreciation, and effects of changes in accounting principles.

5. The process of disclosing information **about foreign operations** involves (1) **grouping** the various foreign countries in which the enterprise operates into meaningful, related geographic areas; (2) applying two tests to each geographic area to determine **whether it is reportable;** and (3) presenting financial information and data for each reportable geo-

graphic area and all other geographic areas combined in such a manner that the amounts shown **tie into the consolidated statements.**

6. The **three major disclosures** for a reportable **geographic area** pertain to **revenues, profitability,** and **identifiable assets** used by each area.

7. **Disposals of segments** (or part of a segment) are reported in the income statement **separately from all other operations,** which are referred to as **continuing operations.**

8. **Losses** projected to occur **after the current year-end** may have to be recorded in the current year.

GLOSSARY OF NEW TERMS

Disposal date   "The disposal date is the date of closing the sale if the disposal is by sale or the date that operations cease if the disposal is by abandonment."[*]

Identifiable assets   "The identifiable assets of an industry segment are those tangible and intangible enterprise assets that are used exclusively by that industry segment and (2) an allocated portion of assets used jointly by two or more industry segments."[†]

Industry segments   "A component of an enterprise engaged in providing a product or service or a group of related products and services primarily to unaffiliated customers (i.e., customers outside the enterprise) for a profit. By defining an industry segment in terms of products and services that are sold primarily to unaffiliated customers, the Statement does not require the disaggregation of the vertically integrated operations of an enterprise."[†]

Measurement date   "The measurement date of a disposal is the date on which management, having authority to approve the action, commits itself to a formal plan to dispose of a segment of the business, whether by sale or abandonment."[*]

Operating profit or loss   "The operating profit or loss of an industry segment is its revenue as defined . . . minus all operating expenses. Operating expenses include expenses that relate to both revenue from sale to unaffiliated customers and revenue from intersegment sales or transfers."[†]

Reportable industry segments   "An industry segment (or, in certain cases, a group of two or more closely related industry segments . . .) for which information is required to be reported by the Statement."[†]

Revenue   "The revenue of an industry segment includes revenue both from sales to unaffiliated customers (i.e., revenue from customers outside the enterprise as reported in the enterprise's income statement) and from intersegment sales or transfers, if any, of products and services similar to those sold to unaffiliated customers."[†]

SELF-STUDY QUESTIONS

(Answers are at the end of this chapter.)

1. Which item is *not* part of the additional information disclosure requirements of *SFAS No. 14?*
   a. Major customers
   b. Different industries
   c. Major suppliers
   d. Foreign operations
   e. Export sales

2. Which item need *not* be disclosed for each reportable industry segment?
   a. Identifiable assets
   b. Capital expenditures
   c. Pretax accounting income

[*]Definitions quoted from *APBO No. 30*, par. 14.
[†]Definitions quoted from *SFAS No. 14*, par. 10.

      d. Depreciation expense

      e. Operating profit or loss

      f. Intersegment revenues

3. For reportable industry segment information, which of the following items need *not* be reconciled to consolidated amounts?

      a. Identifiable assets

      b. Operating profit or loss

      c. Revenues

      d. Depreciation expense

4. Which item *is* used in one of the three 10% tests for determining reportable industry segments?

      a. Consolidated revenues

      b. Nonidentifiable assets

      c. Revenues to unaffiliated customers

      d. Export sales

      e. Segment net income

      f. Segment operating profit

5. Which item *is* to be added or deducted, as the case may be, in computing the operating profit or loss of an industry segment?

      a. Income taxes

      b. General corporate expenses

      c. Nondirectly traceable operating expenses

      d. Extraordinary items

      e. Interest income earned at the corporate level

      f. Interest expense

6. Which item *is* used in determining whether a foreign operation is a reportable foreign operation?

      a. Consolidated sales

      b. Consolidated net income

      c. Sales to unaffiliated customers and intersegment sales

      d. Consolidated pretax income

      e. Major overseas customers

      f. Foreign net income

ASSIGNMENT MATERIAL

REVIEW QUESTIONS

1. Why are consolidated statements alone considered insufficient and inadequate financial reports?
2. What three basic disclosures relate to industry segment reporting?
3. According to *SFAS No. 14*, what is the meaning of *industry segment*?
4. What steps should be taken to distinguish between an industry segment and a reportable segment?
5. What tests determine whether an industry segment is a reportable segment?
6. What amounts for industry segments must be reconciled to consolidated amounts?
7. Under *SFAS No. 14*, how should prices be determined for transfers between segments?
8. What are five items that *cannot* be allocated to industry segments in computing a segment's operating profit or loss?
9. What two tests determine whether foreign operations are reportable?
10. How are foreign countries grouped into geographic areas under *SFAS No. 14*?
11. What three types of information must be disclosed for a reportable *geographic area*?
12. What is the difference between the definition of an *industry segment* under *SFAS No. 14* and under *APBO No. 30*?
13. How do the *measurement date* and the *disposal date* differ as used in *APBO No. 30*?
14. How are revenues, cost of sales, and operating expenses from the beginning of the year to the *measurement date* reported for a segment being disposed of?

EXERCISES

E 15–1   **Treatment of Common Costs**   Patco operates in three different industries, each of which is appropriately regarded as a reportable segment. Segment 1 contributed 60% of Patco's total sales. Sales for Segment 1 were $900,000 and traceable costs were $400,000. Total common costs for Patco were $300,000. Patco allocates common costs based on the ratio of a segment's sales to total sales, an appropriate method of allocation. Assume a 40% income tax rate.

Required   Determine the operating profit presented for Segment 1.   (AICPA adapted)

E 15–2   **Determining Reportable Industry Segments: Revenues Test**   Payco has the following revenues (stated in thousands of dollars) for its industry segments:

Segment	Sales to Unaffiliated Customers	Intersegment Sales	Total Sales
A	$ 170		$ 170
B	150		150
C	75		75
D	300	$125	425
E	80		80
F	125		125
G	200	175	375
	$1,100	$300	$1,400

Required   1. Determine the reportable segments based on the revenues test.
2. Assuming that the other two 10% tests based on operating profit or loss and identifiable assets do not result in any additional reportable segments, perform the 75% test.

E 15–3   **Determining Reportable Geographic Areas: Revenues Test**   Pyeco earns revenues (in thousands of dollars) in the following geographic areas:

Geographic Areas	Sales to Unaffiliated Customers	Transfers Between Geographic Areas	Total
Western Europe	$ 100	$100	$ 200
Africa	200	150	350
South America	300		300
Australia	400	100	500
Middle East	500		500
United States	1,000	150	1,150
	$2,500	$500	$3,000

Required   Determine which foreign geographic areas are reportable areas based on the revenues test.

E 15–4   **Disposal of a Segment: Determining Amounts to Be Reported**   The following condensed income statement for Divesto Inc., a diversified company, is presented for the two years ended 12/31/X7 and X6:

	19X7	19X6
Net sales	$5,000,000	$4,800,000
Cost of sales	(3,100,000)	(3,000,000)
Gross Profit	$1,900,000	$1,800,000
Operating expenses	(1,100,000)	(1,200,000)
Operating Income	$ 800,000	$ 600,000
Gain on sale of division	450,000	
Income Before Income Taxes	$1,250,000	$ 600,000
Provision for income taxes	(500,000)	(240,000)
Net Income	$ 750,000	$ 360,000

On 1/1/X7, Divesto entered into an agreement to sell for $1,600,000 the assets and product line of its separate Data PC division. The sale was consummated on 12/31/X7 and resulted in a pretax gain of $450,000 on disposition. This division's contribution to Divesto's reported pretax operating income for each year was as follows: 19X6, $(250,000) loss; 19X7, $(320,000) loss. Assume an income tax rate of 40%.

Required   Determine the following amounts that Divesto should report in its comparative income statement for 19X7 and 19X6:

1. Income from continuing operations (after income taxes).
2. Discontinued operations.
3. Net income.

E 15–5   **Disposal of a Segment: Determining Loss Related to Discontinued Operations**   On 9/1/X1, Selco decided to dispose of a segment of its business. With respect to this disposal, the following information is given:

Estimated operating loss from the measurement date to 12/31/X1	$200,000
Severance pay	100,000
Relocation costs (for employees)	50,000
Actual operating loss from 1/1/X1 to the measurement date	300,000
Estimated operating loss from 12/31/X1 to the estimated disposal date	400,000
Estimated loss on the sale of the segment's assets in 19X2	500,000

The severance pay and the employee relocation costs are directly associated with the decision to dispose of this segment. Assume a 40% income tax rate.

Required   Prepare the discontinued operations section of the income statement for the current year.

PROBLEMS

P 15–1   **Determining Reportable Industry Segments: Revenues Test, Operating Profit or Loss Test, and Identifiable Assets Test**   Information (in thousands of dollars) with respect to Parco's industry segments for 19X1 follows:

Segment	Total Revenue	Operating Profit (Loss)	Identifiable Assets
A	$ 30	$ (10)	$ 75
B	210	100	400
C	80	(40)	125
D	190	20	100
E	170	(60)	250
F	70	10	100
G	250	110	450
	$1,000	$130	$1,500

The only intersegment revenues were $60,000 from Segment E to Segment D.

Required   1. Determine which industry segments are reportable segments.
2. Perform the 75% test.

P 15–2   **Presenting Industry Segment Information: Intersegment Inventory Sales (Intercompany Profit in Ending Inventory)**   Petco operates in five major industry segments, all of which are reportable segments. Financial information for each segment for 19X8 follows:

			Segment		
	A	B	C	D	E
Total revenues	$70,000	$60,000	$50,000	$40,000	$30,000
Operating profit	30,000	25,000	20,000	15,000	10,000
Identifiable assets	40,000	35,000	30,000	25,000	20,000

Intersegment sales (included in the total revenues above) were as follows:

1. Segment C sold inventory costing $5,000 to Segment D for $8,000. At 12/31/X8, Segment D had sold all of this inventory.
2. Segment A sold inventory costing $6,000 to Segment B for $10,000. At 12/31/X8, Segment B had not sold 20% of this inventory.

Assume that no intercompany inventory was on hand at 12/31/X7 and that a consolidated income tax return is filed. Data related to the corporate offices follow:

Corporate expenses	$12,000
Interest expense	18,000
Interest income	5,000
Corporate assets	15,000
Overall corporate income tax rate	40%

Required Prepare a report presenting industry segment information, reconciling, when required, to amounts that would appear in the consolidated financial statements. (Use the Comprehensive Illustration on pages 515–518 as a guide.)

P 15–3 **Presenting Industry Segment Information: Intrasegment and Intersegment Sales (Intracompany Profit in Beginning and Ending Inventories)** Dubbler operates in two industries, both of which qualify as reportable industry segments. Applicable data follow (amounts are in thousands):

	19X2
Segment A	
Sales to unaffiliated customers	$500
*Inter*segment sales	400
*Intra*segment	200
Operating profit	300
*Inter*segment gross profit that could not be reported at the end of	
19X2	60
19X1	20
*Intra*segment gross profit that could not be reported at the end of	
19X2	10
19X1	–0–
Segment B	
Sales to unaffiliated customers	800
Operating profit	100

Required Determine the proper amounts for revenues and operating profit to be presented in the following industry segment information disclosure schedule for 19X2:

	Segment A	Segment B	Adjustments and Eliminations	Consolidated
Revenues				
Operating profit				

P 15–4 **Presenting Industry Segment Information: Intrasegment and Intersegment Sales (Intercompany Profit in Beginning and Ending Inventories)** Triplex has three industry segments, A, B, and C, each of which is a reportable industry segment. Data (in thousands of dollars) for these segments for 19X2 follow:

	Revenues			
	Intercompany	Unaffiliated Customers	Operating Profit	Identifiable Assets
Segment A				
Company X	$100		$ 30	$240
Company Y		$700	170	660

(continued)

| | Revenues | | | |
	Intercompany	Unaffiliated Customers	Operating Profit	Identifiable Assets
Segment B				
Company M.		300	80	310
Company N.	50	560	120	490
Segment C				
Company T		300	50	200

Additional Information

1. Segment A is a *vertically* integrated operation. Company X sells all of its output to Company Y.
2. Segments B and C are *not* vertically integrated operations. Company N's intercompany sales are to Company T.
3. All intercompany sales are at prices that approximate outside market prices. Assume a 40% gross profit margin on all intercompany sales.
4. At the end of the current reporting year, each company has 10% of its current year intercompany inventory purchases on hand.
5. Data relating to the corporate offices follow:

Corporate expenses	$35,000
Interest expense	29,000
Corporate assets	40,000

6. Assume that a consolidated federal income tax return is filed at a 40% rate.

Required

1. Present the preceding data in a schedule that satisfies the disclosure requirements of *SFAS No. 14*, assuming that no intercompany inventory purchases were on hand at the beginning of the year. The following steps will help:
   a. Prepare the intercompany transaction consolidation entry in consolidating Company X and Company Y.
   b. Post the entry in (a) to a miniworksheet containing the sales and profit data provided in the problem.
2. Present the preceding data in a schedule that satisfies the disclosure requirements of *SFAS No. 14*, assuming that (a) Company Y had $25,000 of intercompany inventory on hand at the beginning of the year and (b) Company T had $4,000 of intercompany inventory on hand at the beginning of the year. (Assume a 40% gross profit rate for the prior year.)

P 15–5   **Presenting Geographic Area Information: Intrageographic and Intergeographic Transfers (Intercompany Profit in Ending Inventory)**   Partex has operations in the United States, Mexico, and England, each of which qualifies as a reportable geographic area. Data (in thousands of dollars) with respect to these areas for 19X3 follow:

| | Revenues | | | |
	Intercompany	Unaffiliated Customers	Operating Profit	Identifiable Assets
United States				
Company A.		$800	$200	$300
Company B.	$150	450	150	200
Company C.	60	600	240	350
Mexico				
Company X.	100		30	180
England				
Company S.		280	110	90

Additional Information

1. Company X is part of a vertically integrated industry and sells all of its output to Company B.
2. Company B is part of a vertically integrated industry and sells part of its output to Company S.
3. Company C's intercompany sales are to Company A.

4. All intercompany sales are at prices that approximate outside market prices. Assume a 40% gross profit margin on all intercompany sales.
5. At the end of the current reporting year, each company has 10% of its current year intercompany inventory purchases on hand.
6. Data as to the corporate offices follow:

General corporate expenses	$37,000
Interest expense	28,000
Corporate assets	65,000

7. Assume a 40% income tax rate.

Required Present the preceding data in a schedule that satisfies the disclosure requirements of *SFAS No. 14,* assuming that no intercompany inventory purchases were on hand at the beginning of the year.

P 15–6 **Disposal of a Segment: Determining Amounts to Report** On 6/30/X1, Zapata Inc. (a calendar year-end–reporting company) announced plans to dispose of several of its segments. Data (in thousands of dollars) gathered at that time for these segments follow:

Segment	Year-to-Date Income (Loss) From Operations	Estimated Future Income (Loss) From Operations Through the Disposal Date 19X1	19X2	Estimated Gain (Loss) on Disposal	Estimated Disposal Date
A	$(400)	$(300)	$(200)	$(100)	2/1/X2
B	(100)	(400)	(300)	800	2/1/X2
C	200	(500)	100	300	2/1/X2
D	(300)	(400)		200	10/1/X1
E	(300)	(200)		400	10/1/X1
F	300	200		(400)	10/1/X1
G	200	200	200	300	3/1/X2
H	200	400	200	(300)	3/1/X2
I	600	300	(100)	(300)	3/1/X2

These amounts do not reflect income taxes.

Required Determine the amounts to be reported in the two categories of the discontinued operations section of the income statement for each segment. Use the following reporting periods:

First and Second Quarters—19X1	Third and Fourth Quarters—19X1	First Quarter— 19X2

For simplicity, assume that future operations and sales of the segments proceed according to plan. Ignore income tax effects.

P 15–7 **Disposal of a Segment: Preparing Income Statement and Statement of Retained Earnings—Variety of Events and Transactions** Multico had the following events and transactions in 19X5:

Sales	$10,000,000[a]
Cost of goods sold (corrected for inventory pricing error at 12/31/X4)	5,700,000[a]
Understatement of 12/31/X4 inventory (pricing error)	250,000
Marketing and administrative expenses	2,000,000[a]
Operating loss for 19X5 related to Gismo Division, $150,000 of which occurred after the decision to dispose of the division	500,000
Estimated 19X6 operating loss for Gismo Division	300,000

(continued)

Estimated loss on sale of Gismo Division's net assets (a separate industry segment), disposal to be completed in 19X6	550,000
Gain on early extinguishment of debt.	600,000
Flood loss, uninsured	700,000[b]
Settlement of lawsuit related to 19X3 activity (not accrued in prior years).	400,000[c]

[a]Excludes Gismo Division.

[b]The last major flood in the area was 60 years ago.

[c]From the time the lawsuit was filed in 19X3, legal counsel believed that the company would not win the lawsuit. Legal counsel could not estimate either the ultimate settlement amount or a likely range within which the settlement amount would fall. Future such lawsuits are possible.

Assume a combined federal and state income tax rate of 40%. Assume that no temporary or permanent differences exist between pretax accounting income and taxable income. Retained earnings were $2,000,000 on 1/1/X5, and cash dividends of $100,000 were declared during 19X5.

Required   Prepare an income statement and a statement of retained earnings for 19X5.

☀ THINKING CRITICALLY ☀

☀ CASES ☀

C 15–1   **Procedures Used to Determine Industry Segments**   Woodco has the following operations: (1) planting and growing trees, (2) harvesting trees, (3) processing cut trees into building materials (lumber and plywood), (4) manufacturing paper and paper products, and (5) manufacturing container and packaging products.
The controller has asked your advice on determining industry segments.

Required   1. How would you determine which operations constitute industry segments?
2. Make several possible assumptions as to the key determinant and proceed accordingly.

C 15–2   **Nonreportable Foreign Geographic Area Having Significant Profits**   A Brazilian subsidiary does *not* satisfy either the 10% or more of consolidated revenues test or the 10% or more of identifiable assets test for determining reportable foreign geographic areas. However, the subsidiary's 19X1 earnings contributed nearly 25% of reported consolidated net income. Furthermore, a significant portion of the subsidiary's 19X1 earnings were the result of currency exchange gains, export subsidies, and income tax considerations.

Required   Need any mention of these facts be made in the financial statements or annual report?

C 15–3   **Treatment of Central Research and Development Costs**   Quadrex operates in four industries, each of which is conducted through subsidiaries. The operations of these subsidiaries are located some distance from the parent's headquarters location. Each subsidiary conducts research and development at its separate location. In addition, the parent maintains a central research department at its own headquarters, which benefits all of the segments in the same manner that top management at the headquarters benefits all segments.

Required   Evaluate the treatment used to record the facilities and expenses of the central research department in preparing segment information disclosures.

C 15–4   **Manner of Reconciling Segment Information to Consolidated Amounts**   Triadco operates in three industry segments, A, B, and C. Industry Segment A comprises three companies (X, Y, and Z), which constitute a vertically integrated operation. Company X sells solely to Company Y, which sells solely to Company Z, which sells solely to unaffiliated customers. In addition, Segment B sells about 10% of its production output to Segment C. Segments B and C are not vertically integrated operations. All of these intercompany sales are at prices approximating outside market prices. Assume that Company Y, Company Z, and Segment C have intercompany inventory purchases on hand at the beginning and end of the current reporting year.

Required How are intercompany sales and intercompany profits on such intercompany inventory sales presented in disclosing industry segment information? Be specific as to the effect on presenting revenues, operating profit or loss, and identifiable assets.

✳ FINANCIAL ANALYSIS PROBLEM ✳

FAP 15–1 **Sale of a Subsidiary in a Leveraged Buyout** On 6/30/X1, Pylox sold its 100% interest in its subsidiary, Sylox Company, to Newco. Sylox had been reported as a separate reportable industry segment prior to the sale. Newco was recently formed by the top management of Sylox and a group of wealthy outside investors. The transaction is a leveraged buyout (LBO). The carrying value of Pylox's investment in Sylox at the sale date was $7,000,000. Newco paid Sylox $10,000,000 cash (virtually all borrowed from a financial institution). The sales agreement provided that Pylox guarantee payment of $2,000,000 of the Newco debt. Furthermore, if Newco's cash flow falls below certain levels, Pylox is obligated to purchase $500,000 of preferred stock of Newco.

Required Determine how Pylox should report its $3,000,000 gain.

ANSWERS TO SELF-STUDY QUESTIONS

1. c **2.** c **3.** d **4.** f **5.** c **6.** a

TRANSLATING FOREIGN CURRENCY TRANSACTIONS

16

The whole art of teaching is only the art of awakening the natural curiosity of young minds for the purpose of satisfying it afterwards.

ANATOLE FRANCE

We begin this chapter by discussing the globalization of business, which entails comparing alternative means of selling U.S. products and services in foreign countries. The significance of the globalization of business is succinctly described in the Business Perspective that follows.

Next we lay the theoretical groundwork for dealing with currency exchange rate changes—including causes of exchange rate changes. We then discuss and illustrate how to translate foreign currency transactions into U.S. dollars. **Foreign currency transactions** require settlement (payment or receipt) in a foreign currency, such as an importing or exporting transaction requiring settlement in British pounds. (When foreign transactions require settlement in U.S. dollars, no accounting issues exist.)

In Chapter 17, we discuss the ways that companies can use certain types of contractual arrangements (generically referred to as *derivatives*) to manage their exposure to adverse changes in exchange rates—an area that has become an integral part of managing international operations in the last two decades.

In Chapters 18, 19, and 20, we discuss and illustrate how to translate the financial statements of foreign subsidiaries (formally called *foreign currency financial statements*) into U.S. dollars. In Chapter 18, we also address special problems associated with intercompany transactions between a domestic company and its foreign subsidiary.

THE GOVERNING FASB PRONOUNCEMENT

FASB *Statement No. 52*, "Foreign Currency Translation," sets forth the accounting principles and procedures for translating (1) foreign currency transactions and (2) foreign currency financial statements. The issues involved in the translation of foreign currency transactions (this chapter's topic) are *not* controversial. The issues pertaining to (1) the manner of accounting for foreign currency derivatives (Chap-

---

BUSINESS PERSPECTIVE

The Globalization of Business

Business no longer knows national boundaries. Capital and human resources can go to work anywhere on the Earth and do a job. . . . If the world operates as one big market, you compete with every person who is capable of doing the same work—and there are a lot of them. And they are hungry!

As (companies) struggle, their methods of operation become history. When you read tens of thousands being laid off, that's a sign of adaption. When a company competes with a counterpart abroad, it can't afford to pay any more on average that its employee productivity warrants. If the competition has lower-paid individuals doing the jobs of those whose long employment history, with many raises, had led to high pay, something has to give. . . . Usually it's least productive.

Accept that no matter where you go to work, you are not an employee—you are a business with one employee, you.

You are in competition with millions of similar businesses. If you want to work, you must dedicate yourself to retaining your competitive advantage.

Nobody owes you a career. You own it, as a sole proprietor.

You must compete with millions of individuals every day of your career. You must enhance your value every day, hone your competitive advantage, learn, adapt, move jobs and industries—retrench so you can advance, learn new skills. And so you do not become one of those statistics in 2015.

And remember: This process starts on Monday.

Source: Andy Grove, Chief Executive Officer, Intel Corporation. Commencement address at the Haas School of Business, University of California, Berkeley, May 1994.

ter 17) and (2) the translation of foreign currency financial statements (Chapters 18–20), however, are highly controversial.

THE FOREIGN CORRUPT PRACTICES ACT OF 1977 (FCPA)

Pervading all aspects of doing business in foreign countries is the Foreign Corrupt Practices Act (FCPA). This act, which is administered by the Securities and Exchange Commission (SEC) and the Justice Department, **prohibits U.S. firms from offering funds (bribes) to foreign officials in an effort to obtain or retain business.** The FCPA also essentially forbids *indirect* payment methods; thus funds may *not* be offered if the firm has reason to believe that any part of them will be used to pay bribes.

An amendment to the FCPA allows small payments to lower-level foreign officials performing routine and lawful duties; however, the amendment does *not* clearly specify who or how much can be paid.

In contrast, bribes are *legal* and *tax deductible* to one degree or another in Austria, Belgium, Canada, Denmark, France, Germany, Greece, Ireland, Luxembourg, the Netherlands, New Zealand, Spain, and Switzerland. The U.S. State Department estimated that this unlevel playing field caused U.S. companies to lose $45 billion in foreign contracts in 1995.

I   GOING INTERNATIONAL: WAYS TO EXPORT

U.S. companies can sell products and services in foreign countries in two ways: They export goods and services from the United States, or they produce goods and services in foreign countries. Any domestic company considering international business must understand the variations within these two general categories to select the alternative that best meets its goals. We first discuss the various exporting alternatives, which are as follows:

- Exporting to an independent distributor.
- Exporting by establishing a foreign commission *agent.*
- Exporting by establishing a foreign marketing *branch.*
- Exporting by establishing a foreign marketing *subsidiary.*
- Exporting by using an export trade vehicle, such as a foreign sales corporation (FSC) or an interest charge-domestic international sales-corporation (IC–DISC).

It is beyond the scope of this text to discuss each of these alternatives in depth because that is more appropriate in an international business or tax course. Because tax considerations are usually of great importance, we also briefly discuss federal income tax consequences pertaining to each alternative.

Doing business in foreign countries also requires an appreciation of cultural differences. In light of the increasing importance of Asia in the world economy during the past decade, we highlight the major differences between the Asian and American cultures in a Cultural Perspective that follows.

ALTERNATIVE 1: EXPORTING TO AN INDEPENDENT DISTRIBUTOR

To demonstrate this first alternative, we use the example of a domestic manufacturer that sells its product to an unrelated, independent distributor in Switzerland. The Swiss distributor takes physical possession and legal title to the inventory, which it sells to the ultimate Swiss consumer using its own marketing efforts. The

---

CULTURAL PERSPECTIVE

Clashing Values

Some of the fundamental differences between Asian and American perspectives:

Order: Having endured periods of chaos over centuries, Asians generally value order and fear the consequences of its absence. This leads them to do as they're told to a degree most Americans would consider repressive. Americans value their independence and resent being told what to do by government or business.

Harmony: Most Asians will do anything possible to avoid confrontation. Instead of saying no, Asians are likely to tell a questioner, "That would be difficult." Saving face is an important concept. Americans thrive on outspokenness and competition. We say we're direct and they're sly. They say they're considerate and we're boorish.

Restraint: Asians keep their emotions to themselves as a sign of strength. Americans love letting it all hang out, which Asians consider childish and weak.

Individual vs. group: Asians respect those who subjugate themselves to the greater good of the group. Americans, reared on the American Revolution and frontier mythology, revere the self-made individual.

Tradition: Asians are part of cultures thousands of years old and are guided by a deep sense of tradition. The United States is a much younger, more fluid society where people move easily to new places for better opportunities and enjoy creating their own traditions. Americans often consider ancient Asian customs quaint and don't understand their importance in setting society's rhythms.

Morality: Asians tend to think of morals as "situational," shifting with the circumstances. Americans think of morals as fixed, universal and applying in all circumstances.

Hierarchy: Asians tend to rank others in terms of status, offering deferences to those more senior or powerful. Even in social situations, social rank determines where people sit and how they are addressed. Americans prefer to believe they think of all people as equals, and have enshrined this principle in their constitution and laws.

Source: Lewis M. Simons, "Clashing Values," *San Jose Mercury News*, March 3, 1996.

U.S. company is subject to U.S. federal, state, and local income taxes on its profit (the sales price minus the cost of goods sold and other related expenses). Because the U.S. company has no *physical presence* in Switzerland, it is *not* subject to the Swiss tax system. Of course, the Swiss distributor is subject to Swiss income taxes on its profit (but the Swiss company is *not* subject to U.S. taxes because it has no business activity in the United States).

ALTERNATIVE 2: EXPORTING BY ESTABLISHING A FOREIGN COMMISSION AGENT

To understand this alternative, assume that a U.S. manufacturer uses a British broker as its commission agent. The broker solicits British customers for the U.S. company and receives a commission on each sale obtained. The commission is tax deductible for the U.S. manufacturer. Generally, the U.S. company is *not* subject to British income taxes under this arrangement because the broker is an independent contractor—not an employee. If the U.S. company establishes a **physical presence** in Great Britain, such as by renting a warehouse or hiring employees, however, the chances of being subject to British income taxes increase. To determine whether the U.S. company is subject to British income taxes requires examining British tax statutes and the U.S.–Great Britain income tax treaty.

ALTERNATIVE 3: EXPORTING BY ESTABLISHING A FOREIGN MARKETING BRANCH

A **branch** can be an office, a warehouse, or U.S. employees conducting activities in a foreign country on behalf of the U.S. home office. These activities are deemed to represent the **physical presence** of the U.S. company in the foreign country and make the branch subject to the foreign country's income taxes. **For U.S. tax purposes, the branch's profits are also currently taxable in the United States.** (Likewise, branch losses are deductible in the United States.) To avoid double taxation on branch profits, U.S. tax laws allow foreign income taxes to be treated as credits against any U.S. income taxes.

For example, assume that a domestic company establishes a branch in France, which has a statutory income tax rate of 42%, compared to the U.S. income tax rate of 35%. If the branch has $100,000 of profit, it pays $42,000 in taxes to the French government. No additional tax must be paid to the U.S. government because $42,000 of tax credits more than offsets the $35,000 of taxes otherwise payable. Thus the domestic company has what is commonly called **"excess foreign tax credits."** This means that the domestic company is paying taxes on its worldwide income at more than the U.S. statutory rate of 35%. Because most foreign countries have income tax rates higher than 35%, many companies operating with foreign marketing branches have this problem.

A highly specialized area of income tax law has developed around **"managing excess foreign tax credits"** for developing strategies designed to minimize and use excess foreign tax credits so that the income taxes on worldwide income are as close as is legally possible to 35%. (At many universities that offer graduate degrees in taxation, one course in the program deals almost exclusively with this topic.)

FAIR TRANSFER PRICING RULES   A domestic company that transfers inventory to its foreign marketing branch must consider the U.S. and foreign country's **arm's-length transfer pricing rules,** so that gross profit is *not* artificially shifted from the *high* income tax rate country to the *low* income tax rate country (thereby depriving one country of its fair share of taxes). To prevent the possibility of later adjustments by taxing authorities, the fairness of the transfer prices must be supportable.

MAJOR CONSIDERATION   A foreign operation conducted as a branch allows foreign tax authorities to examine data not only pertaining to the branch but also to the U.S. home office. Consequently, the *subsidiary* form of organization is usually chosen.

ALTERNATIVE 4: EXPORTING BY ESTABLISHING A FOREIGN MARKETING SUBSIDIARY

To insulate the foreign marketing operation legally from the domestic operation, a foreign subsidiary would be used instead of the branch form of organization. Setting up a foreign **subsidiary** is a more critical consideration for a U.S. company's foreign manufacturing operations, however; we discuss these implications later in the section covering foreign manufacturing subsidiaries. The transfer pricing problem discussed earlier also applies here.

MOST FOREIGN EARNINGS ARE TAXED IN THE UNITED STATES WHEN DIVIDENDS ARE PAID (THE CASH BASIS)   Unlike a foreign marketing *branch* (whose profits are taxed currently in the United States), **the profits of a foreign *subsidiary* are *not* taxed in the United States until paid out in dividends.** Most foreign countries withhold a portion of the dividends being repatriated to the United States (formally called **dividend withholding taxes,** which range generally from 5% to 15%). The system of allowable credits previously explained for branches (to prevent double taxation) is equally applicable to subsidiaries. When dividends are paid, the taxes withheld on dividends by the foreign government are also allowed as credits against U.S. income taxes otherwise payable on the foreign subsidiary's earnings.

SOME FOREIGN EARNINGS ARE TAXED IN THE UNITED STATES WHEN EARNED (DEEMED DISTRIBUTIONS) If a U.S. parent company's foreign subsidiary has certain types of income, the U.S. parent must report that income currently for U.S. tax purposes—even though such earnings remain undistributed. (Exceptions are granted if the subsidiary is unable to distribute its earnings—commonly referred to as having a *blocked funds problem*.) Although the substance of this manner of reporting is as if the Internal Revenue Code were requiring the use of the *equity method* of accounting, the Code instead characterizes this income as being a **deemed distribution** or a **deemed dividend** (as contrasted with a *cash dividend*).

The major types of income that must be reported currently are (1) passive income (interest, dividends, and rents), (2) income earned in tax haven countries, and (3) income from certain foreign sales, services, or shipping subsidiaries.

This type of income is commonly referred to as **"Subpart F"** income. The Subpart F rules of the Internal Revenue Code are part of the tax rules pertaining to **controlled foreign corporations (CFCs),** of which more than 40,000 exist. A **controlled foreign corporation** is defined as a **foreign corporation that has more than half of its common stock owned by 10% U.S. shareholders** (shareholders owning at least 10% of the common stock).[1] (The CFC rules are among the most complex rules of the Code.)

ALTERNATIVE 5: EXPORTING BY USING AN EXPORT TRADE VEHICLE

The Revenue Act of 1971 established a new type of domestic corporation, referred to as a **domestic international sales corporation (DISC).** The purpose of this act was to give tax incentives to U.S. companies to increase their exports. Because the European Community objected to DISCs on the grounds that they resulted in an illegal export subsidy on export income earned in the United States (in violation of tariff and trade agreements), the DISC system was replaced (for the most part) in 1984 with the newly created system of **foreign sales corporations (FSC).**

A domestic company that establishes a foreign corporation (one not chartered in the United States) may elect to have that corporation treated as a foreign sales corporation. Under the FSC system, a portion (15%) of the foreign trade income of an FSC is exempt from U.S. federal income taxes. Although potential tax savings vary with the particular circumstances, the 35% U.S. income tax rate can be reduced by as much as 5.1% (35% × 15%). Numerous requirements must be met for qualification as an FSC. (A "small FSC" having fewer compliance requirements is available for small businesses.) **The foreign trade income of the FSC must result from the foreign presence and activity of the FSC.** Thus a domestic company cannot set up a shell corporation overseas merely to obtain tax benefits. (The system of tax credits discussed earlier for foreign branches is equally applicable to FSCs.)

II GOING INTERNATIONAL: WAYS TO MANUFACTURE OVERSEAS

The various ways to establish a foreign manufacturing operation are as follows:

- Establish a foreign manufacturing *branch.*
- Establish a foreign manufacturing *subsidiary.*
- Establish a domestic *subsidiary* that establishes a foreign manufacturing *branch.*

[1]Note the broadness of this definition in that the U.S. ownership could be by (1) a corporation (the typical case) or (2) one or more individuals. Thus all foreign subsidiaries of U.S. parents are CFCs, but not all CFCs are subsidiaries of U.S. parent companies.

ALTERNATIVE 1: ESTABLISHING A FOREIGN MANUFACTURING *BRANCH*

Earlier we described the use of a foreign marketing branch as a means to generate export sales. A foreign branch can be used to manufacture products as well as to market them. All of the U.S. tax rules discussed earlier for foreign marketing branches (the manner of taxing earnings, the availability of foreign tax credits, and the need to use arm's-length transfer prices) apply equally here as well.

As discussed in Chapter 1, many foreign countries prohibit the establishment of manufacturing branches because they insist that a percentage of the operation be owned locally. This forces the U.S. company to form a foreign *subsidiary* if it intends to manufacture in that particular country.

ALTERNATIVE 2: ESTABLISHING A FOREIGN MANUFACTURING *SUBSIDIARY*

By forming a foreign *subsidiary*, the parent, in theory, has **legally insulated the foreign subsidiary's operations from those of the parent.** For instance, if a major disaster happens at the foreign manufacturing plant, the parent's monetary exposure is limited to the amount it has invested in the subsidiary. As briefly mentioned in Chapter 1, however, sometimes a parent company (possibly for public relations purposes) assumes responsibility for liabilities beyond those the foreign subsidiary can pay.

CASE IN POINT

Union Carbide's Tragic Foreign Disaster

In 1984, at Union Carbide Corporation's manufacturing subsidiary in Bhopal, India, nearly 4,000 people were killed and 20,000 people became disabled as the result of an explosion and a toxic gas leak. Possibly for public relations purposes, Union Carbide subsequently paid $470 million to the government of India to settle claims that its Indian subsidiary was unable to pay.

The tax rules discussed earlier for foreign *marketing* subsidiaries (the manner of taxation, the availability of foreign tax credits, the need to use fair transfer prices, and the CFC rules) apply here as well. *Manufacturing* subsidiaries in certain possessions (such as Puerto Rico) may be exempt from both U.S. federal income taxes and Puerto Rican taxes.

ALTERNATIVE 3: ESTABLISHING A *DOMESTIC* SUBSIDIARY THAT ESTABLISHES A FOREIGN MANUFACTURING BRANCH

Sometimes a domestic company desires to manufacture in a foreign country using the branch form of organization and to insulate the foreign operations from the domestic. It can do so by forming a *domestic* subsidiary, which can then establish a foreign manufacturing branch. A reason for using the branch form of organization overseas is to allow any technology and patents that the foreign operation uses to remain subject to U.S. patent laws. Many foreign countries (such as the Philippines) have virtually no patent laws. If such technology and patents were transferred to a foreign subsidiary, U.S. patent protection would be lost because the foreign subsidiary would be subject to the laws of the foreign country.

III REASONS FOR MANUFACTURING OVERSEAS RATHER THAN EXPORTING

WHAT FOREIGN COUNTRIES HAVE TO OFFER

Historically, the primary reason for a U.S. company to decide to manufacture domestically and export to foreign countries was to keep the technology, as well as the jobs, at home. In the last 35 years, however, many factors have enticed a multitude of companies to build manufacturing plants in foreign countries. These factors, which illustrate *the economic law of comparative advantage,* are as follows:

1. **The lure of cheaper labor.**
2. **The granting of "tax holidays."** Some foreign countries allow a new foreign operation to pay very low or no income taxes overseas. For example, in the 1980s, Ireland granted foreign operations total income tax relief until 1990 and then imposed an income tax rate of only 10% until the year 2010.
3. **The importance of having a visible presence.** Some studies have shown that the most successful way to generate sales in a foreign country is to have a manufacturing presence in that country.
4. **The lack of or nonenforcement of environmental laws.** See the Ethics Perspective.
5. **The lure of a highly literate workforce in a safe environment.** Certain foreign countries have remarkably high literacy rates and safe environments. A few years ago, for example, Apple Computer Inc. established a manufacturing subsidiary in Singapore primarily because more than 95% of its citizens graduate from high school. Singapore also has a very safe working environment because it has virtually no crime or drug problems.

ETHICS PERSPECTIVE

A Way to Avoid Environmental Cleanup Costs

Along the 2,000-mile U.S.–Mexico border are nearly 1,900 maquiladora special assembly plants mostly owned by U.S. firms, including such giants as IBM, General Motors, Kodak, and Zenith. These plants account for approximately 75% of Mexico's manufactured goods exported to the United States. Spawned in 1965 as the Border Industrial Program by the Mexican government (redefined in 1971 as the Maquila Program as the operations later expanded throughout Mexico), these assembly plants import components on consignment (paying no import duties) and export the assembled finished products to the United States. Because no import duties are paid in Mexico and because U.S. Customs laws permit U.S. products to be processed or assembled abroad and returned to the United States with duties paid only on the value of the foreign processing, this border area is loosely referred to as a *free trade zone.*

In 1991, the General Accounting Office (GAO) published several reports concerning a proposed U.S.–Mexico Free Trade Agreement (later enacted as NAFTA).

One report dealt with comparative production wages—$14.31 in the United States to $1.39 in Mexico. (Although Mexico's minimum age for child labor is 14, many children drop out of school by the sixth grade to work.) Another GAO report dealt with Mexico's massive environmental problems caused by air and water pollution and by hazardous waste contamination. Although Mexico has some environmental laws, virtually no enforcement occurs. Contaminated water is routinely used to irrigate farm lands, which grow crops for export to the United States. In 1990, the American Medical Association called the border a "virtual cesspool and breeding ground for infectious disease."

Question

Is it ethical for U.S. companies to move manufacturing operations to countries that have (1) far less stringent environmental laws and enforcement than the United States and (2) virtually no enforcement of child labor laws?

6. **The lure of a large college-educated population.** Often the environment of higher education looms large. For example, more than 300 U.S. companies, including 60 high-technology firms, have established major manufacturing facilities in a 70-mile stretch of Scotland known as "Silicon Glen," whose prime attraction is its 12 universities and more than 60 colleges that produce more college graduates per capita than any other nation in Europe.

7. **The lure of a strong work ethic.** In recent years, the majority of the large U.S. insurance companies moved much of their claims processing offices to Ireland partly because of workers' reputation for accuracy and doing things right the first time.

8. **The lure of loan guarantees, grants, and subsidies.** Often foreign governments make sizable special concessions. For example, in 1995, Advanced Micro Devices Inc. announced that it had received more than $1 billion in loan guarantees and hundreds of millions of dollars in grants and subsidies from the German government in connection with its plan to build a $1.9 billion semiconductor chip factory in Germany.

U.S. TAX LAWS HAVE PROVISIONS THAT ENCOURAGE ESTABLISHING OFFSHORE OPERATIONS

The U.S. income tax laws have several provisions that favor establishing offshore operations instead of onshore operations:

- No payment of U.S. income taxes on earnings of foreign subsidiaries until dividends are received (with some exceptions as discussed earlier)—**a tax deferral benefit.**

- No accumulated earnings tax on undistributed earnings of foreign subsidiaries—**a possible permanent tax savings benefit.** (In general, however, if too much of the income is *passive*, the *undistributed* earnings *will be* taxed under the foreign personal holding company [FPHC] rules.)

- Special tax *credit* allowed (under Section 936) for doing business in a U.S. possession (comprising about 15 islands, with Puerto Rico being the largest)—**a permanent tax savings.**

Because the U.S. possessions have either no or very low income tax rates (Puerto Rico, for example, has about a 4% tax rate), the result of establishing a Section 936 subsidiary is generally a very low effective overall tax rate (the U.S. rate and the U.S. possession rate combined). Pharmaceutical companies have been the biggest beneficiaries of this code section, which saves U.S. corporations an estimated $3.5 billion annually in U.S. taxes. General Electric has been enormously successful in exploiting the benefits of Section 936, managing to report roughly 25% of its pretax income from operations in Puerto Rico in some years.

Interestingly enough, the foreign sales corporation (FSC) section of the U.S. income tax law (discussed earlier) works in the opposite direction of the preceding items because its purpose is to give an incentive to keep jobs in the United States. Recall that under the FSC rules, 15% of a domestic company's *export income* is exempt from U.S. federal income taxes—**a permanent tax savings.** (This section is well-acknowledged as a subsidy to domestic exporters.)

THE FLUCTUATING EXCHANGE RATE PROBLEM: ANOTHER MAJOR INCENTIVE TO MANUFACTURE OVERSEAS

Since 1973, a floating exchange rate system has existed. Under this system (discussed in much detail shortly), exchange rates have fluctuated tremendously. A major problem for domestic exporters under the floating exchange rate system is that when the U.S. dollar strengthens considerably, foreign customers must pay higher prices for U.S. exports because they need to come up with more units of their currency had the dollar *not* strengthened. A *strong* dollar makes it difficult for U.S. companies to sell abroad (unless they are willing to lower their prices and thereby reduce their operating margins). Of course, the ability to sell U.S. products in foreign markets is easier when the dollar *weakens*.

Rather than continually dealing with this roller coaster exchange rate environment, scores of companies have decided to produce products in the country in which they will be sold, thus neutralizing the impact of exchange rate changes. This is just one more reason for U.S. companies to manufacture overseas rather than to export domestically.

THE RISKS OF INVESTING ABROAD

The risks of having U.S. funds invested in foreign countries must be weighed against all of the considerable advantages to manufacturing overseas. An asset held in a foreign country is not the same as an asset held domestically. Assets held in foreign countries entail the following additional risks:

1. **Expropriation,** or the seizure of assets.
2. **Devaluation,** or the diminution of value of the cash flows from future operations because of adverse changes in the exchange rate.
3. **Currency transfer restrictions,** or the limitation on repatriation of foreign profits and invested capital. Many companies must go to extreme lengths to send back earnings to the United States.
4. **Wars and civil disorders.** See the Case in Point.
5. **Government mandated changes in the investment climate.** Sometimes a foreign government enacts legislation that dramatically increases the cost of doing business. For example, in 1985, Spain's economy was booming; however, a new Socialist prime minister undertook to (1) provide free health care and deep subsidies for college education for all citizens and (2) require businesses to provide lifetime contracts for their employees. As a result, tax rates increased every year over the next decade, far surpassing those in the United States. The government and organized labor became virtual partners, and spending on social goals doubled. Eventually, it all began to collapse. Foreign investment plummeted, and big business fled the country—but not after having lost substantial sums on their investments made prior to these dramatic changes. In 1995, Spain's unemployment reached 23%, the highest in Europe.

CASE IN POINT

- In 1959, when Fidel Castro took power in Cuba, he seized approximately $25 billion of properties owned by U.S. firms. No compensation was ever made.
- When Peru nationalized its oil industry, Enron took a $218 million write-off in 1985.
- In the 1980s, Chevron spent more than $1 billion to find and extract oil in the Sudan. After civil war broke out and four of its contract employees were killed, Chevron wrote off hundreds of millions of dollars and sold out to a Sudanese company.

- In 1992, Iran agreed to pay Sun Co. and Atlantic Richfield Co. $260 million in settlement of the 1979 expropriation of their Iranian oil interests. (Such settlements are generally well below the book value or market value of the assets seized.)

Sources: Toni Mack, "Staying at Home," *Forbes*, October 26, 1992, pp. 47–48; James Tanner and Bhushan Bahree, "Iran Will Pay Sun Co., Arco $260 Million," *The Wall Street Journal*, August 19, 1992, p. A2.

PHENOMENAL INCREASE IN WORLD TRADE

Even though U.S. companies have established extensive manufacturing operations overseas, the volume of U.S. importing and exporting transactions is huge for the same reasons that the volume of world trade is huge. World trade has soared from roughly $60 billion in 1950 to more than $4 trillion a year currently, of which $800 billion is for services. This increase was caused primarily by (1) the massive reconstruction required overseas after World War II, (2) the reduction of tariffs (from an average of 40% to 5%) and quotas under the *General Agreement on Tariffs and Trade* (GATT) (signed in 1947, it defines rules for international trade and resolving disputes), (3) the advances in transportation and telecommunications, and (4) the establishment of manufacturing operations in foreign countries that are interdependent with the parent company's operations so that intercompany inventory transfers with the parent company routinely occur.

Currently, U.S. imports of goods total about $670 billion annually, with exports totaling approximately $500 billion—a $170 billion annual *trade deficit*. U.S. exports of services total approximately $180 billion annually, with imports of services worth approximately $120 billion—a $60 billion annual *services surplus*. Accordingly, international transactions have become a higher percentage of total transactions for an increasing percentage of companies. Furthermore, **an estimated 40% of international transactions involves intercompany transactions** (which must be eliminated in consolidation).

Before explaining how to account for foreign currency importing and exporting transactions, we first discuss exchange rates and the floating exchange rate system.

IV CURRENCY EXCHANGE RATES

DISTINGUISHING BETWEEN CONVERSION AND TRANSLATION

CONVERSION Actually exchanging one currency into another is called **conversion.** Foreign currencies may be either purchased or converted into U.S. dollars at commercial banks that have a foreign exchange department.

TRANSLATION In contrast, **translation** (for our purposes) is the process of applying an appropriate *currency exchange rate* (such as 1 British pound = $1.50) to a foreign currency amount (such as 30,000 pounds) so that an amount can be expressed in U.S. dollars (30,000 pounds × $1.50 = $45,000). Hereafter, we use the £ symbol for the British pound in our examples.

METHODS OF EXPRESSING EXCHANGE RATES

The ratio of the number of units of one currency needed to acquire one unit of another currency constitutes the exchange rate between the two currencies. The exchange rate may be expressed either directly or indirectly:

1. **The direct exchange rate.** The number of units of the domestic currency needed to acquire one unit of the foreign currency is the **direct** exchange rate (for example, £1 = $1.50). Accordingly, to determine the U.S. dollar equivalent of an amount stated in a foreign currency, **the foreign currency amount is multiplied by the *direct* exchange rate** (for example, £30,000 × $1.50 = $45,000).

2. **The indirect exchange rate.** The number of units of the foreign currency needed to acquire one unit of the domestic currency is the **indirect** exchange rate (for example, $1 = £.667). Accordingly, to determine the U.S. dollar equivalent of an amount stated in a foreign currency, **the foreign currency amount is divided by the *indirect* exchange rate** (for example, £30,000 ÷ .667 = $45,000).

FINDING THE DIRECT EXCHANGE RATE FROM THE INDIRECT EXCHANGE RATE AND VICE VERSA The indirect exchange rate can always be obtained from the direct exchange rate and vice versa. For example, if the *direct* exchange rate for the British pound is £1 = $1.50, dividing each side of the equation by $1.50 produces the *indirect* exchange rate of £.667 = $1. Likewise, if the *indirect* exchange rate is $1 = £.667, dividing each side of the equation by .667 produces the *direct* exchange rate of $1.50 = £1.

WHICH EXCHANGE RATE TO USE? Banks and daily newspapers in the United States quote exchange rates both directly and indirectly. Translation of amounts stated in foreign currencies is usually performed using *direct* quotations. For this reason and because it is easier to deal with, we use the *direct* exchange rate in all examples and illustrations in this chapter and in the remaining four foreign currency chapters.

SELECTED CURRENCIES AND SYMBOLS The following are the currencies and symbols of a number of foreign countries:

Country	Currency	Symbol	Country	Currency	Symbol
Australia	Dollar	$A	Korea	Won	W
Argentina	Peso	Arg$	Mexico	Peso	Mex$
Canada	Dollar	Can$	Netherlands	Guilder	$f.
China	Renminbi/Yuan	Y	Russia	Ruble	rub
Egypt	Pound	LE	Saudi Arabia	Riyal	SRls
France	Franc	FF	Singapore	Dollar	S$
Germany	Deutsche mark	DM	Spain	Peseta	Ptas
Hong Kong	Dollar	HK$	Sweden	Krona	SKr
Ireland	Punt	£Ir	Switzerland	Franc	SFr
Italy	Lira	Lit	Taiwan	Dollar	NT$
Israel	New shekel	NIS	United Kingdom	Pound	£
Japan	Yen	¥	Vietnam	Dong	D

SPOT AND FORWARD EXCHANGE RATES Exchange rates at which currencies could be *converted* immediately (for settlement in two days) are termed **spot rates.** Exchange rates also exist for transactions whereby conversion could be made at some stipulated date (normally up to 12 months) in the future. These rates are called **forward** or **future rates;** they are discussed in Chapter 17.

THE EXCHANGE RATE SYSTEM: FLOATING VERSUS FIXED EXCHANGE RATES

Currency exchange rates are a function of market conditions (the forces of supply and demand), which in turn are a function of changing economic and political conditions such as (1) the level of the internal inflation rate, (2) the level of interest rates (usually a function of the inflation rate), (3) the level of the federal spending deficit (or surplus), (4) the level of the trade (balance of payments) deficit or surplus, and (5) the imminence of various civil disorders and wars. Exchange rates determined by market conditions are commonly referred to as either **floating** or **free** rates.

Before 1974, the dollar was tied to gold, and most currencies were tied to the dollar. As a result, **fixed** or **official** exchange rates existed. When fixed rates no longer reflected economic conditions, governments were forced to devalue or revalue their currencies (as the U.S. government did in 1973 when it announced a 10% devaluation).

Although devaluations of certain currencies were often expected, it was impossible to determine exactly when they would occur or the amount of the devaluation. This major drawback and the fact that the system could not deal with rapid inflation made the system unsustainable. Accordingly, in 1974, the dollar was taken off the gold standard (that is, it was no longer backed by gold reserves), and most currencies that had not already been allowed to float were allowed to do so. As a result, changing international economic conditions are reflected in the currency exchange rates on a daily basis.

CONSEQUENCES OF A FLOATING EXCHANGE RATE SYSTEM TO U.S. EXPORTERS AND IMPORTERS   When U.S. exporters and importers grant or use credit, respectively, and agree to receive payment or make payment in a foreign currency, respectively, they have **foreign currency exposure.** An entity has foreign currency exposure when it could incur a loss as a result of an adverse change in the exchange rate. A U.S. *exporter* that has a foreign currency *receivable* has an **exposed asset,** that is, an asset exposed to the risk that the exchange rate could change adversely (and thus lose value). A U.S. *importer* that has a foreign currency *payable* has an **exposed liability,** that is, a liability exposed to the risk that the exchange rate could change adversely (and thus gain in value).

STRENGTHENING VERSUS WEAKENING CURRENCIES

A change in a floating exchange rate is appropriately referred to as a *strengthening or weakening of one currency in relation to another currency.*

STRENGTHENING CURRENCIES   A foreign currency that is **strengthening in value in relation to the dollar becomes *more* expensive to purchase** because more dollars are needed to obtain a unit of that foreign currency. Accordingly, the *direct* exchange rate *increases.* A *weakening* of the dollar has the same effect on the direct rate as does the *strengthening* of the foreign currency.

WEAKENING CURRENCIES   A foreign currency that is **weakening in value in relation to the dollar becomes *less* expensive to purchase** because fewer dollars are needed to obtain a unit of it. Accordingly, the *direct* exchange rate *decreases.* A *strengthening* of the dollar has the same effect on the direct exchange rate as does the *weakening* of the foreign currency.

A graphic depiction of the effects of strengthening and weakening is shown in the following table:

Foreign Currency (the British Pound)	Exchange Rates		Domestic Currency (the U.S. Dollar)
	Direct	Indirect	
Strengthens (*more expensive to buy*)	$1.60 ↑	.625£ ↑	Weakens (*less expensive to buy*)
	$1.50 (starting point)	.667£	
Weakens (*less expensive to buy*)	$1.40 ↓	.714£ ↓	Strengthens (*more expensive to buy*)

GOVERNMENT INTERVENTIONS IN THE FLOATING EXCHANGE RATE SYSTEM

Even under the floating exchange rate system, however, governments often intervene (on an unannounced basis) in the foreign currency markets by buying and selling currencies to stabilize exchange rates or bolster a currency to maintain the desired exchange rate. For this reason, the floating exchange rate system is sometimes called a *dirty float.*

RECENT EXAMPLES OF THE U.S. GOVERNMENT'S INTERVENTION   In April 1993, after the U.S. dollar hit a post–World War II low of 109 yen to the dollar, the Federal Reserve Bank of New York (in the Clinton administration's first intervention in the foreign currency markets) repeatedly sold yen for dollars in attempts to halt the yen's continued rise of approximately 12% against the dollar since January 20, 1993. (A rise in the yen is the same as a fall in the dollar.) Just prior to this intervention, the Japanese government was selling yen (thus increasing their supply in the market) for dollars (thus decreasing their supply in the market) in unsuccessful efforts to halt the yen's rise.

This rapid rise in the yen (fall in the dollar) angered many Japanese officials who believed that the Clinton administration was trying to influence the markets and to substantially reduce the approximately $50 billion U.S. trade deficit with Japan by promoting a stronger yen (a weaker dollar). A rule of thumb among economists is that each 1% rise in the yen reduces the U.S. trade deficit with Japan by about $1 billion. A rise in the yen (fall in the dollar) makes Japanese exports more expensive to U.S. customers and U.S. products less expensive to Japanese customers.

The U.S. government intervened because it (1) concluded that the yen had risen too far too fast, (2) desired Japanese cooperation on many other issues, and (3) had concerns over a possible further weakening of Japan's fragile economy, which was in a recession.

This April 1993 intervention temporarily halted the rise in the yen (fall in the dollar). A month later, however, the yen started rising in value again, reaching a high of 85 in April 1995 even though the U.S. government intervened nearly 15 times during this two-year period to try to stop the dollar's fall. One of these interventions occurred in June 1994 and involved a massive but unsuccessful U.S.–led 17-nation effort to stop the dollar's slide. (The Japanese government alone spent more than $20 billion in 1994 trying to prop up the dollar.) In the final analysis, these government interventions are futile because the market is so huge. (Note that at the 85 level, the dollar buys a stunning 64% fewer yen than it did a decade ago.)

THE EUROPEAN EXCHANGE RATE MECHANISM

Of significant interest to U.S. companies having foreign operations in Europe that transact with other European countries is the European monetary system. After the collapse of the Bretton Woods fixed exchange rate system in 1971, the European Community created a narrower "pegged" rate system limited to members of the European Union (EU). Formalized in 1979 as the Exchange Rate Mechanism (ERM), the system provided for pegged exchange rates subject to (1) narrow limits on allowable exchange rate variation for the major currencies (such as the German mark and the French franc) and (2) broader ranges for others. Shifts up and down in the pegged exchange rate ranges were frequent, with 11 *devaluations* or *revaluations* (announced changes in the official pegged rate ranges) occurring from 1979 to 1987.

THE CALM BEFORE THE STORM   From 1987 to September 1992, European currency markets were stable, with predictions that 1992 would be the year of Europe and of European integration, with each country achieving inflation rates and interest rates close to that of Germany. A single European currency and a single central bank were envisioned by the year 2000.

EUROPE'S 1992 CURRENCY CRISIS   In September 1992, after failing to stop the plummeting pound with massive interest rate hikes and central bank intervention,

Britain temporarily suspended its membership in the ERM, allowing the pound to float. Sweden (which had planned to enter the ERM) and Italy did likewise. Thus the system unraveled and a "currency crisis" occurred. The value of the Irish punt and the Spanish peseta also fell sharply as speculators sold these currencies, believing that they also were overvalued. The central banks of Europe lost billions trying to maintain the value of their currencies (the Bank of England lost $7 billion in a single afternoon).[2] As usual, **market forces prevailed,** proving once again that a fixed exchange rate system cannot work when large countries have independent political systems and independent national policies. Interestingly enough, the ERM remains, although it has evolved into a two-tiered system of four strong currencies tightly anchored by the German mark and five weak currencies, the British pound and Italian lira excluded.

The Economic Perspective discusses why exchange rates change.

V THE FOREIGN EXCHANGE MARKET

IT'S AN OVER-THE-COUNTER MARKET

Earlier we stated that a company can buy and sell foreign currencies at commercial banks that have foreign exchange departments. Several hundred banks worldwide maintain foreign exchange departments. The collective buying and selling of foreign currencies at these many dispersed locations compose what is referred to as the **foreign exchange market** (hereafter the **FX market**). Consequently, the FX market is an "over-the-counter market"—the conceptual opposite to an organized exchange (such as the New York Stock Exchange where traders gather in one physical location to quote stock prices and execute trades).

A HUGE 24-HOUR MARKET

Because these banks are spread throughout the world and because their business hours overlap, it is possible to buy or sell currencies 24 hours a day. The major FX trading centers are London, New York, Tokyo, Zurich, Singapore, and Hong Kong, which account for about 80% of the FX trading. The daily volume of the FX market (approximately $1 trillion per day) makes it the world's largest market.

WHO ARE THE PLAYERS IN THE FX MARKET?

In general, the players in the FX market include (1) importers that have agreed to pay for goods in the currency of their vendors, (2) exporters that have agreed to receive payment in the currency of their customers, (3) portfolio managers of funds that invest in foreign stocks and bonds, (4) central banks of governments that intervene (usually unsuccessfully as discussed earlier) to influence market prices, (5) tourists, and (6) commercial banks.[3]

THE IMPORTANCE OF INTERBANK TRADING   The commercial banks, whose currency traders make the FX market, continually trade currencies among themselves in interbank trading, an activity that is an integral part of making the FX market. So integral is interbank trading to "making the market" that roughly 85% of the trading

[2]One U.S. foreign currency trader made more than $1 billion in September 1992, betting the ranch that the ERM would collapse. See "How the Market Overwhelmed the Central Banks," *Forbes*, November 9, 1992, pp. 40–42. (This same trader lost $600 million in a single day of currency speculation six months later.)

[3]Also part of the FX market in a peripheral manner are *FX brokers*, which are commercial firms that earn their profit by matching commercial buyers and sellers. Thus these FX brokers (a small part of the FX market) compete with the FX departments of the commercial banks.

ECONOMIC PERSPECTIVE

What Causes Currency Exchange Rates to Change

Recall that market forces determine exchange rates under a floating exchange rate system. Thus the price of a foreign currency (the exchange rate) is governed by the laws of supply and demand, as is the case for commodities such as corn, cotton, and gold. *Supply* is the quantity of a currency that companies, individuals, and governments are trying to sell. *Demand* is the quantity of a currency that companies, individuals, and governments are trying to buy. Many factors, such as the following, affect supply and demand:

- **The two countries' relative domestic inflation rates**—the major long-term cause. A technical explanation of this major exchange rate change cause (**purchasing power parity theory**) is provided in the appendix to this chapter. For now, realize that (a) **foreign inflation pushes the direct exchange rate down** and (b) **domestic inflation pushes the direct exchange rate up.**
- **Interest rates**—which are usually determined to a large extent by inflation. During Europe's currency crisis in the fall of 1992, the central banks of many weak currency countries (England, Italy, Ireland, and Denmark) increased their interest rates to attract capital, thereby creating a demand for their currencies.
- **Trade deficit or trade surplus**—the difference between the level of a country's merchandise imports and its merchandise exports. This number (approximating $100 billion annually for the United States in recent years) is the focus of much attention in the press (possibly because the United States has had annual trade deficits each year since 1974). The U.S. government reports this statistic monthly.
- **Services deficit or services surplus**—the difference between the level of a country's services rendered to foreign countries and services obtained from foreign countries. Services rendered include (1) fees of U.S. architecture, engineering, and consulting firms (such as Red Adair's firm that extinguishes oil well fires); (2) foreign students attending U.S. colleges (over 400,000 annually, which brings in roughly $5 billion); (3) foreign citizens using U.S. medical facilities; and (4) foreign citizens vacationing in the United States (nearly 40 million foreigners visit the United States annually, spending over $55 billion). In recent years, the United States has had annual service surpluses of roughly $60 billion. This statistic is not as widely reported by the press or followed (possibly because it usually is in a surplus position). The U.S. government counts exports and imports of services in the broader quarterly report on the economy's gross national product.

- **Investment deficit or investment surplus**—the level of investment made domestically by foreign investors versus the level of investment made in foreign countries by domestic investors. For nearly all of the last 25 years, the United States has had sizable annual investment surpluses (foreign investment in the United States exceeding U.S. investment overseas) resulting in the United States changing in the mid-1980s from having been a net creditor nation for decades to becoming the world's largest net debtor nation. (Even though the terms *debtor* and *creditor* are derived from and pertain to debt transactions, economists also use these terms in describing the net investment position of a country. Having more U.S. assets owned by foreign investors than foreign assets owned by U.S. investors is called *being in a net debtor position*.)
- **Federal deficits.** The U.S. federal deficit is an important variable.
- **Government-imposed restrictions on currency transfers.** For example, Ireland and Spain reacted to heavy speculative selling of their respective currencies during Europe's September 1992 currency crisis by reintroducing controls on capital flows (primarily restricting the payment of dividends to foreign parent companies).
- **Civil disorders and wars.** For example, the 1991 attempted coup d'etat in the Soviet Union caused an immediate significant weakening of the German mark (it quickly recovered). Likewise, the 1989 Tiananmen Square massacre in China caused an immediate significant weakening of the Hong Kong dollar because Hong Kong citizens sought a safe haven for their money in the United States.

Some of these factors have only a short-term effect; the effect of others is long term. It is beyond the scope of this book to examine and discuss each of these factors because an entire chapter could be devoted to the topic (as is done in textbooks on international finance). However, we look at some of these factors to give you a fuller understanding of the more important ones.

The Foreign Trade Deficit

For many years, the continuous and substantial foreign trade deficit of the United States, in which imports far exceed exports, has been of considerable concern. Because much of this trade deficit is with Japan (currently $50 billion a year), let us assume for simplicity that (1) the only trading partner of the United States is Japan, (2) trade between the two countries began in 19X1, and (3) exporters in each country demand payment in their own currency.

When a U.S. company imports goods from Japan to sell domestically, it must purchase yen from a foreign currency dealer to pay the Japanese exporter, which creates demand for yen. When a U.S. company exports U.S. goods to sell in Japan, the Japanese importer must purchase dollars from a foreign currency dealer to pay the U.S. exporter, which creates demand for dollars. Therefore, when the United States imports more than it exports, more demand is created for yen than is created for dollars. Disregarding all other factors, one would expect the yen to strengthen and the dollar to weaken when this occurs, resulting in an increase in the direct exchange rate.

Given these circumstances due to foreign trade, at the end of 19X1, the Japanese foreign currency dealers would hold many more dollars than U.S. foreign currency would hold yen. If a trade deficit with Japan continues year after year, the Japanese foreign currency dealers will continue to accumulate substantial sums in dollars. Assuming the dollars can be spent only in the United States, the question arises: Why are the Japanese foreign currency dealers willing to accumulate all those dollars? The answer is that they are convinced that they can sell the dollars to Japanese investors who desire to invest in the United States. This leads to foreign investment as a factor of currency supply and demand.

Foreign Investment

When U.S. companies desire to invest in Japan, they must purchase yen from a foreign currency dealer because they need yen to consummate these investment transactions, which creates a demand for yen. When Japanese companies invest in the United States, they must purchase dollars to consummate their investment transactions in the United States, which creates demand for dollars. Therefore, when Japanese investors invest in the United States more than U.S. investors invest in Japan, more demand is created for dollars than for yen. Disregarding all other factors, we would expect the dollar to strengthen and the yen to weaken when this occurs, thus resulting in a decrease in the direct exchange rate.

Given such circumstances due to foreign investment, at the end of 19X1, the U.S. foreign currency dealers would hold many more yen than Japanese foreign currency dealers would hold dollars. If the investment deficit continues year after year, the U.S. foreign currency dealers will continue to accumulate substantial sums in yen. Assuming that the yen can be spent only in Japan, the question is raised: Why are the U.S. foreign currency dealers willing to accumulate all those

yen? The answer is that they are convinced that they can sell the yen to U.S. companies that desire to import products from Japan. This leads to the interrelationship between trading and investing as a factor of currency supply and demand.

The Interrelationship Between Foreign Trade and Foreign Investment

To make the basic relationship clearer, let us assume that there are no foreign currency dealers (who merely act as intermediaries in matching up buyers and sellers of currencies). Under such a scenario, a U.S. trade deficit with Japan would result in many Japanese companies holding dollars at the end of 19X1. This occurs because the Japanese exporters must accept dollars in payment (otherwise, we would revert to a barter system). Thus the Japanese companies would accumulate substantial sums in dollars each year that the U.S. trade deficit continues. These Japanese exporters, however, are willing to take dollars only if they are convinced that the dollars can be (1) exchanged for something of value from or in the United States or (2) sold to Japanese companies or Japanese citizens who seek to acquire something of value from or in the United States. Japanese companies and Japanese citizens can use dollars obtained from their exports in various ways:

- **To acquire U.S. products.** Unlike automobiles, electronics, and textiles, the United States has large trade surpluses in chemicals, pharmaceuticals, scientific instruments, farm products, software, and entertainment (movies, music, and television).
- **To acquire U.S. services.** One notable service acquired is education. Approximately 24,000 Japanese students attend U.S. schools annually (versus approximately 1,000 U.S. students attending Japanese schools).
- **To acquire U.S. real estate.** Pebble Beach golf course, Squaw Valley ski resort, approximately 30% of the commercial office space in downtown Los Angeles, and most of Hawaii's commercial property are owned by Japanese investors.
- **To acquire U.S. companies.** In one recent year, approximately 175 U.S. companies were acquired by Japanese companies. Recent examples are Columbia Pictures acquired by Sony Corporation for $3.5 billion; MCA, Inc. (the parent of Universal Studios and a colossus of films, records, and television) acquired by Matsushita Electric Industrial Co. for $6.6 billion.
- **To acquire U.S. treasury securities.** Japan is a major lender to the federal government (holds nearly $500 billion of U.S. treasury securities at the end of 1996).

(continued)

The key point is that **no foreign company will accept U.S. dollars unless it is convinced that the dollars can be exchanged for something of value from or in the United States.** Otherwise, countries would be able to import whatever they desired merely by printing money.

This means that when the United States imports from Japan more goods than it exports and this trade deficit is not fully offset by a services surplus with Japan, there is an equal and offsetting effect by Japanese investors. Stated differently, a $50 billion trade deficit with Japan and a $16 billion services surplus with Japan is exactly offset by Japanese investors investing $34 billion more in the United States than was invested in Japan by U.S. investors. This leads to the following equation:

Trade Deficit – Services Surplus* = Investment Surplus

Thus there is offsetting demand, which means that there should be no long-term effect on exchange rates. In the short term, however, there usually is some effect because at any given time or during any short period of time, a perfect balance between trade and investment does not exist. **Note that U.S. trade deficit can last as long as (1) foreign investors are willing to invest in the United States and (2) U.S. companies and citizens are willing to sell their real estate and securities (if they have any left to sell) to foreign investors.** Note also in this case that the result of the U.S. trade deficit with Japan is that U.S. citizens are effectively exchanging ownership in corporate assets to obtain primarily consumer goods (automobiles and electronic entertainment goods, which are Japan's primary exports to the United States).

Since 1980, Japan's overseas net investment has grown from a paltry $25 billion to an estimated $750 billion, much of which is in the United States.

*If services were a deficit, the service deficit would be added to the trade deficit, which would make the investment surplus higher.

that occurs in the FX market is interbank trading, while less than 15% is commercial business. The interbank trading activity keeps the market liquid and keeps prices announced by the various FX traders from diverging greatly from one another.

WHAT DOES *MAKING THE MARKET* MEAN?

The FX traders of the commercial banks "make the market" because they create it by (1) quoting bid and asked prices and (2) executing trades at those prices for orders placed. Thus they make possible the immediate execution of orders from buyers and sellers of currencies because, as market makers, they are willing to take the other side of the transaction themselves. The FX traders, as a group, make a profit because they provide a basic service to the external participants in the market: the importers, exporters, fund portfolio managers, and tourists. As a group, the FX traders also make a profit if a government central bank intervenes in the marketplace and loses money trying to support the price of a currency. Because of interbank trading, the FX traders compete against each other and try to profit from their interbank trading.

VI TRANSLATING IMPORTING AND EXPORTING TRANSACTIONS

The currency in which a transaction is to be settled must be stipulated in each foreign transaction. Whether a foreign transaction is to be settled in a foreign currency or in U.S. dollars is negotiated at the inception of each foreign transaction.[4]

[4]No precise numbers are available as to the percentage of U.S. world trade that requires settlement in foreign currencies versus U.S. dollars. Furthermore, inquiries to foreign exchange traders reveal that no general rule can be given such as the majority of U.S. exports are denominated in dollars and the majority of U.S. imports are denominated in foreign currencies. The reasons that transactions are denominated in dollars versus a foreign currency are numerous and may be found in international finance texts.

MEASURED VERSUS DENOMINATED

When a transaction is to be settled by the receipt or payment of a fixed amount of a specified currency, the receivable or payable, respectively, is said to be *denominated* in that currency. When a transaction is to be settled by the receipt or payment of a fixed amount of currency other than the U.S. dollar, from the perspective of a U.S. reporting entity, the receivable or payable is denominated in a foreign currency. A party to a transaction *measures* and records the transaction in the currency of the country in which that party is located. Thus one of the parties has a transaction that is measured and denominated in its own currency, and the other party has a transaction that is measured in its own currency but denominated in a different currency. The following examples illustrate this distinction:

1. A U.S. importer purchases goods on credit from a Swiss exporter, with payment to be made in a specified number of Swiss francs. The domestic importer measures and records the transaction in dollars, and the Swiss exporter measures and records the transaction in Swiss francs. The domestic importer's liability is denominated in a foreign currency, the Swiss franc. The Swiss exporter's receivable is denominated in Swiss francs. (If the terms of the transaction called for payment to be made in dollars, the transaction would be measured and denominated in dollars, from the perspective of the importer.)

2. A Swiss subsidiary of a U.S. company purchases goods on credit from another Swiss company, with payment to be made in a specified number of Swiss francs. The Swiss subsidiary measures the asset acquired and the liability incurred in Swiss francs. The Swiss subsidiary's liability is *not* denominated in a foreign currency because the liability is denominated in Swiss francs. From the perspective of the U.S. parent, however, the Swiss subsidiary's liability is denominated in a foreign currency because the liability is *not* payable in dollars.

3. A Swiss subsidiary of a U.S. company purchases goods on credit from an Italian company, with the payment to be made in Italian lira. The Swiss subsidiary measures the asset acquired and liability incurred in Swiss francs. The Swiss subsidiary's liability is denominated in a foreign currency. From the perspective of the U.S. parent, the Swiss subsidiary's liability is denominated in a foreign currency because the liability is *not* payable in dollars.

FOREIGN CURRENCY TRANSACTIONS VERSUS FOREIGN TRANSACTIONS

For each international transaction, both parties have a *foreign transaction*. Because payment is usually specified in only one currency, however, only one of the parties can more specifically refer to the transaction as a **foreign currency transaction.** Thus all foreign currency transactions are foreign transactions, but not all foreign transactions can be called foreign *currency* transactions.

DIFFERENTIATING ACCOUNTS REQUIRING SETTLEMENT IN FOREIGN CURRENCY   In discussing accounts requiring settlement in a foreign currency, it is convenient to differentiate these accounts in some manner. Accordingly, in discussions *not* involving a specific example or illustration, we use the designation "FX" (foreign exchange) preceding the amount, such as FX Accounts Payable and FX Accounts Receivable. When dealing with a specific foreign currency as in an illustration, however, we use the symbol for that currency, such as £ for the British pound, instead of FX.

UNDERSTANDING THE RELEVANT DATES

When a U.S. company makes or receives payment in dollars, no special accounting procedures are necessary because no accounting issues exist. When the U.S. company pays or receives in the foreign currency, however, two accounting issues arise. Before discussing these issues, we must define the following four dates that may be involved in a foreign currency transaction:

1. **The order (or commitment) date.** On this date, the purchase or sales order is issued. If noncancellable, a contract effectively has been entered into.

2. **The transaction date.** On this date, the transaction is initially recorded on the books, for example, recording a sale or a purchase of inventory.

3. **The intervening balance sheet (financial reporting) dates.** Such dates occur between the transaction date and the settlement date. A transaction recorded on November 20, 19X5, and settled on January 10, 19X6, has two intervening balance sheet dates, assuming that monthly financial statements are prepared. Such dates exist only for transactions in which credit terms are granted and used.

4. **The settlement date.** On this date, payment is made. The customary payment practice for foreign transactions is to make an international **bank wire transfer.** In a bank wire transfer, the paying party authorizes its bank to subtract the amount being paid from its checking account. The paying party's bank then telexes the receiving party's bank to add to the receiving party's bank account the identical amount, as translated into the receiving party's currency using the spot rate. **Thus, no currency physically changes hands or physically moves in or out of a country in a bank wire transfer.** (Instead of the domestic importer and the foreign vendor having a payable and a receivable, respectively, the two banks now have a payable and a receivable with each other, for which they will settle with each other.)

CONCEPTUAL ISSUES

In foreign currency transactions, the first accounting issue pertains to how the transaction should be recorded in dollars at the transaction date. Accountants generally agree that the transaction should be recorded at the transaction date using the exchange rate in effect at that date. For an importing transaction, therefore, the acquired asset is initially recorded at the dollar amount needed to purchase the amount of foreign currency that would settle the transaction at the transaction date. For an exporting transaction, the export sale is recorded at the dollar amount that would be received from converting the foreign currency into dollars if full payment were made at the transaction date.

If credit terms are *not* granted, no other accounting issues exist.[5] If credit terms *are* granted and used, the following additional accounting issues arise:

1. **Whether to make adjustments at intervening balance sheet dates.** If the exchange rate used to record the transaction at the transaction date has changed between the transaction date and an intervening balance sheet date, should the receivable or payable pertaining to the unsettled portion of the transaction be adjusted to reflect the current rate at such intervening balance sheet date?

---

[5]When credit is *not* granted and cash is not paid in advance (via a bank wire transfer), payment is usually made using either (1) a *letter of credit* (using a bank) or (2) a *draft* (also referred to as a *bill of exchange*), which is an alternative to a letter of credit. Credit is usually given cautiously in foreign transactions because collection efforts in foreign countries can be extremely costly, time consuming, and frustrating.

2. **How to report exchange rate change adjustments.** If the transaction is settled at an amount different from that at which it was initially recorded, how should the difference be recorded.

With respect to the first issue, most accountants agree that any unsettled portion of the transaction represented by a payable or receivable should be adjusted at intervening balance sheet dates to reflect the exchange rate in effect at those dates. It makes sense to carry the receivable or payable at the amount of dollars that would be received or paid, respectively, if the transaction were settled on that date. (**This is essentially current-value accounting—the most relevant of all reporting bases.**) There are two viewpoints concerning the second issue:

1. Under the **one-transaction perspective,** all aspects of the transaction are viewed as part of a single transaction. A company's commitment to pay or receive foreign currency is considered a necessary and inseparable part of the transaction to purchase or sell goods, respectively. The amount initially recorded at the transaction date is considered an estimate until the final settlement. As a result, the initially recorded cost of goods acquired or revenue is subsequently adjusted for any difference between the amount recorded at the transaction date and the amount at which the transaction is ultimately settled.

2. Under the **two-transaction perspective,** the commitment to pay or receive foreign currency is considered a separate transaction from the purchase or sale of goods. The decision to grant or use credit is considered a decision separate from that of purchasing or selling goods. As a result, any difference between the amount initially recorded at the transaction date and the amount at which the transaction is ultimately settled is considered a foreign currency transaction gain or loss—no adjustment is made to the initially recorded cost of goods acquired or revenues recorded pertaining to goods sold, as the case may be.

From either perspective, the risk in a foreign currency transaction from potential adverse exchange rate changes can be eliminated by not granting or using credit or by using a technique called *hedging* (discussed in Chapter 17).

FASB ADOPTS THE TWO-TRANSACTION PERSPECTIVE The Financial Accounting Standards Board rejected the *one-transaction* perspective in *SFAS No. 52* (as it did in *SFAS No. 8*) on the grounds that the consequences of the risks associated with foreign currency transactions should be accounted for separately from the purchase or sale of goods. Thus the requirements of *SFAS No. 52* reflect the *two-transaction perspective,* and a domestic importer or exporter would account for such transactions as follows:

1. At the *transaction date,* measure and record in dollars each asset, liability, revenue, expense, gain, or loss arising from the transaction using the *current exchange rate* (the rate that could be used to settle the transaction at that date).

2. At each *intervening balance sheet date,* adjust the recorded balances of any foreign currency receivable or payable to reflect the current exchange rate (the rate at which the receivable or payable could be settled at that date).

3. Report in the income statement a *foreign currency transaction gain or loss* resulting from (1) adjustments made at any intervening balance sheet dates and (2) any adjustments from settling the transaction at an amount different from that recorded at the latest intervening balance sheet date (or the transaction date when there are no intervening balance sheet dates).

These various dates are shown graphically in Illustration 16–1.

ILLUSTRATION 16–1	Graphic Depiction of Relevant Dates

Order Date	Transaction Date	Intervening Balance Sheet Dates		Settlement Date
Make memo entry	Initially record transaction	Adjust foreign currency receivable or payable to reflect current rate and recognize related gain or loss		Collect or pay cash
10/19/X5	11/20/X5	11/30/X5	12/31/X5	1/10/X6

(Achieves Current Value Accounting)

In summary, **the cost or the revenue arising from a transaction should be determined only once: when the transaction is initially recorded.** The fact that credit terms are granted should *not* result in a later adjustment to the asset or service acquired, or to the revenue initially recorded, if the exchange rate changes between the transaction date and the settlement date. Any higher or lower amount than that initially recorded represents a gain or loss that could have been avoided had the transaction been fully paid for when it occurred. Thus any higher or lower amount payable involves a decision to grant or exercise credit, which should be charged or credited to income in the period in which the exchange rate changes.

ILLUSTRATION	IMPORTING AND EXPORTING TRANSACTIONS

Assume that a domestic company has the following importing and exporting transactions with suppliers and customers in Great Britain:

1. On December 11, 19X1, inventory was acquired from Vendor A for 100,000 pounds. Payment is due in pounds on January 10, 19X2.

2. Inventory is sold to Customer X for 200,000 pounds on December 21, 19X1. Payment is due in pounds on January 20, 19X2.

Illustration 16–2 shows these transactions as initially recorded and as adjusted at the intervening balance sheet date (December 31, 19X1). Payments are made as required. The direct exchange rates (spot rates) for the applicable dates in December 19X1 and January 19X2 (when the pound was strengthening) are as follows:

December 11, 19X1	December 21, 19X1	December 31, 19X1	January 10, 19X2	January 20, 19X2
$1.50	$1.52	$1.55	$1.57	$1.60

REVIEW POINTS FOR ILLUSTRATION 16–2 Note the following:

1. **Netting.** For 19X1, a net FX gain of $1,000 ($6,000 gain on the receivable – $5,000 loss on the payable) is reported in the income statement. For 19X2, the year in which settlement occurred, a net FX gain of $8,000 ($10,000 gain on the receivable – $2,000 loss on the payable) is reported in the income statement.

2. **Apportioning the transaction's gains and losses.** The total gain on the *exporting* transaction is $16,000 (cash of $320,000 received minus the initially recorded sales amount of $304,000). However, the financial reporting requirements cause

ILLUSTRATION 16–2	**Recording Foreign Currency Transactions**	

Entries Related to Vendor A

December 11, 19X1

Inventory (or Purchases)	$150,000	
£ Accounts Payable		$150,000
To record purchase of inventory. (£100,000 × $1.50 = $150,000)		

December 31, 19X1

FX Loss	$5,000	
£ Accounts Payable		$5,000
To adjust foreign currency payable to the current spot rate.		
($1.55 − $1.50 = $.05) ($.05 × £100,000 = $5,000)		

January 10, 19X2

FX Loss	$2,000	
£ Accounts Payable		$2,000
To adjust foreign currency payable to the current spot rate.		
($1.57 − $1.55 = $.02) ($.02 × £100,000 = $2,000)		
£ Accounts Payable	$157,000	
Cash		$157,000
To record payment to vendor **via a bank wire transfer.**		

Shortcut approach at settlement date. Companies often take a shortcut approach of *not* adjusting the FX Accounts Payable account at the settlement date. Thus the following lone entry can be made at the settlement date (rather than the two entries shown for 1/10/X2):

£ Accounts Payable	$155,000	
FX Loss	$2,000	
Cash		$157,000

Entries Related to Customer X

December 21, 19X1

£ Accounts Receivable	$304,000	
Sales		$304,000
To record sale. (£200,000 × $1.52 = $304,000)		

December 31, 19X1

£ Accounts Receivable	$6,000	
FX Gain		$6,000
To adjust foreign currency receivable to the current spot rate.		
($1.55 − $1.52 = $.03) ($.03 × £200,000 = $6,000)		

January 20, 19X2

£ Accounts Receivable	$10,000	
FX Gain		$10,000
To adjust foreign currency receivable to the current spot rate.		
($1.60 − $1.55 = $.05) ($.05 × £200,000 = $10,000)		
Cash	$320,000	
£ Accounts Receivable		$320,000
To record collection from customer **via a bank wire transfer.**		
(£200,000 × $1.60 = $320,000)		

Shortcut approach at settlement date. Companies often take a shortcut approach of *not* adjusting the FX Accounts Receivable account at the settlement date. Thus the following lone entry can be made at the settlement date (rather than the two entries shown for 1/20/X2):

Cash	$320,000	
£ Accounts Receivable		$310,000
FX Gain		$10,000

ILLUSTRATION 16–3	**Conflicting Concerns and Desires of Domestic Importers and Exporters**		
	Account Exposed	**Nature of Concern**	**Desires**
Domestic importers	FX Accounts Payable	Direct rate increases[a]	Direct rate decreases[b]
Domestic exporters	FX Accounts Receivable	Direct rate decreases[b]	Direct rate increases[a]

[a]Caused by foreign currency strengthening and U.S. dollar weakening.
[b]Caused by foreign currency weakening and U.S. dollar strengthening.

the company to recognize $6,000 in 19X1 and $10,000 in 19X2. Likewise, the total loss on the *importing* transaction was $7,000 ($157,000 cash paid – the initially recorded purchase amount of $150,000), of which $5,000 was recognized in 19X1 and $2,000 was recognized in 19X2.

3. **Unrealized nature.** FX gains and losses recognized in the income statement at intervening balance sheet dates (thus, on unsettled accounts) are **unrealized**— a fact deemed irrelevant by the FASB. The FASB concluded that recognizing unrealized gains and losses in the period in which they occur would better serve financial statement users even though reversals might occur in subsequent periods. This is the only area of *SFAS No. 52* in which unrealized gains and losses can be recognized in the income statement.[6]

4. **One-sidedness exposure.** When one of the parties to a foreign transaction incurs an FX gain or loss, the other party does *not* incur an opposite, offsetting FX loss or gain because that other party does *not* transact in a foreign currency. Accordingly, foreign currency transaction gains and losses are one sided.

5. **Tax treatment.** FX *gains* are taxable **when realized,** that is, at the settlement date—the point when the transaction is considered "closed" for tax-reporting purposes. Likewise, FX *losses* are tax deductible when realized (at the settlement date). Thus *temporary differences* between financial reporting and tax reporting will exist at intervening balance sheet dates for unrealized gains and losses recognized for financial reporting purposes.

In Illustration 16–2, in which the direct exchange increased, the domestic importer had a loss, but the domestic exporter had a gain. Thus these parties had different concerns and desires as to the future direction of the direct exchange rate. These conflicting concerns and desires of domestic importers and exporters are summarized in Illustration 16–3.

END-OF-CHAPTER REVIEW

SUMMARY OF KEY POINTS

1. A **floating exchange rate system** is currently used; thus exchange rates are determined daily by the forces of **supply and demand.**

---

[6]In June 1993, the FASB issued *SFAS No. 115*, "Accounting for Certain Investments in Debt and Equity Securities," which constitutes another step forward in the use of current value accounting. Under *SFAS No. 115*, unrealized gains and losses on debt and equity securities that are bought and held principally for the purpose of selling them in the near term ("trading securities") must be recognized in the income statement.

2. **Inflation** is the major long-run cause of exchange rate changes, as explained by the **purchasing power parity theory.**

3. **Foreign inflation** causes the direct exchange rate to **go down. Domestic inflation** causes the direct exchange rate to **go up.**

4. In an international transaction, the party that must make or receive payment in other than its own local currency has a **foreign transaction** that will result in a **foreign currency transaction.** (The other party has only a foreign transaction.)

5. **Foreign currency transaction exposure** effectively begins when a commitment is established as a result of issuing a purchase order or receiving a sales order.

6. The FASB adopted the **two-transaction perspective** for importing and exporting transactions; thus the decision to grant credit or to take advantage of credit **is accounted for separately from the accounting for the item to be received or delivered.**

7. The critical dates for accounting purposes under *SFAS No. 52* are (1) the commitment date, (2) the transaction date, (3) any **intervening balance sheet dates,** and (4) the settlement date.

8. **Between the transaction date and the settlement date,** an FX receivable and an FX payable are *exposed* because they gain or lose value as the exchange rate changes.

9. FX receivables and FX payables are always adjusted at intervening balance sheet dates to the spot rate—**this achieves current-value accounting,** the best of all reporting bases.

10. Adjustments to FX receivables and FX payables at intervening balance sheet dates result in **unrealized FX gains or losses** that are to be **reported currently in the income statement.**

GLOSSARY OF NEW TERMS

Bank wire transfer   A procedure to settle FX receivables and payables by using a bank to electronically make settlement, negating the need to physically handle foreign currencies.

Controlled foreign corporation   A foreign corporation that has more than half of its common stock owned by 10% U.S. shareholders.

Conversion   The physical change of one currency for another currency.

Deemed distribution (deemed dividend)   The IRS characterization of certain undistributed earnings of a controlled foreign corporation so that those earnings are taxed currently in the United States as though a cash dividend had been received.

Exposed asset   A recorded asset that is exposed to the risk that the exchange rate could change adversely.

Exposed liability   A recorded liability that is exposed to the risk that the exchange rate could change adversely.

Foreign currency exposure   The risk that an entity could incur a loss as a result of an adverse change in the exchange rate.

Foreign currency transactions   Transactions whose terms require settlement in a foreign currency.

Foreign exchange market   An over-the-counter market comprising hundreds of currency traders of commercial banks who buy and sell currencies at prices they quote. These FX traders "make the market."

Forward rate (future rate)   A rate quoted for future delivery of currencies to be exchanged (usually up to one year).

Purchasing power parity theory   An explanation of why exchange rates change over long periods of time, the cause being the differential rate of inflation between two countries.

Settlement date   The date at which a receivable is collected or a payable is paid.

Spot rate   The exchange rate for immediate delivery of currencies to be exchanged.

Transaction date   The date at which a transaction (such as the purchase or sale of inventory or services) is recordable in accounting records in accordance with GAAP.

Transaction gain or loss   A gain or loss on a foreign currency payable or receivable that arises because of a change in the exchange rate that occurs between the transaction date and the settlement date.

Translation   Expressing in U.S. dollars amounts denominated in a foreign currency.

SELF-STUDY QUESTIONS

(Answers are at the end of the chapter preceding the appendix.)

1. If *physical presence* exists in a foreign country, it means that
   a. Fair transfer pricing rules may *not* be applicable.
   b. Foreign commission agents may be deemed to be employees.
   c. Foreign tax credits will *not* be available.
   d. A foreign operation may be subject to taxation in the foreign country.
   e. A foreign branch's income will *not* be taxed currently in the United States.

2. A foreign branch is taxed at 20% in the foreign country. All intracompany transactions are priced on an arm's-length basis. The U.S. tax rate is 35%. At what rate should the U.S. home office record income taxes on the branch's pretax earnings?
   a. 0%   **b.** 15%   **c.** 20%   **d.** 35%

3. A domestic exporter sold inventory to a foreign company on credit, with the transaction denominated in the foreign currency. Between the transaction date and the settlement date, the U.S. dollar strengthened. There was no intervening balance sheet date. The exporter should account for the change in the exchange rate as
   a. A decrease to the initially recorded sales amount.
   b. An increase to the initially recorded sales amount.
   c. A gain or loss recognized currently in the income statement.
   d. A gain or loss to be deferred.

4. On 12/10/X1, a domestic importer purchased inventory on credit from a foreign vendor, with payment to be made in the foreign currency. The direct exchange rate was $.80 on 12/10/X1, and $.83 on 12/31/X1, (the importer's year-end). On 1/5/X2 (the settlement date), the direct exchange rate was $.79. At 12/31/X1, the importer should report
   a. An increase to the amount initially recorded for inventory.
   b. A decrease to the amount initially recorded for inventory.
   c. A gain or loss to be deferred.
   d. A gain in its 19X1 income statement.
   e. A loss in its 19X1 income statement.

5. On 11/11/X1, a domestic exporter sold inventory on credit to a Japanese customer for 980,000 yen (the billing currency is yen). On this date, the yen was quoted at 100 to the dollar. On 12/31/X1 (the exporter's year-end), the yen was quoted at 98 to the dollar. At 12/31/X1, the exporter should report
   a. An increase to the initially recorded sales amount.
   b. A decrease to the initially recorded sales amount.
   c. A gain or loss to be deferred.
   d. A gain in its 19X1 income statement.
   e. A loss in its 19X1 income statement.

ASSIGNMENT MATERIAL

REVIEW QUESTIONS

1. In general, when does a domestic company become subject to the income tax laws of a foreign country.
2. In general, how does the IRS treat the earnings of a *foreign branch* of a domestic company?
3. How does the IRS treat the earnings of a *foreign subsidiary* of a domestic company?
4. Do the *arm's-length transfer pricing rules* apply to foreign subsidiaries or foreign branches or both?
5. What are some of the major reasons for domestic exporters to establish overseas manufacturing operations?
6. What is the advantage of using a *subsidiary* versus a *branch* form of organization for an overseas operation?
7. How do fluctuations in the exchange rates impact *domestic exporters?*
8. What is the difference between *conversion* and *translation*?
9. What is the *direct* quotation rate? The *indirect* quotation rate?

10. What are *floating* or *free* exchange rates?
11. What are *fixed* or *official* exchange rates?
12. What is meant when a currency is said to be *strengthening*? When a currency is *weakening*?
13. What are six factors that affect the supply and demand for currencies?
14. Why does the *foreign trade deficit not* affect exchange rates in the long run?
15. What is *purchasing power parity theory*?
16. Is purchasing power parity theory a *cause* of exchange rate changes?
17. What effect does *foreign* inflation have on exchange rates? What effect does *domestic* inflation have on exchange rates?
18. What does *denominated* mean?
19. What is the distinction between a *foreign transaction* and *foreign currency transaction*?
20. What four dates can exist in an importing or exporting foreign currency transaction?
21. Summarize the *two-transaction* perspective.
22. Summarize the *one-transaction* perspective.
23. How do *bank wire transfers* work? Does currency physically move between countries?
24. What are the concerns and desires of a domestic *exporter*? What are they for a domestic *importer*?

EXERCISES

E 16–1 **Expressing Exchange Rates**   On 1/1/X1, 100,000 Mex\$ could be converted into \$40,000. On 12/31/X1, 100,000 Mex\$ could be converted into \$50,000.

Required 1. Express the relationship between the two currencies at each date directly and indirectly.
2. Did the peso strengthen or weaken during 19X1? Did the dollar strengthen or weaken during 19X1?

E 16–2 **Identifying Foreign Currency Exposure**   Comcoe has many importing and exporting transactions that require settlement in foreign currency (often referred to as *local currency units* or LCU). Credit terms are granted and used.

Required 1. Should Comcoe be concerned about whether the direct exchange rate will go up or down?
2. Indicate in the following table what the foreign currency exposure concern should be:

Transaction	Billing Currency	Whether the Dollar Will		Whether the LCU Will	
		Strengthen	Weaken	Strengthen	Weaken
Importing	Dollar	___	___	___	___
Importing	LCU	___	___	___	___
Exporting	Dollar	___	___	___	___
Exporting	LCU	___	___	___	___

E 16–3 **Determining Reportable Amounts on Exporting Transaction**   On 9/9/X1, Sella Inc. accepted a noncancellable merchandise sales order from an Australian firm. The contract price was 100,000 \$A. The merchandise was delivered on 12/14/X1. The invoice was dated 12/11/X1, the shipping date (FOB shipping point). Full payment was received on 1/22/X2. The spot direct exchange rates for the Australian dollar on the respective dates are as follows:

September 9, 19X1	December 11, 19X1	December 14, 19X1	December 31, 19X1	January 22, 19X2
\$.75	\$.78	\$.77	\$.73	\$.725

Required 1. What is the reportable sales amount in the 19X1 income statement?
2. What is the reportable FX gain or loss amount in the 19X1 income statement?
3. What is the reported value of the receivable from the customer at 12/31/X1?

E 16–4 **Determining Reportable Amounts on Importing Transaction**   On 9/3/X1, Bycora placed a noncancellable purchase order with a Swedish company for a custom-built machine. The contract price was 1,000,000

SKr. The machine was delivered on 12/23/X1. The invoice was dated 11/13/X1, the shipping date (FOB shipping point). The vendor was paid on 1/7/X2. The spot direct exchange rates for krona on the respective dates are as follows:

September 3, 19X1	November 13, 19X1	December 23, 19X1	December 31, 19X1	January 7, 19X2
$.20	$.21	$.22	$.23	$.24

Required   1. What amount is the capitalizable cost of the equipment?
2. What is the reportable FX gain or loss amount in Bycora's 19X1 income statement?
3. What is the reported value of the payable to the vendor at 12/31/X1?

PROBLEMS

P 16–1   **Importing and Exporting Transactions**   During July 19X5, Portex had the following transactions with foreign businesses:

Date	Nature of Transaction	Billing Currency	Exchange Rate (Direct)
Vendor A			
July 1, 19X1	Imported merchandise costing 100,000 pesos from Mexico City wholesaler	Pesos	$ .70
July 10, 19X1	Paid 40% of amount owed		.71
July 31, 19X1	Paid remaining amount owed		.66
Customer A			
July 15, 19X1	Sold merchandise for 50,000 francs to French wholesaler	Francs	$.160
July 20, 19X1	Received 20% payment		.150
July 30, 19X1	Received remaining amount owed		.155

Required   Prepare journal entries for these transactions.

P 16–2   **Importing and Exporting Transactions**   During June and July 19X1, Quartex (which reports on a calendar-year basis and issues quarterly financial statements) had the following transactions with foreign businesses:

Date	Nature of Transaction	Billing Currency	Exchange Rate (Direct)
Vendor A			
June 15, 19X1	Imported merchandise costing 100,000 Canadian dollars from Canadian manufacturer	Canadian dollars	$ .80
July 15, 19X1	Paid entire amount owed		.77
Customer A			
June 20, 19X1	Sold merchandise for 200,000 Singapore dollars to Singapore retailer	Singapore dollars	$.650
July 10, 19X1	Received full payment		.640

On 6/30/X1, the spot exchange rate for Canadian dollars was $.79 and for Singapore dollars was $.643.

Required   Prepare journal entries for these transactions. (Be sure to prepare journal entries at 6/30/X1 when necessary.)

P 16–3   **Accounting for a Travel Allowance**   On 12/26/X1, the vice-president of marketing of Travcor was given a $6,000 travel advance for a 10-day trip to the United Kingdom. On that date, the vice-president converted the $6,000 into 12,000 pounds. During this 10-day trip, the pound steadily weakened against the dollar. The exchange rate at 12/31/X1 was 1 pound equals $.48. On 1/5/X2, the vice-president returned and submitted to the company cashier 1,100 pounds and receipts for 10,900 pounds that he had spent. On this date, the exchange rate was 1 pound equals $.42. Of the 10,900 pounds spent during the trip, 5,700 had been spent by 12/31/X1.

Required   Prepare all entries required at 12/31/X1 and 1/5/X2 in connection with this travel advance.

✳ THINKING CRITICALLY ✳

✳ CASES ✳

C 16–1   **Do Economic Gains and Losses Occur on Purchase Orders Outstanding?**   On 10/4/X1, Conrex placed a noncancellable inventory purchase order with a French vendor. On 1/11/X2, Conrex received the inventory. On 2/22/X2, Conrex paid the vendor the full contractual price of 100,000 francs. The spot direct exchange rates for the French franc follow:

October 4, 19X1	December 31, 19X1	January 11, 19X2	February 22, 19X2
$.20	$.23	$.24	$.26

Required   1. What arguments can you make for and against requiring Conrex to record a $3,000 loss at 12/31/X1?
2. In your judgment, did Conrex have a $3,000 economic loss in 19X1?
3. Assume for the dates given that Conrex had also received a noncancellable sales order from a French customer. In your judgment, did Conrex have a $3,000 economic gain in 19X1?

C 16–2   **Just How Many Ways Are There to Describe Gains and Losses?**   Financial accountants characterize gains and losses as *realized* and *unrealized*. Tax accountants use the terms *capital* and *ordinary*. Economists use the terms *real* and *nominal*. Business executives often downplay a loss by saying that it is only a "paper loss."

Required   1. What is the distinction between each of these categories?
2. Would financial reporting be improved if *real* and *nominal* were used instead of *realized* and *unrealized*? Why or why not?

C 16–3   **Theory: How Should Tax Breaks Be Reported?**   When U.S. companies receive a Section 936 tax break for doing business in a U.S. possession, the tax savings is currently reported as a reduction of income tax expense.

Required   1. Does this manner of reporting accurately portray the economic substance of what has occurred?
2. Should special tax breaks (such as this one) be viewed as subsidies and thus reported as a direct credit to equity using an account such as Capital by Government Subsidy? Why or why not?

✳ FINANCIAL ANALYSIS PROBLEM ✳

FAP 16–1   **Determining the Impact of Inflation on Equity**   Consider the population to be composed of the following seven groups:

Group A owns land worth $105,000.
Group B owns land worth $105,000.
Group C owns cash of $105,000.
Group D owns nothing.
Group E owns cash of $100,000.
Group F owns cash of $5,000.
Group G owns nothing but owes $100,000.

On 1/1/X1, the following events and transactions occurred:

1. Group C deposited its $105,000 into Lincoln Savings & Loan, which has no equity capital. (The savings account is fully insured by the federal government.)

2. Lincoln S&L lent the $105,000 to Group D at 5% interest. The note is due in one year.
3. Group D purchased the land from Group B for $105,000 cash.

On 1/2/X1 (one day later), the following events and transactions took place:

4. Inflation of 5% occurred; everything (real estate, commodities, services) now costs 5% more.
5. Because of inflation, the current lending rate is now 10% instead of 5%. Accordingly, Lincoln's $105,000 note receivable fell in value to $100,000.

On 1/3/X1 (another day later), the following events and transactions occurred:

6. The government declared Lincoln insolvent (on a current value basis) and sold the $105,000 note receivable to Group E for $100,000.
7. For simplicity, assume that the government imposed a special savings and loan bailout tax of $5,000 on Group F and deposited the taxes collected in Lincoln. The government then distributed $105,000 cash to Group C in full liquidation of its government insured deposit.

On 1/4/X1 (another day later), the government announced that it expected no future inflation. Accordingly, the lending rate returned to 5%. Prices did *not* return to their previous level, however; they stabilized at the higher level attained on 1/2/X1.

Required

1. Determine the economic gain or loss for each group at the end of 1/4/X1. At the beginning of your solution, include a summary matrix as follows (with amounts inserted in the appropriate columns):

	Asset Held During Inflationary Period	Gained	Lost	Broke Even
Group A				
Group B				
Group C				
Group D				
Group E				
Group F				
Group G				

2. Explain why each group gained, lost, or broke even.
3. Which group did Group F subsidize?
4. Assume that Group A sold its land on 1/5/X1 for $110,250. Assume an applicable income tax rate of 40%. Would your answer to requirement 1 change for Group A? If so, in which way or by how much?
5. How many ways can you think of to label a gain?
6. Are financial statements of U.S. companies adjusted for inflation in any way? Explain either how or why not?
7. In general, who are the winners when inflation occurs?

✳ PERSONAL SITUATIONS: ETHICS AND INTERPERSONAL SKILLS ✳

PS 16–1 **Ethics: Exporting Products Banned in the United States** Tough federal environmental rules and health concerns have largely eliminated lead from gasoline in the United States (gasoline emissions being the greatest single contributor to the buildup of lead in humans, according to the EPA). U.S. laws, however, do *not* bar U.S. companies from exporting leaded gasoline and lead additives. Annual U.S. exports of lead additives are near 125 million pounds. The World Health Organization has warned that chronic exposure to even low levels of lead can reduce birth weight, impair mental development and hearing, lower IQ, and seriously affect a child's ability to learn.

Required

1. Is the exporting of lead an ethical issue or a legal issue?
2. Would you accept a job from a company that exported lead additives to Latin America, Asia, and Africa (areas that currently do not require unleaded gasoline)?

ANSWERS TO SELF-STUDY QUESTIONS

1. d   2. b   3. c   4. e   5. d

■ APPENDIX

DIFFERENTIAL RATES OF INFLATION: THE MAJOR LONG-TERM CAUSE OF EXCHANGE RATE CHANGES

Many economists (as well as the popular press as represented by *The Wall Street Journal*)[7] recognize the **purchasing power parity (PPP) theory** as the best explanation of major changes in exchange rates over long periods. Moreover, financial executives of most multinational corporations understand PPP.

Under PPP (which follows from the "law of one price"), the differential rate of inflation between two countries can be expected to result over the long term in an equal but opposite change in the exchange rate between the two currencies. For example, assume that on January 1, 19X1, the direct exchange rate between the U.S. dollar and the British pound is 1£ equals $1. Also assume that on this date, a bushel of wheat can be purchased in Great Britain for 1£ and in the United States for $1. Thus British citizens will pay the same (one) price (1£) for a bushel of wheat, regardless of whether the wheat is purchased in Great Britain or in the United States.

For 19X1, assume an inflation rate of 100% in Great Britain and zero in the United States. Accordingly, at December 31, 19X1, a bushel of wheat in Great Britain should cost 2£. If the exchange rate does *not* change in 19X1, a British citizen will be able to purchase wheat at two prices: 2£ if purchased in Great Britain and 1£ if purchased in the United States (which would be convertible into $1). Then disregarding the effects of transportation costs, tariffs, taxes, and so on, British citizens will most likely purchase the wheat in the United States, thereby saving 1£ per bushel. This will create more demand for U.S. dollars, however, and will cause the value of the dollar to rise against the pound. Under the theory, the exchange rate by December 31, 19X1, will adjust so that there is only one price to British citizens; 1£ will become equal to $.50. **Because pounds can be spent only in Great Britain, U.S. farmers effectively will demand 2£ per bushel of wheat so that they will have enough pounds to buy something of comparable value that is produced in Great Britain.**

Studies have shown that (1) in the short term, factors other than differential rates of inflation may have greater influence in determining exchange rates[8] and (2) in the long term, the effects of the other factors tend to reverse or cancel out, an eventually exchange rates closely approximate the results expected under PPP. An important question arises: How long is "in the long term"? A recent study found "that purchasing power parity holds in the long run for each of the [16] currencies studied and that the typical half-life of shock to parity is approximately three years.[9] An application of PPP theory for the British pound for the 15 years ended December 31,

---

[7]"Dollar Turmoil" (editorial), *The Wall Street Journal,* May 23, 1989, p. A22.

[8]For many South American countries that have highly inflationary economies, however, inflation (more than 1,000% annually for some countries) is the primary short-term cause of the continual weakening of their currencies. (Inflation became so high in Argentina a few years ago that it became necessary to pay employees at noon and the end of each day.)

[9]Francis X. Diebold, Steven Husted, and Mark Rush, "Real Exchange Rates under the Gold Standard," *Journal of Political Economy* 99, no. 6 (1991), pp. 1253–71. This is a study of 16 exchange rates covering more than a century. For each of the 16 exchange rates, it was found that purchasing power parity theory holds in the long term. Other studies also support PPP. For example, see Gayton's study and Treuherz's study, which are both cited in Appendix E to the FASB's 1973 discussion memorandum that preceded *SFAS No. 8.* Other studies are cited in Professor Thomas W. Hall's 1983 article, "Inflation and Rates of Exchange: Support for *SFAS No.52,*" in the Summer 1983 issue of the *Journal of Accounting, Auditing & Finance.*

ILLUSTRATION 16–4	An Application of PPP Theory to the British Pound for the Fifteen Years Ended December 31, 1995

Date	Annual Inflation U.S.	Annual Inflation U.K.	Actual Direct Exchange Rate	Expected Direct Exchange Rate Under PPP Theory	Actual Rate Over (Under) Expected Rate Amount	Actual Rate Over (Under) Expected Rate Percent
1–1–81			$2.40			
1981	9.6%	11.5%				
12–31–81			1.92	$2.35	$(.43)	(18)%
1982	6.5	7.7				
12–31–82			1.62	2.33	(.71)	(30)
1983	3.8	5.3				
12–31–83			1.45	2.30	(.85)	(37)
1984	3.8	4.6				
12–31–84			1.16	2.27	(1.11)	(49)
1985	3.0	5.7				
12–31–85			1.45	2.22	(.77)	(35)
1986	2.6	3.5				
12–31–86			1.48	2.20	(.72)	(33)
1987	3.1	5.0				
12–31–87			1.89	2.16	(.27)	(12)
1988	3.3	6.5				
12–31–88			1.80	2.10	(.30)	(14)
1989	4.1	6.9				
12–31–89			1.61	2.04	(.43)	(21)
1990	4.1	6.8				
12–31–90			1.93	1.99	(.06)	(3)
1991	4.0	6.2				
12–31–91			1.86	1.95	(.09)	(5)
1992	2.9	4.0				
12–31–92			1.51	1.93	(.42)	(22)
1993	2.7	4.2				
12–31–93			1.48	1.90	(.42)	(22)
1994	2.7	3.7				
12–31–94			1.56	1.88	(.32)	(17)
1995	2.5	3.4				
12–31–95			1.54	1.86	(.32)	(17)
Cum.	58.7%	85.0%	Average annual deviation		$(.47)	(22)%

1995, is shown in Illustration 16–4. A more extensive discussion of PPP theory may be found in textbooks on international finance.

REVIEW POINTS FOR ILLUSTRATION 16–4 Note the following:

1. With Great Britain continually experiencing higher inflation than the United States, the spot rate should trend downward under PPP theory; this has occurred as expected.

2. At December 31, 1990 and 1991, the actual spot rates are relatively close to the expected rates under PPP theory.

3. The absolute average year-end percentage deviation from results expected under PPP theory is 22%, which is not unreasonably high such as to suggest that PPP theory is not valid.

ILLUSTRATION	**ANALYZING AN EXCHANGE RATE CHANGE USING PPP: BOTH COUNTRIES HAVE INFLATION, AND NONINFLATIONARY FACTORS EXIST**

How to analyze and explain a change in the exchange rate for a more realistic situation in which (1) the United States has 5% inflation, (2) a foreign country has 10% inflation, and (3) noninflationary factors exist is shown in Illustration 16–5.

ILLUSTRATION 16–5	**Analyzing an Exchange Rate Change Using PPP—Both Countries Have Inflation and Noninflationary Factors Exist**

	Direct Exchange Rate
I. Handling *Foreign* Inflation First Approach:	
Actual rate, 1/1/X1	$2.20
Less: *Decrease* expected because of the foreign country's 10% inflation rate ($2.20/110% = $2.00; $2.20 − $2.00 = $.20	(.20)
Subtotal	$2.00
Plus: *Increase* expected because of the U.S. 5% inflation rate ($2.00 × 5%)	.10
Expected end-of-year rate (under PPP)	$2.10
Plus or minus: Noninflationary factors (forced)	(.03)[a]
Actual rate, 12/31/X1	$2.07
II. Handling *Domestic* Inflation First Approach:	
Actual rate, 1/1/X1	$2.20
Plus: *Increase* expected because of U.S. 5% inflation rate ($2.20 × 5%)	.11
Subtotal	$2.31
Less: *Decrease* expected because of the foreign country's 10% inflation rate ($2.31/110% = $2.10; $2.31 − $2.10 = $.21)	(.21)
Expected end-of-year rate (under PPP)	$2.10
Plus or minus: Noninflationary factors (forced)	(.03)[a]
Actual rate, 12/31/X1	$2.07

III. Formula Approach:

$$\text{Beginning Rate} \times \frac{1 + \text{Domestic Inflation Rate}}{1 + \text{Foreign Inflation Rate}} = \text{Expected Ending Rate}$$

For the above example, the formula calculation is as follows:

$$\$2.20 \times \frac{1.05}{1.10} = \$2.10$$

[a]In international finance texts, this difference is called **the "real" change in the exchange rate**, even though it may be of a temporary delayed nature (a lag under PPP). The $.10 decrease ($2.20 − $2.10) attributable to inflation effects (both domestic and foreign) is called **the "nominal" (in name only) change**.

REVIEW POINTS   Note the following:

1. *Foreign* inflation drives the direct exchange rate *down.*
2. *Domestic* inflation drives the direct exchange rate *up.*
3. The relationship of the U.S. price index before and after inflation (1.00: 1.05 above) is the relationship that exists between the actual exchange rate prior to inflation and the expected exchange rate under PPP ($2.20: $2.31 above). For foreign countries, this relationship is inverse, not direct.

EXERCISE FOR APPENDIX

E 16–1A **Analyzing an Exchange Rate Change** Information concerning the United States and Mexico for 19X1 follows:

Direct exchange rate on 1/1/X1	$.600
Direct exchange rate on 12/31/X1	$.540
U.S. 19X1 inflation rate	5%
Mexico's 19X1 inflation rate	20%

Required
1. Calculate the expected exchange rate at 12/31/X1 under the purchasing power parity theory.
2. Calculate the *nominal* change in the exchange rate for 19X1.
3. Calculate the *real* change in the exchange rate for 19X1.

USING DERIVATIVES TO MANAGE FOREIGN CURRENCY EXPOSURES

17

LEARNING OBJECTIVES

TO UNDERSTAND

- The types of foreign exchange (FX) exposures that exist.
- The way companies protect against FX exposures.
- The fundamentals of using FX option contracts.
- The fundamentals of using FX forward exchange contracts.
- The accounting treatment prescribed for gains and losses on transactions entered into to protect against FX exposures.
- The nature and risks of derivative financial instruments.
- The disclosures required for FX derivatives.

TOPIC OUTLINE

There are two times in one's life when one should not speculate: when one can't afford it and when one can.

MARK TWAIN

W̅e begin this chapter by showing the many different kinds of foreign exchange (FX) exposures that can exist. Next we describe the technique of hedging, which companies routinely use to protect against FX exposures. We then discuss in detail the two types of derivative financial instruments (foreign currency option contracts and foreign currency forward exchange contracts) that are commonly used to hedge FX exposures. After that, we discuss the accounting treatments for hedging gains and losses that occur in hedging the various types of FX exposures.

We then discuss in general the widespread use, nature, and risks of derivative financial instruments to (1) protect against various kinds of exposures and (2) improve returns. This leads into a discussion of disclosures required for all types of derivative financial instruments.

In June 1996, after ten years of research and study, the FASB published for public comment an exposure draft entitled "Accounting for Derivative and Similar Financial Instruments and for Hedging Activities." This proposed standard could become effective in 1997. Of the three categories of FX exposures discussed in this chapter, substantive rule changes are proposed only for the *hedges of forecasted transactions* category. Accordingly, **our discussion of the treatment of FX gains and losses on** *hedges of forecasted transactions* **is based on this proposed standard.**

THE GOVERNING PRONOUNCEMENTS

The accounting standards for FX derivative financial instruments are set forth in *SFAS No. 52*, "Foreign Currency Translation." Disclosures to be made for *all* financial instruments (including derivatives) are prescribed by several FASB statements (80, 105, 107, and 119). The FASB's proposed 1996 standard mentioned above would (1) amend slightly *SFAS No. 52* and *107* and (2) supersede *SFAS No. 80, 105,* and *119* in their entirety when it becomes effective.

I   TYPES OF FOREIGN EXCHANGE (FX) EXPOSURES

Companies having foreign currency transactions and foreign operations are subject to the risk that exchange rates can change adversely, causing losses, lower revenues, or increased costs. Because of the high potential for such adverse effects under the highly volatile exchange rate movements that occur under the current floating exchange rate system, managing foreign exchange (FX) exposures to minimize or prevent possible FX losses has increasingly become a high-level objective for most companies having international operations.

Many companies have (1) hired FX specialists, (2) invested in technology (computers, commercially available foreign currency software programs, and internally developed foreign currency modeling programs), and (3) built small trading rooms that resemble the FX trading rooms of banks and Wall Street investment firms. In turn, this desire to protect against exchange rate change losses has led to an increase in the number of available financial instruments to accomplish this objective.

Companies can manage any or all of the following types of FX exposures:

1. **Asset and liability positions.**
   a. **A parent's exposed individual assets and liabilities.** Such positions result from transactions recorded but *not* yet settled. Examples are (1) receivables and payables on exporting and importing transactions, respectively, and (2) notes receivable and notes payable on lending and borrowing transactions, respectively.

    b. **A foreign subsidiary's net *asset* position.** This is the subsidiary's total assets minus its total liabilities (which equals the parent's investment balance if the subsidiary was *created* and the parent uses the *equity method* of accounting).

    c. **A foreign subsidiary's net *monetary* position.** This is a foreign subsidiary's monetary assets minus its monetary liabilities. Monetary items are cash and accounts contractually obligated to be settled in cash.

2. **Firm commitments.**

    Examples are (1) noncancelable purchase orders placed or noncancelable sales orders received for which delivery has *not* yet occurred, (2) future interest expense that will be paid on loan contracts, and (3) future lease payments on operating leases.

3. **Forecasted transactions.**

    a. **Budgeted exposures.** Examples are (1) a U.S. company's budgeted export revenues or budgeted import purchases, (2) a foreign subsidiary's budgeted revenues (or a percentage of such revenues as a surrogate for budgeted net income), (3) a foreign subsidiary's budgeted net income or budgeted dividend remittances, and (4) outstanding bids.

    b. **Strategic or competitive exposures.** This is the potential for **loss of** future transactions—as opposed to the potential for **loss on** transactions. Examples are as follows:

        (1) Export sales. Export sales may be lost to foreign competitors if the dollar *strengthens* because foreign customers would find that U.S. products are now *more* expensive.

        (2) Domestic sales. Domestic sales may decline if the dollar *strengthens* because domestic customers would find that foreign products are now *less* expensive.

Companies have different policies as to managing the various possible FX exposures. For example, many companies protect exposed assets and liabilities resulting from exporting and importing transactions, respectively, in all cases—this is a board of director's policy for many companies. Other companies, however, have a policy to protect such exposed assets and liabilities only if management expects the exchange rate to change adversely to a significant extent, which is a "view" aiming at profit enhancement.

We discuss in this chapter how to protect against most of these exposures. In Chapter 18, we discuss how to protect a foreign subsidiary's net *asset* position (item 1[b]). In Chapter 19, we discuss how to protect a foreign subsidiary's net *monetary* position (item 1[c]).

SPECULATING VERSUS MANAGING EXPOSURE

In addition, companies can speculate on the direction of future exchange rates for the sole purpose of making profits. For example, Du Pont expects its FX trading department to operate as a profit center. Many companies prohibit speculation, however, thus limiting their activities to protecting against exchange rate change losses on their FX exposures. For example, Ford Motor Company states in its annual report that "company policy specifically prohibits the use of derivatives for speculative purposes." Speculating is discussed briefly later in the chapter.

II   THE TECHNIQUE OF HEDGING

FX exposures are commonly managed by a technique called *hedging*. By hedging, a company can avoid a loss that may otherwise arise. The idea is to have a counterbalancing gain on the financial instrument used to achieve the hedge if a loss occurs on the item being hedged. As identified earlier, the various FX exposures that can be hedged range from an existing FX receivable or FX payable to an anticipated future revenues stream. A specific FX exposure being hedged is commonly called the **hedged item.** The financial instrument used to achieve the hedge is commonly called the **hedging instrument.**

TYPES OF HEDGING INSTRUMENTS

The two most common types of hedging instruments used to hedge FX exposures are (1) **foreign currency forward exchange contracts**[1] (hereafter *FX forwards*) and (2) **foreign currency option contracts** (hereafter *FX options*).[2]

FX FORWARDS   An FX forward has **"two-sided exposure"** because each party potentially has a favorable or unfavorable outcome, depending on which direction the currency exchange rate moves. Consequently, both the downside risk and the upside potential on the hedged item are counterbalanced. Stated differently, a loss or gain on the hedged item will be offset by a gain or loss, respectively, on the hedging transaction. FX forward hedges, if perfectly matched long (receivable) and short (payable), eliminate a risk and return from FX positions.

FX OPTIONS   An FX option has **"one-sided exposure"** because only the option holder pays for the potential of a favorable outcome and the other party (the option writer) receives payment to run the risk of an unfavorable outcome. Consequently, only the downside risk on the hedged item is counterbalanced. Stated differently, any loss on the hedged item can be offset by a gain on the hedging transaction. A gain on the hedged transaction, however, *cannot* be offset by a loss on the hedging transaction because the option holder will let the option expire and thus *not* incur a loss on the hedging transaction.

Because FX options are much simpler to explain than FX forwards, we discuss them first.

REPORTING THE VALUE OF HEDGING INSTRUMENTS IN THE BALANCE SHEET

As illustrated later, hedging instruments are valued during the contract period, and this value is reported on the balance sheet. General ledger accounts such as FX Contract Value—Option and FX Contract Value—Forward, net are used. These accounts *can* accommodate being in either a *receivable* or *payable* position. Thus when these accounts appear in a company's asset and liability sections of its balance sheet, they convey that entity's favorable or unfavorable position, respectively, in the contract.

---

[1]**Foreign Currency Futures**. A financial instrument that is somewhat similar to an FX forward is a *foreign currency future*. These are contracts *standardized* as to amounts and duration; in contrast, *FX forwards* are *customized* as to amounts and duration. Foreign currency futures are used very infrequently by commercial companies for hedging purposes but are used extensively by (1) banking institutions (to hedge their net position) and (2) speculators. A full discussion may be found in international finance texts.

[2]**Foreign Currency Swaps**. Another type of financial instrument that can be used to hedge foreign currency transactions expected to occur in the future is a foreign currency swap. In swaps, the two parties agree to swap future streams of foreign currency cash flows over a specified period. Although swaps are essentially a series of forward-based contracts, they are much more involved than FX forwards because of interest rate considerations. The use of swaps has become widespread for longer term risk management in recent years; however, FX forwards are much more widely used and represent the essential components of swaps.

HEDGE ACCOUNTING

The accounting issue for hedging is whether the gain or loss on the hedging instrument can be accounted for in a symmetrical manner to the loss or gain on the hedged item. Two symmetrical model possibilities exist: (1) recognize both currently in the income statement (in which case they most likely would be netted against each other for display purposes instead of showing both the gain and the loss) or (2) defer recognition of both (again they offset each other). Accordingly, **hedge accounting** is defined as **a special treatment that achieves both (1) counterbalancing and (2) either concurrent recognition or concurrent deferral of mark-to-market adjustments.**

III FX OPTION CONTRACTS

The use of FX options has increased dramatically since 1983, the year the Philadelphia Stock Exchange began offering exchange-traded FX options. In an FX option, one party has **the right to buy or sell a specific quantity of currency at a specified rate** (the **exercise** or **strike** price) during a specified future period.[3] Consequently, the other party is **obligated to deliver** or **take delivery** of the currency if the FX option is exercised.

By definition, options (in general) need *not* be exercised, enabling the purchaser to "walk away" (and thereby lose only the amount paid to purchase the option). Thus there is **only the possibility of gain** as a result of subsequent changes in the spot rate—*not* both a gain or a loss.

OPTION TERMINOLOGY

TYPES AND PARTIES   An option to buy is a **call**. An option to sell is a **put**. The party having the contractual right to buy or sell is the **holder** of the option. From the perspective of the holder, the option contract is referred to as a **purchased option.** The party that grants the holder this contractual right is the **writer** of the option. From the perspective of the writer, the option contract is referred to as a **written option.** (A corporation that has granted an employee a stock option has *written* a *call* option; the employee is the *holder* of the call option.) Each party has conflicting desires concerning the future movement of the exchange rate for the currency involved.

FEES   Because the writer assumes the responsibility of incurring a potential loss, the writer charges a fee, called a **premium** (ranging from 1.5% to 7% of the spot price). Thus the premium is the price paid to acquire the option. FX options are usually substantially more expensive than FX forwards (discussed later).

WHEN TO EXERCISE VERSUS WALK AWAY   When the relationship between the exercise price and the spot price is **favorable to the holder**—in reverse position for puts than for calls—the FX option is said to be **"in the money"** because the holder would exercise the FX option and have a realized gain. On the other hand, when the relationship between the exercise price and the spot price is **unfavorable to the holder,** the FX option is said to be **"out of the money,"** in which case the holder would *not* exercise the option. When the exercise price and the spot price are the same, the FX option is said to be **"at the money."** These situations are shown in Illustration 17–1.

---

[3]This is an *American* option; options that can be exercised only at the expiration date are called *European* options.

ILLUSTRATION 17–1	FX Option Situations			
	Call FX Option		**Put FX Option**	
	Exercise Price (buying price)	Spot Price (selling price)	Exercise Price (selling price)	Spot Price (buying price)
In the money	$ .98	$1.00	$1.02	$1.00
At the money	1.00	1.00	1.00	1.00
Out of the money	1.02	1.00	.98	1.00

The exercise price need not be the same as the spot price at the inception of the option period. During the option period, the holder can sell the FX option in the open market at its market value, which suggests that the FX option should always be valued at its market value.

ACCOUNTING FOR FX OPTION PREMIUMS— A "SPLIT ACCOUNTING" ISSUE

TIME VALUE If at the inception of the FX option, the option is either **out of the money** (the spot price being either *below* the exercise price for a *call* option or *above* the exercise price for a *put* option) or **at the money** (the spot price equaling the exercise price), the entire premium is called the **time value. The time value is analogous to a prepaid insurance premium** that could be amortized to income over the life of the option period using a systematic and rational method (such as straight line). The **time value** of an option is a function of (1) the length of the option period (increases as the duration becomes longer), (2) the interest rate opportunity, and (3) the volatility of the underlying item. The determination of the time value is beyond the scope of this text.

INTRINSIC VALUE On the other hand, if at the inception of the FX option, the option is **in the money** (the spot price being either *above* the exercise price for a *call* option or *below* the exercise price for a *put* option), the option holder will have paid a higher premium—the incremental amount equaling the difference between the spot price and the exercise price—to be placed in this favorable position. This incremental premium paid is called the FX option's **intrinsic value.** Because the intrinsic value may be viewed as being conceptually different from the time value, it theoretically can be accounted for separately from the time value. Carving out the time value and accounting for it separately from the intrinsic value is often referred to as **split accounting.**

NO CURRENT ACCOUNTING STANDARDS CONCERNING SPLIT ACCOUNTING No authoritative accounting standards currently exist regarding whether FX option premiums should be accounted for using split accounting. In *AICPA Issues Paper 86-2,* "Accounting for Options," which is nonauthoritative, the advisory conclusions of the Accounting Standards Executive Committee (AcSEC) of the American Institute of Certified Public Accountants (AICPA) were mixed.[4] Later we illustrate split accounting.

---

[4]The advisory conclusions of AcSEC in AICPA issues papers (which normally represent the views of at least a majority of the committee members) are *not* enforceable standards under Rule 203 of the AICPA's Code of Professional Conduct. AICPA position papers are sent to the FASB for its consideration.

ACCOUNTING FOR CHANGES IN THE INTRINSIC VALUE

MARK-TO-MARKET ACCOUNTING   Subsequent to the inception date of the FX option, any changes in the spot price of the underlying currency are reflected as an adjustment to the FX option's intrinsic value—**with the limitation that the intrinsic value can never be below zero.** Thus the intrinsic value is marked to market and is always measured by (1) the excess of the spot price over the exercise price for a *call* FX option and (2) the excess of the exercise price over the spot price for a *put* FX option. For FX options purchased for hedging purposes, the accounting issue is whether hedge accounting is allowed, that is, concurrent recognition or concurrent deferral of (1) gains or losses on the option and (2) losses or gains on the hedged item.

THE LIMITATIONS OF *SFAS No. 52*   *SFAS No. 52* does *not* specifically refer to FX options—only to FX forwards. If we apply the spirit of *SFAS No. 52*, however, hedge accounting is appropriate when FX options are used to hedge (1) existing exposed assets and liabilities and (2) firmly committed anticipatory transactions. These are the only items discussed in this chapter that qualify for hedge accounting treatment under *SFAS No. 52*. (Hedge accounting treatment is also allowed for the hedge of a net investment in a foreign subsidiary, which is discussed in Chapter 18.)

HEDGING AN EXPOSED LIABILITY POSITION

A company that has a liability in a foreign currency is said to have an **exposed liability.** The domestic importer in Illustration 16–2 agreed to pay Vendor A £100,000 on January 10, 19X2, for inventory purchased. Thus the domestic importer has an exposed liability. To avoid the risk of an exchange rate increase during the period from the transaction date (December 11, 19X1) to the settlement date (January 10, 19X2), the domestic company could enter into a 30-day *call* FX option on December 11, 19X1. Thus the domestic company can effectively determine now, rather than on January 10, 19X2, how many dollars it needs to obtain £100,000.

SETTLING UP AT THE EXPIRATION DATE UPON EXERCISE   If the FX option is in the money at the end of the contract period, the FX option will be exercised. Accordingly, the bank must make delivery and the FX option holder must take delivery of foreign currency. The FX option holder can take delivery either physically or by instructing the bank to deliver the currency to its overseas vendor via a bank wire transfer. In a **bank wire transfer,** which is the customary practice, the domestic importer's bank would (1) *charge* (debit) the *domestic importer's* bank account (in dollars) at the strike price and (2) then instruct an overseas branch (via telex) to *credit* the *overseas vendor's* bank account (in foreign currency), thereby extinguishing the liability to the foreign vendor (as reflected in the FX Accounts Payable account). All illustrations assume the use of bank wire transfers.[5]

| ILLUSTRATION | HEDGING AN EXPOSED LIABILITY |

Illustration 17–2 shows the entries that would be made under a 30-day call FX option entered into to protect Vendor A's exposed liability of £100,000. For comparative purposes, we also show the entries relating to Vendor A, as shown in

[5]If, however, the company were to physically take delivery of the foreign currency from the FX trader, a *debit* to a £ Cash account would be made. Later when the foreign currency is physically delivered to the vendor, the £ Cash account is *credited* and the £ Accounts Payable account is debited.

ILLUSTRATION 17–2   **Hedging an Exposed Liability Position: Call FX Option Journal Entries**

Transaction With Vendor (same as in Illustration 16–2)		*Hedging Transaction*	

December 11, 19X1
(the transaction date and the inception
of the 30-day *call* FX option period)

Inventory $150,000		FX Contract Value—Option .. $1,500	
£ Accounts Payable . . .	$150,000	Cash	$1,500
To record the		To record the cost of the	
inventory purchase.		call option acquired.	
(£100,000 × $1.50 = $150,000)			

December 31, 19X1
(an intervening balance sheet date)

FX Loss $5,000		FX Contract Value—Option .. $5,000	
£ Accounts Payable . . .	$5,000	FX Gain—Option	$5,000
To adjust the pound payable		To adjust the option's	
to the current spot rate.		intrinsic value to market.	
($1.55 − $1.50 = $.05)		($.05 × £100,000 = $5,000)	
($.05 × £100,000 = $5,000)			
		Hedging Expense $1,000	
		FX Contract Value—	
		Option	$1,000
		To amortize the time value.	
		($1,500 × 20/30 = $1,000)	

January 10, 19X2
(the settlement date)

FX Loss $2,000		FX Contract Value—Option .. $2,000	
£ Accounts Payable . . .	$2,000	FX Gain—Option	$2,000
To adjust the pound payable		To adjust the option's	
to the current spot rate.		intrinsic value to market.	
($1.57 − $1.55 = $.02)		($.02 × £100,000 = $2,000)	
($.02 × £100,000 = $2,000)			
		Hedging Expense $500	
		FX Contract Value—	
		Option	$500
		To amortize the time value.	
		($1,500 × 10/30 = $500)	

£ Accounts Payable $157,000	
FX Contract Value—	
Option	$7,000
Cash	$150,000
To exercise the option and	
pay vendor **via a bank wire**	
transfer. (The bank charges	
the company's checking	
account $150,000 [**the**	
strike price of $1.50 ×	
£100,000].)	

FX CONTRACT VALUE—OPTION

12/11/X1	$1,500	
	5,000	
		1,000
12/31/X1	$5,500[a]	
	2,000	
		500
1/10/X2	$7,000	

[a]Reported as an asset on the importer's 12/31/X1 balance sheet.

Illustration 16–2 on page 551). The direct exchange rates for the applicable dates in December 19X1 and January 19X2 (when the pound was *strengthening*) are as follows:

	December 11, 19X1 (inception date)	December 31, 19X1 (a financial reporting date)	January 10, 19X2 (expiration date)
Spot rate.	$1.50	$1.55	$1.57

REVIEW POINTS FOR ILLUSTRATION 17–2   Note the following:

1. **Independence of transactions.** Although the hedging transaction achieves the desired mirror effect of what occurs on the hedged item, the FX option is a transaction independent of the company's transaction with Vendor A. Accordingly, the accounting entries for each transaction are prepared without regard to the other transaction. Thus the entries for the importing transaction with Vendor A are the same whether or not the company entered into the hedging transaction.

2. **Total offset.** During the 30-day period of the FX option, the pound strengthened from $1.50 to $1.57. Without the FX option, the $7,000 additional amount payable to Vendor A would *not* have been offset by the $7,000 FX gain on the option.

3. **Amounts reported in the income statement.** No compelling reason exists to display the $5,000 loss and the $5,000 gain for 19X1 separately in the income statement. Accordingly, they would be netted against each other.

4. **A perfect hedge.** This hedge is called a *"perfect" hedge* because (1) the amount of currency in the FX option (£100,000) equals the amount of foreign currency owed the vendor and (2) the expiration date of the FX option coincides (by design) with the settlement date on the importing transaction. If the amount of currency on the hedging transaction *exceeded* the amount of currency owed the vendor, such excess would be treated as a speculation (discussed later). A difference in the expiration and settlement dates presents no accounting issues for this exposure category.

5. **Result if the exchange rate had decreased.** If instead of increasing from $1.50 to $1.57 the spot exchange rate had decreased to $1.43, the company would have had (1) a $7,000 gain on its importing transaction and (2) no gain on its FX option because the FX option would *not* have been exercised. The *premium*, however, would be amortized to income over the life of the option period.

HEDGING AN EXPOSED ASSET POSITION

A company that has a receivable in a foreign currency is said to have an **exposed asset.** An **exposed asset** most often results from an exporting transaction in which payment is to be received in the foreign currency. In these situations, the domestic exporter would buy a *put* FX option to hedge its exposed asset position. The accounting for a put FX option is identical to that shown in Illustration 17–2. Thus the FX option holder (1) charges the cost of the FX option (the time value element) to the FX Contract Value—Option account, (2) amortizes this cost over the life of the option period, and (3) adjusts the FX Contract Value—Option account upward if the FX option goes into the money (and thus has intrinsic value). If the option holder exercises the FX option (occurs only if it is in the money), the option holder must now *deliver* foreign currency (that it does *not* have on hand) to the bank. Customarily, this is done when payment is received from the customer via a bank wire transfer.

BANK WIRE TRANSFER PROCEDURES   The foreign customer's payment to the domestic exporter using a bank wire transfer is deemed as having made delivery of the foreign currency to the domestic exporter's bank. Procedurally, the foreign customer instructs its bank to transfer by wire the appropriate amount of foreign currency, say £200,000, to the U.S. domestic exporter's bank account. That foreign bank would then (1) *charge* the *foreign customer's* checking account £200,000 and (2) telex the domestic exporter's U.S. bank with instructions to *credit* the *domestic exporter's* bank account for the spot rate dollar equivalent of the £200,000. Because of the put FX option, however, the bank will credit the domestic exporter's account at the strike price.

IV FX FORWARD EXCHANGE CONTRACTS: BASICS

An *FX forward* is an agreement to buy or sell a foreign currency at (1) **a specified future date** (usually within 12 months) and (2) **a specified exchange rate.** This rate is called the *forward rate*, and it usually is slightly above or below the spot rate for reasons explained more fully later. For now, it is important to realize that one component of this difference is the amount to compensate the FX trader (a bank) for assuming the risk that the exchange rate could change adversely.[6] **Thus eliminating FX exposure involves a cost whether FX forwards or FX options are used.**

FX forwards are widely used because they generally are far less expensive than other types of financial instruments that could be used to transfer FX exposure risk to a FX trader. The FX trader's exposure risk can then be "laid off" (shifted) to other customers, which lowers the FX trader's required commissions.

"LOCKING INTO" A PRICE

By entering into an FX forward, the company "locks into" a price to be paid or received for the foreign currency to be exchanged. Thus a company determines *now* the number of dollars that it (1) needs to acquire foreign currency to settle in the future an FX payable with a foreign vendor or (2) will receive in the future in settlement of an FX receivable from a foreign customer.

AVAILABILITY OF FORWARD MARKETS

Active FX forward markets exist only for the major trading currencies (Japanese yen, German mark, British pound, French franc, Canadian dollar, Swiss franc, Italian lira, Belgian franc, Spanish peseta, and Dutch guilder). FX forward markets for other less developed countries are either limited or nonexistent, with the result that either (1) credit terms may not be as generous or (2) companies take other steps, when possible, to protect their foreign currency exposures. (Some of these other steps are listed later in the chapter.)

THE CUSTOMIZABLE NATURE OF FORWARD EXCHANGE CONTRACTS Newspapers commonly provide daily quotations of FX forward exchange rates for 30-, 90-, and 180-day periods, erroneously implying that FX forwards are available only for these periods. A unique feature of FX forwards, however, is that they can be customized as to both (1) the amount of currency and (2) the time period. Thus a company can obtain, for example, a 44-day FX forward to buy or sell £55,555.

THE REQUIREMENT TO TAKE OR MAKE DELIVERY

Unlike FX options, in which the option holder can chose *not* to exercise the FX option and thus walk away from the contract, **FX forwards require execution by each party at the expiration date of the contract.** In virtually all cases, **execution occurs**

---

[6]Technically, forward exchange contracts can be viewed as bilateral market price risk insurance agreements because each party is both insurer and insured but for opposite directions of price change.

simultaneously. (For compensation, however, FX forwards can be undone prior to execution, as discussed shortly.)

BUYING FORWARD   When the FX forward involves *buying* a foreign currency (commonly referred to as *buying forward*), **the buyer must *take* delivery from the dealer**—either physically or by designating where the foreign currency should be deposited (such as in a foreign vendor's bank account for a bank wire transfer in settlement of an inventory-importing transaction).

SELLING FORWARD   When the FX forward involves *selling* a foreign currency (commonly referred to as *selling forward*), **the seller must *make* delivery to the dealer**—either physically or by having a third party deposit the foreign currency in an overseas bank (as is done for a bank wire transfer in settlement of an inventory-exporting transaction).

THE EXECUTORY NATURE OF FORWARD EXCHANGE CONTRACTS

FX forwards are executory contracts for which no general ledger entries need be recorded on the books at the time they are entered into. This executory nature becomes more evident when considering the fact that FX traders will generally allow their customers to undo FX forwards prior to their execution, providing that the customer pays for transaction costs and any adverse change in the spot rate from the bank's perspective.

Substantively, the company has merely **issued a purchase order to acquire (or accepted a sales order to sell) a foreign currency** (a commodity). Recall that the issuance of inventory purchase orders and the receipt of inventory sales orders are also executory in nature and are *not* recorded on the books until fulfillment of the orders—that is, **until one of the parties has performed** its half of the transaction by shipping the inventory. Thus assets and liabilities are *not* created when an FX forward is entered into. For this reason, in practice, companies do *not* make any general ledger entries at the inception of an FX forward.[7]

The disclosures currently being made in annual reports pursuant to the requirements of *SFAS No 107*, "Disclosures About Fair Values of Financial Instruments," clearly show that companies do *not* make general ledger entries at the inception of forward exchange contracts. They track the FX forwards they have outstanding, however, on a memorandum basis just as they track their sales order backlogs on a memorandum basis.

For pedagogical purposes only, however, it is useful to show entries being made in the general ledger at the inception of the FX forward—a **"gross"** or **"broad"** manner of accounting—to best convey the concept of counterbalancing. Accordingly, we do so for the first FX forward hedging illustration. Later FX forward hedging illustrations (and all solutions to the assignment material) reflect the customary practice of *not* making entries at the inception of the FX forward—a **"net position" manner of accounting.**

---

[7]Paragraph 4.23 (p. 63) of FASB *Discussion Memorandum*, "Recognition and Measurement of Financial Instruments" (1991), states that "in present practice, forward contracts with no consideration paid at inception by either party are generally not recognized."

The illustrative journal entries presented in paragraph A58 of *Exposure Draft E48*, "Financial Instruments" (January 1994), issued by the International Accounting Standards Committee show the customary practice of *not* recording the obligations of each party as assets and liabilities at the inception of the forward contract.

SFAS No. 80, "Accounting for Futures Contracts," also specifically prohibits booking notional values of future contracts.

DISCUSSION ASSUMING THAT THE SPOT RATE EQUALS THE FORWARD RATE

Accounting for the difference between the spot rate and the forward rate slightly complicates the accounting for FX forwards. Accordingly, for simplicity, we assume that the forward rate and the spot rate are identical at the inception of the contract. Later we address accounting for the difference. This allows for the entire focus to be on the concept of counterbalancing.

HEDGING EXPOSED LIABILITIES

The domestic importer in Illustration 16–2 agreed to pay Vendor A £100,000 on January 10, 19X2, for inventory purchased. Thus the domestic importer has an exposed liability. To avoid the risk of an exchange rate *increase* during the period from the transaction date (December 11, 19X1) to the settlement date (January 10, 19X2), the domestic company could enter into a 30-day FX forward on December 11, 19X1, agreeing to purchase £100,000 on January 10, 19X2, at the currently existing forward exchange rate. Consequently, the domestic company determines now, rather than on January 10, 19X2, how many dollars it needs to obtain £100,000 to settle its FX accounts payable balance. Thus the domestic importer is "buying forward." (A domestic exporter "sells forward" to hedge an exposed asset [an FX accounts receivable] as discussed later.)

The contractual obligations under an FX forward in which a domestic importer buys forward are as follows:

1. **Contractual obligation *to* the FX trader.** The domestic importer is obligated to pay the FX trader the agreed upon price (as determined by the forward rate) at the expiration date of the contract. Thus this obligation is a *fixed amount*—regardless of what may happen to the spot rate during the period of the contract. As stated earlier, the result is that the domestic importer has locked into the number of dollars needed to discharge its FX accounts payable to its foreign vendor.

2. **Contractual obligation *of* the FX trader.** The trader is obligated to deliver the agreed upon amount of foreign currency to the domestic importer at the expiration date of the contract. Thus the value of the foreign currency to be received from the FX trader may fluctuate during the period of the contract as a result of changes in the spot rate. The fluctuating nature of the value of this obligation (a future asset of the domestic company) is what creates the counterbalancing to the domestic importer's FX Accounts Payable account that also fluctuates in value as a result of changes in the spot rate.

Assuming that the spot rate and the 30-day forward rate are both $1.50 for the British pound at the inception of the forward contract, a journal entry to record the obligations at the inception of an FX forward for the purchase of £100,000 for delivery in 30 days is as follows:

£ Due *from* FX trader (**a variable amount**)	$150,000[a]	
$ Due *to* FX trader (**a fixed amount**)		$150,000[b]
To record the future obligations under the forward exchange contract.		

[a](£100,000 × $1.50 spot rate)
[b](£100,000 × $1.50 forward rate)

USE OF "DUE TO" AND "DUE FROM" ACCOUNTS   To readily distinguish these two accounts from accounts used to record importing and exporting transactions (FX Accounts Payable and FX Accounts Receivable), we us *due to* and *due from* terminology exclusively for FX forwards. Furthermore, to differentiate between these two accounts (one requiring settlement in U.S. dollars and the other in a foreign currency), we use the account **$ Due to FX Trader** for the fixed obligation to the FX trader and the account **£ Due from FX Trader** for the value of the foreign currency to be received from the FX trader.

SUBSEQUENT ADJUSTMENTS AT INTERVENING BALANCE SHEET DATES At subsequent intervening balance sheet dates before the contract expiration date, the £ Due from FX Dealer account is adjusted to reflect **the spot rate on that date.** These adjustments result in **unrealized** FX gains and losses, which offset the unrealized FX losses or gains, respectively, on the domestic importer's exposed liability to the foreign vendor. Such adjustments may be viewed as adjustments to the **intrinsic value** of the contract. (A **time value** element also exists, but that relates to accounting for the difference between the spot rate and the forward rate, which is discussed later.)

SETTLING UP AT THE EXPIRATION DATE At the end of the contract period, the $ Due to FX Trader account is extinguished by the payment of cash (dollars) to the dealer, and the £ Due from FX Trader account is extinguished by taking delivery of the foreign currency from the foreign currency dealer. In a **bank wire transfer,** which is the customary practice, the FX trader (the domestic importer's bank) (1) *charges* (debits) the *domestic importer's* bank account (in dollars) for the fixed obligation amount due the FX trader and (2) then instructs an overseas branch (via telex) to *credit* the *overseas vendor's* bank account (in foreign currency), thereby extinguishing the liability to the foreign vendor (as reflected in the FX Accounts Payable account). All illustrations assume the use of bank wire transfers.[8]

| **ILLUSTRATION** | **HEDGING AN EXPOSED LIABILITY** |

Illustration 17–3 shows the entries that would be made under an FX forward entered into to protect the exposed liability of the £100,000 inventory purchase transaction with Vendor A. For comparative purposes, we also show the entries relating to Vendor A, as shown earlier in Illustration 17–2. The direct exchange rates for the applicable dates in December 19X1 and January 19X2 (when the pound was strengthening) are as follows:

	December 11, 19X1 (inception date)	December 31, 19X1 (a financial reporting date)	January 10, 19X2 (expiration date)
Spot rate.......	$1.50	$1.55	$1.57
Forward rate....	1.50[a]	1.55[a]	n/a

[a]Recall that the forward rate generally differs from the spot rate but that, for simplicity, we are temporarily assuming that they are identical to focus on the concept of achieving an offsetting gain in the event of a loss on the vendor transaction. Furthermore, as one moves closer to the expiration date, the difference between the spot rate and the forward rate for the remaining period of the contract becomes smaller and smaller so that **at the expiration date, the forward rate will have converged with the spot rate.**

---

[8]If, however, the company were to physically take delivery of the foreign currency from the FX trader, a *debit* to the £ Cash account would be made. Later when the foreign currency is physically delivered to the vendor, the £ Cash account is *credited* and the £ Accounts Payable account is *debited.*

ILLUSTRATION 17–3 Hedging an Exposed Liability : FX Forward—*Gross* or *Broad* Accounting Journal Entries

Transaction With Vendor (same as in Illustration 16–2)	*Hedging Transaction*

December 11, 19X1
(the transaction date and the inception of the FX Forward)

Inventory	$150,000		£ Due from FX Trader	$150,000[a]	
£ Accounts Payable . . .		$150,000	$ Due to FX Trader		$150,000[b]

To record inventory
purchase.
(£100,000 × $1.50 = $150,000)

To record obligations
under forward contract.
[a](£100,000 × $1.50 spot rate)
[b](£100,000 × $1.50 forward rate); **blocking signifies
a fixed amount.**

December 31, 19X1
(an intervening balance sheet date)

FX Loss	$5,000		£ Due from FX Trader	$5,000	
£ Accounts Payable		$5,000	FX Gain—Forward		$5,000

To adjust the pound payable
to the current spot rate.
($1.55 − $1.50 = $.05)
($.05 × £100,000 = $5,000)

To adjust the pound
receivable to the current
spot rate.
($1.55 − $1.50 = $.05)
($.05 × £100,000 = $5,000)

January 10, 19X2
(the settlement date)

FX Loss	$2,000		£ Due from FX Trader	$2,000	
£ Accounts Payable		$2,000	FX Gain—Forward		$2,000

To adjust the pound payable
to the current spot rate.
($1.57 − $1.55 = $.02)
($.02 × £100,000 = $2,000)

To adjust the pound
receivable to the current
spot rate.
($1.57 − $1.55 = $.02)
($.02 × £100,000 = $2,000)

£ Accounts Payable	$157,000		$ Due to FX Trader	$150,000	
Cash		$157,000	Cash	$7,000	
			£ Due from FX Trader . .		$157,000

To record payment to
vendor **via a bank wire
transfer.**

To settle up with the
FX Trader.

Note: Procedurally, the FX trader (a bank) charges the company's checking account at the forward rate, which is the net amount of $150,000 ($157,000 − $7,000). Thus only a single amount appears on the company's bank statement.

Shortcut Approach at the January 10, 19X2, Settlement Date
(not making a separate adjustment to reflect the current spot rate)

FX Loss	$2,000		Cash	$7,000	
£ Accounts Payable	$155,000		$ Due to FX Trader	$150,000	
Cash		$157,000	£ Due from FX Trader . .		$155,000
			FX Gain—Forward		$2,000

REVIEW POINTS FOR ILLUSTRATION 17–3   Note the following:

1. **Independence of transactions.** Although the hedging transaction achieves the desired mirror effect of what occurs on the hedged item, the FX forward is a separate transaction from the company's transaction with Vendor A. Accordingly, the accounting entries for each transaction are prepared without regard to the other transaction. Thus the entries for the importing transaction with Vendor A are the same whether or not the company entered into the hedging transaction.

2. **Total break even.** During the 30-day period of the contract, the pound strengthened from $1.50 to $1.57. Without the FX forward, the $7,000 additional amount payable to Vendor A would *not* have been offset by the $7,000 FX gain on the FX forward.

3. **Amounts reported in the income statement.** No compelling reason exists to display the $5,000 loss and the $5,000 gain for 19X1 separately in the income statement. Accordingly, they would be netted against each other.

4. **A perfect hedge.** This hedge is called a *"perfect" hedge* because (1) the amount of currency in the FX forward contract (£100,000) equaled the amount of foreign currency owed the vendor and (2) the expiration date of the forward exchange contract coincided (by design) with the settlement date of the importing transaction. If the amount of currency on the hedging transaction *exceeded* the amount of currency owed the vendor, such excess would be treated as a speculation (discussed later). A difference in the expiration and settlement dates presents no accounting issues for this category of exposure.

5. **Selling forward instead of buying forward by mistake.** If management had unintentionally and mistakenly *sold forward* instead of *bought forward*, the company would have had two $7,000 losses because the FX forward would have been in the *same* direction as the exposed liability—not the *opposite* direction. Thus there would have been no counterbalancing or offsetting to the exposed liability—an additional future £ liability would have been created instead of an offsetting future £ asset.

6. **Result if the exchange rate had decreased.** If instead of increasing from $1.50 to $1.57 the spot exchange rate had decreased to $1.43, the company would have had (1) a $7,000 FX *gain* on its importing transaction and (2) a $7,000 FX *loss* on its FX forward. Perfect hedging results in a riskless position, but it also results in a profitless, winless outcome, with uncertainty existing only in execution by the counterparty (credit risk).

REPORTING RECEIVABLES AND PAYABLES UNDER FORWARD CONTRACTS AT NET AMOUNTS Because the legal *right of setoff* [9] (which arose as a practical way to eliminate unnecessary transactions between parties holding mutual debts) usually exists in FX forwards, it is customary practice to report in the balance sheet the company's net position in the contract (the fair value of the contract) rather than reporting each party's obligations.[10] Using Illustration 17–3, the net amount that would be reported in the balance sheet at December 31, 19X1, is calculated as follows:

---

[9]A 1913 Supreme Court decision stated that setoff removes "the absurdity of making A pay B when B owes A." *Studley* v. *Boylston National Bank of Boston*, 229 U.S. 523, 57 L.Ed. 1313, 33 S.Ct.806. (1913). (The right of setoff may *not* be available in some situations, such as when the counterparty is in a foreign country that does *not* recognize this right.)

[10]*FASB Interpretation No. 39*, "Offsetting of Amounts Related to Certain Contracts" (an interpretation of *APB Opinion No. 10* and *FASB Statement No. 105* issued in March 1992), clarifies when offsetting is allowed. For an individual contract, reporting the net position in the contract is always allowed). When multiple contracts exist, a net receivable position on *one* contract may or may not be offset against a net payable position on a *different* contract as explained next.

Multiple Contracts with the Same FX Trader. When multiple contracts exist with the *same* FX trader, a net receivable position on one contract *can* be offset against a net payable position on another contract *only* if a master netting arrangement exists. Under a **master netting arrangement,** a default on any one contract enables all of the separate contracts to be treated as one contract. This entitles the other party to terminate the entire arrangement and to demand the net settlement of all of the individual contracts.

Multiple Contracts with Different FX Traders. When multiple contracts exist with *different* traders, offsetting is *not* permitted.

	Dr. (Cr.)
£ Due from FX trader	$155,000
$ Due to FX trader	(150,000)
Net Position (a receivable)	$ 5,000

Because the $5,000 net amount is the fair value of the contract, the requirement of *SFAS No. 107* to disclose the fair value of all financial instruments (either in the balance sheet or in notes to the financial statements) is achieved. Under *SFAS No. 105* (disclosures about off-balance-sheet risk), the contract amount of $155,000 (£100,000 × $1.55 spot rate) must be disclosed.

NET POSITION ACCOUNTING FOR FORWARD CONTRACTS

In Illustration 17–3, the journal entry amounts recorded at the inception of the contract reflected the contractual obligations of both parties—a *gross* or *broad* manner of recording. Although this approach has value for instructional purposes, it is *not* used in practice. Instead, companies make no journal entry at the inception of the contract. At each subsequent reporting date, **adjustments are made to reflect any change in the spot rate.**

Consequently, these procedures result in reflecting in the general ledger only the net position with the FX trader. This manner of accounting is shown in Illustration 17–4.[11] Again for simplicity, we assume that the forward rate and the spot rate are identical at the inception of the contract.

HEDGING AN EXPOSED ASSET

A company that has a receivable in a foreign currency has an **exposed asset.** The accounting for this situation is symmetrical to that shown for exposed liabilities. An exposed asset most often results from an exporting transaction in which payment is to be received in the foreign currency. In these situations, the domestic exporter agrees to **sell a specified number of foreign currency units at a specified future date** to the FX trader. Because the domestic company is *selling* foreign currency under the FX forward, the **amount in dollars that it will receive from the FX trader is fixed.** Thus the domestic exporter "locks into" the number of dollars it will receive from its foreign customer.

COUNTERBALANCING   In exchange for this fixed amount of dollars, the domestic company will deliver foreign currency to the FX trader. Disregarding the exporting transaction, the domestic company would have to buy the foreign currency from the FX trader so that it can deliver it to the FX trader to fulfill its obligation under the FX forward. This obligation (a future liability of the domestic company) creates the counterbalancing position to the domestic exporter's FX Accounts Receivable account balance with its foreign customer. Consequently, any change in the spot rate produces an FX gain or loss on the FX forward, which offsets the FX loss or gain, respectively, on the domestic exporter's FX Accounts Receivable.

SETTLING UP AT THE EXPIRATION DATE   Assume that a domestic exporter (1) has a £200,000 receivable from a foreign customer, (2) sells forward £200,000 at

---

[11]**Net Position Accounting.** This manner of accounting for forward exchange contracts is consistent with the illustrations contained in Arthur Andersen & Co.'s Participant Guide for the foreign exchange management seminars that it periodically conducts. AA & Co. partners who specialize in consulting on managing foreign exchange exposure indicated that their illustrations are based on industry practice. Inquiries to audit partners of other international Big Six accounting firms also confirm that companies account for forward exchange contracts in this manner—no general ledger entry is made on the books at the inception of the forward contract to reflect the obligations of each of the parties. Instead, the prevailing practice is to record a memorandum entry, which serves to track FX forwards (executory contracts) that are outstanding. Also see *SFAS No. 80*, "Accounting for Futures."

ILLUSTRATION 17–4	**Hedging an Exposed Liability: FX Forward—*Net Position* Accounting Journal Entries**

Transaction With Vendor
(same as in Illustration 16–2 and 17–3)   ***Hedging Transaction***

December 11, 19X1
(the transaction date and the inception
of the 30-day FX forward)

Inventory . . . . $150,000   Memorandum entry only.
    £ Accounts Payable . . . $150,000
    To record the
      inventory purchase.
   (£100,000 × $1.50 = $150,000)

December 31, 19X1
(an intervening balance sheet date)

FX Loss . . . . $5,000   *FX Contract Value—*
    £ Accounts Payable . . . $5,000   *Forward, **net** . . . .*   *$5,000*
    To adjust the pound payable   *FX Gain—Forward . . . . . .*   *$5,000*
      to the current spot rate.   *To mark to market the*
   ($1.55 − $1.50 = $.05)   *net position with the*
   ($.05 × £100,000 = $5,000)   *FX Trader.*
                                    ($.05 × £100,000 = $5,000)

January 10, 19X2
(the settlement date)

FX Loss . . . . $2,000   *FX Contract Value—*
    £ Accounts Payable . . . $2,000   *Forward **net** . . . .*   *$2,000*
    To adjust the pound payable   *FX Gain—Forward . . . .*   *$2,000*
      to the current spot rate.   *To mark to market the*
   ($1.57 − $1.55 = $.02)   *net position with the*
   ($.02 × £100,000 = $2,000)   *FX Trader.*
                                      ($.02 × £100,000 = $2,000)

£ Accounts Payable $157,000
    Cash $150,000
    FX Contract Value—
      Forward $7,000
    To record payment to vendor
    via a bank wire transfer.
    (The bank charges the
    company's checking
    account $150,000 [**the**
    forward rate of $1.50 ×
    £100,000].)

FX CONTRACT VALUE—FORWARD, NET

12/11/X1		
	$5,000	
12/31/X1	$5,000[a]	
	2,000	
1/10/X2	$7,000	

[a]Reported as an asset on the importer's 12/31/X1 balance sheet.

---

the forward rate of $1.52 on December 21, 19X1, when the spot rate (direct) was $1.52, and (3) receives payment from the customer via a bank wire transfer on January 20, 19X2, when the spot rate is $1.60. The use of bank wire transfer procedures is considered as the domestic exporter having made delivery to the FX trader. The procedure is for the foreign customer to instruct its bank to wire transfer £200,000 to the U.S. domestic exporter bank account. That foreign bank then (1) *charges* the *foreign customer's* checking account for £200,000 and (2) telexes the domestic exporter's U.S. bank with instructions to *credit* the *domestic exporter's* bank account for the dollar equivalent of £200,000 at the spot rate of $1.60 (the amount is $320,000). Because of the FX forward, however, the bank *credits* the *domestic exporter's* account at the forward rate of $1.52 (the amount is $304,000). Thus the FX trader records a $16,000 gain on the difference.

Illustration 17–5 shows the entries for hedging an exposed asset using the exporting transaction shown for Customer X in Illustration 16–2. For comparative purposes, we also show the entries relating to Customer A, as shown in Illustration 16–2. The direct exchange rates at the applicable dates are repeated here for convenience:

	December 21, 19X1 (inception date)	December 31, 19X1 (a financial reporting date)	January 20, 19X2 (expiration date)
Spot rate	$1.52	$1.55	$1.60
Forward rate . . .	1.52[a]	1.55[a]	n/a

[a]Assumed to be equal to the spot rate.

ILLUSTRATION 17–5   Hedging an Exposed Asset: FX Forward—Net Position Accounting Journal Entries

Transaction With Customer (same as in Illustration 16–2)	Hedging Transaction

December 21, 19X1
(the transaction date and the inception of the 30-day FX forward)

£ Accounts Receivable $304,000
  Sales $304,000
  To record sale.
  (£200,000 × $1.52 = $304,000)

Memorandum entry only.

December 31, 19X1
(an intervening balance sheet date)

£ Accounts Receivable $6,000
  FX Gain $6,000
  To adjust the pound
    receivable to the current
    spot rate.
  ($1.55 – $1.52 = $.03)
  ($.03 × £200,000 = $6,000)

FX Loss—Forward $6,000
  FX Contract—
    Forward, **net** $6,000
  To mark to market the
    net position with the
    FX Trader.
  ($.03 × £200,000 = $6,000)

January 20, 19X2
(the settlement date)

£ Accounts Receivable $10,000
  FX Gain $10,000
  To adjust the pound
    receivable to the current
    spot rate.
  ($1.60 – $1.55 = $.05)
  ($.05 × £200,000 = $10,000)

FX Loss—Forward $10,000
  FX Contract—
    Forward, **net** $10,000
  To mark to market the
    net position with the
    FX Trader.
  ($.05 × £200,000 = $10,000)

Cash $304,000
FX Contract Value—
  Forward, **net** $16,000
    £ Accounts Receivable . $320,000
  To record payment to
    vendor **via a bank wire
    transfer.** (The bank credits
    the company's checking
    account $304,000 [**the
    forward rate of $1.52 ×
    £200,000**].)

FX CONTRACT VALUE—FORWARD, NET

	12/21/X1
$ 6,000	12/31/X1
$ 6,000[a]	
10,000	
$16,000	1/20/X2

[a]Reported as a liability on the exporter's 12/31/X1 balance sheet.

REVIEW POINTS FOR ILLUSTRATION 17–5 Note the following:

1. **Total offset.** The FX gains on the exporting transactions are exactly offset by FX losses on the hedging transaction.

2. **Potential default by the foreign customer.** If the foreign customer does *not* pay the domestic exporter by the expiration date of the contract and does not obtain an extension on the contract, the domestic exporter must purchase £200,000 from its bank so that it has £200,000 to deliver to its bank in fulfillment of its obligation under the FX forward. Procedurally at the January 20, 19X2, expiration date, the bank (1) *charges* the *domestic exporter's* account $320,000 for the purchase of the £200,000 (the current spot rate of $1.60 × £200,000 = $320,000), (2) retains possession of the British pounds (the equivalent of the domestic exporter making delivery to the dealer on the contract), and (3) *credits* the exporter's account at the fixed selling prices of $304,000 (the forward rate of $1.52 × £200,000).

3. **Result if the exchange rate had decreased.** If instead of increasing from $1.50 to $1.57 the spot exchange rate had decreased to $1.43, the company would have had (1) a $7,000 FX *loss* on its exporting transaction and (2) a $7,000 FX *gain* on its FX forward.

COMPARING FORWARD EXCHANGE CONTRACTS TO OPTIONS

Because either a gain or loss can occur on an FX forward, FX forwards differ considerably from FX options, in which only a gain can occur for the FX option's holder. For this reason, FX options are preferred when the occurrence of the FX transaction is uncertain.

CASE IN POINT

The Dramatic Difference Between a Forward Contract and an Option Contract

Many state and corporate pension funds use foreign currency hedges to protect their investments in foreign stocks in the event that the dollar strengthens. The investment managers of Alaska's Permanent Fund (its oil fund) lost $38 million in 1990–1992 using FX forwards to protect against the dollar strengthening; unfortunately, the dollar weakened (and the foreign stocks did *not* appreciate in value to offset the FX losses on the FX forwards). Using FX options instead would have avoided such losses.

Source: "Pension Fund Managers Find Currency Hedge Is Risky Business," *The Wall Street Journal*, August 18, 1992, p. C–1.

THE "TWO-OPTIONS" VIEW The "holder" and "issuer" (or "writer") categories are generally *not* used in the context of FX forwards as they are in the context of FX options. Under the "two-options" view, however, the substance of an FX forward is viewed as being an arrangement in which each party effectively has written an option to the other. Thus each party is considered both a writer *and* a holder (a *call* being *written* in one currency and a *put* being *held* in the other currency). One of the options will always be executed because one of the parties will always be in a favorable position (in the money) while the other party will be in an unfavorable position (out of the money).[12]

---

[12]This would *not* occur, however, in rare instances in which the spot rate at the end of the contract period coincidentally equals the forward rate at the inception of the contract; no sound reason would exist for the parties to exchange currencies in such circumstances.

V   FX FORWARD EXCHANGE CONTRACTS: PREMIUMS AND DISCOUNTS

Earlier we stated that the forward rate usually differs slightly from the spot rate and that one component of this difference is the fee or commission that the FX trader charges for assuming the risk that the exchange rate could change adversely. Before discussing how the FX trader's commission is embedded into the forward rate, we discuss the other component—a time value of money element—that usually accounts for the major portion of the difference.

THE PRIMARY REASON THAT THE SPOT RATE AND FORWARD RATE USUALLY DIFFER: THE INTEREST RATE PARITY SYSTEM

The difference between the spot rate and the forward rate that usually exists is primarily attributable to the difference in interest rates obtainable on the two currencies in the international money market for the duration of the contract.

FOREIGN INTEREST RATE IS *HIGHER* THAN THE U.S. INTEREST RATE   When the interest rate obtainable on the foreign currency is *higher* than the interest rate obtainable on the U.S. dollar, the forward exchange rate is *lower* than the spot rate, and the foreign currency is said to be **selling at a discount on the forward market.**

FOREIGN INTEREST RATE IS *LOWER* THAN THE U.S. INTEREST RATE   On the other hand, when the interest rate obtainable on the foreign currency is *lower* than the interest rate obtainable on the U.S. dollar, the forward exchange rate is *higher* than the spot rate, and the foreign currency is said to be **selling at a premium on the forward market.**

For example, assume that (1) the interest rate obtainable in the United States is 6%, (2) the interest rate obtainable in Great Britain is 11%, (3) the spot rate is $2.00, and (4) a U.S. treasurer has $200,000 available for a one-year money market investment. The one-year forward rate for selling pounds would have to be $1.9099 (a discount to the spot rate) to offset the additional $10,000 of interest earned in Great Britain. The FX traders use the following formula: ($2.00 spot rate × 1.06 / 1.11 = $1.9099). The interest rates obtainable at any point in time must be the same in parity, or capital floods to one or the other countries.

Thus an interest rate parity system exists, which in effect prevents the transfer of money between international money markets merely to obtain a higher interest rate relatively risk free through the use of an FX forward (otherwise, it would be the equivalent of having a money machine).

THE FX TRADER'S COMMISSION

The FX trader earns its commission for assuming the risk of an adverse exchange rate change by adjusting the forward rate that is calculated to offset the effect of the interest rate differentials between the two countries. For example, assume that the 30-day forward rate for the British pound is $1.51 as determined by adjusting the spot rate of $1.50 for the lower interest rate in the United Kingdom. The FX trader provides *bid* (what the FX trader is willing to *buy* at) and *ask* quotes (what the FX trader is willing to *sell* at) slightly different from this $1.51 to earn a commission. For example, the FX trader's **bid quote to *buy* pounds forward** might be $1.505 (for when the *customer* is *selling* forward) and its **ask quote to *sell* pounds forward** might be $1.515 (for when the *customer* is *buying* forward). The $.01 spread is for the FX trader's profit. Thus a commission of $.05 each way is embedded in the forward rate.

CALCULATING THE TOTAL PREMIUM OR DISCOUNT

The difference between the spot rate and the forward rate multiplied by the units of foreign currency to be received or delivered under the contract equals the total amount of the premium or discount on the FX forward. For example, assume that the 30-day forward rate for the domestic importer in Illustrations 17–3 and 17–4 is $1.515 (instead of equaling the $1.50 spot rate). Thus the domestic importer must pay an additional $1,500 (£100,000 × $.015) to the FX trader at the expiration date. The $1,500 is a premium since the domestic importer is buying at *more than* the spot rate.

ACCOUNTING FOR PREMIUMS AND DISCOUNTS

Premiums and discounts are often viewed as the **cost of obtaining the hedge,** which is analogous to an insurance premium that should be accounted for solely based on the passage of time. Thus **premiums and discounts are generally viewed as a time value element of the financial instrument** (the other element being the intrinsic value element, which we discussed earlier).

TO SPLIT OR NOT TO SPLIT   The fundamental issue for all financial instruments is how to best measure their value to be reported in the balance sheet. For FX forwards, two alternative valuation methods exist:

1. **"Split accounting."** Under split accounting, premiums and discounts (the time value element) are accounted for separately. By doing so, however, the intrinsic value must be measured by the change in the spot rate (as shown in previous illustrations in which no premium or discount existed). Consequently, accounting for two distinct elements results in the total valuation amount for the FX forward (on a net basis). Thus an FX forward's value (net) at an intervening balance sheet date comprises the following elements (using assumed amounts):

   FX Contract Value—Forward, net (a receivable)
Time value (expired portion of the $1,500 premium)	$(1,000)
Intrinsic value ($.05 change in the spot rate × £100,000)	5,000
	4,000

2. **Nonsplit accounting.** Under nonsplit accounting, no attempt is made to account for premiums and discounts separately. The value of the FX forward is determined, instead, by continuously valuing the FX forward (on a net basis) using the change in the forward rate for the remaining life of the forward contract. (As explained shortly, the forward rate [1] moves in tandem with the spot rate and [2] converges to the spot rate at the expiration date of the forward period.) Thus an FX forward's value (net) at an intervening balance sheet is determined as follows (using assumed amounts):

   FX Contract Value—Forward, net ($.042 change
in the forward rate × £100,000)	$4,200

SFAS No. 52: SPLIT ACCOUNTING REQUIRED   The valuation results produced under both valuation alternatives usually do *not* differ significantly. Thus which method produces the more realistic valuation is usually *not* a critical issue. *SFAS No. 52* mandates the use of split accounting, however, for FX forwards accounted for as hedges (but not for speculations). Because no journal entry is recorded in the general ledger at the inception of an FX forward, premiums and discounts must be *accrued* onto the books over the life of the contract. As evident from the preceding split accounting example, one side of this journal entry is always to the FX Contract Value—Forward (net) account.

THE OTHER SIDE OF THE TIME VALUE ENTRY: RECOGNIZE IN INCOME OR DEFER?
The account to debit or credit for the other side of the journal entry that adjusts the *time value* element under *split accounting* is mandated by *SFAS No. 52* as follows:

1. **Hedges of exposed assets and liabilities.** The *time value* element offsetting debit or credit must be charged or credited to income over the life of the FX forward. (FX gains and FX losses resulting from accounting for the *intrinsic value* element also are recognized currently in the income statement; thus both elements receive income statement treatment—no deferrals are allowed for either element.)

2. **Hedges of firmly committed transactions.** The *time value* element offsetting debit or credit *need not* be charged or credited to income over the life of the FX forward—it may be deferred and treated as an adjustment to the basis of the item being hedged. (FX gains and losses resulting from accounting for the *intrinsic value* element must be deferred, however, as explained later.)

DETERMINING WHETHER PREMIUMS OR DISCOUNTS EXIST AND WHETHER THEY EVENTUALLY RESULT IN DEBITS OR CREDITS TO EQUITY

THE *IMPORTER'S* SITUATION: *BUYING* A FOREIGN CURRENCY TO HEDGE AN EXISTING EXPOSED LIABILITY   When one buys an asset (whether it be a foreign currency or a personal car) at **more** than its current value, the asset is bought at a **premium.** Buying an asset at a premium impacts stockholders' equity negatively; thus the accounting for the premium should result in a **debit** balance that eventually is charged to equity. Buying an asset at **less** than its current value is buying at a **discount,** which ultimately impacts stockholders' equity favorably; thus the accounting for the buying discount results in a **credit** balance that eventually is credited to equity.

THE *EXPORTER'S* SITUATION: *SELLING* A FOREIGN CURRENCY TO HEDGE AN EXISTING EXPOSED ASSET   When one sells an asset at more or less than its current value, the debits and credits are reversed because selling at **more** than the current value is a favorable event and selling at **less** than the current value is an unfavorable event.

In Illustration 17–6, we summarize the occurrence of premiums and discounts and when a debit or credit balance for the premium or discount results on FX forwards.

SHOULD EQUITY BE ADJUSTED IMMEDIATELY FOR PREMIUMS AND DISCOUNTS?

An entity's purchase or sale forward at more or less than the spot rate raises the question of whether the entity has theoretically suffered an immediate economic loss or obtained an immediate economic gain, as the case may be, at the inception of the FX forward. The answer is no. We give the reasons for a situation in which an entity *buys forward* at *more* than the spot rate:

1. **The FX forward has a value in the marketplace.** Thus minutes after the contract is entered into, the buyer could sell the FX forward in the marketplace for roughly the amount of the premium.

2. **The FX forward can be undone.** A bank usually allows FX forwards to be undone for an amount equal to the sum of (1) closing costs, (2) that portion of the

ILLUSTRATION 17–6	When Premiums and Discounts Occur on FX Forwards Used to Hedge Importing and Exporting Transactions				
		Direct Rate		Result[a]	
Buying or Selling Foreign Currency Forward		Spot Rate[b]	Forward Rate	Premium	Discount
Importer (exposed payable):					
Buying[c]		$1.50	$1.515[d]	x(Debit)	
Buying[c]		1.50	1.485		x(Credit)
Exporter (exposed receivable):					
Selling[e]		1.50	1.515	x(Credit)	
Selling[e]		1.50	1.485		x(Debit)

[a]*Debits* eventually *reduce* stockholders' equity; *credits* eventually *increase* stockholders' equity.

[b]The spot rate is the point of reference.

[c]In the trading vernacular, **buying a currency on the forward market is called being *long* in that currency.**

[d]The entries for this situation are shown in Illustration 17–7.

[e]In the trading vernacular, **selling a currency on the forward market is called being *short* in that currency.**

premium that has expired based on the passage of time, and (3) any loss the bank has occurred as a result of an adverse change in the spot rate. Thus minutes after the contract is entered into, the buyer could undo the FX forward and pay but a fraction of the premium.

ENTRIES FOR ACCRUING THE TIME VALUE ELEMENT ONTO THE BOOKS

Assume that on December 11, 19X1, when the spot rate for the British pound was $1.50, the domestic importer in Illustrations 17–3 and 17–4 bought £100,000 forward at the 30-day forward rate of $1.515. As with the intrinsic value discussed earlier, no entry at the inception of the FX forward is required for the time value element. The entries that would be made to *accrue* the $1,500 premium (£100,000 × $.015) onto the books over the life of the contract are shown in Illustration 17–7.[13]

REVIEW POINTS FOR ILLUSTRATION 17–7   Note the following:

1. **No front-end payment for the time value element.** Unlike FX options, in which the time value element is paid in cash at the *inception* of the option period (thus requiring a subsequent *amortization* process), the time value element for FX forwards is settled up at the *end* of the contract period when each of the two parties executes in cash (thus requiring instead an *accruing* process prior to that time). This difference in when the premium is paid occurs only because of custom and convenience.

[13]**Premium and Discount Accounting.** This manner of accounting for premiums and discounts is consistent with the illustrations contained in Arthur Andersen & Co.'s Participant Guide for the foreign exchange management seminars that it periodically conducts. Responses by audit partners of other international Big Six accounting firms confirm that companies account for premiums and discounts in this manner—no journal entry is made in the books at the inception of the forward contract.

ILLUSTRATION 17–7 | **Journal Entries to *Accrue* a Premium on a Hedge of an Exposed Liability Position**

December 11, 19X1
(the inception of the 30-day FX forward)

No entries are made.

December 31, 19X1
(an intervening balance sheet date)

Hedge Expense	$1,000	
FX Contract Value—Forward, **net**		$1,000
To accrue the premium onto the books over the life of the forward contract.		
($1,500 × 20/30 = $1,000)		

January 10, 19X2
(the expiration date of the FX forward)

Hedge Expense	$500	
FX Contract Value—Forward, **net**		$500
To accrue the premium onto the books over the life of the forward contract.		
($1,500 × 10/30 = $500)		

Recall from Illustration 17–4 that the contract value of the FX forward at January 10, 19X2, as a result of accounting for the intrinsic value, was a net asset position (a receivable) of $7,000. After accounting for the time value element as shown above, the contract value at that date is $5,500 ($7,000 – $1,500). Consequently, the entry to settle up with the FX trader and pay the vendor using a bank wire transfer at the contract expiration date is as follows:

£ Accounts Payable	$157,000	
Cash (the forward rate of 1.515 × £100,000)		$151,500
FX Contract Value—Forward, **net**		$5,500
To settle up with the FX trader who is instructed to make a bank wire transfer		
to Vendor A for £100,000.		

---

2. **What if paid at inception?** If instead it were customary and convenient for the premium or discount to be paid at the *inception* of the contract, an *amortization* process would occur instead of an *accruing* process.

THE RELATIONSHIP BETWEEN THE FORWARD RATE AND THE FUTURE SPOT RATE

Current expectations of future events influence both the spot rate and the forward rate. Both rates move in tandem with the difference between them based on interest rate differentials. Because interest rates reflect expectations about inflation rates, the forward rates effectively forecast future spot rates based on differential rates of expected inflation—**the expected nominal change in the exchange rate.**

Because noninflationary factors have such a major day-to-day (short-term) impact on exchange rates, however, future spot rates rarely coincide with the forward rates—**the difference being the real change in the exchange rate.** If this were not so and instead an extremely high correlation existed between forward rates and future spot rates, little justification for hedging would exist. For example, the spot and 180-day forward rates for the British pound in March 1992 were near $1.80 and $1.75, respectively. Shortly after the European currency crisis of September 1992 occurred, the spot rate was about $1.50—nearly 15% below the 180-day forward rate in March 1992. FX traders having bought pounds 180 days forward in March 1992 lost heavily (they also had huge gains on contracts in which they sold pounds 180 days forward). A fuller discussion of forward rates, expected future spot rates, and interest parity may be found in international finance texts. The basics presented here cannot be observed in FX quotes empirically without allowing for other economic variables.

VI SPECULATING IN FOREIGN CURRENCY

Speculating occurs when a company attempts to make a gain from an expected change in the spot rate without regard to any particular area of FX exposure. Thus there is no intent to create a counterbalancing position to obtain a hedge. To gain from an expected change in the exchange rate, one merely hopes to buy low and sell high.

Assume that the Swiss franc has a current spot rate of $.50 and a 180-day forward rate of $.53. If managers expected the Swiss franc to rise higher than the $.53 forward rate in the next six months and wanted to make a gain if the spot rate rose as they expected, they would *buy* Swiss francs forward (at $.53) now and hope that they could sell them in the open market in 180 days at *more* than $.53. On the other hand, if managers expected the Swiss franc to fall, they would *sell* Swiss francs forward (at $.53) now and hope that they could buy them in the open market in 180 days at *less* than $.53.

ACCOUNTING TREATMENT

Under *SFAS No. 52*, any gains or losses on such speculative FX forwards are recognized currently in the income statement as they arise (no special deferral provisions exist). Furthermore, **split accounting is *not* allowed.** Accordingly, premiums and discounts are *not* carved out and accounted for separately. To accomplish this manner of accounting, the net position with the FX dealer is always valued at each intervening balance sheet **at the change in the forward rate** for the remaining life of the contract—not the change in the spot rate. The rationale for this treatment is that the current forward rate presumably results in a simpler and more realistic estimation of market value, for which symmetry with FX positions at spot rates does *not* exist.

ILLUSTRATION | **SPECULATING IN FOREIGN CURRENCY**

Assume that a domestic company takes the view on November 1, 19X1, that the Swiss franc (SFr) will strengthen within 100 days. Accordingly, it *buys* forward 100,000 SFr at the 100-day forward rate of $.510. Illustration 17–8 shows the entries that would be made for this contract assuming the following direct exchange rates:

	November 1, 19X1 (inception date)	December 31, 19X1 (a financial reporting date)	February 9, 19X2 (expiration date)
Spot rate	$.500	$.550	$.570
Forward rate	.510	.553	n/a

VII HEDGING FIRM COMMITMENTS

Hedging transactions can be entered into *before* the transaction date (the date an FX receivable or FX liability is recorded), a period that is called the *anticipatory transaction period*.

| **ILLUSTRATION 17–8** | **Speculating in Foreign Currency: Net Position Accounting Journal Entries** |

November 1, 19X1
(the inception of the 100-day FX forward)

No general ledger entries are made.

December 31, 19X1
(an intervening balance sheet date)

FX Contract Value—Forward, **net** (a receivable) .... $4,300[a]
     FX Gain—Forward $4,300
  To mark to market the net position with the FX dealer (using the change in the
    forward rate).
  ($.553 × $.510 = $.043)
  ($.043 × 100,000 SFr = $4,300)

[a]For comparative purposes only, the valuation under *split accounting*—which is *not* allowed for
speculations—at 12/31/X1 is as follows:

Time value element (the expired portion of the $1,000 premium
  [$1,000 × 60/100 = $600]) .... $ (600)
Intrinsic value element (the $.05 change in the spot rate ×
  100,000 SFr) 5,000
                                          $4,400

February 9, 19X2
(the expiration date of the FX forward)

FX Contract Value—Forward, **net** (a receivable) $1,700
     FX Gain—Forward $1,700
  To mark to market the net position with the FX trader (using the change in the
    forward rate).
  ($.570 − $.553 = $.017)
  ($.017 × 100,000 SFr = $1,700)

Cash $6,000
     FX Contract Value—Forward, **net** .... $6,000[b]
  To settle up with the FX trader.
  ($.57 ending spot rate − $.051 initial forward rate = $.06)
  ($.06 × 100,000 SFr = $6,000)
  To settle up, the speculator now sells to the FX trader at the $.570 spot rate the
    100,000 SFr it purchased from the FX trader at the forward rate of $.510. The
    FX trader (a bank) credits the speculator's account for the $6,000 net amount.

[a]For comparative purposes only, the valuation under **split accounting**—which is *not* allowed for
speculations—at 2/9/X2 is as follows:

Time value element (the entire $1,000 premium) .... $(1,000)
Intrinsic value element (the $.07 change in the spot rate × 100,000 SFr) 7,000
                                      $ 6,000

Thus at the settlement date, the reported value of the FX forward is the same for both split and nonsplit accounting.
Note that the way to determine the reported value under *split accounting* at any date is always more complicated
than under *nonsplit accounting*.

FIRM COMMITMENT TO PURCHASE

When a domestic importer expects to issue a *purchase order* requiring payment in a
foreign vendor's currency, the domestic company's FX exposure begins when the
expectation arises—not when a liability is recorded later at the transaction date
upon receipt of the inventory. The *anticipatory transaction period* may be separated
into as many as three distinct periods, as shown in Illustration 17–9.

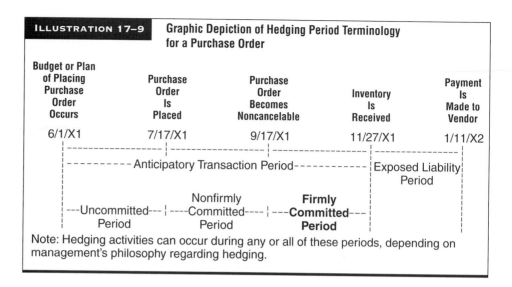

ILLUSTRATION 17–9   Graphic Depiction of Hedging Period Terminology for a Purchase Order

Budget or Plan of Placing Purchase Order Occurs	Purchase Order Is Placed	Purchase Order Becomes Noncancelable	Inventory Is Received	Payment Is Made to Vendor
6/1/X1	7/17/X1	9/17/X1	11/27/X1	1/11/X2

------------- Anticipatory Transaction Period ----------- | Exposed Liability Period

---Uncommitted--- | ----Nonfirmly Committed---- | ---**Firmly Committed**--- |
Period | Period | **Period**

Note: Hedging activities can occur during any or all of these periods, depending on management's philosophy regarding hedging.

We discuss in this section only the accounting for hedges that occur during the *firmly committed* portion of the *anticipatory transaction period*. During the *firmly committed period*, one or more intervening balance sheet (financial reporting) dates may occur, which raises the issue of whether and how to report hedging gains and losses that occur during this period. Illustration 17–10 (an extension of that portion of Illustration 17–9 that concerns us here) shows the accounting to be followed for (1) hedging FX gains and losses that occur during the *firmly committed period* and (2) premium and discount accruals made during the *firmly committed period*.

ACCOUNTING FOR HEDGING FX GAINS AND LOSSES ARISING DURING THE FIRMLY COMMITTED PERIOD   Any FX hedging gain or loss that arises during the firmly committed period must be deferred until the transaction date. The hedging FX gain or loss is then subtracted from or added to the cost of the goods acquired. The rationale for deferring the hedging FX gain or loss is that although the hedging FX gain or loss is recorded on the books, the related purchase executory contract is *not*. Thus the hedging FX gain or loss does *not* offset any FX gain or loss on

ILLUSTRATION 17–10   Graphic Depiction of Relevant Dates: Identifiable Foreign Currency Purchase Commitment

Purchase Order Becomes Noncancelable	Intervening Balance Sheet Date: If Hedged, Defer FX Gain or Loss	Transaction Date: Record Transaction	Intervening Balance Sheet Date: Adjust FX Payable	Settlement Date: Pay Vendor
9/17/X1	9/30/X1	11/27/X1	12/31/X1	1/11/X2

------**Firmly Committed Period**------ | --- Exposed Liability Period-----

-------------------------------------FX Exposure Period--------------------------

_____**Must** Defer Hedging_____ | ___**Must** Recognize Hedging____
FX Gain or Loss | FX Gain or Loss

_____***May*** Defer Premiums_____ | ___**Must** Recognize Premiums___
and Discounts | and Discounts

the executory purchase transaction as is the case for hedging an exposed liability. This leaves no choice but to defer the hedging gain or loss to keep it out of the income statement.

ACCOUNTING FOR PREMIUMS AND DISCOUNTS DURING THE FIRMLY COMMITTED PERIOD   In addition, any premium or discount pertaining to this period may be either (1) charged or credited to income over the life of the contract (as is required in exposed asset or exposed liability situations) (recall that accounting for premiums and discounts as a separate element is split accounting) or (2) treated the same as the hedging FX gain or loss; that is, it may be deferred and added to or subtracted from, respectively, the cost of the goods acquired. The effect of the nonsplit accounting deferral is to record the cost of the goods at the forward rate as locked in by the hedge.

ILLUSTRATION	**HEDGING AN IDENTIFIABLE FOREIGN CURRENCY PURCHASE COMMITMENT**

Assume that a domestic company with a calendar year-end entered into the following transactions on October 2, 19X1:

1. It ordered equipment built to its specifications from a French manufacturer. The purchase price is 1,000,000 francs (FF). Delivery is to be in 120 days (January 30, 19X2), and the payment is due then.

2. It entered into an FX forward with an FX trader to *buy* 1,000,000 FF on January 30, 19X2, at the forward rate of $.098.

Illustration 17–11 shows these transactions as initially recorded and as adjusted at the intervening balance sheet date (December 31, 19X1). Delivery and payments are made as required. The direct exchange rates for the franc at the applicable dates are as follows:

	October 2, 19X1 (inception date)	December 31, 19X1 (a financial reporting date)	January 30, 19X2 (expiration date)
Spot rate	$.100	$.106	$.105
Forward rate	.098	.1057	n/a

REVIEW POINTS FOR ILLUSTRATION 17–11   Note the following:

1. The capitalized cost of the equipment ($98,000) equals the amount of cash committed to the FX trader.

2. In receiving 1,000,000 FF, the vendor received the equivalent of $105,000. Thus the domestic importer's cost is $105,000, which is reduced for the $5,000 FX gain and the $2,000 discount. Accordingly, if the FX forward had *not* been entered into, the capitalized cost would have been $105,000.

3. The $5,000 FX gain can be treated as a reduction to the $105,000 purchase price because the domestic importer's expected purchase price was $100,000 (based on the $.10 spot rate existing when the equipment was ordered). The FX forward merely locks in this price without regard to the existence of a discount. Because of the $2,000 discount, however, the domestic importer has effectively locked itself into paying a maximum price of $98,000.

4. If the spot rate had decreased from $.100 to $.095 (instead of increasing to $.105), the domestic importer would have had a $5,000 FX loss on the FX forward instead of a $5,000 FX gain. Using symmetrical procedures, the initial capitalized cost would be the same $98,000 amount ($95,000 + $5,000 – $2,000). Because the domestic importer would have paid $95,000 cash on January 30, 19X2, if no FX

ILLUSTRATION 17–11	Hedging an Identifiable Foreign Currency Purchase Commitment: Net Position Accounting Journal Entries

October 2, 19X1
(the date of issuing the equipment purchase order entering into the 120-day FX forward)

No general ledger entries are made—only memorandum entries are made.

December 31, 19X1
(an intervening balance sheet date)

FX Contract Value—Forward, **net** (a receivable)	$6,000	
Deferred FX Gain—Forward		$6,000
To mark to market the net position with the FX trader—intrinsic value element only.		
($.106 – $.100 = $.006)		
($.006 × 1,000,000 FF = $6,000)		

FX Contract Value—Forward, **net** (a receivable)	$1,500	
Deferred Hedging income		$1,500
To accrue the $2,000 discount—a time value element. Deferral treatment is assumed.		
(90/120 × $2,000 = $1,500)		

January 30, 19X2
(the transaction date, which coincides with the settlement date, and the expiration date of the FX forward)

Deferred FX Gain—Forward	$1,000	
FX Contract Value—Forward, **net**		$1,000
To mark to market the net position with the FX trader—intrinsic value element only.		
($.105 – $.106 = $.001)		
($.001 × 1,000,000 FF = $1,000)		

FX Contract Value—Forward, **net**	$500	
Deferred Hedging Income		$500
To accrue the $2,000 discount—a time value element. Deferral treatment is assumed.		
(30/120 × $2,000 = $500)		

Equipment (1,000,000 FF × $.105 spot rate)	$105,000	
Cash ($105,000 – $7,000 due from FX trader)		$98,000
FX Contract Value—Forward, **net**		$7,000
To record purchase of equipment and pay vendor **via a bank wire transfer** to the French manufacturer for 1,000,000 FF. The FX trader (a bank) charges the company's bank account $98,000 (1,000,000 FF × $.098 [the forward rate]).		

Deferred FX Gain—Forward	$5,000	
Deferred Hedging Income	$2,000	
Equipment		$7,000
To capitalize previously deferred items.		

forward had been entered into, however, the $3,000 ($98,000 – $95,000) increment over the originally expected acquisition cost raises the issue of whether to recognize an impairment loss pursuant to the requirements of *SFAS No. 121,* "Accounting for the Impairment of Long-Lived Assets and for Long-Lived Assets to Be Disposed Of."

5. The $6,000 deferred FX gain (an unrealized item) should be classified in the December 31, 19X1, balance sheet among liabilities because the $6,000 to be collected from the FX trader will theoretically be used to pay the foreign manufacturer an estimated additional $6,000.

6. Because the French franc was selling at a $.002 discount on the forward market on October 2, 19X1, the domestic importer may prefer to have the transaction denominated in francs rather than dollars to take advantage of this situation and thus be better off by $2,000. Thus premiums and discounts (1) sometimes enter into negotiations concerning which currency a transaction will be denominated in and (2) can reduce transaction costs.

COMMITMENT TO SELL

Parallel accounting procedures are used when (1) the domestic company has entered into a noncancelable agreement to *sell* goods to a foreign customer in the future, with payment to be received in the customer's currency, and (2) the domestic company sells forward to hedge its FX exposure.

QUALIFYING CONDITIONS FOR HEDGE ACCOUNTING TREATMENT

For an FX forward (or other type of hedging instrument) to qualify for hedge accounting treatment of either an identifiable foreign currency commitment or a net investment (hedging a net investment in a foreign subsidiary is illustrated in Chapter 18) under *SFAS No. 52*, it must meet the following:

Condition 1: Be designated a hedge.

Condition 2: Be effective as a hedge.

Condition 3: Be firm.

Thus the intent of the hedge must be identified with the commitment. Whether or not a hedge transaction is effective is **an after-the-fact determination.** Clearly, it is effective if (1) the forward exchange contract is in the same currency as the hedged item and (2) the gain or loss on the hedging transaction is **in the *opposite* direction** to the loss or gain on the hedged item.

SFAS No. 52 does not define the third condition. It implies, however, that the foreign currency commitment is either noncancelable or that the probability of cancellation is remote because of a severe monetary penalty. *Firm* is a term of art in law, which implies enforceability. (See *Black's Law Dictionary.*)

TRANSACTIONS OTHER THAN FORWARDS AND OPTIONS The preceding three conditions are sufficiently broad that foreign currency transactions other than FX forwards and FX options may qualify as hedges of foreign currency commitments. The following are examples:

1. A U.S. company committed to constructing a building in France and receiving payment in francs could borrow francs and designate the borrowing as a hedge of the commitment.

2. A U.S. company committed to purchasing inventory or equipment from a Japanese company could convert dollars into yen, hold or invest the yen, and designate them as a hedge of the commitment.

3. A U.S. company, or its Spanish subsidiary, could designate an FX receivable in Italian lira as a hedge against a foreign currency purchase commitment in Italian lira.

OTHER TECHNICAL POINTS Several technical points regarding foreign currency commitments follow:

1. **Timing.** The hedging transaction need not be entered into at the same time as the commitment, nor must it extend to the anticipated transaction date.

2. **Overlapping.** If the hedging transaction extends beyond the *transaction* date, any hedging FX gain or loss that occurs after that date *cannot* be deferred—it must be reported in the income statement as it arises.

3. **Early termination.** Any deferred FX gain or loss on a hedging transaction terminated *before* the *transaction* date up to that date is still deferred and treated as part of the cost of the asset acquired or as an adjustment to the sales price of the asset sold.

4. **Excess amount.** If the hedging transaction amount exceeds the commitment amount, only the FX gain or loss on the hedging transaction up to the commitment amount may be deferred and treated as an adjustment of the cost of the asset acquired or as an adjustment to the sales price of the asset sold.

5. **Lower-of-cost-or-market problem.** FX losses on hedging transactions related to a commitment *cannot* be deferred (but must be reported currently in the income statement) if such deferral would lead to recognizing losses in a later period.

VIII HEDGING FORECASTED TRANSACTIONS

The collapse of the Bretton Woods fixed exchange rate system in 1971 and the subsequent high volatility of exchange rate fluctuations that continuously occur under the floating exchange rate system have led to (1) the decision by numerous multinational companies to hedge many or all of their FX exposures and (2) an explosive growth in innovative derivatives.

Prior to *SFAS No. 52*'s issuance, FX forwards were used almost exclusively to hedge foreign currency exposures. Furthermore, hedging activities were generally confined to hedging existing balance sheet exposures and firmly committed transactions (identifiable foreign currency commitments). The explosive growth in innovative derivatives to accomplish hedging occurred subsequent to *SFAS No. 52*'s issuance, as did the expansion of hedging activities to cover many other types of exposures. As a result, *SFAS No. 52* is *not* encompassing enough to deal with all of the new types of derivatives and exposures being hedged. As an interim measure, the FASB's Emerging Issue's Task Force addressed several of these areas in 1990 and 1991; its guidance is set forth in EITF Issues 90-17, 91-1, and 91-4. Unfortunately, the result of these EITF documents has been to create patchwork rules for hedging transactions. These rules have been heavily criticized by financial executives and accountants because of their inconsistencies and restrictiveness.

THE FASB'S *PROPOSED* STANDARD FOR HEDGING FORECASTED TRANSACTIONS

As stated in the chapter overview, the FASB's proposed standard on derivative financial instruments and hedging activities (exposed for public comment in mid-1996) will significantly change only the accounting for hedges of forecasted transactions when it becomes effective. Accordingly, **we discuss the FASB's proposed rules for hedges of forecasted transactions—*not* the EITF's guidance in this area that will be superseded when the proposed rules become effective (probably in 1997).**

DELAYED RECOGNITION OF THE FX GAIN OR LOSS The FX gain or loss that occurs as a result in the change in the fair value of a derivative financial instrument (encompassing both FX options *and* FX forwards) that is designated as a hedge of a forecasted transaction is **initially reported as a direct adjustment to stockholders' equity.** On the date when the forecasted transaction was initially identified as expected to occur, however, the FX gain or loss is recognized in the income statement.

CRITERIA FOR DELAYED INCOME STATEMENT RECOGNITION OF FX GAINS AND LOSSES ON FORECASTED TRANSACTIONS

To qualify for this delayed recognition of an FX gain or loss on a hedge of a forecasted transaction, *each* of the following criteria must be met:

1. The use of the derivative must be consistent with the entity's established policy for risk management.

2. The designation must be (a) made prospectively and (b) formally documented.

3. The forecasted transaction must be specifically identified at the time of the designation (identification would include the expected date of the transaction, the type of commodity, asset, or liability involved, the expected dollar amount, and the current price of a forecasted transaction).

4. The forecasted transaction must (a) be probable, (b) be part of an established business activity, and (c) present an exposure to price changes that would (1) produce variations in cash flows and (2) affect reported earnings. (Forecasted dividends from subsidiaries would *not* meet this required characteristic.)

5. The forecasted transaction is an event involving an exchange with an external party—**a party that is *not* consolidated or part of the reporting entity.** (Thus hedges of forecasted transactions between members of the consolidated group do *not* qualify for delayed recognition treatment.)

***NONSPLIT* ACCOUNTING FOR FX OPTIONS**   The proposed standard requires *nonsplit* accounting for FX options. Thus the *time value* element is *not* carved out and accounted for separately. Accordingly, the fair value of the option must be determined by obtaining a quoted price from either (1) an FX trader (for over-the-counter options), (2) a financial newspaper (for exchange-traded options), or (3) a valuation model.

ILLUSTRATION   **HEDGING A DOMESTIC COMPANY'S FORECASTED (NONFIRM) EXPORT SALES USING AN FX OPTION**

To illustrate this type of hedge and the allowable hedge accounting, assume that a domestic company estimated its January 19X2 export sales to the United Kingdom at £4,000,000. On December 2, 19X1, to protect against the pound weakening, the company purchased an **out-of-the-money** FX option **to sell** (a *put*) £4,000,000 at $1.47 (the *exercise price*) with an expiration date of January 31, 19X2. On December 2, 19X1, the *spot rate* was $1.50. The cost of the FX option was $22,000. Accordingly, the premium paid to acquire the FX option represents all *time value* elements. For simplicity, we further assume the following:

1. The only interim financial reporting date was December 31, 19X1, when the spot rate was $1.45 and the option's *market value* was $86,000.

2. The FX option was exercised on January 31, 19X2, when the *spot rate* was $1.41.

Illustration 17-12 shows the entries that would be made under the FX option during 19X1.

REVIEW POINTS FOR ILLUSTRATION 17–12   Note the following:

1. If delayed recognition were *not* permitted, the $64,000 deferred FX gain at December 31, 19X1, would be reported currently in the income statement.

2. The option's value in total at December 31, 19X1, was based on a market quotation; thus separate amounts for the *time value* element and the *intrinsic value* element were *not* used in arriving at a carrying value at that date.

ILLUSTRATION 17–12	**Hedging a Domestic Company's Forecasted (Nonfirm) Export Sales Using FX Options**

December 2, 19X1
(the inception of the *put* FX option period)

FX Contract Value—Option	$22,000	
Cash		$22,000
To record cost of *put* option acquired.		

December 31, 19X1
(an intervening balance sheet date)

FX Contract Value—Option	$64,000	
Deferred FX Gain—Option **(reported as a *direct adjustment* to equity)**		$64,000
To adjust option's carrying value to its market value of $86,000 (a given amount).		
($86,000 – $22,000 = $64,000)		

January 31, 19X2
(the expiration date of the FX option period)

FX Contract Value—Option	$154,000	
FX Gain—Option		$154,000
To adjust option's carrying value to market value of $240,000.		
($1.47 exercise price – $1.41 spot rate = $.06)		
($.06 × £4,000,000 = $240,000)		
($240,000 – $86,000 carrying value at 12/31/X1 = $154,000)		
Deferred FX Gain—Option	$64,000	
FX Gain—Option		$64,000
To recognize previously deferred gain.		
Cash	$240,000	
FX Contract Value—Option		$240,000
To exercise the option and settle up with the FX trader.		
($1.47 strike price – $1.41 spot rate = $.06)		
($.06 × £4,000,000 = $240,000)		

To settle up with the FX trader, the option holder would buy £4,000,000 from the FX trader on the expiration date at the $1.41 spot rate. The FX trader (a bank) would credit the company's bank account for the net $240,000 amount.

IX

DERIVATIVE FINANCIAL INSTRUMENTS: A GENERAL DISCUSSION

Financial instruments are defined to include (1) cash, (2) evidence of an ownership interest in an entity (such as stock certificates), and (3) contracts that contain rights and obligations to exchange cash or other financial instruments (an example is stock options held by employees).[14] In recent years, an explosive increase in the use of a special class of financial instruments (commonly referred to as *derivatives*) has occurred. Derivatives are used as financial tools to better manage business risks and returns.

A **derivative** is an executory (to be executed later) contract between two parties in which the eventual resulting cash flows that take place between the two parties depend on the change in some other measure of value. Thus a derivative "derives"

[14]The formal definition is in *Statement of Financial Accounting Standards No. 105*, "Disclosure of Information About Financial Instruments With Off-Balance-Sheet Risk and Financial Instruments With Concentrations of Credit Risk," para. 6.

its value from another measure of value, which may be any one or combination of the following items:

1. **Financial instruments** (such as common stocks, corporate bonds, and government bonds). An employee who owns a stock option owns a derivative because the stock option's value depends entirely on the value of the company's common stock relative to the stock option's exercise price.

2. **Commodities** (such as corn, cotton, gold, or oil). Likewise, an investor holding an option or a future to buy 1,000 bushels of corn at $3 per bushel for the next 180 days owns a derivative.

3. **Indexes.** Indexes (such as the Dow-Jones index or the Standard and Poors index for common stocks) measure changes in specific markets and represent the values of portfolios of financial instruments and commodities.

4. **Rates** (such as currency exchange rates and interest rates). Rate changes reflect value variations in specific markets (such as currencies or Treasury bonds).

VALUING DERIVATIVES IN THE BALANCE SHEET   Derivatives are recognized in the balance sheet at each financial reporting date at market value. The valuation technique involves determining the net cash flows that are to take place between the two parties by referring to **the change in the underlying financial instrument, commodity, index, or rate.** The result is to report a receivable position for one party and a payable position for the other party. The same types of general ledger accounts (Contract Value—Option and Contract Value—Forward, net) used and shown earlier for FX forwards and FX options are used to convey each entity's favorable or unfavorable position, respectively, in the derivative.

The FASB's definition of a derivative financial instrument follows:

> A financial instrument that by its terms at inception or upon occurrence of a specified event, provides the holder (or writer) with the right (or obligation) to participate in some or all of the price **changes** of an underlying (that is, one or more referenced financial instruments, commodities, or other assets, or other specific items to which a rate, an index of prices, or another market indicator is applied) and . . . does not require the holder to own or deliver the underlying. . . .[15]

More than 1,200 types of derivative products have been created (mostly by investment bankers), a high number of which involve the use of computer programs. Our focus in this chapter has been on derivatives that (1) derive their value from changes in currency exchange rates and (2) are used to manage FX exposures. The AICPA has identified more than 75 derivatives that can be used for hedging exposures, many of which can be used to hedge FX exposures. Almost all of them, however, are variations of (1) FX options and (2) FX forwards.[16]

UNIQUE CONTRACTUAL ELEMENTS OF DERIVATIVES

Unlike traditional financial instruments, such as stocks and bonds, derivatives generally have the following unique elements:

- Neither party initially performs because the eventual dollar amount of the performance is a function of subsequent value *changes*—not the static value of the assets or economic measures that serve as the base.

---

[15]Exposure Draft: *Proposed Statement of Financial Accounting Standards "Accounting for Derivative and Similar Financial Instruments and Hedging Activities"* (FASB: Norwalk, Ct.), June 20, 1996, p. 2.

[16]Some examples of these other types of derivatives are futures, swaps, synthetic forwards, range forwards, participating forwards, options to exchange currencies, deep-in-the-money purchased options, and options purchased and written as a unit.

- No principal cash payments are made at the inception of the contract. No notional balances or other executory fixed amounts are initially recorded as receivables or payables in the balance sheet. Consequently, derivatives are often characterized as being "off-balance-sheet agreements" (even though receivables and payables are recognized later and continuously adjusted throughout the contractual period).
- Cash payments are made during or at the end of the contract.
- If one party has a *favorable* outcome (which results in a favorable position), the other party (the counterparty) has an *unfavorable* outcome (which results in an unfavorable position), a zero-sum game. For most derivatives considered independently, favorable and unfavorable outcomes are characterized as gains and losses, respectively.

UNIQUE CHARACTERISTICS OF DERIVATIVES

Derivatives usually have most of the following unique characteristics:

- Their market value can change quickly.
- Their market value (other than option-based derivatives, as explained shortly) can alternate quickly between a positive value (receivable position) and a negative value (payable position).
- The potential future gains and losses can be huge in relation to the recognized carrying amounts (usually fair values) reported in the balance sheet for the receivable or payable position that currently is reported for the derivative. Thus the reported amounts usually do *not* convey a prudent picture of an entity's latent exposure to market risk.

A ZERO-SUM GAME

The financial press has widely reported numerous examples of entities that have incurred large derivative-related losses in the 1990s from exposed positions subject to latent risk games. Examples include

1. **Orange County (California),** $1.7 billion loss: Bet on the direction of interest rates.
2. **Metallgesellschaft AG,** $1.3 billion loss: Used a flawed hedging strategy subject to timing imbalances.
3. **Barings PLC (investment bank),** $1.3 billion loss: Bet on the direction of the Japanese Nikkei stock index using futures contracts in unauthorized trades by one of its foreign currency traders (resulted in the company's collapse).
4. **Piper Jaffrey,** $700 million loss: Entered into interest rate derivative contracts with mutual funds.
5. **Procter and Gamble Corporation,** $157 million loss: Entered into unfavorable interest rate swaps (sued the investment banker that advised it to use derivatives, claiming it did not understand the risks involved in what it thought was hedging but effectively was speculating).

Because of the "what one party gains, the other party loses" nature, derivatives are examples of a *zero-sum game*. Thus the financial press instead could have written about the spectacular gains obtained using derivatives from the perspective of the counterparty(ies) to this list of five derivative-based losses. The winners (who were also potential losers) on the other side were probably more numerous, prudent, or parties to hedges.

IT'S NOT THE DERIVATIVES—IT'S THE PEOPLE USING THEM The five huge losses cited here did *not* occur merely because derivatives were used. They were the result of (1) using flawed investment or risk management strategies, (2) management's willingness to take excessive risks, (3) individuals purposely circumventing internal controls so that they could execute transactions and take risks in excess of authorized limits, and (4) management's failure to fully understand or control the risks. These spectacular derivative-related losses have awakened many to the potential risks associated with using derivatives, as the Business Perspective reveals.

TYPES OF DERIVATIVES

Derivatives can generally be separated into one of the following two categories:

1. **Option-based derivatives** (examples are option contracts, interest rate caps, and interest rate floors). For this category, only *one* party can potentially have a *favorable* outcome for which it pays a premium at inception; the other party can potentially have only an *unfavorable* outcome for which it is paid the premium at inception.

2. **Forward-based derivatives** (examples are forwards, futures, and swaps). For this category, *either* party (but not both simultaneously) can potentially have a *favorable* outcome and *either* party (but not both simultaneously) can have an *unfavorable* outcome.

TYPES OF RISKS

CREDIT RISK: A CONCERN OF THE PARTY IN THE RECEIVABLE POSITION The possibility of incurring a loss as a result of the counterparty's inability to fulfill its financial obligations under the contract is called **credit risk.** Credit risk exists for only the party in the *receivable* position, and it is limited to the carrying value of the derivative. Credit risk can be volatile because it varies with the market value of the derivative. Credit risk is generally not a major concern, however, unless the receivable position becomes quite large as a result of spectacular gains so that the spectacular losses incurred by the counterparty cause it financial problems. Dealers lay off and balance their positions so that their commercial customers are the usual source of credit risk to the dealers.

As this book goes to print, U.S. international banks that have foreign currency transactions with Japanese banks currently have a major credit risk concern because (1) scores of Japanese banks are in considerable financial difficulty as a result of having nearly $400 billion of nonperforming loans and (2) some of them may collapse and be unable to fulfill their obligations to the U.S. banks.

LIQUIDITY RISK: THE CONCERN OF THE PARTY IN THE PAYABLE POSITION The other side of the coin of credit risk is **liquidity risk,** which is the risk that the party in the *payable* position may not be able to fulfill its obligation because it lacks liquid assets. Thus credit risk and liquidity risk concern the same issue: whether payment can be made when due. Incurring large losses on a derivative can cause liquidity problems, particularly when offset by unrealized gains on assets, which cannot be sold without disrupting operations.

MARKET RISK: A CONCERN OF BOTH PARTIES The risk of incurring losses as a result of future adverse changes in the market value of the derivative is **market risk.** Such losses could lower or reduce to zero one party's receivable position and, in a forward-based derivative, create a payable position for that same party. Thus

---

BUSINESS PERSPECTIVE

Derivatives Could Hedge Career Growth

The derivatives debacles of 1994 continue to reverberate throughout the investment community.

Institutional investors, grilled by directors and pension-fund trustees about their use of derivatives, remain wary of the complex instruments. These investors recall the fate of managers such as Orange County, Calif.'s Robert Citron, whose use of these instruments brought his career to an untimely end.

"After the big derivatives blowups of the last year or two, you don't want to find yourself in a boardroom explaining why you've bought some kind of oddball product," says John Carroll, manager of **GTE** Corp.'s $12 billion pension fund, a veteran investor who acknowledges his reluctance to be a pioneer in the use of derivatives. "If you made the right call and used derivatives, you might get a small additional return. But if you make the wrong call, you could wind up unemployed, with a big dent in your credibility as an investor."

Fear of Embarrassment

The dread of professional humiliation is as powerful a motivation as fear of being fired, says Andrew Turner, director of research at Frank Russell & Co., an investment-advisory firm.

"If you're a treasurer or chief executive, the incentive to just put the lid on all this derivatives stuff is going to be pretty strong," he adds. "Even if you keep your job, you don't want to get labeled as [someone] who got snookered by an investment bank."

Derivatives are financial instruments whose returns are linked to, or derived from, the performance of some underlying asset, such as bonds, currencies or commodities.

Eastman Kodak Co. recently axed its pioneering $300 million investment in managed futures and decided to severely limit the use of derivatives in its pension fund. Just a few weeks ago, **Federal Express** Corp. followed suit, yanking $25 million allocated to managed futures strategies under the aegis of **Mount Lucas Management** Corp., of Princeton, N.J.

Mount Lucas, which also ran the Kodak portfolio, says both investments were profitable, and the Federal Express investment represented one of that company's top-performing assets last year. The decisions, says Mark Stratton, senior vice-president of Mount Lucas, appear to be linked to changes in senior financial personnel at the two companies and to changes in the composition of investment committees.

Mirroring Kodak, Federal Express

Decisions like those by Kodak and Federal Express are just the tip of the iceberg. Similar policies are being adopted quietly by other companies, says one New York banker specializing in risk management, who asked not to be named.

"Trustees have said we shouldn't be investing in derivatives at all," says Russell Meekins, director of finance at the University of South Carolina Educational Foundation, which manages about $50 million. Trustees fearful of offending donors have banned direct investments in even "plain vanilla" products such as exchange-traded futures contracts, Mr. Meekins says. A donor, he adds, doesn't want to read in the newspaper that the university has lost part of its endowment through the use of derivatives.

Furthermore, "career-risk" considerations surface at all levels. For instance, in California and Ohio, where public funds and municipalities have suffered large derivatives-related losses, legislators worried about appearing too lax are responding to public outrage by debating new laws that would ban, or at least limit, this kind of fund's usage of products deemed to be more risky.

Jeremy Grantham, a partner at Grantham Mayo Van Otterloo & Co., a Boston investment management firm, says the misadventures of high-profile investors such as Orange County have rendered even plain derivative products unpalatable.

"If you buy comfortable-looking, well-known, stable stocks like drug companies, or Coca-Cola, you're taking very little career risk because clients will blame a stupid market if things go wrong," Mr. Grantham says. "But if you buy something more risky or unconventional and fail, the response is going to be: 'How could you be so stupid?'"

Source: Suzanne McGee, "Derivatives Could Hedge Career Growth," *The Wall Street Journal*, August 24, 1995, p. C–1.

---

market risk encompasses both (1) *"balance-sheet risk,"* which is **the risk of incurring a loss on a *recorded* asset** and (2) *"off-balance-sheet risk,"* which is **the risk of incurring losses above and beyond an asset or liability's recorded value.** For most derivatives, a party to a contract that can go into a payable position is exposed to incurring unlimited losses. To illustrate, assume that Party A is in a $300,000 receivable position in a derivative contract and that Party B (the counterparty) is thus in a $300,000 payable position.

1. **Option-based derivatives.** In an option-based derivative (recall that only *one* party can have an *unfavorable* outcome), Party A's market risk consists entirely of *balance-sheet risk* and is limited to $300,000 (its receivable). In contrast, Party B's risk consists entirely of *off-balance-sheet risk* and is unlimited because **the potential loss is *not* limited to the recorded amount of a particular asset or liability.** (Note that Party A also has *credit risk* and Party B also has *liquidity risk.*)

2. **Forward-based derivatives.** In a forward-based derivative (recall that *either* party can have an *unfavorable* outcome), Party A's market risk consists of both *balance-sheet risk* and *off-balance-sheet risk* and is thus unlimited because the value of its derivative (a $300,000 receivable position) can become negative (a payable). In contrast, Party B's market risk consists entirely of *off-balance-sheet risk* and is thus unlimited because its $300,000 payable position can become larger.

Thus market risk problems can lead to credit risk and liquidity risk problems so market risk is the major concern of derivative holders. Many believe that latent market risk should be quantified and disclosed in notes to the financial statements. One such way is to give the hypothetical effects of several possible changes in market prices in conjunction with the likelihood of such movements occurring. Value or earnings at risk are latent risks that should be distinguished from realized or unrealized gains or losses.[17]

In this chapter, we discussed and illustrated the use of both an option-based derivative (FX options) and a forward-based derivative (FX forwards). Discussions and illustrations of how to account for other types of derivatives can be found in various professional publications, international finance texts, and specialized books.[18]

X DISCLOSURES REQUIRED FOR FX DERIVATIVES

As stated previously, the use of financial instruments to manage FX exposures has become enormous as a result of the globalization of business. For instance, the contractual value of Ford Motor Company's FX derivatives (forwards, options, and swaps) outstanding at the end of 1995 was $24.5 billion.

When companies use FX derivatives, financial statement readers generally can use the following information (usually disclosed in notes to the financial statements) to assess the firm's risk and return:

1. **Purpose.** The reasons for their use (such as to hedge certain exposures or speculate).

2. **Types.** The classes used (such as forwards, options, and swaps).

---

[17]Various ways to quantify market risk are described in *SFAS No. 119*, "Disclosure About Derivative Financial Instruments and Fair Value of Financial Instruments," para. 69.

[18]Examples are (1) *The Handbook of Derivatives & Synthetics* published by Probus Publishing Company (Chicago), (2) *Statements on Management Accounting (Statement Number 4M)*, "Practices and Techniques: Understanding Financial Instruments," published by the Institute of Management Accountants.

3. **Valuation.** The manner of valuing them in the balance sheet (and their specific location) and their fair value.

4. **Recognition policy.** The policy regarding their recognition versus deferral of FX gains and losses (and the specific location in the statements of recognized and deferred FX gains and losses).

5. **Timing.** When FX gains and losses have been temporarily deferred at the financial reporting date, the period of time until the related hedged anticipated transactions (forecasted and committed) are expected to occur (and thus result in recognition of the deferred FX gains and losses).

6. **Credit risk.** The potential for future losses in the event the other party to the contract fails to make payment.

7. **Market risk.**[19] The potential for future losses if adverse changes in the underlying market prices occur, which the FASB encourages.

8. **Internal controls.** The use of adequate controls to prevent unauthorized transactions that could result in material losses is assumed, but affirmations to that effect are common practice.

THE FASB'S RESPONSE

Because of the increasing use of derivatives and the desire for more information regarding them, the FASB has responded by issuing the following pronouncements:

1. *SFAS No. 105*, "Disclosure of Information About Financial Instruments With Off-Balance-Sheet Risk and Financial Instruments With Credit Risk" (1990).

2. *SFAS No. 107*, "Disclosure About Fair Value of Financial Instruments" (1991).

3. *SFAS No. 119*, "Disclosure About Derivative Financial Instruments and Fair Value of Financial Instruments" (1994). (This pronouncement amended several paragraphs of the two preceding pronouncements.)

These pronouncements (1) *require* disclosures regarding the preceding items 1 through 6 and (2) *encourage* disclosures regarding item 7.

ILLUSTRATIVE DISCLOSURE FOR THE FOREIGN EXCHANGE RISK MANAGEMENT CATEGORY OF DERIVATIVES

An example of required disclosures for an international *nonbanking* entity's FX risk management category of derivatives follows:

The company (1) enters into foreign currency forward exchange contracts to hedge certain firm sales and purchase commitments denominated in foreign currencies (principally the pound and the yen) and (2) purchases foreign currency options to hedge particular anticipated but not yet committed sales in foreign currencies.

The purpose of these hedging activities is to protect against the risk that the future dollar net cash inflows resulting from the sale of products to foreign customers and purchases from foreign suppliers will be adversely affected by changes in exchange rates. The term of these contracts is rarely more than two years.

---

[19]The importance of quantifying latent market risk to make the financial statements more useful to readers as well as the adequacy of the disclosures required in FASB *Statements 105, 107,* and *119* are discussed in depth in the article "Financial Reporting for Foreign Exchange Derivatives," by Stephen R. Goldberg, Charles A. Tritschler, and Joseph H. Godwin, *Accounting Horizons,* June 1995, pp. 1–15.

Information on FX derivatives (FX forwards and purchased FX options) outstanding at December 31, 19X1 (using current market prices provided by outside quotation services), follows (amounts are in millions):

	Carrying Amount[a]	Fair Value	Contractual Amount
Receivable positions	$115	$115	
Liability positions	140	140	
	$255	$255	$7,700

[a]*The separation of these amounts as to the class of financial instruments (FX forwards and FX options) is not required.*

At December 31, 19X1, the company has deferred realized and unrealized FX gains and losses from hedging (1) firm sales and purchase commitments and (2) anticipated but not yet committed sales transactions. The deferred losses (totaling $23 million) are reported as other assets; the deferred gains (totaling $38 million) are reported as other liabilities. These deferred items will be recognized in income in 19X2 and 19X3 either as (1) part of the sale or purchase transaction when those transactions are recognized in the income statement or (2) other gains or losses at the time the forecasted transaction does not materialize.

XI A SUMMARY OF THE FASB'S PROPOSED NEW STANDARD (JUNE 1996) ON DERIVATIVES AND HEDGING ACTIVITIES

In this section, we briefly summarize the FASB's proposed new standard on derivatives and hedging activities (exposed for public comment in June 1996) that we mentioned in the chapter overview. Recall that the FASB has indicated that the ultimate final standard is expected to (1) supersede *SFAS No. 105* and *119* and (2) slightly amend *SFAS No. 52* and *107*. The major elements of the proposed standard follow:

1. **All** derivatives would be valued on the balance sheet as assets and liabilities at their fair value.

2. The designated reason for holding the derivative (to be formally documented) will be the basis for the accounting treatment of the gains and losses.

3. **All** gains and losses on derivatives would be reported in earnings currently with the following two exceptions for which delayed recognition—**by means of a direct credit or charge to stockholders' equity**—is required.

   a. Hedges of forecasted transactions.

   b. Hedges of net investments in foreign subsidiaries.

4. *Purchased options* would qualify as hedging instruments. No distinction is to be made between changes in *time value* and changes in *intrinsic value*.

5. *Written options*—in contrast to *purchased options*—would *not* qualify as hedges of an existing asset, an existing liability, or a firm commitment.

The proposed accounting treatment of FX gains and losses and the way in which current practice would change is shown in Illustration 17–13.

STATEMENT OF COMPREHENSIVE INCOME

In June 1996, the FASB issued an exposure draft, "Reporting Comprehensive Income." In a statement of comprehensive income (which only the United Kingdom

	ILLUSTRATION 17–13	Proposed Accounting Treatment of FX Gains and Losses and the Impact on Current Practice

Purpose of FX Derivative	Accounting Treatment for FX Gains and Losses on FX Derivatives	Impact on Current Practice
To hedge an existing asset or liability.	Recognize in earnings currently. The hedged item (the recorded asset or liability) is marked to market with the FX gain or loss recognized in earnings currently.	None
To hedge a firm commitment.	Recognize in earnings currently. The hedged item (usually a sales order or a purchase order) is marked to market with the FX gain or loss recognized in earnings currently. The offsetting debit or credit is recorded in an FX Receivable or FX Payable account. When delivery occurs, record item acquired or sold net of the position on the FX derivative on that date.	A major procedural change; however, the income statement result is substantively the same as current practice.
To hedge a forecasted transaction.	Report as a direct charge or credit to stockholders' equity. Remove and recognize in earnings on the date the forecasted transaction was designated to occur.	A major change from current practice, which is inconsistent and restrictive as compared to *SFAS No. 80.*
To hedge a foreign subsidiary's net investment position	Report as a direct charge or credit to stockholders' equity. Remove and recognize as earnings upon disposition of the investment.	None
To accomplish something other than the three preceding purposes (such as to speculate).	Recognize in earnings currently.	None

uses), all items that affect stockholders' equity (other than transactions with shareholders) are reported. Thus no items could bypass the income statement as (1) currently occurs under existing GAAP and (2) would occur under the FASB's tentative approach of posting hedging gains and losses on forecasted transactions directly to equity pending occurrence of the forecasted transaction.

Part of the motivation for activating this project was the belief that such a statement may be the best vehicle for reporting unrealized hedging gains and losses on forecasted transactions. This statement, which is discussed and illustrated in Chapter 18 (page 643), is long overdue.

END-OF-CHAPTER REVIEW

SUMMARY OF KEY POINTS

1. **FX exposures** are managed by **hedging**—a technique of deploying financial instruments (primarily FX forwards and FX options) so that a **counterbalancing** gain occurs on the financial instrument in the event of a loss on the hedged item.
2. Refer to Illustration 17–14 for a summary of hedging procedures and hedging terminology.

ILLUSTRATION 17–14	**Summary of Hedging Procedures and Hedging Terminology**			
Inventory Transaction		**To Hedge Inventory Transaction**	**Position Terminology Used in Hedging Contracts**	
Type	**Purpose**		**FX Options**	**FX Forwards**
Importing	To buy inventory	Buy FX	"Call"	"Long"
Exporting	To sell inventory	Sell FX	"Put"	"Short"

3. *SFAS No. 52* allows hedge accounting only for (a) exposed assets and liabilities, (b) identifiable foreign currency commitments, and (c) net investments.
4. In a **hedge of an identifiable foreign currency commitment,** the effect of exchange rate changes that occur during the **commitment period** must be **deferred** and treated as an adjustment to the cost of the item acquired or sales price of the item sold.
5. **Premiums** and **discounts** on FX forwards used in hedging FX receivables and payables are accrued onto the books over the life of the contract (split accounting). For hedges of identifiable foreign currency commitments, accruals occurring *before* **the transaction date may be deferred** and treated as nonsplit adjustments to the cost basis of the related hedged item when that item is recorded onto the books; accruals occurring *after* **the transaction date** of the item being hedged must be reported currently in the income statement.
6. **Premiums** and **discounts** may exist in forward exchange contracts entered into for **speculating**—however, they are *not* given separate accounting recognition because **nonsplit accounting is required.**
7. Extensive disclosures (in the notes) are required for derivatives as to purpose, strategies, classes, recognition and deferral policies, fair values, credit risk, and contractual (or notional) amounts.
8. **Derivatives** are a special type of financial instrument (contracts) that (a) **derive their value from another financial instrument, a commodity, an index, or a rate** and (b) **are used to manage risks** or improve returns.
9. Derivatives are **option based** (one sided in nature) or **forward based** (two sided in nature).
10. Derivatives are reported in the balance sheet **at their fair values. The amounts reported for these contract values are** substantively receivables and payables.
11. **Credit risk** is the risk of not being able to collect a derivative's receivable position.
12. **Market risk** is the potential for incurring losses as a result of adverse changes in the fair value of the derivative.

GLOSSARY OF NEW TERMS

Anticipatory transactions   Transactions expected to occur in the future; they may or may *not* be under contract.

Credit risk   The possibility of *not* collecting a receivable position in a derivative.

Derivative   The term used to refer to a wide variety of financial products whose value depends on changes in (1) a financial instrument (such as stocks and bonds), (2) a commodity, (3) an index representing values of groups of such instruments or assets, or (4) a rate (such as currency exchange rates and interest rates). (The most commonly used derivatives are options, forwards, futures, and swaps.)

Discount (on FX forward)   The amount at which a currency is contractually bought or sold (at the forward rate) *below* its current value (at the spot rate).

Financial instruments   Cash, evidence of ownership interest in an entity, and contracts that involve rights and obligation to exchange cash or other financial instruments.

Firmly committed transactions   Anticipated future transactions that are under contract or have such a severe penalty that nonperformance is remote.

Forecasted transactions   Expected future transactions that are *not* under contract or do *not* have severe potential penalties for nonperformance.

Foreign currency forward contract   See FX forward.

Foreign currency option contract   See FX option.

FX forward   A contractual agreement to exchange currencies of different countries at a specified future date at a specified rate (the forward rate).

FX forward rate   A rate quoted for future delivery of currencies to be exchanged (usually up to one year).

FX option   A contractual agreement giving the holder the right to buy or sell a given amount of currency at a specified price for a period of time or at a point in time.

Hedge accounting   An accounting treatment in which the gain or loss on the hedging instrument and the loss or gain on the hedged item are given concurrent recognition or concurrent deferral.

Intrinsic value (in the context of options)   The value of an option that is "in the money" as represented by the favorable difference between the spot rate and the exercise (strike) price.

Liquidity risk   The possibility that the party in the payable position may *not* be able to fulfill its obligation because it lacks liquid assets.

Market risk   The possibility of incurring losses as a result of adverse changes in the fair value of a derivative.

Master netting arrangement   A contractual arrangement used by traders in which a default on any one contract enables all of the separate contracts with the same party to be treated as one contract. This entitles either party to terminate the entire arrangement and to demand the net settlement of all of the individual contracts.

Premium (on FX forward)   The amount at which a currency is contractually bought or sold (at the forward rate) *above* its current value (at the spot rate).

Purchased option   An option contract viewed from the perspective of the *option holder* who acquires a right from the other party as a result of paying a fee (called a *premium*); as a result, the option holder *can* have a *gain* on the contract but *cannot* incur a *loss*.

Split accounting   Accounting—*as a time value element*—for (1) premiums and discounts on forwards and (2) premiums on options separately from changes in the *intrinsic value element*.

Time value   (in the context of options) That portion of an option's value that is *not* attributable to the contract's intrinsic value.

Written option   An option contract from the perspective of the writer of the option who has granted a right to the other party for a fee (called a *premium*); as a result, the writer *can* incur a *loss* on the contract but *cannot* have a *gain*.

SELF-STUDY QUESTIONS

(Answers are at the end of the chapter.)

1. A domestic entity that enters into an FX forward to *sell* foreign currency when the spot rate (direct) is \$.55 and the forward rate is \$.53 has
   a. A premium that is recorded as a debit.
   b. A premium that is recorded as a credit.
   c. A discount that is recorded as a debit.
   d. A discount that is recorded as a credit.

2. A domestic exporter that enters into an FX forward to hedge an FX receivable must do the following:
   a. Defer any hedging FX gain or loss until the settlement date.
   b. Initially record—at the spot rate—a receivable from the FX trader.
   c. Initially record—at the contractually fixed amount to be paid—a liability to the FX trader.
   d. Continuously carry—at the forward rate—an FX receivable from the FX trader.
   e. Reflect adjustments to its FX position for the change in the spot rate—*not* the change in the forward rate.

3. A domestic importer enters into an FX forward to hedge an identifiable foreign currency commitment. Which of the following is correct?

    a. Any hedging FX gain or loss up to the transaction date for the item being bought must be deferred and treated as an adjustment to the cost of the item being bought.

    b. The foreign currency to be received from the FX trader is to be initially recorded at the fixed contractual amount.

    c. The foreign currency to be received from the FX trader is to be continuously carried at the forward exchange rate.

    d. The hedging FX gain or loss will exactly offset the loss or gain on the purchase contract.

4. On 12/10/X1, Hedlex entered into a 90-day FX forward involving 1,000,000 FF in anticipation that the French franc would weaken. The following direct exchange rates are assumed:

	December 10, 19X1	December 31, 19X1	March 10, 19X2
Spot rate	$.90	$.88	$.91
Forward rate	.86	.87	n/a

The amount of the hedging FX gain or loss that would be reported in the 19X1 income statement, assuming that the FX forward is the hedge of an exposed receivable arising from an exporting transaction, is

a. a $10,000 gain.   f. a $30,000 loss.

b. a $10,000 loss.   g. a $40,000 gain.

c. a $20,000 gain.   h. a $40,000 loss.

d. a $20,000 loss.   i. $–0–.

e. a $30,000 gain.

5. Use the information in Question 4, but assume that the FX forward pertains to the hedge of an identifiable foreign currency commitment involving the sale of special equipment expected to be shipped on 3/10/X2.

6. Use the information in Question 4, but assume that the FX forward was entered into for speculation.

ASSIGNMENT MATERIAL

REVIEW QUESTIONS

1. What is the definition of *hedging*?
2. What is the definition of *hedge accounting*?
3. What is the difference between a *put* option and a *call* option?
4. What is the difference between a *written* option and a *purchased* option?
5. Can a nonbank entity lose money on an *option*?
6. To hedge an exposed asset, should a call or put option be acquired? For an exposed liability?
7. What is *split accounting* as it applies to *options*?
8. In an FX *forward*, which party is the *issuer* and who is the *holder*?
9. What is the *forward rate*? Why does it differ from the *spot rate*?
10. When does a *premium* exist on an FX forward? A *discount*?
11. How does one fulfill an FX forward?
12. How are the *obligations* under FX forwards reported in the balance sheet?
13. What is the distinction between *hedging* and *speculating*?
14. How are FX forwards valued in speculations?
15. What is a hedge of an *identifiable foreign currency commitment*?
16. What three conditions must be met to qualify a forward exchange contract as the hedge of an *identifiable foreign currency commitment*?
17. How do FX options differ from FX forwards?
18. What is meant when it is said that an FX *forward* is substantively two options?

19. What is *split accounting* as it applies to *FX forwards*?
20. Can hedges of *forecasted transactions* be given *hedge accounting* treatment? Give examples.
21. Can a domestic company hedge the *forecasted net income* of a foreign subsidiary?
22. What are *competitive* or *strategic hedges*? Give examples.
23. Can *competitive* or *strategic hedges* be given hedge accounting treatment?
24. What does the term *financial instruments* mean?
25. What does the term *derivative* mean?
26. What are four types of items from which derivatives can derive their value?
27. What are some of the unique *contractual elements* of derivatives?
28. What are some of the unique *characteristics* of derivatives?
29. How do *option-based* derivatives differ from *forward-based* derivatives?
30. What types of risks exist for derivatives?
31. What is *credit* risk? What is *market* risk?

EXERCISES

E 17–1 **Options: Distinguishing Between Hedging and Speculating**   Determine whether the following options contracts are hedging transactions or speculating transactions (assume that the domestic company has transaction exposure in each case):

	Domestic Importer or Exporter	Anticipates	Type of Option Contract
1.	Exporter	U.S. dollar weakening	Call
2.	Importer	U.S. dollar weakening	Call
3.	Exporter	Peso weakening	Put
4.	Importer	Franc strengthening	Call
5.	Exporter	Yen strengthening	Call
6.	Importer	Mark weakening	Put
7.	Exporter	No expectation	Put
8.	Importer	No expectation	Call

E 17–2 **Forwards: Calculating the Expected Forward Rate**   On 1/1/X1, Cashco desires to invest $1,000,000 cash in a one-year CD at the highest possible interest rate. The interest rate obtainable in the United States is 7%. In France, the interest rate obtainable is 10%. The direct exchange rate on 1/1/X1 is $.50.

Required 1. What is the expected forward rate for a one-year FX forward under the interest rate parity system?
2. Would the franc be selling at a premium or a discount on the forward market?

E 17–3 **Forwards: Identifying When to Use Hedging**   Hedglex has importing and exporting transactions and uses forward exchange contracts to hedge its exposure (but never to speculate), depending on management's assessment of whether the exchange rate will move favorably or unfavorably. Hedglex must determine whether it should contract to buy or sell a foreign currency in each of the following situations:

	Area of Foreign Currency Exposure	Direct Rate or Currency	Direction	Buy	Sell	Neither
1.	Exporting	Direct rate	Up	___	___	___
		Direct rate	Down	___	___	___
		U.S. dollar	Strengthen	___	___	___
		U.S. dollar	Weaken	___	___	___
		Foreign	Strengthen	___	___	___
		Foreign	Weaken	___	___	___

(continued)

2. Importing

Direct rate	Up	___	___	___
Direct rate	Down	___	___	___
U.S. dollar	Strengthen	___	___	___
U.S. dollar	Weaken	___	___	___
Foreign	Strengthen	___	___	___
Foreign	Weaken	___	___	___

Required   Place an X in the appropriate Buy, Sell, or Neither column of the table.

E 17–4   **Forwards: Distinguishing Between Hedging and Speculating**   Determine whether the following FX forwards are hedging transactions or speculating transactions (assume that the domestic company has transaction exposure in each case):

	Domestic Importer or Exporter	Anticipates	Buys or Sells in Forward Market
1.	Exporter	U.S. dollar weakening	Buys
2.	Importer	U.S. dollar weakening	Buys
3.	Exporter	Peso weakening	Sells
4.	Importer	Franc strengthening	Buys
5.	Exporter	Yen strengthening	Buys
6.	Importer	Mark weakening	Sells
7.	Exporter	No expectation	Sells
8.	Importer	No expectation	Buys

E 17–5   **Forwards: Matching Accounts With Transactions—"Gross" or "Broad" Accounting**   For each of the following accounts, identify the transaction(s) that would involve their use. For hedging purposes, assume that (1) FX forwards—*not* FX options—are used and (2) the obligations of each party under the FX forward *are* reflected in the general ledger.

		Nature of Transaction			
		Importing	Exporting	Importing Hedge	Exporting Hedge
1.	FX Accounts Receivable	___	___	___	___
2.	FX Accounts Payable	___	___	___	___
3.	Dollars due from FX Trader	___	___	___	___
4.	Dollars due to FX Trader	___	___	___	___
5.	FX due to FX Trader	___	___	___	___
6.	FX due from FX Trader	___	___	___	___

E 17–6   **Forwards: Determining Accounting Treatment of Transactions**

			Foreign Currency Transaction Gains and Losses Are to Be	
	Transaction	Premium or Discount Can Exist	Recognized Currently (in income)	Deferred
1.	Importing and exporting transactions	___	___	___
2.	Hedge of a recorded but unsettled foreign currency transaction	___	___	___
3.	Hedge of an identifiable foreign currency commitment	___	___	___
4.	Speculation in foreign currency	___	___	___

Required   For each of these transactions, place an X in the applicable column(s). For hedging purposes, assume that forward exchange contracts—*not* foreign currency options—are used.

PROBLEMS

P 17–1 **Options: Hedging an Exposed Liability** On 11/1/X1, Callex (which has a 12/31 year-end) took delivery from a French firm of inventory costing 100,000 FF. Payment is due in 90 days. Concurrently, Callex paid $900 cash to acquire a 90-day out-of-the-money *call* option for 100,000 French francs at $.20. Direct exchange rates for the franc on the respective dates are as follows:

	November 1, 19X1	December 31, 19X1	January 30, 19X2
Spot rate	$.20	$.22	$.23

(The symbols for foreign currencies are provided on page 538.)

Required Prepare all journal entries relating to these transactions.

P 17–2 **Options: Hedging an Exposed Asset** On 12/16/X1, Putico (which has a 12/31 year-end) delivered inventory to a Danish firm. Payment of 1,000,000 Danish krones is due in 60 days. Concurrently, Putico paid $4,000 cash to acquire a 60-day out-of-the-money *put* option for 1,000,000 Danish krones at $.16. Direct exchange rates for the krone on the respective dates are as follows:

	December 16, 19X1	December 31, 19X1	February 14, 19X2
Spot rate	$.16	$.15	$.146

Required Prepare all journal entries relating to these transactions.

P 17–3 **Options: Hedging an Exposed Liability** On 12/1/X1, Optix Company (which has a 12/31 year-end) purchased an option to buy 1,000,000 German marks at $.61 during the next 90 days. The cost of the FX option was $9,000 (1.5% of $600,000), which was paid in cash. The FX option was purchased to protect an exposed liability of 1,000,000 German marks relating to an importing transaction recorded on 12/1/X1. At 12/31/X1, Optix had *not* exercised this FX option, and the FX option contract could be sold in the open market for $36,000.

Direct exchange rates for the mark on the respective dates are as follows:

	December 1, 19X1	December 31, 19X1
Spot rate	$.60	$.64

Required 1. Prepare the entry required on 12/1/X1.
2. Prepare the adjusting entries required at 12/31/X1.
3. Perform requirement 2 assuming that (a) the spot rate at 12/31/X1 is $.57 and (b) the FX option can be sold in the open market for only $1,000.

P 17–4 **Forwards: Hedging an Exposed Liability—No Premium or Discount** On 10/17/X1, Bavarotti (which has a 12/31 year-end) took delivery from an Italian firm of inventory costing 40,000,000 Lit. Payment is due in 90 days. Concurrently, Bavarotti entered into an FX forward to *buy* 40,000,000 Lit in 90 days. Direct exchange rates for the lira on the respective dates are as follows:

	October 17, 19X1	December 31, 19X1	January 15, 19X2
Spot rate	$.00065	$.00071	$.00070
Forward rate	.00065	.00071	n/a

Required 1. Prepare all entries relating to these transactions.
2. Indicate the amounts that should be presented in the asset and liability sections of the 12/31/X1 balance sheet, assuming that all of the inventory is still on hand.

P 17–5 **Forwards: Hedging an Exposed Liability—Problem 17–4 With Premium Added** On 10/17/X1, Bavarotti (which has a 12/31 year-end) took delivery from an Italian firm of inventory costing 40,000,000 Lit. Payment is due in 90 days. Concurrently, Bavarotti entered into an FX forward to *buy* 40,000,000 Lit in 90 days.

Direct exchange rates for the lira on the respective dates are as follows:

	October 17, 19X1	December 31, 19X1	January 15, 19X2
Spot rate	$.00065	$.00071	$.00070
Forward rate	.00068	.000715	n/a

Required
1. Prepare all entries relating to these transactions.
2. Indicate the amounts that should be presented in the asset and liability sections of the 12/31/X1 balance sheet, assuming that all of the inventory is still on hand.

P 17–6 **Forwards: Hedging an Exposed Asset**   On 4/1/X1, Fallsey (which has a 6/30 fiscal year-end) delivered to a Canadian firm inventory it sold for 100,000 Can$. Payment is due in 120 days. Concurrently, Fallsey entered into an FX forward to *sell* 100,000 Can$ in 120 days.
Direct exchange rates for the Canadian dollar on the respective dates are as follows:

	April 1, 19X1	June 30, 19X1	July 30, 19X2
Spot rate	$.81	$.825	$.82
Forward rate	.80	.823	n/a

Required
1. Prepare all entries relating to these transactions.
2. Indicate the amounts that should be presented in the asset and liability sections of the 6/30/X1 balance sheet.

P 17–7 **Forwards: Hedging a Noncancelable Purchase Order**   On 10/2/X1, Skeeco (which has a 12/31 year-end) ordered a custom-built aerial tram from a Swiss firm. The purchase order is noncancelable. The purchase price is 1,000,000 SFr, with delivery and payment to be in 180 days. Concurrently, Skeeco entered into an FX forward to *buy* 1,000,000 SFr in 180 days.
On 3/31/X2, the tram was delivered and payment was made. Skeeco desires to *maximize* earnings in 19X1. Direct exchange rates for the Swiss franc on the respective dates are as follows:

	October 2, 19X1	December 31, 19X1	March 31, 19X2
Spot rate	$.47	$.463	$.45
Forward rate	.48	.467	n/a

Required
1. Prepare all entries relating to these transactions.
2. Prepare a T account of the activity in the FX Contract Value—Forward, **net** account through 3/31/X2.
3. Indicate the amounts that should be presented in the asset and liability sections of the 12/31/X1 balance sheet.

P 17–8 **Forwards: Hedging a Noncancelable Sales Order**   On 10/12/X1, Wingex (which has a 12/31 year-end) obtained a noncancelable sales order from a Maltese firm for a custom-made marble statue. The contract price was 100,000 Lm. Concurrently, Wingex entered into an FX forward to *sell* 100,000 Lm in 100 days at the forward rate of $3.15.
The statue was delivered on 12/11/X1. Full payment was received on 1/20/X2. Direct exchange rates for the lira on the respective dates are as follows:

	October 12, 19X1	December 11, 19X1	December 31, 19X1	January 20, 19X2
Spot rate	$3.20	$3.00	$3.09	$2.97
Forward rate	$3.15	n/a	n/a	n/a

Required
1. Prepare a T account of the activity in the FX Contract Value—Forward, **net** account through 1/20/X2.
2. Prepare a partial balance sheet at 12/31/X1.
3. Prepare a partial income statement for 19X1.

P 17–9 **Forwards: Speculating**   On 11/1/X1, Riskco concluded that the French franc would *weaken* during the next six months. To report a gain, Riskco entered into an FX forward to *sell* 1,000,000 FF in 180 days at the forward rate. Direct exchange rates for the franc on the respective dates are as follows:

	November 1, 19X1	December 31, 19X1	April 30, 19X2
Spot rate	$.190	$.180	$.210
Forward rate	.199	.187	n/a

Required   **1.** Prepare all entries required through 12/31/X1 (Riskco's year-end).

2. Show how the amounts relating to the FX forward would be reported in the 12/31/X1 balance sheet.

3. Repeat requirement 2 using *split accounting,* which is *not* allowable GAAP.

4. Prepare all entries required at 4/30/X2.

P 17–10   **Options: Hedging Planned Importing Purchases**   On 1/1/X1, Splitex purchased a *call* FX option involving 1,000,000 FF, with an expiration date of 12/31/X1. The purpose of the option is to hedge 19X1's planned importing purchases of 1,000,000 FF. The option's cost was $16,000. The strike price was $.39. At 6/30/X1 (a financial reporting date), import purchases totaled 600,000 FF, of which $500,000 had been resold to customers. Direct exchange rates for the franc on the respective dates are as follows:

	January 1, 19X1	June 30, 19X1
Spot rate	$.40	$.47

Required   **1.** Calculate the option's time value and intrinsic value at inception.

2. Calculate the option's intrinsic value at 6/30/X1.

3. Calculate the gain that may be deferred at 6/30/X1 as an adjustment to inventory, assuming that hedge accounting is allowed.

4. Prepare all entries relating to the option.

P 17–11   **Forwards: Determining What to Disclose Under *SFAS No. 105 and 107***   Norisko, which has a *master netting arrangement* with each of its FX traders, has the following forward exchange contracts outstanding at 12/31/X1, its year-end:

	Net Position	Contract Amount (at the spot rate as of 12/31/X1)
With FX Trader 1:		
Long positions		
Receivable (gain) position	$4,900,000	$260,000,000
Payable (loss) position	4,100,000	210,000,000
Short positions		
Receivable (gain) position	3,100,000	150,000,000
Payable (loss) position	3,600,000	180,000,000
With FX Trader 2:		
Long positions		
Receivable (gain) position	2,300,000	110,000,000
Payable (loss) position	2,580,000	130,000,000
Short positions		
Receivable (gain) position	1,650,000	82,000,000
Payable (loss) position	1,500,000	77,000,000

Required   **1.** What amount(s) would be reported in the asset and liability sections of the balance sheet at 12/31/X1, assuming that there are no transactions with FX Trader 2?

2. Repeat question 1, but use the information given for both FX traders.

3. What disclosures would be made in the notes to the financial statements under *SFAS No. 105* and *SFAS No. 107*?

✳ THINKING CRITICALLY ✳

✳ CASES ✳

C 17–1   **To Hedge or Not to Hedge Exposed Assets**   A domestic exporter having FX receivables denominated in British pounds expects the British pound to strengthen.

Required   Should the exporter's treasury department hedge the FX receivables?

C 17–2   **To Speculate or Not to Speculate**   A domestic importer has FX payables denominated in French francs, all of which are hedged with FX forwards as called for by company operating policies. The importer is virtually certain that the French franc will strengthen.

Required   Should the importer's treasury department speculate in addition to hedging?

C 17–3   **Forwards: To Offset or Not to Offset**   At 12/31/X1, Hedgem Inc.'s net position in an FX forward that hedges an FX receivable (resulting from an exporting transaction with a French customer) is a $90,000 liability to an FX trader.

Also at this date, Hedgem is in a net asset position (a $70,000 receivable) on an FX forward that hedges an FX payable (resulting from an importing transaction with a Japanese vendor) with an FX trader.

Required   Should these amounts be presented separately or offset in the 12/31/X1 balance sheet? Why or why not?

C 17–4   **Forwards: Is Selling Forward at a Premium an Immediate Economic Gain?**   On 4/1/X1, simultaneously with the recording of a £100,000 receivable from a British customer, Hedgco Inc. entered into a 60-day FX forward to hedge this exposed receivable. The relevant exchange rates follow:

	April 1, 19X1	May 31, 19X1
Spot rate	$1.50	$1.53
Forward rate	1.51	n/a

Required   What arguments can you make for and against immediately recognizing the $1,000 premium on 4/1/X1 as an asset and as income? If not on 4/1/X1, when?

C 17–5   **Evaluating the Propriety of Deferring Hedging Gains and Losses on Forecasted Transactions**   In Illustration 17–12, a $64,000 gain is deferred at December 31, 19X1.

Required   1. What is the rationale for deferring the gain?
2. How does the deferred gain classification fit under the accounting model of Assets = Liabilities + Stockholders' Equity?
3. Would your answers to requirements 1 and 2 differ if the company were deferring a $64,000 loss at 12/31/X1 on a forward contract?

C 17–6   **Strategic Hedge—But How Much?**   On 12/31/X1, Quandree concluded that the French franc will weaken approximately 20% for 19X2. Quandree expects to lose (1) 20% of its domestic sales and (2) 20% of its export sales to France because its products are more expensive to domestic customers and French customers. Accordingly, Quandree has decided to hedge this exposure so that it reports the same gross profit for 19X1.

The spot direct exchange rate at 12/31/X1 is $.25; this rate was also the average rate for 19X1. Quandree had the following sales and costs for 19X1:

	Domestic Sales	Export Sales to France
Sales	$2,000,000	$400,000
Cost of sales	(1,500,000)	(300,000)
Gross Profit	$ 500,000	$100,000

Required   1. What types of FX options and FX forwards should be used to hedge this exposure?

2. What amount of currency should Quandree hedge because the forecasted export sales for 19X2 (forecasted at 20% lower than 19X1's actual export sales) will result in fewer dollars?

3. What amount of currency should Quandree hedge to make up for lost dollar gross profits because of lost sales?

✳ FINANCIAL ANALYSIS PROBLEMS ✳

FAP 17–1   **We Hedged But Lost Money Anyway?**   In Apple Computer's second quarter for the three months ended March 31, 1995, it stated:

> *Included in the Company's pretax results for the quarter were realized and unrealized losses on certain foreign currency hedging activities. As a result of these losses, interest and other income (expense), net for the quarter totaled ($50) million in expense, compared with ($7) million in expense in the year ago period.*
>
> *Apple generates a significant portion of its revenues from international sales and therefore has an ongoing need to exchange foreign currencies for dollars. The Company **attributed** [emphasis added] its foreign currency related expenses to recent dramatic declines in the value of the dollar relative to other currencies, and the impact of that decline on its outstanding foreign exchange contracts undertaken for hedging purposes. As part of its normal business practices, Apple, like many international companies, hedges its identified, and a portion of its anticipated, foreign currency flows against the risk of fluctuations in exchange rates against the U.S. dollar. This hedging is done through the purchase and sale of forward currency contracts and currency options.*
>
> *As a result of the decline in the value of the dollar, the value of the Company's net foreign currency forward and option contracts declined significantly, and the overall cost of hedging increased. The majority of the foreign exchange related expenses included in other income and expense, net for the second quarter is due to the unrealized marked-to-market valuation of sold currency options which Apple typically employs as part of its practice to hedge future anticipated revenues. Although the Company cannot predict movements in currency exchange rates [who can?], or their effect on its overall competitive position (and the situation is very complex), the Company believes that in general, it benefits more by a weaker dollar than by a stronger dollar.*

During a press conference, Apple executives emphasized that (1) the $50 million is mostly a "paper loss" right now, (2) the majority of the $50 million is from unrealized valuations of unclosed currency options in the quarter, and (3) if the dollar gets stronger (against the Japanese yen and the German mark), the unrealized loss goes away.

Required   1. How could Apple have lost $50 million if it were hedging?

2. What was Apple really doing? Be specific as to the exact type of option contracts that Apple entered into.

3. What does Apple mean when it says that most of the $50 million is only a paper loss?

4. What other information does Apple's statement that the loss could reverse reveal to you?

FAP 17–2   **Accounting for the Hedge of a Forecast Transaction**   Expecto Inc. has a calendar year-end. For each of the eight years ended 12/31/X8, a major customer in England placed a noncancelable sales order (£1,000,000) in June (with Expecto shipping the inventory the following month). A similar noncancelable sales order is expected to be placed in June 19X9.

On 1/2/X9, Expecto's foreign currency exchange management department concluded that the British pound would decrease in value from the current direct exchange rate of $1.50 (£1= $1.50) to $1.40 by 6/30/X9.

Thus, instead of the 19X9 sale occurring when the exchange rate is $1.50, it is expected to occur when the exchange rate is closer to $1.40.

Accordingly, on 1/2/X9, management entered into an FX option with a foreign currency dealer to sell £1,000,000 at the current direct exchange rate of $1.50. The cost of the option was $10,000—something that need not be dealt with in this problem. The option expires on 6/30/X9. Thus if the direct exchange rate is below $1.50 on 6/30/X9, Expecto will exercise the FX option. Because it will not have received any pounds from its British customer by 6/30/X9, Expecto will have to buy £1,000,000 in the open market on that date to be able to deliver £1,000,000 to the foreign currency dealer under the FX option.

Assume that on 6/30/X9, the direct exchange rate (spot) was $1.43 and Expecto exercised the option. Consequently, it has a gain (gross) of $70,000 on the FX option (£1,000,000 × $.07), less the $10,000 cost of the option, resulting in a net gain of $60,000. For simplicity, also assume the following:

1. On 3/31/X9, the direct exchange rate was $1.45.
2. On 6/27/X9, the British customer placed a £1,000,000 order that Expecto will fill in July 19X9.

Assume that Expecto could have accomplished its hedging objective using an FX forward instead of an FX option.

Disregarding current GAAP, several theoretical ways to account for the hedging gain (using either an option contract or a forward contract) at the end of the first and second quarters are as follows:

1. Report as **Deferred Income—classified among liabilities** until either realization occurs or the expected inventory sale occurs.
2. Report as **Deferred Income—classified between liabilities and equity** until either realization occurs or the expected inventory sale occurs.
3. Report **as a direct adjustment to equity**—bypassing the income statement until realization occurs or the expected inventory sale occurs.
4. Report in a **Statement of Comprehensive Income—classified as part of Other Changes in Stockholders' Equity until realization occurs** (this statement is illustrated in Chapter 18, on page 643).
5. Report in the income statement—**classified as part of Sales.**
6. Report in the income statement—**classified as part of Other Income.**

Required
1. What (a) underlying rationale, (b) theoretical and practical merits, and (c) theoretical and practical shortcomings exist for each method?
2. Which method do you think is the correct method (regardless of current GAAP)? Why?

ANSWERS TO SELF-STUDY QUESTIONS

1. c   2. e   3. a   4. c   5. i   6. b

TRANSLATING FOREIGN CURRENCY STATEMENTS: THE CURRENT RATE METHOD

18

When you can measure what you are speaking about and express it in numbers, you know something about it; but when you cannot express it in numbers, your knowledge is of a meager and unsatisfactory kind.

LORD KELVIN, 1891

The translation of foreign currency financial statements into U.S. dollars is one of the most complex and controversial of all accounting issues. The complexity exists because currency exchange rates change daily under the floating exchange rate system for both inflationary and noninflationary reasons. Unlike foreign currency importing and exporting transactions in which nearly unanimous agreement exists regarding how to report exchange rate changes, substantial diversity of opinion exists as to (1) which exchange rates to use and (2) whether the favorable or unfavorable effects of exchange rate changes should be reported currently in the income statement.

THE ACCOUNTING ISSUES

Five accounting issues must be addressed for a foreign operation of a domestic company.

1. How should the use of foreign accounting practices that differ from U.S. GAAP be handled?
2. Which translation method should be used to translate the financial statements of foreign units into U.S. dollars?
3. Should the effect of exchange rate changes be reported currently in the income statement?
4. What additional risks must be considered in reporting earnings from foreign operations? Is consolidation appropriate?
5. Should the extent of a company's foreign operations be disclosed as supplementary information?

We begin this chapter by discussing the diversity of accounting practices around the world, ongoing efforts to internationalize GAAP, and the way to restate foreign currency financial statements to U.S. GAAP. We then discuss the first of the two major conceptual issues pertaining to translating foreign currency statements into dollars: which exchange rates to use. In this chapter, we discuss the current rate method of translation, which is by far the predominant of the two translation methods allowed under U.S. GAAP. The other allowable method, the temporal method, is discussed in Chapter 19. Next we discuss the second major conceptual issue pertaining to translating foreign currency statements into dollars: how to report the effect of a change in the exchange rate. Finally, we discuss hedging transactions used to negate the effect of adverse changes in the exchange rate.

THE GOVERNING PRONOUNCEMENTS

TRANSLATION AND REPORTING FASB *Statement No. 52*, "Foreign Currency Translation," was issued in 1981 after three years of intensive research and extensive participation by professionals in industry, public accounting, higher education, and finance. The cornerstone of *SFAS No. 52* is the *functional currency concept*, which is used to determine which of the two translation methods to use for each particular foreign operation.

So that you can better understand and apply this concept, we discuss it in detail in the latter part of Chapter 19—*after* you have become technically proficient with the two allowable translation methods. Furthermore, because of the highly conceptual and controversial nature of the functional currency concept, we do *not* examine its validity until Chapter 20. Delaying this examination enables you to understand more readily the analysis presented. This examination is essential for assessing whether (1) the translated reporting results under GAAP reflect the economics of what has transpired and (2) these numbers should be used for managerial decision making.

ADDITIONAL RISKS AND THE APPROPRIATENESS OF CONSOLIDATION   Recall that the additional risks associated with foreign operations were listed in Chapter 16 in the discussion regarding establishing a foreign operation (page 538). Recall also that (1) the appropriateness of consolidating foreign subsidiaries was addressed in Chapters 1 and (2) the consolidation of foreign subsidiaries *is* mandatory unless control is lacking, in which case consolidation is prohibited.

SUPPLEMENTAL DISCLOSURES   The issue of presenting in financial statements the supplemental information pertaining to the extent of a company's foreign operations is addressed in FASB *Statement No. 14*, "Financial Reporting for Segments of a Business Enterprise." This pronouncement was discussed in detail in Chapter 15, which covers segment reporting.

I   THE DIVERSITY OF WORLDWIDE ACCOUNTING STANDARDS

Each foreign unit of a domestic company (1) keeps its books and records in its own local currency and (2) uses the accounting principles of the country in which it is located—not U.S. generally accepted accounting principles (GAAP). For both internal and external reporting purposes, however, the U.S. parent or home office needs statements in dollars for these foreign units. Furthermore, the statements in dollars must be presented in accordance with U.S. GAAP—not foreign GAAP.

Obviously, it does not make sense to either (1) add together financial statement amounts in dollars and foreign currencies or (2) report worldwide operations using one set of accounting principles for domestic operations and a variety of accounting principles for foreign operations.

Accordingly, it is first necessary to *restate* the foreign currency statements to U.S. GAAP (done on a worksheet). These *restated* foreign currency statements are then *translated* into dollars, using appropriate currency exchange rates (also done on a worksheet). Thus **we restate and then translate**—*not* translate and then restate.[1]

Before showing the worksheet procedures used to restate foreign currency statements to U.S. GAAP, however, we discuss briefly the substantial diversity of accounting systems and practices that exist around the world. Thus you can more fully appreciate that it is often a monumental task to restate foreign currency statements to U.S. GAAP—a task that is usually far more time consuming than translating foreign currency statements into dollars (which usually can be readily done using international accounting software packages and templates).[2]

---

[1]Some accountants (but very few), however, believe that the process should be translate and then restate.

[2]For a description of the more popular software packages designed for handling foreign operations, see "Software That Speaks Your Language" by Marc I. Lebow and Ajay Adhikari, *Journal of Accountancy*, July 1995, pp. 65–72.

DIFFERING REPORTING SYSTEMS

Different accounting standards and systems have evolved throughout the world for many reasons, which are discussed in substantially more detail in international accounting texts.[3] Most countries use one of the following reporting systems.[4]

THE BRITISH-AMERICAN-DUTCH SYSTEM Providing full and accurate financial information to investors is the orientation of this system, which is used by Australia, Canada, India, the Netherlands, the United Kingdom, and the United States.

THE CONTINENTAL SYSTEM Providing creditor protection, using business conservatism, and minimizing income taxes are the orientation of this system, in which creditors (usually banks) are viewed as the primary financial statement users. Accounting standards are usually written into the statutes, and major differences often do *not* exist between financial reporting and tax reporting. The accounting standards are highly conservative, which greatly minimizes income taxes. Furthermore, managements are given wide discretion in many areas, and relevant information is not always provided to shareholders. Most of the European countries and Japan use this system.

A significant competitive advantage of this system compared with the British-American-Dutch system is that firms are *not* burdened with the substantial administrative costs of complying with two distinctly separate reporting systems. (Note that deferred income taxes cannot be an issue if the same reporting system is used for both financial reporting and tax reporting.)

THE SOUTH AMERICAN SYSTEM This system is basically the continental system with the addition of price-level accounting (making periodic adjustments for inflation). It is used by most of the countries in South America, the majority of which have had severe inflation for decades. For instance, Brazil has had annual inflation exceeding 200% in the past decade (the high being 2,567% in 1993); since 1960, its prices have multiplied a staggering 22 billion times.[5]

SELECTED WIDESPREAD DIFFERENCES BETWEEN U.S. GAAP AND FOREIGN GAAP

Certain of the major widespread differences between U.S. GAAP and foreign GAAP are as follows:

1. **LIFO inventory costing.** Although widely used in the United States, this method has limited acceptance in other countries for both financial and tax reporting.

2. **Goodwill.** Although capitalization and mandatory amortization over no more than 40 years is required in the United States, virtually all other countries (1) allow it to be expensed or charged to equity at the business combination date or (2) require it to be amortized over a much shorter period (five years in most cases) if capitalized.

---

[3]For an in-depth discussion of the different accounting systems and standards used overseas, see Gerhard Mueller, Helen Gernon, and Gary Meek, *Accounting: An International Perspective* (Homewood, Ill.: Richard D. Irwin, 1994).

[4]The reporting system for the countries formerly included in the communist bloc is presently evolving from a rigid system in which financial statements were furnished only to government planners to a more open reporting system.

[5]"Why Does Brazil Face Such Woes? Some See a Basic Ethical Lapse," *The Wall Street Journal*, January 4, 1994, p. A1.

3. **Pooling of interests.** Although required in the United States when the specified conditions are met, it is allowed in only a few other countries and then only under rigid constraints. Pooling of interests is unheard of in many countries.

SELECTED INDIVIDUAL COUNTRY-BY-COUNTRY GAAP DIFFERENCES

We show a variation from U.S. GAAP for each of the following selected countries:

AUSTRALIA

- All cost in excess of an acquired business's net assets at book value is usually deemed to be goodwill. Goodwill may be classified as a deduction from capital or charged to capital.

BRAZIL

- A provision for "maintenance of working capital" may be recorded to remove from profit the effect of inflation on current assets, long-term assets (other than fixed assets that are indexed for inflation for both financial and tax reporting purposes), and liabilities.

FRANCE

- No specific accounting standards exist for troubled debt restructurings. In practice, gains and losses on restructurings are recorded in income at the time of the restructuring.

ITALY

- No standards exist as to leases. In practice, all leases are recorded as *operating* leases.

JAPAN

- Research and development costs may be deferred over a maximum of five years.

MEXICO

- Most industrial and retail firms are allowed to write up their fixed assets annually to current appraised value (as opposed to using inflation indices).

SWITZERLAND

- Machinery and equipment may be largely expensed at the time of purchase.

UNITED KINGDOM

- Investments below 20% ownership must be carried at cost.

AN IN-DEPTH LOOK AT GERMANY'S GAAP   To show how the GAAP of one country can differ greatly from U.S. GAAP, we use Germany, for which approximately 50 entries are often needed to restate German financial statements to U.S. GAAP. Germany's GAAP is possibly the most conservative and loose of any of the major industrialized countries. The use of arbitrary reserves for the purpose of smoothing earnings is rampant.

- **Translation of foreign currency statements.** No specific translation method is specified; however, strict consistency is required.

- **Foreign currency transactions.** Anticipated FX losses on FX receivables and payables as a result of *forecasted* adverse exchange rate changes can be expensed currently.
- **Inventory.** Inventory may be valued at amounts lower than that produced by applying the lower-of-cost or market rule (occurs when management believes that *future* price declines will occur).
- **Goodwill.** Goodwill can be written off against stockholders' equity at the business combination date.
- **Pensions.** Actuarial gains and losses must be recognized currently as adjustments of pension expense rather than spread over a number of years.
- **Long-term contracts.** Both the percentage of completion method and the completed contract method are allowed, but in practice the percentage of completion method is rarely used.
- **Contingent liabilities.** Contingent liabilities are recorded if a loss is reasonable and *possible* (not *probable* as in the United States).
- **Accruals and expenses.** Because the books are usually kept in a manner consistent with tax law, expenses not allowed for tax purposes are usually not recorded.
- **Allowances for uncollectibles and warranties.** Because these items are deductible for income tax purposes, firms may arbitrarily accrue the maximum amounts allowed under the tax code so that income taxes are minimized.
- **Prior period adjustments.** Errors discovered that pertain to a prior year must be reported in the current year income statement.

II   EFFORTS TO INTERNATIONALIZE ACCOUNTING STANDARDS

THE INTERNATIONAL ACCOUNTING STANDARDS COMMITTEE

The lack of worldwide uniform accounting principles and practices is unfortunate because it (1) impedes comparability, (2) is costly and inefficient for companies having foreign operations, (3) hinders the ability of firms to raise capital in foreign markets, (4) hinders the ability of firms to list their securities on foreign stock exchanges, and (5) places U.S. firms at a competitive disadvantage to many European firms when U.S. and European firms compete against each other in proposed business combinations.

To promote the development of a "world GAAP," the International Accounting Standards Committee (IASC) was formed in 1973. Based in London, it has members from 79 countries (representing 106 professional accounting bodies). To date, the IASC has issued 31 international accounting standards.

THE SHORTCOMINGS OF THE IASC STANDARDS

Because IASC rules require 11 votes of the 14 board members before issuing a standard, it was usually necessary to provide two alternatives to get the 11 votes. From our U.S. perspective, such standards are not much as standards go. From an international perspective, however, they are better than having three alternatives, so this represents a step forward in achieving the ultimate goal. Unfortunately, almost any company can state in its annual report (as many do) that it is complying with international accounting standards—such a statement does not have much significance.

THE IMPACT OF IASC STANDARDS

Until 1993, one of the two alternatives generally allowed for each standard has always coincided with the U.S. standard. Thus the FASB never had to be concerned about U.S. standards *not* complying with international standards. For many countries, however, the IASC standards *have* served as an incentive to upgrade their standards, and some have done so. Other countries, primarily third world developing countries, use IASC standards rather than incur the cost of maintaining their own private or government standard-setting bodies. China, for example, requires its many joint ventures to report using the IASC standards.

THE IMPACT ON CAPITAL MARKETS   Stock exchanges in several countries—but not in the United States—allow foreign companies to list their securities on the exchange if they furnish financial information using the international standards in lieu of local standards. Consequently, U.S. stock exchanges have pressured the Securities and Exchange Commission (SEC) to do likewise. To date, the SEC has *not* bowed to this pressure. For a foreign company to list on the U.S. stock exchange, the SEC presently requires that the company furnish financial statements that (1) comply with U.S. GAAP or (2) are reconciled to U.S. GAAP.

RECENT EFFORTS MADE TO REDUCE THE ALLOWED ALTERNATIVES

In 1993, the IASC completed an ambitious project begun in 1989, which was aimed at improving comparability and reducing the number of allowable alternatives in 12 of its standards. The major alternatives that the IASC hoped to eliminate were (1) the LIFO inventory method (in IAS 2), (2) deferring research and development costs (in IAS 9), (3) the pooling of interests method (in IAS 22), and (4) charging goodwill directly to stockholders' equity at the combination date (in IAS 22).

RESULTS OF THE RECENT EFFORTS TO REDUCE THE ALLOWED ALTERNATIVES

Although the IASC revised 10 of its standards, it took only a small step forward. Some of the revised standards merely resulted in labeling one of the alternatives as a preferable treatment—called the *benchmark treatment*—with the second alternative labeled as the *allowed alternative treatment*. Of the four major proposed changes, only the alternative of charging goodwill to stockholders' equity at the business combination date was eliminated.

THE SHORTER ALLOWED LIFE FOR GOODWILL: IMPLICATIONS FOR THE FASB
The new goodwill standard in revised IAS 22 allows a maximum amortization period of 5 years—unless a longer life not exceeding 20 years can be justified. Because the allowable life under U.S. GAAP is 40 years, a U.S. standard for the first time does *not* comply with the related international standard. (The FASB has not indicated that it plans to reexamine the U.S. standard in light of this disparity.)

A SPECIAL DISCLOSURE REQUIREMENT WHEN LIFO IS USED   Of interest regarding revised IAS 2 is that if the LIFO method is used, disclosure must be made of the benchmark treatment amount, which is FIFO—a disclosure prohibited by the U.S. Internal Revenue Service when LIFO is used for tax purposes. Thus a disclosure difference now exists between U.S. GAAP and international GAAP.

WORLD GAAP—WILL IT BE ATTAINED?

The goal of having all businesses use a strong world GAAP is not only one of reaching agreement on what standards should exist but also of persuading countries to adopt the standards. This goal often seems unattainable because of the vested interests that many countries have in maintaining their own standards. For example, U.S. companies strongly opposed the proposed elimination of the LIFO inventory method because they would have had to pay sizable "catch-up" income taxes had

INTERNATIONAL PERSPECTIVE

All Accountants Soon May Speak the Same Language

The major roadblock to foreign companies listing their overseas stock on U.S. exchanges has long been the big difference between accounting standards in the U.S. and abroad. For decades, leading accounting theorists have advocated the harmonization of accounting principles worldwide to end the confusion and lack of comparability. But major foreign companies have resisted the move because they've felt that the tougher U.S. accounting rules would likely prevail in formulating global standards.

Suddenly what seemed like an impossible dream appears a bit closer to reality with new moves by key accounting rule-makers—all with the goal of harmonizing disparate accounting rules world-wide.

The boards of the International Accounting Standards Committee, or IASC, which makes international rules, and the International Organization of Securities Commissions, have just agreed to develop accounting standards by mid-1999 for companies seeking stock lists in global markets to raise cross-border capital. And the Financial Accounting Standards Board, the chief rule-making body for U.S. accountants, has joined with standards setters in Canada, Mexico and Chile to explore areas in which the four countries can harmonize their accounting standards.

Even the Securities and Exchange Commission, which has long fought to maintain tough U.S. accounting standards, is easing the barriers somewhat. Last year for the first time the SEC accepted three international accounting standards on cash-flow data, the effects of hyperinflation and business combinations for cross-border stock filings. Such filings are offered by foreign companies in more than one nation, including the U.S.

But Linda Quinn, who heads the SEC's corporation finance division, is adamant that U.S. accounting standards still won't be dropped for domestic companies—a move that would cause a torrent of opposition from financial analysts and academics who feel that U.S. accounting standards should still be the rule rather than the exception.

Whatever the outcome, the stakes are enormous for both U.S. capital markets and the investment community. Big Board officials note that 55 million shares of nonregistered foreign stocks already trade in the U.S. over the counter. And they believe the U.S. stock market may lose world prominence to London and other European exchanges if foreign stocks aren't listed in New York. But financial analysts and accountants say that permitting foreign stocks to be listed here under non-U.S. accounting rules would only confuse and penalize U.S. investors.

Currently, only 204 non-U.S. companies list on the New York Stock Exchange. To the Big Board, this seems like a pittance because there are 2,000 other major foreign companies out there that could qualify for listing. So the exchange has been working quietly to get regulators and rule makers to permit another 200 or more big foreign companies to list here under international standards. This would almost double the Big Board's capitalization to close to $10 trillion from the current $5.4 trillion—enough to make a ticker-tape parade for whoever could push through these proposals.

James L. Cochrane, a senior vice-president and economist for the Big Board, is one of the prime movers behind the scenes to push for opening the door to foreign-stock listings here. Noting that 14% of

LIFO been eliminated. Thus even though scores of companies have much to gain from international GAAP and believe it is a fine idea, they do not want changes made to their local GAAP.

THE CAPITAL MARKETS: A DRIVING FORCE   The increasing practice of companies raising capital in world markets outside their home countries (approximately $400 billion of debt and equity raised in some recent years compared to $50 billion in 1980) has given added emphasis to the desirability of having a common accounting language. This desirability is underscored by the fact that multinational companies that raise capital in world markets and list their securities on foreign stock exchanges are forced to prepare financial statements on several different bases to file in different countries, a needless waste of effort.

THE IOSCO'S PLAN TO ENDORSE IASC STANDARDS IN 1999   In 1995, the International Organization of Securities Commissions (IOSCO), of which the SEC is a member, and the IASC agreed on a timetable for the formal endorsement of a core set of IASC standards as an alternative to national standards. The IASC is to com-

Switzerland's Nestle S.A.'s stock is already owned by Americans, he says that his exchange could "blow London off the map" if more foreign stock listed here under relaxed U.S. accounting standards or international rules.

But some U.S. stock market analysts fear that these benefits wouldn't be worth the price, which is lack of comparable disclosure among U.S. and foreign stocks. Pat McConnell, Bear Stearns & Co.'s accounting guru, maintains that this gap would create "a potential for big lies" in financial statements of companies in foreign countries with weak accounting rules. Indeed, she frets that it would prevent U.S. investors from making meaningful comparisons of U.S. and foreign stocks.

Accountants note, for example, that the U.S. annual report of Daimler-Benz, one of the few German companies to adhere to U.S. GAAP because it was forced to raise money here, shows a $1 billion annual loss. Under German accounting rules, Daimler reports a $100 million profit. In Japan, interest income is overstated, even when not received, and trading-account losses there can be hidden by shifting securities into an investment account—an accounting ploy forbidden in the U.S.

In a computer model set up by two Rider College professors, of an imaginary company with gross operating profit of $1.5 million showed the company had a net profit of $34,600 in the U.S., $260,600 in Britain and $240,600 in Australia.

Some accounting rule-makers seem more willing to permit foreign listings under international standards than under different national standards for overseas companies. But to accomplish this, the U.S. would have to compromise on certain linchpin rules on deferred

taxes, business combinations and foreign currency long used by U.S. companies.

Some accountants fear that SEC relaxation of U.S. rules would be a prelude to the listing of foreign stocks here under accounting rules of other nations.

Without acceptable international accounting rules, most big foreign companies would resist moving to tougher U.S. rules. Rolf Arthur Meyer, chief financial officer of Switzerland's Ciba-Geigy Ltd., strongly urges the U.S. "to be more flexible" on the issue. And Bernd-Joachim Menn, head of the corporate accounting department of Germany's Bayer AG, supports the move to let companies list in New York under non-U.S. accounting standards. "It would spur cross-border investments," he said.

Before any meaningful progress can be made in harmonization, international standard setters need a lot more resources and clout. Consider that IASC, which sets international standards, has only three or four full-time staff members, while the FASB has 45 staff members. And IASC has an annual budget of only $1.7 million compared with $15.8 million for FASB.

With such meager resources, IASC needs more money and staff to help cope with the sizable workload it has undertaken. If it cannot get this support from industry, government and accounting organizations, it will be difficult if not impossible to topple the long-standing Tower of Babel in accounting and produce a lingua franca to dispel the clouds over world-wide financial disclosure.

Source: Lee Berton, "All Accountants Soon May Speak the Same Language," *The Wall Street Journal,* August 29, 1995, p. A–15.

---

plete 16 standards on subjects such as intangibles, financial instruments, interim reporting, segment reporting, and leasing by mid-1999, at which time the IOSCO will endorse the IASC standards as a comprehensive core set of international standards for cross-border offerings and listings of securities. See the International Perspective for more discussion of international standards.

III   METHODOLOGY FOR RESTATING TO U.S. GAAP

Adjusting a foreign unit's financial statements to U.S. GAAP is the equivalent of making correcting entries, a subject covered in intermediate accounting. A simple approach to developing the necessary restatement entries is to (1) compare actual balances ("what was done") to desired balances under U.S. GAAP ("what we wish had been done") and (2) use a step-by-step ("with and without") approach in determining the deferred income tax effects. An example of this methodology is shown in Illustration 18–1.

ILLUSTRATION 18–1   **Manner of Developing Restatement to U.S. GAAP Entries**

I. Assumed Facts:

1. On 1/1/X1, a foreign subsidiary acquired a copyright for 100,000 LCU (local currency units).

2. The foreign subsidiary expensed this cost in accordance with its local GAAP and local income tax laws, even though the copyright's remaining legal life was 10 years.

3. The foreign subsidiary's income tax rate is 40%.

4. A worksheet restatement entry is required at 12/31/X3.

II. Comparison of Actual Balances to Desired Balances:

	Local Currency Units		
	Foreign GAAP (what was done)	U.S. GAAP (what we wish had been done)	Reporting Differences
Balance Sheet—12/31/X3:			
Copyright	–0–	70,000	70,000
Retained earnings, 1/1/X3	(100,000)	(20,000)	80,000
Income Statement—19X3:			
Copyright expense	–0–	(10,000)	(10,000)

III. Worksheet Restatement Entry at 12/31/X3:

	Without Providing Deferred Income Taxes (step 1)		*With* Providing Deferred Income Taxes (step 2)
Copyright	70,000		70,000
Copyright Expense	10,000		10,000
Retained Earnings, 1/1/X3		80,000	48,000[a]
Income Tax Expense			4,000[b]
Deferred Income Taxes Payable			28,000[c]

[a]Reporting difference at 12/31/X2 of 80,000 LCU × 60% = 48,000.
[b]Reporting difference for 19X3 of 10,000 LCU × 40% = 4,000.
[c]Reporting difference at 12/31/X3 of 70,000 LCU × 40% = 28,000

Note: The net effect on retained earnings at 12/31/X3 is 42,000 (48,000 + 4,000 − 10,000 = 42,000). This 42,000 is 60% of the copyright's 70,000 year-end reporting difference.

TRANSLATION CONCEPTUAL ISSUE 1: WHICH EXCHANGE RATES TO USE

The process of translating foreign currency financial statements into dollars is merely a mechanical process once the exchange rate for each account has been determined. For many decades, however, a raging controversy has existed over the following two conceptual issues:

1. Which exchange rates should be used for many of the accounts.

2. Whether to report the effect of a change in the exchange rate currently in the income statement (discussed later).

The first conceptual issue centers around determining the appropriate exchange rates for translating individual assets and liabilities. The translation of the stockholders' equity accounts is *not* part of the issue because the total translated stockholders' equity is a forced residual amount that is the difference between the total translated assets and the total translated liabilities. Once the appropriate exchange rates have been determined for the assets and liabilities, consistency and logic dictate the appropriate exchange rates for translating the income statement accounts.

CRITERIA USED FOR DETERMINING APPROPRIATE EXCHANGE RATES

Accountants have used the following criteria in determining the appropriate exchange rates to use:

1. Does the exchange rate selected for a specific account result in a **meaningful dollar amount?**
2. Does the exchange rate selected for a specific account **change the basis of accounting in translation?** For example, is the historical cost basis for a fixed asset in the foreign currency retained when translation is made into U.S. dollars?
3. When a change in the exchange rate has occurred, do the translated results **reflect the true economic impact of the change?**

Although these criteria seem simple enough, substantial controversy exists in practice because accountants often answer these questions differently for many accounts. Furthermore, the criteria are not always compatible. For instance, in dealing with fixed assets, satisfying the second criterion can prevent satisfying the third criterion.

MAKING GENERALIZATIONS AS TO THE ECONOMIC EFFECTS OF EXCHANGE RATE CHANGES In dealing with the third criterion, it would be convenient to have some *broad generalizations*, such as (1) a *decrease* in the direct exchange rate is always an adverse economic event, which should always result in reporting an *unfavorable* effect on stockholders' equity, or (2) an *increase* in the direct exchange rate is always a *favorable* economic event, which should always result in reporting a *favorable* effect on stockholders' equity. It is *not* possible to make such broad generalizations, however, because the economic effect of an exchange rate change depends on the following three items:

1. **The causes of the exchange rate change.** For instance, foreign inflation, domestic inflation, and noninflationary factors.
2. **The nature of the foreign unit's assets.** For instance, the extent to which the assets are monetary versus nonmonetary.
3. **The extent of debt financing relative to equity financing.**

For **specific situations,** though, **situational generalizations** can be made. For example, when the direct exchange *decreases* (for whatever reason), the economic effect of holding in foreign countries monetary assets that are financed by equity is always an adverse economic event, which should always result in reporting an unfavorable effect on stockholders' equity. As you develop an understanding of this material, you will be able to make situational generalizations.

MONETARY AND NONMONETARY ACCOUNT CLASSIFICATIONS

Assets and liabilities may be conveniently grouped into **monetary accounts** and **nonmonetary accounts** (the same classification scheme used in constant-dollar accounting to adjust for inflation). Monetary items include **cash and accounts that are obligated to be settled in cash** such as:

Assets	**Liabilities**
Accounts receivable	Accounts payable
Long-term receivables	Long-term debt
Deferred income tax receivables	Deferred income tax payables
Intercompany receivables	Intercompany payables
Investments in bonds	Accrued liabilities

All other asset and liability accounts—such as Inventory, Fixed Assets, Intangible Assets—are nonmonetary items. Equity accounts and income statement accounts are neither monetary nor nonmonetary items. This classification scheme is useful in determining the appropriate translation exchange rate to use for each asset and liability.

THE CURRENT RATE VERSUS THE HISTORICAL RATE   Which exchange rate to use for a given asset or liability requires choosing between (1) the exchange rate existing at the balance sheet date—the *current rate* (the spot rate)—and (2) the exchange rate existing when the balance in the account arose—the *historical rate.*

TRANSLATING MONETARY ACCOUNTS   For cash, no controversy exists whatsoever. Accountants agree that the current rate should be used because this produces a current value amount in dollars, the only sensible amount to report. All three criteria listed earlier are satisfied. For each remaining monetary item, accountants almost unanimously agree that only the current rate makes sense because it also results in a largely current value amount in dollars, which again is the only sensible amount to report.[6]

TRANSLATING NONMONETARY ACCOUNTS—THE HIGHLY CONTROVERSIAL AREA
Accountants strongly disagree on the appropriate exchange rates to use to translate nonmonetary accounts. Because of this disagreement, several translation approaches exist.

THE THREE GENERAL TRANSLATION APPROACHES

Three translation approaches have been developed over the years, only two of which are allowed by *SFAS No. 52:* The **foreign currency unit of measure approach** and the **U.S. dollar unit of measure approach.** We discuss and illustrate the first approach in this chapter and the second approach in Chapter 19. In Chapter 20, the third translation approach, a **current value approach using purchasing power parity theory,** is discussed and illustrated. We use this third approach to (1) reveal the characteristics (strengths and weaknesses) of the two allowable translation approaches and (2) evaluate whether the functional currency concept set forth in *SFAS No. 52* is valid.

In illustrating the foreign currency unit of measure approach in this chapter, we *initially* call the effect of the exchange rate change an **economic gain or loss from exchange rate change.** Furthermore, we show this effect as a separate item in equity, which coincidentally happens to be the required treatment under *SFAS No. 52* for this approach. Accordingly, a discussion of the other major controversial issue of how to report the effect of an exchange rate change can be and is delayed until later in the chapter.

---

[6]Prior to the issuance in 1975 of *SFAS No. 8* (the predecessor of *SFAS No. 52*), it was acceptable practice to use historical exchange rates for long-term receivables and long-term payables, a practice that began to lose support in 1956, when Professor Samuel Hepworth (University of Michigan) published a convincing article advocating using the current exchange rate.

V   THE FOREIGN CURRENCY UNIT OF MEASURE APPROACH (THE CURRENT RATE METHOD OF TRANSLATION)

THE RATIONALE

Under this approach, a foreign operation is viewed as a separate business unit whose only factual financial statements are those prepared in its foreign currency. From this premise, it is reasoned that **the item-to-item relationships that exist in the foreign currency statements (such as profitability ratios, liquidity ratios, and specific asset to total asset percentages) must be maintained in translation.** The only way to maintain these relationships is to use a **single exchange rate for all assets and liabilities.** Thus by using a single exchange rate, the translated financial statements in U.S. dollars retain a **"foreign currency feel"** to them.

Managerially, the U.S. parent, in looking at the translated financial statements, is able to view the foreign operation using the same perspective as that of the local management in the foreign country, which uses the foreign currency statements. Thus it is said that even though the amounts are expressed in U.S. dollars, the **unit of measure** is the foreign currency.

THE CURRENT RATE METHOD OF TRANSLATION

Although numerous translation methods have been developed to express foreign currency statements in U.S. dollars, only the **current rate method** achieves the result of retaining the foreign currency as the unit of measure. **For the balance sheet, the current rate is defined as the rate existing at the balance sheet date**—all assets and liabilities are translated at this rate. **For the income statement, the current rate is defined as the exchange rate existing when an item was recognized;** there are conceivably 365 current rates in dealing with the income statement (averages are used to simplify matters).

THE FOCUS: THE NET ASSET POSITION   Under the current rate method, all assets and liabilities are effectively valued (1) higher as a result of a direct rate increase and (2) lower as a result of a direct rate decrease. Because the liabilities offset a portion of the assets—thus constituting what is called a *natural hedge*—it is the subsidiary's assets that are *not* offset by liabilities (the net assets) that are exposed. Thus the effect of the exchange rate change can readily be determined by multiplying the foreign unit's **net asset position** (total assets – total liabilities) by the change in the exchange rate.

Viewed from the *parent's perspective*, the foreign unit's net asset position is really the parent's investment in the subsidiary.[7] Thus, in substance, the parent's *Investment account* is effectively exposed to the risk of exchange rate changes. As shown later, a parent using the *equity method* adjusts its Investment account upward or downward for exchange rate changes (as is done for an FX Accounts Receivable account on the parent's books).

REPORTED EFFECTS OF EXCHANGE RATE CHANGES   When the foreign unit is in a net asset position, an increase in the direct exchange rate causes a favorable result to be reported (a presumed economic gain from the exchange rate change). A decrease in the direct exchange rate causes an unfavorable result to be reported (a

---

[7]The infrequent case in which a foreign unit is in a **net liability position** (total liabilities exceeding total assets) would be considered a *negative investment* position from the parent's perspective only if the parent is obligated to make an additional investment (usually because of having guaranteed the subsidiary's debt). In such cases, the parent reports a liability on its books (as discussed in Chapter 2).

ILLUSTRATION 18–2	**The Foreign Currency Unit of Measure Approach: Reporting Effects of Exchange Rate Changes**		
Translation Method Used	**Possible Relevant Financial Positions**	**Increase[a] (Foreign Currency Has Strengthened or Dollar Has Weakened)**	**Decrease[b] (Foreign Currency Has Weakened or Dollar Has Strengthened)**
Current rate	Net asset (assets exceed liabilities)[c]	Favorable	Unfavorable
Current rate	Net liability (liabilities exceed assets)[d]	Unfavorable	Favorable

[a]In all situations, the effect is *favorable* on the assets and *unfavorable* on the liabilities.

[b]In all situations, the effect is *unfavorable* on the assets and *favorable* on the liabilities.

[c]From the parent's perspective, the subsidiary's net asset position constitutes the parent's investment.

[d]From the parent's perspective, it has an investment that has been written down to zero (and a liability to the subsidiary if obligated to the subsidiary in some manner).

presumed economic loss from the exchange rate change). These effects are summarized in Illustration 18–2.

KEY OBSERVATIONS AS TO THE CURRENT RATE METHOD This approach makes no distinction as to the nature of the assets and liabilities (monetary versus nonmonetary) or their longevity (current versus noncurrent). Nor is any attempt made to understand why the change in the exchange rate occurred. Any distortions that exist in the foreign currency statements (such as fixed assets being substantially undervalued because of inflation) are perpetuated and carried over to the translated financial statements. Thus the status quo is preserved.

INTRODUCTORY ILLUSTRATION | **TRANSLATION USING THE CURRENT RATE METHOD**

Assume that in late 19X1, a U.S. company created a 100%-owned subsidiary in Mexico, making a $1,000,000 cash equity investment at that time when the direct exchange rate was $.50. For simplicity, assume that this direct exchange rate did *not* fluctuate through December 31, 19X1. The subsidiary's first sales were on January 1, 19X2.

Additional assumptions are that (1) no dividends were declared or paid in 19X2; (2) fixed asset additions of 200,000 pesos (equal to 19X2's depreciation expense) occurred on January 3, 19X2, when the exchange rate was $.50; (3) Mexico had 25% inflation for 19X2; (4) the United States had 10% inflation for 19X2; and (5) the direct exchange rates were $.50 at December 31, 19X1, $.44 at December 31, 19X2, and $.47 for 19X2 as an average.

The subsidiary's balance sheets at the end of 19X1 and 19X2 and its 19X2 income statement are shown in Illustration 18–3.

The current rate method of translation for the 19X2 is shown in Illustration 18–4.

IS THE TRANSLATED AMOUNT FOR FIXED ASSETS HISTORICAL COST? The most difficult result to understand under the foreign currency unit of measure approach is whether the amount expressed in U.S. dollars for fixed assets should be considered historical cost or some form of current value. Unlike domestic fixed assets, foreign fixed assets are reported at different amounts at each financial reporting date under the current rate method because of exchange rate changes (as if they

ILLUSTRATION 18–3	Foreign Currency Financial Statements	

	Pesos	
	December 31, 19X1	December 31, 19X2
Balance Sheets:		
Monetary assets	2,200,000	2,500,000
Inventory	1,000,000	1,250,000
Fixed assets, net	4,800,000	4,800,000[a]
Total Assets	8,000,000	8,550,000
Monetary liabilities	6,000,000	6,250,000
Common stock	2,000,000[b]	2,000,000
Retained earnings	–0–	300,000
Total Liabilities and Equity	8,000,000	8,550,000
Net Asset Position	**2,000,000**	**2,300,000**
Income Statements (19X2):		
Revenues		5,300,000
Cost of sales		(4,300,000)
Depreciation		(200,000)
Expenses		(500,000)
Net Income		300,000

[a]Because of the 25% inflation in Mexico during 19X2, these assets are undervalued 25%.

[b]This amount is the peso equivalent of the $1,000,000 cash investment made by the parent when it created the subsidiary in late 19X1 ($1,000,000/$.50 = 2,000,000 pesos).

were marketable securities being accounted for at market prices). Advocates of this approach contend that the amounts in U.S. dollars *do* constitute historical cost **using the foreign currency as the unit of measure.** Critics of this approach contend that this is merely an abandonment of historical cost. Other critics contend that it produces amounts that are difficult to interpret and *not* meaningful. In our opinion, the amounts are meaningful—**but only to the extent that the local currency statements are meaningful.** If fixed assets are undervalued by 25% because of inflation, which causes total assets to be undervalued by 15%, this same percentage level of distortion is reflected in the translated statements. Thus consistency is maintained with the way U.S. domestic assets are valued (no adjustment for inflation). Perhaps the best way to look at it is to say that the translated amounts are historical cost amounts that have been adjusted for exchange rate changes—adjustments that are made to monetary assets as well.

THE DISAPPEARING PLANT PROBLEM Many countries (primarily in South America) currently have highly inflationary economies (sometimes exceeding 2,000% annually for some countries). The use of the foreign currency unit of measure approach (current rate method) can quickly result in reporting meaningless fixed asset amounts in these situations. To illustrate, consider the following example of a manufacturing plant in Argentina that cost 10,000,000 pesos when it was purchased on December 31, 19X4, using $2,000,000 of the parent's money:

	Amount (pesos)	December 31, 1974		December 31, 1995	
		Rate	Amount	Rate	Amount
Plant	10,000,000	$.20	$2,000,000	$.00000001	$.10

Clearly, the application of the December 31, 1995, current exchange rate to the historical cost in pesos produces an amount that bears no relationship to current value or a reasonable historical cost amount. The use of the current rate would produce a meaningful amount only if it were applied to the inflation-adjusted historical cost in pesos. This procedure, however, would depart from historical cost in the foreign currency. Even though the $.10 is the historical cost using the foreign currency as the unit of measure, it obviously makes no sense to use this method when foreign inflation has caused the direct exchange rate to decrease so severely. Unfortunately, the problem exists for all foreign countries because they all have inflation. The problem is just more readily evident in highly inflationary economies. Even in rel-

---

ILLUSTRATION 18–4	**The Current Rate Method**
	for the Year Ended December 31, 19X2

		Exchange		U.S.
	Pesos	**Code**	**Rate**	**Dollars**
Income Statement (19X2):				
Revenues	5,300,000	A	$.47	$2,491,000
Cost of sales	(4,300,000)	A	$.47	(2,021,000)
Depreciation	(200,000)	A	$.47	(94,000)
Expenses	(500,000)	A	$.47	(235,000)
Net Income	300,000			$ 141,000
Balance Sheet (12/31/X2):				
Monetary assets	2,500,000	C	$.44	$1,100,000
Inventory	1,250,000	C	$.44	550,000
Fixed assets, net	4,800,000	C	$.44	2,112,000
Total Assets	8,550,000			$3,762,000
Monetary liabilities	6,250,000	C	$.44	$2,750,000
Common stock	2,000,000	H	$.50	$1,000,000
Retained earnings	300,000	(Per above)		141,000
Economic loss from				
exchange rate change		(See below)		(129,000)
Total Equity	2,300,000			$1,012,000
Total Liabilities and Equity	8,550,000			$3,762,000

Calculation of Economic Loss from Exchange Rate Change:

Net asset (stockholders' equity) position at 1/1/X2 of	
2,000,000 pesos × $.06 decrease in the direct exchange	
rate equals	$ (120,000)
Net income of 300,000 pesos × $.03 difference between the	
average rate and the year-end rate ($.47 − $.44) equals.	(9,000)
Total Economic Loss from Exchange Rate Change	$ (129,000)

Key Review Points:

1. **Note how ratios and relationships *are* maintained after translation:**

	Pesos	U.S. Dollars
Debt-to-equity ratio	2.71:1	2.71:1
Gross profit margin ratio	19%	19%
Net income to sales ratio	6%	6%
Fixed assets to total assets percent	56%	56%
Undervaluation of fixed assets	25%	25%

2. **Note the increase in the stockholder's equity:**

Ending stockholder's equity (per above)	$1,012,000
Less—Beginning stockholder's equity (parent's initial	
capital investment per Illustration 18–3)	1,000,000
Increase in Stockholder's Equity	$ 12,000

Code: A = Average rate; C = Current rate; H = Historical rate.

atively low inflationary economies, the reporting results can lose meaning fairly quickly. This inability to deal with the effects of foreign inflation is the Achilles' heel of this translation method. More about this in Chapter 20.

We now provide a more comprehensive illustration of the current rate method that shows (1) the use of the **Cumulative Translation Adjustment** account, which is the name assigned to the equity account to which the effect of a change in the exchange rate is charged or credited; (2) beginning balances for the Retained Earnings account and the Cumulative Translation Adjustment account; (3) the translation treatment for a cash dividend payment to the parent; and (4) all of the individual asset and liability accounts.

In addition, we discuss (1) certain pretranslation procedures, (2) the finer points of this method, and (3) certain post-translation procedures. This comprehensive illustration is for 19X3, the year following the year in Illustration 18–4.

BASIC PROCEDURES *BEFORE* TRANSLATION

Certain fundamental procedures must be performed before the financial statements of foreign subsidiaries (and branches) may be translated into dollars.

ADJUSTMENTS TO CONFORM TO GAAP   Operations conducted in a foreign country must be accounted for using that country's accounting principles. When foreign currency financial statements use accounting principles that are different from U.S. generally accepted accounting principles, appropriate adjustments must be made to those statements before translation so that they conform to U.S. generally accepted accounting principles. These adjustments, which are **made on a worksheet,** are never posted to the general ledger of the foreign accounting entity. The adjustments are necessary regardless of (1) the organizational form through which foreign operations are conducted and (2) whether or not the foreign operation's statements are consolidated (if a subsidiary) or combined (if a division or a branch) with the financial statements of the domestic accounting entity.

Similarly, when a domestic company has a 20% to 50% interest in a foreign operation, which must be accounted for under the equity method of accounting if significant influence exists, the investee's foreign statements must be adjusted to conform to U.S. generally accepted accounting principles before translation into dollars. The equity method is then applied after the translation process in accordance with *SFAS No. 52.*

ADJUSTMENTS TO RECEIVABLES AND PAYABLES   A foreign operation's receivables or payables in other than its local currency must be adjusted to reflect the current rate between the local currency (of the foreign country) and the currency in which the receivable or payable is stated. Recall that the way to make and account for such adjustments was discussed in Chapter 16. In the illustration of the translation process in this section, we assume that any such adjustments have already been made.

RECONCILIATION OF INTER- OR INTRACOMPANY RECEIVABLE AND PAYABLE ACCOUNTS   Inventory and cash are commonly transferred between domestic and foreign operations. Such transactions are usually recorded in separate inter- or intracompany receivable and payable accounts by each accounting entity. Such accounts must be reconciled to each other before translation to ensure that no clerical errors or unrecorded in-transit items exist. Only by performing this reconciliation will these accounts completely offset each other after translation.

Furthermore, when the inter- or intracompany account is to be settled in dollars (rather than in the foreign unit's local currency), the foreign unit's accounts must be adjusted as described in the preceding section. If settlement is to be made in the foreign unit's local currency, the domestic operation must adjust its books. Such adjustments are illustrated later in the chapter where the fine points of intercompany transactions with foreign subsidiaries are discussed.

EXCHANGE RATES USED IN TRANSLATION

CURRENT EXCHANGE RATE Recall that *SFAS No. 52* has a dual definition of the current exchange rate. For the balance sheet, this is the exchange rate existing at the balance sheet date. For the income statement, this is the exchange rate in effect when an item is recognized in the income statement.

AVERAGE EXCHANGE RATES Because it is impractical to translate the various income statement items at the numerous exchange rates that could apply throughout a period, *SFAS No. 52* allows firms to use appropriately weighted average exchange rates for the period.

MULTIPLE (OFFICIAL) EXCHANGE RATES In addition to the floating rates, many countries declare one or more official rates for certain types of currency conversions. For example, to discourage the repatriation of dividends to a foreign parent company, a country would use a rate whereby the parent company would receive a lower amount of its own currency than it otherwise would receive had the free rate been used. When such multiple rates exist, the current exchange rate is the rate **that could be used for dividend remittances.**

SPECIFIC TRANSLATION PROCEDURES

BALANCE SHEET ACCOUNTS The following procedures translate the individual balance sheet accounts:

1. All assets and liabilities are translated at the exchange rate existing at the balance sheet date.
2. Common stock and additional paid-in capital are translated at historical exchange rates (to isolate the effect of the change in the exchange rate for the current period).
3. Beginning retained earnings is the dollar balance in the Retained Earnings account at the end of the prior period.
4. Dividend payments, if any, are translated using the exchange rate in effect at the time of the declaration.

REVENUE, COST OF GOODS SOLD, AND EXPENSE ACCOUNTS All revenues, costs of sales, and expenses (as well as gains and losses) are translated using exchange rates that were in effect when these items were **recognized** in the income statement. Thus exchange rates **in effect during the current period** are used. (The following two paragraphs explain how this process can be simplified.) For income statement account balances that come *directly from the balance sheet* (Cost of Sales, Depreciation Expense, and Amortization Expenses), the result is to use an **"exit date" rate** (as opposed to the rate when the item "entered" the balance sheet).

THE USE OF AVERAGE EXCHANGE RATES When translating income statement accounts, average exchange rates may be used provided that approximately the same results can be obtained from translating each individual transaction into dollars using the exchange rate that was in effect when the transaction occurred. If the item being translated occurred evenly throughout the period (month, quarter, or year), a simple average is sufficient. Otherwise, a weighted average is necessary. (Most publicly owned companies achieve a weighted average result by multiplying each individual month's amount by each month's average exchange rate.) Average exchange rates must be calculated using the direct exchange rates that existed during the period; indirect exchange rates would not give the proper translated amounts.

THE SUBSTITUTION TECHNIQUE   A simplifying technique commonly used to translate income statement accounts that arise from activity with the parent or home office is to **substitute the amount in the domestic company's account for the subsidiary's or branch's account.** For example, the Intercompany Interest Expense account on the foreign subsidiary's books would be translated at the amount recorded in the Intercompany Interest Income account on the parent company's books. Likewise, the Intercompany Sales account on the foreign subsidiary's books would be translated at the amount recorded in the Intercompany Purchases account on the parent's books. This procedure automatically translates these items at the rates in effect on each transaction date, thus negating the need to use average rates. This technique cannot be used in the translation process for downstream sales because it would result in a cost of goods sold amount based on exchange prices in existence when the inventory was acquired by the foreign unit rather than when the foreign unit sold the inventory. The latter is required under the translation process.

In most cases, inter- or intracompany revenue and expense accounts need not be reconciled before doing the substitution. By reconciling the inter- or intracompany receivable and payable accounts before this substitution is made (as discussed on page 631), any clerical errors or unrecorded in-transit items affecting these income statement accounts would have been detected.

<table>
<tr><td>COMPREHENSIVE
ILLUSTRATION</td><td>**TRANSLATION USING THE CURRENT RATE METHOD**</td></tr>
</table>

Assume the following information for this 100%-owned subsidiary located in Mexico:

1. **Conformity with U.S. GAAP:** The financial statements in pesos already have been adjusted to conform with U.S. GAAP.

2. **Intercompany Receivable and Payable accounts:** The parent company and the subsidiary have no intercompany transactions (other than dividends declared by the subsidiary). Accordingly, no Intercompany Receivable and Payable accounts exist, and no adjustments must be made at the balance sheet date prior to the translation process relating to changes in the exchange rate.

3. **Exchange rates:** The direct exchange rate at December 31, 19X2, was $.44. The peso weakened or the dollar strengthened during 19X3 such that the direct exchange rate at December 31, 19X3, was $.40. The average rate for 19X3 was $.42.

4. **Common stock:** The subsidiary was created in late 19X1 when the direct exchange rate was $.50. No additional capital stock changes have occurred since then.

5. **Retained earnings—beginning of year:** The translated amount of retained earnings at the end of the prior year was $141,000 (the balance at December 31, 19X2, was shown in Illustration 18–4 on page 630).

6. **Dividends declared:** The subsidiary declared and paid a cash dividend of 100,000 pesos on November 11, 19X3, when the direct exchange rate was $.41.

7. **Sales, costs, and expenses:** All sales, costs, and expenses occurred evenly throughout 19X3.

8. **Cumulative translation adjustment—beginning of year:** The amount of the cumulative translation adjustment at the end of the prior year was a *debit* balance of $129,000 (as shown in Illustration 18–4).

9. **Current year translation adjustment:** The current year translation adjustment is a *debit* of $100,000. The manner of calculating this amount is shown in a supporting schedule to this illustration.

10. At January 1, 19X3, the subsidiary's assets exceeded its liabilities by 2,300,000 pesos (as shown in Illustration 18–4).

Illustration 18–5 uses the preceding information to translate the foreign subsidiary's financial statements into dollars. The calculation of the current year translation adjustment is shown in supporting Illustration 18–6.

ILLUSTRATION 18–5   Translation Worksheet: The Current Rate Method—for the Year Ended December 31, 19X3

	Foreign Currency (Pesos)	Code	Rates	Dollars
Income Statement (19X3):				
Sales	6,000,000	A	$.42	$2,520,000
Cost of sales	(4,600,000)	A	$.42	(1,932,000)
Depreciation expense	(200,000)	A	$.42	(84,000)
Operating expenses	(600,000)	A	$.42	(252,000)
Income before Taxes	600,000			$ 252,000
Income tax expense at 25%	(150,000)	A	$.42	(63,000)
Net Income	450,000			$ 189,000
Statement of Retained Earnings:				
Balance, 1/1/X3	300,000			$ 141,000
+ Net income	450,000	(Per above)		189,000◄
– Dividends	(100,000)	H	$.41	(41,000)
Balance, 1/1/X3	650,000			$ 289,000
Balance Sheet (12/31/X3):				
Cash	400,000	C	$.40	$ 160,000
Accounts receivable, net	1,600,000	C	$.40	640,000
Inventory	1,500,000	C	$.40	600,000
Land	1,000,000	C	$.40	400,000
Buildings and equipment	4,000,000	C	$.40	1,600,000
Accumulated depreciation	(400,000)	C	$.40	(160,000)
Total Assets	8,100,000			$3,240,000
Payables and accruals	1,950,000	C	$.40	$ 780,000
Long-term debt	3,500,000	C	$.40	1,400,000
Total Liabilities	5,450,000			$2,180,000
Common stock	2,000,000	H	$.50	$1,000,000
Retained earnings	650,000	(Per above)		289,000◄
Cumulative translation adjustment				
Prior years				(129,000)
Current year		(Per Illus. 18–6)		(100,000)
Total Equity	2,650,000			$1,060,000
Total Liabilities and Equity	8,100,000			$3,240,000

Beginning Net Assets 2,300,000 pesos

Ending Net Assets 2,650,000 pesos

Code:
C = Current rate existing at the balance sheet date.
A = Average rate, as given in the introduction to this illustration.
H = Historical rate.

ILLUSTRATION 18–6	Calculation of Current Year Translation Adjustment: Supporting Schedule to Illustration 18–5

Method I: Analysis of the Net Asset Position

	Pesos	Decrease in Direct Exchange Rate	Increase (decrease in dollars)
Net Assets at 1/1/X3:	2,300,000[a]		
Portion that lost $.04 of valuation ($.44 – $.40): 2,200,000 pesos		$(.04)	$ (88,000)
Portion (assumed used to pay the dividend) that lost $.03 of valuation ($.44 – $.41): 100,000 pesos	(100,000)	(.03)	(3,000)
+ Increase in net assets from earnings—a loss of $.02 of valuation ($.42 average rate – $.40 year-end rate)	450,000	(.02)	(9,000)
Net Assets at 12/31/X3	2,650,000		$(100,000)

[a]By making a **FIFO assumption** that the 100,000 pesos dividend was paid out of *beginning* retained earnings (part of *beginning* net assets), it can be assumed that (1) 2,200,000 pesos of the beginning net assets existed for the entire year (losing $.04 of valuation) and (2) the remaining 100,000 pesos of beginning net assets existed only through the dividend declaration date (11/1/X3) (losing only $.03 of valuation).

Method II: Residual Force Out

1.		Translated assets	$3,240,000
2.	Less	Translated liabilities	2,180,000
3.	Equals	Total stockholders' equity	$1,060,000
4.	Less	Translated common stock and additional paid-in capital accounts	1,000,000
5.	Equals	Total retained earnings and the cumulative translation adjustment	$ 60,000
6.	Less	Ending retained earnings	289,000
7.	Equals	The cumulative translation adjustment	$ (229,000)
8.	Less	The cumulative translation adjustment at the beginning of the year (a known amount from the prior year)	(129,000)
9.	Equals	The Current Period Translation Adjustment	$ (100,000)

Comparative Note: In practice, most companies perform their translations using templates on electronic spreadsheet software. The templates are designed so that the current period translation adjustment is forced out.

PARENT'S PROCEDURES *AFTER* TRANSLATION

Under the equity method of accounting, the parent company makes the following entries:

Investment in Subsidiary	189,000	
Equity in Net Income of Subsidiary		189,000
To record equity in net income.		

Cumulative Translation Adjustment	100,000	
Investment in Subsidiary		100,000
To record effect of change in exchange rate.		

Note: These entries always maintain the book value element of the Investment account balance at the difference between the subsidiary's assets and liabilities.

The analysis of the parent's Investment account is updated in 19X3 as follows:

	Parent's Investment Account	=	Common Stock	+	Retained Earnings	+	Cumulative Translation Adjustments
			Subsidiary's Equity Accounts				
Balances, 1/1/X3	$1,012,000[a]		$1,000,000		$141,000		$(129,000)
Equity in net income	189,000				189,000		
Dividends declared	(41,000)				(41,000)		
Translation adjustment ...	(100,000)						(100,000)
Balances, 12/31/X3	$1,060,000		$1,000,000		$289,000		$(229,000)

[a]There is no cost in excess of book value because the subsidiary was created by the parent company.

The basic elimination entry to consolidate the subsidiary at December 31, 19X3, is developed from the preceding analysis and is as follows:

		Dr.	Cr.
WORKSHEET ENTRY ONLY	Common Stock	1,000,000	
	Retained Earnings, 1/1/X3	141,000	
	Equity in Net Income of Subsidiary	189,000	
	Dividends Declared		41,000
	Cumulative Translation Adjustment		229,000
	Investment in Subsidiary		1,060,000

The equity accounts on the consolidation worksheet appear as follows:

	P Company	S Company	Consolidation Entries Dr.	Consolidation Entries Cr.	Consolidated
P Company					
Common stock	5,000,000[a]				5,000,000
Retained earnings	4,330,000[a]				4,330,000
Cumulative translation adjustment ..	(229,000)				(229,000)
S Company					
Common stock		1,000,000	1,000,000(1)		–0–
Retained earnings		289,000	330,000[b]	41,000[b]	–0–
Cumulative translation adjustment ..		(229,000)		229,000(1)	–0–

(1) This posting comes from the basic elimination entry.
[a]Assumed amount.
[b]Carried forward from the statement of retained earnings.

TRANSLATING A STATEMENT OF CASH FLOWS

Foreign units that are consolidated will also have their translated statement of cash flows consolidated. We purposely do not illustrate this statement because that would take away the opportunity to learn how to deal with the unique aspects of this statement. Information for preparing this statement is presented in many of the problems in the chapter.

INCOME TAX CONSEQUENCES OF EXCHANGE RATE CHANGES

The income tax consequences of exchange rate changes are discussed in the appendix to this chapter.

DISPOSITION OF TRANSLATION ADJUSTMENTS

The translation adjustments reported as a separate component of stockholders' equity are removed from that component (along with any income taxes) and reported in the income statement as part of the gain or loss on (1) complete or substantially complete liquidation or (2) sale of the investment. To illustrate, assume that on January 2, 19X4, the parent company sold all of its common stock holdings in the subsidiary for $1,090,000 cash ($30,000 more than the $1,060,000 carrying value of its investment at December 31, 19X3, as shown in the analysis of the Investment account).

The entry to record the sale and remove the $229,000 debit balance in the Cumulative Translation Adjustment account follows:[8]

Cash	1,090,000	
Loss on Sale of Subsidiary	199,000	
Investment in Subsidiary		1,060,000
Cumulative Translation Adjustment		229,000

A company that has foreign operations in more than one country must, of course, maintain the separate translation component of equity for each such foreign operation that has translation adjustments.

INTERCOMPANY TRANSACTIONS WITH FOREIGN UNITS

Certain procedures must be followed when a parent has intercompany transactions with a foreign unit.

ADJUSTMENTS TO INTERCOMPANY RECEIVABLES AND PAYABLES   When intercompany receivables and payables exist, the entity that makes or receives payment in the foreign currency (that is, in other than its own currency) must adjust its intercompany receivable or payable to reflect the current (spot) exchange rate at the financial reporting date. Otherwise, these accounts will *not* agree in dollars and would *not* be eliminated in consolidation. These accounts are adjusted using the identical procedures shown in Chapter 16 for FX receivables and FX payables arising from exporting and importing transactions, respectively. The treatment of the offsetting FX gain or loss, however, depends on whether the account is expected to be settled in the foreseeable future:

1. **Expected to be settled in the foreseeable future.** In these cases, the FX gain or loss is recognized currently in the income statement.

2. *Not* **expected to be settled in the foreseeable future.** A parent's Long-Term Intercompany Receivable account is, in substance, an *addition* to its Investment account. Likewise, a parent's Long-Term Intercompany Payable account is, in substance, a *reduction* of its investment. When such receivables and payables are denominated in a foreign currency and settlement is *not* planned or anticipated in the foreseeable future, *SFAS No. 52* requires that FX gains and losses from adjusting these accounts be treated as translation adjustments. Thus they are **charged or credited to the Cumulative Translation Adjustment account rather than reported currently in the income statement.** This provision ensures that the entire effect of an exchange rate change on the parent's true investment in a foreign unit is shown as part of the separate component of stockholders' equity.

INTERCOMPANY DIVIDEND RECEIVABLE   When a subsidiary declares a dividend, the parent uses the exchange rate existing at the dividend declaration date

---

[8]*SFAS Interpretation No. 37* requires such treatment on a pro rata basis when only *part* of the ownership in a foreign operation is sold.

to record its dividend receivable. Any changes in the exchange rate between the declaration date and the remittance date result in an FX gain or loss that is recognized currently in the income statement. Which entity incurs the FX gain or loss depends on the currency in which the dividend is denominated. (Such FX gains and losses can be avoided, of course, if dividends are remitted at their declaration date.)

UNREALIZED INTERCOMPANY PROFIT TO BE DEFERRED IN CONSOLIDATION Recall from Chapter 9 that all intercompany transactions are eliminated in consolidation. In preparing the matrix analysis for determining the amount of unrealized intercompany profit to be deferred, **the exchange rate at the transfer date**—*not* the exchange rate at the financial reporting date—is used. This procedure is required even though any remaining intercompany-acquired inventory (or fixed asset) is translated in the balance sheet at the current rate, which usually differs from the rate that existed at the transfer date.

To do otherwise produces nonsensical results in relation to the physical proportion of the inventory resold versus still on hand. Stated differently, if the subsidiary's records show that 20% of the intercompany-acquired inventory is still on hand, 20% of the parent's gross profit must be deferred; using the current (spot) rate at the balance sheet date in preparing the analysis instead produces a percentage other than 20%.

SPECIAL DISCLOSURES REQUIRED REGARDING THE CUMULATIVE TRANSLATION ADJUSTMENT ACCOUNT

For the Cumulative Translation Adjustment (CTA) account, an analysis must be presented (in either notes, in a separate statement, or as part of a statement of changes in stockholders' equity) of the following items:

1. The beginning and ending balance of the CTA account.
2. The aggregate adjustment for the period to the CTA account resulting from (a) translation adjustments, (b) adjustments to long-term intercompany receivables and payables, and (c) FX gains and losses arising from hedges of the net asset position (discussed shortly).
3. The amount of income taxes for the period charged or credited to the CTA account as a result of the current period translation adjustment.
4. The amounts transferred from the CTA account and recognized in the income statement as a result of the sale or complete or substantially complete liquidation of the investment in the foreign subsidiary.

MAINTAINING RELATIONSHIPS IS A CRITICAL ELEMENT OF INTERPERSONAL SKILLS—BUT IS IT THE CRITICAL FACTOR IN DETERMINING HOW TO TRANSLATE FINANCIAL STATEMENTS?

Recall that the foreign currency unit of measure approach results in maintaining in translation the relationships that exist in the foreign currency. These are fair questions to ask:

1. Is maintaining the relationships important? To whom? Why?
2. Are foreign managers evaluated using local currency statements or dollar statements?
3. If dollar statements are used to evaluate foreign managers, do firms use for this evaluation the results produced under the current rate method or the results produced under one of the other methods (discussed in the following two chapters)?

4. Do the results reflect the true economic consequences of an exchange rate change?

We deal with these questions in Chapter 20.

VI · HEDGING A FOREIGN SUBSIDIARY'S NET ASSET POSITION

Recall that (1) a subsidiary's net asset position (total assets – total liabilities) is what is exposed to the effect of exchange rate changes and (2) a subsidiary's net asset position is effectively the equivalent of the parent's Investment account from the parent's perspective. Thus hedging the subsidiary's net asset position accomplishes the same result as though the parent hedged its Investment account (which fluctuates in value merely as a result of exchange rate changes).

When the parent uses the current rate method of translation and hedges a foreign unit's net asset position, the FX gain or loss on the hedge (net of the related tax effects) must be credited or debited, respectively, to the Cumulative Translation Adjustment account. This requirement allows the hedging of FX gain or loss to offset partially or fully the FX translation adjustment for the year. For the hedging FX gain or loss to be treated in this manner, the transaction must be (1) designated as a hedge of the net asset position and (2) effective.

ILLUSTRATION · **HEDGING A NET ASSET POSITION WHEN THE PARENT USES THE CURRENT RATE METHOD**

Assume that on December 31, 19X2, the parent of the 100%-owned Mexican subsidiary used in the earlier example expected the Mexican peso to weaken by the end of 19X3. Accordingly, the parent contracted with an FX trader on December 31, 19X2, to *sell* 2,300,000 pesos (the subsidiary's net asset position at that date) in 365 days at the forward rate of $.43. Illustration 18–7 shows this special accounting treatment for this hedging transaction. (For simplicity, we do *not* deal with interim quarterly reporting dates.) The following direct exchange rates are assumed:

	December 31, 19X2 (the inception date)	December 31, 19X3 (the expiration date and financial reporting date)
Spot rate	$.44	$.40
Forward rate	.43	n/a

REVIEW POINTS FOR ILLUSTRATION 18–7 Note the following:

1. The net change in the CTA account. Recall that a $100,000 *unfavorable* translation adjustment occurred for 19X3 in Illustration 18–5. Accordingly, the activity in the CTA account for 19X3 is as follows:

CUMULATIVE TRANSLATION ADJUSTMENT

Balance, 1/1/X3 (per Illustration 18–5)	$129,000
Translation adjustment for 19X3	100,000
Hedging discount	23,000
Balance, 12/31/X3	$160,000

92,000 Hedging gain

Obviously, the hedge was effective.

ILLUSTRATION 18–7	**Hedging the Subsidiary's Net Asset Position: Net Position Accounting**	

December 31, 19X2
(the date the 365-day FX forward was entered into)

No general ledger entries are made—only memorandum entries are made.

December 31, 19X3

FX Contract Value—Forward, **net**	$92,000	
Cumulative Translation Adjustment		$92,000
To mark to market the net position with the		
FX trader—intrinsic value element only.		
($.44 − $.40 = $.04)		
($.04 × 2,300,000 pesos = $92,000)		
Cumulative Translation Adjustment	$23,000	
FX Contract Value—Forward, **net**		$23,000
To accrue the discount—a time value element.		
($.44 − $.43 = $.01)		
($.01 × 2,300,000 pesos = $23,000)		
Cash	$69,000	
FX Contract Value—Forward, **net**		$69,000
To settle up with the FX trader. The FX trader		
(a) **Credits** the company's bank account $989,000		
(2,300,000 pesos × $.43 [the contracted forward rate]).		
(b) **Debits** the company's bank account $920,000		
(2,300,000 pesos × .40 [the spot rate]) because the company has to buy		
2,300,000 pesos at the spot rate of $.40 on 12/31/X3 to make delivery to		
the FX trader on the FX forward. ($989,000 − $920,000 = $69,000).		

2. **Realized versus unrealized.** The net $69,000 gain on the FX forward is a *cash* gain and thus has been realized. The adverse translation adjustment of $100,000, however, is unrealized. Furthermore, it will reverse itself in later periods if the direct exchange rate increases by $.04.

3. **What if the exchange rate had *increased from $.44 to $.48?*** If the direct exchange rate had *increased* by $.04 instead of decreasing by $.04, the company would have incurred a $115,000 loss on its FX forward ($.48 − $.43 = $.05; $.05 × 2,300,000 pesos = $115,000), which would have been mostly offset by a $100,000 *favorable* translation adjustment. The favorable translation adjustment will reverse itself in later periods if the exchange rate decreases by $.04. The $115,000 loss on the FX forward, however, is a *cash* loss that will *not* reverse itself in later periods.

Thus hedging a net asset position presents a dilemma that does *not* exist when hedging FX receivables and FX payables because these balances are settled at the expiration of the FX forward and cease to exist. In contrast, the net asset position continues to exist.

WHAT ARE THE ECONOMIC CONSEQUENCES ON HEDGING EXPOSED POSITIONS OF FOREIGN UNITS AS A RESULT OF *SFAS NO. 52* ALLOWING TRANSLATION ADJUSTMENTS TO BE CHARGED OR CREDITED DIRECTLY TO EQUITY?

Prior to *SFAS No. 52*'s issuance in 1981, it was *not* possible to charge or credit translation adjustments directly to equity (income statement recognition was required in all cases). Also, substantial volatility occurred in the income statement. To eliminate potential income statement volatility, managements often hedged a foreign unit's exposed position. Some studies have shown that since the issuance of *SFAS No. 52*, managements that now use the current rate method (a method *not* allowed prior to the issuance of *SFAS No. 52*) have decreased—but not eliminated altogether—their hedging of the exposed position of their foreign units. As one unidentified executive put it (in one such study), "There's less need to play around [to hedge a foreign unit's exposed position] under *SFAS No. 52* because the P&L isn't getting hammered."[9]

WHETHER TO HEDGE THE NET ASSET POSITION, THE NET MONETARY POSITION, OR PROJECTED CASH FLOWS

Differing views exist as to what the true FX exposure is for a foreign unit. Some companies using the current rate method hedge the net asset position with the objective of canceling out some or all of the translation adjustment. Other companies using the current rate method view their true economic exposure as being either (1) the **net *monetary* position** (the difference between monetary assets and monetary liabilities) or (2) the projected cash flows (usually from dividends). Accordingly, these companies may choose to hedge one of these items. (Hedging a *net monetary position* is explained in Chapter 19 in the discussion of the *temporal method* in which the focus is on the *net monetary position* rather than the *net asset position*).

Possibly for competitive reasons, disclosures in virtually all annual reports of multinational companies are presently too general and vague to determine either the extent or the exact exposure being hedged of foreign units. Which exposure to hedge is (1) discussed more fully in international finance texts and (2) usually a high-level finance decision.

VII TRANSLATION CONCEPTUAL ISSUE 2: HOW TO REPORT THE EFFECT OF AN EXCHANGE RATE CHANGE

We now discuss the controversial issue of how the effect of an exchange rate change should be theoretically reported (even though *SFAS No. 52* requires translation adjustments arising under the current rate method to be credited or charged directly to equity).

CRITERIA USED AS A FRAME OF REFERENCE

Accountants use the following criteria to evaluate how to report the effects of exchange rate changes:

1. Do the reported effects relate to day-to-day operations?
2. Do the reported effects impact cash flows?
3. Are the reported effects realized or unrealized in nature?

SOME READILY APPARENT MANNERS OF REPORTING

The effects of exchange rate changes can be reported in many ways, the most readily apparent being the following:

1. **Report as a deferred gain or loss in the balance sheet** and then amortize to income in some rational manner to minimize the volatility that otherwise would occur in the income statement. This was the general practice prior to the issuance of *SFAS No. 8* in 1975 (the predecessor to *SFAS No. 52*). Under *SFAS Con-*

[9]Business International Corporation, *BIMR Handbook on Global Treasury Management* (New York: Business International Corporation, 1984), p. 68.

cepts Statement 6, "Elements of Financial Statements" (paragraphs 35 and 25), however, such gains are *not* liabilities (probable future sacrifices of economic benefits) and such losses are not assets (probable future economic benefits).

2. **Report currently in the income statement** (in accordance with the all-inclusive income statement concept). This was the required practice under *SFAS No. 8* from 1975 to 1981. Under *SFAS No. 52*, this practice must be used if the temporal method of translation is used (as discussed in Chapter 19).

3. **Report as a direct adjustment to equity—bypassing the income statement temporarily.** Under *SFAS No. 52*, this practice must be used if the current rate method is used.

The fact that the rule makers have tried three different approaches attests to the diversity of opinion that exists. Most revealing is that the current FASB position (reached by a mere 4–3 vote) requiring the income statement to be bypassed in most cases is the opposite of its position just six years earlier in *SFAS No. 8* (reached in a 6–1 vote). This hardly inspires confidence that a sound solution was found in *SFAS No. 52*.

THE *SFAS No. 8* EXPERIENCE

What may have driven the FASB to its current position was the disastrous experience with *SFAS No. 8* (whereby only the temporal method was allowed), which by fate was issued in 1975 shortly after the relatively new floating exchange rate system began in 1971. *SFAS No. 8* had two problems. First, it usually reported exchange gains or losses when the events indicated that no economic gain or loss had occurred and vice versa. Second, it required such exchange gains or losses to be reported currently in the income statement, which greatly increased the volatility of earnings. As an example of the volatility, consider the experience of ITT under *SFAS No. 8* for the first three quarters of 1981 in comparison to the prior year amounts:

	Exchange Gains or Losses	
	Included	Excluded
First quarter	(45)%	—
Second quarter	109%	(29)%
Third quarter	(119)%	2%
Full nine months	(53)%	(8)%

The volatility problem cannot be overemphasized. In financial reporting, it is well known that companies try to "manage their earnings" to report smooth quarter-to-quarter and year-to-year earnings gains that security analysts treasure. Few things are more upsetting to chief executives than accounting rules that result in reporting wildly fluctuating amounts over which they have absolutely no control and cannot predict. Such reporting experiences resulted in the quick reconsideration of *SFAS No. 8*. In the process that led to *SFAS No. 52*, the business community strongly opposed reporting the effects of exchange rate changes in the income statement.

VIII REPORTING THE EFFECT OF AN EXCHANGE RATE CHANGE IN A STATEMENT OF COMPREHENSIVE INCOME

Statement of Financial Concepts No. 3, "Elements of Financial Statements of Business Enterprises" (1980) introduced the concept of a **statement of comprehensive income.**[10] The bottom line of such a statement reports the total change in a company's

---

[10]This pronouncement was superseded by *SFAS Concepts Statement No. 6*, "Elements of Financial Statements," in 1985.

equity exclusive of transactions (investments and distributions) with owners. Thus the statement would report items that now bypass the income statement—such as (1) mark-to-market adjustments on investments in marketable equity securities classified as "available for sale" and (2) the cumulative effect of a change to FIFO from LIFO, which is currently reported as an adjustment to beginning retained earnings).

In our opinion, the statement of comprehensive income is long overdue and is essential to a full understanding of foreign operations. The effects of exchange rate changes would be reported in this statement, thereby eliminating the controversy of whether translation adjustments should be made directly to equity. The reporting format of this statement is shown in Illustration 18–8.

ILLUSTRATION 18–8	Statement of Income and Comprehensive Income—Format A: One-Statement Approach

Enterprise
Statement of Income and Comprehensive Income
Year Ended December 31, 19X7

Revenues	$140,000
Expenses	(25,000)
Other gains and losses	8,000
Gain on sale of securities	2,000
Income from Operations before Tax	$125,000
Income tax expense	(31,250)
Income before Extraordinary Item and Cumulative Effect of Accounting Change	$ 93,750
Extraordinary item, net of tax	(28,000)
Income before Cumulative Effect of Accounting Change	$ 65,750
Cumulative effect of accounting change, net of tax	(2,500)
Net Income	$ 63,250
Other comprehensive income:[a]	
Foreign currency translation adjustments, net of tax[b]	8,000
Unrealized gains on securities:[c]	
Unrealized holding gains arising during period, net of tax ... $13,000	
Less: reclassification adjustment, net of tax, for gain included in net income ... (1,500)	11,500
Minimum pension liability adjustment, net of tax[d]	(2,500)
Other comprehensive income	$ 17,000
Comprehensive Income	$ 80,250
Earnings per common share (*simple* capital structure assumed):	
Income before extraordinary item and cumulative effect of accounting change	$ 3.75
Extraordinary item	(1.12)
Cumulative effect of accounting change	(.10)
Net income	$ 2.53
Comprehensive Income	$ 3.21

[a]The FASB exposure draft also displays a "two-statement approach" whereby this section is presented in a *separate* financial statement.
[b]It is assumed that there is no reclassification adjustment this period.
[c]This illustrates the required gross display for this classification.
[d]This illustrates the required net display for this classification.

Source: Exposure Draft: *Proposed Statement of Financial Accounting Standards*, "Reporting Comprehensive Income" (FASB: Norwalk, Ct.), June 20, 1996, p. 30, adapted.

As mentioned in Chapter 17, the FASB issued an exposure draft of a proposed standard, "Reporting Comprehensive Income," in June 1996.[11]

END-OF-CHAPTER REVIEW

SUMMARY OF KEY POINTS

1. Foreign currency financial statements must be **restated** to U.S. GAAP **before translation.**
2. The London-based International Accounting Standards Committee establishes international accounting standards, with which U.S. standards comply in virtually all respects.
3. The **economic effect** of **an exchange rate change** on a foreign unit depends on (a) the causes of the exchange rate change, (b) the nature of the foreign unit's assets (monetary versus nonmonetary), and (c) the extent of debt financing relative to equity financing.
4. **Monetary items** are cash and accounts that are **obligated** to be settled in cash.
5. In translating the balance sheet, the **current rate** is defined as the spot exchange rate existing at the balance sheet date, whereas the **historical rate** is the exchange rate existing when the balance in the account arose.
6. Under the **foreign currency unit of measure approach,** the foreign currency relationships are maintained in translation, the **current rate method** is used, and the financial position focus is on the **subsidiary's net asset position** (total assets – total liabilities).
7. The **effect of an exchange rate change** under the current rate method is (a) called a **translation adjustment** and (b) charged or credited **directly to stockholders' equity.**
8. FX gains or losses from adjusting intercompany receivable and payable balances **expected to be settled in the foreseeable future** are reported currently in the income statement. If the parent uses the current rate method, FX gains and losses from adjusting **long-term** receivables and payables that are *not* **expected to be settled in the foreseeable future** are charged or credited **directly to the CTA account.**
9. When **intercompany-acquired inventory exists** at a financial reporting date, the amount of any unrealized intercompany profit to be deferred is the gross profit recorded **on that inventory at the transfer date** (requires using the exchange rate at the transfer date to calculate that gross profit).
10. If the parent uses the current rate method, FX gains and losses arising from **hedging a net asset position** are charged or credited **directly to the CTA account.**

GLOSSARY OF NEW TERMS

Current rate method   The only translation method that achieves a foreign currency unit of measure in translation.

Current value approach using PPP   A translation approach in which nonmonetary assets are adjusted for inflation before translation at the current rate. See Chapter 20.

Foreign currency unit of measure approach   A way to translate foreign currency financial statements that maintains the financial relationships in the foreign currency (accomplished by using a single exchange rate for all assets and liabilities).

Monetary accounts   Cash and all asset and liability accounts that are obligated to be settled in cash.

Net asset position   Having assets in excess of liabilities.

Net liability position   Having liabilities in excess of assets.

Net monetary position   The difference between monetary assets and monetary liabilities (discussed in Chapter 19).

---

[11]For a thorough discussion of comprehensive income, see "The Time Has Come to Report Comprehensive Income" by Loudell Ellis Robinson, *Accounting Horizons,* June 1991, pp. 107–112.

Nonmonetary accounts   All asset and liability accounts that are *not* monetary accounts.

Statement of comprehensive income   A financial statement in which the bottom line reports the change in stockholders' equity excluding transactions with owners.

Translation adjustments   The name given to the effects of exchange rate changes reported under the current rate method.

Unit of measure   The currency that serves as a perspective from which a foreign unit's financial statements are measured when expressing amounts in U.S. dollars.

U.S. dollar unit of measurement approach   A manner of translating foreign currency financial statements that changes the unit of measure to the U.S. dollar (financial relationships *are* changed).

SELF-STUDY QUESTIONS

(Answers are at the end of this chapter preceding the appendix.)

1. Under the foreign currency unit of measure approach, the focus is on which of the following?
   a. Net current position
   b. Net asset position
   c. Net monetary position
   d. Net exposed position

2. Which exchange rates should be used in expressing the following accounts in dollars under the *current rate* method?

	Additional Paid-in Capital	Deferred Income Taxes Payable
a.	Current	Historical
b.	Historical	Current
c.	Historical	Historical
d.	Current	Current

3. Which exchange rates should be used in expressing the following accounts in dollars under the *current rate* method?

	Cost of Sales	Depreciation Expense
a.	Current	Historical
b.	Historical	Current
c.	Historical	Historical
d.	Current	Current

4. A parent's long-term intercompany receivable from its Japanese subsidiary (denominated in yen) is *not* expected to be settled in the foreseeable future. During 19X1, the direct exchange rate increased. The parent uses the *current rate* method. At year-end, the parent should do which of the following?
   a. Adjust the receivable and *debit* an income statement account.
   b. Adjust the receivable and *credit* an income statement account.
   c. Adjust the receivable and *debit* the Cumulative Translation Adjustment account.
   d. Adjust the receivable and *credit* the Cumulative Translation Adjustment account.

5. During 19X1, a parent sold inventory costing $70,000 to its British subsidiary for $100,000. At 12/31/X1, the subsidiary reported in its balance sheet £40,000 of this inventory. At the transfer date, the direct exchange rate was $.50. At 12/31/X1, the direct exchange rate was $.40. How much intercompany profit must be deferred at 12/31/X1?
   a. $6,000
   b. $4,800
   c. $12,000
   d. $18,000

ASSIGNMENT MATERIAL

REVIEW QUESTIONS

1. Restate and then translate or translate and then restate—which is correct?
2. How have the IASC's international accounting standards impacted the development of accounting standards in the United States?
3. What is the general procedure for *restating* foreign GAAP to U.S. GAAP?
4. What is meant by the term *monetary accounts*?
5. As to foreign units, is a *decrease* in the direct exchange rate a favorable or unfavorable economic event? Is an *increase* favorable or unfavorable?
6. What is meant by the *current exchange rate*? What is meant by the *historical exchange rate*?
7. What is the *foreign currency unit of measure approach*? Summarize it.
8. What is the *financial position focus* under the *foreign currency unit of measure approach*?
9. Is the translated amount for fixed assets historical cost under the *foreign currency unit of measure approach*?
10. What is the major shortcoming of the *current rate method*?
11. What is the effect of an exchange rate change called when the *current rate method* is used?
12. When the *current rate method* is used, how is the effect of an exchange rate change reported under *SFAS No. 52*?
13. If the *current rate method* were used, how is the effect of an exchange rate change reported in a *statement of comprehensive income*?
14. What are the *basic procedures* required before the translation process begins?
15. What eventually happens to accumulated translation adjustments?
16. How are exchange rate change adjustments relating to a parent's *long-term* receivables and payables reported? Why?
17. How are exchange rate change adjustments relating to a parent's intercompany *dividend* receivable reported?
18. Which exchange rate is used to calculate the amount of unrealized intercompany profit?
19. How are FX gains and losses on hedging a net asset position treated?

EXERCISES

E 18–1   **Restating to U.S. GAAP for Deferred Taxes**   A foreign subsidiary of a U.S. parent does not record deferred income taxes because this does not follow local GAAP. The subsidiary's income tax rate is 30%. The following temporary differences relating to the use of accelerated depreciation for income tax reporting purposes exist:

	Cumulative Excess Depreciation Claimed for Tax Reporting
At 12/31/X7	200,000 Local currency unit (LCU)
At 12/31/X8	240,000 LCU

Required   Prepare the worksheet adjusting entry necessary to restate to U.S. GAAP at 12/31/X8.

E 18–2   **Restating to U.S. GAAP for Foreign Inflation Adjustment**   To comply with local GAAP, a foreign subsidiary adjusts its fixed assets for inflation every 10 years. Inflation adjustments for depreciable fixed assets are depreciable for income tax–reporting purposes. The foreign country's income tax rate is 40%. The first such adjustment for the subsidiary occurred 1/1/X1. *Separate* general ledger accounts are used for these adjustments. The balances in these *separate* general ledger accounts at 12/31/X5 (except for one account) follow:

	Debit	Credit
Land—revaluation	500,000	
Building—revaluation	800,000	
Accumulated depreciation—revaluation		200,000
Depreciation expense—revaluation	40,000	

Required   1. What account did the subsidiary credit when it wrote up its fixed assets for inflation? You must determine this before you can proceed.

2. Prepare the worksheet adjusting entry necessary to restate to U.S. GAAP at 12/31/X5.

E 18–3 **Calculating the Effect of an Exchange Rate Change**   Pondox has a foreign subsidiary in a country in which the direct exchange rate decreased from $.25 to $.20 during 19X2. The average balances of the individual assets and liabilities during 19X2 follow:

	Local Currency Units
Cash	80,000
Accounts receivable	220,000
Inventory	275,000
Fixed assets, net	425,000
Total Assets	1,000,000
Accounts payables and accruals	325,000
Current portion of long-term debt	25,000
Intercompany payable	100,000
Long-term debt	300,000
Deferred income taxes payable	50,000
Total Liabilities	800,000

Assume that the carrying value of the parent's Investment account on 1/1/X2 was $50,000 for this 100%-owned subsidiary that was created in late 19X1 when the direct exchange rate was $.25.

Required   Determine the effect of the exchange rate change for 19X2 under the current rate method.

E 18–4 **Calculating the Effect of an Exchange Rate Change**   Kobb Inc. has a 100%-owned foreign subsidiary. The average balances of the subsidiary's assets and liabilities during 19X1 follow:

	Local Currency Units
Monetary assets	4,000,000
Nonmonetary assets	6,000,000
Total Assets	10,000,000
Liabilities (all monetary)	9,000,000
Stockholders' equity	1,000,000
Total Liabilities & Equity	10,000,000

The direct exchange rate decreased steadily during 19X1 from $.40 at 1/1/X1 to $.30 at 12/31/X1.

Required   Determine the effect of the change in the exchange rate for 19X1 under the current rate method.

E 18–5 **Selecting Proper Exchange Rates: Balance Sheet Accounts**   The following accounts exist in a foreign subsidiary's books:

1. Allowance for Doubtful Accounts.
2. Inventory (carried at *cost*).
3. Inventory (carried at *market,* which is *below* cost).
4. Inventory (carried at *market,* which *exceeds* cost).
5. Marketable Equity Securities (carried at *market* [readily determinable], which *exceeds* historical cost).
6. Marketable Bonds (*expected* to be held to maturity).
7. Marketable Bonds (*not* expected to be held to maturity).
8. Patents.
9. Equipment.
10. Accumulated Depreciation.
11. Intercompany Payable.
12. Long-Term Debt.
13. Income Taxes Payable.
14. Deferred Income Taxes Payable.
15. Common Stock.
16. Additional Paid-in Capital.

17. Retained Earnings.
18. Revaluation Capital (from inflation adjustments).

Required   Determine whether the historical exchange rate, the current exchange rate, an average exchange rate, or some other procedure should be used to translate these accounts.

E 18–6   **Selecting Proper Exchange Rates: Income Statement Accounts**   The following accounts exist in a foreign subsidiary's books:

1. Revenues.
2. Intercompany Sales to Parent Company.
3. Purchases.
4. Intercompany Purchases from Parent Company.
5. Cost of Sales.
6. Marketing Expenses.
7. Depreciation Expense.
8. Income Tax Expense.
9. Goodwill Amortization Expense.
10. Loss on Abandonment of Fixed Assets.
11. Gain on Sale of Equipment.
12. Intercompany Interest Expense.
13. Depreciation Expense (incremental amount resulting from adjusting assets for inflation).
14. Inventory Loss from Flood Damage.

Required   Determine whether the historical exchange rate, the current exchange rate, an average exchange rate, or some other procedure should be used to translate these accounts.

E 18–7   **Forcing Out the CTA**   Following are certain items (accounts or account totals) that have been translated into dollars at or for the year ended 12/31/X2:

Total assets	$200,000
Total liabilities	110,000
Common stock	20,000
Revenues	80,000
Expenses	50,000
Amounts reported **in dollars** at the end of the prior year (12/31/X1)	
Retained earnings	$ 12,000
Cumulative translation adjustment (credit)	15,000

The subsidiary did *not* declare any dividends in 19X2.

Required   Use the "forcing out" process to determine the following items:

1. Ending balance for the Retained Earnings account at 12/31/X2.
2. Current period effect of the change in the exchange rate.

E 18–8   **Adjusting Intercompany Accounts**   Pond Inc. created a foreign subsidiary on 12/31/X1. The parent lent the subsidiary $90,000 at that time when the direct exchange rate between the dollar and the LCU was $.10. The subsidiary immediately converted the $90,000 into LCUs and used the entire amount to purchase land on 12/30/X1. At 12/31/X1, the year-end of the parent and the subsidiary, the direct exchange rate was $.09.

Required   1. Make the appropriate adjustments at 12/31/X1, assuming that the loan is denominated in LCUs.
2. Make the appropriate adjustments at 12/31/X1, assuming that the loan is denominated in dollars.
3. Express in dollars the effect of the adjustments made in requirement 2. (Show the calculations for the two ways to determine this amount.)

E 18–9   **Accounting for Intercompany Dividend**   For the year ended 12/31/X5, a 100%-owned foreign subsidiary had net income of 60,000,000 LCU, which was appropriately translated into $5,900,000. On 7/25/X5, when the exchange rate was 10 LCU to $1, the subsidiary declared a dividend of 27,000,000 LCU. The dividend represented the subsidiary's net income for the six months ended 6/30/X5, during which time the weighted average of the exchange rate was 11 LCU to $1. The dividend was paid on 8/3/X5 when the exchange rate was 9 LCU to $1. The exchange rate existing at 12/31/X5 was 8.5 LCU to $1. The parent uses the *equity* method of accounting for the foreign subsidiary.

Required 1. Prepare the parent company's entry to record the dividend receivable.
2. Prepare the entry related to the receipt of the dividend on 8/3/X5.

PROBLEMS

P 18–1 **Restating to U.S. GAAP for Patent Life Difference** On 1/1/X1, a foreign subsidiary of a U.S. parent company acquired a patent for 150,000 LCU. The foreign country's GAAP requires amortization over no more than 5 years. Accordingly, the subsidiary uses a 5-year life even though the patent has a remaining legal life of 15 years. The foreign subsidiary's income tax rate is 40%.

Required Prepare the worksheet adjusting entry necessary at 12/31/X2 to restate the foreign subsidiary's financial statements to U.S. GAAP.

P 18–2* **Translation Worksheet** The financial statements of Maginot Inc., a foreign subsidiary domiciled in France, for the year ended 12/31/X2 follow:

		Francs
Income Statement (19X2)		
Sales		10,000,000
Cost of sales		
Beginning inventory	1,500,000	
Purchases	6,000,000	
	7,500,000	
Less—Ending inventory	(2,000,000)	(5,500,000)
Depreciation expense (total)		(200,000)
Operating and interest expenses		(3,300,000)
Income before Income Taxes		1,000,000
Income tax expense		(400,000)
Net Income		600,000
Balance Sheet (12/31/X2)		
Cash		300,000
Accounts receivable, net		1,000,000
Inventory		2,000,000
Land		1,000,000
Buildings and equipment		5,200,000
Accumulated depreciation		(500,000)
Total Assets		9,000,000
Payables and accruals		2,500,000
Income taxes payable		200,000
Long-term debt		2,800,000
Total Liabilities		5,500,000
Common stock		1,500,000
Retained earnings		2,000,000
Total Equity		3,500,000
Total Liabilities & Equity		9,000,000

Additional   **1. Conformity with U.S. GAAP.** Assume that the financial statements in francs have been adjusted
Information   to conform with U.S. GAAP.

*The financial statement information presented for problems accompanied by asterisks is also provided on MODEL 18 of the software file disk (filename: MODEL18) that is available for use with the text, allowing the problem to be worked on the computer.

2. **Exchange rates** (direct):

Current rate at 12/31/X1	$.15
Average rate for 19X2	.12
Current rate at 12/31/X2	.10

3. **Inventory.** The ending inventory is valued at the lower of cost or market in francs; however, no write-down to market was necessary on the subsidiary's books. Assume that the inventory at 12/31/X2 was acquired when the exchange rate was $.11. Inventory at 12/31/X1 was acquired when the exchange rate was $.16.
4. **Property, plant, and equipment.** All were acquired in prior years when the exchange rate was $.16, except equipment costing 200,000 francs, which was acquired in late December 19X2 when the exchange rate was $.11. (No depreciation was recorded on this equipment for 19X2.)
5. **Sales, purchases, and operating expenses.** All occurred evenly throughout the year.
6. **Common stock.** The subsidiary was created two years ago when the direct exchange rate was $.16. No additional capital transactions have occurred since that time.
7. **Dividends.** The subsidiary did *not* declare any dividends during the year.
8. **Information for statement of cash flows.** The beginning-of-year cash balance was 600,000 francs. Cash collections from customers (9,800,000 francs), cash payments to suppliers and employees (8,600,000 francs), and cash payments to lenders for interest (400,000 francs) were made evenly throughout the year. A cash payment for income taxes (300,000 francs) was made on 5/30/X2 when the direct exchange rate was $.13. The only cash flows pertaining to investing activities were for the purchase of equipment in late 19X2 when the direct exchange rate was $11. The only activity in the Long-Term Debt account during the year was a principal repayment (600,000 francs) on 3/31/X2 when the direct exchange rate was $.14. No dividends were paid during 19X2.

Required 1. Calculate the translation adjustment for 19X2 using the analysis of the net asset approach. Approximately how much of this amount is the result of lowering the value of (a) assets and (b) liabilities?
2. Translate the financial statements into dollars assuming the following:
    a. Retained earnings at 12/31/X1 (per the translated financial statements) were $217,000.
    b. The cumulative translation adjustment at 12/31/X1 was $(22,000).
3. Prepare the parent's entry or entries at 12/31/X2 relating to the *equity* method of accounting.
4. Prepare a T-account analysis of the parent's Investment account since the subsidiary's creation.
5. Qualitatively assess whether the subsidiary had a good year or a bad year. Do you think the parent's price-earnings ratio is based on net income or net income plus the current year translation adjustment?
6. Prepare the general ledger entry that would be made if the subsidiary were sold for $400,000 cash on 1/3/X3.
7. **Optional** (check with your instructor): Prepare a translated statement of cash flows for 19X2 using the *direct* method.

P 18–3*   **Translation Worksheet**   The financial statements of Tipperary Inc., a foreign subsidiary domiciled in Ireland, for the year ended 12/31/X4 follow:

		Punts
Income Statement (19X4)		
Sales		4,000,000
Cost of sales		
Beginning inventory	800,000	
Purchases	3,200,000	
	4,000,000	
Less—Ending inventory	(900,000)	(3,100,000)
Depreciation expense (in total)		(50,000)
Operating and interest expenses		(450,000)
Income before Income Taxes		400,000
Income tax expense @ 25%		(100,000)
Net Income		300,000

(continued)

Balance Sheet (as of 12/31/X4)

Cash	200,000
Accounts receivable	500,000
Allowance for doubtful accounts	(50,000)
Inventory (FIFO)	900,000
Land	300,000
Buildings and equipment	1,100,000
Accumulated depreciation	(250,000)
Total Assets	2,700,000
Payables and accruals	700,000
Accrued income taxes payable	100,000
Intercompany payable (to parent)	500,000
Long-term debt	600,000
Total Liabilities	1,900,000
Common stock	100,000
Retained earnings	700,000
Total Equity	800,000
Total Liabilities & Equity	2,700,000

Additional Information

1. **Conformity with U.S. GAAP.** Assume that the financial statements in punts are in accordance with U.S. GAAP; thus no adjustments are required.
2. **Exchange rates** (direct):

Current rate at 12/31/X3	$1.25
Average rate for 19X4	1.40
Current rate at 12/31/X4	1.50

3. **Inventory.** The ending inventory is valued at the lower of cost or market in punts; however, no write-down to market was necessary on the subsidiary's books. Assume that the inventory at 12/31/X4 was acquired evenly during the last quarter of 19X4 (which had an average exchange rate of $1.45).

   The beginning inventory was all acquired when the exchange rate was $1.20, and no market adjustment in punts was necessary.

4. **Fixed assets.** The land, buildings, and equipment were acquired in 19X2 when the exchange rate was $1.60, except for some office equipment costing 100,000 punts that was acquired in late December 19X4 when the exchange rate was $1.49. (No depreciation was recorded on this equipment for 19X4).
5. **Sales and operating expenses.** Assume that they occurred evenly throughout the year.
6. **Purchases.** Assume that purchases occurred evenly throughout the year.
7. **Intercompany payable.** The intercompany payable is denominated in punts.
8. **Common stock.** The subsidiary was created in 19X2 when the direct exchange rate was $1.60. No additional capital transactions have occurred since then.
9. **Dividends.** Dividends of 200,000 punts were declared and paid in 19X4 when the direct exchange rate was $1.45. No dividends were declared in 19X2 or 19X3.
10. **Information for statement of cash flows.** The beginning-of-year cash balance was 250,000 punts. Cash collections from customers (4,100,000 punts), cash payments to suppliers and employees (3,300,000 punts), and cash payments to lenders for interest (90,000 punts) were made evenly throughout the year. A cash payment for income taxes (60,000 punts) was made on 4/1/X4 when the direct exchange rate was $1.30. The only cash flow pertaining to investing activities was for the purchase of equipment in late 19X4 when the direct exchange rate was $1.49. The only activity in the long-term debt account during the year was a principal repayment (400,000 punts) on 6/3/X4 when the direct exchange rate was $1.35. The cash dividend (200,000 punts) was paid on 11/1/X4 when the direct exchange rate was $1.45.

Required

1. Calculate the translation adjustment for 19X4 using the analysis of net assets approach. Approximately how much of this amount is the result of lowering the value of (a) assets and (b) liabilities?

2. Translate the financial statements into dollars assuming the following:
   a. From the dollar financial statements, retained earnings at 12/31/X3 were $840,000.
   b. The cumulative translation adjustment at 12/31/X3 was $(125,000).
3. Prepare the parent's entry or entries at 12/31/X4 under the *equity* method of accounting.
4. Prepare a T-account analysis of the parent's Investment account since the subsidiary's creation.
5. Prepare the general ledger entry that would be made if the subsidiary were sold for $1,240,000 on 1/3/X5.
6. **Optional** (check with your instructor): Prepare a translated statement of cash flows for 19X4 using the *direct* method.

P 18–4   **Adjusting Intercompany Accounts and Calculating Unrealized Intercompany Profit**   The following are certain accounts of PBX and its 100%-owned foreign subsidiary SBX for the year ended 12/31/X5.

	PBX (in dollars)	SBX (in pounds)
Intercompany sales	$500,000	
Intercompany cost of sales	(300,000)	
Intercompany receivable	500,000	
Intercompany payable		250,000 pounds
Inventory		
Vendor acquired		700,000 pounds
Intercompany acquired		50,000 pounds
Direct Exchange Rates for 19X5		
December 31, 19X4		$2.40
December 31, 19X5		1.20
Average rate for 19X5		1.80
Exchange rate at time of intercompany sale. . .		2.00

Additional Information
1. SBX's intercompany payable is denominated in pounds.
2. At year-end, SBX still owes PBX the entire amount relating to this inventory purchase (of 100 widgets).
3. No adjustment has been made at year-end because of the change in the exchange rate.

Required
1. Make the necessary adjustment at 12/31/X5 to the appropriate intercompany receivable or intercompany payable account balance.
2. What adjusting entry would be made if the intercompany payable were denominated in dollars?
3. Complete the following analysis:

	Total	Sold	On Hand
Intercompany sales	$500,000		
Intercompany cost of sales	(300,000)	_____	_____
Gross Profit	$200,000	_____	_____

4. What is the translated amount for inventory in the 12/31/X5 balance sheet under the current rate method?
5. Prepare the universal intercompany elimination entry or entries (discussed in Chapter 10) required in consolidation at 12/31/X5 relating to the preceding intercompany transaction.
6. Repeat requirement 3 assuming that the $1.20 direct exchange rate at year-end is to be used in determining the inventory on hand at year-end in dollars.
7. Repeat requirement 3 assuming the following:
   a. The 12/31/X5 direct exchange rate is $.10.
   b. This exchange rate is to be used in determining the inventory on hand at year-end in dollars.
8. Note that the amount of gross profit deferred at year-end using a year-end exchange rate (as in requirements 6 and 7) can differ significantly from the amount deferred using the exchange rate prescribed by *SFAS No. 52*. Which exchange rate makes the most sense to use? Why?
9. How many widgets does SBX still have on hand?

P 18–5 **Determining the Net Effect of Adjustments to Intercompany Account**   Pyox created Syox, a German subsidiary, on 12/31/X1. On that date, Pyox made a $360,000 noninterest-bearing loan to Syox. Syox immediately converted the $360,000 into marks and used all of them to purchase land. For simplicity, assume that Syox was so thinly capitalized that we can ignore the capital accounts. The direct exchange rate was $.40 at 12/1/X1 and $.45 at 12/31/X1. The loan is denominated in marks.

Required   1. Make the appropriate adjusting entry at 12/31/X1 relating to the intercompany loan.
2. Translate the subsidiary's 12/31/X1 balance sheet into dollars using the current rate method.
3. What is the net effect of the change in the exchange rate as reported in the equity section of the consolidated balance sheet at the end of 19X1?
4. Is the effect on the parent's equity calculated in requirement 3 the result of the adjustment to the intercompany account?

P 18–6*   **COMPREHENSIVE: Translation Worksheet, Consolidation Worksheet and Intercompany Transactions**   The financial statements of Piper Inc. and its 100%-owned British subsidiary, Swan Inc., for the year ended 12/31/X5 follow:

	Piper (dollars)	Swan (pounds)
Income Statement (19X5)		
Sales	$7,000,000	£1,500,000
Cost of sales	(4,000,000)	(800,000)
Depreciation expense	(86,000)	(30,000)
Expenses	(1,900,000)	(470,000)
Intercompany Accounts		
Sales	465,000	
Cost of sales	(279,000)	
Net Income	$1,200,000	£ 200,000
Balance Sheet (as of 12/31/X5)		
Cash	$ 569,000	£ 50,000
Accounts receivable	800,000	300,000
Intercompany receivable	472,000	
Inventory		
Vendor acquired	700,000	400,000
Intercompany acquired		100,000
Investment in Swan	$ 359,000	
Land	200,000	£ 150,000
Buildings and equipment	1,000,000	500,000
Accumulated depreciation	(300,000)	(100,000)
Total Assets	$3,800,000	£1,400,000
Accounts payable	$ 700,000	£ 160,000
Accrued liabilities	500,000	40,000
Intercompany payable		300,000
Long-term debt	1,500,000	500,000
Total Liabilities	$2,700,000	£1,000,000
Common stock	$ 500,000	£ 60,000
Retained earnings	609,000	340,000
Cumulative translation adjustment	(9,000)	
Total Equity	$1,100,000	£ 400,000
Total Liabilities & Equity	$3,800,000	£1,400,000
Dividends declared	$ 900,000	£ 100,000

Additional Information   **1. Conformity with U.S. GAAP.** Assume that the financial statements of the subsidiary are in accordance with U.S. GAAP.

2. **Exchange rates** (direct):

Current rate at 12/31/X4	$1.70
Average rate for 19X5	1.60
Current rate at 12/31/X5	1.50

3. **Inventory.** The ending inventory was acquired during the last quarter of 19X5 when the average exchange rate was $1.55. (No intercompany-acquired inventory was on hand at the beginning of 19X5.)
4. **Fixed assets.** The fixed assets were acquired when the subsidiary was created in 19X2, at which time the exchange rate was $1.75.
5. **Sales and operating expenses.** These occurred evenly throughout the year.
6. **Intercompany accounts.** All intercompany transactions are denominated in pounds. No adjustment has been made at year-end because of changes in the exchange rate during the year. The activity in the intercompany accounts for 19X5 follows:

	SUBSIDIARY'S INTERCOMPANY PAYABLE (IN POUNDS)			PARENT'S INTERCOMPANY RECEIVABLE (IN DOLLARS)			
		£ 60,000	Bal., 1/1/X5	Bal., 1/1/X5	$102,000		
6/30X5	60,000[a]					$ 96,000[a]	7/1/X5
		300,000[b]	11/20/X5	11/15/X5	465,000[b]		
		100,000[c]	12/20/X5	12/20/X5	151,000[c]		
12/30/X5	100,000[d]					$150,000[d]	12/30/X5
		£300,000	Bal., 12/31/X5	Bal., 12/31/X5	$472,000		

[a]Cash payment to parent when direct rate was $1.60.

[b]Inventory transfer.

[c]Dividend declaration.

[d]Dividend payment.

7. **Common stock.** No common stock transactions have occurred since the creation of the subsidiary by the parent in 19X2.
8. **Retained earnings.** From the dollar financial statements, the subsidiary's Retained Earnings account at 12/31/X4 was $414,000.
9. **Cumulative translation adjustment.** The cumulative translation adjustment at 12/31/X4 was $(9,000).
10. **Dividends.** The subsidiary declared its 19X5 dividends on 12/20/X5 (when the direct exchange rate was $1.51), and paid the dividend on 12/30/X5 (when the direct exchange rate was $1.50). (Intercompany dividends are recorded in the Intercompany Payable and Intercompany Receivable accounts and were properly recorded by both entities.)
11. **Income taxes.** For simplicity, ignore income tax considerations.
12. **Equity method of accounting.** The parent uses the *equity* method of accounting but has yet to record the earnings of the subsidiary for 19X5. No adjustment has been made to the parent's books for unrealized intercompany profit.
13. **Information for statement of cash flows.** The beginning-of-year cash balance was £250,000. Cash collections from customers (£1,400,000), cash payments to suppliers and employees (£1,410,000), and cash payments to lenders for interest (£40,000) were made evenly throughout the year. A cash payment for income taxes (£50,000) was made on 4/15/X5 when the direct exchange rate was $1.64. There were no cash flows pertaining to investing activities nor was there activity in the long-term debt account during the year. A short-term borrowing (£200,000) was made on 4/1/X5 when the direct exchange rate was $1.65. This borrowing was repaid on 11/15/X5 when the direct exchange rate was $1.45. The cash dividend (£100,000) was paid on 12/30/X5 when the direct exchange rate was $1.50.

Required 1. Calculate the translation adjustment for 19X5 using the analysis of net assets approach. Approximately how much of this amount is the result of lowering the value of (1) assets and (2) liabilities?

2. Translate the subsidiary's financial statements into dollars.
3. Prepare the appropriate adjusting entry to bring the Intercompany Receivable and Intercompany Payable accounts into agreement.
4. Prepare an analysis showing the amount of intercompany profit that is unrealized at year-end.
5. Prepare the entries the parent would record under the *equity* method of accounting.
6. Prepare an analysis of the Investment account as of 12/31/X4 and update it through 12/31/X5. (*Hint:* The components at 12/31/X4 total $510,000.)
7. Prepare all consolidation entries needed at 12/31/X5 to consolidate the subsidiary's financial statements properly.
8. Prepare a consolidation worksheet.
9. **Optional** (check with your instructor): Prepare a translated statement of cash flows for 19X5 using the direct method. Why does the amount calculated for the translation adjustment in requirement 1 differ from the $78,000 amount that is supposed to appear in the translated statement of cash flows?

P 18–7 **Hedging a Net Asset Position** Pemco uses the current method of translation for its 100%-owned foreign subsidiary, Semco (created in 19X1). For 19X2, Semco's net income as 100,000 LCUs, which translated into $33,000. (Earnings occurred evenly throughout the year and were remitted to Pemco monthly.) An *unfavorable* translation adjust of $64,000 resulted for 19X2. At 12/31/X1, the Cumulative Translation Adjustment account had a *credit* balance of $18,000.

On 12/31/X1, in expectation that the LCU would weaken throughout 19X2, management entered into a one-year forward exchange contract to *sell* 600,000 LCUs (Semco's net asset position at 12/31/X1) on 12/31/X2 at the forward rate of $.39. (No hedging was done in 19X1.) The following direct exchange rates are assumed:

	December 31, 19X1 (inception date)	June 30, 19X2 (a financial reporting date)	December 31, 19X2 (expiration date)
Spot rate	$.40	$.36	$.30
Forward rate	.39	.355	n/a

Required
1. Prepare the journal entries pertaining to the forward exchange contract.
2. Determine the amount to be charged or credited to the CTA account for 19X2.

※ THINKING CRITICALLY ※

※ CASES ※

C 18–1 **Determining How to Report the Effect of an Exchange Rate Change** A foreign subsidiary has only cash as an asset and no liabilities. During 19X1, the direct exchange rate changed 10%.

Required
1. Disregarding *SFAS No. 52*'s requirements, what is the most meaningful way to report the effect of the exchange rate change? Use the criteria listed in the chapter for conceptual issue 2, and consider the possible different causes of the exchange rate change in arriving at your answer.
2. Repeat requirement 1, but assume that the subsidiary's only asset is land.

C 18–2 **Evaluating Translated Amounts** A foreign subsidiary has the following balance sheet at year-end:

	LCUs
Cash	100,000
5% Note receivable	200,000
Land	500,000
	800,000

Additional Information
1. The land has a current value of 750,000 LCUs.
2. The note receivable has a current value of 150,000 LCUs as a result of the current interest rate being substantially higher than the 5% fixed interest rate.

3. The current exchange rate at year-end is $1.00.
4. The land was acquired when the direct exchange rate was $1.40.

Required   Evaluate whether the translated amounts under the *current rate* method are meaningful.

C 18–3   **Evaluating Reporting Results**   On 11/10/X1, a domestic company transferred inventory costing $150,000 to its 100%-owned foreign subsidiary at cost. At 12/31/X1, the subsidiary had all of this inventory on hand. The direct exchange rates were $1.50 at 11/10/X1 and $1.60 at 12/31/X1.

Required   Economically, at what amount should the inventory be valued in the 12/31/X1 consolidated balance sheet?

C 18–4   **Determining How to Report the Effect of an Exchange Rate Change**   Kalla Inc. has a 100%-owned foreign subsidiary. Annual inflation in the foreign country is generally about 5%. Consequently, the subsidiary's local lender, a bank, charges the subsidiary an additional 5% interest above and beyond the 4% that it otherwise would charge on its 1,000,000 LCU loan to the subsidiary. This loan is the sole financing for a manufacturing plant. During 19X1, the direct exchange rate decreased from $1.05 to $1.00 as a result of inflation in the foreign country.

Required   1. Disregarding the requirements of *SFAS No. 52,* what is the most appropriate manner of reporting the economics of this situation?
2. Would your answer to requirement 1 change if the lender indexed the debt for inflation and instead charged a lower interest rate?
3. Under the current rate method, what would be reported?

C 18–5   **Issuing Partially Price-Level–Adjusted Statements: How Is It Routinely Done and Concealed?**   Some foreign countries, such as Brazil and Italy, allow companies to adjust periodically their fixed assets for inflation. In the United States, one side of the balance sheet is effectively adjusted for inflation for the large majority of companies. This is not evident, however, from the financial statements and disclosures made.

Required   How is one side of the balance sheet effectively adjusted for inflation in the United States?

C 18–6   **Determining Just How Many Equity Accounts There Are**   Some accountants favor using fewer than the at least eight equity accounts that currently can be used.

Required   Try to identify the existing eight equity accounts. Can you think of any new ones that you have not been exposed to in your accounting courses?

C 18–7   **Hedging Net Asset Exposures: What Is There to Lose?**   On 12/31/X1, Parrex hedged its Belgian subsidiary's 500,000 krone net asset position (using a one-year forward exchange contract) because it thought the krone would weaken during 19X2. The forward rate was $.19. During 19X2, the direct exchange rate *increased* from $.20 to $.24. Disregard the change in net assets from 19X2's operations in responding to the requirements.

Required   1. What is the translation adjustment for 19X2 under the *current rate method*?
2. What is the change in the cumulative translation adjustment account for 19X2?
3. Evaluate economically the outcome of Parrex's actions in light of the krone *strengthening* instead of *weakening.*

C 18–8   **A Proposed Way to Get Hedge Accounting Treatment: Will It Fly?**   A foreign unit's budgeted net income for 19X2 is 50,000 LCUs per quarter (200,000 LCUs total), which is expected to be distributed to the parent at the end of each quarter. The parent believes that the direct exchange rate will decrease significantly by 12/31/X2. Accordingly, the parent wishes to hedge this projected cash inflow using FX forwards.

Under *SFAS No. 52,* hedging budgeted net income or expected cash flows from dividends will *not* qualify for hedge accounting treatment. Thus the expected hedging gain cannot be credited to the CTA account to offset the expected adverse translation adjustment for 19X2. At 12/31/X1, the foreign unit's net asset position is 1,000,000 LCUs.

Required   1. Would hedge accounting treatment be allowed if the parent hedged to the extent of 200,000 LCUs but designated it a hedge of a portion of the net asset position?
2. What type of FX forward should be acquired and for what term?

❋ FINANCIAL ANALYSIS PROBLEM ❋

FAP 18–1 **Calculating Parent's AROI: Subsidiary Disposed of After Three Years** PDX created a 100%-owned foreign subsidiary (SDX) on 1/1/X1, with a capital investment of $400,000 when the direct exchange rate was $.50. Selected data for SDX follow:

Year	Net Income LCU	Net Income Dollars	Dividends Declared LCU	Dividends Declared Dollars	Current Year Translation Adjustment	Direct Exchange Rate at Year-End
19X1	200,000	$100,000	–0–	$ –0–	$ –0–	$.50
19X2	200,000	90,000	200,000	80,000	(110,000)	.40
19X3	200,000	70,000	200,000	80,000	(90,000)	.30

Additional Information
1. SDX declared and paid its 19X2 dividend at the *end* of 19X2 and its 19X3 dividend at the *beginning* of 19X3.
2. On 12/31/X3, PDX sold its entire interest in SDX to a group of local investors for cash of 1,120,000 LCUs.
3. SDX's reported net income each year was earned evenly throughout the year.
4. PDX used the *current rate* method of translation.

Required
1. Prepare a T-account analysis of PDX's Investment in Subsidiary account for 19X1 through 19X3.
2. Calculate PDX's annual return on investment (AROI) for 19X1, 19X2, and 19X3 using SDX's reported net income—*without* the current period translation adjustment included in the numerator.
3. Repeat requirement 2, but *with* the current period translation adjustment included in the numerator.
4. Which manner of calculation—requirement 2 or 3—is consistent with *SFAS No. 52*?
5. Calculate an average AROI for the three years first using the percentages in requirement 2 and then the percentages in requirement 3. Which average reflects the economic reality of what occurred?
6. Explain whether it is correct to use the *beginning-of-year* investment balance or the *average* investment balance for the year in the denominator in requirements 2 and 3.
7. Calculate the internal rate of return (IRR) over the life of the investment. (You may readily obtain this answer using the IRR function available in EXCEL or LOTUS 1–2–3 by merely setting up a cash flow table and then programming the IRR function with the cursor in the cell in which you want your answer to appear.)
8. Explain why the IRR in requirement 7 differs from the AROI calculations in requirements 2, 3, and 5. Which should be used in evaluating the profitability of SDX?

❋ PERSONAL SITUATION: ETHICS AND INTERPERSONAL SKILLS ❋

PS 18–1 **Ethics: Can You Tell the Truth About Former Accountants?** You are an accounting supervisor at Oldco Inc. The accounting supervisor at Newco Inc. has called you in reference to an accountant whom Newco is considering for employment. The accountant was terminated from Oldco several months ago for embezzling small amounts of money.

Required
1. What can you say to the accounting supervisor at Newco?
2. If Newco hires the accountant who then embezzles large sums of money, does Newco have any legal recourse against Oldco if Oldco concealed the accountant's embezzlement while in its employment?

ANSWERS TO SELF-STUDY QUESTIONS

1. b 2. b 3. d 4. d 5. a

INCOME TAX CONSEQUENCES OF EXCHANGE RATE CHANGES

Deferred income taxes may have to be recorded on translation adjustments. The governing pronouncements in this regard are *SFAS No. 109*, "Accounting for Income Taxes" and *APB Opinion No. 23*, "Accounting for Income Taxes—Special Areas."

I PROCEDURES WHEN THE TRANSLATION ADJUSTMENT IS *POSITIVE*

If the translation adjustment is positive, a deferred tax liability is recorded; the off-setting debit is made to the Cumulative Translation Adjustment account. This requirement becomes inoperable, however, if the parent is using the loophole available in *APBO No. 23* that allows no income taxes to be provided on foreign earnings (discussed in depth in an appendix to Chapter 19). Such deferred income taxes are in addition to any deferred income taxes that are recorded on the subsidiary's undistributed earnings (the subject of the appendix to Chapter 19).

THE NATURE OF THE CTA

Think of a CTA *credit* balance as an "unrecognized unrealized gain" and a CTA *debit* balance as an "unrecognized unrealized loss." Realization and recognition of a CTA balance occur (for financial reporting and tax reporting) only as a result of cash distributions to the parent resulting from either (1) distributions of earnings (dividends) or (2) liquidation of the subsidiary (a return of some or all of the initial invested capital). To illustrate the procedures for calculating deferred income taxes on a CTA balance, assume that

1. Parr Inc. created a British subsidiary, Subb Inc., by investing cash of $100,000 on January 1, 19X1, when the direct exchange rate was £1 = $1.
2. Subb's net income for 19X1 was £20,000 and occurred evenly throughout the year.
3. Subb did *not* declare any dividends in 19X1.
4. The average direct exchange rate for 19X1 was £1 = $1.05. The direct exchange rate on December 31, 19X1, was £1 = $1.10.
5. The CTA account had a credit balance of $11,000 at December 31, 19X1.
6. Subb declared and paid a cash dividend of £20,000 on January 1, 19X2, when the direct exchange rate was £1 = $1.10.

Illustration 18–9 shows how the CTA account is analyzed for calculating deferred income taxes to be recorded at the parent level on the $11,000 CTA credit balance when a subsidiary's undistributed earnings are *not* intended to be invested indefinitely. An assumed U.S. income tax rate of 40% is used.[12] The procedures are symmetrical when the CTA account balance is a debit instead of a credit.

II PROCEDURES WHEN THE TRANSLATION ADJUSTMENT IS *NEGATIVE*

If the translation adjustment is *negative,* the parent must make the appropriate calculations under *SFAS No. 109* to determine whether a deferred tax *asset* can be recorded; if one is recorded, the offsetting credit is made to the CTA account.

---

[12]Foreign tax credits in the foreign taxing jurisdiction relating to U.S. dollar translation adjustments do not apply to the CTA. Thus the full 40% rate is used because foreign tax credits apply only to the discussion in the Appendix to Chapter 19.

| **ILLUSTRATION 18–9** | **Calculating Deferred Income Taxes Relating to the CTA Balance** |

I. Selected Accounts from the Translation Worksheet at 12/31/X1

	Pounds	Direct Exchange Rate	Dollars
Common stock	100,000	$1.00 (H)	$100,000
Retained earnings	20,000	$1.05 (A)	21,000
Cumulative translation adjustment		(Given)	11,000
	120,000		$132,000ᵃ

H = Historical rate.
A = Average rate.
ᵃNote that $132,000 = £120,000 × $1.10, the direct exchange rate at 12/31/X1.

II. Components of the CTA Balance

Common stock—the increase in value of the beginning net assets
(£100,000 × $.10 [ending rate of $1.10 – 1.00 beginning rate]) $10,000
Retained earnings—the increase in value of the added net assets
(£20,000 × $.05 [ending rate of $1.10 – $1.05 average rate]) 1,000
$11,000

Note: These components constitute the amount by which the translated amounts for the common stock and retained earnings accounts are "undervalued" in relation to the direct exchange rate of $1.10 on 12/31/X1.

III. Calculation of Deferred Income Taxes on the CTA Balance

Retained earnings component of CTA $1,000
U.S. income tax rate (assumed) 40%
Income Taxes to Be Recorded by Parent . . . . $ 400

Parent's Entry at 12/31/X5

Cumulative Translation Adjustment 400
   Deferred Income Taxes Payable 400

Note: No deferred income taxes are recognized on the $10,000 common stock component because the investment in the subsidiary is deemed to be essentially permanent in duration. If the parent had plans to liquidate the subsidiary in the foreseeable future, however, income taxes would be recognized relating to this component.

P 18–1A **Liquidating a Subsidiary: Cumulative Translation Adjustment Tax Consequences** In late 19X5, Parr Inc. decided to liquidate its 100%-owned British subsidiary, Subb Inc. Accordingly, Subb (1) sold all of its noncash assets for cash, (2) paid off all of its creditors in full, and (3) distributed the remaining cash to Parr (in two steps as explained below). Subb's translation worksheet for its balance sheet at 12/31/X5 (just prior to the two cash distributions to Parr) follows:

	Pounds	Direct Exchange Rate	Dollars
Cash	160,000	$1.50	$240,000
Common stock	100,000	$1.00	$100,000
Retained earnings	60,000	(Given)	72,000
Cumulative translation adjustment		(Given)	68,000
	160,000		$240,000

Additional Information
1. Parr has never recorded on its books any income tax liabilities relating to Subb's earnings because Parr had expected Subb's earnings to be invested indefinitely.
2. Parr's balance in its Investment in Subsidiary account (under the equity method) just prior to the two cash distributions was $240,000.
3. For simplicity, assume that the U.S. income tax rate is 40% and Great Britain has (a) a zero income tax rate and (b) no dividend withholding tax (thus no foreign tax credits exist).

4. The components of the cumulative translation adjustment of $68,000 follow:

Common stock (£100,000 × [$1.50 − $1.00]) $50,000
Retained earnings (£60,000 × $1.50 = $90,000;
  $90,000 − $72,000 = $18,000) .... <u>18,000</u>
                                                                          <u>$68,000</u>

5. On 1/1/X6, when the direct exchange rate was £1 equals $1.50, Subb declared and paid a cash dividend of £60,000.
6. On 1/2/X6, when the direct exchange rate was £1 equals $1.50, Subb distributed the remaining cash of £100,000 to Parr in exchange for all of its outstanding common stock.
7. Parr has never recorded any deferred income taxes on its books relating to Subb because it always had considered undistributed earnings to be invested permanently.

Required
1. What unified entry (without considering income taxes) should Parr make upon receipt of the two cash distributions in 19X6?
2. What amount will Parr pay in U.S. income taxes upon the first cash (dividend) distribution?
3. What amount will Parr pay in U.S. income taxes upon the second cash (return of the initial capital investment) distribution?
4. What entry should Parr make to recognize deferred income taxes payable at 12/31/X5?
5. What unified entry should Parr make upon receipt of the two cash distributions in 19X6, assuming that Parr made the entry in requirement 4 at 12/31/X5?
6. At what amount would the Cumulative Translation Adjustment account be reported in Parr's 12/31/X5 balance sheet under each of the following assumptions?
   a. Parr is liquidating Subb (as explained above).
   b. Parr has no intention to liquidate Subb (contrary to above) and intends to reinvest Subb's earnings permanently.
   c. Parr has no intention of liquidating Subb (contrary to above) but intends to have Subb's earnings distributed in the near future.

TRANSLATING FOREIGN CURRENCY STATEMENTS: THE TEMPORAL METHOD & THE FUNCTIONAL CURRENCY CONCEPT

19

LEARNING OBJECTIVES

TO UNDERSTAND

- The procedures for applying the temporal method of translation.
- The way to hedge a foreign operation's exposed monetary position.
- The objectives of translation under *SFAS No. 52*.
- The functional currency concept and its underlying rationale.
- When and how to record U.S. income taxes on earnings of foreign subsidiaries.

TOPIC OUTLINE

The first panacea for a mismanaged nation is inflation of the currency; the second is war. Both bring a temporary prosperity; both bring a permanent ruin.

ERNEST HEMINGWAY

CHAPTER OVERVIEW

In this chapter, we first discuss and illustrate the other translation approach allowed under FASB *Statement No. 52:* The U.S. dollar unit of measure, which is implemented using the temporal method of translation. Next we discuss hedging a foreign operation's exposed *monetary* position. After that, we review the objectives of translation under *SFAS No. 52*. Finally, we explain the functional currency concept, which is the underlying foundation conceived to support the use of (1) the current rate method of translation in certain situations and (2) the temporal method of translation in all other situations.

The validity of the functional currency concept is addressed in Chapter 20. That discussion reveals the characteristics (strengths and weaknesses) of the current rate method and the temporal method under the existing floating exchange rate system.

I THE U.S. DOLLAR UNIT OF MEASURE APPROACH (THE TEMPORAL METHOD)

THE RATIONALE

Under the U.S. dollar unit of measure approach, no consideration is given to trying to preserve the relationships that exist in the foreign currency statements. Instead, **the objective is to translate the nonmonetary assets** (with one exception mentioned later) **at rates that produce the equivalent number of dollars that would have been needed to acquire the nonmonetary assets when they were purchased.** Thus it is said that the nonmonetary assets are not only expressed in U.S. dollars but also are "remeasured" in the process (to the dollars that would have been needed to acquire the item). Only historical rates achieve these results. In the income statement, depreciation and amortization expenses are likewise translated at historical rates.

By using historical rates for nonmonetary items and the current rate for monetary items, the item-to-item relationships that exist in the foreign currency statements are *not* maintained in translation—**an entirely different set of relationships is produced.** Thus the translated financial statements in U.S. dollars **do *not* have a "foreign currency feel" to them.** Managerially, the U.S. parent, in looking at the translated financial statements, views the foreign operation using a different perspective than that of the local management in the foreign country that uses the foreign currency statements.

Some claim that this remeasuring is tantamount to simulating what the cost of a foreign plant would have been had it been located in the United States. Some claim that it results in treating foreign operations as though all of the transactions had occurred in U.S. dollars. Others disagree with these views and believe that it merely results in expressing in U.S. dollars the cost of a foreign plant.[1]

TRANSLATION METHODS FOR ACHIEVING A U.S. DOLLAR UNIT OF MEASURE

Three translation methods exist for achieving a U.S. dollar unit of measure: the **temporal method,** the **monetary-nonmonetary method,** and the **current-noncurrent method.**

---

[1]*SFAS No. 52*, pp. 20–21.

1. **The temporal method.** Under this method, **the measurement basis of an asset or liability determines the exchange rate used in translating that asset or liability.** Accordingly, different exchange rates are used for different measurement bases (for example, historical exchange rates for fixed assets and the current exchange rate for receivables). Consequently, a foreign currency measurement is changed into a dollar measurement without changing the basis. Thus the accounting principles are not changed (even though the unit of measure has been changed to the dollar). The temporal method can accommodate any measurement basis (historical cost, current replacement price, or current market price). This highly flexible method developed in 1968 by Leonard Lorenson attracted such wide support that it was adopted in 1975 in *SFAS No. 8* (superseded by *SFAS No. 52* in 1981), which allowed only this method of translation.

2. **The monetary-nonmonetary method.** Under this method, **monetary assets are translated using the current rate, and nonmonetary assets are translated using historical rates.** This is merely a classification scheme. The results of the temporal method and the monetary-nonmonetary method coincide except for the translation of (1) inventories carried at market (below cost) and (2) certain debt and equity securities having readily determinable fair values and classified as either "trading securities" or "available-for-sale" securities (under *SFAS No. 115*, "Accounting for Certain Investments in Debt and Equity Securities"). Thus inventory valued at market (below cost) is translated using (1) the *current rate* under the *temporal method* and (2) the *historical rate* under the *monetary-nonmonetary method*. Consequently, the temporal method accommodates current market valuation of nonmonetary assets; the monetary-nonmonetary method does *not* because the measurement basis is *not* maintained in translation.

3. **The current-noncurrent method.** Under this method, **current assets and current liabilities are translated using the current rate, and noncurrent assets and noncurrent liabilities are translated using historical rates.** This is also merely a classification scheme. This method was general practice from the early 1930s until 1975 when *SFAS No. 8* was issued.[2]

For simplicity, in discussing the U.S. dollar unit of measure approach hereafter, we refer only to the temporal method because it is the soundest of the three translation methods that achieve a U.S. dollar unit of measure.

THE FOCUS: THE NET MONETARY POSITION   Under the temporal method, the composition of the individual assets and liabilities is critical in determining whether a favorable or unfavorable result is reported as a consequence of an exchange rate change. An excess of monetary assets over monetary liabilities is referred to as a **net monetary asset position;** an excess of monetary liabilities over monetary assets is referred to as a **net monetary liability position.**

REPORTED EFFECTS OF EXCHANGE RATE CHANGES   If a foreign unit is in a net monetary *asset* position, an increase in the direct exchange rate causes a *favorable* result to be reported (an economic gain from the exchange rate change); however, if it is in a net monetary *liability* position, it reports an *unfavorable* result (an economic loss from the exchange rate change). On the other hand, if a foreign unit is in a net monetary *asset* position, a *decrease* in the direct exchange rate causes an *unfavorable* result to be reported; however, if it is in a net monetary *liability* position, a *favorable* result is reported. These reporting results are summarized in Illustration 19–1.

---

[2]The death knell for this method was sounded with Hepworth's historic turning point article in 1956 that advocated translating noncurrent receivables and noncurrent payables based on their *nature* (which would result in using the current rate)—not on their *classification.*

ILLUSTRATION 19–1	The U.S. Dollar Unit of Measure Approach: Reporting Effects of Exchange Rate Changes		
Translation Method Used	Possible Relevant Financial Positions	Increase[a] (foreign currency has strengthened or dollar has weakened)	Decrease[b] (foreign currency has weakened or dollar has strengthened)
Temporal	Net monetary asset	Favorable	Unfavorable
Temporal	Net monetary liability	Unfavorable	Favorable

[a]In all situations, the effect is *favorable* on the assets and *unfavorable* on the liabilities.
[b]In all situations, the effect is *unfavorable* on the assets and *favorable* on the liabilities.

KEY OBSERVATIONS OF THE TEMPORAL METHOD This approach considers only the monetary assets (with the two exceptions discussed earlier) and monetary liabilities to be exposed to the economic consequences of exchange rate changes—not the foreign unit's net assets (total assets – total liabilities). As was true for the current rate method (discussed in Chapter 18), no attempt is made to understand why a change in the exchange rate occurred. Because historical exchange rates are used for nonmonetary assets—**effectively freezing the values of these items in dollars**—any distortions that exist in the foreign currency statements resulting from nonmonetary assets being undervalued because of inflation are negated in translation. (This problem is discussed fully in Chapter 20.)

INTRODUCTORY ILLUSTRATION	**TRANSLATION USING THE TEMPORAL METHOD**

For convenience, we repeat the factual data given in Chapter 18 for illustrating the two translation approaches allowed by *SFAS No. 52*.

Assume that in late 19X1, a U.S. company created a 100%-owned subsidiary in Mexico when the direct exchange rate was $.50, making a $1,000,000 cash equity investment at that time. For simplicity, assume that this direct exchange rate did *not* fluctuate through December 31, 19X1. The subsidiary's first sales were on January 1, 19X2.

Additional assumptions are that (1) no dividends were declared or paid in 19X2; (2) fixed asset additions of 200,000 pesos (Mex$) (equal to 19X2's depreciation expense) occurred on January 3, 19X2, when the exchange rate was $.50; (3) Mexico had 25% inflation for 19X2; (4) the United States had 10% inflation for 19X2; and (5) the direct exchange rates were $.50 at December 31, 19X1, $.44 at December 31, 19X2, and $.47 for 19X2 as an average.

The subsidiary's balance sheets at the end of 19X1 and 19X2 and its 19X2 income statement are shown in Illustration 19–2.

The temporal method of translation is shown in Illustration 19–3.

We now provide a more comprehensive illustration of the temporal method that shows (1) the use of the *Remeasurement Gain or Loss* account, which is the name assigned to the *income statement* account to which the effect of a change in the exchange rate change is charged or credited under this translation method (pursuant to *SFAS No. 52*), (2) beginning balances for the Retained Earnings account, (3) the treatment for a cash dividend payment to the parent, and (4) all of the individual

ILLUSTRATION 19–2	**Foreign Currency Financial Statements**	
	Pesos	
	12/31/X1	**12/31/X2**
Balance Sheets		
Monetary assets	2,200,000	2,500,000
Inventory	1,000,000	1,250,000
Fixed assets, net	4,800,000	4,800,000[a]
Total Assets	8,000,000	8,550,000
Monetary liabilities	6,000,000	6,250,000
Common stock	2,000,000[b]	2,000,000
Retained earnings	–0–	300,000
Total Liabilities and Equity	8,000,000	8,550,000
Net Monetary liability position		
At 12/31/X1 (6,000,000 – 2,200,000)	**3,800,000**	
At 12/31/X2 (6,250,000 – 2,500,000)		**3,750,000**
Average for 19X2		3,875,000[c]
Income Statements (19X2)		
Revenues		5,300,000
Cost of sales		(4,300,000)
Depreciation		(200,000)
Expenses		(500,000)
Net Income		300,000

[a]Because of the 25% inflation in Mexico during 19X2, these assets are undervalued 25%.

[b]This amount is the peso equivalent of the $1,000,000 cash investment made by the parent when it created the subsidiary in late 19X1 ($1,000,000/$.50 = 2,000,000 Mex$)

[c]3,800,000 Mex$ + 200,000 Mex$ for the equipment acquired on 1/1/X2 = 4,000,000 Mex$; (4,000,000 Mex$ + 3,750,000 Mex$)/2 = 3,875,000 Mex$.

asset and liability accounts. (As explained later, *SFAS No. 52* refers to translation under the temporal method as the *remeasurement process*.)

In addition, we discuss (1) certain pretranslation procedures, (2) the finer points of this method, and (3) certain post-translation procedures. This comprehensive illustration is for 19X3, the year following the year in Illustration 19–3.

BASIC PROCEDURES BEFORE TRANSLATION

The same basic pretranslation procedures discussed in Chapter 18 (restating to U.S. GAAP, adjusting FX Receivable and Payable accounts to the spot rate, and reconciling intercompany account balances) must be performed prior to translation.

SPECIFIC TRANSLATION PROCEDURES

BALANCE SHEET ACCOUNTS   *SFAS No. 52* identifies the specific balance sheet accounts that must be translated at the *historical exchange rate*—the exchange rate existing **when the item *entered* the balance sheet.** All other accounts are translated at the current exchange rate (the spot rate at the balance sheet date). The balance sheet accounts for which historical exchange rates are to be used are listed in Illustration 19–4. It is not necessary to memorize this list. An easier way to readily

ILLUSTRATION 19–3	Translation Worksheet: The Temporal Method for the Year Ended December 31, 19X2

	Pesos	Code	Rate	U.S. Dollars
Income Statement (19X2)				
Revenues	5,300,000	A	$.47	$2,491,000
Cost of sales	(4,300,000)	H	$.483	(2,078,500)
Depreciation	(200,000)	H	$.50	(100,000)
Expenses	(500,000)	A	$.47	(235,000)
Net Income	300,000			$ 77,500
Balance Sheet (as of 12/31/X2)				
Monetary assets	2,500,000	C	$.44	$1,100,000
Inventory	1,250,000	H	$.448	560,000
Fixed assets, net	4,800,000	H	$.50	2,400,000
Total Assets	8,550,000			$4,060,000
Monetary liabilities	6,250,000	C	$.44	$2,750,000
Common stock	2,000,000	H	$.50	$1,000,000
Retained earnings	300,000	(Per above)		77,500
Economic gain from exchange rate change		(See below)		232,500
Total Equity	2,300,000			$1,310,000
Total Liabilities and Equity	8,550,000			$4,060,000

Calculation of Economic Gain from Exchange Rate Change

Average net monetary liability position of 3,875,000 Mex$
   × $.06 decrease in the exchange rate $232,500

Note: Because the nonmonetary assets are translated at historical rates (effectively being held constant), an economic gain or loss is reported only on the monetary accounts. In this case, the exchange rate decreased by $.06. Thus a valuation loss occurs on monetary assets; a valuation gain occurs on monetary liabilities. Monetary liabilities exceeded monetary assets, thus a net gain.

Key Review Points

  1. Note how ratios and relationships are *not* maintained after translation:

	Pesos	U.S. Dollars
Debt to equity ratio	2.71:1	2.10:1
Gross profit margin ratio	19%	17%
Net income to sales ratio	6%	3%
Fixed assets to total assets ratio	56%	59%
Undervaluation of fixed assets	25%	10%

  2. Note the increase in the stockholder's equity:

Ending stockholders' equity (per above)	$1,310,000
Less—Beginning stockholders' equity (parent's initial capital investment per Illustration 19–2)	1,000,000
Increase in Stockholders' Equity	$ 310,000

Code: A = Average rate; C = Current rate; H = Historical rate.

determine the exchange rate to use for translating each asset or liability is to use the monetary-nonmonetary distinction, which works for all accounts other than those related to (1) marketable securities and (2) inventory valued at market (below cost).

INCOME STATEMENT ACCOUNTS   *SFAS No. 52* identifies the specific income statement accounts that must be translated at the *historical exchange rate*—the exchange rate existing **when the item *entered* the balance sheet.** Thus consistency occurs between the balance sheet and the income statement for related accounts (such as

---

ILLUSTRATION 19–4	**Accounts Translated (Remeasured) Using Historical Exchange Rates**

Assets
Marketable securities carried at cost:[a]
  Equity securities
  Debt securities *not* intended to be held until maturity
Inventories carried at cost
Prepaid expenses, such as insurance, advertising, and rent
Property, plant, and equipment
Accumulated depreciation on property, plant, and equipment
Patents, trademarks, licenses, and formulas
Goodwill
Deferred charges and credits
Other intangible assets

Liabilities
Deferred income

Equity
Common stock
Additional paid-in capital
Preferred stock carried at issuance price

Revenues, Costs, and Expenses (examples of accounts related to nonmonetary items)
Cost of sales
Depreciation of property, plant, and equipment
Amortization of intangible items, such as goodwill, patents, licenses, and so on
Amortization of deferred charges or credits

[a]Those *not* carried at fair value pursuant to the requirements of *SFAS No. 115*, "Accounting for Certain Investments in Debit and Equity Securities" because they do *not* have a "readily determinable fair market value."

Note: The Retained Earnings account is not listed because it represents a "forced out" amount—not because the current rate is used.

Note: Under *SFAS No. 109*, "Accounting for Income Taxes," deferred income taxes reported in the balance sheet are *not* deferred charges or deferred credits; they are receivables and payables. Accordingly, they are translated using the current exchange rate.

Source: Based on *SFAS No. 52*, par. 48.

---

depreciation expense and equipment). All other accounts are translated at the current exchange rate—**the spot rate when the item *entered* the income statement.** The income statement accounts for which historical exchange rates are to be used are also listed in Illustration 19–4.

COMPREHENSIVE ILLUSTRATION	**TRANSLATION USING THE TEMPORAL METHOD**

Assume the following information for this 100%-owned subsidiary located in Mexico (much of which is identical to the information used for the comparable comprehensive illustration using the current rate method presented in Chapter 18).

1. **Conformity with U.S. GAAP.** The financial statements in pesos have already been adjusted to conform with U.S. GAAP.

2. **Intercompany receivable and intercompany payable accounts.** The parent and subsidiary *do* have intercompany transactions (other than dividends declared by the subsidiary), a condition that often leads to the use of the temporal method (as explained later). All necessary adjustments to reflect the spot

rate at year-end have already been made to the Intercompany Receivable and Intercompany Payable accounts. (These accounts are included with other accounts on the worksheet.)

3. **Exchange rates.** The direct exchange rates were $.44 at December 31, 19X2, $.40 at December 31, 19X3, and $.42 for 19X3 as an average.

4. **Inventory.** The 19X3 beginning inventory was translated (remeasured) at $560,000 in the December 31, 19X2, balance sheet (as shown in Illustration 19–3, which shows an average historical exchange rate of $.448). The 19X3 ending inventory cost was *below* market pesos; thus no adjustments in pesos for valuation purposes were needed. The 19X3 ending inventory was acquired when the exchange rates were as follows:

Pesos	Rate	Dollars
200,000	$.42	$ 84,000
500,000	.41	205,000
800,000	.40	320,000
1,500,000	.406[a]	$609,000

[a]This is the average rate ($609,000 ÷ 1,500,000 Mex$).

5. **Fixed assets.** All fixed assets were acquired in prior years when the exchange rate was $.50. No fixed assets were retired during 19X3.

6. **Common stock.** The subsidiary was formed in late 19X1 when the exchange rate was $.50. No additional capital stock changes have occurred since then.

7. **Retained earnings—beginning of year.** The translated retained earnings amount at the end of the prior year was $310,000 (the 19X2 increase in equity shown in Illustration 19–3).

8. **Dividends declared.** The subsidiary declared and paid a cash dividend of 100,000 Mex$ on November 11, 19X3, when the direct exchange rate was $.41.

9. **Sales, purchases, and expenses.** All sales, purchases, and expenses occurred evenly throughout 19X3.

10. **Certain monetary information.** At the beginning of 19X3, the subsidiary had monetary assets of 2,500,000 Mex$ and monetary liabilities of 6,250,000 Mex$ (the amounts shown at December 31, 19X2, in Illustration 19–3). During 19X3, cash disbursements in payment of liabilities totaled 6,400,000 Mex$ (excluding the 100,000 Mex$ cash dividend payment).

Illustration 19–5 uses this information to translate the foreign subsidiary's financial statements into dollars. The calculation of the remeasurement gain is shown in supporting Illustration 19–6.

REVIEW POINTS FOR ILLUSTRATION 19–5   Note the following:

1. **Applying the equity method.** The equity method of accounting is applied to the subsidiary's net income of $260,000 as follows:

Investment in Subsidiary	260,000	
Equity in Net Income (of subsidiary)		260,000

Recall that the $143,000 remeasurement gain *is* included in determining net income.

2. **Managing the monetary position.** The $143,000 remeasurement gain would *not* have resulted if the company had kept monetary assets and monetary liabilities at approximately the same level during 19X3. Doing this merely to minimize remeasurement gains and losses, however, counteracts the long-standing practice

ILLUSTRATION 19–5	**Translation Worksheet: The Temporal Method for the Year Ended December 31, 19X3**			
	Foreign Currency (Pesos)	Exchange Code	Rates	Dollars
Income Statement (19X3)				
Sales	6,000,000	A	$.42	$2,520,000
Cost of sales:				
Beginning inventory	1,250,000	H	$.448	560,000
+ Purchases	4,850,000	A	$.42	2,037,000
= Goods available for sale	6,100,000			$2,597,000
− Ending inventory	1,500,000	H	$.406	609,000
= Cost of sales	(4,600,000)			$(1,988,000)
Depreciation expense	(200,000)	H	$.50	(100,000)
Operating expenses	(600,000)	A	$.42	(252,000)
Income before Taxes	600,000			$ 180,000
Income tax expense @ 25%	(150,000)	A	$.42	(63,000)
Subtotal	450,000			$ 117,000
Remeasurement gain		(Per Illus. 19–6)		**143,000**
Net Income	450,000			$ 260,000
Statement of Retained Earnings				
Balance, 1/1/X3	300,000		(Given)	$ 310,000
+ Net income	450,000		(Per above)	260,000
− Dividends	(100,000)	H	$.41	(41,000)
Balance, 12/31/X3............	650,000			$ 529,000
Balance Sheet (as of 12/31/X3)				
Cash	400,000	C	$.40	$ 160,000
Accounts receivable, net	1,600,000	C	$.40	640,000
Inventory	1,500,000	H	$.406	609,000
Land	1,000,000	H	$.50	500,000
Buildings and equipment	4,000,000	H	$.50	2,000,000
Accumulated depreciation.......	(400,000)	H	$.50	(200,000)
Total Assets	8,100,000			$3,709,000
Payables and accruals	1,950,000	C	$.40	$ 780,000
Long-term debt	3,500,000	C	$.40	1,400,000
Total Liabilities	5,450,000			$2,180,000
Common stock	2,000,000	H	$.50	$1,000,000
Retained earnings	650,000		(Per above)	529,000
Total Equity	2,650,000			$1,529,000
Total Liabilities and Equity ...	8,100,000			$3,709,000

Code:

C = Current rate existing at the balance sheet date.

A = Average rate, as given in the introduction to this illustration.

H = Historical rate.

of minimizing the risks associated with foreign operations by financing them with foreign borrowings (payable in the foreign currency of the foreign unit) to the maximum extent possible. Obviously, firms must carefully weigh these conflicting objectives. Later we discuss other ways to minimize remeasurement gains and losses.

3. **Realization review procedures for nonmonetary assets.** Because of the use of historical exchange rates for nonmonetary assets, the results under the temporal method create a special problem that does *not* arise with the current rate

---

ILLUSTRATION 19–6	Calculation of the Transaction Gain from Remeasurement: Supporting Schedule to Illustration 19–5

Method I: Analysis of Monetary Assets and Liabilities for 19X3

	Pesos		
	Monetary Assets	Monetary Liabilities	Net Monetary Liability Position
Monetary items, 1/1/X3 (per Illustration 19–3 on p. 666)	2,500,000	6,250,000	3,750,000
Sales	6,000,000		(6,000,000)
Purchases		4,850,000	4,850,000
Operating expenses (excluding depreciation expense)		600,000	600,000
Income tax expense		150,000	150,000
Payment of liabilities	(6,400,000)	(6,400,000)	
Dividend payment (cash)	(100,000)		100,000
Monetary Items, 12/31/X3	2,000,000	5,450,000	3,450,000

Calculating the Transaction Gain from Remeasurement Using the Preceding Analysis of the Monetary Accounts

	U.S. Dollars		
	Loss of Valuation		Transaction Gain (Loss) from Remeasurement
	Monetary Assets (a Loss)	Monetary Liabilities (a Gain)	
Monetary assets at 1/1/X3 (100,00 Mex$ assumed used for the dividend shown separately)			
2,400,000 Mex$ × $.04 ($.44 − $.40)[a]	$ (96,000)		$ (96,000)
100,000 Mex$ × $.03 ($.44 − $.41)[b]	(3,000)		(3,000)
Monetary liabilities at 1/1/X3			
6,250,000 Mex$ × $.04 ($.44 − $.40)[a]		$250,000	250,000
Sales (6,000,000 Mex$ × $.02 [$.42 − $.40][c])	(120,000)		(120,000)
Purchases (4,850,000 Mex$ × $.02 [$.42 − $.40][c])		97,000	97,000
Operating expenses (600,000 Mex$ × $.02 [$.42 − $.40][c])		12,000	12,000
Income tax expense (150,000 Mex$ × $.02 [$.42 − $.40][c])		3,000	3,000
	$(219,000)	$362,000	$143,000

[a]Beginning-of-Year Rate − End-of-Year Rate.

[b]Beginning-of-Year Rate − Rate at Dividend Declaration Date.

[c]Average Rate − End-of-Year Rate.

Method II: Residual Force Out

1.		Remeasured assets	$3,709,000
2.	Less	Remeasured liabilities	2,180,000
3.	Equals	Total Stockholders' Equity	$1,529,000
4.	Less	Remeasured common stock and additional paid-in capital	1,000,000
5.	Equals	Total Retained Earnings	$ 529,000
6.	Less	Beginning retained earnings in dollars as reported in the prior period's remeasured financial statements reduced for any dividends declared ($310,000 − $41,000)	269,000
7.	Equals	Current Period Net Income	$ 260,000
8.	Less	Remeasured revenues and expenses (as shown in Illustration 19–5)	117,000
9.	Equals	The Current Period Foreign Currency Transaction Gain from Remeasurement	$ 143,000

method. Namely, nonmonetary assets translated (remeasured) at historical rates are *not* necessarily realizable in dollars—even though no realizability problem exists in the foreign currency. **This problem arises only when (1) the direct exchange rate has *decreased* and (2) the decrease is for reasons other than inflation in the foreign country.**

Accordingly, a lower-of-cost-or-market test is required **in dollars** for inventory (using identical procedures shown in intermediate accounting texts) and fixed assets, with adjustments made to the dollar amounts in the translation worksheet prior to consolidation. In Illustration 19–5, if the nonmonetary assets *cannot* be sold for more than their book value of 6,100,000 Mex$, their net realizable value in dollars is only $2,440,000 (6,100,000 Mex$ × $.40). This $2,440,000 is $469,000 below the $2,909,000 amount shown in dollars ($609,000 + $500,000 + $2,000,000 − $200,000 = $2,909,000). An adjustment of this magnitude would be more than the $143,000 remeasurement gain (which by itself would be illusory if such a lower-of-cost-or-market adjustment were necessary).

4. **Comparison to Illustration 18–5 (the current rate method).** Total assets and total equity are both higher by $469,000 in Illustration 19–5 than in Illustration 18–5 (on page 634) in which the current rate method was used. This difference is the result of using historical exchange rates for inventory (a $9,000 difference) and fixed assets (a $460,000 difference) rather than the rate existing at the balance sheet date (the current rate). Thus these two methods can often produce dramatically different reporting results.

5. **What if the exchange rate had *increased*?** If the direct exchange rate had *increased* rather than decreased during 19X3, a remeasurement *loss* would have resulted (the loss from revaluing monetary liabilities higher would have been more than the gain from revaluing monetary assets higher). The loss would be imaginary, however, if the nonmonetary assets can be sold for *at least* their book values. If so, their realizable value in dollars would be much higher than the amounts reported in dollars under the temporal method. Unfortunately, no upward mark-to-market provision exists for revaluing inventory and fixed assets upward in dollars to obtain an offsetting effect (as is possible when the direct exchange decreases). Accordingly, the reporting of a current period remeasurement loss would be offset in later periods as the nonmonetary assets are realized (transformed into monetary assets).

SPECIAL DISCLOSURES CONCERNING REMEASUREMENT GAINS AND LOSSES

The total of all remeasurement gains and losses, along with any FX gains and losses that are to be reported in the income statement (such as those resulting from importing and exporting transactions), must be **disclosed as a net amount** either in the income statement or in notes to the financial statements. Remeasurement gains and losses are *not* considered extraordinary items, no matter how material they might be.

II HEDGING A NET MONETARY POSITION

When the temporal method of translation is used, a company that desires to negate the potential negative effect of an adverse change in the exchange rate (that will be reported in the income statement) must hedge the net monetary position (whether it be a net monetary *asset* position or a net monetary *liability* position).

One of the criticisms leveled at the temporal method of translation when *SFAS No. 8* required it to be used for all foreign operations was that it caused firms to focus their attention on hedging the net *monetary* position—even when they believed that (1) the net *asset* position was their true economic exposure or (2) the net *asset* position was *not* at risk and thus did not need to be hedged. Because the temporal method is still permitted, firms using it may be influenced by *SFAS No. 52* to focus their hedging on the net *monetary* position.

Hedging a net monetary *asset* position presents no dilemma. In contrast, hedging an exposed monetary *liability* position does present one. The following discussion assumes the use of forward exchange contracts (FX forwards).

HEDGING AN EXPOSED NET MONETARY *ASSET* POSITION

In this situation, the entity treats the net monetary asset position the same way it would an FX Accounts Receivable. Its concern is that the direct exchange will *decrease;* thus it *sells forward.* If the direct exchange rate does *decrease,* the gain on the FX forward (an actual cash gain) offsets the remeasurement loss from translation, which is unquestionably a true economic loss because the net monetary assets are liquid. If instead the direct exchange rate *increases,* the loss on the FX forward (an actual cash loss) is offset by the remeasurement gain from translation, which again is unquestionably a true economic gain because the net monetary assets are liquid. Thus the results of hedging a net monetary asset position reflect the economic consequences of the change in the exchange rate.

HEDGING AN EXPOSED NET MONETARY *LIABILITY* POSITION: DIRECT EXCHANGE RATE *INCREASES*

In this situation, the entity treats the net monetary liability position the same way it would an FX Accounts Payable. Its concern is that the direct exchange rate will *increase;* thus it *buys forward.* If the direct exchange rate does *increase,* the gain on the FX forward (an actual cash gain) offsets the remeasurement loss from translation. The remeasurement loss, however, may *not* be a true economic loss because the nonmonetary assets being financed with the net monetary liability position may have gained in value and be worth more than their translated dollar amounts as a result of the increase in the direct exchange rate. Furthermore, the remeasurement loss will reverse itself in later periods if the direct exchange rate decreases. This scenario is ideal.

HEDGING AN EXPOSED NET MONETARY *LIABILITY* POSITION: DIRECT EXCHANGE RATE *DECREASES*

In this situation, if the direct exchange rate *decreases,* the loss on the FX forward (an actual cash loss) is offset by the remeasurement gain from translation. The remeasurement gain, however, may not be a true economic gain because the nonmonetary assets being financed by the net monetary liability position may have lost value and be worth less than their translated dollar amounts as a result of the decrease in the direct exchange rate. Furthermore, the remeasurement gain will reverse itself in later periods if the direct exchange rate increases. The loss on the FX forward, however, is an actual cash loss that will *not* reverse itself in later periods. This scenario points out the dilemma that exists in hedging a net monetary liability position because the direct exchange rate could decrease (resulting in a cash loss) rather than increase (resulting in a cash gain).

III THE OBJECTIVES OF TRANSLATION UNDER *SFAS NO. 52*

SFAS No. 52 states that the objectives of translation are to

    a. Provide information that is generally compatible with the expected economic effects of a rate change on an enterprise's cash flows and equity.

b. Reflect in consolidated statements the financial results and relationships of the individual consolidated entities as measured in their *functional currencies* in conformity with U.S. generally accepted accounting principles.[3]

THE FIRST OBJECTIVE

Note that this objective does *not* use unequivocal wording such as "provide information that reports the **true economic effect** of an exchange rate change." Instead, it uses the words "provide information that is **generally compatible** with the expected economic effects of a rate change." This raises questions such as this one: If the true economic effect of an exchange rate change is $800,000 *favorable,* is the reporting of a $500,000 *favorable* result using one translation method generally compatible enough? Certainly, reporting a $300,000 *unfavorable* effect using the other translation method generally would *not* be compatible.

The looseness of this objective apparently is an acknowledgment that the translation methods required in *SFAS No. 52* are incapable of reflecting the true economic effect of an exchange rate change—**probably because of the constraints of having to maintain historical cost in translating nonmonetary assets.** Reflecting the true economic effect of an exchange rate change is shown in Chapter 20.

THE SECOND OBJECTIVE

Concerning *nonmonetary* accounts, this objective effectively requires the use of translation methods that produce dollar amounts that can be considered historical cost to conform with U.S. GAAP. This raises a critical question: Can the general compatibility goal of the first objective be attained using translation methods that are presumed to preserve the historical cost basis of accounting? In other words, are these objectives compatible?

In less abstract terms, are these two objectives the equivalent of having the objective of valuing a building at its near market value (based on economic conditions) using the straight-line or double declining-depreciation methods? (Such a result would occur only by coincidence.) Chapter 20 addresses these questions. For now, it is important to understand that *SFAS No. 52* makes a major presumption that the two translation methods that it allows (1) preserve historical cost for non-monetary assets and (2) achieve results that are generally compatible with the economic effects of exchange rate changes.

IV THE FUNCTIONAL CURRENCY CONCEPT

SFAS No. 52 presumes that foreign operations may be conducted in one or more economic and currency environments. The primary economic environment must be determined for each separate foreign operation; however, *SFAS No. 52* does *not* specifically define the economic environment concept. Each foreign country has its own economic environment composed of taxation policies, currency controls, government policies toward intervention in the international currency markets, economic stability, and inflation. The primary economic environment concept, however, pertains to the manner in which the foreign unit conducts its operations—**the currency it primarily uses to generate and expend cash.** This concept presumes that each foreign operation has a primary currency.

---

[3]*Statement of Financial Accounting Standards No. 52*, "Foreign Currency Translation" (Stamford: Financial Accounting Standards Board, 1981), par. 4.

The currency of the primary economic environment is then designated as that foreign unit's functional currency. The FASB has developed some economic factors that are to be considered individually and collectively in determining the functional currency for each foreign operation of an enterprise. A list of these factors appears in Illustration 19–7. The functional currency determined for each foreign operation is the basis for the method of translation into dollars. If the foreign currency is the functional currency, the foreign unit of measure is required (imple-

ILLUSTRATION 19–7	**Economic Factors to Be Considered in Determining the Functional Currency**	
Type of Factor	Factors Pointing to a Foreign Functional Currency	Factors Pointing to a Dollar Functional Currency
Cash flows	Cash flows related to the foreign entity's individual assets and liabilities are primarily in the foreign currency and do not directly impact the parent company's cash flows.	Cash flows related to the foreign entity's individual assets and liabilities directly impact the parent's cash flows on a current basis and are readily available for remittance to the parent company.
Sales prices	Sales prices for the foreign entity's products are not primarily responsive on a short-term basis to changes in exchange rates but are determined more by local competition or local government regulation.	Sales prices for the foreign entity's products are primarily responsive on a short-term basis to changes in exchange rates: for example, sales prices are determined more by worldwide competition or by international prices.
Sales market	An active local sales market exists for the foreign entity's products, although significant amounts of exports might also be available.	The sales market is mostly in the parent's country, or sales contracts are denominated in the parent's currency.
Cost and expenses	Labor, materials, and other cost for the foreign entity's products or services are primarily local costs, even though imports from other countries might also be available.	Labor, materials, and other costs for the foreign entity's products or services, on a continuing basis, are primarily costs for components obtained from the country in which the parent company is located.
Financing	Financing is primarily denominated in foreign currency, and funds generated by the foreign entity's operations are sufficient to service existing and normally expected debt obligations.	Financing is primarily from the parent or other dollar-denominated obligations, or funds generated by the foreign entity's operations are not sufficient to service existing and normally expected debt obligations without the infusion of additional funds from the parent company. Infusion of additional funds from the parent company for expansion is not a factor, provided that funds generated by the foreign entity's expanded operations are expected to be sufficient to service that additional financing.
Intercompany transactions and arrangements	There is a low volume of intercompany transactions, and an extensive interrelationship does not exist between the operations of the foreign entity and the parent company. However, the foreign entity's operations may rely on the parent's or affiliates' competitive advantages such as patents and trademarks.	There is a high volume of intercompany transactions, and an extensive interrelationship exists between the operations of the foreign entity and the parent company. Additionally, the parent's currency generally would be the functional currency if the foreign entity is a device or shell corporation for holding investments, obligations, intangible assets, and so on, that could readily be carried on the parent's or an affiliate's books.

Source: Adapted from *Statement of Financial Accounting Standards, No. 52*, "Foreign Currency Translation" (Stamford: Financial Accounting Standards Board, 1981), Appendix A, par. 42.

mented using the *current rate method*). If the U.S. dollar is the functional currency, the U.S. dollar unit of measure is required (implemented using the *temporal method*).

THE TWO DIFFERENT TYPES OF FOREIGN OPERATIONS

In reviewing Illustration 19–7, realize that *SFAS No. 52* presumes that each foreign operation fits into one of two categories.

CATEGORY 1: RELATIVELY AUTONOMOUS FOREIGN UNITS   These foreign units primarily generate and expend the local currency of the country in which they are located. One example is a French subsidiary that (1) pays its employees and vendors in francs, (2) sells its products for francs in France, (3) has its debt denominated in francs, and (4) has no intercompany inventory purchases or sales with the domestic parent. Thus the subsidiary is relatively **independent and self-contained.** Obviously, the French franc is the functional currency.

CATEGORY 2: RELATIVELY NONAUTONOMOUS FOREIGN UNITS   These units primarily generate and expend U.S. dollars. One example is an assembly plant on the Mexican side of the Rio Grande that (1) purchases parts from the U.S. parent (paying in dollars), (2) pays its employees in dollars, (3) sells the processed product back to the U.S. parent (billing in dollars), and (4) has its debt denominated in dollars. Thus the operation is viewed as **an extension of the parent's operations**—not a relatively self-contained and independent operation. In these cases, the dollar is the functional currency.

NO ARBITRARY SELECTION ALLOWED

The determination of the functional currency is to be based on the economic facts—it cannot be an arbitrary selection. Because significant differences in reported net income can occur as a result of choosing the foreign currency or the dollar as the functional currency, the intent is to prevent managements from arbitrarily choosing one of the two translation methods. When the economic factors listed in Illustration 19–7 do *not* clearly indicate the functional currency, management must weigh the individual economic factors and use its judgment, considering the stated objectives of translation.

WHAT OCCURS IN PRACTICE   In practice, determining the functional currency is largely a management call; in effect, managements may choose the translation method they desire. This might explain why the six largest U.S. oil companies are split evenly as to the functional currencies of most of their foreign units.[4] Otherwise, one must conclude that three of them conduct foreign operations quite differently than the other three. Considering that these companies are in the same industry and several operate in the same foreign countries, the fact that they have different functional currencies raises serious questions as to whether they conduct their operations that differently. Some rigorous studies are needed to determine just how much differently competing companies conduct foreign operations in common countries; the FASB has not commissioned any such studies.[5] The

[4]See "Plenty of Opportunity to Fool Around," *Forbes*, June 2, 1986, p. 139.

[5]In 1986, the FASB published a research report, *Determining the Functional Currencies under Statement 52*, by Thomas G. Evans and Timothy Doupnik. However, this was a more general study based on questionnaires received from 180 firms having 543 foreign units. The responses to the questionnaires by the managements indicated that they determine their functional currencies "consistent with the guidelines presented in Appendix A of Statement 52." As the report's authors pointed out, these responses could not be independently verified, nor was there any interaction with the respondents. Thus it was not a rigorous analytical study along the lines suggested here.

potential for abuse and arbitrary selection of translation methods is quite high. Beyond the *SFAS No. 52* indicators, the large public accounting firms have developed additional indicators, some of which are rather novel and could well serve a client that desires a certain translation method. For instance, one that puts emphasis on repatriating earnings instead of on currencies used in generating earnings is found in Price Waterhouse's foreign currency booklet, which states:

> Accordingly, it would seem that a foreign operation's policy of converting its available funds into dollars for current or near-term distribution to the parent may be one of the most significant indicators suggesting a dollar functional currency.[6]

HIGHLY INFLATIONARY ECONOMIES: FUNCTIONAL CURRENCY CONCEPT TO BE DISREGARDED (REPORTING RESULTS UNDER THE CURRENT RATE METHOD ARE NOT MEANINGFUL)

An exception to the approach of determining the functional currency from the economic factors specified in *SFAS No. 52* is made for operations in highly inflationary economies. *SFAS No. 52* defines a highly inflationary economy as "one that has cumulative inflation of approximately 100 percent or more over a three-year period.[7] In these cases, the dollar is used as the functional currency. The purpose of the exception is to deal with the "disappearing plant" problem discussed in Chapter 18. Recall that applying the current exchange rate to historical cost amounts in foreign currency financial statements can produce meaningless dollar amounts for fixed assets in such economies. The problem is the foreign currency's lack of stability, which makes it completely unsuitable for use as a functional currency.

In the exposure draft that preceded *SFAS No. 52*, the FASB proposed restating the historical cost amounts for inflation prior to translation (and then allowing the use of the current rate method). The proposal was dropped, however, because of conceptual objections to mixing historical cost with inflation-adjusted amounts and the inadequacy of published indices for several countries. As a practical alternative, which is an acknowledged conceptual compromise, the FASB designated the dollar as the functional currency in highly inflationary economies (whereby the historical cost amounts are translated at historical exchange rates). The results are more reasonable dollar amounts for the fixed assets of these foreign operations. Numerous countries, primarily in South America, have cumulative inflation rates near or exceeding 100% over three-year periods. Although 100% may seem high, an annual inflation rate of only 26% results in 100% inflation cumulatively over a three-year period.

THE JUDGMENT FACTOR IN HIGHLY INFLATIONARY ECONOMIES The use of 100% is arbitrary, but the use of the modifier "approximately" in the pronouncement allows management some latitude in judgment. Thus a cumulative inflation rate of 90%, for example, could be sufficient grounds for using the dollar as the functional currency, whereas a foreign unit operating with a cumulative inflation rate of 110% could still use the foreign currency as the functional currency. We must also consider management's latitude when the economic facts do not clearly indicate the functional currency. In such a case and when the cumulative inflation rate is high but below 100%, management may lean toward using the dollar as the functional currency.

---

[6]Price Waterhouse, *Foreign Currency Translation—Understanding and Applying SFAS 52* (New York: 1981), p. 14.

[7]*SFAS No. 52*, par. 11.

DISTINGUISHING *TRANSLATION* FROM *REMEASUREMENT*

For simplicity, we have referred to the process of applying exchange rates to a foreign operation's financial statements to arrive at dollar amounts as *translation*. Historically, this has been the definition of the term. The use of the functional currency concept, however, has resulted in a narrower definition of the term in *SFAS No. 52*.

TRANSLATION: GOING FROM THE FUNCTIONAL CURRENCY (A FOREIGN CURRENCY) TO THE REPORTING CURRENCY (THE DOLLAR)

In *SFAS No. 52*, **translation** refers to the process of **expressing functional currency amounts in the reporting currency.** Accordingly, the term is restricted to situations in which the foreign currency is the functional currency. Recall that when the foreign currency is the functional currency, the current rate method is required, and it merely *expresses* the foreign currency financial statements in dollars—it does not "remeasure" the nonmonetary accounts to obtain their dollar equivalents at the time the transactions were recorded.

REMEASUREMENT: GOING FROM A NONFUNCTIONAL CURRENCY (A FOREIGN CURRENCY) TO THE FUNCTIONAL (AND REPORTING) CURRENCY (THE DOLLAR)

In *SFAS No. 52*, **remeasurement** is the process of expressing nonfunctional currency amounts in the functional (and reporting) currency. Accordingly, the term almost always refers to situations in which the foreign currency is *not* the functional currency but the U.S. dollar is. Foreign operations normally maintain their books and prepare their financial statements in the currency of the country in which they are located—regardless of whether the dollar is their functional currency. Recall that when the dollar is the functional currency, historical exchange rates are used so that the **nonmonetary assets are remeasured into the dollar equivalent of the transactions at the time of the purchase.** Thus the remeasurement process in *SFAS No. 52* refers to the remeasuring that takes place in expressing amounts in the functional currency. Note that when the dollar is the functional currency, translation (as narrowly defined in the preceding paragraph) is not necessary because the functional currency is also the reporting currency.

REMEASUREMENT AND TRANSLATION SITUATIONS

Infrequently, a foreign operation's functional currency is a foreign currency that is different from the currency it uses to maintain its books and prepare its financial statements. An example would be a Swiss operation that keeps its books in Swiss francs (most likely because of tax laws) but uses the French franc as its functional currency. In such a case, the Swiss financial statements must be "remeasured" and expressed in French francs. Then, the French franc financial statements must be "translated" into dollars. Thus, a two-step process is required to obtain amounts in dollars. Most foreign operations require only a one-step process, however—either the translation process *or* the remeasurement process.

V CONCLUDING COMMENTS

Even though corporations have expressed hardly any dissatisfaction with *SFAS No. 52* (unlike *SFAS No. 8*, and possibly only because income statement volatility is largely eliminated), it is unfortunate that more of those who studied and voted on this issue did not agree, suggesting that the solution that most closely reflects economic reality was *not* found.

Proponents of the functional currency concept contend that the economic exposure differs for *autonomous* foreign units versus *nonautonomous* foreign units and that the functional currency is intended to deal with these differences.

INTERNATIONAL PERSPECTIVE

Worldwide Translation Practices

A review of the translation practices employed by the most significant 50 countries reveals the following:

Translation Methods	Number or Percentage of Countries Using This Particular Translation Method
Current rate method	Nearly 50% (including almost all of Western Europe and Japan)
Temporal method or its monetary-nonmonetary method equivalent	Nearly 50%
Current-noncurrent method	Very few (no major countries)
Both the current rate method and the temporal method	Three (United States, United Kingdom, Canada)

In 1983, the International Accounting Standards Committee (discussed in Chapter 14) issued *International Accounting Standard No. 21,* "Accounting for the Effects of Changes in Foreign Exchange Rates." This pronouncement (revised slightly in 1993) mirrors *SFAS No. 52* in that it allows the use of either the current rate method or the temporal method, depending on the circumstances.

In Chapter 20, we present the *current value approach using PPP.* This approach revolves around the causes of exchange rate changes—not whether the foreign unit uses a foreign currency or the U.S. dollar in conducting its operations. Under this approach, **the economic exposure for all foreign units is competition** (the same risk that domestic operations face). Thus the *autonomous* versus *nonautonomous* distinction made in *SFAS No. 52* is deemed artificial, irrelevant, and misguided.

Also in Chapter 20, the financial reporting results under the *current value approach using PPP* are compared to the financial reporting results under both the *current rate method* and the *temporal method.* Accordingly, you will be able to evaluate whether (1) the functional currency concept in *SFAS No. 52* is theoretically sound (2) management should use the *SFAS No. 52* financial reporting results for internal decision-making purposes, and (3) stockholders should rely on *SFAS No. 52* financial reporting results.

A summary of worldwide translation practices is shown in the International Perspective.

END-OF-CHAPTER REVIEW

SUMMARY OF KEY POINTS

1. Under the **U.S. dollar unit of measure approach,** the foreign currency relationships are **not** maintained in translation (a new set of relationships is produced), the **temporal method of translation** is used, and the financial position focus is on the **net monetary (asset or liability) position.**
2. *SFAS No. 52* is built on the **functional currency concept,** which presumes that the currency in which a foreign unit **primarily generates and expends cash** reflects whether the foreign unit is relatively autonomous or nonautonomous.

3. **Autonomous** foreign units have the **foreign currency** as the functional currency—their financial statements are translated using the **current rate method.**
4. **Nonautonomous** foreign units have the **U.S. dollar** as the functional currency—their financial statements are translated using the **temporal method.**
5. Illustration 19–8 contains a summary of accounting for the translation of foreign currency financial statements once the functional currency has been determined.

GLOSSARY OF NEW TERMS

Current-noncurrent method   One of three translation methods that achieves a U.S. dollar unit of measure. An asset or liability's classification as to current or noncurrent determines the exchange rate to use.

Monetary-nonmonetary method   One of three translation methods that achieves a U.S. dollar unit of measure (an asset or liability classification as to monetary or nonmonetary determines the exchange rate to use).

ILLUSTRATION 19–8	Summary of Accounting for the Translation of Foreign Currency Financial Statements	
	Functional Currency	
	Foreign Currency	**U.S. Dollar**
Approach/unit of measure to be used	Foreign Currency	U.S. Dollar
Translation method to be used	Current rate	Temporal
Exchange rates to be used for: Assets and liabilities	Current rate[a]	Combination of current[a] and historical rates
Income statement accounts	Current rate[b]	Combination of current[b] and historical rates
Treatment to be accorded the effect of a change in the exchange rate	Direct charge or credit to special account in stockholders' equity (pending liquidation or disposal of the investment)	Immediate recognition in the income statement
Terms used in *SFAS No. 52* to describe: The translation process	Translation	Remeasurement
The effect of a change in the exchange rate	Translation adjustment	Foreign currency transaction gain or loss from remeasurement
Deemed functional currency for operations in highly inflationary economies		U.S. Dollar

[a]*Current rate* here means the exchange rate existing at the balance sheet date.

[b]*Current rate* here means the exchange rate existing when the items were recognized in the income statement.

Net monetary asset position   Having monetary assets in excess of monetary liabilities.

Net monetary liability position   Having monetary liabilities in excess of monetary assets.

Remeasurement   The process of going from a nonfunctional currency (a foreign currency) to the functional (and reporting) currency (the dollar).

Remeasurement gains and losses   The name given to the effects of exchange rate changes reported under the temporal method (formally called foreign currency transaction gains and losses in *SFAS No. 52*).

Temporal method   One of three translation methods that achieves a U.S. dollar unit of measure (an asset or liability basis of valuation determines the exchange rate to use).

Translation (distinguished from remeasurement)   The process of going from the functional currency (a foreign currency) to the reporting currency (the dollar).

U.S. dollar unit of measure approach   A manner of translating foreign currency financial statements that changes the unit of measure to the U.S. dollar (changes financial relationships).

SELF-STUDY QUESTIONS

(Answers are at the end of this chapter preceding the appendix.)

1. Which of the following is a translation method that does *not* fit under the U.S. dollar unit of measure approach?
   a. Current rate method
   b. Monetary-nonmonetary method
   c. Current-noncurrent method
   d. Temporal method

2. Under the U.S. dollar unit of measure approach, the focus is on which of the following?
   a. Net monetary asset position
   b. Net monetary liability position
   c. Net exposed asset position
   d. Net exposed liability position
   e. Net monetary position

3. When the direct exchange rate *decreases* during the year and a *favorable* effect for this change in the exchange rate is reported in the income statement, the foreign unit had to be in which position?
   a. Net asset
   b. Net current
   c. Net monetary
   d. Net monetary asset
   e. Net monetary liability

4. The effect of a change in the exchange rate should be reported as a charge or credit to which of the following?

	Under the U.S. Dollar Unit of Measure Approach	Under the Foreign Currency Unit of Measure Approach
a.	The income statement	The income statement
b.	Stockholders' equity	The income statement
c.	The income statement	Stockholders' equity
d.	Stockholders' equity	Stockholders' equity

5. A subsidiary located in a foreign country having a *highly inflationary economy* should use which of the following methods in expressing the financial statements in dollars?
   a. The current rate method
   b. The temporal method
   c. The monetary-nonmonetary method
   d. The functional currency method

6. Which of the following methods should be used for expressing in dollars the financial statements of a foreign operation that is relatively *self-contained* and *independent* of the parent's operations?

a. The current rate method
b. The monetary-nonmonetary method
c. The temporal method
d. The current-noncurrent method

7. A subsidiary's functional currency is the local currency, which has *not* experienced significant inflation. Which exchange rate should be used in expressing the following accounts in dollars?

	Depreciation Expense	Plant and Equipment
a.	Current	Current
b.	Historical	Historical
c.	Current	Historical
d.	Historical	Current

8. Assume the same information in Question 3, except that the functional currency is the dollar.

9. Which exchange rates should be used in expressing cost of sales in dollars for a foreign subsidiary under each of the following methods?

	Current Rate Method	Temporal Method
a.	Current	Current
b.	Historical	Historical
c.	Current	Historical
d.	Historical	Current

ASSIGNMENT MATERIAL

REVIEW QUESTIONS

1. What is the *U.S. dollar unit of measure approach*? Summarize it.
2. What translation methods achieve a *U.S. dollar unit of measure approach*?
3. What is the theory underlying the *temporal method*?
4. What is the financial focus of the *U.S. dollar unit of measure approach*?
5. When the *temporal method* is used, how is the effect of the exchange rate change reported under *SFAS No. 52*?
6. When the *temporal method* is used, what is the effect of the exchange rate change called under *SFAS No. 52*?
7. What are six balance sheet accounts for which *historical exchange rates* are used under the *temporal method*?
8. What are five income statement accounts for which *historical exchange rates* are used under the *temporal method*?
9. When is it necessary to address *realization* of a foreign unit's *nonmonetary* assets in dollars?
10. What dilemma exists in considering whether to hedge a net monetary liability position?
11. On what critical assumption is *SFAS No. 52* constructed?
12. Are the two *SFAS No. 52 objectives of translation* incompatible? Why or why not?
13. What purpose does the *functional currency concept* serve?
14. Is the *functional currency concept* necessary to use *multiple units of measure*?
15. What are the *factors* used to determine the functional currency?
16. What *two categories* of foreign operations are presumed to exist under the functional currency concept?
17. When the *economic factors* set forth in *SFAS No. 52* do not clearly indicate the functional currency, which currency must be used?
18. How are *highly inflationary economies* dealt with in *SFAS No. 52*?
19. What is the definition of a *highly inflationary economy*?
20. What is the difference between *translation* and *remeasurement*?
21. How are the effects of exchange rate changes treated in *remeasurement* situations?

22. What two essential elements are necessary for achieving meaningful translated reporting results?
23. How is the *true economic effect* of an exchange rate change determined?

EXERCISES

E 19–1   Determining the Financial Position from the Effect and Direction of Exchange Rate Changes   Information for the overseas subsidiaries of Hubb Inc. for 19X1 follows:

Country	Translation Method	Direction of Direct Exchange Rate in 19X1	Effect of Change in Exchange Rate
Brazil	Temporal	Decreased	Favorable
Mexico	Temporal	Decreased	Unfavorable
Sweden	Current rate	Increased	Favorable
Belgium	Current rate	Increased	Unfavorable
Ireland	Current rate	Decreased	Unfavorable
Spain	Current rate	Decreased	Favorable
Saudi Arabia	Temporal	Increased	Favorable
Japan	Temporal	Increased	Unfavorable

Required   Determine the appropriate financial position that each of these foreign operations was in during the year for the listed effect to have resulted.

E 19–2   Calculating the Effect of an Exchange Rate Change   Pondox has a foreign subsidiary in a country in which the direct exchange rate decreased from $.25 to $.20 during 19X2. The average balances of the individual assets and liabilities during 19X2 follow:

	Units of Foreign Currency
Cash	80,000
Accounts receivable	220,000
Inventory	275,000
Fixed assets, net	425,000
Total Assets	1,000,000
Accounts payables and accruals	325,000
Current portion of long-term debt	25,000
Intercompany payable	100,000
Long-term debt	300,000
Deferred income taxes payable	50,000
Total Liabilities	800,000

Assume that the carrying value of the parent's Investment account on 1/1/X2 was $50,000 for this 100%-owned subsidiary that was created in late 19X1 when the direct exchange rate was $.25.

Required   1. Determine the effect of the exchange rate change for 19X2 under the *temporal method*.
2. Repeat requirement 1 using the *current rate method*.

E 19–3   Calculating the Effect of an Exchange Rate Change   Kobb Inc. has a 100%-owned foreign subsidiary. The average balances of the subsidiary's assets and liabilities during 19X1 follow:

	LCU
Monetary assets	4,000,000
Nonmonetary assets	6,000,000
Total Assets	10,000,000
Liabilities (all monetary)	9,000,000
Stockholders' equity	1,000,000
Total Liabilities & Equity	10,000,000

The direct exchange rate decreased steadily during 19X1 from $.40 at 1/1/X1 to $.30 at 12/31/X1.

Required   1. Determine the effect of the change in the exchange rate for 19X1 under the temporal method.
         2. Repeat requirement 1 using the current rate method.
         3. Which reporting result best reflects economic reality?

E 19–4   **Selecting Proper Exchange Rates: Balance Sheet Accounts**   The following accounts exist in a foreign subsidiary's books:

    1. Allowance for Doubtful Accounts.
    2. Inventory (carried at *cost*).
    3. Inventory (carried at *market,* which is *below* cost).
    4. Inventory (carried at *market,* which *exceeds* cost).
    5. Marketable Equity Securities (carried at *market,* which *exceeds* historical cost).
    6. Marketable Bonds (*expected* to be held to maturity).
    7. Marketable Bonds (*not* expected to be held to maturity).
    8. Patents.
    9. Equipment.
   10. Accumulated Depreciation.
   11. Intercompany Payable.
   12. Long-Term Debt.
   13. Income Taxes Payable.
   14. Deferred Income Taxes Payable.
   15. Common Stock.
   16. Additional Paid-in Capital.
   17. Retained Earnings.
   18. Revaluation Capital (from inflation adjustments).

Required   Determine whether the historical exchange rate, the current exchange rate, an average exchange rate, or some other procedure should be used to translate these accounts under the *temporal method*.

E 19–5   **Selecting Proper Exchange Rates: Income Statement Accounts**   The following accounts exist in a foreign subsidiary's books:

    1. Revenues.
    2. Intercompany Sales to Parent Company.
    3. Purchases.
    4. Intercompany Purchases from Parent Company.
    5. Cost of Sales.
    6. Marketing Expenses.
    7. Depreciation Expense.
    8. Income Tax Expense.
    9. Goodwill Amortization Expense.
   10. Loss on Abandonment of Fixed Assets.
   11. Gain on Sale of Equipment.
   12. Intercompany Interest Expense.
   13. Depreciation Expense (incremental amount resulting from adjusting assets for inflation).
   14. Inventory Loss from Flood Damage.

Required   Determine whether the historical exchange rate, the current exchange rate, an average exchange rate, or some other procedure should be used to translate these accounts under the *temporal method*.

E 19–6   **Translating Depreciation Expense**   Kona Inc. owns a foreign subsidiary with 3,600,000 local currency units (LCU) of property, plant, and equipment before accumulated depreciation at 12/31/X5. Of this amount, 2,400,000 LCU were acquired in 19X3 when the exchange rate was 5 LCU to $1; 1,200,000 LCU were acquired in 19X4 when the exchange rate was 8 LCU to $1.

    The exchange rate in effect at 12/31/X5 was 10 LCU to $1. The average of exchange rates that were in effect during 19X5 was 12 LCU to $1. Assume that the property, plant, and equipment are depreciated using the straight-line method over a 10-year period with no salvage value.

Required   1. Are these exchange rates given the direct rates or the indirect rates?

2. Determine the dollar amount of depreciation expense for 19X5 assuming that the foreign operation's functional currency is the
   a. LCU.
   b. Dollar.

E 19–7 **Translating a Gain on a Fixed Asset Disposal**   A Mexican subsidiary sold equipment acquired in prior years costing 6,000,000 Mex$ on 4/1/X1 for 2,500,000 Mex$ when the exchange rate was $.008. (The exchange rate existing when the equipment was purchased several years ago was $.04.) A 1,000,000 Mex$ gain relating to this disposal is recorded in the general ledger.

The exchange rate at 12/31/X1 is 200 Mex$ to $1; however, the average relationship for 19X1 was 150 Mex$ to $1.

Required   Determine the amount of the gain in dollars assuming the following:

1. The peso is the functional currency.
2. The dollar is the functional currency.

E 19–8 **Translating and Performing a Lower-of-Cost-or-Market Test in Dollars for Inventory**   The following selected information is provided in connection with the translation of a Mexican subsidiary's 12/31/X1 financial statements. The 12/31/X1 inventory was acquired when the following exchange rates existed:

Pesos	Direct Rate
1,000,000	$.009
3,000,000	.008
7,000,000	.007
10,000,000	.006
15,000,000	.005
36,000,000	

The replacement cost of the inventory is 38,000,000 Mex$; the net realizable value is 60,000,000 Mex$; and the net realizable value less a normal profit margin is 40,000,000 Mex$.

The exchange rate at 12/31/X1 is 200 Mex$ to $1; however, the average relationship for 19X1 was 150 Mex$ to $1.

Required   Perform a lower-of-cost-or-market test in dollars assuming the following:

1. The peso is the functional currency.
2. The dollar is the functional currency.

E 19–9 **Determining When to Hedge Balance Sheet Exposure**   Ponder Inc. often enters into forward exchange contracts to hedge its exposure on its foreign operations. Ponder must determine whether it should contract to buy or sell a foreign currency in each of the following situations:

Area of Foreign Currency Exposure	Direct Rate or Currency	Future Expectation Direction	Buy	Sell	Neither
1. Net investment in a foreign subsidiary	U.S. dollar	Strengthen	_____	_____	_____
	U.S. dollar	Weaken	_____	_____	_____
	Foreign	Strengthen	_____	_____	_____
	Foreign	Weaken	_____	_____	_____
2. Net monetary asset position of a foreign subsidiary	U.S. dollar	Strengthen	_____	_____	_____
	U.S. dollar	Weaken	_____	_____	_____
	Foreign	Strengthen	_____	_____	_____
	Foreign	Weaken	_____	_____	_____
3. Net monetary liability position of a foreign subsidiary	U.S. dollar	Strengthen	_____	_____	_____
	U.S. dollar	Weaken	_____	_____	_____
	Foreign	Strengthen	_____	_____	_____
	Foreign	Weaken	_____	_____	_____

Required   Put an X in the appropriate column in the table.

PROBLEMS

P 19–1 **Comparing Reporting Results** On 12/3/X1 Pella created a 100%-owned real estate development subsidiary, Sella, in France. Pella paid $2,500,000 cash for common stock of Sella on this date. Also on this date, Sella converted the $2,500,000 into 5,000,000 FF. It immediately acquired land for 4,000,000 FF and left the remaining 1,000,000 FF in a checking account for all of 19X2 (earning no interest). Sella had no expenses in 19X2. The exchange rate at 12/31/X2 is 1 FF equals $.40. France had 25% inflation during 19X2, which caused the 19X2 exchange rate decrease.

Required
1. Translate Sella's balance sheet at 12/31/X2 under the *current rate method*.
2. Translate Sella's balance sheet at 12/31/X2 under the *temporal method*.
3. Calculate the parent's increase or decrease in cash for 19X2 if the subsidiary were liquidated at 12/31/X2 (with the land being sold at its current value of 5,000,000 FF). Compare this reporting result to the results in requirement 1 and 2. Comment accordingly.

P 19–2* **Translation (Remeasurement) Worksheet** Assume the information provided in Problem 18–2 (page 648).

Required
1. Calculate the remeasurement gain or loss for 19X2 by analyzing the monetary items. (Assume that at the beginning of 19X2, the subsidiary had monetary assets of 1,400,000 FF and monetary liabilities of 5,700,000 FF. Also assume that cash disbursed in payment of liabilities during 19X2 was 9,900,000 FF [excluding the 200,000 FF paid for the equipment purchase]).
2. Remeasure the financial statements into dollars, assuming the following:
   a. The dollar is the functional currency.
   b. From the dollar financial statements, the retained earnings amount at 12/31/X1 was $267,000.
3. Prepare the parent company's entry or entries at 12/31/X2 relating to the *equity method* of accounting.
4. Prepare a T-account analysis of the parent's Investment account since the creation of the subsidiary.
5. Qualitatively assess whether the subsidiary had a good year or a bad year, considering whether its nonmonetary assets are realizable in dollars.
6. Prepare the general ledger entry that would be made if the subsidiary were sold for $400,000 cash on 1/3/X3.
7. **Optional** (check with your instructor): Prepare a translated statement of cash flows for 19X2 using the direct method.

P 19–3* **Translation (Remeasurement) Worksheet** Assume the information provided in Problem 18–3 (page 650).

Required
1. Calculate the remeasurement gain or loss for 19X4 by analyzing the monetary items. (Assume that at the beginning of 19X4, the subsidiary had monetary assets of 800,000 punts and monetary liabilities of 2,000,000 punts. Also assume that cash disbursed in payment of liabilities during 19X4 was 3,850,000 punts.)
2. Remeasure the financial statements into dollars assuming the following:
   a. The dollar is the functional currency.
   b. From the dollar financial statements, the retained earnings amount at 12/31/X3 was $1,060,000.
3. Prepare the parent company's entry or entries at 12/31/X4 under the equity method of accounting.
4. Prepare a T-account analysis of the parent's Investment account from inception of the subsidiary.
5. Evaluate whether the subsidiary is likely to have a realizability problem in dollars for its nonmonetary assets.
6. Prepare the general ledger entry that would be made if the subsidiary were sold for $1,240,000 cash on 1/3/X5.
7. **Optional** (check with your instructor): prepare a translated statement of cash flows for 19X4 using the direct method.

P 19–4 **Translating a Statement of Cash Flows** Use the information provided in Illustrations 19–5 and 19–6. In addition, assume that cash receipts from collections on accounts receivable totaled 6,200,000 Mex$.

*The financial information presented for problems accompanied by asterisks is also provided on Model 19 of the software file disk (filename: MODEL19) that is available for use with the problem, allowing the problem to be worked on the computer.

during 19X3. Also assume that cash receipts and cash disbursements (other than the cash dividend paid to the parent) occurred evenly throughout the year. There were no borrowings or repayments of debt in 19X3—only debt interest payments totaling 300,000 Mex$.

Required   1. Calculate the subsidiary's 1/1/X3 balances in pesos for its Cash account and its Accounts Receivable account. (See if you can find the *two* ways to determine the cash balance.)

2. Prepare a translated statement of cash flows for 19X3 using the *direct* method. (*Hint:* Think about what amount would appear in the translated statement of cash flows if [a] the subsidiary's only asset or liability during all of 19X3 was a noninterest-bearing checking account having a balance of 400,000 Mex$ throughout the year and [b] the subsidiary had no revenues or expenses for 19X3.)

3. Assuming that the average balance of the subsidiary's assets for 19X3 was 8,000,000 Mex$, calculate the approximate loss of valuation on the *total* assets for 19X3 under the *current rate method*. To what amount in the translated statement of cash flows does this amount relate? Explain the relationship.

P 19–5   **Hedging Net Asset and Net Monetary Positions**   Puntex's foreign subsidiary had the following average account balances for 19X1 expressed in its local currency (LCUs):

Monetary assets	400,000	Monetary liabilities	300,000
Nonmonetary assets	400,000	Stockholders' equity	500,000

Net income for 19X1 was 100,000 LCUs earned evenly throughout the year and remitted to the parent monthly. During 19X1, the LCU weakened 25%, the direct (spot) rate going from $.40 to $.30. Various assumptions for different situations follow:

Situation	Functional Currency	Item Hedged
A	LCU	Net investment
B	LCU	Net monetary asset position
C	U.S. dollar	Net investment
D	U.S. dollar	Net monetary asset position
E	U.S. dollar	Net monetary liability position
		(For situation E, assume that average monetary liabilities were 500,000 LCUs and average stockholders' equity was 300,000 LCUs.)

For situations A, B, C, and D, assume that management expected the LCU to weaken during 19X1 and hedged the item indicated using forward exchange contracts entered into on 1/1/X1 and terminated 12/31/X1. For situation E, assume that management expected the LCU to strengthen during 19X1 and hedged accordingly. (For simplicity, assume that the forward rate on 1/1/X1 for a one-year forward exchange contract was $.40.)

Required   For each situation, determine the following and indicate how the amounts should be reported for 19X1:

1. The hedging gain or loss.
2. The translation adjustment or the gain or loss from the remeasurement process, as appropriate.

P 19–6   **Highly Inflationary Economy: Recording a General Price-Level Change**   Subco is a 100%-owned foreign subsidiary located in a country that wishes to prepare financial statements that are (a) restated for general price-level changes and (b) in accordance with U.S. GAAP (except for price-level adjustments). Assume that

1. Subco has just completed its first year of operations (19X1).
2. On 1/1/X1, Subco acquired land at a cost of 100,000 LCUs.
3. The inflation rate for 19X1 was 50%.
4. The foreign government, which has a 25% corporate income tax rate, will allow the tax basis of fixed assets to be restated by 40% for 19X1.

Required   1. What entry(ies) should be made on the foreign subsidiary's books to restate for general price-level changes?

2. Record the related deferred tax adjustment required under *SFAS No. 109*, "Accounting for Income Taxes." Assume that it is proper GAAP to record deferred taxes relating to this item for this particular subsidiary.
3. What entry(ies) would be made if the land were sold for 150,000 LCUs on 1/2/X2?

✳ THINKING CRITICALLY ✳

✳ CASES ✳

C 19–1   **Analyzing an Annual Report Disclosure**   In its 1995 annual report, Ford Motor Company stated that the remeasurement gains reported in the 1995 income statement from operations in highly inflationary economies were mostly offset by higher cost of sales that resulted from the use of historical exchange rates for inventories sold during 1995.

Assume that (1) the direct exchange rate decreased in 1995 for the countries in which these operations were located and (2) each foreign operation's total assets were composed of 20% monetary items, 30% inventory, and 50% fixed assets.

Required   1. For this to occur, what had to be the financial position of these foreign units?
2. What was the percentage of debt to total assets for these operations?

C 19–2   **Crediting the Remeasurement Gain to Interest Expense: Why Would They Do That?**   Some companies having foreign subsidiaries in highly inflationary economies report their foreign currency transaction gains from remeasurement as a reduction of interest expense.

Required   What justification might exist for this treatment?

C 19–3   **Evaluating One of the FASB Objectives of Translation**   *SFAS No. 52* states that translation should accomplish the objective of providing "information that is generally compatible with the expected economic effects of a rate change on an enterprise's cash flows and equity." For simplicity, assume that the foreign unit's monetary assets equal its monetary liabilities and that its fixed assets are financed entirely by equity.

Required   1. If the direct exchange rate *decreases* solely because of *foreign* inflation.
2. If the direct exchange rate *increases* solely because of *domestic* inflation.
3. If the direct exchange rate *decreases* solely because of *noninflationary* factors.

Determine whether the current rate method accomplishes the preceding objective.

C 19–4   **Determining the Functional Currency**   Handy Company manufactures soap domestically and in a foreign country, which has low labor costs. The foreign operation (conducted through a wholly owned subsidiary) purchases all of its raw materials from the parent company, which can obtain volume discounts because of its size. (Were it not for the volume discount, the foreign subsidiary would purchase the raw materials directly from suppliers.) The foreign subsidiary's purchases from the parent company are denominated in dollars.

All of the subsidiary's sales are in its local currency, the mun, and all employees are paid in muns. The parent company has established that the subsidiary's dividend policy is to convert its available funds into dollars as quickly as possible each month for current or near-term distribution to the parent.

Required   Determine whether the functional currency is the dollar or the mun.

C 19–5   **Translating Land When No Functional Currency Exists**   Puzzlex Inc. formed a foreign manufacturing subsidiary in 19X1. In 19X8 an earthquake destroyed the subsidiary's manufacturing facility. Because the subsidiary had become marginally profitable in recent years, the parent decided not to rebuild the manufacturing plant. The parent decided to maintain the subsidiary as a passive investment, however, with the subsidiary having land as the only asset because the location was highly desirable and the opportunity for significant appreciation in the near future existed. All liabilities were paid off with the insurance proceeds. Until the earthquake, the subsidiary's functional currency had been the local currency.

Required   1. Should the balance in the Cumulative Translation Adjustment account be taken into income?
2. How should the land be translated in future periods?

3. How would you translate the land in future periods if the land has been purchased outright as a passive investment in 19X8?

※ FINANCIAL ANALYSIS PROBLEMS ※

FAP 19–1 **Evaluating the Impact of a Weakening Dollar**   Zell Inc. is a domestic company that established a manufacturing subsidiary in Belgium in 19X1. In establishing this foreign operation, Zell minimized the number of dollars taken out of the United States by financing the subsidiary's manufacturing plant through a loan obtained from a Belgian financial institution. This loan is being repaid over 25 years. As a result, the subsidiary is thinly capitalized.

During 19X4 the dollar weakened approximately 20% against the mark as concerns arose over the sizable U.S. foreign trade deficit, the federal spending deficit, and the inability to control inflation. (The franc held steady against the other major currencies of the world.) In francs, the subsidiary had a profit for the current year comparable to that of the prior year. In dollars, the subsidiary had a loss for the current year, compared with a profit for the prior year.

Required   1. Considering the following, how is it possible to report a loss on the foreign operation for the current year?
   a. The parent minimized its dollars at risk by financing the foreign plant with local borrowings.
   b. The operation was run as efficiently this year as in the prior year.
2. Is this an economic loss or a paper loss? Explain your answer.
3. Is there any way the loss could have been avoided?

FAP 19–2 **Evaluating the Impact of a Weakening Foreign Currency**   Assume that you are the controller of a domestic company that established operations in Mexico two years ago. These foreign operations are conducted through a Mexican subsidiary. The subsidiary has three operational manufacturing plants, all of which cost approximately the same amount and were financed as follows:

1. The first plant was financed entirely from the parent's *capital stock investment* in the subsidiary.
2. The second plant was financed entirely from a *long-term loan from a local Mexican bank*, none of which has been repaid.
3. The third plant was financed entirely from an interest-bearing, *long-term loan from the parent*, none of which has been repaid. (The loan is payable in dollars.)

During the month preceding the annual shareholders' meeting, the Mexican peso declined approximately 30% in value. You are sure a question will arise at the shareholders' meeting concerning the financial consequences of this decline.

Required   1. Without regard to using a particular translation method, prepare a brief summary of the impact of the decline in the value of the peso on the company's foreign operations.
2. Indicate the effect of the exchange rate change that will be reported for the current year for each of the plants under the *current rate* method.
3. Repeat requirement 2 using the *temporal* method.

※ PERSONAL SITUATION: ETHICS AND INTERPERSONAL SKILLS ※

PS 19–1 **Ethics: Should "Corporate Welfare" Be Reported as Income?**   Many newspaper columnists use the term *corporate welfare* to characterize the tax breaks that corporations receive under various provisions of the Internal Revenue Code (such as Section 936, which allows tax credits for doing business in a U.S. possession, as discussed in Chapter 16). Under current financial reporting standards, such tax savings are reported in the income statement as a reduction of income tax expense.

Required   1. Is it ethical to report as income the positive effect that can result from such legislative provisions?
2. What might be a better and more informative way of reporting this effect?

ANSWERS TO SELF-STUDY QUESTIONS

1. a   2. e   3. e   4. c   5. b   6. a   7. a   8. b   9. c

■ **APPENDIX**

U.S. TAXATION OF FOREIGN SUBSIDIARY EARNINGS

I THE POSSIBLE TAXATION OF A FOREIGN SUBSIDIARY'S EARNINGS AT THE PARENT LEVEL IN ADDITION TO TAXATION AT THE SUBSIDIARY LEVEL

As discussed in the Appendix to Chapter 3, the intent of the Internal Revenue Code is to tax earnings of subsidiaries (domestic or foreign) only once in the United States at the corporate level. Recall further from that appendix that (1) a foreign subsidiary **cannot** file a consolidated income tax return with its U.S. parent and (2) the "dividend received deduction" applies only to dividends received from domestic subsidiaries. (Also recall from Chapter 1 that the earnings of a foreign subsidiary are taxed in the United States only when dividends are received.[8])

Because of these two limitations, a domestic parent's *dividend income* from its *foreign subsidiary* is taxed at the corporate level in the United States. Thus without some comparable special tax provisions for foreign subsidiaries, a *double corporate tax* would result—something that is easily avoided for domestic subsidiaries.

Due to the heavy double corporate tax that would result on a foreign subsidiary's earnings (which would border on a system of "confiscation" rather than taxation), the Internal Revenue Code provisions allow the parent-level tax to be either (1) entirely avoided or (2) substantially lessened, as explained in detail shortly.

DIFFERENCES IN INCOME TAX RATES

For all practical purposes, the *parent-level tax* on dividend income received from a foreign subsidiary is paid only when the subsidiary pays income-related taxes to the foreign government at a lower tax rate than the U.S. tax rate. Thus the parent-level tax becomes a problem only when a parent has a subsidiary in a low tax-bracket country (relative to the United States), such as Ireland, which has a 10% income tax rate, or Singapore, which has a zero tax rate. (The statutory corporate income tax rates of the major trading companies range from 34% [France] to 56.5% [Germany].)

Thus the parent-level tax does *not* result in fully taxing the same income twice (once abroad and once domestically). Instead, it merely makes up for income taxes that otherwise would have been paid if the income had been earned in the United States. Keep in mind that the U.S. income tax system—unlike the tax system of most foreign countries—taxes worldwide income, not just income earned within the United States.[9]

---

[8]Some exceptions exist (most notably on foreign income characterized as passive), and such foreign income is taxed as it is earned—whether it is distributed. Such income is referred to as a *deemed dividend* or *deemed distribution* by the IRS. In financial reporting, it is merely the equity method of accounting.

The ability of the parent to choose when a foreign subsidiary's earnings become taxable in the United States allows the parent to have a planning strategy at its disposal if it becomes necessary to report taxable income to prevent certain net operating losses or tax credit carryforwards from expiring.

[9]In contrast, many foreign countries (such as Britain, Germany, and the Netherlands) tax only income earned in their country—not worldwide income.

AVOIDING THE PARENT-LEVEL TAX ON A FOREIGN SUBSIDIARY'S EARNINGS: INSTRUCTING THE SUBSIDIARY TO REINVEST RATHER THAN DISTRIBUTE ITS EARNINGS

Because the parent-level tax is paid only if the foreign subsidiary pays dividends, the parent-level tax can be entirely avoided merely by instructing the foreign subsidiary to reinvest rather than distribute its earnings.[10]

THE CRITICAL FINANCIAL REPORTING ISSUE— IF AND WHEN TO RECORD THE PARENT-LEVEL TAXES

Even if a foreign subsidiary's earnings are reinvested rather than distributed, whether deferred income tax expense and deferred income taxes payable should be recorded for financial reporting purposes is an issue. The concern is that at some point the foreign subsidiary's accumulated earnings may be partially or fully distributed to the parent, thus triggering the payment of the parent-level taxes. After all, the parent controls the foreign subsidiary's dividend policy, and changed economic conditions could cause a reversal of the "pay no dividends policy."

Thus the issue is whether the parent-level taxes should be recorded (1) **in any event,** (2) **only if it is reasonably expected that the taxes will actually have to be paid,** or (3) **only when actually paid.** This issue is addressed in *APB Opinion No. 23.*

II THE REQUIREMENTS OF *APB OPINION NO. 23*

APBO No. 23, "Accounting for Income Taxes—Special Areas," is the governing pronouncement on recording parent-level taxes on a subsidiary's earnings, and it requires that the parent-level income taxes be recorded when the subsidiary's earnings are earned (consistent with the *accrual basis*)—not when the earnings are distributed (consistent with the *cash basis*). (*SFAS No. 109,* "Accounting for Income Taxes," did *not* supersede this pronouncement.) However, **if certain reinvestment conditions are met** (discussed shortly), the parent-level income taxes need not be recorded. Accordingly, *APBO No. 23's* approach is *not* fully consistent with either the accrual basis or the cash basis. Instead, *APBO No. 23* takes a pragmatic in-between approach of recording the parent-level taxes only to the extent that they are **reasonably expected to be paid.** *APBO No. 23* sets forth two conditions in this regard. If *neither* condition is met, the parent-level tax must be recorded when the subsidiary earnings are earned even though some or all of such taxes may be deferred income taxes.

CONDITION 1: PLANNED TAX-FREE LIQUIDATION

As mentioned in the Appendix to Chapter 3, Section 332 of the Internal Revenue Code allows a subsidiary to remit its **undistributed** earnings to its parent in a tax-free liquidation, providing certain conditions are met. Under *APBO No. 23,* a parent *need not* provide income taxes on such undistributed earnings if the earnings could be remitted tax free. Note that this provision pertains solely to undistributed earnings. In contrast, earnings that have been distributed prior to the actual tax-free liquidation date are taxed as dividend income and require the parent-level tax to be provided.

---

[10]Note that the accumulated earnings tax does not apply to foreign subsidiaries.

CONDITION 2: INDEFINITE INVESTMENT OF UNDISTRIBUTED EARNINGS

If evidence shows that **some** or **all** of the *undistributed earnings* have been or will be invested indefinitely, parent companies do *not* have to record parent-level income taxes on their share of their subsidiaries' *undistributed earnings. Indefinitely* does *not* mean *permanently.* Thus parent companies are *not* required to invest the undistributed earnings of their subsidiaries forever but **only for the foreseeable future.**

EXAMPLES OF EVIDENCE   Two examples of evidence to satisfy this "invested indefinitely" condition are (1) *historical experience* and (2) *planned future programs of operations.*

THE FINAL ANALYSIS   In effect, the parent records income taxes only to the extent that their payment is reasonably expected to be made. Possible scenarios include

1. **Total reinvestment.** The intention is to reinvest indefinitely 100% of the foreign subsidiary's earnings (**no** parent-level taxes need be recorded).

2. **Partial reinvestment.** The intention is to reinvest less than 100% of the foreign subsidiary's earnings indefinitely (**some** parent-level taxes must be recorded).

3. **No reinvestment.** The intention is to distribute in the foreseeable future 100% of the foreign subsidiary's earnings (**full** parent-level taxes must be recorded).

WHAT IF CIRCUMSTANCES CHANGE?   With respect to changing circumstances, *APBO No. 23* requires that income tax expense **for the current year** be adjusted to reflect any change in such estimated taxes payable. This manner of reporting is a **change in accounting estimate** treatment, as opposed to either (1) a correction of an error treatment (for which prior period statements would be restated) or (2) a change in accounting principle treatment. Two changed-circumstance scenarios are possible:

1. **Undistributed earnings are no longer planned to be** *reinvested indefinitely.* Income taxes which in retrospect should have been accrued in prior periods, must now be accrued. The Income Tax Expense account is debited (restatement of the prior period financial statements is *not* allowed).

2. **Undistributed earnings are no longer planned to be** *distributed.* Previously recorded accrued income taxes payable must now be adjusted downward. The offsetting credit is to the Income Tax Expense account. Restatement of the prior period financial statements is *not* allowed—nor can the offsetting credit be reported as an extraordinary item.

RATIONALE OF *APB OPINION NO. 23*

The rationale of *APBO No. 23* is that a subsidiary may not distribute all of its earnings because the capital is needed to finance internal growth. Thus the parent views all or a large portion of the subsidiary's retained earnings as *permanent capital.* From this viewpoint, no U.S. income taxes would ever be paid on the amount deemed permanent capital because it would never be distributed as dividends. Consequently, it would not be sensible to record parent-level taxes on that portion of a subsidiary's earnings that is invested in the subsidiary indefinitely.

OBSERVATION   Not recording parent-level income taxes on a foreign subsidiary's undistributed earnings is an **implicit form of discounting**—if the parent-level taxes will *not* be paid until far into the future, the present value of the deferred tax liability is effectively zero.

III CALCULATING PARENT-LEVEL TAXES ON FOREIGN SUBSIDIARIES' EARNINGS

A foreign subsidiary files an income tax return in the country in which it is domiciled (that is, incorporated). Although a U.S. parent must report as dividend income on its tax return any dividends received from its foreign subsidiary, no income taxes may be owed at the parent level on this dividend income if the subsidiary paid taxes at a rate equal to or higher than the U.S. tax rate. To determine whether taxes should be recorded at the parent level for financial reporting purposes, the following procedures are used:

1. Determine how much of the subsidiary's earnings do **not** qualify for either of the two conditions of *APBO No. 23.*
2. Gross up these "nonqualifying" earnings to a **pretax** income amount.
3. Apply the U.S. statutory income tax rate to this pretax income. This is in the nature of a **pro forma calculation**—it shows what income taxes would have been owed had these foreign earnings been earned in the United States.
4. Subtract from these **pro forma income taxes** any available **foreign tax credits** allowed. If a **positive** balance exists, record that amount as the parent-level taxes on the subsidiary's "nonqualifying" earnings. If a **zero or negative** balance exists, no parent-level taxes need be recorded. Two kinds of foreign tax credits exist:
   a. **Foreign income taxes.**
   b. **Dividend withholding taxes.** The foreign government withholds these taxes when a dividend is remitted. One of the avowed purposes of this tax is to collect taxes that otherwise would have been collected at the individual taxpayer level had local citizens owned the corporation. (The dividend withholding tax rates of most of the major trading countries range from 5% to 15%.)

The Internal Revenue Code has limitations on the credit amount allowable against the pro forma income taxes—both on a per country basis and an overall basis. The specific limitations are beyond the scope of this text, but you should be aware that they exist.

WHY IT IS ALSO NECESSARY TO RECORD THE DIVIDEND WITHHOLDING TAXES ON THE PARENT'S BOOKS?

In addition to the parent-level income taxes, the parent must record on its books the dividend withholding tax payable. The dividend withholding tax is **a tax to the recipient;** accordingly, it is *never* recorded as an expense on the foreign subsidiary's books.

REQUIRED DISCLOSURES

When a deferred tax liability has *not* been recognized because the "invested indefinitely" assumption is used, *SFAS No. 109* requires disclosure of either (1) the amount of the unrecognized deferred tax liability if that amount is determined to be practicable or (2) a statement that determination is *not* practicable. See the Case in Point for an example of such disclosure.

Illustrations 19–9 and 19–10 show how to calculate and record parent-level taxes on "nonqualifying" earnings of foreign subsidiaries under differing assumptions.

CASE IN POINT

Chevron Corporation's 1995 Annual Report

"Undistributed earnings of international consolidated subsidiaries and affiliates for which no deferred income tax provision has been made for possible future remittances totaled approximately $3.7 billion at December 31, 1995. Substantially all of this amount represents earnings reinvested as part of the company's ongoing business. It is not practical to estimate the amount of taxes that might be payable on the eventual remittance of such earnings.

On remittance, certain countries impose withholding taxes that, subject to certain limitations, are then available for use as tax credits against a U.S. tax liability, if any. The company estimates withholding taxes of approximately $207 million would be payable upon remittance of these earnings."

ILLUSTRATION 19–9 Calculating and Recording U.S. Income Taxes on a 100%-Owned Foreign Subsidiary's Earnings: 100% of Earnings Distributed

I. Assumed Information Regarding Parco Inc.'s 100%-Owned Foreign Subsidiary, Subco Inc., for 19X1

Foreign Income Tax Rate	20%
Dividend Withholding Tax Rate	5%
Percentage of 19X1 Net Income Distributed as Dividends in 19X1	100%

Income before Income Taxes (pretax income)	$1,000,000
Income tax expense @ 20%	(200,000)
Net Income	$ 800,000
Less—Dividend withholding taxes at 5%	(40,000)
Cash Received by Parco	$ 760,000

Taxes Recorded Versus Taxes Owed

Taxes **Recorded** on Subco's Books in 19X1	$ 200,000
Taxes **Owed** to the Foreign Government for 19X1	$ 240,000

II. Calculation of Income Taxes to Be Recorded by Parco in 19X1 That Pertain to Subco's 19X1 Earnings

Subco's 19X1 pretax income	$1,000,000
U.S. income tax rate	35%
Pro Forma U.S. Income Taxes	$ 350,000
Less allowable foreign tax credits:	
Foreign income taxes ($1,000,000 × 20%)	(200,000)
Dividend withholding taxes ($800,000 × 5%)	(40,000)
Taxes Owed to the U.S. Government	$ 110,000

Taxes Recorded Versus Taxes Owed

Taxes **Recorded** on Parco's Books in 19X1	$ 150,000
Taxes **Owed** to the U.S. Government for 19X1	$ 110,000

III. Parco's 19X1 Entries Relating to Subco's 19X1 Earnings

(1) Investment in Subsidiary	800,000	
Equity in Net Income (of subsidiary)		800,000
To apply the equity method of accounting.		

(2) Income Tax Expense	150,000	
Income Taxes Payable—IRS		110,000
Income Taxes Payable—Foreign		40,000
To record income taxes on Subco's 19X1 earnings (100% **currently** payable because 100% of the 19X1 net income was distributed in 19X1).		

(3) Cash	760,000	
Income Taxes Payable—Foreign	40,000	
Investment in Subsidiary		800,000
To record receipt of dividend.		

Parco's journal entries shown in Illustration 19–9 are presented in T-account fashion:

INVESTMENT IN SUBSIDIARY	EQUITY IN NET INCOME (OF SUBSIDIARY)	CASH
(1) 800,000 800,000 (3)	800,000 (1)	(3) 760,000

INCOME TAX EXPENSE	INCOME TAXES PAYABLE—IRS	INCOME TAXES PAYABLE—FOREIGN
(2) 150,000	110,000 (2)	40,000 (2)
	(3) 40,000	

ILLUSTRATION 19–10   **Calculating and Recording U.S. Income Taxes on a 100%-Owned Foreign Subsidiary's Earnings: 20% of Earnings Expected to Be Reinvested Indefinitely**

I. Assumed Information Concerning Parco Inc.'s 100%-Owned Foreign Subsidiary, Subco Inc., for 19X1

Foreign Income Tax Rate	20%
Dividend Withholding Tax Rate	5%
Income before Income Taxes (pretax income)	$1,000,000
Income tax expense @ 20%	(200,000)
Net Income	$ 800,000

	Breakdown of 19X1 Earnings		
	Expected to Be		Actually
	Reinvested Indefinitely (20%)	Distributed as Dividends After 19X1 (30%)	Distributed as Dividends in 19X1 (50%)
Subco's Pretax Income	$200,000	$300,000	$500,000
Income taxes @20%	(40,000)	(60,000)	(100,000)
Net Income	$160,000	$240,000	$400,000

II. Calculation of Income Taxes to Be Recorded by Parco in 19X1 That Pertain to Subco's 19X1 Earnings

	Expected to Be		Actually
	Reinvested Indefinitely (20%)	Distributed as Dividends After 19X1 (30%)	Distributed as Dividends in 19X1 (50%)
Subco's Pretax Income	$200,000	$300,000	$500,000
U.S. income tax rate		35%	35%
Pro Forma U.S. Income Taxes		$105,000	$175,000
Less allowable foreign tax credits:			
Foreign income taxes @ 20%			
of Subco's **pretax** income		(60,000)	(100,000)
Dividend withholding taxes @ 5%			
of Subco's **net** income		(12,000)	(20,000)
Taxes Owed to the U.S. Government		$ 33,000	$ 55,000

Taxes Recorded Versus Taxes Owed

Taxes **Recorded** on Parco's Books in 19X1 ($12,000 + $20,000 + $33,000 + $55,000)	$120,000
Taxes **Owed** to the U.S. Government for 19X1 ($33,000 + $55,000)	$88,000

Note: Observe that these amounts are 80% of the comparable amounts shown in Illustration 19–9.

(continued)

ILLUSTRATION 19–10 (continued)

III. Parco's 19X1 Entries Relating to Subco's 19X1 Earnings

(1) Investment in Subsidiary	800,000	
Equity in Net Income (of subsidiary)		800,000
To apply the equity method of accounting.		
(2) Income Tax Expense	120,000	
Income Taxes Payable—IRS		55,000
Deferred Income Taxes Payable—IRS		33,000
Income Taxes Payable—Foreign		20,000
Deferred Income Taxes Payable—Foreign		12,000
To record income taxes on foreign subsidiary's earnings.		
(3) Cash	380,000	
Income Taxes Payable—Foreign	20,000	
Investment in Subsidiary		400,000
To record receipt of dividend.		

IV. Calculation of Parent-Level Income Taxes That Would Have to Be Recorded on Subco's 19X1 Earnings Being Reinvested Indefinitely If this Reinvestment Assumption Were Changed

Subco's 19X1 pretax earnings currently intended to be reinvested Indefinitely	$200,000[a]
U.S. income tax rate	35%
Pro Forma U.S. Income Taxes	$70,000
Less allowable foreign tax credits:	
Foreign income taxes ($200,000 × 20%)	(40,000)
Dividend withholding taxes ($160,000 × 5%)	(8,000)
Income Taxes That Would Be Owed to the U.S. Government	$ 22,000
Parent-Level Taxes That Would Have to Be Recorded If the "Being Reinvested Indefinitely"	
Assumption Were Changed.	$ 30,000[b]

[a]Companies commonly disclose this amount in the notes to the financial statements.

[b]Companies generally do not calculate or disclose this amount because it is impractical to calculate.

SUMMARY OF KEY POINTS FOR APPENDIX

1. Under *APBO No. 23*, the parent-level tax must be recorded in the year in which the subsidiary earns the income—not when the dividends are paid. To the extent that the income taxes **are not expected to be paid,** however, they need not be recorded.
2. Conditions that allow the parent-level tax **not** to be recorded are (1) **indefinite investment** (supported by history or planned programs of operations) and (2) the possibility that the earnings could be remitted in a **tax-free liquidation.**
3. In computing the parent-level taxes on a foreign subsidiary's earnings, a **pro forma calculation** is made as if the earnings had been earned and then taxed in the United States. **Foreign tax credits** and **dividend withholding taxes** can be used to reduce the amount of parent-level taxes otherwise payable to the IRS.

SELF-STUDY QUESTIONS FOR APPENDIX

(The answers are at the end of the appendix.)

1. For financial reporting purposes, under what circumstances must parent companies record income taxes on earnings of foreign subsidiaries?
   a. If a tax-free liquidation is planned.
   b. If the earnings have been or will be invested indefinitely.
   c. If a consolidated income tax return *cannot* be filed.
   d. If the dividend received deduction is *not* applicable.
   e. If some or all of the earnings are expected to be distributed.

2. Paxe Inc. owns 100% of the common stock of Sax Inc., a foreign subsidiary located in a country that has a 20% income tax rate and a 10% dividend withholding tax. The U.S. income tax rate is 35%. Saxe reported net income of $400,000 for 19X1 and remitted $250,000 of these earnings as dividends to Paxe in 19X2. The remaining earnings are expected to be remitted in 19X2. What is the total amount of income taxes relating to Saxe that Paxe should record on its books for 19X1?
   a. $–0–   **b.** $25,000   **c.** $35,000   **d.** $40,000   **e.** $75,000

3. Use the information in Question 2. What amount of parent-level income taxes will eventually be paid to the IRS?
   a. $–0–   **b.** $25,000   **c.** $35,000   **d.** $40,000   **e.** $75,000

4. Use the information in Question 2. What will be the total taxes eventually paid to the foreign government?
   a. $100,000   **b.** $125,000   **c.** $135,000   **d.** $140,000   **e.** $175,000

REVIEW QUESTIONS FOR APPENDIX

1. When and to what extent does *APBO No. 23* require the parent-level taxes on a *foreign* subsidiary's earnings to be recorded?
2. What conditions allow for *not* recording the parent-level taxes?
3. What are two examples of evidence to support the invested indefinitely condition?
4. What are the general procedures used to calculate the parent-level tax on a foreign subsidiary's earnings?
5. What two types of foreign tax credits exist?
6. Which entity records as an expense the dividend withholding tax paid or payable? Why?
7. How is the effect of a change in assumption regarding indefinite investment of a foreign subsidiary's undistributed earnings reported?

EXERCISES FOR APPENDIX

E 19–1A **100% Reinvestment of Earnings**   Pikee Inc. owns 100% of the outstanding common stock of Sikee Inc., a foreign subsidiary that consistently does *not* declare dividends on its common stock because the earnings are used each year for internal expansion, which is expected to continue into the foreseeable future. For 19X1, Sikee had net income of $140,000. Assume a 30% foreign income tax rate, a 5% dividend withholding tax rate, and a 40% U.S. income tax rate.

Required   Prepare Pikee's 19X1 entries relating to its investment in Sikee assuming that Pikee uses the equity method.

E 19–2A **Planned Tax-Free Liquidation: No Dividends Declared**   Probco Inc. owns 100% of the outstanding common stock of Solvco Inc., a foreign subsidiary domiciled in a country that has a 25% corporate income tax and a 5% dividend withholding tax. Probco expects Solvco to be operational for 8 years, after which its undistributed earnings will be remitted to Probco in a tax-free liquidation. For 19X1, Solvco (1) reported net income of $300,000 and (2) declared no dividends. Assume a 40% U.S. income tax rate.

Required   Prepare Probco's 19X1 entries related to its investment in Solvco assuming that Probco uses the equity method.

PROBLEMS FOR APPENDIX

P 19–1A **Planned Tax-Free Liquidation: Dividends Declared**   Putco Inc. owns 100% of the outstanding common stock of Sutco Inc., a foreign subsidiary domiciled in a country that has a 25% corporate income tax and a 15% dividend withholding tax. Putco expects Sutco to be operational for 10 years, after which its undistributed earnings will be remitted to Putco in a tax-free liquidation. For 19X1, Sutco (1) reported net income of $450,000 and (2) declared and paid cash dividends of $240,000. Assume a 40% U.S. income tax rate.

Required   1. Prepare Putco's 19X1 entries related to its investment in Sutco assuming that Putco uses the equity method.
   2. What amount is reported on Putco's 19X1 federal corporate income tax return relating to its investment in Sutco?

P 19–2A   **Temporary Partial Reinvestment of Earnings**   Pavco Inc. owns 100% of the outstanding common stock of Savco Inc., a foreign subsidiary domiciled in a country that imposes a 20% corporate income tax and a 5% dividend withholding tax. For 19X1, Savco (1) reported net income of $200,000 and (2) declared and paid cash dividends of $120,000. Savco's $80,000 of undistributed 19X1 earnings are expected to be distributed within 5 years. Assume a 40% U.S. income tax rate.

Required   1. Prepare Pavco's 19X1 entries relating to its investment in Savco assuming that Pavco uses the equity method.
   2. What amount is reported on Pavco's 19X1 federal corporate income tax return relating to its investment in Savco?

P 19–3A   **Temporary Partial Reinvestment of Earnings**   Ponex Inc. owns 100% of the outstanding common stock of Sonex Inc., a foreign subsidiary domiciled in a country that imposes a 25% corporate income tax and a 15% dividend withholding tax. For 19X1, Sonex (1) reported net income of $600,000 and (2) declared cash dividends of $420,000 ($360,000 of which was paid in 19X1 and $60,000 was paid in early 19X2). The remaining $180,000 of 19X1 net income is expected to be distributed as soon as cash becomes available. Assume a 40% U.S. income tax rate.

Required   1. Prepare Ponex's 19X1 entries related to its investment in Sonex assuming that Ponex uses the equity method.
   2. What amount is reported on Ponex's 19X1 federal corporate income tax return relating to its investment in Sonex?

P 19–4A   **Indefinite Partial Reinvestment of Earnings**   Punco Inc. owns 100% of the outstanding common stock of Sunco Inc., a foreign subsidiary domiciled in a country that imposes a 30% corporate income tax and a 10% dividend withholding tax. For 19X1, Sunco (1) reported net income of $350,000 and (2) declared cash dividends of $210,000 ($150,000 of which was paid in 19X1 and $60,000 of which was paid in early 19X2). The remaining $140,000 of 19X1 net income is expected to be used for internal expansion. Assume a 40% U.S. income tax rate.

Required   1. Prepare Punco's 19X1 entries related to its investment in Sunco assuming that Punco uses the equity method.
   2. What amount is reported on Punco's 19X1 federal corporate income tax return relating to its investment in Sunco?

ANSWERS TO APPENDIX SELF-STUDY QUESTIONS

1. e   2. e   3. c   4. d

TRANSLATING FOREIGN CURRENCY STATEMENTS: EVALUATING THE VALIDITY OF THE FUNCTIONAL CURRENCY CONCEPT

20

One may go wrong in many different directions, but right in only one.

ARISTOTLE

In this chapter, we show the third possible approach to translating foreign currency financial statements that was mentioned in Chapter 18: the current-value approach using purchasing power parity theory (hereafter the PPP current-value approach). We then use this approach to reveal the characteristics (strengths and weaknesses) of the current rate and temporal methods of translation. Next, we address the environment and thinking that gave rise to the functional currency concept and whether it is a valid concept. Last, we discuss how to evaluate and manage foreign operations when the reporting results of *SFAS No. 52* are so unrealistic that the translated statements cannot be relied upon.

I THE CURRENT-VALUE APPROACH USING PURCHASING POWER PARITY THEORY

In the appendix to Chapter 16, we discussed that long-term exchange rate changes are best explained by purchasing power parity theory, which states the following: **The differential rate of inflation between two countries can be expected to result over the long term in an equal but opposite change in the exchange rate between the two currencies.** Recall further that foreign inflation drives the direct exchange rate down and that domestic inflation has the opposite result.

THE RATIONALE

The premise of the PPP current-value approach is that it makes little sense to apply an exchange rate that has been impacted downward for foreign inflation to amounts that likewise **have not been adjusted upward for the same inflation.** To do so is to deal with only half of accounting for the exchange rate change problem. Accordingly, under this approach, **nonmonetary assets** that have increased in value because of foreign inflation are adjusted for the foreign inflation and then translated at the **current rate.** This approach largely achieves current-value accounting.[1] All remaining assets and liabilities are also translated at the current rate. All income statement accounts are translated using exchange rates in effect when the items were recognized (the current rate).

Managerially, a foreign currency unit of measure is achieved only if local management internally uses the inflation-adjusted foreign currency statements to manage the subsidiary.

THE FOCUS: THE NET ASSET POSITION

This approach assumes that all of the foreign unit's assets and liabilities are exposed to the risk of exchange rate changes. Thus the exposure pertains to the net asset position (which equals the parent's net investment)—the same focus used for the foreign currency unit of measure approach discussed in Chapter 18. Because a single exchange rate is used in translating all assets and liabilities, the relationships that exist in the inflation-adjusted foreign balance sheet are maintained in translation (as under the foreign currency unit of measure approach shown in Chapter 18).

---

[1]The modifier *largely* is used because no general price level index can exactly achieve current values on a company-by-company basis. Also, the base to which the general price index is applied could be unreliable inasmuch as the depreciable life used and/or the depreciation method used could be inappropriate.

KEY OBSERVATIONS REGARDING THE PPP CURRENT-VALUE APPROACH

This approach eliminates the *"disappearing plant" problem* that can occur in the foreign currency unit of measure approach (current rate method). To fully understand the reporting results of the PPP current-value approach, it is necessary to analyze the exchange rate change for the period using PPP. We will do this shortly.

To illustrate translation under this approach, we will use the same set of assumptions used in illustrating the other two approaches in Chapters 18 and 19. For convenience, we list those assumptions again here.

ASSUMED FACTUAL DATA FOR ILLUSTRATIONS OF THE THREE POSSIBLE TRANSLATION APPROACHES

Assume that in late 19X1, a U.S. company created a 100%-owned subsidiary in Mexico when the direct exchange rate was $.50, making a $1,000,000 cash equity investment at that time. For simplicity, assume that this direct exchange rate did *not* fluctuate through December 31, 19X1. The subsidiary's first sales were on January 1, 19X2. The subsidiary's balance sheets at the end of 19X1 and 19X2 and its 19X2 income statement are shown in Illustration 20–1.

Additional assumptions are that (1) no dividends were declared or paid in 19X2; (2) fixed asset additions of 200,000 Mex$ (equal to 19X2 depreciation expense) occurred on January 3, 19X2, when the exchange rate was $.50; (3) Mexico had 25% inflation for 19X2; (4) the United States had 10% inflation for 19X2; and (5) the direct exchange rates were $.50 at December 31, 19X1, $.44 at December 31, 19X2, and $.47 for 19X2 as an average.

ILLUSTRATION 20–1	Foreign Currency Financial Statements	
	Pesos	
	12/31/X1	12/31/X2
Balance Sheets		
Monetary assets	2,200,000	2,500,000
Inventory	1,000,000	1,250,000
Fixed assets, net	4,800,000	4,800,000[a]
Total Assets	8,000,000	8,550,000
Liabilities	6,000,000	6,250,000
Common stock	2,000,000[b]	2,000,000
Retained earnings	–0–	300,000
Total Liabilities and Equity	8,000,000	8,550,000
Income Statements (19X2)		
Revenues		5,300,000
Cost of sales		(4,300,000)
Depreciation		(200,000)
Expenses		(500,000)
Net Income		300,000

[a]Because of the 25% inflation in Mexico during 19X2, these assets are undervalued 25%.

[b]This amount is the peso equivalent of the $1,000,000 cash investment made by the parent when it formed the subsidiary in late 19X1 ($1,000,000/$.50 = 2,000,000 Mex$).

Because Mexico had 25% inflation in 19X2, the 19X2 inflation adjustment on the fixed assets is 1,200,000 Mex$ (historical cost of 4,800,000 Mex$ × 25%). The translation worksheet using the inflation-adjusted values and the current exchange rate is shown in Illustration 20–2.

To explain the $399,000 economic gain reported under the PPP current-value approach as shown in Illustration 20–2, it is necessary to analyze the change in the exchange rate using PPP. This analysis is shown in Illustration 20–3.

The inflation effects shown in Illustration 20–3 are used in Illustration 20–4 to explain the $399,000 economic gain reported in Illustration 20–2.

ILLUSTRATION 20–2 **The Current-Value Approach Using PPP**

	Inflation Adjusted (Pesos)	Exchange Code	Exchange Rate	U.S. Dollars
Income Statement (19X2)				
Revenues	5,300,000	A	$.47	$2,491,000
Cost of sales	(4,300,000)	A	$.47	(2,021,000)
Depreciation	(200,000)	A	$.47	(94,000)
Expenses	(500,000)	A	$.47	(235,000)
Net Income	300,000			$ 141,000
Balance Sheet (as of 12/31/X2)				
Monetary assets	2,500,000	C	$.44	$1,100,000
Inventory	1,250,000	C	$.44	550,000
Fixed assets, net	6,000,000(1)	C	$.44	2,640,000
Total Assets	9,750,000			$4,290,000
Liabilities	6,250,000	C	$.44	$2,750,000
Common stock	2,000,000	H	$.50	$1,000,000
Retained earnings	300,000	(Per above)		141,000
Revaluation capital	1,200,000			n/a
Economic gain from exchange rate change		(forced)		399,000(2)
Total Equity	3,500,000			$1,540,000
Total Liabilities and Equity	9,750,000			$4,290,000

(1) Includes a 1,200,000 Mex$ inflation adjustment (the historical cost at 1/1/X2 of 4,800,000 Mex$ × 25%).
(2) This amount can be forced out or calculated. The calculation is shown later in Illustration 20–4.

Key Review Points:
1. Note how ratios and relationships *are* maintained after translation:

	Pesos	U.S. Dollars
Debt-to-equity ratio	1.78:1	1.78:1
Gross profit margin ratio	19%	19%
Net income to sales ratio	6%	6%
Fixed assets to total assets ratio	62%	62%
Undervaluation of fixed assets	0%	0%

2. Note the increase in the stockholders' equity (which we later compare to the change under the other two approaches):

Ending stockholders' equity (per above)	$1,540,000
Less—Beginning stockholders' equity (parent's initial capital investment per Illustration 20–1)	1,000,000
Increase in stockholders' equity	$ 540,000

Code: A = Average rate; C = Current rate; H – Historical rate.

ILLUSTRATION 20–3	Analyzing the Change in the Exchange Rate	

	Direct Exchange Rate
Actual rate, 1/1/X2	$ .50
Plus: Increase expected because of U.S. 10% inflation ($.50 × 10%) ...	.05
Subtotal	$ .55
Less: Decrease expected because of 25% Mexican inflation ($.55/125% = $.44; $.55 − $.44 = $.11)	(.11)
Expected end-of-year rate under PPP	**$ .44**
Plus or minus: Noninflationary factors	.00[a]
Actual rate, 12/31/X2	$ .44

[a]For simplicity, it is assumed that there are no noninflationary factors. Later, noninflationary factors are addressed.

ILLUSTRATION 20–4	Using the Exchange Rate Analysis in Illustration 20–3 to Explain the Increase in the Subsidiary's Equity in Illustration 20–2

(1) Unrealized Nominal[a] Inflationary Holding Gain Resulting from U.S. Inflation (calculated on parent's beginning net investment position):

	Pesos	Dollars
Subsidiary's equity at 1/1/X2 (per Illustration 20–1)	2,000,000	
Effect of domestic inflation on the exchange rate ($.55 − $.50)	$.05	$100,000

(2) Unrealized Inflationary Holding Gain Resulting from Mexico's Inflation (calculated on nonindexed debt financing of fixed assets):

	Pesos	Dollars
Fixed assets at 1/1/X2 (per Illustration 20–1)	4,800,000	
Less—Equity financing at 1/1/X2	(2,000,000)	
Net Debt Financing	2,800,000	
Effect of Mexico's inflation on the exchange rate ($.55 − $.44)	$.11	$308,000

(3) Exchange Rate Change Effect on 19X2 Earnings:

	Pesos	Dollars
Reported earnings (per Illustration 20–2)	300,000	
Difference between the average rate and the year-end rate ($.47 − $.44)	$.03	$ (9,000)
Total Effect of Exchange Rate Changes (a net gain)		$399,000

(4) Subsidiary's net income (per Illustration 20–2) .... | 141,000
    Reported Number of U.S. Dollars the Parent Is Ahead $540,000

Calculation of Parent's Increase in Purchasing Power:

Reported (nominal) number of U.S. dollars ahead	$540,000
Less—Loss of purchasing power on beginning investment ($1,000,000 × 10%)	(100,000)
Real Increase in Purchasing Power	$440,000

[a]A **"nominal" gain** in the parlance of economics means a gain "in name only" as contrasted to a **"real" gain.** In this case, the $100,000 unrealized gain does not result in any increased purchasing power to the parent. In a real gain, the parent would have increased purchasing power. In this chapter, a gain is assumed to be a real gain unless it is labeled as a *nominal gain.*

II WHICH OF THE THREE TRANSLATION APPROACHES REFLECTS ECONOMIC REALITY?

One of the objectives in foreign currency translation is to properly reflect the economic impact of exchange rate changes. Each of the three approaches shown produces significantly different results, as summarized:

	Economic Gain or (Loss) from Exchange Rate Change	Increase in Subsidiary's Equity
1. Current rate method, per Illustration 18–4 (page 630)	$(129,000)	$ 12,000
2. Temporal method, per Illustration 19–3 (page 666)	232,500	310,000
3. PPP current value, per Illustration 20–2 (page 702)	399,000	540,000

They all cannot reflect economic reality because there can be only one economic reality. Only the PPP current-value approach reflects the economic effect of the exchange rate change. The only sensible way to manage the foreign subsidiary and evaluate its results—both at the local level and the parent level—is to use the inflation-adjusted financial statements shown under the PPP current-value approach.

Because both the current rate method and the temporal method are permitted by *SFAS No. 52* (specific conditions determining when to use one or the other), it is necessary to fully understand them. We now compare the current rate method and the temporal method to the PPP current-value approach to isolate the reasons that the reporting differences occur and thus gain insight into the strengths and weaknesses of each method. Interwoven in this analysis is the issue of adjusting for inflation foreign fixed assets but not domestic fixed assets.

III THE CHARACTERISTICS OF THE CURRENT RATE METHOD

A comparison of the reporting results of the current rate method and the PPP current-value approach is shown in Illustration 20–5.

THE CURRENT RATE METHOD PROPERLY REPORTS THE ECONOMIC EFFECT OF DOMESTIC INFLATION

Illustration 20–5 shows that the current rate method properly reports the $100,000 economic effect of the upward inflationary effect of $.05 caused by the 10% U.S. inflation—an **unrealized nominal inflationary holding gain.** If noninflationary factors were present, their economic effect would also be properly reported because they are dealt with as is the U.S. inflation effect.

THE CURRENT RATE METHOD DOES *NOT* PROPERLY REPORT THE ECONOMIC EFFECT OF FOREIGN INFLATION

Illustration 20–5 also shows that the current rate method does not properly report the $308,000 economic effect of Mexico's 25% inflation—an **unrealized inflationary holding gain.** Under the current rate method, translating the fixed assets at the $.44 current rate means that both the upward inflationary effect of $.05 (Illustration 20–3) and the downward inflationary effect of $.11 (Illustration 20–3) were considered in

ILLUSTRATION 20–5	Comparison of the Current Rate Method to the Current-Value Approach Using PPP		
	Current Rate Method (per Illustration 18–4)	Current-Value Approach (per Illustration 20–2)	Reporting Difference
Earnings (excluding effects of exchange rate changes)	$141,000	$141,000	$ –0–
Economic gain (loss) from exchange rate changes	(129,000)	399,000	528,000
Parent's Reported Economic Gain	$ 12,000	$540,000	$528,000

Comparison of Reported Effects of Exchange Rate Changes

	Current Rate Method	Current-Value Approach (per Illustration 20–4)	Reporting Difference
Effect of U.S. inflation:			
Beginning investment of 2,000,000 Mex$ × $.05 upward inflationary effect	$ 100,000	$100,000	$ –0–
Effect of Mexican Inflation:			
Beginning investment of 2,000,000 Mex$ × $.11 downward inflationary effect	(220,000)		220,000
Debt financing of fixed assets of 2,800,000 Mex$ × $.11 downward inflationary effect		308,000	308,000
Effect of exchange rate change on net income	(9,000)	(9,000)	–0–
Total Effect of Exchange Rate Change	$(129,000)	$399,000	$528,000

Explanation of $528,000 Reporting Difference:

Suppressed Valuation of Fixed Assets (4,800,000 Mex$ × $.11)			$528,000

the translation process. This approach's shortcoming—in relation to the PPP current-value approach—is that the downward inflationary effect of $.11 (for Mexico's 25% inflation) should not have been considered in the translation of the fixed assets. The result is $528,000 of suppressed valuation of fixed assets (4,800,000 Mex$ × $.11).

Applying an exchange rate that has decreased because of Mexico's inflation to historical cost amounts in pesos that have not likewise been adjusted upward for the same inflation is illogical from an economic perspective and produces an amount that is difficult to interpret. The resulting dollar amount of $2,112,000 (Illustration 18–4, page 630) is not the $2,400,000 U.S. dollar equivalent needed to acquire the fixed assets when they were acquired (4,800,000 pesos at 1/1/X2 as shown in Illustration 20–1 × the $.50 exchange rate existing when the assets were acquired in late 19X1). Nor is this the current value of the fixed assets—that amount being $2,640,000 (Illustration 20–2). The amount can be described only as historical cost that has been adjusted for the exchange rate change. This difficult-to-interpret problem is not unique to fixed assets. The translated amount for a note receivable or payable having a fixed interest rate different from the current market rate is also neither the initial dollar equivalent nor a current value amount.

Applying current exchange rates to historical costs does result in fixed assets being maintained at the same percentage of total assets that existed in the foreign currency statements (the preservation of the functional currency relationship). Accordingly, the dollar amounts are no less meaningful or unclear than the foreign currency amounts from which they were derived. Stated differently, if the foreign fixed assets are undervalued by 25% because of inflation, both sets of financial statements reflect this undervaluation.

SFAS No. 52 acknowledges the inability of the current rate method to deal properly with the effects of foreign inflation in dealing with highly inflationary economies. The FASB's solution to this problem was to have companies (1) disregard all of the economic factors that are prescribed (in *SFAS No. 52*) to determine the functional currency and (2) instead always use the U.S. dollar as the functional currency. This by itself should raise serious questions as to the validity and conceptual merits of the functional currency concept.

The foreign inflation problem exists for all economies, however, not just highly inflationary ones. For instance, Great Britain had approximately 5.7% annual inflation for the 15 years ended 1995, a cumulative change of 128% for 15 years. Under PPP, the exchange rate would *decrease* 56% for this period. U.S. inflation during this period averaged 3.9%, a cumulative change of 76%. Accordingly, the *expected decrease* in the exchange rate was only 23% instead of 56%. As shown in Illustration 20–6, the suppressed valuation of British fixed assets acquired in 1981 is substantial for this relatively low inflationary economy even when one considers the countereffect of U.S. inflation during this period.

Accordingly, the "disappearing plant" problem discussed in Chapter 18 can also occur in relatively low inflationary economies. Thus, given a choice between valuing foreign fixed assets at current values versus values based on preserving foreign currency relationships that can have the disappearing plant problem, users will likely choose current values every time.

ILLUSTRATION 20–6   **The Effects of Inflation in a Low Inflationary Economy: Great Britain (1981–1995)**

	Direct Exchange Rate
Actual rate for the British Pound, 1/1/81	$2.40
Less: Decrease expected because of 128% British cumulative inflation for 1981–1995	
($2.40/228% = $1.05; $2.40 − $1.05 = $1.35)	(1.35)
Subtotal	$1.05
Plus: Increase expected because of 76% U.S. cumulative inflation for 1981–1995	
($1.05 × 76% = $.80)	.80
Expected Rate at 12/31/95 under PPP	$1.85
Less: Noninflationary factors	(.31)
Actual Rate for the British Pound, 12/31/95	$1.54

Valuations at 12/31/95 for Land Costing 1,000,000 Pounds Acquired on 1/1/81	Pounds		Rate		U.S. Dollars
Temporal method	1,000,000	×	$2.40	=	$2,400,000
Current rate method	1,000,000	×	$1.54	=	$1,540,000[a]
PPP current-value approach	2,280,000[d]	×	$1.54	=	$3,511,000
Current rate method—assuming that no U.S. inflation had occurred	1,000,000	×	$ .74[b]	=	$ 740,000[c]
PPP current-value approach—assuming that no U.S inflation had occurred	2,280,000[d]	×	$1.05	=	$2,394,000
	2,280,000[d]	×	$ (.31)	=	(707,000)
	2,280,000[d]	×	$ .74	=	$1,687,000

[a]The **disappearing plant problem** occurs here to the extent of $550,000 (£1,000,000 × the $.55 decrease ($2.40 − $1.85) in the exchange rate because of higher foreign inflation than domestic inflation).

[b]The expected rate of $1.05 − $.31 for the noninflationary factors.

[c]Note how severe the **disappearing plant problem** would have been had *no* offsetting inflation occurred in the United States.

[d]Includes a 128% inflation adjustment of £1,280,000.

IV THE CHARACTERISTICS OF THE TEMPORAL METHOD

A comparison of the reporting results of the temporal method and the PPP current-value approach is shown in Illustration 20–7.

THE TEMPORAL METHOD PROPERLY REPORTS THE ECONOMIC EFFECT OF FOREIGN INFLATION

Illustration 20–7 shows that the temporal method properly reports the $308,000 economic effect of Mexico's 25% inflation—an unrealized inflationary holding

---

ILLUSTRATION 20–7 **Comparison of the Temporal Method to the PPP Current-Value Approach**

	Temporal Method (per Illustration 19–3)	Current-Value Approach (per Illustration 20–2)	Reporting Difference
Earnings (excluding effects of exchange rate changes)	$ 77,500	$141,000	$63,500
Economic gain from exchange rate change	232,500	399,000	166,500
Parent's Reported Economic Gain	$310,000	$540,000	$230,000

Comparison of Reported Effects of Exchange Rate Changes

	Temporal Method	Current-Value Approach (per Illustration 20–4)	Reporting Difference
Effect of U.S. Inflation:			
Beginning investment of 2,000,000 Mex$ × $.05 upward inflationary effect		$100,000	$100,000
Debt financing of fixed assets (2,800,000[a] Mex$ × $.05 upward inflationary effect)	$(140,000)		140,000
			$240,000
Debt financing of inventory of 1,075,000[a] Mex$ × $.05 upward inflationary effect	(53,750)		53,750
Effect of Mexico's Inflation:			
Debt financing of fixed assets of 2,800,000[a] Mex$ × $.11 downward inflationary effect	308,000	308,000	–0–
Debt financing of inventory of 1,075,000 Mex$ × $.11 downward inflationary effect	118,250		(118,250)
Effect of exchange rate change on net income		(9,000)	(9,000)
Reported effect of exchange rate change	$232,500	$399,000	$166,500
Difference in reported amounts for depreciation and cost of sales	(63,500)[b]		63,500
Corrected Reported Effect of Exchange Rate Change	$ 169,000	$399,000	$230,000

Explanation of $230,000 Reporting Difference:

Suppressed valuation of fixed assets (4,800,000 Mex$ × $.05)	$240,000
Overvaluation of inventory ($560,000 – $550,000)	(10,000)
Net Overvaluation	$230,000

[a]The average net monetary liability position for 19X2 was 3,875,000 Mex$, which is separated here between fixed assets and inventory.

[b]These additional income statement charges under the temporal method largely offset the $64,500 net inflationary holding gain reported for the debt financing of the inventory ($118,250 – $53,750). Because the inventory turned over in 19X2, there is no real inflationary holding gain. The inventory effectively is a monetary item.

gain. This occurs because the same $2,400,000 fixed asset amount in U.S. dollars is obtained under the temporal method whether or not the subsidiary adjusts its fixed assets for inflation as shown:

		December 31, 19X2	
	Pesos	Exchange Rate	U.S. Dollars
Fixed assets, net (as shown in Illustration 20–1)	4,800,000 ×	$.50	= $2,400,000
Inflation adjustment @ 25%	1,200,000	(.10)[a]	
Fixed assets, as adjusted	6,000,000 ×	$.40	= $2,400,000

[a]($.50/125% = $.40; $50 – $.40 = $.10)

The $.40 rate is the exchange rate that would have existed if U.S. inflation had been zero.

THE TEMPORAL METHOD ACHIEVES INFLATIONARY ACCOUNTING REPORTING RESULTS FOR FOREIGN INFLATION

As shown in Illustration 20–7, the temporal method always reports inflationary holding gains when local inflation has caused the direct exchange rate to decrease. Management cannot conclude otherwise than the subsidiary had an inflationary holding gain. Thus, the temporal method achieves a form of inflationary accounting. Under *SFAS No. 52*, such inflationary holding gains are reported as "foreign currency transaction gains."

In dealing with highly inflationary economies, the FASB stated in its basis for conclusions that the mandatory use of the U.S. dollar as the functional currency in these situations did not introduce a form of inflation accounting.[2] Quite to the contrary, inflation adjustment accounting is effectively being used in these situations because inflationary holding gains are always reported under the temporal method when local inflation has caused the direct exchange rate to decrease. Ironically, this is one aspect of *SFAS No. 52* that is sound because the reporting of inflationary holding gains reflects the underlying economics of these situations.[3]

Thus, whenever foreign inflation occurs, *SFAS No. 52* is inconsistent in a major respect because (1) inflationary holding gains are reported currently in the income statement if the U.S. dollar is the functional currency and (2) inflationary holding gains are not reported currently (neither in the income statement nor as a direct adjustment to equity) if a foreign currency is the functional currency (an erroneous zero net effect is reported).

THE TEMPORAL METHOD DOES *NOT* PROPERLY REPORT THE ECONOMIC EFFECT OF DOMESTIC INFLATION

Illustration 20–7 shows that the temporal method does *not* properly report the $100,000 economic effect of the upward inflationary effect of $.05 caused by the 10% U.S. inflation—an unrealized **nominal** inflationary holding **gain.** Clearly, the use of the $.50 historical exchange rate to translate fixed assets means that the upward factor of $.05 was not considered in determining the fixed asset amount in U.S. dollars. Consequently, $240,000 of suppressed fixed asset valuation exists (4,800,000 Mex$ ×

---

[2] *SFAS No. 52,* paragraph 107.

[3] If the liabilities of a foreign operation in a highly inflationary economy are indexed for inflation, the indexing adjustment results in a charge to the income statement. In U.S. dollars, the effect of that charge is to partially or fully negate the inflationary holding gain that otherwise would be reported.

$.05) in comparison to the PPP current-value approach. If noninflationary factors were present, their economic effect also would not be properly reported because they are dealt with in the same manner as the U.S. inflation effect.

The inability of the temporal method to produce realistic translation results for the effects of **domestic inflation** on exchange rates is **not** addressed in *SFAS No. 52* (as **was** the inability of the current rate method to produce realistic translation results for **highly inflationary economies**). An interesting situation arises when (1) **domestic inflation** consistently **exceeds** foreign inflation and (2) the economic factors set forth in *SFAS No. 52* point to the U.S. dollar as the functional currency. In this situation, high domestic inflation causes the U.S. dollar to weaken against foreign currencies, pushes the direct exchange rate up, and results in the reporting of large exchange rate change losses under the temporal method.[4] Economically, such reported losses would be nonexistent.

These unusual reporting results have *not* occurred under *SFAS No. 52* only because (1) the annual domestic inflation rates after 1981 (the year *SFAS No. 52* was issued) have not been high relative to the annual inflation rates of the majority of foreign countries[5] and (2) *SFAS No. 52*'s requirements are such that the current rate method is used for most foreign operations. If domestic inflation were again to reach the high levels of 1978–1981 and a fair number of companies changed their manner of doing business resulting in their having to use the temporal method instead of the current rate method, however, *SFAS No. 52* would produce the same misleading results as the severely criticized *SFAS No. 8*, and the business community again would be clamoring, and justifiably so, for a reexamination of the foreign currency rules as it did with *SFAS No. 8*.

To be consistent with its approach in dealing with a high foreign inflation problem, the FASB's likely solution to high domestic inflation would be to amend *SFAS No. 52* so that companies operating overseas in low-inflationary economies (relative to the United States) would be required to use the current rate method instead because this would produce more realistic reporting results. Thus the underlying rationale of the approach in *SFAS No. 52* used for determining whether to use the current rate method versus the temporal method again would have to be disregarded.

Thus the temporal method is no more able to produce realistic results when high domestic inflation is the dominant exchange rate change factor than the current rate method is able to produce reliable results when high overseas inflation is the dominant exchange rate change factor. So the state of affairs is that the functional currency concept is so theoretically lacking that it must be cast aside when the reporting results do *not* make sense. Furthermore, the temporal method is unable to produce realistic results when the exchange rate has changed because of noninflationary factors.

V   THE FUNCTIONAL CURRENCY CONCEPT: IS IT VALID?

The functional currency concept must be able to withstand the test of both (1) being sound theoretically and (2) being able to produce results that reflect the economic effects of changes in exchange rates.

---

[4]This reporting result occurs in the typical situation in which the foreign unit has long-term debt. If fixed assets are financed solely by the parent's equity investment, it does not occur.

[5]For the period 1978–1981, the United States did experience a much higher inflation rate than many foreign countries (averaging 10.5%), and the U.S. dollar weakened considerably against virtually all of these currencies during this period.

THE THEORETICAL SOUNDNESS TEST

Without question, the true economics revolve around causes of exchange rate changes. Accordingly, the development of translation methodologies based on any other economic factors must be misguided. Only one true set of economic factors can exist. Consequently, the "economic factors" set forth in Appendix A of *SFAS No. 52* (indicators of cash flow, sales price, sales market, expense, financing, and intercompany transactions and arrangements) must be illusory and irrelevant both individually and collectively.

THE RESULTS-PRODUCED TEST

Because the reporting results under both the current rate method and the temporal method can reflect the true economic effect of changes to the exchange rate only by coincidence, their reporting results must be artificial. Thus the functional currency concept cannot be valid. After all, the concept calls for the use of these translation methods. Therefore, which particular currency a foreign unit uses to conduct its day-to-day operations is irrelevant—especially in a world in which currencies are readily convertible into each other.

IMPROPER LINKAGE

Any linkage between the **manner of conducting operations** and **how to value fixed assets** is tenuous at best. Nobody would suggest that the fixed assets of an **autonomous** subsidiary in Texas should be valued differently than the fixed assets of a **nonautonomous** subsidiary in New York or that the *economic exposure* of the two operations should be measured differently. This is what the functional currency concept requires be done, however, for autonomous versus nonautonomous foreign operations. (The true economic exposure is competition, which exists for all operations—whether or not they are autonomous.)

The rationale set forth for making this assumption is that the economic exposure is different for each type of operation, an assertion that was soundly rejected in *SFAS No. 8* (by a 6-to-1 vote) but barely accepted in *SFAS No. 52* (by a 4-to-3 vote).[6] Because two FASB board members voting on *SFAS No. 8* were also board members when *SFAS No. 52* was issued, 12 different individuals served as board members and voted on the autonomous versus nonautonomous argument. Of these 12 individuals, 7 rejected the autonomous versus nonautonomous argument, 4 voted for it, and 1 person voted against it in *SFAS No. 8* but for it in *SFAS No. 52*.

In our opinion, the focus should be on selecting the translation method that most realistically values fixed assets—not on which particular perspective (foreign currency versus U.S. dollars) should be used.

UNJUSTIFIABLE REPORTING RESULTS OF THIS IMPROPER LINKAGE   IBM has "determined" that all of its foreign operations have local currencies as their functional currencies. Hewlett-Packard has "determined" that all of its foreign opera-

---

[6]In 1992, we showed our analysis of the characteristics of the current rate and temporal methods and our conclusions regarding the functional currency concept presented in this chapter to Ralph Walters, one of the four FASB members who voted in favor of *SFAS No. 52*. Walters stated that at the time he was not aware of the strengths and weaknesses of these two translation methods and that he strongly doubted that the other six board members were aware either. Furthermore, Walters stated that he agreed with our conclusions that the functional currency concept was not valid, and he suggested that we send the analysis and the conclusions to the FASB for the purpose of having it possibly reexamine *SFAS No. 52*.

tions have the U.S. dollar as their functional currency. Both companies have extensive operations in western Europe. From a commonsense perspective, it is illogical for these competing companies to be translating their European fixed assets so differently. This problem may be largely the result of the substantial latitude managements have in deciding between the two allowable translation methods—a problem in implementing the concept. Thus inconsistencies in applying this ill-conceived concept can exacerbate the inherent reporting problems resulting from the concept itself.

INABILITY TO MEANINGFULLY DEAL WITH THE SIMPLEST OF SITUATIONS

The weakness of the functional currency concept is evident in even the simplest of situations. For example, if a U.S. company purchased a parcel of land in a foreign city as a long-term investment, there would be no true functional currency because there would be no day-to-day operations. An arbitrary selection between the local currency and the U.S. dollar would have to be made. Another example would be the acquisition of land in a foreign country that has natural resources, with the extraction to take place in the future. Again, an arbitrary selection would be necessary. It should not be necessary to make a completely arbitrary decision between two alternatives that in reality are totally artificial in terms of determining the translated valuation of such assets.

VI HOW THE FUNCTIONAL CURRENCY CONCEPT CAME INTO EXISTENCE

SFAS No. 52 was issued in 1981 as a solution to the perceived deficiencies of *SFAS No. 8*, "Accounting for the Translation of Foreign Currency Transactions and Foreign Currency Financial Statements," which was issued in 1975. The main criticism of *SFAS No. 8* was that the reporting results did not reflect the underlying economic events. This problem was attributed to **using only a single unit of measure** (the U.S. dollar), which allegedly could not deal well with significantly **different economic facts.** (*SFAS No. 8* required the use of the **temporal method** to achieve a U.S. dollar unit of measure.)

Specifically, the complaints focused on (1) the reporting of exchange gains or losses when the events indicated that either no economic gain or loss had occurred or vice versa and (2) the requirement to report such exchange gains or losses currently in the income statement, which greatly increased the volatility of reported earnings. Prior to *SFAS No. 8*, exchange gains and losses could be deferred and then amortized to income, a practice followed by most firms.

These complaints were loud and many. In a nutshell, industry was furious with the reporting results of *SFAS No. 8*. In response, in 1978 the FASB formed the largest task force ever assembled to reexamine what had proved to be the most complex of all accounting issues. Clearly, the FASB was under enormous pressure to find a politically acceptable improvement to *SFAS No. 8*.

THE *SFAS No. 52* SOLUTION

SFAS No. 52 (1981) made three major changes that were intended to correct the perceived deficiencies of *SFAS No. 8*.

MAJOR CHANGE 1: ALLOWING MULTIPLE UNITS OF MEASURE The first major change was to allow multiple units of measure so that different economic facts would be accounted for differently. Accordingly, the **foreign currency unit of measure approach was sanctioned** (implemented using the current rate method).[7] The U.S. dollar unit of measure approach was retained (implemented using the temporal method).

MAJOR CHANGE 2: BYPASSING THE INCOME STATEMENT IN MOST CASES The second major change required exchange rate change effects under the current rate method to be (1) called *translation adjustments*[8] and (2) reported as **adjustments to be made directly to stockholders' equity**—bypassing the income statement. Largely because the current rate method has since become the most widely used translation method,[9] the earnings volatility problem that occurred under *SFAS No. 8* (as discussed in Chapter 18) has substantially declined. Thus the business community's acceptance of *SFAS No. 52* may rest largely on the reduced income volatility.

MAJOR CHANGE 3: ADDING THE FUNCTIONAL CURRENCY CONCEPT The third major change created the functional currency concept to serve as a framework for determining whether the foreign currency unit of measure (current rate method) or the U.S. dollar unit of measure (temporal method) is to be used for a particular foreign operation.

LINKAGE BETWEEN THE FUNCTIONAL CURRENCY CONCEPT AND USING MULTIPLE UNITS OF MEASURE

It is unknown whether (1) the FASB first decided to allow multiple units of measure as a solution to *SFAS No. 8* and then, as an afterthought, created the functional currency concept as a means to determine when the current rate method or the temporal method should be used for a given foreign operation or (2) the FASB first created the functional currency concept in the process of trying to identify different economic facts, which, in turn, led to the decision to use multiple units of measure. In any event, **the functional currency concept is not a necessary condition to allow the use of multiple units of measure;** the FASB could have implemented the use of multiple units of measure simply by allowing firms to **judgmentally select** either the current rate method or the temporal method.

WHAT IF JUDGMENTAL SELECTION HAD BEEN ALLOWED IN CHOOSING BETWEEN THE CURRENT RATE METHOD AND THE TEMPORAL METHOD?

If judgmental selection had been allowed, managements would have been free to decide between the two allowable translation methods based on any rationale they deemed appropriate, such as (1) the functional currency used in the foreign operation, (2) the assessment of the causes of exchange rate changes, (3) whether the exchange rate changes are expected to be temporary or permanent, (4) the method

---

[7]Prior to being sanctioned in *SFAS No. 52*, the current rate method had never been permitted in a U.S. generally accepted accounting principle, even though it was used widely in Europe.

[8]Prior to the issuance of *SFAS No. 52*, "exchange gains and losses" was the commonly used term (in *SFAS No. 8* and elsewhere) to describe the effect of exchange rate changes. *SFAS No. 52* drops this term and uses "translation adjustments" (current rate method) and "foreign currency transaction gain or loss from remeasurement" (temporal method).

[9]Thomas G. Evans and Timothy Doupnik, *Determining the Functional Currency under Statement 52* (Stamford: Financial Accounting Standards Board, 1986), pp. 34–35.

that avoids income statement volatility, (5) the method that most closely produces current values for nonmonetary assets, (6) whether local managers are rewarded based on foreign currency statement results or U.S. dollar results, or (7) some other rationale (sound or unsound) of which there could be many.

Considering such potential latitude in choosing between the two allowable translation methods, it appears worthwhile that the FASB should prohibit judgmental selection and instead identify the relevant different economic facts so that uniformity is achieved in using one translation method or the other.

The Importance of Identifying the Proper Economic Facts

When two accounting alternatives are allowed, the decision to identify the economic facts for deciding between the two alternatives must be done with extreme care—if it is even possible. For instance, it may be impossible to determine the economic facts that indicate when to use LIFO versus FIFO.[10] If this is possible for foreign currency exchange translation (*SFAS No. 52* presumes that it is) and the wrong economic facts are identified, the wrong alternative may be selected, producing nonmeaningful reporting results.

Compounding the problem is the fact that the two allowable alternative practices must be capable of achieving the stated objective. Otherwise, any attempt to decide when to use one method or the other based on economic facts is senseless. As an analogy, assume that the objective is to value a building at its fair market value, which may be above cost. If only the straight-line depreciation method and the double declining-balance method can be used, no amount of effort in trying to determine the economic facts as to when to use one depreciation method or the other will achieve the objective (although one method will always achieve a closer result than the other). In summary, achieving meaningful translated reporting results requires both (1) proper identification of economic facts and (2) the selection of appropriate related translation methods.

Unfortunately, the FASB improperly diagnosed the problem with *SFAS No. 8*. The problem with *SFAS No. 8* was not that it did *not* account differently for different economic facts, as the four members voting in favor of *SFAS No. 52* claimed, but that it was *not* based on addressing the causes of exchange rate changes. *SFAS No. 52* has the same major shortcoming.

VII Why the PPP Current-Value Approach Was Not Chosen

SFAS No. 52 does *not* allow the use of the PPP current-value approach (nor did *SFAS No. 8*). Two possible explanations for this exist.

The First Possible Explanation: Not Addressing the Proper Issue

One possible explanation is that the FASB did not adequately address the most important issue in foreign currency translation: causes of exchange rate changes. There appears to be substantial support for this explanation. There is no discussion of this issue in *SFAS No. 52* or in *SFAS No. 8*. In the 1974 discussion memorandum that preceded *SFAS No. 8*, a single page (in Appendix C) is devoted to some of the fundamental and technical causes of exchange rate changes. However, no

---

[10]In light of the IASC's recent proposal to eliminate LIFO, it would be interesting to see what economic facts the FASB could identify for choosing between LIFO and FIFO.

methodology based on causes of exchange rate changes that would fit into the relatively new (at that time) floating exchange rate system was developed.[11]

NO REVISED DISCUSSION MEMORANDUM The FASB did not prepare a revised discussion memorandum preceding the issuance of *SFAS No. 52*. A revised discussion memorandum might have been useful if it had explored the floating exchange rate system, which was then nearly 10 years old. Thus the process that led to *SFAS No. 52* (as with *SFAS No. 8*) focused on whether to use (1) a single unit of measure (the U.S. dollar or a foreign currency) or (2) multiple units of measure. Thus this process was a virtual "rounding up of the usual suspects."

THE FIRST EXPOSURE DRAFT The first exposure draft (1980) would have required using the current rate method almost exclusively—**even in highly inflationary economies.** This further supports the conclusion that causes of exchange rate changes were *not* adequately addressed because the translated financial statements would quickly become of limited value for such operations. As shown earlier, high inflation would drive down the direct exchange rate so severely that the foreign fixed assets quickly would be reduced to near zero balances in the translated balance sheets (the "disappearing plant" problem shown earlier).

THE SECOND EXPOSURE DRAFT Many companies operating in highly inflationary economies noted this problem, and in the revised exposure draft (1981), the FASB proposed that companies in such environments adjust their fixed assets for inflation prior to translation at the current exchange rate. This proposal (later withdrawn) was a clear attempt to address the causes of exchange rate changes. Even so, the consideration was narrowly focused on highly inflationary economies.

ERRONEOUS CONCLUSIONS REGARDING CONSTRUCTED EXCHANGE RATES Appendix D of the 1974 discussion memorandum contains a three-page discussion of **constructed exchange rates** based on PPP.[12] In the process that led to *SFAS No. 8*, the use of constructed exchange rates was disregarded as a viable alternative because (1) the basic approach (incorrectly) was assumed to be a possibility only under the former **fixed exchange rate system** and (2) the methodology that was offered did *not* allow for the consideration of **noninflationary** causes of exchange rate changes.

As shown later, however, the PPP current-value approach can be applied within the framework of the floating exchange rate system. Also, the effect of noninflationary causes of exchange rate changes can be isolated and adjusted for in the translation process. Later we show how to update fixed assets for a period of several years using the PPP current-value approach when noninflationary factors exist.

THE SECOND POSSIBLE EXPLANATION: TRYING TO STAY WITHIN THE BOUNDS OF HISTORICAL COST

Regardless of its ability to reflect the economics, the primary objection to using the PPP valuation technique is the perceived inappropriateness of mixing foreign fixed

---

[11]The fixed exchange rate system existed from 1944 to August 15, 1971, under the Bretton Woods agreement. An attempt to use a similar "pegged" exchange rate system began in December 1971; this pegged rate system lasted until February 1973. Thus the floating exchange rate system was in its infancy during the time leading to the issuance of *SFAS No. 8*.

[12]Dealing with disparities in price levels when translating foreign currency financial statements was recommended in *NAA Research Report 36*, "Management Accounting Problems in Foreign Operations" (New York: NAA, 1960). This report recommended the use of constructed exchange rates as an alternative to fixed exchange rates when a wide disparity in relative purchasing powers at the current exchange rate exists.

assets valued at current values with domestic fixed assets valued at historical costs—a departure from historical cost. Accordingly, to stay within the bounds of historical cost, the PPP current-value approach may have been dismissed out of hand. An influencing factor may have been the lack of reliable price indices for some countries that have highly inflationary economies. For these situations, however, the temporal method could have been mandated as a practical matter, with the PPP current-value approach being used for other countries.

As shown earlier, however, the temporal method results achieve inflationary reporting results as foreign fixed assets had been adjusted for inflation. Accordingly, its use automatically results in mixing different valuation bases; this was either not understood or merely not acknowledged by the FASB. Furthermore, the use of the current rate method results in adjusting foreign fixed assets for the effects of domestic inflation—a different kind of mixing result.

VIII EVALUATING AND MANAGING A FOREIGN OPERATION USING THE REPORTING RESULTS OF *SFAS NO. 52*

Besides not being designed to reflect the *true economic effect* of exchange rate changes, *SFAS No. 52* often does *not* achieve its stated objective of attaining *general compatibility.* Recall from Chapter 19 that the FASB did not define what it meant by *general compatibility.* For simplicity, let us assume that the term means reporting a positive effect when a positive effect should be reported and reporting a negative effect when a negative effect should be reported—a directional quality rather than a materiality quality. Illustration 20–8 shows various exchange rate change causes and outlines the situations in which *SFAS No. 52* achieves or does *not* achieve its general compatibility objective.

Accordingly, because the translated amounts produced under *SFAS No. 52* are not always reliable, great care must be taken in using such results and operationally

ILLUSTRATION 20–8	**Reporting Results Under Various Exchange Rate Change Causes**			
Assumed Sole Cause of Exchange Rate Change	Achieves "General Compatibility" with the Economic Effect of the Exchange Rate Change[a]		Reflects the "True Economic Effect" of the Exchange Rate Change	
	Current Rate Method	Temporal Method	Current Rate Method	Temporal Method
Foreign inflation	No	Yes	No	Yes
Domestic inflation	Yes	No	Yes	No
Noninflationary factors	Yes	No	Yes	No
Offsetting foreign and domestic inflation (no net change)	No[b]	No[b]	No	No
Domestic inflation > foreign inflation	Yes	No	No	No
Foreign inflation > domestic inflation	No	Yes	No	No

[a]This means that a favorable result is reported when a favorable result should be reported and an unfavorable result is reported when and unfavorable result should be reported. Thus the answer is based only on the direction of the reported effect—not its materiality relative to the true economic effect of the exchange rate change.

[b]In this situation, a zero effect is reported under *SFAS No. 52,* whereas economically the effect is favorable.

trying to manage foreign performance based on such results. For each individual foreign operation, the most that can be hoped for within the confines of *SFAS No. 52* is that companies use the method that best deals with exchange rate change causes. Except for highly inflationary economies, this occurs only by coincidence under *SFAS No. 52*. Thus it is necessary to prepare more meaningful translated amounts for nonmonetary assets in certain circumstances (we show how shortly). The importance of this cannot be overemphasized. We now discuss in more detail the specific situations in which *SFAS No. 52* does and does *not* produce reliable results.

In terms of the causes of exchange rate changes under the floating exchange rate system, foreign operations can be grouped into three categories:

1. **Highly inflationary economies.**

2. **Nonhighly inflationary economies** for which domestic and foreign inflation **are** consistently approximately the same.

3. **Nonhighly inflationary economies** for which domestic and foreign inflation **are not** consistently approximately the same.

These categories are useful in determining when *SFAS No. 52*'s results can be relied upon.

HIGHLY INFLATIONARY ECONOMIES

Perhaps the soundest part of *SFAS No. 52* is its requirement to use the *temporal method* when operating in a highly inflationary economy. This is because *foreign inflation* is by far the **dominant exchange rate change factor.** For many of these countries, the annual inflation rate is over 100%, with some countries exceeding 2000% annually. Accordingly, *SFAS No. 52* consistently produces sensible reporting results in these situations. However, such operations account for only a small percentage of foreign operations of U.S. companies.

NONHIGHLY INFLATIONARY ECONOMIES

For these economies, the **dominant exchange rate change factor involves noninflationary factors,** for which the noninflationary factors can cause as much as a 30–40% change in the exchange rate in any given year.

RESULTS UNDER THE CURRENT RATE METHOD   As shown earlier, only the current rate method can properly deal with the effects of *noninflationary* causes of exchange rate changes. Because the current method is the translation method that is used predominantly in these situations, sensible reporting results usually occur when the current rate method is used. However, when the *foreign inflation rate* is consistently slightly **higher** than our domestic inflation rate, the *disappearing plant problem* occurs under the current rate method (although it occurs very gradually in comparison to what would occur if the current rate method were used in a highly inflationary economy). This was shown earlier in Illustration 20–6 in which the cumulative inflation of 128% in Great Britain substantially exceeded the cumulative U.S. inflation of 76% for the 15-year-period 1981–1995. Thus the current rate method does *not* produce sensible reporting results in such situations. To properly evaluate and soundly manage operations facing this differential inflation rate problem, it is necessary to use the PPP current-value approach internally to obtain meaningful translated amounts for fixed assets.

RESULTS UNDER THE TEMPORAL METHOD   Using the temporal method in nonhighly inflationary economies (as do Hewlett-Packard and Du Pont, for instance) makes little sense because it produces the bizarre and volatile reporting results so heavily criticized in *SFAS No. 8*. Furthermore, when *domestic inflation* is consistently slightly **higher** than foreign inflation, the *disappearing plant problem* occurs here as well (although it also occurs very gradually). To properly evaluate and soundly manage operations facing this differential inflation rate problem, it is necessary to use the PPP current-value approach internally to obtain meaningful translated amounts for fixed assets.

We now show how to update fixed assets for several years using the PPP current-value approach.

IX   UPDATING FIXED ASSET VALUATIONS USING THE PPP CURRENT-VALUE APPROACH

The procedures for updating fixed asset valuations using PPP for several years are shown in Illustration 20–9, which continues the example used earlier in later years. This example also shows the way to deal with the effects of *noninflationary factors*. Note that even when noninflationary factors are present, adjustments are made to achieve largely current-value reporting results. Accordingly, the PPP current-value approach can be applied within the framework of the floating exchange rate system.

ILLUSTRATION 20–9	Procedures for Valuing Fixed Assets in U.S. Dollars Using Purchasing Power Parity Theory							
	Annual Inflation		**Effect of Noninflationary**			**Direct Exchange**		**U.S.**
Date	**Mexico**	**U.S.**	**Factors**	**Pesos**[a]		**Rate**		**Dollars**
12/31/X1				4,800,000	×	$.50	=	$2,400,000
		10%		4,800,000	×	.05	=	240,000
				4,800,000	×	$.55	=	$2,640,000
	25%			1,200,000	×	(.11)	=	n/a
12/31/X2				6,000,000	×	$.44	=	$2,640,000
			$(.02)	6,000,000	×	(.02)	=	(120,000)[b]
12/31/X3				6,000,000	×	$.42	=	$2,520,000
				6,000,000	×	.02	=	120,000[c]
				6,000,000	×	$.44	=	$2,640,000
	10%			600,000	×	(.04)	=	n/a
				6,600,000	×	$.40	=	$2,640,000
			$ .05	6,600,000	×	.05	=	330,000[d]
12/31/X4				6,600,000	×	$.45	=	$2,970,000

Valuation at 12/31/X4 under *SFAS No. 52*

Current rate method				4,800,000	×	$.45	=	$2,160,000
Temporal method				4,800,000	×	$.50	=	$2,400,000

[a]For simplicity, fixed asset additions were assumed to be made on January 3 of each year at amounts equal to depreciation expense for the year.

[b]This adjustment reflects a decrease in economic value that results from a $.02 decrease in the exchange rate attributable to noninflationary factors. If the fixed assets are sold on 12/31/X3 for cash of 6,000,000 Mex$ (the inflation-adjusted book value on this date), the realizable amount in U.S. dollars is $2,520,000.

[c]This is a reversal of the 19X3 noninflationary factor decrease of $.02 to get back to the $.44 exchange rate expected at 12/31/X3, under PPP. The $.44 is the constructed exchange rate that must be used for dealing with future inflation.

[d]This is the same type of adjustment as that made on 12/31/X3, only it goes in the opposite direction.

Note: Significant differences can occur between the expected rate under PPP and the actual year-end rate. For the British pound, the average of the absolute annual year-end differences between the expected rate under PPP and the actual rate for 1981–1995 was 22%; the cumulative difference at 12/31/95 was 17%. Similar differences were found for the French franc, the German mark, and the Japanese yen for these years.

END-OF-CHAPTER REVIEW

SUMMARY OF KEY POINTS

1. The only way to correctly determine the **true economic effect** of exchange rate changes is to use the **PPP current-value approach.**
2. Under the **PPP current-value approach,** nonmonetary assets that have increased in value because of foreign inflation are **adjusted for inflation** and then translated at the **current rate.**
3. The **current rate method** (as used in the foreign currency unit of measure approach) **cannot reflect the economic effect of exchange rate decreases caused by foreign inflation**—this method properly reflects only the effects of domestic inflation and noninflationary effects.
4. The **temporal method** (used under the U.S. dollar unit of measure approach) **cannot reflect the economic effect of exchange rate changes caused by domestic inflation or noninflationary effects**—this method properly reflects only the effects of foreign inflation.
5. The **characteristics** of the current rate method and temporal method are such that their reporting results do not always reflect either (a) the **true expected economic effects** of exchange rate changes or (b) **general compatibility** with the expected economic effects of an exchange rate change.
6. The **functional currency concept** came into existence because the problem with *SFAS No. 8* was improperly diagnosed. The concept is not valid.
7. To properly evaluate and soundly manage foreign operations, it may be necessary to use **fixed asset valuations based on the PPP current-value approach** in certain situations.

GLOSSARY OF NEW TERMS

Constructed exchange rates   Exchange rates calculated based on the effects of foreign and domestic inflation.

Nominal gain   An illusory gain when considering purchasing power.

Real gain   A gain that results in an increase in purchasing power.

SELF-STUDY QUESTIONS

(Answers are at the end of this chapter.)

1. The disappearing plant problem can occur
   a. Only under the current rate method.
   b. Only under the temporal method.
   c. Under both the current rate and temporal methods.
   d. Only under the PPP current-value approach.
2. The current rate method properly accounts for
   a. Only domestic inflation.
   b. Only foreign inflation.
   c. Only noninflationary factors.
   d. Both domestic inflation and noninflationary factors.
   e. Both foreign inflation and noninflationary factors.
3. The temporal method properly accounts for
   a. Only domestic inflation.
   b. Only foreign inflation.
   c. Only noninflationary factors.
   d. Both domestic inflation and noninflationary factors.
   e. Both foreign inflation and noninflationary factors.
4. An inflationary holding gain can occur when fixed assets are financed with
   a. Nonindexed debt.   c. Debt or equity.
   b. Equity.   d. Indexed debt.

5. On 1/1/X1, the direct exchange rate is $.24. Management forecasts that the United States will have 5% inflation during 19X1 and that the foreign country will have 20% inflation during 19X1. Under PPP theory, what is the expected exchange rate at 12/31/X1?
   a. $.20   c. $.274
   b. $.21   d. $.208

ASSIGNMENT MATERIAL

REVIEW QUESTIONS

1. What is an explanation of the current-value approach using purchasing power parity theory?
2. What are the strengths and weaknesses of the *current rate method*?
3. What are the strengths and weaknesses of the *temporal method*?
4. If the exchange rate has changed solely because of *foreign* inflation, what are the true economic effect and the effect reported under the *current rate method*?
5. What is the answer to Question 4 using the *temporal method*?
6. If the exchange rate has changed solely because of *domestic* inflation, what are the true economic effect and the effect reported under the *current rate method*?
7. What is the answer to Question 6 using the *temporal method*?
8. What are the two situations in which the disappearing plant problem occurs?
9. What is the relationship between conducting a foreign unit's transactions in a certain currency and the way to value the foreign unit's fixed assets?
10. In which situations might it be necessary to evaluate and manage a foreign unit using fixed asset valuations determined by the PPP current-value approach?

EXERCISES

E 20-1   *Foreign* **Inflation: Determining Reporting Results**   Following are several assumed asset composition and related financing situations of a foreign subsidiary:

Subsidiary's Assets		
Nature	**Amount**	**Type of Financing**
1. Monetary assets	100,000 LCUs	All equity
2. Monetary assets	100,000 LCUs	All debt (nonindexed)
3. Monetary assets	100,000 LCUs	All debt (indexed for inflation)
4. Nonmonetary assets	100,000 LCUs	All equity
5. Nonmonetary assets	100,000 LCUs	All debt (nonindexed)
6. Nonmonetary assets	100,000 LCUs	All debt (indexed for inflation)

Required   For each situation, determine the dollar effect on the subsidiary's stockholders' equity of a $.20 *decrease* in the direct exchange rate (from $1.00 to $.80) caused solely by *foreign* inflation of 25%. For *favorable* effects, indicate whether the effect is a *nominal* gain or a *real* gain. Use the following answer format:

	Reporting Result Under	
Correct Economic Reporting Result in Dollars	**Current Rate Method**	**Temporal Method**
1. _____	_____	_____
2. _____	_____	_____
3. _____	_____	_____
4. _____	_____	_____
5. _____	_____	_____
6. _____	_____	_____

E 20–2 *Domestic* **Inflation: Determining Reporting Results** Following are several assumed asset composition and related financing situations:

Subsidiary's Assets		
Nature	**Amount**	**Type of Financing**
1. Monetary assets	100,000 LCUs	All equity
2. Monetary assets	100,000 LCUs	All debt (nonindexed)
3. Monetary assets	100,000 LCUs	All debt (indexed for inflation)
4. Nonmonetary assets	100,000 LCUs	All equity
5. Nonmonetary assets	100,000 LCUs	All debt (nonindexed)
6. Nonmonetary assets	100,000 LCUs	All debt (indexed for inflation)

Required For each situation, determine the dollar effect on the subsidiary's stockholders' equity of a \$.25 *increase* in the direct exchange rate (from \$1.00 to \$1.25) caused solely by *domestic* inflation of 25%. For *favorable* effects, indicate whether the effect is a *nominal* gain or a *real* gain. Use the following answer format:

	Reporting Result Under	
Correct Economic Reporting Result in Dollars	**Current Rate Method**	**Temporal Method**
1. _____	_____	_____
2. _____	_____	_____
3. _____	_____	_____
4. _____	_____	_____
5. _____	_____	_____
6. _____	_____	_____

E 20–3 **Determining When Nominal and Real Gains Are Reported** Following are four possible scenarios for the reason that the exchange rate changed:

1. Foreign inflation—current rate method used.
2. Foreign inflation—temporal method used.
3. Domestic inflation—current rate method used.
4. Domestic inflation—temporal method used.

Assume that the foreign operations' fixed assets are financed with 50% **nonindexed** debt and 50% equity.

Required For each scenario, indicate the following:

1. Is a favorable or unfavorable result reported under *SFAS No. 52*?
2. If a favorable or unfavorable result is reported, is that result a *nominal gain*, a *real gain*, a *real loss*, or an *imaginary loss*?

E 20–4 **Translating Fixed Assets** Mirage Inc., created a foreign subsidiary on 1/1/X1 by making a \$920,000 cash investment in exchange for 1,000 shares of the subsidiary's common stock. The subsidiary used the money to buy land on the same day. During 19X1, the foreign country had 15% inflation, and the United States had 5% inflation. Direct exchange rate information follows:

January 1, 19X1	\$2.30
December 31, 19X1	\$2.05

Required Determine the translated amount at year-end for the fixed assets for (1) the current rate method, (2) the temporal method, and (3) the PPP current-value approach.

E 20–5 **Calculating the Projected Exchange Rate** On 1/1/X1, the direct exchange rate was 1 local currency unit equals \$.60. For 19X1, management expects 5% inflation for the United States and 20% inflation for the foreign country.

Required Calculate the expected exchange rate at 12/31/X1 under PPP theory.

PROBLEMS

P 20–1 **Evaluating Reporting Results: U.S. Dollar Is the Functional Currency**   Ten years ago, Golli Inc. created a 100%-owned subsidiary in Mexico and invested $1,000,000 in the subsidiary. The subsidiary purchased a farm in Mexico for $500,000 cash and designated the remaining $500,000 to be used for working capital. The U.S. dollar is the functional currency because employees and vendors are paid in dollars and the produce is sold in the United States for dollars. Other assumptions are as follows:

1. When the farm was purchased, 1 Mex$ equaled $.50.
2. During the past 10 years, the United States had cumulative inflation of 100% and Mexico had zero cumulative inflation. As a result, the direct exchange rate is now $1.00. For simplicity, we assume that no noninflationary factors exist that could affect the exchange rate.
3. All earnings are distributed to the parent monthly.
4. The typical balance sheet at year-end is as follows:

	Pesos
Cash	1,000,000
Land	1,000,000
	2,000,000
Common Stock	2,000,000

Required 1. Prepare a translated balance sheet under the temporal method at the end of the 10th year.
2. What are the long-term consequences of using the temporal method, assuming a continuation of each country's assumed 10-year inflation history?
3. If the farm were sold at the end of the 10th year for its book value in pesos, how many dollars would be available for distribution to the parent?

P 20–2 **Determining Translated Fixed Asset Valuations**   On 1/1/X1, Cola Inc. purchased a parcel of land in a foreign country at a cost of $1,440,000. Exchange rate and inflation information follows:

	Direct Exchange Rate
January 1, 19X1	$.60
December 31, 19X1	.65
December 31, 19X2	.57
December 31, 19X3	.52

	Inflation Rates	
	U.S.	Foreign
19X1	10%	—
19X2		20%
19X3	6	10

Required 1. Calculate the inflation-adjusted carrying value of the land in foreign currency at 12/31/X3.
2. Calculate the translated amount in dollars at 12/31/X3 under the current-value approach using PPP theory.
3. Calculate the translated amounts in dollars at 12/31/X3 under the current rate method and the temporal method.

P 20–3 **Evaluating Translated Financial Statement Results**   Assume that on 10/1/X1, Pana Inc. created a 100%-owned subsidiary, Sonic Inc., in England when the direct exchange rate was $1.10. Pana made a $1,100,000 cash equity investment at that time. For simplicity, assume that this direct exchange rate did *not* fluctuate through 12/31/X1. Sonic's first sales were on 1/1/X2. Sonic's balance sheets at the end of 19X1 and 19X2 and its 19X2 income statement are shown in Exhibit 1 to Problem 20–3. Additional assumptions follow:

1. No dividends were declared or paid in 19X2.

2. Fixed assets additions of 100,000 pounds (equal to the 19X2 depreciation expense) occurred on 1/3/X2.
3. England had 10% inflation for 19X2.
4. The United States had 2% inflation for 19X2.
5. The direct exchange rates were as follows:

December 31, 19X1	$1.10
Average rate for 19X2	1.06
December 31, 19X2	1.02

The properly prepared translated financial statements for the subsidiary for 19X2 in dollars under both functional currency possibilities (using the procedures prescribed in *SFAS No. 52*) are also shown in Exhibit 1 to Problem 20–3.

Exhibit 1 to Problem 20–3
Pound Financial Statements and *SFAS No. 52* Translated Financial Statements
(under both functional currency posssibilities)

	Pounds		Functional Currency	
			Pound (Current Rate)	U.S. Dollar (Temporal)
	12/31/X1	12/31/X2	12/31/X2	12/31/X2
Balance Sheets				
Monetary assets	500,000	900,000	$ 918,000[a]	$ 918,000[a]
Inventory	1,000,000	1,100,000	1,122,000[a]	1,133,000[b]
Fixed assets, net	3,000,000	3,000,000	3,060,000[a]	3,300,000[b]
	4,500,000	5,000,000	$5,100,000	$5,351,000
Liabilities	3,500,000	3,600,000	$3,672,000[a]	$3,672,000[a]
Common stock	1,000,000	1,000,000	1,100,000[b]	1,100,000[b]
Retained earnings	–0–	400,000	424,000	579,000
Cumulative translation adjustment	n/a	n/a	(96,000)[c]	n/a
	4,500,000	5,000,000	$5,100,000	$5,351,000
Income Statements (19X2)				
Revenues		5,150,000	$5,459,000[d]	$5,459,000[d]
Cost of sales		(4,150,000)	(4,399,000)[d]	(4,468,000)[b]
Depreciation		(100,000)	(106,000)[d]	(110,000)[b]
Expenses		(500,000)	(530,000)[d]	(530,000)[d]
Subtotal		400,000	$ 424,000	$ 351,000
Remeasurement gain		n/a	n/a	228,000[e]
Net Income		400,000	$ 424,000	$ 579,000
Parent's Reported Economic Gain				
Subsidiary's reported net income			$ 424,000	$ 579,000
Less—Translation adjustment			(96,000)	n/a
Parent's Reported Economic Gain			$ 328,000	$ 579,000

[a]The current (year-end) exchange rate of $1.02 was used.

[b]The historical rate was used ($1.10 for fixed assets, depreciation, and common stock; $1.077 for cost of sales; and $1.03 for inventory).

[c]Net asset position at 1/1/X2 of £1,000,000 × $.08 decrease in the direct exchange rate equals ..... $(80,000)
Net income of £400,000 × $.04 difference between the average rate and the year-end rate
($1.06 – $1.02) equals ..... (16,000)
Total Translation Adjustment ..... $(96,000)

[d]The average exchange rate of $1.06 was used (it is assumed that sales, expenses, and purchases occurred fairly evenly throughout the year).

[e]Average net monetary liability position of £2,850,000 × $.08 decrease in the exchange rate equals $228,000.

Required   **1.** Adjust Sonic's fixed assets at 12/31/X2 for 19X2 inflation and *then* translate the 12/31/X2 financial statements using the current rate method.

2. Analyze and explain the economic gain calculated in requirement 1.

3. Reconcile the economic gain calculated in requirement 1 to the economic gain shown for the current rate method under *SFAS No. 52*. In other words, explain what accounts for the difference.

4. Optional—Very Challenging: Repeat requirement 3 but for the temporal method under *SFAS No. 52*.

5. Assume that the United States had 0% inflation in 19X2—instead of 2%. How would this change your answer in requirement 2?

P 20–4   **Evaluating Translated Financial Statement Results**   Assume that on 10/30/X1 Pane Inc. created a 100%-owned subsidiary, Sill Inc., in England when the direct exchange rate was $1.10. Pane made a $1,100,000 cash equity investment at that time. For simplicity, assume that this direct exchange rate did *not* fluctuate through 12/31/X1. Sill's first sales were on 1/1/X2. Sill's balance sheets at the end of 19X1 and 19X2 and its 19X2 income statement are shown in Exhibit 1 to Problem 20–4. Additional assumptions follow:

1. No dividends were declared or paid in 19X2.

2. Fixed-asset additions of £100,000 (equal to 19X2 depreciation expense) occurred on 1/3/X2.

3. England had 10% inflation for 19X2.

4. The United States had 2% inflation for 19X2.

5. The direct exchange rates were as follows:

December 31, 19X1	$1.10
Average rate for 19X2	1.06
December 31, 19X2	1.01

The properly prepared translated financial statements for the subsidiary for 19X2 in dollars under both functional currency possibilities (using the procedures prescribed in *SFAS No. 52*) are also shown in Exhibit 1 to Problem 20–4.

Required   **1.** Adjust Sill's fixed assets at 12/31/X2 for 19X2 inflation and *then* translate the 12/31/X2 financial statements using the current rate method.

2. Analyze and explain the economic gain calculated in requirement 1.

3. Reconcile the economic gain calculated in requirement 1 to the economic gain shown under the current rate method set forth in *SFAS No. 52*. In other words, explain what accounts for the difference.

4. Optional—Very Challenging: Repeat requirement 3 but for the temporal method set forth in *SFAS No. 52*. For simplicity, assume that the noninflationary effect on the exchange rate change occurred on 12/31/X2.

✳ THINKING CRITICALLY ✳

✳ CASES ✳

C 20–1   **Evaluating the Current Rate Method: *Domestic* Inflation**   Assume that the *current rate method* is used. If *domestic* inflation is the sole cause of the exchange rate change, the direct exchange rate will *increase* and a foreign subsidiary's fixed assets will be valued at a higher amount in translation, resulting in an increase in reported equity. Assume fixed assets are financed with equity.

Required   **1.** Evaluate the logic of valuing foreign fixed assets higher as a result of *domestic* inflation and reporting a corresponding increase in equity under the *current rate method*.

2. Evaluate the reporting result described in requirement 1 with the manner of accounting for the parent's domestic fixed assets when domestic inflation occurs.

C 20–2   **Evaluating the Current Rate Method: *Foreign* Inflation**   Assume that the *current rate method* is used. If *foreign* inflation is the sole cause of the exchange rate change, the direct rate will decrease and a foreign subsidiary's fixed assets will be valued at a lower amount in translation, resulting in reporting a decrease in equity. Assume that fixed assets are financed with equity.

Exhibit 1 to Problem 20–4
Pound Financial Statements and *SFAS No. 52* Translated Financial Statements
(under both functional currency possibilities)

| | Pounds | | Functional Currency | |
	12/31/X1	12/31/X2	Pound (Current Rate) 12/31/X2	U.S. Dollar (Temporal) 12/31/X2
Balance Sheets				
Monetary assets	500,000	900,000	$ 909,000[a]	$ 909,000[a]
Inventory	1,000,000	1,100,000	1,111,000[a]	1,133,000[b]
Fixed assets, net	3,000,000	3,000,000	3,030,000[a]	3,300,000[b]
	4,500,000	5,000,000	$5,050,000	$5,342,000
Liabilities	3,500,000	3,600,000	$3,636,000[a]	$3,636,000[a]
Common stock	1,000,000	1,000,000	1,100,000[b]	1,100,000[b]
Retained earnings	–0–	400,000	424,000	606,000
Cumulative translation adjustment	n/a	n/a	(110,000)[c]	n/a
	4,500,000	5,000,000	$5,050,000	$5,342,000
Income Statements (19X2)				
Revenues		5,150,000	$5,459,000[d]	$5,459,000[d]
Cost of sales		(4,150,000)	(4,399,000)[d]	(4,468,000)[b]
Depreciation		(100,000)	(106,000)[d]	(110,000)[b]
Expenses		(500,000)	(530,000)[d]	(530,000)[d]
Subtotal		400,000	$ 424,000	$ 351,000
Remeasurement gain		n/a	n/a	255,000[e]
Net Income		400,000	$ 424,000	$ 606,000
Parent's Reported Economic Gain				
Subsidiary's reported net income			$ 424,000	$ 606,000
Less—Translation adjustment			(110,000)	n/a
Parent's Reported Economic Gain			$ 314,000	$ 606,000

[a]The current (year-end) exchange rate of $1.01 was used.

[b]The historical rate was used ($1.10 for fixed assets, depreciation, and common stock; $1.077 for cost of sales; and $1.03 for inventory).

[c]Net asset position at 1/1/X2 of £1,000,000 × $.09 decrease in the direct exchange rate equals . . . . $(90,000)
Net income of £400,000 × $.05 difference between the average rate and the year-end rate
($1.05 – $1.00) equals . . . . (20,000)
  Total Translation Adjustment . . . . $(110,000)

[d]The average exchange rate of $1.06 was used (it is assumed that sales, expenses, and purchases occurred fairly evenly throughout the year).

[e]Average net monetary liability position of £2,850,000 × $.08 decrease in the exchange rate = $228,000; year-end net monetary position of £2,700,000 × $.01 decrease due to noninflationary effect = $27,000; $228,000 + $27,000 = $255,000.

Required   **1.** Should an unfavorable economic event be reported in translation as a result of foreign inflation?
   2. Evaluate the reporting result described in requirement 1 with the manner of accounting for the parent's domestic fixed assets when domestic inflation occurs.

ANSWERS TO SELF-STUDY QUESTIONS

   1. c   **2.** d   **3.** b   **4.** a   **5.** b

INTERIM REPORTING

21

LEARNING OBJECTIVES

TO UNDERSTAND

- The importance of the quarterly reporting process.
- The conceptual issues peculiar to interim reporting.
- The requirements of the various professional pronouncements, particularly the latitude that exists in several areas.
- The role of certified public accountants in the interim reporting process.
- The high potential for arbitrarily shifting profits between interim periods, often called *managing the earnings*.

TOPIC OUTLINE

   I. Conceptual Issues
  II. Current Reporting Standards: The Requirements of *APBO No. 28*
 III. Involvement of Certified Public Accountants in Interim Reporting

Time has no divisions to mark its passage; there is never a thunderstorm or blare of trumpets to announce the beginning of a new month or year. Even when a new century begins, it is only we mortals who ring bells and fire off pistols.

THOMAS MANN

CHAPTER OVERVIEW

APPLICABILITY

Users of financial data need continuous, timely information about the performance of an enterprise to make investment or credit-related decisions. Although it has the benefit of an independent audit, an annual report is inadequate by itself in meeting these needs. Accordingly, the reporting of quarterly financial data has become a basic part of the corporate reporting process. Quarterly periods are sufficiently short to reveal business turning points, which may be obscured in annual reports. For companies that have significant seasonal variations in their operations, quarterly financial reports may give investors a better understanding of the nature of the business.

No official accounting pronouncement of the Financial Accounting Standards Board (FASB) or of any of its predecessor organizations requires quarterly financial reporting. The New York Stock Exchange and the American Stock Exchange, however, require their listed companies to furnish interim quarterly operating results to their stockholders. Companies not subject to these stock exchange listing requirements usually furnish such reports voluntarily. In fact, many privately owned companies furnish financial information to their stockholders as often as monthly.

REQUIREMENTS OF THE SECURITIES AND EXCHANGE COMMISSION Publicly owned companies that are subject to the continuous reporting requirements of the Securities and Exchange Commission (SEC) must file with it interim financial statements on Form 10-Q. This form must be filed for each of the first three quarters of each fiscal year within 45 days after the end of each such quarter.[1] Furthermore, the SEC requires specified quarterly financial data pertaining to operations for the latest two years to be presented in the annual report sent to stockholders and in the annual financial statements that must be filed with the SEC on Form 10-K.[2] (Forms 10-Q and 10-K are discussed in detail in Chapter 22.) Such disclosures inform investors of the pattern of corporate activities throughout the year.

THE IMPORTANCE OF FURNISHING ACCURATE QUARTERLY REPORTS

The ramifications of *not* issuing truthful quarterly reports can be costly and embarrassing. Frequently, shareholders sue companies (often successfully so) for allegedly issuing false and misleading quarterly reports. (See the "Case in Point.")

MANNER OF FURNISHING QUARTERLY INFORMATION

In general, publicly owned companies automatically mail hard copy quarterly reports to their shareholders. Some companies (Apple Computer Inc. and Intel Corporation, for instance) have discontinued this practice, however, to save money and to enable their shareholders to obtain the information more quickly by tapping into computerized information services (such as America Online, Prodigy, and the Internet). Shareholders who desire a hard copy must write for one each quarter.

---

[1]Companies whose securities are listed on a stock exchange and companies meeting certain size tests whose securities are traded in the over-the-counter market are subject to the continuous reporting requirements of the SEC.

[2]Proxy and Information Statement Rule 14a-3(b)(3): Form 10-K, Item 8 and Regulation S-K, Item 302 (a) (Washington, D.C.: Securities and Exchange Commission).

OFFICIAL ACCOUNTING PRONOUNCEMENTS

The first and still current pronouncement specifically dealing with interim reports is *APB Opinion No. 28*, "Interim Financial Reporting" issued in 1973. This pronouncement has been amended by FASB *Statement No. 3*, "Reporting Accounting Changes in Interim Financial Statements," and interpreted by FASB *Interpretation No. 18*, "Accounting for Income Taxes in Interim Periods." Also, slight amendments were made to the pronouncement by FASB *Statement No. 109*, "Accounting for Income Taxes." *APBO No. 28* is divided into the following two major parts:

1. Part I does *not* require interim financial reports to be issued but sets accounting standards to be used in preparing them.

2. Part II sets minimum disclosures to be included in interim financial reports issued by publicly owned companies.

Interim financial statements filed with the SEC on Form 10-Q must be prepared in accordance with the provisions of *APBO No. 28* and any amendments. Before discussing the detailed requirements of this pronouncement and the related amendment and interpretation, we discuss the conceptual issues associated with interim reporting.

I CONCEPTUAL ISSUES

The fundamental conceptual issue concerning *interim* financial statements (whether complete or condensed) is whether or not they should be prepared in accordance with the same accounting principles and practices used to prepare *annual* financial statements. This issue pertains almost solely to the recognition of costs and expenses because accountants generally agree that for interim reporting purposes, no sensible alternatives exist to the long-established practice of recognizing revenue when it is earned. The following examples of costs and expenses illustrate the problems associated with their treatment for interim reporting purposes:

1. **Major advertising expenditures.** Suppose that a major advertising campaign is launched early in the year. For interim reporting purposes, should the cost be deferred as an asset and amortized throughout the year, even though no portion of advertising costs can be deferred and reported as an asset at the end of the annual reporting period?

2. **Seasonal repairs.** Suppose that a company historically makes major annual repairs late in the year. Accruing liabilities for future repair costs (other than warranty-related costs) is *not* proper at the end of an annual reporting period. Is it proper, therefore, to spread total estimated repairs throughout the year by accruing such costs in interim periods prior to their incurrence?

3. **Depreciation and rent.** In most cases, depreciation and rent expenses are computed for annual reporting purposes based on the passage of time. Should a year's depreciation and rent expense associated with nonmanufacturing activities be assigned to interim periods for interim reporting purposes on this same basis, or should some other basis (such as sales) be used?

4. **Social security taxes.** The employer pays social security taxes only during a portion of the year for employees who have incomes higher than the maximum amount on which employer's social security taxes must be paid. Should the employer's social security taxes for these employees be charged to expense over the entire year, using deferrals?

5. **Year-end bonuses.** Should year-end bonuses be anticipated and accrued for interim reporting purposes?

There are three schools of thought concerning the approach used in interim reporting: the *discrete view,* the *integral view,* and the *combination discrete-integral view.*

THE DISCRETE VIEW

Under the **discrete view,** an interim period is a discrete, **self-contained segment of history,** as is an annual period; therefore, an interim period must stand on its own. From this perspective, the results of operations for each interim period are determined employing the same accounting principles and practices used to prepare annual reports. No special deferral or accrual practices are used for interim reporting purposes unless they can be used for annual reporting purposes. As a result, the components of assets, liabilities, revenues, expenses, and earnings are defined for interim reporting purposes the same way they are for annual reporting purposes. Under the discrete view, the function of accounting is to record transactions and events as they occur. Thus the period of time for which results of operations are determined should not influence how such transactions and events are reported.

This approach is unacceptable to most accountants because it does not allow accruals, deferrals, and estimations at interim dates for annual items.

THE INTEGRAL VIEW

Under the **integral view,** an interim period is an integral **part of an annual period.** From this perspective, the expected relationship between revenues and expenses for the annual period should be reflected in the interim periods so that reasonably constant operating profit margins can be reported throughout the year. Under this "pure form" of the integral view, annual expenses are estimated and assigned to interim periods in proportion to revenues recognized. Special deferral and accrual practices are used for interim reporting purposes that may not be used for annual reporting purposes. As a result, the components of assets, liabilities, revenues, expenses, and earnings are defined differently for interim reporting purposes than for annual reporting purposes. The costs of unforeseen events and certain other nonoperating items—such as settlement of litigation, discontinued operations, and asset disposals—are recorded in the interim period in which they occur.

This approach is also unacceptable to most accountants because of the artificial assumption that each dollar of revenue attracts the same rate of operating profit margin. Such an assumption is no more appropriate for periods within a year than it is over a company's entire life cycle.

THE COMBINATION DISCRETE-INTEGRAL VIEW

Between the extremes of the discrete view and the pure form of the integral view are various **combination discrete-integral approaches.** Under these approaches, the integral view is used for some costs and the discrete view is used for the remaining costs. All methods of deciding which costs are treated with integral techniques and which are treated under the discrete view are arbitrary. The remainder of this chapter discusses *APBO No. 28,* which prescribes a combination discrete-integral approach.

II   CURRENT REPORTING STANDARDS: THE REQUIREMENTS OF *APBO NO. 28*

REVENUES

> Revenue from products sold or services rendered should be recognized as earned during an interim period on the same basis as followed for the full year.[3]

This provision, which requires that each interim period be viewed as an annual period, produces the following results:

1. Companies that have *seasonal* revenues must report such revenues in the interim period in which they are earned as opposed to allocating them over the full year.

2. When receipts at an interim date precede the earning process, the revenues are deferred until the interim period in which the product is delivered or the service is rendered.

3. Companies using the percentage-of-completion method for long-term construction-type contracts must recognize revenues in interim periods using the same procedures that are used at the end of the annual period.

COSTS ASSOCIATED WITH REVENUES (PRODUCT COSTS)

> Those costs and expenses that are associated directly with or allocated to the products sold or to the services rendered for annual reporting purposes (including for example, material costs, wages and salaries and related fringe benefits, manufacturing overhead, and warranties) should be similarly treated for interim reporting purposes.... Companies should generally use the same inventory pricing methods and make provisions for write-downs to market at interim dates on the same basis as used at annual inventory dates....[4]

Although this provision appears to treat each interim period as though it were an annual period, the following four specified exceptions allow each interim period to be viewed as part of an annual period:

1. Estimated gross profit rates may be used to determine the cost of goods sold during interim periods. This procedure is merely a practical modification because complete physical inventories are usually not taken at interim dates.

2. Liquidation at an interim date of LIFO base-period inventories that the company expects to replace by the end of the annual period does *not* affect interim results; that is, cost of goods sold for the interim reporting period *should* include the expected cost of replacing the liquidated LIFO base.

3. Declines in market price at interim dates that will probably be recovered by the end of the annual period (temporary declines) "need not" be recognized at the interim date. If inventory losses from market declines are recognized at an interim date, any subsequent recoveries should be recognized as gains in those periods but only to the extent of previously recognized losses.

---

[3]*Opinions of the Accounting Principles Board, No. 28*, "Interim Financial Reporting" (New York: American Institute of Certified Public Accountants, 1973), par. 11.
[4]*APBO No. 28*, pars. 13–14.

4. For companies using standard cost accounting systems, purchase price variances or volume or capacity variances of costs that are inventoriable "should ordinarily" be deferred at interim reporting dates, providing that such variances are planned and expected to be absorbed by the end of the annual period.

With respect to the third exception, assume that a company has on hand at the beginning of the year 15,000 units of a particular inventory item, each of which is valued at its historical FIFO cost of $20. For simplicity, we assume that no additional purchases of this item are made during the year. Assumed sales for each quarter and replacement costs (assumed to be market) at the end of each quarter are as follows:

Quarter	Units Sold During Quarter	Replacement Cost at End of Quarter
1	1,000	$16 (not considered a temporary decline)
2	2,000	14 (considered a temporary decline)
3	3,000	17
4	4,000	21

Illustration 21–1 shows the adjustments that would be made to the Inventory account for this item during the year for market changes.

In reviewing Illustration 21–1, note that *no* market adjustment was made at the end of the second quarter. The market decline during that quarter was considered a *temporary decline* that was reasonably expected to disappear by the end of the annual period.

Note also that the use of the language "need not" in the pronouncement (rather than the mandatory term "should") permits companies to recognize temporary market declines in the interim period in which they occur if they choose to do so. Thus alternative treatments for temporary market declines are sanctioned.

With respect to the fourth exception dealing with companies using standard cost accounting systems, the use of "should ordinarily" in the pronouncement (rather

---

ILLUSTRATION 21–1	**Analysis of the Inventory Account for the Year**			
	Units			**Amount**
Balance, January 1	15,000	×	$20	= $300,000
First-quarter sales	(1,000)	×	20	= (20,000)
				$280,000
First-quarter market adjustment	14,000	×	(4) [$20 – $16]	= (56,000)
Balance, March 31	14,000	×	16	= $224,000
Second-quarter sales	(2,000)	×	16	= (32,000)
Balance, June 30	12,000	×	16	= $192,000
Third-quarter sales	(3,000)	×	16	= (48,000)
				$144,000
Third-quarter market adjustment	9,000	×	1 [$17 – $16]	= 9,000
Balance, September 30	9,000	×	17	= $153,000
Fourth-quarter sales	(4,000)	×	17	= (68,000)
				$ 85,000
Fourth-quarter market adjustment	5,000	×	3 [$20 – $17]	= 15,000
Balance, December 31	5,000	×	20	= $100,000

than an unqualified "should") permits alternative treatments for purchase price and volume variances that are planned and expected to be absorbed by year-end. In summary, *APBO No. 28* allows substantial leeway for dealing with certain aspects of inventory costing and manufacturing cost variances in interim reports.

ALL OTHER COSTS AND EXPENSES

The Accounting Principles Board (APB) developed the following standards for all costs and expenses other than product costs:

a. Costs and expenses other than product costs should be charged to interim periods as incurred, or be allocated among interim periods based on an estimate of time expired, benefit received or activity associated with the periods. Procedures adopted for assigning specific cost and expense items to an interim period should be consistent with the bases followed by the company in reporting results of operations at annual reporting dates. However when a specific cost or expense item charged to expense for annual reporting purposes benefits more than one interim period, the cost or expense item may be allocated to those interim periods.

b. Some costs and expenses incurred in an interim period, however, cannot be readily identified with the activities or benefits of other interim periods and should be charged to the interim period in which incurred. Disclosure should be made as to the nature and amount of such costs unless items of a comparable nature are included in both the current interim period and in the corresponding interim period of the preceding year.

c. Arbitrary assignment of the amount of such costs to an interim period should not be made.

d. Gains and losses that arise in any interim period similar to those that would not be deferred at year-end should not be deferred to later interim periods within the same fiscal year.[5]

These standards do the following:

1. They prohibit "normalizing" or "spreading" expenditures over a fiscal year on a revenue basis as under a pure integral approach.

2. They require that most expenditures be treated as though each interim period were an annual reporting period.

3. They permit certain expenditures that clearly benefit more than one interim period to be allocated among the interim periods benefited. Note that this treatment is **permissive, not mandatory.** Some examples of expenditures that may qualify for allocation among interim periods are major annual repairs, costs of periodic advertising campaigns, social security taxes, and charitable contributions.

In addition to the preceding standards, estimation procedures must be used at interim dates for items that historically have resulted in year-end adjustments (usually charges to income) or that can be reasonably approximated at interim dates. Examples are allowances for uncollectible accounts, inventory shrinkage, quantity discounts, and accruals for discretionary year-end bonuses. The purpose is to prevent the reporting of material fourth-quarter adjustments that cast a shadow on the reliability of prior interim reports and undermine the integrity of the interim reporting process.

SEASONAL REVENUES, COSTS, AND EXPENSES

Many businesses—such as amusement parks, professional sports teams, farming corporations, department stores, and toy manufacturers—receive all or a major

---

[5]*APBO No. 28*, par. 15.

portion of their revenues in one or two interim periods. As a result, these companies report wide fluctuations in revenues and profitability in their interim reports. Such companies must disclose the seasonal nature of their activities to avoid misleading inferences about revenues and profitability for the entire year. Furthermore, these companies should consider providing supplemental financial information for the 12-month periods ended at the interim date for the current and prior years.

INCOME TAX PROVISIONS

The basic provision for the computation of income taxes for interim periods is as follows:

> At the end of each interim period the company should make its best estimate of the effective tax rate expected to be applicable for the full fiscal year. The rate so determined should be used in providing for income taxes on a current year-to-date basis. The effective tax rate should reflect anticipated investment tax credits, foreign tax rates, percentage depletion, capital gains rates, and other available tax planning alternatives.[6]

The following points concerning this provision should be understood:

1. Each interim period is *not* a separate taxable period.
2. If the estimated tax rate for the year changes as the year proceeds, the effect of the change is included in the appropriate interim period as a **change in estimate.** No retroactive restatement of prior interim periods is made. The provision for income taxes for the third quarter of a company's fiscal year, for example, is the result of applying the expected tax rate to year-to-date earnings and subtracting the provisions reported for the first and second quarters.

The basic provision as stated here is supplemented for the tax effects of unusual or extraordinary items as follows:

> However, in arriving at this effective tax rate no effect should be included for the tax related to significant unusual or extraordinary items that will be separately reported or reported net of their related tax effect in reports for the interim period or for the fiscal year.[7]

Illustration 21–2 shows how to calculate the income tax expense for the first interim quarter and subsequent interim quarters using assumed estimates of the effective annual income tax rate at the end of each interim quarter.[8]

Illustration 21–3 then shows how to calculate the estimated effective annual income tax rate at the end of the first interim quarter.

MORE COMPLEX SITUATIONS   For simplicity, the facts assumed in Illustrations 21–2 and 21–3 did not involve any complexities. Computing interim period income taxes is more involved when one or more of the following elements is present:

1. Unusual items reported separately.
2. Extraordinary items reported net of related tax effects.

---

[6]*APBO No. 28*, par. 19.

[7]*APBO No. 28*, par. 19.

[8]*SFAS No. 109* has made estimating the annual effective tax rate more difficult (than under its predecessor) because it uses the *liability method* (instead of the "with-and-without" method). Under the *liability method*, companies must (1) project the deferred tax effects of expected year-end temporary differences and (2) take into consideration the tax effect of a valuation allowance expected to be necessary at the end of the year for deferred tax assets related to originating deductible temporary differences and carryforwards. For simplicity, we assume in illustration 21–3 that no originating temporary differences are expected at year-end.

ILLUSTRATION 21–2	Calculation of Interim Income Tax Expense		
	First Quarter	Second Quarter	Third Quarter
Estimated **annual** pretax earnings made at the end of each quarter	$600,000	$700,000	$750,000
Estimated **annual** income tax rates made at the end of each quarter	36%[a]	34%	37%
Actual **cumulative** pretax earnings at the end of each quarter	$100,000	$300,000	$650,000
Income tax rate to be used at the end of each quarter	36%	34%	37%
Cumulative income tax expense to be reported at the end of each quarter	$36,000	$102,000	$240,500
Income tax expense to be reported			
For the first quarter	$36,000		
For the second quarter ($102,000 − $36,000)		$66,000	
For the third quarter ($240,500 − $102,000)			$138,500
Actual **quarterly** pretax earnings	$100,000	$200,000	$350,000
Effective income tax rate for each quarter	36%	33%[b]	39.6%[c]

[a]The calculation of this **estimated annual** income tax rate is shown in Illustration 21–3.

[b]$66,000/$200,000 = 33%. Note that 34% of $200,000 is $68,000. The $2,000 difference between this amount and the $66,000 amount calculated here is the 2% decrease in the estimated annual income tax rate multiplied by the first-quarter pretax earnings of $100,000. Thus the $66,000 amount is net of this $2,000 downward correction (a "catch-up" adjustment) of the first quarter's previously reported income tax expense of $36,000. Accordingly, **no retroactive restatement** was made to the first quarter's previously reported income tax expense of $36,000.

[c]$138,500/$350,000 = 39.6%. Note that 37% of $350,000 is $129,500. The $9,000 difference between this amount and the $138,500 amount calculated above is the 3% increase in the estimated annual income tax rate multiplied by the first- and second-quarter combined pretax earnings of $300,000. Thus the $138,500 amount includes a $9,000 upward correction (a "catch-up" adjustment) of the first- and second-quarter previously reported combined income tax expense of $102,000. Accordingly, **no retroactive restatement** was made to the first- and second-quarter previously reported income tax expense of $36,000 and $66,000, respectively.

3. Losses in one or more interim periods.

4. Prior year operating loss carryforwards available.

5. Discontinued operations.

6. Changes in accounting principles.

7. Effects of new tax legislation.

FASB *Interpretation No. 18*, "Accounting for Income Taxes in Interim Periods," clarifies the application of *APBO No. 28* with respect to accounting for income taxes. This interpretation, containing more than 20 detailed examples spread over more than 40 pages, shows how to compute income taxes involving these more complex areas, which, except for a brief discussion of seasonal businesses, are beyond the scope of this chapter.

SEASONAL BUSINESSES HAVING LOSSES DURING EARLY INTERIM PERIODS
Frequently, a seasonal business has a loss during an early interim period, but management expects the *annual* results to be profitable. In these cases, the tax effects of

---

ILLUSTRATION 21–3 | **Calculation of Estimated Effective Annual Income Tax Rate at End of First Quarter**

1. Assumptions

Income before income taxes for 19X1:

First quarter **(actual)**	$100,000
Remainder of the year **(estimated)**	$500,000
Statutory federal income tax rate	35%
Statutory state income tax rate	5%
Estimated federal research and development tax credits for 19X1	$ 17,325
Estimated officers' life insurance premiums *not* deductible for state or federal income tax	$ 10,000

2. Calculation of Estimated Effective Annual Income Tax Rate

Calculation of estimated state income taxes for 19X1:

Estimated annual income before income taxes ($100,000 + $500,000)	$600,000
Add—Officers' life insurance premiums	10,000
Estimated State Taxable Income for 19X1	$610,000
Statutory state income tax rate	5%
Estimated State Income Taxes for 19X1	$ 30,500

Calculation of estimated federal income taxes for 19X1:

Estimated annual income before income taxes ($100,000 + $500,000)	$600,000
Add—Officers' life insurance premiums	10,000
Less—State income taxes	(30,500)
Estimated Federal Taxable Income for 19X1	$579,500
Statutory federal income tax rate	35%
	$202,825
Less—Research and development tax credits	(17,325)
Estimated Federal Income Taxes for 19X1	$185,500

Calculation of estimated effective annual income tax rate for 19X1:

Combined estimated federal and state income taxes for 19X1 ($185,500 + $30,500)	$216,000
Estimated income before income taxes for 19X1	$600,000
Estimated effective annual income tax rate ($216,000 ÷ 600,000)	36%

Note: Similar calculations would be made at the end of the second and third quarters.

---

losses arising in the early portion of a fiscal year are recognized only when the **tax benefits** are expected to be realized. A historical pattern of losses in early interim periods offset by profits in later interim periods normally constitutes sufficient evidence that realization is more likely than not (the *SFAS No. 109* criterion for reporting a deferred tax asset), unless other facts indicate that the historical pattern will *not* repeat.

Illustration 21–4 shows the income tax expense or benefit reported in each interim reporting period for an enterprise engaged in a seasonal business that shows a loss for the first interim reporting period. We assume that the enterprise anticipates being profitable for the entire year and that this expectation proves to be correct. For simplicity, we also assume that (1) the estimated effective annual tax rate is 40%, (2) this rate does not change during the year, and (3) no unusual or extraordinary items are present.

| ILLUSTRATION 21–4 | Income Tax Expense or Benefit to Be Reported for a Seasonal Business (in thousands of dollars) |

	Reporting Quarter				Fiscal Year
	1	2	3	4	
Income (loss) before income taxes	$(200)	$100	$150	$950	$1,000
Income tax benefit (expense) @ 40% .	80	(40)	(60)	(380)	(400)
Net Income (loss)	$(120)	$ 60	$ 90	$570	$ 600

DISPOSAL OF A SEGMENT OF A BUSINESS AND EXTRAORDINARY, UNUSUAL, INFREQUENTLY OCCURRING, AND CONTINGENT ITEMS

The effects of the disposal of a business segment and extraordinary, unusual, and infrequently occurring items are reported in the period in which they occur. If the effects are material in relation to the operating results of the interim period, they are reported separately.

The basic thrust of *APBO No. 28* concerning contingencies is a discrete approach; that is, disclosures are made in interim reports in the same manner that they are made in annual reports, except that the significance of a contingency should be judged in relation to annual financial statements. FASB *Statement No. 5*, "Accounting for Contingencies," was issued after *APBO No. 28*. The application of FASB *Statement No. 5* provisions to interim periods as though each interim period were an annual period is consistent with the basic thrust of *APBO No. 28* in this area. Thus the **probable** and **reasonably estimable** criteria of FASB *Statement No. 5* are used to determine the interim period in which a loss contingency should be accrued.

ACCOUNTING CHANGES

Interim financial reports must disclose any **changes in accounting principles or practices.** The basic provisions of APB *Opinion No. 20*, "Accounting Changes," apply to interim reporting. Changes in accounting principles that require **retroactive restatement** of previously issued annual financial statements result in the similar restatement of previously issued interim financial statements when such accounting changes are made in other than the first interim reporting period. (*APBO No. 20* specifically sets forth the few changes that can be accorded retroactive restatement, such as a change in the method of accounting for long-term construction contracts.)

The **cumulative effect** of a change in accounting principles is reported as an adjustment in the current year income statement as prescribed by *SFAS 3*, an amendment to *APBO No. 28*. If such a change is made during the *first* interim reporting period, the cumulative effect as of the beginning of that year is included in the net income of that first interim reporting period. If such a change is made in *other than the first* interim reporting period, however, the prior interim reporting periods of the current year are restated by applying the new accounting principles, and the cumulative effect as of the beginning of that year is included in the restated net income of the first interim reporting period of the current year. The end result, therefore, is as though all such changes had been made in the first interim reporting period.

Changes in accounting estimates must be accounted for in the interim period in which the change is made on a *prospective basis*, regardless of the interim period of the change. Thus restatement of previously reported interim information is prohibited for such changes.

Previously issued *interim* reports may be restated for **corrections of an error** just as previously issued *annual* financial statements may be restated for such items.

DISCLOSURES OF SUMMARIZED INTERIM FINANCIAL DATA BY PUBLICLY OWNED COMPANIES

The following minimum disclosures must be furnished to stockholders in interim reports (including fourth-quarter reports):

a. Sales or gross revenues, provision for income taxes, extraordinary items (including related income tax effects), cumulative effect of a change in accounting principles or practices, and net income.
b. Primary and fully diluted earnings per share data for each period presented. . . .
c. Seasonal revenue, costs or expenses.
d. Significant changes in estimates or provisions for income taxes.
e. Disposal of a segment of a business and extraordinary unusual or infrequently occurring items.
f. Contingent items.
g. Changes in accounting principles or estimates.
h. Significant changes in financial position.[9]

Most publicly owned companies exceed these requirements by furnishing either a condensed or a complete income statement. These income statements (condensed or complete) are usually presented in comparative form. For reports other than the first quarter, quarterly data and **year-to-date** amounts are usually presented. Many companies also furnish complete or condensed balance sheets (usually in comparative form) in their interim reports. In addition to financial data, these interim reports usually contain a narrative discussion of interim period highlights.

Many publicly traded companies do *not* issue a separate report covering fourth-quarter results. Such companies often disclose fourth-quarter results (as outlined in paragraph 30 of *APBO No. 28*) in the annual report. If the results of the fourth quarter are *not* furnished in a separate report or in the annual report, a company must disclose the following items recognized in the fourth quarter in a note to the annual financial statements:

1. Disposals of segments.

2. Extraordinary items.

3. Unusual or infrequently occurring items.

4. The aggregate effect of year-end adjustments that are material to the results of the fourth quarter.

In addition, the effects of accounting changes made during the fourth quarter are disclosed in a note to the annual financial statements in the absence of a separate fourth-quarter report or other disclosure in the annual report.

A COMPARISON OF THE REQUIREMENTS OF *APBO No. 28* AND OF SEC FORM 10-Q

The disclosure requirements of SEC Form 10-Q are more extensive than those of *APBO No. 28*. Form 10-Q requires that the following condensed financial statements be included in interim reports filed with the SEC:

1. **Balance sheets.** Balance sheets are presented for the end of the most recent fiscal quarter and for the end of the preceding fiscal year.

---

[9]*APBO No. 28*, par. 30.

2. **Income statements.** Income statements are presented for the most recent fiscal quarter, for the period between the end of the last fiscal year and the end of the most recent fiscal quarter (year-to-date amounts in second- and third-quarter reports), and for corresponding periods of the preceding fiscal year.

3. **Statements of cash flows.** Statements of cash flows are presented for the period between the end of the last fiscal year and the end of the most recent fiscal quarter and for the corresponding period of the preceding fiscal year.

As stated earlier, financial statements included in Form 10-Q reports are prepared in accordance with *APBO No. 28* provisions and any amendments to the opinion that may be adopted by the FASB. Disclosures must be complete enough so that none of the information presented is misleading. Furthermore, management must provide an analysis of the quarterly results of operations. Information required in Form 10-Q may be omitted from that form if such information is contained in a quarterly report to the stockholders and a copy of that quarterly report is filed with Form 10-Q.

III   INVOLVEMENT OF CERTIFIED PUBLIC ACCOUNTANTS IN INTERIM REPORTING

Audited interim financial reports are virtually nonexistent. For many years prior to 1975, common deficiencies in unaudited reports included a preponderance of unusual charges and, less often, credits to income late in the year and corrections to previously issued interim financial data. In recognition of such significant, continuing deficiencies and abuses in the interim reporting process, the SEC took steps in 1975 to improve the quality of interim financial reports by effectively forcing the accounting profession to accept auditor involvement in the interim reporting process. At that time, most members of the profession did not want to be associated with interim financial reports on anything less than a complete audit basis, fearing potential lawsuits in the event that interim financial report data proved to be false or misleading. The SEC obtained auditor involvement in quite an interesting way. First, it passed a rule requiring that quarterly financial data appear in a note to the annual financial statements included in the annual 10-K report filed with the SEC. This requirement caused auditors to be "associated" with these data by virtue of reporting on the financial statements in which the note was included. This occurred even though the SEC allowed the note to be labeled "unaudited" and the auditors had not audited the data in the note.

Second, the SEC passed a rule informing auditors that the SEC presumed that auditors applied "appropriate professional standards and procedures with respect to the data in the note." Thus auditors had to perform some form of "review" of the data included in this note. Furthermore, the SEC indicated that unless the American Institute of Certified Public Accountants (AICPA) developed professional standards and procedures in connection with reviewing the data in this note, the SEC would do so. The AICPA chose to develop them and issued review standards in 1979. The current review standards (several revisions have been made since 1979) are contained in *Statement on Auditing Standards No. 71,* "Interim Financial Information."[10] Because this pronouncement is the subject of an auditing course, it is not discussed in detail here. Briefly, auditors must perform certain procedures that are **substantially less than an audit.**

---

[10]*Statement on Auditing Standards No. 71,* "Interim Financial Information" (New York: American Institute of Certified Public Accountants, 1992).

Auditors are not specifically required as part of the interim reporting process to perform these review procedures during the year. Thus the review can be made at year-end. The SEC took these steps, however, in the belief that companies would have the reviews made as part of the interim reporting process for the following reasons:

1. The likelihood of having to revise quarterly data when the annual statements are published should decrease.
2. The likelihood of discovering needed adjustments on a timely basis should increase, so that unusual charges and credits are less frequent in the last month of the year.
3. The added expertise of professional accountants increases the quality of the interim reporting process.[11]

To encourage auditors to be more involved in the interim reporting process, the SEC in 1979 adopted a rule that exempts interim financial reports from a federal securities law provision automatically making certified public accountants liable for a client's false and misleading financial statements unless such accountants can prove that they were diligent. (Certified public accountants are not exempted, however, from the section of the federal securities law that deals with fraud.) Even before the adoption of this rule, the opposition of auditors to involvement in the interim reporting process had, for the most part, dissipated. Most auditors of publicly held companies now encourage their clients to have the review performed as part of the interim reporting process rather than at year-end.

In 1980, the SEC revised its reporting requirements so that (1) quarterly financial data may be presented outside of the notes to the annual financial statements and (2) auditors must follow the AICPA's review standards and procedures regardless of the placement of the quarterly financial data.[12]

END-OF-CHAPTER REVIEW

SUMMARY OF KEY POINTS

1. Interim reporting raises the fundamental issue of whether interim financial statements should be prepared using the same accounting principles and practices used in preparing annual financial statements.
2. Under the **discrete view,** each interim period must stand on its own without regard to the fact that it is part of an annual reporting period.
3. Under the **integral view,** the fact that an interim period is part of an annual reporting period is a basis for assigning the total estimated annual costs and expenses to interim periods based on revenues to report reasonably constant operating margins.
4. *APBO No. 28* adopted a **combination discrete-integral approach.**
5. **Revenues, extraordinary items,** gains or losses from the disposal of a segment, unusual items, and infrequently occurring items are treated under the discrete view.
6. For **costs associated with revenue** (product costs), the *discrete view* is used—four specified exceptions to this rule produce integral results.
7. The *discrete view* must be used for **all other costs and expenses** unless an item meets specified standards for *integral* treatment. If the standards are met, the company may use *integral* techniques.
8. For **income taxes,** the *integral view* is prescribed.

[11]*Accounting Series Release No. 177* (Washington, D.C.: Securities and Exchange Commission, 1975).

[12]*Regulation S-K,* Item 302(a)(1) and (4) (Washington, D.C.: Securities and Exchange Commission, 1980).

GLOSSARY OF NEW TERMS

Discrete view   A manner of measuring interim period earnings by viewing each interim period as an independent period that must stand on its own.

Integral view   A manner of measuring interim period earnings by viewing each interim period as an integral part of an annual reporting period. Under this view, each interim period should bear part of the annual expenses that are incurred in generating revenues for the entire year.

Combination discrete-integral view   A manner of measuring interim period earnings by accepting the integral view for certain costs and expenses and using the discrete view for all other costs and expenses.

SELF-STUDY QUESTIONS

(Answers are at the end of this chapter.)

1. Under the *discrete view*
   a. An interim period *cannot* stand on its own.
   b. The period of time for which results of operations are being determined influences how such transactions and events are reported.
   c. Accounting procedures that result in reasonably constant operating profit margins throughout the year are used.
   d. Events and transactions are recorded as they occur.
2. Under *APBO No. 28*
   a. Revenues may be artificially smoothed over the four quarters, providing that full disclosure is made of the procedures used.
   b. *Unplanned* capacity variances arising at an interim date should *not* be deferred at interim reporting dates.
   c. Certain expenditures (other than product costs) that clearly benefit more than one interim period are required to be allocated among interim periods benefited.
   d. Extraordinary items must be prorated over the current and remaining interim periods.
3. Under *APBO No. 28*
   a. *Temporary* declines in inventory market prices are to be recognized at interim reporting dates.
   b. Inventory price declines at interim dates that are considered *not* to be *temporary* need not be recognized at the interim date.
   c. Physical inventories must be taken at the end of each interim quarter.
   d. *Temporary* and *nontemporary* declines in inventory market prices are to be recognized at interim reporting dates.
   e. None of the above.
4. Under *APBO No. 28*, if annual major repairs made in the first quarter and paid for in the second quarter clearly benefit the entire year, they
   a. Must be expensed in the first quarter.
   b. Must be expensed in the second quarter.
   c. Must be expensed in each of the four quarters using allocation procedures.
   d. May be expensed in the first quarter or allocated over the four quarters.

ASSIGNMENT MATERIAL

REVIEW QUESTIONS

1. Do the principles and practices that apply to interim reporting apply only to publicly owned companies?
2. What is the fundamental issue pertaining to interim reporting?
3. Are the issues associated with interim reporting primarily related to revenues or to costs and expenses?
4. What are the three schools of thought that exist concerning the approach to interim reporting?
5. Under which approach must each interim period stand on its own?

6. Does *APBO No. 28* impose *integral* techniques for costs and expenses not associated with revenue? Explain.

7. What factors could cause the estimated annual income tax rate to change from quarter to quarter?

8. If fourth-quarter results are not furnished in a separate report or in the annual report, which items recognized in the fourth quarter must be disclosed in a note to the annual financial statements?

EXERCISES

E 21-1   **Inventory Loss from Market Decline**   A $420,000 inventory loss from market declines occurred in April 19X6. At that time, the market decline was not considered temporary. Of this loss, $100,000 was recovered in the fourth quarter ended 12/31/X6.

Required   How should this loss be reflected in the quarterly income statements for 19X6?   (AICPA adapted)

E 21-2   **Annual Major Repairs and Property Taxes**   On 1/1/X6, Luca Company paid property taxes of $40,000 on its plant for calendar year 19X6. In March 19X6, Luca made its annual-type major repairs to its machinery amounting to $120,000. These repairs benefit the entire calendar-year operations.

Required   How should these expenditures be reflected in the quarterly income statements for 19X6?   (AICPA adapted)

E 21-3   **Year-End Bonuses**   In January 19X7, Gelt Company estimated that its 19X7 year-end bonuses to executives would be $240,000. The actual amount paid for 19X6 year-end bonuses was $224,000. The 19X7 estimate is subject to year-end adjustment.

Required   What amount of expense, if any, should be reflected in the quarterly income statement for the three months ended 3/31/X7?   (AICPA adapted)

E 21-4   **Percentage-of-Completion Method on Long-Term Contracts**   For annual reporting purposes, Candu Company appropriately accounts for revenues from long-term construction contracts under the percentage-of-completion method. In December 19X5, for budgeting purposes, Candu estimated that these revenues would be $1,600,000 for 19X6. As a result of favorable business conditions in October 19X6, Candu recognized revenues of $2,000,000 for the year ended 12/31/X6. If the percentage-of-completion method had been used for the quarterly income statements on the same basis as followed for the year-end income statement, revenues would have been as follows:

Three months ended 3/31/X6	$ 300,000
Three months ended 6/30/X6	400,000
Three months ended 9/30/X6	200,000
Three months ended 12/31/X6	1,100,000
Total	$2,000,000

Required   What amount of revenues from long-term construction contracts should be reflected in the quarterly income statement for the three months ended 12/31/X6?   (AICPA adapted)

E 21-5   **Severance Pay**   During the second quarter of its current reporting year, Shears Company announced that it would trim its workforce by 7% as a result of below-normal demand for its products. Employees being laid off are given three to six weeks' severance pay, depending on their length of employment.

Required   Assuming that the severance pay was paid in the second quarter, how should it be accounted for in the quarterly reports for the current year?

PROBLEMS

P 21-1   **Incentive Compensation Plan for Sales Personnel**   Pavlov Inc. uses an incentive system for its sales personnel whereby each salesperson receives

1. A base salary of $1,000 per month.
2. A commission of 2% of the individual salesperson's sales.

3. A bonus of 10% on the individual salesperson's annual sales in excess of $1,200,000. (This bonus is paid in the first quarter of the year following the year on which the bonus is based.)

The company's sales do *not* occur in a seasonal pattern. Sales generated by certain sales personnel for the first and second quarters of 19X3 are as follows:

	First Quarter	Second Quarter	Cumulative
Buffet	$ 400,000	$ 370,000	$ 770,000
Cook	360,000	210,000	570,000
Dillon	260,000	380,000	640,000
Holly	280,000	290,000	570,000
Total	$1,300,000	$1,250,000	$2,550,000

Payments made during the first quarter of 19X3 for bonuses based on total 19X2 sales are as follows:

Buffet	$24,000
Holly	3,000

Required   Determine the compensation expense to be reported for the *first* and *second* quarters of 19X3 using two different approaches for the bonuses.

P 21–2   **Income Taxes: Calculating Interim Expense**   Reviso Inc. had the following pretax income for the first two reporting quarters of 19X2:

First quarter	$500,000
Second quarter	700,000

Reviso's actual annual effective income tax rate for 19X1 was 40%. For budgeting purposes, Reviso estimated that the effective annual income tax rate for 19X2 would also be 40%. Near the end of the second quarter, Reviso changed its estimated effective annual income tax rate for 19X2 to 35%. Reviso issues its quarterly reports within 45 days of the end of the quarter.

Required   Determine the income tax expense to be reported for the *first* and *second* quarters of 19X2.

P 21–3   **Income Taxes: Calculating Estimated Annual Rate and Interim Expense**   Antax has developed the following data for 19X2 at the end of its first reporting quarter:

Income before income taxes:	
First quarter (actual)	$200,000
Remainder of year (estimated)	$800,000
Statutory federal income tax rate	40%
Statutory state income tax rate	10%
Estimated federal research and development tax credits	$ 44,600
Officers' life insurance premiums *not* deductible for state or federal purposes	10,000
Excess of accelerated depreciation over straight-line depreciation for state and federal purposes	50,000

Required   1. Calculate the estimated effective *annual* income tax rate at the end of the *first* quarter.
2. Calculate the income tax provision for the *first* quarter.
3. Calculate the estimated effective *annual* income tax rate at the end of the *second* quarter assuming that
   a. Income before income taxes for the second quarter was $400,000.
   b. The estimated income before income taxes for the *third* and *fourth* quarters is $500,000 in total.
4. Calculate the income tax provision for the *second* quarter.

✳ THINKING CRITICALLY ✳

✳ CASES ✳

C 21–1 **Thinking of Ways to "Manage Earnings"** The president of Manipulex has instructed you, the controller, to report quarterly profits within 2% of budgeted profits.

Required 1. See how many ways you can think of to shift profits between quarters or arbitrarily report profits.
  2. If you were the company's outside auditor performing a quarterly review and you became aware of such practices, would you require disclosure of these practices in the quarterly financial report?

C 21–2 **Treatment of Annual Furnace Relining Costs** Harthco was formed in 19X1 to produce steel. Production commenced in October 19X2, and sales began in November 19X2. The company expects to close down its furnaces each September to reline them, which takes about a month. Members of the controller's staff disagree on how the costs of relining the furnaces should be reported. The following approaches are advocated:

  1. Expense the costs in the period in which they are incurred.
  2. Expense the costs over the company's calendar reporting year.
  3. Expense the costs over a period from September to August of the following year.

Required Evaluate the theoretical soundness of these proposed treatments and comment on their conformity with the provisions of *APBO No. 28*.

C 21–3 **Treatment of Accounting and Legal Fees** Callex reports on a calendar year-end basis. The accounting firm that performs the annual year-end audit renders approximately one-third of its audit-related services in the fourth quarter of each calendar year and approximately two-thirds of its audit-related services in the first quarter of each calendar year. The accounting firm renders an interim billing in the fourth quarter for services performed during that quarter.

The legal firm that assists the company in preparing its annual 10-K report, which must be filed with the SEC within 90 days after year-end, renders all of its 10-K related services in the first calendar quarter of each year. The legal firm renders its billing sometime in the second quarter.

Required Determine how these accounting and legal fees should be reported in the quarterly financial statements.

C 21–4 **Material Year-End Physical Inventory Adjustment** Pilferex uses a *periodic* inventory system and takes an annual physical inventory at year-end. Historically, the company's adjustments from book value to physical inventory have been insignificant. Current year sales and production increased substantially over the prior year, and a material book to physical inventory adjustment (a shortage) occurred. Management has not determined the cause of the physical inventory adjustment.

The market price of the company's common stock rose during the year due to the favorable sales and earnings pattern reported for the first three quarters. The market price declined sharply when the company announced that the annual earnings would be below estimated amounts as a result of the large physical inventory adjustment.

Required 1. How should the physical inventory adjustment be reported?
  2. What are the possible consequences of large *fourth-quarter* adjustments?

C 21–5 **Revising Previously Issued Quarterly Results** In November 1982, Tandem Computers, Inc. announced results for its fourth quarter (ended 9/30/82) prior to the completion of its annual audit. (The company assumed that its outside auditors would not have any proposed adjustments.) In December 1982, after the auditors had completed their work, the company announced a *restatement* of third- and fourth-quarter results because (1) recorded sales included shipments that had occurred after the end of these quarters and (2) previously recorded sales did not have sufficient documentation. Reported results (in millions of dollars) follow:

	Initially Reported	Restated	Decrease Amount	Decrease Percent
Sales	$336.9	$312.1	$(23.8)	(7)
Net income	37.3	29.9	(7.4)	(20)

After this announcement, the price of the company's common stock immediately fell 6 points, a 20% decline.

Required 1. What are the ramifications of restating results for these quarters?
2. If the auditors reviewed quarterly information at the end of each quarter, why did they *not* discover this problem at the end of the third quarter?

C 21–6 **Treatment of Unresolved Item**   During its second quarter, Newtex entered into a new type of transaction, which will result in the immediate reporting of substantial income. The company believes that its proposed accounting treatment is in accordance with GAAP. Its outside auditors have been noncommittal, however, as to whether the company's interpretation of the applicable FASB accounting standard is proper. At the end of the *second* quarter, the auditors indicate that they need more time to study the issue and do research. (Assume that the auditors review quarterly results at year-end.)

Required 1. Should the company record the transaction and report the income in the second quarter? State the reasons for your position.
2. What steps might the outside auditors take in doing research?
3. What other steps should the auditors consider?

✳ FINANCIAL ANALYSIS PROBLEM ✳

FAP 21–1 **Identifying Weaknesses in an Interim Report and Evaluating Treatment of Selected Items**   Budgco, which is listed on the American Stock Exchange, budgeted activities for 19X5 as follows:

	Amount	Units
Sales, net	$6,000,000	1,000,000
Cost of sales	(3,600,000)	1,000,000
Gross Margin	$2,400,000	
Selling, general, and administrative expenses	(1,400,000)	
Operating Income	$1,000,000	
Nonoperating revenue and expenses	–0–	
Income before Income Taxes	$1,000,000	
Estimated income taxes (current and deferred)	(400,000)	
Net Income	$ 600,000	
Earnings per share of common stock	$6.00	

Budgco has operated profitably for many years and has experienced a seasonal pattern of sales volume and production similar to the ones forecasted for 19X5. Sales volume is expected to follow a quarterly pattern of 10%, 20%, 35%, and 35%, respectively, because of the seasonality of the industry. Because of production and storage capacity limitations, production is expected to follow a pattern of 20%, 25%, 30%, and 25% per quarter, respectively.

At the conclusion of the *first* quarter of 19X5, the controller prepared and issued the following interim report for public release:

	Amount	Units
Sales, net	$ 600,000	100,000
Cost of sales	(360,000)	100,000
Gross Margin	$ 240,000	
Selling, general, and administrative expenses	(260,000)	
Operating Loss	$ (20,000)	
Loss from warehouse fire	(140,000)	
Loss before Income Taxes	$ (160,000)	
Estimated income taxes	–0–	
Net Loss	$ (160,000)	
Loss per share of common stock	$(1.60)	

The following additional information is available for the *first* quarter just completed but was not included in the information released to the public:

1. Budgco uses a *standard costing system,* in which standards are set annually at currently attainable levels. At the end of the first quarter, a $50,000 underapplied fixed factory overhead (volume

variance) was treated as an asset at the end of the quarter. Production during the quarter was 200,000 units, of which 100,000 units were sold.

2. The selling, general, and administrative expenses were budgeted on the basis of $800,000 fixed expenses for the year plus $.50 variable expenses per unit of sales. (A $10,000 unfavorable variance was incurred in the first quarter.)

3. Assume that the warehouse fire loss met the conditions of an *extraordinary loss*. The warehouse had an undepreciated cost of $320,000; $180,000 was recovered from insurance on the warehouse. No other gains or losses are anticipated this year from similar events or transactions, nor has the company had any similar losses in preceding years; thus the full loss is deductible as an *ordinary loss* for income tax purposes.

4. The effective annual income tax rate, for federal and state taxes combined, is expected to average 40% of earnings before income taxes during 19X5. No differences exist between pretax accounting earnings and taxable income.

5. Earnings per share was computed on the basis of 100,000 shares of capital stock outstanding. Budgco has only one class of stock issued, no long-term debt outstanding, and no stock option plan.

Required
1. Without reference to the specific situation described, what standards of disclosure exist for interim financial data (published interim financial reports) for publicly traded companies? Explain.

2. Identify the form and content weaknesses of the interim report without reference to the additional information.

3. Indicate for interim reporting purposes the preferable treatment for each of the five items of additional information and explain why that treatment is preferable. (AICPA adapted)

✳ PERSONAL SITUATIONS ✳

PS 21–1 **Ethics: Booking Sales Before Their Normal Time?** Near the end of Fudgco's third quarter, it became evident that actual sales for the quarter would be significantly below those budgeted. Accordingly, Fudgco offered discounts and extended payment terms (no payments necessary for 120 days) to many of its distributors to induce them to take delivery in the third quarter. As a result, Fudgco was able to meet its third-quarter sales budget.

Required Is this practice ethical? Should this practice be disclosed to stockholders in the third quarter's interim report?

ANSWERS TO SELF-STUDY QUESTIONS

1. d **2.** b **3.** e **4.** d

SECURITIES AND EXCHANGE COMMISSION REPORTING

. . . one's judgment cannot be better than the information on which it is based. Given the truth, one may still go wrong when one has the chance to be right. But given no news, or presented only with distorted or incomplete data, with ignorant, sloppy or biased reporting, with propaganda and deliberate falsehoods, you destroy one's whole reasoning process. . . .

ARTHUR HAYS SULZBERGER

This chapter discusses the manner by which the Securities and Exchange Commission (SEC) regulates (1) the sale of corporate securities to the public, (2) the trading of securities of publicly owned companies, and (3) the financial reporting process of all *publicly owned* companies and the larger *privately owned* companies.

Companies subject to this federal regulatory process must have an extensive understanding of a host of statutory laws, SEC regulations, releases, interpretations, and forms. Often they seek expert legal counsel.

We also discuss the SEC's statutory-given powers to (1) establish GAAP, (2) enforce its rules and decisions on companies, (3) take various disciplinary actions against auditors of publicly owned companies, and (4) recommend that the Justice Department begin a criminal investigation into the conduct of publicly owned companies, their officers, or their auditors.

I THE PURPOSE OF THE SEC

HISTORICAL BACKGROUND

The nature of securities is such that their purchase and sale can create substantial opportunities for misrepresentation, manipulation, and other fraudulent acts. In reaction to a rapidly increasing number of flagrant abuses in this area, all but one state enacted some form of legislation between 1911 and 1933 to regulate the purchase and sale of corporate securities. Commonly referred to as the **blue sky laws,** these laws vary widely among the states. In addition, because these laws apply only to intrastate transactions, they have proved to be ineffective from an overall standpoint of protecting the public. The stock market crash of 1929, testimonial to the inadequacy of this type of regulation, was preceded by (1) the issuance of billions of dollars of securities during the preceding decade that proved to be worthless, (2) the excessive use of credit to purchase stocks on margin, (3) the extensive manipulation of stock prices by various means, (4) the extensive use of inside information by officers and directors for purposes of self-enrichment, and (5) lax standards governing the solicitation of votes from shareholders whereby managements were often able to perpetuate themselves in power. The magnitude of the inadequate financial reporting and questionable ethical standards that led to this financial collapse substantially undermined the integrity of the capital markets and thus raised serious questions concerning the survival of our system of free capital markets.

To restore investor confidence and reestablish integrity in the capital markets, Congress passed the Securities Act of 1933 (the 1933 Act) and the Securities Exchange Act of 1934 (the 1934 Act). These two acts do not replace the intrastate regulation provided by the blue sky laws but merely supplement them. The 1933 Act applies to the initial distribution of securities to the public. The purpose of this act, as expressed in its preamble, is

> to provide full and fair disclosure of the character of securities sold in interstate and foreign commerce and through the mails, and to prevent frauds in the sale thereof. . . .

This required disclosure is accomplished by "registering" securities with the SEC before they may be offered to the public. The registration procedure involves filing specified financial and nonfinancial information with the SEC for examination.

The 1934 Act applies to the subsequent trading in outstanding securities that are listed on organized stock exchanges and in the over-the-counter markets. The purpose of this act, as expressed in its preamble, is

> to provide for the regulation of securities exchanges and of over-the-counter markets operating in interstate and foreign commerce and through the mails to prevent inequitable and unfair practices on such exchanges and markets. . . .

Companies that come under the provisions of the 1934 Act must file with the SEC periodic reports of specified financial and nonfinancial information. In addition, certain practices are prohibited.

Because each act constitutes a major piece of legislation, we cannot discuss them in great detail in one chapter. Accordingly, this chapter provides a general familiarity with selected portions of each act and the means to comply with the financial reporting requirements established by the SEC.

The Functions of the SEC

Before discussing the two acts, we must examine the functions and organization structure of the Securities and Exchange Commission. Created in 1934 to administer the 1933 Act and the 1934 Act, the SEC is a quasi-judicial agency of the U.S. government. Since its creation, the SEC's responsibilities have broadened so that it now administers and enforces the following additional acts:

1. **The Public Utility Holding Company Act of 1935,** which requires geographic integration of operations and simplification of unduly cumbersome and complex capital structures of public utility holding companies. Because these objectives were accomplished many years ago through the registration process, current efforts are directed toward maintaining the status quo.

2. **The Trust Indenture Act of 1939,** which requires the use of a trust indenture that meets certain requirements for debt securities offered to the public to protect the rights of investors in such securities. Although a separate act, it is substantively an amendment to the 1933 Act.

3. **The Investment Company Act of 1940,** which regulates investment companies, that is, companies engaged primarily in the business of investing, reinvesting, owning, holding, or trading in securities. Mutual funds are the most visible investment companies. Regulation is effected through the registration process.

4. **The Investment Advisers Act of 1940,** which regulates the conduct of investment advisers similarly to the manner in which the 1934 Act regulates the conduct of brokers and dealers. Regulation is effected through the registration process.

5. **The Foreign Corrupt Practices Act of 1977 (FCPA),** which prohibits U.S. firms from offering funds (bribes) to foreign officials in an effort to obtain or retain business. The FCPA also essentially forbids *indirect* payment methods in that funds may not be offered if the firm has reason to believe that any part of these funds will be used to pay bribes. Although an amendment to the FCPA allows small payments to be made to lower-level foreign officials performing routine and lawful duties, the amendment does *not* clearly specify whom or how much can be paid. (In 1995, the SEC requested IBM Corporation to furnish information on its Argentine operations because of published reports of a possible massive bribery scandal involving several high-level government officials.)

6. **The Insider Trading Sanctions Act of 1984 and the Insider Trading and Securities Fraud Enforcement Act of 1988,** which substantially increased

(1) *monetary penalties* for those who profit by trading securities using inside information—**the penalty is now the higher of $1 million or three times the profit gained or loss avoided** (rather than merely the profit gained or loss avoided)—and (2) *criminal penalties* for securities fraud, market manipulation, and other violations—**individuals can now be fined up to $1 million and receive prison sentences of up to 10 years.**

THE RELATIONSHIP OF THE FEDERAL SECURITIES LAWS TO THE STATE SECURITIES LAWS

DUAL COMPLIANCE IS NECESSARY The federal government and each state government have separate autonomous securities laws and regulations. Compliance with the laws and rules of one does *not* constitute compliance with the laws and regulations of the other. An entity selling securities must comply with federal securities laws as well as with the laws of each state in which it intends to offer its securities. In addition, the fact that a particular offering may be exempt from certain provisions of the federal securities laws does *not* necessarily mean that it is exempt from the notice and filing requirements of state laws.

JUDGING THE MERIT OF AN OFFERING In certain states, the law permits a state official to judge the merits of an offering. In these "merit states," even though a company complies with the registration or filing procedures, the state may prohibit the offering because the state official does not consider it to be "fair, just, and equitable" for purchase by citizens of that state. Consequently, an issuer of securities must be careful to make sure there is compliance with all the appropriate state requirements as well as with the federal securities laws.[1]

In enforcing the 1933 Act, the SEC has no authority to evaluate the quality of securities offered or to pass judgment on the merits of each offering. Rather, the "disclosure" approach permits a company to offer its securities for sale if it has disclosed sufficient and accurate information about the business it conducts or proposes to conduct. In this respect, the SEC requires the following disclaimer be prominently shown on the cover page of each prospectus or offering circular given to potential investors:

> **These securities have not been approved or disapproved by the Securities and Exchange Commission nor has the Commission passed upon the accuracy or adequacy of this prospectus. Any representation to the contrary is a criminal offense.**

II THE ORGANIZATION STRUCTURE OF THE SEC

The SEC is composed of five members appointed by the president of the United States, with the advice and consent of the Senate, for a five-year term, with one term expiring each year. No more than three members may be of the same political party. An extensive professional staff—primarily comprising lawyers, accountants, economists, and financial analysts—has been organized into numerous separate offices and divisions. We list the more important ones:

---

[1]We know of one case in which the State of New York would not allow an issuer to sell its securities in New York unless the issuer's president made full restitution to the creditors of a former New York company that (1) the president had owned and (2) had gone bankrupt 15 years earlier.

OFFICES

Administrative Law Judges

Chief Accountant

Compliance, Inspections, and Examinations

Economic Analysis

Executive Director

Filings and Information Services

Freedom of Information and Privacy Act Operations

General Counsel

Information Technology

International Affairs

Legislative Affairs

Municipal Securities

Secretary

DIVISIONS

Corporation Finance

Enforcement

Investment Management

Market Regulation

Each office and each division is responsible to the commissioners and carries out its orders and legal responsibilities. In addition to this bureaucracy located in Washington, D.C., five regional offices and six district offices are located in major cities throughout the country. The roles of the Office of Chief Accountant and the Division of Corporation Finance are pertinent to this chapter.

THE DIVISION OF CORPORATION FINANCE   The division of Corporation Finance reviews the registration statements and reports that registrants file with the SEC. The review determines (1) that all required financial statements and supporting schedules have been included and (2) that such financial statements apparently have been prepared in accordance with GAAP, as well as the rules, regulations, and policies issued by the SEC. Because the SEC does *not* perform audits of registrants' financial statements, it cannot absolutely determine whether they have been prepared in accordance with GAAP. For this it relies on the reports of registrants' outside certified public accountants (discussed later in the chapter).

THE CHIEF ACCOUNTANT   The Chief Accountant is the commission's chief accounting officer for all accounting and auditing matters in connection with the administration of the various acts. The Chief Accountant advises the commission of accounting problems and recommends courses of action. For example, in 1986 the Chief Accountant proposed that the full cost method used by oil- and gas-producing companies be abolished. Following an outcry by two cabinet members and 10 senators from oil- and gas-producing states, the SEC's commissioners voted to abandon the proposal. Thus **the power to establish accounting standards** (discussed in detail in the following section) **resides with the SEC's commissioners**— not with the Chief Accountant. Administratively, the Chief Accountant drafts rules and regulations governing the form and content of the financial statements that must be filed with the commission under the various acts.

III   THE ROLE OF THE SEC IN RELATION TO THE FASB

THE STATUTORY AUTHORITY OF THE SEC

Under the 1933 Act and the 1934 Act, the SEC has the power to do the following:

1. Adopt, amend, and rescind rules and regulations as necessary to carry out the provisions of these acts.

2. Prescribe the form or forms on which required information is filed with the SEC.

3. Prescribe the accounting methods to be followed in the financial statements filed with the SEC.

4. Prescribe the items or details to be shown in the financial statements filed with the SEC.

In relation to item 3, the SEC has the statutory authority to prescribe accounting principles for companies falling under its jurisdiction. Recognizing the expertise and substantial resources of the public accounting profession, however, the SEC has usually looked to the accounting profession's standard-setting bodies to establish and improve accounting and reporting standards. When the Financial Accounting Standards Board (FASB) was established in 1973, for example, the SEC specifically announced that

> principles, standards and practices promulgated by the FASB in its Statements and Interpretations will be considered by the Commission as having substantial authoritative support and those contrary to such FASB promulgations will be considered to have no such support.[2]

This policy of looking to the private sector to establish and improve standards is by no means an abdication of its responsibilities or authority. When the SEC has concluded that such bodies were moving too slowly or in the wrong direction, it has not hesitated to take one of the following courses of action:

1. Establish its own additional financial reporting requirements (calling for additional disclosures).

2. Impose a moratorium on accounting practices.

3. Overrule a pronouncement of the FASB.

Concerning items 1 and 2, in most instances the SEC has later rescinded its own action as a result of the passage of new or revised accounting principles or disclosure requirements by the profession's standard-setting bodies. The following two paragraphs present examples of the most recent major actions of the SEC along these lines.

EXAMPLES OF ADDITIONAL DISCLOSURES REQUIRED   The SEC imposed line-of-business disclosure requirements long before the 1976 issuance of FASB *Statement No. 14*, "Financial Reporting for Segments of a Business Enterprise." Shortly after this statement was issued, the SEC modified its previous line-of-business disclosure requirements to conform in most respects with the requirements of *SFAS No. 14*. In 1976, the SEC required certain large companies to disclose replacement cost data (*Accounting Series Release No. 190*). After FASB *Statement No. 33*, "Financial Reporting and Changing Prices," was issued in 1979, the SEC rescinded its requirements in this area. (In 1986, FASB *Statement No. 89*, "Financial Reporting and Changing Prices," superseded *SFAS No. 33* and made voluntary the supplementary disclosure of current cost/constant purchasing power information.)

EXAMPLES OF PROHIBITING ACCOUNTING PRACTICES   In 1974, the SEC imposed a moratorium on the capitalization of interest (*Accounting Series Release No. 163*). It had noted with concern an increase in the number of companies changing their accounting methods to a policy of capitalizing interest cost. Because no authoritative statement on this subject existed at that time (except for two specific

---

[2]*Accounting Series Release No. 150*, "Statement of Policy on the Establishment and Improvement of Accounting Principles and Standards" (Washington, D.C.: Securities and Exchange Commission), 1973. In April 1982, *Accounting Series Release No. 150* was codified in *SEC Financial Reporting Release No. 1*, Section 101.

industries), this action stopped a developing trend until the FASB could deal with the issue. In 1979, after the FASB issued FASB *Statement No. 34*, "Capitalization of Interest Cost," the SEC rescinded its moratorium.

In another action, the SEC moved in 1983 to halt the spread of a controversial accounting method that more than a dozen computer software companies were using to increase their earnings. The SEC had noticed a trend in the industry toward capitalization without adequate criteria—the accounting standards and related interpretation that existed then were somewhat fuzzy. Therefore, the SEC imposed a moratorium on the capitalization of software development costs for companies that had not publicly disclosed the practice of capitalizing those costs prior to April 14, 1983 (*Financial Reporting Release No. 12*). In 1985, after the FASB issued *Statement No. 86*, "Accounting for the Costs of Computer Software to Be Sold, Leased, or Otherwise Marketed," the SEC rescinded its moratorium.

The SEC has *not* deemed it necessary to issue a moratorium since 1984, the year that the FASB created the Emerging Issues Task Force (discussed shortly).

OVERRULING THE FASB   Only once has the SEC overruled a pronouncement of the FASB. This ruling occurred in 1978 when the SEC rejected the standards set forth in FASB *Statement No. 19*, "Financial Accounting and Reporting for Oil and Gas Producing Companies." The SEC favored developing a new system of "reserve recognition accounting" (RRA). The conflict between the requirements of *SFAS No. 19* and those of the SEC (as set forth in *Accounting Series Release No. 253*) resulted in an untenable situation. Privately owned companies were subject to *SFAS No. 19* and publicly owned companies were subject to *ASR No. 253*. Lack of comparability resulted. Accordingly, the FASB voluntarily (and to be practical) issued *SFAS No. 25*, which suspended the effective dates of most requirements in *SFAS No. 19*. In 1981, the SEC abandoned its efforts to develop RRA and announced that it would support FASB's efforts to develop disclosure requirements for oil and gas producers. In 1982, the FASB issued *Statement No. 69*, "Disclosures about Oil and Gas Producing Activities," which amended *SFAS No. 19* and *25*. Shortly thereafter, the SEC amended its disclosure requirements for oil and gas producers to require compliance with the provisions of *SFAS No. 69*.

CURRENT WORKING RELATIONSHIP   The Securities and Exchange Commission and the FASB now try to maintain a close working relationship to prevent any future conflicts. The full FASB board meets annually or biennially with all of the commissioners to exchange information on the status of projects and plans and to discuss other matters of mutual interest. The FASB staff meets quarterly in Washington with the SEC staff. Members of the Chief Accountant's staff are responsible for keeping track of the development of specific FASB technical projects. SEC staff members participate in advisory task force meetings on those projects and frequently observe FASB meetings. When the SEC proposes changes to its rules and regulations, the FASB has occasionally expressed its views on such proposals. In summary, **both organizations strive for a climate of mutual cooperation and no surprises.**

THE SEC'S PUSH FOR MARKET VALUE ACCOUNTING   The SEC was the driving force behind the issuance of both (1) FASB *Statement No. 107*, "Disclosures About Fair Value of Financial Instruments" (1991), which requires companies to disclose in notes the fair values of their financial instruments and (2) FASB *Statement No. 115*, "Accounting for Certain Investments in Debt and Equity Securities" (1993), which requires companies to account for certain debt and equity investments at their fair value. In 1993, the SEC encouraged the FASB to require financial institutions to value their investment securities (in their financial statements) at current market prices—something that banks, bank regulators, the secretary of the treasury, the chairman of the FDIC, and the chairman of the Federal Reserve System strongly oppose. The FASB is currently studying this issue as part of its project dealing with financial instruments.

SEC INVOLVEMENT IN THE FASB'S EMERGING ISSUES TASK FORCE The Chief Accountant is a member of the FASB's Emerging Issues Task Force (EITF) that conducts an open meeting every six weeks to discuss emerging issues on a timely basis. The consensus views of the EITF constitute generally accepted accounting principles for public and nonpublic companies. Thus the SEC has a very active and direct role in establishing GAAP.[3]

THE OPEN DOOR POLICY The SEC encourages registrants to bring novel accounting treatments and new types of accounting transactions to its attention for immediate resolution before reporting the accounting effects to stockholders. Unfortunately, many registrants do not avail themselves of this opportunity (possibly fearing that the answer will be no). Instead, they try to slip liberal accounting practices and interpretations past the SEC—hoping that it will not notice these practices when making its reviews—and placing themselves in the position of having enforcement actions brought against them.

IV THE SEC'S ENFORCEMENT POWERS

ENFORCEMENT ACTIONS AGAINST REGISTRANTS

The SEC has at its disposal several enforcement weapons in its efforts to prevent violations of the federal securities laws.

1. **Instituting administrative proceedings with the SEC's Office of Administrative Law Judges.** Under this course of action, which is generally used **for less egregious violations,** the Enforcement Division notifies the entity that the Enforcement Staff intends to recommend to the SEC commissioners (who must approve initiation of all enforcement actions) that an enforcement action be brought against the entity. The entity usually is given 14 days to respond and submit an offer of settlement (which usually includes willingness to accept a cease and desist order to refrain from violating the securities laws in the future).

    The Enforcement Division's recommendations and the entity's response are then sent to the SEC commissioners. If the commissioners approve the Enforcement Division's recommendation, the Enforcement Division begins administrative proceedings (also commonly referred to as *cease-and-desist proceedings*) by filing a complaint with the SEC's Office of Administrative Law Judges.

    An administrative law judge then holds a hearing with Enforcement Division lawyers and the entity's legal counsel to determine whether a cease and desist order should be issued. (If the issues are complex, the hearing essentially becomes a trial that can last several weeks.) A cease and desist order against an individual may (1) require the disgorgement of ill-gotten gains and (2) result in a suspension (for up to one year) or a bar (for longer than one year) from practicing before the commission. (If barred, the person must reapply to the SEC to practice before it again.)

---

[3]In 1992, the consensus views of the EITF officially became part of GAAP as a result of being added to category c of the GAAP hierarchy applicable to nongovernmental entities. This GAAP hierarchy is set forth in *Statement on Auditing Standards No. 69*, "The Meaning of Present Fairly in Conformity With Generally Accepted Accounting Principles" (issued by the AICPA's Auditing Standards Board in 1992). (Abstracts of all EITF issues can be obtained from the FASB in either a loose-leaf or an annual softbound format.)

If the administrative law judge issues a cease and desist order, the entity can appeal the decision to the SEC commissioners. If the commissioners uphold the order, the entity can appeal the decision to a federal district court.

The advantage to this course of action is that it usually is swifter, more efficient, and more flexible than the alternative of seeking a federal district court injunction.

2. **Obtaining an injunction in a federal district court.** Under this course of action, which is usually used **for egregious violations,** the SEC files a complaint with the district court seeking a court order that (1) enjoins the defendant **from future violations of specified sections of the federal securities laws,** (2) may impose **monetary penalties,** (3) may require **disgorgement of unlawful gains,** or (4) **bars or suspends a person(s) from serving as an officer(s) or director(s) of a public company.** (Bars and suspensions are usually sought only when a defendant has engaged in fraudulent conduct while serving in a corporate or other fiduciary capacity.) A future violation of a judge's order (the SEC monitors) can result in court-ordered civil penalties for being in contempt of court.

   Consenting. When an entity chooses *not* to litigate the SEC action in court (as usually occurs), the entity consents to a court order, usually without admitting or denying liability, and the court enters an order based on the consent. In these cases, the SEC actions can have other major consequences to the entity because its shareholders usually sue it to recover related losses that they suffered. The monetary amounts recovered are often astronomical compared with any court-imposed penalties. (See the "Case in Point" below.)

3. **Suspending stock trading for a 10-day period.** Under this course of action, the SEC can—**without the permission of either a federal district court judge or an SEC administrative law judge**—suspend trading in an entity's stock for 10 days. (In 1978, the Supreme Court outlawed the SEC's practice of stringing together 10-day suspensions to keep a stock from trading for months at a time, a practice the court called "flagrantly abusive.") In these cases, seeking a district court injunction is usually sought as well.

CASE IN POINT

The SEC Versus Oracle Systems Corporation: Accounting and Auditing Enforcement Release No. 494 (9/24/93)

The SEC filed a complaint seeking injunctive relief and civil penalties against Oracle Systems Corporation (Oracle) alleging that Oracle committed violations of Sections 13(1), 13(b)(2)(A), and 13(b)(2)(B) of the Exchange Act and Rules 12b-20, 13a-1, and 13a-13 promulgated thereunder. The commission's complaint alleged that Oracle filed with the commission reports that included financial statements that materially misstated revenues, net income (by as much as 159%), and related captioned line items for the periods ended August 31, 1989, through November 1990. The complaint further alleged that Oracle's materially inaccurate financial reports resulted from an inadequate internal accounting control system that failed to detect double invoicing of customers for products and/or technical support services, invoicing of customers for work that was not performed, failure to credit customers for product returns, booking revenues that were contingent, and premature recognition of other revenue. Finally, the complaint alleged that Oracle **failed to maintain accurate books and records.**

Oracle consented to the entry of a permanent injunction prohibiting future violations of the named sections of the Exchange Act and to the entry of an order imposing civil penalties pursuant to Section 21(d) of the Exchange Act in the amount of $100,000, without admitting or denying the commission's allegations. In 1993, Oracle paid $24 million to settle civil lawsuits filed by its shareholders to recover losses as a result of having relied on these false and misleading financial statements.

ACTIVELY QUESTIONING ACCOUNTING PRACTICES The SEC does not hesitate to question the accounting and reporting practices of the financial statements filed with it, regardless of whether a registrant's outside auditors concur with the registrant's accounting treatment. The SEC pays great attention to ensuring that substance prevails over form. Countless instances have occurred in which the SEC has cast aside a registrant's literal interpretation of generally accepted accounting principles that the SEC deemed superficial and unreflective of the economics. Some of the more notable and recent of such actions are as follows:

1. Financial Corp. of America had to restate its net income for the first half of 1984 to a loss of $79.9 million from the previously reported profit of $73.3 million. The SEC required the company to change its method of accounting for its reverse repurchase agreement transactions. (FCA is also discussed in FAP 4-2.)

2. BankAmerica Corp. had to reclassify as an extraordinary item a $30.8 million gain from a debt-equity exchange that it previously had reported as part of operating income.

3. Aetna Life & Casualty Co. was prohibited from giving tax effects to an operating loss carryforward.

4. Alexander and Alexander Services Inc. had to report as an extraordinary loss the unanticipated $40 million it had proposed to add to goodwill and amortize over 40 years. The registrant had purchased a target company and shortly after the consummation discovered that the acquired company's liabilities had been understated by $40 million.

5. Several financial institutions were ordered to reduce their goodwill amortization lives from 40 years to 25 years or less because of SEC's perception that artificial income was being reported in the use of 40 years for goodwill and a much shorter life for loan discounts (the amortization of which increased income). (Partly as a result of SEC pressure, the FASB subsequently addressed the issue in *Statement No. 72*, "Accounting for Certain Acquisitions of Banks or Thrift Institutions," with similar conclusions.)

6. Numerous companies having contractual arrangements with their research and development limited partnerships were required to recognize a liability for the eventual acquisition of the R&D product and charge a like amount to income as R&D expense. (The FASB later addressed the issue in *Statement No. 68*, "Research and Development Arrangements" with similar conclusions concerning if and when a liability should be recognized.)

7. Several companies that had formed "nonsubsidiary subsidiaries" (discussed in Chapter 3) to avoid recognition of expenses or losses in their statements during the early years of the affiliates' operations were ordered to consolidate such companies.

During economically troubled times, the SEC usually scrutinizes financial reports closely because fraudulent and deceptive practices are much more likely when companies attempt to conceal their financial difficulties. Overall, the SEC is given high marks and has won the reputation as a tough police officer of corporate conduct.

DISCIPLINARY ACTIONS AGAINST AUDITORS

If the SEC finds that a registrant's certified public accountants are not qualified, lack integrity, have engaged in unethical or improper professional conduct, or have willfully violated or aided and abetted the violation of any provision of the federal securities laws or rules thereunder, the SEC is empowered to take the following steps:

1. Bar the auditor(s) from practicing before the SEC either permanently or for a specified period of time.
2. Bar the auditor(s) from accepting new publicly owned companies as clients for a stipulated period of time.
3. Censure the auditor(s).
4. Require the auditor(s) to submit to a peer review.
5. Recommend criminal proceedings against the auditor(s) (as the SEC did in the well-publicized *Continental Vending* case and the *National Student Marketing* case of the early 1970s in which partners of two large accounting firms were convicted and sent to prison).

THE S&L CRISIS: GOVERNMENT ACTION AGAINST S&L OUTSIDE AUDITORS

Because Congress created the Resolution Trust Corporation (RTC) to deal with the S&L crisis of the late 1980s, the SEC had no role in bringing enforcement actions against auditors of S&Ls that issued false and misleading financial statements. The RTC, as a surrogate for the SEC, however, exacted more than $1 billion in settlements (in total) from most of the Big Six international accounting firms regarding their role (grossly incompetent auditing that, in the minds of some, often bordered on collusion with management) in auditing dozens of S&Ls that committed massive frauds. (To the surprise of some in light of the publicity regarding the well below par manner of conducting these audits, the RTC brought no criminal charges against any of these S&L auditors as it brought against many of the S&L managements.)

V SEC PROMULGATIONS

To carry out its responsibilities, the SEC issues various rules, regulations (a group of rules), releases, and staff accounting bulletins, and prescribes certain forms that companies must use in filing registration statements and reports. The 1933 Act and the 1934 Act have their own regulations, rules, releases, and forms. In addition, certain regulations and releases apply to both the 1933 Act and the 1934 Act. The Staff Accounting Bulletins also apply to both acts. An understanding of all of these items is essential to comply with the registration and reporting requirements of these acts.

THE GENERAL RULES AND REGULATIONS, FORMS, AND RELEASES

GENERAL RULES AND REGULATIONS   The Securities Act of 1933 is divided into 26 sections, and the Securities Exchange Act of 1934 is divided into 35 sections. The SEC has adopted rules pertaining to the 1933 Act, which are assigned three-digit numbers starting with 100. The rules are grouped into various categories, most of which are designated *regulations*. For example, Rules 400–494 make up *Regulation C*, which deals with the mechanics of registering securities with the SEC.

Rules and regulations pertaining to the 1934 Act are assigned numbers that correspond to the section of the act to which they relate. The major sections are referred to as *regulations,* and the detailed rules within each regulation are *rules.* For example, Section 10(b) of the act is called *Regulation 10B*, and the individual rules within that section are referred to as Rule 10b-1 through Rule 10b-17.

FORMS   The **forms** are enumerations of the form and content of the information included in registration statements and reports. (They are *not* blank forms to be filled out, as the Internal Revenue Service and other taxing authorities use the term.) Each act has its own forms.

RELEASES *Releases* are announcements pertaining to the various rules, regulations, and forms. Releases are numbered sequentially as issued. To date, approximately 7,000 releases have been issued under the 1933 Act and approximately 36,000 under the 1934 Act. A release is formally designated as follows: Securities Act of 1933, Release No. 5307. A release is informally referred to simply as *Release 33-5307*, for example, under the 1933 Act, and *Release 34-9310*, for example, under the 1934 Act. Some SEC releases under the 1934 Act also apply under the 1933 Act. In these cases, a release is assigned a number under the 1933 Act and a different number under the 1934 Act. Except for Interpretative Releases, they are subject to the Administrative Procedures Act and must be exposed for public comment before becoming effective. The primary matters to which these releases pertain are as follows:

1. **Proposals to amend or adopt new rules and forms.** Changes are often necessary to keep up with the times. In some instances, better ways of disclosure are found. For example, to improve the readability of information provided to investors, the SEC issued Release 33-5164, which proposed certain amendments to Rules 425A and 425 of the Securities Act of 1933.

   Interested companies and certified public accountants usually make comments and suggestions to the SEC. The final adopted amendment or new rule or form probably reflects many of these comments and suggestions. Sometimes a proposed item is not adopted for various reasons.

2. **Adoption of amendments or new rules and forms.** To continue with the preceding example, the proposals contained in Release 33-5164 were revised to reflect the comments and suggestions that the SEC considered significant and were subsequently adopted in Release 33-5278.

REGULATION S-K, REGULATION S-X, AND REGULATION S-T

All nonfinancial disclosure requirements are contained in *Regulation S-K*. All financial disclosure requirements are contained in *Regulation S-X*. Each form under the 1933 Act and the 1934 Act specifies the disclosures contained in *Regulations S-K* and *S-X* that are to be made for that form.

REGULATION S-K (NONFINANCIAL STATEMENT DISCLOSURE REQUIREMENTS) The major disclosure requirements contained in *Regulation S-K* deal with (1) a description of the company's business, (2) a description of the company's properties, (3) a description of the company's legal proceedings, (4) selected financial data for the last five years (including sales, income from continuing operations, cash dividends per common share, total assets, and long-term obligations, (5) supplementary financial information (quarterly financial data and information on the effects of changing prices), (6) information about the company's directors and management (including management remuneration), and (7) management's discussion and analysis (commonly referred to as the *MDA*) of financial condition and results of operations.

REGULATION S-X (FINANCIAL STATEMENT DISCLOSURE REQUIREMENTS) *Regulation S-X*, which accountants deal with most often, not only lists the **specific financial statements** that must be filed under all acts administered by the SEC but also details the **form and content of such financial statements.** The term *financial statements* as used in this regulation includes all notes to the financial statements and all related financial statement supporting schedules. The financial statements filed under *Regulation S-X* are (1) audited balance sheets as of the end of the two most recent fiscal years and (2) audited statements of income and cash flows for the three fiscal years preceding the date of the most recent audited balance sheet being filed. (Variations from these requirements are permitted for certain specified filings.) In addition, the regulation contains requirements for filing interim financial statements. (*Regulation S-X* is discussed in more detail later in the chapter.)

REGULATION S–T: ELECTRONIC DATA GATHERING AND RETRIEVAL SYSTEM (EDGAR) The SEC has designed an electronic database (named *EDGAR*) to keep track of financial documents filed with it by publicly traded companies. When fully operational by 1997, all 15,000 of the nation's public corporations and investment firms will be required to file their reports electronically. *Regulation S-T* set forth the rules prescribing requirements for filing electronically and the procedures for making such filings.

In addition to serving the SEC's internal needs, EDGAR is expected to increase the efficiency and fairness in the securities markets by allowing a means for quick public distribution of corporate information. EDGAR can be accessed using the internet. It is also the centerpiece of the SEC's home page on the worldwide web; the page offers to investors a wide range of SEC information formerly available only from dispersed sources.

FINANCIAL REPORTING RELEASES

The Financial Reporting Releases (FRRs), numbered sequentially, pertain solely to accounting matters. Nearly 50 Financial Reporting Releases have been issued. Prior to 1982, such accounting matters (as well as enforcement matters) were dealt with in the now discontinued Accounting Series Releases (of which 307 had been issued). *Financial Reporting Release No. 1* is the codification of the earlier releases that had continuing relevance to financial reporting. This codification (with its topical index) makes thousands of pages of material available in a concise and much more accessible format. These releases pertain to the following major areas of accounting:

1. **Adoption of amendment or revision of** *Regulation S-X.* Many FRRs include financial reporting requirements that go beyond the pronouncements of the FASB and its predecessor organizations. In addition to setting forth an amendment or revision to *Regulation S-X*, such FRRs also discuss the purpose of the new reporting requirements and comments received in response to the SEC's proposed revisions to *Regulation S-X* (including the SEC's reaction to those comments). In some cases, an FRR contains exhibits and examples to assist companies in understanding and complying with the new reporting requirements of *Regulation S-X*.

   Many FRRs have been rescinded as a result of the issuance of subsequent accounting pronouncements. The SEC rescinds such requirements, however, only when it concurs with an accounting pronouncement.

2. **Policy/interpretive statements regarding particular accounting areas.** *Accounting Series Release Nos. 130, 135, 146,* and *146A* (now part of *FRR No. 1*), for example, deal with the way that the SEC interprets certain provisions of APB *Opinion No. 16,* "Accounting for Business Combinations." Accountants must be familiar with such releases in addition to the provisions of the professional pronouncements. (Recall that *Accounting Series Release Nos. 146* and *146A* were discussed in Chapter 7 in connection with pooling of interests accounting.)

ACCOUNTING AND AUDITING ENFORCEMENT RELEASES (AAERs)

Accounting and Auditing Enforcement Releases (AAERs) announce accounting and auditing matters related to the SEC's enforcement activities that have been finalized. Because of their nature, AAERs are not codified. (A separate series of releases, *Litigation Releases*, announces litigation actions.)

STAFF ACCOUNTING BULLETINS (SABs)

The Staff Accounting Bulletins (SABs) represent interpretations and practices followed by certain departments of the SEC that are responsible for reviewing the disclosure requirements of the federal securities laws. These bulletins do not constitute official rules or regulations, nor do they have the official approval of the SEC. The bulletins essentially accomplish on an informal basis what otherwise would be dealt with formally through releases. Much of the subject matter of the bulletins arises from specific questions raised by registrants. The dissemination of answers to these questions in this manner rather than solely to the company making an inquiry avoids needless repetition of inquiries pertaining to the same subject. Nearly 100 SABs have been issued to date. In 1981, the staff codified by topic all bulletins issued to date in *Staff Accounting Bulletin No. 40*, making the SABs substantially more easy to use. (Recall from Chapter 8 that push-down accounting was implemented as a result of the issuance of *Staff Accounting Bulletin No. 54*.)

VI THE SECURITIES ACT OF 1933

REGISTRATION

The Securities Act of 1933 prohibits sales of, or offers to sell, securities to the public (in interstate commerce or through the use of the mails) by an **issuer** or an underwriter unless the securities have been registered with the SEC. Certain exemptions to this prohibition are discussed later in the chapter. A **security** is defined broadly as

> any note, stock, treasury stock, bond, debenture, evidence of indebtedness, certificate of interest or participation in any profit-sharing agreement, . . . transferable share, investment contract, voting trust certificate . . . or in general any interest or instrument commonly known as a security. . . .

To avoid having a technical loophole in the law, the prohibition also applies to underwriters. An **underwriter** is defined as

> any person who has purchased from an issuer with a view to, or offers or sells for an issuer in connection with, the distribution of any security, or participates [directly or indirectly] . . . in any such undertaking. . . .

It is important at this point to understand that registration under the 1933 Act refers only to the **actual quantity of securities being registered,** not to the registration of an **entire class of securities.** This is just the opposite of the 1934 Act, which is discussed in detail later in the chapter.

THE ESSENCE OF REGISTRATION   **Registration** of a security offering under the 1933 Act begins with the filing of specified financial and nonfinancial information with the SEC using the appropriate form. The appropriate SEC form in a particular case is a legal determination. All specified financial and nonfinancial information submitted as set forth in the appropriate form is called a **registration statement.** The SEC examines the registration statement and almost always issues a **letter of comments** (commonly referred to as a **deficiency letter**). The registrant must respond to this letter of comments to the SEC's satisfaction before it may sell the securities to the public. Responding to a letter of comments usually involves a combination of direct written responses to the SEC in a letter, revision of certain information in the registration statement, and addition of information to the statement. The revised registration statement, called an **amended registration**

statement, is filed with the SEC for reexamination. When the SEC is satisfied that the items in its letter of comments have been appropriately addressed, it permits the amended registration statement to become "effective," and the securities being offered are deemed registered under the 1933 Act and may be sold to the public.

PROSPECTUSES   Prospective investors in a security being registered with the SEC under the 1933 Act must be furnished a **prospectus.** The registration statement is divided into two basic parts:

- Part I Information required to be included in the prospectus.
- Part II Information not required to be included in the prospectus.

Part I is the major part of the registration statement. It includes all required financial statements and related notes (according to the provisions of *Regulation S-X*), as well as reports by the registrant's auditors on financial statements that must have been audited. Part I also includes, among other things, such nonfinancial information as an extensive description of the registrant's business (including risk factors associated with the purchase of the securities offered) and properties, an explanation of how the proceeds are to be used, a description of any current legal proceedings, the names of the registrant's directors and officers (including their backgrounds), and the amount of their remuneration. The financial and nonfinancial disclosures included in the prospectus should provide potential investors with an adequate basis for deciding whether to invest in the securities offered. Preliminary prospectuses, which may be distributed to potential investors before the effective date, are commonly referred to as *red herrings* because certain information on the cover is printed in red ink.

Part II of the registration statement lists all exhibits filed with the registration statement and includes specified financial statement supporting schedules and other miscellaneous information not deemed necessary for distribution to potential investors.

REGULATION C   *Regulation C* deals with the mechanics of registering securities under the 1933 Act. A company's legal counsel usually assumes responsibility for ensuring that the registration statement complies with *Regulation C.*

EXEMPTIONS FROM REGISTRATION

Certain types of securities and securities transactions, which have no practical need for registration or for which the benefits of registration are too remote, are exempt from the registration requirements of the 1933 Act. The major categories of exemptions are discussed in the following sections.

1. **The intrastate offering exemption** [Section 3(a)(11) of the 1933 Act]. This statutory exemption is intended to facilitate the local financing of local business operations. To qualify, the security must be offered and sold only to the residents of the state in which the corporate issuer is incorporated and doing business. No fixed limits exist on (1) the size of the offering or (2) the number of purchasers.

2. **The private offering exemption** [Section 4(2) of the 1933 Act]. This statutory exemption applies to offerings made to so-called sophisticated investors, those who have access to information about the company and are able to fend for themselves. Examples of **private offerings** are (1) bank loans; (2) *private placements* of securities with institutions such as venture capital firms, insurance companies, and pension funds; (3) offerings to individuals directly managing the business; and (4) offerings for the promotion of a business venture by a few closely related persons. To qualify, each buyer must (1) have sufficient knowledge and experience in financial and business matters so that he or she is

capable of evaluating the risks and merits of the investment or is able to bear the economic risk of the investment, (2) have access to the type of information normally provided in a prospectus, and (3) agree not to resell or distribute the securities for a specified number of years.

Substance versus form. If the investor were to turn around and immediately sell the securities purchased, the sale is considered a distribution of securities to the public because the investor is acting as a conduit for sale to the public on behalf of the issuer—that is, *as an underwriter.* In such cases, the resale of the security to the public must be registered. Because of these restrictions on the buyer, the securities are referred to as **restricted securities.**

Rule 144. Rule 144 of the 1933 Act sets the conditions that must be satisfied to resell restricted securities to the public other than through registration. This rule emphasizes that (1) the investor must have paid for and held the security for a reasonable period of time (a minimum of two to four years, depending on the category of issuer) and (2) adequate current public information with respect to the issuer of the securities must be available.

3. **The *Regulation A* exemption.** [Rules 251–263 adopted by the SEC under authority granted by Section 3(b) of the 1933 Act]. This statutory authorized exemption is a *conditional exemption* for security offerings that involve relatively small dollar amounts. To qualify, the offering, together with other exempt offerings within a one-year period, cannot exceed $5,000,000. Although Regulation A is technically an exemption from the registration requirements of the 1933 Act, it is often referred to as a *short form* of registration because (1) an **offering circular** (similar in content to a prospectus) must be given to each purchaser, (2) the securities are freely tradable in an aftermarket, and (3) an offering statement (consisting of a notification, an offering circular, and exhibits) must be filed with the closest SEC regional office.

    Advantages. The major advantages of *Regulation A* offerings, as opposed to full registration on Form S-1, SB-2 or SB-3 (SB is for small business) are that (1) the required financial statement disclosures are less extensive, (2) the issuer does *not* become subject to the continuous reporting requirements of the 1934 Act (discussed later) unless assets exceed $5 million and the number of shareholders exceeds 500, and (3) three offering circular formats are permitted, one of which is a relatively simple question-and-answer document.

4. **The *Regulation D* exemption** [Rules 501–506 adopted by the SEC pursuant to authority granted under Sections 4(2) and 3(b) of the 1933 Act]. This regulation was established in 1982 **to facilitate the capital-raising process for small businesses.** Three types of statutory authorized exemptions are available: (1) offerings not exceeding $500,000, (2) offerings not exceeding $5,000,000, and (3) unlimited offerings. Extensive detailed conditions (beyond the scope of this text) must be satisfied to meet each type of exemption. Compared to the *Regulation A* exemption, the *Regulation D* exemption is generally much less time consuming and costly to prepare. Only a notice of the sale (using Form D, which is in questionnaire format) must be filed with the SEC (within 15 days of the first sale).

5. **The "accredited investor" exemption: Section 4(6)** [pursuant to **The Small Business Investment Incentive Act of 1980**]. This statutory exemption (1) is limited to offerings of $5,000,000, (2) is intended for offerings to six specified types of investors (such as insiders, certain institutional investors, and persons having a net worth of at least $1,000,000), and (3) does *not* contain any specific disclosure requirements. The issuer must file a notice of the sale on Form D within 15 days of the sale.

WHO DECIDES WHETHER A SECURITIES OFFERING OR TRANSACTION IS EXEMPT?   Whether a security offering or transaction is exempt from registration under the 1933 Act is strictly a legal and factual determination and outside the expertise of accountants. Accordingly, an entity's legal counsel usually makes this determination. If all conditions of the exemption are *not* met, purchasers may seek to have their purchase price refunded. (As stated earlier, a determination is also necessary to decide whether the offering is exempt from state laws.)

ANTIFRAUD PROVISIONS STILL APPLY   Regardless that a security offering qualifies as being exempt from the registration requirements of the 1933 Act, the sale of these securities is subject to the antifraud provisions of the federal securities laws. This means that issuers are responsible for false or misleading statements (whether written or oral), which may be redressed through private or government legal action, including criminal sanctions.

FORMS USED IN REGISTRATION

The Securities and Exchange Commission has devised numerous forms to deal with the diverse companies (and their maturity) seeking to offer securities to the public. Although the general contents of a registration statement have already been described, each form has its own detailed table of contents and related instructions. (Recall that the financial statement requirements for these forms are set forth in *Regulation S-X.*) Two categories of forms are used under the 1933 Act: general forms and special forms.

GENERAL FORMS   The SEC has three *general forms:* S-1, S-2, and S-3. These three forms are set up on a tier system based on the issuer's following in the stock market. Although all three forms basically require the same information to be furnished to potential investors, the method of furnishing that information varies. Form S-1, the most widely used of the forms, is required when one of the special forms is not authorized or prescribed, or when a company eligible to use Form S-2 or S-3 chooses to use Form S-1 instead. Basically, Form S-1 is used by new registrants and by companies that are already registered under the 1934 Act but have been filing reports with the SEC for less than 36 months. All financial and nonfinancial disclosures must be included in the prospectus. The detailed table of contents to Form S-1 appears in Illustration 22–1.

To be eligible to use Forms S-2 and S-3, a company must have been subject to the reporting requirements of the 1934 Act for at least 36 months and satisfy other conditions. Form S-3 is used by large companies having a wide following in the stock market; accordingly, such firms must meet an additional requirement based on annual trading volume and outstanding voting stock. The advantage to these forms is time and effort; that is, financial and nonfinancial information need not be included in the prospectus; it may simply be incorporated by reference to reports already filed with the SEC under the 1934 Act. Thus these forms are effectively a simplified Form S-1.

SPECIAL FORMS   The SEC has 12 *special forms,* 6 of which are commonly used:

1. **Form S-4,** for registration of securities issued in connection with most business combinations and reofferings. (Substantial information may be incorporated by reference.)

2. **Form S-8,** for securities offered to employees pursuant to employee benefit plans, such as stock option plans.

3. **Form S-11,** applicable to real estate investment trusts and real estate companies.

ILLUSTRATION 22–1	Table of Contents of Form S-1

The following is the table of contents from Form S-1, the most widely used of the SEC's forms. It is reprinted here to provide a more complete look at what is called for in a registration statement.

I. Information Required in Prospectus

Item

1. Forepart of the registration statement and outside front cover page of prospectus
2. Inside front and outside back cover page of prospectus
3. Summary information, risk factors, and ratio of earnings to fixed charges
4. Use of proceeds
5. Determination of offering price
6. Dilution
7. Selling security holders
8. Plan of distribution
9. Description of securities being registered
10. Interest of named experts and counsel
11. Information with respect to the registrant.[a] This item represents the bulk of the registration statement and consists of the following categories of information (those that are generally prepared by accountants are shown in bold):
    - Description of Business
    - Description of Property
    - Legal Proceedings
    - Market Price and Dividends
    - **Financial Statements and Financial Statement Schedules**
    - **Selected Financial Data**
    - **Supplementary Financial Information**
    - Management's Discussion and Analysis (MDA) of Financial Condition and Results of Operations
    - **Changes in and Disagreements With Acccountants on Accounting and Financial Disclosure**
    - Directors and Executive Officers
    - Executive Compensation
    - Security Ownership of Certain Beneficial Owners and Management
    - Certain Relationships and Related [-Party] Transactions
12. Disclosure of commission position on indemnification for securities act liabilities

II. Information Not Required in Prospectus

13. Other expenses of issuance and distribution
14. Indemnification of directors and officers
15. Recent sales of unregistered securities
16. Exhibits and financial statement schedules
17. Undertakings

Signatures

Instructions as to Summary Prospectuses

[a]This item specifies (1) the nonfinancial disclosure requirements in *Regulation S-K* and (2) the financial statement requirements of *Regulation S-X* that are to be included.

---

4. **Form S-15,** for securities issued in certain business combinations (involving a large company and a much smaller company). This streamlined form requires only an abbreviated prospectus.

5. **Form SB-1,** for *small business issuers,* which are entities with revenues of less than $25 million and with a *public float* (the aggregate market value of its voting stock held by nonaffiliates) of less than $25 million. This form gives small initial registrants (including limited partnerships) a fast and simple method to raise capital in public markets because (1) the disclosure requirements are less extensive than under Form S-1 and (2) the filing may be made at an SEC regional office rather than in Washington, D.C. The exemption limit is $10 million worth of securities in a fiscal year.

6. **Form SB-2,** for *small business issuers.* An unlimited dollar amount of securities may be sold.

LEGAL LIABILITY FOR FILING A FALSE REGISTRATION STATEMENT

Section 6 of the Securities Act of 1933 requires that the registration statement be signed by the following persons:

1. The principal executive officer or officers.
2. The principal financial officer.
3. The controller or principal accounting officer.
4. The majority of the board of directors or persons performing similar functions.

The 1933 Act sets forth the following civil liabilities for a false registration:

In case any part of the registration statement, when such part became effective, contained an untrue statement of a material fact or omitted to state a material fact required to be stated therein or necessary to make the statements therein not misleading, any person acquiring such security (unless it is proved that at the time of such acquisition he knew of such untruth or omission) may . . . sue [for recovery of losses suffered]—

1. every person who signed the registration statement;
2. every person who was a director of . . . the issuer . . .;
3. every person who, with his consent, is named in the registration statement as being or about to become a director . . .;
4. every accountant, engineer, appraiser, or any person whose profession gives authority to a statement made by him, who has with his consent been named as having prepared or certified part of the registration statement, . . . with respect to the statement in such registration statement, report, or valuation, which purports to have been prepared or certified by him;
5. every underwriter with respect to such security [Section 11].

In addition to these civil proceedings whereby a purchaser may recover damages suffered, Section 24 of the 1933 Act provides for criminal penalties (monetary fines and imprisonment) if the untrue statement of a material fact or omission thereof was "willful."

SHAREHOLDERS OFTEN SUE IF STOCK PRICES FALL   Countless instances have occurred in which stock prices have substantially declined from the offering price within 6 to 12 months of the offering. In such cases, it is common for disgruntled stockholders to file class action lawsuits alleging that unfavorable information was purposely omitted from the prospectus. Such information could include known problems in developing anticipated new products or shipping and order delays. In fact, many attorneys actively search out investors who have sustained losses on public offerings, hoping to represent them in such lawsuits, which have a high settlement potential.

RAMIFICATIONS TO OUTSIDE AUDITORS   This section of the 1933 Act has special significance to certified public accountants of companies registering securities. When securities are not registered, *gross negligence* must be proved for a company's certified public accountant to be held liable for civil damages. When a company registers securities under the 1933 Act, however, the focal point is not whether the outside auditors were grossly negligent in the performance of their duties. Instead, the issue is merely whether or not the financial statements and related notes in the registration statement **contained an untrue statement of a material fact or omitted a material fact.** Thus, the 1933 Act imposes an additional potential liability on the certified public accountants of companies registering securities. Certain defenses are available to the outside auditors, however, under Section 11 of the 1933 Act that relate to their having made a "reasonable investigation" and having "reasonable grounds for belief."

VII THE SECURITIES EXCHANGE ACT OF 1934

The Securities Exchange Act of 1934, which deals with the trading in (exchange of) securities, has two broad purposes:

1. To require publicly held companies to disclose on a continual basis current information to holders and prospective purchasers of their securities comparable to the information that must be disclosed in a registration statement under the 1933 Act. In this respect, the 1934 Act supplements the 1933 Act, which applies only to public offerings of securities, not to subsequent trading in such securities.

2. To regulate the public trading markets (organized exchanges and over-the-counter markets) and the broker-dealers who operate in such markets.

MAJOR PROVISIONS OF THE 1934 ACT

Unlike the 1933 Act, which is a unified piece of legislation, the 1934 Act covers a wide range of areas. Its major provisions are discussed in the following paragraphs.

REGISTRATION OF SECURITIES EXCHANGES Securities exchanges (such as the New York Stock Exchange) must be registered with the SEC, which has supervisory control over them.

REGISTRATION OF SECURITIES ON SECURITIES EXCHANGES Securities exchanges cannot effect transactions in any security unless that security is registered on the exchange. The registration process involves filing a registration statement on Form 10 (or another appropriate form) with the securities exchange and with the SEC. Form 10 requires information comparable to that required in Form S-1 under the 1933 Act. A security that is traded on a securities exchange is referred to as a *listed security*. Companies having securities registered on a securities exchange are referred to as *Section 12(b) companies*.

REGISTRATION OF OVER-THE-COUNTER SECURITIES The *over-the-counter* market encompasses all securities transactions that do not take place on organized securities exchanges. The 1934 Act was amended in 1964 to require registration of securities traded in the over-the-counter market that meet certain size tests. Companies that have total assets exceeding $10 million *and* a class of equity security with 500 or more stockholders must register such security with the SEC by filing a registration statement (usually Form 10). Securities traded in the over-the-counter market are referred to as *unlisted*. Companies meeting these tests are referred to as *Section 12(g) companies*. Once a company meets these size tests, it is subject to all the requirements of the 1934 Act that are imposed on listed companies. **Thus an entity that has never registered the sale of securities under the 1933 Act may be subject to the 1934 Act by virtue of the entity's size and number of its stockholders.**

A Section 12(g) company may deregister when it has (1) less than 500 shareholders for the class of equity security and total assets of less than $10 million at the end of each of its last three fiscal years or (2) fewer than 300 shareholders.

FILING PERIODIC AND OTHER REPORTS   Issuers of securities that must be registered under the 1934 Act must file annual and quarterly reports with the SEC containing specified financial and nonfinancial information. In addition, reports describing specified important events must be filed promptly after they occur. These periodic reports are discussed in detail shortly.

PROXY REGULATIONS   For companies subject to the registration requirements of the 1934 Act, the SEC is authorized to prescribe regulations and rules governing the solicitation of proxies by management from shareholders regarding matters to be voted on by shareholders. A **proxy** is merely a document empowering one person to vote for another. Because all shareholders do not normally attend annual or special shareholders' meetings, companies typically request each shareholder to sign a proxy empowering management to vote either as the shareholder indicates or in accordance with the recommendations of management. When soliciting proxies, a **proxy statement** containing information specified by the SEC must be furnished to the stockholders. Furthermore, preliminary proxy material must be filed with the SEC for review at least 10 days before the proposed mailing date.

ANTIFRAUD AND INSIDER TRADING PROVISIONS   Section 10 of the 1934 Act makes it unlawful for any person directly or indirectly to use deceptive or fraudulent practices or to misstate or omit any material fact in connection with the purchase or sale of a security. Criminal fines up to $100,000 can be imposed. Persons suffering losses as a result of fraud are entitled to sue for recovery of actual losses.

Corporate "insiders" are prohibited from trading in a corporation's securities using material information that has not been disseminated to the public. Inside traders can be forced to give up their profits and be fined up to the higher of $1,000,000 or three times the profit gained or loss avoided. Also, criminal fines of $1,000,000 can be imposed. An **insider** is any person who has *material nonpublic information*, including any officer or director or any person who obtains such information from others. In addition, under the *short-swing profit* rule in Section 16(b), any profit realized from any purchase and sale (or from any sale and purchase) of any such issuer's equity security within any period of less than six months by certain persons accrues to the issuer and is recoverable by the issuer, with certain exceptions. These certain persons are officers, directors, or any person who is the beneficial owner of more than 10% of any security that is registered under the 1934 Act. Under Section 16(a), officers, directors, and such 10% security holders must report to the SEC any changes in their beneficial ownership of registered securities. Changes in ownership are reported using either Form 3 (Initial Statement of Ownership) or Form 4 (Changes in Ownership). The form must be filed within 10 days after the end of the month in which the transaction occurs.

The definition of *officer* is not based on title but instead **focuses on individuals who have access to inside information** that may allow them to profit from securities transactions. Officers now include a company's CEO; president; CFO; vice presidents in charge of principal business units, divisions, or functions; other persons who perform policy-making decisions; and executive officers of parents or subsidiaries who perform policy-making functions.

BROKERS AND DEALERS   The 1934 Act requires brokers and dealers to register with the SEC and to comply with regulations imposed on them. Certain trading practices are prohibited. Specific sections of the 1934 Act deal with unlawful representations, liability for misleading statements, and criminal penalties.

FORMS USED IN REPORTING

The SEC has devised approximately 20 forms to be used by companies whose securities are registered under the 1934 Act. Because most of these forms are of a specialized nature, a complete list is not presented. By far the most commonly used forms (for domestic companies) are the following:

- Form 8-K, current reports.
- Form 10-K, annual report.
- Form 10-Q, quarterly report.

Regulation 12B of the 1934 Act sets forth the mechanics of reporting in the same manner that *Regulation C* does under the 1933 Act. *Small business issuers* (defined earlier) use periodic reporting forms 10-KSB and 10-QSB.

FORM 8-K, CURRENT REPORTS

Form 8-K provides certain information to investors on a reasonably current basis. A report on this form must be filed when one of the following events occurs:

1. Changes in control of the registrant.
2. Significant acquisitions or dispositions of assets (including business combinations).
3. Bankruptcy or receivership.
4. Changes in the registrant's outside auditors. (The disclosures here are designed to discourage "opinion shopping." We discuss this event more fully in the following section.)
5. Other events (that the registrant deems important to its security holders).
6. The resignation of a director.
7. Illegal acts.

Form 8-K reports must be filed within 15 days after the occurrence of the earliest event (5 days for item 4).

CHANGES IN OUTSIDE AUDITORS Companies must report to the SEC when their auditors are fired, resign, or inform the company that they do not intend to seek reappointment for the following year. **The report must state whether the company and its auditor disagreed about accounting principles or practices, financial statement disclosures, or auditing scope or procedures.** Form 8-K elaborates on what circumstances are deemed to be disagreements. Within 10 days after the 8-K report is filed, the former auditor must submit a letter to the SEC stating whether he or she agrees or disagrees with the company's statement. Furthermore, **if the company has held discussions with its new auditors concerning accounting and financial reporting matters within the two years prior to their appointment, the issues discussed must be reported.**

ILLEGAL ACTS The *Private Securities Litigation Reform Act of 1995* requires auditors to report certain illegal acts to a client's board of directors if management fails to take appropriate remedial action. In turn, the board must notify the SEC that it has received such a report. If the auditor is *not* furnished a copy of the client's notice to the SEC **within one business day after giving the report to the board,** the auditor must provide the SEC with a copy of the report given to the board. Thus auditors, for the first time, are placed in the position of having to be "whistle-blowers" to a federal agency.

FORM 10-K, ANNUAL REPORT

Within 90 days after the end of the fiscal year, a company must file an annual report with the SEC, using Form 10-K if no other form is prescribed. Although it must be furnished to stockholders on request, this report is in addition to the company's annual report to its stockholders. Form 10-K must include substantially all *nonfinancial statement information* set forth in *Regulation S-K* (the major items were indicated on page 756) and the *financial statement information* specified in *Regulation S-X* (described on page 769).

FORM 10-K COMPARED WITH THE ANNUAL REPORT TO STOCKHOLDERS Substantially all the information called for in the 10-K annual report also must be included in the annual report sent to the stockholders. Companies may omit information from the 10-K annual report if it is included in the annual report sent to the stockholders. A copy of the annual report sent to the stockholders must be filed with the 10-K annual report, and the 10-K annual report must indicate that the omitted information is included in the annual report sent to the stockholders. (This is known as *incorporation by reference*.)

FORM 10-K COMPARED WITH A FORM S-1 The bulk of the information called for in a 10-K annual report is identical to the information called for in a Form S-1 registration statement (discussed earlier).

FORM 10-Q, QUARTERLY REPORT

Within 45 days of the end of each of the first three fiscal quarters of each fiscal year, a company must file a quarterly report with the SEC on Form 10-Q. No report is necessary for the fourth quarter. Form 10-Q calls for the interim financial statements specified in Regulation S-X. These financial statements, which may be condensed, are as follows:

1. An interim **balance sheet** as of the end of the most recent fiscal quarter and a balance sheet at the end of the preceding fiscal year.

2. Interim **income statements** for the most recent fiscal quarter; for the period between the end of the last fiscal year and the end of the most recent fiscal quarter (year-to-date amounts in second- and third-quarter reports) and corresponding periods of the preceding fiscal year.

3. Statements of **cash flows** for the period between the end of the last fiscal year and the end of the most recent fiscal quarter and for the corresponding period of the preceding fiscal year.

Detailed notes to these statements are not required; however, disclosures must be complete enough so that the information presented is not misleading. In this respect, companies may presume that users of the interim financial information have read or have access to the audited financial statements for the preceding fiscal year. Thus disclosures deal primarily with events after the end of the most recent fiscal year. The interim financial information need not be audited or reviewed by an independent public accountant.

Form 10-Q also calls for a *management discussion and analysis* (MDA) of the financial condition and results of operations pursuant to the nonfinancial statement disclosure requirements of *Regulation S-K*.

FORM 10-Q COMPARED WITH THE QUARTERLY REPORT TO STOCKHOLDERS As with the rules concerning the 10-K annual report, information called for on Form 10-Q may be omitted if such information is contained in a quarterly report to the stockholders and a copy of that report is filed with Form 10-Q.

MAJOR DISTINCTION BETWEEN THE 1933 ACT AND THE 1934 ACT

As stated earlier, the 1933 Act deals with **registering a quantity of securities,** and the 1934 Act deals with **registering a class of securities** (such as common stock, preferred stock, and debenture bonds).

ILLUSTRATION 22–2	**Shares Registered for Sale Versus Shares Tradable**

Parrco Inc. common shares outstanding on 7/6/X5

Shares issued to founders on 1/1/X1 (**restricted securities**)	200,000
Shares issued to employees in 19X3 pursuant to stock options granted in 19X1 (**restricted securities**)	60,000
Shares issued to an insurance company in a private placement on 4/4/X4 (**restricted securities**)	40,000
Common Shares Outstanding on 7/6/X5	300,000
Primary offering on 7/7/X5 (registered under the **1933 Act** using Form S-1)	100,000
Common Shares Outstanding on 7/7/X5	**400,000**
Common shares that may be publicly traded on 7/7/X5 (assuming that the common stock was registered with the SEC on 7/7/X5 under the **1934 Act** using Form 10)	100,000
Secondary offering on 12/12/X5 of common shares held by founders, employees, and the insurance company (registered under the **1933 Act** using Form S-1)	50,000
Common Shares That May Be Publicly Traded on 12/12/X5	**150,000**[a]

[a]A very small percentage of the 250,000 common shares that have not been registered under the 1933 Act are also tradable at this time as allowed under Rules 144 and 145.

PRIMARY OFFERINGS: TO RAISE CAPITAL   To show the difference between the two acts, assume that Parrco Inc. is a privately owned company with 300,000 common shares outstanding as a result of shares issued to its founders, its employees (pursuant to a stock option plan), and an insurance company (as a result of a private placement). Assume also that Parrco desires to become a publicly owned company and, therefore, registers the sale of 100,000 new shares of its common stock with the SEC under the 1933 Act. The sale of these shares, in which the proceeds go to the company, is characterized as a **primary offering.**

THE INITIAL RESULT   For any of Parrco's common stock to be publicly tradable, however, the common stock—**as a class of securities**—must also be registered under the 1934 Act. Doing so does *not* mean that all of Parrco's 400,000 common shares outstanding become immediately tradable—only the 100,000 common shares registered under the 1933 Act do so. Thus the result **at the time that an entity first becomes publicly owned,** however, **is as if** the 100,000 common shares were actually registered under the 1934 Act (even though a quantity of shares is *not* registered under that act).

AS TIME GOES BY   Subsequent to the primary offering date, however, the remaining 300,000 common shares become tradable slowly over time pursuant to Rules 144 and 145—without having to be registered with the SEC. The purpose of not allowing these 300,000 common shares to become immediately tradable is to limit the ability of the owners of these shares to immediately dump all of their holdings on the public, which might cause a sharp drop in the price of the stock and cause the new owners to believe that they were defrauded.

SECONDARY OFFERINGS: TO ENABLE MORE SHARES TO BE PUBLICLY TRADED
The only way to enable the 300,000 common shares to become publicly tradable more quickly is to register some or all of these shares under the 1933 Act in a **secondary offering,** which process allows them to become publicly traded under the 1934 Act. In a secondary offering, the proceeds go to the selling shareholders—not

to the company. Thus the company acts merely as a conduit between these shareholders and the public.

Illustration 22–2 is a summary of the example used in the preceding discussion, with a secondary offering of 50,000 shares included.

VIII REGULATION OF FOREIGN SECURITIES TRADED IN THE UNITED STATES

The U.S. capital market is the largest of the world's capital markets. The market capitalization of the companies listed on the New York Stock Exchange alone is approximately $5,000 billion, which about equals the market capitalization of the four largest foreign stock exchanges (Tokyo, London, Paris, and Frankfurt) combined.

Foreign firms desiring access to the U.S. capital market must comply with federal securities laws. The SEC has a separate category of forms for these entities to use in their filings that are identified with an *F* for *foreign* (for example, Form F-1 is used for the sale of securities under the 1933 Act instead of Form S-1 used by domestic companies).

Approximately 700 foreign companies have their stocks traded in the U.S. either in (1) **direct** form (less than 100 companies, most of which are Canadian) in which the U.S. investor buys the actual common shares or (2) **American Depository Receipt (ADR)** form in which the U.S. investor buys a "negotiable certificate of ownership" (using a bank as an intermediary) that serves as a surrogate for the actual common shares. ADRs (discussed in detail in international finance texts) are generally considered a more convenient form of ownership than the direct form.

In lieu of filing a 10-K annual report, these foreign firms must file a Form 20-F annual report, which requires inclusion of a **reconciliation of net income using foreign GAAP to U.S. GAAP.** A copy of the annual report prepared for the stockholders must also be filed (using Form 6-K) with the SEC.

IX *REGULATION S-X:* A CLOSER LOOK

Recall from the introduction to *Regulation S-X* on page 756 that this regulation sets forth not only the financial statements filed with the SEC under the various acts but also the form and content of those financial statements. As a result of recent revisions to modernize *Regulation S-X* and integrate the various reporting requirements of companies, the regulation also applies to annual reports to stockholders. Accordingly, the financial statements included in the Form 10-K annual report are now identical to the financial statements in annual reports to stockholders.

Because this regulation is approximately 100 pages long, a detailed discussion is beyond the scope of this book. The objective here is to provide a general familiarity with the contents of *Regulation S-X*.

Regulation S-X is composed of the following articles, each of which has its own rules:

Article	Description
1	Application of *Regulation S-X*
2	Qualifications and reports of accountants
3	General instructions as to financial statements
3A	Consolidated and combined financial statements

(continued)

4	Rules of general application
5	Commercial and industrial companies
6	Registered investment companies
6A	Employee stock purchase, savings, and similar plans
7	Insurance companies
9	Bank holding companies
10	Interim financial statements
11	Pro forma financial information
12	Form and content of schedules

Because Articles 6, 6A, and 7 have at most only limited application to most companies, they are not discussed in this chapter. The remaining articles are discussed briefly.

ARTICLE 1: APPLICATION OF *REGULATION S-X*

Article 1 specifies the nature of *Regulation S-X*, states the acts to which it applies, and defines the terms used in the regulation.

ARTICLE 2: QUALIFICATIONS AND REPORTS OF ACCOUNTANTS

Article 2 discusses (1) the qualification of certified public accountants (primarily conditions necessary for their independence) and (2) specific requirements concerning the content of a certified public accountant's report on audited financial statements included in one of the designated forms filed with the SEC.

ARTICLE 3: GENERAL INSTRUCTIONS AS TO FINANCIAL STATEMENTS

Article 3 specifies the balance sheets, income statements, and statements of cash flows to be included in registration statements and reports filed with the SEC.

ARTICLE 3A: CONSOLIDATED AND COMBINED FINANCIAL STATEMENTS

Article 3A deals with the presentation of consolidated and combined financial statements. It specifies which subsidiaries should not be consolidated and requires, in general, that all intercompany items and transactions be eliminated.

ARTICLE 4: RULES OF GENERAL APPLICATION

Article 4, the rules of general application, pertains to a variety of items regarding the form, classification, and content of notes to the financial statements. Rule 4–08, "General Notes to Financial Statements," composes most of this article. It is an extensive rule specifying certain information to be set forth in notes to the financial statements. This rule is not a duplication of FASB disclosure requirements. Instead, the requirements pertain to items not specifically addressed in FASB pronouncements and those of its predecessor organizations. Generally, preparing the additional disclosures called for by this article is not a major task.

ARTICLE 5: COMMERCIAL AND INDUSTRIAL COMPANIES

Article 5 applies to all companies that are not required to follow Articles 6, 6A, 7, and 9. Rules 5-02 and 5-03 set forth the various line items and certain additional disclosures that should appear in the balance sheet, income statement, or related notes.

Rule 5-04 is a list and description of 5 financial statement supporting schedules (commonly referred to as **schedules**) that are filed in support of the basic financial statements. These schedules pertain to such things as analyses of property, plant, and equipment and of valuation accounts for specified periods of time. In most cases, only four or five schedules apply. The exact form and content of the schedules are specified by Article 12.

ARTICLE 9: BANK HOLDING COMPANIES

This article is discussed in Chapter 2, page 47.

ARTICLE 10: INTERIM FINANCIAL STATEMENTS

Article 10 deals with the form and content of presentation of interim financial statements (quarterly reports under the 1934 Act and interim financial statements in registration statements filed under the 1933 Act).

ARTICLE 11: PRO FORMA FINANCIAL INFORMATION

Article 11 specifies when pro forma financial statements must be presented. Such financial statements are required when business combinations have occurred or are probable.

ARTICLE 12: FORM AND CONTENT OF SCHEDULES

Article 12 prescribes the form and content of the financial statement supporting schedules required by Rule 5-04 under Article 5 and certain rules in other articles. The exact columnar headings used for each schedule are specified, along with detailed instructions on how to prepare each schedule.

END-OF-CHAPTER REVIEW

SUMMARY OF KEY POINTS

1. The Securities Act of 1933 and the Securities Exchange Act of 1934 protect investors from fraudulent actions and unethical practices by the promoters of securities and the managements of companies issuing securities.
2. The Securities and Exchange Commission administers the 1933 Act and the 1934 Act, as well as several other acts.
3. The SEC has the **statutory authority** (granted by Congress) to establish GAAP, but to date, it has allowed the private sector to establish them. The SEC works closely with the FASB and the Emerging Issues Task Force in establishing GAAP.
4. Unlike the FASB, the SEC has **enforcement powers** that it uses as necessary to order a company to change its interpretation of GAAP. Also, the SEC is empowered to take **disciplinary actions** against auditors.
5. Companies subject to the registration and reporting requirements of these statutes must be familiar with a labyrinth of regulations, rules, releases, forms, and bulletins to comply with these statutes. For the disclosure of nonfinancial information, companies usually rely heavily on their legal counsel for assistance and guidance. For the disclosure of financial information, company accountants must be intimately familiar with the detailed requirements of *Regulation S-X*.
6. In some areas, *Regulation S-X* imposes significant additional reporting requirements beyond those required under generally accepted accounting principles.

GLOSSARY OF NEW TERMS

American Depository Receipt (ADR) A "negotiable certificate of ownership" (bought through a bank intermediary) that serves as a surrogate for the actual common shares owned in a foreign firm. (ADRs are generally considered a more convenient form of ownership than the *direct* form of ownership.)

Blue sky laws State laws dealing with the purchase and sale of securities.

Exempt offering An offering of securities that need not be registered with the SEC because of an available statutory exemption.

Forms Specific enumerations of the form and content of information included in registration statements and reports filed with the SEC.

Offering circular A scaled down version of a *prospectus* (used in *Regulation A* exempt offerings).

Primary offering The sale of new (previously unissued) securities to the public.

Private offering "Transactions by an issuer not involving a public offering."*

Prospectus The portion of a registration statement that must be furnished to prospective investors in connection with an offering of securities being registered with the SEC.

Proxy A document empowering a person to vote for another person.

Proxy statement A statement containing specified information furnished to stockholders in connection with the solicitation of proxies for use at an annual meeting (or special meetings) of shareholders.

Registration The process of submitting certain specified financial and nonfinancial information to the SEC for the purpose of obtaining approval to sell securities to the public.

Registration statement All of the specified financial and nonfinancial information filed with the SEC (set forth according to an appropriate form) for purposes of registering an offering of securities to the public.

Restricted security Securities acquired by means that did not involve a public offering.

Secondary offering The sale of restricted securities (securities that were issued by means other than a *primary offering*) to the public.

Security "Any note, stock, treasury stock, bond, debenture, evidence of indebtedness, certificate of interest or participation in any profit-sharing agreement. . . . transferable share, investment contract, voting trust certificate. . . . or in general any interest or instrument commonly known as a security. . . ."*

Underwriter "Any person who has purchased from an issuer with a view to, or offers or sells for an issuer in connection with, the distribution of any security, or participates [directly or indirectly] . . . in any such undertaking. . . ."*

SELF-STUDY QUESTIONS

(Answers are at the end of this chapter.)

1. Which of the following is the SEC *not* empowered to do?
   a. Require additional disclosures
   b. Prohibit accounting practices
   c. Overrule the FASB
   d. Establish GAAP
   e. Rescind FASB pronouncements

2. With which body does the statutory authority to establish GAAP reside?
   a. The SEC Commissioners
   b. The Chief Accountant of the SEC
   c. The Division of Corporate Finance
   d. The FASB
   e. The SEC staff

3. Which of the following actions can the SEC *not* take against auditors?
   a. Censure the auditors
   b. Require the auditors to submit to a peer review
   c. Institute criminal proceedings

*Securities Act of 1933.

    d. Bar the auditors from practicing before the SEC either temporarily or permanently

    e. Require the auditors to take continuing education courses

4. Where can one find interpretations and practices followed by certain departments of the SEC that are responsible for reviewing the disclosure requirements of the federal securities law?

    a. *Regulation S-K*

    b. *Regulation S-X*

    c. Financial Reporting Releases

    d. Staff Accounting Bulletins

    e. Accounting and Auditing Enforcement Releases

    f. SEC releases

5. Which of the following must a company desiring to issue common stock to the public file with the SEC?

    a. Prospectus

    b. Registration statement

    c. Proxy statement

    d. Offering circular

    e. S-1 registration statement

6. The Securities Act of 1933, in general, exempts certain stock offerings from full registration. Which of the following is *not* exempt from full registration?

    a. Private offerings

    b. *Regulation A* offerings

    c. Strictly intrastate issues

    d. Securities of governmental units

    e. Securities registered using Form S-1

7. In which of the following are the financial statements in filings with the SEC to be included in the material being filed?

    a. The appropriate form being used

    b. *Regulation S-X*

    c. *Regulation S-K*

    d. Staff Accounting Bulletins

    e. Financial reporting releases

8. Which form is used to report a change in auditors?

    a. Form S-1

    b. Form 10-K

    c. Form 8-K

    d. Form F-4

    e. Form S-X

    f. Form 10

ASSIGNMENT MATERIAL

REVIEW QUESTIONS

1. How does the Securities Exchange Act of 1934 differ from the Securities Act of 1933?
2. What purpose do the SEC's Staff Accounting Bulletins serve?
3. What purpose do SEC releases serve?
4. What is the SEC's role in the formation and improvement of generally accepted accounting principles?
5. How do a registration statement and a prospectus differ?
6. What is the distinction between Form S-1 and Form 10-K?
7. What do Regulations A and D have in common?
8. What do Forms 8-K, 10-K, and 10-Q have in common?
9. How is *Regulation C* under the 1933 Act similar to *Regulation 12B* under the 1934 Act?
10. What is the distinction between *Regulation S-X* and *Regulation S-K*?
11. How do a proxy and a proxy statement differ?

12. How are financial statements prepared in accordance with *Regulation S-X* requirements different from financial statements prepared in accordance with GAAP?

EXERCISES

E 22–1   **The Role of the SEC in Relation to the FASB**   Indicate whether each of the following statements is true or false. Discuss the reasons for your answers.

1. The pronouncements of the FASB must be formally approved by the SEC before they can be issued.
2. The accounting-related pronouncements of the SEC must be formally approved by the FASB before they are issued.
3. The SEC has given the FASB the statutory authority to prescribe accounting principles.
4. Publicly owned companies are subject to the SEC and FASB financial reporting requirements.
5. Privately owned companies are *not* subject to the SEC financial reporting requirements.
6. The SEC automatically rescinds a pronouncement when the FASB issues a Statement of Financial Accounting Standards involving a particular accounting issue.
7. When the SEC notices an emerging accounting practice that the FASB has not addressed, it most likely will establish accounting standards in that area until the FASB or the EITF can address the issue.
8. Unlike the FASB, the SEC can order a company subject to its reporting requirements to alter its financial statements.

E 22–2   **SEC Promulgations**   Complete the following statements:

1. The form and content of financial statements included with filings with the SEC are set forth in _____.
2. The pronouncements that announce the SEC's proposed revisions to its rules and regulations are called _____.
3. Nonfinancial statement disclosure requirements are set forth in _____.
4. An SEC regulation is merely a collection of _____.
5. The SEC rules and regulations that pertain to the various sections of the 1933 Act and the 1934 Act are referred to as the _____ rules and regulations.
6. The regulation that specifies the financial statements included in SEC filings is _____.
7. The interpretations and practices followed by certain departments of the SEC are called _____.
8. Accounting-related releases used to be announced in _____, but now they are set forth in _____.
9. The promulgation of the SEC that accountants deal with more than any other is _____.
10. A list of instructions concerning what is included in a particular SEC filing is called a _____.

E 22–3   **The 1933 and 1934 Acts: Terminology**   Complete the following statements:

1. Under the 1933 Act, issuers of securities must furnish potential investors with a(n) _____.
2. A registration statement is divided into the following two basic parts:
   a. Information _____.
   b. Information _____.
3. A "red herring" is a(n) _____.
4. Stocks and bonds are _____.
5. A person who purchases an issuer's stock with a view to distributing that stock to the public is a(n) _____.
6. Security offerings that need not be registered with the SEC are considered _____ offerings.
7. All the information filed with the SEC using an appropriate form under the 1933 Act is called a(n) _____.
8. The Securities Act of 1933 pertains to the _____ of securities.
9. The Securities Exchange Act of 1934 pertains to _____ of issued securities.
10. Securities acquired by means that did not involve a public offering are called _____.
11. A document authorizing one person to vote for another person is a _____.
12. A statement furnished to stockholders in connection with soliciting their votes is called a _____.

TROUBLED DEBT RESTRUCTURINGS, BANKRUPTCY REORGANIZATIONS, AND LIQUIDATIONS

Some debts are fun when you are acquiring them, but none are fun when you set about retiring them.

OGDEN NASH

CHAPTER OVERVIEW

OPTIONS FOR FINANCIALLY DISTRESSED COMPANIES

Any type of economic entity (including corporations, partnerships, sole proprietorships, and municipalities) can encounter financial difficulties. Business entities in financial difficulty first usually retrench and undertake cost-cutting steps to conserve cash and reduce operating losses. Such steps may include revamping the organization structure to eliminate or consolidate functions (often resulting in the termination of a substantial number of personnel), seeking wage and fringe-benefit concessions from employees, seeking relaxation of restrictive union work rules, and disposing of unprofitable segments. In addition, the entity may eventually need to (1) raise additional capital, (2) dispose of profitable segments, (3) combine with another business, (4) restructure its debt outside the bankruptcy courts, (5) reorganize through the bankruptcy courts, or (6) liquidate.

This chapter deals with corporations that select the last three options. Option 4, restructuring debt outside the bankruptcy courts, usually consists of extending due dates, forgiving some portion of debt, and reducing the interest rate on the debt. This option gives the business a reasonable chance to continue as a viable entity and recover from the financial difficulties, thereby avoiding liquidation, at least for the time being. Although option 5, reorganization through the bankruptcy courts, is identical in its objective to that of option 4, it is considered less desirable even though it usually results in a substantial forgiveness of debt. Option 6, **liquidation,** consists of converting all noncash assets into cash, paying creditors to the extent possible, and ending the legal existence of the corporation. In discussing the options of restructuring debt and reorganizing through the bankruptcy courts, we exclude railroads and municipalities because of their special nature. We also exclude these special entities from the discussion of liquidation because public policy dictates that these entities not be liquidated.

I BANKRUPTCY STATUTES

THEIR PURPOSE

Debt capital markets would be inhibited without some provisions for ensuring fair and equitable means to resolve rights and protect public interests. This is the purpose of the bankruptcy laws. Distressed companies and their creditors must decide whether it is necessary to resort to the bankruptcy process. Accordingly, we now discuss the federal bankruptcy statutes.

THEIR SUBSTANCE

Under the bankruptcy statutes, a company or an individual is placed under the protection of the court, whereby creditors (including creditors possessing security interests, unsecured creditors, tax collectors, and public utilities) are prevented from taking other legal action (such as foreclosing on loans, filing lawsuits, repossessing or seizing assets, and placing padlocks on the doors of the company's real property). When a company's rehabilitation and future viable operations are feasible, its debt is restructured under the supervision and control of the court in such a manner that the debtor may be legally freed from the payment of certain past debts. When rehabilitation and recovery are not feasible, an orderly liquidation takes place under the supervision and control of the bankruptcy court. Approximately 1,000,000 bankruptcy filings occur each year (almost double the number a decade ago).

THE FEDERAL BANKRUPTCY CODE

The U.S. Constitution grants to the Congress the power to establish uniform laws throughout the United States pertaining to the subject of bankruptcies. The federal bankruptcy statutes are set forth in title 11 of the United States Code. These laws are commonly referred to as the **Bankruptcy Code.** Federal statutes pertaining to bankruptcy prevail over state laws that conflict with federal laws.

The Bankruptcy Code is periodically amended (as it was in 1994 and 1984). Under the Bankruptcy Code, separate bankruptcy courts (adjuncts to the district courts) are required, along with special judges (commonly referred to as *bankruptcy judges*) who supervise and review all bankruptcy petitions and proceedings. (If a case involves broad bankruptcy issues, however, such issues are decided by district judges, not the bankruptcy judges.)

The Bankruptcy Code consists of the following nine chapters (even-numbered chapters do not exist except for Chapter 12):

Chapter 1	General provisions
Chapter 3	Case administration
Chapter 5	Creditors, the debtor, and the estate
Chapter 7	Liquidation
Chapter 9	Adjustment of debts of a municipality
Chapter 11	Reorganization
Chapter 12	Adjustment of the debts of a family farmer with regular annual income
Chapter 13	Adjustment of debts of an individual with regular income

The general provisions of Chapters 1, 3, and 5 pertain to Chapters 7, 9, 11, 12, and 13, unless otherwise indicated. In this section, we discuss certain basic aspects of Chapters 1, 3, and 5. Chapters 9, 12, and 13 do *not* pertain to corporations organized to make a profit; accordingly, they are not discussed in this chapter. (Chapter 9 applies only to municipalities that seek relief voluntarily; a municipality cannot be forced into bankruptcy proceedings against its will by its creditors.) Chapter 7 is discussed later in this chapter in the section dealing with *liquidations.* Chapter 11 is also discussed later in this chapter in the section dealing with *bankruptcy reorganizations.*

In the Bankruptcy Code, the subject of the bankruptcy proceedings is referred to as a **debtor.** The commencement of a bankruptcy case creates an **estate.** The estate includes all of the debtor's property no matter where located (Section 541).[1]

APPLICABILITY OF THE BANKRUPTCY CODE

The Bankruptcy Code applies to individuals, partnerships, corporations (all of which are collectively referred to as *persons*), and municipalities. Insurance companies and certain financial institutions (such as banks, savings and loan associations, building and loan associations, and credit unions) are excluded because they are subject to alternative regulations. Railroads may not use the liquidation provisions of Chapter 7 and may use only the reorganization provisions of Chapter 11. Stockbrokers and commodity brokers are not eligible for the reorganization provisions of Chapter 11 and may use only the liquidation provisions of Chapter 7 (Section 109[b]).

---

[1]This reference is to the Bankruptcy Code. Hereafter, only the section number of the code is provided.

VOLUNTARY PETITIONS

An eligible corporation (that is, a corporation other than an insurance company or certain financial institutions) may file a voluntary petition with the bankruptcy courts under Chapter 7 or 11 and thereby obtain the benefits available under the statutes (Section 109). Filing a voluntary petition constitutes an **order for relief,** which has the full force and effect as if the bankruptcy court had issued an order that the debtor be granted relief under the statutes (Section 301). The court can dismiss a voluntary filing, however, if it is in the best interests of creditors (Section 707 and 112[b]).

The **voluntary petition** initiates bankruptcy proceedings and is an official form that must be accompanied by a summary of the debtor's property (at market or current values) and debts, including supporting schedules, all on official forms. The supporting schedules for property consist of separate schedules for real property, personal property, and property not otherwise scheduled. The supporting schedules for debts consist of separate schedules for *creditors with priority* (a special class of creditors explained later in the book), creditors holding security, and creditors having unsecured claims without priority. Information must also include each creditor's address (if known), when the debt was incurred, and whether the debt is contingent, disputed, or subject to setoff. In addition, the petitioner must respond to a questionnaire regarding all aspects of its financial condition and operations. Although this questionnaire is called the *statement of affairs,* it should not be confused with the statement of affairs that accountants prepare regarding asset values and debts owed, which is explained later in the chapter.

INVOLUNTARY PETITIONS

Under Chapter 7 or 11, an eligible corporation may be forced into bankruptcy proceedings against its will by its creditors. One or more creditors may file an **involuntary petition** with the bankruptcy court. If a debtor has 12 or more creditors, at least 3 of them who have claims totaling a minimum of $10,000 more than the value of any lien on the property of the debtor securing such claims must sign the petition (Section 303[b][1]). If a company has fewer than 12 creditors, one or more creditors having such claims of at least $10,000 must sign the petition (Section 303[b][2]). These dollar amounts apply to both liquidation and reorganization cases.

For an involuntary petition filed under Chapter 7 or 11, the bankruptcy court enters an order for relief against the debtor only if either of the following conditions pertains:

1. The debtor is generally not paying its debts as they become due.
2. A custodian was appointed or took possession of the debtor's property within 120 days before the date of the filing of the petition. (This does not apply to a trustee, receiver, or agent appointed or authorized to take charge of less than the majority of the debtor's property for the purpose of enforcing a lien against such property.) (Section 303[h]).

The first test listed is an equity insolvency test; that is, the debtor's assets equitably belong to the creditors to the extent of their claims. In the second test, the appointment of a custodian presumes that the debtor cannot pay its debts as they mature.

In practice, *voluntary* bankruptcies occur much more frequently than *involuntary* bankruptcies. Regardless of whether a company enters bankruptcy proceedings voluntarily or involuntarily, it should immediately obtain the assistance of an attorney who specializes in bankruptcy proceedings.

CREDITORS WITH PRIORITY

A company entering bankruptcy proceedings can have two general classes of creditor—secured and unsecured. **Secured creditors** have been pledged certain of the company's assets as security on their claims. Creditors that have no right to any of the company's specific assets are **unsecured creditors.** In addition to these two general classes of creditors, the Bankruptcy Code creates a special class of creditor termed **creditors with priority.** Nine categories of debt are given priority status. We list the major ones in the order of their priority, as follows:

1. **Administrative expenses, fees, and charges assessed against the estate.** Administrative expenses are the actual and necessary costs and expenses of preserving the estate after the petition has been filed. This includes trustee's fees, legal, accounting, and appraisal fees incurred in connection with the bankruptcy proceedings, filing fees paid by creditors in an involuntary bankruptcy petition, and expenses incurred in recovering assets that were concealed or fraudulently transferred.

2. **Certain postfiling "gap" claims.** This category, which exists only for involuntary filings, includes unsecured claims arising in the ordinary course of the debtor's business after the involuntary filing but before the appointment of a trustee or an order of relief is entered, whichever occurs first.

3. **Wages, salaries, and commissions.** Wages, salaries, and commissions are limited to unsecured amounts earned by an individual within 90 days before the filing date or the date of the cessation of the debtor's business, whichever occurs first, but only up to $4,000 for each individual. This category includes vacation, severance, and sick leave pay.

4. **Employee benefit plans.** This category pertains to unsecured claims for contributions to employee benefit plans arising from services rendered by employees within 180 days before the date of the filing of the petition or the date of the cessation of the debtor's business, whichever occurs first. The claims are limited to the number of employees covered by each such plan multiplied by $4,000, minus (a) the total amount paid to such employees as items in priority 3 and (b) the total amount paid by the estate on behalf of such employees to any other employee benefit plan.

5. **Deposits by individuals.** This category includes unsecured claims of up to $900 for each such individual, arising from the deposit of money before the commencement of the case in connection with the purchase, lease, or rental of property, or the purchase of services for the personal, family, or household use of such individuals, which were not delivered or provided.

6. **Taxes.** This category includes income taxes, property taxes, withholding taxes, employer payroll taxes, excise taxes, and customs duties. Most of these taxes are limited to amounts relating to a specified period of time preceding the date of the filing, usually one or three years, depending on the item.

Creditors with priority are given a statutory priority over the claims of other unsecured creditors with regard to payment. Later in the chapter, we illustrate this priority in a liquidation through the bankruptcy courts.

II | TROUBLED DEBT RESTRUCTURINGS

In troubled debt restructurings, steps are taken outside the bankruptcy courts to give the distressed company a reasonable chance to survive. This option is considered much more desirable than a Chapter 11 reorganization.

ADVANTAGES OF RESTRUCTURING VERSUS REORGANIZING

One advantage of restructuring outside the bankruptcy courts is that the restructuring can be completed in far less time than a Chapter 11 reorganization, which takes a minimum of approximately 18 months. Of greater importance, however, is the desire to avoid the stigma associated with being or having been subject to bankruptcy proceedings. More uncertainty is associated with Chapter 11 reorganizations concerning the distressed company's chances of survival—many companies that file for Chapter 11 reorganizations are unable to work out a successful plan of reorganization and are liquidated instead. Thus filing for reorganization under Chapter 11 is considered the last resort, short of liquidation.

Needless to say, filing for a Chapter 11 reorganization has far greater consequences to the distressed company in terms of its impact on suppliers, competitors, customers, and employees than does a restructuring outside the bankruptcy courts. For example, a distressed company that is restructuring may be able to obtain some credit from suppliers; when a company reorganizes under Chapter 11, suppliers usually require payment on delivery. During restructuring, competitors tend to get sales leverage from a distressed company's problems; during a Chapter 11 reorganization, competitors have that much more ammunition. (Competitors often show customers press clippings of the distressed company's financial problems.)

When a company has filed for reorganization under Chapter 11, customers have that much less ensurance that the company will survive—this can be critical for a distressed company that sells products requiring the company's continued existence for purposes of providing service and stocking spare parts. Employees are more likely to look for greener pastures once a company files for reorganization under Chapter 11 because of the uncertainty associated with bankruptcy proceedings. (Personnel placement firms tend to zero in on distressed companies to hire away their employees; their chances of success increase when a company files for a Chapter 11 reorganization.)

Working out a troubled debt restructuring agreement is usually a substantial and difficult undertaking, especially when major differences exist among various groups of creditors as to the sacrifices each is willing to make. A distressed company often resorts to a Chapter 11 reorganization when it is impossible to work out a troubled debt restructuring agreement with its creditors, when its lenders refuse to lend any more money, or when suppliers begin requiring payment on delivery. Although the advantages of restructuring debt outside the bankruptcy courts are considerable, there are certain advantages to filing for reorganization under Chapter 11. These advantages are discussed later in the chapter when reorganization under Chapter 11 is discussed in detail.

NATURE OF TROUBLED DEBT RESTRUCTURINGS

The accounting procedures for most debt restructurings are prescribed by FASB *Statement No. 15*, "Accounting by Debtors and Creditors for Troubled Debt Restructurings."[2] Before discussing the accounting issues and procedures in detail, we (1) define *troubled debt restructuring*, (2) show transactions that may be considered troubled debt restructurings, and (3) show some ways in which a distressed company can restructure its debt.

---

[2]This statement was amended slightly by FASB *Statement No. 114*, "Accounting by Creditors for Impairment of a Loan" (discussed later) and FASB *Statement No.121*, "Accounting for the Impairment of Long-Lived Assets and for Long-Lived Assets to Be Disposed Of."

DEFINITION   *SFAS No. 15* defines a troubled debt restructuring as follows:

> A restructuring of debt constitutes a **troubled debt restructuring** for purposes of this Statement if the creditor for economic or legal reasons related to the debtor's financial difficulties grants a concession to the debtor that it would not otherwise consider.[3]

The statement expounds on this definition as follows:

> Whatever the form of concession granted by the creditor to the debtor in a troubled debt restructuring, the creditor's objective is to make the best of a difficult situation. That is, the creditor expects to obtain more cash or other value from the debtor, or to increase the probability of receipt, by granting the concession than by not granting it.[4]

CATEGORIES OF TRANSACTIONS   The statement lists the following types of transactions that may constitute troubled debt restructurings:

a. Transfer from the debtor to the creditor of receivables from third parties, real estate, or other assets to satisfy fully or partially a debt (including a transfer resulting from foreclosure or repossession).
b. Issuance or other granting of an equity interest to the creditor by the debtor to satisfy fully or partially a debt unless the equity interest is granted pursuant to existing terms for converting the debt into an equity interest.
c. Modification of terms of a debt, such as one or a combination of:
    1. Reduction (absolute or contingent) of the stated interest rate for the remaining original life of the debt.
    2. Extension of the maturity date or dates at a stated interest rate lower than the current market rate for a new debt with similar risk.
    3. Reduction (absolute or contingent) of the face amount or maturity amount of the debt as stated in the instrument or other agreement.
    4. Reduction (absolute or contingent) of accrued interest.[5]

INDIVIDUAL CREDITOR AGREEMENTS   The most frequently used manner to restructure debt is the **individual creditor agreement** between a debtor and a creditor whereby the payment terms are restructured pursuant to negotiated terms. Within the past 15 years, dozens of large companies have restructured their debt in this manner or have at least attempted to do so. Typically, the creditors involved are banks. The most major, widely publicized and completed restructurings in the past 15 years were those of Chrysler Corp., which owed $4.4 billion to more than 400 banks, and International Harvester Corp., which owed $3.4 billion to more than 200 banks.

COMPOSITION AGREEMENTS   A **composition agreement** is a formal agreement between a debtor and its creditors (and among the creditors) whereby the creditors collectively agree to accept a percentage of their claims—such as 60 cents on the dollar—in full settlement of their claims. For example, a composition agreement may include only the debtor's major creditors, with all other creditors still entitled to full payment. The payment terms of the composition agreement may require immediate, partial, or full payment of the reduced amount. To the extent that payment of the reduced amount is deferred, a debtor may execute notes payable bearing interest on the deferred amount.

Composition agreements are usually negotiated when a company's filing for a Chapter 11 reorganization is imminent. As a result of the agreement, the company

---

[3]*Statement of Financial Accounting Standards No. 15*, "Accounting by Debtors and Creditors for Troubled Debt Restructurings" (Stamford: Financial Accounting Standards Board, 1977), par. 2.
[4]*SFAS No. 15*, par. 3.
[5]*SFAS No. 15*, par. 5.

does not suffer the taint of having gone through a bankruptcy proceeding, a potentially lengthy and involved bankruptcy process is avoided, and the creditors expect to recover more than they would in a Chapter 11 reorganization.

CONCEPTUAL ISSUES

Troubled debt restructurings usually result in the creditors' substantial reduction of the debtor's financial obligations (required payments for principal and interest). This procedure requires a comparison of (1) the total amount owed (including unpaid interest) immediately *before* the restructuring, which is commonly referred to as the **carrying amount of the debt,** with (2) the **total future payments** (including amounts designated as interest) to be made pursuant to the restructuring agreement. If the carrying amount of the debt *exceeds* the total future payments, the debtor's liabilities must be reduced. This reduction constitutes a **forgiveness of debt.** If the debtor's total future payments exceed the carrying amount of the debt, the excess is reported as interest expense in future periods. This situation presents no accounting issue. The accounting issues pertain solely to the forgiveness of debt and are as follows:

1. **How should any forgiveness of debt be measured?** The focus of this issue is primarily whether the new (postrestructuring) liability amount should be measured and reported at (a) the *undiscounted* total future payments to be made or (b) the present value of total future payments. The difference between (a) or (b) and the carrying amount of the debt is the amount of the forgiveness. Obviously, the choice between (a) and (b) affects the amount of forgiveness that is reported.

2. **How should a forgiveness of debt be classified and reported?** This issue is concerned with whether a forgiveness of debt should be considered (a) a **gain** and, therefore, reported in the **income statement** or (b) a **capital contribution** by the creditor or creditors and, therefore, credited directly to an **equity account.**

The resolution of these issues should be based on the *substance* of the restructuring rather than its *form.* Varying perceptions exist, however, as to what constitutes the substance.

CONCEPTUAL ISSUE 1: CALCULATION OF FORGIVENESS OF DEBT

In some situations, the calculation of forgiveness of debt is quite simple. For example, assume that a creditor that is owed $100,000 agrees to cancel $40,000 of the debt in return for the immediate payment of the remaining $60,000. Obviously, the amount of debt forgiven is $40,000. Most situations, however, are more complex. For example, assume that (1) a creditor is owed $100,000 of principal related to a delinquent loan bearing interest at 10% (for simplicity, we assume that no interest is owed) and (2) the creditor agrees to be paid in full in two years with no interest to be charged. Two approaches have been advocated for such situations—one that **imputes interest** and one that **does not impute interest.** When interest is *not* imputed, the calculation to determine any forgiveness of debt is as follows:

Carrying amount of debt	$100,000
Total future payments	100,000
Amount of Forgiveness	$ –0–

Under this approach, the liability reported in the balance sheet immediately after the restructuring is $100,000, and it bears a zero interest rate. No interest expense is reported in either year.

When interest is imputed (using present value techniques), the amount of forgiveness, if any, depends on the imputed interest rate used. Assuming that the 10%

prerestructuring interest rate is appropriate, the calculation to determine any forgiveness of debt is as follows:

Carrying amount of debt		$100,000
Total future payments	$100,000	
Present value factor (10%, 2 years)	0.82645	
Present value of total future payments		82,645
Amount of Forgiveness		$ 17,355

Under this approach, the liability reported in the balance sheet immediately after the restructuring is $82,645, and it bears interest at 10%. Interest expense of $8,264 (10% of $82,645) would be reported in Year 1, and $9,091 [10% of ($82,645 + $8,264)] would be reported in Year 2.

RATIONALE FOR *NOT* IMPUTING INTEREST   Arguments for *not* imputing interest are as follows:

1. Troubled debt restructurings *are not* "exchanges of debt" and, therefore, *do not* require the use of present value techniques as set forth in *APB Opinion No. 21,* "Interest on Receivables and Payables," which deals with "exchanges."

2. A creditor does not grant any forgiveness under the restructuring so long as the total future payments to be received equal or exceed the recorded investment in the receivable; that is, the *recoverability* of the recorded investment in the receivable is not affected.

3. A reduction of the debtor's financial obligations (before the restructuring) to the amount of the recorded investment in the receivable merely changes the creditor's *future profitability* on the loan. Thus a creditor's effective interest rate after the restructuring could vary from the *prerestructuring interest rate* of 10%, for example, down to zero.

Recall from the *nonimputing* example that no forgiveness of debt existed because the total future payments of $100,000 were not below the $100,000 carrying amount of the debt. Thus, from the creditor's perspective, the future profitability on the loan had been reduced to zero, but the *recoverability* of the recorded amount of the receivable had not been affected.

RATIONALE FOR IMPUTING INTEREST   Arguments for imputing interest are as follows:

1. The debtor's liability after restructuring ($82,645 in the imputing example) is reported on the same basis as the borrowings of all debtors—that is, the present value of the future cash outflows for principal and interest.

2. The debtor's future income statements reflect a reasonable amount of interest expense, which should enhance comparability of those statements with the debtor's past income statements and with future income statements of other companies.

An implementation issue under this approach is whether the **prerestructuring interest rate** or a **current market interest rate** should be used. Most accountants believe that the debtor's obligation after the restructuring results from a modification of an existing loan. Therefore, the prerestructuring rate should be used. Other accountants who view the debtor's obligation after restructuring as arising from the execution of a new lending agreement conclude that a current market interest rate should be used. An advantage of the prerestructuring approach is that the interest rate is known. However, the current market rate approach involves determining the interest rate at which a debtor in a precarious financial position might be able to borrow when, in fact, no lenders may be available.

CONCEPTUAL ISSUE 2: REPORTING FORGIVENESS OF DEBT

One alternative is to report the forgiveness of debt in the income statement. In this approach, **a forgiveness of debt is a gain on restructuring,** which is **similar to a gain on extinguishment of debt.** Under *APB Opinion No. 26,* "Early Extinguishment of Debt," gains on extinguishments of debt must be reported in the income statement either as an *ordinary* or *extraordinary item,* as appropriate. In most cases, such gains are reported as an *extraordinary item* because the criteria of *unusual* and *infrequent* are met.

In a second alternative, **a forgiveness of debt may be reported as a direct addition to paid-in capital.** The arguments for this approach are as follows:

1. Because the transaction infuses capital to the debtor, in substance, the debtor has received a capital contribution from the creditor.

2. It should make no difference whether the additional capital needed to keep the debtor in business comes from stockholders or creditors.

3. A company in serious financial difficulty, which has probably reported substantial operating losses, should not report income on a transaction intended to assist it in eventually returning to profitable operations.

REQUIREMENTS OF FASB *STATEMENT NO. 15*

After considering the various viewpoints on imputing or not imputing interest, the Financial Accounting Standards Board (FASB) concluded that (1) **interest should *not* be imputed** in the calculation to determine whether any forgiveness of debt exists; (2) the amount of debt forgiven should be **reported as a gain on restructuring;** and (3) such gain, if material, should be **reported as an extraordinary item,** net of its related income tax effect. Accordingly, in calculating the amount of debt forgiven, the carrying amount of the debt is compared with any one (or more) of the following that was included in the restructuring plan:

1. The total future cash payments specified in the new terms **not discounted** back to their present value.

2. The fair value of the noncash assets transferred.

3. The fair value of the equity interest granted.

To the extent that the carrying amount of the debt exceeds these relevant factor(s), a gain on restructuring is reportable.

We now define in detail certain terms used in *SFAS No. 15.*

1. **The carrying amount of the debt** is the face, or principal amount, plus any accrued interest payable, less any unamortized discount (or plus any premium), finance charges, or debt issuance costs.

2. **Total future cash payments** include amounts that are designated principal and interest. Thus the labels traditionally assigned to amounts to be paid to creditors lose their significance for purposes of determining whether a gain on restructuring of debt exists.

3. **Fair value** is defined as "the amount that the debtor could reasonably expect to receive . . . in a current sale between a willing buyer and a willing seller, that is, other than in a forced or liquidation sale."[6]

In most respects, this approach for calculating the amount of debt forgiven is relatively simple to apply. Subsequent income statements, however, reflect either no

---

[6]*SFAS No. 15, par. 13.*

interest expense (when a forgiveness of debt is reportable) or unrealistically low interest expense (when no forgiveness of debt is reportable) until the maturity date of the restructured debt. Consequently, reported earnings are higher than the earnings reported if the company paid interest (or at least measured interest expense) at the current rate. Because of the potentially misleading inferences that can be made from subsequent income statements immediately after a complex restructuring, it is important to disclose in the notes to the financial statements of the appropriate subsequent periods the fact that reported interest expense is artificially low because the restructuring was accounted for in this manner.

OTHER IMPORTANT TECHNICAL AND PROCEDURAL POINTS Other important technical and procedural points of *SFAS No. 15* are the following:

1. The *date of consummation* is the point in time at which the restructuring occurs.

2. The restructuring of each payable is accounted for individually, even if the restructuring was negotiated and restructured jointly.

3. When a noncash asset is transferred to a creditor in full settlement of a debt, the difference between the carrying amount of the noncash asset and its fair value is recognized as a gain or loss in the transfer of the asset. (Such gain or loss is reported in the income statement in the period of transfer as provided in *APB Opinion No. 30*, "Reporting the Results of Operations.")

4. To the extent that the total future cash payments specified in the new terms exceed the carrying amount of the debt, the difference is reported as interest expense between the restructuring date and the maturity date.

5. The "interest" method prescribed by *APBO No. 21* is used to calculate the amount of the interest expense for each year between the restructuring date and the maturity date. This method causes a constant effective interest rate to be applied to the carrying amount of the debt at the beginning of each period between the restructuring date and the maturity date.

6. When a gain on restructuring has been recognized, all future cash payments are charged to the carrying amount of the payable. In other words, if a gain on restructuring is reported, there *cannot* be any future interest expense with respect to that debt.

7. For determining whether a gain on restructuring exists, the total future cash payments include amounts that may be contingently payable.

8. When a debtor grants an equity interest to a creditor to settle fully a payable, the equity interest is recorded in the debtor's capital accounts at its fair value, and any remaining liability in excess of this fair value is recognized as a gain on restructuring of payables.

9. When either noncash assets or an equity interest is given to a creditor in partial settlement of a payable and the payment terms of the remaining payable are modified, the fair value of the assets transferred or the equity interest granted is first subtracted from the carrying amount of the payable. The residual amount of the payable is then compared with the total future cash payments specified in the new terms to determine whether a gain on restructuring exists.

ILLUSTRATION | **APPLICATION OF FASB *STATEMENT NO. 15***

Assume that the financially distressed Never-Quit Company consummated a troubled debt restructuring with substantially all of its unsecured creditors on August 31, 19X1. Never-Quit's August 31, 19X1, balance sheet before the restructuring is shown in Illustration 23–1. We assume that all notes payable (secured and unsecured) are currently due and payable as a result of defaults under related loan agreements.

The following items are part of the restructuring. For each of these items (except the last one), the application of *SFAS No. 15* is explained and the journal entry to reflect the restructuring is given. (All solutions ignore income tax effects.)

1. **Payment of cash in full settlement.** Never-Quit owes $600,000 to 80 vendors. These vendors have collectively agreed to settle their claims fully for 40 cents on the dollar. Payment of $240,000 was made on August 31, 19X1. Because the carrying amount of the $600,000 debt exceeds the total future cash payments of $240,000, a $360,000 gain on restructuring of debt is reportable in the 19X1 income statement, recorded as follows:

Accounts Payable	600,000	
Cash		240,000
Gain on Restructuring of Debt		360,000
To record payment to vendors and gain on restructuring of debt.		

ILLUSTRATION 23–1	**Balance Sheet Before Restructuring of Debt**

Never-Quit Company
Balance Sheet as of August 31, 19X1
(immediately before restructuring)

Assets

Current Assets		
Cash		$ 450,000
Accounts receivable	$ 650,000	
Less—Allowance for uncollectibles	(240,000)	410,000
Inventories		800,000
Total Current Assets		$ 1,660,000
Noncurrent Assets		
Property, plant, and equipment	$2,700,000	
Less—Accumulated depreciation	(1,500,000)	$ 1,200,000
Other assets		140,000
Total Assets		$ 3,000,000

Liabilities and Stockholders' Deficiency

Current Liabilities		
Note payable, secured by land and buildings		$ 1,000,000
Notes payable, unsecured		2,050,000
Accrued interest (all on unsecured notes)		540,000
Accounts payable		925,000
Other accrued liabilities		75,000
Total Liabilities		$ 4,590,000
Stockholders' Deficiency		
Common stock, $1 par value, 200,000 shares issued and		
outstanding		$ 200,000
Additional paid-in capital		1,850,000
Accumulated deficit		(3,640,000)
Total Stockholders' Deficiency		$(1,590,000)
Total Liabilities in Excess of Stockholders' Deficiency		$ 3,000,000

2. **Transfer of receivables in full settlement.** The company owes $325,000 to a vendor who has agreed to accept certain of the company's accounts receivable totaling $280,000. The company has an allowance of $100,000 recorded on the books against these receivables. The receivables were assigned to the creditor on August 31, 19X1. The company has *not* guaranteed the collectibility of these receivables.

   Because the $325,000 carrying amount of the debt exceeds the $180,000 fair value of the assets (the net amount expected to be collectible by the debtor), a gain of $145,000 on restructuring is reportable in the 19X1 income statement, recorded as follows:

Accounts Payable	325,000	
Allowance for Uncollectibles	100,000	
Accounts Receivable		280,000
Gain on Restructuring of Debt		145,000
To record transfer of assets to vendor and		
gain on restructuring of debt.		

3. **Grant of an equity interest in full settlement.** The company owes $500,000 ($430,000 principal and $70,000 interest) to a financial institution that has agreed to cancel the entire amount owed in exchange for 100,000 shares of the debtor's common stock. The market value of the common stock on August 31, 19X1, is $3.50 per share. The company issued the 100,000 shares of common stock to the creditor on this date.

   Because the $500,000 carrying amount of the debt exceeds the $350,000 fair value of the equity interest granted (100,000 shares × $3.50 per share), a gain on restructuring of debt of $150,000 is reportable in the 19X1 income statement, recorded as follows:

Notes Payable	430,000	
Accrued Interest Payable	70,000	
Common Stock		100,000
Additional Paid-in Capital		250,000
Gain on Restructuring of Debt		150,000
To record grant of equity interest and gain		
on restructuring of debt.		

4. **Modification of debt terms (no contingent interest).** The company owes $260,000 ($220,000 principal and $40,000 interest) to a financial institution that has agreed to cancel $20,000 of principal and the $40,000 of accrued interest and reduce the interest rate on the remaining principal to 5% for five years, at the end of which time the note is to be paid in full.

   Because the $260,000 carrying amount of the debt exceeds the $250,000 total future cash payments as specified in the terms of the agreement ($200,000 designated as a principal payment and $50,000 designated as interest payments), a gain of $10,000 on restructuring of debt is reportable in the 19X1 income statement, recorded as follows:

Notes Payable	220,000	
Accrued Interest Payable	40,000	
Restructured Debt		250,000
Gain on Restructuring of Debt		10,000
To record the restructuring of the debt and the resultant gain.		

Because a gain on restructuring of debt exists, no interest expense is reported for the next five years on this debt.

5. **Modification of debt terms (contingent interest).** The company owes a total of $750,000 ($500,000 principal and $250,000 interest) to a financial institution that has agreed to the following:

   a. The $250,000 accrued interest is canceled.

   b. The due date of the $500,000 principal is extended six years from August 31, 19X1.

   c. The interest rate for the first three years is 5% (a reduction of 5% from the old rate).

   d. The interest rate for the following three years is 10%.

   e. If the debtor's cumulative earnings for the next six years exceed $1,000,000, interest for the first three years must be paid at 10% rather than 5%. (The cumulative earnings will probably not exceed $1,000,000 for the next six years.)

   The total minimum and maximum future payments are determined as follows:

Principal	$500,000
Interest—Years 1, 2, and 3 @ 5%	75,000
Interest—Years 4, 5, and 6 @ 10%	150,000
Minimum Total Future Payments	$725,000
Contingent interest—Years 1, 2, and 3	75,000
Maximum Total Future Payments	$800,000

   The $750,000 carrying value of the debt does *not* exceed the $800,000 total maximum future payments that may be made under the new terms. Thus no gain on restructuring of debt is reportable in 19X1:

Notes Payable	500,000	
Accrued Interest Payable	250,000	
Restructured Debt		750,000
To record the restructuring of the debt.		

   If at the end of the sixth year the cumulative earnings have *not* exceeded $1,000,000, a $25,000 gain on restructuring is reported at that time. If it becomes probable during the six years that the cumulative earnings will exceed $1,000,000, additional interest expense of $50,000 ($800,000 – $750,000 carrying amount of the debt) must be provided over the remaining life of the loan.

6. **Combination grant of equity interest and modification of debt terms.** Never-Quit owes $1,080,000 ($900,000 principal and $180,000 interest) to some of its major stockholders, who have agreed to the following:

   a. Accrued interest of $80,000 is canceled.

   b. Principal of $400,000 is canceled in exchange for the issuance of 4,000 shares of 6%, $100 par value, convertible preferred stock with cumulative dividends. (We assume that the articles of incorporation were amended to approve the authorization for this new class of stock, which was issued on August 31, 19X1.)

   c. The remaining principal of $500,000 and the uncanceled interest of $100,000 bear interest at 5%, with $300,000 to be paid in six months and the remaining $300,000 to be paid in 18 months.

   Because no established market price is available for the preferred stock, we assume that the fair value of the preferred stock equals the $400,000 amount of the principal canceled. This assumed fair value of the preferred stock is subtracted from the $1,080,000 carrying value of the debt to arrive at an *adjusted carrying value* of $680,000. The adjusted carrying value of $680,000 is then compared with the total future payments to determine whether a gain on restructuring exists. The total future payments are $630,000 ($600,000 designated as principal and $30,000 designated as interest). Accordingly, a gain on restructuring of debt of $50,000 ($680,000 – $630,000) is reportable in the 19X1 income statement, recorded as follows:

Notes Payable	900,000	
Accrued Interest Payable	180,000	
Preferred Stock		400,000
Restructured Debt		630,000
Gain on Restructuring of Debt		50,000
To record the restructuring of the debt.		

7. **Reclassification by secured creditor.** None of the preceding items pertain to the company's secured creditor (who is owed $1,000,000) because a secured creditor is under no economic compulsion to make concessions. Because of the preceding restructurings, however, this creditor agrees to allow Never-Quit to repay $960,000 of the $1,000,000 owed after August 31, 19X2, leaving only $40,000 as a current liability as of August 31, 19X1. (The interest rate was not changed.)

Never-Quit's August 31, 19X1, balance sheet, which reflects the financial terms of the restructurings, is shown in Illustration 23–2. In comparing Illustration 23–2 with Illustration 23–1, note that the stockholders' deficiency has been almost eliminated as a result of the restructuring. Although a substantial portion of the stockholders' deficiency is usually eliminated in a troubled debt restructuring, the entire deficiency need not be eliminated for the rehabilitation efforts to be successful.

Never-Quit's 19X1 income statement would reflect the gain on restructuring as an extraordinary item, part of the period's income but separate from income (loss) from operations. The illustration has omitted tax effects, which we address in a later section.

NONAPPLICABILITY OF FASB *STATEMENT NO. 15* TO QUASI-REORGANIZATIONS

Although a debt restructuring may eliminate most or all of the stockholders' deficiency, some companies try to eliminate the accumulated deficit by using the "quasi-reorganization" procedures provided by many state laws.

Recall from intermediate accounting that adjustments made to restate (usually write down) assets in a **quasi-reorganization** are charged directly to equity.[7] Adjustments to restate (reduce) liabilities in a quasi-reorganization are similarly credited directly to equity. Treating such adjustments to assets and liabilities as capital transactions is desirable because otherwise asset write-downs would be reported as capital transactions and liability reductions would be reported (per the general rule of *SFAS No. 15*) as noncapital (income statement) transactions.

SFAS No. 15 does *not* apply to a troubled debt restructuring that coincides with quasi-reorganization procedures if the debtor "restates its liabilities generally" in that quasi-reorganization. The phrase **"restates its liabilities generally"** is a new

---

[7]This procedure is required pursuant to the provisions of *Accounting Research Bulletin No. 43*, Chapter 7, Section A, "Capital Accounts," par. 6. This position was reaffirmed in *Opinions of the Accounting Principles Board, No. 9*, "Reporting the Results of Operations," par. 28.

ILLUSTRATION 23–2	**Balance Sheet After Restructuring of Debt**

Never-Quit Company
Balance Sheet as of August 31, 19X1
(after the restructuring)

Assets

Current Assets

Cash		$ 210,000
Accounts receivable	$ 370,000	
Less—Allowance for uncollectibles	(140,000)	230,000
Inventories		800,000
Total Current Assets		$ 1,240,000

Noncurrent Assets

Property, plant, and equipment	$2,700,000	
Less—Accumulated depreciation	(1,500,000)	$ 1,200,000
Other assets		140,000
Total Assets		$ 2,580,000

Liabilities and Stockholders' Deficiency

Current Liabilities

Other accrued liabilities	$ 75,000
Current portion of secured note payable	40,000
Current portion of restructured debt, unsecured	300,000
Total Current Liabilities	$ 415,000

Long-Term Debt

Secured note payable	$ 960,000
Restructured debt, unsecured	1,330,000
Total Long-Term Debt	$ 2,290,000

Stockholders' Deficiency

Preferred stock, 6%, $100 par value, cumulative, 40,000 shares issued and outstanding	$ 400,000
Common stock, $1 par value, 300,000 shares issued and outstanding	300,000
Additional paid-in capital	2,100,000
Accumulated deficit	(2,925,000)
Total Stockholders' Deficiency	$ (125,000)
Total Liabilities in Excess of Stockholders' Deficiency	$ 2,580,000

term introduced into the accounting literature by *SFAS No. 15*. Although the pronouncement does not define the term, it means a restructuring that encompasses most of a company's liabilities, as usually occurs when restructuring is part of the quasi-reorganization plan. Although *SFAS No. 15* does not explain why it does not apply to these situations, we may assume that the FASB wants to allow consistent treatment for both asset and liability adjustments in quasi-reorganizations.

This explanation does not help in the more common situation in which the stockholders' deficiency resulted from several years of large operating losses—that is, *not* from a restatement of the assets. Regardless of what caused the accumulated deficit (whether from restating assets or from operating losses), the following question is raised: Why should the decision to eliminate the accumulated deficit using quasi-reorganization procedures (a mere formality under state law) change the perception of forgiveness of debt from an income statement gain (in *SFAS No. 15*) to a capital transaction? The answer evidently lies in the "fresh start" objective of a quasi-reorganization. A restructuring not involving a quasi-reorganization maintains the company's basic continuity. A quasi-reorganization results in the assumed death of the old company and the assumed creation of a new one. A "break" exists that usually destroys any pre- versus postincome statement comparability. Because of this fresh-start objective, treating the forgiveness as a capital transaction makes more sense.

TAX CONSEQUENCES OF GAINS ON RESTRUCTURINGS

The Internal Revenue Code treats gains on troubled debt restructurings as taxable only to the extent that such restructurings result in a positive balance in total stockholders' equity (not retained earnings). Any income taxes provided are netted against the gain on the restructuring because in financial reporting, the gain must be reported as an extraordinary item net of income tax effects.

ACCOUNTING BY CREDITORS

Although this chapter concerns accounting by a debtor, *SFAS No.15* applies to creditors as well. Prior to May 1993, accounting by a creditor was *symmetrical* to the accounting by a debtor. Thus, if the debtor reported a gain on restructuring, the creditor simultaneously reported an offsetting loss on restructuring of its receivables, except to the extent that such loss had already been provided for in allowances for uncollectibles or write-offs, or both.

It is interesting that the banking industry uniformly and vehemently opposed the imputed interest (discounted present value) approach of calculating the amount of debt forgiven as presented in the FASB discussion memorandum that preceded *SFAS No. 15*. This approach would have had creditors reporting much larger losses than under the "no-discount" alternative adopted by the FASB. How the banking industry's strong vocal opposition influenced the FASB in its deliberations is conjecture. It is interesting to note, however, that the FASB's first exposure draft on troubled debt restructurings (dated November 7, 1975, and encompassing only accounting by debtors) called for the imputed interest approach. Because of the obvious implications to creditors—that is, if a debtor reports a gain, the creditor should simultaneously report a loss—the project was expanded to include accounting by creditors as well.

In May 1993, the FASB issued *Statement No. 114*, "Accounting by Creditors for Impairment of a Loan." This standard amended *SFAS No. 15* by requiring creditors to account for a troubled debt restructuring involving a modification of terms **at fair value**—using *discounting* of expected future cash flows at the loan's *effective* interest rate—as of the restructuring date.[8] Thus **asymmetry between creditors' and debtors' accounting for such restructuring now occurs.**

SUBSEQUENT PERIOD INTEREST EXPENSE IN "NO REPORTABLE GAIN" RESTRUCTURINGS

Procedural points 4 and 5 of *SFAS No. 15* (see page 789) indicate that when the total future payments exceed the carrying amount of the debt, the *excess* is reported as interest expense between the restructuring date and the maturity date using the interest method prescribed by *APBO No. 21*. In such cases, the effective interest rate must be calculated. Assume the following information:

---

[8]As a practical expedient, the FASB allows a creditor to measure an impairment based on a loan's observable market price or the fair value of the collateral if the loan is collateral dependent.

1. Carrying amount of the debt at January 1, 19X1:

Principal owed	$1,100,000
Interest owed	33,947
	$1,133,947

2. Cancellation of debt per restructuring agreement consummated January 1, 19X1:

Principal	$ 100,000
Interest	33,947
	$ 133,947

3. Total future payments to be made:

Amount designated as principal (due December 31, 19X2)	$1,000,000
Amounts designated as interest (10% of $1,000,000 payable annually at year-end for two years)	200,000
	$1,200,000

Because the $1,200,000 of total future payments exceeds the $1,133,947 carrying amount of the debt, $66,053 of interest expense ($1,200,000 – $1,133,947) is reported in the income statements during the two years following the restructuring. What interest rate is needed for the total future payments of $1,200,000 to equal the present value of the carrying amount of the debt of $1,133,947? A trial-and-error approach to the present value tables reveals that the effective interest rate is 3%. The present value calculations follow:

Designation	Total Future Payments	Present Value Factor at 3%	Present Value
Principal	$1,000,000	.94260	$ 942,600
Interest	200,000	1.91347[a]	191,347
	$1,200,000		$1,133,947

[a]Obtained from an annuity present value table (applied to the $100,000 annual amount).

This example was designed so that the effective interest rate would be an even number to avoid the additional complexity of interpolating. In practice, of course, interpolating is usually necessary.

The following entries would be made for the restructuring, the recording of interest using the effective interest rate, and the payments made under the restructuring agreement:

1. January 1, 19X1:

Notes Payable	1,100,000	
Interest Payable	33,947	
Restructured Debt		1,133,947
To record the effect of the restructuring.		

2. December 31, 19X1:

Interest Expense	34,018	
Restructured Debt	65,982	
Cash		100,000
To record (1) interest expense at 3% of $1,133,947 and (2) the first payment of $100,000.		

3. December 31, 19X2:

Interest Expense	32,035	
Restructured Debt	67,965	
Cash		100,000

To record (1) interest expense at 3% of $1,067,965
($1,133,947 − $65,982) and (2) the second payment
of $100,000.

Restructured Debt	1,000,000	
Cash		1,000,000

To record the $1,000,000 payment at its maturity date.

The entries affecting the Restructured Debt account are recorded in the following T account to illustrate how the use of the exact effective interest rate results in a zero balance after the last required payment.

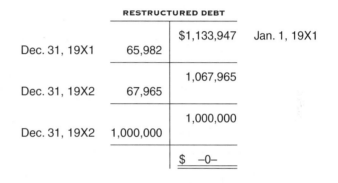

RESTRUCTURED DEBT

		$1,133,947	Jan. 1, 19X1
Dec. 31, 19X1	65,982		
		1,067,965	
Dec. 31, 19X2	67,965		
		1,000,000	
Dec. 31, 19X2	1,000,000		
		$ −0−	

III BANKRUPTCY REORGANIZATIONS

Although Chapter 11 of the Bankruptcy Code is the reorganization chapter, the statutes do not define the term *reorganization*. We may assume from Chapter 11's purpose and procedures, however, that the chapter intends that the term have a broad meaning. Basically, a **reorganization** encompasses the development of a plan—called a *plan of reorganization*— to alter the company's liability and/or equity structure so that the company has a reasonable chance of surviving bankruptcy proceedings and prospering on its own.

Most reorganization plans involve a negotiated settlement between the company and its unsecured creditors to repay debts, usually at so many cents on the dollar. Thus the company is provided with a "fresh start," a unique opportunity in business. Approximately 10 to 20% of all business bankruptcy filings are Chapter 11 filings (the remainder being Chapter 7 filings).

ADVANTAGES AND DISADVANTAGES OF REORGANIZING UNDER CHAPTER 11 VERSUS RESTRUCTURING OUTSIDE THE BANKRUPTCY COURTS

ADVANTAGES The primary advantages of a Chapter 11 reorganization to a distressed company are as follows:

1. **Achieving sanctuary status.** Creditors cannot sue or take other steps to collect amounts owed while a debtor is under Chapter 11 protection. Thus distressed companies have some "breathing room" to develop a plan of reorganization.

2. **Freezing amounts owed for interest.** For unsecured debt, no interest accrues while the company is in Chapter 11, thus allowing the debtor to conserve

substantial amounts of cash. Some companies have saved several hundred millions of interest while under Chapter 11 protection. Competitors of such debtors often complain (as did the competitors of Eastern Airlines and Braniff Airlines a few years ago) that the debtors have an unfair advantage because of this feature.

3. **Obtaining a massive reduction in debt.** Companies usually are able to obtain a massive reduction of the debtor's liabilities (forgiveness of debt) compared with the amount of debt forgiven in a restructuring outside of the bankruptcy courts.

4. **Obtaining modifications to collective bargaining agreements.** Companies usually are more effective in obtaining wage reductions or modifications to collective bargaining agreements than when not under Chapter 11 protection.

DISADVANTAGES Historically, the stigma typically associated with having gone through bankruptcy was a prime motivator to avoid filing for Chapter 11 bankruptcy protection. In recent years, however, having filed for Chapter 11 bankruptcy protection has lost some of its stigma. Many executives and management consultants now view Chapter 11 as merely a strategic weapon.

WHAT PERCENTAGE SURVIVES CHAPTER 11? To file for reorganization under Chapter 11 is to flirt with extinction. Of all Chapter 11 filings (about 20,000 per year), only about 15% emerge as viable companies (and then usually with new top management); the remainder is transferred to Chapter 7 and liquidated.

THE SEQUENCE OF EVENTS IN A CHAPTER 11 FILING

The typical sequence of events in a Chapter 11 filing is as follows:

1. **Filing the petition.** Either a voluntary or an involuntary petition can initiate bankruptcy proceedings. The company in question may prepare a statement showing asset values and amounts that would be paid to each class of creditor in the event of liquidation. As noted earlier, accountants called this a *statement of affairs*. We illustrate the preparation of this statement later in the chapter in connection with *liquidations*.

2. **Management of the company.** The debtor company's management usually continues to control and operate the debtor's day-to-day activities. Under certain conditions, however, and for just cause (such as fraud, incompetence, or gross mismanagement of the company), and if in the best interests of creditors, the court may appoint a trustee to manage the debtor's business (Section 1104[a]). **The appointment of a trustee in a Chapter 11 filing is infrequent.** We discuss the duties of trustees later in the chapter in connection with *liquidations,* for which trustees are always appointed.

3. **Creditors' and equity security holders' committees.** After an order for relief has been entered, the court appoints a committee of *unsecured* creditors. (The court may also appoint additional committees of creditors, or of equity security holders if necessary, to ensure adequate representation of these groups. Such a court-appointed committee may

   a. select and authorize [with the court's approval] the employment by such committee of one or more attorneys, accountants, or other agents to represent or perform services for such committee [Section 1103(a)];

   b. consult with the trustee or debtor in possession concerning the administration of the case;

   c. investigate the acts, conduct, assets, liabilities and financial condition of the debtor, the operation of the debtor's business and the desirability of the continuance of such business, and any other matter relevant to the case or to the formulation of a plan;

   d. participate in the formulation of a plan [of reorganization], advise those represented by such committee of such committee's determinations as to any plan formulated, and collect and file with the court acceptances or rejections of a plan;

e. request the appointment of a trustee or examiner . . . and

f. perform such other services as are in the interest of those represented [Section 1103(c)].

4. **Plan of reorganization.** Under Chapter 11 of the Code, a plan of reorganization may alter the legal, equitable, and contractual rights of any class of creditors' claims, secured or unsecured, or of equity interests. Such an alteration is known as **impairment** of a claim or an interest (Section 1124). In a common plan of reorganization, all unsecured creditors agree to accept payment at a percentage of their respective claims—for example, 25 cents on the dollar—with the remainder of the debt canceled.

The debtor has the exclusive right to propose a plan during the 20 days after the order for relief. At the end of this period, any party of interest—such as the trustee, committee, a creditor, or an equity security holder—may file a plan, provided certain conditions are met (Section 1121). The role of the Securities and Exchange Commission (SEC) is quite limited:

> The Securities and Exchange Commission may raise and may appear and be heard for any issued . . . but the SEC may not appeal from any judgment, order, or decree entered in the case [Section 1109].

Fast track for small businesses. A significant new provision enacted in 1994 is the special fast-track option for debtors that (1) have debts of $2 million or less and (2) are prepared to reorganize immediately upon filing. Among other things, this treatment (1) entitles the debtor to an exclusive 100-day period for filing a plan of reorganization, (2) the obligation to file the plan within 160 days and the right to request that no creditors' committee be appointed.

5. **Disclosure statement.** Before acceptance of a plan of reorganization can be solicited, the debtor must furnish the plan or a summary of the plan to the various classes of creditors and equity interests, along with a written disclosure statement approved by the court as containing *adequate information* (Section 1125[b]). Adequate information is defined as "information of a kind, and in sufficient detail, as far as is reasonably practicable in light of the nature and history of the debtor and the condition of the debtor's books and records, that would enable a hypothetical reasonable investor . . . to make an informed judgment about the plan" (Section 1125[a][1]). This is obviously determined on a case-by-case basis.

6. **Acceptance of plan.** Each class of creditor and equity interest then votes to accept or reject the plan of reorganization. The requirements for approval are as follows:

a. **Creditors' claims.** "A class of *claims* has accepted a plan if such plan has been accepted by creditors . . . that hold at least **two-thirds in amount and more than one-half in number** [emphasis added] of the allowed claims of such class . . ." (Section 1126[c]).

b. **Equity interests.** "A class of *interest* has accepted a plan if such plan has been accepted by holders of such interests . . . that hold at least **two-thirds in amount** [emphasis added] of the allowed interests of such class . . ." (Section 1126[d]).

7. **Confirmation of the plan by the court.** After the plan of reorganization has been submitted to the court, a hearing is held. A plan must meet 13 specific requirements to be approved by the court. The overriding requirement is that the debtor must be unlikely to be liquidated or have need for further financial reorganization after the plan is confirmed. In other words, the plan of reorganization must be feasible. Another major requirement is that each class of claims or equity

interests must have accepted the plan or must not be impaired under the plan. A provision in the law (referred to in House committee reports as *cram down*), however, allows the court to confirm the plan (if requested by the proponent of the plan) even if each class of claims or equity interests has *not* accepted it. For this to occur, the plan must not discriminate unfairly and must be fair and equitable with respect to each class of claims or equity interests that is impaired or has not accepted the plan (Section 1129).

If the court does *not* confirm the plan of reorganization, it may, on request of a party of interest and after notice and a hearing, either *dismiss* the case or *convert* it to a Chapter 7 case (whereby the debtor is forced out of business through liquidation). Such action depends on which course is in the best interest of creditors and the estate (Section 1112).

8. **Discharge of indebtedness.** After the court confirms the plan of reorganization, the debtor is discharged of certain indebtedness as set forth in the plan. If the debtor has committed certain acts, however, discharge of indebtedness does *not* occur even though a plan has been confirmed (Section 1141[d]). In general, discharge of indebtedness is *not* granted if (a) the debtor has not fully cooperated with the court (for example, by not making all properties and records available to the court's representative, failing to explain losses satisfactorily, or refusing to obey court orders) and (b) the debtor has performed certain specified acts involving the debtor's properties and records to hinder, delay, or defraud creditors (for example, concealing property, destroying records, failing to keep or preserve records, or obtaining money or property fraudulently) (Section 727[a]). A discharge is not granted if the debtor was granted a discharge in a case commenced within *six* years before the filing date of the petition (Section 727[a]).

9. **Exceptions to discharge of indebtedness.** Certain types of indebtedness cannot be discharged under the bankruptcy statutes. These debts, which eventually must be paid if the debtor survives Chapter 11 proceedings, are as follows:

   a. Taxes owed to the United States or any state, county, district, or municipality, and customs duties.

   b. Debts incurred in obtaining money, property, services, an extension renewal, or refinance of credit by either:

      (1) False pretenses, a false representation, or actual fraud, other than a statement concerning the debtor's financial condition.

      (2) Use of a written statement that is materially false with respect to the debtor's financial condition on which the creditor reasonably relied and that the debtor made or published with intent to deceive.

   c. Debts that have not been duly scheduled in time for proof and allowance because a creditor had no notice or knowledge of bankruptcy proceedings.

   d. Debts for fraud or defalcation while acting in a fiduciary capacity, embezzlement, or larceny.

   e. Debts related to willful and malicious injury by the debtor to another entity or to the property of another entity.

   f. Fines, penalties, and forfeitures payable to and for the benefit of a governmental unit (Section 523).

ACCOUNTING ISSUES

The accounting issues in bankruptcy reorganizations are the same as those discussed earlier for troubled debt restructurings—that is, how to calculate and report the amount of debt forgiven. After some initial confusion about the application of *SFAS No. 15* to bankruptcy reorganizations, FASB *Technical Bulletin No. 81-6* was issued to clarify the matter. This bulletin states that *SFAS No. 15* does *not* apply to bankruptcy reorganizations that result in a "general restatement of the debtor's liabilities" (defined earlier as a restructuring of most of the amount of a company's liabilities). Because this usually occurs in bankruptcy reorganizations, *SFAS No. 15* rarely applies. Consequently, the following questions must be addressed:

- What is meaningful accounting for a reorganized company?
- What, if any, guidance is contained in promulgated accounting standards?

SOP No. 90–7 Plugs a Gaping Hole in the Accounting Literature In 1990, the AICPA issued *Statement of Position No. 90-7*, "Financial Reporting by Entities in Reorganization under the Bankruptcy Code." *SOP No. 90-7* brought much needed uniformity to an area for which widely diverse accounting practices existed. The areas of diverse practices were (1) whether the restructured liabilities should be reported at *discounted* or *undiscounted* amounts—this issue greatly determines the reported amount of debt forgiven, (2) whether the amount of debt forgiven should be reported as an *extraordinary item* (as a gain from forgiveness of debt) or credited *directly to capital* (as a capital contribution), (3) whether a deficit in retained earnings should be eliminated or carried forward, and (4) whether *assets* should be adjusted *upward* to their fair values.

Key Characteristics of Typical Chapter 11 Reorganizations

Before discussing the requirements of *SOP No. 90-7*, it is important to note that in the typical Chapter 11 reorganization, the following two items are present:

1. The former owners *lose control* because they receive less than 50% of the voting shares of the emerging entity. Thus a **change in ownership** occurs because the creditors effectively acquire the company as a result of now owning more than 50% of the voting shares.
2. The *fair value* of the emerging entity's assets immediately *before* the date of confirmation is less than the total of its existing liabilities (includes both allowed claims and postpetition liabilities). Thus a substantial forgiveness of debt—called a **discharge of indebtedness** in Chapter 11—occurs.

The Requirements of *SOP No. 90-7*

In Chapter 11 reorganizations, in which both of these two items are present, *SOP No. 90-7* requires the following:

1. The entity that emerges from Chapter 11 is deemed to be a **new entity** for which **fresh-start financial statements** should be prepared. One major feature of fresh-start reporting is that **no beginning retained earnings or deficit is reported.**
2. Comparative financial statements that straddle a confirmation date *cannot* be presented because it would be an inappropriate comparison of a former entity and a new entity.
3. The discharge of indebtedness should be reported as an extraordinary item in the predecessor entity's final statement of operations.
4. The discharge of indebtedness should be calculated using the *present values* of amounts to be paid, determined by using appropriate current interest rates.
5. All *assets* are to be restated to reflect their *fair value* at the date of reorganization.
6. Prior to the confirmation date, the "old entity" is to (a) report bankruptcy-related losses and expenses in a separate "reorganization items" category in its statement of operations and (b) report its liabilities in specified categories in any balance sheets issued.

Procedurally, item 5 is accomplished by (1) first determining the *reorganization value* of the entity—an amount that approximates what a willing buyer would pay for the assets of the emerging entity immediately after the restructuring (done generally by discounting expected future cash flows), (2) allocating the reorganization value to the entity's tangible and intangible assets using the purchase accounting procedures specified in *APB Opinion No. 16,* "Business Combinations," and (3) reporting any unallocated reorganization value as "reorganization value in excess of amounts allocable to identifiable assets" (goodwill), which is to be subsequently amortized over no more than 40 years. Determining the reorganization value often requires arm's-length negotiations or litigation between the interested parties. A summary depiction of the *SOP No. 90-7* requirements appears in Illustration 23–3.

ILLUSTRATION **TYPICAL ENTRIES IN A CHAPTER 11 REORGANIZATION**

Assume that Emergco Inc. has the following capitalization immediately before the confirmation of the plan of reorganization:

Prepetition Liabilities Subject to Compromise	$ 900,000[a]
Prepetition Liabilities Not Subject to Compromise	$ 72,000[b]
Postpetition Liabilities	$ 300,000[b]
Stockholders' equity (deficiency)	
Preferred stock ($100 par value)	$ 250,000
Common stock ($5 par value)	50,000
Additional paid-in capital	105,000
Accumulated deficit	(555,000)
	$(150,000)

[a]Includes partially secured liabilities.
[b]These liabilities would be paid in full.

The entries to reflect the plan of reorganization, using assumed amounts as appropriate, follow:

1. To record discharge of indebtedness— creditors having liabilities subject to compromise receive cash, notes, and a 93% controlling equity interest:

Liabilities Subject to Compromise	900,000	
Cash		200,000
Senior Debt (a new issue)		180,000
Subordinated Debt (a new issue)		120,000
Common Stock—new issue		
(93,000 shares × $1 par)		93,000
Gain on Discharge of Debt		307,000

2. To record cancellation of preferred and common stock issues in exchange for new common stock issue—preferred and common stockholders receive a 7% equity interest:

Preferred Stock	250,000	
Common Stock—old issue ($5 par)	50,000	
Common Stock—new issue		
(7,000 shares × $1 par)		7,000
Additional Paid-in Capital		293,000

Note: Although it would seem that the old stockholders should receive nothing by virtue of the fact that Chapter 11 provides creditors with the right to enforce the **absolute priority rule,** whereby equity claims can be wiped out using the allowable "cram-

ILLUSTRATION 23–3	**Summary Depiction of Typical Chapter 11 Reorganization**

Chapter 11 Petition Filed (3-17-X1)	Plan of Reorganization Confirmed (9-1-X2)
──────── Old Entity ────────▶	──────── New Entity ────────

Old Entity	New Entity

1. Reports gain on discharge of debt in final statement of operations as an **extraordinary item.**
 	
2. Classifies liabilities between:
  a. **Prepetition** liabilties **subject to compromise—** at the expected amount of the allowed claims.[a]
  b. **Prepetition** liabilities **not subject to compromise**—at the expected amount of the allowed claims.
  c. **Postpetition** liabilities.
 	
3. Reports bankruptcy-related items in a special **reorganization items** category in its statement of operations:
  a. Loss of disposal of facilities.
  b. Professional fees relating to bankruptcy proceeding.
  c. Interest earned on cash accumulated during bankruptcy proceeding.
	1. Begins with **fresh-start** reporting:
	  a. No beginning retained earnings or deficit.
	  b. Assets adjusted to fair values.
	  c. Excess of reorganization value over amounts allocated to assets effectively reported as goodwill.
	  d. Liabilties adjusted to present values (other than Deferred Taxes).
	
	2. Never presents financial statements of old entity for comparison purposes.

[a]Even though these liabilities (which consist of both **unsecured claims** and **undersecured claims**) most likely will be settled at amounts substantially below the amount of allowed claims, the full amount of the claims expected to be allowed by the court is to be reported up until the confirmation date at which time any discharge of debt is reported.

down" procedure, creditors normally give up this right because it is costly to pursue and they can end up worse off than if they provide some payment to old stockholders.

3. To adopt fresh-start reporting by revaluing assets to fair values and eliminating the accumulated deficit:

Inventory	30,000	
Property, Plant, and Equipment	180,000	
Reorganization Value in Excess of Amounts Allocable to Identifiable Assets	40,000	
Additional Paid-in Capital (residual amount to balance)	203,000	
Goodwill (old)		205,000
Accumulated Deficit ($555,000 – $307,000 gain on debt discharge)		248,000

The stockholders' equity on a *fresh-start basis* follows:

Emergco Inc.
Stockholders' Equity on Fresh-Start Basis

Common stock (100,000 shares × $1 par value)	$100,000
Additional paid-in capital	195,000
Retained earnings (accumulated deficit)	–0–
Total Stockholders' Equity	$295,000
Fresh-start book value per common share	$2.95

COMPANIES *NOT* QUALIFYING FOR FRESH-START REPORTING

Some companies file for Chapter 11 protection merely to seek relief from creditors with no expectation that existing stockholders will lose control, as was the case for Texaco's Chapter 11 filing in 1987. Fresh-start reporting is allowed only for companies in which a loss of control and change in ownership occurs, which occurs in most cases. The small percentage of companies emerging from Chapter 11 that do *not* qualify for fresh-start reporting must (1) report liabilities subject to compromise at present values of amounts to be paid using appropriate interest rates, (2) report any discharge of indebtedness as an extraordinary item, and (3) report bankruptcy-related costs and expenses in the special reorganization items category in its statement of operations.

THE ROLE OF ACCOUNTANTS IN BANKRUPTCY REORGANIZATIONS

Certified public accountants are commonly employed in varying capacities in bankruptcy proceedings. Many accounting firms can generate substantial (and often lucrative) fees for their services in this area. (Bankruptcy assistance is *not* considered charity work.) The most common capacity for outside accountants is that of rendering advice and assistance on financial projections used in developing a reorganization plan. Both the distressed company and its creditors' committee commonly hire their own outside accountants. Occasionally, outside accountants are responsible for determining the quality of the distressed company's accounts receivable. If management is suspected of improper actions, bankruptcy judges may need to appoint outside accountants to investigate such charges. The creditors' committee often hires outside accountants to determine the following:

1. Has the debtor made any transfers of assets that would constitute preferences to certain creditors?
2. Has management committed any acts that would constitute fraud, deception, or bad faith?
3. Has management committed any acts that would bar it from obtaining a discharge of certain indebtedness?
4. In what condition are the company's books and records?
5. What would be obtained in liquidation? Answering this question requires the preparation of a statement of affairs, which is discussed and illustrated later in the chapter.

The creditors' accountants need not perform an audit of the debtor's financial statements to be of assistance in these areas; a limited special-purpose examination is usually sufficient. Obviously, the scope of any such limited examination must be worked out with the creditors' committee.

Ⅳ LIQUIDATIONS

Large companies with common stock publicly traded on the New York Stock Exchange are seldom liquidated because they usually have adequate capital and managerial talent to deal with adverse developments. The growing trend toward diversification also works against liquidation. A large, diverse business is less apt to be affected overall by an adverse development resulting from poor management decisions in one of its industry segments. Furthermore, if management cannot deal effectively with such problems in one of its industry segments, that segment will most likely be disposed of through sale (or possibly abandonment), but the remainder of the business will continue. Consequently, liquidation is generally associated with small and moderate size businesses. The smaller and more unseasoned a company is, the more likely it is to face liquidation.

LIQUIDATION *OUTSIDE* THE BANKRUPTCY COURTS

In some instances, liquidation may take place *outside* the bankruptcy courts. In these situations, a formal **general assignment for the benefit of creditors** usually is executed, whereby the debtor's property is transferred to a designated assignee or assignees (who are often the debtor's creditors) for the purpose of converting the assets into cash and making appropriate distributions of cash to the creditors. Any assets that remain after creditors have been paid in full are returned to the debtor for ultimate distribution to its stockholders. If the proceeds from the conversion of assets into cash are insufficient to pay creditors in full, however, the creditors have no other recourse and the stockholders receive nothing.

There are three possible advantages to liquidating outside the bankruptcy court:

1. Legal fees are usually lower.
2. The debtor can designate the assignee or assignees.
3. The conversion of assets into cash is more flexible.

Under an *involuntary* proceeding, a general assignment for the benefit of creditors is considered grounds for the bankruptcy court to enter an order for relief. Accordingly, to avoid liquidation through the bankruptcy court, a general assignment must be agreed to by all of the creditors for all practical purposes. If a sufficient number of qualified creditors subsequently file an involuntary petition of bankruptcy, the general assignment for the benefit of creditors is null and void, and the bankruptcy court then supervises and controls the liquidation of the company.

LIQUIDATION THROUGH BANKRUPTCY COURT

After a company has filed for liquidation under Chapter 7, one of the court's first duties is to determine whether the case should be dismissed. As we mentioned at the beginning of the chapter, filing a *voluntary* petition constitutes an order for relief. Dismissals of voluntary filings are infrequent. When the debtor does not dispute an involuntary petition, the court enters an order for relief against the debtor. Dismissals of uncontested involuntary filings are also infrequent. If the debtor disputes an involuntary petition, however, a trial must be held to determine whether the case should be dismissed or an order for relief should be entered.

THE ROLE OF THE TRUSTEE   After an order for relief has been entered, the bankruptcy court must promptly appoint an interim trustee (Section 701[a]). In an involuntary filing, the debtor may continue to operate the business from the filing date until an order for relief is entered, just as though the petition had not been filed (Section 303[f]). The court may appoint an interim trustee during this period, however, if necessary to preserve the property of the estate or to prevent loss to the estate, providing certain procedures are followed (Section 303[g]).

After an order for relief has been entered, the court must also call a meeting of the debtor's creditors (Section 341). In this meeting, the creditors first vote for a trustee and then select a creditors' committee that consults with the trustee in connection with the administration of the estate. If the creditors are unable to select a trustee, the interim trustee becomes the trustee (Section 702[d]). Trustees are usually professionals, mostly practicing lawyers, who specialize in this type of work. The following duties of trustees are set forth under Section 704:

1. Collect and reduce to money the property of the estate for which such trustee serves, and close up such estate as expeditiously as is compatible with the best interests of parties of interest.
2. Be accountable for all property received.
3. Ensure that the debtor shall perform [certain] intentions [that the debtor specifies].
4. Investigate the financial affairs of the debtor.
5. If a purpose would be served, examine proofs of claims and object to the allowance of any claim that is improper. . . .

6. If advisable, oppose the discharge of the debtor.

7. Unless the court orders otherwise, furnish such information concerning the estate and the estate's administration as is requested by a party of interest.

8. If the business of the debtor is authorized to be operated, file with the court, with the United States trustee, and with any governmental unit charged with responsibility for collection or determination of any tax arising out of such operation, periodic reports and summaries of the operation of such business, including a statement of receipts and disbursements, and such other information as the United States trustee or the court requires.[Under Section 721 "The court may authorize the trustee to operate the business of the debtor for a limited period, if such operation is in the best interest of the estate and consistent with the orderly liquidation of the estate."]

9. Make a final report and file a final account of the administration of the estate with the court and with the United States trustee.

Accounting by trustees is discussed in detail later in the chapter.

TECHNICAL ASPECTS OF THE DUTIES OF TRUSTEES   The following technical aspects of the trustee's duties should be noted:

1. **Employment of professionals.** With the court's approval, the trustee may employ attorneys, accountants, appraisers, auctioneers, or other professional persons to represent or assist the trustee in carrying out his or her duties (Section 327).

2. **Avoidance powers.** A trustee is authorized to void both *fraudulent* and *preferential* transfers made by the debtor within certain specified periods preceding the filing date. (Such transfers include giving a security interest in a property.) Creditors, therefore, may be required to return monies and/or properties recovered or may lose their security interest, or both. The section of the act dealing with preferences is intended to prevent a debtor from giving certain creditors preferential treatment over other creditors. The Bankruptcy Code sets forth the conditions that must exist for a trustee to void a property transfer to a creditor. It also sets forth certain transfers that a trustee cannot void (Sections 544–550).

3. **Setoffs.** With respect to mutual debts between the debtor and allowable claims of a creditor, the amount owed the debtor by the creditors is subtracted from or *offset* (thus the term **setoff**) against the amount owed to the creditor (Section 553). (There are certain technical exceptions to this rule that we need not deal with now.)

DISTRIBUTION OF CASH TO CREDITORS   The sequence of payments to creditors is as follows:

1. The proceeds from the sale of assets that have been pledged to secured creditors are applied to satisfy those claims. Note that the bankruptcy proceedings do not alter the rights of the secured creditors to the assets that have been pledged to them; these rights are only temporarily suspended.

2. If the proceeds exceed the secured creditors' claims, such excess is available to pay creditors with priority and unsecured creditors.

3. If the proceeds are insufficient to satisfy the claims of the secured creditors, the secured creditors become unsecured creditors to the extent of the deficiency.

4. The proceeds from the sale of unpledged assets are used to pay creditors with priority.

5. After creditors with priority have been paid, payments are made to the unsecured creditors. Payments are always stated as a percentage of all allowed claims.

6. To the extent that any creditors are not paid in full, the deficiency represents a loss.

After the final payment has been made to the unsecured creditors, the corporation is a *shell* corporation without any assets or liabilities. In most instances, the corporation then ceases its legal existence. The bankruptcy court is *not* authorized to grant a formal discharge of indebtedness with respect to any unpaid claims when the debtor is other than an individual (Section 727[a][1]). According to House of Representatives Bankruptcy Committee reports, this change is intended to prevent trafficking in corporate shells and bankrupt partnerships.

Selling assets and paying proceeds to the debtor's various creditors does not always conclude a liquidation. Trustees may file suit against former directors and officers, asking for monetary damages on the grounds of gross negligence in the management of certain aspects of the business. When the sudden collapse of a company occurs shortly after its outside auditors have issued an unqualified ("clean") audit report on the company's financial statements, serious questions may be raised concerning the performance of the audit. In such situations, the auditors may be sued for alleged breach of performance.

THE ROLE OF THE ACCOUNTANT IN LIQUIDATIONS Bankruptcy trustees often employ certified public accountants to assist them in preserving the assets of the bankrupt's estate. The extent of the accountant's services usually depends on the complexity of the estate. If the debtor's in-house accountants have not resigned before the bankruptcy petition is filed, they generally leave shortly thereafter. A certified public accountant can provide the following types of services to the bankruptcy trustee:

1. Determining what accounting books and records exist at the debtor's offices.
2. Determining the condition of the accounting records, including the filing status of all tax reports.
3. Updating the debtor's accounting records as necessary.
4. Preparing current year tax reports and informational forms.
5. Comparing creditors' claims (as filed with the court) with the debtor's books and records and with the schedule of liabilities filed with the court by the debtor.
6. Examining certain of the debtor's books and records in detail and submitting a formal report to the trustee in certain instances, if fraud is suspected or known.

This list is not exhaustive; the accountant may be called on to perform any service within the realm of accounting expertise.

THE STATEMENT OF AFFAIRS

Regardless of whether liquidation takes place outside or through bankruptcy court, a special **statement of affairs** is prepared showing the company's financial condition. The statement of affairs is prepared on the basis that the company is going out of business. Because the company is not considered a going concern, the historical cost basis for carrying assets loses its significance, and the amount expected to be realized in liquidation is the relevant valuation basis.

The statement of affairs **provides information concerning how much money each class of creditors can expect to receive on liquidation of the company,** assuming that assets are converted into cash at the estimated realizable values used in preparing the statements. Thus conventional classifications such as current assets and current liabilities lose their significance. Instead, assets are classified as to whether they are pledged with creditors or not pledged with creditors; **liabilities are classified by category of creditor**—namely, creditors with priority, secured creditors, and unsecured creditors. Stockholders' equity also loses its significance because companies in the process of liquidation usually have a negative net worth. The specific categories of assets and liabilities in the statement of affairs are as follows.

ASSETS

1. **Assets pledged with fully secured creditors** are expected to realize an amount at least sufficient to satisfy the related debt.

2. **Assets pledged with partially secured creditors** are expected to realize an amount below the related debt.

3. **Free assets** are not pledged and are available to satisfy the claims of creditors with priority, partially secured creditors, and unsecured creditors.

LIABILITIES

1. **Liabilities with priority** have priority under the bankruptcy statutes (explained earlier in the chapter).

2. **Fully secured creditors** expect to be paid in full as a result of their having sufficient collateral (pledged assets) to satisfy the indebtedness.

3. **Partially secured creditors** have collateral (pledged assets), the proceeds of which are expected to be insufficient to satisfy the indebtedness.

4. **Unsecured creditors** have no collateral (pledged assets) relating to their indebtedness.

Contingent liabilities that are reasonably calculable and probable as to payment (the criteria under FASB *Statement No. 5*, "Accounting for Contingencies") are shown in the statement of affairs. Contingent liabilities that do not meet these criteria should be disclosed in a note to the statement of affairs.

ILLUSTRATION   **THE STATEMENT OF AFFAIRS**

The balance sheet of Fold-Up Company, which filed a voluntary bankruptcy petition (for liquidation under Chapter 7) on September 23, 19X5, is shown in Illustration 23–4. Additional information regarding realization follows:

1. **Receivables.** The notes and accounts receivable are considered to have been adequately provided for in preparing the balance sheet; thus the company expects to realize the amounts shown.

2. **Finished goods.** The finished goods can be sold for $47,000; however, the company expects to incur $4,000 of direct selling and shipping costs.

3. **Work in process.** The work in process can be completed if $3,000 of direct costs are incurred for labor. On completion, this inventory can be sold for $37,000; however, the company expects to incur $2,000 of direct selling and shipping costs.

4. **Raw materials.** The raw materials can be converted into finished goods if $7,000 of direct costs are incurred for labor. On completion, this inventory can be sold for $19,000; however, the company expects to incur $1,000 of direct selling and shipping costs.

5. **Supplies.** The supplies will be substantially consumed in the completion of the work in process and the conversion of raw materials into finished goods. The estimated realizable value of the remaining supplies after completion and conversion is $1,000.

6. **Prepayments.** The prepayments are expected to expire during the liquidation period.

7. **Land.** The land has a current market value of $90,000.

8. **Building.** The building has a current market value of $135,000.

9. **Equipment.** The equipment can be sold at auction for an estimated $35,000.

ILLUSTRATION 23–4	A Balance Sheet for a Company in Chapter 7 Bankruptcy Proceedings

Fold-Up Company
Balance Sheet as of September 23, 19X5

Assets

Current Assets

Cash	$ 2,000
Notes receivable	5,000
Accounts receivable, net	25,000
Inventory:	
Finished goods	40,000
Work in process	30,000
Raw materials	20,000
Supplies	5,000
Prepayments	8,000
Total Current Assets	$135,000

Noncurrent Assets

Land	70,000
Building, net	110,000
Equipment, net	60,000
Deferred charges	15,000
Total Assets	$390,000

Liabilities and Stockholders' Deficiency

Current Liabilities

10% Notes payable to bank, secured by accounts receivable	$ 35,000
Accounts payable	246,000
Accrued liabilities:	
Interest ($2,000 to bank, $6,000 to insurance company)	8,000
Salaries and wages	7,000
Payroll taxes	2,000
Total Current Liabilities	$298,000

Long-Term Debt

8% Notes payable to insurance company, secured by land and building	175,000
Total Liabilities	$473,000

Stockholders' Deficiency

Common stock, no par	$100,000
Accumulated deficit	(183,000)
Total Stockholders' Deficiency	$ (83,000)
Total Liabilities in Excess of Stockholders' Deficiency	$390,000

---

10. **Deferred charges.** Deferred charges include organization costs, issuance expenses relating to the notes payable to the insurance company, and plant rearrangement costs.

11. **Salaries and wages.** All salaries and wages were earned within the last 90 days, and no employee is owed more than $4,000.

12. **Liquidation expenses.** The company estimates that $15,000 in court and filing fees, appraisal fees, and legal and accounting fees will be incurred in connection with the liquidation. No amounts have been provided in these expenses at September 23, 19X5.

13. **Accounts payable.** Accounts payable include $6,000 to the company's attorneys for legal work incurred in connection with patent research and collection efforts

ILLUSTRATION 23–5	A Statement of Affairs for a Company in Bankruptcy Proceedings

Fold-Up Company
Statement of Affairs as of September 23, 19X5

Book Value	Assets	Estimated Current Value	Estimated Amount Available for Unsecured Creditors	Gain or Loss on Realization
	Assets Pledged with Fully Secured Creditors			
$ 70,000	Land	$ 90,000		$ 20,000
110,000	Building	135,000		25,000
		$225,000		
	Less—Fully secured claims **(contra—from liability side)**	(181,000)	$ 44,000	
	Assets Pledged with Partially Secured Creditors			
25,000	Accounts receivable .... (deducted on liability side)	$ 25,000		
	Free Assets			
2,000	Cash	$ 2,000	2,000	
5,000	Notes receivable	5,000	5,000	
	Inventory			
40,000	Finished goods	43,000[a]	43,000	3,000
30,000	Work in process	32,000[b]	32,000	2,000
20,000	Raw materials	11,000[c]	11,000	(9,000)
5,000	Supplies	1,000	1,000	(4,000)
8,000	Prepayments			(8,000)
60,000	Equipment	35,000	35,000	(25,000)
15,000	Deferred charges			(15,000)
	Estimated amount available for unsecured creditors, including creditors with priority		$173,000	
	Less—Liabilities with priority **(contra—from liability side)**		(24,000)	
	Estimated amount available for unsecured creditors		$149,000	
	Estimated deficiency to unsecured creditors (plug)		109,000	
$390,000				$(11,000)
	Total Unsecured Debt		$258,000	

[a]Net of $4,000 of estimated disposal costs.
[b]Net of $3,000 of estimated labor to complete and $2,000 of disposal costs.
[c]Net of $7,000 of estimated labor to convert into finished goods and $1,000 of disposal costs.

on certain accounts receivable that have been written off. Accounts payable also include $5,000 owed to the company's certified public accountants in connection with the December 31, 19X4, audit of the company's financial statements.

A statement of affairs prepared using this information is shown in Illustration 23–5. The following points are important for understanding Illustration 23–5.

1. The Book Value column is shown only for purposes of tying into the September 23, 19X5, balance sheet, which was prepared in the conventional manner.

2. Each asset and liability is assigned to its appropriate descriptive category. The categories themselves are the key to producing the desired information—that is, how much money can the unsecured creditors expect to receive in liquidation?

3. Accrued interest payable is classified with the debt to which it relates because the pledged assets are security for both the principal and the interest.

ILLUSTRATION 23–5 *(Continued)*

Fold-Up Company
Statement of Affairs as of September 23, 19X5

Book Value	Liabilities and Stockholders' Deficiency		Amount Uncensored
	Liabilities with Priority		
$ –0–	Estimated liquidation expenses	$ 15,000	
7,000	Salaries and wages	7,000	
2,000	Payroll taxes	2,000	
	(deducted from amount available for unsecured creditors		
	on asset side	$ 24,000	
	Fully Secured Creditors		
175,000	Notes payable to insurance company	$175,000	
6,000	Accrued interest on notes	6,000	
	Total (deducted on asset side)	$181,000	
	Partially Secured Creditors		
35,000	Note payable to bank	$ 35,000	
2,000	Accrued interest on note	2,000	
		$ 37,000	
	Less—Pledged accounts receivable		
	(contra—from asset side)	(25,000)	$ 12,000
	Unsecured Creditors		
246,000	Accounts payable and accruals		246,000
(83,000) ←	**Stockholders' deficiency**		
$390,000			
	Total Unsecured Debt		$258,000

4. Although the company has *not* recorded the $15,000 of estimated liquidation expenses in its general ledger at September 23, 19X5, the statement of affairs should reflect this estimate so that it is as useful as possible.

5. Legal and accounting fees incurred in connection with matters *not* related to the bankruptcy are *not* considered debts with priority under the bankruptcy statutes.

6. The bank is an unsecured creditor to the extent of $12,000, the amount by which the $25,000 collateral is insufficient to satisfy its $37,000 claim.

7. The unsecured creditors are estimated to receive $149,000 of the $258,000 owed them. This figure is often expressed in terms of recovery per dollar owed. In this situation, it would be 58 cents on the dollar ($149,000 ÷ $258,000).

Once a liquidation has occurred, no accounting issues exist for the former company. An accountant performing services for a trustee in liquidation, however, should have a basic familiarity with the liquidation process.

V ACCOUNTING BY TRUSTEES

The accountability of trustees to the bankruptcy court was stated earlier in the discussion of liquidations under Chapter 7 of the Bankruptcy Code. The same accountability exists in reorganizations under Chapter 11 of the code in which a trustee is appointed to operate the debtor's business. The code sets specific requirements concerning the type of report or reports rendered to the courts by trustees only when the debtor's business is operated by a trustee. In most liquidation cases, normal operations cease immediately. Accordingly, we discuss accounting by trustees in liquidations separately from reorganizations (when normal operations continue).

ACCOUNTING IN LIQUIDATION

When normal operations immediately cease, the preparation of an operating statement for the period covering the trustee's administration of the estate is inappropriate. This holds true even when a trustee, with the court's permission, continues the operations necessary to convert work in process (and possibly raw materials) into finished goods. Such activities by themselves do *not* constitute normal operations; accordingly, costs incurred in this regard are treated as bankruptcy administration costs. Because the Bankruptcy Code does not prescribe the type of report or reports rendered by trustees when normal operations are not conducted (as was the case under the old law), each bankruptcy court establishes its own requirements. Most bankruptcy courts simply require a written explanation as to the disposition of the various assets and a statement of cash receipts and disbursements. Such a statement typically shows the following: (1) cash balances of the debtor that were turned over to the trustee at the trustee's appointment, (2) the proceeds from the conversion of noncash assets into cash, (3) cash disbursements (which are usually limited to bankruptcy administration costs), (4) the remaining cash balance available for distribution to creditors, and (5) a summary of how the remaining cash balance should be distributed to the various classes of creditors (including creditors with priority). In most cases, only one report (called the *final report*) is rendered. In some cases, cash is distributed to creditors on an interim basis, after an interim report proposing such a distribution is filed with and approved by the court. Some courts require the cash disbursements in summary form only; others require detail by check number, payee, and purpose of disbursement.

Most trustees find it expedient to (1) open a separate checking account for each estate they administer and (2) use the related cash receipts and disbursement records to prepare the required statement of cash receipts and disbursements. Trustees usually do not use the debtor's general ledger or any of the debtor's journals to record transactions and events. If the court or creditors desire information that relates the trustee's activity with the book balances existing when the trustee was appointed, a **statement of realization and liquidation** can be prepared. Such a statement for Fold-Up Company is shown in Illustration 23–6. The beginning balances are taken from Illustration 23–5. The activity during the assumed period that the trustee administers the estate is consistent with the estimated amounts and information provided in the data used to prepare the statement of affairs in Illustration 23–5.

In some cases, a trustee may be authorized to operate the debtor's business. This is often done when a larger amount may be realized by selling the business in its entirety rather than in piecemeal and when a larger amount may be realized by selling an active business rather than one that has been shut down. The accounting reports rendered during the time that a trustee operates the debtor's business are the same as those required in reorganizations, which are discussed in the following section.

ACCOUNTING IN REORGANIZATION

When a trustee is appointed in a Chapter 11 reorganization, the Bankruptcy Code requires trustees to submit

> periodic reports and summaries of the operation of such business, including a statement of receipts and disbursements, and such other information as the court requires [Sections 704 and 1106].

A Statement of Realization and Liquidation

Fold-Up Company
Statement of Realization and Liquidation
For the Period September 23, 19X5, to May 18, 19X6

	Assets		Liabilities				Stockholders' Deficiency
	Cash	Noncash	With Priority	Fully Secured	Partially Secured	Unsecured	
Book balances, September 23, 19X5 (from the Book Value column in Illustration 23–5)	$ 2,000	$388,000	$ 9,000	$181,000	$37,000	$246,000	$ (83,000)
Cash Receipts							
Collection of note receivable and related interest	5,200	(5,000)					200
Proceeds from sale of inventory, net of $16,700 "actual" direct costs	85,800[a]	(90,000)					(4,200)
Proceeds from sale of supplies	1,100[a]	(5,000)					(3,900)
Proceeds from sale of equipment	35,400[a]	(60,000)					(24,600)
Proceeds from sale of land and building, net of $181,000 withheld by title company to pay off fully secured creditor	45,500[a]	(180,000)		(181,000)			46,500
Cash Disbursements							
Payment of bankruptcy administration costs, net of $16,700 "actual" inventory conversion and selling costs shown above	(2,000)						(2,000)
Other							
Amortization of prepaids		(8,000)					(8,000)
Write-off of deferred charges		(15,000)					(15,000)
Release of accounts receivable to partially secured creditor		(25,000)			(25,000)		
Reclassification of residual amount to unsecured status					(12,000)	12,000	
Accrual of bankruptcy administration costs			12,600				(12,600)
Book Balances, May 18, 19X6	$173,000	$ –0–	$21,600	$ –0–	$ –0–	$258,000	$(106,600)
Proposed distribution	$173,000		$21,600			$151,400	
			(100%)			(58.7%)	

[a]The actual proceeds here are purposely slightly different from the "estimated" current values shown in Illustration 23–5 because it is highly unlikely that the actual proceeds would agree with the estimated proceeds in a real-world situation.

In addition to these items, the courts usually require that a balance sheet be presented when operating statements or summaries are furnished. In most cases, trustees find it practical to use the debtor's books and records to record transactions and events. The date the trustee was appointed is usually recorded, however, so that the activity during the trustee's administration can be reported separately. Also, a distinction is usually made between (1) assets on hand and liabilities owed at the trustee's appointment and (2) assets acquired and liabilities incurred during the trustee's administration. This distinction is necessary because trustees are responsible for the acquisition and realization of new assets as opposed to only the realization of old assets and for the incurrence and liquidation of new liabilities as opposed to only the liquidation of old liabilities.

The preparation of required reports and statements presents no unusual problems when the trustee uses the debtor's books and records. In some cases, a trustee may account for some or all of the debtor's assets and operations in a new set of books. In this case, the transfer of assets to the new set of books and the accounting for subsequent operations parallel the accounting for a home office and a branch. Accordingly, the balances and activity on each set of books must be combined to the extent necessary in preparing financial reports. Traditionally, advanced accounting textbooks have included a discussion and illustration of a somewhat involved statement of realization and liquidation encompassing assets, liabilities, and operations. Current practice favors the use of the separate conventional financial statements, however, and we do not present a discussion and illustration of this single comprehensive statement.

VI CONCLUDING COMMENTS

Most companies in serious financial difficulty never recover and must be liquidated. A company that can feasibly effect a successful recovery must show complete honesty and good faith with its creditors during this difficult period. Creditors should realize that often they can minimize their losses if a successful troubled debt restructuring can be achieved. The use of professionals in insolvency proceedings can minimize the procedural problems and help the company and its creditors to be realistic in arriving at an acceptable plan of recovery.

Not all proposed troubled debt restructurings succeed. Many are rejected as infeasible, with liquidation best serving the creditors' interests. Others are rejected as the result of evidence of management fraud, deception, or bad faith—again, liquidation best serves the creditors' interests. Consequently, an accountant furnishing assistance to a debtor or a creditors' committee must be skeptical, alert, and imaginative in carrying out this difficult assignment.

END-OF-CHAPTER REVIEW

SUMMARY OF KEY POINTS

1. The accounting issues involved with **troubled debt restructurings** include how to calculate whether any debt has been forgiven and how to report a forgiveness of debt. *SFAS No. 15* does *not* **allow the imputing of interest** in making this calculation.
2. The total amount owed (the **carrying amount of the debt**) is compared with the total amount to be paid back (the **total future payments**).
3. If the **total future payments** *exceed* the carrying amount of the debt, the excess is reported **as interest expense** between the restructuring date and the maturity date. If the carrying amount of the debt *exceeds* the total future payments, however, a forgiveness of debt results. *SFAS No. 15* treats a forgiveness of debt as a gain reported as an extraordinary item, if material.

4. As a result of these procedures, the debtor's future income statements reflect either no interest expense (when a forgiveness of debt results) or unrealistically low interest expense (when no forgiveness of debt results) until the maturity date of the debt.

5. In most all instances, *SFAS No. 15* does *not* apply to either *quasi-reorganizations* or *formal bankruptcy reorganizations* under Chapter 11 of the Bankruptcy Code.

6. For bankruptcy reorganizations under Chapter 11, the AICPA's *SOP No. 90-7* specifies the manner of accounting whereby **fresh-start reporting** is implemented when the plan of reorganization is confirmed—providing a **change in ownership** has occurred and the fair value of the debtor's assets is less than its liabilities.

7. Under fresh-start reporting of *SOP No. 90-7*, a **new reporting entity** exists. Accordingly, no beginning retained earnings or accumulated deficit is reported. Also, **assets** are adjusted to their **fair values** and **liabilities** are reported at their **present values.** Comparative statements with the old entity are never presented.

8. Adjusting assets to their fair values first requires determining the **reorganization value** of the company, which generally involves **discounting expected future cash flows.** An **excess of reorganization value over the amount allocated to specific tangible and intangible assets** is effectively treated as goodwill and amortized over no more than 40 years.

9. The **discharge of indebtedness** in a Chapter 11 reorganization is reported as an **extraordinary item** in the **old entity's** final statement of operations. Bankruptcy-related costs and losses are presented in a special **reorganization items** category in the old entity's statement of operations.

GLOSSARY OF NEW TERMS

Bankruptcy Code The federal bankruptcy statutes set forth in Title 11 of the United States Code.

Creditors with priority A special class of creditors created by the bankruptcy statutes. These creditors are entitled to payment before a debtor's other unsecured creditors may be paid.

Debtor Under the bankruptcy statutes, the party that is the subject of a bankruptcy proceeding.

Estate Under the bankruptcy statutes, all of a debtor's property.

Impairment The alteration of the rights of a creditor or equity holder in a bankruptcy reorganization case.

Involuntary petition A petition filed by the creditors of a company in financial distress to have the distressed company liquidated or financially reorganized under the control and supervision of the bankruptcy court.

Liquidation The process of converting a company's assets into cash, paying off creditors to the extent possible, and ceasing operations.

Quasi-reorganization A process outside bankruptcy court to eliminate a deficit balance in Retained Earnings (properly called an *accumulated deficit*) to give the entity a "fresh start."

Reorganization The altering of a distressed company's liability and/or equity structure under Chapter 11 of the bankruptcy statutes for purposes of financially rehabilitating the company to avoid liquidation.

Restate liabilities generally Restructuring or modifying debt that encompass most of the debtor's liabilities coincidentally with either a *reorganization* under Chapter 11 of the bankruptcy statutes or a *quasi-reorganization.*

Setoff In a bankruptcy proceeding, offsetting amounts owed to a debtor by a creditor against amounts owed to that creditor by the debtor.

Troubled debt restructuring Granting a creditor's concession because of a debtor's financial difficulties.

Voluntary petition A petition filed with the bankruptcy court by a company in financial distress to have the company liquidated or financially reorganized under the control and supervision of the bankruptcy court.

SELF-STUDY QUESTIONS

(Answers are at the end of this chapter.)

A. Bankruptcy Law: Filing the Petition and Debts with Priority

1. Which of the entities listed are entitled to file a *voluntary* bankruptcy petition under Chapter 7 or 11?
   a. A banking corporation
   b. A partnership
   c. A corporation that manufactures consumer goods
   d. A corporation that provides personal services
   e. A municipal corporation
   f. A railroad
   g. An insurance corporation

2. Which entities in Question 1 may have an *involuntary* bankruptcy petition filed against them?

3. In which of the following situations could an involuntary bankruptcy petition be filed?
   a. The debtor has debts of at least $10,000.
   b. The appropriate number of creditors required to sign the petition are owed at least $10,000.
   c. The debtor has committed a fraudulent act.
   d. The debtor has recently appointed a custodian.
   e. The debtor has made asset transfers that constitute a preference to one or more creditors.
   f. Wages are owed to employees for more than 90 days.
   g. The debtor is not paying its debts as they mature.
   h. The debtor has entered into discussions with its creditors to restructure its debt.
   i. The debtor's net worth is negative as a result of operating losses.

4. Which of the following debts have priority under the Bankruptcy Code?
   a. Amounts owed to secured creditors
   b. In an involuntary petition, amounts owed to the creditors who signed the petition
   c. Costs of administering the bankruptcy proceedings
   d. Debts incurred by issuing materially false statements as to financial condition
   e. All wages owed to employees that were earned within 90 days prior to filing the bankruptcy petition
   f. Wages of up to $4,000 per employee, no matter when earned
   g. Taxes owed to the United States or any state or subdivision thereof

B. Bankruptcy Law: Reorganization under Chapter 11

5. Which of the following statements is false?
   a. In a Chapter 11 *reorganization*, management usually continues to operate the business.
   b. The legal and contractual rights of any class of creditors may be altered or impaired under a plan of reorganization.
   c. A *plan of reorganization* must be approved by the Securities and Exchange Commission.
   d. A simple majority of creditors in a class of claims is required to approve a *plan of reorganization*.
   e. None of the above.

6. Which of the following statements is true?
   a. A simple majority in the amount of claims in a class of creditors is required to approve the dollar amount of claims in a *plan of reorganization*.
   b. The bankruptcy court usually imposes a *plan of reorganization* on the creditors.
   c. The rights of secured creditors are eliminated when a company files for *reorganization* under Chapter 11.
   d. In a *reorganization* under Chapter 11, the discharge provisions have no meaningful application.
   e. None of the above.

C. Bankruptcy Law: Liquidation under Chapter 7

7. Which of the following statements is true?
   a. In *involuntary* filings under Chapter 7, the case is dismissed if the debtor contests the filing.

   b. In a Chapter 7 filing, the bankruptcy court usually appoints a trustee.
   c. In a Chapter 7 filing, management usually continues to operate the business until the liquidation is completed.
   d. The primary function of a trustee in Chapter 7 filings is to settle disputes between the debtor and the debtor's creditors.
   e. None of the above.
8. Which of the following statements is false?
   a. When a company is liquidated under Chapter 7, all unpaid debts (except those specified in the bankruptcy statutes) are discharged by the bankruptcy court.
   b. In a Chapter 7 filing, trustees have the authority to dispose of the debtor's assets.
   c. Trustees are authorized to void preferential transfers made to certain creditors.
   d. The concept of creditors with priority applies to both Chapter 7 and Chapter 11 filings.
   e. None of the above.

ASSIGNMENT MATERIAL

REVIEW QUESTIONS

1. Between what two broad categories is the bankruptcy code divided (pertaining to business corporations)?
2. What fundamental objectives does the Bankruptcy Code accomplish?
3. Under what conditions may an involuntary petition be filed?
4. What is meant by the term *creditors with priority*?
5. What is the order of priority of creditors with priority?
6. In an *involuntary* bankruptcy filing, do secured creditors lose their right to their security?
7. Why do companies try to restructure their debt outside Chapter 11 of the Bankruptcy Code if at all possible?
8. What are the advantages of filing for reorganization under Chapter 11 of the Bankruptcy Code?
9. What are the general procedures for determining whether a gain on the restructuring of debt exists as set forth in *SFAS No. 15*?
10. How are material gains on the restructuring of debt reported in the income statement?
11. To what extent are the present procedures discussed in *APBO No. 21* used to determine a gain on the restructuring of debt under *SFAS No. 15*?
12. What is the essence of a *composition agreement*?
13. What is meant by a *discharge of indebtedness* in a bankruptcy reorganization?
14. Which debts *cannot* be discharged in a bankruptcy reorganization?
15. Is a discharge of indebtedness automatic in a *liquidation* proceeding? In a *reorganization* proceeding?
16. On what basis is the *statement of affairs* prepared?
17. What are two purposes for which a statement of affairs may be used?
18. How does the statement of affairs differ from the balance sheet?
19. What are four classifications of liabilities that can appear in a statement of affairs?

EXERCISES

E 23–1 **Troubled Debt Restructuring: Modification of Terms**   A company having serious financial difficulty executed an agreement with its bank whereby the currently due $500,000 note payable to the bank was extended for five years. The old interest rate of 10% was lowered to 4%. Interest is to be paid annually in arrears. Accrued interest of $20,000 as of the restructuring date was canceled.

Required   1. Determine whether a gain on restructuring of debt has resulted.
2. Prepare the journal entry related to the restructuring.

E 23–2 **Troubled Debt Restructuring: Modification of Terms**   A company having serious financial difficulty executed an agreement with one of its major vendors whereby the $800,000 account payable to the vendor was converted into a $600,000 note payable, all due and payable in two years. The interest rate on the note is 10%, with interest payable annually in arrears. The remaining $200,000 of the original note payable was canceled.

Required   1. Determine whether a gain on restructuring of debt has resulted.
2. Prepare the journal entry related to the restructuring.
3. How would your answer be different if the due date of the note payable were four years from the restructuring date?

E 23–3   **Troubled Debt Restructuring: Modification of Terms—Use of Present Value Concepts**   A company having serious financial difficulty has entered into a restructuring agreement with a creditor owed $1,000,000 of principal (now due and payable) and $28,000 of interest. In the restructuring agreement, the company agrees to pay the principal in three years, with interest paid annually in arrears at 4%. The accrued interest of $28,000 is canceled.

Required   1. Determine whether a gain on restructuring of debt has resulted.
2. Determine the total amount of interest expense reported over the next three years.
3. Using present value tables, calculate the approximate effective interest rate.
4. Prepare the journal entries made between the restructuring date and the maturity date, assuming that all required payments are made on time.

E 23–4   **Troubled Debt Restructuring: Equity Interest Granted**   A company having serious financial difficulty executed an agreement with one of its note holders whereby a $100,000 note payable was converted into 30,000 shares of the company's $1 par value common stock. The common stock was traded at $2 per share on the date of the agreement.

Required   1. Determine whether a gain on restructuring of debt has resulted.
2. Prepare the journal entry related to the restructuring.

E 23–5   **Troubled Debt Restructuring: Transfer of Noncash Assets**   A company having serious financial difficulty executed an agreement with one of its creditors whereby a $200,000 note payable and the $25,000 related accrued interest was canceled in exchange for a parcel of land. The land had cost the company $100,000 and has a current appraised value of $150,000.

Required   1. Determine the amount of "gain on restructuring" to be reported.
2. Prepare the required journal entry or entries.

E 23–6   **Bankruptcy Reorganization: Settlement for Cash and Stock**   New Life Company's plan of reorganization under Chapter 11 of the Bankruptcy Code calls for a cash payment of $4,000,000 and the issuance of 800,000 shares of its $1 par value common stock to its unsecured creditors on a pro rata basis. These unsecured creditors are composed of vendors (owed $8,000,000) and a bank (owed $3,500,000 principal and $500,000 interest). New Life's common stock has a value of $1.25 per share based on the reorganization value of the company.

Required   Prepare the journal entry related to this settlement.

E 23–7   **Bankruptcy Reorganization: Settlement for Cash and Notes**   Skiddex Company's plan of reorganization under Chapter 11 of the Bankruptcy Code calls for a cash payment of $1,500,000 and the issuance of $2,000,000 of 14% notes payable to its unsecured creditors on a pro rata basis. These unsecured creditors are composed of vendors (owed $2,300,000) and a bank (owed $3,300,000 principal and $400,000 interest). (The 14% interest rate on the notes is considered reasonable under the circumstances.) The notes are to be paid in full in three years.

Required   Prepare the journal entry related to this settlement.

E 23–8   **Statement of Affairs: Calculating Expected Settlement Amounts**   The statement of affairs for Defuncto Company reflects the following amounts:

	Book Value	Estimated Current Value
Assets		
Assets pledged with fully secured creditors	$150,000	$180,000
Assets pledge with partially secured creditors	80,000	60,000
Free assets	220,000	150,000
	$450,000	$390,000

(continued)

Liabilities

Liabilities with priority	$ 20,000
Fully secured creditors	130,000
Partially secured creditors	100,000
Unsecured creditors	260,000
	$510,000

Required   Compute the amount that each class of creditors can expect to receive if assets are converted into cash at their estimated current values.   (AICPA adapted)

PROBLEMS

P 23–1   **Troubled Debt Restructuring: Modification of Terms**   Stallex Company, which is having serious financial difficulty, entered into an agreement with its major lender on 12/31/X4. The amount owed to the lender was restructured as follows:

1. Of the $2,000,000 of principal owed to the lender (all of which was then due), 10% was canceled.
2. Accrued interest of $300,000 was canceled.
3. The due date on the remaining principal amount was extended to 12/31/X8.
4. The interest rate on the remaining principal amount was reduced from 12% to 3% for 19X5 and 19X6. For 19X7 and 19X8, the interest rate was set at 6%. All interest at these new rates is to be paid annually in arrears.

Required   1. Determine whether a gain on restructuring of debt has resulted.
2. Prepare the journal entry to record the restructuring.
3. Calculate the total amount of interest expense, if any, reported from the restructuring date to the maturity date.

P 23–2   **Troubled Debt Restructuring: Combination of Equity Interest Granted and Modification of Terms**   Ganes Company, which is having serious financial difficulty, entered into an agreement with holders of its notes payable on 12/31/X5. The debt was restructured as follows:

1. Of the total of $14,000,000 of notes payable (all of which was currently due), $7,000,000 of principal was canceled in exchange for 300,000 shares of the company's $1 par value common stock. (The common stock had a market value of $20 per share on 12/31/X5.)
2. The remaining $7,000,000 of principal is to bear interest at 5%, payable annually in arrears. The maturity date of this $7,000,000 was extended to 12/31/X8.
3. Accrued interest of $350,000 was canceled.

Required   1. Determine whether a gain on restructuring of debt has resulted.
2. Prepare the journal entry to record the restructuring.
3. Calculate the total amount of interest expense, if any, reported from the restructuring date to the maturity date.

P 23–3   **Troubled Debt Restructuring: Combination of Equity Interest Granted and Modification of Terms**   Lossco Company, which is having serious financial difficulty, entered into an agreement with its bondholders on 12/31/X1. The debt was restructured as follows:

1. Of the total $25,000,000 in face value of bonds outstanding (which bear interest at 12%), $5,000,000 was canceled in exchange for 50,000 shares of a new class of preferred stock having a par value of $100.
2. The maturity date of the remaining $20,000,000 of bonds was extended to 12/31/X3.
3. The interest rate on the $20,000,000 is 3% until maturity.
4. Of the $2,000,000 interest payable accrued at 12/31/X1, $1,500,000 was canceled. The remaining $500,000 was paid when the restructuring agreement was signed (at the close of business on 12/31/X1).

Additional Information   1. The bonds were issued at a $700,000 premium eight years ago. The *straight-line method* of amortization had been used.
2. The bonds had an original life of 10 years. They were due in full during 19X1 as the result of a default in the interest payments.

Required   1. Determine whether a gain on restructuring of debt has resulted.

2. Prepare the journal entry to record the restructuring.

3. Calculate the total amount of interest expense, if any, reported from the restructuring date to the maturity date.

P 23–4 **Troubled Debt Restructuring: Combination of Equity Interest Granted and Modification of Terms Involving Contingent Interest**   Futura Company, which is having serious financial difficulty, entered into an agreement with its major lender on 12/31/X3. The amount owed to the lender was restructured as follows:

1. Of the $100,000,000 of principal owed to the lender (all of which was currently due), $40,000,000 was canceled in exchange for 400,000 shares of a new class of preferred stock, having a par value of $100 per share.

2. The maturity date of the remaining $60,000,000 of principal was extended to 12/31/X8.

3. The interest rate on the $60,000,000 of principal was reduced to 4% from 8%, with interest payable annually in arrears.

4. If the company's cumulative earnings before interest expense and income taxes from 1/1/X4 through 12/31/X8 exceed $25,000,000, the interest rate reverts to 8% retroactive to 1/1/X4. (As of 12/31/X3, it is not probable that cumulative earnings during this period will exceed $25,000,000.)

5. Accrued interest payable of $15,000,000 as of 12/31/X3 was forgiven.

Required   **1.** Determine whether a gain on restructuring of debt has resulted.

2. Prepare the journal entry to record the restructuring.

3. Determine the total amount of interest expense, if any, reported during the next five years, assuming that the company's cumulative earnings before interest expense and taxes during that period

   a. Did not exceed $25,000,000.

   b. Did exceed $25,000,000 as of 9/30/X7.

P 23–5 **Troubled Debt Restructuring: Modification of Terms—Use of Present Value Concepts**   Defaulto Company, which is having serious financial difficulty, entered into a restructuring agreement with a creditor owed $3,000,000 of principal (now due and payable) and $427,000 of interest. The terms of the restructuring agreement (dated 1/1/X1) call for

1. Cancellation of $277,000 of accrued interest, with payment of the remaining $150,000 on signing the agreement. (This payment was indeed made at that time.)

2. Principal payments of $1,000,000 per year beginning 1/1/X2 (one year from now), until the loan is paid in full on 1/1/X4.

3. Interest to be paid annually in arrears, beginning 1/1/X2 at 10% on the unpaid balance. (The interest rate prior to the restructuring was 14%.)

Required   **1.** Determine whether a gain on restructuring of debt has resulted.

2. Prepare the journal entry to record the restructuring.

3. Determine the total amount of interest expense reported over the next three years.

4. Using present value tables, calculate the approximate effective interest rate.

5. Prepare the journal entries made between the restructuring date and the maturity date, assuming that all required payments are made on time.

P 23–6 **Comprehensive: Troubled Debt Restructuring**   On 7/1/X2, TDR Company entered into a troubled debt restructuring agreement with its creditors. Data pertaining to the various classes of creditors and equity interests prior to the restructuring are as follows:

Accounts payable, unsecured	$1,800,000
10% Note payable to bank, currently due and payable	3,000,000
Accrued interest on note payable	400,000
8% Debenture bonds (subordinated to bank loan)	2,000,000
Accrued interest on debenture bonds	100,000
6% Preferred stock, $100 par value, cumulative, dividends in arrears of $90,000; 5,000 shares outstanding	
Common stock, no-par value, 200,000 shares outstanding	

The terms of the restructuring are as follows:

1. Accounts payable of $400,000 are canceled outright. Accounts payable of $600,000 are canceled in exchange for 80,000 shares of common stock. Trading in the company's common stock was suspended on 1/15/X2. Just before that time, the common stock was selling at $2 per share. Trading was resumed on 7/2/X2, and the stock closed at 50 cents per share on that day. All remaining payables are to be paid within 180 days.

2. Principal of $500,000 on the bank note, along with all accrued interest, is canceled. The due date on the remaining principal is extended to 7/1/X5. The interest rate is reduced to 5%. If TDR's cumulative earnings exceed $2,000,000 during the three years ended 6/30/X5, however, the interest rate reverts to 10% retroactively. (It appears unlikely that TDR's earnings will exceed $2,000,000 during this period.)

3. Principal of $1,000,000 on the debenture bonds is exchanged for a new class of 7% preferred stock. This new preferred stock designated Series A is senior to the existing preferred stock with respect to dividends and distributions in the event of liquidation. The existing preferred stock (which was issued at par) is designated Series B. All accrued interest on the debentures is canceled. The 6/30/X7 due date is unchanged. The interest rate on the remaining $1,000,000 of principal is reduced to 5% until maturity.

4. The dividends in arrears on the existing preferred stock is canceled, and the future dividend rate is reduced to 3% for a period of five years.

Required   1. Prepare the accounting entries related to these restructurings, assuming that 7/1/X2 is the consummation date.

2. What entry, if any, would be made on 6/30/X5 if TDR's earnings do *not* exceed $2,000,000 from 7/1/X2 to 6/30/X5?

3. Calculate the total amount of interest expense reported in the income statement for the next five years with respect to the debenture bonds.

P 23–7   **Bankruptcy Reorganization under Chapter 11**   The following balance sheet was prepared for Newcoe Inc. *immediately before* its plan of reorganization under Chapter 11 was confirmed:

	Book Value (preconfirmation)	Fair Value
Cash	$ 270,000	$ 270,000
Accounts receivables, net	130,000	130,000
Inventory, LIFO	280,000	440,000
Fixed assets, net	400,000	510,000
Patents	80,000	60,000
Goodwill	40,000	–0–
	$1,200,000	$1,410,000
Postpetition liabilities:		
Accounts payable and other	$ 280,000	$ 280,000
Short-term borrowings	90,000	90,000
	$ 370,000	$ 370,000
Prepetition Liabilities *Not* Subject to Compromise	$ 60,000	$ 60,000
Prepetition Liabilities Subject to Compromise	$1,300,000	
Shareholders' deficiency:		
Preferred stock	$ 100,000	
Common stock, $1 par value	5,000	
Additional paid-in capital	215,000	
Retained earnings (deficit)	(850,000)	
	$ (530,000)	
	$1,200,000	

Details of the confirmed plan of reorganization follow:

1. Creditors having liabilities subject to compromise agree to forgive debt of $1,300,000 in exchange for
   a. A pro rata cash payment of $150,000.
   b. Senior debt of $650,000 bearing 12% interest, repayable over five years. The 12% interest rate is deemed reasonable.

   c. Eighty thousand shares of the existing common stock issue; the existing common stock issue is to have a fresh-start book value of $2.70 per share.

2. The preferred stock issue is canceled in exchange for 15,000 shares of the existing common stock issue.

3. The reorganization value of the company's assets was deemed to be $1,500,000.

Required 1. Prepare the entry to record the discharge of indebtedness.

2. Prepare the entry to record cancellation of the preferred stock.

3. Prepare the entry to adopt fresh-start reporting.

4. Prepare the stockholders' equity section on a fresh-start basis.

P 23–8 **Bankruptcy Reorganization: Settlement with Unsecured Creditors—Use of Present Value Concepts**
Debtorex Corporation's plan of reorganization was confirmed by the bankruptcy court on 6/30/X1. Under the plan, unsecured creditors (who are owed $850,000,000) are to receive the following:

Cash	$300,000,000
12% Unsecured notes	$300,000,000
Common stock, $1 par value	10,000,000 shares

The company's investment bankers have determined that the 12% unsecured notes will trade at a discount on issuance to yield a return of approximately 15%. These notes are to be paid off at $60,000,000 per year beginning 6/30/X2 until their maturity five years from now. Interest is to be paid annually in arrears each June 30.

The company's common stock (2,000,000 shares now outstanding) traded at $1.50 per share when the company's plan of reorganization was confirmed.

Assume that *APBO No. 21* applies to the 12% unsecured notes. Selected present value factors follow:

	Present Value Factors	
Periods	**12%**	**15%**
1	0.89286	0.86957
2	0.79719	0.75614
3	0.71178	0.65752
4	0.63552	0.57175
5	0.56743	0.49718
Five payments (annuity)	3.60478	3.35216

Required 1. Prepare the journal entries related to the discharge of indebtedness.

2. Prepare the journal entries made for the first two years following confirmation of the plan, assuming that all required payments are made on time. (Assume that the company has a June 30 fiscal year-end.)

P 23–9* **Liquidation: Preparing a Statement of Affairs**   As Die-Hard Corp.'s CPA, you are aware that it is facing bankruptcy proceedings. Its balance sheet at 6/30/X1 and supplementary data are as follows:

Assets

Cash	$ 2,000
Accounts receivable, less allowance for uncollectibles	70,000
Inventory, raw materials	40,000
Inventory, finished goods	60,000
Marketable securities	20,000
Land	13,000
Buildings, net of accumulated depreciation	90,000

(continued)

*The financial statement information presented for problems accompanied by asterisks is also provided on Model 23 (filename: MODEL23) of the software file disk that is available with the text, allowing the problem to be worked on the computer.

Machinery, net of accumulated depreciation	120,000
Goodwill	20,000
Prepaid expenses	5,000
Total Assets	$440,000

Liabilities and Equity

Accounts payable	$ 80,000
Notes payable	135,000
Accrued wages	15,000
Mortgages payable	130,000
Common stock	100,000
Accumulated deficit	(20,000)
Total Liabilities and Equity	$440,000

Additional Information

1. Cash includes an expended $500 travel advance.
2. Accounts receivable of $40,000 have been pledged to bank loans of $30,000. Credit balances of $5,000 are netted in the accounts receivable total.
3. Marketable securities consist of government bonds costing $10,000 and 500 shares of Bumm Company stock. The market value of the bonds is $10,000 and the stock is $18 per share. The bonds have accrued interest due of $200. The securities are collateral for a $20,000 bank loan.
4. Appraised value of raw materials is $30,000 and of finished goods is $50,000. For an additional cost of $10,000, the raw materials would realize $70,000 as finished goods.
5. The appraised value of fixed assets is land, $25,000; buildings, $110,000; and machinery, $75,000.
6. Prepaid expenses will be exhausted during the liquidation period.
7. Accounts payable include $15,000 of withheld payroll taxes and $6,000 owed to creditors who had been reassured by Die-Hard's president that they would be paid. Unrecorded employer's payroll taxes total $500.
8. Wages payable are not subject to any limits under bankruptcy laws.
9. Mortgages payable consist of $100,000 on land and buildings and $30,000 chattel mortgages on machinery. Total unrecorded accrued interest for these mortgages amounts to $2,400.
10. Estimated legal fees and expenses connected with the liquidation are $10,000.
11. Probable judgment on a pending damage suit is $50,000.
12. You have not rendered a $5,000 invoice for last year's audit, and you estimate a $1,000 fee for liquidation work.

Required

1. Prepare a statement of affairs. (The Book Value column should reflect adjustments that properly should have been made at 6/30/X1 in the normal course of business.)
2. Compute the estimated settlement per dollar of unsecured liabilities.   (AICPA adapted)

P 23–10* **Liquidation: Preparing a Statement of Affairs**   Last-Legg Corporation is in financial difficulty because of low sales. Its stockholders and principal creditors want an estimate of the financial results of the liquidation of the assets and liabilities and the dissolution of the corporation.

Last-Legg Corporation
Postclosing Trial Balance
December 31, 19X3

	Debit	Credit
Cash	$ 5,000	
Accounts receivable	82,000	
Allowance for uncollectibles		$ 3,000
Inventories	160,000	
Supplies inventory	12,000	
Investment in Hye-Flyer Company's 5% bonds (at face value)	20,000	
Accrued bond interest receivable	3,000	
Advertising	24,000	
Land	16,000	
Building	120,000	

(continued)

	Debit	Credit
Accumulated depreciation—Building		$ 20,000
Machinery and equipment	$184,000	
Accumulated depreciation—Machinery and equipment		32,000
Accounts payable		104,000
Notes payable—Bank		100,000
Notes payable—Officers		80,000
Payroll taxes payable		3,000
Wages payable		6,000
Mortgage payable		168,000
Mortgage interest payable		2,000
Capital stock		200,000
Accumulated deficit	117,000	
Estimated liability for product guarantees		25,000
	$743,000	$743,000

The following information has been collected for a meeting of the stockholders and principal creditors to be held on 1/10/X4:

1. Cash includes a $2,000 protested check from a customer. The customer stated that funds to honor the check will be available in about two weeks.
2. Accounts receivable include accounts totaling $40,000 that are fully collectible and have been assigned to the bank in connection with the notes payable. Included in the unassigned receivables is an uncollectible account of $1,000. The Allowance for Uncollectibles account of $3,000 now on the books will adequately provide for other doubtful accounts.
3. Purchase orders totaling $36,000 are on hand for the corporation's products. Inventory with a book value of $24,000 can be processed at an additional cost of $2,000 to fill these orders. The balance of the inventory, which includes obsolete materials with a book value of $4,000, can be sold for $41,000.
4. In transit at December 31 but not recorded on the books is a shipment of defective merchandise being returned by a customer. The president of the corporation authorized the return and the refund of the $1,000 purchase price after the merchandise had been inspected. Other than this return, the president knows of no other defective merchandise that would affect the Estimated Liability for Product Guarantees account. The merchandise being returned has no salvage value.
5. The supplies inventory comprises advertising literature, brochures, and other sales aids, which could not be replaced for less than $14,000.
6. The investment in 10% bonds of Hye-Flyer Company is recorded at face value (two bonds each having a $10,000 face value). They were purchased in 19X1 for $8,500, and the adjustment to face value was credited to the Retained Earnings account. At 12/31/X3 the bonds were quoted at 30.
7. The Advertising account represents the future benefits of a 19X3 advertising campaign. The account contains 10% of certain advertising expenditures. The president stated that this figure was too conservative and that 20% would be a more realistic measure of the market that was created.
8. The land and building are in a downtown area. A $200,000 firm offer has been received for the land, which would be used as a parking lot; the building would be razed at a cost of $48,000 to the buyer. Another offer of $160,000 was received for the real estate, which the bidder stated would be used for manufacturing that would probably employ some employees of Last-Legg.
9. The highest offer received from used machinery dealers was $72,000 for all of the machinery and equipment.
10. One creditor, whose account for $16,000 is included in the accounts payable, confirmed in writing that he would accept 75 cents on the dollar if the corporation paid him by January 10.
11. Wages payable are for amounts earned within the last 30 days.
12. The mortgage payable is secured by the land and building. Neither of the last two monthly principal payments of $800 was made.
13. Estimated liquidation expenses amount to $13,000.
14. For income tax purposes, the corporation has the following net operating loss carryovers (the combined federal and state tax rate is 40%): 19X1, $40,000; 19X2, $48,000; and 19X3, $32,000.

Required   1. Prepare a statement of affairs. (The Book Value column should reflect adjustments that should have been made at 12/31/X3 in the normal course of business. Assume that the company has a June 30 fiscal year-end.)
2. Prepare a schedule that computes the estimated settlement per dollar of unsecured liabilities.

(AICPA adapted)

✳ THINKING CRITICALLY ✳

✳ CASES ✳

C 23–1   **Troubled Debt Restructuring: Theory**   Debtco Company has recently completed restructuring a substantial portion of its debt with one of its major lenders, which was owed $1,000,000 principal and $100,000 interest as of the date the restructuring was consummated. Under the terms of the restructured debt agreement, the $100,000 accrued interest is forgiven and the $1,000,000 principal is to be paid two years hence, with no interest to be paid for these two years.

Debtco Company's controller has indicated to you that the company intends to value the debt owed at $826,446, which is the present value of $1,000,000 using a discount rate of 10% (the interest rate before the restructuring). This valuation results in reporting (1) a $273,554 gain on restructuring debt in the current year, (2) $82,645 interest expense in the first year following the restructuring, and (3) $90,909 interest expense in the second year following the restructuring. The controller gives you the following reasons that this approach best reflects the economics of the restructuring.

1. The creditor's $1,000,000 note receivable is worth no more than what the note receivable can be sold for or discounted to on a nonrecourse basis.
2. If the creditor sold the note receivable to a financial institution on a nonrecourse basis, it certainly would not sell it for more than its present value using an interest rate commensurate with the issuing company's risk.
3. Considering the company's poor financial condition, a rate higher than 10% probably would be justified. The controller decided not to use a rate higher than 10%, however, to be conservative in the computation of the gain on restructuring of the debt.
4. If the value of the note receivable on the creditor's books cannot be worth more than $826,446, the excess of the carrying amount of the note payable (including accrued interest) over this amount must represent the true value of the debt forgiveness.

Required   1. Disregarding the requirements of *SFAS No. 15,* evaluate the soundness of the controller's approach.
2. Is the controller's approach conservative? What other reason might have prompted the controller to use a low interest rate?
3. What impact will this approach have on retained earnings at the end of the two years? What impact will the approach set forth in *SFAS No. 15* have on retained earnings?

C 23–2   **Troubled Debt Restructuring: Theory**   Assume that *SFAS No. 15* required that income statements of periods subsequent to a troubled debt restructuring reflect interest expense related to restructured debt based on an interest rate commensurate with the risk associated with the restructured debt.

Required   How would you determine an appropriate interest rate "commensurate with the risk"?

C 23–3   **Bankruptcy Reorganization: Theory**   You are the controller of a company that has been attempting to work out a troubled debt restructuring at lengthy meetings with its major creditors. At the last meeting, the company's president told the creditors that if they did not agree to the restructuring plan proposed by the company, management would file for *reorganization* under Chapter 11 of the bankruptcy statutes.

Required   1. How would the accounting change as a result of restructuring the debt through the bankruptcy courts versus outside the bankruptcy courts?
2. What is the rationale for having different rules for restructuring debt in bankruptcy reorganizations?

✳ **PERSONAL SITUATIONS: ETHICS AND INTERPERSONAL SKILLS** ✳

PS 23–1 **Ethics: Bankruptcy on the Horizon—Start Draining the Subsidiary** If PS 2–1 was not assigned when Chapter 2 was covered, it can be assigned in this chapter instead.

ANSWERS TO SELF-STUDY QUESTIONS

1. b, c, d, f   **2.** b, c, d, f   **3.** a, b, d, g   **4.** c, g   **5.** c   **6.** e   **7.** b   **8.** a

GOVERNMENTAL ACCOUNTING: BASIC PRINCIPLES AND THE GENERAL FUND

Nobody spends somebody else's money as wisely as they spend their own.

MILTON FRIEDMAN
NOBEL PRIZE WINNER
IN ECONOMICS

In this chapter, we first discuss the Governmental Accounting Standards Board (GASB), which establishes accounting standards for state and local governmental units and is a sister organization of the Financial Accounting Standards Board (FASB). We then discuss (1) the nature and diversity of governmental activities, (2) the objectives of governmental financial reporting, (3) the two different kinds of flow statements that present operating statements for governmental activities, and (4) the basic principles used in governmental financial reporting.

Last, we discuss the General Fund of governmental units, which is the fund that accounts for most of the operations of governmental units. All other funds, which are specialized funds, are discussed in Chapter 25. Likewise, accounting for capitalizable fixed assets and long-term debt—both those that are (1) reported *within* certain funds and those that are (2) reported *outside* any of the funds in two categorical lists called *account groups*—are discussed in Chapter 25. Chapter 25 discusses the manner of reporting all of the funds and these two account groups in a quasi-combined manner to present an overall picture of the governmental unit.

In the Chapter 25 appendix, we discuss two major changes that the GASB hopes to implement in 1999 (at the earliest), namely, changes in (1) the financial reporting model and (2) the measurement focus and basis of accounting used in the financial reporting model.

Although entire textbooks are devoted to accounting for state and local governmental units, the coverage in this and the following chapter is sufficiently broad and deep to prepare for the governmental portion of the CPA examination.

I THE GOVERNMENTAL ACCOUNTING STANDARDS BOARD

ITS PURPOSE, STRUCTURE, AND LOCATION

In 1984, the Governmental Accounting Standards Board was created as an arm of the Financial Accounting Foundation (FAF) to establish state and local governmental accounting standards. Thus the FAF now oversees both the FASB and the GASB. The GASB has a five-member board (appointed for five-year terms), with a full-time chairperson. The GASB is located in the same Norwalk, Connecticut, headquarters as the FASB.

NO AUTHORITY TO ESTABLISH STANDARDS FOR THE FEDERAL GOVERNMENT
The GASB does *not* have authority to establish financial reporting standards for the federal government. The Federal Accounting Standards Advisory Board (FASAB), which functions independently of the FAF, the FASB, and the GASB, however, proposes reporting standards to (1) the Office of Management and Budgets (OMB), (2) the General Accounting Office (GAO), and (3) the Treasury department, all of which issue their own standards.

STATUS OF PRE-GASB STANDARDS

Prior to GASB's creation, state and local governmental accounting standards were established by various bodies (the last one being the National Council on Governmental Accounting—NCGA—that made some major reporting improvements during its existence from 1978 to 1984). These various bodies were sponsored by the Government Finance Officers Association (GFOA), which is for the governmental sector what the American Institute of Certified Public Accountants (AICPA) is for the private sector.[1]

State and local governmental accounting standards in force at the time of GASB's creation continue in force until their status is changed by a subsequent GASB pronouncement (as mandated by GASB *Statement No. 1*, "Authoritative Status of NCGA Pronouncements and AICPA Audit Guide").

THE JURISDICTIONAL ARRANGEMENT FOR THE GASB AND THE FASB

The current jurisdictional arrangement (effective since November 30, 1989) for the GASB and the FASB is that each board has primary responsibility for setting standards for the reporting entities within its jurisdiction. Under this arrangement, an entity subject to the jurisdiction of one board

1. **Is** *not* required to change its reporting methods as a result of a standard issued by the *other* board.

2. **Must** follow a pronouncement of the *other* board if required to do so by the *primary* board.

3. **May** elect to follow the pronouncements of the *other* board (or look to other sources for guidance) when the *primary* board has *not* addressed a specific issue. Furthermore, a governmental unit that elects to use such FASB standards must use them on an all-or-nothing basis; thus a governmental unit *cannot* pick and choose among those FASB standards (the ones that do *not* conflict with or contradict GASB pronouncements).

THE GOVERNMENTAL GAAP HIERARCHY

Auditors of private companies and governmental units that issue unqualified opinions usually use wording as follows in their audit reports:

> In our opinion, the financial statements referred to above present fairly, in all material respects, the financial position of X Company or X City as of December 31, 19X1, and the results of its operations and its cash flows for the year then ended, in conformity with generally accepted accounting principles [hereafter GAAP].

The Auditing Standards Board of the AICPA has issued an auditing standard that (1) requires the auditor's judgment concerning "fairness" be applied within the framework of GAAP and (2) sets forth a hierarchy of GAAP for both nongovernmental and governmental entities.[2] The governmental GAAP hierarchy (in which Level 1 is the highest authoritative source) is presented in Illustration 24–1.

***GAAFR:* "THE BLUE BOOK"**   Note that in footnote d of Illustration 24–1 we mention the 1994 (6th) edition of *GAAFR*, the acronym for *Governmental Accounting, Auditing and Financial Reporting*, which the GFOA publishes. With more than 30,000

---

[1]Prior to 1984, the GFOA was called the *Municipal Finance Officers Association.* In this chapter, we use its new name. The GFOA, as does the AICPA for the private sector, offers the governmental sector a wide range of (1) publications (including 85 books, periodicals, and a monthly newsletter), (2) services, and (3) software, all of which are designed to enhance and promote the professional management of governmental units.

[2]This guidance is set forth in *Statement on Auditing Standards No. 69,* "The Meaning of *Present Fairly in Conformity With Generally Accepted Accounting Principles,*" issued in 1992 and in paragraphs 1.16–18 of the AICPA's audit guide, *Audits of State and Local Governmental Units,* which was issued in 1994 (the third edition).

ILLUSTRATION 24-1	**Summary of Hierarchy of Governmental GAAP**			
		Source		
Level	GASB	FASB	AICPA	Other
1	Statements and Interpretations	Applicable[a] pronouncements[b]	Applicable[a] pronouncements[b]	
2	Technical Bulletins		Applicable[c] Industry Audit and Accounting Guides Applicable[c] Statements of Position	
3	Emerging Issues Task Force Consensus Positions (if and when a GASB EITF is formed)		Applicable[c] Practice Bulletins	
4	Implementation Guides (Questions and Answers published by the GASB staff)			Industry Practices[d]
5[e]				Other Accounting Literature[f]

[a]*Applicable* at this level means if designated as applying to state and local governmental entities by a GASB Statement or Interpretation.

[b]Proprietary funds of governmental units (which are the funds that report in the same manner as for-profit entities as explained later) are subject to private-sector authoritative guidance issued prior to 11/30/89 (through *SFAS No. 102*), unless it is inconsistent with GASB guidance. Furthermore, proprietary funds retain the option of following pronouncements of the FASB issued subsequent to that date if (1) they do so consistently and (2) the guidance is *not in*consistent with GASB guidance.

[c]*Applicable* at this level means those designated by the AICPA as applying to state and governmental entities and cleared by the GASB (no formal objection given to the issuance of the pronouncement).

[d]Must be widely recognized and prevalent. (The 1994 edition of *GAAFR* would be a useful reference at this level.)

[e]This is referred to as *Other Sources* in *SAS No. 69* rather than as Level 5.

[f]Includes GASB Concepts Statements, FASB and AICPA pronouncements *not* specifically made applicable to state and local governmental units, Technical Information Service Inquiries and Replies included in AICPA Technical Practice Aids, accounting textbooks, articles (such as *GAAFR Review*, a monthly publication by the GFOA).

copies in print, government finance practitioners use *GAAFR* widely as a *nonauthoritative* source of practical guidance on properly applying GAAP to state and local governments. The 1994 edition (570 pages) includes updated guidance on all facets of governmental accounting and auditing, including detailed discussions and extensive examples of governmental reporting standards.[3]

THE GASB'S ACCOMPLISHMENTS TO DATE

Since its inception in 1984, the GASB has issued one Concepts Statement (1987), 30 Statements of Governmental Accounting Standards (hereafter we use *SGAS* in

---

[3]Prior to the formalization of the governmental standard-setting process through the NCGA, *GAAFR* was *the* authoritative source of governmental GAAP.

referring to specific standards), four Interpretations, and three Technical Bulletins. The GASB statements have simplified or upgraded governmental financial reporting, but none has resulted in a substantial upgrading of governmental financial reporting as did *NCGA Statement 1* in 1979.

Several major projects are currently in progress, however, the most important by far being a complete reexamination of the financial reporting model. In the Chapter 25 appendix, we discuss (1) this major project and (2) a completed project (measurement focus and basis of accounting) for which a GASB standard was issued (*SGAS No. 11*) but is not scheduled to become effective until a new standard on the financial reporting model is issued and becomes effective.

THE GAO URGES THE GASB TO QUICKLY UPGRADE STATE AND LOCAL GOVERNMENT FINANCIAL REPORTING

A letter from the comptroller general of the General Accounting Office (GAO) to the chairman of the GASB in 1991 underscored the need to significantly upgrade state and local governmental financial reporting further. In that letter, the comptroller general

1. Stated that several annual financial reports of state and local governments reviewed by the GAO contained "little or no warning of the severe financial difficulties the press subsequently reported."

2. Suggested that the GASB "move quickly to revise state and local government financial reporting."

3. Concluded that "the deteriorating financial conditions in a large number of our cities and states give these suggestions a degree of urgency."[4]

You will be able to more fully appreciate the degree to which governmental reporting needs to be improved after you have (1) covered Chapters 24 and 25 and (2) read the Chapter 25 appendix, which discusses the major improvements the GASB hopes to propose in final form in 1997 and to become effective in 1999 (at the earliest).

THE GASB *CODIFICATION* OF GOVERNMENTAL GAAP

In 1984, the GASB codified all existing governmental accounting and financial reporting standards, interpretations, and technical bulletins in a joint effort with the GFOA. This book, *Codification of Governmental Accounting and Financial Reporting Standards*, is periodically updated for subsequent changes.[5]

In referring to governmental GAAP, the AICPA's governmental audit guide cites the GASB Codification rather than the various GASB and NCGA statements and interpretations in force at the time of the *Codification*. This makes the most sense, and for this reason we do the same, citing the *Codification* in the same manner as in the audit guide (for example, "GASB *Cod.*, sec xxx") after first citing it in full.

II   THE NATURE AND DIVERSITY OF GOVERNMENTAL ACTIVITIES

Governmental operations are unique for several reasons: (1) their absence of a profit motive, (2) their extensive legal requirements, (3) their diverse activities, and (4) their use of fund accounting.

---

[4]*Journal of Accountancy*, November 1991, p. 26.
[5]The most recent update was effective June 30, 1995.

THE ABSENCE OF A PROFIT MOTIVE: WHAT TO MEASURE?

The fundamental difference between the private sector and the governmental sector is that the former is organized and operated to make a profit for its owners while the latter exists to provide services to its citizens on a substantially nonprofit basis. In the private sector, profit measurement is possible because a causal relationship exists between expenses and revenues: costs and expenses are incurred to generate revenues. As a result, it is appropriate to compare these categories and determine profitability. The services of governmental units, however, are *not* intended to generate revenues. Thus revenues are *not* earned; they stand alone. This circumstance raises two key questions:

- Should revenues be compared with the costs of providing services?
- Is some other comparison of inflows and outflows more appropriate?

We discuss this issue in depth in Section IV, Measurement Focus and Basis of Accounting.

EXTENSIVE LEGAL REQUIREMENTS

Constitutions, charters, and statutes regulate governmental units. Many legal provisions pertain to financial accounting areas. For example, certain activities or specified revenues must frequently be accounted for separately from all other operations. The uses of certain revenues may be limited. In some instances, a certain method of accounting—such as the cash basis—may be stipulated. We discuss the accounting ramifications of these requirements later in the chapter.

Many governmental units are required by law to follow GAAP and be audited annually by outside CPA firms or governmental audit agencies.

DIVERSITY OF ACTIVITIES

Governmental activities are tremendously diverse and are classified into three broad categories:

1. **Governmental.** Activities that do *not* resemble commercial activities are classified in this category. These operations provide primary services and are normally financed from tax revenues. Examples are education, public safety, the judicial system, social services, and administration.

2. **Proprietary.** These activities resemble commercial activities. Usually financed wholly or partially from user charges, these operations may be considered secondary services. Examples are utilities, public transportation, parking facilities, and recreational facilities. Proprietary operations usually have the objective to earn a profit or recover a certain level of operating costs from fees charged the public for their use.

3. **Fiduciary.** These activities pertain to accounting for assets held by a governmental unit as trustee or agent. The most common example is a pension fund for current and former public employees.

THE USE OF FUND ACCOUNTING

Because of the legal requirements pertaining to financial accounting areas and the diversity of governmental activities, the use of a single set of accounts to record and summarize all the financial transactions of a governmental unit is neither legally possible nor practical. As a result, **fund accounting,** whereby certain activities are accounted for separately from other operations, is predominant in governmental accounting. The GASB *Codification* defines a **fund** as follows:

A fund is . . . a fiscal and accounting entity with a self-balancing set of accounts recording cash and other financial resources, together with all related liabilities and residual equities or balances, and changes therein, which are segregated for the purpose of carrying on activities or attaining certain objectives in accordance with special regulations, restrictions, or limitations.[6]

FUND EQUITY   The difference between a fund's assets and liabilities is the *fund's equity*. Different terms are used, however, to describe this section of the balance sheet for governmental and fiduciary-type funds than for proprietary funds. Also, different general ledger accounts are used as well. This section of the balance sheet is presented as follows:

Governmental and Fiduciary-Type Funds	Proprietary Funds
Fund balance:	Equity:
Reserved for encumbrances[a]	Contributed capital
Unreserved[a]	Retained earnings

[a]The nature of these accounts is explained later.

III THE OBJECTIVES OF GOVERNMENTAL FINANCIAL REPORTING

GASB Concepts Statement No. 1, "Objectives of Financial Reporting," sets forth three overall objectives of governmental financial reporting and nine additional ones that flow from the three overall ones. We list the three overall objectives and selected additional ones in Illustration 24–2.

IV MEASUREMENT FOCUS AND BASIS OF ACCOUNTING

MEASUREMENT FOCUS: WHAT FLOWS TO MEASURE FOR OPERATIONS

The concept of *measurement focus* pertains to presenting in an operating statement information concerning flows for a *period* of time. Thus measurement focus is exclusively an operating statement concept pertaining to "what to measure for operations."[7] Consequently, the concept of measurement focus does *not* apply to the reporting of assets and liabilities, which are reported at a *point* in time.

Because of the diversity of governmental activities, the reporting issue is raised as to whether (1) the same flows should be measured for all three types of activities or (2) different flows should be measured.

As a point of reference, recall that business enterprises (proprietary in nature) present an operating statement called an *income statement*. An income statement measures *the flow of economic resources and claims against those resources* that have occurred for a period of time. In addition, business enterprises present a statement of

---

[6]*Codification of Governmental Accounting and Financial Reporting Standards* (Norwalk, CT: Governmental Accounting Standards Board, 1995), sec. 1100.102.

[7]The word *operations* in the private sector refers exclusively to transactions and events that impact equity. For nonproprietary-type activities of government, operations has (1) a broader meaning in some respects because it *includes* borrowings, repayments of debt, and expenditures for the acquisition of capital assets and (2) a narrower meaning in some respects because it *excludes* both (a) depreciation expense and (b) long-term liabilities and pension obligations not expected to be funded currently. This becomes evident as you read this section of the chapter.

ILLUSTRATION 24–2	**Objectives of Governmental Financial Reporting**

"1. Financial reporting should assist in fulfilling a government's duty to be publicly accountable and enable users to assess that accountability (the paramount objective from which all other objectives must flow). Financial reporting should
   a. Provide information to determine whether current-year revenues were sufficient to pay for current-year services.
   b. Demonstrate whether revenues were obtained and used in accordance with the entity's legally adopted budget.
"2. Financial reporting should assist users in evaluating the operating results of the governmental entity for the year. Financial reporting should
   a. Provide information about sources and uses of financial resources.
   b. Determine whether the entity's financial position improved or deteriorated as a result of the year's operations.
"3. Financial reporting should assist users in assessing the level of services that can be provided by the governmental entity and its ability to meet its obligations as they become due."

Source: GASB *Cod.*, sec. 100.177–179.

---

cash flows, which has a much more limited measurement focus than that of an income statement. Thus business enterprises present *two* flow statements.

PROPRIETARY-TYPE ACTIVITIES OF GOVERNMENT Some governmental activities are managed in a manner similar to those of business enterprises because the objective is to recover either all or a majority of the cost of providing services through user charges. For such activities, it is sensible to measure economic flows and thus present an operating statement that shows revenues, gains, expenses (including depreciation expense), and losses. Rather than calling this operating statement an income statement, however, *statement of revenues and expenses* is deemed more appropriate in view of the fact that the intent is *not* to generate income or maximize profits as in the private sector. Thus a statement of revenues and expenses for proprietary-type activities answers the following questions:

1. What revenues were generated during the year?
2. What expenses were incurred during the year?
3. What was the improvement or deterioration in the governmental unit's overall *economic condition* as a result of events and transactions that occurred during the year?

It is also sensible to present a statement of cash flows for proprietary-type activities, as the private sector does. Partly because of this manner of reporting (presenting two flow statements), the issues involved in reporting the proprietary-type activities of governmental units are minuscule in comparison to those that exist for reporting governmental-type activities (in which only one flow statement is presented).

GOVERNMENTAL-TYPE ACTIVITIES The GASB deems it inappropriate to prepare a statement of revenues and expenses for governmental-type activities. Accordingly, a measurement focus other than the **flow of economic resources** (and claims against those resources) must be used. Possible alternative flows are as follows:

1. **Cash flows.** (This is considered too narrow a measurement focus.)
2. **Flows of *current* financial resources** (essentially cash and receivables) **and claims against those items that will be *paid* in the current period or shortly thereafter.**
3. **Flows of *total* financial resources** (essentially cash, receivables, prepaids, and inventories) **and claims against those items that will be *paid* in the current pe-**

riod or shortly thereafter. (This alternative is only a slightly broader measurement focus than alternative 2.)

4. **Flows of** *current* **financial resources** (essentially cash and receivables) **and claims against those items that were** *incurred* **in the current period**—regardless of when paid. (This alternative is a substantially broader measurement focus than alternatives 2 and 3.)

5. **Flows of** *total* **financial resources** (essentially cash, receivables, prepaids, and inventories) **and claims against those items that were** *incurred* **in the current period**—regardless of when paid. (This alternative is only a slightly broader measurement focus than alternative 4.)

None of these alternatives produces a result that would come close to the result obtained if the flow of economic resources measurement focus were used (which produces a statement of revenues and expenses [or costs of providing services]). Also, alternatives 2 and 3 generally produce results that are somewhat close to those that would be obtained using cash flows as the measurement focus. (The last two alternatives do so as well but to a lesser extent.) Note that the following cash flows (but *not* depreciation expense, which is *not* a cash flow) are reported in the operating statement under each of these five alternatives:

- Proceeds from borrowings.
- Repayments of debt.
- Interest payments on debt.
- Acquisitions of capital assets.
- Proceeds from the sale of capital assets.

The GASB requires use of the first alternative, the **flow of current financial resources.**[8] The rationale is that users are best served with a statement that revolves around receiving and spending resources rather than one that shows whether the governmental unit's economic condition has improved or deteriorated. Thus an operating statement using the flow of current financial resources answers the following questions:

1. What financial resources were **received** during the year?
2. What financial resources were **expended** during the year?
3. What increase or decrease occurred in the net financial resources that can be spent in the near future?

To facilitate reporting using this measurement focus, fixed assets and long-term liabilities are excluded from the balance sheets of the funds used to account for governmental-type activities. They are reported instead in account groups, which are mere lists of these items.

A MAJOR FINANCIAL REPORTING DEFICIENCY: A "STATEMENT OF REVENUES AND EXPENSES/COSTS OF PROVIDING SERVICES" SHOULD ALSO BE PRESENTED   Many accountants believe, as we do, that a statement of revenues and expenses/costs of providing services should be presented either in addition to or instead of a statement that measures the flow of current financial resources. Their reasoning is that (1) it is equally important to show the change in the overall economic condition of the governmental unit, (2) the concept of interperiod equity is an essential aspect of accountability, and (3) a measure of interperiod equity is *not* achieved using the flow of current financial resources as the measurement focus.

---

[8]As you can deduce later, the second alternative also is permitted as a result of the allowable option of using the *consumption method* to account for prepaids and inventories.

ACHIEVING INTERPERIOD EQUITY The concept of interperiod equity focuses on whether financial resources received during the year were sufficient to cover claims incurred during that year. Stated more simply, it focuses on **whether current year citizens received services for which future year citizens will be required to pay.** From a broader perspective, realize that the concept of interperiod equity is also **an intergenerational equity issue.**

BALANCED BUDGET LAWS The concept of interperiod equity is also consistent with the balanced-budget laws required by most governmental units, the intent of which is to require governments to live within their means. Many accountants believe that this manner of reporting (presenting only a statement that measures the flows of *current financial resources*) is merely a way for politicians to circumvent the intent of these laws. Thus it is a form versus substance reporting issue.

A SECOND MAJOR FINANCIAL REPORTING DEFICIENCY: PENSION BENEFIT OBLIGATIONS GREATLY EXCEED AMOUNTS RECOGNIZED TO DATE IN THE OPERATING STATEMENTS The interperiod equity problem is enormous and is mainly caused by (1) an unrealistic manner of calculating pension costs and (2) the manner of reporting unfunded annual required contributions (a liability) in the financial statements. (Other causes are postemployment health care benefits, compensated absences, and claims.) The GASB *Codification* requires that the manner of funding the pension benefit obligation be used to determine the pension liabilities to be recorded.[9] Unfortunately, much of the past service costs and retroactive benefit enhancements are funded during the years that the employees are in retirement (rather than *totally* during their working years when they rendered services). As a result, a liability is reported in the governmental unit's financial statements only to the extent that the current and prior years' required contributions (the *unfunded* annual required contributions) have *not* been paid.

Even then, to the extent that these required contributions are unpaid at year-end and are *not* expected to be paid from available financial resources (as reported in the balance sheet), an expenditure is *not* reported in the operating statement. Instead this liability is reported in a list of general long-term debt (discussed later). Furthermore, no disclosure of the pension benefit obligation need be made for comparison with the amounts set aside to show the amount by which the pension plan is underfunded.

If governmental units were required to follow the much more demanding *SFAS No. 87*, "Accounting for Pensions" (which separates the manner of calculating pension costs from the funding of those costs and requires that a liability be reported for the unfunded pension benefit obligation), governmental financial statements would report a staggering additional amount of liabilities. (One recent estimate is $125 billion.)[10] Consequently, current year citizens are now receiving substantial benefits for which they are shifting the burden of payment to future year citizens. Note that this problem is both a GAAP deficiency problem and a measurement focus problem.

Refer to the Business Perspective that follows for a discussion of the political factors causing (1) an accelerating and serious interperiod equity problem and (2) serious liquidity problems for a high percentage of public pension funds.

---

[9]Accounting for governmental pensions is set forth in *GASB No. 27*, "Accounting for Pensions by State and Local Governmental Employers," issued in 1994. It is patterned after *APB Opinion No. 8*, "Accounting for the Cost of Pension Plans," which was superseded by the substantially more rigorous *SFAS No. 87*, "Employers' Accounting for Pensions."

[10]Public Pension Plans Are So Underfunded That Trouble Is Likely," *The Wall Street Journal*, April 6, 1994, p. A1.

BUSINESS PERSPECTIVE

Votes Today, Taxes Tomorrow

In 1989 unions for Minnesota's schoolteachers and other public employees wanted to do something for their members, but they knew taxpayers weren't in a giving mood.

Never mind. A little pressure here, a little hint there, and lo! the state legislature handed the unions a gift worth as much as $1 billion that the taxpayers scarcely noticed.

The lawmakers instructed the Minnesota State Retirement System and four teachers' retirement systems to give roughly 200,000 public servants a juicy new early retirement package. The "Rule of 90" package allowed an employee whose age and years of service totaled 90 to retire without a reduction in benefits for early retirement. Thus a teacher who started working at 22 could retire at 56, several years earlier than the normal retirement age for the plans.

We're talking big money here: One estimate puts the cost of the early retirement package at $5,000 per employee. Minnesotans had just been put on the hook for perhaps $1 billion without being consulted.

But no one called it a raise, and the media scarcely noticed. To make the Rule of 90 look like a free lunch, the state legislators simply extended the period to amortize the retirement plans' already huge unfunded liabilities from 20 years to 30 years. The investment returns that the actuaries assumed the plans would earn were also raised, from 8% to 8.5%. The legislature used the "gains" to offset the cost of the pension grab.

To call such ploys phony bookkeeping is to put it mildly. Governmental Accounting Standards Board, where is thy sting?

"It is much easier for public employees to negotiate higher pension benefits than salary increases, which come out of current budgets," says Minnesota State Representative Phyllis Kahn, who has sponsored legislation to oversee her state's public pension funds more closely.

About 9,000 public pension plans cover some 16 million working or retired teachers, firemen, garbagemen, tax assessors and other state and local government employees. Together these plans have assets of $1.1 *trillion*. That compares with $3.4 trillion for private-sector pension funds covering over 40 million workers.

The public pension plans are very different animals from the private-sector plans. Corporate plan sponsors increasingly are shifting to so-called defined *contribution* plans. The benefits they pay out depend on how much the worker pays in, and how well the plan's assets are managed.

By contrast, virtually all public pension schemes are defined *benefit* plans. Most of these public plans cap employee contributions at around 5% of salary but guarantee retirees a predetermined amount of pension income, almost always with fat cost-of-living adjustments.

Jonathan Schwartz, who served as chief actuary for New York City's five pension funds from 1973 until 1986, well understands the game politicians play with these plans. "The challenge of being a public-sector actuary," he says, "is that by definition actuaries are concerned with long-range implications; but, for the principals you report to, the definition of long range is the four-year election cycle."

As a result of all this fun and games, public-sector plans are grossly underfunded. According to a recent survey by the Public Pension Coordinating Council, plans covering 76% of state and local government employees fell $164 billion short of the $812 billion that actuarial assumptions say they need. Such are the consequences of permitting legislatures to impose pension burdens on future taxpayers.

Corporate executives can't use this dodge. The 1974 Employee Retirement Income Security Act requires them to fully fund their pension liabilities within a reasonable period. Erisa also requires uniform financial reporting and disclosure by corporate pension plans. State and local politicians are not subject to Erisa. Besides, they probably won't be in office when the bills finally come due.

In Illinois the unfunded liability for its five retirement systems covering state employees (total assets, $20 billion) nearly doubled in the five years through 1994, from $8.6 billion to a current $17 billion. Assets cover barely half of liabilities, one of the country's worst coverage ratios. In effect, the state owes $17 billion that does not count as debt but must be paid.

Gregory Wass is the director of research at Chicago's Civic Federation, a taxpayers' group. Here's how he describes the process: "In Illinois, public unions go to the state legislature and attach benefit [increase] provisions to labor bills, which result in unfunded mandates for local property taxpayers." In other words, local taxpayers are ordered by their "representatives" to fork out.

Until recently, South Carolina's employees had to work for 30 years or reach age 65 to receive maximum pension benefits. But in 1991 associations representing about 225,000 public employees pressed the state's politicians for an early retirement package that would allow them to work just 25 years and retire. They got it, with only minor modifications.

South Carolina's statewide public pension plan is now underfunded by $2.1 billion, and the employee associations are back in Columbia, demanding elimination of the small concessions they made.

(continued)

Robert A.G. Monks, a principal at Washington, D.C.-based investment firm Lens, Inc., recently chaired a pension study committee for the Maine legislature. Monks shakes his head. "You have a [public pension fund] system that on the surface involves bargaining by equals and a level of openness and accountability," he says. "In truth, none of those phenomena actually exist in Maine."

Nor anywhere else in the country. The general rule is: Never mind the cost; we gain votes today and the bill doesn't come in until tomorrow. In most states the government is by law the guarantor of last resort for a local pension, oftentimes under the state constitution itself. Thus, according to the recent survey by the Public Pension Coordinating Council, only 57% of the country's public fund sponsors made the contributions that actuaries told them were needed to cover liabilities in 1992; only 77% covered at least 80% of obligations. Why bother? Let future taxpayers do it.

As if all this weren't bad enough, the potential burden on taxpayers is worsened by the slovenly way many of the pension funds are managed. In many cases, political considerations win out over sound investment management. That has become a particular concern lately thanks to Labor Secretary Robert Reich's program of encouraging funds to sink money into politically favored investments. Congressman Jim Saxton (R–N.J.) submitted a bill last month to prevent the government from promoting so-called economically targeted investments. But most states' taxpayers don't have a Jim Saxton to watch out for their interests, or if they do their watchdogs are outgunned and outmaneuvered by the public employees' unions and the elected officials in their pockets.

The Kansas Public Employees Retirement System, covering 195,000 workers and retirees, invested heavily in Kansas-based firms in the late 1980s, including an ailing savings and loan and a troubled steel mill. The plan's losses on these two investments alone came to over $70 million.

In California the giant California Public Employees' Retirement System (assets, $82 billion) has devoted $375 million to a program to promote single-family housing construction since 1992. Two similar programs were set up last year, with $150 million going to single-family and low-income housing construction and $145 million to support midsize California firms that have difficulty raising capital elsewhere. Such programs are useful to politicians. They enable them to deliver pork to favored constituents, snug in the knowledge that any losses will be picked up by future taxpayers.

According to research by Robert Monks and his colleague Nell Minow, the New York State United Teachers Fund sold its shares of the Tribune Co. a few years ago, after workers at the Tribune's New York *Daily News* went on strike. The fund cited a policy of not investing in "antiunion" companies. Tribune Co.'s stock has nearly doubled since the teachers' fund sold it.

Roberta Romano, a Yale Law School professor, took a hard look at the results of such politically motivated investments. Her conclusion: They cost public funds $5.6 billion *annually* from 1985 to 1989, the period her study examined. The figure is probably higher today.

Maybe the worst fiddling involves playing around with actuarial assumptions. By raising return assumptions the trustees can hide the costs of benefit increases and the losses that result from politically motivated investments—and even from fraud. A recent study by Wilshire Associates found that funds with high levels of unfunded liabilities tended to make the highest future rate-of-return assumptions. That is to say, the worse a fund's present finances are, the better that

Illustration 24–3 summarizes the measurement focus differences between governmental-type activities and proprietary-type activities.

BASIS OF ACCOUNTING: WHEN SHOULD TRANSACTIONS AND EVENTS BE RECOGNIZED?

The concept of *basis of accounting* refers to "when a transaction or event is recognized in the financial statements" (both the balance sheet and the operating statement). Only by being recognized can they be included in the measurement of the flow that has been selected for the operating statement. The possible alternative bases of accounting are

1. **The cash basis.**
2. **The accrual basis.**

fund's trustees claim they'll be able to do with the assets in the future.

As an example, the West Virginia Teachers' Retirement System is about broke, with only $376 million in assets and a $3.7 billion unfunded liability, according to Wilshire Associates. Yet it assumes its investment income will outpace salary gains by 3.7% per year, the second-highest such assumption among the 82 statewide funds Wilshire tracks. The only fund that is more optimistic is the Louisiana State Employees' Retirement System, the 73rd-worst-funded plan, with $3.2 billion in assets and $2.6 billion in unfunded liabilities. The Louisiana fund assumes its investment income will grow by 3.75% per annum faster than salaries will grow.

In the past five years, almost two-thirds of the states have "cut" budget deficits with increasingly optimistic assumptions about future returns on investments. From 1992 to 1994 California Governor Pete Wilson withheld about $700 million in pension plan contributions. A court recently declared the diversion unconstitutional and ordered repayment.

Struggling to create the appearance of balance in the New York State budget in 1990, then-Governor Mario Cuomo and the state legislature changed the accounting methods for plans covering most state and local government employees so adroitly that they eliminated for a few years the nearly $1 billion a year required to fund the plans.

Quick to demand ever more generous pensions, New York's public servants were even quicker to charge Cuomo and company with endangering their plans. Public unions sued to have the accounting changes reversed, and the New York State Court of Appeals sided with the workers in 1993. By then, however, the pension funds had lost $4 billion in contributions and Cuomo was on his way to being retired into private life by tax-weary voters. The problem of coming up with the money now falls to his successor, George Pataki.

Here's the bottom line: Between 1990 and 1994 the stock market rose 56% and bond prices rose, too. Yet at the end of the period, unfunded liabilities for the 82 statewide pension systems surveyed by Wilshire Associates still totaled $70 billion. The investment gains, in short, had been handed out to public employees to make sure they voted the right way.

What happens if the assumptions turn out to be far too optimistic? In a bear market, for example? For an idea of what a bear market or inflation might do to these funds, take a look at the District of Columbia Retirement Board, which covers 12,300 active and 11,400 retired policemen, firefighters, teachers and judges. It began operating in 1981 with $150 million in assets and $2.6 billion in liabilities, giving it a $2.45 billion unfunded liability. Since then, assets have grown to $2.5 billion, but the unfunded liability has doubled, to $5.2 billion—a stunning $8,700 per city resident.

Woe betide the politician who tries to stem this profligate tide. Donald Moe, a former Minnesota state senator who served on Minnesota's Legislative Commission on Pensions and Retirement for 20 years, tried. He resisted many proposed benefit increases, pointing out the cost of such generosity. Public employee unions got revenge by bankrolling Moe's opponent in the 1990 Democratic primary, and again when he ran for state auditor in 1994. "Don Moe wants to cut your pension," ran one union-financed radio ad.

In both races, Moe lost. So did most of the citizens. They are potentially liable now for close to $5 billion in unfunded pension liabilities in what is already among the highest-taxed states in the union.

Source: Neil Weinberg, "Votes Today, Taxes Tomorrow," *Forbes,* June 5, 1995, pp. 88–98. Reprinted by permission of *Forbes* magazine, June 5, 1995, © Forbes Inc., 1995.

3. **The modified accrual basis.** Under this alternative, some liabilities are recognized in the governmental funds on a delayed basis rather than when the liability is incurred. Until such recognition occurs, they are recorded in the General Long-Term Debt Account Group (discussed briefly later in the chapter and illustrated in Chapter 25). Thus such liabilities are temporarily *excluded* from the measurement focus of the governmental funds.

REPORTING FLOWS IN THE OPERATING STATEMENT For the operating statement, significantly different measurement results usually occur for each of the alternative bases of accounting. Consequently, it is important to select (1) the most meaningful measurement focus *and* (2) the basis of accounting that produces the most informative and realistic measurement results. The GASB requires the use of the modified accrual basis of accounting for governmental-type activities, and we

ILLUSTRATION 24–3	**Summary of Measurement Focus–Related Differences**	
	Governmental-Type Activities	**Proprietary-Type Activities**
Measurement focus	Flow of *current financial* resources	Flow of *economic* resources
Information provided	Financial resources *received*	Revenues generated
	Financial resources *spent*	Expenses incurred
	Increase or decrease in net financial resources available for spending in the near future	Extent of improvement in or deterioration of economic condition
Terminology used for *increases*	Revenues Other financing *sources*	Revenues Gains
Terminology used for *decreases*	Expenditures Other financing *uses*	Expenses Losses

discuss it in detail shortly. The GASB requires the use of the accrual basis of accounting for proprietary-type activities.

REPORTING ASSETS AND LIABILITIES

Although measurement focus is *not* an issue for reporting assets and liabilities, whether to use the cash basis, the accrual basis, or the modified accrual basis to determine when to recognize assets and liabilities is an issue because vastly different amounts would be reported under each of these alternatives (usually more so for liabilities than for assets).

MANNER OF DISPLAYING   An additional major reporting issue for assets and liabilities that are reported regardless of the particular basis of accounting selected is whether they should be reported/displayed (1) in individual funds, (2) partly in individual funds and partly in account group lists (split), or (3) in some form of aggregated manner comparable to a consolidated balance sheet used by business enterprises. For governmental-type activities, the display issue for assets and liabilities is quite controversial, and we discuss it near the end of Chapter 25 and in the Chapter 25 appendix .

V   BASIC PRINCIPLES OF THE GASB *CODIFICATION*

We have grouped the 12 basic principles in the GASB *Codification* into the following seven broad categories:

Category	
1	Accounting and Reporting Capabilities (GAAP, Legal Provisions, and Conflicts)
2	Types of Funds and Account Groups
3	Basis of Accounting
4	Financial Reporting (presented in three subcategories)
5	Long-Term Liabilities
6	Fixed Assets
7	Budgets and Budgetary Accounting

funds) have the objective of profit measurement or capital maintenance. Thus the accrual basis of accounting as conceived for private businesses is entirely suitable for these funds. Also, Pension Trust Funds (fiduciary funds) exhibit the same characteristics as pension funds established in the private sector. Thus the accrual basis also lends itself to use with Pension Trust Funds. Accordingly, for each of these funds, revenues earned and expenses incurred may be accrued and recognized in the period to which they relate in essentially the same manner as in the private sector. For these reasons, the GASB *Codification* recommends the use of the accrual basis for these funds.

MODIFIED ACCRUAL BASIS FUNDS For all remaining funds (the four governmental funds, Expendable Trust Funds, and Agency Funds), the GASB *Codification* recommends the use of the **modified accrual basis** of accounting, which is described as follows:

> Revenues should be recognized in the accounting period in which they become **available and measurable** [emphasis added]. Expenditures should be recognized in the accounting period in which the fund liability is incurred, if measurable, except for unmatured interest on general long-term debt, which should be recognized when due.[16]

The reason for using the *modified accrual basis* of accounting for these funds may be attributed to the nature of governmental revenue sources and activities. We discuss the modified accrual basis first concerning revenues and then expenditures.

REVENUES Governmental-type activities do not "earn" revenues as do business enterprises. Accordingly, a more appropriate revenue recognition criteria than the "when earned" criteria of the private sector is used. The objective is to try to record revenues in the period to which they relate to the extent that it is practical to do so. **To accrue revenue (and the related receivable), it must be susceptible to accrual.** To be susceptible to accrual, it must be *available and measurable*. The term *available* means that a revenue source is **collectible within the current period or soon enough thereafter to be used to pay liabilities of the current period.**[17] These revenue recognition criteria apply to *all* revenue sources. Revenues can be categorized as follows:

1. **Revenues generally accrued using the available and measurable criteria.** Property taxes, taxpayer-assessed taxes (sales taxes, gross receipts taxes, income taxes), grants, and interfund transfers. The GASB *Codification* gives specific guidance about applying the "availability" criterion only for **property taxes— collection must occur within 60 days.** For revenues *other than* property taxes, some governmental units use a 60-day cutoff date. Other cutoff dates (such as 90 days) are also used.

2. **Revenues generally accounted for on the cash basis.** Fines, forfeits, fees, inspection charges, parking fees, parking meter receipts, licenses, and permits. For practical reasons, the GASB *Codification* recommends accounting for these items on the *cash basis,* even though some of them could be accrued.

3. **Revenues accrued when earned.** Interest income. The susceptible-to-accrual criteria is generally *not* applied to investment income. Similarly, bond discount is amortized to income without application of the susceptible to accrual criteria.

Cash received *before* the period to which it relates should be reported as deferred revenues (such as an overpayment of taxes that the taxpayer instructs the city to apply to the following year's tax bill).

---

[16]GASB *Cod.*, sec. 1100.108.
[17]GASB *Cod.*, sec. 1600.106.

EXPENDITURES   For many items (such as the monthly payroll), expenditures and the related liability are recognized in governmental funds when the liability is incurred. For several items, however, this is *not* the case. These items are

1. **Liabilities that *may* first be recognized in the General Long-Term Debt Account Group (GLTDAG).** The GASB *Codification* calls for **expenditures** recognition **when the *fund* liability is incurred**—this does *not* mean the same thing as recognizing an expenditure **when the liability is incurred.** Many liabilities are incurred for which no intent exists to liquidate them with the available resources existing at the balance sheet date. Accordingly, such liabilities are first recorded *outside* the governmental funds in the GLTDAG, which is discussed later in the chapter, until there is an intent to liquidate them.

   Later when they are intended to be liquidated (using available financial resources), the liability is transferred *from* the GLTDAG *to* the governmental fund, and an expenditure is recognized in the governmental fund. The liabilities that *can* be first recorded in the GLTDAG *before* being recognized in a governmental fund are (1) compensated absences, (2) claims and judgments, (3) unfunded pension contributions, (4) special termination benefits, and (5) landfill closure and postclosure care costs. (These items give rise to the *interperiod equity* problem discussed earlier.)

2. **Liabilities *always* first recorded in the GLTDAG before being recognized as an expenditure and liability in a governmental fund.** General long-term debt is *always* first recorded in the GLTDAG when the money is borrowed. It is later transferred to a governmental fund when it is due (we illustrate this manner of accounting in Chapter 25).

3. **Liabilities not recognized *at all* until due.** One exception to recognizing liabilities when incurred exists: the recognizing of interest on general long-term debt as an expenditure *when due* rather than as the liability arises (we discuss this exception in Chapter 25).

4. **Liabilities recognized in a governmental fund *before* expenditures are recognized.** When inventories are accounted for using the *consumption method*, the Inventory account rather than the Expenditures account is charged when the liability is incurred. (Under the *purchases method*, however, the Expenditures account is charged when the liability is incurred.)

CATEGORY 4 (A): FINANCIAL REPORTING—THE BASICS

THE BALANCE SHEET   As discussed earlier, the accounts used within the fund equity section for the governmental funds are different than those used within the fund equity section of the proprietary funds. For the governmental funds, a unique aspect of the balance sheet is the manner of reporting the Fund Balance in the fund equity section. If no restrictions exist, the Fund Balance account may be viewed as a "surplus" (a term often used in newspapers) that is available for spending in the new fiscal year. In most cases, however, restrictions that earmark a portion of the fund balance for a specific purpose exist. These restrictions are reflected in the Fund Equity section as reservations of the fund balance. For example, a restriction pertaining to outstanding (unfilled) purchase orders of $33,000 at year-end would be presented as follows:

Fund balance:	
Reserved for encumbrances[a]	$ 33,000
Unreserved	427,000
	$460,000

[a]Encumbrances are explained shortly.

ILLUSTRATION 24–4	Statement of Revenues, Expenditures, and Changes in Fund Balance	
Revenues (an inflow of resources)		$550,000
Expenditures (an outflow of resources)		(450,000)
Excess of Revenues over Expenditures		$100,000
Fund Balance, January 1, 19X1		360,000
Fund Balance, December 31, 19X1		$460,000

Certain proprietary funds also have some unique balance sheet features; however, we delay their discussion until Chapter 25.

THE OPERATING STATEMENT In governmental accounting, the **operating statement** presents the financial results of operations in conformity with GAAP. For *proprietary funds* and *nonexpendable trust funds*, the operating statement is an income statement (to which an analysis of retained earnings is appended). For *governmental funds* and *expendable trust funds*, income statements are *not* prepared, and the operating statement presents the inflows and outflows of resources (the measurement focus in these funds). Recall that although this statement is called the *statement of revenues, expenditures, and changes in fund balance*, substantively it is merely a statement of sources and uses of resources. Note that the format of this statement (shown in Illustration 24–4) includes the beginning and ending fund balance amounts, thereby requiring all changes in the fund balance for the period to be shown. This "all-inclusive" format makes it unnecessary to present a separate statement of changes in fund balance (similar to a statement of changes in stockholders' equity for a commercial enterprise). The statement format is modified slightly when (1) bond proceeds are recorded in a governmental fund and (2) a fund has certain types of transactions with other funds. These modifications are discussed and illustrated in the following section.

CATEGORY 4 (B): FINANCIAL REPORTING OF BOND PROCEEDS AND INTERFUND TRANSACTIONS

The GASB *Codification* recommends the following classification reporting practices:

> Interfund transfers and proceeds of general long-term debt issues [that are not recorded as fund liabilities] should be classified separately from fund revenues and expenditures or expenses.[18]

Classifying proceeds of general long-term debt separately from fund revenues is a substantial improvement over the former practice of showing such proceeds as revenues. Such proceeds must be shown under a separate section of the operating statement of the recipient fund. This section is called **Other Financing Sources and Uses.** Reporting interfund transfers separately from fund revenues and expenditures or expenses is also a substantial improvement over the former practice of showing these items as revenues and expenditures or expenses. Before showing the operating statement, as revised for the inclusion of the Other Financing Sources and Uses section, it is necessary to discuss the types of interfund transactions.

TYPES OF INTERFUND TRANSACTIONS In the GASB *Codification*, all interfund transactions fall into one of the following four categories:

- Loans (short-term) and advances (long-term).
- Quasi-external transactions.

[18]GASB *Cod.*, sec. 1800.

- Residual equity transfers.
- Operating transfers.

1. **Loans and Advances.**
   Often the General Fund makes a loan or advance to another fund. If the borrowing is to be repaid within a relatively short period (one year or less is commonly used), the borrowing is called a *loan*. For longer periods, the borrowing is called an *advance*. **Loans and advances affect only the balance sheet.** The lending fund reports a receivable, and the borrowing fund reports a liability. Special descriptive terminology is used for the accounts reported in the balance sheet as follows:

	Receivable Accounts	**Liability Accounts**
Loans	Interfund Receivable	Interfund Payable
Advances	Advance to XXXX Fund	Advance from XXXX Fund

2. **Quasi-External Transactions.**
   Often one fund provides a service to another fund. An example is a city's water utility (which would be accounted for in an Enterprise Fund) that supplies water to the city. The most meaningful form of reporting for such transactions is to report expenditures in the fund receiving the services and report revenues in the fund providing the services because the fund receiving the services would have had to charge expenditures if it had obtained the services from an organization external to the governmental unit. Furthermore, recording revenues in the fund providing the services is essential to the proper determination of that fund's operating results when such fund is a proprietary fund. The entries that would be recorded in the General Fund and the Municipal Water Utility Enterprise Fund for supplying water to the city are as follows:

General Fund

Expenditures	45,000	
Due to Municipal Water Utility Enterprise Fund.		45,000

Municipal Water Utility Enterprise Fund

Due from General Fund	45,000	
Revenues		45,000

These *Due to* and *Due from* accounts are used only for **interfund transactions that do *not* involve loans or advances,** such as in this case in which services are provided by an Enterprise Fund to the General Fund. (They may also be used in setting up liabilities and receivables involving residual equity transfers and operating transfers, which are discussed shortly.)

Other examples of quasi-external transactions are as follows:

- Payments in lieu of taxes from an Enterprise Fund to the General Fund.
- Internal Service Fund billings for services to departments of other funds.
- Routine service charges for inspection, engineering, utility, or similar charges.
- Routine employer contributions from the General Fund to a Pension Trust Fund.

Quasi-external transactions are the only type of interfund transactions that may be recorded as revenues, expenditures, or expenses.

3. **Residual Equity Transfers.**
   Residual equity transfers are **nonrecurring** or **nonroutine** transfers of equity between funds made in connection with the formation, expansion, contraction, or discontinuance of a fund (usually involving the General Fund and one of the Proprietary Funds). **Because such transfers are of a *nonoperating* nature, they are reported as direct additions to or subtractions from the fund equity ac-**

counts (Fund Balance, Contributed Capital, or Retained Earnings, as appropriate). For example, assume that the General Fund transferred $300,000 to a newly *established* Municipal Golf Course Enterprise Fund as a capital contribution in its start-up period. The entries to be made by each fund are as follows:

General Fund

Residual Equity Transfer Out	300,000	
Cash		300,000

Municipal Golf Course Enterprise Fund

Cash...	300,000	
Contributed Capital—Government		300,000

For the General Fund to make such a transfer, it must, of course, have an unreserved fund balance of at least $300,000.

Assume that 15 years later, the golf course is sold to a real estate developer. At the time that the Municipal Golf Course Enterprise Fund is *discontinued,* assume that it has $300,000 in its Contributed Capital account and $50,000 in its Retained Earnings account. The entries to record the transfer of the discontinued fund's residual equity to the General Fund is recorded as follows:

General Fund

Cash...	350,000	
Residual Equity Transfer In		350,000

Municipal Golf Course Enterprise Fund

Contributed Capital	300,000	
Retained Earnings	50,000	
Cash		350,000

COMPARATIVE PRACTICE NOTE

In showing the entries for the General Fund, we used Residual Equity Transfer Out and Residual Equity Transfer In accounts. In practice, some governmental units shortcut the procedures slightly by debiting or crediting directly the Unreserved Fund Balance account (in the same manner that commercial enterprises charge dividends declared directly to retained earnings rather than to a separate Dividends Declared account, which later must be closed out to the Retained Earnings account).

---

4. **Operating Transfers.**

   Operating transfers are made in connection with the **normal operations of the recipient fund.** In comparison to residual equity transfers (which are made in connection with the formation and discontinuance of a fund), operating transfers are conceptually the opposite. An example of an operating transfer is subsidizing the operations of a Municipal Golf Course Enterprise Fund each year, as necessary, when expenses exceed revenues. Operating transfers are presented in the operating statements as a separate line item. The manner of presentation differs slightly for governmental funds than for proprietary funds as shown here:

Governmental Funds	**Proprietary Funds**
Revenues	Revenues
Expenditures	Expenses
Other Financing Sources and Uses:	Operating Transfers In
Operating Transfers In	Operating Transfers Out
Operating Transfers Out	

The difference in presentation of these two fund types is attributable to the difference in the nature of the operating statement used (an *income statement* for the *proprietary funds* and a *source and use of resources statement* for *governmental funds*). As a result, the presentation in the respective operating statements dictates the description of the accounts used in the general ledgers. The following entries assume that the General Fund made an operating transfer to the Municipal Golf Course Enterprise Fund:

General Fund

Other Financing Uses—Operating Transfers Out	20,000	
Cash		20,000

Municipal Golf Course Enterprise Fund

Cash.......................................	20,000	
Operating Transfer In		20,000

Other examples of operating transfers are as follows:

1. Transfers of tax revenues from a Special Revenue Fund to a Debt Service Fund or the General Fund.

2. Transfers from the General Fund to a Capital Projects Fund to help pay for construction costs.

3. Transfers from the General Fund to a Debt Service Fund to enable interest and principal payments to be made on general long-term debt.

4. Transfers from an Enterprise Fund to the General Fund *other than* payments in lieu of taxes to finance General Fund expenditures.

THE OPERATING STATEMENT FOR GOVERNMENTAL FUNDS: MODIFIED FOR RE-PORTING BOND PROCEEDS AND INTERFUND TRANSFERS In Illustration 24–5, we present the statement of revenues, expenditures, and changes in fund balance

---

ILLUSTRATION 24–5	**Statement of Revenues, Expenditures, and Changes in Fund Balance—Format for Reporting Bond Proceeds and Interfund Transfers**

General Fund
Statement of Revenues, Expenditures,
and Changes in Fund Balance
For the Year Ended December 31, 19X1

Revenues	$550,000
Expenditures	(495,000)[a]
Excess of Revenues over Expenditures	$ 55,000
Other financing sources and uses:	
Bond proceeds	–0–
Operating transfers in	–0–
Operating transfers out	(20,000)
Excess of Revenues and Other Financing Sources over	
Expenditures and Other Financing Uses	$ 35,000
Fund Balance, January 1, 19X1	360,000
Residual equity transfer out to Municipal Golf Course	
Enterprise Fund	(300,000)
Fund Balance, December 31, 19X1	$ 95,000

[a]Includes $45,000 for purchase of water from Municipal Water Enterprise Fund (a quasi-external transaction).

used by governmental funds when bond proceeds have been received in such a fund and both residual equity transfers and operating transfers exist. To enhance understanding of this illustration, we used the amounts shown in Illustration 24–4 plus the following previously illustrated interfund transactions:

1. **Quasi-external transaction.** The purchase of water by the General Fund from the Municipal Water Utility Fund for $45,000.
2. **Residual equity transfer.** The transfer of $300,000 from the General Fund at the inception of the Municipal Golf Course Enterprise Fund.
3. **Operating transfer.** The transfer of $20,000 from the General Fund to subsidize the day-to-day operations of the Municipal Golf Course Enterprise Fund.

Because the illustration is for the General Fund, no amount is shown on the bond proceeds line because virtually all bond proceeds of governmental funds are recorded in Capital Projects Funds. (Most governmental units are prohibited by law from issuing bonds to finance current operations; thus it is rare for the General Fund to report bond proceeds.) We also omit an amount on the Operating transfers in line because the General Fund rarely has operating transfers in—it usually has numerous operating transfers out.

ADDITIONAL ITEMS TO BE CLASSIFIED UNDER THE OTHER FINANCING SOURCES AND USES CATEGORY When a governmental unit sells some of its General Fixed Assets (discussed shortly), the proceeds are to be reported under the other financing sources and uses category. Also, when a governmental unit enters into a capital lease, the present value of the lease payments is deemed to be the equivalent of proceeds from a loan, an amount that is to be reported under the other financing sources and uses category. Accordingly, this category of the operating statement could appear as follows if all types of transactions occur:

Other Financing Sources and Uses

Bond proceeds	xxx
Operating transfers in	xxx
Operating transfers out	(xxx)
Proceeds from sale of general fixed assets	xxx
Proceeds from capital lease	xxx

No other types of transactions are reportable under the other financing sources and uses category.

CATEGORY 4 (C): FINANCIAL REPORTING: GENERAL-PURPOSE FINANCIAL STATEMENTS AND THE COMPREHENSIVE ANNUAL FINANCIAL REPORT (CAFR)

The annual financial report for governmental units is called the *comprehensive annual financial report (CAFR)*. Three distinct types of financial statements are presented in the CAFR:

1. **Combined financial statements.** These are five specific financial statements that are collectively referred to as the **general-purpose financial statements.** They **present an overview** much in the same manner as consolidated financial statements serve for corporations. The five specific financial statements are as follows:
   a. *Combined Balance Sheet*—All fund types, account groups, and discretely presented component units.

b. *Combined Statement of Revenues, Expenditures, and Changes in Fund Balance*—All governmental fund types and discretely presented component units.

c. *Combined Statement of Revenues, Expenditures, and Changes in Fund Balances—Budget and Actual*—General and special revenue fund types (and similar governmental fund types for which annual budgets have been legally adopted).

d. *Combined Statement of Revenues, Expenses, and Changes in Retained Earnings (or Equity)*—All Proprietary Fund types and discretely presented component units.

e. *Combined Statement of Cash Flows*—All Proprietary Fund types and discretely presented component units.[19]

(Illustrations of the first four of the five combined statements are shown in Chapter 25 on pages 919–924. At this point, we suggest you briefly review those illustrations before proceeding.)

2. **Combining financial statements by fund type.** In these statements, all funds of a given type are shown individually, along with a "combining" total. For example, if a government has three special revenue funds, they are shown along with the combining total. (The combining total is presented in the combined financial statements.)

3. **Individual fund and account group statements.** The individual statements are presented when it is desirable to present additional detailed information not provided in the combining statements (such as budgetary or prior year comparative data).

Although not normally subject to audit by outside auditors, the combining financial statements and the individual fund and account group statements are required by the GASB *Codification* to follow the identical format of the more significant combined financial statements (the general-purpose financial statements) on which the outside auditors express an opinion. (The only exception to this is a utility operated as an Enterprise Fund, whereby the individual financial statements may be presented in the regulatory format.)

In discussing each of the seven funds and the two account groups, we illustrate the individual financial statements. The combined financial statements (the general-purpose financial statements) are discussed at the conclusion of the discussion of the seven funds and two account groups in Chapter 25.

COMPONENT UNITS A primary government's **component units** are reported in the *combined* financial statements. Component units are legally separate organizations; however, the elected officials of the primary government are financially accountable for them. A component unit's financial data is presented in two possible manners:

1. **Discrete presentation.** The data is presented in one or more columns *separate* from the primary government's financial data. (State universities are component units of state governments that are typically presented in this manner.)

2. **Blended presentation.** The data is combined—called "blending" in the GASB *Codification*—with the data of the primary government in the *combining* statements (Level 2). This manner of presentation is required when (1) the component unit's governing body is substantively the same as that of the primary government or (2) the component unit's activities serve or benefit entirely or almost exclusively the government. (The component unit's General Revenue Fund must be reported as a Special Revenue Fund, however, rather than being combined with the primary government's General Fund.)

[19]GASB *Cod.*, sec. 2200.108.

CATEGORY 5: LONG-TERM LIABILITIES

According to the GASB *Codification,* long-term debt should be accounted for as follows:

> Long-term liabilities of proprietary funds and trust funds should be accounted for through those funds. All other unmatured general long-term liabilities of the governmental unit, which includes special assessment debt for which the government is obligated in some manner, should be accounted for through the General Long-Term Debt Account Group.[20]

General long-term debt (GLTD) (as opposed to liabilities of proprietary funds and trust funds) is the liability of the governmental unit as a whole, *not* that of any specific fund. As such, it is secured by the taxing powers of the governmental unit, *not* by the resources available in a specific fund.

Because the **General Long-Term Debt Account Group (GLTDAG)** is merely a listing of certain long-term debt, it *cannot* properly be said to have operations. Thus the GLTDAG is *not* the equivalent of a fund and does *not* report operations.

The GLTDAG is a "self-balancing" set of accounts because the list of liabilities, maintained in account form, is balanced by accounts showing (1) amounts, if any, set aside in Debt Service Funds for repayment of the GLTD and (2) amounts yet to be provided for repayment of the GLTD. The GLTDAG is discussed in detail in Chapter 25.

CATEGORY 6: FIXED ASSETS

ACCOUNTING FOR FIXED ASSETS   The nature of governmental operations is such that more meaningful financial reporting results if certain fixed assets are accounted for in fund accounts and all other fixed assets (referred to collectively as **general fixed assets**) are accounted for outside the funds in *account groups.* The GASB *Codification* recommends the following:

> Fixed assets related to specific proprietary funds or trust funds should be accounted for through those funds. All other fixed assets of a governmental unit should be accounted for through the General Fixed Assets Account Group.[21]

Fixed assets are excluded from the governmental funds because such assets do *not* constitute financial resources available for spending purposes. Because one of the reporting objectives of the governmental funds is to reflect the financial resources available for spending purposes, fixed assets must be excluded from governmental funds to accomplish this objective.

The **General Fixed Assets Account Group (GFAAG)** is simply a list of certain fixed assets. Thus it *cannot* properly be said to have operations. Consequently, it is *not* the equivalent of a fund and does *not* report operations.

The list of a governmental unit's general fixed assets is maintained in account form. These accounts are complemented by credit accounts showing the *sources* by which the assets were obtained. Because of the manner of making entries, the GFAAG is also a "self-balancing" set of accounts. The GFAAG is discussed in detail in Chapter 25.

VALUATION OF FIXED ASSETS   With respect to the valuation of fixed assets, the GASB *Codification* specifies the following:

> Fixed assets should be accounted for at cost or, if the cost is not practicably determinable, at estimated cost. Donated fixed assets should be recorded at their estimated fair value at the time received.[22]

[20]GASB *Cod.,* sec. 1100.105.
[21]GASB *Cod.,* sec. 1100.105.
[22]GASB *Cod.,* sec. 1100.106.

DEPRECIATION OF FIXED ASSETS With respect to depreciating fixed assets, the GASB *Codification* recommends the following:

> Depreciation of general fixed assets should not be recorded in the accounts of governmental funds. Depreciation of general fixed assets may be recorded in cost accounting systems or calculated for cost finding analysis; and accumulated depreciation may be recorded in the General Fixed Assets Account Group [an optional treatment].
>
> Depreciation of fixed assets accounted for in a proprietary fund should be recorded in the accounts of that fund. Depreciation is also recognized in those Trust Funds where expenses, net income, and/or capital maintenance are measured.[23]

Commercial businesses record depreciation expense to match revenues with expenses to determine net income properly. Fixed assets accounted for in proprietary funds and certain trust funds also have the objectives of profitability or capital maintenance (cost recovery). Accordingly, depreciation expense is properly recorded in these funds because income statements are prepared.

For all other funds, income statements are *not* presented, nor is a statement presented comparing revenues with the costs of providing services (which would include depreciation expense). Instead, only a statement of revenues, expenditures, and changes in fund balance based on the "flow of *current financial* resources" measurement base is presented. Accordingly, when a general fixed asset is acquired, it is reflected as an expenditure in the fund at the time of acquisition. Depreciation expense would *not* be recorded in this statement because it does *not* constitute a flow of resources.

The absence of depreciation expense in the statement of revenues, expenditures, and changes in fund balance should not be considered a departure from the accrual basis of accounting. The GASB *Codification* makes an important clarification regarding what is encompassed by the accrual basis of accounting:

> Unfortunately, the terms "accrual" and "accrual accounting" often are interpreted to mean "income determination accounting," and thus to connote the recognition of depreciation in the course of expense measurement. This misunderstanding likely has arisen because most literature centers on income determination and uses the terms "accrual" and "accrual accounting" in that context. It should be recognized, however, that depreciation and amortization are allocations, not accruals, and that "accrual" in a governmental fund accounting context does not mean that depreciation, amortization, and similar allocations should be recognized.[24]

CATEGORY 7: BUDGETS AND BUDGETARY ACCOUNTING

BUDGETS Budgets are used in the public sector for planning, controlling, and evaluating operations just as they are used in the private sector. A **budget** is merely a plan of financial operations covering a specified period of time. For all governmental, proprietary, and fiduciary funds (other than Agency Funds), the GASB *Codification* recommends that "an annual budget(s) should be adopted by every governmental unit."[25]

Prepared under the direction of the governmental unit's chief executive officer, the *annual* budget is submitted to the legislative body for review, possible modification, and formal adoption. The significance of the budget for each of these funds is as follows:

[23]GASB *Cod.*, sec. 1100.107.
[24]GASB *Cod.*, sec. 1600.104.
[25]GASB *Cod.*, sec. 1100.109.

Fund Type	Significance
Governmental funds and certain fiduciary funds	The statutory authorization for spending an estimated amount during the subsequent fiscal year. The authorization is referred to as an **appropriation.**
Proprietary funds and certain fiduciary funds	The approval of a proposed operating plan (as distinct from a statutory authorization to spend a certain amount in dollars).

A *long-term* budget covers a period of several years. Long-term budgets restricted to major capital additions and improvements are referred to as *capital* budgets.

BUDGETARY ACCOUNTING   Because legal limitations are imposed on certain of the funds (primarily the governmental funds) as to the amount that may be spent during a fiscal year, it is exceedingly important to monitor and control spending so that expenditures do not exceed this limitation. The GASB *Codification* recommends that "the accounting system should provide the basis for appropriate budgetary control."[26]

The GASB *Codification* specifies the following two areas in which **budgetary accounts** should be used to monitor and control spending: (1) recording the annual budget in the general ledger and (2) recording purchase order commitments in the general ledger, which is referred to as *encumbrance accounting.*

To enhance the understanding of budgetary integration in the general ledger, we use the technique, illustrated in the 1994 edition of *GAAFR*, of **printing budgetary account descriptions in all capital letters.** As a result, we can consider all budgetary accounts as a separate trial balance from the regular general ledger accounts. We also use the same account descriptions for budgetary and actual accounts used in the 1994 edition of *GAAFR* because these descriptions are now used by both the AICPA (in its official solutions to the CPA examinations) and the CPA examination review courses (in their course materials).

RECORDING THE ANNUAL BUDGET: SIMPLIFIED SITUATION INVOLVING NO INTERFUND TRANSFERS   The budget for the General Fund and Special Revenue Funds is recorded in the general ledger. (The annual budget pertaining to Capital Projects Funds and Debt Service Funds is recorded in the general ledger only if it serves a useful purpose, determined on a case-by-case basis.) Assuming that a governmental unit expects its General Fund revenues to exceed its General Fund appropriations for the new fiscal year, the budget is recorded in the General Fund's general ledger as follows:

ESTIMATED REVENUES	1,000,000	
APPROPRIATIONS		980,000
BUDGETARY FUND BALANCE		20,000
To record the legally adopted annual operating budget.		

The ESTIMATED REVENUES account is a control account. Actual revenues are usually recorded in individual subsidiary Revenue accounts (and in a Revenues Control account). The detail making up the ESTIMATED REVENUES account is also recorded directly in the individual subsidiary Revenue accounts at the start of the year. As a result, estimated revenues may be compared readily with actual revenues throughout the year. Although revenues cannot be "controlled" in the manner that expenditures can be controlled, a governmental unit may be able to curtail

[26]GASB *Cod.*, sec. 1100.109.

spending if it appears that revenue inflows will not be reasonably close to estimated revenues.

Likewise, the APPROPRIATIONS account is a control account. Actual expenditures are usually recorded in individual subsidiary Expenditures accounts (and in an Expenditures Control account). The detail making up the APPROPRIATIONS account is also recorded directly in the individual subsidiary Expenditures accounts at the start of the year. As a result, expenditures to date may be readily compared with the authorized spending limitation, revealing how much more may be spent.

A governmental unit's budget for the coming fiscal year may reflect an intention to increase (as in the preceding example) or decrease the fund balance amount existing at the beginning of the year. Most governmental units (with the notable exception of the federal government) try to accumulate a reasonable "surplus" in the Fund Balance account in case unforeseen adverse events occur. In recording the budget in the general ledger, the difference between the debit to ESTIMATED REVENUES and the credit to APPROPRIATIONS is credited (as in the preceding example) or debited to BUDGETARY FUND BALANCE.

Recording the budget in the general ledger does not affect the year-end balance in the Fund Balance account because the budget entry is reversed at year-end as part of the normal closing process.

RECORDING THE ANNUAL BUDGET: TYPICAL SITUATION INVOLVING INTERFUND TRANSFERS When interfund transfers exist, up to four additional budgetary accounts may be used to record the budget. The budgetary accounts can be classified as either those that pertain to *inflows* or those that pertain to *outflows* as shown here:

Budgetary Accounts Pertaining to Estimated *Inflows* (recorded as *debits*):

ESTIMATED REVENUES
ESTIMATED OPERATING TRANSFERS IN
ESTIMATED RESIDUAL EQUITY TRANSFERS IN

Budgetary Accounts Pertaining to Legally Authorized *Outflows* (recorded as *credits*):

APPROPRIATIONS (a general category)
APPROPRIATIONS—OPERATING TRANSFERS OUT
APPROPRIATIONS—RESIDUAL EQUITY TRANSFERS OUT

The budgetary account BUDGETARY FUND BALANCE is *not* listed in either of these categories because it is merely used to balance the entry recording the budget. Later in the chapter, we illustrate the use of some of these additional budgetary accounts that pertain to interfund transfers.

ENCUMBRANCE ACCOUNTING As stated earlier, expenditures are recognized when the fund liability is incurred, which is usually when goods are received or

---

COMPARATIVE PRACTICE NOTE

The illustrative entries shown in the 1994 edition of *GAAFR* use the accounts ESTIMATED OTHER FINANCING SOURCES—OPERATING TRANSFERS IN and APPROPRIATIONS: OTHER FINANCING USES—OPERATING TRANSFERS OUT. The use of the additional descriptive terminology OTHER FINANCING SOURCES and OTHER FINANCING USES (the category in the operating statement under which operating transfers are to be reported) is unnecessary and cumbersome in our opinion. Inquiries to numerous cities and counties reveal that almost all governmental units bypass this additional descriptive terminology in recording their annual budgets.

services are rendered. Many expenditures involve the issuance of purchase orders, whereby goods are received or services are rendered at a later date. Outstanding purchase orders are commitments for future expenditures. To monitor and control spending properly, governmental units must keep track of the amount of each purchase order (including the amount of contracts entered into) in the general ledger at the time of issuance. For example, assuming that a purchase order for $50,000 is issued, the following budgetary entry is made:

```
ENCUMBRANCES ................................    50,000
     BUDGETARY FUND BALANCE RESERVED
          FOR ENCUMBRANCES ....................             50,000
     To record encumbrances for purchase orders issued.
```

The ENCUMBRANCES account may be thought of as an "expenditure-to-be" account. Likewise, the BUDGETARY FUND BALANCE RESERVED FOR ENCUMBRANCES account may be thought of as a "liability-to-be" account. At a later date, when the goods are received or services are rendered, the entry is reversed and the expenditure and liability are recorded. Assume that in the preceding example that the actual cost of the goods received under the purchase was $49,000. The following entries are made:

```
BUDGETARY FUND BALANCE RESERVED
     FOR ENCUMBRANCES .........................    50,000
          ENCUMBRANCES ...........................             50,000
     To cancel encumbrances of $50,000 upon receipt
          of materials and rendering of services totaling $49,000.

Expenditures .....................................    49,000
     Vouchers Payable ...........................             49,000
     To record expenditures of $49,000 for goods and
          services that were previously encumbered for $50,000.
```

Like the APPROPRIATIONS account, the ENCUMBRANCES account is a control account. Each encumbrance is usually recorded in the individual subsidiary Expenditures accounts. As a result, the remaining amount that may be legally spent at a given time is readily determined by subtracting expenditures to date and encumbrances outstanding from appropriations. (Because an Expenditures Control account is also maintained, this calculation can be done at the control level or at the detail level using the individual subsidiary accounts.)

Illustration 24–6 shows what a subsidiary ledger might look like at the departmental level. Note that the format indicates the spendable amount remaining at the end of each month. (Only two months' activities are illustrated.) If an Encumbrances column were not included, the department supervisor might erroneously conclude that $94,000 ($100,000 appropriations – $6,000 expenditures)

ILLUSTRATION 24–6	**Example of a Department's Subsidiary Ledger Account**			
	Department No. 34			
Date	**Appropriation**	**Expenditures**	**Encumbrances**	**Remaining Spendable Amount**
July 1, 19X1	$100,000			$100,000
July 19X1		$ 6,000	$7,000	(13,000)
July 31, 19X1	$100,000	$ 6,000	$7,000	$ 87,000
August 19X1		11,000	(3,000)	(8,000)
August 31, 19X1	$100,000	$17,000	$4,000	$ 79,000

was available for spending at July 31, 19X1. This figure is incorrect because purchase orders outstanding at July 31, 19X1, total $7,000. Thus, of the $94,000 not yet spent at July 31, 19X1, $7,000 is earmarked for the outstanding purchase orders. This leaves only $87,000 available for spending at July 31, 19X1. The objective of the procedure, of course, is to prevent spending more than has been authorized (appropriated).

From the preceding discussion and analysis, you should realize that only the debit entry recording the encumbrance is used in controlling spending. The credit to the BUDGETARY FUND BALANCE RESERVED FOR ENCUMBRANCES account serves no control function other than to provide a credit for double-entry bookkeeping. Thus it is merely a *contra account*. The steps in the process of using financial resources may be summarized as follows:

1. **Appropriation** (legal authorization to spend by governing body).
2. **Encumbrances** (commitment to spend by issuing purchase orders or signing contracts).
3. **Expenditures** (liability incurred upon vendor or contractor performance).
4. **Disbursement** (actual payment of liability).

BUDGETARY COMPARISONS   A financial reporting requirement of the GASB *Codification* is the preparation of "budgetary comparison statements or schedules" (as appropriate) in which budgeted data are compared with actual data for the year. Under GAAP reporting, encumbrances outstanding at year-end are not reported in the statement of revenues, expenditures, and changes in fund balance. They would become expenditures in the following year and be reported as expenditures in that year. To present a meaningful comparison of actual expenditures with the budgeted expenditures, the budgeted expenditures must be prepared on a basis consistent with GAAP. To do this, amounts must be included in the following year's budget for encumbrances outstanding at the current year-end. Thus it can be said that **encumbrances outstanding at the end of the current year "lapse" but are then "rebudgeted" and "reappropriated" in the following year.** Without this procedure, the following year's expenditures would include amounts relating to the encumbrances outstanding at the end of the prior year, but no amount would appear in the following year's budget for these expenditures, resulting in a meaningless comparison.

To illustrate this comparison process, we assume the following data:

1. For 19X1, a governmental unit expects routine expenditures of $500,000 and the purchase of a new fire truck for $30,000. Thus it budgets $530,000 for 19X1 expenditures.
2. Actual spending occurs according to budget, except that the fire truck is received in early 19X2 rather than 19X1.
3. The governmental unit expects routine expenditures of $500,000 for 19X2. It also "reappropriates" or "rebudgets" an additional $30,000 to cover the fire truck for 19X2. Thus the total budget for 19X2 expenditures is $530,000.
4. Actual spending for 19X2 occurs according to budget.

The budgetary comparison is as follows:

	Budget	Actual	Variance Favorable (Unfavorable)
19X1:			
Expenditures	$530,000	$500,000	$30,000
19X2:			
Expenditures	530,000	530,000	–0–

VI THE GENERAL FUND

Recall that (1) the General Fund is a governmental fund, (2) governmental funds use the modified accrual basis of accounting, and (3) the measurement focus for governmental funds is the flow of resources.

NATURE AND SCOPE OF ACTIVITIES

The **General Fund** accounts for all revenues and expenditures of a governmental unit that are not accounted for in one of the special-purpose funds. Because all other funds are special-purpose funds, most activities and current operations of governmental units are financed from the General Fund. For instance, general government administration, public safety, judicial system, health, sanitation, welfare, and culture-recreation are usually accounted for in this fund.

Normally, more types of revenues flow into this fund than any other fund. For example, property taxes, sales taxes, income taxes, transfer taxes, licenses, permits, fines, penalties, and interest on delinquent taxes commonly flow into the General Fund. In addition, the General Fund may receive monies from other governmental units; such receipts are classified by the GASB *Codification* as follows:

> **Grant.** A contribution or gift of cash or other assets from another government to be used or expended for a specified purpose, activity, or facility.
>
> **Capital grant.** A contribution or gift of cash or other assets restricted by the grantor for the acquisition and/or construction of fixed (capital) assets [which would be accounted for in a Capital Projects Fund].
>
> **Operating grant.** Grants that are intended to finance operations or that may be used for either operations or capital outlays at the discretion of the grantee.
>
> **Entitlement.** The amount of payment to which a state or local government is entitled as determined by the federal government (e.g., the Director of the Office of Revenue Sharing) pursuant to an allocation formula contained in applicable statutes.
>
> **Shared revenue.** A revenue levied by one government but shared on a predetermined basis, often in proportion to the amount collected at the local level, with another government or class of government.[27]

ILLUSTRATION	COMPREHENSIVE: JOURNAL ENTRIES AND FINANCIAL STATEMENTS

The June 30, 19X1, balance sheet for Funn City's General Fund is shown in Illustration 24–7.

Before proceeding with assumed transactions for the subsequent fiscal year, the following points should be understood with regard to Illustration 24–7:

1. **Inventory.** We assume that the consumption method (discussed in more detail later) is used to account for the supplies inventory. Under this method, the inventory is viewed as a resource as are cash and property tax receivables. Although the $10,000 of inventory cannot be "spent" in a cash sense, it can be "expended" in the sense that its eventual use (consumption) will result in a future charge to the expenditures account.

2. **Deferred revenues.** Of the $40,000 net amount expected to be collected for property taxes ($43,000 – $3,000), $30,000 is expected to be collected *after* 60 days. Accordingly, deferred revenues of $30,000 are reported at June 30, 19X1.

---

[27]GASB *Cod.*, sec. G60. 501–505.

```
ILLUSTRATION 24-7
                                Funn City
                     Balance Sheet—General Fund
                            June 30, 19X1
─────────────────────────────────────────────────────────────────────
                                 Assets

Cash  . . . . . . . . . . . . . . . . . . . . . . . . . . . . . . . . . . . . . . . . . . . .    $120,000
Property taxes receivable—delinquent . . . . . . . . . . . . . . . . . . . . . . . . . .        43,000
Less: Allowance for estimated uncollectible taxes—delinquent  . . . . . . . . .       (3,000)
Inventory . . . . . . . . . . . . . . . . . . . . . . . . . . . . . . . . . . . . . . . . . . . .    10,000
        Total Assets . . . . . . . . . . . . . . . . . . . . . . . . . . . . . . . . . . . . .    $170,000

                        Liabilities and Fund Equity

Vouchers payable . . . . . . . . . . . . . . . . . . . . . . . . . . . . . . . . . . . . . .    $ 35,000
Deferred revenues  . . . . . . . . . . . . . . . . . . . . . . . . . . . . . . . . . . . . .      30,000
Fund balance:
    Unreserved . . . . . . . . . . . . . . . . . . . . . . . . . . . . . . . . . . . . . . . .     105,000
        Total Liabilities and Fund Balance . . . . . . . . . . . . . . . . . . . . . . . .    $170,000
```

3. **Unreserved fund balance.** The entire fund balance of $105,000 is designated as being "unreserved." This signifies that the fund has $105,000 of financial resources available for incurring expenditures in the following fiscal year.

4. **Reserving a portion of the fund balance for inventory.** Theoretically, no reservation of the fund balance should be made for inventory when the consumption method is used. In practice, however, some governmental units *do* reserve a portion of the fund balance for inventory reported under the consumption method. If this had been done at June 30, 19X1 (by *debiting* Unreserved Fund Balance for $10,000 and *crediting* Fund Balance Reserved for Inventory for $10,000), the Unreserved Fund Balance account would have been $95,000 (instead of $105,000). As a result, the $95,000 would have signified the amount of *liquid* financial resources available for incurring expenditures in the following fiscal year—this would be the amount available to "spend" in the cash sense.

Assumed transactions and related journal entries for the fiscal year July 1, 19X1, through June 30, 19X2, are discussed in the following paragraphs.

1. ADOPTION OF THE BUDGET   The city council approved and adopted the budget for the year. The budget contained the following amounts:

```
Estimated revenues  . . . . . . . . . . . . . . . . . . . . . . . . . . . . . . . . . . . . .    $700,000
Authorized expenditures  . . . . . . . . . . . . . . . . . . . . . . . . . . . . . . . . . .     660,000
Authorized operating transfer out
    to the Library Debt Service Fund . . . . . . . . . . . . . . . . . . . . . . . . . . .     30,000
Authorized residual equity transfer out to establish
    a Central Motor Pool Internal Service Fund . . . . . . . . . . . . . . . . . . . . .     25,000
```

As explained earlier, the adoption of the budget for the General Fund involves the use of budgetary accounts, as follows:

	Dr.	Cr.
ESTIMATED REVENUES	700,000	
BUDGETARY FUND BALANCE	15,000	
APPROPRIATIONS		660,000[a]

(continued)

APPROPRIATIONS— OPERATING TRANSFERS OUT	30,000	
APPROPRIATIONS— RESIDUAL EQUITY TRANSFER OUT	25,000	

To record the legally adopted annual operating budget.

[a]In practice, this amount is often broken down by category, such as General Government, Public Safety, Sanitation, and so forth.

2. PROPERTY TAXES Property taxes for the period July 1, 19X1, through June 30, 19X2, were levied in the amount of $515,000. Of this amount $5,000 was estimated to be uncollectible. During the year, $485,000 was collected ($41,000 of which pertained to delinquent taxes of the prior fiscal year), and $2,000 of prior year delinquent balances was written off as uncollectible.

At June 30, 19X2, it was estimated that (1) a $9,000 allowance for uncollectibles was necessary and (2) $45,000 of the net amount expected to be collected would be collected after 60 days. Property taxes unpaid at the end of the fiscal year become delinquent.

As explained earlier, the accrual basis of accounting is usually appropriate for property taxes. In this case, the city's fiscal year coincides with the period to which the property taxes relate; accordingly, the property tax levy is appropriately recorded on the first day of the new fiscal year. In recording the property taxes, the estimated uncollectible amount is netted against the revenues, and the use of the Bad Debts Expense account is avoided. The Bad Debts Expense account would be inappropriate because the General Fund has expenditures, not expenses. At the end of the fiscal year, remaining property tax receivables and the related allowance for uncollectible accounts are transferred to accounts that designate these items as relating to delinquent taxes. Thus tax levies of the following fiscal year may be separated from the delinquent taxes.

(1)	Property Taxes Receivable—Current	515,000	
	Allowance for Uncollectibles—Current		5,000
	Deferred Revenues		510,000
	To record the property tax levy.		
(2)	Cash	485,000	
	Property Taxes Receivable—Current		444,000
	Property Taxes Receivable—Delinquent		41,000
	To record the collection of property taxes.		
(3)	Deferred Revenues	485,000	
	Revenues		485,000
	To recognize revenues.		
(4)	Allowance for Uncollectibles—Delinquent	2,000	
	Property Taxes Receivable—Delinquent		2,000
	To write off accounts determined to be uncollectible.		
(5)	Allowance for Uncollectibles—Delinquent	1,000	
	Revenues		1,000
	To eliminate the remaining balance in the Allowance for Uncollectibles—Delinquent account as a result of collections of $41,000 being in excess of the $40,000 net amount estimated to be collected at the end of the prior year.[a]		
(6)	Deferred Revenues	4,000	
	Allowance for Uncollectibles—Current		4,000
	To increase the allowance for uncollectibles—current at year-end from $5,000 to $9,000.		

| (7) | Deferred Revenues .... | 6,000 | |
| | Revenues .... | | 6,000 |

To adjust the Deferred Revenues account at year-end to
the $45,000 amount estimated to be collected *after*
60 days ($51,000 – $45,000 = $6,000).

(8)	Property Taxes Receivable—Delinquent	71,000	
	Allowance for Uncollectibles—Current	9,000	
	Property Taxes Receivable—Current		71,000
	Allowance for Uncollectibles— Delinquent		9,000

To transfer the fiscal year-end balances to the
delinquent accounts.

[a]The beginning of year balance in the Allowance for Uncollectibles—Delinquent
account was $3,000.

COMPARATIVE PRACTICE NOTE

Some governmental units (1) initially credit Revenues (instead of Deferred Revenues) and (2) make an adjusting entry at year-end to debit Revenues and credit Deferred Revenues for the amount to be deferred at year-end.

---

3. REVENUES OTHER THAN PROPERTY TAXES The total estimated revenues for the year include an estimated $22,000 *entitlement* from the federal government. We assume that these funds are used for purposes normally financed through the General Fund. The amount is assumed to be susceptible to accrual; the actual amount received midway through the year is $23,000. Revenues of $181,000 are collected from sales taxes, business licenses, permits, and miscellaneous sources. Because these revenues are not susceptible to accrual, they are accounted for on the cash basis.

| (1) | Entitlement Receivable .... | 22,000 | |
| | Revenues .... | | 22,000 |

To record entitlement from the federal government.

(2)	Cash...	23,000	
	Entitlement Receivable		22,000
	Revenues		1,000

To record collection of entitlement.

| (3) | Cash... | 181,000 | |
| | Revenues .... | | 181,000 |

To record revenues accounted for on the cash basis.

4. EXPENDITURES AND ENCUMBRANCES FOR ITEMS OTHER THAN INVENTORY During the year, $115,000 of encumbrances on purchase orders (pertaining to other than inventory) and contracts were recorded. For $103,000 of these encumbrances, the city received billings of $102,000, which it approved for payment. Additional expenditures of $524,000 (which did not involve the use of purchase orders or contracts) were incurred.

(1)	ENCUMBRANCES	115,000	
	BUDGETARY FUND BALANCE RESERVED		
	FOR ENCUMBRANCES		115,000

To record encumbrances on purchase orders issued.

(2)	BUDGETARY FUND BALANCE RESERVED FOR		
	ENCUMBRANCES	103,000	
	ENCUMBRANCES		103,000

To cancel encumbrances of $103,000 upon receipt of
goods and services totaling $102,000.

(3)   Expenditures   102,000
       Vouchers Payable   102,000
       To record expenditures of $102,000 for goods and
         services that were previously encumbered for $103,000.

(4)   Expenditures   524,000
       Vouchers Payable   524,000
       To record expenditures for items not previously encumbered.

5. ACQUISITION AND CONSUMPTION OF INVENTORY   During the current year, purchase orders totaling $15,000 for supplies were issued. All of these purchase orders were filled by year-end, with billings of $15,000 having been received and approved. The government uses the "consumption" method of accounting for supplies inventories whereby the inventory account is charged upon acquisition. As the supplies are used, the Inventory account is relieved and the Expenditures account is charged. (Note that this manner of accounting parallels the accounting for inventories for commercial enterprises). During the year, $11,000 of supplies were consumed.

(1)   ENCUMBRANCES   15,000
       BUDGETARY FUND BALANCE RESERVED
         FOR ENCUMBRANCES   15,000
       To record encumbrances on purchase orders
       issued for supplies.

(2)   BUDGETARY FUND BALANCE RESERVED
       FOR ENCUMBRANCES   15,000
         ENCUMBRANCES   15,000
       To cancel encumbrances of $15,000 upon receipt
       of goods totaling $15,000.

(3)   Inventory   15,000
       Vouchers Payable   15,000
       To record acquisition of supplies received.

(4)   Expenditures   11,000
       Inventory   11,000
       To record consumption of supplies used during the year.

COMPARATIVE PRACTICE NOTE

Some governmental units simplify the procedures under the consumption method by assuming throughout the year that the supplies received will always approximate the supplies used. Accordingly, they charge the Expenditures account as the supplies are received instead of charging the Inventory account. At year-end, a physical count is taken and the Inventory account is adjusted to its proper balance (the offsetting adjustment being to the Expenditures account).

If significant amounts of inventory exist at the balance sheet date, the GASB *Codification* requires such inventory to be reported in the balance sheet. This automatically occurs under the consumption method. Note that under the consumption method, the acquisition of inventory is viewed merely as **the conversion of resources (from cash to inventory)—not the use of resources.** The GASB *Codification* also sanctions the use of the "purchases" method, which takes the opposite position and, therefore, results in charging the Expenditures account upon acquisition of inventory. The purchases method, however, is outdated and has lost much support in recent years. *SGAS No. 11* (which is not yet effective) prohibits the purchases method. At the end of the chapter, we discuss the purchases method in detail and show its procedures for reporting significant amounts of inventory in the balance sheet.

6. DISBURSEMENTS (OTHER THAN INTERFUND) Cash disbursements totaled $606,000.

Vouchers Payable	606,000	
Cash		606,000
To record cash disbursements other than interfund disbursements.		

7. INTERFUND TRANSACTIONS The city had the following interfund transactions:

A. Quasi-External Transactions

During the year, the city's electric utility, which is operated as an Enterprise fund, rendered billings in the amount of $21,000 for electricity supplied to the General Fund. Of this amount, $19,000 was paid during the fiscal year. These billings qualify for treatment as **quasi-external transactions.** Accordingly, they are treated as expenditures in the General Fund (and as revenues in the Enterprise Fund).

(1)	Expenditures	21,000	
	Due to Electric Utility Enterprise Fund		21,000
	To record as expenditures electricity acquired from the Electric Utility Enterprise Fund.		
(2)	Due to Electric Utility Enterprise Fund	19,000	
	Cash		19,000
	To record payment made to Electric Utility Enterprise Fund.		

B. Operating Transfer

The operating transfer of $30,000 to be made to the Library Debt Service Fund is recorded on the first day of the fiscal year because the amount is susceptible to being accrued.

(1)	Other Financing Uses—Operating Transfers Out	30,000	
	Due to Library Debt Service Fund		30,000
	To record operating transfer to be made to the Library Debt Service Fund.		

The following entry assumes that the payment was made in accordance with the authorized amounts.

(2)	Due to Library Debt Service Fund	30,000	
	Cash		30,000
	To record payment of operating transfer to the Library Debt Service Fund.		

C. Residual Equity Transfer

The Central Motor Pool Internal Service Fund was established in September 19X1. A residual equity transfer was made from the General Fund.

Residual Equity Transfer Out	25,000	
Cash		25,000
To record residual equity transfer to the newly established Central Motor Pool Internal Service Fund.		

The General Fund preclosing trial balances after recording the preceding items are shown in Illustration 24–8.

8. CLOSING ENTRIES (EXCLUDING ENCUMBRANCES) The closing entries at June 30, 19X2, are as follows:

	Dr.	Cr.
(1) APPROPRIATIONS	660,000	
APPROPRIATIONS—OPERATING TRANSFER OUT . . .	30,000	
APPROPRIATIONS—RESIDUAL EQUITY TRANSFER OUT	25,000	
ESTIMATED REVENUES		700,000
BUDGETARY FUND BALANCE		15,000
To reverse the entry previously made to record the legally adopted annual operating budget.		
(2) Revenues	696,000	
Expenditures		658,000
Other Financing Uses—Operating Transfers Out . .		30,000
Unreserved Fund Balance		8,000
To close operating statement accounts.		
(3) Unreserved Fund Balance	25,000	
Residual Equity Transfer Out		25,000
To close residual equity transfer out (a nonoperating statement account to be shown as a direct adjustment to the beginning fund balance).		

ILLUSTRATION 24–8

Funn City
Preclosing Trial Balances—General Fund
June 30, 19X2

	Debit	Credit
Actual (nonbudgetary) Accounts		
Cash	$129,000	
Property taxes receivable—delinquent	71,000	
Allowance for estimated uncollectibles—delinquent		$ 9,000
Inventory	14,000	
Vouchers payable		70,000
Due to Electric Utility Enterprise Fund		2,000
Deferred revenues		45,000
Unreserved fund balance		105,000
Revenues		696,000
Expenditures	658,000	
Other financing uses—Operating transfers out	30,000	
Residual equity transfer out	25,000	
Totals	$927,000	$927,000
Budgetary Accounts		
ESTIMATED REVENUES	$700,000	
BUDGETARY FUND BALANCE	15,000	
APPROPRIATIONS		$660,000
APPROPRIATIONS—OPERATING TRANSFER OUT . . .		30,000
APPROPRIATIONS—RESIDUAL EQUITY TRANSFER OUT		25,000
ENCUMBRANCES	12,000	
BUDGETARY FUND BALANCE RESERVED FOR ENCUMBRANCES		12,000
Totals	$727,000	$727,000

9. CLOSING ENTRY RELATING TO ENCUMBRANCES When encumbrances are outstanding at year-end, the encumbrances budgetary accounts must be closed as follows:

BUDGETARY FUND BALANCE RESERVED FOR ENCUMBRANCES	12,000	
ENCUMBRANCES		12,000
To close encumbrances outstanding at year-end by reversing the entry that previously recorded them.		

10. ADJUSTING ENTRY TO RESERVE A PORTION OF THE FUND BALANCE If the governmental unit intends to honor purchase orders and commitments outstanding at year-end (the customary practice), the encumbrances outstanding must be disclosed as a reservation of the Fund Balance account (similar to an appropriation of retained earnings for a commercial corporation). This requires the following adjusting entry:

Unreserved Fund Balance	12,000	
Fund Balance Reserved for Encumbrances		12,000
To record *actual* fund balance reserve account to indicate the portion of the year-end fund balance segregated for expenditure upon vendor performance.		

At the start of the new year, the preceding two $12,000 journal entries would be reversed to reestablish budgetary control over encumbrances outstanding in the normal manner. These reversing entries are as follows:

(1)	Fund Balance Reserved for Encumbrances	12,000	
	Unreserved Fund Balance		12,000
	To reverse appropriation of fund balance made at the end of the prior year.		

(2)	ENCUMBRANCES	12,000	
	BUDGETARY FUND BALANCE RESERVED FOR ENCUMBRANCES		12,000
	To reestablish budgetary control over encumbrances outstanding at the end of the prior year that will be honored during the current year.		

The individual financial statements for the fiscal year ended June 30, 19X2, are shown in Illustrations 24–9 and 24–10.

MANNER OF CLASSIFYING EXPENDITURES

The operating statement for Funn City classifies expenditures by **character** and **function.** *Character* refers to the fiscal period that the expenditures are presumed to benefit. Virtually all of Funn City's expenditures were presumed to benefit the current fiscal year. Other major categories of character classification are *Capital Outlay* (which benefits primarily future periods) and *Debt Service* (which benefits the period encompassing the useful life of the related fixed assets acquired or constructed with the proceeds of the borrowing).

Note that the operating statement shows a minor amount for the Capital Outlay category and no Debt Service category. In Chapter 25, which covers the other types of funds, the Capital Outlay category is also encountered in Capital Projects Funds (in which the amounts are usually not minor); the Debt Service category is encountered in Debt Service Funds.

When desirable, the major functions may be subdivided into **activities** and **objects.** For example, the sanitation function could be subdivided into sewage treatment and disposal, garbage collection, garbage disposal, and street cleaning. Al-

ILLUSTRATION 24-9

Funn City
Balance Sheet—General Fund
June 30, 19X2

Assets

Cash	$129,000
Property taxes receivable—Delinquent	71,000
Less: Allowance for estimated uncollectible taxes—Delinquent	(9,000)
Inventory	14,000
Total Assets	$205,000

Liabilities and Fund Balance

Vouchers payable	$ 70,000
Due to Electric Utility Enterprise Fund	2,000
Deferred revenues	45,000[a]
Total Liabilities	$117,000
Fund balance:	
Reserved for encumbrances	$ 12,000
Unreserved	76,000
Total Fund Balance	$ 88,000
Total Liabilities and Fund Balance	$205,000

[a]This amount is that portion of the $62,000 net realizable amount of the property taxes ($71,000 − $9,000) that is *not* expected to be collected within 60 days.

---

ternatively, the sanitation function could be subdivided into employee salaries, contracted services, materials, and supplies. These other ways to classify expenditures may be presented in the financial statements, in supporting schedules to the financial statements, or in notes to the financial statements.

MANNER OF REPORTING INVENTORY UNDER THE *PURCHASES* METHOD

Recall that under the *purchases* method, inventory is charged to the Expenditures account upon acquisition, regardless of when actually consumed. Thus the use of resources is deemed to occur upon the *acquisition*—*not* the *consumption*. To report significant amounts of inventory in the balance sheet when the purchases method is used, the following entry is used:

Inventory of Supplies	xxx	
Fund Balance Reserved for Inventory of Supplies		xxx
To report supplies inventory in the balance sheet.		

This entry, which is made only in the balance sheet, superimposes inventory into the balance sheet—no adjustment is made to the Expenditures account. If the amount of inventory on hand changes from the preceding balance sheet date, these two accounts are adjusted accordingly. Note that the credit side of the entry is to Fund Balance Reserved for Inventory of Supplies, not to the Unreserved Fund Balance Account. The reason for this is that it would be improper to credit the Unreserved Fund Balance account because that would indicate an additional amount available for spending, when in fact the inventory has already been reported as an expenditure in the operating statement. Thus it *cannot* be "spent" twice.

ILLUSTRATION 24–10

Funn City
Statement of Revenues, Expenditures, and
Changes in Fund Balance—Budget and Actual—General Fund
For the Fiscal Year Ended June 30, 19X2

Classified by		Budget	Actual	Variance Favorable (Unfavorable)
	Revenues			
	Property taxes	$495,000	$492,000	$(3,000)
	Intergovernmental grant	22,000	23,000	1,000
Source	Sales taxes[a]	130,000	124,000	(6,000)
	Licenses and permits[a]	45,000	38,000	(7,000)
	Miscellaneous[a]	8,000	19,000	11,000
	Total Revenues	$700,000	$696,000	$(4,000)
	Expenditures			
Character——	Current:			
	General government[a]	$103,000	$101,000	$ 2,000
	Public safety[a]	215,000	220,000	(5,000)
Function	Sanitation[a]	50,000	49,500	500
	Health[a]	40,000	41,500	(1,500)
	Welfare[a]	70,000	62,700	7,300
	Education[a]	175,000	176,300	(1,300)
	Subtotal	$653,000	$651,000	$ 2,000
Character——	Capital outlay	7,000	7,000	—
	Total Expenditures	$660,000	$658,000	$ 2,000
	Excess of Revenues over Expenditures	$ 40,000	$ 38,000	$(2,000)
	Other Financing Sources (Uses)			
	Operating transfers out	$ (30,000)	$ (30,000)	—
	Total Other Financing Sources (Uses)	$ (30,000)	$ (30,000)	—
	Excess of Revenues and Other Sources over Expenditures and Other Uses	$ 10,000	$ 8,000	$(2,000)
	Fund Balance (in total)—July 1, 19X1	105,000	105,000[b]	—
	Residual equity transfer out to establish Internal Service Fund	(25,000)	(25,000)	—
	Fund Balance (in total)—June 30, 19X2	$ 90,000	$ 88,000[b]	$(2,000)

Note: Some governmental units use only the *Unreserved Fund Balance* rather than the *total* Fund Balance in the changes in fund balance section of the statement. Inquiries made to the GFOA revealed that only about 10% of the governmental units use this manner of reporting. However, the GFOA does deem this manner of reporting to be GAAP.

[a]These assumed amounts were not given in the transactions and journal entries.

[b]This is the total fund balance (reserved and unreserved portions).

END-OF-CHAPTER REVIEW

SUMMARY OF KEY POINTS

1. The Governmental Accounting Standards Board (GASB) establishes accounting standards for state and local governments.
2. The major deficiency of current financial reporting by governmental units is that practices are allowed that do not fully achieve **interperiod equity.**
3. **Fund accounting** is used extensively by government.
4. **Governmental funds** are accounted for on the **modified accrual basis,** which, for certain liabilities that have been incurred, results in the recognition of expenditures in the oper-

ating statement when financial resources become available for their liquidation rather than when the liability was incurred. For **proprietary funds,** the accrual basis is used because activities accounted for in these funds resemble commercial activities.

5. The **operating statement for governmental funds** is a "flow" of current financial resources statement called *the statement of revenues, expenditures, and changes in fund balance* (an all-inclusive approach)—this is *not* an income statement. The **operating statement for proprietary funds** *is* an income statement.

6. **Interfund transactions** may be categorized as (a) **loans and advances** (shown as receivables and payables in the balance sheets), (b) **quasi-external transactions** (shown as revenues in the fund providing the service and shown as expenditures in the fund receiving the services), (c) **residual equity transfers** (shown as direct adjustments to the opening fund balance), and (d) **operating transfers** (shown as an other financing source or use in governmental funds).

7. **Budgetary accounts** are used to control spending. All budgetary accounts are closed at year-end.

8. Unfilled purchase orders and uncompleted contracts at year-end that are intended to be honored in the following year require a **reservation of the fund balance** in the balance sheet.

GLOSSARY OF NEW TERMS

Appropriation "A legal authorization granted by a legislative body to make expenditures and to incur obligations for specific purposes. An appropriation usually is limited in amount and time it may be expended."*

Budget A plan of financial operations covering a specified period of time.

Budgetary Accounts "Accounts used to enter the formally adopted annual operating budget into the general ledger as part of the management control technique of formal budgetary integration."*

Component units "Legally separate organizations for which elected officials of the primary government are financially accountable."*

Encumbrances "Commitments related to unperformed (executory) contracts for goods or services. Used in budgeting, encumbrances are not GAAP expenditures or liabilities but represent the estimated amount of expenditures ultimately to result if unperformed contracts in process are completed."*

Expenditures "Decreases in net financial resources. . . ."*

Financial resources "Cash and other assets that, in the normal course of operations, will become cash."*

Flow of current financial resources "A measurement focus that recognizes the net effect of transactions on current financial resources by recording accruals for those revenue and expenditure transactions which have occurred by year end that are normally expected to result in cash receipt or disbursement early enough in the following year either (a) to provide financial resources to liquidate liabilities recorded in the fund at year end or (b) to require the use of available expendable financial resources reported at year end."*

Flow of economic resources "The measurement focus used in the commercial model and in proprietary and similar trust funds to measure economic resources, the claims to those economic resources and the effects of transactions, events and circumstances that change economic resources and claims to those resources. This focus includes depreciation of fixed assets, deferral of unearned revenues and prepaid expenses, and amortization of the resulting liabilities and assets. Under this measurement focus, all assets and liabilities are reported on the balance sheet, whether current or noncurrent. Also, the accrual basis of accounting is used, with the result that operating statements report expenses rather than expenditures."*

Fund "A fiscal and accounting entity with a self-balancing set of accounts in which cash and other financial resources, all related liabilities and residual equities, or balances, and changes therein, are recorded and segregated to carry on specific activities or attain certain objectives in accordance with special regulations, restrictions or limitations."*

*GAAFR, 1994 edition, Appendix B.

Fund accounting   Accounting for certain activities separately from other operations.

Fund balance   "The difference between fund assets and fund liabilities of governmental and similar trust funds."*

General fixed assets   "Capital assets that are not assets of any fund, but of the government unit as a whole. Most often these assets arise from the expenditure of the financial resources of governmental funds."*

General Fixed Assets Account Group (GFAAG)   "A self-balancing group of accounts established to account for fixed assets of a government not accounted for through specific proprietary funds or trust funds."*

General Fund   "The fund used to account for all financial resources, except those required to be accounted for in another fund."*

General long-term debt (GLTD)   "Long-term debt [including special assessment debt for which the governmental unit is obligated] expected to be repaid from governmental funds."*

General Long-Term Debt Account Group (GLTDAG)   "A self-balancing group of accounts established to account for the unmatured general long-term debt of a government. . . ."*

General-purpose financial statements   "Five combined financial statements that, together with the accompanying notes, constitute the minimum financial reporting needed for fair presentation in conformity with GAAP."*

Modified accrual basis   Recognizing revenues when they become available and measurable. Recognizing expenditures when the *fund* liability is incurred (which may be subsequent to when the liability is incurred and recognized in the balance sheet).

Operating statement   "The financial statement disclosing the financial results of operations of an entity during an accounting period in conformity with GAAP. In governmental financial reporting, operating statements and statements of changes in fund equity are combined into 'all-inclusive' operating statement formats."*

Operating transfers   "All interfund transfers other than residual equity transfers (e.g., legally authorized transfers from a fund receiving revenue to the fund through which the resources are to be expended)."*

Other financing sources   "Governmental fund general long-term debt proceeds, amounts equal to the present value of minimum lease payments arising from capital leases, proceeds from the sale of general fixed assets, and operating transfers in. Such amounts are classified separately from revenues on the governmental operating statement."*

Other financing uses   "Governmental fund operating transfers out and the amount of refunding bond proceeds deposited with the escrow agent. Such amounts are classified separately from expenditures on the governmental operating statement."*

Quasi-external transactions   "Interfund transactions that would be treated as revenues, expenditures or expenses if they involved organizations external to the government unit (e.g., payments in lieu of taxes from an enterprise fund to the general fund; internal service fund billings to departments; routine employer contributions to a pension trust fund and routine service charges for inspection, engineering, utilities or similar services provided by a department financed from one fund to a department financed from another fund). These transactions should be accounted for as revenues, expenditures or expenses in the funds involved."*

Residual equity transfers   "Nonrecurring or nonroutine transfers of equity between funds (e.g., contribution of enterprise fund or internal service fund capital by the general fund, subsequent return of all or part of such contribution to the general fund and transfers of residual balances of discontinued funds to the general fund or a debt service fund)."*

SELF-STUDY QUESTIONS

(Answers are at the end of this chapter.)

A. Theory and Basic Principles
   1. Which of the following is *not* a fund type?
      a. Budgetary

    b. Fiduciary

    c. Governmental

    d. Proprietary

2. Which of the following is the appropriate basis of accounting for a *governmental fund*?

    a. Accrual basis

    b. Cash basis

    c. Modified accrual basis

    d. Modified cash basis

3. Which of the following is the appropriate basis of accounting for a *proprietary fund*?

    a. Accrual basis

    b. Cash basis

    c. Modified accrual basis

    d. Modified cash basis

4. Under the *modified accrual basis,* revenues are recognized in which accounting period?

    a. When they are collected

    b. When they are measurable

    c. When they become available

    d. When they become available and measurable

5. Under the *modified accrual basis,* expenditures are recognized in which accounting period?

    a. When the liability becomes susceptible to accrual

    b. When the fund liability is paid

    c. When the fund liability is incurred

    d. When the liability becomes measurable

6. To what is the use of *financial resources* of a fund broadly referred?

    a. Encumbrance

    b. Expenditure

    c. Appropriation

    d. Disbursement

7. What are commitments related to *unperformed* contracts and purchase orders called?

    a. Appropriations

    b. Encumbrances

    c. Expenditures

    d. Reservations of the fund balance

8. Which of the following can the statement of revenues, expenditures, and changes in fund balance not be called in substance?

    a. Statement of Where Got and Where Gone

    b. Statement of Sources and Uses of Resources

    c. Statement of Cash Flows

    d. Statement of Changes in Financial Position

9. Which of the following is *not* one of the four types of *interfund transactions*?

    a. All-inclusive external transactions

    b. Residual equity transfers

    c. Operating transfers

    d. Loans and advances

10. How are each of the following *interfund transactions* classified in the operating statement of a governmental fund?

	Under Other Financing Sources and Uses	As an Increase to or a Subtraction from the Beginning Fund Balance
a.	Residual equity transfers	Operating transfers
b.	Quasi-external transactions	Residual equity transfers
c.	Operating transfers	Loans and Advances
d.	Operating transfers	Residual equity transfers

11. Which of the following items is *not* reportable under the category Other Financial Sources and Uses in the operating statement of a *governmental fund*?

    a. Bond proceeds

    b. Quasi-external transactions

    c. Operating transfers

    d. Proceeds from sale of general fixed assets

12. In which of the following categories can *expenditures* not be classified?

    a. Character

    b. Function

    c. Activity

    d. Object

    e. Source

13. Which of the following statements is true?

    a. General long-term debt is a liability of the General Fund.

    b. General Fixed Assets refer to fixed assets that are recorded in the General Fund as assets.

    c. The practice of not recording depreciation in the governmental funds is a departure from the accrual basis of accounting.

    d. It is appropriate for a proprietary fund to report long-term debt.

B. Revenues

14. For the four *governmental funds,* when are revenues recognized?

    a. In the period to which they relate

    b. When they become susceptible to accrual

    c. When earned

    d. When the related expenditures are recognized

15. For the four *governmental funds,* revenues are

    a. Matched against the cost of providing services

    b. Generated by expenditures

    c. Earned

    d. Reported in a quasi-income statement

    e. None of the above

16. Under the *modified accrual basis,* which of the following would be a revenue *susceptible to accrual?*

    a. Income taxes

    b. Business licenses

    c. Sales taxes

    d. Property taxes

    e. Parking meter receipts

    f. None of the above

17. At the end of the fiscal year, a governmental unit *increased* its allowance for uncollectible accounts relating to property tax receivables. The entry resulted in a charge to

    a. Unreserved fund balance

    b. ENCUMBRANCES

    c. Bad debts expense

    d. Deferred revenues

    e. ESTIMATED REVENUES

    f. APPROPRIATIONS

C. Expenditures and Encumbrances

18. When are *expenditures* (other than the exceptions) recognized under the *modified accrual basis?*

    a. When the vendor or contractor submits a bill

    b. When paid

    c. When the related revenues are recognized

    d. When the goods or services are ordered or contracted for

    e. When the goods are received or the services are performed

19. Which of the following defines *expenditures?*

    a. The cost of providing services

    b. Costs incurred to generate revenues

    c. An outflow of resources

    d. Amounts arising from encumbrances

    e. None of the above

20. When a fire truck is received by a governmental unit, it should be recorded in the General Fund as which of the following?
    a. Appropriation
    b. Encumbrance
    c. Expenditure
    d. Expense
    e. Fixed asset
    f. Transfer to the General Fixed Assets Account Group
21. When supplies are ordered out of the General Fund, they should be recorded as which of the following?
    a. Appropriation
    b. Encumbrance
    c. Expenditure
    d. Estimated expenditure
    e. Reduction of the fund balance
22. Which of the following terms refers to an *actual* cost rather than to an *estimate* in reporting for the four *governmental funds*?
    a. Appropriation
    b. Encumbrance
    c. Expenditure
    d. Expense
    e. None of the above
23. Wages that have been earned by the employees of a governmental unit but *not* paid should be recorded in the General Fund as which of the following?
    a. Appropriation
    b. Encumbrance
    c. Expenditure
    d. Expense
    e. None of the above

D. **Budgetary Accounting**
24. Which of the following is a *budgetary account* in governmental accounting?
    a. Fund balance reserved for encumbrances
    b. Unreserved fund balance
    c. APPROPRIATIONS
    d. Estimated uncollectible property taxes
    e. Expenditures
25. Authority granted by a legislative body to make expenditures and to incur obligations during a fiscal year is the definition of which of these?
    a. Appropriation
    b. Authorization
    c. Encumbrance
    d. Expenditure
    e. None of the above
26. The *actual* general ledger account Fund Balance—Reserved for Encumbrances is which of the following?
    a. Liability of substance
    b. Budgetary account
    c. Contra account
    d. Appropriation of the fund balance
    e. None of the above
27. An *encumbrance* could not be thought of as which of the following?
    a. Commitment
    b. Contingent liability
    c. Future expenditure
    d. Eventual reduction of the fund balance
    e. Liability of the period in which the encumbrance was created
28. Which of the following General Fund accounts would be *credited* when a purchase order is issued?
    a. APPROPRIATIONS

     b. ENCUMBRANCES
     c. Estimated expenditures
     d. Vouchers payable
     e. Fund balance
     f. None of the above
  29. At the end of 19X1, a governmental unit has unfilled purchase orders. In 19X2, these purchase orders are filled. In the 19X2 operating statement, which of the following is reported?
     a. Encumbrances
     b. Expenditures
     c. Neither encumbrances nor expenditures
     d. Expenditures only if the items were rebudgeted for in the 19X2 budget

ASSIGNMENT MATERIAL

REVIEW QUESTIONS

1. What is the difference between the Governmental Finance Officers Association (GFOA), the National Council on Governmental Reporting (NCGA), and the Governmental Accounting Standards Board (GASB)?
2. For governmental units, what is the relationship of the pronouncements of the GASB and the FASB?
3. Where does *GAAFR* (the "blue book") fit into the governmental GAAP hierarchy?
4. Must all state and local governmental units prepare their financial statements in accordance with GASB pronouncements?
5. What are some of the unique aspects of the governmental sector compared with the private sector?
6. For *governmental-type activities*, what account(s) are used to describe a fund's equity? What account(s) is(are) used for *proprietary-type activities*?
7. What is the relationship between revenues and expenditures?
8. What is meant by *fund accounting*?
9. What is meant by *measurement focus*?
10. What are the alternative measurement focuses?
11. What measurement focus is used for *governmental-type activities*? What measurement focus is used for *proprietary-type activities*?
12. What is meant by *interperiod equity*?
13. To what does *basis of accounting* refer?
14. What are the two major reporting deficiencies that currently exist for governmental units?
15. What are the seven major types of funds?
16. Are *general fixed assets* and *general long-term liabilities* accounted for in funds? Why or why not?
17. When is it appropriate to depreciate a governmental unit's fixed assets?
18. Is the *modified accrual basis of accounting* in accordance with GAAP? Why or why not?
19. What is meant by *budgetary accounting*?
20. What are the two major types of *interfund transfers*? What is the difference between the two?
21. How are *operating transfers* classified in the operating statement of *governmental funds*? In *proprietary funds*?
22. What is the difference between a *quasi-external transaction* and an *operating transfer*?
23. What is the difference between and *expenditure* and an *encumbrance*?

EXERCISES

E 24-1 **Revenue Recognition** The City of Potterville, which has a calendar year-end, was awarded a $300,000 federal job development grant on 12/3/X1. The grant is expected to be disbursed by the federal government in May 19X2. In 19X1, the city levied property taxes of $800,000. At year-end, $100,000 remains uncollected, of which $75,000 is expected to be collected within 60 days. An allowance for uncollectibles of $10,000 is deemed adequate at year-end.

Required Determine the amount to be reported for revenues for 19X1 for these items.

E 24–2   **Revenue Recognition**   Wilbur Whoops mistakenly paid his tax bill for the fiscal year ended 6/30/X4 twice. He noticed this in June 19X4 and contacted the governmental unit. Rather than requesting a refund, he told the governmental unit to apply the overpayment of $3,000 to his taxes for the fiscal year ended 6/30/X5. The governmental unit (which had credited the Accounts Receivable account $6,000) agreed to do this.

Required   Prepare the entry or entries required by the General Fund, if any, at 6/30/X4 relating to the overpayment.

E 24–3   **Revenue Recognition**   The City of Joy has the following tax assessment–related accounts at its fiscal year-end, 6/30/X7:

Property taxes receivable—Delinquent	$470,000
Allowance for uncollectibles—Delinquent	(20,000)

The net amount expected to be collected at year-end is usually collected within 60 days of the fiscal year-end. At 6/30/X7, however, only about $300,000 is expected to be collected within 60 days, with the remaining $150,000 expected to be collected after that time over many months. The reason for the delay is a severe recession in the city's economy. The total property tax assessment is $1,000,000. No property tax receivables existed at 6/30/X6.

Required   **1.** Prepare the entry or entries required for the General Fund at 6/30/X7, if any.
         2. Determine the amount to be reported for property tax revenues for the year ended 6/30/X7.

E 24–4   **Interfund Transactions: Preparing Journal Entries**   The City of Mityville had the following interfund transactions during the year ended 12/31/X5:

1. The General Fund received a billing of $11,000 from its city-owned Water Fund, which is accounted for in an Enterprise Fund.
2. The General Fund disbursed $22,000 to its Library Debt Service Fund so that interest could be paid to bondholders.
3. The General Fund disbursed $33,000 to start a central purchasing fund, which is accounted for in an Internal Service Fund.
4. The General Fund disbursed $44,000 to its Municipal Transit Fund (accounted for in a Special Revenue Fund) as its annual subsidy.
5. The General Fund disbursed $55,000 to its Convention Center Enterprise Fund. Repayment is to be made in three years.
6. The General Fund received $66,000 from its Library Capital Projects Fund in repayment of money the General Fund had advanced to the architectural firm designing the library. The General Fund had charged the Expenditures account when the advance was made.

Required   Prepare the entries required in the General Fund.

E 24–5   **Preparation of a General Fund's Operating Statement From Year-End Trial Balance**   The following are selected *preclosing* account balances of Borrowsville Township's General Fund at 6/30/X2:

	Dr.	Cr.
Expenditures	600,000	
Residual Equity Transfers Out	70,000	
Operating Transfers Out	50,000	
Subsidy to Airport Enterprise Fund	80,000	
Amount Paid to Internal Service Fund for Printing Services	10,000	
Advance to City Transit Enterprise Fund	90,000	
Due to City Water Fund		20,000
Bond Proceeds Received		100,000
Revenues		650,000
Residual Equity Transfers In		15,000
Unreserved Fund Balance		200,000

In some cases, the bookkeeper was not sure which was the proper account and used a description of the transaction instead. Encumbrances of $25,000 are outstanding at 6/30/X2, whereas there were no encumbrances outstanding at 6/30/X1.

Required Prepare a statement of revenues, expenditures, and changes in fund balance for the year ended 6/30/X2.

E 24–6 **Recording the Budget** A city's legislative body approved the budget for the coming fiscal year. The details of the budget follow:

1. Estimated revenues of $500,000.
2. Estimated expenditures of $450,000.
3. Authorized transfer of $30,000 to Debt Service Fund to pay interest on bond indebtedness.
4. Estimated receipt of $15,000 from closure of Municipal Swimming Pool Enterprise Fund.
5. Authorized transfer of $5,000 to Capital Projects Fund to pay for cost overrun on construction of new civic center.
6. Estimated receipt of $50,000 subsidy from Electric Utility Enterprise Fund to help finance General Fund expenditures (this is not a payment in lieu of taxes).

Required Prepare the General Fund's entry to record the budget.

E 24–7 **Budgetary Control** The following balances are included in the subsidiary records of Tylersville's fire department at 5/31/X2:

Appropriation—Supplies	$33,000
Expenditures—Supplies	27,000
Encumbrances—Supply orders	2,000

Required Determine how much the fire department has available for additional purchases of supplies.

E 24–8 **Presentation of Financial Statements: Expenditures and Encumbrances** The City of Thrillsville has the following accounts in its *preclosing* trial balance at 6/30/X5:

	Account	
Amount	**Dr.**	**Cr.**
Expenditures—Current Year	800,000	
Expenditures—Prior Year	60,000	
ENCUMBRANCES	28,000	
APPROPRIATIONS		902,000
BUDGETARY FUND BALANCE RESERVED FOR ENCUMBRANCES		28,000

The encumbrances outstanding at each year-end ($62,000 at 6/30/X4) are reappropriated in the following year's budget. The city council has requested that expenditures relating to such encumbrances be kept separate in the accounting records.

Required Prepare the applicable section of the budgetary comparison statement for the year ended 6/30/X5.

E 24–9 **Preparing Budgetary Comparison Statements from Selected Data** The following information is given for the City of Budgetville:

Fund Balance at 12/31/X1:	
Reserved for encumbrances	$ 30,000
Unreserved	70,000
Total Fund Balance	$100,000
Budgeted items for 19X2:	
Estimated revenues	$500,000
Appropriations (including $30,000 rebudgeted for encumbrances outstanding at 12/31/X1)	480,000
Actual amounts for 19X2:	
Revenues	503,000
Expenditures (including $29,000 relating to encumbrances outstanding at 12/31/X1)	473,000
Encumbrances outstanding at 12/31/X2	5,000

Required   Prepare a budgetary comparison statement of revenues, expenditures, and changes in fund balance for 19X2.

PROBLEMS

P 24–1   **General Fund: Preparing Transaction and Closing Entries—Fundamentals**   The City of Smileyville had the following activities pertaining to its General Fund for the fiscal year ended 6/30/X6:

1. **Adoption of the budget.** Revenues were estimated at $1,000,000, and authorized expenditures were $950,000. (Assume that no encumbrances were outstanding at 6/30/X5.)
2. **Property taxes.** Property taxes were billed in the amount of $800,000, of which $25,000 was expected to be uncollectible. Collections were $750,000. A $22,000 allowance for uncollectibles is deemed adequate at year-end. All uncollected property taxes at year-end are delinquent. All but $11,000 of the net realizable amount at year-end is expected to be collected within 60 days.
3. **Other revenues.** Cash collections of $210,000 were received from sales taxes, licenses, fees, and fines.
4. **Purchase orders.** Purchase orders totaling $300,000 were issued to vendors and contractors during the year. For $270,000 of these purchase orders and contracts, billings totaling $268,000 were received. Cash payments totaling $245,000 were made.
5. **Payroll and other operating costs.** Expenditures for payroll and other operating costs not requiring the use of purchase orders and contracts totaled $631,000. Cash payments of $590,000 were made on these items.

Required   1. Prepare the journal entries relating to these items.
2. Prepare the year-end closing entries, assuming that encumbrances outstanding at year-end will be honored in the following year.
3. Prepare the entry or entries that must be made on the first day of the following fiscal year.

P 24–2   **General Fund: Preparing Financial Statements from Preclosing Trial Balance**   Following is the trial balance of Ponder City at 6/30/X2, prior to adjusting and closing entries. The bookkeeper was not certain of the exact account to use in some cases and merely used an account that was most descriptive of the nature of the transaction.

Cash	$ 550,000
Taxes receivable—Current	80,000
Allowance for uncollectibles—Current	(90,000)
Inventory	20,000ᵃ
BUDGETARY FUND BALANCE	220,000
ESTIMATED REVENUES	920,000
ENCUMBRANCES	80,000
Expenditures	790,000
Residual equity transfer out to New Golf Course Enterprise Fund	230,000
Quasi-External payment to City Utility Enterprise Fund	40,000
Annual subsidy to City Transit Enterprise Fund	60,000
	$2,900,000
Vouchers payable	$ 280,000
Due to Internal Service Fund	30,000
APPROPRIATIONS	840,000
APPROPRIATIONS—OPERATING TRANSFERS OUT	70,000
APPROPRIATIONS—RESIDUAL EQUITY TRANSFER OUT	230,000
Revenues	870,000
Unreserved fund balance	300,000
Bond proceeds received	200,000
BUDGETARY FUND BALANCE RESERVED FOR ENCUMBRANCES.	80,000ᵇ
	$2,900,000

ᵃThe *consumption method* is used.

ᵇAt 6/30/X1 (the end of the *prior year*), encumbrances outstanding totaled $25,000.

Required   1. Prepare a balance sheet and an operating statement (*no* comparison to budget required).
2. Prepare a T-account analysis of the Unreserved Fund Balance account as it should have been posted for the year (inclusive of any year-end adjusting entries *and* the year-end closing entries).

P 24–3   **General Fund: Preparing Transaction and Closing Entries and an Operating Statement**   Ledgerville had the following events and transactions for its fiscal year ended 6/30/X2:

1. **Adoption of the budget.** The budget for the year was approved. It provided for (a) $620,000 of estimated revenues, (b) $565,000 of expenditures, (c) $40,000 for servicing general long-term debt (principal and interest), and (d) $30,000 to establish a central printing department that will provide services to all city departments. (The $30,000 will not be repaid to the General Fund.)
2. Items (c) and (d) above were expended in accordance with authorizations.
3. **Property taxes.** Property taxes totaling $450,000 were levied, of which $8,000 was estimated to be uncollectible. Property tax collections totaled $405,000. At year-end, the estimated allowance for uncollectibles was increased from $8,000 to $12,000. Unpaid taxes at year-end become delinquent. The net realizable amounts at 6/30/X1 and X2 were expected to be collected within 60 days.
4. **Other revenues.** City income taxes, sales taxes, business licenses, and fines totaled $162,000.
5. **Equipment sale.** Some equipment accounted for in the General Fixed Assets Account Group was sold for $11,000. This transaction was not included in the budget.
6. **Cost overrun.** A Capital Projects Fund was short $3,000 as a result of changes to contracts issued in connection with certain street improvements being charged to certain property owners. Authorization was given during the year to transfer funds to this fund to make up the shortage. The amount was *not* budgeted and will *not* be repaid.
7. **Purchase orders.** Purchase orders and contracts totaling $280,000 were entered into. For $255,000 of this amount, invoices for goods and services totaling $254,000 were rendered. (Assume that no encumbrances were outstanding at 6/30/X1.)
8. **Nonpurchase orders.** Payroll and other operating costs *not* involving the use of purchase orders and contracts totaled $282,000.
9. **Cash payments.** Cash disbursements (other than to other funds) totaled $507,000.

Required   1. Prepare the General Fund entries for these items.
2. Prepare the closing entries at 6/30/X2, assuming that encumbrances outstanding at year-end will be honored in the following year.
3. Prepare a statement of revenues, expenditures, and changes in fund balance for the year ended 6/30/X2 for the General Fund that compares budgeted amounts with actual amounts. (Assume that the General Fund had a total fund balance of $100,000 at 6/30/X1.)
4. Prepare the fund equity section of the balance sheet at 6/30/X2.

P 24–4   **COMPREHENSIVE: Preparing Transaction and Closing Entries and a Budgetary Comparison Statement (Several Interfund Transactions)**   The City of Postville had the following items and transactions pertaining to its General Fund for the fiscal year ended 6/30/X3:

1. **Adoption of the budget.** The budget for the year was as follows:

Estimated revenues	$800,000
Authorized expenditures (including $55,000 reappropriated	
for encumbrances outstanding at 6/30/X2, which lapsed)	725,000
Authorized operating transfers to other funds	50,000
Estimated inflow from discontinuance of Central Motor Pool	
Internal Service Fund	25,000

2. **Property taxes.** Property taxes totaling $550,000 were levied. Of this amount, $10,000 was estimated to be uncollectible. Collections during the year were $535,000, of which $12,000 pertained to property tax levies of the prior year that had been declared delinquent at the end of the prior year. All remaining property tax receivables at the beginning of the current year totaling $4,000 were written off as uncollectible. The net realizable amounts at 6/30/X2 ($11,000) and X3 were expected to be collected within 60 days.
3. **Entitlement.** The estimated revenues for the year include a $34,000 entitlement from the federal government. During the year, $36,000 was received.
4. **Other revenues.** City income taxes, sales taxes, licenses, permits, and miscellaneous revenues totaled $222,000.
5. **Encumbrances at 7/1/X2.** Encumbrances outstanding at the *beginning* of the year totaled $55,000. The goods and services relating to these encumbrances were received along with invoices totaling $53,000.

6. **Purchase orders.** Purchase orders and contracts totaling $370,000 were entered into during the year. For $330,000 of this amount, invoices totaling $326,000 for goods and services were rendered. Assume that the city generally allows encumbrances outstanding at year-end to lapse but *reappropriates* amounts in the following year to honor the encumbrances. Of the $326,000 amount, $76,000 was for the acquisition of supplies inventory. The city uses the *consumption method* of accounting for supplies.

7. **Nonpurchase orders.** Payroll and other items *not* involving the use of purchase orders and contracts totaled $280,000. (This amount *excludes* interfund billings.)

8. **Cash payments.** Cash disbursements (other than to other funds) totaled $740,000.

9. **Interfund transactions.** Interfund transactions consisted of the following:
   a. The Central Motor Pool Internal Service Fund was discontinued pursuant to authorization of the legislative body at the beginning of the year. The actual amount disbursed to the General Fund during the year when the fund was discontinued was $17,000.
   b. A $30,000 payment was made to the Electric Utility Enterprise Fund to make up its operating deficit, initially estimated to be $35,000.
   c. A payment of $15,000 made to a Capital Projects Fund to finance a portion of certain street improvements equaled the amount budgeted.
   d. The Electric Utility Enterprise Fund rendered billings to the city totaling $26,000 for electricity supplied to the city by the Enterprise Fund. Cash disbursements to this fund during the year in payment of such billings totaled $22,000.
   e. An $80,000 disbursement was made to the City Center for Performing Arts Enterprise Fund. Repayment is expected in three years.

10. **Inventory.** A physical inventory of supplies inventory at year-end shows that the supplies inventory *decreased* during the year from $44,000 to $42,000.

Required
1. Prepare General Fund journal entries only for the preceding items.
2. Prepare the closing entries at 6/30/X3 for the General Fund.
3. Prepare a statement of revenues, expenditures, and changes in fund balance for the year ended 6/30/X3 that compares *budgeted* amounts with *actual* amounts. (Assume that the fund balance at the beginning of the year was $100,000.)
4. Prepare the fund equity section of the balance sheet at 6/30/X3.

P 24-5   **COMPREHENSIVE: Preparing Transaction and Closing Entries and a Budgetary Comparison Statement**   The City of Solna's General Fund trial balance at 12/31/X2 follows:

	Dr.	Cr.
Cash	$ 62,000	
Taxes receivable—Delinquent	46,000	
Allowance for uncollectible taxes—Delinquent		$ 8,000
Stores inventory—Program operations	18,000	
Vouchers payable		28,000
Fund balance reserved for encumbrances		12,000
Unreserved fund balance		78,000
	$126,000	$126,000

Collectible delinquent taxes are expected to be collected within 60 days after the end of the year. Solna uses the *consumption method* to account for stores inventory. The following data pertain to 19X3 General Fund operations:

1. **Budget adopted** (*including* reappropriation of 19X2 items):

Revenues and Other Financing Sources

Taxes	$220,000
Fines, forfeits, and penalties	80,000
Miscellaneous revenues	100,000
Share of bond issue proceeds	200,000
	$600,000

(continued)

Expenditures and Other Financing Uses

Program operations	$312,000
General administration	120,000
Stores—program operations	60,000
Capital outlay	80,000
Periodic transfer to Special Revenue Fund	20,000
	$592,000

2. **Property taxes.** Taxes were assessed at an amount that would result in revenues of $220,800, after deduction of 4% of the tax levy as uncollectible. The net realizable amounts at 12/31/X2 and X3 were expected to be collected within 60 days.

3. **Orders placed but not received:**

Program operations	$176,000
General administration	80,000
Capital outlay	60,000
	$316,000

4. **Future capital outlay.** The city council designated $20,000 of the unreserved fund balance for possible future appropriation for capital outlay.

5. **Cash collections and transfer:**

Delinquent taxes	$ 38,000
Current taxes	226,000
Refund of overpayment of invoice for purchase of equipment	4,000
Fines, forfeits, and penalties	88,000
Miscellaneous revenues	90,000
Share of bond issue proceeds	200,000
Transfer of remaining fund balance of a discontinued fund	18,000
	$664,000

6. **Canceled encumbrances:**

	Estimated	Actual
Program operations	$156,000	$166,000[a]
General administration	84,000	80,000
Capital outlay	62,000	62,000
	$302,000	$308,000

[a]Includes $36,000 of stores inventory purchases.

7. **Additional vouchers:**

Program operations	$182,000
General administration	38,000
Capital outlay	18,000
Transfer to Special Revenue Fund	20,000
	$258,000

8. **Tax overpayment.** Alberta Alberts, a taxpayer, overpaid her 19X3 taxes by $2,000. She applied for a $2,000 credit against her 19X4 taxes. The city council granted her request.

9. **Cash payments.** Vouchers paid amounted to $580,000 (including $20,000 paid to the Special Revenue Fund).

10. **Inventory.** Stores inventory on 12/31/X3 amounted to $12,000.

Required
1. Prepare General Fund *journal* entries only for these items.
2. Prepare any required year-end *adjusting* entries.
3. Prepare the *closing* entries at 12/31/X3.
4. Prepare a balance sheet at 12/31/X3.

5. Prepare a statement of revenues, expenditures, and changes in fund balance for 19X3 that compares budgeted amounts with actual amounts.
6. Qualitatively evaluate the city's financial statements. (AICPA adapted)

P 24–6 **General Fund: Reconstructing Transaction and Closing Entries; Preparing a Budgetary Comparison Statement**
The following data were obtained from the general ledger for the General Fund of the City of Hope *after* the general ledger had been closed for the fiscal year ended 6/30/X6:

	Balances June 30, 19X5	Fiscal 19X5–19X6 Activity Debit	Fiscal 19X5–19X6 Activity Credit	Balances June 30, 19X6
Cash	$180,000	$ 955,000	$ 880,000	$255,000
Taxes receivable	20,000	809,000	781,000	48,000
Allowance for uncollectible taxes	(4,000)	6,000	9,000	(7,000)
	$196,000			$296,000
Vouchers payable	$ 44,000	813,000	822,000	$ 53,000
Due to Internal Service Fund	2,000	7,000	10,000	5,000
Due to Debt Service Fund	10,000	60,000	100,000	50,000
Fund balance reserved for encumbrances	40,000	40,000	47,000	47,000
Unreserved fund balance	100,000	47,000	88,000	141,000
	$196,000	$2,737,000	$2,737,000	$296,000

Additional Information
1. The budget for fiscal 19X5–19X6 included estimated revenues of $1,000,000, appropriations of $905,000 (including $40,000 pertaining to encumbrances outstanding at 6/30/X5), and $100,000 to be transferred to a debt service fund.
2. Expenditures totaled $832,000, of which $37,000 pertained to encumbrances outstanding at 6/30/X5.
3. Purchase orders issued during 19X5–19X6 totaled $170,000.
4. The city does not use delinquent accounts for delinquent taxes.
5. The net realizable amount for taxes receivable at each year-end was expected to be collected within 60 days.

Required
1. Using the given data, reconstruct the original detailed journal entries that were required to record all transactions for the fiscal year ended 6/30/X6, including the recording of the current year budget. (*Hint:* Using T accounts will help.)
2. Prepare the year-end *closing* entries from the entries you have reconstructed.
3. Prepare a budgetary comparison statement of revenues, expenditures, and changes in fund balance for the current year. (AICPA adapted)

P 24–7 **General Fund: Reconstructing Transactions and Preparing Closing Entries and Preparing an Operating Statement** The following transaction summary is from the accounts of the Good Times School District General Fund *before* the books had been closed for the fiscal year ended 6/30/X5:

	Postclosing Balances June 30, 19X4	Preclosing Balances June 30, 19X5
Actual Accounts		
Cash	$400,000	$ 630,000
Property taxes receivable—Delinquent	150,000	180,000
Allowance for uncollectibles—Delinquent	(40,000)	(80,000)
Expenditures	—	2,900,000
	$510,000	$3,630,000
Vouchers payable	$ 80,000	$ 408,000
Due to other funds	210,000	62,000
Fund balance reserved for encumbrances	60,000	—
Unreserved fund balance	160,000	220,000

(*continued*)

	Postclosing Balances June 30, 19X4	Preclosing Balances June 30, 19X5
Revenues from property taxes	—	2,800,000
Miscellaneous revenues	—	140,000
	$510,000	$3,630,000

Budgetary Accounts

ESTIMATED REVENUES	$3,000,000
ENCUMBRANCES	91,000
	$3,091,000
APPROPRIATIONS	$2,980,000
BUDGETARY FUND BALANCE	20,000
BUDGETARY FUND BALANCE RESERVED FOR ENCUMBRANCES	91,000
	$3,091,000

Additional Information

1. The property tax levy for the year ended 6/30/X5 was $2,870,000. Taxes collected during the year totaled $2,810,000, of which $100,000 pertained to delinquent balances as of 6/30/X4. Of the 6/30/X4 delinquent balances, $30,000 was written off as uncollectible. Unpaid taxes become delinquent at the end of the fiscal year. The net realizable amount at each year-end was expected to be collected within 60 days.

2. Encumbrances outstanding at each year-end are *always* honored in the following year; they are re-budgeted or reappropriated in the following year. During the current year, invoices totaling $58,000 were rendered on encumbrances outstanding at the *beginning* of the year. On 5/2/X5, commitment documents were issued to purchase new textbooks at a cost of $91,000. Only this encumbrance is outstanding at 6/30/X5. Other purchase orders issued during the year totaled $850,000, with invoices having been rendered for $847,000.

3. An analysis of the transactions in the Vouchers Payable account for the year ended 6/30/X5 follows:

Balance, 6/30/X4	$ 80,000
Expenditures	2,758,000
Cash disbursements	(2,430,000)
Balance, 6/30/X5	$ 408,000

4. During the year, the General Fund was billed $142,000 for services performed on its behalf by other city funds.

Required

1. Using these data, reconstruct the original detailed journal entries required to record all transactions for the fiscal year ended 6/30/X5, including the recording of the current year's budget. (*Hint:* Using T accounts will help.)
2. Prepare the *closing* entries at 6/30/X5.
3. Prepare a statement of revenues, expenditures, and changes in fund balance for fiscal 19X4–19X5.

(AICPA adapted)

P 24–8 **Challenger: Preparing Adjusting and Closing Entries; Preparing Balance Sheet and Budgetary Comparison Statement—Nongeneral Fund Transactions *Improperly* Recorded in General Fund** The General Fund trial balances of the ABC School District at 6/30/X7 follow:

ABC School District
General Fund Trial Balances
June 30, 19X7

	Dr.	Cr.
Actual Accounts		
Cash	$ 60,000	
Taxes Receivable—Current Year	31,800	
Allowance for Uncollectibles—Current Year Taxes		$ 1,800
Inventory of Supplies	10,000	
Buildings	1,300,000	

(continued)

Bonds Payable		500,000
Vouchers Payable		12,000
Operating Expenses:		
Administration	25,000	
Instruction	602,000	
Other	221,000	
Capital Outlays (equipment)	22,000	
Debit Service (interest)	30,000	
State Grant Revenue		300,000
Revenues from Tax Levy, Licenses, and Fines		1,008,000
Unreserved Fund Balance		480,000
Totals	$2,301,800	$2,301,800

Budgetary Accounts

Estimated Revenues	$1,007,000	
Appropriations		$1,000,000
Budgetary Fund Balance		7,000
Totals	$1,007,000	$1,007,000

Additional Information

1. The recorded allowance for uncollectible current year taxes is considered sufficient. Unpaid taxes become delinquent at year-end. The net realizable amount for taxes receivable at each year-end was expected to be collected within 60 days.
2. During the year, the local governmental unit gave the school district 20 acres of land for a new grade school and a community playground. The unrecorded estimated value of the land donated was $50,000. In addition, a state grant of $300,000 was received, and the full amount was used to pay contracts pertaining to the construction of the grade school. Purchases of classroom and playground equipment costing $22,000 were paid from general funds of the school district.
3. On 7/1/X2, a 5%, 10-year serial bond issue in the amount of $1,000,000 for constructing school buildings was issued. Principal payments of $100,000 must be made each June 30, along with interest for the year. All payments required through 6/30/X7 have been made. (Serial bonds have annual principal payments over the life of the bond issue, whereas term bonds are repaid in total at the maturity date.)
4. Outstanding purchase orders for operating expenses not recorded in the accounts at year-end follow:

Administration	$1,000
Instruction	1,400
Other	600
Total	$3,000

    The school district honors encumbrances outstanding at each year-end and *reappropriates* amounts in the following year's budget. No encumbrances were outstanding at 6/30/X6.

5. Appropriations for the year consisted of the following:

Current

Administration	$ 25,000
Instruction	600,000
Other	222,000
Capital Outlay	23,000

Debt Service

Principal	100,000
Interest	30,000
	$1,000,000

6. The *consumption method* is used for the supplies inventory ($9,000 balance at 6/30/X6).

Required

1. Prepare the appropriate adjusting entry to eliminate the activities and accounts that the school district should account for in separate funds or account groups outside the General Fund. (It is not

necessary to prepare the entries that would be made in these other funds or account groups to account properly for these items.) (*Note: Problem 24–8 will be used in the requirement for Problem 25–9.*)

2. Prepare any adjusting entries to accounts that are properly part of the General Fund.
3. Prepare the closing entries relating to the General Fund.
4. Prepare a balance sheet at 6/30/X7.
5. Prepare a statement of revenues, expenditures, and changes in fund balance for the year ended 6/30/X7, comparing budgeted amounts with actual amounts. (The beginning fund balance amount must be "forced" as though a correcting entry had been made at 6/30/X6.)

(AICPA adapted)

✳ THINKING CRITICALLY ✳

✳ CASES ✳

C 24–1 **Did They Submit a Balanced Budget?** Mirage City's finance director is required to submit a balanced budget to the city council each year. For 19X2, the following budget was submitted:

Estimated revenues	$1,000,000
Appropriations	960,000

In November 19X1, the city concluded three days of negotiations with its employees' union. Immediately prior to these negotiations, the city's pension fund was fully funded. Thus the city had no pension obligation. The revised union contract, however, increased pension benefits for all current active employees by 2%, a retroactive increase. As a result, the city's pension obligation immediately went from zero to $3,000,000; which will be funded over the next 30 years. The 19X2 budgeted appropriations include $100,000 for funding this increase in pension benefits. For simplicity, assume that the average age of the city's union employees is 50 and that all union employees retire at age 60.

Required   1. Did the city manager submit a balanced budget for 19X2?
2. How does the concept of interperiod equity apply here?

C 24–2 **Modified Accrual Basis of Accounting** As an accountant for the city of Tulipville, you assist the city manager in answering questions raised at city council meetings. At one meeting, a taxpayer asks why the city uses the *modified accrual basis* of accounting for its General Fund rather than the *accrual basis*, which is required for public corporations in the private sector. Furthermore, the taxpayer would like to know "the magnitude of the misstatement at the end of the recently concluded fiscal year as a result of not using the accrual basis." Assume that the city has an income tax, a sales tax, a property transfer tax, a property tax, and annual business licenses.

Required   Respond to these questions.

C 24–3 **What Is It?** In May 19X1, a city incurred $2,000 of legal fees directly traceable to the Airport Enterprise Fund. The legal fees were paid out of the General Fund and charged to the Expenditures account. In June 19X1, the Airport Enterprise Fund sent a $2,000 check to the General Fund.

Required   1. How would you report these transactions in the operating statement of the General Fund and the Airport Enterprise Fund?
2. How would you classify the June 19X1 transaction between the two funds?

C 24–4 **Accruing Vested Sick Leave: It Seems Too Simple** On 1/1/X1, Lynn began work at Funn City at an annual salary of $52,000. City policy allows unused sick leave to be converted into a cash payment upon termination. The city does *not* have a pension plan; its employees are covered by social security.

Lynn was *not* sick on any day during 19X1. If Lynn's employment at Funn City were terminated on 12/31/X1 (for whatever reason), Lynn would be entitled to receive one week's salary.

Required   Determine the liability to be accrued at 12/31/X1 relating to this compensated absence.

✳ FINANCIAL ANALYSIS PROBLEM ✳

FAP 24–1 **Developing Financial Statements Without Referring to the Chapter Material** The City of Twin Hills was incorporated on 1/1/X1. The city had the following transactions and events during 19X1:

1. **Property taxes.** Property taxes of $650,000 for calendar-year 19X1 were assessed. Collections totaled $580,000. At 12/31/X1, $10,000 is expected to be uncollectible.
2. **Bond issuance.** On 1/1/X1, the city issued 7% general obligation bonds (face value of $1,000,000) for $1,000,000. The proceeds were used to build a city hall, which was completed on 6/30/X1 and is expected to last 50 years.
3. **Bond principal payments.** The 10% bond issue is to be repaid $40,000 per year beginning 12/31/X1. The 19X1 year-end principal payment was made on time.
4. **Bond interest payments.** Interest is due semiannually on July 1 and January 1 with a five-day grace period. The 7/1/X1 interest payment of $35,000 was made on time. The 1/1/X2 interest payment of $35,000 was made *on* that date.
5. **Supplies inventories.** Of the $90,000 of supplies ordered, $77,000 worth were received, $65,000 of which had been paid for by year-end. The physical inventory at year-end totals $20,000.
6. **Sidewalk improvements.** The city incurred $60,000 of costs (paid for by year-end) for making sidewalk improvements.
7. **Payroll costs.** City employees were paid $300,000. At 12/31/X1, $23,000 is owed but unpaid to these employees.
8. **Compensated absences—vacation.** Two of the city's employees did *not* take vacations during 19X1. Unused vacation pay vests ($4,000 for these two employees).
9. **Compensated absences—sick leave.** Unused sick leave days also vest. At 12/31/X1, $16,000 would be paid to the city's employees if their employment with the city were terminated.

Required

1. Determine how these transactions should be meaningfully reported (if at all) in the city's balance sheet at 12/31/X1. Make this determination independently of the chapter material (which may not necessarily be the best manner of reporting). Accordingly, do *not* refer to the material in the chapter.
2. Prepare a balance sheet at 12/31/X1. (It may be helpful to record the transactions in T accounts for the more frequently used accounts, such as Cash and Accounts/Vouchers Payable for ease to determine the ending balances).
3. Consider how the increase in the city's net assets for the year should be reported in an operating statement that you deem meaningful. Again, do *not* refer to the material in the chapter to determine your answer.
4. Prepare an operating statement for the year ended 12/31/X1. Compare the operating statement you developed with the one used by governmental units.

FAP 24–2   **The Social Security "Trust" Fund: Real or Imaginary—Will a Consolidated Perspective Reveal the Truth?**   If FAP 1–1 was *not* assigned while covering Chapter 1, it can be assigned in this chapter instead.

✳ PERSONAL SITUATION: ETHICS AND INTERPERSONAL SKILLS ✳

PS 24–1   **Ethics: Telling It Like It Is or Is Not?**   The operating statement is defined as the statement that discloses the results of operations for an entity in conformity with GAAP.

Required

1. Is it misleading for governmental units to use the title *operating statement* when such statement is so narrowly defined that it excludes depreciation expense and many liabilities incurred during the period?
2. If so, can you think of a more informative title? (Can you think of a more misleading title?)

ANSWERS TO SELF-STUDY QUESTIONS

1. a   2. c   3. a   4. d   5. c   6. b   7. b   8. c   9. a   10. d   11. b   12. e   13. d
14. b   15. e   16. d   17. d   18. e   19. c   20. c   21. b   22. c   23. c   24. c   25. a
26. d   27. e   28. f   29. b

GOVERNMENTAL ACCOUNTING: THE SPECIAL-PURPOSE FUNDS AND ACCOUNT GROUPS

LEARNING OBJECTIVES

TO UNDERSTAND

- When to record a transaction in one of the special funds or account groups.
- The way to account for transactions in the remaining funds and in the related account groups.
- The financial reporting pyramid concept.
- The financial statements to be included in the general-purpose financial statements.
- The major GASB project currently in process that could greatly change governmental financial reporting.

TOPIC OUTLINE

Deficit spending is simply a scheme for the "hidden" confiscation of wealth.

ALAN GREENSPAN
CHAIRMAN, FEDERAL
RESERVE BOARD

CHAPTER OVERVIEW

In Chapter 24, we discussed the General Fund. In this chapter, we discuss the remaining six types of funds used for governmental accounting, the General Fixed Asset Account Group (GFAAG), and the General Long-Term Debt Account Group (GLTDAG). Concerning the number of funds to be used by a governmental unit, the GASB *Codification* states:

> Only the minimum number of funds consistent with legal and operating requirements should be established . . . since unnecessary funds result in inflexibility, undue complexity and inefficient financial administration.[1]

Certain governmental revenues, functions, or activities often must be accounted for in a designated fund separate from all others. In some situations, greater accounting control may be obtained by using a separate fund, even though it is not required by law. In most cases, the type of fund to be used to account for the specific revenues, functions, or activities is readily determinable. In a few instances, selecting the most appropriate type of fund requires greater scrutiny.

Certain transactions or events require entries in one or more funds or account groups. For example, the decision to build a new civic center to be financed by issuing general obligation bonds eventually results in entries being made in a Capital Projects Fund, a Debt Service Fund, the GFAAG, the GLTDAG, and in some cases the General Fund.

THE REMAINING GOVERNMENTAL FUNDS AND THE ACCOUNT GROUPS

I SPECIAL REVENUE FUNDS

Special Revenue Funds account for **"the proceeds of specific revenue sources (other than expendable trusts or for major capital projects) that are legally restricted to expenditure for specified purposes."**[2] Special Revenue Funds may be used for such small activities as the maintenance of a municipal swimming pool or such gigantic ones as operating a state highway system. The distinguishing feature of a Special Revenue Fund is that its revenues are obtained primarily from tax and nontax sources not directly related to services rendered or facilities provided for use. In other words, revenues are *not* obtained primarily from direct charges to the users of the services or facilities. Conceptually, therefore, Special Revenue Funds are the opposite of *most* Enterprise Funds, which recover the majority of their operating costs from charges to users.

The GASB *Codification* requires the use of Enterprise Funds when the costs of providing goods or services are recovered primarily from user charges. In addition, **under certain circumstances,** which we discuss later, Enterprise Funds may be used for activities that do not recover their costs primarily from user charges. The following activities could be accounted for in either Special Revenue Funds or Enterprise Funds, depending on the individual facts, circumstances, and operating policies: off-street parking facilities, transportation systems, turnpikes, golf courses, swimming pools, libraries, and auditoriums.

---

[1] *Codification of Governmental Accounting and Financial Reporting Standards* (Stamford, CT: Governmental Accounting Standards Board, 1987), sec. 1100.104.

[2] GASB *Cod.*, sec. 1300.104.

Special Revenue Funds may derive their revenues from one or several sources, commonly (1) specified property tax levies, (2) state gasoline taxes, (3) licenses, (4) grants, and (5) shared taxes from other governmental units (including federal revenue sharing).

Unless legal provisions specify the contrary, Special Revenue Funds are accounted for using the same accounting principles, procedures, and financial statements shown for the General Fund in Chapter 24. Accordingly, we do *not* illustrate any journal entries for Special Revenue Funds.

II PREVIEW OF INTERRELATIONSHIP OF CAPITAL PROJECTS FUNDS, DEBT SERVICE FUNDS, AND RELATED ACCOUNT GROUPS

Virtually all governmental buildings are constructed by governmental units and are financed by bond offerings. In commercial accounting, all of this activity (constructing the building, subsequently capitalizing and accounting for the building, and servicing the debt incurred to finance the construction of the building) is accounted for using one general ledger. In government, four general ledgers are used—two of which are funds and two of which are account groups.

This separation into four general ledgers results in the following arrangement:

1. **Capital Projects Fund.** Receives cash from bond offerings and uses cash to construct fixed assets (reporting the outflow of resources as expenditures).

2. **General Fixed Assets Account Group.** Accounts for fixed assets during and after construction.

3. **General Long-Term Debt Account Group.** Accounts for unmatured general long-term debt (GLTD). At the maturity date, the liability is transferred to a Debt Service Fund.

4. **Debt Service Fund.** Services GLTD, making both interest and principal payments using money obtained from tax levies or operating transfers from the General Fund.

This system is somewhat cumbersome and can be confusing when first trying to learn it. Accordingly, in Illustration 25–1, we present a simplified number of events and transactions. To highlight the effect on the asset and liability accounts (one of which is used in each journal entry), the other half of each entry is shown in a shaded format. These shaded portions of each entry involve either (1) a "flow" account (describing the nature of the inflow or the nature of the outflow) in the two funds or (2) a "balancing" account in the two account groups. The flow accounts used in the two funds were discussed and illustrated in Chapter 24. The balancing accounts are discussed in detail later in this chapter.

III CAPITAL PROJECTS FUNDS

Capital Projects Funds account for

> financial resources to be used for the acquisition or construction of major capital facilities (other than those financed by proprietary funds and Trust Funds).[3]

Examples of major capital facilities are administration buildings, auditoriums, civic centers, and libraries. These funds do not account for the purchase of fixed assets having comparatively limited lives, such as vehicles, machinery, and office

---

[3]GASB *Cod.*, sec. 1300.104.

ILLUSTRATION 25–1 — Overview of Interrelationship of Capital Projects Fund, Debt Service Fund, General Fixed Assets Account Group, and General Long-Term Debt Account Group—Flow and Balancing Accounts Shown in Shaded Format

Event or Transaction	Capital Projects Fund Dr.	Capital Projects Fund Cr.	General Fixed Assets Account Group Dr.	General Fixed Assets Account Group Cr.	General Long-Term Debt Account Group Dr.	General Long-Term Debt Account Group Cr.	Debt Service Fund Dr.	Debt Service Fund Cr.
1. Issue bonds.	Cash.... 50,000	Other Financing Sources— Bond Proceeds... 50,000			Amount to Be Provided... 50,000	Bonds Payable... 50,000		
2. Construct new building.			Buildings 50,000	Investment in General Fixed Assets 50,000				
3. Bond matures.					Bonds Payable.... 50,000	Amount to Be Provided.. 50,000	Expenditures.. 50,000	Bonds Payable ... 50,000
4. Operating transfer made from General Fund.[a]							Cash........ 50,000	Other Financing Sources— Operating Transfer In.. 50,000
5. Redeem bonds.							Bonds Payable 50,000	Cash........ 50,000

[a]The General Fund debits Other Financing Uses—Operating Transfer Out for $50,000.

equipment, which are normally budgeted for and acquired through the General Fund or a Special Revenue Fund and recorded as expenditures.

Capital Projects Funds **do *not* account for the fixed assets acquired—only for the construction of the fixed assets.** The fixed assets constructed are accounted for in the GFAAG, which is discussed in Chapter 24 and later in the chapter. Furthermore, Capital Projects Funds do not account for the repayment and servicing of any debt obligations issued to raise money to finance the acquisition of capital facilities. Such debt and related servicing is accounted for in the GLTDAG and a Debt Service Fund, both of which we discuss later in the chapter.

Capital Projects Funds are categorized as governmental funds. Recall that the measurement basis for governmental funds is sources and uses (and balances) of current financial resources. Accordingly, the same financial statements used for the General Fund are used for Capital Projects Funds. Likewise, the modified accrual basis of accounting is used.

ESTABLISHMENT AND OPERATION

Capital Projects Funds are usually established on a project-by-project basis because legal requirements may vary from one project to another. (Some governmental units include capital budgets as part of their annual appropriated budget, in which case the annual capital budget is recorded in the general ledgers of the various Capital Projects Funds.) Most capital facilities are financed by issuing general obligation bonds, the liability for which is recorded in the GLTDAG. In many cases, some portion is financed by the General Fund or a Special Revenue Fund. Such transfers are **operating transfers,** which we discussed in Chapter 24. Federal and state grants are another major source of funds.

Contracted labor usually constructs major capital facilities. Because encumbrance accounting procedures alone are usually deemed sufficient for control purposes, recording the budgeted amounts in the general ledger is usually considered unnecessary. Construction costs incurred are charged to expenditures. At each year-end, expenditures are closed out to the Unreserved Fund Balance account, as are any amounts recorded in accounts pertaining to bond proceeds and operating transfers in for the year. Each Capital Project Fund is terminated upon completion of the project for which it was created.

At the completion of the project, the cost of the facility is recorded as a fixed asset in the GFAAG. Until then, any costs incurred are shown as Construction Work in Progress in the GFAAG. Generally, the year-end closing entry in the Capital Projects Fund triggers the recording of an amount in the GFAAG equal to the credit to the Expenditures account. (We explain more fully later in the chapter that the GASB *Codification* makes optional recording certain types of improvements constructed through Capital Projects Funds in the GFAAG.

ISSUING BONDS AT A PREMIUM Bond premiums (and discounts, discussed shortly) arise because of adjustments to the interest rate. The bond indenture agreements usually specify that any bond premium is to be set aside in the related Debt Service Fund. This is desirable because it removes the incentive to spend more on a project than is authorized merely by raising additional cash by increasing the interest rate. In the Capital Projects Fund, the proceeds of the bond offering—including the premium—are reported as an Other Financing Source—Bond Proceeds in the operating statement. The transfer of the premium to the Debt Service Fund is reported as an operating transfer out in the Capital Projects Fund and an operating transfer in in the Debt Service Fund. Regardless of whether the bonds are issued at a premium (or a discount), the bond issue is recorded at its face amount in the GLTDAG.

ISSUING BONDS AT A DISCOUNT Bond discounts are rare because the stated interest rate is usually set high enough so that no discount results. (Many governmental units are legally prohibited from issuing bonds at a discount.) If a discount does result, theoretically there should be a transfer from the related Debt Service Fund to the Capital Projects Fund to cover the shortfall. In practice, such a transfer may not be possible because money may not be available in the related Debt Service Fund or because of legal restraints. In such cases, the size of the project may be curtailed or the shortage may be covered by an operating transfer from the General Fund.

INVESTING EXCESS CASH UNTIL NEEDED All the money necessary to pay for the capital project is usually raised at or near the inception of the project, but contractors are paid as work progresses. Excess cash, therefore, may be temporarily invested in high-quality, interest-bearing securities. In such cases, the interest income on the investments is credited to revenues in the Capital Projects Fund. This inflow of resources may be spent on the project or transferred to the related Debt Service Fund (an operating transfer), depending on legal requirements.

DISPOSING OF CASH REMAINING AT COMPLETION DATE Any cash remaining at the completion date is disposed of in accordance with legal requirements. In most cases, the remaining cash is transferred to the related Debt Service Fund, with the transfer reported as a residual equity transfer.

PAYING FOR COST OVERRUNS The source of additional money to pay for cost overruns is specified by legal requirements or operating policy. In most cases, an operating transfer is made from the General Fund to pay for the cost overrun.

ILLUSTRATION | **JOURNAL ENTRIES AND FINANCIAL STATEMENTS**

Assume that Funn City established a Capital Projects Fund during the fiscal year ended June 30, 19X2, to construct a new city hall. Assumed transactions pertaining to the establishment and operation of the fund, along with the related journal entries, follow:

1. **Fund establishment.** The new city hall is expected to cost $5,000,000. The city obtained a **capital grant** of $1,500,000 from the state government, of which $600,000 was contributed at the inception of the project. The remaining $900,000 is deemed to be susceptible to accrual. The General Fund contributes $500,000, of which $200,000 was contributed at the inception of the project.

Cash	600,000	
Grant Receivable from State Government	900,000	
Revenues		1,500,000
To record amounts received and due		
from the state government.		
Cash	200,000	
Due from General Fund	300,000	
Other Financing Sources—Operating Transfer In		500,000
To record amounts received and due		
from the General Fund.		

2. **Bond sales.** The remaining $3,000,000 was obtained from the sale of general obligation bonds at 101. The bond indenture agreement requires any premium to be set aside in the related Debt Service Fund.

| Cash | 3,030,000 | |
| Other Financing Sources—Bond Proceeds | | 3,030,000 |

To record the sale of general obligation bonds.

| Other Financing Uses—Operating Transfers Out | 30,000 | |
| Cash | | 30,000 |

To transfer bond premium to Debt Service Fund.

Recall that the bond liability must also be recorded in the GLTDAG. That entry is as follows:

| Amount to Be Provided for Payment of Bonds | 3,000,000 | |
| Bonds Payable | | 3,000,000 |

An additional entry must be made in the GLTDAG as follows:

| Amount Available for Payment of Bonds | 30,000 | |
| Amount to Be Provided for Payment of Bonds | | 30,000 |

3. **Construction-related activity.** A construction contract for $4,600,000 is authorized and signed. During the year ended June 30, 19X2, billings of $2,700,000 were rendered, and payments totaling $2,200,000 were made.

| ENCUMBRANCES | 4,600,000 | |
| BUDGETARY FUND BALANCE RESERVED FOR ENCUMBRANCES | | 4,600,000 |

To record encumbrance on construction contract.

| BUDGETARY FUND BALANCE RESERVED FOR ENCUMBRANCES | 2,700,000 | |
| ENCUMBRANCES | | 2,700,000 |

To cancel part of encumbrance for project contract with general contractor for completions to date.

| Expenditures | 2,700,000 | |
| Contracts Payable | | 2,700,000 |

To record *actual* expenditures to date on contract with general contractor for completions to date.

| Contracts Payable | 2,200,000 | |
| Cash | | 2,200,000 |

To record payments to contractor.

In addition to the preceding construction contract, $390,000 was incurred for the services of architects and engineers. Of this amount, $310,000 was paid. (For simplicity, we assume that encumbrance accounting procedures were *not* used.)

| Expenditures | 390,000 | |
| Vouchers Payable | | 390,000 |

To record fees for architects and engineers.

| Vouchers Payable | 310,000 | |
| Cash | | 310,000 |

To record payment of architect and engineering fees.

4. **Closing entries.** The appropriate closing entries at June 30, 19X2, are as follows:

Revenues	1,500,000	
Other Financing Sources—Bond Proceeds	3,030,000	
Other Financing Sources—Operating Transfer In	500,000	

(continued)

Expenditures ($2,700,000 + $390,000)		3,090,000
Other Financing Uses—Operating Transfers Out		30,000
Unreserved Fund Balance		1,910,000

To close out *actual* revenues, other financing
sources and uses, and expenditures into
unreserved fund balance.

BUDGETARY FUND BALANCE RESERVED		
FOR ENCUMBRANCES	1,900,000	
ENCUMBRANCES		1,900,000

To close encumbrances outstanding at year-end by
reversing the entry that previously recorded them.

Unreserved Fund Balance	1,900,000	
Fund Balance Reserved for Encumbrances		1,900,000

To record *actual* fund balance reserve account to
indicate the portion of year-end balance segregated
for expenditure upon contractor performance.

In addition to the preceding closing entries, the partially completed capital facility must be reflected in the GFAAG at June 30, 19X2. These accounts are discussed in detail later in the chapter. For now, you should know that the following entry would be made:

Construction Work in Progress	3,090,000	
Investment in General Fixed Assets		
from Capital Projects		3,090,000

To record city hall construction in progress.

FINANCIAL STATEMENTS   The financial statements that would be prepared for the fiscal year ended June 30, 19X2, as a result of the preceding journal entries are shown in Illustrations 25–2 and 25–3.

COMPLETION OF PROJECT IN FOLLOWING YEAR   Assume that the project is completed in the following fiscal year. The journal entries made during the fiscal year ended June 30, 19X3, follow.

ILLUSTRATION 25–2

Funn City
Capital Projects Fund—City Hall
Balance Sheet
June 30, 19X2

Assets

Cash	$1,290,000
Grant receivable	900,000
Due from General Fund	300,000
Total Assets	$2,490,000

Liabilities and Fund Balance

Vouchers payable	$ 80,000
Contracts payable	500,000
Total Liabilities	$ 580,000
Fund Balance:	
Reserved for encumbrances	$1,900,000
Unreserved	10,000
Total Fund Balance	$1,910,000
Total Liabilities and Fund Balance	$2,490,000

ILLUSTRATION 25–3

Funn City
Capital Projects Fund—City Hall
Statement of Revenues, Expenditures,
and Changes in Fund Balance
For the Fiscal Year Ended June 30, 19X2

Revenues
Intergovernmental—state grant . . . . $ 1,500,000

Expenditures
Capital outlay . . . . (3,090,000)
Revenues under Expenditures . . . . $(1,590,000)

Other Financing Sources (Uses)
Proceeds of general obligation bonds . . . . $ 3,030,000
Operating transfer in from General Fund 500,000
Operating transfer out to Debt Service Fund . . . . (30,000)
Total Other Financing Sources (Uses) . . . . $ 3,500,000
Excess of Revenues and Other Sources over Expenditures
and Other Uses . . . . $ 1,910,000
Fund Balance, July 1, 19X1 . . . . –0–
Fund Balance, June 30, 19X2 . . . . $ 1,910,000

---

1. **Reestablishment of budgetary control over outstanding encumbrances.** Budgetary control must be reestablished over outstanding encumbrances on July 1, 19X2. This is done by reversing the prior year-end closing entries related to encumbrances.

ENCUMBRANCES	1,900,000	
BUDGETARY FUND BALANCE RESERVED		
FOR ENCUMBRANCES		1,900,000
To reestablish budgetary control on remainder		
of construction contract.		
Fund Balance Reserved for Encumbrances	1,900,000	
Unreserved Fund Balance		1,900,000
To reverse appropriation of fund balance made at		
6/30/X2 relating to encumbrances outstanding at		
6/30/X2, which will be honored during the current year.		

2. **Cash receipts.** All receivables were collected.

Cash	900,000	
Grant Receivable		900,000
To record collection of grant receivable.		
Cash	300,000	
Due from General Fund		300,000
To record collection of amounts received from the General Fund.		

3. **Construction-related activity.** The contractor submitted bills for the remainder of the contract. Additional engineering services totaled $6,000. All liabilities were paid.

BUDGETARY FUND BALANCE RESERVED		
FOR ENCUMBRANCES	1,900,000	
ENCUMBRANCES		1,900,000
To cancel remainder of encumbrance for project contract		
with general contractor upon completion of contract.		

Expenditures	1,900,000	
Contracts Payable		1,900,000
To record expenditures relating to billings on		
remainder of contract.		
Contracts Payable	2,400,000	
Cash		2,400,000
To record payments to contractor.		
Expenditures	6,000	
Vouchers Payable		6,000
To record fees for engineering services.		
Vouchers Payable	86,000	
Cash		86,000
To record payment of engineering fees.		
($6,000 + $80,000 owed at 6/30/X2).		

4. **Disposition of remaining cash.** After payment of all liabilities, $4,000 of remaining cash was transferred to the Debt Service Fund.

Residual Equity Transfer Out	4,000	
Cash		4,000
To record transfer of remaining cash to Debt Service Fund.		

5. **Closing entry.** The appropriate closing entry at June 30, 19X3, follows:

Unreserved Fund Balance	1,910,000	
Expenditures		1,906,000
Residual Equity Transfer Out		4,000
To close out expenditure and residual equity transfer		
out into Unreserved Fund Balance.		

In addition to the preceding closing entry, the fully completed capital facility would be reflected in the GFAAG at June 30, 19X3, as a result of the following entry in these accounts:

Buildings	4,996,000	
Construction Work in Progress		3,090,000
Investment in General Fixed Assets		
from Capital Projects		1,906,000
To record completed city hall in the GFAAG.		

FINANCIAL STATEMENTS FOR YEAR ENDED JUNE 30, 19X3   Because all liabilities were paid by June 30, 19X3, and no assets remained, a balance sheet at June 30, 19X3, is not necessary. The operating statement for the year ended June 30, 19X3, is shown in Illustration 25–4.

ILLUSTRATION 25–4

Funn City
Capital Projects Fund—City Hall
Statement of Revenues, Expenditures,
and Changes in Fund Balance
For the Fiscal Year Ended June 30, 19X3

Revenues	$ –0–
Expenditures:	
Capital outlay	(1,906,000)
Excess of Expenditures over Revenues	$(1,906,000)
Fund Balance, 7/1/X2	1,910,000
Residual equity transfer out to Debt Service Fund	(4,000)
Fund Balance, 6/30/X3	$ –0–

IV GENERAL FIXED ASSETS ACCOUNT GROUP

The GFAAG is created to account for a governmental unit's fixed assets not accounted for in an Enterprise Fund, an Internal Service Fund, or a Trust Fund. This group of accounts is not a fund but a self-balancing group of accounts. Each asset recorded in the group of accounts has a corresponding offsetting credit descriptive of the asset's source. The following are the five asset accounts generally used:

1. Land.

2. Buildings.

3. Improvements other than buildings.

4. Equipment.

5. Construction work in progress.

A statement of general fixed assets classified by type of asset is the basic financial statement for this group of accounts. This statement may be supplemented with (1) a statement showing these assets broken down by function, activity, or department and (2) a statement showing the changes in the account balances for the year. A typical statement of general fixed assets classified by type of account and source is shown in Illustration 25–5.

As mentioned previously, not all improvements constructed through Capital Projects Funds must be recorded in the GFAAG. According to the GASB *Codification*,

> Reporting public domain or "infrastructure" fixed assets— roads, bridges, curbs and gutters, streets and sidewalks, drainage systems, lighting systems, and similar assets that are immovable and of value only to the governmental unit—is optional.[4]

ILLUSTRATION 25–5

Funn City
Statement of General Fixed Assets
June 30, 19X2

General Fixed Assets

Land	$ 1,300,000
Buildings	12,900,000
Improvements other than buildings	1,100,000
Equipment	450,000
Construction work in progress	3,600,000[a]
Total General Fixed Assets	$19,350,000

Investment in General Fixed Assets from:

Capital Projects Funds—	
General obligation bonds	$15,300,000
Federal grants	1,000,000
State grants	800,000
County grants	600,000
General Fund revenues	560,000
Special Revenue Fund revenues	310,000
Gifts	180,000
Special assessments	600,000
Total Investment in General Fixed Assets	$19,350,000

[a]This is work in progress in the Capital Projects Funds.

---

[4]GASB *Cod.*, sec. 1400.109.

In practice, only a small percentage of governmental units capitalize and report "infrastructure" fixed assets in the GFAAG.

ACCOUNTING PROCEDURES

Most high-dollar general fixed assets originate from Capital Projects Funds. Most of the equipment shown in this account group originates from expenditures made through the General Fund and Special Revenue Funds. When such assets are constructed or acquired, each of these three funds debits Expenditures. At the same time or at the end of the fiscal year, entries are made in the GFAAG debiting the appropriate asset category and crediting the appropriate source investment accounts.

Entries relating to the construction of a new city hall that would be made in the GFAAG were shown earlier in the discussion of the Capital Projects Funds. A typical entry pertaining to the acquisition of equipment by the General Fund is as follows:

Equipment	47,000	
Investment in General Fixed Assets from		
General Fund Revenues		47,000
To record equipment purchased through the General Fund.		

General fixed assets acquired through purchase or construction are recorded at cost. Assets arising from gifts or donations are recorded at their estimated current fair values at the time of donation. On abandonment, the entry is reversed. On sale, the entry is reversed, and the sales proceeds are recorded as an inflow of resources in the General Fund (typically) using the account Other Financing Sources—Proceeds from Sale of Fixed Assets. As discussed in Chapter 24, accumulated depreciation may be reflected for general fixed assets in the GFAAG at the option of the governmental unit. Depreciation expense, however, may not be reported in the operating statements of the governmental funds.

The GASB *Codification* covers accounting for lease agreements and requires that FASB *Statement No. 13*, "Accounting for Leases," be followed.

V DEBT SERVICE FUNDS

For discussion purposes, long-term debt of governmental units may be categorized as follows:

1. **Revenue bonds.** Revenue bonds are issued to finance the establishment or expansion of activities accounted for in Enterprise Funds. These bonds are shown as liabilities of the Enterprise Funds because their repayment and servicing can come only from money generated from the operations of those funds.

2. **General obligation bonds serviced from Enterprise Funds.** General obligation bonds also are issued to finance establishment or expansion of activities accounted for in Enterprise Funds. They bear the full faith and credit of the governmental unit. When such bonds are to be repaid and serviced from money generated from the operations of an Enterprise Fund, the bonds should be shown as liabilities of the Enterprise Fund and as a contingent liability of the GLTDAG. (We discuss these bonds more fully later in the chapter.)

3. **All other long-term debt.** All long-term debt not fitting into one of the two preceding categories is shown as a liability of the GLTDAG.

Debt Service Funds are **created for long-term debt that is shown as a liability of the GLTDAG.** Remember that the GLTDAG is not a fund but merely a self-balancing group of accounts that keep track of all unmatured long-term debt in category 3. Debt Service Funds account for the *matured* **portion of and the payment of principal and interest on such long-term debt.** Although notes payable occasionally are encountered, substantially all long-term debt of governmental units consists of one of the following two major types of bonds:

1. **Term bonds'** principal is repaid in a lump sum at their maturity date. Such a lump-sum payment is usually made possible by accumulating money in the Debt Service Fund on an actuarial basis over the life of the bond issue ("sinking fund"). Term bonds are less prevalent than they once were.

2. The principal of **serial bonds** is repaid at various predetermined dates over the life of the issue. **Regular** serial bonds are repaid in equal annual installments. **Deferred serial bonds** also are repaid in equal annual installments, but the first serial payment is delayed a specified number of years. **Irregular serial bonds** are repaid in other than equal principal repayments.

On the date that a principal payment relating to GLTD is to be made, a liability is established in the Debt Service Fund for the amount of the payment. Simultaneously, the amount of the debt as recorded in the GLTDAG is reduced by a like amount. Thus liabilities recorded in this group are effectively transferred at their maturity dates to a Debt Service Fund for their liquidation.

AN UNUSUAL FEATURE   The only unusual feature of Debt Service Funds is the method of accounting for interest on the GLTD. **Interest is not reflected as a liability in the Debt Service Fund until the date it is due and payable.** This use of the cash basis of accounting is the major exception to the accrual of expenditures in the period to which they relate. As a result, interest for the period from the last payment date to the end of the fiscal year is not reflected as a liability at the end of the fiscal year. This is so because governmental units generally budget for interest on the cash basis instead of the accrual basis.

Debt Service Funds are categorized as governmental funds. Accordingly, the modified accrual basis of accounting is used, and the financial statements used for the General Fund are also used for Debt Service Funds.

ESTABLISHMENT AND OPERATION

The legal provisions of a specific debt issue may require the establishment of a separate Debt Service Fund solely for that debt issue. In other cases, several debt issues may be accounted for using a single Debt Service Fund. Concerning the appropriateness of recording budgeted amounts in the general ledger, the GASB *Codification* states that

> it would not be necessary [to record the budget] in controlling most Debt Service Funds, where the amounts required to be received and expended are set forth in bond indentures or sinking fund provisions and few transactions occur each year.[5]

Encumbrance accounting is not appropriate because contracts are not entered into and purchase orders are not issued.

SOURCES OF REVENUES   Debt Service Funds may obtain their revenues from one or several sources. The most common is property taxes. A separate rate is levied for each bond issue or group of bond issues. In these situations, the revenues are recognized on the accrual basis. (The accounting procedures are identical to those used by the General Fund in accounting for property taxes.) Revenues obtained from sources such as shared sales taxes are customarily recorded at the time of

---

[5]GASB *Cod.*, sec. 1700.119.

receipt. When money is to be transferred from the General Fund, a receivable from the General Fund may be recorded at the start of the fiscal year for the amount authorized to be transferred to the Debt Service Fund.

Recall from Chapter 24 that an interfund transfer made in connection with the routine operation of the recipient fund is an *operating transfer.* In this case, the General Fund debits the outflow account, Other Financing Uses—Operating Transfers Out; the Debt Service Fund credits the inflow account, Other Financing Sources—Operating Transfers In. Payments made for principal and interest are recorded as expenditures.

Governmental units commonly use designated fiscal agents to make the payments to the bondholders. In such cases, money is transferred from the Debt Service Funds to the fiscal agents, who submit reports and canceled coupons (if used) to the governmental unit. The fee charged for such services is recorded as an expenditure of the Debt Service Fund.

The operation of Debt Service Funds pertaining to issues of *regular serial bonds* essentially involves collecting revenues and transferring monies to the fiscal agent. Significant accumulations of money requiring investment do *not* occur. In these cases, the journal entries to record the revenues, the expenditures, and the closing of the books parallel those used in the General Fund. Accordingly, an illustration of journal entries and financial statements for this type of Debt Service Fund is not presented.

The operation of Debt Service Funds is more complex when *deferred serial bonds* and *term bonds* are involved. Accumulated money must be invested, and bond premiums and discounts may exist on such investments. Actuarial computations are used to determine additions and earnings. The journal entries and financial statements for a Debt Service Fund pertaining to term bonds are illustrated in the following section.

ILLUSTRATION | **JOURNAL ENTRIES AND FINANCIAL STATEMENTS: TERM BONDS**

Assume that Funn City established a Debt Service Fund on October 1, 19X1, for an 8%, $400,000 general obligation bond issue due in 20 years (the proceeds of which will be used to construct a new civic center). Interest is to be paid semiannually on March 31 and September 30. We assume that all required additions to the fund will come from the General Fund and a specific tax levy. Assumed transactions pertaining to the operation of the fund for the fiscal year ended June 30, 19X2, along with related journal entries, follow:

Transaction or Event	Journal Entry		
The required fund transfer from the General Fund is recorded on 10/1/X1.	Due from General Fund .... Other Financing Sources—Operating Transfer In	5,000	5,000
The required fund transfer is received from the General Fund.	Cash.. Due from General Fund	5,000	5,000
Property taxes are levied.[a]	Property Tax Receivables .... Allowance for Uncollectibles .... Revenues	23,000	1,000 22,000
Property taxes are collected.[b]	Cash.. Property Tax Receivables	20,000	20,000

(continued)

An investment of $8,500 is made.	Investment	8,500	
Cash		8,500
Cash is transferred to the fiscal agent for the 3/31/X2 interest payment.	Cash with Fiscal Agent	16,000	
Cash		16,000
Interest of $16,000 and the fiscal agent's fee of $100 is charged as an expenditure on the interest due date 3/31/X2.	Expenditures	16,100	
Interest Payable		16,000
Accrued Liability		100
Interest is paid by the fiscal agent, and the fiscal agent's fee is paid.	Interest Payable	16,000	
Accrued Liability	100	
Cash with Fiscal Agent		16,000
Cash		100
Interest earned on investments is accrued at 6/30/X2.	Interest Receivable	500	
Revenues		500
The fiscal year-end closing entry is made.	Other Financing Sources—Operating Transfer In	5,000	
Revenues	22,500	
Expenditures		16,100
Fund Balance Reserved for Debt Service		11,400

[a]For simplicity, we (1) credit Revenues initially rather than Deferred Revenues and (2) assume that the entire carrying value at year-end will be collected within 60 days.

[b]For simplicity, we ignore the establishment of delinquent accounts at year-end.

FINANCIAL STATEMENTS   The financial statements that would be prepared for the fiscal year ended June 30, 19X2, as a result of the preceding journal entries are shown in Illustrations 25–6 and 25–7.

The following points are important to understand the financial statements:

1. A liability for interest for the period April 1, 19X2, through June 30, 19X2, is not reflected in the balance sheet at June 30, 19X2, in accordance with the modified accrual basis of accounting. This interest will be shown as an expenditure in the following year when the September 30, 19X2, interest payment is due and payable.

ILLUSTRATION 25–6

Funn City
Debt Service Fund—Civic Center
Balance Sheet
June 30, 19X2

Assets

Cash	$ 400
Property tax receivables	3,000
Less: Allowance for uncollectible taxes	(1,000)
Investments	8,500
Interest receivable	500
Total Assets	$11,400

Fund Balance

Fund balance reserved for debt service	$11,400[a]

[a]The actuarial requirement at 6/30/X2 is $10,200.

ILLUSTRATION 25–7

Funn City
Debt Service Fund—Civic Center
Statement of Revenues, Expenditures,
and Changes in Fund Balance
For the Fiscal Year Ended June 30, 19X2

Revenues	
Property taxes	$22,000
Interest on investments	500
Total Revenues	$22,500
Expenditures	
Interest on bonds	$16,000
Fiscal agent's fees	100
Total Expenditures	$16,100
Revenues over Expenditures	$ 6,400
Other Financing Sources	
Operating transfer in from General Fund	5,000
Excess of Revenues and Other Sources over Expenditures	$11,400[a]
Fund Balance, 7/1/X1	–0–
Fund Balance, 6/30/X2	$11,400

[a]The actuarial requirement for the year was $9,300.

2. If all required additions are made on time and earnings on investments earn the rate assumed in the actuarial calculations, $400,000 will be accumulated in the Debt Service Fund by the maturity date of the bonds (19¼ years from June 30, 19X2).

3. At the maturity date of the bonds, the entire $400,000 is recorded as a liability in the Debt Service Fund by debiting the Expenditures account and crediting Bonds Payable. Simultaneously, this debt is removed from the GLTDAG.

4. Making all required additions and earning interest at rates at least equal to the actuarially assumed interest rate is critical to the accumulation of the $400,000 required to redeem the bonds. If a lower interest rate is actually earned, additional money must be contributed to the fund to make up the shortage. To the extent that earnings exceed the actuarially assumed rate, future contributions may be reduced accordingly.

5. The following essential disclosures for Debt Service Funds pertain to term bonds: (a) the actuarially computed amount that should exist in the Fund Balance account as of the statement of financial position date and (b) the actuarially computed amount of earnings that should have been earned during the current fiscal year.

VI GENERAL LONG-TERM DEBT ACCOUNT GROUP

The GLTDAG presents a governmental unit's debt that (1) has a maturity date of more than one year at the time of issuance and (2) is not properly shown in proprietary funds (Enterprise Funds and Internal Service Funds) or Trust Funds. Such debt is shown as a liability in this account group until its maturity date, when the liability is effectively transferred to the appropriate Debt Service Fund. For governmental purposes, *long-term debt* includes the portion of long-term debt that is due and payable in the coming fiscal year.

As previously discussed, the GLTDAG does *not* include the following types of long-term debt:

1. **Revenue bonds of Enterprise Funds,** which are recorded as liabilities of the applicable Enterprise Funds.
2. **General obligation bonds to be repaid and serviced from Enterprise Fund operations,** which are recorded as liabilities of the applicable Enterprise Funds. (The contingent liability must be disclosed in a footnote.)

When GLTD is created, an entry is made in the GLTDAG crediting a descriptive liability account—for example, Serial Bonds Payable—and debiting an offsetting account, Amount to Be Provided for Payment of Bonds (Serial or Term). As money accumulates in the Debt Service Fund, the Amount to Be Provided for Payment of Bonds account is reduced to that extent, and the account Amount Available for Payment of Bonds is debited to signify the availability of these monies. (The proceeds are recorded in the appropriate fund authorized to use the borrowings.) For financial reporting purposes, a statement of GLTD is used. A typical one is shown in Illustration 25–8.

ACCOUNTING PROCEDURES

Typical entries made in the GLTDAG follow:

```
Amount to Be Provided for Payment
   of Bonds (serial or term)  ........................  3,500,000
         Bonds Payable (serial or term)  .................             3,500,000
      To record the issuance of bonds for the
         new community center.
```

(continued)

ILLUSTRATION 25–8

Funn City
Statement of General Long-Term Debt
June 30, 19X2

Amount available and to be provided for the payment of general long-term debt		
Term bonds—		
Amount available in Debt Service Fund	$ 11,400[a]	
Amount to be provided	388,600	
		$ 400,000
Serial bonds—		
Amount available in Debt Service Fund	$ 14,000	
Amount to be provided	2,386,000	
		2,400,000
Total Amount Available and to Be Provided		$2,800,000
General long-term debt payable:		
Term bonds payable		$ 400,000
Serial bonds payable		2,400,000
Total General Long-Term Debt Payable		$2,800,000

[a]This amount agrees with the amount in the Fund Balance account of the Civic Center Debt Service Fund balance sheet in Illustration 25–6. Thus it was assumed that no other Debt Service Funds involving term bonds exist.

Note: Footnote disclosure is required for the contingent liability that exists for general obligation bonds recorded in Enterprise Funds.

Amount Available in Debt Service Fund	100,000	
Amount to Be Provided for Repayment		
of Serial Bonds		100,000
To record increase in assets available for		
retirement of serial bonds.		
Serial Bonds Payable	100,000	
Amount Available in Debt Service Fund		100,000
To transfer liability to Debt Service Fund.		

VII   SPECIAL ASSESSMENTS (*NOT* A FUND)

Some government activities involve constructing **public improvements that benefit a specific geographical area rather than the community as a whole.** The most common examples are residential streets, sidewalks, street lighting, and sewer lines. In these cases, governmental units usually charge all or most of the costs of the improvements directly to the owners of the properties benefited. In most cases, money is collected from the appropriate property owners in installments over a period of years. In some cases, the General Fund contributes monies for part of the improvements. Such transfers are *operating transfers.*

Although construction may be started after all the necessary money has been collected, it is more common to (1) borrow money (usually by issuing bonds), (2) use the borrowed funds to pay for the improvements, (3) collect money in installments from property owners in succeeding years, and (4) use the collected money to make principal and interest payments on the borrowings. In these cases, the borrowings are generally serial bonds, which may be either special assessment bonds or general obligation bonds. The former may be repaid only from assessments made against the applicable properties benefited, whereas the latter bear the full faith and credit of the governmental unit. To pay for the interest on outstanding bonds, the assessment payers are charged interest in installments.

MANNER OF ACCOUNTING

Prior to the 1987 issuance of GASB *Statement No. 6,* "Accounting and Financial Reporting for Special Assessments," special assessments were accounted for in Special Assessment Funds. *SGAS No. 6* eliminated this type of fund because a much criticized nonsensical reporting result occurred with them and it was believed that the other fund types could readily accommodate special assessments.

CONSTRUCTION ACTIVITY   Under *SGAS No. 6,* **all construction activity is to be accounted for and reported as any other capital improvement—in a Capital Projects Fund.** No illustrations of entries are provided here because they would be identical to those shown earlier for Capital Projects Funds. The capital improvements (depending on their nature) may have to be reported in the General Fixed Assets Account Group.

FINANCING ACTIVITY: THE CRITICAL DETERMINANT IS THE GOVERNMENT'S OBLIGATION TO ASSUME THE DEBT   The manner of accounting for Special Assessment Receivables from the property owners and the Special Assessment Bonds depends on whether the governmental unit is "obligated in some manner" to make good the repayment of the special assessment bonds in the event of default by the assessed property owners. According to *SGAS No. 6,*

> The phrase *obligated in some manner* as used in this Statement is intended to include all situations *other than* those in which (a) the government is *prohibited* (by constitution, charter, statute, ordinance, or contract) from assuming the debt in the event of default by the

property owner or (b) the government is not legally liable for assuming the debt and makes no statement, or gives no indication, that it will, or may, honor the debt in the event of default.[6]

In the vast majority of cases, the governmental unit *is* obligated in some manner. We discuss these situations in the following paragraphs. In the section on Agency Funds later in the chapter, we discuss the situation in which the governmental unit is *not* obligated in any manner (and, consequently, the financing activity must be accounted for in an Agency Fund).

WHEN THE GOVERNMENT *Is* OBLIGATED IN SOME MANNER In situations in which the governmental unit is obligated in some manner, *SGAS No. 6* requires that a Debt Service Fund be used to account for the servicing of any Special Assessment debt and the collection of Special Assessment Receivables. The Special Assessment debt is initially recorded in the GLTDAG. To the extent that such debt is to be repaid from Special Assessment Receivables, a special classification, Special Assessment Debt with Governmental Commitment, is to be used in the GLTDAG. Other than this special designation, accounting and reporting for this debt is the same as for general obligation debt recorded in the GLTDAG and serviced through a Debt Service Fund.

The accounting procedures for Special Assessment Receivables in a Debt Service Fund are nearly the same as for other property tax receivables accounted for in Debt Service Funds (illustrated earlier). **The one significant difference is that the deferred portion of the assessment cannot be recognized as revenues until later periods because the amounts are not "available to pay current period liabilities"** (the revenue-recognition criteria discussed in Chapter 24). To illustrate, assume that a street lighting project has an estimated cost of $500,000. On July 1, 19X1, certain property owners are assessed $500,000 to be collected in five equal installments of $100,000 per year beginning April 1, 19X2. Interest at 12% is to be charged on the deferred portion of the assessment ($400,000). Also on July 1, 19X1, special assessment bonds having a face value of $500,000 are issued at par, with interest at 8% to be paid annually. The entries pertaining to the assessment (but *not* the bonds) for the years ended June 30, 19X2, and June 30, 19X3, follow.

For the year ended June 30, 19X2:

Special Assessment Receivables—Current	100,000	
Special Assessment Receivables—Deferred	400,000	
Revenues		100,000
Deferred Revenues		400,000
To record levy of assessments on 7/1/X1.		
Cash	100,000[a]	
Special Assessment Receivables—Current		100,000
To record collection of current assessment receivables due on 4/1/X2.		

[a]These proceeds would be used to retire a portion of the special assessment bonds.

For the year ended June 30, 19X3:

Special Assessment Receivables—Current	100,000	
Special Assessment Receivables—Deferred		100,000
To reflect the current portion at 7/1/X2.		
Deferred Revenues	100,000	
Revenues		100,000
To recognize revenues.		

[6]*SGAS No. 6*, par. 16.

Cash..	148,000[a]	
Special Assessment Receivables—Current		100,000
Revenues		48,000

To record collection of current assessment receivables
due on 4/1/X3 along with interest of $48,000
($4,000,000 × 12%).

[a]These proceeds would be used to retire a portion of the special assessment bonds
and pay related interest.

MANNER OF RECORDING INTEREST   Recall from the discussion of Debt Service
Funds that (1) they are used to service debt recorded in the GLTDAG and (2) interest is recognized when due rather than in the period to which the interest relates.
Because of this manner of accounting for interest, *SGAS No. 6* allows interest on
Special Assessment Receivables to be recognized when due because the amounts
usually offset each other approximately. If the amounts do not, interest is to be recognized in the period to which it relates.

SERVICE-TYPE SPECIAL ASSESSMENTS

Governmental units provide many routine services that are financed from general
revenues, such as street cleaning and snow plowing. Sometimes these services are
provided at more frequent intervals or provided outside the normal service area.
In these cases, the affected property owners may be assessed for the incremental
services. Under *SGAS No. 6*, such assessment revenues and the related expenditures (expenses) for which the assessments were levied are to be accounted for and
reported

> in the fund type that best reflects the nature of the transactions, usually the general fund,
> a special revenue fund, or an enterprise fund, giving consideration to the "number of
> funds" principle. . . .[7]

THE PROPRIETARY FUNDS

VIII INTERNAL SERVICE FUNDS

In this section and the next, we discuss the two proprietary types of funds: Internal Service Funds and Enterprise Funds, the accounting for which parallels that of
commercial businesses. The primary distinction between an Internal Service Fund
and an Enterprise Fund is that **the former provides services to departments
within a governmental unit or to related governmental units, and the latter provides services primarily to the general public.**

Various departments of a governmental unit usually require common services.
Each department may hire people to perform these services, or it may contract with
outside vendors. It is usually cheaper, however, for the governmental unit to establish one or more separate operations to provide these services to its various departments. Internal Service Funds account for each of these separate operations in a
manner that charges the total cost of an operation to the various user departments.
Internal Service Funds commonly are established for motor pool operations, central
purchasing and stores, maintenance services, printing and reproduction services,
and data processing services.

[7]*SGAS No. 6*, par. 14.

The objective of an Internal Service Fund is to recover the total cost of an operation from billings to the various user departments. Generally, billings are not set at levels intended to generate significant profits—only to recover costs or generate a slight profit. The accounting principles and procedures used in private industry also lend themselves to use with Internal Service Funds, even though billings are not made to independent parties. Accordingly, the accrual basis of accounting is used, depreciation expense is recorded, and any earnings are closed out at year-end to a Retained Earnings account. The following financial statements are used:

1. A balance sheet.
2. A statement of revenues, expenses, and changes in retained earnings (or equity).
3. A statement of cash flows.

Simply because all costs are recovered through billings, it does not automatically follow that the services are being provided at a lower cost than would be incurred if the Internal Service Fund were not used. This determination may be made only by comparing the total cost incurred with amounts that would have been incurred if the Internal Service Fund had not been established.

ESTABLISHMENT AND OPERATION OF INTERNAL SERVICE FUNDS

Internal Service Funds are normally established by contributions or advances from the General Fund. Contributions are credited to a Contributed Capital account (considered the equivalent of a private corporation's capital stock accounts). Recall from Chapter 24 that this type of interfund transfer is a *residual equity transfer.* Recall also from Chapter 24 that if an advance is made by the General Fund (rather than a contribution), the General Fund records a receivable (Advance to Internal Service Fund) and the Internal Service Fund records a liability (Advance from General Fund). Cash is then used to purchase materials, parts, supplies, and equipment as needed to fulfill the fund's objectives.

A significant managerial accounting issue is that of developing a cost accounting system for charging the various user departments for the costs of the operation as reflected in the statement of revenues and expenses. When billings exceed costs, some or all of the retained earnings may need to be transferred to the General Fund. When billings are below cost, an accumulated deficit may be made up through additional charges to the user departments or a transfer from the General Fund. These interfund transfers must be substantively evaluated as to whether they are **operating transfers** or **residual equity transfers.** As discussed in Chapter 24, **nonrecurring** or **nonroutine** transfers are considered **residual equity transfers,** and all other transfers are treated as **operating transfers.**

ILLUSTRATION   **JOURNAL ENTRIES AND FINANCIAL STATEMENTS**

Assume that Funn City established a Central Printing and Reproduction Fund during the fiscal year ended June 30, 19X2. Assumed transactions pertaining to the establishment and operation of the fund, along with related journal entries, follow:

1. **Establishment of the fund.** A contribution of $40,000 from the General Fund established the fund. The operation is conducted in a facility leased on a month-to-month basis from a privately owned company.

Cash	40,000	
Contributed Capital—General Fund		40,000
To record contribution from the General Fund.		

2. **Purchase and depreciation of equipment.** Equipment costing $30,000 was acquired on July 3, 19X1. The equipment is assigned a 10-year life and no salvage value.

Equipment	30,000	
Vouchers Payable		30,000
To record purchase of equipment.		
Operating Expenses	3,000	
Accumulated Depreciation		3,000
To record depreciation expense.		

3. **Purchase and use of supplies inventory.** Supplies costing $65,000 were acquired. A physical inventory taken on June 30, 19X2, was valued at $11,000.

Inventory of Supplies	65,000	
Vouchers Payable		65,000
To record purchase of supplies.		
Operating Expenses	54,000	
Inventory of Supplies		54,000
To record cost of supplies used.		

Note that inventories are accounted for in the same manner as in a private corporation.

4. **Incurrence of operating expenses and payment of liabilities.** Various operating expenses were incurred. Of these expenses, $7,000 represented charges from the city's electric utility (an Enterprise Fund).

Operating Expenses	67,000	
Vouchers Payable		60,000
Due to Electric Utility Fund		7,000
To record operating expenses.		
Vouchers Payable	138,000	
Due to Electric Utility Fund	5,000	
Cash		143,000
To record partial payment of liabilities.		

5. **Billings and collections.** Billings to the city's various departments totaled $125,000. Of this amount, $9,000 pertained to services performed for the city's electric utility and $5,000 pertained to services performed for the city's central garage (an Internal Service Fund).

Due from General Fund	111,000	
Due from Electric Utility Fund	9,000	
Due from Central Garage Fund	5,000	
Operating Revenues		125,000
To record billing to departments for services rendered.		
Cash	110,000	
Due from General Fund		102,000
Due from Electric Utility Fund		5,000
Due from Central Garage Fund		3,000
To record partial collection of amounts due from other funds.		

Because closing entries are identical to those made for a private enterprise, they are not shown.

FINANCIAL STATEMENTS   The balance sheet and operating statement prepared for the fiscal year ended June 30, 19X2, are shown in Illustrations 25–9 and 25–10.

ILLUSTRATION 25–9

Funn City
Central Printing and Reproduction Fund
Balance Sheet
June 30, 19X2

Assets

Cash	$ 7,000
Due from General Fund	9,000
Due from Electric Utility Fund	4,000
Due from Central Garage Fund	2,000
Inventory of supplies	11,000
Equipment	30,000
Accumulated depreciation	(3,000)
Total Assets	$60,000

Liabilities and Fund Equity

Vouchers payable	$17,000
Due to Electric Utility Fund	2,000
Total Liabilities	$19,000
Contributed capital	$40,000
Retained earnings:	
Unreserved	1,000
Total Fund Equity	$41,000
Total Liabilities and Fund Equity	$60,000

ILLUSTRATION 25–10

Funn City
Central Printing and Reproduction Fund
Statement of Revenues, Expenses, and
Changes in Retained Earnings
For the Year Ended June 30, 19X2

Operating revenues:		
Charges for services		$125,000
Operating expenses:		
Supplies	$54,000	
Salaries and wages	42,000	
Lease expense	18,000	
Utilities	7,000	
Depreciation	3,000	124,000
Net Income		$ 1,000
Retained Earnings, 7/1/X1		–0–
Retained Earnings, 6/30/X2		$ 1,000

Note: A statement of cash flows would also be prepared.

IX   ENTERPRISE FUNDS

According to the GASB *Codification,* Enterprise Funds account for

operations (a) that are financed and operated in a manner similar to private business enterprises—where the intent of the governing body is that the costs (expenses, including depreciation) of providing goods or services to the general public on a continuing basis be financed or recovered primarily through user charges; or (b) where the governing body has decided that periodic determination of revenues earned, expenses incurred, and/or net income is appropriate for capital maintenance, public policy, management control, accountability, or other purposes.[8]

The most common type of activity accounted for in an Enterprise Fund is the public utility providing water services, electricity, or natural gas. Other activities commonly accounted for in Enterprise Funds are offstreet parking facilities, recreational facilities (principally golf courses and swimming pools), airports, hospitals, and public transit systems. The language of the GASB *Codification* is so broad that a governmental unit may establish an Enterprise Fund for almost any activity regardless of the extent of financing obtained from user chargers. In practice, however, only a small percentage of governmental units use Enterprise Funds for activities that recover less than 50% of their costs from user charges, with public transit systems probably being the most common.

Because Enterprise Funds evaluate operations from a profit-and-loss perspective, the results of operations are reported in an income statement (using the accrual basis of accounting), which includes depreciation expense. At year-end, earnings are closed out to a retained earnings account. The following financial statements are prepared:

1. A balance sheet (which includes all of the fund's assets and liabilities).

2. A statement of revenues, expenses, and changes in retained earnings (or equity).

3. A statement of cash flows.

Although evaluated from a profit-and-loss perspective, the activities accounted for in Enterprise Funds are not engaged in to maximize profits, as in the private sector. Instead, the intent is to raise sufficient revenues to either (1) recover costs to break even or (2) generate profits so that capital is effectively raised to finance expansion of operations.

ESTABLISHMENT AND EXPANSION

Some of the more common ways to establish an operation to be accounted for as an Enterprise Fund or to expand the operations of an existing Enterprise Fund follow:

1. **Contribution from the General Fund.** An interfund transfer from the General Fund is categorized as a *residual equity transfer.* Accordingly, the Enterprise Fund debits the Cash account and credits a Contributed Capital account. Contributed capital accounts are similar to the capital stock accounts used by private corporations in that both reflect the value of assets contributed. Thus Enterprise Funds do not use a Fund Balance account. Contributed capital accounts are normally shown by the source of the contribution—for example, Contributed Capital from Municipality.

2. **Loan from the General Fund.** When the General Fund makes a loan, it *debits* the Advance to Enterprise Fund account and *credits* the Cash account. The Enterprise Fund *debits* Cash and *credits* Advance from General Fund (a liability account). If interest is paid on the advance, the Enterprise Fund has interest expense and the General Fund has interest revenue.

3. **Issuance of revenue bonds.** Revenue bonds are issued by an Enterprise Fund and are repayable, with interest, only from the earnings of the operations accounted for in the Enterprise Fund. (If the bonds also have a security interest in the fixed assets of the Enterprise Fund, they are called *mortgage revenue bonds.*) Revenue bonds require accounting entries only in the Enterprise Fund. Bond in-

---

[8]GASB *Cod.*, sec. 1300.104.

denture agreements frequently restrict the use of bond proceeds to specific capital projects; therefore, the bond proceeds are deposited in a separate checking account called, for example, *Construction Cash.* Using a separate account provides greater accounting control to ensure that the proceeds are spent only on authorized projects. The offsetting credit is to the Revenue Bonds Payable account.

4. **Issuance of general obligation bonds.** General obligation bonds are issued by a governmental unit with its full faith and backing. The proceeds are transferred to the Enterprise Fund, which uses the cash in accordance with the bond indenture agreement. General obligation bonds fall into the following two categories, based on the source of their repayment and payment of related interest:

   a. **Repayable from earnings of the enterprise.** When the governmental unit intends to repay the principal and related interest from Enterprise Fund earnings, the GASB *Codification* recommends that such debt be reflected as a liability in the Enterprise Fund.

   b. **Repayable from taxes and general revenues.** When the bonds and related interest are to be repaid from taxes and general revenues of the governmental unit, the bond liability is shown as a liability of the GLTDAG. The Enterprise Fund treats the money received as a contribution and credits the Contributed Capital from Municipality account. Thus a liability is not reflected in the Enterprise Fund.

Unique Features of Financial Statements

Because the financial statements of Enterprise Funds are similar to those of private enterprises engaged in comparable activities, typical transactions, related journal entries, and a complete set of illustrative financial statements are not presented. Instead, we discuss the unique features of Enterprise Fund financial statements and then illustrate the balance sheet for a water utility. (The balance sheet has certain unique classification features.)

1. **Contributed capital accounts.** As mentioned previously, Enterprise Funds use contributed capital accounts rather than capital stock accounts.

2. **Restricted assets.** Assets restricted as to use are shown separately. The most common examples are these:

   a. **Construction cash.** Construction cash is not available for normal operating purposes and must be identified as usable only for its designated purpose—for example, plant expansion.

   b. **Customer deposits.** For public utilities that require their customers to make deposits to ensure payment of final statements, the deposits constitute restricted assets that are not available for normal operations. When such deposits are invested in allowable investments, the investments should also be shown as restricted assets.

   c. **Debt-related accumulations.** Some bond indenture agreements require that certain amounts of cash provided from operations be set aside in separate accounts for retiring and servicing bonds. In some cases, monies must be set aside to cover potential future losses.

3. **Appropriation of retained earnings.** When money relating to retiring debt and servicing bonds has been set aside pursuant to bond indenture agreements, it may be necessary to appropriate a portion of retained earnings. The appropriation indicates that a portion of the retained earnings is not available for normal operations, internal expansion, or cash transfers to the General Fund; that is, cash that might otherwise be used for such purposes has been

set aside for other purposes. This practice differs from customary practice in private industry, where showing the restricted assets separately is deemed sufficient disclosure.

Technically, at any balance sheet date, the appropriation should equal only the amounts set aside to cover (a) future interest expense, (b) future principal payments (above and beyond amounts deemed to have been generated from operations to date), and (c) potential future losses.

4. **Depreciation expense.** For public utilities, depreciation expense is usually a major expense because of the large capital investment required. Depreciation expense is customarily shown on a separate line of the income statement.

5. **Income taxes.** Because governmental units do not pay income taxes, no income tax expense is shown in the statement of revenues and expenses.

6. **Payments to the General Fund.** Payments to the General Fund in lieu of taxes are **quasi-external transactions,** discussed in Chapter 24. Accordingly, such payments are recorded as **expenses in the Enterprise Fund** and as **revenues in the General Fund.** Payments to the General Fund not in lieu of taxes but to finance General Fund expenditures are *operating transfers.*

7. **Inverted balance sheet format.** Some governmental utilities use an inverted format for their balance sheets. (Many state Public Utility Commissions require it.) Under this presentation, fixed assets, long-term debt, and capital balances are shown before current items to emphasize the relative importance of the investment in fixed assets and the related financing sources. The conventional format, which places current items first, is still more prevalent, however, than the inverted format. A utility fund balance sheet using the conventional format is shown in Illustration 25–11.

THE FIDUCIARY FUNDS

Agency Funds and Trust Funds are created to account for money and property received but not owned.

X AGENCY FUNDS

Agency Funds act as conduits for the transfer of money. Thus they are purely custodial in nature. Money deposited with such a fund is generally disbursed shortly after receipt to authorized recipients, such as other governmental funds, other governmental units, and private corporations. Common examples of Agency Funds are tax collection funds and employee benefit funds.

1. **Tax collection funds.** When overlapping governmental units collect tax revenues from the same source, it is usually more practical and economical for only one of the governmental units to collect the taxes and then to distribute them to the various taxing authorities. Counties commonly collect all property taxes and then distribute amounts collected to the various cities, school districts, water districts, and any other special districts.

2. **Employee benefit funds.** When governmental employees have premiums for medical and dental insurance plans withheld from their paychecks, the withholdings are deposited in such funds. Periodically, the governmental unit makes a lump-sum payment from these funds to an insurance company. (The alternative to using employee benefit funds is to set up liabilities in the appropriate funds.)

Agency Funds have no unusual operating characteristics or unique accounting issues. Usually, cash is the only asset, which is completely offset by liabilities to

ILLUSTRATION 25–11

Funn City
Water Fund
Balance Sheet
June 30, 19X2

Assets

Current Assets

Cash		$ 330,000
Customer's accounts receivable, less $185,000 allowance for uncollectible accounts		2,490,000
Due from other funds		55,000
Unbilled accounts receivable		670,000
Inventories of materials and supplies		240,000
Prepaid expenses		34,000
Total Current Assets		$ 3,819,000

Restricted Assets

Customer's deposits:		
Cash	$ 23,000	
Investments	512,000	$ 535,000
Revenue bond construction account:		
Cash		188,000
Revenue bond current debt service reserve account:		
Cash	$ 10,000	
Investments	1,130,000	1,140,000
Revenue bond future debt service reserve account:		
Cash	$ 70,000	
Investments	1,200,000	1,270,000
Total Restricted Assets		3,133,000

Property, Plant, and Equipment

Land	$ 1,511,000	
Buildings	4,477,000	
Improvements other than buildings	38,870,000	
Machinery and equipment	18,440,000	
Construction in process	2,900,000	
	$66,198,000	
Less: Accumulated depreciation	(12,450,000)	53,748,000
Total Assets		$60,700,000

(continued)

the authorized recipients. Thus it has no Fund Balance account. Because cash disbursements are made frequently, on many occasions throughout the year these funds have no assets or liabilities at all.

BASIS OF ACCOUNTING AND FINANCIAL STATEMENTS

Agency funds do *not* report operations. A balance sheet is presented, the assets and liabilities of which are recognized using the modified accrual basis. Because no operating statement is presented, a **statement of changes in assets and liabilities** (a statement unique to this fund) is presented to report the changes in the governmental unit's custodial responsibilities. In light of their simplicity, we do not illustrate journal entries and financial statements for Agency Funds beyond the journal entries shown in the following discussion of special assessment debt for which the governmental unit is not obligated in any manner.

ILLUSTRATION 25-11	(continued)		

Funn City
Water Fund
Balance Sheet
June 30, 19X2

Liabilities and Fund Equity

Current Liabilities (payable from current assets)

Vouchers payable		$ 1,347,000	
Accrued wages and taxes		73,000	
Accrued interest payable on advance from municipality		26,000	
Advance from municipality		50,000	
Total			$ 1,496,000

Current Liabilities (payable from restricted assets)

Customer deposits		$ 535,000	
Construction contracts payable		172,000	
Accrued revenue bond interest payable		400,000	
Revenue bonds payable		1,000,000	
Total			2,107,000
Total Current Liabilities			$ 3,603,000

Liabilities Payable after One Year

Revenue bonds payable		$28,000,000	
Advance from municipality		650,000	
Total			28,650,000
Total Liabilities			$32,253,000

Fund Equity

Contributions:			
Contributions from municipality		$ 5,000,000	
Contributions from subdividers		7,880,000	
Total Contributions			$12,880,000
Retained Earnings:			
Reserved for revenue bond future debt service reserve account		$ 1,270,000	
Unreserved		14,297,000	
Total Retained Earnings			15,567,000
Total Fund Equity			$28,447,000
Total Liabilities and Fund Equity			$60,700,000

SPECIAL ASSESSMENT DEBT FOR WHICH THE GOVERNMENT IS *NOT* OBLIGATED IN ANY MANNER

In situations in which the governmental unit is *not* obligated in any manner to pay off special assessment debt in the event of a default by the property owners, *SGAS No. 6* requires that the collection activity pertaining to the special assessment receivables and the debt service activity pertaining to the special assessment debt be accounted for in an Agency Fund. The rationale here is that the governmental unit is acting merely as an agent for the assessed property owners and the debtholders. Accordingly, the special assessment debt is not reflected as a liability in the financial statements of the governmental unit. Nor is the special assessment levy accrued as a receivable in the governmental unit's financial statements. Only the cash collections of the levy and the disbursement of this money to the debtholders are recorded in the Agency Fund.

To illustrate the entries related to the collection of the first annual installment of $100,000 due April 1, 19X2, from the property owners (the same information used earlier in the chapter in the discussion and illustration of special assessments) are as follows:

Cash	100,000	
Due to Special Assessment Bondholders		100,000
To record collection of first annual		
installment from property owners.		
Due to Special Assessment Bondholders	100,000	
Cash		100,000
To distribute money to bondholders.		

Because the bonds are not reported as a liability in the governmental unit's financial statements, *SGAS No. 6* requires the following:

> The source of funds in the capital projects fund should be identified by a description other than "bond proceeds," such as "contribution from property owners."[9]

XI   TRUST FUNDS

Most Trust Funds involve investing and using money in accordance with stipulated provisions of trust indenture agreements or statutes. Common examples of Trust Funds include the following:

1. **Public employee pension and retirement systems.** These Trust Funds account for employer and employee retirement contributions, the investment of such contributions, and the payments to retired employees.

2. **Nonexpendable Trust Funds.** These funds account for **endowments,** the money and property given to a governmental unit. The principal must be preserved intact; only the Trust Fund income may be expended or completely used in the course of operations.

3. **Expendable Trust Funds.** These funds also account for endowments. The principal does not have to be preserved intact, however; the trust principal and income may be expended or completely used in the course of operations. State and federal grant programs that establish a continuing trustee relationship are to be accounted for in this type of fund under the requirements of the GASB *Codification*.

CLASSIFICATION FOR ACCOUNTING MEASUREMENT PURPOSES

The GASB *Codification* states:

> Each Trust Fund is classified for accounting measurement purposes as either a governmental fund or a proprietary fund. Expendable Trust Funds are accounted for in essentially the same manner as governmental funds. Nonexpendable Trust Funds and Pension Trust Funds are accounted for in essentially the same manner as proprietary funds.[10]

Because the nature of the activities accounted for in Expendable Trust Funds resembles the nature of the activities accounted for in the *governmental funds*, operations are reported in a statement of revenues, expenditures, and changes in fund balance (using the *modified accrual basis* of accounting). Because the nature of the activities accounted for in Nonexpendable Trust Funds and Pension Trust Funds resembles the nature of the activities accounted for in the *proprietary funds*,

[9]*SGAS No. 6*, par. 19.
[10]GASB *Cod.*, sec. 1300.102.

operations are reported in a statement of revenues, expenses, and changes in retained earnings (using the *accrual basis* of accounting).

ESTABLISHMENT AND OPERATION

Public employee pension and retirement trust funds have the same operation characteristics and accounting issues as private pension and retirement plans that are funded with a trustee. Accordingly, journal entries and financial statements for these funds are *not* illustrated. As mentioned in Chapter 24, a major shortcoming of many such trust funds is the lack of a sound actuarial basis in accounting for contributions to meet retirement payments.

No significant accounting issues exist for state and federal grant programs accounted for in **expendable Trust Funds.** As the creators of trusts, donors of **nonexpendable Trust Funds** have the right to specify in the trust agreement the accounting treatment to be accorded specific items. Such instructions prevail over GAAP. In the absence of specific accounting instructions, the governing authorities are state statutes, which usually conflict with GAAP in several respects. For example, most state statutes require gains and losses on the sale of trust investments to be credited or charged, respectively, to trust principal rather than to trust income. For nonexpendable trusts, separate trust funds may be established for the principal and for the income generated by the principal. (The latter fund is essentially treated as a Special Revenue Fund.) We illustrate journal entries and financial statements for this type of fund next.

ILLUSTRATION   **JOURNAL ENTRIES AND FINANCIAL STATEMENTS**

Assume that Funn City received $100,000 from a citizen, who specifies that the principal amount should remain intact. Earnings on the principal are to be used for park beautification projects. Assumed transactions pertaining to the establishment and operation of these funds, along with related journal entries, are as follows:

**ENDOWMENT PRINCIPAL
NONEXPENDABLE TRUST FUND**

Transaction or Event	Journal Entry		
The endowment principal fund is established.	Cash	100,000	
	Operating Revenues		100,000
Investment of cash.	Investments	96,000	
	Cash		96,000
Accrual of interest on investments.	Interest Receivable	8,000	
	Operating Revenues		8,000
Amortization of bond discount on investments.	Investments	700	
	Operating Revenues		700
Collection of interest on investments.	Cash	4,500	
	Interest Receivable		4,500
To reflect liability to Endowment Revenues Fund.	Operating Transfers Out	8,700	
	Due to Endowment Revenues Fund		8,700
To close operating revenues and operating transfer out accounts.	Operating Revenues	108,700	
	Operating Transfers Out		8,700
	Fund Balance Reserved for Endowments		100,000

(continued)

| Payment of part of amount due to Endowment Revenues Fund. | Due to Endowment Revenues Fund .... | 7,500 | |
| | Cash .... | | 7,500 |

ENDOWMENT REVENUES
EXPENDABLE TRUST FUND

Transaction or Event	**Journal Entry**		
To reflect revenues earned by and payable from Endowment Principal Fund.	Due from Endowment Principal Fund	8,700	
	Other Financing Sources—Operating Transfer In		8,700
Receipt of part of amount due from Endowment Principal Fund.	Cash	7,500	
	Due from Endowment Principal Fund		7,500
Payment of administrative expenses.	Expenditures	300	
	Cash		300
Costs incurred on park beautification projects are paid.	Expenditures	6,300	
	Cash		6,300
To close other financing sources and expenditures into Fund Balance Reserved for Endowments.	Other Financing Sources—Operating Transfer In	8,700	
	Expenditures		6,600
	Fund Balance Reserved for Endowments		2,100

FINANCIAL STATEMENTS

The balance sheets and operating statements prepared at June 30, 19X2, for each of these funds are shown in Illustrations 25–12, 25–13, and 25–14. (Nonexpendable Trust Funds must also present a statement of cash flows.)

ILLUSTRATION 25–12

Funn City
Endowment Trust Funds
Balance Sheets
June 30, 19X2

	Principal Fund (Nonexpendable)	Revenue Fund (Expendable)
Assets		
Cash	$ 1,000	$ 900
Due from Endowment Principal Fund		1,200
Investments	96,700	
Interest receivable	3,500	
Total Assets	$101,200	$2,100
Liabilities and Fund Balances		
Due to Endowment Revenues Fund	$ 1,200	
Fund balances		
Reserved for endowments	$100,000	$2,100
Total Fund Balance	$100,000	$2,100
Total Liabilities and Fund Balances	$101,200	$2,100

ILLUSTRATION 25–13

Funn City
Endowment Principal Funds (Nonexpendable)
Statement of Revenues, Expenses,
and Changes in Fund Balance
For the Year Ended June 30, 19X2

Operating revenues:	
Gifts	$100,000
Interest income	8,700
Total Revenues	$108,700
Operating expenses	–0–
Income before Operating Transfers	$108,700
Operating transfers out	(8,700)
Net Income	$100,000
Fund Balance, 7/1/X1	–0–
Fund Balance, 6/30/X2	$100,000

ILLUSTRATION 25–14

Funn City
Endowment Revenues Funds (Expendable)
Statement of Revenues, Expenditures,
and Changes in Fund Balance
For the Year Ended June 30, 19X2

Revenues	$ –0–
Expenditures:	
Park beautification	$ 6,300
Administrative	300
Total Expenditures	$ 6,600
Revenues under expenditures	$(6,600)
Other financing sources:	
Operating transfer in	8,700
Excess of Revenues and Other Financing Sources over	
Expenditures	$ 2,100
Fund Balance, 7/1/X1	–0–
Fund Balance, 6/30/X2	$ 2,100

FINANCIAL REPORTING TO THE PUBLIC: GENERAL-PURPOSE FINANCIAL STATEMENTS

XII THE FINANCIAL REPORTING PYRAMID CONCEPT

The annual financial report for governmental units is called *the comprehensive annual financial report (CAFR)*. The GASB *Codification* requires that financial statements be presented using a "reporting pyramid" concept. The reporting pyramid consists of four levels of financial information, each of which provides more detailed information than the previous level. Illustration 25–15 shows how this reporting pyramid might appear.

The reporting pyramid includes the following levels of financial information:

Level 1: Combined financial statements—Overview (General-purpose financial statements). The financial statements in the first level present the overall

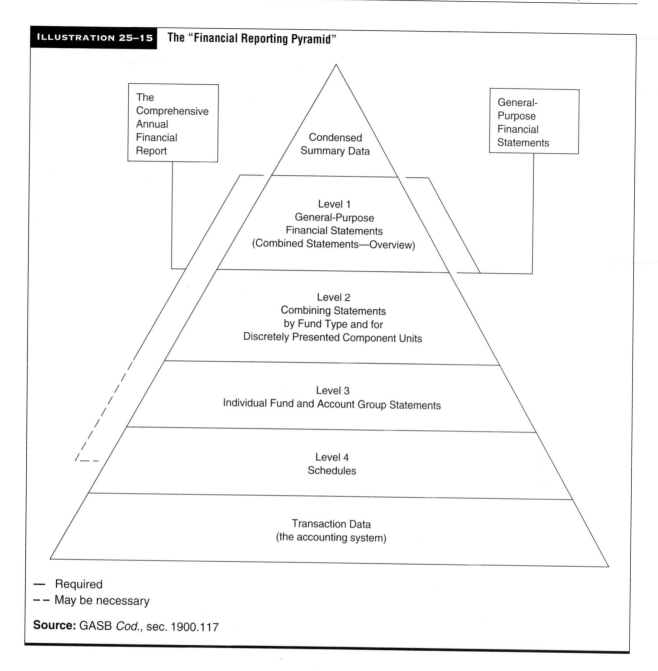

ILLUSTRATION 25–15 The "Financial Reporting Pyramid"

The
Comprehensive
Annual
Financial
Report

General-
Purpose
Financial
Statements

Condensed
Summary Data

Level 1
General-Purpose
Financial Statements
(Combined Statements—Overview)

Level 2
Combining Statements
by Fund Type and for
Discretely Presented Component Units

Level 3
Individual Fund and Account Group Statements

Level 4
Schedules

Transaction Data
(the accounting system)

— Required
– – May be necessary

Source: GASB *Cod.*, sec. 1900.117

financial position and operating results of a governmental unit as a whole. They are referred to as the *General-Purpose Financial Statements*. Level 1 contains

1. Combined Balance Sheet—All Fund Types and Account Groups and Discretely Presented Component Units.
2. Combined Statement of Revenues, Expenditures, and Changes in Fund Balances—All Governmental Fund Types and Discretely Presented Component Units.
3. Combined Statement of Revenues, Expenditures, and Changes in Fund Balances—Budget and Actual—General and Special Revenue Fund Types (and

similar governmental fund types for which annual budgets have been legally adopted).

4. Combined Statement of Revenues, Expenses, and Changes in Retained Earnings (or Equity)—All Proprietary Fund Types and Discretely Presented Component Units. [Segment financial information for major nonhomogeneous Enterprise Funds must also be presented.]

5. Combined Statement of Cash Flows—All Proprietary Fund Types and Discretely Presented Component Units.

6. Notes to the financial statements.

   Trust Fund operations may be reported in items 2, 4, and 5, as appropriate, or separately.)[11]

   The combined balance sheet in item 1 shows data for each fund type and account group in columnar format. The combined statement in item 2 shows data only for each fund type. Both statements may present a Total column, which may or may not reflect interfund and similar eliminations. If a Total column is presented, it is described as "Memorandum Only." For the combined statements in items 3, 4, and 5, a Total Memorandum Only column is used. Illustrations of these five general-purpose financial statements are presented in Illustrations 25–16 through 25–20. (A general familiarity with these statements is required of CPA candidates.)

   Level 2: Combining statements by fund type. In preparing combined financial statements for the first reporting level, individual funds of a given type must be combined. The financial statements in level 2 present the individual funds that have been combined, along with a Total column that ties into the appropriate column of the combined financial statements in level 1. Note that this level would be completely bypassed if a governmental unit had no more than one fund for each type of fund.

   Level 3: Individual fund and account group statements. Level 3 presents data for (a) individual funds not shown in level 2 and (b) individual funds for which additional detailed information is provided—such as budgetary and prior year comparative data. Illustrations of individual fund and account group financial statements were presented earlier in the chapter and in Chapter 24. Recall from Chapter 24 that the individual financial statements must follow the same format as the combined financial statements.

   Level 4: Schedules. Level 4 primarily presents data in connection with demonstrating legal compliance for finance-related matters. Other useful information may also be presented at this level.

In presenting operating statements at any level in the reporting pyramid and for any fund or fund type, the GASB *Codification* recommends that such statements incorporate changes in fund balance or retained earnings (as appropriate).

In addition to financial statements and notes required for adequate disclosure, governmental units generally include in their annual reports substantial statistical tables and data covering such items as population, number of employees, assessed values, and principal taxpayers.

---

[11]GASB *Cod.*, sec. 1900.113.

ILLUSTRATION 25–16 The *First* of the Five General-Purpose Financial Statements

Name of Government
Combined Balance Sheet—All Fund Types and Account Groups
December 31, 19X2
With Comparative Totals for December 31, 19X1
(amounts expressed in thousands)

	Governmental Fund Types				Proprietary Fund Types		Fiduciary Fund Type	Account Groups		Totals (Memorandum Only)	
	General	Special Revenue	Debt Service	Capital Projects	Enterprise	Internal Service	Trust and Agency	General Fixed Assets	General Long-Term Debt	19X2	19X1
Assets and Other Debits											
Assets											
Cash	$1,369	$ 211	$ 10	$ 552	$ 1,164	$ 100	$ 293	$ —	$ —	$ 3,699	$ 1,893
Investments	2,091	1,577	1,513	11,051	15,523	50	17,327	—	—	49,132	36,301
Receivables (net of allowances for uncollectibles):											
Interest	92	2	30	411	420	2	434	—	—	1,391	1,014
Taxes	952	—	10	—	—	—	—	—	—	962	897
Accounts	72	—	—	—	2,622	—	—	—	—	2,694	2,386
Special assessments	—	—	4,230	—	—	—	—	—	—	4,230	—
Intergovernmental	215	—	—	199	—	4	—	—	—	418	422
Due from other funds	105	—	—	335	39	126	—	—	—	605	382
Inventories	39	—	—	—	308	23	—	—	—	370	498
Prepaid items	—	—	—	—	—	38	—	—	—	38	—
Advances to other funds	78	—	—	—	—	—	—	—	—	78	50
Restricted assets	—	—	—	—	27,454	—	—	—	—	27,454	5,290
Deferred charges	—	—	—	—	651	—	—	—	—	651	581
Fixed assets (net, where applicable, of accumulated depreciation)	—	—	—	—	120,053	2,904	—	$58,912	—	181,869	167,074
Other debits											
Amount available in debt service fund	—	—	—	—	—	—	—	—	$ 1,384	1,384	10
Amount to be provided for retirement of general long-term debt	—	—	—	—	—	—	—	—	41,473	41,473	39,256
Total Assets and Other Debits	$5,013	$1,790	$5,793	$12,548	$168,234	$3,247	$18,054	$58,912	$42,857	$316,448	$256,054

ILLUSTRATION 25-16 (continued)

Liabilities, Equity, and Other Credits

	Governmental Fund Types — General	Special Revenue	Debt Service	Capital Projects	Proprietary — Enterprise	Internal Service	Fiduciary — Trust and Agency	Account Groups — General Fixed Assets	General Long-Term Debt	Totals (Memorandum Only) 19X2	19X1
Liabilities:											
Vouchers payable	$ 772	$ 340	$ —	$ —	$ 1,469	$ 242	$ —	$ —	$ —	$ 2,581	$ 1,378
Accounts payable	165	76	—	784	336	242	38	—	—	1,641	1,001
Compensated absences payable	225	—	—	—	390	28	—	—	2,242	2,885	2,414
Intergovernmental payable	—	—	—	—	—	—	—	—	—	—	11
Due to other funds	476	—	—	—	87	42	—	—	—	605	382
Matured bonds payable	—	—	8	—	123	—	—	—	—	131	—
Accrued interest payable	—	—	—	—	1,201	—	—	—	—	1,201	1,261
Deferred revenue	240	—	4,240	—	—	—	—	—	—	4,480	230
General obligation bonds payable—current	—	—	—	—	1,641	—	—	—	—	1,641	1,523
Capital leases—current	—	—	—	—	23	—	—	—	—	23	—
Liabilities payable from restricted assets	—	—	—	—	4,358	—	—	—	—	4,358	2,177
Advances from other funds	—	—	—	—	—	78	—	—	—	78	50
General obligation bonds payable	—	—	—	—	32,934	—	—	—	35,790	68,724	65,000
Special assessment debt with government commitment	—	—	—	—	—	—	—	—	4,700	4,700	—
Revenue bonds payable	—	—	—	—	32,828	—	—	—	—	32,828	8,580
Capital leases payable	—	—	—	—	78	—	—	—	125	203	—
Deferred compensation benefits payable	—	—	—	—	—	—	1,216	—	—	1,216	900
Total Liabilities	$1,878	$ 416	$4,248	$ 784	$ 75,468	$ 390	$ 1,254	$ —	$42,857	$127,295	$ 85,069
Equity & Other Credits:											
Investment in general fixed assets	$ —	$ —	$ —	$ —	$ —	$ —	$ —	$58,912	$ —	$ 58,912	$ 59,377
Contributed capital	—	—	—	—	59,395	2,486	—	—	—	61,881	52,152
Retained earnings:											
Reserved	—	—	—	—	3,817	—	—	—	—	3,817	2,590
Unreserved	—	—	—	—	29,554	371	—	—	—	29,925	28,252
Fund balances:											
Reserved for encumbrances	320	361	—	6,563	—	—	—	—	—	7,244	840
Reserved for advances	78	—	—	—	—	—	—	—	—	78	50
Reserved for debt service	—	—	1,545	—	—	—	—	—	—	1,545	10
Reserved for perpetual care	—	—	—	—	—	—	1,193	—	—	1,193	1,102
Reserved for employees' retirement system	—	—	—	—	—	—	16,670	—	—	16,670	14,248
Unreserved, undesignated	2,737	1,013	—	5,201	—	—	(1,063)	—	—	7,888	12,364
Total Equity & Other Credits	$3,135	$1,374	$1,545	$11,764	$ 92,766	$2,857	$16,800	$58,912	$ —	$189,153	$170,985
Total Liabilities, Equity & Other Credits	$5,013	$1,790	$5,793	$12,548	$168,234	$3,247	$18,054	$58,912	$42,857	$316,448	$256,054

Source: Adapted from *Governmental Accounting, Auditing and Financial Reporting* (Chicago: Government Finance Officers Association, 1994), pp. 442–443.

ILLUSTRATION 25-17	The *Second* of the Five General-Purpose Financial Statements

Name of Government
Combined Statement of Revenues, Expenditures, and Changes in Fund Balances—All Government Fund Types and Expendable Trust Funds
For the Fiscal Year Ended December 31, 19X2
With Comparative Totals for the Fiscal Year Ended December 31, 19X1 (amounts expressed in thousands)

	Governmental Fund Types				Fiduciary Fund Type	Totals (Memorandum Only)	
	General	Special Revenue	Debt Service	Capital Projects	Expendable Trust	19X2	19X1
Revenues							
Taxes	$25,068	$1,528	$1,650	$ —	$—	$28,246	$24,271
Licenses and permits	2,041	—	—	—	—	2,041	1,820
Intergovernmental	5,770	100	—	462	—	6,332	5,674
Charges for services	2,300	—	—	—	—	2,300	2,335
Fines	808	—	—	—	—	808	521
Special assessments	—	—	470	—		470	—
Interest	623	116	280	844	6	1,869	807
Miscellaneous	345	149	—	—	82	576	605
Total Revenues	$36,955	$1,893	$ 2,400	$ 1,306	$88	$42,642	$36,033
Expenditures							
Current:							
General government	$ 4,244	$ —	$ —	$ —	$86	$ 4,330	$ 3,850
Public safety	13,438	—	—	—	—	13,438	12,150
Highways and streets	3,735	742	—	—	—	4,477	3,389
Sanitation	3,726	—	—	—	—	3,726	3,404
Culture and recreation	5,882	1,001	—	—	—	6,883	5,972
Capital outlay	—	—	—	5,461	—	5,461	2,501
Debt service:							
Principal	15	—	2,045	—	—	2,060	1,470
Interest and fiscal charges . .	150	—	2,993	—	—	3,143	1,865
Total Expenditures	$31,190	$1,743	$ 5,038	$ 5,461	$86	$43,518	$34,601
Excess (Deficiency) of Revenues over (under) Expenditures	$ 5,765	$ 150	$(2,638)	$ (4,155)	$ 2	$ (876)	$ 1,432
Other Financing Sources (Uses)							
Operating transfers in	$ —	$ —	$ 4,173	$ 1,210	$—	$ 5,383	$ 6,154
Operating transfers out	(4,537)	—	—	(846)	—	(5,383)	(6,154)
General obligation bond proceeds	—	—	—	—	—	—	7,500
Special assessment bond proceeds	—	—	—	4,690	—	4,690	—
Sale of general fixed assets . . .	145	—	—	—	—	145	—
Total Other Financing Sources (Uses)	$(4,392)	$ —	$4,173	$ 5,054	$—	$ 4,835	$ 7,500
Excess of Revenues and Other Financing Sources over Expenditures and Other Financing uses	$ 1,373	$ 150	$1,535	$ 899	$ 2	$ 3,959	$ 8,932
Fund Balances, January 1	1,807	1,224	10	10,865	49	13,955	5,023
Residual equity transfers out	(45)	—	—	—	—	(45)	—
Fund Balances, December 31. . .	$ 3,135	$1,374	$1,545	$11,764	$51	$17,869	$13,955

Source: Adapted from *Governmental Accounting, Auditing, and Financial Reporting* (Chicago: Government Finance Officers Association, 1994), p. 444.

Name of Government

Combined Statement of Revenues, Expenditures, and Changes in Fund Balances—
Budget and Actual, General, Special Revenue and Debt Service Funds
For the Fiscal Year Ended December 31, 19X2 (amounts expressed in thousands)

	General Fund			Special Revenue Funds			Debt Service Fund		
	Budget	Actual	Variance Favorable (Unfavorable)	Budget	Actual	Variance Favorable (Unfavorable)	Budget	Actual	Variance Favorable (Unfavorable)
Revenues									
Taxes	$25,566	$25,068	$ (498)	$ 1,307	$1,528	$ 221	$ 1,500	$ 1,650	$ 85
Licenses and permits	1,827	2,041	214	—	—	—	—	—	—
Intergovernmental	5,661	5,770	109	100	100	–0–	—	—	—
Charges for services	2,158	2,300	142	—	—	—	—	—	—
Fines	810	808	(2)	—	—	—	—	—	—
Special assessments	—	—	—	—	—	—	470	470	–0–
Interest	555	623	68	73	116	43	220	280	60
Miscellaneous	345	345	–0–	23	149	126	—	—	—
Total Revenues	$36,922	$36,955	$ 33	$ 1,503	$1,893	$ 390	$ 2,190	$ 2,400	$145
Expenditures									
Current:									
General government	$ 4,628	$ 4,244	$ 384	$ —	$ —	$ —	$ —	$ —	$ —
Public safety	13,645	13,453	192	—	—	—	—	—	—
Highways and streets	3,866	3,735	131	1,437	742	695	—	—	—
Sanitation	3,848	3,726	122	—	—	—	—	—	—
Culture and recreation	5,950	5,882	68	1,095	1,001	94	—	—	—
Capital outlay	—	—	—	—	—	—	—	—	—
Debt service:									
Principal	—	—	—	—	—	—	2,054	2,045	24
Interest and fiscal charges	150	150	–0–	—	—	—	3,006	2,993	13
Total Expenditures	$32,087	$31,190	$ 897	$ 2,532	$1,743	$ 789	$ 5,075	$ 5,038	$ 37
Excess (Deficiency) of Revenues over (under) Expenditures	$ 4,835	$ 5,765	$ 930	$(1,029)	$ 150	$1,179	$(2,885)	$(2,638)	$182
Other Financing Sources (Uses)									
Operating transfers in	$ —	$ —	$ —	$ —	$ —	$ —	$ 3,500	$ 4,173	$673
Operating transfers out	(4,700)	(4,537)	163	—	—	—	—	—	—
Other	34	145	111	—	—	—	—	—	—
Total Other Financing Sources (Uses)	$ (4,666)	$ (4,392)	$ 274	$ —	$ —	$ —	$ 3,565	$ 4,173	$673
Excess (deficiency) of Revenues and Other Financing Sources over (under) Expenditures and Other Financing Uses	$ 169	$ 1,373	$1,204	$(1,029)	$ 150	$1,179	$ 680	$ 1,535	$855
Fund Balances, January 1	1,807	1,807	–0–	1,224	1,224	–0–	10	10	–0–
Residual equity transfers out	(60)	(45)	15	—	—	—	—	—	—
Fund Balances, December 31	$ 1,916	$ 3,135	$1,219	$ 195	$1,374	$1,179	$ 690	$ 1,545	$855

Source: Adapted from *Governmental Accounting, Auditing and Financial Reporting* (Chicago: Government Finance Officers Association, 1994), p. 445.

ILLUSTRATION 25–19	The *Fourth* of the Five General-Purpose Financial Statements

Name of Government
Combined Statement of Revenues, Expenses, and Changes in Retained Earnings/Fund Balances
All Proprietary Fund Types and Similar Trust Funds
For the Fiscal Year Ended December 31, 19X2
With Comparative Totals for the Fiscal Year Ended December 31, 19X1
(amounts expressed in thousands)

	Proprietary Fund Types		Fiduciary Fund Types		Totals (Memorandum Only)	
	Enterprise	Internal Service	Non-expendable Trust	Pension Trust	19X2	19X1
Operating Revenues						
Charges for sales and service	$17,676	$1,857	$ —	$ —	$19,533	$14,729
Interest	—	—	41	774	815	867
Employer contributions	—	—	—	1,051	1,051	1,047
Employee contributions	—	—	—	729	729	511
Total Operating Revenues	$17,676	$1,857	$ 41	$ 2,554	$22,128	$17,154
Operating Expenses						
Costs of sales and services	$ 7,797	$1,145	$ 13	$ —	$ 8,955	$ 7,127
Administration	3,148	134	—	160	3,442	3,048
Benefits	—	—	—	455	455	380
Refunds	—	—	—	15	15	34
Depreciation	2,507	511	—	—	3,018	2,415
Total Operating Expenses	$13,452	$1,790	$ 13	$ 630	$15,885	$13,004
Operating Income	$ 4,224	$ 67	$ 28	$ 1,924	$ 6,243	$ 4,150
Nonoperating Revenues (Expenses)						
Interest revenue	$ 1,823	$ 8	$ —	$ —	$ 1,831	$ 1,944
Interest expense	(3,734)	—	—	—	(3,734)	(3,098)
Other	(35)	—	138	—	103	47
Total Nonoperating Revenues (Expenses)	$ (1,946)	$ 8	$ 138	$ —	$ (1,800)	$ (1,107)
Net Income before Extraordinary Items	$ 2,278	$ 75	$ 168	$ 1,924	$ 4,443	$ 3,043
Extraordinary gain (loss) on advance refunding	$ 547	$ —	$ —	$ —	$ 547	$ (76)
Net Income	$ 2,825	$ 75	$ 166	$ 1,924	$ 4,990	$ 2,967
Retained Earnings/Fund Balances, January 1	30,546	296	1,887	12,772	45,501	42,534
Retained Earnings/Fund Balances, December 31	$33,371	$ 371	$2,053	$14,696	$50,491	$45,501

Source: Adapted from *Governmental Accounting, Auditing and Financial Reporting* (Chicago: Government Finance Officers Association, 1994), p. 446.

ILLUSTRATION 25–20   The *Fifth* of the Five General-Purpose Financial Statements

Name of Government
Combined Statement of Cash Flows
All Proprietary Fund Types and Nonexpendable Trust Fund
For the Fiscal Year Ended December 31, 19X2
(amounts expressed in thousands)

	Proprietary Fund Types		Fiduciary Fund Type	Totals (Memorandum Only)	
	Enterprise	Internal Service	Nonexpendable Trust	19X8	19X7
Cash flows from operating activities:					
Cash received from customers and users	$ 17,408	$1,839	$ —	$ 19,247	$14,742
Cash paid to suppliers	(7,342)	(1,050)	(18)	(8,410)	(6,962)
Cash paid to employees	(3,608)	(116)	—	(3,724)	(2,954)
Net Cash Provided (Used) by Operating Activities	$ 6,458	$ 673	$ (18)	$ 7,113	$ 4,826
Cash flows from noncapital financing activities:					
Capital contributions and advances	$ 4,294	$ 105	$ —	$ 4,399	$ 6,744
Net Cash Flows from Noncapital Financing Activities	$ 4,294	$ 105	$ —	$ 4,399	$ 6,744
Cash flows from capital and related financing activities:					
Proceeds from issuance of long-term debt	$ 41,155	$ —	$ —	$ 1,155	$ 3,617
Principal payments—bonds	(9,945)	—	—	(9,945)	(4,885)
Principal payments—capital leases	(12)	—	—	(12)	—
Interest paid	(3,258)	—	—	(3,258)	(3,217)
Proceeds from sales of fixed assets	5	—	—	5	—
Purchase of fixed assets	(55)	(639)	—	(694)	(327)
Capital lease obligation down payment	(6)	—	—	(6)	—
Construction (including capitalized interest costs)	(10,759)	—	—	(10,759)	—
Net Cash Provided by Capital and Related Financing Activities	$ 17,125	$ (639)	$ —	$ 16,486	$ (4,812)
Cash flows from investing activities:					
Proceeds from sales of investments	$ 1,930	$ 31	$1,788	$ 3,749	$ 1,524
Purchase of investments	(24,259)	(81)	(1,555)	(25,895)	(8,708)
Interest received	1,416	6	—	1,422	1,973
Net Cash Provided (Used) by Investing Activities	$(20,913)	$ (44)	$ 233	$(20,724)	$ (5,211)
Net Increase in Cash and Cash Equivalents ...	$ 6,964	$ 95	$ 215	$ 7,274	$ 1,547
Cash and cash equivalents, January 1	2,811	5	16	2,832	1,285
Cash and Cash Equivalents, December 31	$ 9,775	$ 100	$ 231	$ 10,106	$ 2,832

Source: Adapted form *Governmental Accounting, Auditing and Financial Reporting* (Chicago: Government Finance Officers Association, 1994), p. 447.

END-OF-CHAPTER REVIEW

SUMMARY OF KEY POINTS

Illustrations 25–21 and 25–22 summarize the major key points of this chapter.

SELF-STUDY QUESTIONS

(Answers are at the end of this chapter preceding the appendix.)

A. Differentiation of Types of Funds: Activities

1. Recreational facilities run by a governmental unit and financed on a user-charge basis most likely would be accounted for in which fund?
   a. General Fund
   b. Trust Fund
   c. Enterprise Fund
   d. Capital Projects Fund
   e. Special Revenue Fund
2. The activities of a municipal golf course that receives *most* of its revenues from a special tax levy should be accounted for in which fund?
   a. Capital Projects Fund
   b. Internal Service Fund

| ILLUSTRATION 25–21 | Summary Comparison of All Funds and Account Groups | | | | | |

Fund Type or Account Group	Measurement Focus Is on the Flow of	Basis of Accounting	Records Annual Budget in General Ledger	Uses Encumbrances Accounting	Reports Fixed Assets and Long-Term Debt in Its Own Balance Sheet	Does Not Have a Fund Equity
Government Funds						
General Fund	CFR	MA	X	X		
Special Revenue Funds	CFR	MA	X	X		
Capital Projects Funds	CFR	MA	(1)	X		
Debt Service Funds	CFR	MA	(1)			
Fiduciary Funds						
Agency Funds	n/a	MA				X
Trust Funds						
Expendable	CFR	MA				
Nonexpendable	ER	A			X	
Pension trusts	ER	A			X	
Proprietary Funds						
Internal Service Funds	ER	A			X	
Enterprise Funds	ER	A			X	
Account Groups						
General Fixed Assets	n/a	n/a			(2)	n/a
General Long-Term Debt	n/a	n/a			(3)	n/a

(1) This depends on whether the governmental unit has legally adopted an annual budget for this fund—some governmental units do and some do not.

(2) General Fixed Assets are reported in a statement of general fixed assets (level 3 of the financial reporting pyramid) and in the combined balance sheet—all fund types and account groups (level 1 of the financial reporting pyramid).

(3) GLTD is reported in a statement of GLTD (level 3 of the financial reporting pyramid) and in the combined balance sheet—all fund types and account groups (level 1 of the financial reporting pyramid).

Code: CFR = Current Financial Resources
      ER = Economic Resources
      MA = Modified Accrual
       A = Accrual

ILLUSTRATION 25–22 **Summary of Required General-Purpose Financial Statements (level 1 of the financial reporting pyramid)**

Fund Type or Account Group	Combined Balance Sheet	Combined Statement Revenues, Expenditures, and Changes in Fund Balances	Revenues, Expenditures, and Changes in Fund Balances— Budget Versus Actual	Revenues, Expenses, and Changes in Retained Earnings/ Fund Balance	Cash Flows
Governmental Funds					
General Fund	X	X	X		
Special Revenue Funds	X	X	X		
Capital Projects Funds	X	X	(1)		
Debt Service Funds	X	X	(1)		
Fiduciary Funds					
Agency Funds	X				
Trust Funds—					
Expendable	X	X			
Nonexpendable	X			X	X
Pension trusts	X			X	
Proprietary Funds					
Internal Service Funds	X			X	X
Enterprise Funds	X			X	X
Account Groups					
General Fixed Assets	X				
General Long-Term Debt	X				

(1) This depends on whether the governmental unit has legally adopted an annual budget for this fund.

    c. Special Revenue Fund
    d. General Fund
    e. Enterprise Fund

3. A data processing center established by a governmental unit to service all agencies within the unit should be accounted for in which fund?
    a. Capital Projects Fund
    b. Internal Service Fund
    c. Agency Fund
    d. Trust Fund
    e. Enterprise Fund

4. The activities of a municipal employees' retirement and pension system should be recorded in which fund?
    a. General Fund
    b. Special Revenue Fund
    c. Debt Service Fund
    d. Agency Fund
    e. Trust Fund

5. Receipts from taxes levied in connection with a special assessment for sidewalk improvements (involving a bond issuance for which the governmental unit has guaranteed repayment) should be accounted for in which fund?
    a. Special Revenue Fund
    b. General Fund
    c. Internal Service Fund
    d. Capital Projects Fund
    e. Debt Service Fund

6. A city collects property taxes for the local sanitary, park, and school districts and periodically remits collections to these units. This activity should be accounted for in which fund?
   a. Agency Fund
   b. General Fund
   c. Internal Service Fund
   d. Special Revenue Fund
   e. None of the above

7. The operations of a public library receiving the majority of its support from property taxes levied for that purpose should be accounted for in which fund?
   a. General Fund
   b. Special Revenue Fund
   c. Enterprise Fund
   d. Internal Service Fund
   e. None of the above

8. The proceeds of a federal grant to help finance the future construction of an adult training center should be recorded in which fund?
   a. General Fund
   b. Special Revenue Fund
   c. Capital Projects Fund
   d. Internal Service Fund
   e. None of the above

9. The receipts from a special tax levy to retire and pay interest on general obligation bonds issued to finance the construction of a new city hall should be recorded in which fund?
   a. Debt Service Fund
   b. Capital Projects Fund
   c. General Fund
   d. Special Revenue Fund
   e. None of the above

10. The lump-sum monthly remittance to an insurance company for hospital-surgical insurance premiums collected as payroll deductions from employees should be recorded in which fund?
    a. General Fund
    b. Agency Fund
    c. Special Revenue Fund
    d. Internal Service Fund
    e. None of the above

11. The activities of a central motor pool that supplies and services vehicles for the use of municipal employees on official business should be accounted for in which fund?
    a. Agency Fund
    b. General Fund
    c. Internal Service Fund
    d. Special Revenue Fund
    e. None of the above

12. To provide for the retirement of general obligation bonds, a city invests a portion of its general revenue receipts in marketable securities. This investment activity should be accounted for in which fund?
    a. Trust Fund
    b. Enterprise Fund
    c. Special Revenue Fund
    d. General Long-Term Debt Account Group
    e. Debt Service Fund

B. **Understanding the Interrelationship Among the Funds and Account Groups for Fixed Assets**

13. A new fire truck was purchased out of a city's General Fund. An entry is also required in which of the following?
    a. Internal Service Fund
    b. Capital Projects Fund

    c. Special Revenue Fund

    d. General Fixed Assets Account Group

    e. None of the above

14. A city sells an unused fire station previously accounted for in its GFAAG. An entry is also required in which of the following?

    a. General Fund

    b. Special Revenue Fund

    c. Trust Fund

    d. Debt Service Fund

    e. None of the above

15. A city built a new city hall, the construction of which was accounted for in a Capital Projects Fund. Entries relating to the new building are also required in which of the following?

    a. General Fund

    b. Enterprise Fund

    c. Internal Service Fund

    d. General Fixed Assets Account Group

    e. None of the above

16. A city made certain public improvements from a special assessment. Entries relating to the improvements are optional in which of the following?

    a. Capital Projects Fund

    b. Internal Service Fund

    c. Enterprise Fund

    d. General Fixed Assets Account Group

    e. None of the above

17. A city's water utility, which is accounted for in an Enterprise Fund, acquired some new fixed assets. An entry is also required in which of the following?

    a. Agency Fund

    b. Internal Service Fund

    c. General Fund

    d. General Fixed Assets Account Group

    e. No additional entry required

18. A city's purchasing and stores department is properly accounted for in an Internal Service Fund. When fixed assets are acquired for this department, accounting entries are required in which of the following?

    a. General Fixed Assets Accounting Group

    b. Internal Service Fund

    c. General Fixed Assets Account Group and an Internal Service Fund

    d. General Fund and the General Fixed Assets Account Group

    e. Enterprise Fund

    f. Enterprise Fund and the General Fixed Assets Account Group

C. Understanding the Interrelationship of the Funds and Account Groups for Long-Term Debt

19. A transaction in which a municipal electric utility issues bonds (to be repaid from its own operations) requires accounting recognition in which of the following?

    a. Enterprise Fund

    b. Debt Service Fund

    c. Enterprise and Debt Service Funds

    d. Enterprise Fund, a Debt Service Fund, and the General Long-Term Debt Account Group

    e. None of the above

20. The liability for general obligation bonds issued for the benefit of a municipal electric company and serviced by its earnings should be recorded in which of the following?

    a. Enterprise Fund

    b. General Fund

    c. Enterprise Fund and the General Long-Term Debt Account Group

    d. Enterprise Fund and disclosed in a footnote in the statement of General Long-Term Debt

e. None of the above

21. The liability for special assessment bonds that carry a secondary pledge of a municipality's general credit should be recorded in which of the following?
    a. Debt Service Fund
    b. General Long-Term Debt Account Group
    c. Agency Fund
    d. Only disclosure would be made in a footnote in the statement of General Long-Term Debt
    e. None of the above

22. The liability for special assessment bonds when the municipality is *not* obligated in any manner in the event of default by the property owners should be recorded in which of the following?
    a. Debt Service Fund
    b. General Long-Term Debt Account Group
    c. Agency Fund
    d. Only disclosures would be made in a footnote in the statement of General Long-Term Debt
    e. None of the above

23. A transaction in which a municipality issues general obligation serial bonds to finance the construction of a fire station requires accounting recognition in which of the following?
    a. General Fund
    b. Capital Projects and General Funds
    c. Capital Projects Fund and the General Long-Term Debt Account Group
    d. General Fund and the General Long-Term Debt Account Group
    e. None of the above

24. Several years ago, a city established a sinking fund to retire an issue of general obligation bonds. This year, the city made a $50,000 contribution to the sinking fund from general revenues and realized $15,000 in revenue from sinking fund securities. The bonds due this year were retired. These transactions require accounting recognition in which of the following?
    a. General Fund
    b. Debt Service Fund and the General Long-Term Debt Account Group
    c. Debt Service Fund, the General Fund, and the General Long-Term Debt Account Group
    d. Capital Projects Fund, a Debt Service Fund, the General Fund, and the General Long-Term Debt Account Group
    e. None of the above   (AICPA adapted. nos. 19–24)

D. **Familiarity with General-Purpose Financial Statements**

25. In the comprehensive annual financial report (CAFR), the combined balance sheet should include which of the following?

	Governmental Funds	Proprietary Funds	Account Groups
a.	Yes	Yes	Yes
b.	Yes	Yes	No
c.	Yes	No	Yes
d.	Yes	No	No
e.	No	Yes	Yes

26. The CAFR should include a combined statement of revenues, expenses, and changes in retained earnings (or equity) for which of the following?

	Governmental Funds	Proprietary Funds	Account Groups
a.	Yes	Yes	Yes
b.	Yes	Yes	No
c.	Yes	No	Yes
d.	No	Yes	Yes
e.	No	Yes	No

27. The CAFR should include a combined statement of revenues, expenditures, and changes in retained earnings (or equity) for which of the following?

	Governmental Funds	Proprietary Funds	Account Groups
a.	Yes	Yes	Yes
b.	No	No	No
c.	Yes	No	No
d.	No	Yes	No
e.	Yes	Yes	No

28. The CAFR should include a combined statement of cash flows for which of the following?

	Governmental Funds	Proprietary Funds	Account Groups
a.	No	Yes	Yes
b.	Yes	Yes	No
c.	No	Yes	No
d.	Yes	No	No
e.	Yes	No	Yes

29. Which financial statement is *not* one of the five general-purpose financial statements?
   a. A combined balance sheet—all funds and account groups and discretely presented component units.
   b. A combined statement of revenues, expenditures, and changes in fund balances—all governmental fund types and discretely presented component units.
   c. A combined statement of revenues, expenses, and changes in retained earnings—all proprietary fund types and discretely presented component units.
   d. A combined statement of cash flows—all fund types and discretely presented component units.
   e. None of the above
30. The CAFR is required to include a statement of cash flows for which of the following?
   a. Agency Fund
   b. General Fixed Assets Account Group
   c. General Long-Term Debt Account Group
   d. Expendable Trust Fund
   e. Pension Trust Fund
   f. Internal Service Fund

ASSIGNMENT MATERIAL

REVIEW QUESTIONS

1. When is a Special Revenue Fund used instead of the General Fund?
2. What is the relationship between a Capital Projects Fund and the GFAAG?
3. Does the GFAAG include all fixed assets of a governmental unit? Why or why not?
4. What is the relationship between the Debt Service Funds and the GLTDAG?
5. What is the difference in meaning of the term *general long-term debt* as used in the GLTDAG and as used in private industry?
6. Does the GLTDAG include all long-term debt? Why or why not?
7. What determines whether special assessment receivables are recorded in a Debt Service Fund or in an Agency Fund?
8. Which fund is used to account for construction activity to be financed from a special assessment to certain property owners?
9. What is the distinction between an Agency Fund and a Trust Fund?

10. What are the two types of Trust Funds?

11. In what way are Enterprise Funds and Internal Service Funds similar to commercial operations?

12. What significance may be attributed to the fact that the billings of an Internal Service Fund or an Enterprise Fund exceed its costs and expenses?

EXERCISES

E 25–1 **GLTD: Preparing Journal Entries**   The following transactions occurred during Bondsville County's fiscal year ended 6/30/X2:

1. On 10/1/X1, general obligation term bonds having a face value of $1,000,000 and an 8% interest rate were issued. Interest is payable semiannually on April 1 and October 1. The $980,000 proceeds were used to construct a new courthouse.
2. On 1/1/X2, the county transferred $16,000 from the General Fund to a Debt Service Fund for sinking fund purposes.
3. The Debt Service Fund immediately invested this money, and by 6/30/X2, the county's fiscal year-end, $1,000 of interest had been earned on these investments.
4. On 3/27/X2, $40,000 was transferred from the General Fund to the Debt Service Fund to meet the first interest payment.
5. On 4/1/X2, the Debt Service Fund made the required interest payment of $40,000. (A fiscal agent is not used.)

Required   Prepare the journal entries that should be made in all of the appropriate funds and account groups for these transactions.

E 25–2 **Debt Service Fund and GLTDAG: Preparing Journal Entries**   The city of Promises had the following transactions during its fiscal year ended 6/30/X4:

1. General obligation serial bonds having a face value of $100,000 matured during the year and were redeemed. (Money was transferred from the General Fund to the Debt Service Fund to redeem this debt.)
2. Total interest paid on serial bonds during the year was $80,000. (Money was transferred from the General Fund to the Debt Service Fund to pay this interest.)
3. General obligation term bonds having a face value of $500,000 were issued for $505,000. The proceeds are for construction of a new fire station, which is expected to cost $500,000. The $5,000 premium, which will not be used for construction purposes, was properly transferred to the Debt Service Fund.
4. A cash transfer of $10,000 was made from the General Fund to a Debt Service Fund in connection with a sinking fund requirement pertaining to general obligation term bonds.
5. Special assessment bonds having a face value of $400,000 were issued at par. The proceeds are for residential street improvements. (The city *is* liable for this debt in the event of default by the assessed property owners.)

Required   Prepare journal entries for each of these transactions in all appropriate funds or account groups. Use the following headings for your workpaper:

Transaction Number	Account Titles and Explanations	Amount		Fund or Account Group
		Dr.	Cr.	

E 25–3 **COMPREHENSIVE: Matching Transactions With Possible Ways to Record Transactions**   Each item in the left-hand column represents various transactions pertaining to a city that uses encumbrance accounting. The right-hand column lists possible ways to record the transactions.

Transactions

1. General obligation bonds were issued at par.
2. Approved purchase orders were issued for supplies.
3. These supplies were received and the related invoices were approved.

Possible Ways to Record the Transactions

A. Credit Appropriations.
B. Credit Budgetary Fund Balance— Unreserved.
C. Credit Expenditures.
D. Credit Deferred Revenues.
E. Credit Interfund Revenues.

4. General Fund salaries and wages were incurred.
5. The Internal Service Fund had interfund billings.
6. Revenues were earned from a previously awarded grant.
7. Property taxes were collected in advance.
8. Appropriations were recorded on adoption of the budget.
9. Short-term financing was received from a bank, secured by the city's taxing power.
10. There was an excess of estimated inflows over estimated outflows.

F. Credit Tax Anticipation Notes Payable.
G. Credit Other Financing Sources.
H. Credit Other Financing Uses.
I. Debit Appropriations.
J. Debit Deferred Revenues.
K. Debit Encumbrances.
L. Debit Expenditures.

Required   For each of the transactions, what is the appropriate recording of the transaction? A method to record the transactions may be selected once, more than once, or not at all.   (AICPA adapted)

E 25–4   **COMPREHENSIVE: Matching Funds, Accounts, and Account Groups with Possible Accounting and Reporting Methods**   Each item in the left-hand column represents the funds, accounts, and account groups used by a city. The right-hand column lists possible accounting and reporting methods.

Funds, Accounts, and Account Groups	**Possible Accounting and Reporting Methods**
1. Enterprise Fund Fixed assets.	A. Accounted for in a fiduciary fund.
2. Capital Projects Fund.	B. Accounted for in a proprietary fund.
3. General Fixed Assets.	C. Accounted for in a quasi-endowment fund.
4. Infrastructure Fixed Assets.	D. Accounted for in a self-balancing account group.
5. Enterprise Fund Cash.	E. Accounted for in a special assessment fund.
6. General Fund.	F. Accounts for major construction activities.
7. Agency Fund Cash.	G. Accounts for property tax revenues.
8. General Long-Term Debt.	H. Accounts for payment of interest and principal on tax supported debt.
9. Special Revenue Fund.	I. Accounts for revenues from earmarked sources to finance designated activities.
10. Debt Services Fund.	J. Reporting is optional.

Required   For each of the city's funds, accounts, and account groups, what is the appropriate accounting and reporting method? Each method may be selected once, more than once, or not at all.

(AICPA adapted)

PROBLEMS

P 25–1   **Capital Projects Fund: Preparing Journal Entries and Financial Statements**   On 8/1/X2, the City of Atlantis authorized the issuance of 6% general obligation serial bonds having a face value of $8,000,000. The proceeds will be used to construct a new convention center estimated to cost $8,300,000. Over the past several years, the Unreserved Fund Balance account in the city's General Fund has been approximately $300,000 higher than is prudently needed. Accordingly, this excess accumulation will be used to pay for the remainder of the construction cost. A Capital Projects Fund, designated the Convention Center Construction Fund, was established to account for this project.

The following transactions occurred during the fiscal year ended 6/30/X3:

1. On 8/4/X2, a $180,000 payment was made from the General Fund to Ace Architecture Company for the design of the convention center. (This $180,000 for architect's fees was part of the $8,300,000 total estimated cost of the convention center.) The Expenditures account was charged on the books of the General Fund.
2. On 9/5/X2, a $8,100,000 construction contract was entered into with Nautilus Construction Company.
3. On 10/2/X2, the city deposited $120,000 ($300,000 – $180,000 paid to the architect) to the Convention Center Construction Fund.

4. On 12/1/X2, one-half of the authorized bond issue was sold at 101. The bond premium was properly transferred to a Debt Service Fund.
5. On 4/30/X3, Nautilus submitted a $2,100,000 bill for work completed to date. Only $1,900,000 was paid.
6. On 6/1/X3, the first semiannual interest payment on the bonds was made. (Principal payments are deferred until 12/1/X4.)
7. On 6/20/X3, the city was awarded an irrevocable federal grant totaling $1,000,000 to help finance the cost of the convention center. Payment will be received within 60 days. The city had applied for this grant in May 19X1, with slight expectation of receiving it. Accordingly, it obtained authorization for a bond issue of $8,000,000 instead of $7,000,000.

Additional Information
1. The city intends to use a Special Revenue Fund to account for the operations of the convention center upon completion of the project.
2. The city does not record budgets for capital projects in Capital Projects Funds.

Required
1. For these transactions, prepare the entries that should be made in the Convention Center Construction Fund for the year ended 6/30/X3. (Also, show the appropriate General Fund entry for items 1 and 3.)
2. Prepare the appropriate closing entries at 6/30/X3.
3. Prepare a balance sheet at 6/30/X3.
4. Prepare a statement of revenues, expenditures, and changes in fund balance for the year ended 6/30/X3.

P 25–2 **Debt Service Fund: Preparing the Operating Statement from Selected Information** The following information relating to the City of Debtville's Debt Service Fund is provided for the year ended 12/31/X2:

Interest

Interest owed at 12/31/X1 (none past due)	$ 160,000
Interest payments made at due dates during 19X2	700,000
Interest owed at 12/31/X2 (none past due)	130,000
Cash received from the General Fund to pay interest	700,000

Property Taxes

Property tax assessments made in 19X2 (to be collected by the Debt Service Fund)	566,000
Property tax collections by the Debt Service Fund	550,000
Allowance for uncollectible accounts	
12/31/X1	4,000
12/31/X2	5,000
Accounts written off during 19X2 (from 19X1 assessments)	2,000
Property tax receivables	
12/31/X1	26,000[a]
12/31/X2	40,000[b]

Long-Term Debt

Cash received from the General Fund to pay for the retirement of debt principal	400,000
GLTD that matured during 19X2 and was paid off	1,000,000

Miscellaneous

Gain on sale of investments	11,000
Interest on investments	75,000
Fund balance, 12/31/X1 (all reserved for debt service)	621,000

[a]At 12/31/X1, the entire net realizable amount of the property tax receivables was expected to be collected within 60 days, the time period the city uses to determine whether revenues are "available."

[b]At 12/31/X2, $25,000 of the net realizable amount of the property tax receivables are expected to be collected *after* 60 days.

Required Prepare a statement of revenues, expenditures, and changes in fund balance for 19X2. (*Hint:* Use T accounts for calculations pertaining to property tax revenues.)

P 25–3   **Special Assessments: Preparing Journal Entries and *Combined* Financial Statements**   Sunn City had the following transactions pertaining to street improvements for which a special assessment was made:

1. On 9/1/X1, a special assessment levy of $200,000 was made against properties on Main Street for street improvements. The $200,000 is to be paid in four annual installments beginning 3/1/X2. No uncollectible accounts are expected. Concurrently, a $200,000 bond issue was authorized, which carries a secondary pledge by the city. The proceeds can be used only on the project.
2. On 10/1/X1, $203,000 was received from the sale of 10% special assessment serial bonds. The bond indenture requires any premium to be set aside for servicing the bonds.
3. On 10/5/X1, a construction contract for $195,000 was signed with a general contractor who is to be paid at the completion of the work.
4. On 12/5/X1, the contractor completed the work and was paid in full.
5. In February 19X2, the first installment of the special assessment levy was collected in full.
6. On 3/31/X2, the city retired $50,000 of the special assessment bonds and made the $10,000 semi-annual interest payment. The city council authorized all interest payments on the bonds to be the responsibility of the General Fund.

The city does *not* capitalize infrastructure fixed assets.

Required   1. Prepare the journal entries that should be made in all of the appropriate funds and account groups for these transactions.
2. Prepare any appropriate year-end adjusting entries.
3. Prepare a combined statement of revenues, expenditures, and changes in fund balance for the fiscal year ended 6/30/X2—omit the General Fund.
4. Prepare a combined balance sheet at 6/30/X2 for all funds and account groups—omit the General Fund. (Assume that the city follows customary practice in reporting street improvements.)
5. Prepare the entry to close the books at year-end.

P 25–4   **Capital Projects Fund and Debt Service Fund: Preparing Journal Entries and *Combined* Financial Statements**   River City, whose citizens were troubled by the lack of recreational facilities for its youth, entered into the following transactions during its fiscal year ended 12/31/X1:

1. On 1/3/X1, a $600,000 serial bond issue having an 8% stated interest rate was authorized to acquire land and construct a youth recreation center thereon. The bonds are to be redeemed in 10 equal annual installments beginning 2/1/X2.
2. On 1/10/X1, the city made a $50,000 nonrefundable deposit on the purchase of land for the youth recreation center. The contracted price for the land is $150,000, which is $40,000 below the city's estimate.
3. On 3/1/X1, the city issued serial bonds having a $450,000 face value at 102. The bond indenture requires any premium to be set aside for servicing bond indebtedness. The General Fund was repaid $50,000.
4. On 3/10/X1, the city paid the remaining amount on the land contract and took title to the land.
5. On 3/17/X1, the city signed a $400,000 construction contract with Rover Construction Company.
6. On 7/10/X1, the contractor was paid $200,000 for work completed to date.
7. On 9/1/X1, a semiannual interest payment was made on the outstanding bonds. (The source of the money was the General Fund.)
8. On 12/1/X1, the city issued serial bonds having a $100,000 face value at par.
9. On 12/2/X1, the contractor completed the recreation center and submitted a final billing of $210,000, which includes $10,000 of additional work authorized by the city in October 19X1. The $210,000 was paid to the contractor on 12/12/X1.
10. Through 12/10/X1, the city had invested excess cash (from the bond offering) in short-term certificates of deposit. The amount collected on these investments totaled $12,000. (For this item, you need to make an entry only for the investment income.)

Required   1. Prepare the journal entries for the preceding transactions.
2. Prepare any appropriate year-end adjusting entries.
3. Prepare a combined statement of revenues, expenditures, and changes in fund balance for 19X1—omit the General Fund.
4. Prepare a combined balance sheet for all funds and account groups at 12/31/X1—omit the General Fund.

P 25–5 **Internal Service Funds: Preparing Journal Entries and Financial Statements**   The City of Paradise had the following transactions relating to its newly established Central Printing Internal Service Fund during the fiscal year ended 6/30/X1:

1. It received a $100,000 contribution from the General Fund to establish the Internal Service Fund.
2. Machinery and equipment costing $80,000 were purchased and paid for by the Internal Service Fund. These items were placed in service on 1/4/X1 and have an estimated useful life of 10 years. (All machinery and equipment in the GFAAG is depreciated using a 10-year life.)
3. Materials and supplies of $18,000 were ordered using purchase orders. For $14,000 of these purchase orders, the materials and supplies were received at a cost of $14,300. Payments totaling $9,500 were made on these billings.
4. Total billings for the year were $60,000. Of this amount, $7,000 was billed to the city's water utility, which is operated in an Enterprise Fund. The remaining amount was billed to various departments in the General Fund. Of these billings, $32,000 was collected from the General Fund and $5,500 from the water utility.
5. Salaries and wages totaling $49,000 were paid.
6. The city's electric utility, operated as an Enterprise Fund, billed the Internal Service Fund $900. Of this amount, $700 was paid.
7. Materials and supplies on hand at 6/30/X1 were counted and costed at $3,800.
8. A $5,000 subsidy was received from the General Fund near the end of the fiscal year, recognizing that the first year of operations was a start-up year at a loss. In addition, $10,000 was received from the General Fund near the end of the fiscal year as a temporary advance to be repaid (without interest) during the following fiscal year.

Required   1. Prepare the appropriate journal entries for these transactions in the Internal Service Fund.
2. Prepare the year-end closing entry.
3. Prepare a balance sheet at 6/30/X1.
4. Prepare a statement of revenues, expenses, and changes in retained earnings for the year ended 6/30/X1.

P 25–6 **Enterprise Fund: Preparing Journal Entries**   The following activities pertain to Enterprise Funds:

1. City A contributed $1,000,000 to a newly established Enterprise Fund formed to provide off-street parking facilities.
2. City B established an Enterprise Fund to account for the building of a municipal golf course using the $3,000,000 proceeds of general obligation bonds to be repaid from golf course earnings. The bonds were issued at a $50,000 premium.
3. City C established an Enterprise Fund to account for its municipal swimming pools to be built using the $2,000,000 proceeds of general obligation serial bonds to be repaid from taxes and general revenues. The bonds were issued at a $25,000 discount.
4. City D operates a water utility in an Enterprise Fund. To expand operations, the city issued $5,000,000 of revenue bonds at a $40,000 premium.
5. City E operates an electric utility in an Enterprise Fund, which made a $500,000 payment in lieu of taxes to the city's General Fund.
6. City F operates an airport in an Enterprise Fund, which made a $600,000 payment to the city to finance General Fund expenditures.
7. City G discontinued its municipal golf course, which was accounted for in an Enterprise Fund. It sold the land to a residential home developer. All outstanding liabilities were paid, and the remaining $750,000 cash was disbursed to the General Fund. (The Enterprise Fund had $300,000 in its Capital Contribution from Municipality account and $450,000 in its Retained Earnings account just before the disbursement.)
8. City H operates a public transit system in an Enterprise Fund. The transit system usually recovers approximately 60% of its costs and expenses from user charges. During the current year, the Enterprise Fund received an $800,000 subsidy from the General Fund.
9. City I operates an electric utility in an Enterprise Fund. During the year, the city redeemed $500,000 of its electric utility's revenue bonds.
10. City J operates a gas utility in an Enterprise Fund. During the year, the city redeemed $1,000,000 of its general obligation serial bonds, issued many years ago to finance the gas utility expansion. The bonds were to be repaid from taxes and general revenues.

Required For each transaction, prepare the necessary journal entries for all the funds and account groups involved. Use the following headings for your workpaper:

Transaction Number	Account Titles and Explanations	Amount		Fund or Account Group
		Dr.	Cr.	

P 25–7 **Agency Fund (Resulting from a Special Assessment)** On 1/2/X1, the city council of Walkerville approved a six-year special assessment project for a sidewalk improvement program. Transactions during 19X1 and other information pertaining to this project follow:

1. 1/2/X1: Issued 10% serial bonds having a face amount of $500,000 at their face amount. (The city is *not* obligated in any manner in the event of default.)
2. 1/2/X1: Signed a construction contract having a fixed price of $600,000.
3. 1/2/X1: Levied special assessments totaling $660,000, of which $60,000 is expected to be uncollectible. Beginning 7/1/X1, interest at 10% is to be charged on the deferred installments of $550,000, of which $110,000 is due annually each July 1 beginning 7/1/X2, along with accrued interest.
4. 7/1/X1: Collected $101,000 on the current portion of the $110,000 assessment that became due.
5. 7/1/X1: Disbursed $100,000 to the Capital Projects Fund.

Required Prepare the entries required in the Agency Fund for 19X1.

P 25–8 **Comprehensive: (All Funds and Account Groups) Preparing Journal Entries for Typical Transactions** The Village of Starville had the following transactions for the year ended 12/31/X3:

1. Property taxes of $500,000 were levied. Of this amount, $100,000 was a special levy for servicing and retiring serial bonds issued 15 years ago to construct a fire station. Of the total amount levied, 2% was estimated to be uncollectible. An Agency Fund was used.
2. The village received its share of state sales taxes on gasoline. The $33,000 share can be used only for street improvements and maintenance. During the year, the village spent $31,000 for this purpose. (The village used its own workforce.)
3. On 3/31/X3, general obligation bonds bearing 6% interest were issued in the face amount of $500,000. The proceeds were $503,000, of which $500,000 was authorized to be spent on a new library. The remaining $3,000 was set aside for the eventual retirement of the debt. The bonds are due in 20 years, with interest to be paid each year on March 31 and September 30.
4. A $490,000 construction contract was entered into with Booker Construction Company to build the new library. Of the $240,000 bill submitted, $216,000 was paid.
5. On 9/30/X3, the interest due on the library bonds was paid using money from the General Fund.
6. On 11/30/X3, the fire station serial bonds referred to in item 1 were paid off ($60,000), along with interest due at that time ($36,000).
7. On 7/31/X3, 8% special assessment bonds having a face value of $90,000 were issued at par; the proceeds will be used for a street lighting project. Interest is paid annually each July 31. (The village has pledged to pay off these bonds in the event that the assessed property owners default.)
8. Assessments of $100,000 were levied for a residential street lighting project, the village contributed $7,000 from the General Fund as its share. Of the $100,000 assessed, $10,000 was collected, with the remaining $90,000 to be collected in succeeding years.
9. An $8,000 General Fund transfer was made to establish an Internal Service Fund to provide for a central purchasing and stores function.
10. During the year, the Internal Service Fund purchased various supplies costing $6,500. Of this amount, $4,400 was billed to the city's various departments at $5,500.
11. A Capital Projects Fund having a $2,000 fund balance was terminated. The cash was sent to the General Fund as required.
12. A local resident donated marketable securities with a market value of $80,000 (the resident's cost was $44,000) under the terms of a trust agreement. The principal is to remain intact. Earnings on the principal are to be used for college scholarships to needy students. Revenues earned during 19X3 totaled $7,500, of which $7,000 was disbursed for scholarships.
13. The village water utility billed the General fund $6,600.
14. A new fire truck costing $22,000 was ordered, received, and paid for. The old fire truck (which had cost $8,000) was sold for $1,500.

Required For each transaction, prepare the necessary journal entries for all of the appropriate funds and account groups involved. Use the following headings for your workpaper:

Transaction Number	Account Titles and Explanations	Amount		Fund or Account Group
		Dr.	Cr.	

P 25–9 **Additional Requirement for Problem 24–8 in Chapter 24**

Required Prepare the entries that would be made in the other funds and account groups in Problem 24–8 to account properly for the items that should *not* be accounted for in the General Fund.

P 25–10 **Comprehensive: Preparing a *Combined* Balance Sheet from Trial Balances** Following is the trial balance of all of the funds and account groups for Nerf City at 6/30/X6, just *prior* to the adjusting and closing entries. All depreciation adjustments have been made.

General Fund

Cash	$ 150,000	Vouchers Payable	$ 75,000
Taxes Receivable—Current	130,000	Due to Internal Service Fund	15,000
Inventory	20,000	BUDGETARY FUND BALANCE	
ESTIMATED REVENUES	900,000	RESERVED FOR	
ENCUMBRANCES	30,000	ENCUMBRANCES	30,000
Expenditures	770,000	BUDGETARY FUND BALANCE	100,000
		Unreserved Fund Balance	50,000
		APPROPRIATIONS	800,000
		Revenues	930,000
	$2,000,000		$2,000,000

New Fire Station Capital Projects Fund[a]

Cash	$ 10,000	Unreserved Fund Balance	$100,000
Expenditures	90,000		
	$100,000		$100,000

[a]This project was completed by year-end. The money raised can be spent only on the fire station.

New Fire Station Debt Service Fund

Cash	$22,000	Revenues	$ 2,000
Investments	20,000	Unreserved Fund Balances	40,000
	$42,000		$42,000

Internal Service Fund

Cash	$ 85,000	Revenues	$ 90,000
Due from General Fund	15,000	Accumulated Depreciation	50,000
Equipment	200,000	Retained Earnings	260,000
Expenses	100,000		
	$400,000		$400,000

Trust and Agency Funds

Cash	$ 80,000	Accumulated Depreciation	$ 30,000
Office Building	300,000	Revenues	30,000
Expenses	10,000	Liability to Federal Government	14,000
		Liability to State Government	6,000
		Unreserved Fund Balance	310,000
	$390,000		$390,000

General Fixed Assets Account Group

Buildings	$390,000	Investment in GFA-CPF	$430,000
Equipment	50,000	Investment in GFA-GF	70,000
Construction W.I.P.	60,000		
	$500,000		$500,000

General Long-Term Debt Account Group

Amount Available in Debt		Bonds Payable	$350,000
Service Fund	$ 40,000		
Amount to Be Provided	310,000		
	$350,000		$350,000

Required   Prepare a combined balance sheet for all funds and account groups.

✳ THINKING CRITICALLY ✳

✳ CASES ✳

C 25–1   **Expenditure Recognition on Construction Contract**   On 1/1/X1, the city council of Centersville approved the construction of a new civic center. It immediately signed a construction contract having a fixed price of $10,000,000. The terms of the contract follow:

1. A $2,000,000 payment is to be made to the contractor at the time of the signing. (The city made the payment.)
2. Progress billings are to be made each December 20 based on the percentage of completion times $7,000,000.
3. Progress payments are to be made within 10 days after bills are submitted.
4. Upon completion of the project, the $1,000,000 final payment is to be made.

On 12/20/X1, the contractor submitted a progress billing for $2,800,000 (40% of $7,000,000). The city paid it on 12/30/X1.

Required   1. What amount should the city report for expenditures in its Capital Projects Fund for 19X1?
2. Assuming that the contractor uses the percentage of completion method of accounting, what amount should the contractor report for sales for 19X1?
3. Explain the disparity between requirements 1 and 2.

C 25–2   **Accounting for General Fund Overhead Allocation to an Enterprise Fund**   Crystal City has an Electric Utility Enterprise Fund. The city believes that some of its general overhead (accounted for in the General Fund) should be allocated to the Electric Utility Enterprise Fund because it obtains benefits. If the utility were a private corporation, its overhead would be higher than it is now. A cash payment will be made from the Electric Utility Enterprise Fund to the General Fund for the amount of the overhead allocation.

Required   How should the overhead allocation and cash payment be reported in each fund's financial statements?

ANSWERS TO SELF-STUDY QUESTIONS

1. c   **2.** c   **3.** b   **4.** e   **5.** e   **6.** a   **7.** b   **8.** c   **9.** a   **10.** b   **11.** c   **12.** e   **13.** d
14. a   **15.** d   **16.** d   **17.** e   **18.** b   **19.** a   **20.** d   **21.** b   **22.** c   **23.** c   **24.** c   **25.** a
26. e   **27.** b   **28.** c   **29.** d   **30.** f

■APPENDIX

THE GASB'S MAJOR CURRENT PROJECT REEXAMINING GOVERNMENTAL FINANCIAL REPORTING: MAJOR NEW STANDARDS COULD BECOME EFFECTIVE IN 1999 (AT THE EARLIEST)

As stated earlier, the GASB has in process a major project to completely reexamine accounting and financial reporting for governmental units. This examination involves two broad areas:

1. The Financial Reporting Model: Dual-Perspective Reporting Versus Single-Perspective Reporting.
2. Measurement Focus and Basis of Accounting.

I THE FINANCIAL REPORTING MODEL: DUAL-PERSPECTIVE REPORTING VERSUS SINGLE-PERSPECTIVE REPORTING

In June 1994, the GASB issued the *Invitation to Comment*, "Governmental Financial Reporting Model," whose purpose was to solicit comments on issues involving the display and disclosure requirements for the external general-purpose financial statements of state and local governmental units. In June 1995, the GASB issued a *Preliminary Views* document in which it proposed to (1) discard the current pyramid approach to financial reporting and (2) require a dual-perspective manner of reporting in which governments present two different types of information to meet the needs of different users as follows:

1. **Highly aggregated information from an entitywide perspective** (with one or two columns for all of a government's activities) to meet the needs of users concerned with a government's operational accountability and *interperiod equity.* The measurement focus would be on the flow of **economic resources,** and the full **accrual basis of accounting** would be used.
2. **Fund level financial statements for each type of fund category** (governmental, proprietary, and fiduciary) to meet the needs of financial statements users concerned with a government's accountability for its *current financial resources.*

The GASB's current timetable is to (1) issue a final statement in 1997 at the earliest and (2) allow at least two years from the issuance date to ensure adequate time for implementation (which would be 1999 at the earliest if the standard indeed is issued in 1997).

II MEASUREMENT FOCUS AND BASIS OF ACCOUNTING

In 1990, the GASB concluded its reexamination of the **measurement focus** (what to measure) and **basis of accounting** (when to recognize a transaction or event) project. As a result, it issued GASB *Statement No. 11*, "Measurement Focus and Basis of Accounting—Governmental Fund Operating Statements."

This standard originally had an effective date for periods beginning after June 15, 1994. In 1993, however, the GASB indefinitely postponed the effective date of *SGAS No. 11* because of the inability to resolve certain related reporting issues initially thought to be resolvable by 1994. If and when *SGAS No. 11* becomes effective, it will mandate the use of the *accrual basis* of accounting, which will cause a massive change in financial reporting by governmental units.

LINKAGE OF *SGAS NO. 11* TO THE EFFECTIVE DATE OF THE EXPECTED NEW FINANCIAL REPORTING MODEL STANDARD

The GASB plans to have *SGAS No. 11* become effective at the same time that the expected new standard pertaining to the financial reporting model becomes effective (1999 at the earliest). Also, the GASB has stated that it plans to issue an implementation guide two years prior to the effective date of *SGAS No. 11*. This guide has *not* been issued as this book goes to print.

SGAS No. 11 will substantially change financial reporting because it requires liabilities for compensated absences, pensions, and claims to be reported as expenditures in the operating statement in the year in which the liability is incurred (to achieve a measure of interperiod equity, discussed shortly). *SGAS No. 11* does *not*, however, address the manner that these liabilities are to be reported in the balance sheet.

The alternatives are to report these liabilities in (1) the appropriate fund(s), (2) the GLTDAG, or (3) both the funds and the GLTDAG (split reporting). This issue is being resolved in the examination of the financial reporting model.

THE MAJOR CONCEPT OF *SGAS NO. 11*: ACHIEVING INTERPERIOD EQUITY Underlying *SGAS No. 11* is the concept that interperiod equity is an essential aspect of accountability. The concept of interperiod equity focuses on whether financial resources obtained during a period are sufficient to cover claims incurred during that period. Stated more simply, it focuses on **whether current year citizens receive services for which future year citizens will be required to pay**—a major deficiency of current financial reporting by governmental units.

OVERVIEW OF THE MAJOR *SGAS NO. 11* CHANGES

When it becomes effective, *SGAS No. 11* will change current practice in three major respects:

1. **Measurement focus.** It retains but modifies the flow of **financial resources** concept as the measurement focus.
2. **Basis of accounting.** It requires use of the full **accrual basis** of accounting rather than the modified accrual basis.
3. **Emphasis on achieving a measurement of interperiod equity.** It results in the current reporting of expenditures for items that previously were reported as expenditures long after the services were performed, primarily enabling the determination of whether current year citizens receive services for which part of the payment burden is shifted to future year citizens (comparing expenditures to revenues allows this determination to be made).

Note that the current reporting practice is inconsistent with the spirit of balanced-budget laws and that achieving a measure of interperiod equity is consistent with that spirit.

WHAT *SGAS NO. 11* DOES *NOT* ACCOMPLISH

Even though *SGAS No. 11* will change current practice in major respects, the operating statement for governmental funds under *SGAS No. 11* **will *not* and is not intended to measure the "cost of providing services."** The only significant remaining changes necessary in this regard would be (1) reporting depreciation expense in the operating statement (rather than reporting an expenditure for the fixed asset at the time of acquisition) and (2) *not* reporting in the operating statement long-term debt borrowings as inflows and repayments of long-term debt as expenditures.[12]

Even though *SGAS No. 11* will not change these two reporting practices, however, it takes a gigantic step in the direction of providing information that measures the cost of providing services.

MEASUREMENT FOCUS: WHAT SHOULD BE MEASURED AND REPORTED IN GOVERNMENTAL FUND OPERATING STATEMENTS?

Recall that under current practice, the measurement focus is on the "flow of **current** financial resources" (and **current claims** incurred during the period against the current financial resources). *SGAS No. 11* retains the "flow of financial resources" as the measurement focus, which has been broadened slightly, however, from **current** financial resources to **total** financial resources (and **total claims**). The GASB considered but rejected the "flow of **economic** resources" concept (similar to private-sector accounting). Consequently, the flow of total financial resources (for simplicity now referred to in *SGAS No. 11* as the "flow of financial resources" concept) is both a new concept and an intermediate position between the other two concepts. **Financial resources** are defined as follows:

> Cash, claims to cash (for example, debt securities of another entity and accounts and taxes receivable), claims to goods or services (for example, prepaid items), consumable goods (for example supplies inventories), and equity securities of another entity obtained or controlled as a result of past transactions or events.[13]

Thus under *SGAS No. 11*, assets are viewed as comprising two categories:

1. **Financial Resources.**

2. **Capital assets** (long-lived tangible assets).

THE FOUR CHANGES *SGAS No. 11* makes four changes concerning the measurement focus in the operating statement.

1. **Supplies inventory, a minor change.** Under the flow of financial resources concept, the acquisition of inventory is deemed merely a conversion from one financial resource (cash) to another financial resource. Expenditures are recognized when the supplies are used. Thus the **consumption method** is made mandatory for inventories. The **purchases method** is prohibited. Because supplies inventories are generally minor and the consumption method is already allowed under current GAAP, eliminating the purchases method will *not* significantly change the operating statement reporting results.

2. **Prepaid items, a minor change.** Under the flow of financial resources concept, payments for prepaid items are considered payments in advance of the receipt of goods or services. Viewed as such, they constitute a conversion of cash into another type of financial resource that will be used to pay future liabilities as they arise. When the related services are received, expenditures are recognized. This recognition method is known as the **consumption method.**

---

[12]Note that if a fixed asset is acquired solely by issuing long-term debt and that debt is repaid over the useful life of the fixed asset, the amount reported as expenditures for the repayment of that debt in future years can serve as a surrogate for depreciation expense. In such situations, the operating statement would effectively show the cost of providing services.

[13]*SGAS No. 11*, "Measurement Focus and Basis of Accounting—Governmental Fund Operating Statements" (Norwalk, CT: GASB, 1990), p. 96.

3. **Claims incurred against financial resources, a major change.** Under *SGAS No. 11*, total claims incurred during the period against financial resources will now be reported in the operating statement instead of current claims incurred during the period (claims paid during the current period or expected to be paid shortly thereafter).

4. **Operating debt, a major change.** Under *SGAS No. 11*, operating debt borrowings and repayments are **excluded** from the operating statement. **Operating debt** is defined as follows:

> Debt that provides financial resources to and is expected to be repaid from the financial resources of governmental funds but that is not related to the acquisition of capital assets, including infrastructure, or the financing of certain nonrecurring projects or activities that have long-term economic benefit.[14]

Operating debt borrowings and repayments (classified in the category Other Financing Sources and Uses under current GAAP) are excluded from the operating statement under *SGAS No. 11* so that governmental units cannot appear to have achieved a measure of interperiod equity (showing inflows approximating outflows) merely by borrowing money to finance current operations.

BASIS OF ACCOUNTING: WHEN SHOULD TRANSACTIONS AND EVENTS BE RECOGNIZED IN GOVERNMENTAL FUND OPERATING STATEMENTS?

SGAS No. 11 requires the use of the full accrual basis of accounting. (Thus, the modified accrual basis of accounting takes its place on the ash-heap of history where it rightfully belongs.) Under *SGAS No. 11*, the occurrence of the underlying transaction or event as the basis of recognition is the sole criterion—the timing of the inflow or outflow of cash or financial resource is no longer a consideration. The greatest impact of this change affects accounting for property taxes, sales taxes, and compensated absences.

PROPERTY TAXES The "measurable and **available**" standard has been replaced by a "measurable and **demanded**" standard. Property taxes have been demanded **if the due date falls within the current year.** Accordingly, property taxes accrued but not expected to be collected within 60 days of the balance sheet date will no longer be reported as deferred revenues but as revenues (net of an allowance for uncollectibles as under current practice). Thus implementing *SGAS No. 11* will result in a one-time increase in the Unreserved Fund Balance account initially as a result of eliminating the Deferred Revenues account. Property tax revenues relating to a given year that are collected *prior* to the beginning of that year are reported as deferred revenues in the balance sheet.

SALES TAXES Sales taxes are to be recognized as revenues when the sale takes place—regardless of when the taxing government collects them. For sales that occur before the end of the period, taxes are deemed to have been demanded **if the due date is within two months after the end of the period.** This provision allows a reasonable time for the taxpayer to administratively calculate and remit the sales tax because it is unreasonable for governments to establish a due date that coincides with or is prior to the end of the period. For many governmental units, the implementation of this change will result in a one-time increase to the Unreserved Fund Balance account to capture the two-month lag.

---

[14]*SGAS No. 11*, p. 98.

This two-month lag provision also applies to taxpayer-assessed taxes such as income taxes. Because most governmental units have a June 30 year-end and income taxes for individuals are due by April 15, income taxes cannot be deemed to have been demanded by June 30 since payment is *not* due until 9½ months later. Accordingly, *SGAS No. 11* will not have a significant impact in this area.

NOT-FOR-PROFIT ORGANIZATIONS: INTRODUCTION AND *PRIVATE* NPOS

26

LEARNING OBJECTIVES

TO UNDERSTAND

- The types of not-for-profit organizations (NPOs) that exist.
- The salient characteristics of NPOs.
- The uniform manner of reporting contributions and valuing investments required for all *private* NPOs.
- The types of long-lived assets that *private* NPOs must depreciate or need *not* depreciate.
- The unique, uniform manner to display financial information in financial statements for all *private* NPOs.

TOPIC OUTLINE

The important thing is to not stop questioning.

ALBERT EINSTEIN

CHAPTER OVERVIEW

We begin this chapter by describing (1) the various types of not-for-profit organizations (NPOs) that exist, (2) the unique characteristics of NPOs, and (3) certain aspects of *nongovernmental* NPOs. Nongovernmental NPOs (hereafter *private* NPOs) fall under the jurisdiction of the Financial Accounting Standards Board (FASB) and must follow its guidance.

Governmental NPOs (hereafter *public* NPOs), however, fall under the jurisdiction of the Governmental Accounting Standards Board (GASB) and must follow GASB guidance. This chapter discusses FASB guidance. GASB guidance for public NPOs is discussed in detail in Chapter 27. The major substantive financial reporting differences between the FASB guidance and the GASB guidance exist primarily for only one type of NPO—colleges and universities—and are discussed in Chapter 27.

Concerning the FASB guidance discussed in this chapter, we discuss (1) reporting contributions (a major source of funds for many NPOs); (2) valuing investments in debt and equity securities, investments that are often quite sizable for many NPOs; (3) recognizing depreciation on long-lived assets; and (4) presenting in the financial statements amounts used for external reporting purposes.

INTRODUCTION

I TYPES OF NOT-FOR-PROFIT ORGANIZATIONS

Traditionally, NPOs have been grouped into the following four categories:

- Health care organizations (HCOs).
- Colleges and universities (C&Us).
- Voluntary health and welfare organizations (VHWOs).
- Certain (or "all other") nonprofit organizations (CNOs).

CATEGORY 1: HEALTH CARE ORGANIZATIONS

This category includes hospitals (other than those at the federal level such as veterans hospitals), health maintenance organizations, nursing homes, continuing care retirement communities, intermediate care facilities, medical group practices, clinics, and other ambulatory care organizations.

CATEGORY 2: COLLEGES AND UNIVERSITIES

This category includes all state and private colleges and universities, as well as two-year colleges. Commercial business and technical schools—"for-profit" enterprises—are excluded.

CATEGORY 3: VOLUNTARY HEALTH AND WELFARE ORGANIZATIONS

This category includes NPOs that provide a broad range of public services in the areas of health, social welfare, and community services. Such organizations include the American Red Cross, the American Cancer Society, the American Heart Association, the United Way of America, Goodwill Industries, the Salvation Army, the Girl Scouts, the Boy Scouts, and many others dedicated to serving human needs and the public good. In terms of the size of VHWOs, more than 90% of them are almost minuscule in comparison to the large VHWOs such as the United Way or the American Red Cross.

CATEGORY 4: CERTAIN NOT-FOR-PROFIT ORGANIZATIONS

This category includes cemetery organizations, civic and community organizations, fraternal organizations, performing arts organizations, private and community foundations, professional associations,[1] political parties, political action committees, public broadcasting stations, religious organizations, research and scientific organizations, social and country clubs, trade associations, and zoological and botanical societies.

EXCLUDED ENTITIES   Excluded from the CNO category are entities whose purpose is to serve the economic interests of their owners, members, participants, or trust beneficiaries by paying dividends, lowering costs, or providing other economic benefits directly and proportionately to these parties. Examples of such excluded entities are credit unions, employee benefit and pension plans, mutual insurance companies, mutual banks, farm and rural cooperatives, and trusts.

Ⅱ CHARACTERISTICS OF NOT-FOR-PROFIT ORGANIZATIONS

NPOs usually possess the following characteristics (in varying degrees) that distinguish them from commercial business enterprises:

- An absence of an ownership interest such as that for business enterprises.
- A mission to provide services to their users, patients, society as a whole, or members—but *not* at a profit.
- A dependence on significant levels of contributions (from resource providers who do *not* expect commensurate or proportionate monetary return) to carry out the stated mission.
- A significant level of assets that are restricted as to their use as a result of donor stipulations—something that has major financial reporting implications.
- Tax-exempt status (avoids income taxes *and* enables many NPOs to obtain greater contributions than otherwise possible).

ABSENCE OF AN OUTSIDE OWNERSHIP INTEREST

NPOs are *not* owned by an individual proprietor, partners, or common and preferred stock investors but by the general public or the NPO's members. Accordingly, success is *not* measured by achieving acceptable rates of profitability on an equity interest as for business enterprises.

CONVERTING TO A FOR-PROFIT ENTITY OR GOING OUT OF EXISTENCE   Private NPOs sometimes (1) convert to a for-profit business, (2) are acquired by a private for-profit business (many *private* hospitals were acquired by health maintenance organizations in the last few years), or (3) cease their activities and go out of existence. Under state laws, such NPOs must (1) given their remaining assets to an appropriate governmental unit or (2) donate their remaining assets to a public charity or public purpose. (See the "Case in Point" on page 948.)

FINANCIAL REPORTING FOR PRIVATE NPOs   Because managements of *private* NPOs are *not* responsible to shareholders (who do *not* exist), they are responsible instead to (1) the NPO's board of directors or board of trustees and (2) state agencies (which require annual reports to be filed).

---

[1]In accounting, the professional organizations are the Financial Accounting Standards Board (FASB), the American Institute of Certified Public Accountants (AICPA), the Institute of Management Accountants (IMA), the Government Finance Officers Association (GFOA), the American Accounting Association (AAA), the National Association of College and University Business Officers Organization (NACUBO), and Beta Alpha Psi (BAP).

THE MISSION TO PROVIDE SERVICES

Because the mission is to provide services rather than maximize stockholders' equity, a comparison of revenues to costs and expenses does *not* have the same meaning to NPOs as it does for business enterprises. For business enterprises, revenues are compared to costs and expenses to determine net income. Furthermore, a causal relationship exists between these items for business enterprises because costs and expenses are incurred to generate revenues.

For NPOs, however, no such causal relationship exists between costs and expenses incurred and revenues. Even though revenues of NPOs are *not* "earned" as is the case for business enterprises, it is still just as important to compare revenues with costs and expenses. Such a comparison merely tells a different story—that is, **the extent to which the NPO is covering its costs and expenses incurred to provide services during the period.** To prevent any potential misunderstanding that an NPO's operating statement is an income statement, *private* NPOs are required to call their operating statement a *statement of activities*. (*Public* NPOs also use this or other descriptive titles to describe the operating statement to avoid any implication that it is an income statement.)

DEPENDENCE ON CONTRIBUTIONS (MORE IMPORTANT FOR SOME NPOS THAN OTHERS)

The amounts charged to the users of NPO services often are *less* than the costs and expenses incurred to provide the services. For example, many hospitals and *private* C&Us *cannot* meet their operating costs and expenses from patient fees and student tuition alone. The difference must be provided by private and public funding such as that from federal and state governments, philanthropic organizations, and individuals. These *external providers* perceive the NPO as a public-service agency accomplishing goals for the public good.

The type of NPO that depends most heavily on contributions is by far VHWOs. Most of their financial resource inflows are from others who do *not* receive direct benefits. Their principal financial resource inflows are public contributions made either directly to them or through the United Way[2] and government grants. Collectively, these inflows from outside sources are commonly referred to as *outside money*, as contrasted with inflows from investment earnings and user fees, which collectively are commonly referred to as *inside money*. Many NPOs, however, receive no contributions, most notably the majority of CNOs, which serve their members.

ASSETS RESTRICTED AS TO USE

An NPO's assets may be restricted by stipulations that donors make (*external* restrictions) or by the NPO's board of directors' action (*internal* restrictions).

---

[2] As a condition of granting money, the United Way almost always requires recipient VHWOs to (1) be audited and (2) follow GAAP.

DONOR RESTRICTIONS   Many contributors to NPOs stipulate (1) the specific program or manner in which the contributed asset is to be used, (2) the time period in which the contributed asset is to be used, or (3) the specific program for which the income earned on the contributed asset (for contributed assets required to be invested) is to be used. **Donor-imposed restrictions** limit management's ability to (1) use the NPO's assets as it pleases and (2) respond to unexpected needs and opportunities—something the FASB refers to as an NPO's "financial flexibility."

Donor restrictions must be fully disclosed. These disclosures are so important that *SFAS No. 117* requires that the format of the financial statements themselves (shown shortly) rather than the notes reveal these restrictions.

DONOR-RESTRICTED ENDOWMENT FUNDS   Often donors stipulate that the contributed asset (whether received by gift or bequest) *cannot* be expended either (1) in perpetuity or (2) for a specified period. For control purposes, the NPO must account for the donated asset(s) separately to comply with the donor's stipulations in future periods. Accordingly, it is said that the donor has created an **endowment fund.** An endowment fund is merely an established fund of cash, securities, or other assets that is accounted for separately from all other assets either by using (1) separate general ledger accounts or (2) a separate set of books. *Private* C&Us usually have quite sizable donor-restricted endowment funds.

CASE IN POINT

Harvard University's Endowment Fund

Harvard University has nearly $5 billion in its donor-restricted endowment fund.

Historically, such assets usually have been accounted for in separate sets of books for control purposes (doing so results in fund accounting), although this is *not* absolutely necessary unless the donor so stipulates. (The manner of accounting for endowment funds using a separate set of books is illustrated in Chapter 27.)

BOARD-DESIGNATED ENDOWMENT FUNDS   Far less sizable and prevalent than donor-restricted endowments are **board-designated endowments** (often called *quasi-endowments*). These endowments are created by action of the NPO's board of directors, such as a board designation that certain assets be set aside and used only for a capital addition project. Board-designated assets may be disclosed in the financial statements *or* in the notes.

TAX-EXEMPT STATUS

Most *private* NPOs of any size seek and receive tax-exempt status from the IRS.[3] Upon determination that the NPO is a qualifying organization (such as a charity,

---

[3]Internal Revenue Code Section 501(c) classifies NPOs into 25 categories, each of which is dealt with in a separate subsection. Some of the NPOs may be eligible for tax-deductible donations under Section 170 of the Code. NPOs exempt under Section 501(c)(3) receive the largest part of tax-deductible donations. These are NPOs whose purpose is charitable, educational, religious, scientific, or related to public safety testing. Their activities are restricted in that they must further one or more of these exempt purposes. Examples of these NPOs include public charities, nonprofit hospitals, nonprofit universities and schools, youth organizations, community fund-raising campaigns, and environmental support groups. They are also restricted from activities to influence legislation, and they cannot participate in any political campaign on behalf of, or in opposition to, any candidate for political office.

an educational institution, a religious organization), the IRS sends a letter stating that the entity qualifies as a Section 501 (c) corporation of the Internal Revenue Code). A tax-exempt *private* NPO for income tax–reporting purposes (1) pays no income taxes on the excess of its revenues (including its contribution revenues) over its costs and expenses (with certain exceptions discussed shortly) and (2) files annually with the IRS an information return on Form 990, 990A, or 990PF. Also, most states allow *private* NPOs that have 501 (c) status to be exempt from paying state income and state sales taxes. More than 300,000 NPOs file tax returns with the IRS annually.

Scores of *private* colleges and hospitals have changed to nonprofit status over the years to greatly increase their ability to obtain federal grants and contributions from donors that are tax deductible only if made to an NPO qualifying as such for tax-reporting purposes. (Of course, *not* having to pay income taxes is an additional bonus.)

WHAT IF SOME OF THE *PRIVATE* NPOS ACTIVITIES ARE BUSINESS RELATED?

If some of a *private* NPO's activities are business related or if any of its investments are *not* passive in nature, however, it must report such business-related income on a separate tax return and pay income taxes on that income and at the *highest* corporate rate. Tax law on this subject is somewhat vague and thus leaves wide latitude for interpretation as to whether a specific activity is taxable. Further complicating the matter is that the tax law has several categories of NPOs, each of which has its own rules. Thus social welfare organizations and charities are held to different standards.

Overall, more than 50% of the total revenues of all NPOs comes from the sale of goods, services, and endorsements, as opposed to donations, bequests, and members' dues. Often, these sales are in direct competition with private for-profit businesses.

CASE IN POINT

The American Association of Retired Persons (AARP), a lobby for the nation's older people and one of Washington's most formidable lobbies, is a tax-exempt NPO. Roughly 45% of its 1994 revenues of $382 million (excluding federal grants) came from endorsing products of commercial companies. These commercial operations, which AARP claims should be nontaxable, have been so successful that AARP is currently embroiled in a dispute with the IRS. In 1994, AARP paid the IRS $135 million to resolve claims over tax returns for 1985–1993.

III FASB GUIDANCE VERSUS GASB GUIDANCE

Because C&Us and HCOs exist widely in both the private sector and the *public sector*, the different reporting requirements of the FASB and the GASB are easily dealt with by sequencing our remaining discussion of NPOs as follows:

Chapter 26 (FASB Guidance)	Chapter 27 (GASB Guidance)
Private HCOs	Public HCOs
Private C&Us	Public C&Us
VHWOs	
CNOs	

Furthermore, the major substantive financial reporting difference between the FASB guidance and the GASB guidance concerns C&Us—not both HCOs *and* C&Us. These differences are discussed in detail in Chapter 27.

PRIVATE NPOs

IV | THE FASB'S 1993 STANDARDS FOR *PRIVATE* NPOs— A HISTORIC ACHIEVEMENT IN BRINGING ABOUT UNIFORMITY, SIMPLIFICATION, AND PROPER FOCUS

In 1993, the FASB completed two major projects that addressed the major financial reporting issues for private NPOs: (1) when and how to report contributions received and (2) whether to present financial statements for external reporting purposes that focus on (a) the NPO as a whole (an aggregated basis) or (b) individual funds (a disaggregated basis). The completion of these projects resulted in the 1993 issuance of the following two FASB financial reporting standards:

1. *SFAS No. 116*, "Accounting for Contributions Received and Made."
2. *SFAS No. 117*, "Financial Statements of Not-for-Profit Organizations."

These standards (1) eliminated numerous financial reporting inconsistencies between the various types of *private* NPOs, (2) require financial statement reporting that focuses on the NPO as a whole (aggregated) rather than on a fund-by-fund basis (disaggregated), and (3) apply to all *private* NPOs. Even though these standards constitute a giant step forward in financial reporting for *private* NPOs, the manner of reporting fund-raising costs for VHWOs is another important reporting issue to financial statement users that warrants addressing, as discussed in the Business Perspective.

REVISIONS TO THE AICPA'S FOUR OLD NPO AUDIT GUIDES

The AICPA published two new audit guides in 1996 that (1) are based on the four FASB NPO standards (*Nos. 93, 116, 117,* and *124*) and (2) supersede four of its old NPO audit guides.

A unique aspect of the AICPA audit guides is that *SFAS No. 117* allows them to provide more detailed guidance than that set forth in *SFAS No. 117*. Accordingly, the specific guidance in these audit guides can and does differ from that in *SFAS No. 117*. The major differences that exist for HCOs—both *private* and *public*—are discussed in the HCO section of Chapter 27. (The differences for other types of NPOs are *not* significant.)

THE NEW COMPREHENSIVE NPO AUDIT GUIDE (EXCLUDING HCOs) One new audit guide is titled "Not-for-Profit Organizations"; it superseded three of the AICPA's old NPO audit guides (the C&U audit guide issued in 1975, the VHWO audit guide issued in 1988, and the CNO audit guide issued in 1987) concerning *private* NPOs.

To accommodate the GASB, which is currently reexamining the reporting model for C&Us, these three old NPO audit guides were *not* superseded concerning *public* NPOs. Accordingly, our discussion of *public* C&Us in Chapter 27 centers around the 1975 C&U audit guide.

THE NEW HCO AUDIT GUIDE The other new audit guide is titled "Health Care Organizations"; it superseded the AICPA's old HCO audit guide issued in 1990 concerning *all* HCOs, that is, for-profit HCOs, *private* not-for-profit HCOs, and *public* HCOs (automatically not for profit).

The Accounting Games Charities Play

Last year St. Labre Indian School, an Ashland, Montana, Catholic charity that runs schools on Indian reservations, collected nearly $17 million from the public. It spent over $5 million to raise that amount. Thus only 68 cents of every dollar raised actually made it to the classrooms.

But to make the operation look more efficient, the charity reported that it raised only $14.6 million and spent only $2 million on fund-raising. Through book-keeping magic, the group's ratio of charitable spending to total expenses suddenly jumped from 66% to 76%. That higher ratio looks better when hitting up potential donors for contributions.

Was St. Labre bending the rules? Not really. Under some obscure guidelines set by something called the National Catholic Development Conference, the school may reduce its reported fund-raising costs by the amount raised from *new* donors—$2 million in St. Labre's case.

St. Labre isn't unusual. Hundreds of tax-exempt organizations that have turned charity into a huge business use similar accounting practices. Nonprofit organizations took in $125 billion last year, with 88% of that contributed by individual donors. Yet, unlike for-profit companies, which must adhere to fairly strict accounting rules, charities are subject only to the vaguest of rules. As a result, donors often can't tell whether a charity is efficient at collecting and disbursing money for worthy causes or just good at cooking its books.

"Charities are toying with the credibility and integrity of their financial statements," says Kenneth L. Albrecht, head of the National Charities Information Bureau, a New York–based industry watchdog. "We have an epidemic."

Adds Russy Sumariwalla, a charities accounting expert who heads United Way International: "The system is not designed to honestly disclose to the donor the real picture."

The basic problem: The people who run charities like to be able to show that most of the money they raise goes to fund the worthy programs their donors like—saving dolphins, say, or promoting health awareness. To make their reported program expenses as high as possible, they try to make the amounts spent on fund-raising, highly paid administrators and other overhead as low as possible.

Until 1987 charities didn't have much leeway when reporting their fund-raising costs to state governments. A rule followed by most auditors held that if the primary purpose of an activity was to raise money, it had to be accounted for as a fund-raising expense. Period.

That changed in 1987. Several of the country's biggest charities—among them the American Lung Association and the March of Dimes—convinced the American Institute of Certified Public Accountants to write a new rule and state regulators to accept it. This one says that part of fund-raising costs can be classified as "educational" costs, as long as the charity can prove the audience is specifically interested in its cause and the message motivates the recipient to act rather than just contribute.

That's the theory. The practice? Practically every charitable solicitation now comes with a newsletter, sticker or some other "educational" material that lets the charity's executives deflate their reported fund-raising costs and inflate the percentage they disburse to the programs they're supposed to support. Says charities watchdog Albrecht: "Public education has become the toxic dump of charity accounting."

Take $3 million (direct public support 1991 fiscal year) American Heart Disease Prevention Foundation. It says it spent 29% of its expenses on charity last year—an unusually small percentage. Eliminating education expense, the amount spent directly on charity drops to just 5%. Most of the rest went for fund-raising. . . .

Big charities play the education allocation game, too. Consider the American Lung Association, which uses a sophisticated sweepstakes billed as an "old-fashioned" raffle. The charity assigns 20% of the cost of its sweepstakes mailings to education.

Where is the "educational" material? A spokesperson for the charity notes that on the back of each sweepstakes ticket is a picture and text about people helped by donations.

Does this information serve any purpose other than making you want to enter the sweepstakes? The American Lung Association people and their auditors say it does, and under the current accounting rules, their judgment usually is all that matters.

"When donors call us," says Steve Arter, a senior financial investigator specializing in charities at the Pennsylvania Attorney General's office, "we'll say such and such a charity spends 80% [of the money it raises] on programs. But what that doesn't tell you is that the charity may be spending 2 cents on research and the remaining 78 cents on what you're holding in your hand."

Yielding to pressure from state officials like Arter, the American Institute of Certified Public Accountants is studying ways to tighten the rules on what can be charged to education. A decision is expected next year.

Meanwhile, some charities are turning for guidance to a book coauthored by Robert Frank, a Washington, D.C.–area accountant who advocates the "physical units" method of allocating costs. What Frank means is counting words. So if a charity spent $100,000 to mail a 500-word solicitation attached to a 5,000-word "educational" newsletter, 90% of the cost could be considered money spent on programs.

"Word counting is theoretically appropriate," says Richard Larkin, a director at Price Waterhouse and head of an AICPA task force on nonprofits. "But it's subject to abuse by charities that pad the mailings with fluff."

A lot of charities' expenses for administrative costs end up as program costs, too. "We're seeing charities that report administrative costs of only 1% or 2%," says Pennsylvania charities investigator Arter. "It's rare now to see anyone reporting costs over 5%. It's not that they've become any more efficient, but they're writing off the costs to programs, including legal and accounting fees."

Compassion International, an agency that arranges sponsorship of children, raised over $35 million from the public in fiscal 1991. Compassion books nearly half of its accounting costs under spending on its programs. Says Scott Noll, one of Compassion's internal accountants: "There are no real standards for what can be included in programs. Each organization is flexible in what it calls 'programs.'"

More headaches arise in accounting for donated goods. Charities can record the fair market value of goods received as contributions, and then as program costs unless the goods are just passed on to other charities. But that rule is often abused.

In August Connecticut and Pennsylvania filed lawsuits, accusing four charities of booking worthless goods at inflated prices and passing them on to other charities, which put them on their books at the same inflated values. The states' attorneys general charged that Knoxville, Tenn.–based Cancer Fund of America falsely claimed in 1990 that it had spent $7.4 million on "patient services." But of that amount, $2.5 million was the value asserted by the charity of unsalable vegetable seeds CFA had allegedly purchased for a mere $25,462 and passed on to another relief organization, which in turn donated the seeds to a South Dakota Indian reservation.

Another of the charities under investigation by Connecticut is Feed the Children, based in Oklahoma City. Out of total program expenses of $102 million last year, this charity recorded $86 million as the value of in-kind gifts. Investigators are looking into whether Feed the Children reported the value of used books it passed on to other charities to makes its ratio of expenses to program spending look more efficient. John Schantz, Feed the Children's controller, says he isn't aware of any probe.

Here's yet another twist: Many charities sell merchandise—gifts, cards, T shirts and the like—to supplement their donations. The cost of producing those products can be considered a program expense—if the products are "program-related."

The National Wildlife Federation, for instance, considers the production and distribution of Christmas cards and toys with conservation themes a part of its charitable program activity. "Getting people excited about nature is exactly what our mission is all about," says Lynn Bowersox, National Wildlife's media relations manager.

The wildlife group has no qualms about adding around $12 million a year in merchandise production costs to its reported expenditures on charitable programs. But the National Charities Information Bureau, which evaluates charities, thinks this is one accounting gimmick too many. Excluding these merchandise costs, National Wildlife spent 64%, not 69%, of its total expenses on charitable programs in fiscal 1991.

Some charities are awash with cash but hold back charitable spending. Shriners Hospitals for Crippled Children, for example, took in revenues of $500 million last year, but spent less than 50% on programs, tucking most of the rest away for investment. Shriners has been criticized by the Better Business Bureaus' philanthropic advisory service for not spending enough of its income on programs.

And some charities use multiple accounting gimmicks to make program expenditures look impressive. Example: World Vision, the Christian charity that provides health, disaster and poverty assistance around the world.

World Vision claims that 80% (or $187 million) of its total expenditures goes to charitable activities. The figure is inflated in several ways. First, about $73 million is goods, not cash, that were passed on to other charities or its independent field offices. Second, nearly $9 million is booked as a public awareness and education expense incurred with fund-raising costs; charity industry watchdogs at the NCIB believe all that $9 million should be reported as fund-raising expenses.

We're down to actual program expenses of $105 million. But only $4 million of that went to evangelism in the United States, and another $97 million was actually sent to World Vision's international headquarters for charitable uses. And not even that much made it to the charity's programs. Nearly 6% of every dollar received by headquarters goes to administration; figure another 3% is taken out for administration in the organization's Third World offices.

(continued)

Bottom line: Of the $187 million World Vision says it spent last fiscal year, only $92 million was spent directly on the group's various charitable programs.

Some modest protection for donors is on the way. The Financial Accounting Standards Board, the country's chief rule-setter, is finally getting ready to issue two proposals based on its eight-year effort to write better rules for nonprofit organizations. But don't hold your breath. The FASB proposals deal mostly with presentation and measurement, as opposed to how charities should be allocating costs.

If better accounting from charities is on the horizon, we may have the Internal Revenue Service's growing interest in the industry to thank. This summer the IRS went to Tax Court to defend its September 1990 decision

to rescind the tax exemption of the United Cancer Council, a former client of direct mail fundraiser Watson & Hughey. The charity claimed that 43% to 55% of its direct mail expenses went to public education. But the IRS rejected the charity's accounting and found that only about 4% of the UCC's expenses went for exempt purposes. The IRS deemed that percentage is insufficient and concluded that the charity was in effect working for the benefit of Watson & Hughey, not cancer patients. A court decision isn't expected before next year, but lots of charities are keeping their eyes glued to the case.

Source: Adapted from Roula Khalaf, "The Accounting Games Charities Play," *Forbes,* October 26, 1992, pp. 252–254. Reprinted by permission of *Forbes* magazine, October 26, 1992, © Forbes, Inc., 1992.

V ACCOUNTING FOR CONTRIBUTIONS

SFAS No. 116, "Accounting for Contributions," which encompasses contributed services, requires *private* NPOs to (1) report almost all *unrestricted* and *restricted* contributions, including contributions that establish endowments, as contributions in the Revenues, Gains, and Other Support category of the statement of activities **when received** and (2) value both the contributions revenue and the related contribution receivables at their fair value when received.

CONTRIBUTIONS DEFINED

In *SFAS No. 116,* **contributions** are defined as

> An **unconditional** [emphasis added] transfer of cash or other assets to an entity or a settlement or cancellation of its liabilities in a voluntary nonreciprocal transfer by another entity acting other than as an owner.[4]

For clarification purposes, *unconditional* means with no conditions (or strings) attached. *Nonreciprocal transfers* are transactions in which value is *not* received or given in exchange. Therefore, transfers of assets under contract that are in substance the purchase of goods or services are outside the scope of *SFAS No. 116.*

WHAT DOES *TRANSFER* MEAN? The preceding definition of *contributions* implies that the transfer of cash or other assets must have been made to qualify as a contribution. However, **unconditional promises[5] to give**—which may be written or oral— cash or other assets in the future are considered to be unconditional transfers. Accordingly, such unconditional promises to give can be accrued as Contributions

---

[4] *Statement of Financial Accounting Standards No. 116,* "Accounting for Contributions Received and Contributions Made" (Norwalk, CT: Financial Accounting Standards Board, 1993), p. 67.

[5] The four nonprofit AICPA audit guides that predate *SFAS No. 116* use the term *pledge* instead of *contribution. SFAS No. 116* does *not* use *pledge* because that term describes not only promises to give but also plans or intentions to give that are *not* promises.

Receivable in the balance sheet **when received** and thus can be concurrently recognized in the statement of activities as revenues from contributions. (Other terms used to describe promises to give are *awards, grants, subscriptions,* and *appropriations.*)

To recognize unconditional promises in the financial statements, however, sufficient evidence in the form of verifiable documentation that a promise was made and received must exist. A communication that is unclear as to whether it constitutes an unconditional promise is deemed an unconditional promise if it is legally enforceable.

Note that besides cash, the preceding definition of contributions includes the transfer of *other assets,* defined in *SFAS No. 116* as follows:

> securities, land, buildings, use of facilities or utilities, materials and supplies, intangible assets, services, and unconditional promises to give those items in the future.[6]

CONDITIONAL PROMISES TO GIVE

The conceptual opposite of the unconditional promise to give is the **conditional promise to give,** which depends on the occurrence of a specified future and uncertain event that must occur to bind the promisor and thus transform the promise from conditional to unconditional status. For example, the promisor may stipulate that the NPO must first raise at least 50% of the $1 million needed for the expansion project. Being conditional, such promises to give automatically fall outside the definition of contributions. If the possibility that the condition will *not* be met is remote, such promises are considered unconditional.

If assets have been received and the retention and use of such assets is conditional on a future event, the offsetting credit is made to the Refundable Advance account (in the Liabilities section of the balance sheet) until the conditional future event occurs.

CONTRIBUTIONS OF MONETARY AND NONMONETARY ASSETS

With certain limited exceptions, contributions of monetary and nonmonetary assets are recognized as revenues when received. (The exceptions are [1] assets received on conditional status for which the possibility of the conditional future event occurring is remote, as mentioned previously, and [2] collection items that are *not* recognized in the financial statements, which are discussed in detail later.)

MEASUREMENT AT FAIR VALUE

Contributions of monetary and nonmonetary assets are valued at the fair value of the assets received, which may require (1) obtaining quoted market prices (usually the best evidence of fair value, if available), (2) using independent appraisals, or (3) using other appropriate methods, such as determining the present value of estimated future cash flows—for unconditional promises to give expected to be collected over *more* than one year. When present value procedures are used, the subsequent recognition of the interest element is reported as *contribution income* by the donee—*not* as interest income. Allowances for uncollectibles should be recorded as necessary so that the contribution revenues and related receivables are both valued at their fair value.

The journal entry to recognize unconditional promises of $5,000 cash that (1) are estimated to be 80% collectible and (2) can be spent for any purpose, is as follows:

Contributions Receivable	5,000	
Allowance for Uncollectibles		1,000
Contribution Revenues—Unrestricted[a]		4,000

[a]This unrestricted designation is explained more fully shortly.

---

[6]*SFAS No. 116,* para. 5.

CONTRIBUTIONS OF SERVICES

Contributed services are recognized as revenues in the period received if

> the services received **(a) create or enhance nonfinancial assets** [emphasis added] or **(b) require specialized skills** [emphasis added], are provided by individuals possessing those skills, and would typically need to be purchased if not provided by donation. Services requiring specialized skills are provided by accountants, architects, carpenters, doctors, electricians, lawyers, nurses, plumbers, teachers, and other professionals and craftsmen. Contributed services and promises to give services that do not meet the above criteria shall not be recognized.[7]

For contributed services, disclosures must be made of (1) the nature and extent of the contributed services received during the period, (2) the amount recognized as revenues in the financial statements, and (3) the programs or activities in which those services were used. When the conditions for recognition are *not* satisfied, *SFAS No. 116* encourages disclosures of the fair value of contributed services received that have *not* been recognized in the financial statements, if practicable.

MEASUREMENT AT FAIR VALUE Recognizable contributed services that do *not* create or enhance nonfinancial assets, such as a CPA performing a free audit or a lawyer giving free legal advice, are recorded at the fair value of the services contributed. For recognizable contributed services that create or enhance nonfinancial assets, such as refurbishing a building by either lay volunteers or volunteer carpenters, the fair value of the asset or asset enhancement may be recognized instead of the fair value of the contributed services.

A journal entry to recognize the $4,000 fair value of free legal services follows:

```
Expenses—Management and General . . . . . . . . . . . . . . . .    4,000
        Contribution Revenues—Unrestricted  . . . . . . . . . . .           4,000
```

Note that the result is the same as if (1) the lawyer had contributed $4,000 cash to the NPO and (2) the NPO used the $4,000 cash to pay the lawyer for the legal services.

CONTRIBUTED WORKS OF ART, HISTORICAL TREASURES, AND SIMILAR ASSETS RECEIVED (COLLECTION ITEMS)

Collection items received **need not** be capitalized as assets and concurrently recognized as revenues in the statement of activities. Specifically, collection items need not be capitalized if all of the following conditions are satisfied:

a. [They] are held for public exhibition, education, or research in furtherance of public service rather than financial gain
b. [They] are protected, kept unencumbered, cared for, and preserved
c. [They] are subject to an organizational policy that requires the proceeds from sales of collection items to be used to acquire other items for collections.[8]

If a *private* NPO chooses to capitalize and recognize such collections, however, either **retroactive capitalization** or **prospective capitalization** is permitted— selective capitalization is *not* permitted.

REPORTING CONTRIBUTIONS IN THE STATEMENT OF ACTIVITIES

As discussed in more detail shortly, *SFAS No. 117* requires a statement of activities that shows the changes in three categories of net assets (or equity):

[7]*SFAS No. 116*, para. 9.
[8]*SFAS No. 116*, para. 11.

1. Unrestricted net assets.

2. Temporarily restricted net assets.

3. Permanently restricted net assets.

Accordingly, contributions relating to each category must be displayed separately in the statement of activities.

UNRESTRICTED CONTRIBUTIONS   Contributions received *without* donor restrictions increase *unrestricted net assets*. Accordingly, in the statement of activities, such contributions are reported in the Unrestricted category.

RESTRICTED CONTRIBUTIONS   A restriction on the use of contributed assets can result from either (1) a donor's explicit stipulations or (2) the circumstances surrounding the contribution that clearly show the donor's intent to restrict use of the contributed assets. In the statement of activities, such contributions are reported in one of the restricted categories (*temporarily restricted* or *permanently restricted*, as appropriate).

As a practical matter, however, donor-restricted contributions whose conditions are *fulfilled in the same period in which the contribution is recognized* may be reported in the Unrestricted category provided that the entity (1) consistently follows this policy and (2) discloses it.

For simplicity, we hereafter usually use the following abbreviations for these three net asset categories:

1. For unrestricted net assets: *UR net assets.*

2. For temporarily restricted net assets: *TR net assets.*

3. For permanently restricted net assets: *PR net assets.*

PERMANENTLY RESTRICTED CONTRIBUTIONS

Contributions having stipulations that prohibit spending the contributed asset (the principal) in perpetuity create **permanent endowments.**

REPORTING INCOME EARNED ON INVESTED PRINCIPAL   As to income earned on the invested principal, the donor may stipulate that it be used for (1) any purpose (thus being classified in the Unrestricted category), (2) certain purposes (thus being classified in the Temporarily Restricted category), (3) increasing the principal, for example, to maintain purchasing power or reach a specified dollar amount (thus being classified in the Permanently Restricted category), or (4) any combination of these.

TEMPORARILY RESTRICTED CONTRIBUTIONS

A donor may stipulate that the contributed asset be expended (1) on a specific program or activity, (2) in a later time period, or (3) to acquire fixed assets. Thus unlike a permanently restricted asset, the **temporarily restricted** contributed asset eventually will be expended (or used up for depreciable fixed assets) as the donor intended. The following items are also usually classified as temporarily restricted contributions:

1. **Promises with future payment dates.** Sometimes donors make unconditional promises to give with payments due over several periods. To the extent that future payments have been recorded as Contributions Receivable, the offsetting credit is usually reported as increasing *temporarily restricted* **net assets** (or equity). The unavailability of the funds usually means that the use of the asset is effectively restricted to the future period(s). If the donor intended the contribution to be used to support activities of the current period (whether by explicit

stipulations or circumstances surrounding the receipt of the promise), however, the contribution may be shown as increasing **UR** *net assets*.

2. **Term endowments.** The principal of term endowments may be expended at some future point in time.

CLASSIFYING CONTRIBUTIONS OF FIXED ASSETS: IT DEPENDS ON WHETHER DONOR STIPULATIONS EXIST OR THE NPO'S ACCOUNTING POLICY

EXPLICIT DONOR STIPULATIONS EXIST   When a donor stipulates that the contributed fixed asset must be used for a specified time period, the contribution is reported as increasing either **TR** *net assets* or **PR** *net assets,* as appropriate. For example, land contributed for use as an open space preserve to be held in perpetuity is reported as increasing **PR** *net assets.* Assuming that the land has a fair value of $600,000, the journal entry is

Land	600,000	
Contribution Revenues—Permanently Restricted . . .		600,000

On the other hand, a depreciable fixed asset that must be held for at least 10 years is classified as increasing **TR** *net assets.* After the 10th year, a **reclassification** from **TR** *net assets* to **UR** *net assets* must be reported separately in the statement of activities. (More about this shortly.)

EXPLICIT DONOR STIPULATIONS DO *NOT* EXIST   In the absence of explicit donor stipulations, each NPO must establish an accounting policy as to whether an implied time restriction exists. If the NPO's accounting policy is to imply a time restriction, the contribution of a fixed asset is reported as though the donor had stipulated a time period restriction. Such policy is based on the presumption that the donor intended to have the NPO use the fixed asset over its useful life.

If the NPO's policy is *not* to imply a time restriction, the contribution of a fixed asset is reported as increasing unrestricted net assets. Such a policy is based on the presumption that the donor most likely did *not* intend to prevent the NPO from selling or disposing of the fixed asset at any point in time if it was in the best interest of the NPO; thus the NPO has the financial flexibility to dispose of the fixed asset at will.

If a donor contributes a fixed asset with the intent to have the NPO sell it and use the proceeds for any purpose, its contribution is always reported as increasing **UR** *net assets* (or equity).

EXPIRATION OF DONOR-IMPOSED TIME OR PURPOSE RESTRICTIONS

As expenditures are made according to a donor's stipulations (for a specific purpose or in a specific time period), the NPO fulfills the donor's wishes. Accordingly, the donor's restrictions "expire." The statement of activities must reflect the expiration of a donor-imposed restriction. This is done by showing separately from other transactions a *reclassification* in the statement of activities between (1) the *temporarily restricted* category (a decrease) and (2) the *unrestricted category* (an increase). The journal entry to reflect the expiration of a $70,000 *purpose* restriction follows (we use the account descriptions illustrated in the AICPA's 1996 audit guide for NPOs as abbreviated for simplicity):

TR Net Assets—Transfer Out	70,000	
UR Net Assets—Transfer In		70,000

Note: These amounts, which are displayed as reclassifications in the statement of activities as shown later, are closed to the appropriate equity accounts when the accounts in the statement of activities are closed to the equity accounts at year-end.

A *purpose* restriction is deemed to have expired when an expense has been incurred for that purpose, regardless of whether unrestricted resources are also available for that expense. In other words, a liability could be incurred and cash might *not* be available at that time to pay the liability, but the purpose restriction is still deemed to have expired when the liability was incurred.

EXPIRATION OF RESTRICTIONS ON LONG-LIVED ASSETS

Restrictions on contributed long-lived assets classified as temporarily restricted net assets (due either to donor stipulations or the NPO's accounting policy of implying a time restriction) expire over the estimated useful lives of the assets as they are exhausted or used up. Thus as depreciation expense is recognized on such *temporarily restricted* assets, a reclassification between the *TR Net Asset* category (a decrease) and the *UR Net Asset* category (an increase) must be reflected or recognized in the statement of activities. Assuming that the annual depreciation expense is $12,000, the year-end journal entry to reflect such a restriction expiration is as follows:

TR Net Assets—Transfer Out	12,000	
UR Net Assets—Transfer In		12,000

Assume also that (1) a building having a fair value of $360,000 at the time of the donation had to be kept for 10 years, (2) it is depreciated over 30 years, and (3) its carrying value is $240,000 at the end of the tenth year. The journal entry at the end of the tenth year to reflect this restriction expiration is as follows:

TR Net Assets—Transfer Out	240,000	
UR Net Assets—Transfer In		240,000

In the absence of donor-imposed restrictions or an accounting policy specifying how long contributed long-lived assets must be used, restrictions on long-lived assets and cash to acquire them expire when the long-lived assets are placed in service.

VI ACCOUNTING FOR INVESTMENTS

Under *SFAS No. 124*, "Accounting for Certain Investments Held by Not-for-Profit Organizations," the following investments of *private* NPOs must be valued at their fair value **in the statement of financial position:**

1. Investments in *equity securities* that have a **readily determinable fair value** (excluding investments accounted for under the *equity method*).
2. All investments in *debt securities.*

Interest, dividends, and other investment income on all investments are reported in the statement of activities (1) in the periods in which they are earned and (2) as increasing **UR** *net assets,* **TR** *net assets,* or **PR** *net assets,* as appropriate.

Gains and losses—both realized and unrealized—on all investments are reported in the statement of activities (1) in the periods in which they occur and (2) as increases or decreases in **UR** *net assets* unless their use is temporarily or permanently restricted by explicit donor stipulations or by law (which applies only if no donor stipulations exist).

GAINS AND LOSSES OF DONOR-RESTRICTED ENDOWMENT FUNDS

Gains and losses of donor-restricted endowment funds are classified as changes in the appropriate category of net assets. The hierarchy for determining the appropriate category of net assets in which to report gains and losses is as follows:

1. **First:** Determine whether the donor stipulated the treatment to be accorded gains and losses. If so, follow that treatment. (In a high percentage of cases, donors specify the treatment of gains—but not losses.)

2. **Second:** If no donor stipulations exist, determine the requirements of state law. If specified, follow that treatment.

3. **Third:** If donor stipulations do *not* exist and state law is silent, follow the requirements of *SFAS No. 124*, which are discussed next.[9]

***SPECIFIC* DONATED ASSETS MUST BE HELD IN PERPETUITY**   Assume that an individual donated an equity security with the stipulation that it be held in perpetuity. This stipulation implies that the enhancements and diminishments in value of the equity security (unrealized gains and losses) are subject to the same permanent restriction. Accordingly, unrealized gains and losses on that investment are reported as changes to *PR net assets*. If instead the donor had stipulated that the equity security be held at least 10 years, however, the unrealized gains and losses are reported as changes to *TR net assets* because the equity security is *temporarily* restricted rather than *permanently* restricted.

PRINCIPAL (CORPUS) (BUT *NOT* ANY SPECIFIC ASSET) MUST BE HELD IN PERPETUITY   Assume that a donor (1) contributed an equity security having a $100,000 fair value on May 3, 19X1, to an NPO (having a calendar year-end) and (2) the donor stipulated that (a) the NPO may sell the equity security at any time and make other suitable investments, (b) the $100,000 endowment must remain intact in perpetuity, and (c) the income and gains may be spent only on cancer research. Thus the donor is silent regarding the treatment of unrealized losses. We first discuss unrealized gain situations.

1. **Unrealized *gain*.** Assume that the donated asset's fair value is $105,000 at December 31, 19X1. The $5,000 unrealized gain is treated as an *increase* to *TR net assets*. As this $5,000 amount is spent as specified (on cancer research in this example), *TR net assets* are decreased dollar for dollar. (This treatment is consistent with the donor's stipulation and always results in reporting $100,000 for *PR net assets* on the balance sheet. If this donor stipulation did *not* exist, however, the increase would be to *UR net assets* because the increase in value could be spent for any purpose.

2. **Unrealized *loss*—no prior net appreciation.** In this case, unrealized losses are treated as *decreases* to *UR net assets*. For example, if the endowment fund assets had a market value of $93,000 at December 31, 19X1 ($7,000 below the fair value at the donation date), the Equity section of the statement of financial position reflects $100,000 for *PR net assets* and $(7,000) for *UR net assets*. Theoretically, $7,000 of unrestricted *assets* (not *net assets*) should be transferred to the endowment fund assets to make up the $7,000 shortfall.

3. **Unrealized *loss*—prior net appreciation has *not* yet been fully expended.** In this case, the unrealized loss is first applied to any net gain appreciation recognized prior to the loss—but only to the extent that this appreciation has *not* been expended on the stipulated purpose. Any remaining (unapplied) loss *decreases*

---

[9]All states have laws regarding the treatment of gains and losses on endowment funds. Furthermore, the states are nearly equally divided as to treating them as *restricted* versus *unrestricted*. Thus the FASB treatment is consistent with state law roughly 50% of the time.

UR net assets. For example, assume that (1) the endowment fund investments have (a) a $105,000 fair value at December 31, 19X1 ($5,000 more than at the donation date) and (b) an $88,000 fair value at December 31, 19X2 (one year later), and (2) the NPO spent $4,000 on cancer research in 19X2. The $17,000 decrease in the investment's fair value ($105,000 – $88,000) during 19X2 results in decreasing *TR net assets* by $1,000 and decreasing *UR net assets* by $16,000. (At both December 31, 19X1 and 19X2, the amount reported for *PR net assets* is $100,000, the amount of the endowment to be held in perpetuity.)

4. **Subsequent gains.** Subsequent gains that restore the fair value of the endowment fund investments to the required $100,000 level are reported as increases in *UR net assets.* (Subsequent gains that increase the fair value above and beyond $100,000 increase *TR net assets.*)

DISCLOSURES

SFAS No. 124 also requires a variety of disclosures, including the following:

1. The methods and significant assumptions used to estimate the fair values.
2. The basis for determining the carrying value of investments that are *not* required to be valued at fair value.
3. The aggregate carrying value of the investments by major type (for example, equity securities, U.S. Treasury securities, corporate debt securities, mortgage-backed securities, oil and gas, and real estate).
4. The aggregate amount of the shortfall in the fair value of donor-restricted endowment funds below the amount required to be maintained by donor stipulations or law.
5. The composition of return on investment.
6. A reconciliation of the investment return to amounts reported in the statement of activities in certain situations.

Other investment-related FASB standards that also apply to all *private* NPOs are *SFAS No. 105,* "Disclosure of Information About Financial Instruments With Off-Balance-Sheet Risk and Financial Instruments With Concentration of Credit Risk"; *SFAS No. 107,* "Disclosures About Fair Values of Financial Instruments"; and *SFAS No. 119,* "Disclosure About Derivative Financial Instruments and Fair Value of Financial Instruments."

The Business Perspective discusses how an accounting instructor at a small private college (1) questioned one of the college's investments and (2) subsequently uncovered a massive fraud perpetrated on scores of C&Us and VHWOs.

VII   RECOGNIZING DEPRECIATION ON LONG-LIVED ASSETS

SFAS No. 93, "Recognition of Depreciation by Not-for-Profit Organizations," requires that (1) **long-lived tangible assets be depreciated,** (2) the depreciation method(s) and expense for the period be disclosed, and (3) information on the major classes of depreciable assets and accumulated depreciation be disclosed.

WORKS OF ART OR HISTORICAL TREASURES

Works of art or historical treasures *need not* be depreciated so long as certain conditions are met. In this respect, *SFAS No. 93* states:

Consistent with the accepted practice for land used as a building site, depreciation need not be recognized on individual works of art or historical treasures whose economic

---

BUSINESS PERSPECTIVE

Unlikely Hero: A Persistent Accountant Brought New Era's Problems to Light

As a hero, Albert J. Meyer is an unlikely figure: a mild-mannered, chess-playing accountant who teaches business at a tiny Christian college in a Michigan farming community.

But investigators for the Securities and Exchange Commission and others say that Mr. Meyer, 44 years old, is exactly that: He persevered for nearly two years, despite efforts to discourage him, and eventually blew the lid off a massive case of alleged fraud.

The target of Mr. Meyer's persistence was the Foundation for New Era Philanthropy, which authorities believe was operating a scam that sucked in hundreds of individuals and organizations, (including Mr. Meyer's own college) and took in up to $200 million on the promise of a double-your-money return.

It was purely accidental that Mr. Meyer stumbled upon New Era in the first place. He and his wife, Melenie, 39, moved to bucolic Spring Arbor, Mich., from their native South Africa four years ago. "We wanted the excitement of being in another country," he says, "but not the excitement of being in 30 minutes of traffic jams." Devout Baptists, they also wanted to find a close-knit Christian community in which to bring up their three sons.

Mr. Meyer took a tenure-track job teaching accounting at Spring Arbor College, but because the college had only three accounting majors at the time, he worked part-time in the business office, balancing the college's books.

It was in this job that Mr. Meyer found a $294,000 bank transfer, dated July 8, 1993, from Spring Arbor to a foundation called the Heritage of Values Foundation Inc. The word "Heritage" caught his eye, reminding him of fallen TV evangelist Jim Bakker and his Heritage USA theme park. "It was the play on those words," Mr. Meyer recalls. "I guess I'm a cynic."

He dashed to the library to look up Heritage of Values and realized it wasn't connected to the Bakker scam, but could find nothing else. The next day, he approached Janet M. Tjepkema, the college's vice president for business affairs, and told her he felt compelled to query the transfer.

Mr. Meyer says Ms. Tjepkema told him Heritage of Values was connected to a consultant who had introduced the college to New Era and that the money was earmarked for New Era.

He rushed to the library again, but was unable to find anything on New Era. When he returned to campus, "I could sense annoyance" from administrators, he says. "I was biting the hand that was feeding us."

For most of the time that it took Mr. Meyer to amass financial documents and to help bring the alleged scam to light, he worked alone at night and on weekends, with his wife as his only sounding board. He also told a few students, saying, "This is what auditing is all about. This is a real-life case study."

He telephoned all over the country and amassed three thick files of correspondence, with labels like "Ponzi-File: If it quacks like a duck, walks like a duck and looks like a duck, could it really be a duck?" He operated quietly at first, fearing that, as an untenured foreigner on a temporary work visa, he might lose his job.

But Mr. Meyer also tried—repeatedly—to warn Spring Arbor. The associate business professor attempted to rally faculty colleagues, called administrators, sent a cautionary letter to Glenn E. White, the trustees' chairman, and alerted the college's president, Allen Carden.

While most of the faculty eventually came to agree with Mr. Meyer, the administrators never did, and by April, he had begun to sense a coldness that led him to avoid social situations such as Spring Arbor's annual staff appreciation dinner.

At one point, Mr. Meyer thought he had succeeded in persuading the college not to trust New Era. In a mid-March meeting with President Carden and Neil E. Veydt, vice president for planning and advancement, he was told that the college was prepared to plunk down $1 million—but hadn't sent it yet. "As I walked

---

benefit or service potential is used up so slowly that their estimated useful lives are extraordinarily long. A work of art or historical treasure shall be deemed to have that characteristic only if verifiable evidence exists demonstrating that (a) the asset individually has cultural, aesthetic, or historical value that is worth preserving perpetually and (b) the holder has the technological and financial ability to protect and preserve essentially undiminished the service potential of the asset and is doing that.[10]

[10]*SFAS No. 93*, "Recognition of Depreciation by Not-for-Profit Organizations" (Norwalk, CT: Financial Accounting Standards Board, 1987), para. 6.

out, I thought, 'That's it, I'm saving the college money,' I was over the moon," he says.

Then he learned that administrators had ignored his advice and sent the money—part of a $1.5 million New Era investment that Spring Arbor (which has only a $6 million endowment) now stands to lose.

"I couldn't believe it. I said, 'OK, if I'm not able to protect them, I'll protect anyone else I can. I will become a crusader,'" he says.

He began to identify with the sleuth in "Scoundrels & Scalawags," a book about Charles Ponzi's turn-of-the-century pyramid scheme in Boston. "By this time . . . I felt that I would have to carry the whole burden of exposing Ponzi," he says.

Mr. Meyer might have kept working inconspicuously, but on March 15, he received tenure. In the tenure letter, the college saluted him for his "strong Christian faith" and for "outstanding qualities that exemplify the kind of faculty members needed at Spring Arbor College." The next day, Mr. Meyer told his wife he was going to "test the limits of tenure."

She knew he wasn't kidding; he's never done anything halfway. He didn't simply play chess: He competed in the national U.S. Open tournament. He didn't simply cut down on TV-watching in his house: He gave away the television. "He's a very focused guy," his wife says. "He's a pit bull. He never daydreams. He's always thinking about things and working things out."

Mr. Meyer launched a full-scale attack on New Era, believing he was the only person who fully understood what was happening, and knowing he would never be able to face faculty members if he backed off. He contacted some of the institutions that had invested money in New Era, including Wheaton College in Illinois and the Moody Bible Institute in Chicago. When they ignored him, he went to the Internal Revenue Service and the American Institute of Certified Public Accountants, among others.

"I spoke to so many people who said, 'Yes, yes, yes,

you might be right,' but they didn't do anything because it's a burden," he says.

It was his letter to the SEC last month that prompted the SEC to start investigating New Era, setting off the chain of events that led to the collapse of New Era.

Mr. Meyer says he is "overwhelmed" that the alleged New Era scam is as big as it now appears. "I actually earned my salary," he says, returning to one of his sources of motivation: his sense of obligation to employers and to his host country. "I always count the credit hours—what the students pay, what they pay me, and am I earning $2 or $3 for every $1 I'm being paid? I have to pay my way . . . I'm a visitor," he says.

The campus's reaction has been mixed. Just two weeks before the scandal broke, Dr. Carden assured the Spring Arbor community of the trustees' "business savvy" and warned faculty members that "a healthy skepticism" was commendable, but a "crusading zeal" was often "counterproductive."

Dr. Carden said in an interview Tuesday that he was "not going to give up hope" of recovering the $1.5 million that Spring Arbor stands to lose, but said he believed the college had "acted in an appropriate fashion."

But late Wednesday, Mr. Meyer received a letter from Dr. Carden that said, "I believe you did something heroic. You followed your professional instincts when many of us believed you to be wrong." Ms. Tjepkema, Dr. Carden, Mr. White, Mr. Veydt and Wheaton College couldn't be reached for comment Thursday.

And faculty members and students are showing their support for Mr. Meyer. Former student Virgie Ammerman-Warner says, "I think it's great that he went on. Some people would have sat back and said, 'If my bosses aren't going to support me, I'm not going to go any further.'

"But he didn't. He went anyway," she says.

Source: Barbara Carton, "Unlikely Hero: A Persistent Accountant Brought New Era's Problems to Light," *The Wall Street Journal*, May 19, 1995, p. B1. Copyright © 1995 *The Wall Street Journal*. Reprinted with permission.

VIII FINANCIAL STATEMENTS FOR EXTERNAL REPORTING

REQUIRED FINANCIAL STATEMENTS: A FOCUS ON THE ORGANIZATION AS A WHOLE

Unlike *SFAS No. 116* (contributions), which focuses on recognition and measurement issues, *SFAS No. 117* (financial statements of NPOs) specifies (1) **what** financial statements to present for external reporting purposes and (2) **what specific information,**

as a minimum, to show in those statements. *Private* NPOs are required to present financial statements that focus on the **organization as a whole;** these are

- A statement of financial position.
- A statement of activities (the "operating" statement).
- A statement of cash flows.

SUBSTANTIAL FORMATTING LATITUDE ALLOWED *SFAS No. 117* imposes no more stringent reporting standards than those for commercial for-profit entities. Thus even though these statements must include certain minimum information (discussed later), it neither prescribes nor prohibits particular formats for the financial statements. No requirement exists to distinguish "operating" items from "nonoperating" items. Thus *SFAS No. 117* allows the same formatting flexibility in preparing financial statements that for-profit entities have.

Accordingly, if an NPO desires to report an intermediate measure of "operations" (for example, the excess of operating revenues over operating expenses), it may do so under *SFAS No. 117*. (*SFAS No. 117* requires that such measure be reported, however, in a statement that at a minimum reports the change in **UR** *net assets* for the period.)

PROVIDING MORE RELEVANT INFORMATION AND ACHIEVING IMPROVED UNDERSTANDABILITY AND COMPARABILITY

Donors make financial decisions in the context of NPOs as a whole, not of their individual parts. Accordingly, reporting on a fund-by-fund basis does *not* provide the most relevant information for external users to assess an NPO's ability to take appropriate actions to alter the amounts and timing of cash flows, often in response to rapidly changing needs and opportunities. For this reason, *SFAS No. 117* emphasizes providing financial information for the entity as a whole.

REQUIRING CLASSIFICATIONS BASED ON DONOR-IMPOSED RESTRICTIONS To provide information on financial flexibility, *SFAS No. 117* requires classifications of an entity's net assets (equity) **based on (1) whether donor-imposed restrictions exist and (2) the type of donor-imposed restrictions.** Accordingly, the required statement of financial position must display three classes of net assets (or equity)— which are the same as those discussed earlier in the section on contributions: (1) **unrestricted,** (2) **temporarily restricted,** and (3) **permanently restricted.** Likewise, the statement of activities must display information showing the changes in these three classes of net assets (equity).

Donors' stipulations pertaining to endowments *usually* permit the NPO to (1) pool the donated assets with other assets and (2) sell or exchange the donated assets and make other suitable investments (providing that the economic benefits of the donated assets are *not* consumed or used for a purpose that does *not* comply with the donors' stipulations). Consequently, the terms **PR** *net assets* and **TR** *net assets* as used in the Net Assets section of the balance sheet generally refer to amounts of *net assets* restricted by donors—***not* to *specific* assets.** If a donor stipulated that a *specific* asset (such as shares of XYZ common stock) be held in perpetuity, however, the **PR** *net assets* amount *does* relate to a *specific* asset.

STANDARD FORMAT FOR THE STATEMENT OF CASH FLOWS The required statement of cash flows is to be formatted in a manner consistent with the provisions of *SFAS No. 95*, "Statement of Cash Flows," and with the other statements and accompanying notes assist external users in assessing a private NPO's

- Liquidity and financial flexibility.
- Ability to meet its obligations.
- Management in discharging its stewardship responsibilities.

IX   ILLUSTRATED FINANCIAL STATEMENTS

THE STATEMENT OF FINANCIAL POSITION

The minimal display requirements for the statement of financial position follow:

- The statement should focus on the NPO as a whole and show amounts for its **total assets, total liabilities,** and **total net assets** (or equity).
- The net assets/equity section should show total amounts for each of the three classifications of net assets: **unrestricted, temporarily restricted,** and **permanently restricted.**
- The nature and amounts of **donor-imposed restrictions** should be disclosed.
- Information about **liquidity** should be shown in any of several ways in the statement and in its notes.

Illustration 26–1 presents a sample statement of financial position that meets the minimum disclosure requirements of *SFAS No. 117*.

ILLUSTRATION 26–1	Statement of Financial Position

The Foundation for the Needy
Statement of Financial Position
December 31, 19X1

Assets

Current Assets

Cash and cash equivalents	$ 42,000
Accounts and interest receivable	51,000
Inventories and prepaid expenses	41,000
Contributions receivable	33,000
Short-term investments	24,000
Total Current Assets	$ 191,000

Noncurrent Assets

Long-term investments	1,420,000
Land, buildings, and equipment	583,000
Assets restricted to investment in land, buildings, and equipment	36,000
Total Assets	$2,230,000

Liabilities

Current Liabilities

Accounts payable	$ 32,000
Refundable advance	3,000
Grants payable	2,000
Notes payable	14,000
Total Current Liabilities	$ 51,000

Noncurrent Liabilities

Annuity obligations	11,000
Long-term debt	45,000
Total Liabilities	$ 107,000

Net Assets (or Equity)

Unrestricted[a]	$ 990,000
Temporarily restricted[a] (Note A)	373,000
Permanently restricted[a] (Note B)	760,000
Total Net Assets (Equity)	$2,123,000
Total Liabilities and Net Assets (Equity)	$2,230,000

[a]This is an *actual* general ledger account—not merely a classification category. Amounts shown in the applicable column of the statement of activities in Illustration 26–3 (discussed shortly) were closed to this account.

REVIEW POINTS FOR ILLUSTRATION 26–1 Note the following:

1. Like the balance sheets of for-profit business enterprises, the statement format assists the user in assessing **liquidity.** For ease of understanding, we show a **classified** statement of financial position, that is, with current and noncurrent asset and liability categories. An allowable alternative (the one illustrated in *SFAS No. 117*) is to use an **unclassified** format with assets and liabilities sequenced based on relative liquidity.

2. The statement **purposely does *not* use the description "Fund Balance."** *SFAS No. 117* does *not* use this description because it is considered appropriate only for reporting on a fund-by-fund basis, not on an overall organization basis. (Also, the term is more appropriate for *governmental* NPOs whether they report on an overall basis or a fund-by-fund basis.)

3. The unique feature of this statement relates to the three categories shown in the Net Assets (or Equity) section. (More about these categories shortly.)

4. Although not shown in the illustrated statement, a private NPO could also disclose **board-designated assets** in this statement by subdividing the unrestricted category into a board-designated category and an undesignated category. Such disclosures could also be made in the notes.

IMPORTANT REQUIRED NOTES TO THE STATEMENT OF FINANCIAL POSITION

Important financial statement notes concerning the *TR net asset* and *PR net asset* categories in the statement of financial position are shown in Illustration 26–2.

THE STATEMENT OF ACTIVITIES

The minimal information to be shown in the statement of activities—certain exceptions apply to HCOs, as discussed later—follows:

- Revenues, gains, and other support **by category** (unrestricted, temporarily restricted, or permanently restricted).
- Revenues, gains, and other support in the unrestricted category unless donor-imposed requirements limit the use of the assets. Contributions are presumed to be unrestricted in the absence of explicit donor stipulations or particular circumstances that indicate a donor's implicit restrictions on use.
- Other events that simultaneously increase one class of net assets while decreasing another—**expirations of restrictions**—reported separately from revenues, gains, expenses, and losses.
- **All expenses** in the unrestricted category.
- **Expenses by functional classification (such as major classes of program services and supporting activities),** unless shown in notes to the financial statements. Reporting expenses by natural classification in a supplementary schedule is optional, except for VHWOs, which must also report by natural classifications (such as salaries, rent, utilities, interest expense, depreciation) in a matrix format in a separate financial statement.
- For the organization as a whole, the amount of change in *UR net assets, TR net assets,* and *PR net assets.*
- **Gross amounts for revenues and expenses**—including special events that often are ongoing and major activities, as opposed to being peripheral or incidental transactions. (However, investment revenues may be shown net of custodial fees and investment advisory fees.)

An example of a statement of activities meeting these minimum information disclosure requirements is shown in Illustration 26–3.

ILLUSTRATION 26–2	Key Notes for the Statement of Financial Position

Note A

Temporarily restricted net assets are restricted to the following:
Spending only for the following purposes or periods

Community services	$111,000[a]
Public education	109,000[a]
Acquisition of buildings and equipment	26,000[b]
For community services after 19X3 (pursuant to a **term endowment**)	20,000[a]
For any purpose after 12/31/X1	6,000[a]
	$272,000
Buildings and equipment (already acquired)	101,000[b]
	$373,000

Note B

Permanently restricted net assets are restricted to the following:
Perpetual endowments for which the principal must be invested in perpetuity, the income from
which is expendable for the following purposes

Community services	$211,000
Public education	89,000
Any activities of the organization	422,000
	$722,000
Perpetual endowment requiring income to be added to the original gift until the principal is $50,000	33,000
Land required to be used as a public recreation area that by donor stipulation cannot be sold	5,000
	$760,000

[a]As funds are expended in accordance with the wishes of donors, these restrictions expire.

[b]As depreciation is recognized over the useful lives of these assets (the assets substantively being used up), these restrictions expire because the assets are being used in accordance with the donors' intent. During 19X1, $12,000 depreciation expense was recognized on net assets restricted to investment in buildings and equipment.

REVIEW POINTS FOR ILLUSTRATION 26–3   Note the following:

1. The statement of activities is in *columnar format*. A *"layering" format* (not illustrated here) is also acceptable.

2. Contributions are assumed to have been received for all three net asset categories (the typical situation for most NPOs). The $13,000 contribution in the Permanently Restricted column is to **establish an endowment.**

3. Investment income from interest and dividends on endowments is also reported in all three net asset categories. All but $2,000 of the $62,000 of income earned on the endowments, however, **may be expended.** (Endowments are the bulk if not all of the $760,000 of permanently restricted net assets at year-end.) The $2,000 reported in the Permanently Restricted column signifies that this amount is being used to either (1) maintain purchasing power of some portion of the endowment principal or (2) increase the amount of some portion of the endowment principal for other reasons stipulated by a donor(s).

4. Expirations of donor-imposed temporary restrictions are reflected or recognized by showing separately **a reclassification** between the temporarily restricted category and the unrestricted category.

5. The statement shows expenses as decreases only in the Unrestricted column. Expenses are shown by function.

6. By requiring a format that shows the change in an NPO's net assets, the FASB has effectively required NPOs to present the **equivalent of a *statement of***

ILLUSTRATION 26–3	Statement of Activities—Separate Columns Format

The Foundation for the Needy
Statement of Activities
For the Year Ended December 31, 19X1

	Unrestricted	Temporarily Restricted	Permanently Restricted	Total
Revenues, Gains, and Other Support				
Contributions	$137,000	$ 32,000	$ 13,000	$ 182,000
Fees	64,000			64,000
Investment income (interest and dividends):				
Endowments	38,000	22,000	2,000	62,000
Other than endowments	23,000	16,000		39,000
Investment gains (realized and unrealized), net:				
Endowments	41,000	29,000	44,000	114,000
Other than endowments	27,000			27,000
Miscellaneous	16,000			16,000
	$346,000	$ 99,000	$ 59,000	$ 504,000
Net Assets Released from Restrictions as a Result of:				
Program expenditures	**76,000**	**(76,000)**		**–0–**
Equipment acquisitions	**11,000**	**(11,000)**		**–0–**
Time expirations	**26,000**	**(26,000)**		**–0–**
Total Revenues, Gains, and Other Support	$459,000	$ (14,000)	$ 59,000	$ 504,000
Expenses and Losses				
Community services	$122,000			$122,000
Public education	84,000			84,000
Research	52,000			52,000
Management and general	94,000			94,000
Fund-raising	23,000			23,000
Total Expenses	$375,000	$ –0–	$ –0–	$ 375,000
Hurricane Loss	18,000			18,000
Actuarial loss on annuity obligations		3,000		3,000
Total Expenses and Losses	$393,000	$ 3,000	$ –0–	$ 396,000
Change in Net Assets	**$ 66,000**	**$ (17,000)**	**$ 59,000**	**$ 108,000**
Net assets—12/31/X0	924,000	390,000	701,000	2,015,000
Net assets—12/31/X1	$990,000	$373,000	$760,000	$2,123,000

comprehensive income for a commercial for-profit entity. Such statement was discussed and illustrated in Chapter 18 (reporting foreign operations).

SPECIAL RULES APPLICABLE TO HCOs   For HCOs, the operating statement must (1) be called a *statement of operations* (rather than a *statement of activities*), (2) report a *measure of operations* (such as *operating income or loss*), (3) **report amounts only for the *unrestricted* category of net assets,** and (4) report **expirations of restrictions** in *two* categories (those pertaining to *operations* are reported in the revenues section, and those pertaining to *fixed asset contributions* are reported *below* the measure of operations line). Except for this unique manner of reporting restriction expirations, the operating statement for a *private* HCO is substantially the same as that for a *public* HCO, which we show in Illustration 27–2 (page 986) in Chapter 27. (This special manner of reporting for HCOs exists because of the specific guidance set forth in the AICPA's 1996 HCO audit guide, discussed in detail in Chapter 27.)

ILLUSTRATION 26–4	Statement of Cash Flows (Direct Method)

The Foundation for the Needy
Statement of Cash Flows
For the Year Ended December 31, 19X1

Cash Flows from Operating Activities

Cash collected from contributors	$ 171,000	
Cash collected from fees charged to service recipients	61,000	
Cash received from interest and dividends	54,000	
Miscellaneous receipts	14,000	
Cash paid to employees and suppliers	(323,000)	
Grants paid	(7,000)	
Interest paid	(4,000)	
Net Cash Used by Operating Activities		$(34,000)

Cash Flows from Investing Activities

Proceeds from sales of investments	$ 122,000	
Purchase of investments	(81,000)	
Purchase of equipment	(6,000)	
Insurance proceeds from hurricane loss	3,000	
Net Cash Obtained by Investing Activities		$ 38,000

Cash Flows from Financing Activities

Proceeds from contributions restricted for the following:

Investment in endowments	$ 13,000	
Investment in equipment	6,000	
	$ 19,000	

Other financing activities

Cash received for interest and dividends which is restricted for reinvestment	$ 2,300	
Payments of principal on notes payable	(4,000)	
Payments of principal on long-term debt	(5,000)	
Payments of annuity obligations	(300)	
	$ (7,000)	
Net Cash Obtained by Financing Activities		$ 12,000
Net Increase in Cash and Cash Equivalents		**$ 16,000**

Cash and Cash Equivalents at 12/31/X0	26,000
Cash and Cash Equivalents at 12/31/X1	$ 42,000

Supplemental data for items not reportable in this statement:

Gifts of equipment received	$ 4,000	
Gift of paid-up life insurance, cash surrender value	5,000	

THE STATEMENT OF CASH FLOWS

To assess the ability of an NPO to continue to provide services, users must have a complete set of financial statements, including a statement of cash flows. *SFAS No. 117* amends *SFAS No. 95*, "Statement of Cash Flows," so that it is also applicable to *private* NPOs. This statement can be prepared using the **direct** method (the preferred method) or the **indirect** method. An example of a cash flow statement for a private NPO using the direct method is shown in Illustration 26–4.

IMPLICATIONS OF THE NEW FASB STANDARDS ON THE CONTINUED USE OF FUND ACCOUNTING

Prior to the issuance of the FASB's new NPO Standards in 1993, *private* NPOs used fund accounting internally and reported *externally* on a fund-by-fund basis (pursuant to the requirements of then existing GAAP). Because *external* financial reporting now requires information on an aggregated basis, this question is raised: Will *private* NPOs continue to use fund accounting for *internal* record-keeping purposes?

Unless mandated by donors (rarely done) or the board of directors for internal control purposes, no requirements exist to use fund accounting. Furthermore, *SFAS No. 117* neither encourages nor discourages the continued use of fund accounting because this is an *internal* bookkeeping matter.

Knowledgeable individuals associated with finance officers of colleges and universities have indicated to us that (1) they believe that fund accounting will slowly fade away and (2) some NPOs that recently installed new accounting information systems have designed their new chart of accounts to conform with the external reporting requirements of *SFAS No. 117* rather than tailoring them to fund accounting. Certainly, externally imposed stipulations, internal control, practicality, and economic cost considerations are key factors in determining the extent to which fund accounting continues to be used *internally*.

DOES FUND ACCOUNTING ENTAIL PHYSICAL SEGREGATION OF ASSETS?

The use of fund accounting for *internal* record-keeping purposes does *not* mean that the various assets accounted for in each of the separate funds must be physically segregated from assets accounted for in the other funds. Often the assets accounted for in the various funds are *not* kept separate. For example, it is common to use only one checking account for cash reported in several funds, thereby eliminating the need to prepare multiple bank account reconciliations each month. The fact that the assets are commingled suggests that NPOs may discontinue fund accounting.

COMPLYING WITH *SFAS No. 117* WHEN USING FUND ACCOUNTING

If fund accounting is used for *internal* record-keeping purposes, however, some form of "aggregating worksheet" (similar in concept to a consolidated worksheet) to determine the aggregated amounts to present in the financial statements issued for *external* reporting purposes must be prepared.

Furthermore, footnote 5 to *SFAS No. 117* does *not* preclude the presentation of *disaggregated* data (by fund groups) so long as the required *aggregated* information is presented (a presentation we have not seen any NPOs use). Some funds will fall entirely within one of the three net asset categories. Other funds may have to be split into two or more of the three net asset categories to arrive at the required *aggregated* data.

END-OF-CHAPTER REVIEW

SUMMARY OF KEY POINTS

A. Contributions

1. With certain specified exceptions, contributions (including endowments) are to be recognized **in the statement of activities when received.**

2. Contributions affecting a particular class of net assets recognized in the statement of activities must be reported as unrestricted support or restricted support **in that class** of net assets.

3. Contributions received are to be measured at their **fair values.** Receivables for **long-term (beyond one year) unconditional promises to give** may be reported at the **present value** of the estimated cash inflows.

4. **Unconditional promises to give** with payments due in future periods are reported as restricted support unless the contribution is intended to support unrestricted operations in the period in which the promise is received.

5. **Conditional promises to give** are *not* recognized in the financial statements until the conditional promise becomes **unconditional.**

6. Contributions received **to acquire long-lived assets** are reported as restricted support. Contributions of long-lived assets are reported as **restricted support** or **unrestricted support,** depending on (a) donor stipulations or (b) the NPO's accounting policy regarding an implied time period restriction in the absence of donor restrictions.

7. **Expirations of donor-imposed time and purpose restrictions** are reflected in the statement of activities by showing a reclassification of amounts between the temporarily restricted category (a decrease) and the unrestricted category (an increase).

8. **For long-lived depreciable assets classified as part of temporarily restricted net assets,** a time-period restriction expiration is reported in the statement of activities over the depreciable life of the assets.

9. **Contributed services** are recognized only if they (1) create or enhance nonfinancial assets or (2) are obtained from individuals or organizations possessing specialized skills and typically would otherwise be purchased.

10. **Contributed works of art, historical treasures,** and similar assets (collection items) received need not be capitalized in the balance sheet and concurrently recognized in the statement of activities.

B. **Investments and Depreciation of Long-Lived Assets**
1. Investments in equity securities that have a **readily determinable fair value** and all investments in debt securities are to be valued **at their fair value.**

2. Interest, dividends, and other investment income are reported **in the statement of activities when earned** as increases in the appropriate category of net assets.

3. Gains and losses on investments are reported **in the statement of activities (a) when they occur** and (b) as increases or decreases, respectively, to the appropriate category of net assets.

4. Depreciable long-lived tangible assets **must be depreciated** and depreciation expense for the period must be disclosed.

5. Individual works of art and historical treasures **need not be depreciated** if the NPO can demonstrate that verifiable evidence exists that the asset (1) is and can be maintained by the NPO in a manner that preserves its value and (2) the asset individually has cultural, aesthetic, or historical value worth preserving perpetually.

C. **Financial Statements**
1. **Specified financial statements.** *SFAS No. 117* specifies that for external reporting purposes, private NPOs must present for the organization as a whole (a) a statement of **financial position,** (b) a statement of **activities,** and (c) a statement of **cash flows.** (Thus this is an aggregated reporting manner as though a single set of books were used rather than several sets of books as in fund accounting.)

2. **Reporting specified financial statement information.** For the statement of financial position, total assets, total liabilities, and total net assets (or equity) for the NPO as a whole must be reported.

3. **Classified reporting.** For the statement of financial position, the **total net assets** (or equity) must be classified based on **donor-imposed restrictions.** For the statement of activities, **all accounts—except expenses—**are also to be classified on this basis.

4. **Required classification categories.** Three classification categories are to be used: **unrestricted, temporarily restricted,** and **permanently restricted.**

5. The statement of activities must report the **changes** in each of the three classes of equity or net assets. This is done either by "layering" or using separate columns.

6. The standards specify only minimal information and category display requirements, thus allowing flexibility in the use of reporting formats.

GLOSSARY OF NEW TERMS

Board-designated endowment   An endowment created as the result of the board of directors' action (classified as unrestricted net assets in the statement of financial position). Also called a *quasi-endowment.*

Conditional promise to give   "A promise to give that depends on the occurrence of a specified future and uncertain event to bind the promisor."*

Contribution   "An unconditional transfer of cash or other assets to an entity or a settlement or cancellation of its liabilities in a voluntary nonreciprocal transfer by another entity acting other than as an owner."*

Donor-imposed condition   "A donor stipulation that specifies a future and uncertain event whose occurrence or failure to occur gives the promisor a right of return of the assets it has transferred or releases the promisor from its obligation to transfer its assets."*

Donor-imposed restriction   "A donor stipulation that specifies a use for the contributed asset that is more specific than broad limits resulting from the nature of the organization, the environment in which it operates, and the purposes specified in its articles of incorporation or bylaws or comparable documents for an unincorporated association. A restriction on an organization's use of the asset contributed may be temporary or permanent."*

Endowment   A type of restricted contribution in which the donor stipulates that the principal be maintained intact either in perpetuity or for a specified period. Thus only the income from the investment of the principal (the corpus) may be spent. Endowments require the establishment of endowment funds.

Endowment fund   An established fund of cash, securities, or other assets accounted for separately from all other assets for control purposes either by (1) using separate general ledger accounts or (2) a separate set of books.

Financial flexibility   The freedom to use assets (resources) for various purposes to be able to respond to unforeseen events and opportunities.

Nonreciprocal transfer   "A transaction in which an entity incurs a liability or transfers an asset to another entity (or receives an asset or cancellation of a liability) without directly receiving (or giving) value in exchange."*

Permanent endowment   A type of restricted contribution in which the principal must remain intact in perpetuity (classified as permanently restricted net assets in the statement of financial position).

Permanent restriction   "A donor-imposed restriction that stipulates that resources be maintained permanently but permits the organization to use up or expend part or all of the income (or other economic benefit) derived from the donated assets."*

Permanently restricted net assets   "The part of the net assets of a not-for-profit organization resulting (a) from contributions and other inflows of assets whose use by the organization is limited by donor-imposed stipulations that neither expire by passage of time nor can be fulfilled or otherwise removed by actions of the organization, (b) from other asset enhancements and diminishments subject to the same kinds of stipulations, and (c) from reclassifications from (or to) other classes of net assets as a consequence of donor-imposed stipulations (*Concepts Statement 6*, paragraph 92)."*

Promise to give   "A written or oral agreement to contribute cash or other assets to another entity. A promise to give may be either conditional or unconditional."*

Restricted support   "Donor-restricted revenues or gains from contributions that increase either temporarily restricted net assets or permanently restricted net assets."*

Temporarily restricted net assets   "The part of the net assets of a not-for-profit organization resulting (a) from contributions and other inflows of assets whose use by the organization is limited by donor-imposed stipulations that either expire by passage of time or can be fulfilled and removed by actions of the organization pursuant to those stipulations, (b) from other asset enhancements and diminishments subject to the same kinds of stipulations, and (c) from reclassifications to (or from) other classes of net assets as a consequence of donor-imposed stipulations, their expiration by passage of time, or their fulfillment and removal by actions of the organization pursuant to those stipulations" (*Concepts Statement 6*, paragraph 93).*

Temporary restriction   "A donor-imposed restriction that permits the donee organization to use up or expend the donated assets as specified and is satisfied either by the passage of time or by actions of the organization."*

*Definition quoted from *SFAS No. 116*, Appendix D.

Term endowment   A type of restricted contribution in which the principal becomes expendable at a future date (classified as temporarily restricted net assets in the statement of financial position).

Unconditional promise to give   "A promise to give that depends only on passage of time or demand by the promisee for performance."*

Unrestricted net assets   "The part of net assets of a not-for-profit organization that is neither permanently restricted nor temporarily restricted by donor-imposed stipulations" (*Concepts Statement 6* paragraph 94).*

Unrestricted support   "Revenues or gains from contributions that are not restricted by donors."*

SELF-STUDY QUESTIONS

1. Under *SFAS No. 116*, promises to give cash for which stipulations exist as to the use of the cash are recorded as which of the following?
   a. Revenues or other support when received.
   b. Revenues or other support when collected.
   c. Revenues or other support when the expenditures are made to satisfy the intended purpose.
   d. Direct additions to equity.

2. Under *SFAS No. 116*, contributions that are *endowments* are recorded as which of the following?
   a. Revenues or other support when received.
   b. Revenues or other support when collected.
   c. Revenues or other support when the expenditures are made to satisfy the intended purpose.
   d. Direct additions to equity.

3. Under *SFAS No. 116*, which of the following types of contributed services would *not* be reported in the statement of activities?
   a. A CPA performs the NPO's annual audit at no charge.
   b. A board member of the NPO is a lawyer and performs some legal work for the NPO at no charge.
   c. An employee of the NPO having an annual salary of $40,000 per year for working 2,000 hours works 2,300 hours, volunteering the 300 extra hours.
   d. A plumber makes free repairs to the NPO facility.

4. Under *SFAS No. 116*, the recognition of contributed *collection items* is which of the following?
   a. Mandatory   b. Prohibited   c. Optional

5. Under *SFAS No. 116*, recognition in the statement of activities of the receipt of a conditional promise to give is which of the following?
   a. Mandatory
   b. Prohibited
   c. Optional
   d. Depends on the probability of the condition occurring

6. A *private* NPO received promises of $600,000 in 19X6 from local citizens, half of which were payable in 19X6, the other half payable in 19X7 for use in 19X7. Only 90% of the amount is expected to be collectible. What amount should be reported for Contribution Revenues (in total) for 19X6?
   a. $–0–   b. $270,000   c. $540,000   d. $600,000

7. Use the information in Question 6. What amount should be reported for Contribution Revenues—Unrestricted for 19X6?
   a. $–0–   b. $270,000   c. $540,000   d. $600,000

8. On 4/1/X1, a *private* NPO received a gift of equity securities having an $80,000 fair value. The donor's cost was $30,000. At 12/31/X1, the securities had a readily determinable fair value of $95,000. The securities cannot be sold for five years. What is the gain reported in the statement of activities for 19X1?
   a. $–0–   b. $15,000   c. $65,000

9. On 1/1/X1, a *private* NPO received the gift of an office building having an estimated useful life of 10 years and no salvage value. The donor's cost was $300,000 and the fair value at the donation date was $500,000. The building cannot be sold for five years. What amount should be reported for depreciation expense for 19X1?
    a. $–0–   **b.** $30,000   **c.** $50,000   **d.** $60,000   **e.** $100,000

10. During 19X1, a *private* NPO (1) incurred an $8,000 charge for printing its annual report and (2) spent $22,000 for merchandise sent to potential contributors on an unsolicited basis. What amount should be classified as fund-raising costs for 19X1?
    a. $–0–   **b.** $8,000   **c.** $22,000   **d.** $30,000

11. During 19X1, a labor union incurred (1) $50,000 of administrative costs, (2) $2,000 of fund-raising costs, (3) $30,000 of labor negotiation costs, and (4) $4,000 of membership development costs. What amount should be reported for program services for 19X1?
    a. $30,000   **b.** $32,000   **c.** $34,000   **d.** $36,000   **e.** $80,000

ASSIGNMENT MATERIAL

REVIEW QUESTIONS

1. What are the four categories of NPOs?
2. What are the five main characteristics of NPOs?
3. When a *private* NPO ceases its operations, what happens to its remaining assets after all liabilities are settled?
4. Is it appropriate to compare an NPO's revenues with its costs and expenses? Why or why not?
5. What title is used for the operating statement of *private* NPOs? Why is this title used instead of statement of income?
6. What does the term *financial flexibility* mean?
7. How does an entity *officially* become an NPO?
8. What are the two categories of restrictions used in *SFAS No. 116* and *SFAS No. 117*?
9. How are contributions of works of art, historical treasures, and similar assets accounted for under *SFAS No. 116*?
10. How are *contributed (donated) services* accounted for under *SFAS No. 116*?
11. Why are certain contributed (donated) services *not* recognized in the statement of activities under *SFAS No. 116*?
12. Under what conditions are gifts of long-lived assets *not* reported as *restricted support* under *SFAS No. 116*?
13. How are *conditional promises to give* reported under *SFAS No. 116*?
14. How are investments in debt and equity securities valued under *SFAS No. 124*?
15. Which long-lived assets must be depreciated under *SFAS No. 93*?
16. What are the three classifications of net assets required in the statement of financial position under the *SFAS No. 117*?
17. How is the expiration of a *temporary restriction* reported in the statement of activities under *SFAS No. 117*?
18. Revenues and expenses are generally reported at their *gross* amounts in the statement of activities. Under what exception may revenues be reported *net* of related expenses under *SFAS No. 117*?

EXERCISES

E 26–1 **Manner of *Reporting* Contributions**   Each of the items in the left column represents various contribution transactions pertaining to a private NPO. The right column lists possible manners of reporting.

Contribution Transactions	Possible Manners of Reporting
1. Receipt of a conditional promise to give.	A. Recognize when received.
2. Receipt of a contributed fixed asset.	B. Recognize when collected.
3. Receipt of an *unconditional* cash contribution.	C. Recognize at a later date.
4. Receipt of cash to use for a specific purpose.	D. Recognize when received or do *not* recognize at all.
5. Receipt of an art collection.	

6. Receipt of a long-term unconditional promise to give.
7. Receipt of free legal services.
8. Receipt of services from volunteer fund-raisers.

E. Recognize in the balance sheet but not in the statement of activities.
F. Do *not* recognize at all.
G. Recognize when placed in service.

Required   What is the appropriate manner to report each of these transactions? A reporting manner may be selected once, more than once, or not at all.

E 26–2   **Manner of *Recording* Contributions**   Each of the items in the left column represents various contribution transactions pertaining to a *private* NPO. The right column lists possible manners of recording.

Contribution Transactions

1. A donor contributed cash.
2. A donor contributed cash, specifying that it be used for medical research.
3. A donor contributed cash, specifying that it be used for operating purposes in the following year.
4. A donor contributed cash, specifying that it be used for medical research in the following year.
5. A donor contributed cash, specifying that only the income earned on the investment of the cash can be spent.
6. A donor contributed cash, specifying that it is to be used for adding a new wing to the hospital.
7. A lawyer gives free legal advice.

Possible Manners of Recording

A. Credit Fund Balance.
B. Credit Contribution Revenues— Unrestricted.
C. Credit Contribution Revenues— Restricted.
D. Credit Contribution Revenues— Temporarily Restricted.
E. Credit Contribution Revenues— Permanently Restricted.
F. Credit Deferred Contribution Revenue.
G. No entry.

Required   What is the proper manner to record each of these transactions? A reporting manner may be selected once, more than once, or not at all.

E 26–3   **Classifying Transactions in the Statement of Activities**   Each of the items in the left column represents various transactions. The right column lists possible—both appropriate and inappropriate—reporting categories in the statement of activities.

Transactions

1. Transfer of cash from an unrestricted fund to a restricted fund to repay debt.
2. Transfer of cash from an unrestricted fund to a restricted fund to pay interest on debt.
3. Recording depreciation.
4. Receipt of cash to establish an endowment fund.
5. Receipt of cash for fixed asset additions.
6. Receipt of cash for operations.
7. Expenditure of cash received in the prior year designated for fixed asset additions.
8. Receipt of free legal advice from a lawyer.

Category of Presentation in the Statement of Activities

A. Revenues, Gains, and Other Support.
B. Net Assets Released from Restrictions.
C. Interfund Transfers.
D. Expenses and Losses.
E. Residual Equity Transfers.
F. Between Net Assets at Beginning of Year and Net Assets at End of Year.
G. Operating Transfers.
H. As Expenses and Losses and as Revenues, Gains, and Other Support (offsetting debits and credits).
I. None of the above.

Required   What is the appropriate category in the statement of activities in which to report each transaction? A category may be selected once, more than once, or not at all.

E 26–4   **Categorizing Transactions in the Statement of Activities**   Each of the items in the left column represents various transactions. The right column lists possible—both appropriate and inappropriate—classification categories in the statement of activities.

Transactions	Classification Category in the Statement of Activities

Transactions

1. Transfer of cash from an *unrestricted* fund to a restricted fund to repay debt.
2. Transfer of cash from an *unrestricted* fund to a restricted fund to pay interest on debt.
3. Recording depreciation on a fixed asset contributed to the NPO.
4. Receipt of cash to establish an endowment fund.
5. Receipt of cash for fixed asset additions.
6. Receipt of cash for operations.
7. Expenditure of cash received in the prior year designated for fixed asset additions.

Classification Category in the Statement of Activities

A. Unrestricted.
B. Temporarily Restricted.
C. Permanently Restricted.
D. Interfund Transfers.
E. Unrestricted and Temporarily Restricted.
F. Unrestricted and Permanently Restricted.
G. None of the above.

Required   For each transaction, in which classification category or categories in the statement of activities should an amount be reported? A classification category may be selected once, more than once, or not at all.

E 26–5   **Private C&U: Determining Whether Certain Fund Accounting Transactions Are Reported Under *SFAS No. 117***
A private university that uses fund accounting had the following transactions during 19X1:

1. A $900,000 cash disbursement was made from the Current Unrestricted Fund to the Retirement of Indebtedness Fund.
2. The Retirement of Indebtedness Fund retired $200,000 of its bonded indebtedness.
3. The Retirement of Indebtedness Fund disbursed $700,000 cash on 9/30/X1 in payment of interest on its bonds.

Required   Should these transactions be reported in the 19X1 statement of activities?

E 26–6   **Private HCO: Determining Whether Certain Fund Accounting Transactions Are Reported Under *SFAS No. 117***
A private hospital that uses fund accounting had the following transactions during 19X1:

1. Pursuant to the board of directors' authorization, $100,000 was disbursed from the General Funds to the Plant Replacement and Expansion Funds.
2. The investments of a term endowment established by a donor were sold at the termination date. All cash on hand ($222,000) was transferred to the General Funds.
3. The Specific-Purpose Funds reimbursed the General Funds $300,000 in connection with spending on donor-stipulated purposes.

Required   How should these transactions be reported in the 19X1 statement of activities?

PROBLEMS

P 26–1   **Private C&U: Recording Transactions and Preparing a Statement of Activities**   During 19X1, Ivory Tower College, a private NPO, had the following transactions and events in 19X1:

1. A wealthy citizen donated $500,000 cash, which can only be invested. Net investment income (dividends and interest) can be used only for granting scholarships.
2. Investment income (interest) on the investment in item 1 totaled $33,000. Of this amount, $21,000 was expended on scholarships. Investment advisory fees of $1,000 were paid.
3. A wealthy citizen donated 10,000 shares of BT&T common stock. The citizen's cost basis was $12 per share. The market price was $30 per share at the donation date. The common stock cannot be sold for 10 years. After 10 years, the university has total discretion as to investing or spending the proceeds from the sale of the stock.
4. Concerning the donation in item 3, dividends of $44,000 were declared, of which $22,000 was collected by year-end. The investment income (dividends) can be used for any purpose.
5. Concerning the donation in item 3, the common stock had a market price of $35 per share at year-end.
6. Interest of $6,000 was earned on an investment made with a $100,000 cash donation in the prior year. None of the income can be spent until the market value of the investment reaches $200,000.

7. The college's engineering school employs a retired engineer who teaches engineering classes and is paid a nominal stipend of $3,000 per year. Other faculty in the engineering school are paid $60,000 per year.
8. Cash of $80,000 from contributions in the preceding year and restricted as to a specific program purpose was expended as intended.
9. Cash of $90,000 received from contributions in the preceding year solely to buy new equipment was expended as intended.

Required
1. Prepare the journal entries to record these transactions. Assume that fund accounting is not used.
2. Prepare the revenues, gains, and other support section of the 19X1 statement of activities (including restriction expirations) using the columnar format. (Code your amounts to the related transaction number.)

P 26-2   **Private HCO: Recording Transactions and Preparing a Statement of Activities**   During 19X1, Clean Sheets Hospital, a private NPO, had the following transactions or events:

1. Cash of $110,000 received in the preceding year and restricted to a specific program purpose was expended.
2. In connection with desired expansion plans, a prominent citizen purchased land adjacent to the hospital at a cost of $220,000 and donated it to the hospital to use as it pleases consistent with its mission.
3. A wealthy citizen donated $300,000 cash that can only be invested. Income earned on the investment in excess of $10,000 can be used for any purpose. The first $10,000 must be reinvested.
4. The cash received in item 2 was invested and earned $14,000 (interest and dividends).
5. Local citizens volunteered 10,000 hours as candy-stripers (working at the hospital's information desk, gift shop, and nurses stations). The minimum wage is $5 per hour.
6. A wealthy citizen donated $600,000 cash, of which $500,000 is to be used to establish a kidney dialysis unit. The remaining $100,000 is to be used to run the unit.
7. Depreciation of $700,000 was recognized. Of this amount, $80,000 pertained to equipment that had been donated to the hospital two years ago on the condition that the equipment be used for at least seven years. The remaining depreciation pertains to assets acquired with unrestricted funds.

Required
1. Prepare the journal entries to record these transactions. Assume that fund accounting is not used.
2. Prepare the revenues, gains, and other support section of the 19X1 statement of activities (including restriction expirations) using the columnar format. (Code your amounts to the related transaction number.)

P 26-3   **Private VHWO: Recording Transactions and Preparing a Statement of Activities**   During 19X1, Free Food Foundation, a VHWO serving needy families, had the following transactions or events:

1. Cash contributions of $111,000 were received.
2. Unconditional promises to give, which are legally enforceable, total $22,000 at the end of 19X1. The promissors made no stipulations regarding when or how the money could be spent. At the end of 19X0, $16,000 of unconditional promises existed, all of which were collected in 19X1.
3. At year-end, a citizen promised in writing to contribute $30,000 cash if the local baseball team, which finished in last place in 19X1, wins the World Series in 19X2.
4. A wealthy citizen donated a van to deliver meals to disabled citizens. Its fair value is $24,000. If the van is not used as intended, it must be returned to the donor.
5. A wealthy citizen donated $500,000 cash with the stipulation that it can only be invested. Income on the investment can be spent only to provide counseling.
6. During 19X1, income (interest and dividends) on the investment in item 5 totaled $36,000. Investment advisory fees totaling $1,000 were paid.
7. A gift of common stock received on 12/30/X0 (valued at $200,000), appreciated in value by $22,000 in 19X1. Investment income and appreciation gains beyond what is needed to maintain the original economic value can be spent for any purpose. Inflation in 19X1 was 5%. Dividends of $72,000 were declared on this stock in 19X1, of which $54,000 had been collected by year-end.
8. A local CPA audited the NPO's 19X1 financial statements at no charge, which normally would have been $8,000.
9. A biannual special fund-raising event resulted in $660,000 of cash contributions. The event incurred costs of $60,000. The board of directors designated $300,000 for spending in 19X2.

10. For the $300,000 in item 9 that could be spent in 19X1, $280,000 was spent.
11. Depreciation expense of $4,000 on the van in item 4 was recognized.
12. Volunteers contributed 1,200 hours of time delivering meals to elderly people. Assume that the minimum wage is $5.

Required   1. Prepare the journal entries to record these transactions. Assume that fund accounting is *not* used.
2. Prepare the revenues, gains, and other support section of the 19X1 statement of activities (including restriction expirations) using the columnar format. (Code your amounts to the related transaction number.) Show multiple lines for contribution revenues for ease of coding the transactions.

P 26–4 **Private VHWO: Manner of Reporting Certain Transactions**

1. The board of directors designated $600,000 to refurbish one of its buildings.
2. An endowment fund had an $80,000 unrealized gain on one of its common stock investments. The donor stipulated that any holding gains need *not* be added to the principal—they could be spent for any purpose. Accordingly, the VHWO sold a sufficient number of shares of the common stock holding to obtain $70,000 cash that it could spend.
3. A building having a $700,000 carrying value was sold at a $90,000 gain.
4. An endowment fund created by a board designation had a market valuation loss of $44,000.
5. A common stock investment, which must be held in perpetuity and is classified as *permanently restricted,* decreased in value by $55,000 during the year.

Required   How should each of these transactions be reported in the statement of activities?

✳ THINKING CRITICALLY ✳

✳ CASES ✳

C 26–1 **Determining How to Report Aggregated and Disaggregated Data** *SFAS No. 117* emphasizes reporting for the organization as a whole, not by fund.

Required   How might a *private* NPO present disaggregated data on a fund basis for the statement of financial position and still comply with the requirement to show aggregated data?

C 26–2 **Evaluating Continued Use of Fund Accounting for Internal Record-Keeping Purposes** *SFAS No. 117* does *not* address how a private NPO should internally maintain its books and records.

Required   If you were the controller of a private NPO, would you continue to use fund accounting internally? Why or why not?

ANSWERS TO SELF-STUDY QUESTIONS

1. a   2. a   3. c   4. c   5. d   6. c   7. b   8. b   9. c   10. c   11. a

NOT-FOR-PROFIT ORGANIZATIONS: *PUBLIC* NPOS

27

There's a better way to do it. Find it.

THOMAS EDISON

Recall from Chapter 26 that of the four types of not-for-profit organizations (NPOs), only these two types exist to a significant degree as governmental (public) NPOs:

1. Health-care organizations (HCOs).
2. Colleges and universities (C&Us).

Recall further that (1) these *public* NPOs must follow the guidance of the Governmental Accounting Standards Board (GASB) and (2) the substantive differences between the GASB guidance and the FASB guidance for HCOs and C&Us concerns C&Us—not C&Us *and* HCOs. This chapter discusses the GASB guidance for *public* HCOs and *public* C&Us.

Because the GASB guidance for *public* HCOs closely resembles the FASB guidance for *private* HCOs in virtually all major respects and, therefore, is simpler to deal with than *public* C&Us, we discuss *public* HCOs before we discuss *public* C&Us.

THE AICPA'S AUDIT AND ACCOUNTING GUIDES

The GASB guidance (with one execption for C&Us mentioned later) for both *public* HCOs and *public* C&Us requires these NPOs to follow the applicable audit and accounting guides issued by the American Institute of Certified Public Accountants (AICPA)—except to the extent that they conflict with or contradict a GASB pronouncement. Recall that we discussed these audit and accounting guides in Chapter 26.

THE REVISIONS TO THE ACCOUNTING AND AUDIT GUIDES Recall also from Chapter 26 that both the 1990 HCO Audit and Accounting guide and the 1975 C&U Audit guide were revised in 1996 to reflect the requirements of *SFAS No. 116*, "Accounting for Contributions Received and Made"; *SFAS No. 117*, "Financial Statements for Not-for-Profit Organizations"; and *SFAS No. 124*, "Accounting for Certain Investments Held by Not-for-Profit Organizations."[1]

Unique to the updated guides is that *SFAS No. 117* (in paragraph 3) specifically allows these AICPA guides to provide more specific reporting guidance than it provides. As mentioned in Chapter 26, the financial reporting guidance in the 1996 HCO Audit and Accounting guide differs from the financial reporting guidance in *SFAS No. 117* in several respects.

THE FOCUS OF OUR DISCUSSION

The discussion in this chapter focuses on the requirements of the specific guides that apply to *public* HCOs and *public* C&Us.

PUBLIC HCOs Recall from Chapter 26 that the revised HCO Audit and Accounting guide (which for convenience we hereafter refer to as the *1996 HCO guide*) superseded the 1990 HCO guide insofar as *all HCOs* are concerned, that is, *private* for-profit HCOs, *private* not-for-profit HCOs, and *public* HCOs (automatically not for profit). Accordingly, our discussion of *public* HCOs centers around the 1996 HCO guide, which requires that *external* financial reporting be on an *aggregated*

---

[1] *SFAS No. 93*, "Recognition of Depreciation by Not-for-Profit Organizations" (issued in 1987), was incorporated into both of the revised audit guides. (Previously, it had been incorporated into only the 1990 HCO audit guide.)

basis (consistent with *SFAS No. 117*) rather than on a *disaggregated* basis (fund accounting based).

PUBLIC C&Us   Also recall from Chapter 26 that the successor guide to the C&U guide superseded the 1975 C&U guide *only* concerning *private* C&Us. Thus the 1975 C&U guide remains in effect concerning *public* C&Us, pending the GASB's completion of its current project involving a complete reexamination of the financial reporting model for *public* C&Us. Accordingly, our discussion of *public* C&Us centers on the 1975 C&U guide, which requires external financial reporting on a *disaggregated* basis (fund accounting based) rather than on an *aggregated* basis.

PUBLIC HEALTH-CARE ORGANIZATIONS

Before discussing *public* HCOs, we briefly discuss (1) health-care costs in general and (2) *private* managed care organizations as a frame of reference.

Health-care costs are currently spiralling out of control, having increased at a rate of 8% to 13% yearly over the past decade. In 1995, health-care costs equalled 14% of the gross national product (GNP), a 27% increase from 11% in 1985. The current concern is whether the projected increases can be pulled back to 17% of the GNP by the year 2000. Because of these rapidly increasing costs, employers, health insurers, and the government have demanded changes. The health-care industry has responded with efforts to reduce medical care costs by using *managed care organizations*.

I MANAGED CARE ORGANIZATIONS

TYPES OF MANAGED CARE ORGANIZATIONS

Managed care organizations can be (1) self-insured health maintenance organizations (HMOs), such as Kaiser Permanente and U.S. Healthcare; (2) preferred provider organizations (PPOs), organized networks of physicians who sell their services to insurance companies; and (3) businesses founded solely to manage health care.

In the past decade, managed care evolved from a corporate experiment into the dominant form of health-care delivery in the United States. Nationwide, 130 million people (including 71% of insured employees) now belong to some kind of managed-care plan. Of these 130 million people, nearly 50% belong to HMOs, which wield the tightest control over costs.

THE WAY MANAGED CARE ORGANIZATIONS OPERATE

Managed care organizations are companies that oversee providers (doctors, clinics, and hospitals) in a manner that causes the providers to seriously evaluate the costs of their services. In essence, a physician's practice behavior is manipulated to make the system more profitable for the managed care organizations.

Under this system, most medical care must be pre-approved. Patients and their physicians must jump through many administrative hoops to obtain authorization for discounted fee-for-service care from the managed care organization (often referred to as "the gatekeeper"). These systems control costs by managing physicians through efficiently utilizing resources and establishing practice guidelines that save money. As a result, fewer test and treatments are ordered, and fewer services are sought from specialists.

Doctors can be on salary, supplemented by bonuses for cost-saving care. These financial incentives serve to cause physicians to restrict their patients' access to medical services in exchange for money.

With such an emphasis on controlling costs, the term *the bottom line* has taken on a new meaning in the private health-care industry. Accordingly, the need for accounting and financial reporting standards of the highest quality is paramount. Controlling health-care costs in the *public* sector is equally as important.

II APPLICABILITY OF THE AICPA'S 1996 HCO AUDIT AND ACCOUNTING GUIDE

As stated earlier, our discussion of the GASB guidance for *public* HCOs centers on the AICPA's 1996 HCO guide. This guide applies to the separate financial statements issued by the following categeories of health-care providers:

1. Private for-profit HCOs.
2. Private nonprofit HCOs.
3. **Nonfederal** government HCOs (automatically nonprofit), such as state, county, and city hospitals. (The Veterans Administration hospitals are excluded because they are at the federal level.)

These three categories include the following types of HCOs:

Hospitals (almost all are in categories 2 and 3).
Nursing homes (almost all are in category 1).
HMOs and other prepaid care providers (almost all are in category 2).
Continuing-care retirement communities.
Home health agencies.
Medical group practices.
Clinics.
Other ambulatory care organizations.

FOCUS ON *PUBLIC* HOSPITALS

In almost all cases, the only nonfederal government HCOs that exist are public hospitals; accordingly, we limit our discussion of *public* HCOs to *public* hospitals.

A state, county, or city hospital may be (1) part of another organization (called the *primary* governmental unit) or (2) deemed a "component unit" of the primary governmental unit. Consequently, the financial statements of a state, county, or city hospital may be presented in one of two manners, depending on whether the HCO is deemed a component unit of the primary governmental unit. The 1996 HCO guide applies to each of these two manners of *external* reporting of a *public* HCO's financial statements, which are now described in more detail.

AS A *PART OF* THE PRIMARY GOVERNMENTAL UNIT   If the *public* hospital *is* part of another organization, such as a county hospital of a general-purpose government or a medical school of a public university, it is (1) accounted for as an Enterprise Fund of the primary governmental unit, (2) its financial statements are combined with other Enterprise Funds of the primary governmental unit, and (3) the combined amounts are reported in the combined financial statements of the primary governmental unit's general-purpose financial statements—this is at **Level 1 of the financial reporting pyramid** discussed in Chapter 25.

In addition, many primary governmental units report separately in their annual reports the individual financial statements of their hospitals—this is at **Level 3 of the financial reporting pyramid**.

AS A *COMPONENT UNIT* OF THE PRIMARY GOVERNMENTAL UNIT   If the public hospital is a *component unit* of the *primary governmental unit*, however, its financial statements are either (1) shown in separate columns added to the general-purpose financial statements prepared by the governmental unit (a *discrete presentation*) or (2) "blended in" as explained in Chapter 24.

III THE FINANCIAL REPORTING MODEL FOR *PUBLIC* HCOS

The financial reporting model for *nonprofit* HCOs (both public and private), as set forth in the 1996 HCO guide, is based on the commercial accounting model, that is, the model used by *for-profit* businesses. Recall from Chapter 24 that under this model, (1) the **measurement focus is on the flow of all *economic* resources** (requires recognizing depreciation) and (2) **the *accrual basis* of accounting is used.**

Nonprofit HCOs are required to use the same financial reporting model as that used by *for-profit* HCOs because the activities of *nonprofit* HCOs are characterized as **proprietary-type activities,** that is, **activities that are similar to those often found in the private (for-profit) sector.** Thus a city, county, or state hospital of a governmental unit is a proprietary-type activity. (A public utility is another example of a governmental proprietary-type activity.) Recall from Chapter 24 that a focus of proprietary-type activities is maintaining capital—*not* maximizing the excess of revenues over expenses relative to the capital employed.

PROPRIETARY ACTIVITY ACCOUNTING AND FINANCIAL REPORTING

Under *SGAS No. 20*, "Accounting and Financial Reporting for Proprietary Funds and Other Governmental Entities That Use Proprietary Fund Accounting," governmental proprietary-type activities are required to follow (1) all applicable GASB pronouncements and (2) all private-sector standards issued on or before November 30, 1989[2] (except to the extent that those pronouncements conflict with or contradict GASB pronouncements). Furthermore, governmental proprietary-type activities are given the option to follow all FASB standards issued after November 30, 1989 (except to the extent that those pronouncements conflict with or contradict GASB pronouncements). If this option is selected, however, it must be on an "all-or-none" basis—selecting only those standards the NPO wishes to follow is *not* allowed.

Furthermore, *SGAS No. 29*, "The Use of Not-for-Profit Accounting and Financial Reporting Principles by Governmental Entities" clarifies *SGAS No. 20* by stating that this option pertains only to FASB standards that apply to *for-profit* entities. Consequently, proprietary-type activities are prohibitied from applying *SFAS Nos. 116, 117,* and *124*, unless the GASB allows them to do so (which the GASB has not done).

However, the reporting model for *public* HCOs set forth in the 1996 HCO guide differs from the reporting model mandated by *SFAS No. 117* in only one major respect, which we discuss later in the chapter.

IV FINANCIAL STATEMENTS USED FOR *EXTERNAL* FINANCIAL REPORTING

Because the measurement focus for all HCOs is the flow of all *economic* resources and because the accrual basis is mandated for all HCOs, the financial statements of

---

[2]This is the date of the revised structural agreement between the FASB and the GASB regarding jurisdiction (as discussed in Chapter 24).

all HCOs are quite similar. The slight differences that exist pertain to the descriptive terms (labels) used. These differences are as follows:

Type of HCO	Appropriate Terminology
Private for-profit HCO	Statement of income
	Stockholders' equity:
	Common stock
	Retained earnings
Private not-for-profit HCO	Statement of operations
	Net assets:
	Unrestricted
	Temporarily restricted
	Permanently restricted
Public HCO	Statement of operations
	Fund balance:
	Unrestricted
	Temporarily restricted
	Permanently restricted
	or
	Unrestricted
	Restricted

Because of the use of (1) the flow of economic resources (requires recognizing depreciation) and (2) the accrual basis of accounting, for each of the three categories of HCOs, the appropriate financial statements for all *public* HCOs are as follows:

- A balance sheet.
- A statement of operations (includes depreciation).
- A statement of changes in fund balances.
- A statement of cash flows.

Recall that the guidance set forth in the 1996 HCO guide (for both private and public HCOs) is based on the use of aggregated financial reporting—not disaggregated (fund accounting–based) financial reporting.

THE BALANCE SHEET

The balance sheet for a *public* hospital includes fund balance categories of either (1) *unrestricted, temporarily restricted,* and *permanently restricted* or (2) *unrestricted* and *restricted.* Illustration 27–1 shows a balance sheet for a *public* hospital using the three categories of fund balance.

REVIEW POINTS FOR ILLUSTRATION 27–1   Note the following:

1. The 1996 HCO guide states that it is more appropriate to classify assets and liabilities as to current and noncurrent than by liquidity (unclassified).

2. A special classification of assets called *assets limited as to use* shows those assets *not* available for day-to-day operations. Internally designated amounts result from board actions. Amounts held by a trustee could result from either a malpractice funding arrangement and/or an indenture agreement.

THE STATEMENT OF OPERATIONS

Historically, hospitals are viewed more as businesses than as NPOs because they focus on their viability as a going concern and the maintenance of capital (thus the use of Enterprise Funds when they are part of the primary governmental unit). Accordingly, the operating statement format is similar in most respects (no income tax

ILLUSTRATION 27–1

Hope City Hospital
Balance Sheets—As of December 31, 19X2 and 19X1

Assets	19X2	19X1
Current Assets:		
Cash and cash equivalents	$ 3,700,000	$ 3,850,000
Short-term investments	4,250,000	4,100,000
Assets limited as to use	1,120,000	980,000
Patient accounts receivable, net of estimated uncollectibles of $2,150,000 in 19X2 and $2,050,000 in 19X1	19,110,000	18,775,000
Supplies and other current assets	1,515,000	1,250,000
Total Current Assets	$29,695,000	$28,955,000
Assets Limited as to Use:		
Internally designated	$ 4,500,000	$ 3,100,000
Held by trustees	2,055,000	2,175,000
	$ 6,555,000	$ 5,275,000
Less amount required to meet current obligations	(722,000)	(830,000)
Total Assets Limited as to Use	$ 5,833,000	$ 4,445,000
Properties and Other:		
Property and equipment, net	54,482,000	53,350,000
Other assets	1,520,000	970,000
Total Assets	$91,530,000	$87,720,000
Total Liabilities and Fund Balance		
Current Liabilities:		
Current maturities of long-term debt	$ 1,100,000	$ 875,000
Accounts payable and accrued expenses	6,050,000	4,605,000
Estimated third-party payor settlements	1,750,000	1,225,000
Other current liabilities	1,468,000	1,297,000
Total Current Liabilities	$10,368,000	$ 8,002,000
Noncurrent Liabilities:		
Long-term debt, net of current maturities	19,750,000	20,850,000
Other liabilities	4,202,000	3,568,000
Total Liabilities	$34,320,000	$32,420,000
Fund Balance:		
Unrestricted	$52,640,000	$52,770,000
Temporarily restricted	2,210,000	720,000
Permanently restricted	2,360,000	1,810,000
Total Fund Balance	$57,210,000	$55,300,000
Total Liabilities and Fund Balance	$91,530,000	$87,720,000

expense, for example) to an income statement for a *for-profit* entity. Illustration 27–2 shows a statement of operations for a *public* hospital.

REVIEW POINTS FOR ILLUSTRATION 27–2   Note the following, which (other than item 4) apply to *all* HCOs—both *private* and *public:*

1. **Net patient service charges.** This account shows the primary source of revenues for public hospitals. It is always shown **net of provisions for contractual and other adjustments—but *not* net of the provision for** *bad debts,* which are classified as part of expenses.
2. **Other revenues.** The illustrated financial statements in the AICPA's HCO guide show a single amount for all types of other revenues. We present it in detail to convey the nature of the many types of items that this category includes.

ILLUSTRATION 27–2

Hope City Hospital
Statement of Operations
For the Years Ended December 31, 19X2 and 19X1
(*excludes* amounts pertaining to *restricted* items)

	19X2	19X1
Revenues:		
Net patient service charges	$62,576,000	$60,755,000
Other revenues:		
Gift shop, snack bar, cafeteria and vending machine sales	4,770,000	4,390,000
Fees charged for educational programs, lab services, and X-ray technology	1,660,000	1,580,000
Fees charged to lawyers, insurance companies, and others for incidental services	610,000	440,000
Rental income from the use of the facilities by others	640,000	570,000
Parking lot revenues	460,000	390,000
Scrap (X-ray film) sales	180,000	170,000
Ad valorem (property) taxes	18,844,000	18,185,000
Grants	510,000	1,020,000
Contributions (other than fixed asset contributions)	350,000	220,000
Total Revenues	$90,600,000	$87,720,000
Expenses:		
Salaries and benefits	$46,195,000	$42,605,000
Medical supplies and drugs	14,072,000	11,685,000
Insurance	8,650,000	8,025,000
Other supplies	13,114,000	12,430,000
Provision for bad debts	5,466,000	4,233,000
Depreciation and amortization	4,280,000	3,966,000
Interest	1,493,000	1,566,000
Total Expenses	$93,270,000	$84,510,000
Operating Income (Loss)	$ (2,670,000)	$ 3,210,000
Nonoperating Income:		
Investment income (interest & dividends)	630,000	570,000
Excess of Revenues & Nonoperating Income over Expenses	$ (2,040,000)	$ 3,780,000
Change in net unrealized gains (losses) on available-for-sale securities	(90,000)	170,000
Transfers from (to) county	2,000,000	(3,000,000)
Increase (Decrease) in Unrestricted Fund Balance	$ (130,000)	$ 950,000

3. **Charity care.** Charity care represents health-care services that are provided but are *never* expected to result in cash flows. For this reason, charity care does *not* qualify for recognition as a receivable or a revenue. Thus patient service revenues do *not* include any *imputed* amounts for charity care. The level of charity care provided (based on the HCO's rates, costs, units of service, or other statistical measure) must be disclosed in the notes, along with the HCO's policy for providing charity care.

4. **Restriction expirations.** The expiration of restrictions is reported in the Revenues category using natural account descriptions (such as grant revenue or contributions)—they are *not* reported as a separate line item called *net assets released from restrictions*—which is the reporting manner under *SFAS No. 117* for *private* HCOs.

In this illustration, we assumed that *all* restriction expirations for 19X1 and 19X2 resulted solely from fulfilling conditions on grants received. Accordingly, the amounts shown for grant revenues tie directly to the statement of changes in fund balances, which is shown later in Illustration 27–3.

Such a tie-in usually is *not* possible when either (1) expirations pertain to more than one type of inflow (such as the expiration of both grants and temporary endowments) or (2) unrestricted inflows also occur in the reporting year.

5. **Contributions.** *Public* HCOs usually do *not* receive or rely on significant annual contributions (as do many C&Us and most VHWOs) to sustain their operations. Contributions are recognized when received and are discussed further using the following two categories:

   a. **Contributions other than fixed assets.** *Unrestricted* contributions are reported as contribution revenues in the operating statement when received. *Restricted* contributions are reported as a *direct credit* to one of the *Restricted* Fund Balance accounts, as appropriate. If and when the restriction expires, the contributed amount is reported as contribution revenues in the operating statement (requires a *debit* to the appropriate *Restricted* Fund Balance account).

   b. **Contributions of fixed assets.** These contributions are reported as a *direct credit* to the *Unrestricted* Fund Balance account or one of the *Restricted* Fund Balance accounts. *Direct credits* to the Unreserved Fund Balance account (and later credits resulting from restriction expirations) are reported *below* the operating income or loss line.

6. **Operating income or loss.** A measure of operations must be reported. The meaning of the term *operations* must be either (a) apparent from the details reported on the face of the statement or (b) described in the notes.

7. **Nonoperating items.** Operating results must be reported separately from the following items:

   a. Extraordinary items, the cumulative effect of accounting changes, and discontinued operations.

   b. Receipt of restricted contributions (both temporary and permanent).

   c. Contributions of *unrestricted* long-lived assets (reported as a direct addition to the *Unrestricted* Fund Balance account).

   d. Equity transfers to or from entities that (1) control the HCO, (2) are controlled by the HCO, or (3) are under common control with the HCO.

   e. Changes in unrealized gains and losses on investments.

8. **The limited scope of the statement of operations.** Items that increase or decrease the *Temporarily Restricted* Fund Balance account and the *Permanently Restricted* Fund Balance account are *not* reported in the statement of operations—they are reported in the statement of changes in fund balance. **This manner of reporting is the major difference between the guidance set forth in *SFAS No. 117* and the AICPA HCO guide.** (This different manner of reporting is also required for *private* HCOs).

STATEMENT OF CHANGES IN FUND BALANCES

All changes in the HCO's fund balance are reported in this statement, which serves the same purpose as a statement of changes in stockholder's equity for a *for-profit* corporation.

Illustration 27–3 shows such a statement.

STATEMENTS OF CASH FLOW

Public HCOs must follow the requirements of *SGAS No. 9*, "Reporting Cash Flows of Proprietary and Nonexpendable Trust Funds and Governmental Entities That Use Proprietary Fund Accounting." The required format for this statement differs

ILLUSTRATION 27-3

Hope City Hospital
Statement of Changes in Fund Balances
For the Years Ended December 31, 19X2 and 19X1

	Unrestricted	Temporarily Restricted	Permanently Restricted	Total
Fund Balance, 1/1/X1	$51,820,000	$ 440,000	$1,000,000	$53,260,000
+ Excess of revenues and nonoperating income over expenses	3,780,000			3,780,000
+ Unexpended research grants received		1,300,000		1,300,000
− Amounts released from restrictions		(1,020,000)		(1,020,000)
+ Endowment funds received			810,000	810,000
+ *Favorable* change in unrealized gain or loss on available-for-sale securities	170,000			170,000
− Transfers *to* county	(3,000,000)			(3,000,000)
Fund Balance, 12/31/X1	$52,770,000	$ 720,000	$1,810,000	$55,300,000
− Excess of expenses over revenues and nonoperating income	(2,040,000)			(2,040,000)
+ Unexpended research grants received		1,400,000		1,400,000
− Amounts released from restrictions		(510,000)		(510,000)
+ Endowment funds received		600,000	550,000	1,150,000
− *Unfavorable* change in unrealized gain or loss on available-for-sale securities	(90,000)			(90,000)
+ Transfers *from* county	2,000,000			2,000,000
Fund Balance, 12/31/X2	$52,640,000	$2,210,000	$2,360,000	$57,210,000

from the format required under *SFAS No. 95*, "Statement of Cash Flows" (illustrated in Chapter 26) because it requires the presentation of two categories of cash flows from financing activities. (The format under *SGAS No. 9* is presented in Chapter 25 in Illustration 25–20, which was the fifth of the five general-purpose financial statements presented at Level 1 of the financial reporting pyramid concept for a governmental unit.)

The two categories of financing, along with the types of cash flows associated with each for a *public* HCO, are as follows:

Cash flows from *noncapital* financing activities:
    Proceeds from contributions restricted for specific expenditure
    Transfers to county
Cash flows from capital and related financing activities:
    Proceeds from contributions restricted for investment in equipment
    Principal paid on long-term debt
    Interest paid on long-term debt
    Purchase of property and equipment

OTHER REQUIRED DISCLOSURES

A *public* HCO must not only follow the specific guidance in the AICPA 1966 HCO guide but also must comply with all applicable GASB statements, interpretations, and technical bulletins. Examples of additional probable disclosures for *public* HCOs to comply with GASB pronouncements are as follows:

1. *SGAS No. 3* (on investments) requires certain disclosures about credit risk and market risks of investments.

2. *SGAS No. 12* (on postemployment benefits) requires certain disclosures about postemployment benefits provided to employees.

3. *SGAS No. 27* on pensions requires certain disclosures about pension benefits.

A *public* HCO that *elects* to follow FASB standards issued after November 30, 1989, that pertain to *for-profit* entities also must comply with standards such as the following if the HCO had financial instruments and derivative financial instruments:

1. *SFAS No. 105*, "Disclosure of Information About Financial Instruments With Off-Balance-Sheet Risk and Financial Instruments with Concentrations of Credit Risk."

2. *SFAS No. 107*, "Disclosure About Fair Value of Financial Instruments."

3. *SFAS No. 119*, "Disclosure About Derivative Financial Instruments and Fair Value of Financial Instruments."

ACCOUNTING FOR INVESTMENTS

Public HCOs that elect to apply paragraph 7 of *SGAS No. 20* (choosing to follow all FASB pronouncements issued after November 30, 1989) are required under the AICPA HCO guide to follow *SFAS No. 115*, "Accounting for Certain Investments in Debt and Equity Securities" (which requires the use of fair values in the balance sheet). Recall that *SGAS No. 29* prohibits *public* HCOs from applying *SFAS No. 124*.

THE GASB'S PROPOSED STANDARD   In early 1996, the GASB issued for comment the exposure draft of a proposed financial reporting standard dealing with certain investments and external investment pools. Under this proposal, most governmental entities (including governmental external investments pools, *public* HCOs, and *public* C&Us) would report (1) investments at fair value in the balance sheet and (2) changes in the fair value of investments as part of investment income in the operating statement or other statement of activites of all entities or funds.

When this proposed standard becomes effective (most likely in 1997), *public* HCOs will become subject to this standard rather than *SFAS No. 115*.

PUBLIC COLLEGES AND UNIVERSITIES

Colleges and universities (both *public* and *private*) provide educational services and conduct research. As noted earlier, some medical C&Us have hospitals. All *public* C&Us are nonprofit institutions (as are virtually all **private** C&Us[3]).

THE TWO ALLOWABLE FINANCIAL REPORTING MODELS FOR *PUBLIC* C&US

SGAS No. 15, "Governmental College and University Accounting and Financial Reporting Models" (issued by the GASB in 1991) requires *public* C&Us to use either of the following two financial reporting models:

1. **The AICPA College Guide model.** This model is discussed and illustrated in the AICPA's 1975 audit guide, "Audits of Colleges and Universities." As stated earlier, this guide was superseded in late 1996 as it applies to *private* C&Us, but

---

[3]Colleges and universities are institutions that offer degrees. Commercial business schools, which do *not* offer degrees, are *for-profit* institutions that use commercial accounting reporting practices.

it (1) still applies to *public* C&Us and (2) continues to be published by the AICPA until the GASB completes its reexamination of the C&U financial reporting model that is currently underway and is discussed shortly.

2. **The Governmental model.** This model is the manner of reporting discussed and illustrated for state and local governmental units in Chapters 24 and 25.

The substantive reporting differences between the model used in the FASB guidance (for *private* C&Us) and the two allowable models used in the GASB guidance (for *public* C&Us) are shown in Illustration 27–4.

ILLUSTRATION 27–4	**Substantive Reporting Differences Between the FASB Guidance and the GASB Guidance for Colleges and Universities**		
	Colleges and Universities		
	FASB Guidance (for *Private* NPOs)	**GASB Guidance (for *Public* NPOs)**	
		AICPA Model	**Governmental Model**
Measurement focus on the flow of	Economic resources	Predominantly economic resources	Current financial resources
Basis of accounting	Accrual basis	Accrual basis	Modified accrual basis
Manner of presenting financial statements	Aggregated	Disaggregated (by fund)	Disaggregated (by fund)
Depreciation expense reported	Yes	No	No
Includes the term *expenditures* in the operating statement	No	Yes	Yes
Reports the acquisition of fixed assets as an *expenditure* in the operating statement	No	No	Yes
Reports the proceeds of borrowings as an *inflow* in the operating statement	No	No	Yes
Reports debt repayments as an *expenditure* in the operating statement	No	No	Yes
Timing of reporting contributions	When received	When expended	No guidance
Manner of valuing investments	Fair value	Cost or market value[a]	Amortized cost for debt investments (equity investments are rare)

[a]In March 1996, the GASB issued the exposure draft of a proposed standard that would require *public* NPOs to value many of their investments at fair value. This standard is expected to be finalized by the end of 1996.

REVIEW POINTS FOR ILLUSTRATION 27-4.   Note the following:

1. Because of their many similarities, the AICPA College Guide model can be characterized as a "cousin" of the model used in the FASB guidance.

2. The AICPA College Guide model produces an operating statement that can best be described as a *statement of revenues and nondepreciation expenses.* Accordingly, this statement comes much closer to measuring the change in net assets resulting from operations than does the operating statement produced using the Governmental model.

3. Even though it would be more informative and less confusing to use the title *statement of revenues and nondepreciation expenses* for the AICPA College Guide model, the AICPA's 1975 C&U guide uses the less descriptive term *statement of revenues and expenditures.*

4. The substantive difference between the two *public* C&U models is that *expenditures* are defined quite differently.

WHICH OF THE ALLOWABLE GASB GUIDANCE REPORTING MODELS TO USE

SOVEREIGNTY OF STATES   *Public* C&Us must use the reporting model mandated by their state governments. States are sovereign entities; accordingly, they can mandate whatever reporting model they choose. Some states (California and Washington, for instance) use their own internally developed reporting model. Other states require the use of one of the two allowable GASB reporting models.

THE AICPA COLLEGE MODEL IS THE PREDOMINANT PRACTICE   In practice, most *public* C&Us that choose to follow the GASB guidance use the AICPA College Guide model. Very few *public* C&Us that follow the GASB guidance use the Governmental model because it is less informative and useful than the AICPA College Guide model. In general, only C&Us that have taxing authority and thus resemble governmental units in this respect (as do many two-year colleges) use the governmental model.

REPORTING MODEL FOCUS FOR OUR REMAINING DISCUSSION OF *PUBLIC* C&US
The remaining discussion focuses on the *AICPA College Guide model.* Accordingly, remember that (1) depreciation expense is *not* reported in the operating statement and (2) the operating statement title uses the term *expenditures* rather than *expenses* solely because depreciation is *not* reported.

VI THE VARIOUS FUNDS USED UNDER THE AICPA COLLEGE GUIDE MODEL

The individual funds used under the AICPA College Guide model, as listed in the order in which they are usually presented in the balance sheet, are as follows:

Current Funds (the only funds reported in the operating statement)
   Current Unrestricted Fund
   Current Restricted Fund

Plant Funds
   Unexpended Plant Fund
   Renewals and Replacement Funds
   Retirement of Indebtedness Funds
   Investment in Plant

(continued)

Loan Funds

Endowment and Similar Funds

   Endowment Funds (permanent endowments)
   Term Endowment Funds
   Quasi-Endowment Funds

Other

   Annuity Funds
   Life Income Funds

Agency Funds

Before discussing each of these funds individually, we (1) describe the financial statements used for *external* financial reporting purposes and (2) present an illustrative balance sheet that includes *all* of these funds.

VII FINANCIAL STATEMENTS USED FOR *EXTERNAL* FINANCIAL REPORTING

The following financial statements are prepared for external financial reporting:

- A balance sheet (all funds).
- A statement of revenues, **expenditures**, and other changes (Current Funds only).
- A statement of changes in fund balances (**all funds**).

A *statement of revenues, expenditures, and other changes* is prepared only for the Current Funds because the other funds do *not* report revenues and expenditures—all of their transactions are posted directly to their Fund Balance account, as explained in more detail shortly.

The balance sheet is usually presented in layered or "pancake" form, as shown in Illustration 27–5 in which each fund appears stacked on another. (The alternative to layering is using a column for each fund, as is done in presenting the combined balance sheet in governmental accounting.)

VIII THE NATURE OF EACH SPECIFIC FUND

THE CURRENT FUNDS GROUP

The **Current Funds Group** (the Current Unrestricted Fund and the Current Restricted Fund) accounts for resources expendable for operating purposes and, therefore, includes the asset, liability, revenue, expenditure, and other accounts needed to record daily operations. For example, expenditures for instructions, research, extension programs, and auxiliary enterprise activities are accounted for in the Current Funds Group. In many ways, these two funds serve the same function as the General Fund of a state or local government.

THE CURRENT *UNRESTRICTED* FUND   The assets of this fund may be (1) used for operating purposes or (2) transferred by the governing board to other funds for loan, investment, or plant purposes. For example, the governing board may transfer cash to (1) a **Quasi-Endowment Fund,** in which the cash is invested until some other more suitable purpose is determined, (2) a **Loan Fund** for supplemental governmental appropriation, (3) the **Plant Funds Group** for expansion, refurbishment, or debt retirement. For these board-designated transfers—which are *internally* restricted amounts—the receiving fund credits its *Unrestricted* Fund Balance account—not the *Temporarily Restricted* Fund Balance account or the *Permanently Restricted* Fund Balance account. These latter two accounts are used only in connection with *externally* restricted amounts.

THE CURRENT *RESTRICTED* FUND   The assets of this fund are also available for operating purposes. The assets are restricted, however, by donors or other outside agencies as to the specific purpose for which they may be expended. The inflows into this fund can come from a variety of sources, such as gifts, bequests, investment income from Endowment Funds, contracts, grants, appropriations from governments (for research, public service, or other restricted purposes). The fund also usually has investment income gains. Inflows having restrictions are initially credited to the Fund Balance account. Later, as the amounts are expended for the intended purpose, revenues are credited and the Fund Balance account is debited.

Illustration 27–6 shows the statement of revenues, expenditures (nondepreciation expenses), and other changes for the Current Unrestricted Fund and the Current Restricted Fund (the only funds for which an operating statement is prepared).

REVIEW POINTS FOR ILLUSTRATION 27–6   Note the following:

1. **Recognizing revenues in the Current Restricted Fund.** Revenues for the Current Restricted Fund are recognized only to the extent that expenditures were made for the intended purpose. Thus revenues *always* equal expenditures for this fund.

2. **Interfund transfers.** Cash transfers to other funds (usually pertaining to debt service) are called *mandatory transfers* in this statement. (The net assets of the transferring fund *decrease* and the net assets of the receiving fund *increase*.) The inclusion of interfund transfers in this statement (rather than only in the statement of changes in fund balances) is such that they are given the same treatment as *operating transfers* (as opposed to *residual equity transfers* of governmental funds as discussed in Chapter 24).

3. **Remissions and student aid.** All student tuition and fees are recognized as revenues. To the extent that students are granted remissions (generally in connection with scholarships or financial aid), the waived amounts are recorded both as (1) student tuition/fees revenues and as (2) expenditures for scholarships or financial aid. Thus offsetting revenues and expenditures are reported. The result is as though the students actually paid their tuition/fees and the C&U simultaneously awarded a cash scholarship or gave financial aid.

4. **Cash transfers being returned.** Unrestricted resources that had previously been transferred to Plant Funds or Quasi-Endowment Funds and are returned are reported as transfers—not revenues.

5. **Not recognizing depreciation expense.** Unlike *private* C&Us, *public* C&Us do *not* recognize depreciation expense.

Illustration 27–7 shows a statement of changes in fund balances for all of the funds.

REVIEW POINTS FOR ILLUSTRATION 27–7   Note the following:

1. All funds are included.

2. This statement is more revealing for the funds other than the Current Funds because it is the only statement that reveals inflows and outflows that occurred in

ILLUSTRATION 27–5

Rocky State University
Balance Sheets as of June 30, 19X1 and 19X0

Assets	19X1	19X0	Liabilities and Fund Balances	19X1	19X0
Current Funds			**Current Funds**		
Unrestricted:			Unrestricted:		
Cash	$ 210,000	$ 110,000	Accounts payable	$ 125,000	$ 100,000
Investments	450,000	360,000	Accrued liabilities	20,000	15,000
Accounts receivable, less allowance of			Students' deposits	30,000	35,000
$18,000 both years	228,000	175,000	Due to other funds	158,000	120,000
Inventories, at lower of cost (first-in,			Deferred credits	30,000	20,000
first-out basis) or market	90,000	80,000	Fund balance	643,000	455,000
Prepaid expenses and deferred charges	28,000	20,000	Total Unrestricted Liabilities		
Total Unrestricted Assets	$1,006,000	$ 745,000	and Fund Balance	$1,006,000	$ 745,000
Restricted:			Restricted:		
Cash	$ 145,000	$ 101,000	Accounts payable	$ 14,000	$ 5,000
Investments	175,000	165,000	Fund balances	446,000	421,000
Accounts receivable, less allowance of			Total Restricted Liabilities		
$8,000 both years	68,000	160,000	and Fund Balance	460,000	426,000
Unbilled charges	72,000	–0–	Total Current Funds Liabilities		
Total Restricted Assets	$ 460,000	$ 426,000	and Fund Balance	$1,466,000	$1,171,000
Total Current Funds Assets	$1,466,000	$1,171,000			
Loan Funds			**Loan Funds**		
Cash	$ 30,000	$ 20,000	Fund balances:		
Investments	100,000	100,000	U.S. government grants refundable	$ 50,000	$ 33,000
Loans to students, faculty, and staff, less			University funds:		
allowance of $10,000 current year and			Restricted	483,000	369,000
$9,000 prior year	550,000	382,000	Unrestricted	150,000	100,000
Due from unrestricted funds	3,000	–0–	Total Loan Funds	$ 683,000	$ 502,000
Total Loan Funds Assets	$ 683,000	$ 502,000			
Endowment and Similar Funds			**Endowment and Similar Funds**		
Cash	$ 100,000	$ 101,000	Fund balances:		
Investments	13,900,000	11,800,000	Endowment	$ 7,800,000	$ 6,740,000
			Term endowment	3,840,000	3,420,000
			Quasi-endowment—unrestricted	1,000,000	800,000
Total Endowment and Similar			Quasi-endowment—restricted	1,360,000	941,000
Funds Assets	$14,000,000	$11,901,000	Total Endowment and Similar Funds	$14,000,000	$11,901,000
Annuity and Life Income Funds			**Annuity and Life Income Funds**		
Annuity funds:			Annuity funds:		
Cash	$ 55,000	$ 45,000	Annuities payable	$ 2,150,000	$ 2,300,000
Investments	3,260,000	3,010,000	Fund balances	1,165,000	755,000
Total Annuity Funds Assets	$ 3,315,000	$ 3,055,000	Total Annuity Funds	$ 3,315,000	$ 3,055,000

ILLUSTRATION 27-5 (continued)

Assets

Life Income Funds:		
Cash	15,000	15,000
Investments	2,045,000	1,740,000
Total Life Income Funds	$ 2,060,000	$ 1,755,000
Total Annuity and Life Income Funds Assets	$ 5,375,000	$ 4,810,000
Plant Funds		
Unexpended Plant Funds:		
Cash	$ 275,000	$ 410,000
Investments	1,285,000	1,590,000
Due from unrestricted current funds	150,000	120,000
Total Unexpended Assets	$ 1,710,000	$ 2,120,000
Renewals and Replacements Funds:		
Cash	$ 5,000	$ 4,000
Investments	150,000	286,000
Deposits with trustees	100,000	90,000
Due from unrestricted current funds	5,000	–0–
Total Renewals and Replacements Assets	$ 260,000	$ 380,000
Retirement of Indebtedness Funds:		
Cash	$ 50,000	$ 40,000
Deposits with trustees	250,000	253,000
Total Retirement of Indebtedness Assets	$ 300,000	$ 293,000
Investment in Plant:		
Land	$ 500,000	$ 500,000
Land improvements	1,000,000	1,110,000
Buildings	25,000,000	24,060,000
Equipment	15,000,000	14,200,000
Library books	100,000	80,000
Total Investment in Plant Assets	$41,600,000	$39,950,000
Total Plant Funds Assets	$43,870,000	$42,743,000
Agency Funds		
Cash	$ 50,000	$ 70,000
Investments	60,000	20,000
Total Agency Funds Assets	$ 110,000	$ 90,000

Liabilities and Fund Balances

Life Income Funds:		
Income payable	5,000	5,000
Fund balances	2,055,000	1,750,000
Total Life Income Funds	$ 2,060,000	$ 1,755,000
Total Annuity and Life Income Funds	$ 5,375,000	$ 4,810,000
Plant Funds		
Unexpended Plant Funds:		
Accounts payable	$ 10,000	$ –0–
Notes payable	100,000	–0–
Bonds payable	400,000	–0–
Fund balances:		
Restricted	1,000,000	1,860,000
Unrestricted	200,000	260,000
Total Unexpended	$ 1,710,000	$ 2,120,000
Renewals and Replacements Funds:		
Fund balances:		
Restricted	25,000	180,000
Unrestricted	235,000	200,000
Total Renewals and Replacements	$ 260,000	$ 380,000
Retirement of Indebtedness Funds:		
Fund balances:		
Restricted	185,000	125,000
Unrestricted	115,000	168,000
Total Retirement of Indebtedness	$ 300,000	$ 293,000
Investment in Plant:		
Notes payable	790,000	810,000
Bonds payable	2,200,000	2,400,000
Mortgages payable	400,000	200,000
Net investment in plant	38,210,000	36,540,000
Total Investment in Plant	$41,600,000	$39,950,000
Total Plant Funds	$43,870,000	$42,743,000
Agency Funds		
Deposits held in custody for others	$ 110,000	$ 90,000
Total Agency Funds	$ 110,000	$ 90,000

Source: Adapted from *Audits of Colleges and Universities*, 2nd ed. (New York: American Institute of Certified Public Accountants, 1975), Exh. 1, pp. 108–110.

ILLUSTRATION 27–6

Rocky State University
Statement of Revenues, Expenditures, and Other Changes—Current Funds
For the Year Ended June 30, 19X1, with Comparative Figures for 19X0

	19X1			19X0
	Unrestricted	Restricted	Total	Year Total
Revenues				
Educational and general:				
Student tuition and fees [at 100%]	$2,600,000		$2,600,000	$2,300,000
Governmental appropriations	1,300,000		1,300,000	1,300,000
Governmental grants and contracts	35,000	$ 425,000	460,000	595,000
Gifts and private grants	850,000	380,000	1,230,000	1,190,000
Endowment income	325,000	209,000	534,000	500,000
Sales and services of educational departments ..	90,000		90,000	95,000
Organized activities related to				
educational departments	100,000		100,000	100,000
Other sources (if any)				
Total Educational and General	$ 5,300,00	$1,014,000	$ 6,314,00	$6,080,000
Auxiliary enterprises				
[residence halls, bookstore, parking]	2,200,000		2,200,000	2,100,000
Expired term endowment	40,000		40,000	
Total Revenues	$7,540,000	$1,014,000	$8,554,000	$8,180,000
Expenditures and Mandatory Transfers				
Educational and general:				
Instruction and departmental research	$2,820,000	$ 300,000	$3,120,000	$2,950,000
Organized activities related to				
educational departments	140,000	189,000	329,000	350,000
Sponsored research		400,000	400,000	500,000
Other separately budgeted research	100,000		100,000	150,000
Other sponsored programs		25,000	25,000	50,000
Extension and public service	130,000		130,000	125,000
Libraries	250,000		250,000	225,000
Student services	200,000		200,000	195,000
Operation and maintenance of plant	220,000		220,000	200,000
General administration	200,000		200,000	195,000
General institutional expense	250,000		250,000	250,000
Student aid	90,000	100,000	190,000	180,000
Educational and General Expenditures	$4,400,000	$1,014,000	$5,414,000	$5,370,000
Mandatory transfers for:				
Principal and interest	90,000		90,000	50,000
Renewals and replacements	100,000		100,000	80,000
Loan fund matching grant	2,000		2,000	
Total Education and General	$4,592,000	$1,014,000	$5,606,000	$5,500,000
Auxiliary enterprises [residence halls,				
bookstore, parking]				
Expenditures	$1,830,000		$1,830,000	$1,730,000
Mandatory transfers for—				
Principal and interest	250,000		250,000	250,000
Renewals and replacements	70,000		70,000	70,000
Total Auxiliary Enterprises	$2,150,000		$2,150,000	$2,050,000
Total Expenditures and Mandatory				
Transfers	$6,742,000	$1,014,000	$7,756,000	$7,550,000
Other Transfers and Additions/(Deductions)				
Excess of restricted receipts over				
transfers to revenues		$ 45,000	$ 45,000	$ 40,000
Refunded to grantors		(20,000)	(20,000)	
Unrestricted gifts allocated to other funds	$ (650,000)		(650,000)	(510,000)
Portion of quasi-endowment gains appropriated ...	40,000		40,000	
Net Increase in Fund Balances	$ 188,000	$ 25,000	$ 213,000	$ 160,000

Source: Adapted from *Audits of Colleges and Universities,* 2nd ed. (New York: American Institute of Certified Public Accountants, 1975), Exh. C., pp. 66–67.

these other funds. Recall that all transactions in these other funds are recorded as direct additions to or subtractions from the Fund Balance account.

3. For the Current Unrestricted Fund and the Current Restricted Fund, the amounts in this statement are merely amounts from the statement of revenues, expenditures, and other changes for the Current Funds, as shown in Illustration 27–6. The formatting is different, however, and amounts were condensed (the usual practice).

LOAN FUNDS

Loan funds are usually established to provide loans to a C&U's students, faculty, and staff. Loan Funds are generally revolving, that is, repayments of principal and interest are loaned to other individuals. The following table shows their sources and uses.

Sources and Uses of Loan Funds

Sources	Uses
Gifts, bequests, and government advances	Loans written off
Interest on loan notes	Deductions to provide allowances for
Income from endowment funds	uncollectible loans
Interfund transfers	Interfund transfers
Income, gains, and losses on investments	Refunds to grantors
of Loan Funds	Administrative and collection costs

Notes receivable are carried at face value, less an allowance for doubtful notes. Provisions for doubtful notes are charged directly to the Loan Fund's Equity account. All other transactions that affect this fund's Equity account are also credited or charged directly to that account.

ENDOWMENT FUNDS AND SIMILAR FUNDS

This funds group includes *permanent* endowment funds, *term* endowment funds, and Quasi-Endowment Funds (established by board action). The income **generated from the** endowment usually may be expended by the Current Unrestricted Fund. **Term Endowment Fund principal becomes expendable at some specified time or after a designated event.** These funds are then available for operating needs. Quasi-Endowment Funds are *internally designated* by the board rather than *externally restricted*. The board may expend the principal at any time.

Legal restrictions in the endowment instrument determine the accounting for each fund's principal, income, and investments. Each endowment is accounted for as a separate fund, but the resources are generally pooled for investment purposes unless restrictive covenants limit investments to certain types of securities.

ANNUITY FUNDS AND LIFE INCOME FUNDS

Annuity Funds and Life Income Funds consist of assets contributed to them with the stipulation that the C&U, in turn, promise to pay a certain sum periodically to a designated individual, usually for the remainder of his or her life. Upon that person's death, the unexpended assets of the Annuity Fund are transferred to the Current Unrestricted Fund, the Current Restricted Fund, or the Endowment Fund, as specified by the donor.

ILLUSTRATION 27-7

Rocky State University
Statement of Changes in Fund Balances—All Funds
For the Year Ended June 30, 19X1

	Current Funds		Loan Funds	Endowment and Similar Funds	Annuity and Life Income Funds	Plant Funds			
	Unrestricted	Restricted				Unexpended	Renewal and Replacement	Retirement of Indebtedness	Investment in Plant
Revenues and Other Additions									
Educational and general revenues	$5,300,000								
Auxiliary enterprises revenues	2,200,000								
Expired term endowment revenues	40,000								
Expired term endowment—Restricted						$ 50,000			
Gifts and bequests—Restricted		$ 370,000	$100,000	$1,500,000	$800,000	115,000		$65,000	$ 15,000
Grants and contracts—Restricted		500,000							
Governmental appropriations—Restricted						50,000			
Investment income—restricted		224,000	12,000	10,000		5,000	$ 5,000	5,000	
Realized gains on investments—Unrestricted				109,000					
Realized gains on investments—Restricted			4,000	50,000		10,000	5,000	5,000	
Interest on loans receivable			7,000						
U.S. government advances			18,000						
Expended for plant facilities (including $100,000 charged to current funds expenditures)									1,550,000
Retirement of indebtedness									220,000
Accrued interest on sale of bonds								3,000	
Matured annuity and life income funds restricted to endowment				10,000					
Total Revenues and Other Additions	$7,540,000	$1,094,000	$141,000	$1,679,000	$800,000	$230,000	$10,000	$78,000	$1,785,000

ILLUSTRATION 27-7 (continued)

Expenditures and Other Deductions

	(1)	(2)	(3)	(4)	(5)	(6)	(7)	(8)	(9)
Educational and general expenditures	$4,400,000	$1,014,000							
Auxiliary enterprises expenditures	1,830,000								
Indirect costs recovered		35,000							
Refunded to grantors		20,000							
Loan cancellations and write-offs			$10,000						
Administrative and collection costs			1,000					$1,000	
Adjustment of actuarial liability for annuities payable					$75,000				
Expended for plant facilities (including noncapitalized expenditures of $50,000)						$1,200,000	$300,000		
Retirement of indebtedness								220,000	
Interest on indebtedness								190,000	
Disposal of plant facilities									$115,000
Expired term endowments ($40,000 unrestricted, $50,000 restricted to plant)				$90,000					
Matured annuity and life income funds restricted to endowment					10,000				
Total Expenditures and Other Deductions	**$6,230,000**	**$1,069,000**	**$12,000**	**$90,000**	**$85,000**	**$1,200,000**	**$300,000**	**$411,000**	**$115,000**

Transfers Among Funds—Additions/(Deductions)

	(1)	(2)	(3)	(4)	(7)	(8)
Mandatory:						
Principal and interest	$ (340,000)					$340,000
Renewals and replacements	(170,000)				$170,000	
Loan fund matching grant	(2,000)		$ 2,000			
Unrestricted gifts allocated	(650,000)	$ 550,000	50,000			
Portion of unrestricted quasi-endowment funds investment gains appropriated	40,000	(40,000)		$ 50,000		
Total Transfers	**$(1,122,000)**	**$ 510,000**	**$ 52,000**	**$ 50,000**	**$170,000**	**$340,000**

	(1)	(2)	(3)	(4)	(5)	(6)	(7)	Total
Net increase/(decrease) for the year	$ 188,000	$181,000	$ 2,099,000	$ 715,000	$ (920,000)	$(120,000)	$ 7,000	$ 1,670,000
Fund Balance at Beginning of Year	455,000	502,000	11,901,000	2,505,000	2,120,000	380,000	293,000	36,540,000
Fund Balance at End of Year	$ 643,000	$683,000	$14,000,000	$3,220,000	$1,200,000	$ 260,000	$ 300,000	$38,210,000

Source: Adapted from *Audits of Colleges and Universities*, 2nd ed. (New York: American Institute of Certified Public Accountants, 1975), pp. 112–113.

At the date of the contribution (1) the assets are accounted for at their fair market value, (2) the Annuities Payable account is credited for the current value of the liability (based on life expectancy tables), and (3) the balance is credited to the annuity's Fund Balance account.

Investment income and gains or losses are credited or charged to the Liability account. Annuity payments are also charged to Liability. The liability and the fund balance are periodically adjusted to record the actuarial gain or loss due to recomputation of the liability based on the donor's revised life expectancy.

The essential difference between *Annuity Funds* and *Life Income Funds* is that the principal of the latter remains intact, and all income is distributed to the beneficiary. *Annuity Fund* distributions are fixed, whereas distributions of *Life Income Funds* reflect all fund earnings.

THE PLANT FUNDS GROUP

C&Us include investment in plant within a **Plant Funds Group,** which accounts for both *unexpended* and *expended* resources. This group consists of the following subfunds:

1. **The Unexpended Plant Funds.** These funds are used to accumulate assets to acquire physical properties—only *unexpended* amounts are reported.

2. **The Renewals and Replacement Funds.** These funds are used to accumulate assets to renew and replace institutional properties.

3. **The Retirement of Indebtedness Fund.** These funds are used to accumulate assets to service debt (interest and principal payments) on institutional properties.

4. **Investment in Plant.** Technically, this is not a fund but the equivalent of the General Fixed Assets Account Group of a governmental unit, which we discussed in Chapter 25.

Illustration 27–8 discloses in more detail the nature of the funds flows for the accounts in the Plant Funds Group.

The illustrated balance sheet shown in Illustration 27–5 (pages 994–995) shows how a college's Plant Funds Group is presented. The following points are important to understand the Plant Funds Group section of Illustration 27–5:

1. The first two funds are, in effect, *unexpended* plant funds. Frequently, they are summarized or combined and disclosed as Unexpended Funds for financial reporting purposes.

2. Unexpended plant funds include both *externally restricted* and *internally designated* funds.

3. The Investment in Plant is, in effect, the *Expended* Plant Fund. The resources are carried at cost. This fund's residual equity is referred to as *Net Investment in Plant,* not *Fund Balance.*

Illustrated transaction entries for the various funds are presented and explained in the appendices to this chapter.

AGENCY FUNDS

Often a C&U is simply a fiscal agent for assets that are *not* actually its property. An **Agency Fund** accounts for these assets. For example, a college may act as fiscal agent for the assets of student government and of faculty and staff organizations. The net assets of such a fund appear as a liabilitiy because the college has no equity in the fund.

ILLUSTRATION 27–8	**Plant Funds Group for Colleges and Universities: Subgroup Funds Flows**

Unexpended Plant Funds

Inflows	Outflows
Bond sales proceeds	Disbursements
Private donations	Investment losses
Restricted government appropriations	Return of unrestricted amounts to
Income and gains from the investment of	unrestricted current funds
unexpended funds	Transfers: Investment in plant
Transfers from other fund groups	

Renewals and Replacement Funds

Inflows	Outflows
Mandatory and voluntary transfers from	Investment losses
current funds	Return of unrestricted amounts to
Income and gains from the investment of	unrestricted current funds
funds	Expenditures not capitalized
	Capitalized expenditures for renewals and
	replacements

Retirement of Indebtedness Funds

Inflows	Outflows
Transfers from current funds for principal	Payments on principal and interest
and interest payments	Trustees' fees and expenses
Income and gains from the investment of	Investment losses
funds	
Gifts, grants, and government	
appropriations restricted to debt	
retirement	
Transfers from other fund groups as	
directed by donors (such as expired	
term endowments, annuity and life	
income funds)	

Investment in Plant

Inflows	Outflows
Current fund equipment replacements	Investment losses
Gifts of plant assets	Abandonments
Transfers from unexpended plant and	Sales of plant assets
renewals and replacement funds	
Debt retirement	

ACCOUNTING FOR PLEDGES

Gifts and bequests are generally not a major source of resources for *public* C&Us. Pledges[4] of gifts may be (1) disclosed in the notes to the financial statements or (2) reported within the financial statements. When reported in the financial statements, the pledge receivables are (1) initially (and subsequently) valued at their net realizable value and (2) presented net of an appropriate allowance for uncollectible pledges.

Depending on whether conditions are attached to the pledge, the credit side of the entry is to (1) the Pledge Revenues account of the Current Unrestricted Fund, (2) the Fund Balance account of the Current Restricted Fund, or (3) the Unrestricted

---

[4]The AICPA's 1975 C&U audit guide uses the more restrictive term *pledges* rather than *promises*, which *SFAS No. 117* uses.

Fund Balance account or the Restricted Fund Balance account of either the (a) Unexpended Plant Funds or (b) the Renewals and Replacement Funds.

ACCOUNTING FOR A PLEDGE COLLECTED OVER SEVERAL YEARS Pledge revenues should be recognized in the year in which the pledge or installment of the pledge is received. The donor's intention determines its future accounting. For example, assume that (1) several donors agreed in 19X1 to give a total of $35,000 a year for four years for normal operating expenses and (2) $5,000 of the annual amount is *not* expected to be collected. The appropriate entry to record these pledges is as follows:

Pledges Receivable	140,000	
Allowance for Uncollectible Pledges		20,000
Pledge Revenues		30,000
Deferred Pledge Revenues		90,000

ACCOUNTING FOR INVESTMENTS

Public C&Us generally account for investments (exclusive of those in physical plant) at either cost or market value if they are received as gifts. The AICPA's 1975 C&U guide, however, allows the alternative of using market value if all funds use this valuation basis. *Unrealized* gains and losses measured using this alternative basis are reported in the same manner as *realized* gains and losses. *SFAS No. 124,* "Accounting for Certain Investments Held by Not-for-Profit Organizations," superseded this specialized practice concerning *private* C&Us; thus the specialized practice continues to apply to *public* C&Us. As mentioned earlier, however, in early 1996 the GASB issued the exposure draft of a proposed standard that will require the use of fair values for substantially all investments; this standard probably will be finalized by the end of 1996.

IX DIVERGENT *EXTERNAL* FINANCIAL REPORTING FOR *PRIVATE* AND *PUBLIC* C&US: PERMANENT OR TEMPORARY?

As stated earlier, the GASB currently has underway a project that involves reexamining the financial reporting model for C&Us. In 1995, the GASB issued a preliminary views document that proposes the use of a "dual-perspective" reporting approach that would require presentation of financial statements on both (1) an aggregated basis (an "entitywide" perspective) and (2) a disaggregated basis (a "fund group" perspective). The aggregated basis is virtually identical to the FASB guidance. The fund group basis—which is *not* called for in the FASB guidance—is virtually identical to the AICPA College Guide model currently allowed.

If this proposed approach becomes a GASB standard, the divergence between FASB guidance and GASB guidance would continue; however, it would *not* be as major because the fund group basis financial statements would be viewed merely as supplementary financial statements from the FASB guidance perspective.

END-OF-CHAPTER REVIEW

SUMMARY OF KEY POINTS

PUBLIC HCOs

1. Financial statements for *public* HCOs are prepared using the GASB guidance that encompasses both (a) the AICPA's 1996 HCO accounting and audit guide and (b) GASB pronouncements.

2. *SFAS No. 117* allows the AICPA's 1996 HCO guide to provide more specific accounting guidance than that set forth in *SFAS No. 117*. Thus *allowable* differences exist between the two documents.

3. Under the AICPA's 1996 HCO guide, all HCOs (public and private) (a) use the **flow of economic resources** measurements focus, (b) use the **accrual basis** of accounting, and (c) **recognize depreciation** in the operating statement.

4. All HCOs (public and private) must disclose information concerning their fund balance (or net assets) as to the unrestricted and restricted portions thereof.

5. A major difference between the *SFAS No. 117* and the AICPA's 1996 HCO guide is that inflows and outflows pertaining to *temporarily restricted* net assets and *permanently restricted* net assets are *not* reported in the operating statement under the AICPA's 1996 HCO guide.

6. The four required financial statements for HCOs are a balance sheet, a statement of operations, a statement of changes in fund balances, and a statement of cash flows (with two categories of cash flows from financing activities [capital and related financing activities and noncapital financing activities]).

PUBLIC C&US

1. The GASB guidance allows *public* C&Us to use either (a) the **AICPA College Guide model** or (b) the **Governmental model.**

2. The most substantive difference between the two models is that the definition of expenditures is much more broadly defined in the *Governmental* model because **it encompasses borrowings, repayments of debt, and acquisitions of fixed assets.**

3. Under the AICPA College Guide model (the predominant model used in practice), (a) *fund accounting* **is used for** *external* **financial reporting purposes** (a *disaggregated* manner of reporting), (b) the **accrual basis of accounting is used,** and (c) **depreciation is** *not* **recognized.**

4. The operating statement under the AICPA College Guide model (a) is called a *statement of revenues, expenditures, and other changes* and (b) **includes only the two current funds** (the Current Unrestricted Fund and the Current Restricted Fund). (This statement could more properly be called a *statement of revenues and* nondepreciation *expenses.*)

5. A **statement of changes in fund balances is prepared for** *all* **of the funds**—this is the only statement that shows activities of the funds other than the two current funds.

6. A unique aspect of the Current Restricted Fund is that (a) inflows are initially credited to the Fund Balance account and (b) as amounts are expended for the intended purpose, the Fund Balance account is debited and the Revenues account is credited. Thus **revenues** *always* **equal expenditures.**

7. **Pledges** may be (a) recorded as pledge receivables (net of an allowance for uncollectibles) or (b) merely disclosed in the notes.

GLOSSARY OF NEW TERMS

Agency Fund   The fund of a *public* C&U that accounts for assets owned by others.

Annuity Funds and Life Income Funds   Consist of assets of a *public* C&U contributed with the stipulation that the C&U in turn promise to pay a certain sum periodically to a designated individual, usually for the remainder of his or her life.

Current Funds Group   Resources of a *public* C&U that are expendable for operating purposes and that include the assets, liabilities, and activity accounts necessary to record daily operations.

Current Restricted Funds   Funds of a *public* C&U that are available for operating purposes but are restricted by donors or other outside agencies as to the specific purpose for which they may be expended.

Loan Funds   Funds established by *public* C&Us to provide loans to students, faculty, and staff. Loan Funds are generally revolving; that is, cash received from repayments of principal and interest is loaned to other individuals.

Mandatory transfers   A category presented in the operating statement of *public* C&Us under the AICPA College Guide model that is used to report transfers contractually obligated to be made.

Plant Funds Group A group of funds that accounts for both unexpended and expended resources of *public* C&Us.

Proprietary-type activity A governmental organization or activity that is similar to those often found in the private sector.

Quasi-Endowment Fund Funds of a *public* C&U that serve as endowments as a result of board action until some other more suitable purpose is determined.

SELF-STUDY QUESTIONS

(Answers are at the end of this chapter, preceding Appendix A.)

1. A *public* HCO

	Uses the Accrual Basis of Accounting	Recognizes Unrestricted Nonfixed Asset Contributions as Revenues Upon Receipt	May Classify Its Net Assets As to Unrestricted, Temporarily Restricted, and Permanently Restricted
a.	Yes	Yes	Yes
b.	Yes	Yes	No
c.	Yes	No	Yes
d.	No	Yes	Yes
e.	No	No	Yes
f.	No	Yes	No
g.	Yes	No	No
h.	No	No	No

2. A *public* HCO reports the following items in its operating statement:

Repayment of Principal on Debt	Capital Asset Acquisitions	Depreciation Expense

Use the a–h choices provided in Question 1.

3. A *public* HCO reports the following items in its operating statement:

Fair Value of Charitable Care Provided	Contractual Adjustments	Adjustments for Uncollectible Accounts

Use the same a–h choices provided in Question 1.

4. A *public* HCO's statement of cash flows includes which of the following classifications?

Cash Flows Relating to		
Capital and Investing Activities	Noncapital Financing Activities	Capital and Related Financing Activities

Use the same a–h choices provided in Question 1.

5. For *nonprofit* HCOs, which statement is presented?

	Statement of Operations		Statement of Income	
	Public HCO	*Private* HCO	*Public* HCO	*Private* HCO
a.	Yes	Yes	No	No
b.	No	No	Yes	Yes
c.	Yes	No	Yes	No

(continued)

d.	No	Yes	Yes	No
e.	No	Yes	No	Yes
f.	No	No	No	Yes
g.	Yes	Yes	Yes	No
h.	Yes	No	No	No

6. For *public* C&Us, which of the following models requires recognition of depreciation expense in the operating statement?

	AICPA College Guide Model	Governmental Model
a.	Yes	Yes
b.	Yes	No
c.	No	No
d.	No	Yes

7. For *public* C&Us, which of the following models reports the acquisition of fixed assets as an expenditure in the operating statement?

	AICPA College Guide Model	Governmental Model
a.	Yes	Yes
b.	Yes	No
c.	No	No
d.	No	Yes

8. For *public* C&Us, which of the following contributions are recognized as revenues in the Current Funds Group upon receipt?

	Unrestricted Cash Contributions	Restricted Cash Contributions	Unrestricted Fixed Asset Contributions
a.	Yes	No	Yes
b.	Yes	Yes	No
c.	Yes	No	No
d.	No	No	Yes
e.	No	No	No
f.	Yes	Yes	Yes
g.	No	Yes	Yes

9. At 6/30/X8, the end of its fiscal year-end, a *public* C&U reported in its balance sheet both the following amounts and their intended uses:

Renewal and replacement of college properties	$200,000
Retirement of indebtedness on college properties	300,000
Purchase of physical properties for college purposes but unexpended at year-end	400,000

What total amount should be included in the Plant Funds group?

a. $200,000   **c.** $400,000   **e.** $600,000   **g.** $900,000
b. $300,000   **d.** $500,000   **f.** $700,000

10. For *public* HCOs and *public* C&Us, are *expenses* rather than *expenditures* reported in the operating statement?

	Public HCOs	*Public* C&Us
a.	Yes	Yes
b.	Yes	No
c.	No	No
d.	No	Yes

11. For *public* HCOs and C&Us, which of the following NPOs presents a statement of cash flows?

	Public HCOs	Public C&Us
a.	Yes	Yes
b.	Yes	No
c.	No	No
d.	No	Yes

ASSIGNMENT MATERIAL

REVIEW QUESTIONS

PUBLIC HCOS

1. What special status does *SFAS No. 117* give to the AICPA's 1996 HCO audit and accounting guides? What are the financial reporting ramifications of this special status?
2. Into what three categories can health-care providers be classified?
3. What are the two possible manners of financial reporting for use by *public* HCOs?
4. How are the financial statements of a *public* HCO presented when it is *not* a *component unit* of the primary governmental unit?
5. How are the financial statements of a *public* HCO presented when it is a *component unit* of the primary governmental unit?
6. What are the *measurement focus* and *basis of accounting* for public HCO's?
7. What does the term *proprietary-type activities* mean?
8. What is the focus of accounting for *proprietary-type activities*?
9. Are *proprietary-type activities* required to follow the pronouncements of the FASB that apply to *for-profit* entities? Explain.
10. Are *proprietary-type activities* required to follow FASB pronouncements that apply to *not-for-profit* organizations?
11. What financial statements are required for *public* HCOs?
12. How are amounts pertaining to *uncollectible accounts* reported in the operating statement of a *public* HCO?
13. How are amounts pertaining to *contractual adjustments* reported in the operating statement of a *public* HCO?
14. How are amounts pertaining to *charity care* reported in the operating statement of a *public* HCO?
15. What items must be reported as a line item separate from operations in the operating statement of a *public* HCO?
16. What is the major format difference between a statement of cash flows for a *public* HCO and a *private* HCO?

PUBLIC C&US

17. Under the AICPA College Guide model, what are the *measurement focus* and *basis of accounting*?
18. Under the Governmental model, what are the *measurement focus* and *basis of accounting*?
19. What are the major differences between the AICPA College Guide model and the Governmental model for *public* C&Us?
20. What financial statements are required for *public* C&Us under the AICPA College Guide model?
21. Which specific funds are reported in the statement of revenues, expenditures, and other changes for *public* C&Us under the AICPA College Guide model?
22. How do the accounting and reporting of fixed assets by *public* HCOs differ from those of *public* C&Us that use the AICPA College Guide model?
23. When are revenues recognized for the Current Restricted Funds for *public* C&Us?
24. What are the major differences between the operating statements of a *public* HCO and a *public* C&U that uses the AICPA College Guide model?

EXERCISES

E 27–1 *Public* HCO: **Manner of Reporting Transactions**   Needles County Hospital, a *public* HCO, had the following transactions:

1. The board of directors designated $1,000,000 to purchase investments whose income will be used for capital improvements.
2. Income from investments in item 1, which was *not* previously accrued, is received.
3. A benefactor provided funds for building expansion.
4. The funds in item 3 were used to purchase a building in the fiscal period following the period in which the funds were received.
5. An accounting firm prepared the HCO's financial statements free of charge.
6. Investments received were subject to the donor's requirement that the investment income be used to pay for outpatient services.

Required   1. Indicate the manner in which the transactions affect the hospital's financial statements—use the following choices:
    a. Increase in *unrestricted* revenues.
    b. Decrease in expenses.
    c. Increase in *temporarily restricted* fund balance.
    d. Increase in *permanently restricted* fund balance.
    e. No required reportable event.
  2. Would your answers change if the HCO were a *private* HCO?   (AICPA adapted)

E 27–2 *Public* HCO: **Classification of Items in the Operating Statement**   Carbo County's general hospital billed patients $9,500,000 in 19X1. Information concerning this amount follows:

Amount deemed charity care at the time of treatment for which no payment was expected (bills were sent only to inform patients of the value of the services rendered)	$2,400,000
Discounts granted to third-party payors pursuant to contracts	700,000
Noncharity basis accounts written off because the patients were unable to pay	300,000
Cash collections	4,600,000
Allowance for uncollectibles deemed needed at 12/31/X1 for *noncharity* basis accounts	100,000
Billing waived on Patient 133 who had the wrong leg amputated (this patient was also given a $500,000 cash settlement on the related malpractice claim, which the hospital did not litigate because it did not have a leg to stand on)	5,000

Required   What amounts should be reported in the specific revenue and expense accounts of the operating statement for 19X1 for these items?

E 27–3 *Public* HCO: **Reporting Donated Supplies**   In May 19X1, Lemon County's general hospital purchased medicines from Delta Drug Inc. for $3,000. Before payment was made, however, Delta notified the HCO that the invoice was being canceled and the medicines (which had cost Delta $1,000) were being donated.

Required   How should the HCO record this donation of medicine?

1. Credit Other Revenues for $3,000.
2. Credit Other Revenues for $1,000.
3. Credit Operating Expenses for $3,000.
4. Credit Operating Expenses for $1,000.
5. Credit Nonoperating Gains for $3,000.
6. Credit Nonoperating Gains for $1,000.
7. Credit Unrestricted Fund Balance.
8. Make a memorandum entry.

E 27–4 *Public* **HCO: Reporting Donated Gifts and Bequests** In 19X1, York City's general hospital had the following transactions:

1. Unrestricted cash gifts of $100,000.
2. Unrestricted cash bequests of $200,000.
3. A kidney dialysis machine that cost the manufacturer $600,000 and sells for $900,000.
4. A $400,000 cash gift that can be used only to operate the kidney dialysis unit.
5. A $500,000 cash gift that *cannot* be spent but for which the investment income can be used only to operate the kidney dialysis unit.
6. The HCO incurred $166,000 of costs to operate the kidney dialysis unit.
7. The HCO earned $7,000 of interest on the investment in item 5.

Required How should these amounts be reported in the 19X1 financial statements?

E 27–5 *Public* **C&U: Reporting Tuition and Fees** For fiscal 19X1–19X2, Solo State University billed its students $7,700,000 for tuition and fees. The net amount contractually to be paid was only $7,000,000, however, because of the following items:

Refunds resulting from class cancellations and withdrawals	$400,000
Scholarships awarded	200,000
Tuition remissions granted to faculty members' families	100,000
Total	$700,000

Required 1. What amount should Solo report for revenues from tuition and fees for the year?
2. What amount(s) should Solo report in its expenditures category relating to these items?

E 27–6 *Public* **C&U: Reporting Endowment Income** Information concerning interest earned by Saddle State University's Endowment Fund investments for 19X1 follows:

Type of Endowment	Interest Earned	Amount Expended for Current Operations
Quasi-endowment (board designated)	$900,000	$500,000
Term endowment	300,000	70,000
Permanent endowment	100,000	–0–

Also, a five-year term endowment of $250,000 expired during 19X1.

Required What amounts should be reported in the operating statement for 19X1 under the AICPA College Guide model?

E 27–7 *Public* **C&U: Reporting Contributions** Shady State University received the following cash contributions during 19X1:

Principal specified by the donor as	
Nonexpendable	$8,000,000
Expendable after the year 2005	3,000,000
Expendable for any purpose (received on 12/30/X1)	2,000,000
Expendable only for the renovation of the business classroom building (work is scheduled to begin in 19X2)	1,000,000
Expendable only on accounting scholarships ($60,000 was awarded in 19X1)	700,000

Required 1. What amount should be reported as contributions in the 19X1 statement of operations?
2. What amount is reported in the Fund Balance section of the various affected funds at 12/31/X1?

PROBLEMS

P 27–1 **Public HCO: Preparing a Statement of Operations** Candu County's hospital had the following items for its fiscal year ended 6/30/X1:

Patient revenues, gross	$26,600,000
Contractual adjustments granted on amounts billed to patients	1,200,000
Charity care provided, valued using standard rates for services provided . .	7,600,000
Provision for uncollectible accounts	400,000
Property tax revenues (all deemed collectible)	5,800,000
Gift shop and cafeteria sales	1,400,000
Interest income earned on investments for which the use of the income is	
Unrestricted	200,000
Temporarily restricted (100% spent in 19X1 in accordance with donor stipulations)	220,000
Permanently restricted	380,000
Fund balance released from restrictions (includes the preceding $220,000 interest income item and $700,000 from grants)	920,000
Expenses, excluding depreciation	35,100,000
Depreciation expense	1,500,000
Term endowment received in 19X1	2,000,000
Annual subsidy received from the Candu County General Fund	4,000,000
Interest expense on hospital bonds	900,000
Change (favorable) in net unrealized gains (losses) on available-for-sale securities (*none* of these securities involve specific assets that must be held in perpetuity)	240,000

Required   Prepare the operating statement for 19X1.

P 27–2   *Public* **C&U: Analyzing Current Funds Transactions and Preparing a Statement of Changes in Fund Balances**
A partial balance sheet for Sonora State University at the end of its fiscal year (7/31/X4) follows:

Sonora State University
Balance Sheet—Current Funds
July 31, 19X4

Assets

Current Unrestricted Fund:	
Cash	$200,000
Accounts receivable—student tuition and fees, less $15,000 allowance for uncollectibles	360,000
Prepaid expenses	40,000
Total Unrestricted Assets	$600,000
Current Restricted Fund:	
Cash	$ 10,000
Investments	210,000
Total Restricted Assets	$220,000
Total Current Funds Assets	$820,000

Liabilities and Fund Balances

Current Unrestricted Fund:	
Accounts payable	$100,000
Due to other funds	40,000
Deferred revenue—tuition and fees	25,000
Fund balance	435,000
Total Unrestricted Liabilities and Fund Balance	$600,000
Current Restricted Fund:	
Accounts payable	$ 5,000
Fund balance	215,000
Total Restricted Liabilities and Fund Balance	$220,000
Total Current Funds Liabilities and Fund Balances	$820,000

The following financial events and transactions occurred during the fiscal year ended 7/31/X5.

1. Cash collected from student tuition totaled $3,000,000. Of this amount, $362,000 was outstanding at 7/31/X4; $2,500,000 was for current year tuition, and $138,000 was for tuition applicable to the semester beginning in August 19X5.
2. Deferred revenue at 7/31/X4 was earned during the year ended 7/31/X5.
3. Accounts receivable at 7/31/X4 that were *not* collected during the year ended 7/31/X5 were declared uncollectible and were written off against the allowance account. At 7/31/X5, the Allowance for Doubtful Accounts was an estimated $10,000.
4. During the year, a $60,000 unrestricted grant was awarded by the state. This state grant was payable to Sonora State sometime in August 19X5.
5. During the year, unrestricted cash gifts of $80,000 were received from alumni. Sonora State's board of trustees allocated $30,000 of these gifts to the student loan fund.
6. During the year, investments costing $25,000 were sold for $31,000. Restricted fund investments were purchased for $40,000. Investment income of $18,000 was earned and collected during the year.
7. Unrestricted general expenses of $2,500,000 were recorded in the voucher register. At 7/31/X5, the unrestricted Accounts Payable balance was $75,000.
8. The restricted Accounts Payable balance at 7/31/X4 was paid.
9. The $40,000 due to other funds at 7/31/X4 was paid to the Plant Fund as required.
10. One-quarter of the prepaid expenses at 7/31/X4, which pertain to general education expenses, expired during the current year. No additions to prepaid expenses were made during the year.

Required
1. Prepare general journal entries for these transactions for the year ended 7/31/X5. Number each entry to correspond to the transaction number. Organize your answer as follows:

| | | Current Funds | | | |
| | | Unrestricted | | Restricted | |
Entry Number	Account	Dr.	Cr.	Dr.	Cr.

2. Prepare a statement of changes in fund balances for the year ended 7/31/X5.

P 27–3 *Public* **C&U: Preparing Entries Under the AICPA Audit Guide Model and the Governmental Model**   The following are selected transactions of Salinas State University:

Fiscal Year Ended 6/30/X4

1. Student tuition and fees billed for the year were $10,000,000, which was used for educational and general purposes. Prior experience shows that $100,000 of this billing will be uncollectible. At year-end, $700,000 remains uncollected.
2. Unrestricted gifts and private grants received during the period amounted to $500,000.
3. The trustees have specified that certain Current Fund revenues must be transferred to meet the debt service provisions relating to the university's institutional properties, including amounts set aside for debt retirement and interest. For this year, the mandatory transfers totaled $300,000.
4. A $1,000,000 federal government grant was received to construct a new science building.
5. Bonds were sold at par to finance the new science building. The proceeds were $5,000,000.
6. The contract was signed for the science building construction. The contract price was $6,000,000.
7. The science building was completed at a cost of $5,800,000, and the contractor was paid.

Fiscal Year Ended 6/30/X5

8. The new science building was estimated to have a useful life of 40 years with no salvage value. Trustees' action designated $150,000 for eventual replacement of the building.
9. Restricted gifts of $400,000 were received from the Marla Foundation.
10. Expenses of $50,000 were incurred in connection with fund-raising activities for the new science building equipment.

Required
1. Prepare the necessary entries under the *Governmental* model.
2. Prepare the necessary entries under the *AICPA College Guide* model.

For each entry in requirements 1 and 2, specify the affected funds.

P27–4 *Public* **C&U: COMPREHENSIVE Comparing GASB Guidance With FASB Guidance—Recording Transactions Involving More Than One Fund Under the AICPA College Guide Model and Determining How to Report Them Under** *SFAS No. 117* The following transactions of a *public* college that uses the AICPA college guide model involve more than one fund:

1. A *term* endowment fund was terminated. The investment, consisting of bondholdings, was sold at a loss of $17,000 below the preceding year-end carrying value. The $133,000 cash proceeds from the sale were properly transferred to the Current Unrestricted Fund.
2. Cash of $200,000 was transferred from the Current Unrestricted Fund to the Plant Funds Group to pay interest ($120,000) and principal ($80,000) on its bonds.
3. Excess land was sold at a $30,000 gain. The $350,000 proceeds were deposited in the Cash bank account of the Current Unrestricted Fund.
4. The Unexpended Plant Fund reimbursed the Current Unrestricted Fund for $400,000 that it had paid an architect to design a new student union (the Unexpended Plant Fund had not yet received the proceeds of the related bond offering).
5. The Current Unrestricted Fund voluntarily transferred $500,000 cash to its Renewals and Replacement Fund to use on various renewal projects.
6. The Unexpended Plant Fund expended $6,000,000 on a new residence hall.

Required
1. Prepare the journal entries to record these transactions using the AICPA College Guide model.
2. Describe how these transactions should be reported in a statement of activities required by *SFAS No. 117* (an aggregated basis of reporting rather than the disaggregated manner of reporting under the AICPA College Guide model).

ANSWERS TO SELF-STUDY QUESTIONS

1. a **2.** e **3.** d **4.** d **5.** a **6.** c **7.** d **8.** c **9.** g **10.** b **11.** b

■ APPENDIX A

PUBLIC C&US: ILLUSTRATED TRANSACTIONS FOR THE CURRENT FUNDS GROUP

The following sections illustrate the accounting for Current Funds Group transactions.

ILLUSTRATION   **CURRENT UNRESTRICTED FUNDS SUBGROUP TRANSACTIONS**

The following journal entries pertain to financial events and transactions of Andover University's Current Unrestricted Funds for the year ended June 30, 19X2.

1. Student tuition and fees billed for the year were $8,000,000, which was used for educational and general purposes. Prior experience shows that $100,000 of this billing will be uncollectible. At year-end, $800,000 remains uncollected.

Cash	7,200,000	
Accounts Receivable	800,000	
Expenditures—Education and General	100,000	
Revenue—Student Tuition and Fees		8,000,000
Allowance for Bad Debts		100,000

2. Unrestricted government appropriations for the year amounted to $5,000,000, all of which have been collected.

Cash	5,000,000	
Revenue—Government Appropriations		5,000,000

3. Unrestricted gifts and private grants received during the period amounted to $50,000.

Cash	50,000	
Revenue—Gifts and Private Grants		50,000

4. Unrestricted income from endowment and similar funds amounted to $185,000.

Cash	185,000	
Revenue—Endowment Income		185,000

5. Auxiliary enterprise included $175,000 from student residence halls, $200,000 from cafeterias, and $750,000 from the college store sales. All billed amounts have been collected except for $50,000 in student residence fees. Of this amount, an estimated $5,000 will be uncollectible.

Cash	1,075,000	
Accounts Receivable	50,000	
Expenditures—Auxiliary Enterprises	5,000	
Revenue—Auxiliary Enterprises		1,125,000
Allowance for Bad Debts		5,000

6. Term endowment funds that are now available for unrestricted use amount to $300,000.

Cash	300,000	
Revenue—Endowment Income		300,000

7. Purchases of materials and supplies amounted to $800,000 for the year. A perpetual inventory is used. Purchases of $150,000 remain unpaid at year-end.

Materials and Supplies Inventory	800,000	
Cash		650,000
Vouchers Payable		150,000

8. Operating expenditures are incurred and assigned as shown in the following journal entry. Note that $2,250,000 of these expenditures is for unpaid vouchers payable at year-end.

Expenditures—Instruction	3,500,000	
Expenditures—Research	1,200,000	
Expenditures—Academic Support	3,000,000	
Expenditures—Student Services	380,000	
Expenditures—Operation and Maintenance of Plant	1,120,000	
Expenditures—Institutional Support	500,000	
Cash		7,450,000
Vouchers Payable		2,250,000

9. Use of materials and supplies is assigned as shown in the following journal entry:

Expenditures—Instruction	300,000	
Expenditures—Research	150,000	
Expenditures—Academic Support	50,000	
Expenditures—Student Services	25,000	
Expenditures—Institutional Support	120,000	
Materials and Supplies Inventory		645,000

10. The university's student aid committee granted student tuition and fee reductions of $200,000.

| Expenditures—Student Aid | 200,000 | |
| Accounts Receivable | | 200,000 |

11. The trustees have specified that certain Current Fund revenues must be transferred to meet the debt service provisions relating to the university's institutional properties, including amounts set aside for debt retirement, interest, and required provisions for renewal and replacement. For this year, these mandatory transfers total $550,000.

| Mandatory Transfers—Plant Funds | 550,000 | |
| Cash | | 550,000 |

12. Auxiliary enterprises' expenditures amount to $650,000.

| Expenditures—Auxiliary Enterprises | 650,000 | |
| Vouchers Payable (Cash). | | 650,000 |

13. Closing entries are not illustrated. Revenues, expenditures, and transfers are merely closed to the Fund Balance account.

ILLUSTRATION   **CURRENT RESTRICTED FUNDS SUBGROUP TRANSACTIONS**

The following journal entries pertain to financial events and transactions of Andover University's Current Restricted Funds for the year ended June 30, 19X2.

1. Restricted gifts of $100,000 were received from the Wollaston Foundation for student aid.

Cash	100,000	
Fund Balance[a]		100,000

[a]Subsidiary accounts usually show the sources, purposes, and applications of restricted resources.

2. A $750,000 federal government grant was received for library acquisitions in science and engineering.

Cash	750,000	
Fund Balance		750,000

3. Federal government contracts were awarded to certain academic departments to develop training programs and instructional institutes for child care and development. These contracts totaled $1,500,000 and included a provision to reimburse the university for indirect costs of $75,000. The contract payments were collected.

Cash	1,500,000	
Fund Balance		1,500,000

Fund Balance	75,000	
Cash		75,000

The latter entry transfers the indirect cost recovery to the Current Unrestricted Fund, which acknowledges receipt of the payment with the following entry:

Cash	75,000	
Revenue—General		75,000

4. Expenditures incurred were for student aid, $85,000; instruction (library acquisitions), $700,000; training programs and instructional institutes, $1,425,000. At year-end, 10% of the expenditures remain unpaid.

Expenditures—Student Aid	85,000	
Expenditures—Instruction	700,000	
Expenditures—Instruction	1,425,000	
Cash		1,989,000
Vouchers Payable		221,000

Fund Balance	2,210,000	
Revenue—Gifts		85,000
Revenue—Governmental Grants and Contracts		2,125,000

5. Closing entries are not illustrated. (Because total revenues equal total expenditures, these accounts offset each other in the closing entry.)

■ APPENDIX B

PUBLIC C&US: ILLUSTRATED TRANSACTIONS FOR PLANT FUNDS GROUP

ILLUSTRATION   **PLANT FUNDS GROUP TRANSACTIONS**

The following journal entries pertain to transactions of Andover University's Plant Funds Group for the year ended June 30, 19X2.

I. The Unexpended Plant Fund:

1. A major fund-raising drive for new laboratory equipment generated $300,000 cash and $250,000 in marketable securities.

Cash	300,000	
Marketable Securities	250,000	
Fund Balance—Restricted		550,000

2. The university received a $1,000,000 federal grant to construct a new classroom wing for the science department. The grant requires the university to match the government appropriation.

Cash	1,000,000	
Fund Balance—Restricted		1,000,000

3. The university's governing board directed a transfer from Current Unrestricted Funds for the construction of the new classroom wing for the science department. The $1,000,000 transfer complied with the government's building grant.

Cash	1,000,000	
Fund Balance—Restricted		1,000,000

4. The addition to the science department building was completed during the year and cost the university $2,500,000. A mortgage was signed for $500,000.

Cash	500,000	
Mortgage Payable		500,000
Construction in Progress	2,500,000	
Cash		2,500,000
Mortgage Payable[a]	500,000	
Fund Balance—Restricted	2,000,000	
Construction in Progress		2,500,000

[a]This entry transfers the building cost and mortgage to the Investment in Plant Fund account.

5. Income from pooled investments totaled $25,000.

Cash	25,000	
Fund Balance—Unrestricted		25,000

6. A planned expansion of the university's sports stadium was abandoned because of cutbacks in available federal funds. The governing board directed the return of $400,000 to Current Unrestricted Funds.

Fund Balance—Unrestricted	400,000	
Cash[a]		400,000

[a]The Current Unrestricted Fund credits the Transfers—Unexpended Plant Fund account.

7. Expenses of $20,000 were incurred in connection with fund-raising activities for the new science department classroom wing and laboratory equipment.

Fund Balance—Unrestricted	20,000	
Cash		20,000

II. The Renewals and Replacement Fund:

1. Income from pooled investments totaled $15,000.

Cash	15,000	
Fund Balance—Unrestricted		15,000

2. The governing board transferred $80,000 cash to the Renewals and Replacements Fund for equipment replacement in the science department.

Cash[a]	80,000	
Fund Balance—Unrestricted		80,000

[a]The Current Unrestricted Fund charges the Transfers—Plant Funds Renewals and Replacements account.

3. Replacement equipment was purchased for the science department for $78,000.

Fund Balance—Unrestricted[a]	78,000	
Cash		78,000

[a]This entry transfers the equipment cost to the Investment in Plant Fund account.

III. The Retirement of Indebtedness Fund:

1. Income earned from pooled investments amounts to $10,000.

Cash	10,000	
Fund Balance—Unrestricted		10,000

2. The governing board transferred $250,000 to the Retirement of Indebtedness Fund for interest and principal payments on debt. The debt payments were made.

Cash	250,000	
Fund Balance—Unrestricted		250,000
Fund Balance—Unrestricted	250,000	
Cash		250,000

IV. The Investment in Plant Fund:

1. Completed science building is transferred from Unexpended Plant Fund (see transaction 4, Unexpended Plant Fund).

Building (science)	2,500,000	
Mortgage Payable		500,000
Net Investment in Plant		2,000,000

2. Replacement equipment is tranferred from the Renewals and Replacement Fund (see transaction 3, Renewals and Replacement Fund).

Equipment (science)	78,000	
Net Investment in Plant		78,000

3. Mortgage payable is reduced (see transaction 2, Retirement of Indebtedness Fund).

Mortgage Payable	250,000	
Net Investment in Plant		250,000

4. The university received an art collection and several rare books for its library. The appraised values were $325,000 and $200,000, respectively.

Valued Collections—Art	325,000	
Valued Collections—Rare Books	200,000	
Net Investment in Plant		525,000

5. The laboratory equipment that was replaced was sold for $30,000. The recorded value of the equipment was $55,000.

Net Investment in Plant[a]	55,000	
Equipment (science)		55,000

[a]The sales proceeds could be accounted for by the Current Unrestricted Fund or by the Unexpended Plant Funds, depending on the disposition of the funds.

■ **APPENDIX C**

PUBLIC C&US: ILLUSTRATED TRANSACTIONS FOR ENDOWMENT AND SIMILAR FUNDS, LOAN FUNDS, ANNUITY FUNDS, LIFE INCOME FUNDS, AND AGENCY/CUSTODIAL FUNDS

ILLUSTRATION   **ENDOWMENT AND SIMILAR FUNDS GROUP TRANSACTIONS**

The following journal entries pertain to transactions of Andover University's Endowment and Similar Funds Group.

1. The Quincy family established an endowment fund, the income from which should be used to maintain the university's rare books collection. This permanent endowment does not restrict the investment of the funds.

Cash	350,000	
Fund Balance—Endowment		350,000

2. The university's board of trustees directed the accounting officer to establish a Quasi-Endowment Fund of $200,000. The income is to be used to maintain the campus theater. No restrictions were imposed on the investment of the funds. The transfer was made from Current Unrestricted Fund.

Cash	200,000	
Fund Balance—Endowment		200,000
Current Unrestricted Fund:		
Transfers—Endowment and Similar Funds	200,000	
Cash		200,000

3. Coulomb Corporation established an endowment fund in the amount of $150,000, the income from which will augment a professorial chair in electrical engineering. The endowment instrument stipulates that all income and investment gains are expendable for salary augmentation for five years. At the end of the fifth year, the principal is to be used to replace equipment in the engineering laboratories.

Cash	150,000	
Fund Balance—Term Endowment		150,000

4. Investment earnings from pooled investments totaled $19,500, received as shown:

Cash	19,500	
Revenues—Endowment Income		
(Current Unrestricted Fund)		6,500
Revenues—Endowment Income		
(Current Restricted Fund)		8,000
Fund Balance (unexpended plant fund)		5,000

5. Salary augmentation payments for the professorial chair in electrical engineering amounted to $6,500.

Fund Balance—Term Endowment	6,500	
Cash		6,500
Current Restricted Fund:		
Cash	6,500	
Fund Balance—Endowment Fund		6,500
Then, as expended:		
Fund Balance—Endowment Fund	6,500	
Revenue—Instruction		6,500

ILLUSTRATION   **LOAN FUND TRANSACTIONS**

The following journal entries show Andover University's Loan Fund transactions.

1. A fund-raising drive for student loan funds generated $750,000.

Cash	750,000	
Fund Balance—Loan		750,000

2. The board of trustees directed the use of $200,000 of Current Unrestricted Funds for low interest real estate loans to the faculty.

Cash	200,000	
Fund Balance—Loan		200,000
Current Unrestricted Funds:		
Transfers—Endowment Fund	200,000	
Cash		200,000

3. Loans to students and faculty totaled $500,000. An allowance for uncollectible loans was established for 1% of this amount.

Notes Receivable	500,000	
Cash		500,000
Fund Balance—Loan	5,000	
Allowance for Doubtful Loans		5,000

4. Excess cash of $400,000 was invested in marketable securities.

Investments	400,000	
Cash		400,000

5. Investment income earned amounted to $8,000.

Cash	8,000	
Fund Balance—Loan		8,000

6. Certain notes having a face amount of $25,000 proved to be uncollectible and were written off.

Allowance for Doubtful Loans	25,000	
Notes Receivable		25,000

7. Administrative and collection costs for the period amounted to $4,000.

Fund Balance—Loan	4,000	
Cash		4,000

ILLUSTRATION   **ANNUITY FUNDS GROUP TRANSACTIONS**

The following journal entries show Andover University's Annuity Funds Group transactions.

1. Phyllis Sims donated $250,000 to the university with the stipulation that she receive $20,000 per year for the rest of her life. Thereafter, the principal should be used to provide student aid. The actual value of the annuity is $85,000.

Cash	250,000	
Annuities Payable		85,000
Fund Balance—Annuity		165,000

2. Net investment gains for the period were $24,000, and investment income was $14,000.

Cash	38,000	
Annuities Payable		38,000

3. Payments to annuitant Phyllis Sims were $20,000.

Annuities Payable	20,000	
Cash		20,000

4. A periodic adjustment for the actuarial gain was due to recomputation of the liability based on the revised life expectancies of all annuitants.

Annuities Payable	53,500	
Fund Balance—Annuity		53,500

5. Annuitant Josh Gaylord died. The annuity was transferred to the Endowment Funds Group according to the provisions of the gift instrument.

Annuities Payable	1,500	
Fund Balance—Annuity	23,000	
Cash		24,500

ILLUSTRATION | **LIFE INCOME FUNDS GROUP TRANSACTIONS**

The following journal entries show Andover University's Life Income Fund Group transactions.

1. Gerald Baumann established a Life Income Fund, which specified that at his death the principal is to be transferred to the Current Unrestricted Fund group and used at the discretion of the board of trustees.

Cash	50,000	
Investments	150,000	
Fund Balance—Life Income		200,000

2. Income earned on investments amounted to $15,000.

Cash	15,000	
Income Payable		15,000

3. Life Income Fund distributions amounted to $15,000.

Income Payable	15,000	
Cash		15,000

4. The Erika Meagher Life Income Fund was transferred to Endowment Funds in accordance with the provisions of the gift instrument.

Fund Balance—Life Income	100,000	
Cash		100,000

ILLUSTRATION | **AGENCY/CUSTODIAL FUND TRANSACTIONS**

The following journal entries pertain to Andover University's Agency Fund transactions.

1. Student government fees collected during the registration process are deposited in the student government fund.

Cash   25,000
    Deposits Held in Custody for Others   25,000

2. Income earned from student government fund investments amounted to $2,000.

Cash   2,000
    Deposits Held in Custody for Others   2,000

3. Authorized disbursements for the period amounted to $7,500.

Deposits Held in Custody for Others   7,500
    Cash   7,500

4. Fund maintenance charges were $350.

Deposits Held in Custody for Others   350
    Cash   350

PARTNERSHIPS: FORMATION AND OPERATION

LEARNING OBJECTIVES

TO UNDERSTAND

- The various types of partnerships that can be formed.
- The distinguishing features of partnerships.
- The way to form a partnership.
- The various ways to share partnership profits and losses.
- The financial reporting issues peculiar to partnerships.
- The fundamental income tax aspects of partnerships.

TOPIC OUTLINE

Be nice to people on the way up. They're the same people you'll pass on the way down.

JIMMY DURANTE

A **partnership** is an association of two or more persons who contribute money, property, or services to operate as co-owners of a business, the profits and losses of which are shared in an agreed-upon manner. The term *person* refers to *individuals, corporations,* and even *other partnerships.*

Partnerships that are owned by one or more partnerships or corporations usually are formed to combine managerial talent and financial resources to conduct a specific undertaking—for example, designing and developing a large shopping center. Such partnerships are commonly referred to as *joint ventures.* Regardless of whether the partners are individuals, corporations, or other partnerships, the accounting and tax issues are the same.

According to the latest Internal Revenue Service (IRS) publications, more than 1.5 million partnerships exist (nearly 16 million partners), an increase of more than 50% in the last 25 years. Of all business income tax returns filed, nearly 8% are partnership returns.

In this chapter, we discuss the formation and operation of partnerships. Changes in ownership are discussed in Chapter 29, and liquidations of partnerships are discussed in Chapter 30.

ALTERNATIVES TO THE PARTNERSHIP FORM OF ORGANIZATION

The alternatives to the partnership form of organization are (1) a *regular corporation* (known as a C corporation for federal tax-reporting purposes), which in some ways is the most complex form of organization; (2) a *professional corporation* (a special corporation type for state statutory purposes but *not* for federal tax-reporting purposes; thus they are C corporations for federal tax purposes); (3) an *S corporation* (a small business company that elects special tax status with the result that its income is taxed only at the shareholder level); and (4) a *limited liability company (LLC),* a hybrid form of organization that (a) has a corporation's limited liability feature but is taxed as a partnership for federal purposes and (b) is generally a stronger version of a limited liability partnership, discussed shortly.

Determining the form of organization that is most appropriate for a particular entity requires an in-depth understanding of each of these alternatives, which is beyond the scope of this text. Some of the major accounting firms have prepared lengthy booklets that discuss (1) the advantages and disadvantages of these alternatives and the partnership form of organization and (2) the conditions that must be met to use these various forms of organization.[1]

I TYPES OF PARTNERSHIPS

GENERAL PARTNERSHIPS

Chapters 28–30 deal with **general partnerships**—that is, those in which each partner is personally liable to the partnership's creditors if partnership assets are insufficient to pay such creditors. Such partners are referred to as *general partners.* Two other types of partnerships exist, however: limited partnerships and limited liability partnerships.

---

[1]For example, see *Choosing a Business Entity in the 1990s* (Coopers and Lybrand L.L.P., Washington, D.C., 1994).

LIMITED PARTNERSHIPS

In a **limited partnership,** only *one* partner need be a general partner. The remaining partners can be limited partners, which means that their obligations to creditors are limited to their capital contributions. Thus their personal assets are *not* at risk. Furthermore, they play no role in the partnership management, which is the complete responsibility of the general partner.

Limited partnerships can be used for almost any business venture. During the 1970s and 1980s, passive investors widely used such partnerships as investment vehicles for various types of ventures such as (1) real estate (by far, the most popular investment), (2) oil and gas explorations, (3) research and development, (4) leveraged buyouts, (5) motion pictures, (6) cable television, and (7) horse breeding. Because of the much publicized staggering losses that investors had in these ventures overall, they are no longer widely used.[2]

LIMITED LIABILITY PARTNERSHIPS (LLPs)

In **limited liability partnerships,** a partner's personal assets are *not* at risk for the negligence and wrongdoings of the *other partners*. They *are* at risk, however, for (1) his or her own negligence and wrongdoing and (2) the negligence and wrongdoing of those under his or her direction and control. Of course, *all* partners could lose their *entire* partnership investment as a result of the negligence or wrongdoing (malpractice and torts) of any *one* partner.

In the accounting profession, many general partnerships (including all of the Big Six accounting firms) changed to limited liability partnerships in the mid-1990s to protect their partners' personal assets.

LLPs, which debuted in the mid-1990s, came about because the accounting profession heeded the unfortunate consequences of the bankruptcy and liquidation of the then seventh largest accounting partnership (Laventhol and Horwath—L&H) in 1991 (discussed in detail in Chapter 30), in which the 350 L&H partners lost $47 million of their personal assets (in addition to all of their partnership capital of approximately $60 million). In response, the American Institute of Certified Public Accountants (AICPA) (1) changed its rules in 1992 so that accounting firm members no longer had to be general partnerships—they could use whatever business form was available to them by their state governments—and (2) conducted an extensive effort to pass LLP legislation in each state. So successful were these efforts that nearly 40 states subsequently enacted legislation that allows LLPs.

The accompanying Business Perspective looks at the environment that led to the creation of LLPs. This relatively new form of organization (1) is expected to become quite popular and (2) may result in reversing the massive shift from the partnership form of organization to the professional corporation form of organization that occurred in the 1970s.

---

[2]In 1994, Prudential Securities Inc. reached a settlement with the Justice Department over its role in promoting the sale of limited partnerships in the 1980s. Under the terms of the settlement, Prudential (1) admitted criminal wrongdoing for the first time, (2) agreed to pay $330 million into a restitution fund for investors (in addition to the $371 million settlement it reached with state and federal regulators in 1993), and (3) agreed to be put on probation for three years. By doing so, the firm avoided a potentially crippling criminal indictment, which might have brought the firm down. Also in 1994, Paine Webber Inc. agreed to pay $303 million to settle regulators' charges that it had defrauded customers by luring them into highly risky limited partnership investments by describing them as safe investments.

Seeking Shelter: Partnership Structure Is Called in Question As Liability Risk Rises

Edward Nickles was elated when his small accounting firm made him a partner. "I thought it was the culmination of my entire life," the 37-year-old Bostonian says.

But his joy didn't last. After his firm, Pannell Kerr Forster, had to pay $1 million of a $5 million legal settlement that it could ill afford in the midst of a business slump, it slashed the young accountant's compensation to $65,000 from $145,000.

And the toll went beyond that. "I'd wake up at three or four in the morning and start worrying about my job." His wife, Ellen, says she would suddenly burst into tears for no apparent reason and was short-tempered with their two preschoolers.

But things are looking up. In April, Pannell Kerr jettisoned its partnership structure, reorganizing itself into six separate professional corporations in five states.

Out From Under

Because of the restructuring, Mr. Nickles no longer bears personal responsibility for any negligence on the part of his colleagues, and no liability for court judgments against them. Sharing the risks—and the repercussions—of any partner's misdeeds long had been an accepted part of partnership arrangements. Today, Mr. Nickles's earnings are climbing back toward what they were two years ago before being slashed. And he is getting more sleep.

The perils of partnership have become a hot issue, not merely among many accountants but also among attorneys, architects, investment bankers and others who once coveted a partner's perks, power and share of the profits. They are now asking: Do partnerships still make sense?

Many partnerships are scurrying to limit their shared liability. Others are abandoning the partnership setup altogether in favor of a corporate structure, even though corporations generally pay an income tax and partnerships don't. (Partners pay income taxes as individuals.)

Some skeptics see partners' complaints as mere sour grapes. "It's outrageous that partners so well paid for their firms' opinions are asking for liability protection," says U.S. Rep. Ron Wyden, an Oregon Democrat. "They want it both ways: Get rich from their professional credentials but avoid being culpable for the acts of their partners. They're saying, 'To heck with people who depend on our work and opinions.'"

Less to Sue For

Clients, too, may well take a different view of the reorganizations. The changes can mean clients are less able to get at partners' personal assets in suits over malpractice and bum advice. Clients could lose the reassurance of knowing that they've retained professionals willing to stake all they have on the work they and their partners do. It's possible the cost of professional services could go up as more partnerships incorporate and pass along the expense of their higher taxes.

On the other hand, if partnerships aren't able to somehow limit their liability, it will be tougher to find a lawyer or accountant willing to take on risky business. Some law and accounting firms may stop expanding in highly litigious states such as California. They also may stop handling business from some higher-risk banks, savings and loan associations, brokerage houses and real estate operations. More than half the 500 accountants recently surveyed by Johnson & Higgins Financial Group said they already are limiting their services or shunning certain business to protect themselves from suits.

Double Whammy

Professional partnerships suffer from two threats at once. First, many accounting, law and architectural firms have grown much bigger in recent years and have lost much of their collegial atmosphere. At the same time, a slew of big court damage awards—totaling close to a record $1 billion against U.S. accountants and attorneys in the past year alone—is raising some doubts about whether the nation's once-dominant form of business organization can survive.

In May, the prestigious accounting firm Price Waterhouse was hit by a record $338 million negligence award. An Arizona state court levied the award in favor of Standard Chartered PLC for negligence related to the accounting firm's audits of an Arizona bank before it was purchased by the London bank. The award represents about three times Price Waterhouse's insurance coverage.

Some negligence attorneys and Price Waterhouse competitors suggest the giant accounting firm could have real trouble staying afloat because its 950 partners may wind up paying $200 million or more out of their own pockets if courts uphold the award.

The firm, which intends to appeal, says it isn't in any danger of sinking. But if Price Waterhouse were a corporation and not a partnership, the award would come from its own coffers and from a few presumably culpable executives. As it is, hundreds of uninvolved partners face the possibility of losing much of what they own.

That explains why at least 10 partners of Laventhol & Horwath, a major accounting firm that collapsed two years ago, have filed for personal bankruptcy. They are trying to protect their savings and their homes because partners and principals of the now-defunct firm owe creditors $47.3 million.

As a result, some observers worry about the very future of partnerships. "With such risks, the partnership may go the way of the dodo," says Belverd Needles, former director of DePaul University's 2,000-student school of accountancy in Chicago.

Of all partnerships, accountants are the most jittery about their rising liability exposure, a product of the recession and the thrift-industry debacle. "There are currently more than 3,000 suits filed against accounting firms alleging negligence and asking up to $10 billion in damages," estimates Dan Goldwasser, an attorney who advises the New York State Society of Certified Public Accountants. That's twice the number of suits and five times the damages sought five years ago, he adds. "It's conceivable that one or two major accounting firms will seek bankruptcy-law protection over the next five years unless their legal status is changed."

Costly Buy-Out

Other professional partners also are losing their shirts over litigation awards. In April, John Burgee Architects, a major New York partnership that with Philip Johnson designed American Telephone & Telegraph Co.'s striking headquarters in midtown Manhattan, sought bankruptcy-law protection after a partner who had left the firm won a $16 million arbitration judgment. The sum represented much of the firm's past and projected profit, which the arbitrator agreed belonged to the man because of his contributions to the bottom line as a partner in the enterprise.

"Partnership is unfair because it offers me no protection," says Mr. Burgee, who worked out a payment plan that allows the firm to continue operating after halving its staff, to 30.

Lawyers are complaining, too. "You have to be out of your mind to be a partner in a law firm today," contends Peter Fass, a partner at New York's Kaye, Scholer, Fierman, Hays & Handler, a blue-chip law firm still reeling from a recent $41 million settlement. It reached the settlement in mid-March after federal regulators had sought a stunning $275 million over its alleged concealment of damning information about the firm's client Lincoln Savings & Loan Association, the country's most famous failed thrift. Mr. Fass and his 109 partners must fork over $16 million, the portion not taken care of by insurance.

Kaye Scholer's staggering settlement—and a $24 million settlement this spring by Cleveland law firm Jones, Day, Reavis & Pogue—may push up legal-malpractice premiums paid by partners of large law firms by as much as 50% in the next two years.

Little wonder that professional partners are campaigning hard to reduce their personal vulnerabilities to litigation. Last January, members of the American Institute of Certified Public Accountants agreed to let accountants create professional corporations whose principals would have limited liability. The 300,000-member institute previously had resisted such state action because it believed that accountants should jointly stand behind their work.

But with the recent huge negligence awards, the institute has launched a drive in 37 states for laws limiting professionals' liability. Thirteen states, including Florida, Texas, and Virginia, provide certain protection for the personal assets of partners not involved in wrongdoing committed by their firms' other members.

"A partner in Boston shouldn't have all of his assets at risk because another partner in Dallas made a mistake," says John Hunnicutt, the institute's top lobbyist in Washington, D.C. "It's simply unfair."

Other professionals are joining accountants to seek state legislative change. In New York, accounting firms, bar associations and Goldman Sachs & Co., one of the few major investment houses that remain partnerships, are pressing for limits on the use of partners' personal assets to settle claims against their firms.

Yet with such state protection, a true partnership ceases because each partner no longer collectively shares the risks for other partners' errors. Some big corporate clients might demand additional safeguards if partners' liability is lessened. Clients "are going to say, 'Come up with the [extra negligence] insurance or come up with a personal guarantee,'" says Lawrence A. Salibra, senior counsel for Alcan Aluminum Corp. in Cleveland.

But without limits on partners' personal liability, tougher management of legal risks is "going to absolutely be unavoidable for any professional partnership," says attorney Eugene Pinover. Mr. Pinover, a partner at Willkie Farr & Gallagher, was a top Kaye Scholer partner until May 1. He must contribute a six-figure sum to Kaye Scholer's settlement. "It's a major part of my life savings," he says.

At least one of the six biggest U.S. accounting firms has hired consultants to help determine whether it should drop partnerships for parts or all of the firm's activities. A leading alternative: spinning off the consulting practice as a separate professional corporation in each state. A professional corporation's principals aren't liable for one another's blunders.

(continued)

While the differences in state laws would make such a shift difficult for big law and accounting firms doing business all over the country, most leading architectural firms have become professional corporations because most operate in but a few states. To raise capital, nearly all big U.S. investment-banking firms dropped their partnerships, incorporated and sold stock to the public in the 1980s.

But partnerships that want to stay that way are nevertheless trying to make partners' lives less stressful. Nelson, Trimble & Co., an accounting firm in Bend, Ore., hired a psychiatrist to mediate arguments about who's the boss among nine partners.

Dropping Like Flies

The nation's top 100 law firms have eliminated between 5% and 10% of their partnership positions during the past two years, estimates Leslie Corwin, a partnership specialist with Morrison Cohen Singer & Weinstein, a New York law firm. The cuts are unprecedented in size. Major accounting firms have gotten rid of between 5% and 14% of their partners over the past 18 months—far above the 2% reductions seen a decade ago.

Law firms are going out of business at a steady clip, and a few major accounting firms have collapsed in re-

cent years. "At least a dozen [major law] firms have failed in the past three to four years," figures Bradford W. Hildebrandt, chairman of a legal consulting firm in Somerville, N.J. "In the next year or two, there could be another half-dozen."

Dissolving a 75-year-old partnership is particularly painful. Ask Mr. Hodes, who oversaw the liquidation of his father's firm in late March and currently is a senior partner in Chicago's Ross & Hardies. The younger attorney had spent three years searching for a merger partner for the midsized firm, which was established by Col. Jacob M. Arvey, a Democratic powerhouse in Chicago.

"I helped turn out the lights" on the firm's last day, Mr. Hodes says. "I was very upset. It was part of history in this city. . . . It did give me a great sense of sadness" to close the firm. At its peak, Arvey Hodes employed 75 lawyers. Mr. Hodes adds: "It was just as painful to see Arvey Hodes dissolved as it is to get divorced."

Source: Adapted from Lee Berton and Joann S. Lublin, "Partnership Structure Is Called in Question as Liability Risk Rises," *The Wall Street Journal*, June 10, 1992, pp. A1, A6. Copyright © 1992 by *The Wall Street Journal.* Reprinted by permission.

II   MAJOR FEATURES OF THE PARTNERSHIP FORM OF BUSINESS

EASE OF FORMATION   Forming a partnership is a relatively simple process. The partners merely put their agreement into writing concerning who contributes assets or services, who performs which functions in the business, and how profits and losses are shared. The written document is called the **partnership agreement.**

Thus, compared with the corporation form of business, a partnership need not prepare articles of incorporation, write bylaws, print stock certificates, prepare minutes of the first meeting of the board of directors, pay state incorporation fees, or register stocks.

POTENTIAL *NONCONTINUITY OF EXISTENCE*   Historically, the possibility that the operations of a partnership could not continue after the death or withdrawal of a partner (with the business subsequently liquidated) was considered a major disadvantage of this form of organization. In practice, this problem occurs only for small partnerships. Even then, some steps can be taken to minimize the impact of the loss of a partner. For example, life insurance proceeds on the death of a partner can be used to settle with the deceased partner's estate, thus conserving the assets of the business so that the remaining partners can continue the operation. For larger partnerships, this feature usually is not significant. Some of the largest partnerships have more than 1,000 partners. Obviously, the loss of one or even several partners in a partnership of such size has minimal impact on the day-to-day operations of the business.

DIFFICULTY IN DISPOSING OF INTEREST　An ownership interest in a partnership is a personal asset, as is the ownership of stock in a corporation. No formal established marketplace exists for the sale of a partnership interest, however, as exists for the sale of stock in a publicly owned corporation. Accordingly, a partner who wishes to sell or assign his or her partnership interest has more difficulty finding a buyer than a shareholder who wishes to sell stock in a publicly owned corporation. To make this process even more difficult, the person buying a partnership interest does *not* have the automatic right to participate in the business management—the consent of the remaining partners is necessary.

UNLIMITED LIABILITY　If a partnership's assets are insufficient to pay its creditors, the creditors have recourse to the personal assets of any and all general partners of the partnership. This characteristic contrasts sharply with the corporate form of organization, in which the personal assets of the shareholders are insulated from the corporation's creditors. This is undoubtedly the major disadvantage of the partnership form of organization.

MUTUAL AGENCY　The partnership is bound by each partner acting within the scope of partnership activities. Thus each partner acts as an agent for the partnership in dealing with persons outside the partnership. Furthermore, partners have a duty to conduct every transaction in full view of their partners.

SHARING PROFITS AND LOSSES　Profits and losses are shared among the partners in any manner to which they agree.

NONTAXABLE STATUS　Unlike a corporation, a partnership does *not* pay income taxes. Instead, partnerships must file with the IRS information on Form 1065, which shows the partnership's taxable income and each partner's share of such income. Each partner then reports and pays taxes on his or her share of the partnership's taxable income. These procedures eliminate the undesirable "double taxation," a feature of corporations. That is, a corporation's earnings are taxed and then its dividends are also taxed—whereas partnership income is taxed only once, at the individual partner level. Thus partnerships serve as *conduits* through which income flows to the partners.

CONCLUDING COMMENTS　For professionals, the partnership form of organization is simple and flexible compared with that of a professional corporation, which is generally considered complex and cumbersome. The partnership form is still common largely because it is a more effective way for partners to relate to each other.

　Partnerships often begin with great enthusiasm and rosy expectations. Keeping the partnership going is much harder. In many cases, the partners must seek help of a professional business therapist (often a psychologist) because they cannot work together harmoniously.

INCORPORATING A PARTNERSHIP

Many corporations began as partnerships. Then at some point in the enterprise's existence, the advantages of incorporation outweighed the advantages of the partnership form of organization. When a partnership incorporates, its assets are transferred to the corporation, which assumes the partnership's liabilities. One technical point should be noted: The corporation's board of directors is responsible for valuing the assets transferred to the corporation. In theory, the assets can be revalued to their current values, which is often done. If the corporation ever decides to register its common stock with the Securities and Exchange Commission, however, the SEC will insist that assets transferred to the corporation be carried at the partnership's historical cost, adjusted for depreciation and amortization. In other words, no *upward* revaluation of assets on incorporation is allowed. (Presumably, a *downward* revaluation would be permitted if appropriate.)

III   FORMATION OF A PARTNERSHIP

THE UNIFORM PARTNERSHIP ACT

Before discussing the partnership agreement in detail, some understanding of the laws that govern partnerships is necessary. Although each of the 50 states has laws pertaining to partnerships, most states have adopted the Uniform Partnership Act (UPA) or a variation thereof to govern partnerships. In this text, we consider the UPA the governing statute.

The UPA is reasonably comprehensive in defining the consequences of a partnership relationship. For our purposes, its more relevant sections pertain to the following:

1. Relations of partners to one another.
2. Relations of partners to persons dealing with the partnership.
3. Dissolution and winding up of the partnership.

Several parts of the UPA are effective only if the partnership agreement is silent on an issue. For example, item (d) of Section 18 of the UPA states that a partner shall receive interest on his or her capital contribution only from the date when repayment should be made. Inserting a contrary provision into the partnership agreement overrides this provision. In contrast, other sections of the UPA *cannot* be overridden by having contrary provisions in the partnership agreement.

The UPA is not so comprehensive, however, that it provides for every possible provision that otherwise could be included in a partnership agreement. For example, Section 27 discusses certain consequences of a partner's sale of his or her partnership interest. Although a partner need not give the remaining partners the first opportunity to acquire the partnership interest, neither does the UPA prevent a partnership agreement from containing a clause to the effect that if a partner desires to sell any or all of his or her interest, the remaining partners must be given the right of first refusal.

Selected sections of the UPA appear in Appendix B of this chapter to give you a general idea of this act.

THE PARTNERSHIP AGREEMENT

The partnership agreement is merely a written expression of what the partners have agreed to. Because state laws govern the consequences of partnership relationships, an attorney who is experienced in partnership law should prepare the partnership agreement. This is essential for the following reasons:

1. Mandatory provisions of the UPA may be included or referred to, so that the partners are aware of and somewhat familiar with partnership law.
2. Provisions that conflict with the UPA can be avoided.
3. Optional provisions that do *not* conflict with the UPA can be considered for possible inclusion.

A well-written partnership agreement should be a guide to the partners' relationship and any allowable variations from the UPA to which they have agreed. It should also minimize potential disputes among the partners.

In addition to essential legal provisions, the partnership agreement should address the following:

1. **Noninvolved provisions.**
   a. The partnership's exact name and designated place of business.
   b. The partners' names and addresses.
   c. The date that the partnership was formed.
   d. The partnership's business purpose.
   e. The partnership's duration.
   f. The basis of accounting to be used (for example, the accrual basis, the cash basis, the tax basis).
   g. The partnership's accounting year-end.
2. **Assets contributed.** A list of the assets contributed by each partner and their agreed-upon valuation to the partnership.
3. **Profit sharing.** The specific procedures for sharing profits and losses.
4. **Withdrawals.** The amounts that partners can periodically withdraw from the business and any conditions for withdrawals (for example, a certain amount per month or an amount up to a percentage of current period earnings).
5. **Additional capital contributions.** Provisions for making future capital infusions should the firm have financial difficulties.
6. **Rights of partners.** Provisions detailing the rights of partners (such as to accept clients, incur incidental expenses in connection with professional activities, and perform certain tasks).
7. **Avoidance of conflicts of interest.** A requirement that each partner is obligated to (a) bring all business opportunities to the partnership and (b) refrain from activities that create a conflict of interest.
8. **Designation of a managing partner or executive committee.** Provisions for designating a managing partner or an executive committee and the authority granted to such partner and committee (managing partners are commonly used in all but the smallest of firms).
9. **Tax matters.** Procedures to follow to comply with Internal Revenue Code requirements pertaining to partnerships.
10. **Notice of withdrawal.** The minimum time period for giving notice prior to withdrawing.
11. **Settling with withdrawing partners.** Provisions for settling with a partner (or a partner's estate) who withdraws from the partnership through choice, retirement, or death.
12. **Expulsion of a partner.** Causes for expulsion and manners of expelling and settling with (a) a partner who breaches the terms of the partnership agreement and (b) an unwanted partner. Larger firms usually empower executive committees to expel a partner *without* a vote of all of the partners. The alternative to omitting expulsion provisions is to allow the other partners vote to dissolve the firm and then reestablish it, *minus one member.* Even so, partners forced out in this manner sometimes file troublesome civil lawsuits against the firm, which take time and money to defend.
13. **Nonsolicitation.** Provisions that (a) either permit or prohibit a departing partner's solicitation of the partnership's clients and (b) set the compensation to be

---

CASE IN POINT

Recently, KPMG Peat Marwick "dropped" 265 weak-performing partners from its 1,876 partners. The cost was $52 million in severance pay and benefits.

given the firm if clients are taken. Not having such provisions sometimes leads to civil lawsuits between the firm and the departing partner.

14. **Noncompetition.** Provisions regarding whether a departing partner can or cannot compete against the partnership for a specified period of time in a specified geographic area. (Prohibitions must be reasonable or the courts will *not* enforce them.)

15. **Forfeitures.** Provisions specifying whether any termination or retirement payments shall be forfeited if a withdrawing partner violates any nonsolicitation or noncompetition provisions.

Many partnerships that (1) have a significant number of partners, (2) admit new partners annually, and (3) do business in more than one state have fashioned their partnership agreements so that they can operate in the same general manner as corporations. Thus such partnerships exhibit the corporate characteristics of (1) centralized management and decision making, (2) continuity of life (in substance but not form), and (3) an annual meeting of the owners (the partners) to vote on various matters. For additional information on partnerships, refer to *Management of an Accounting Practice,* which the AICPA publishes.

An accountant can assist persons who are in the preliminary stages of forming a partnership in the following ways:

1. By explaining the cash basis and accrual basis of accounting.

2. By explaining and illustrating the numerous alternative methods available to share profits and losses and the appropriateness of each. (A significant portion of this chapter is devoted to this subject.)

3. By discussing the tax ramifications compared with other methods of organizing the business. (This subject is discussed in Appendix A.)

THE PARTNERSHIP AS AN ENTITY

The business of the partnership should logically be accounted for separately from the personal transactions of the partners. Although partnerships are not separate legal entities with unlimited lives, as are corporations, this does not prevent partnerships from being accounted for as separate, operating business entities.

Although partners legally must contribute additional cash or property to the partnership to satisfy creditors' claims, this does *not* mean that the partnership is inseparable from the partners. It is a common banking practice for certain top officers of corporations to guarantee personally loans made to the corporation. Thus the fact that additional collateral for creditors exists is irrelevant.

Income tax laws do *not* determine sound accounting theory. They do treat partnerships as separate reporting entities, although *not* as separate tax-paying entities. Most partnerships are considered separate business entities in that they prepare monthly financial statements for internal use. Some of the large public accounting firms even publish annual reports, complete with financial statements, for their partners, employees, and other interested parties to use.

APPLICABILITY OF GENERALLY ACCEPTED ACCOUNTING PRINCIPLES

To study partnerships, we must make an important transition from corporate accounting (in which GAAP is almost always followed) to partnership accounting (in which GAAP need not be and often is not followed). The professional pronouncements of the AICPA and the Financial Accounting Standards Board (FASB) apply to businesses that present their financial statements in accordance with GAAP. Such businesses include (1) publicly held corporations, which must present their financial statements in accordance with GAAP; (2) nonpublicly held corporations, which usually present their financial statements in accordance with GAAP (often pursuant to requirements of loan agreements with financial institutions); and (3) partnerships and sole proprietorships that choose to present their financial statements in accordance with GAAP.

When a partnership does *not* maintain its books in accordance with GAAP, such a departure usually falls into one of the following categories:

1. *Cash basis* **instead of** *accrual basis.* The *cash basis* of recording receipts and expenses is often more efficient and economical than the *accrual basis.*

2. **Prior period adjustments.** To achieve greater equity among the partners, prior period adjustments are often made even though the items do not qualify as such under FASB *Statement No. 16*, "Prior Period Adjustments."

3. *Current values* **instead of** *historical cost.* When the ownership of the partnership changes, it is sometimes more expedient to reflect assets at their *current values* than to continue to value them at their *historical cost.*

4. **Recognition of goodwill.** To accommodate a partner's wishes, goodwill may be recognized on the admission or retirement of a partner, even though a business combination has not occurred.

Categories 3 and 4 are discussed and illustrated in Chapter 29 on changes in ownership.

PARTNERS' ACCOUNTS

CAPITAL ACCOUNTS Each partner has a **capital account,** created when the partner contributes assets to the partnership. The account is increased for subsequent capital contributions and decreased for withdrawals. In addition, the account is increased for the partner's share of earnings and decreased for the partner's share of losses.

Traditionally, accountants have not attempted to maintain a balance sheet distinction between contributed capital and earnings that have been retained in the partnership, as is customary for corporations. This is primarily because the partnership's earnings do *not* reflect any salary expense for the partners (they are owners, *not* employees), and therefore they must be evaluated carefully. If the corporate form of business were used rather than the partnership form, the corporation's earnings would be *lower* than those reported by the partnership because the services performed by the partners would be performed by salaried officers and employees of the corporation. Earnings under the corporate form of business would also be *lower* because of income taxes. To avoid the implication that the earnings retained in the partnership are comparable to the retained earnings of a corporation, a retained earnings account is considered inappropriate for partnerships. Accordingly, a partnership's earnings or losses are added or subtracted, respectively, to the capital accounts of the individual partners.

DRAWING ACCOUNTS Typically, partners do not wait until the end of the year to determine how much of the profits they wish to withdraw from the partnership. To meet personal living expenses, partners customarily withdraw money on a periodic basis throughout the year. Such withdrawals could be charged directly to the capital accounts of the individual partners. A special account called the **drawing account** is used, however, to charge current year withdrawals. In substance, drawing accounts are contra capital accounts. At year-end, each partner's drawing account is closed to that partner's capital account. The maximum amount partners may withdraw during the year is usually specified in the partnership agreement.

LOAN ACCOUNTS Partners may make loans to the partnership in excess of their required capital contributions. Section 18 of the UPA provides that unless the partners agree otherwise, "a partner, who in aid of the partnership makes any payment or advance beyond the amount of capital which he agreed to contribute, shall be paid interest from the date of the payment or advance." Interest on partners' loans to the partnership is a bona fide borrowing expense of the business, is treated as interest expense in the general ledger, and enters into the determination of profit or loss.

If a partnership loans money on an interest-bearing basis to a partner, the interest is recorded as interest income in the general ledger. It also enters into the determination of the profit or loss.

RECORDING THE INITIAL CAPITAL CONTRIBUTIONS

The following two fundamental principles are deeply rooted in partnership accounting:

1. Noncash assets contributed to a partnership should be valued at their *current values*.

2. Liabilities assumed by a partnership should be valued at their *current values*.

These principles achieve equity among the partners, an objective repeatedly stressed in partnership accounting. If these principles are not followed, the subsequent operations do not reflect the true earnings of the partnerships, and certain partners are treated inequitably.

For example, assume that a partner contributed to a partnership marketable securities with a $10,000 current market value and a $7,000 cost basis to the individual partner. If the partnership later sells the marketable securities for $12,000, the recorded gain on the partnership's books is $2,000, the amount of appreciation that occurred during the period that the partnership held the asset. If the marketable securities had been valued on the partnership's books at the partner's cost basis of $7,000, however, the recorded gain is $5,000. This results in the other partner's sharing in an additional $3,000 of profit, the appreciation that occurred *before* the asset was contributed to the partnership. *Current values* must be used to prevent such inequities. The partnership agreement normally indicates the agreed-upon valuation assigned to noncash assets contributed and liabilities assumed. (Alternatively, the partnership agreement can specify that the first $3,000 of profit go to the contributor with the balance distributed in the profit and loss sharing ratio.)

The entry to record initial capital contributions for an assumed two-person partnership follows using these assumed facts:

Assets Contributed and Liabilities Assumed	Adjusted Basis[a]	Current Value
By Partner A		
Cash	$23,000	$23,000
Marketable securities	7,000	10,000
	$30,000	$33,000
By Partner B		
Cash	$ 5,000	$ 5,000
Land	15,000	20,000
Building, net	25,000	35,000
Note payable, secured by land and building	(20,000)	(20,000)
	$25,000	$40,000

(continued)

Entry to Record Initial Contributions

Cash	28,000	
Marketable securities	10,000	
Land	20,000	
Building	35,000	
Notes payable		20,000
Capital, Partner A		33,000
Capital, Partner B		40,000

[a]*Adjusted Basis* means each partner's historical cost, as adjusted for depreciation and amortization previously allowed (or allowable) for income tax reporting purposes.

The Adjusted Basis column is completely irrelevant for recording the initial capital contributions in the general ledger, but it is significant for income tax reporting. Income tax aspects are discussed in Appendix A.

IV METHODS TO SHARE PROFITS AND LOSSES

Section 18 of the UPA specifies that profits and losses be shared equally unless the partnership agreement provides otherwise. Because the sharing of profits and losses is such an important aspect of a partnership relationship, it would be rare to find a partnership agreement that did not spell out the divisions of profits and losses in detail. The formula used to divide profits and losses is determined through negotiations among the partners. Whether it is fair does *not* concern the accountant.

Profits and losses can be shared in many ways. Partners should select a formula that is sensible, practical, and equitable. Most profit and loss sharing formulas include one or more of the following features or techniques:

1. Equal shares or some other agreed-upon ratio.
2. Imputed salary allowances to acknowledge time devoted to business.
3. Imputed interest on capital investments to recognize capital invested.
4. Expense-sharing arrangements.
5. Performance criteria to recognize above- or below-average performance.

Note that the computations determining the profit and loss allocation among the partners are made on worksheets. The only journal entry that results from this process is to close the Profit and Loss Summary account to the partners' capital accounts, using the amounts determined from the worksheet computations.

RATIOS

Under the *ratio method*, each partner is allocated a percentage of the profits and losses. For example, partner A receives 60% and partner B receives 40% of the profits and losses. These percentages are then expressed as a ratio. Thus profits and losses are shared between A and B in the ratio 3:2, respectively. If the A and B partnership had profits of $100,000, the entry to record the division of the profits is as follows:

Profit and Loss Summary	100,000	
Capital, Partner A		60,000
Capital, Partner B		40,000

An infrequently used variation of this method specifies one ratio for profits and a different ratio for losses. Because profit and loss years may alternate, it is extremely important that profit or loss for each year be determined accurately in all material respects when this variation is used.

SALARY ALLOWANCES AND RATIOS

Sometimes certain partners devote more time to the business than do other partners. In these cases, a frequently used method for sharing profits and losses provides for salary allowances, with any residual profit or loss allocated in an agreed-upon ratio. For example, assume that partner A devotes all of her time to the business, and partner B devotes only one-third of his time to the business. The partners could agree to salary allowances in relation to the time devoted to the business—for example, $30,000 to partner A and $10,000 to partner B. All remaining profits or losses could then be divided in the agreed-upon ratio—that is, 3:2, respectively.

Using these salary allowances and a residual sharing ratio of 3:2 for partner A and partner B, respectively, the partnership divides $100,000 in profits in the following way:

		Allocated to	
	Total	Partner A	Partner B
Total profit	$100,000		
Salary allowances	(40,000)	$30,000	$10,000
Residual Profit	$ 60,000		
Allocate 3:2	(60,000)	36,000	24,000
	$ –0–	$66,000	$34,000

The general ledger entry to divide the profits follows:

Profit and Loss Summary	100,000	
Capital, Partner A		66,000
Capital, Partner B		34,000

Remember that partners are owners, *not* employees. Accordingly, it is *not* appropriate to charge a Salary Expense account and credit Accrued Salary Payable. Some partnerships do record salary allowances in this manner, however. Although not technically correct, it does *not* affect the final profit and loss allocations. In these cases, cash distributions that relate to salary allowances are charged to Accrued Salary Payable. Any remaining credit balance in a partner's Accrued Salary Payable account at year-end is then transferred to that partner's capital account.

In the preceding example, the total profit was higher than the total salary allowances of $40,000. What if that were not the case? Profit of only $25,000 is shared as follows:

		Allocated to	
	Total	Partner A	Partner B
Total profit	$ 25,000		
Salary allowances	(40,000)	$30,000	$10,000
Residual Loss	$(15,000)		
Allocate 3:2	15,000	(9,000)	(6,000)
	$ –0–	$21,000	$ 4,000

The general ledger entry to divide the profits follows:

Profit and Loss Summary	25,000	
Capital, Partner A		21,000
Capital, Partner B		4,000

Another way to handle this situation would be if the partners agreed not to use a residual sharing ratio in the event profits were less than the total salary allowances. In this case, the first $40,000 of profit is divided in the ratio of the salary allowances. Using the same example, a $25,000 profit is divided as follows:

	Total	Allocated to Partner A	Partner B
Total profit	$ 25,000		
Salary allowances—up to			
$40,000 in a 3:1 ratio	(25,000)	$18,750	$6,250
	$ –0–	$18,750	$6,250

Large and moderate sized partnerships usually function with an administrative hierarchy. Partnership positions within such a hierarchy have greater responsibilities than do positions outside the hierarchy. To compensate the partners who assume these greater responsibilities, salary allowances commonly are used; their amounts are correlated to the various levels of responsibility within the hierarchy.

IMPUTED INTEREST ON CAPITAL, SALARY ALLOWANCES, AND RATIOS

When partners' capital investments are *not* equal, the profit-sharing formula frequently includes a feature that recognizes the larger capital investment of certain partners. Accordingly, interest is imputed on each partner's capital investment. For example, a profit and loss sharing formula could specify that interest be imputed at 10% of each partner's average capital investment. To illustrate this procedure's application, assume the following profit-sharing formula and *average* capital investments:

	Partner A	Partner B
Profit sharing formula:		
Salary allowances	$30,000	$10,000
Interest on average capital balance	10%	10%
Residual profit or loss (3:2)	60%	40%
Average capital investments	$10,000	$40,000

Profits of $100,000 are divided as follows:

	Total	Allocated to Partner A	Partner B
Total profit	$100,000		
Salary allowances	(40,000)	$30,000	$10,000
Interest on average capital investments	(5,000)	1,000	4,000
Residual Profit	$ 55,000		
Allocate 3:2	(55,000)	33,000	22,000
	$ –0–	$64,000	$36,000

The general ledger entry to divide the profits follows:

Profit and Loss Summary	100,000	
Capital, Partner A		64,000
Capital, Partner B		36,000

Remember that the partners' capital investments are just that—they are *not* loans to the partnership. Accordingly, it is *not* appropriate to charge an Interest Expense account and an Accrued Interest Payable account. Some partnerships do record imputed interest in this manner, however. This procedure is not technically correct, but it does *not* affect the final profit and loss allocations. In these cases, cash distributions that relate to imputed interest are charged to Accrued Interest Payable. Any remaining credit balance in a partner's Accrued Interest Payable account at year-end is then transferred to that partner's capital account.

In this example, the profit was higher than both the $40,000 total of the salary allowances and the $5,000 total of imputed interest. A profit of only $25,000 is divided as follows:

| | | Allocated to | |
	Total	Partner A	Partner B
Total profit	$ 25,000		
Salary allowances	(40,000)	$30,000	$10,000
Interest on average capital investments	(5,000)	1,000	4,000
Residual Loss	$(20,000)		
Allocate 3:2	20,000	(12,000)	(8,000)
	$ –0–	$19,000	$ 6,000

The general ledger entry to divide the profits follows:

Profit and Loss Summary	25,000	
Capital, Partner A		19,000
Capital, Partner B		6,000

ORDER OF PRIORITY PROVISION   Alternatively, the partners could agree not to use a residual sharing ratio if profits do not exceed the total of the salary allowances and the imputed interest on average capital balances. In this case, the partners must agree on **the priority of the various features.** If the partnership agreement gives salary allowances priority over imputed interest on capital balances, the first $40,000 of profit is divided in the ratio of the salary allowances, and the next $5,000 is divided in the ratio of the imputed interest amounts. Using the profit-sharing formula and data from the preceding example, a profit of only $42,000 is divided as follows:

| | | Allocated to | |
	Total	Partner A	Partner B
Total profit	$ 42,000		
Salary allowances	(40,000)	$30,000	$10,000
Available for Interest on Capital	$ 2,000		
Interest on average capital investment 1:4	(2,000)	400	1,600
	$ –0–	$30,400	$11,600

Note: If interest on capital had priority over salary allowances, the $42,000 profit division results in Partner A being allocated $28,750 ($1,000 for interest and $27,750 for salary) and Partner B being allocated $13,250 ($4,000 for interest and $9,250 for salary).

In these examples, interest is imputed on the *average* capital investments. Although this is apparently the most equitable method, using the *beginning* or *ending* capital investments is another option. When this imputed interest on capital feature is used, the partnership agreement should specify whether the beginning, average, or ending capital balances should be used. Furthermore, if the partnership agreement calls for using *average* or *ending* capital investments, it should define specifically how these are determined. Only the capital account or the capital account and the drawing account of each partner may be used. For the *average* capital balance method, the method to compute the average must be selected—that is, using *daily* balances, *beginning-of-month* balances, or *end-of-month* balances.

The following assumptions and capital account activities illustrate the computation of an *average* capital investment:

1. The drawing account activity is considered in arriving at the annual *average* capital investment.

2. An *average* capital investment for each month is used to arrive at the annual *average* capital investment.

CAPITAL, PARTNER X				DRAWINGS, PARTNER X	
$50,000	1/1/X5	6/30/X5	$6,000		
10,000	4/1/X5	9/15/X5	6,000		
2,000	11/15/X5	12/31/X5	6,000		

Computation Month	Monthly Averages
January	$ 50,000
February	50,000
March	50,000
April	60,000
May	60,000
June	60,000
July	54,000
August	54,000
September	51,000
October	48,000
November	49,000
December	50,000
	$636,000
Average Capital Investment for 19X5 ($636,000 ÷ 12)	$ 53,000

CAPITAL BALANCES ONLY

Many international accounting firms allocate profits and losses *solely* on the basis of capital balances. In these cases, each partner must maintain a specified capital balance, which is correlated to the level of responsibility assumed in the partnership. This method not only is easy to apply but also can prevent certain inequities from occurring among partners if the partnership is liquidated. These potential inequities are discussed in Chapter 30, which deals with partnership liquidations.

EXPENSE-SHARING ARRANGEMENTS

Sometimes a small partnership operates as a confederation of sole proprietorships, in that the profit-sharing formula entitles each partner to all net billings he or she generates. Expenses are then allocated to partners on the basis of total floor space, amount of billings, or some other arbitrary method. This arrangement is common when two or more sole proprietorships form a partnership, with each partner maintaining former clients. Any net billings from clients obtained after the formation of the partnership may be assigned either to the partner responsible for obtaining the client or to a common pool to be allocated to all partners on some arbitrary basis.

PERFORMANCE METHODS

Many partnerships use profit and loss sharing formulas that give some weight to the specific performance of each partner to provide incentives to perform well. Some examples of the use of performance criteria are listed here:

1. **Chargeable hours.** These are the total number of hours that a partner incurred on client-related assignments. Weight may be given to hours in excess of a norm.

2. **Total billings.** The total amount billed to clients for work performed and supervised by a partner constitutes total billings. Weight may be given to billings in excess of a norm.

3. **Write-offs.** Write-offs consist of the amount of uncollectible billings. Weight may be given to a write-off percentage below a norm.

4. **Promotional and civic activities.** Time devoted to developing future business and enhancing the partnership name in the community is considered promotional and civic activity. Weight may be given to time spent in excess of a norm or to specific accomplishments resulting in new clients.

5. **Profits in excess of specified levels.** Designated partners commonly receive a certain percentage of profits in excess of a specified level of earnings.

An additional allocation of profits to a partner on the basis of performance is frequently referred to as a **bonus.** As with salary allowances and imputed interest, a bonus should not be charged to an expense account in the general ledger, although some partnerships improperly do this. For example, assume that the A and B partnership has a bonus provision whereby partner A is to receive 50% of partnership income in excess of $100,000, with all remaining profits and losses to be shared 60%–40%, respectively. Partnership income of $110,000 is shared as follows:

	Total	Allocated to	
		Partner A	Partner B
Total profit	$110,000		
Bonus (50% × $10,000)	(5,000)	$ 5,000	
Residual profit	$105,000		
Allocate 3:2	(105,000)	63,000	$42,000
	$ –0–	$68,000	$42,000

Many types of bonus provisions can exist. Also, the bonus feature can be applied at any level of partnership income, for example, a bonus based on a percentage of the remaining profits after salary allowances and imputed interest on capital have been allocated.

SUBSEQUENT CHANGES IN METHODS TO SHARE PROFITS AND LOSSES

If the partners subsequently agree to change the method to share profits and losses, equity dictates that assets be revalued to their current values at the time of the change. To illustrate, assume that partners A and B shared profits and losses equally but that at a later date agree to share profits and losses in a 3:2 ratio, respectively. Suppose also that the partnership holds a parcel of land carried on the books at $60,000, but with an $80,000 current value. Partner A would receive a larger share of the profit on the land (when it is later sold) than had the land been sold *before* the change in the method to share profits and losses. This is *not* equitable because the land appreciated $20,000 while the profits and losses were shared equally.

An alternative to revaluing the land to its current value is to stipulate in the new profit-sharing formula that the first $20,000 of profit on the sale of that parcel of land is to be shared in the *old* profit and loss sharing ratio. Under this method, the partnership avoids making an entry that is at variance with GAAP. This is not a major reason for selecting this alternative, however, if revaluing assets is more practical.

When the profit and loss sharing formula is revised, the *new* formula should contain a provision specifying that the *old* formula applies to certain types of subsequent adjustments arising out of activities that took place before the revision date. Examples are as follows:

1. Unrecorded liabilities existing at the revision date.
2. Settlements on lawsuits not provided for at the revision date, even though the liability may not have been probable as to payment or reasonably estimable at that time.
3. Write-offs of accounts receivable existing as of the revision date.

Regardless of the fact that some of these items do *not* qualify as prior period adjustments under FASB *Statement No. 16*, "Prior Period Adjustments," greater equity usually is achieved among the partners by using the old sharing formula. Because partnerships need *not* follow GAAP, the will of the partners may prevail.

V   FINANCIAL REPORTING ISSUES

Because partnerships are not publicly owned, their financial statements are prepared primarily for internal use. Such statements normally include all of those that a corporation prepares, except for the statement of changes in stockholders' equity, for which a statement of changes in partners' equity is substituted.

One common reason for making partnership financial statements available to outside parties is to borrow money from financial institutions. (Under the UPA, partnerships can hold debt in the partnership name rather than in the names of its individual partners.) Financial statements made available to outside parties should be converted to the accrual basis if the cash basis is used for book purposes. (Most partnerships use the cash basis as a matter of convenience.) Because partnership earnings are not comparable to what they would have been had the business been organized as a corporation, an indication to this effect should be made in the notes to the financial statements.

Some accountants have suggested that a partnership's income statement should reflect an imputed amount for salaries that would have been paid to the partners had the corporate form of business been used. Presumably, such an approach would state the "true earnings" of the partnership. In our opinion, this is a somewhat futile exercise involving substantial subjectivity. Furthermore, from a technical standpoint, consideration should also be given to (1) additional payroll taxes; (2) deductions for fringe benefits (primarily pension and profit-sharing plans), which are not available to partners; and (3) income taxes. It seems sufficient to state in a note that, because the partnership form of organization is used, the earnings must be evaluated carefully because, conceptually, earnings should provide for equivalent salary compensation, return on capital invested in the partnership, retirement, and payroll-type fringe benefits.

Virtually all partnerships maintain strict confidentiality of their financial statements. Financial statements issued by international public accounting partnerships to interested parties are commonly characterized as follows:

1. Conversion from the *cash basis* to the *accrual basis* of accounting.
2. No imputed amount for salaries in the income statement.
3. A note to the financial statements indicating that the firm's earnings are *not* comparable to those of a corporation.

4. Preparation of the financial statements in accordance with GAAP, with the notes to the financial statements complete as to required disclosures—for example, of accounting policies, lease commitments, and segment information.

The income statement of small partnerships commonly shows how the profit or loss is divided. The allocation can be shown immediately below net income, as follows:

A & B Partnership
Income Statement
For the Year Ended December 31, 19X1

Revenues	$1,000,000
Expenses	(900,000)
Net Income	$ 100,000

Allocation of Net Income to Partners:

	Partner A	Partner B
Salary allowances	$30,000	$10,000
Imputed interest on capital	1,000	4,000
Residual (3:2)	33,000	22,000
Total	$64,000	$36,000

Furthermore, a small partnership's statement of changes in partners' equity is often shown *by partner* as follows:

A & B Partnership
Statement of Changes in Partners' Equity
For the Year Ended December 31, 19X1

	Partner A	Partner B	Total
Beginning capital	$25,000	$ 85,000	$110,000
Contributions	5,000	–0–	5,000
Drawings	(10,000)	(15,000)	(25,000)
Net income	64,000	36,000	100,000
Ending Capital	$84,000	$106,000	$190,000

END-OF-CHAPTER REVIEW

SUMMARY OF KEY POINTS

1. In **general partnerships,** each partner is personally liable to the partnership's creditors if partnership assets are insufficient to pay such creditors. In **limited partnerships,** the limited partners are *not* personally liable to the partnership creditors.
2. In **limited liability partnerships,** a partner is personally liable to creditors only as a result of (a) his or her own actions and (b) the actions of those under his or her supervision and control.
3. The partnership agreement governs the manner of operating the partnership, including the manner of dividing profits and losses and withdrawing earnings and capital.
4. Partnerships are accounted for as separate business entities, with the primary accounting objective being **to achieve equity** among the partners.
5. Partnership accounting often deviates from GAAP to achieve equity.
6. Upon formation of a partnership, assets and liabilities contributed into the partnership are recorded at their **current values,** which usually results in a **new basis of accounting** for financial reporting purposes. For tax purposes, no change in basis occurs.

GLOSSARY OF NEW TERMS

Drawing account   A contra capital account used to keep track of amounts withdrawn during the year by a partner.

General partnerships   Partnerships in which *all* of the partners are personally liable to the partnership's creditors.

Limited liability partnerships (LLPs)   Partnerships in which each partner is *not* personally liable to the partnership's creditors as a result of actions by other partners.

Limited partnerships   Partnerships in which certain partners (called *limited partners*) are *not* personally liable to the partnership creditors (there must be at least one general partner).

SELF-STUDY QUESTIONS

(Answers are at the end of this chapter, preceding the appendices.)

1. Don Doss and Kim Keyes form a partnership. Doss contributes into the partnership a personal computer that he has used at home in nonbusiness-related activities. He paid $10,000 for the computer two years ago. Its replacement cost is $9,000. The partners, after reviewing IRS rules, assigned the computer a remaining life of six years. For financial reporting purposes, at what amount should the computer be recorded in the partnership's general ledger?

   a. $10,000   **b.** $9,000   **c.** $7,500   **d.** $6,750

2. For income tax–reporting purposes, at what amount should the computer in Question 1 be accounted for by the partnership?

   a. $10,000   **b.** $9,000   **c.** $7,500   **d.** $6,750

3. Partners Harry and Sally share profits and losses of their business equally after (a) annual salary allowances of $25,000 for Harry and $20,000 for Sally and (b) 10% interest is provided on average capital balances. During 19X1, the partnership had earnings of $50,000; Harry's average capital balance was $60,000, and Sally's average capital balance was $90,000. How should the $50,000 of earnings be divided?

	Harry	Sally
a.	$26,000	$24,000
b.	$27,000	$23,000
c.	$25,000	$25,000
d.	$27,500	$22,500

4. Assume the same information in Question 3 and that an order of priority is specified whereby salary allowances have a higher priority than interest on capital.

5. Kelly, a partner in the Kelly and Green partnership, is entitled to 40% of the profits and losses. During 19X1, Kelly contributes land to the partnership that cost her $50,000 but has a current value of $60,000. Also during 19X1, Kelly has drawings of $80,000. The balance in Kelly's capital account was $120,000 at the beginning of the year and is $150,000 at the end of the year. What are the partnership's earnings for 19X1?

   a. $(75,000)   **b.** $(50,000)   **c.** $150,000   **d.** $125,000

6. Contrera and Badgez have just formed a partnership. Contrera contributed $50,000 cash and some equipment that cost him $45,000. The equipment had been used in his sole proprietorship and had been depreciated $20,000. The replacement cost of the equipment is $30,000. Contrera also contributed a $10,000 note payable. Contrera is to receive 60% of the profits and losses. Badgez contributed only $90,000 cash. Determine the following items for Contrera:

	Capital Account Balance	Tax Basis
a.	$80,000	$69,000
b.	$80,000	$71,000
c.	$70,000	$71,000
d.	$70,000	$69,000
e.	$70,000	$79,000

ASSIGNMENT MATERIAL

REVIEW QUESTIONS

1. What is a *general partnership*?
2. How is *partnership* defined?
3. What is a *limited partnership*?
4. What is a *limited liability partnership*?
5. Why is it advisable to use an attorney's services in preparing a partnership agreement?
6. What is the function of the *partnership agreement*?
7. What essential items should be set forth in the *partnership agreement*?
8. Must partnerships follow GAAP? Why or why not?
9. What common features may be structured into a profit and loss sharing formula?
10. Can partners be paid *salaries*?
11. What performance criteria may be incorporated into a profit-sharing formula?
12. What is the function of the *drawing* account? Is it really necessary?
13. How are loans *from* a partner to a partnership accounted for on the partnership's books?
14. Why might it be appropriate to use the *old* profit and loss sharing formula in certain transactions instead of the *new* formula?
15. In what broad areas do partnerships commonly deviate from GAAP?
16. Should partnership financial statements be prepared so that partnership earnings are comparable to what they would have been had the corporate form of business been used? Why or why not?

EXERCISES

E 28-1   **Dividing the Profit or Loss: Partnership Agreement Is Silent**   The partnership of Reed and Wright had earnings of $40,000 for the year. Reed devotes all of her time to the business, and Wright devotes 50% of his time to it. The average capital balance for Reed was $60,000, and Wright's was $30,000. The partnership agreement is silent regarding profit distribution.

Required   1. Prepare a schedule showing how the profit should be divided.
2. Prepare the entry to divide the profit.

E 28-2   **Dividing the Profit or Loss: Performance Features and Ratio**   The partnership of Monte and Carlo has the following provisions:

1. Monte, who is primarily responsible for obtaining new clients, is to receive a 30% bonus on revenues in excess of $200,000.
2. Carlo, who is primarily responsible for administration, is to receive a 30% bonus on profits in excess of 50% of revenues, as reflected in the general ledger.
3. All remaining profits or losses are to be divided equally.

Additional Information

Revenues for the year	$280,000
Operating expenses	120,000

Required   1. Prepare a schedule showing how the profit or loss should be divided for the year.
2. Prepare the entry to divide the profit or loss for the year.

E 28-3   **Dividing the Profit or Loss: Ratio and Salary Allowances**   The partnership of Bunn and Frye shares profits and losses in a 7:3 ratio, respectively, after Frye receives a $10,000 salary allowance.

Required   1. Prepare a schedule showing how the profit or loss should be divided, assuming the profit or loss for the year is
   a. $30,000.
   b. $6,000.
   c. $(10,000).
2. Prepare the entry to divide the profit or loss in situations a to c of requirement 1.

E 28-4   **Dividing the Profit or Loss: Ratio, Salary Allowance, and Imputed Interest on Capital**   The partnership of Agee and Begee has the following provisions:

1. Agee and Begee receive salary allowances of $19,000 and $11,000, respectively.
2. Interest is imputed at 10% of the average capital investments.
3. Any remaining profit or loss is shared between Agee and Begee in a 3:2 ratio, respectively.

Additional Information

Average capital investments
   Agee .... $ 60,000
   Begee 100,000

Required
1. Prepare a schedule showing how the profit would be divided, assuming the partnership profit or loss is
   a. $76,000.
   b. $42,000.
   c. $(14,000).
2. Prepare the entry to divide the profit or loss in situations a to c of requirement 1.

E 28–5   **Dividing the Profit or Loss: Ratio, Salary Allowances, and Imputed Interest on Capital—Order of Priority Specified**   Assume the information provided in Exercise 28–4, except that the partnership agreement stipulates the following **order of priority** in the distribution of profits:

1. *Salary allowances* (only to the extent available).
2. *Imputed interest* on average capital investments (only to the extent available).
3. Any remaining profit in a 3:2 ratio. (No mention is made regarding losses.)

Required   The requirements are the same as for Exercise 28–4.

E 28–6   **Recording Initial Capital Contributions**   On 5/1/X7, Booker and Page formed a partnership. Each contributed assets with the following agreed-upon valuations:

	Booker	Page
Cash	$80,000	$ 20,000
Machinery and equipment	50,000	60,000
Building	–0–	240,000

The building is subject to a $100,000 mortgage loan, which the partnership assumes. The partnership agreement provides that Booker and Page share profits and losses 40% and 60%, respectively.

Required
1. Prepare the journal entry to record each partner's capital contributions.
2. *Optional:* Assuming that no difference exists between the agreed-upon valuation of each asset contributed and its related adjusted basis, determine the *tax basis* of each partner on 5/1/X7.

PROBLEMS

P 28–1   **Dividing Profits: Interest on Capital, Bonuses, and Salary Allowances**   Horn and Sax are in partnership. The activity in each partner's capital account for 19X1 follows:

		HORN				SAX	
		$20,000	1/1			$30,000	1/1
		8,000	2/12	3/23	5,000		
5/25	4,000			7/10	5,000		
		7,000	10/19	9/30	5,000		
12/10	2,000					18,000	12/5
		1,000	12/30	12/30	23,000		
		$30,000	12/31			$10,000	12/31

A *drawing* account is *not* used. The profit for 19X1 is $200,000.

Required   Divide the profit for the year between the partners using each of the following formulas:

1. *Beginning* capital balances.

2. *Average* capital balances. (Investments and withdrawals are assumed to have been made as of the beginning of the month if made *before* the middle of the month, and assumed to have been made as of the beginning of the following month if made *after* the middle of the month.)
3. *Ending* capital balances.
4. *Bonus* to Horn equal to 20% of profit in excess of $150,000; remaining profit divided equally.
5. *Salary allowances* of $45,000 and $35,000 to Horn and Sax, respectively; interest on average capital balances imputed at 10%; any residual balance divided equally. (Investments and withdrawals are treated as explained in item 2.)

P 28-2 **Dividing Profits: Revision of Profit-Sharing Agreement—Prior Period Adjustments**   The partnership agreement of Archer, Bowes, and Cross written in 19X5 specifies that profits and losses are determined on the *accrual basis* and are divided as follows:

	Archer	Bowes	Cross	Total
Salary allowances	$15,000	$15,000	$5,000	$35,000
Bonuses (percentage of profits in excess of $90,000)	20%	20%		
Residual profit or loss	40%	40%	20%	

On 1/1/X9, the partnership agreement was revised to provide for the sharing of profits and losses in the following manner:

	Archer	Bowes	Cross	Total
Salary allowances	$20,000	$20,000	$15,000	$55,000
Bonuses (percentage of profits in excess of $110,000)	20%	20%	10%	
Residual profit or loss	35%	35%	30%	

The partnership books show a profit of $145,000 for 19X9 before the following errors were discovered:

1. Inventory at 12/31/X7 was overstated by $7,000.
2. Inventory at 12/31/X8 was understated by $8,000.
3. Inventory at 12/31/X9 was understated by $18,000.
4. Depreciation expense for 19X9 was understated by $5,000.

Required
1. Divide the profit among the partners for 19X9, assuming that the partnership agreement calls for any prior years errors to be treated as *prior period adjustments*.
2. Assuming that the reported profits for 19X7 and 19X8 were $85,000 and $110,000, respectively, prepare the proper adjusting entry to correct the capital balances as of 1/1/X9. The old profit-sharing agreement is used for these items.

P 28-3 **Combining Two Partnerships: Recording the Initial Capital Contributions**   The partnerships of Altoe & Bass (A&B) and Sopra & Tennor (S&T) began business on 7/1/X1; each partnership owns one retail appliance store. The two partnerships agree to combine as of 7/1/X4, to form a new partnership, Four Partners Discount Stores.

Additional Information
1. **Profit and loss ratios.** The profit and loss sharing ratios for the *former* partnerships were 40% to Altoe and 60% to Bass, and 30% to Sopra and 70% to Tennor. The profit and loss sharing ratio for the *new* partnership is Altoe, 20%; Bass, 30%; Sopra, 15%; and Tennor, 35%.
2. **Capital investments.** The opening capital investments for the new partnership are to be in the same ratio as the profit and loss sharing ratios for the new partnership. If necessary, certain partners may have to contribute additional cash and others may have to withdraw cash to bring the capital investments into the proper ratio.
3. **Accounts receivable.** The partners agreed to set the new partnership's allowance for bad debts at 5% of the accounts receivable contributed by A&B and 10% of the accounts receivable contributed by S&T.
4. **Inventory.** The new partnership's opening inventory is to be valued by the FIFO method. A&B used the FIFO method to value inventory (which approximates its current value), and S&T used the LIFO method. The LIFO inventory represents 85% of its FIFO value.

5. **Property and equipment.** The partners agree that the land's current value is approximately 20% *more than* its historical cost, as recorded on each partnership's books.

 The depreciable assets of each partnership were acquired on 7/1/X1. A&B used *straight-line depreciation* and a 10-year life. S&T used *double-declining-balance depreciation* and a 10-year life. The partners agree that the current value of these assets is approximately 80% of their historical cost, as recorded on each partnership's books.

6. **Unrecorded liability.** After each partnership's books were closed on 6/30/X4, an unrecorded merchandise purchase of $4,000 by S&T was discovered. The merchandise had been sold by 6/30/X4.

7. **Accrued vacation.** The A&B accounts include a vacation pay accrual. The four partners agree that S&T should make a similar accrual for their five employees, who will receive a one-week vacation at $200 per employee per week.

The 6/30/X4 *postclosing* trial balances of the partnerships follow:

	Altoe & Bass Trial Balance—June 30, 19X4		Sopra and Tennor Trial Balance—June 30, 19X4	
Cash	$ 20,000		$ 15,000	
Accounts receivable	100,000		150,000	
Allowance for doubtful accounts		$ 2,000		$ 6,000
Merchandise inventory	175,000		119,000	
Land	25,000		35,000	
Buildings and equipment	80,000		125,000	
Accumulated depreciation		24,000		61,000
Prepaid expenses	5,000		7,000	
Accounts payable		40,000		60,000
Notes payable		70,000		75,000
Accrued expenses		30,000		45,000
Altoe, capital		95,000		
Bass, capital		144,000		
Sopra, capital				65,000
Tennor, capital				139,000
Totals	$405,000	$405,000	$451,000	$451,000

Required

1. Prepare the journal entries to record the initial capital contribution after considering the effect of this information. Use separate entries for each of the combining partnerships.

2. Prepare a schedule computing the cash contributed or withdrawn by each partner to bring the initial capital account balances into the profit and loss sharing ratio. (AICPA adapted)

P 28–4 **Combining Three Sole Proprietorships: Dividing the Profit for the First Year of Operations** Arby, Bobb, and Carlos, attorneys, agree to consolidate their individual practices as of 1/1/X3. The partnership agreement includes the following features:

1. Each partner's capital contribution is the net amount of the assets and liabilities assumed by the partnership, which are as follows:

	Arby	Bobb	Carlos
Cash	$ 5,000	$ 5,000	$ 5,000
Accounts receivable	14,000	6,000	16,000
Furniture and library	4,300	2,500	6,200
	$23,300	$13,500	$27,200
Allowance for depreciation	$ 2,400	$ 1,500	$ 4,700
Accounts Payable	300	1,400	700
	$ 2,700	$ 2,900	$ 5,400
Capital Contribution	$20,600	$10,600	$21,800

Each partner guaranteed the collectibility of receivables.

2. Carlos had leased office space and was bound by the lease until 6/30/X3; the monthly rental is $600. The partners agree to occupy Carlos's office space until the expiration of the lease and to pay the rent. The partners concur that the rent is too high for the space and that a fair rental value is $450 per month. The excess rent is charged to Carlos at year-end. On July 1, the partners move to new quarters with a $500 monthly rental.

3. No salaries are paid to the partners. The individual partners receive 20% of the *gross fees* billed to their respective clients during the first year of the partnership. After deducting operating expenses (including the excess rent), the balance of the fees is credited to the partners' capital accounts in the following ratios: Arby, 40%; Bobb, 35%; and Carlos, 25%.

    On 4/1/X3, Mack is admitted to the partnership, receiving 20% of the fees from new business obtained *after* April 1, after deducting expenses applicable to that new business. Expenses (including the excess rent) are apportioned to the new business in the same ratio that total expenses, other than bad debt losses, bear to total gross fees.

4. The following information pertains to the partnership's 19X3 activities:

    a. Fees are billed as follows:

Arby's clients	$ 44,000
Bobb's clients	24,000
Carlos's clients	22,000
New business:	
Prior to April 1	6,000
After April 1	24,000
Total	$120,000

    b. Total expenses, excluding depreciation and bad debt expenses, are $29,350, including the total amount paid for rent. Depreciation is computed at the rate of 10% on original cost. Depreciable assets purchased during 19X3, on which one-half year's depreciation is taken, total $5,000.

    c. Cash charges to the partners' accounts during the year are as follows:

Arby	$ 5,200
Bobb	4,400
Carlos	5,800
Mack	2,500
	$17,900

    d. Of Arby's and Bobb's receivables, $1,200 and $450, respectively, proved to be uncollectible. A new client billed in March for $1,600 went bankrupt, and a settlement of 50 cents on the dollar was made.

Required
1. Determine the profit for 19X3.
2. Prepare a schedule showing how the profit for 19X3 is to be divided.
3. Prepare a statement of the partners' capital accounts for the year ended 12/31/X3.

(AICPA adapted)

P 28–5* **Converting From Cash to Accrual Basis** The partnership of Arfee, Barker, and Chow engaged you to adjust its accounting records and convert them uniformly to the accrual basis in anticipation of admitting Pupp as a new partner. Some accounts are on the *accrual basis*, and others are on the *cash basis*. The partnership's books were closed at 12/31/X6 by the bookkeeper, who prepared the following trial balance:

Arfee, Barker, and Chow
Trial Balance 12/31/X6

	Debit	Credit
Cash	$ 10,000	
Accounts receivable	40,000	

(continued)

---

*The financial statement information presented for problems accompanied by asterisks is provided on Model 28 (filename: MODEL28) of the software disk that is available for use with the text, allowing the problem to be worked on the computer.

Inventory	$ 26,000	
Land	9,000	
Buildings	50,000	
Accumulated depreciation—Buildings		$ 2,000
Equipment	56,000	
Accumulated depreciation—Equipment		6,000
Goodwill	5,000	
Accounts payable		55,000
Allowance for future inventory losses		3,000
Arfee, capital		40,000
Barker, capital		60,000
Chow, capital		30,000
Totals	$196,000	$196,000

The partnership was organized on 1/1/X5, with no provision in the partnership agreement for the distribution of partnership profits and losses. During 19X5, profits were distributed equally among the partners. The partnership agreement was amended effective 1/1/X6, to provide for the following profit and loss ratio: Arfee, 50%; Barker, 30%; and Chow, 20%. The amended partnership agreement also stated that the accounting records should be maintained on the *accrual basis* and that any adjustments necessary for 19X5 should be allocated according to the 19X5 distribution of profits.

1. The following amounts were *not* recorded as prepayments or accruals:

	December 31	
	19X6	**19X5**
Prepaid insurance	$700	$ 650
Advances from customers	200	1,100
Accrued interest expense		450

Customers' advances were recorded as sales in the year the cash was received.

2. In 19X6, the partnership recorded a $3,000 provision for anticipated declines in inventory prices. You convinced the partners that the provision was unnecessary and should be removed from the books.
3. The partnership charged equipment purchased for $4,400 on 1/3/X6 to expense. This equipment has an estimated life of 10 years. The partnership depreciates its capitalized equipment under the *double-declining-balance method* at twice the straight-line depreciation rate.
4. The partners want to establish an allowance for doubtful accounts at 2% of current accounts receivable and 5% of past due accounts. At 12/31/X5, the partnership had $54,000 of accounts receivable, of which only $4,000 was past due. At 12/31/X6, 15% of accounts receivable were past due, of which $4,000 represented sales made in 19X5 that were generally considered collectible. The partnership had written off uncollectible accounts in the year the accounts became worthless, as follows:

	Accounts Written Off in	
	19X6	**19X5**
19X6 accounts	$ 800	
19X5 accounts	1,000	$250

5. Goodwill was recorded on the books in 19X6 and credited to the partners' capital accounts in the profit and loss ratio in recognition of an increase in the value of the business resulting from improved sales volume. The partners agreed to write off the goodwill *before* admitting the new partner.

Required Prepare a worksheet showing the adjustments and the adjusted trial balance for the partnership on the accrual basis at 12/31/X6. All adjustments affecting income should be made *directly* to partners' capital accounts. Number your adjusting entries. (Prepare formal journal entries and show supporting computations.)

(AICPA adapted)

P 28–6*   **Preparing Worksheets to Determine Current Trial Balance**   Pace & Runn is a partnership that has *not* maintained adequate accounting records because it has been unable to employ a competent book-keeper. The company sells hardware items to the retail trade and sells wholesale to builders and contractors. As Pace & Runn's CPA, you prepare the company's financial statements as of 6/30/X2.

The company's records provide the following postclosing trial balance at 12/31/X1:

Pace & Runn
Postclosing Trial Balance—12/31/X1

	Debit	Credit
Cash	$10,000	
Accounts receivable	8,000	
Allowance for bad debts		$ 600
Merchandise inventory	35,000	
Prepaid insurance	150	
Automobiles	7,800	
Accumulated depreciation—Automobiles		4,250
Furniture and fixtures	2,200	
Accumulated depreciation—Furniture and fixtures ..		650
Accounts payable		13,800
Bank loan payable (due 1/2/X2)		8,000
Accrued liabilities		200
Pace, capital		17,500
Runn, capital		18,150
Totals	$63,150	$63,150

You collect the following information at 6/30/X2:

1. Your analysis of cash transactions, derived from the company's bank statements and checkbook stubs, follows:

Deposits:		
Cash receipts from customers		$65,000
($40,000 of this amount represents collections on receivables including redeposited protested checks totaling $600)		
Bank loan, 1/2/X2 (due 5/1/X2, 5%)		7,867
Bank loan, 5/1/X2 (due 9/1/X2, 5%)		8,850
Sale of old automobile		20
Total Deposits		$81,737
Disbursements:		
Payments to merchandise creditors		$45,000
Payment to IRS on Runn's 19X2 declaration of estimated income taxes		3,000
General expenses		7,000
Bank loan, 1/2/X2		8,000
Bank loan, 5/2/X2		8,000
Payment for new automobile		7,200
Protested checks		900
Pace, withdrawals		5,000
Runn, withdrawals		2,500
Total Disbursements		$86,600

2. The protested checks include customers' checks totaling $600 that were redeposited and an employee's check for $300 that was redeposited.
3. At 6/30/X2, accounts receivable from customers for merchandise sales amount to $18,000 and include accounts totaling $800 placed with an attorney for collection. Correspondence with the client's attorney reveals that one of the accounts for $175 is uncollectible. Experience indicates that 1% of credit sales will prove uncollectible.

4. On 4/1/X2, a new automobile was purchased. Its list price was $7,500, and $300 was allowed for the trade-in of an old automobile, even though the dealer stated that its condition was so poor that he did not want it. The client sold the old automobile, which cost $1,800 and was fully depreciated at 12/31/X1, to an auto wrecker for $20. The old automobile was in use up to the date of its sale.

5. Depreciation is recorded by the *straight-line method* and is computed on acquisitions to the nearest full month. The estimated life for furniture and fixtures is 10 years and for automobiles is 3 years. (Salvage value is ignored in computing depreciation. No asset other than the car in item 4 was fully depreciated prior to 6/30/X2.)

6. Other data as of 6/30/X2 follow:

Merchandise inventory	$37,500
Prepaid insurance	80
Accrued expenses	166

7. Accounts payable to merchandise vendors total $18,750. A $750 credit memorandum was received from a merchandise vendor for returned merchandise; the company will apply the credit to July merchandise purchases. Neither the credit memorandum nor the return of the merchandise had been recorded on the books.

8. Profits and losses are divided *equally* between the partners.

Required   Prepare a worksheet that provides, on the *accrual basis*, information regarding transactions for the six months ended 6/30/X2, the results of the partnership operations for the period, and the financial position of the partnership at 6/30/X2. (Do *not* prepare formal financial statements or formal journal entries, but show supporting computations when necessary.)   (AICPA adapted)

✳ THINKING CRITICALLY ✳

✳ CASES ✳

C 28–1   **Planning for Settlement in the Event of a Partner's Death**   Cross and Penn are in the process of forming a partnership. Each partner desires to obtain control of the business in the event of the death of the other partner and to make settlement with the deceased partner's estate in an orderly manner with little conflict and minimal taxation.

Required   How might the partners accomplish these objectives?

C 28–2   **Preparing the Partnership Agreement**   Nichols and Dimer have formed a partnership. They personally prepared the partnership agreement to save legal costs, but they ask you to study the agreement for completeness when you record the initial capital contributions in the general ledger.

Required   How would you respond to this request?

C 28–3   **Dividing Profits and Losses**   Barr and Courtner, both lawyers, have decided to form a partnership. They have asked your advice on how the profits and losses should be divided and have provided you with the following information:

1. Initial capital contributions

Barr	$20,000
Courtner	80,000

2. Time devoted to the business

Barr	75%
Courtner	100%

3. Personal facts

Barr has an excellent reputation in the community. Substantially all new clients will come from her efforts.

Courtner is strong technically and is an excellent supervisor of staff lawyers who are expected to do most of the detailed legal research and initial preparation of legal documents.

Required   How would you advise the partners to share profits and losses?

C 28–4 **Recording the Initial Capital Contributions** Hye and Lowe have agreed to form a partnership in which profits are divided equally. Hye contributes $100,000 cash, and Lowe contributes a parcel of land, which the partnership intends to subdivide into residential lots on which to build custom homes for sale. Data regarding the parcel of land follow:

Cost of land to Lowe (acquired three years ago)	$100,000
Current market value, based on most recent county property tax assessment notice	120,000
Appraised value, based on recent appraisal by independent appraiser	150,000

Hye believes that the land should be recorded on the partnership books at $120,000. Lowe believes that the land should be recorded at $100,000 so that the *tax basis* to Lowe carries over to the partnership. Neither believes that the *current appraised value* is appropriate because an objective, verifiable transaction has not occurred. They have asked your advice on how to record the land.

Required 1. How would you respond?
2. Assuming that the land is sold two years later for $140,000 (the land having been *over*appraised by $10,000), would this change your answer in requirement 1?

C 28–5 **Selecting the Form of Business Organization** Sandy Seeker has invested $600,000 in a new business venture, in which two, possibly three, former business associates will join him. He has purchased the patent rights to a revolutionary adhesive substance known as "sticko." He is considering the various forms of business organization he might use in establishing the business. You have been engaged to study the accounting and business problems he should consider in choosing either a *general partnership* or a *corporation*. Seeker requests specific advice on the following aspects as they relate to one of these two forms of business organization.

1. Personal liability if the venture is a disaster.
2. The borrowing capacity of the entity.
3. Requirements for operating a multistate business.
4. The recognition of the entity for income tax–reporting purposes and major income tax considerations in selecting one of these forms of business organization.

Required Discuss the legal implications of each form of organization mentioned for each specific aspect on which Seeker requests advice.

ANSWERS TO SELF-STUDY QUESTIONS

1. b　　2. c　　3. a　　4. b　　5. d　　6. c

INCOME TAX ASPECTS

Other than dividing the profits and losses among the partners in accordance with the profit-sharing formula, accounting for the operations of a partnership presents no unusual problems. The income tax aspects of partnerships, however, are much more involved. An accountant providing services to a partnership must have a solid grasp of partnership tax concepts to serve his or her clients adequately. The following discussion will not make you an expert in partnership taxation; it provides only a basic understanding of partnership taxation.

I EQUITY VERSUS TAX BASIS

A partner's interest in a partnership is a *personal, capital asset* that can be sold, exchanged, assigned, or otherwise disposed of. From a financial accounting viewpoint, a partner's equity in the partnership is the balance in his or her capital account net of any balance in his or her drawing account. If a partner were to sell his or her interest in the partnership, the gain or loss from a partnership accounting viewpoint would be determined by comparing the *proceeds* to his or her *equity* at the time of sale. The gain or loss from an accounting viewpoint, however, is *not* important. The sale is a *personal transaction;* therefore, any gain or loss is *not* reflected in the partnership's general ledger. In this respect, it is similar to the sale of stock by a shareholder of a corporation—it does *not* enter into the operations of the business entity. From the selling partner's viewpoint, the relevant objective is to determine the amount of the *taxable* gain or loss.

CONTRIBUTING ASSETS The tax laws are *not* structured around a partner's equity as recorded in the partnership general ledger. Thus, to determine for tax purposes the amount of gain or loss on the sale of a partner's interest in a partnership, we must be familiar with the concept of tax basis. For tax purposes, a partner's interest in a partnership is referred to as that partner's **tax basis.** It is an *asset-related* concept; if a partner contributed $5,000 cash to a partnership, his or her tax basis in the partnership is $5,000. (Coincidentally, this is the amount credited to his or her capital account in the general ledger, but this fact is irrelevant from a tax standpoint.) If a partner contributes equipment to a partnership, that partner's tax basis in the partnership increases by the *adjusted tax basis* of the equipment *immediately before* the contribution or transfer. The adjusted tax basis of the equipment is the partner's *historical cost* less (1) any depreciation previously *allowed* (deducted) for income tax–reporting purposes or (2) any depreciation *allowable* for income tax–reporting purposes if no previous depreciation deduction had been taken. Thus, if equipment that cost the partner $10,000 had been depreciated $2,000 in the partner's business before the contribution or transfer, the *adjusted tax basis* is $8,000. Accordingly, the partner's tax basis in the partnership increases by $8,000.

If the equipment were completely paid for at the time of the contribution or transfer to the partnership, the amount credited to the partner's capital account in the general ledger depends on the *current value* assigned to the equipment and agreed to by the partners. This *current value* could be more or less than the $8,000 *adjusted tax basis.* Thus it would be only a coincidence that the credit to the partner's capital account increases by the amount of the *adjusted tax basis* at the time of the contribution or transfer.

NO STEP-UP OR STEP-DOWN IN TAX BASIS For tax purposes, any difference between the *current value* and the *adjusted tax basis* at the time of the contribution or transfer to the partnership is *not* recognized. In other words, no gain or loss must be reported. The *adjusted tax basis* of the asset (in the hands of the partner immediately before the contribution or transfer) is not stepped up or stepped down on transfer to the partnership. Accordingly, the *adjusted tax basis* of each asset contributed to a partnership merely carries over to the partnership for tax-reporting purposes. To the extent that future depreciation and amortization expenses are different for book (general ledger) reporting purposes than for tax-reporting purposes, the book income or loss must be adjusted (on a worksheet) to arrive at taxable income.

CONTRIBUTING LIABILITIES This concept of tax basis is slightly more involved if the contributed asset has a debt attached to it that the partnership assumed. Suppose that the equipment had a $3,000 installment note payable attached to it, for which the partnership assumed responsibility. The contributing partner's tax basis still increases by $8,000 (the amount of the adjusted tax basis of the asset at the time of the contribution or transfer). The fact that the partnership has assumed responsibility for payment of the debt, however, is significant from a tax viewpoint. The tax law says that the other partners (by becoming *jointly responsible* for the payment of this debt) in substance have given money to this partner. Accordingly, their tax bases should be *increased* and the tax basis of the partner who contributed the liability should be *decreased* by the amount of money deemed to have been given constructively to the partner. The profit and loss sharing ratio determines this deemed amount. For example, if a three-person partnership shared profits *equally*, the tax basis of the partner contributing the equipment and the related $3,000 liability would be *reduced* from $8,000 to $6,000 (two-thirds of $3,000) and the tax basis of each of the other partners would be *increased* by $1,000 (one-third of $3,000). This procedure is used although the creditor could seek personal recourse from the partner who contributes the liability to the partnership.

KEEPING TRACK OF EACH PARTNER'S BASIS Because a **partner's tax basis can-not be determined by using the amounts recorded *in* the general ledger capital accounts,** each partner must determine his or her own individual tax basis in the partnership on a memorandum tax basis *outside* the general ledger. In summary, each partner's tax basis can be determined when the partnership is formed by adding the first three of the following categories and subtracting the fourth category.

- Cash contributed to the partnership by a partner.
- *Add*—A partner's adjusted tax basis in any noncash property contributed or transferred to the partnership.
- *Add*—A partner's share of any liabilities assumed by the partnership that were contributed by other partners.
- *Subtract*—The other partners' share of any liabilities assumed by the partnership that the partner contributed to the partnership.

COMPREHENSIVE ILLUSTRATION To further demonstrate the application of these procedures for determining tax basis, we assume the same facts related to the formation of a partnership as in the example on page 1053. In addition, we assume that partners A and B share profits and losses in a 3:2 ratio, respectively. The *adjusted tax basis* of each partner follows:

	Adjusted Tax Basis		
	Partner A	**Partner B**	**Total**
Cash contributed	$23,000	$ 5,000	$28,000
Noncash assets contributed			
Marketable securities	7,000		7,000
Land		15,000	15,000
Building		25,000	25,000
	$30,000	$45,000	$75,000
Adjustments to **tax** basis for liabilities			
of $20,000 assumed by the partnership[a]	12,000	(12,000)	
Basis	$42,000	$33,000	$75,000

[a]The adjustment to each partner's tax basis is 60% of $20,000, because partner A assumes a 60% responsibility for the $20,000 liability contributed by partner B.

In reviewing this illustration, you should understand one major point. Partner A's $42,000 tax basis plus partner B's $33,000 tax basis equal the partnership's tax basis in the assets of $75,000 for tax-reporting purposes. This equality always exists. Note also that the sum of the tax bases of the assets immediately before the transfer ($30,000 for partner A's assets and $45,000 for partner B's assets) also equals the partnership's tax basis in the assets for tax-reporting purposes.

II SUBSEQUENT ADJUSTMENTS TO EACH PARTNER'S TAX BASIS

The personal tax basis of each partner's interest in the partnership is adjusted as subsequent partnership activity takes place. Such activities can be grouped as follows:

1. **Contributions and distributions (withdrawals).** If a partner subsequently *contributes* additional assets to the partnership, the tax basis of that partner's interest in the partnership *increases*. If the partner *withdraws* assets from the partnership, the tax basis of that partner's interest in the partnership *decreases*. (It can never be less than zero.)

2. **Profits and losses.** To the extent that *profits* exist, each partner's tax basis in the partnership *increases* by that partner's share of the partnership's taxable income. To the extent that there are *losses,* each partner's tax basis in the partnership *decreases* by that partner's share of the partnership's loss for tax-reporting purposes.

3. **Changes in partnership liabilities.** Tax laws effectively treat partnership liabilities as *personal liabilities* of the partners. For example, if a partnership borrowed $1,000 from a financial institution, its assets would increase by $1,000. The same result could be produced if one of the partners were personally to borrow the $1,000 from the financial institution and then make an additional capital contribution of $1,000. The form of each transaction is different, but the substance is the same.

Thus the partners treat an *increase* in a partnership's liabilities as an *additional capital contribution*. This increase is shared among the partners, and each partner's tax basis in the partnership increases.[1] A *decrease* in a partnership's liabilities is treated

[1]If one ratio exists for profits and a different one exists for losses, the IRS uses the loss ratio (unless the debt is nonrecourse debt in which case the IRS uses the profit ratio). The rationale for using the loss ratio for recourse debt is that if the partnership were unable to repay the debt, it would be because of operating losses.

as a *distribution of partnership assets* to its partners. This decrease also is shared among the partners, and each partner's tax basis in the partnership decreases.

In the example given in the preceding illustration, we showed a $12,000 adjustment to the tax bases of partners A and B as a result of partner B's contributing a $20,000 liability to the partnership. In a different approach to this adjustment, we assume that (1) instead of partner B's contributing the $20,000 liability to the partnership, the partnership borrowed $20,000 from a financial institution and (2) it then distributed that $20,000 to partner B, who paid off his personal loan of $20,000. The adjustments to the tax basis of each partner follow:

	Adjustments to Tax Basis	
	Partner A	**Partner B**
Borrowing of $20,000 by the partnership (60% to partner A and 40% to partner B)	$12,000	$ 8,000
Distribution of $20,000 to partner B		(20,000)
Net Change to Basis	$12,000	$(12,000)

Note that the net effect on each partner's tax basis is still $12,000.

The determination of a partner's tax basis in a partnership is relevant when a partner disposes of some or all of his or her partnership interest. This situation is discussed more fully in Chapter 29 on ownership changes.

III ⬛ NET OPERATING LOSS CARRYBACKS AND CARRYFORWARDS

Because partnerships are *not* taxable entities, they do *not* have net operating loss carrybacks or carryforwards. When a partner's share of a partnership's loss for a given year exceeds the excess of the partner's *nonbusiness income* over *nonbusiness deductions* (excluding personal exemptions as deductions), however, this net amount is a net operating loss that can be carried back three years and then forward seven years on the partner's individual tax return. The excess of *nonbusiness deductions* (excluding personal exemptions as deductions) over *nonbusiness income* does *not* increase the net operating loss because it is *not* business related.

⬛ ASSIGNMENT MATERIAL FOR APPENDIX A

REVIEW QUESTIONS

1. What is the purpose of keeping track of a partner's tax basis?
2. What does the term *adjusted tax basis* mean?
3. Is it possible to use a partner's capital account balance to determine that partner's tax basis? Why or why not?
4. How does each of the following items affect a partner's tax basis?
   a. Contributions
   b. Distributions
   c. Profits
   d. Losses
   e. Partnership borrowings
   f. Repayments of partnership debt
5. Why do partnership loans result in an *increase* in partners' tax bases?
6. Do partnerships have net operating loss carrybacks and carryforwards? Explain.
7. When a partner *contributes* into a partnership an *asset* that has a fair value *more than* the partner's cost of that asset, does the partnership get to step up the asset's tax basis? Does the partner report a gain for tax purposes on his or her individual tax return?
8. How are *liabilities contributed* into a partnership treated for tax purposes?

EXERCISES

E 28–1 A **Determination of Each Partner's Tax Basis**   Evers, Glade, and Marsh have formed a partnership by combining their respective sole proprietorships. The profit and loss sharing ratio is 4:3:3, respectively. The assets and liabilities contributed to the partnership follow:

	Adjusted Basis	Current Value
Evers		
Cash	$50,000	$50,000
Accounts receivable	20,000	20,000
Glade		
Land	30,000	40,000
Marsh		
Equipment	20,000[a]	25,000
Equipment note payable	10,000	10,000

[a]Original cost of $27,000 minus $7,000 of depreciation taken to date.

Required
1. Determine the tax basis of each partner's interest in the partnership.
2. What is the tax basis of each noncash asset in the hands of the partnership?
3. Prepare the *general ledger* entry to record these contributions.
4. Assume that Glade decided to quit the partnership one day after it was formed and received cash in full satisfaction of his capital account balance. What gain or loss, if any, should Glade report for tax purposes?

E 28–2A **Subsequent Changes in Each Partner's Tax Basis**   The tax basis of Reed, Storey, and Teller at the *beginning* of their partnership year was $50,000, $35,000, and $65,000, respectively. Profits and losses are shared equally.

Additional Information

Additional capital contributions	
Reed	$18,000
Storey	10,000
Teller	4,000
Withdrawals during the year	
Reed	6,000
Storey	12,000
Teller	5,000
Profits for the year	
From the general ledger	30,000
From the tax return	33,000

Required
1. Determine each partner's tax basis at *year-end*, assuming no change in partnership liabilities.
2. Determine each partner's tax basis at *year-end*, assuming that the only change in liabilities during the year was a $24,000 bank loan obtained at year-end. (The $24,000 borrowed, along with $6,000 cash on hand, was used to purchase equipment costing $30,000.)

■ APPENDIX B

THE UNIFORM PARTNERSHIP ACT: SELECTED SECTIONS

The Uniform Partnership Act has 45 sections separated into the following seven parts:

Part I	Preliminary provisions
Part II	Nature of partnerships
Part III	Relations of partners to persons dealing with the partnership
Part IV	Relations of partners to one another
Part V	Property rights of a partner
Part VI	Dissolution and winding up
Part VII	Miscellaneous provisions

The UPA is approximately 14 pages long and can be found in law library books that contain all of the various uniform acts. Because of its length, the UPA is not set forth here in its entirety. Two of the sections are presented here, however, to give you an idea of the UPA's content.

I PART III: RELATIONS OF PARTNERS TO PERSONS DEALING WITH THE PARTNERSHIP

Sec. 15. (Nature of Partner's Liability.)
All partners are liable:
a. Jointly and severally for everything chargeable to the partnership under sections 13 and 14.
b. Jointly for all other debts and obligations of the partnership; but any partner may enter into a separate obligation to perform a partnership contract.

II PART IV: RELATIONS OF PARTNERS TO ONE ANOTHER

Sec. 18. (Rules Determining Rights and Duties of Partners.)
The rights and duties of the partners in relation to the partnership shall be determined by the following rules:
a. Each partner shall be repaid his contributions, whether by way of capital or advances to the partnership property and share equally in the profits and surplus remaining after all liabilities, including those to partners, are satisfied; and must contribute toward the losses, whether of capital or otherwise, sustained by the partnership according to his share in the profits.
b. The partnership must indemnify every partner in respect of payments made and personal liabilities reasonably incurred by him in the ordinary and proper conduct of its business, or for the preservation of its business or property.
c. A partner, who in aid of the partnership makes any payment or advance beyond the amount of capital which he agreed to contribute, shall be paid interest from the date of the payment or advance.
d. A partner shall receive interest on the capital contributed by him only from the date when repayment should be made.
e. All partners have equal rights in the management and conduct of the partnership business.
f. No partner is entitled to remuneration for acting in the partnership business, except that a surviving partner is entitled to reasonable compensation for his services in winding up the partnership affairs.

g. No person can become a member of a partnership without the consent of all the partners.

h. Any difference arising as to ordinary matters connected with the partnership business may be decided by a majority of the partners; but no act in contravention of any agreement between the partners may be done rightfully without the consent of all the partners.

PARTNERSHIPS: CHANGES IN OWNERSHIP

29

Never tell people how to do things. Tell them what to do and they will surprise you with their ingenuity.

GENERAL GEORGE S. PATTON

A business conducted as a partnership usually has changes in ownership during its existence. In this chapter, we discuss the changes in ownership that do not result in the termination of the partnership's business activities. Such changes in ownership may be categorized as follows:

1. **An increase in the number of partners.**
   a. **Admission of a new partner.** More partners may be needed to serve clients properly, or additional capital may be required above and beyond existing partners' personal resources.
   b. **Business combinations.** Two partnerships may combine, resulting in a *pooling of interests*—that is, the partners of each individual partnership become partners in a larger, combined business.
2. **A decrease in the number of partners.**
   a. **Willful or forced withdrawal.** A partner may withdraw from a partnership to (1) engage in another line of work, (2) continue in the same line of work but as a sole proprietor, or (3) retire. In addition, a partner may be forced out of a partnership for economic reasons or for not having performed adequately the responsibilities entrusted to him or her.
   b. **Death or incapacity.** A partner may die or become so seriously ill that he or she cannot continue partnership duties.
3. **Purchase of an existing partnership interest.** A partner may decide to sell his or her partnership interest to someone outside the partnership.

The first two categories may generate issues of how to treat each partner equitably when (1) *tangible* assets have *current values* different from *book values* and (2) *intangible* elements exist. For simplicity, we discuss these issues separately. The third category consists entirely of personal transactions conducted outside the partnership. Because no partnership accounting issues are associated with this category, we discuss it only briefly at this point before discussing the first two categories.

PURCHASE (BUYOUT) OF AN EXISTING PARTNER'S INTEREST

The purchase of an interest from one or more of a partnership's existing partners is a *personal transaction* between the incoming partner and the selling partner(s). No additional money or properties are invested in the partnership. In this respect, the transaction is similar to individuals' sale of a corporation's stock. The only entry made on the partnership's books transfers an amount from the selling partner's capital account to the new partner's capital account. For example, assume the following information:

1. A and B are in partnership and share profits and losses equally.
2. A and B have capital account balances of $30,000 each.
3. C purchases B's partnership interest for $37,500, making payment *directly* to B.

The entry to record the transaction on the books of the partnership follows:

Capital, Partner B	. . . .	30,000
Capital, Partner C	. . . .	30,000

The purchase price paid by C is completely irrelevant to the entry recorded on the books, regardless of why C paid more than the book value of the partnership interest. The fact that the partnership may have undervalued tangible assets or possible superior earnings power is *not* relevant to the accounting issues. A *personal transaction* has occurred, which is independent of accounting for the business of the partnership.

Alternatively, C could purchase a portion of each existing partner's interest in the partnership. For example, assume that C purchased one-third of A's interest for $12,500 and one-third of B's interest for $12,500, making payments *directly* to A and B. The entry to record the transaction on the books follows:

Capital, Partner A	10,000	
Capital, Partner B	10,000	
Capital, Partner C		20,000

Again, the purchase of an existing partnership interest is a personal transaction between the old and the new partners.

AN *INCREASE* OR *DECREASE* IN THE NUMBER OF PARTNERS: METHODS TO PREVENT INEQUITIES

The number of partners in a partnership may *increase* or *decrease* without the purchase of an existing partner's interest. Recall that in Chapter 28 we stated that to prevent partners from being treated inequitably as a result of revisions to the profit and loss sharing formula, either the partnership assets should be revalued to their current values or the new profit and loss sharing formula should include a special provision whereby the old profit and loss sharing formula is used in specified instances. Because a change in ownership of a partnership produces a new profit and loss sharing formula, the same techniques to prevent inequities may be applied to situations of changes in ownership. In addition, we introduce a new method—the **bonus method**—that also may be used to prevent inequities.

The determination of the journal entry to reflect a change in the ownership of a partnership is to some extent an after-the-fact mechanical process using the terms and methods selected by the partners. A far more important role for the accountant when a change in ownership is contemplated involves explaining and illustrating the various methods (and their ramifications) of dealing with situations in which assets have current values different from book values and/or intangible elements exist. The accountant may even assist partners in determining the amount of any goodwill by demonstrating some of the common methods used to calculate goodwill. Remember that in these situations, the accountant is only an adviser. It is not his or her role to select a method to determine the amount of goodwill or to select one of the three methods available for achieving equity among the partners.

⬛ I　*TANGIBLE* ASSETS HAVING CURRENT VALUES DIFFERENT FROM BOOK VALUES

ADMISSION OF A NEW PARTNER

In most cases, a partner is admitted into a partnership by making a capital contribution to it. In accountant and attorney partnerships, virtually all partners admitted make substantial contributions after spending years in lower levels of the business obtaining the necessary training and experience. A capital contribution creates a new partner's interest. In substance, this is similar to a corporation's issue of additional shares of its stock to new stockholders.

One of the three methods available to prevent an inequity must be applied when a new partner is admitted. Each method, although different procedurally, produces the same result. To illustrate how each method is applied to a situation in which a new partner is admitted into a partnership by making a capital contribution, assume the following facts:

1. The partnership of A and B desires to admit C.
2. A's capital account is $25,000, as is B's.
3. Profits and losses are shared *equally* between A and B. On admission of C, profits and losses are **shared equally** among the three partners.
4. All partnership assets have carrying values equal to their current values, except for a parcel of land worth $12,000 *more than* its book value of $100,000.
5. Because the current value of the existing partners' equity is $62,000 ($25,000 + $25,000 + $12,000), A and B agree to admit C into the partnership on contribution of $31,000 cash.

The credit to the *new* partner's capital account regarding the $31,000 capital contribution is determined only *after* the partners agree on one of the following three methods.

REVALUING OF ASSETS METHOD   Under the **revaluing of assets method,** the parcel of land merely is written up to its *current value* using the following entry:

Land	12,000	
Capital, Partner A		6,000
Capital, Partner B		6,000

Because the *old* partners shared profits and losses *equally* until C was admitted, each of their capital accounts increases by 50% of the upward revaluation. The entry to record C's contribution follows:

Cash	31,000	
Capital, Partner C		31,000

The revaluing of assets method is the simplest of the three methods. Although it is *not* in accordance with GAAP, this disadvantage is usually not important to the partnership form of business. If the partners agree to this method, the new partnership agreement should specify that the new partner is to receive a one-third interest in the new net assets of the partnership **after the land has been written up by $12,000,** thus receiving a full credit to her capital account for the $31,000 capital contribution ($62,000 + $31,000 = $93,000; $93,000 × ⅓ = $31,000).

SPECIAL PROFIT AND LOSS SHARING PROVISION METHOD   Under the **special profit and loss sharing provision** approach, the land is carried at its *historical cost*. The new profit and loss sharing formula contains a provision, however, that (1) acknowledges that the land's *current value* is $12,000 in excess of its book value at the time of C's admission and (2) specifies that the *old* partners are entitled to share equally in the first $12,000 profit on the sale of the land. Assuming that the land is sold for a $15,000 profit several years after C's admission to the partnership, the profit on the sale is divided as follows:

	Total	Partner A	Partner B	Partner C
First $12,000	$12,000	$6,000	$6,000	
Excess over $12,000	3,000	1,000	1,000	$1,000
	$15,000	$7,000	$7,000	$1,000

The entry to record C's contribution is the same as shown for the preceding method. If the partners agree to this method, the new partnership agreement should state that the *new* partner is to receive a full credit to her capital account for the $31,000 capital contribution, **with no revaluation made to the assets of the partnership.**

THE BONUS METHOD Under the **bonus method,** no adjustment is made to the carrying amount of the land, nor is any special provision included in the new profit and loss sharing formula because the land is worth *more than* its book value. When the land is subsequently sold, C will receive one-third of the *entire* profit. From an equity viewpoint, C is *not* entitled to one-third of the first $12,000 profit; therefore, C's capital account is *reduced* at her admission by the amount that will be credited to her capital account in the event the land is sold for $12,000 in excess of its current book value. Thus one-third of $12,000, or $4,000, of C's $31,000 initial capital contribution is *not* credited to her capital account. Instead, the $4,000 is credited to the *old* partners' capital accounts. The $4,000 is shared by partners A and B in the *old* profit and loss sharing ratio. The entry to record C's admission into the partnership is as follows:

Cash	31,000	
Capital, Partner A		2,000
Capital, Partner B		2,000
Capital, Partner C		27,000

Note that the total partnership capital is now $81,000 ($50,000 + $31,000) and that the $27,000 amount is one-third of $81,000.

Assuming that the land is sold for a $15,000 profit several years *after* C's admission to the partnership, the profit on the sale is divided as follows:

	Total	Partner A	Partner B	Partner C
Total Profit	$15,000	$5,000	$5,000	$5,000

In this situation, C initially gives up part of her capital contribution, only to recover the amount given up at a later date. The *old* partners initially receive a bonus, but on the subsequent sale of the land, they are *not* allocated all of the first $12,000 profit. In this sense, *bonus* is a misnomer because it is *not* permanent. If the partners agree to the bonus method, the new partnership agreement should state that the *new* partner is to receive a one-third interest in the *new* assets of the partnership of $81,000 ($50,000 + $31,000), **with *no* revaluation to be made to the partnership assets.**

REVIEW POINTS REGARDING THE THREE METHODS Note the following:

1. If the land subsequently is sold for $112,000 ($12,000 *more than* its $100,000 book value immediately *before* C was admitted into the partnership), the individual capital account balances are identical under each method. Thus each method ensures that partners A and B share equally in the first $12,000 of profit on the sale of the land. Furthermore, each method ensures that partners A, B, and C share equally on any profit on the sale of the land *in excess* of $12,000.

2. The method chosen depends on the partners' personal whims. Often an incoming partner desires to have the full amount of his or her capital contribution credited to his or her capital account, if only for psychological reasons. The *new* partnership agreement should specify the method agreed upon by the partners.

3. If the *new* profit and loss sharing formula includes a feature providing for imputed interest on capital investments, the second method results in an inequity to the *old* partners because their individual capital accounts are less than that of the *new* partner.

4. The key to achieve the same result with each method is the assumption that the partnership assets actually are worth the agreed-upon amounts. If they are not, these methods do not always prevent inequities from occurring. We discuss this situation more fully next.

WHAT IF AGREED-UPON CURRENT VALUES ARE ERRONEOUS? Because the determination of the current value of assets is so subjective, the possibility exists that the land is *not* really worth $12,000 *more than* its book value. What if shortly after C's admission into the partnership, the land is sold for only $9,000 *more than* its book value immediately *before* C was admitted? Does each method still treat each partner equitably? The answer is no. Partner C is *not* treated equitably under the **revaluation of assets method** because she is allocated one-third of the book loss of $3,000; she effectively loses $1,000 of her initial $31,000 capital contribution. Partner C is *not* treated equitably under the **bonus method** because she does *not* recoup all of the $4,000 bonus she initially gave to the *old* partners. She recoups only $3,000 (one-third of the $9,000 book profit) and, therefore, loses $1,000 of her initial $31,000 capital contribution. Under the **special provision in the new profit and loss sharing method,** however, C *cannot* lose any of her initial capital contribution; she is best protected under this method.

The land may actually have a current value $12,000 *more than* its book value *immediately before* C is admitted into the partnership but subsequently declines in value *afterward*. The same question must be asked: Does each method treat each partner equitably? Under the special provision in the *new* profit and loss sharing formula, partners A and B are treated inequitably because they share the *entire loss* of value that occurred *after* C's admission. From an equity standpoint, C should share in this loss of value, which she does only under the revaluation of assets method and the bonus method.

Obviously, each partner strives to select the method that best protects his or her personal interest. Often there is a conflict between an incoming partner and the old partners concerning which method to use. The ultimate resolution takes place through negotiation. In large partnerships—such as the national accounting firms—differences between current values and book values usually are ignored for the sake of simplicity. Of course, such partnerships usually do *not* have significant amounts of land and depreciable assets, which are most likely to have current values different from book values.

BUSINESS COMBINATIONS

Historically, business combinations are considered to occur only between corporations. A large number of business combinations involve partnerships, however, especially public accounting partnerships. Business combinations in the public accounting sector range from a two-person partnership combining with a sole proprietorship to a large international firm combining with another large international firm (as occurred in 1989 when Arthur Young & Company, the sixth largest accounting firm, combined with Ernst & Whinney, the third largest accounting firm, to form Ernst & Young, the largest accounting firm). Although *APB Opinion No. 16,* "Accounting for Business Combinations," was intended primarily for combinations among corporations, paragraph 5 of that pronouncement states that "its provisions should be applied as a general guide" when two or more unincorporated businesses combine.[1] Accordingly, business combinations among unincorporated accounting entities may be classified as either purchases or pooling of interests. Whether the substance of a combination is one or the other depends on whether the owners of the combining businesses continue as owners in the new, enlarged business.

If the owners of one business do *not* continue as owners of the enlarged business, a *purchase* has occurred. Purchases do *not* increase the number of partners. Thus no change in ownership of the acquiring partnership occurs, and such transactions do not concern us here. The acquiring firm merely applies the provisions of

---

[1] *Accounting Principles Board Opinion No. 16,* "Accounting for Business Combinations" (New York: American Institute of Certified Public Accountants, 1970), par. 5.

APBO No. 16 with respect to the assets acquired. The assets of the acquiring business are *not* revalued to their current values.

If the owners of both businesses continue as owners of the enlarged business, a *pooling of interests* has occurred. Pooling of interests results in an *increase* in the number of partners; thus the issues associated with changes in ownership exist. If the assets of either or both of the combining firms have current values different from their book values, one of the methods to prevent inequities from occurring must be used (revaluing the assets, using a special provision in the new profit and loss sharing formula, or the bonus method). A strict application of the pooling of interests procedures does *not* permit the revaluing of assets of either combining firm. If the partners revalue the assets, however, they may do so and depart from GAAP. These three methods are procedurally the same as when a new partner is admitted, other than through a business combination.

A unique aspect of business combinations is that both entities can have (1) under- or overvalued assets and (2) goodwill. Under the bonus method, this situation requires that these sequential steps be followed so that the proper set of partners receives the proper bonus:

1. For each partnership, calculate the bonus that the partnership would receive or give, assuming that the other partnership had no under- or overvalued assets or goodwill.
2. If both partnerships are to *receive* or *give* bonuses, use the *difference* between the two bonus amounts in step 1 to adjust for the bonuses. Thus the bonus that one set of partners is to receive (or give) is more than offset by the bonus to be received (or given) by the other set of partners, who receive (or give) a net bonus amount in total.
3. If one partnership is to *receive* a bonus and the other partnership is to *give* a bonus, use the *sum* of the two bonus amounts in step 1 to adjust for the bonuses.

Remember that the objective is to prevent partners from *not* sharing in what they are *not* entitled to share.

DECREASE IN NUMBER OF PARTNERS

If a partnership's assets have current values different from their book values when a partner withdraws from the partnership, the partners are *not* treated equitably unless this difference in value is considered in settling with the withdrawing partner or his estate. In these situations, all methods of preventing an inequity are available. To illustrate how each method is applied in such a situation, we assume the following facts:

1. A, B, and C are in partnership.
2. The capital account of each partner is $25,000.
3. Carrying values of the partnership's tangible assets equal their current values, except for a parcel of land worth $12,000 *more than* its book value.
4. Profits and losses are shared *equally.*
5. C decides to withdraw from the partnership.

REVALUING OF ASSETS METHOD   Under the revaluing of assets method, the land is merely written up to its current value using the following entry:

Land	12,000	
Capital, Partner A		4,000
Capital, Partner B		4,000
Capital, Partner C		4,000

Each partner's capital account is increased by one-third of the upward revaluation because the partners shared profits and losses equally until C decided to withdraw from the partnership. The entry to record C's withdrawal from the partnership is as follows:

```
Capital, Partner C  . . . . . . . . . . . . . . . . . . . . . . . . . . . . . . . . . . . .    29,000
        Payable to Partner C  . . . . . . . . . . . . . . . . . . . . . . . . . . . . .              29,000
```

As indicated previously, this is the simplest of the three methods. The fact that it departs from GAAP may be of little concern to a partnership.

SPECIAL PROFIT AND LOSS SHARING PROVISION METHOD   Under the special profit and loss sharing provision approach, the land is carried at its historical cost. The *new* profit and loss sharing formula contains a provision, however (1) acknowledging that the land's estimated current value is $12,000 in excess of its current book value and (2) specifying that the withdrawing partner is entitled to one-third of the first $12,000 profit on the sale of the land. The entry to record C's withdrawal from the partnership follows:

```
Capital, Partner C  . . . . . . . . . . . . . . . . . . . . . . . . . . . . . . . . . . . .    25,000
        Payable to Partner C  . . . . . . . . . . . . . . . . . . . . . . . . . . . . .              25,000
```

Effectively, a contingent liability exists with respect to the amount to be paid to C upon sale of the land. This method has limited application in situations involving withdrawing partners. If different appraisals of current value of partnership assets exist, this method may be a practical alternative to the other two methods, especially if such assets are expected to be sold within a relatively short period of time. Normally, however, this method is impractical because a withdrawing partner does *not* want to wait until such assets are disposed of to obtain his or her final settlement from the partnership.

THE BONUS METHOD   Under the bonus method, no adjustment is made to the carrying amount of the land, nor is any special provision included in the *new* profit and loss sharing formula because the land is worth more than its book value. Consequently, when the land is later sold, A and B share *all* the profit. From an equity viewpoint, A and B are *not* entitled to one-third of the first $12,000 profit; therefore, their capital accounts are reduced at C's withdrawal by the amount that represents C's share of the $12,000 of unrealized profit. Thus one-third of $12,000, or $4,000, is charged to the capital accounts of A and B in their respective profit and loss sharing ratio. A and B will recoup this bonus to C later if the land is sold for $12,000 in excess of its current book value. The entry to record the bonus and C's withdrawal from the partnership follows:

```
Capital, Partner A  . . . . . . . . . . . . . . . . . . . . . . . . . . . . . . . . . . . .    2,000
Capital, Partner B  . . . . . . . . . . . . . . . . . . . . . . . . . . . . . . . . . . . .    2,000
        Capital, Partner C  . . . . . . . . . . . . . . . . . . . . . . . . . . . . . . .              4,000
   To record the bonus to the *withdrawing* partner.

Capital, Partner C  . . . . . . . . . . . . . . . . . . . . . . . . . . . . . . . . . . . .    29,000
        Payable to Partner C  . . . . . . . . . . . . . . . . . . . . . . . . . . . . .              29,000
   To record the withdrawal of Partner C.
```

In this situation, A and B gave up part of their capital account balances, expecting to recover the amounts given up at a later date. Thus the bonus is *not* permanent because it will be recovered later.

REVIEW POINTS REGARDING THE THREE METHODS   Note the following:

1. If the land is later sold for $112,000 ($12,000 *more than* its $100,000 book value immediately before C withdrew from the partnership), the settlement to C is the same under each method. Also, the capital account balances of A and B are identical under each method. Thus each method ensures that the withdrawing partner receive one-third of the first $12,000 profit on the sale of the land. Furthermore, each method ensures that C not share in any of the profit on the sale of the land in excess of $12,000.

2. The real problem is obtaining a reasonable assurance of the current value of partnership assets. If the agreed-upon values are *overstated,* the revaluing the asset method and the bonus method result in an excess settlement to the withdrawing partner. Under the special profit and loss sharing provision method, however, no such excess payment is possible; thus A and B are best protected under this method. If the agreed-upon values are *understated,* one method protects the withdrawing partner. The remaining partners share the entire increase above the agreed-upon value.

3. If the land declined in value *after* C withdrew, C is *not* treated equitably under the special profit and loss sharing provision method because she is sharing in a loss that occurred *after* she withdrew.

In all of the preceding examples, the partnership's tangible assets were undervalued. When tangible assets have current values less than their book values, the first method—which writes down the assets—makes the most sense. (This procedure is in accordance with GAAP.) The second choice is the bonus method. The use of the special profit and loss sharing provision method is usually impractical.

II INTANGIBLE ELEMENT EXISTS: RECORDING METHODS AND ALTERNATIVE APPROACHES

We restricted our discussion in the preceding section to situations in which the current values of a partnership's tangible assets differ from their book values. In this section, we discuss situations in which either the existing partnership or an incoming partner possesses an intangible element. In discussing these situations, we assume that all partnership tangible assets have current values equal to their book values. Although this assumption is not necessarily realistic, it allows us to concentrate on the issue of accounting for this intangible element.

The discussion of intangible elements usually has wider application than the earlier discussion of tangible assets because most partnerships—other than those engaged in real estate development—do not have substantial investments in the types of assets that appreciate or depreciate, such as inventory, land, buildings, and equipment. The largest asset for such partnerships is usually accounts receivable.

Intangible elements are usually associated with an *existing* partnership. The most common intangible element is a partnership's *superior earnings.* Obviously, a partner's interest in such a partnership is worth *more than* its book value. Even when a partnership has only average earnings, a partner's interest may be worth *more than* its book value to an incoming partner merely because the organization already has clients and the potential to develop superior earnings.

An *incoming* partner may also possess intangible elements. For example, the incoming partner may have a successful sole proprietorship with superior earnings power. He or she may have individual potential for which the existing partners are willing to pay. This is similar to situations in which corporations pay one-time bonuses to executives to induce them to accept a position and in professional sports when a rookie may receive a one-time bonus just for signing with a particular team.

In these situations, whether the existing partnership or an incoming partner possesses the intangible element, the intangible element is referred to as *goodwill.* The accounting issue is to how to compensate the partner or partners who created or possess the goodwill. If there is no compensation, the other partner or partners share unfairly in a portion of the partnership's future earnings.

RECORDING METHODS

The general approach to compensating the appropriate partners parallels that for situations in which tangible assets have current values different from book values—that is, we may apply the same three methods that we discussed and illustrated in the preceding section of the chapter. The first method is called *recording the goodwill* however, rather than *revaluing assets*. Other than this descriptive change, the three methods are procedurally the same.

The larger the partnership, the less likely are the partners to compute the value of goodwill. For example, in the interest of simplicity, most national public accounting firms completely ignore goodwill for all changes in ownership situations. Instead, a simpler approach is for an *incoming* partner to accept a lower-than-normal profit and loss sharing percentage; that percentage increases on a sliding scale over a period of years until the *incoming* partner eventually shares profits and losses equally with other partners. Such an approach has the same overall effect as the three mechanical methods of dealing with goodwill, although the exact effect on each partner is different.

ASSUMED EQUALITY OF PROFIT-SHARING PERCENTAGE AND INTEREST IN PARTNERSHIP NET ASSETS

In examples used later involving the admission of a partner when goodwill exists, we assume that the incoming partner's agreed-upon profit and loss sharing percentage equals his or her agreed-upon ownership interest in the partnership's net assets. In practice, this is common.[2]

ALTERNATIVE APPROACHES FOR ILLUSTRATING GOODWILL SITUATIONS

Apart from the three methods (recording the goodwill method, the bonus method, and the special profit and loss sharing method), two pedagogical approaches can be used to discuss and illustrate these methods. The difference between the two pedagogical approaches is the information furnished:

The Working-Forward Approach. The negotiated value of goodwill **is** given.

The Working-in-Reverse Approach. The negotiated value of goodwill **is not** given.

Understanding both of these approaches enables you to understand this material both forward and backward because that is the conceptual difference between the two approaches. In each of the later examples dealing with goodwill, we present both approaches. Before presenting these examples, however, we briefly discuss these approaches in general.

THE WORKING-FORWARD APPROACH: THE VALUE OF GOODWILL IS GIVEN

When a partner is admitted into a partnership, the normal process among the parties involves negotiating the following four items (the sequence of which may vary):

---

[2]If these percentages do not coincide, the partners are financially impacted differently (in comparison to when the percentages are the same) only if the agreed-upon value of goodwill does not materialize. Situations in which these percentages are different have not been tested on past CPA examinations to any significant extent.

1. The value of the existing goodwill is agreed upon between the *old* partners and the *new* partner.
2. The capital contribution of the *incoming* partner is agreed upon.
3. The profit or loss ratio is agreed upon.
4. One of the available accounting methods designed to compensate the partner who created or possesses the goodwill is selected.

Once these items are agreed upon, each partner's capital account balance may be adjusted or recorded using the accounting method selected. After determining each partner's capital account balance, we may express each partner's interest as a percentage of the partnership's net assets (as defined to either include or exclude goodwill). Thus each partner's ownership percentage in the partnership's net assets is a *derived* amount—not the value of the goodwill agreed upon during negotiations.

THE WORKING-IN-REVERSE APPROACH: THE VALUE OF GOODWILL IS NOT GIVEN Under this approach, the following information is furnished:

1. The total of the capital balances of the *old* partners.
2. The capital contributed by the *new* partner.
3. The percentage interest the *new* partner receives in the partnership's net assets (the *old* partners have the remaining interest).
4. Whether the net assets in that percentage interest include or exclude the value of the goodwill.

Given all this information, one then determines (as though trying to solve a puzzle) which method the partners used to compensate the partner or partners who created or possess the goodwill. Under the valuing of the goodwill method, the value of the goodwill may then be determined and recorded on the books of the partnership. Under the bonus method, the amount of the bonus given to the *old* partners or their *new* partner may then be determined and recorded on the partnership's books. Thus one works in reverse—**from the given ownership percentages**—to find the value of the goodwill.[3] This approach can be reduced to a step-by-step process, as shown in Illustration 29–1.

III *INTANGIBLE* ELEMENT EXISTS: SPECIFIC SITUATIONS

In each of the following examples involving goodwill, we first show the working-forward approach and then the working-in-reverse approach.

ADMISSION OF A NEW PARTNER: *EXISTING* PARTNERSHIP POSSESSES GOODWILL

In the first illustration, the partnership possesses the goodwill. To illustrate the application of the three methods to compensate the *old* partners for the goodwill they have created, we assume the following information:

1. A and B are in partnership, **sharing profits equally.**
2. C is to be admitted into the partnership.

---

[3]An understanding of this approach is required for taking the CPA examination because most CPA examination questions regarding ownership changes can be answered using only this approach.

| **ILLUSTRATION 29–1** | **The Working-in-Reverse Approach: Step-by-Step Process** |

I. Calculating the *Negotiated* Value of Goodwill

1. Divide the *new* partner's tangible capital contribution by his or her ownership percentage in the net assets of the partnership (for example, $35,000 ÷ 20% = $175,000).
2. Divide the total recorded capital balances of the *old* partners by their total **ownership interest in the net assets** of the partnership (for example, $120,000 ÷ 80% = $150,000).
3. Add the numerators used in steps 1 and 2 ($35,000 + $120,000 = $155,000) to arrive at the total recorded net assets of the *new* partnership excluding goodwill.
4. Select the larger of the amounts calculated in steps 1 and 2 ($175,000). From this amount, subtract the total calculated in step 3 ($155,000) to obtain the *negotiated* value of goodwill ($20,000).
5. If the amount calculated in step 1 is selected, the *old* partners possess goodwill; if the amount calculated in step 2 is selected, the *new* partner possesses goodwill.

II. Calculating the Bonus (for the bonus method)

A. **Using the negotiated value of the goodwill** (calculated above):
   Multiply the goodwill amount calculated in step 4 by the **profit and loss sharing percentage(s)** of the partner(s) **not** possessing goodwill (for example, $20,000 × 20% = $4,000).
B. **Using the ownership percentage of tangible net assets** (must be given—implicit amount of goodwill is not given):
   1. Multiply the sum of the numerators in step 3 by the ownership percentage the *new* partner has in the net assets (for example, $155,000 × 20% = $31,000). (The 20% is a given.)
   2. Compare the amount calculated in step B1 ($31,000) to the *new* partner's *tangible* capital contribution (the same amount used in step 1 [35,000]) to determine the bonus to be given by the *incoming* partner ($4,000 in this example) or received.

   Note: If desired, the implicit amount of goodwill can then be calculated from the bonus amount and the profit and loss sharing percentages.

---

3. A, B, and C agreed that the existing partnership will generate superior earnings of $10,000 for one year *after* C's admission.

4. C contributes $30,000 cash to the partnership.

5. Profits and losses are to be shared among A, B, and C in a ratio of 4:3:3, respectively. (Thus the *old* partners are to receive 70% of the profits and losses and the *new* partner is to receive 30%.)

6. A and B have capital account balances of $45,000 and $15,000, respectively (for a total of $60,000), *immediately before* admitting C.

RECORDING THE GOODWILL METHOD Under the **recording the goodwill method,** C's admission into the partnership results in recording the entire amount of the agreed-upon goodwill in the partnership's books, as follows:

Goodwill	10,000	
Capital, Partner A		5,000
Capital, Partner B		5,000
To record the agreed-upon value of the goodwill, shared equally between the *old* partners using their *old* profit and loss sharing ratio.		

The entry to record C's $30,000 capital contribution follows:

```
Cash  .............................................  30,000
      Capital, Partner C  ...............................        30,000
   To record C's capital contribution.
```

The following points are important for understanding the preceding entries:

1. C has a 30% interest in the net assets of the partnership ($30,000 ÷ $100,000 total of the capital accounts).

2. Recording goodwill in this manner is not in accordance with GAAP because the goodwill did not result from the purchase of a business.

3. The goodwill will be amortized over a one-year period because the partnership is expected to produce superior earnings only for one year.

4. Because of the goodwill amortization in the year after C's admission, earnings will be $10,000 lower than if goodwill had not been recorded on the books.

5. Effectively, $10,000 of future profits has been capitalized into the *old* partners' capital accounts. In this respect, the partners have guaranteed that they alone will receive the first $10,000 of future earnings (determined without regard to the goodwill amortization expense).

6. If $10,000 of superior earnings results in the following year, such superior earnings completely absorb the $10,000 goodwill amortization.

7. If the superior earnings in the following year are less than $10,000, C effectively loses a portion of her initial capital contribution of $30,000. This happens because the partnership's normal earnings must absorb a portion of the goodwill amortization, and C *cannot* share in a portion of the normal earnings.

To illustrate how this method may favor the *old* partners over the *new* partner if the entire amount of the superior earnings does *not* materialize, assume that during the year *after* C's admission, only $8,000 of superior earnings materialize. These superior earnings absorb only $8,000 of goodwill amortization. The remaining $2,000 of goodwill amortization is absorbed by normal earnings. Thus, C does not share in $2,000 of normal earnings. Because C's profit and loss sharing percentage is 30%, she effectively loses $600 (30%, or $2,000) of her $30,000 initial capital contribution.

SPECIAL PROFIT AND LOSS SHARING PROVISION METHOD   Under the special profit and loss sharing provision method, no entry is made on the partnership's books with respect to the goodwill. As under the previous method, C's capital account is credited with the full amount of her $30,000 capital contribution. It can be stated that C has a one-third interest in the partnership's net assets ($30,000 ÷ $90,000 total of the capital accounts). The *new* profit and loss sharing formula stipulates that the *old* partners are entitled to share (in accordance with their *old* profit and loss sharing ratio) in the first $10,000 of earnings in excess of a specified amount, which is the expected normal earnings for the year of C's admission into the partnership.

If the superior earnings of $10,000 do *not* materialize during this year, the *old* partners will have credited to their capital accounts only those amounts that *do* materialize. Of course, the normal earnings and any earnings above the $10,000 of superior earnings during the next year are shared in accordance with the *new* profit and loss sharing ratio. This method protects the *new* partner's initial capital contribution of $30,000 in the event that superior earnings of $10,000 do *not* materialize. Obviously, the *old* partners would prefer the previous method, under which they are assured of the first $10,000 of earnings, regardless of whether such earnings are superior.

THE BONUS METHOD   Under the bonus method, no entry is made on the partnership books with respect to goodwill. Unlike the previous two methods, C does not receive full credit to her capital account for her $30,000 capital contribution because she must give a bonus to the old partners. The amount of the bonus to the old partners is C's profit and loss sharing percentage of 30% times the agreed-upon value of the $10,000 goodwill. Thus the bonus to the old partners is $3,000, which they share in their old profit and loss sharing ratio as follows:

Cash	. . . .	30,000
Capital, Partner A	. . . .	1,500
Capital, Partner B	. . . .	1,500
Capital, Partner C	. . . .	27,000
To record C's capital contribution and to record the *bonus* to the *old* partners.		

The following points are important to understand this entry:

1. C has a 30% interest in the partnership's net assets ($27,000 ÷ $90,000 total of the capital accounts).
2. GAAP is followed by not recording goodwill on the books.
3. If superior earnings of $10,000 materialize in the year following C's admission, C shares in them ($3,000, or 30% of $10,000). Consequently, she recoups the bonus she initially gave the *old* partners.
4. The bonus method compensates the *old* partners currently for the portion of the superior earnings that will later be credited to the *new* partner's capital account. Thus if all the superior earnings materialize, the bonus is temporary.
5. If the superior earnings in the year following C's admission are *less than* $10,000, C effectively loses a portion of her initial $30,000 capital contribution. This happens because she does *not* share in the amount of superior earnings she expected to materialize and for which she was willing to give a bonus to the *old* partners.

To illustrate how the bonus method may favor the *old* partners over the *new* partner if the entire amount of superior earnings does *not* materialize, assume that during the year following C's admission, only $8,000 of superior earnings materialized. Her share of the $8,000 that did materialize is $2,400 (30% of $8,000). Because she gave a bonus of $3,000, she recouped only $2,400 of the bonus, effectively losing $600 of her initial $30,000 capital contribution.

APPROACH IF THE VALUE OF GOODWILL IS NOT GIVEN   Assume that the partners in their negotiations agree upon an amount for the goodwill, but that they do *not* state this amount in the *new* partnership agreement. Instead, knowing the amount of agreed-upon goodwill, they merely calculate the percentage that the incoming partner has in the partnership's net assets. In these situations, the accountant may determine the goodwill using the available information regarding the individual ownership percentage the new partner has in the partnership's net assets. We demonstrate this approach using the information in our example.

If the value of the goodwill is to be recorded on the partnership's books and the *new* partner has a 30% interest in the net assets (tangible and intangible) of the partnership, the goodwill implicit in the transaction can be determined as follows:

1. Divide C's $30,000 capital contribution by her 30% interest in the net assets to arrive at $100,000.
2. Subtract from the amount determined in step 1 the sum of the old partners' capital account balances *immediately before* C is admitted ($60,000) plus her capital contribution ($30,000). Thus the goodwill is $10,000 ($100,000 − $90,000).

Alternatively, if goodwill is *not* to be recorded on the partnership's books and the *new* partner has a 30% interest in the net assets (tangible assets only) of the partnership, the bonus and the related goodwill implicit in the transaction can be determined as follows:

1. Determine the total tangible net assets of the partnership including C's contribution ($60,000 + $30,000).

2. Multiply the amount determined in step 1, $90,000, by C's given ownership percentage in the partnership's net assets ($90,000 × 30% = $27,000).

3. Subtract the $27,000 determined in step 2 from C's $30,000 capital contribution to determine the $3,000 bonus to be given to the *old* partners.

4. Divide the $3,000 bonus by C's profit and loss sharing percentage of 30% to obtain the value of the goodwill implicit in the transactions, $10,000.

ADMISSION OF A NEW PARTNER POSSESSING GOODWILL

Although in most situations the existing partnership has created the goodwill, an incoming partner may possess goodwill. To illustrate the three methods of compensating an incoming partner for goodwill, assume the following information:

1. A and B are in partnership, **sharing profits equally.**

2. C is to be admitted into the partnership.

3. A,B, and C agree that C is expected to generate superior earnings of $10,000 for one year following her admission.

4. C contributes $30,000 cash to the partnership.

5. Profits and losses are to be shared among A, B, and C in a ratio of 3:3:4, respectively.

6. A and B have capital account balances of $45,000 and $15,000, respectively (a total of $60,000), *immediately before* admitting C.

RECORDING THE GOODWILL METHOD   Under the recording the goodwill method, the entire amount of the agreed-upon value of the goodwill is credited to C's capital account, along with her capital contribution of $30,000, as follows:

Goodwill	10,000	
Cash	30,000	
Capital, Partner C		40,000
To record the agreed-upon value of the goodwill and C's		
capital contribution.		

Compared with the situation in which the *old* partners created the goodwill, the roles are now reversed. The *new* partner receives the first $10,000 of future earnings (determined without regard to the goodwill amortization expense), even if superior earnings do *not* materialize. If the superior earnings of $10,000 do not materialize, the old partners lose the anticipated increases to their capital accounts. In this situation, C has a 40% interest in the partnership's net assets ($40,000 ÷ $100,000 total of the capital accounts).

SPECIAL PROFIT AND LOSS SHARING PROVISION METHOD   Under the special profit and loss sharing provision method, no entry is made on the partnership's books with respect to the goodwill. C receives a credit to her capital account equal to her $30,000 capital contribution. C has a one-third interest in the partnership's net assets ($30,000 ÷ $90,000 total of the capital accounts). The *new* profit and loss sharing formula stipulates that the *new* partner is entitled to receive the first $10,000 of earnings in excess of a specified amount. That amount is the expected normal earnings for the year after C's admission into the partnership. If superior earnings of $10,000 do *not* materialize during this year, C will have credited to her capital account only the amount that *does* materialize. In this situation, this method protects the old partners' capital balances that existed when C was admitted into the partnership.

THE BONUS METHOD   Under the bonus method, no entry is made on the partnership's books with respect to goodwill. Because the *new* partner possesses the goodwill, the *old* partners give her a bonus. Its amount is the total of the old partners' profit and loss sharing percentage of 60% times the agreed-upon value of the goodwill, which is $10,000. Thus the bonus to the new partner is $6,000, recorded as follows:

Cash	30,000	
Capital, Partner A	3,000	
Capital, Partner B	3,000	
Capital, Partner C		36,000
To record C's capital contribution and to record the bonus		
given to her.		

C has a 40% interest in the partnership's net assets ($36,000 ÷ $90,000). Compared with the situation in which the *old* partners created the goodwill, the roles now are reversed. The *old* partners will recoup the bonus they gave to the *new* partner only if superior earnings of $10,000 materialize. To the extent that they are *less than* $10,000, the *old* partners will lose a portion of the balances that existed in their capital accounts immediately before C was admitted.

APPROACH IF THE VALUE OF GOODWILL IS NOT GIVEN   If the agreed-upon value of the goodwill is *not* available (an unusual situation), the accountant may determine this amount so long as information is available regarding the individual ownership percentage the *new* partner has in the partnership's net assets. We demonstrated the general approach using the information in our example.

If the value of the goodwill is to be recorded on the partnership's books and the *new* partner has a 40% interest in the net assets (tangible and intangible) of the partnership, the goodwill implicit in the transaction can be determined as follows:

1. Divide the total of the *old* partners' capital accounts by their total interest in the net assets ($60,000 ÷ 60%) to arrive at $100,000.

2. Subtract from the amount determined in step 1 the sum of the *old* partners' capital account balances immediately before C is admitted ($60,000) plus her $30,000 tangible capital contribution. Thus the goodwill is $10,000 ($100,000 − $90,000).

Alternatively, if goodwill is *not* to be recorded on the partnership's books and the *new* partner has a 40% interest in the net assets (tangible assets only), the bonus to be given by the *old* partners and the goodwill implicit in the transaction can be determined as follows:

1. Determine the total net assets of the partnership, including C's tangible contribution ($60,000 + $30,000).

2. Multiply the amount determined in step 1, $90,000, by C's given ownership percentage in the partnership's net assets ($90,000 × 40% = $36,000).

3. Subtract from the $36,000 amount determined in step 2 C's $30,000 *tangible* capital contribution to determine the $6,000 bonus that C receives from the *old* partners.

4. Divide the $6,000 bonus by the *old* partners' combined profit and loss sharing percentage of 60% to obtain the value of the goodwill implicit in the transaction, $10,000. (Recall the profit and loss sharing ratio of 3:3:4.)

BUSINESS COMBINATIONS

When two businesses combine so that the owners of each separate business continue as owners in the enlarged business (substantively, a pooling of interests) and when one of the businesses possesses goodwill, we may apply the same three methods that have been illustrated in this section to compensate the partners of the business possessing the goodwill. Procedurally, these three methods are the same as in situations in which a new partner is admitted other than through a business combination. The mechanics become more involved, however, as the number of combining partners increases.

A DECREASE IN THE NUMBER OF PARTNERS

If a partnership possesses unrecorded goodwill when a partner withdraws from it, the withdrawing partner is *not* treated equitably unless this difference in value is considered in settling with the withdrawing partner or his estate. In these situations, each method to compensate the partner is available—the recording the goodwill method, the special profit and loss sharing provision method, and the bonus method. To illustrate the application of each method, assume the following facts:

1. A, B, and C are in partnership, sharing profits *equally.*
2. The capital accounts of A, B, and C are $40,000, $30,000, and $20,000, respectively.
3. All the partnership's *tangible* assets have carrying values equal to their current values.
4. C withdraws from the partnership.
5. The partners agree that the partnership currently has unrecorded goodwill of $15,000.

RECORDING THE GOODWILL METHOD   Under the recording the goodwill method, goodwill is recorded on the books and shared among the partners in their profit and loss ratio, as follows:

Goodwill	15,000	
Capital, Partner A		5,000
Capital, Partner B		5,000
Capital, Partner C		5,000
To record the agreed-upon value of goodwill existing at the time of C's withdrawal from the partnership.		

The entry to record C's withdrawal follows:

Capital, Partner C	25,000	
Payable to Partner C		25,000

An alternative to recording all the goodwill is to record only C's share of the goodwill, which is $5,000, as follows:

Goodwill	5,000	
Capital, Partner C		5,000

Whether all or a portion of the goodwill is recorded is irrelevant from an equity standpoint; both methods produce the same result for the withdrawing partner. As previously indicated, the goodwill method is *not* in accordance with GAAP, which the partners need not follow. If superior earnings of $15,000 do *not* materialize after C's withdrawal, the remaining partners lose a portion of their capital balances existing when C withdraws as a result of writing off the goodwill.

SPECIAL PROFIT AND LOSS SHARING PROVISION METHOD   Under the special profit and loss sharing provision method, goodwill is *not* recorded on the books. Instead, C's withdrawal is conditional on the *new* profit and loss sharing formula between A and B, which contains a provision that C is to share in one-third of future earnings in excess of a specified level for a certain time period. If past superior earnings have largely depended on C's efforts, the partnership may not be able to generate superior earnings after she withdraws. Accordingly, this method best protects the remaining partners in the event that superior earnings do *not* materialize during the stipulated period of time after C's withdrawal.

THE BONUS METHOD   Under the bonus method, the old partners give the withdrawing partner a bonus. The bonus equals C's share of the agreed-upon value of the goodwill, which is one-third of $15,000, or $5,000. The bonus is shared between the remaining partners in their respective profit and loss sharing ratio as follows:

Capital, Partner A	2,500	
Capital, Partner B	2,500	
Capital, Partner C		5,000
To record the bonus to C on her withdrawal from the partnership.		

This method does *not* deviate from GAAP. If $15,000 of above-normal earnings does *not* materialize during the stipulated time period *after* C withdraws, however, the remaining partners do *not* recoup all of the bonus they gave her.

SPIN-OFF SITUATIONS   A partner may withdraw from a partnership and immediately commence business in the same line of work as a sole proprietor. In this situation, the *withdrawing* partner often requests the partnership's clients and customers that he or she personally has been serving to give their future business to the newly formed sole proprietorship. When this happens, the method selected for equitably treating the withdrawing partner should be accompanied by provisions that protect the remaining partners from any loss of clients and customers as result of the withdrawing partner's forming a sole proprietorship. In other words, the remaining partners must guard against recording goodwill or paying a bonus and losing clients or customers to the newly formed sole proprietorship.

IV   LEGAL ASPECTS OF CHANGES IN OWNERSHIP

Although a thorough discussion of the legal aspects of a change in ownership of a partnership is properly the subject of an upper-division course on business law, a brief discussion of the major legal aspects is appropriate at this point.

Section 29 of the Uniform Partnership Act (UPA) states that "the dissolution of a partnership is the change in the relation of the partners caused by any partner ceasing to be associated in the carrying on as distinguished from the winding up of the business." This definition implies that **dissolution** occurs only when a partner withdraws from a partnership. Section 41(1) of the UPA (also concerned with dissolution) refers to a partnership that admits a partner as being the "first or dissolved partnership." Accordingly, any change in ownership (whether by withdrawal of a partner, admission of a new partner, or a business combination that is in substance a pooling of interests) legally dissolves the existing partnership. Because we are dealing with changes in ownership that do *not* terminate the business activities of the partnership, a *new* partnership must be formed immediately to continue the business of the *dissolved* partnership.

The fact that a legal dissolution has occurred is meaningless in terms of continuity of existence; the business continues to operate as though no change in ownership had occurred. A legal dissolution does have personal significance, however, to new partners, withdrawing partners, continuing partners, and creditors of the dissolved partnership.

ADMISSION OF A PARTNER

With respect to an incoming partner, Section 17 of the UPA provides that "a person admitted as a partner into an existing partnership is liable for all the obligations of the partnership arising before his admission as though he had been a partner when such obligations were incurred, except that his liability shall be satisfied only out of partnership property." This provision insulates the personal assets of the *new* partner from creditors' claims existing at his or her admission.

In practice, the existing partners usually insist that an *incoming* partner be jointly responsible for all such preexisting partnership debts. If the *new* partner agrees to this, Section 17 of the UPA may be circumvented by including a provision to that effect in the *new* partnership agreement. Because of the possibility of undisclosed liabilities (actual or contingent), the *new* partner in these situations should limit his or her responsibilities to the liabilities that are set forth in a scheduled exhibit to the partnership agreement.

WITHDRAWAL OF A PARTNER

With respect to a withdrawing partner, Section 36(1) of the UPA provides that "the dissolution of the partnership does not of itself discharge the existing liability of any partner." Section 36(2), however, provides that a withdrawing partner may be relieved of his or her responsibility for such debt if and only if the creditor expressly releases the partner from this responsibility by entering into an agreement to that effect between the withdrawing partner and the person or partnership continuing the business. Some court cases have held that a withdrawing partner may be liable for debts incurred after his or her withdrawal unless prior notice was given of that withdrawal. Notice usually must be given directly to persons who have dealt with the partnership. For persons who have not dealt with the partnership, a notice usually may be given by publication in a newspaper or some other appropriate manner.

END-OF-CHAPTER REVIEW

SUMMARY OF KEY POINTS

1. The **bonus method** may be applied when

$$\begin{array}{ccccc} \text{New} & & \text{Old} & & \text{New} \\ \text{Partnership} & = & \text{Partners'} & + & \text{Partner's Asset} \\ \text{Capital} & & \text{Capital} & & \text{Investment} \end{array}$$

2. The **goodwill method** is applied when

$$\begin{array}{ccccc} \text{New} & & \text{Old} & & \text{New} \\ \text{Partnership} & > & \text{Partners'} & + & \text{Partner's Asset} \\ \text{Capital} & & \text{Capital} & & \text{Investment} \end{array}$$

3. Both methods attempt to achieve equity among the partners; however, both methods result in an inequity to one or more partners if goodwill does *not* materialize.

GLOSSARY OF NEW TERMS

Bonus method   A method to achieve equity among partners upon a change in the number of partners when partnership assets are *undervalued* or goodwill exists. Adjustments are made within the partners' equity accounts to the extent of the undervaluation or the agreed-upon value of goodwill, thereby neither changing the recorded amounts of the partnership assets nor recording goodwill as an asset.

Dissolution   The change in the relationship of the partners caused by a change in ownership.

Goodwill method   A method to achieve equity among partners upon a change in the number of partners when goodwill is deemed to exist. Goodwill is recorded on the books of the partnership with an offsetting credit made to the partner(s) who possesses or created the goodwill.

SELF-STUDY QUESTIONS

(Answers are at the end of this chapter preceding the appendix.)

1. Flutie and Harper are partners with capital balances of $90,000 and $60,000, respectively. They share profits and losses in a 2:1 ration, respectively. Tuba is *admitted* into the partnership for a cash contribution of $50,000. Tuba receives a 20% capital interest and a 20% interest in profits and losses. What is the *implied* goodwill in the transaction? Do the *old* partners or the *new* partner possess the goodwill?

   a. $10,000   a. New partner
   b. $12,500   b. Old partners
   c. $40,000
   d. $50,000

2. Horne and Picolo are partners with capital balances of $140,000 and $100,000, respectively. They share profits and losses in a 2:1 ratio, respectively. Sax is *admitted* into the partnership for a $60,000 cash contribution. Sax shares in 25% of the profits and losses and is to have a 25% capital interest. Assuming that goodwill *is* recorded, how much should be credited to Sax's capital account?

   a. $60,000   b. $75,000   c. $80,000   d. $100,000

3. Use the data in the preceding question, but assume that goodwill is *not* recorded. How much should be credited to Sax's capital account under the *bonus method*?

   a. $60,000   b. $75,000   c. $80,000   d. $100,000

4. Bell, Ring, and Toner are partners having capital balances of $72,000, $48,000, and $40,000, respectively. Their profit and loss sharing ratio is 5:3:2, respectively. Toner is *withdrawing* from the partnership. The partners agree that the partnership possesses $50,000 of goodwill, which is *not* to be recorded. What is the total cash payment to Toner in full settlement of his partnership interest?

   a. $40,000   b. $50,000   c. $52,500   d. $53,333

5. What is Bell's capital balance, assuming that all of the goodwill *is* recorded? Use the information in the preceding question.

   a. $72,000   b. $88,667   c. $94,500   d. $97,000

6. What is Bell's capital balance assuming that the *bonus method* is used? Use the information in Question 4.

   a. $65,750   b. $66,000   c. $67,000   d. $72,000

7. Drummer decides to *retire* from a partnership in which she has 20% of the profits and losses and a 25% capital interest. Just prior to this decision, her capital balance is $60,000. The partnership agrees that she should receive a cash bonus of $7,000 upon retirement. The partnership has liabilities of $150,000 at the retirement date. Drummer's *tax basis* just prior to retirement is $85,000. What is her taxable gain or loss?

   a. $18,000 loss   b. $25,000 loss   c. $5,000 gain   d. $12,000 gain

ASSIGNMENT MATERIAL

REVIEW QUESTIONS

1. What is the primary objective of accounting for changes in the ownership of a partnership?
2. What three methods are available to achieve equity among partners when a change in ownership occurs?

3. Does each method to achieve equity always treat each partner equitably?

4. Under the *bonus method,* is the bonus temporary or permanent?

5. Is recognizing goodwill on a partner's admission into a partnership considered to be in accord with GAAP?

6. How would you describe a business combination of two partnerships that is in substance a *pooling of interests*?

7. Is a business combination that is in substance a *purchase* (as opposed to a *pooling of interests*) deemed a change in ownership with respect to the acquiring partnership?

8. How does an accountant know whether the *bonus method,* the *special profit and loss sharing provision method,* or the *recording the goodwill method* should be used to reflect a change in ownership?

9. Under the *recording the goodwill method,* what substantively has occurred?

10. Under the *bonus method,* what substantively has occurred?

11. What is the significance of a legal dissolution when a partner is admitted into a partnership? When a partner withdraws?

12. When a partner withdraws from a partnership after many years and has a gain on the liquidation of his or her interest, is such gain treated as a capital gain for income tax–reporting purposes?

EXERCISES

E 29–1 **Admission: Calculation of Required Contribution**   Partners Angel, Bird, and Crow share profits and losses 50:30:20, respectively. The 4/30/X5 balance sheet is as follows:

Cash	$ 40,000
Other assets	360,000
	$400,000
Accounts payable	$100,000
Capital, Angel	74,000
Capital, Bird	130,000
Capital, Crow	96,000
	$400,000

The assets and liabilities are recorded and presented at their respective fair values. Dove is to be *admitted* as a new partner with a 20% capital interest and a 20% share of profits and losses in exchange for a cash contribution. No goodwill or bonus is to be recorded.

Required   1. Determine how much cash Dove should contribute.

2. Prepare the entry to record Dove's admission.

(AICPA adapted)

E 29–2 **Admission: Recording the Goodwill Method**   Abbey and Landly are partners with capital balances of $80,000 and $40,000 and they share profits and losses in the ratio of 2:1, respectively. Deere invests $36,000 cash for a one-fifth interest in the capital and profits of the *new* partnership. The partners agree that the *implied* partnership goodwill *is* to be recorded simultaneously with the admission of Deere.

Required   1. Calculate the firm's total implied goodwill.

2. Prepare the entry or entries to record the admission of Deere.

(AICPA adapted)

E 29–3 **Admission: The Bonus Method**   Cord and Stringer are partners who share profits and losses in the ratio of 3:2, respectively. On 8/31/X4 their capital accounts are as follows:

Cord	$ 70,000
Stringer	60,000
	$130,000

On that date, they agreed to admit Twiner as a partner with a one-third interest in the capital and profits and losses, for an investment of $50,000. The *new* partnership will begin with a total capital of $180,000.

Required   Prepare the entry or entries to record the admission of Twiner.

(AICPA adapted)

E 29–4   **Admission: Recording the Goodwill Method and the Bonus Method**   Waters is *admitted* into the partnership of Dunes, Kamel, and Sanders for a $40,000 total cash investment. The capital accounts and respective percentage interests in profits and losses *immediately before* Waters' admission are as follows:

	Capital Accounts	Percentage Interests in Profits and Losses
Dunes	$ 80,000	60
Kamel	40,000	30
Sanders	20,000	10
	$140,000	100

All tangible assets and liabilities are fairly valued. Waters receives a one-fifth interest in profits and losses and a 20% interest in the *new* partnership's net assets.

Required   1. Prepare the entry to record Waters' admission into the partnership, assuming that goodwill *is* to be recorded.
2. Prepare the entry to record Waters' admission into the partnership, assuming that goodwill is *not* to be recorded.

E 29–5   **Admission: Determining Bonus and Goodwill from Interest in Net Assets**   Ball and Batt are partners, share profits and losses equally, and have capital balances of $30,000 and $20,000, respectively. All *tangible* assets have current values equal to book values. Glover is admitted into the partnership.

Required   Determine the entry to record Glover's admission in each of the following independent situations:

1. Glover contributes $10,000 cash for a 10% interest in the *new* net assets of the partnership of $60,000.
2. Glover contributes $10,000 cash for a 10% interest in the *new* net assets of the partnership and receives a credit to his capital account equal to his full cash contribution.
3. Glover contributes $10,000 for a one-sixth interest in the *new* net assets of the partnership of $60,000.
4. Glover purchases 10% of each existing partner's interest for a total cash payment of $10,000 to the existing partners.
5. Glover contributes $10,000 cash for a 20% interest in the *new* net assets of the partnership of $60,000.
6. Glover contributes $10,000 cash for a 20% interest in the *new* net assets of the partnership, with the old partners' capital accounts not to decrease.

E 29–6   **Retirement**   On 6/30/X1, the balance sheet for the Oakley, Pine, and Woods partnership, together with their respective profit and loss ratios, was as follows:

Assets, at cost	$180,000
Oakley, loan	$ 9,000
Capital, Oakley (20%)	42,000
Capital, Pine (20%)	39,000
Capital, Woods (60%)	90,000
	$180,000

Oakley has decided to *retire* from the partnership. By mutual agreement, the assets are to be adjusted to their current value of $216,000 and the partnership is to pay Oakley $61,200 for her partnership interest, including her loan, which is to be repaid in full.

Required   1. Prepare the required entries, assuming that goodwill *is* to be recorded on the partnership's books. (*Note:* Two alternative amounts may be recorded for goodwill. Prepare entries under each alternative.)
2. Prepare the entries, assuming that goodwill is *not* to be recorded on the partnership's books.

(AICPA adapted)

E 29–7   **Calculation of Gain on Sale of Partnership Interests**   The capital accounts of the partnership of Fender, Hood, and Shields on 5/31/X5 follow with their respective profit and loss ratios:

Fender	$200,000	1/2
Hood	150,000	1/3
Shields	100,000	1/6
	$450,000	

On 5/31/X5, Wheeler was admitted into the partnership when she purchased for $120,000 an interest from Fender in the net assets and profits of the partnership. As a result of this transaction, Wheeler acquired a one-fifth interest in the net assets and profits of the firm. Assume that *implied* goodwill is *not* to be recorded. Fender's *tax basis* just prior to the sale was $180,000.

Required   1. What gain does Fender realize on the sale of a portion of this interest in the partnership to Wheeler?
2. Is the gain calculated in requirement 1 for book purposes, for tax purposes, or both?
3. Prepare the entry required on the partnership's books.
4. *Optional:* What is Fender's taxable gain or loss if he retires on 6/1/X5 and receives cash equal to the balance in his capital account at this date? (Assume that the partnership had no liabilities at this date.)

PROBLEMS

P 29–1   **Admission: Tangible Assets Are *Undervalued* and Goodwill Exists**   Fields and Hill are in partnership, share profits and loses in the ratio 4:1, respectively, and have capital balances of $22,500 each. The partnership's tangible assets have a fair value of $15,000 in excess of book value. Mounds is admitted into the partnership for a cash contribution of $30,000. The *new* profit and loss sharing formula is Fields, 56%; Hill, 14%; and Mounds, 30%. The value of the partnership's existing goodwill is agreed to be $10,000.

Required   1. Prepare the required entries, assuming that the *tangible* assets are to be revalued and the goodwill *is* to be recorded on the partnership's books.
2. Prepare the required entries, assuming that the *bonus method* is to be used with respect to the undervalued tangible assets and the goodwill.

P 29–2   **Retirement: Tangible Assets Are *Undervalued* and Goodwill Exists**   The 4/30/X5 balance sheet of the partnership of Arbee, Karle, and MacDonald follows. The partners share profits and losses in the ratio of 2:2:6, respectively.

Assets, at cost	$100,000
	$100,000
Arbee, loan	$ 9,000
Capital, Arbee	15,000
Capital, Karle	31,000
Capital, MacDonald	45,000
	$100,000

Arbee *retires* from the partnership. By mutual agreement, the assets are to be adjusted to their fair value of $130,000 at 4/30/X5. Karle and MacDonald agree that the partnership will pay Arbee $37,000 cash for his partnership interest, exclusive of his loan, which is to be paid in full. No goodwill is to be recorded.

Required   1. Prepare the entry to record the revaluation of assets to their fair value.
2. Prepare the entry to record Arbee's retirement.
3. What is the *implicit* goodwill?   (AICPA adapted)

P 29–3   **Business Combination: Each Partnership Has *Undervalued* Tangible Assets and Goodwill**   The partnership of A, B, C, and D has agreed to combine with the partnership of X and Y. The individual capital accounts and profit and loss sharing percentage of each partner follow:

	Capital Accounts	Profit and Loss Sharing Percentages	
		Now	Proposed
A	$ 50,000	40	28
B	35,000	30	21
C	40,000	20	14
D	25,000	10	7
	$150,000	100	70
X	$ 60,000	50	15
Y	40,000	50	15
	$100,000	100	30

A, B, C, and D's partnership has undervalued *tangible* assets of $20,000, and the X and Y partnership has undervalued *tangible* assets of $8,000. All the partners agree that (1) the partnership of A, B, C, and D possesses goodwill of $30,000 and (2) the partnership of X and Y possesses goodwill of $10,000. (Assume that the combined businesses will continue to use the general ledger of A, B, C, and D.)

Required   **1.** Prepare the entries required to reflect the combination, assuming that tangible assets are to be revalued and goodwill *is* to be recorded.
2. Prepare the entries required to reflect the combination, assuming that the *bonus method* is to be used with respect to the undervalued tangible assets *and* the goodwill.

P 29–4 **Admission: Tangible Assets Are *Overvalued* and Goodwill Exists**   Diamond and Hart are in partnership and have (1) capital balances of $110,000 and $75,000, respectively, and (2) a profit and loss sharing ratio of 3:2, respectively. Klubb is to be admitted with a $60,000 cash contribution. The parties agree that the partnership possesses goodwill of $65,000 and its equipment is *overvalued* by $10,000. Klubb will share in 20% of the profits and losses.

Required   **1.** Prepare the required entries, assuming that the equipment *is* to be written down and goodwill *is* to be recorded.
2. Prepare the required entries, assuming that the equipment is *not* to be written down and goodwill is *not* to be recorded.

P 29–5 **Retirement: Tangible Assets Are *Overvalued* and Goodwill Exists**   Acres, Barnes, and Cowes are in partnership and have (1) capital balances of $200,000, $60,000, and $210,000, respectively, and (2) a profit and loss sharing ratio of 4:1:5, respectively. Cowes is retiring. The parties agree that the partnership possesses goodwill of $100,000 and its equipment is *overvalued* by $20,000.

Required   **1.** Prepare the required entries, assuming that the equipment *is* to be written down and goodwill *is* to be recorded.
2. Prepare the required entries, assuming that the equipment is *not* to be written down and goodwill is *not* to be recorded.

P 29–6 **COMPREHENSIVE: Admission of New Partners—Withdrawal of Old Partner and Division of Profits**   You have been engaged to prepare the 6/30/X2 financial statements for the partnership of Ash, Cherry, and Douglas. You have obtained the following information from the partnership agreement, as amended, and from the accounting records.

1. Ash and Burch originally formed the partnership on 7/1/X1 when
   a. Burch contributed $400,000 cash.
   b. Ash contributed land, a building, and equipment with fair market values of $110,000, $520,000, and $185,000, respectively. The land and buildings were subject to a mortgage securing an 8% per annum note (interest rate of similar notes at 7/1/X1). The note is due in quarterly payments of $5,000 plus interest on January 1, April 1, July 1, and October 1 of each year. Ash made the 7/1/X1 principal and interest payment *personally*. The partnership then assumed the obligation of the remaining $300,000 balance.
   c. The agreement further provided that Ash had contributed a certain *intangible* benefit to the partnership because of her many years of business activity in the area serviced by the new partnership. The assigned value of this intangible asset plus the net tangible assets she contributed gave her a 60% initial capital interest in the partnership.

d. Ash was designated the only active partner, at an annual salary of $24,000 plus an annual bonus of 5% of net income after deducting her salary but before deducting interest on partners' capital investments (see below). Both the salary and the bonus are to be recorded as operating expenses of the partnership.

e. Each partner is to receive a 10% return on *average* capital investment; such interest is to be an *expense* of the partnership.

f. All remaining profits or losses are to be shared *equally*.

2. On 10/1/X1, Burch sold his partnership interest and rights as of 7/1/X1, to Cherry for $370,000. Ash agreed to accept Cherry as a partner if he would contribute sufficient cash to meet the 10/1/X1 principal and interest payment on the mortgage note. Cherry made the payment from personal funds.

3. On 1/1/X2, Ash and Cherry *admitted* a new partner, Douglas. Douglas invested $150,000 cash for a 10% capital interest based on the initial investments (tangible and intangible) at 7/1/X1 of Ash and Burch, plus Douglas' capital contribution of $150,000. At 1/1/X2, the book values of the partnership's assets and liabilities approximated their fair market values. Douglas contributed no intangible benefit to the partnership.

   Similar to the other partners, Douglas is to receive a 10% return on his average capital investment. His investment also entitles him to 20% of the partnership's profits or losses as defined above. For the year ended 6/30/X2, however, Douglas receives one-half his pro rata share of the profits or losses.

4. The accounting records show that on 2/1/X2, the Other Miscellaneous Expenses account had been charged $3,600 for hospital expenses incurred by Ash's eight-year-old daughter, Fern.

5. All salary payments to Ash have been charged to her drawing account. On 6/1/X2, Cherry made a $33,000 withdrawal. These are the only transactions recorded in the partners' drawing accounts.

6. The following is a trial balance summarizing the partnership's general ledger balances at 6/30/X2. The general ledger has *not* been closed.

	Debit	Credit
Current assets	$ 307,000	
Fixed assets	1,285,000	
Current liabilities		$ 104,100
8% Mortgage note payable		285,000
Capital, Ash		515,000
Capital, Cherry		400,000
Capital, Douglas		150,000
Drawing, Ash	24,000	
Drawing, Cherry	33,000	
Drawing, Douglas	–0–	
Sales		946,900
Cost of sales	695,600	
Administrative expenses	28,000	
Other miscellaneous expenses	11,000	
Interest expense	17,400	
Totals	$2,401,000	$2,401,000

Net income $194,900 (bracket covering Sales, Cost of sales, Administrative expenses, Other miscellaneous expenses, Interest expense)

Required Prepare a worksheet to adjust the net income (loss) and partners' capital accounts for the year ended 6/30/X2, and to close the net income (loss) to the partners' capital accounts at 6/30/X2. Supporting schedules should be in good form. Amortization of goodwill, if any, is to be over a 10-year period. (Ignore all tax considerations.) Use the following column headings and begin with balances from the books as shown:

	Net Income (Loss)	Partners' Capital			Other Accounts	
		Ash	Cherry	Douglas	Amount	
Description	(Dr.) Cr.	(Dr.) Cr.	(Dr.) Cr.	(Dr.) Cr.	Dr. (Cr.)	Name
Book balances at 6/30/X2	$194,900	$515,000	$400,000	$150,000		

(AICPA adapted)

✳ **CASES** ✳

C 29–1   **Admission: Evaluation of the Bonus Method**   Gentry and Royals are in partnership and are contemplating admitting Squires. Gentry and Royals have proposed that Squires give them a $20,000 bonus as a condition of admittance. Squires believes that this bonus is ridiculous considering that (1) all *tangible* assets have fair market values equal to their book values, (2) all partners are to devote 100% of their time to the partnership business, (3) future profits and losses are to be shared *equally*, (4) Squires' capital contribution is to be 50% of the existing partnership capital of $100,000 *immediately before* his admission, and (5) his *tax basis* would be reduced by $20,000. Squires has asked you as his accountant to counsel him on this matter.

Required   How would you respond to this request?

C 29–2   **Admission: Adherence to Generally Accepted Accounting Principles**   Castle and Hurst are partners negotiating with Randolph regarding his admission into the partnership. They have reached agreement regarding the value of goodwill that the existing partnership possesses. The partners disagree, however, as to whether the goodwill should be recorded on the books. Castle and Hurst believe that goodwill should be recognized and recorded on the books at Randolph's admission. Randolph believes that it is improper to record goodwill because it was *not* bought and paid for. Furthermore, Randolph contends that recording goodwill is senseless because it would *not* be deductible for income tax purposes in this situation. They have asked you as the partnership's accountant to settle this disagreement.

Required   How would you respond to this request?

C 29–3   **Admission: Role of the Accountant**   Disnee and Walters are partners contemplating Duckett's admission as a partner. They have requested that you, the partnership's accountant, determine how this should be done.

Required   How would you respond to this request? Be specific about the advice you would give them.

C 29–4   **Admission: Role of the Accountant**   Berry and Knott are partners contemplating Farmer's admission into the partnership. Berry and Knott believe that the partnership possesses goodwill of $60,000, whereas Farmer believes that it possesses goodwill of only $20,000. As the partnership's accountant, you have been asked to determine the amount of goodwill that the partnership possesses.

Required   How would you respond to this request?

ANSWERS TO SELF-STUDY QUESTIONS

1. d, b   **2.** c   **3.** b   **4.** b   **5.** d   **6.** a   **7.** d

■ APPENDIX

TAX ASPECTS OF CHANGES IN OWNERSHIP

The general ledger entries to the partners' capital accounts in connection with the revaluation of assets, recording the goodwill, or the bonus method are *not* significant from a tax viewpoint. The only tax significance of such entries is the existence of *unrealized gains* (when partners' capital accounts *increase*) and *unrealized losses* (when partners' capital accounts *decrease*). In general, until the partnership interest is disposed of, such gains and losses are *not* reportable for tax purposes.

I WITHDRAWAL OF A PARTNER

When a *withdrawing* partner receives cash from either the partnership or persons to whom his or her partnership interest is sold, the determination of the withdrawing partner's gain or loss for income tax–reporting purposes is made by comparing the *proceeds* to his or her tax basis. The *proceeds* are the sum of cash received plus the share of existing partnership liabilities for which he or she is relieved of responsibility. (The assumption of the partner's share of the liabilities by the remaining partners is treated as a distribution of money to the withdrawing partner.) To illustrate, we assume the following:

1. The withdrawing partner has a capital balance of $20,000.
2. The withdrawing partner is to receive a $5,000 bonus.
3. The partnership has liabilities of $24,000.
4. The partnership shares profits and losses *equally* (three partners).
5. The withdrawing partner's *tax basis* is $27,000.

The withdrawing partner's taxable gain is calculated as follows:

Proceeds:	
Cash distribution ($20,000 + $5,000 bonus)	$25,000
Relief of partnership liabilities (⅓ × $24,000)	8,000
Total Proceeds	$33,000
Withdrawing partner's tax basis	27,000
Taxable Gain	$ 6,000

When a withdrawing partner receives noncash consideration, the tax laws are complex; a discussion of these laws is beyond the scope of this chapter.

II ADMISSION OF A PARTNER

The procedures for determining an *incoming* partner's tax basis are the same as those illustrated in Chapter 28 on the formation of partnerships. The incoming partner's tax basis equals the sum of (1) the amount of cash contributed, (2) the adjusted basis of any noncash assets contributed, and (3) the share of any partnership liabilities for which he or she is jointly responsible, (4) less the old partners' share of any liabilities the new partner contributes to the partnership. As with the formation of a partnership, the profit and loss sharing ratios are used to adjust each partner's tax basis for any liabilities relieved of or assumed.

When a partner is admitted by directly purchasing a partner's interest, his or her tax basis is the sum of the cash paid plus the share of any partnership liabilities for which he or she is jointly responsible. The *incoming* partner's tax basis need not coincide with the selling partner's tax basis because the amount paid is a negotiated amount. The partnership may elect to adjust the tax basis of its assets to reflect the difference between the tax basis of the incoming partner and that of the selling partner. (No entries are made in the general ledger—the difference is kept on a *memorandum basis*.)

The amount of the increase or decrease in tax basis affects only the incoming partner. For example, assume that an incoming partner's tax basis exceeds that of the selling partner and this difference is allocable to merchandise inventory, a building, unrealized receivables, and goodwill. In future years, the incoming partner's share of earnings is adjusted by (1) treating the amount allocable to inventory as additional cost of goods sold (as the inventory is sold), (2) treating the amount allocable to the building as additional depreciation expense, (3) treating the amount allocable to the unrealized receivables as a reduction of revenues (as the accounts receivable are collected), and (4) treating the amount allocable to goodwill as goodwill expense (over a 15-year life).

This election to adjust the tax basis of the assets is much more common in small partnerships than in large partnerships because the partnership—not the individual incoming partner—must do the record keeping, and most large partnerships do *not* bother with this record-keeping function. If the election is made to adjust the tax basis of the partnership assets, the sum of the tax bases of each partner will equal the partnership's tax basis in its assets. If the election is *not* made, this equality will *not* exist, and the difference will exist until the partner disposes of his or her interest.

ASSIGNMENT MATERIAL FOR APPENDIX

PROBLEMS

P 29-1A   **Calculation of New Partner's Tax Basis and Adjustment to Old Partners' Tax Bases: Admission by Capital Contribution into the Partnership**   Bishop and Knight are in partnership; share profits and losses in the ratio 5:3, respectively; and have capital balances of $80,000 and $60,000, respectively. They admit Rook into the partnership for a cash contribution of $50,000, of which $16,000 is to be credited to the capital accounts of the old partners as a *bonus*. The *new* profit and loss sharing percentages are Bishop, 50%; Knight, 30%; and Rook, 20%. The partnership has $120,000 of liabilities at Rook's admission. Rook became jointly responsible for these liabilities at her admission pursuant to a provision in the new partnership agreement. Bishop's *tax basis* just prior to Rook's admission was $138,000.

Required   **1.** Prepare the entry required on the partnership's books.
          2. Calculate the tax basis of Rook's interest in the partnership.
          3. Calculate the required adjustment to the tax basis of each of the old partners as a result of Rook's admission.
          4. What is Bishop's tax basis after Rook's admission?
          5. What is the tax significance of the bonus received by Bishop and Knight?
          6. Calculate Bishop's taxable gain or loss assuming (1) he quits the partnership one day after Rook is admitted and (2) Bishop receives cash in full liquidation of this capital interest equal to the balance in his capital account.

P 29-2A   **Calculation of New Partner's Tax Basis and Determination of Old Partner's Proceeds and Taxable Gain: Admission by Purchase of Existing Partner's Interest**   Board and Checker are in partnership, share profits and losses equally, and have capital balances of $60,000 and $40,000, respectively. Kingmee purchases all of Checker's interest for $50,000 and agrees to be jointly responsible for all existing partnership liabilities, which total $14,000.

Required   **1.** Prepare the entry required on the partnership's books.
          2. Calculate the tax basis of Kingmee's interest in the partnership.
          3. Calculate the adjustment, if any, to Board's tax basis as a result of Kingmee's purchase of Checker's interest.
          4. Assuming that Checker's tax basis was $47,000 when he sold his interest, determine the proceeds he received on the sale of his interest and his taxable gain, if any.

PARTNERSHIPS: LIQUIDATIONS

30

Nothing endures but personal qualities.

WALT WHITMAN

The termination of a partnership's business activities is known as **liquidation.** A partnership may be liquidated for many reasons, for example, its original agreed-upon term of existence has expired, it is marginally profitable, or it is in serious financial difficulty.

A partnership in serious financial difficulty may attempt rehabilitation either by (1) filing under Chapter 11 of the federal bankruptcy statutes or (2) restructuring its debt outside bankruptcy court. Such alternatives for partnerships, however, do *not* entail any significant special problems not already discussed for corporations in Chapter 23. Consequently, we restrict our discussion in this chapter to the liquidation process.

EVEN THE BIG ONES CAN FALL

The Business Perspective discusses the liquidation of Laventhol & Horwath (L&H) in 1990, the then seventh-largest accounting partnership (350 partners), as a result of financial difficulties resulting from litigation and overexpansion. The unfortunate personal consequences of L&H's demise (which we list at the end of the Business Perspective) has probably motivated many accounting general partnerships to become limited liability partnerships (LLPs)—*all* of the Big Six accounting firms changed from being general partnerships to LLPs in 1994.

Recall that LLPs were discussed in Chapter 28 and that an LLP partner is *not* subject to personal liability for any tort or malpractice liability of another partner in the partnership. In this chapter, the discussion and illustrations focus on the liquidation of *general partnerships*—not LLPs. Much of the chapter, however, applies to LLPs—only the material that discusses and illustrates partners having to make additional capital contributions because a partner is personally insolvent does *not* apply to LLPs.

"QUITTING CONCERN" INSTEAD OF "GOING CONCERN"

In the liquidation process, the entity is a "quitting concern"—not a "going concern." As explained in the bankruptcy liquidation section of Chapter 23, income statements are *not* prepared for periods in which an entity is liquidating; thus no need exists to match asset costs into the proper time period. Furthermore, all assets and liabilities become current.

THE LIQUIDATION PROCESS IN A NUTSHELL

The liquidation process for partnerships is in several respects identical to the liquidation process for corporations. Over a period of time, (1) the entity's noncash assets are converted to cash (the realization process), (2) creditors are paid to the extent possible, and (3) remaining funds, if any, are distributed to the owners (partners). Partnership liquidations, however, differ from corporate liquidations in the following respects:

1. Because **partners have unlimited liability,** any partner may be asked to contribute additional funds to the partnership if its assets are insufficient to satisfy creditors' claims.

2. To the extent that a partner does *not* make good a deficit balance in his or her capital account, the remaining partners must absorb that deficit balance. Absorption of a partner's deficit balance gives the absorbing partners legal recourse against him or her.

The special problems created by these two situations are discussed throughout this chapter.

TYPES OF LIQUIDATIONS

Liquidations may be categorized broadly as lump-sum liquidations and installment liquidations.

1. In *lump-sum liquidations,* no distributions are made to the partners until the realization process is completed when the full amount of the realization gain or loss is known.
2. In *installment liquidations,* distributions are made to some or all of the partners as cash becomes available. Thus cash distributions are made to partners before the full amount of the realization gain or loss is known.

Within each category, a variety of situations may arise concerning the ability of the partnership and the individual partners to satisfy the claims of partnership creditors. Before discussing each situation in detail, we discuss some fundamental procedures in liquidations.

I   FUNDAMENTAL PROCEDURES IN LIQUIDATIONS

PROCEDURES FOR MINIMIZING INEQUITIES AMONG PARTNERS

SHARING OF GAINS AND LOSSES   Gains and losses incurred on the realization of assets may be allocated among the partners in the manner they have agreed to in the partnership agreement. If the partnership agreement is silent with respect to sharing gains and losses during liquidation, the Uniform Partnership Act (UPA) treats such gains and losses in the same way as it does preliquidation profits and losses—that is, gains and losses are allocated in accordance with the profit and loss sharing formula. Most partnerships follow the profit and loss sharing formula in distributing gains and losses incurred during liquidation. This is the most equitable manner for the following reasons:

1. The cumulative profit and loss of a partnership during its existence is the difference between total capital contributions and total capital withdrawals. Accordingly, a partnership's cumulative profit or loss during its existence should include *start-up periods, normal operating periods,* and *wind-down periods.*
2. Certain gains and losses recognized during the liquidation process actually may have occurred during normal operating periods. This is the case when (a) land or buildings have been held for several years and appreciated in value prior to the liquidation and (b) certain accounts receivable should have been written off as uncollectible *before* liquidation. The use of a method other than the profit and loss sharing formula results in inequities among the partners.

If a partner's capital account is not sufficient to absorb his or her share of the losses incurred in liquidation, Section 18 of the UPA provides that "each partner . . . must contribute toward the losses . . . sustained by the partnership according to his share in the profits." In other words, a partner must contribute additional funds to the partnership to eliminate any deficit balance in his or her capital account created by losses incurred through normal operations or in the liquidation process. If such a partner does *not* have the personal resources to eliminate this deficit, the remaining partners must absorb the capital deficit, resulting in inequities to them. A basic procedure that may minimize such potential inequities is discussed in the next section.

BUSINESS PERSPECTIVE

Behind the Fall of Laventhol

It was a fitting farewell. The Sunday after the top partners of Laventhol & Horwath had voted to break up their 75-year-old firm, Chief Executive Robert N. Levine was in the corner of a crowded ballroom at the Houston Airport Marriott when his 350 partners rose to offer a standing ovation for his ill-fated yearlong turnaround effort. But he couldn't respond with words of thanks. Like so much else about the firm, his microphone failed him.

Eventually, Levine walked to another mike and got his message across. But there was nothing he could do to stop Laventhol from filing for bankruptcy three days later, on Nov. 21. Slipshod client screening and a tidal wave of malpractice suits had helped seal L&H's fate long before the partnership turned to Levine in November 1989 for a rescue. Nor could Levine single-handedly revive the once-lucrative tax-shelter business, killed off by tax reform, or resuscitate the real estate and leveraged-buyout booms of the 1980s that had fueled dizzying growth at the nation's seventh-largest accounting firm.

Cash Hits

L&H's cash squeeze, Levine says, resulted from high litigation defense costs, a dramatic downturn in key industries, and the softening of the general economy. Other factors that now plague national accounting firms also played a part: cutthroat competition that leads to underbidding of audits, a shrinking client pool, and an overdependence on distressed industries. Thus, days after Laventhol became the largest professional-services firm to collapse into Chapter 11, a smaller rival, Spicer & Oppenheim, disbanded. The firm had never recovered from the 1987 crash that crushed its Wall Street client base. And giants KPMG Peat Marwick and Deloitte & Touche are cutting staff.

Above all, the industry suffers from the ravages of a five-year epidemic of malpractice suits. Creditors and investors in failed companies like to sue auditors because those firms are often the only participants left with any cash. This, plus the growing use of antiracketeering laws against professionals, has inflicted huge litigation expenses, even when the firms eventually win the cases.

Now, savings and loan failures are fueling more suits and boosting the potential liability. Ernst & Young has just had to mount a public-relations blitz to reassure clients of its solvency. Rumors of an impending bankruptcy had been swirling, partly because of the $560 million suit filed by the Federal Deposit Insurance Corp. over E&Y's audits of a Dallas thrift. "I fear for the profession," says Levine.

Merger Binge

Nonetheless, Laventhol's tale is unique because of its excesses. Hot to compete with the Big Six, the scrappy second-tier firm went on a merger binge. Starting in 1984, L&H added 65 smaller practices, which helped double revenues, to $345.2 million, by fiscal 1990. At its peak, L&H had over 50 offices and 460 partners.

But the lack of a distinct culture—a code of values and practices that knit together other far-flung firms—often left some L&H partners placing profit above other concerns. The management by numbers ultimately killed morale, says Ronald A. Gunn, a former principal in L&H's Washington office. After Laventhol expanded its D.C. presence by buying a local rival, he says, it boosted rates so high that partners "spent more time apologizing about what was happening than serving the clients."

The drive for growth brought on heavy pressures. And, concedes Jeffrey L. Lefcourt, chairman of L&H's policy-setting national council: "We may not have looked as carefully at the people we were doing business with as we should have." This resulted in a client roster that often looked like a rogues' gallery. It included jailed San Diego swindler J. David Dominelli, and Blinder, Robinson & Co., the defunct Denver penny-stock firm repeatedly attacked by regulators for defrauding investors. Best known is defrocked TV evangelist Jim Bakker, whose PTL spawned a $184 million fraud claim against L&H and the far larger Deloitte & Touche. Only L&H's bankruptcy filing spared it from the risk of a judgment now. But the claim can be refiled in bankruptcy court.

In the end, L&H's legacy is an object lesson on how a business can go awry. Beginning in 1988, litigation expenses and settlements sharply cut into earnings. By this year, the profit decline twice forced the firm to curtail monthly partnership draws, which had averaged $7,500 per partner. By March, when L&H had borrowed $85 million for operating costs, the banks said: No more. Now, L&H faces claims of $2 billion, say its bankruptcy papers.

'The Darkest Day'

The final chapter in L&H's destruction began with the woes of Grabill Corp., the Chicago manufacturing and real estate empire built by college dropout William J. Stoecker. In the late 1980s, audits by L&H's Chicago office of Grabill's financial statements and a review of Stoecker's finances persuaded banks to lend millions. But by early 1989, Grabill was in Chapter 11, and Stoecker was soon indicted for bankruptcy fraud.

Stoecker was found innocent. His lawyer, Thomas A. Durkin, argues that L&H's audits were designed to ease the banks' concerns about the complex Grabill corporate structure and the risk that Stoecker might be double-pledging assets as collateral. "They were pushing money on him. He knew he was getting into trouble, but [the banks] didn't want to hear anything about it," he asserts.

Laventhol admitted some procedural mistakes with its Grabill audits and quietly paid the banks $40 million, and the publicity over the case shook public confidence. The U.S. Bankruptcy Trustee continues to search for some $30 million in cash and $70 million in real estate missing from Grabill, although it's listed in L&H-audited financial statements.

Grabill marked "the darkest day in the history of our firm," Levine says. The affair tossed L&H's leadership into upheaval. Kenneth Solomon, the hardcharging head of the Chicago office who had overseen the Grabill work, was national-council chairman and heir apparent to CEO George L. Bernstein, whose 10-year tenure ended in June. Instead, desperate to shake off Grabill, the L&H partners tapped the mild-mannered Levine, a popular national-council member who ran the San Francisco office. And when Solomon quit as council chairman, they chose Lefcourt, a Miami partner. Solomon refused to comment.

The tumult in the executive suite compounded L&H's other management woes. Gunn of the Washington office says it never was clear who was in charge—the relatively independent branches, the weak national council, or the executive office in Philadelphia. The uncertainty, he adds, "brought out the worst in people: fiefdomism, lack of cooperation, and avarice on the part of some." Responds Bernstein: "That is nonsense."

Laventhol's problems may have gone deeper. Much of the litigation, which now totals more than 100 suits, alleges that L&H audits failed to spot problems with clients' finances. Some claim they missed fraudulent activity, a charge L&H disputes and its defenders say is easier to lodge in hindsight. But L&H's fundamental flaw was a lust for growth at all costs. Only belatedly did L&H try to stop its downward spiral. Early this year, Levine moved to tighten client screening. But as he struggled to improve operations, he was overwhelmed by business pressures beyond his control.

Fleeing partners and staff made the turnaround tougher still. Earnings slipped so badly that L&H boosted its borrowings from First Fidelity, Chase Manhattan Bank, and State Street Bank—until they cut off credit. With legal bills between $700,000 and $1 million a month, says Levine, L&H cut partner payouts by 80% and salaries by 10%.

Despite warning signs, few partners heading for the Houston meeting suspected—or sought—what occurred. Rather, Douglas McGregor, a Boston partner, says management had come up with what it viewed as a viable plan to raise cash. It proposed selling off its consulting practices to partners, plus selling or closing some offices. But when the idea was presented to lenders before the weekend, they rejected it.

Cost of Carelessness

On Friday, the national council met for 12 hours in Houston. When Levine met with all his partners the next day, he offered a last-ditch rescue option, calling for each partner to contribute $50,000 to tide the firm over until big first-quarter billings came in. Levine said it could work, but even he couldn't recommend it. By late Saturday, the sentiment for liquidation was nearly unanimous.

For L&H partners, the firm's fall hardly puts an end to their litigation woes. It just transfers them to another arena: Manhattan bankruptcy court. Under partnership law, individual partners, including retirees, are personally liable for all debts incurred during their stay at the firm. Already, many partners have hired lawyers in anticipation of fighting claims by creditors—and by partners.

L&H's demise also offers some hard lessons for the industry. Failing to check out clients and business partners, for one, can be costly. "If you lie down with dogs, you get up with fleas," says one accounting executive. And it presents a tough challenge for policymakers. Arthur Andersen Chief Executive Lawrence A. Weinbach says bluntly: "The liability system for professionals needs to be rethought." And one more thing is clear: With L&H as a fresh case study in disaster, the profession could use a bit of scrutiny.

Source: Joseph Weber, Michele Galen, Catherine Yang, and David Greising, "Behind the Fall of Laventhol," *Business Week*, December 24, 1990, pp. 54–55. Reprinted by permission of *Business Week* magazine, December 24, 1990. © 1990.

The Aftermath

1. The partners lost their entire capital investment (approximately $60 million in total, which averaged $175,000 per partner).
2. The active partners and all partners who had retired in the preceding seven years were assessed $47.3 million (averaging $76,000 per partner, with some paying nearly $400,000).
3. Retired partners stopped receiving pension payments (ranged from $20,000 to $80,000 per year).
4. Several partners declared personal bankruptcy.

ADVANCED PLANNING WHEN THE PARTNERSHIP IS FORMED   Although every partnership commences business under the "going concern" concept, the partners' failure to acknowledge the possibility that the partnership may have to be liquidated at some time is unrealistic. It is in the interest of each partner, therefore, to take prudent steps to minimize the possibility of inequities occurring in liquidation. Inequities among partners may arise during liquidation if a deficit balance is created in a partner's capital account (as a result of losses incurred during the conversion of noncash assets into cash), and that partner cannot contribute capital to eliminate the deficit. The partners who do not have deficit balances in their capital accounts must absorb the deficit balance of the partner who does. In other words, they must absorb losses larger than their agreed-upon profit and loss sharing percentage.

Because a partnership has no control over its partners' personal affairs, it has no assurance that its partners will have sufficient personal funds to contribute if a deficit balance is created during liquidation. Accordingly, the partnership should be operated in a manner that minimizes the possibility of a deficit balance occurring. If the partnership agreement specifies that all partners' capital balances are to be maintained in the profit and loss sharing ratio, a partnership may incur losses on the conversion of noncash assets into cash up to the total equity of the partnership, without creating a deficit balance in any partner's capital account. This safeguard is so important that many partnerships (including most of the international accounting partnerships) require capital accounts to be maintained in the profit and loss sharing ratio. Furthermore, as cash is available for distribution to the partners (a situation that occurs only if losses during liquidation are less than the total partnership equity), such cash may be distributed to the partners in the profit and loss sharing ratio with complete assurance that no inequities will result. In such situations, the liquidation process is quite simple. Unfortunately, not all partnerships use such a provision. Partners in such partnerships needlessly expose themselves to potential inequities in the event of liquidation, making the liquidation process much more complex.

Although the potential for inequities occurring during liquidation *cannot* be completely eliminated, a partnership that requires maintaining capital accounts in the profit and loss sharing ratio has taken a big step toward minimizing any potential inequities that may arise.

RULE OF SETOFF   When a partnership has a loan outstanding **to a partner,** the partnership receivable should be subtracted, or *set off*, from the partner's capital account. It is not equitable to assume that the receivable is uncollectible (even though the partner may not have sufficient personal assets to repay the loan) and thereby to allocate the loss among all the partners. The partner's capital account less the receivable represents the partner's true capital investment.

When a partner has a loan outstanding **to the partnership,** the loan does *not* rank on an equal level with other partnership liabilities. Section 40 of the UPA states that the *order of payment* to creditors and partners during liquidation is as follows:

   (I)   Those owing to creditors other than partners.
   (II) Those owing to partners other than for capital and profits (loans).
   (III) Those owing to partners in respect of capital.
   (IV) Those owing to partners in respect of profit.

When profits and losses are closed in the partners' capital accounts at each year-end, the last two categories may be considered one amount, which is the balance in each partner's capital account. Although this section of the UPA implies that partners' loans are paid off *before* any cash distributions are made to partners in liquidation of their capital balances, a strict application of this order of payment could result in inequities among the partners. For example, a partner with a loan to the partnership could be repaid the loan, a deficit balance could be created in his or her capital account at a later date because of losses on the realization of assets, and the partner might not be able to make a capital contribution to eliminate that deficit balance. The other partners would have to absorb such partner's deficit balance and thus incur a larger portion of the losses during liquidation than they originally agreed to. The legal doctrine of **setoff**—whereby a deficit balance in a partner's capital account may be set off against any balance existing in his or her loan account—has been incorporated into accountants' procedures for determining which partners would receive cash as it becomes available. **These procedures effectively treat the loan as an additional capital investment.** The mechanical procedures, which are different in lump-sum liquidations and installment liquidations, are discussed and illustrated later in the chapter.

THE STATEMENT OF REALIZATION AND LIQUIDATION

Because normal operations do not take place during the liquidation period, traditional financial statements are not appropriate. Instead, the partners prefer to have a statement that provides information on the following:

1. Gains and losses on the realization of assets, including the impact of such gains and losses on the partners' capital accounts.
2. Payments that have been made to creditors and partners.
3. The noncash assets still to be converted into cash.

Accordingly, accountants have devised the **statement of realization and liquidation** to provide this information. The statement is *entirely* historical; it reflects only the *actual* transactions that have occurred *during* the liquidation period up to the date of the statement. If the liquidation process takes place over several months, the statement is updated periodically as noncash assets are converted into cash and payments are made to creditors, partners, or both. Other than the allocation of realization gains and losses among the partners and the exercising of the right of setoff, the statement is essentially a summary of cash inflows and outflows.

LIQUIDATION EXPENSES

Certain costs incurred during the liquidation process should be treated as a reduction of the proceeds from the sale of noncash assets—for example, costs to complete inventory, sales commissions and shipping costs related to the disposal of inventory, escrow and title transfer fees associated with the sale of real property, and costs of removing equipment. Other liquidation costs should be treated as expenses. Making a reasonable estimate of these expenses at the beginning of the liquidation process and recording an estimated liability in the general ledger at that time are preferable, adjusting the liability as necessary during the liquidation process. **Recording the estimated liability at the inception of the liquidation process minimizes the possibility of making excess cash distributions to partners.** Any cash available for distribution to partners should be set aside in an amount equal to the remaining estimated liability so that it is *not* distributed to partners.

ⅠⅠ LUMP-SUM LIQUIDATIONS

In a **lump-sum liquidation,** all noncash assets are converted to cash and outside creditors are paid in full before cash is distributed to the partners. Thus the full amount of the gain or loss on realization of assets is known before the partners receive any cash distributions. Lump-sum liquidations are rare or nonexistent because partners liquidate their loan and capital accounts as cash becomes available for distribution. Usually, partners have personal needs for cash, and there is no sound business reason to wait until the very last asset is converted to cash before distributing any cash to the partners. We illustrate several lump-sum liquidations for instructional purposes only.

PARTNERSHIP IS SOLVENT AND ALL PARTNERS ARE PERSONALLY SOLVENT

In the first three illustrations in this section, (1) the partnership is solvent (the fair value of its assets is sufficient to satisfy outside creditors' claims) and (2) all partners who must make capital contributions have either sufficient loans to the partnership (for exercising the right of setoff) or are personally solvent so that the capital deficit from losses incurred during the realization process is eliminated by contributions.

ILLUSTRATION | **LOSS ON REALIZATION DOES NOT CREATE A DEFICIT BALANCE IN ANY PARTNER'S CAPITAL ACCOUNT**

To illustrate the preparation of the statement of realization and liquidation in a lump-sum liquidation, assume that partners A and B share profits and losses in the ratio 3:2, respectively, and the balance sheet of the partnership is as follows:

A and B Partnership
Balance Sheet
May 31, 19X5

Cash	$ 5,000	Liabilities	$20,000
Noncash assets	70,000	Loan, Partner B	3,000
		Capital:	
		Partner A	37,000
		Partner B	15,000
	$75,000		$75,000

Also assume that during June 19X5, (1) the $70,000 noncash assets are converted into $40,000 cash, resulting in a $30,000 loss, which is distributed 60% to partner A ($18,000) and 40% to partner B ($12,000); (2) outside creditors are paid in full; and (3) the remaining cash is distributed to the partners. The statement of realization and liquidation covering the entire liquidation period is prepared as in Illustration 30–1.

ILLUSTRATION 30–1 | Lump-Sum Liquidation: Partnership and All Partners Personally *Solvent*

A and B Partnership
Statement of Realization and Liquidation
June 19X5

	Cash	Noncash	Outside Liabilities	Loan B	A(60%)[a]	B(40%)[a]
Preliquidation Balances	$ 5,000	$70,000	$20,000	$3,000	$37,000	$15,000
Realization of assets and allocation of loss	40,000	(70,000)			(18,000)	(12,000)
Subtotal	$45,000	$ –0–	$20,000	$3,000	$19,000	$ 3,000
Cash distributions:						
Outside creditors	(20,000)		(20,000)			
Partner's loan	(3,000)			(3,000)		
Partner's capital	(22,000)				(19,000)	(3,000)
Postliquidation Balances	$ –0–		$ –0–	$ –0–	$ –0–	$ –0–

[a]Denotes profit and loss sharing percentage.

REVIEW POINTS FOR ILLUSTRATION 30–1   Note the following:

1. The statement format does *not* combine the loan account of partner B with his capital account. The loan is a bona fide loan, *not* a capital investment.
2. Cash distributions were made in accordance with the priority set forth in Section 40 of the UPA.

ILLUSTRATION	LOSS ON REALIZATION CREATES A DEFICIT BALANCE IN ONE PARTNER'S CAPITAL ACCOUNT: RIGHT OF SETOFF EXERCISED

Assume the information in the preceding illustration except that partner B's loan account is $10,000 instead of $3,000 and his capital account is $8,000 instead of $15,000. The statement of realization and liquidation is prepared as shown in Illustration 30–2.

REVIEW POINTS FOR ILLUSTRATION 30–2   Note the following:

1. The fact that partners' loans are assigned a higher priority for repayment than partnership capital accounts under Section 40 of the UPA is not significant if a partner with a loan account also has a deficit balance in his or her capital account—that is, the full amount of the loan is not paid before payments are made to partners in liquidation of their capital accounts.
2. The $4,000 deficit in partner B's capital account after the $30,000 realization loss on the noncash assets means that partner B must contribute $4,000 to the partnership so that he can fully absorb his share of the loss on realization.
3. Partner B did not contribute $4,000 to the partnership to eliminate his capital account deficit because he exercised the right of setoff whereby he transferred $4,000 from his loan account to his capital account.
4. Each partner received the same amount of cash in Illustration 30–1 and 30–2. For all practical purposes, partner B's loan account is the equivalent of an additional capital investment for liquidation purposes.

ILLUSTRATION 30–2	Lump-Sum Liquidation: Partnership and All Partners Personally *Solvent*

A and B Partnership
Statement of Realization and Liquidation
June 19X5

	Assets		Outside Liabilities	Loan	Partners' Capital	
	Cash	Noncash		B	A(60%)[a]	B(40%)[a]
Preliquidation Balances	$ 5,000	$70,000	$20,000	$10,000	$37,000	$ 8,000
Realization of assets and allocation of loss	40,000	(70,000)			(18,000)	(12,000)
Subtotal	$45,000	$ –0–	$20,000	$10,000	$19,000	$ (4,000)
Right of setoff exercised				(4,000)		4,000
Subtotal	$45,000		$20,000	$ 6,000	$19,000	$ –0–
Cash distributions:						
Outside creditors	(20,000)		(20,000)			
Partner's loan	(6,000)			(6,000)		
Partner's capital	(19,000)				(19,000)	
Postliquidation Balances	$ –0–		$ –0–	$ –0–	$ –0–	

[a]Denotes profit and loss sharing percentage.

ILLUSTRATION	**LOSS ON REALIZATION CREATES A DEFICIT BALANCE IN ONE PARTNER'S CAPITAL ACCOUNT: RIGHT OF SETOFF EXERCISED AND ADDITIONAL CAPITAL CONTRIBUTION IS REQUIRED AND MADE**

Assume the information in the preceding illustration except that the loss on the re-alization of the noncash assets is $50,000, *not* $30,000. This additional $20,000 loss causes partner B to have a capital deficit, which is not completely eliminated when he exercises the right of setoff. Assume that partner B is personally solvent and makes the required capital contribution to eliminate the remainder of his capital deficit. The statement of realization and liquidation is prepared as shown in Illustration 30–3.

PARTNERSHIP IS SOLVENT AND AT LEAST ONE PARTNER IS PERSONALLY INSOLVENT

In the next two illustrations, at least one partner is personally insolvent and unable to make a capital contribution to eliminate his or her capital deficit. In such circumstances, the remaining partners must absorb the capital deficit of the insolvent partner in their respective profit and loss sharing ratio. If this, in turn, causes a capital deficit for an absorbing partner, that partner must make a capital contribution to eliminate the deficit. If such partner also is personally insolvent, his or her capital deficit must be absorbed by the remaining partners, using their respective profit and loss sharing ratio.

The absorption of a partner's deficit capital balance by other partners violates the UPA, in that the partner who cannot eliminate his or her deficit capital balance has broken the terms of the partnership agreement. The other partners have legal recourse against the personal assets of the defaulting partner. This situation raises the question of how such claims against the defaulting partner's personal assets are treated in relation to claims of his or her personal creditors. In the next section

ILLUSTRATION 30–3	**Lump-Sum Liquidation: Partnership and All Partners Personally *Solvent***

A and B Partnership
Statement of Realization and Liquidation
June 19X5

| | Assets | | Outside | Loan | Partners' Capital | |
	Cash	Noncash	Liabilities	B	A(60%)[a]	B(40%)[a]
Preliquidation Balances	$ 5,000	$70,000	$20,000	$10,000	$37,000	$ 8,000
Realization of assets						
and allocation of loss	20,000	(70,000)			(30,000)	(20,000)
Subtotal	$25,000	$ –0–	$20,000	$10,000	$ 7,000	$(12,000)
Right of setoff exercised				(10,000)		10,000
Subtotal	$25,000		$20,000	$ –0–	$ 7,000	$ (2,000)
Cash contribution by B	2,000					2,000
Subtotal	$27,000		$20,000		$ 7,000	$ –0–
Cash distributions:						
Outside creditors	(20,000)		(20,000)			
Partner's capital	(7,000)				(7,000)	
Postliquidation Balances	$ –0–		$ –0–		$ –0–	

[a]Denotes profit and loss sharing percentage.

of the chapter, we answer this question and discuss situations in which the **partnership is insolvent** and at least one partner is personally insolvent.

ILLUSTRATION	LOSS ON REALIZATION CREATES A DEFICIT BALANCE IN ONE PARTNER'S CAPITAL ACCOUNT: RIGHT OF SETOFF EXERCISED AND ADDITIONAL CAPITAL CONTRIBUTION IS REQUIRED BUT NOT MADE

Assume that partners A, B, C, and D share profits in the ratio 4:2:2:2, respectively. The partnership's balance sheet at the beginning of the liquidation process is as follows:

A, B, C, and D Partnership
Balance Sheet—June 30, 19X5

Cash	$ 10,000	Liabilities	$157,000
Noncash assets	290,000	Loan:	
		Partner B	10,000
		Partner C	5,000
		Partner D	2,000
		Capital:	
		Partner A	70,000
		Partner B	30,000
		Partner C	20,000
		Partner D	6,000
	$300,000		$300,000

Assume also that during July 19X5, the noncash assets realize $210,000 cash, resulting in an $80,000 realization loss, which is shared among the partners (using the profit and loss sharing ratio 4:2:2:2) as follows: A, $32,000; B, $16,000; C, $16,000; and D, $16,000. The realization loss creates a deficit in D's capital account, which her exercise of the right of setoff does not completely eliminate. D must make an additional $8,000 capital contribution but is unable to do so. As a result, her $8,000 capital deficit must be allocated to partners A, B, and C in their profit and loss sharing ratio of 4:2:2, respectively. Assuming that all cash was distributed in July 19X5, the statement of realization and liquidation is prepared as shown in Illustration 30–4.

REVIEW POINTS FOR ILLUSTRATION 30–4   Note the following:

1. Because partner D was unable to eliminate the deficit balance in her capital account, the remaining partners had to bear a higher percentage of the realization loss than their individual profit and loss sharing percentages. For example, partner A suffered a total loss of $36,000 ($32,000 + $4,000). This represents 45% of the $80,000 total realization loss, which is higher than her stipulated profit and loss sharing percentage of 40%. Partners A, B, and C needlessly exposed themselves to this additional $8,000 loss by not employing the fundamental safeguard provision of maintaining capital accounts in the profit and loss sharing ratio.

2. The illustration assumes that partner D was unable to make any of the required contribution. If a partner contribution had been made, the remaining partners would have had to absorb a smaller deficit balance.

3. A partner with a deficit balance may indicate that he or she is unable to completely eliminate the deficit balance when it is created, but that he or she might be able to make a capital contribution at a later date (which may or may not be specified). If partner D had indicated this, the available $220,000 cash could have been distributed to the outside creditors and the remaining partners. The partnership

ILLUSTRATION 30–4   Lump-Sum Liquidation: Partnership and All but One Partner Personally *Solvent*

A, B, C, and D Partnership
Statement of Realization and Liquidation
July 19X5

	Assets		Outside Liabilities	Partners' Loans			Partners' Capital			
	Cash	Noncash		B	C	D	A(40%)[a]	B(20%)[a]	C(20%)[a]	D(20%)[a]
Preliquidation Balances, 6/30/X5	$ 10,000	$290,000	$157,000	$10,000	$5,000	$2,000	$70,000	$30,000	$20,000	$ 6,000
Realization of assets and allocation of loss	210,000	(290,000)					(32,000)	(16,000)	(16,000)	(16,000)
Subtotal	$220,000	$ –0–	$157,000	$10,000	$5,000	$2,000	$38,000	$14,000	$ 4,000	$(10,000)
Right of setoff exercised						(2,000)				2,000
Subtotal	$220,000		$157,000	$10,000	$5,000	$ –0–	$38,000	$14,000	$ 4,000	$ (8,000)
Absorption of D's capital deficit							(4,000)	(2,000)	(2,000)	8,000
Subtotal	$220,000		$157,000	$10,000	$5,000		$34,000	$12,000	$ 2,000	$ –0–
Cash distributions:										
Outside creditors	(157,000)		(157,000)							
Partners' loans	(15,000)			(10,000)	(5,000)					
Partners' capital	(48,000)						(34,000)	(12,000)	(2,000)	
Postliquidation Balances, 7/31/X5	$ –0–		$ –0–	$ –0–	$ –0–		$ –0–	$ –0–	$ –0–	

[a]Denotes profit and loss sharing percentage.

books then could be kept open until partner D makes a capital contribution or subsequently determines that she cannot make a payment after all. This procedure could result in a lengthy delay in completing the partnership liquidation. There is no sound reason for keeping the partnership books open indefinitely, thereby delaying the completion of the liquidation process, merely because of partner D's uncertain financial situation. When partner D's capital account deficit was created (and *not* completely eliminated by exercising the right of setoff), she became liable for her deficit to the other partners. Accordingly, if partner D later makes a capital contribution, she makes the payment directly to the other partners. Consequently, in situations involving lump-sum liquidations in which a partner cannot immediately eliminate his or her capital deficit, the accountant should complete the liquidation process by transferring the capital deficit to the capital accounts of the remaining partners (using their respective profit and loss sharing ratios). The partnership books may then be closed, and the liquidation process can be completed.

ILLUSTRATION	**LOSS ON REALIZATION CREATES A DEFICIT BALANCE IN ONE PARTNER'S CAPITAL ACCOUNT; ABSORPTION BY OTHER PARTNERS CREATES A DEFICIT BALANCE IN ANOTHER PARTNER'S CAPITAL ACCOUNT**

Assume the information in the preceding illustration except that the noncash assets are sold for only $170,000. This results in a realization loss of $120,000 rather than $80,000. The $120,000 realization loss is allocated among the partners (using the profit and loss sharing ratio 4:2:2:2) as follows: A, $48,000; B, $24,000; C, $24,000; and D, $24,000. In addition to the previously described consequences to partner D, the greater loss results in partner C's inability to absorb fully his share of partner D's deficit balance. Thus, partner C has a deficit balance that he cannot eliminate through setoff or contribution. His capital deficit, in turn, must be allocated to partners A and B in their respective profit and loss sharing ratio of 4:2. (Partners A and B have legal recourse against the personal assets of partners C and D—such recourse is discussed in the next section.) Assuming that all cash was distributed in July 19X5, the statement of realization and liquidation is prepared as shown in Illustration 30–5.

PARTNERSHIP IS INSOLVENT AND AT LEAST ONE PARTNER IS PERSONALLY SOLVENT

In the next two illustrations, the partnership is insolvent— that is, the loss on the realization of noncash assets is higher than the total of the partners' capital (including their loan accounts). Because unlimited liability is a feature of the partnership form of organization, creditors may seek payment from any or all of the partners as individuals.

ILLUSTRATION	**LOSS ON REALIZATION CREATES A DEFICIT BALANCE IN CERTAIN PARTNERS' CAPITAL ACCOUNTS: ALL PARTNERS ARE PERSONALLY SOLVENT**

In this situation, all partners are personally solvent, and those with deficit capital balances contribute funds to the partnership to eliminate their capital deficits, enabling the partnership to pay creditors in full. Using the same preliquidation balances given for Illustration 30–5, assume that the $290,000 noncash assets are sold for $130,000, resulting in a $160,000 realization loss. The realization loss is shared among the partners (using the profit and loss sharing ratio 4:2:2:2) as follows:

ILLUSTRATION 30-5   Lump-Sum Liquidation: Partnership Solvent and Some Partners Personally *Insolvent*

A, B, C, and D Partnership
Statement of Realization and Liquidation
July 19X5

	Assets			Partners' Loans			Partners' Capital			
	Cash	Noncash	Outside Liabilities	B	C	D	A(40%)[a]	B(20%)[a]	C(20%)[a]	D(20%)[a]
Preliquidation Balances, 6/30/X5	$ 10,000	$290,000	$157,000	$10,000	$5,000	$2,000	$70,000	$30,000	$20,000	$ 6,000
Realization of assets and allocation of loss	170,000	(290,000)					(48,000)	(24,000)	(24,000)	(24,000)
Subtotal	$180,000	$ -0-	$157,000	$10,000	$5,000	$2,000	$22,000	$ 6,000	$ (4,000)	$(18,000)
Right of setoff exercised					(4,000)	(2,000)			4,000	2,000
Subtotal	$180,000		$157,000	$10,000	$1,000	$ -0-	$22,000	$ 6,000	$ -0-	$(16,000)
Absorption of D's capital deficit							(8,000)	(4,000)	(4,000)	16,000
Subtotal	$180,000		$157,000	$10,000	$1,000		$14,000	$ 2,000	$ (4,000)	$ -0-
Right of setoff exercised					(1,000)				1,000	
Subtotal	$180,000		$157,000	$10,000	$ -0-		$14,000	$ 2,000	$ (3,000)	
Absorption of C's capital deficit							(2,000)	(1,000)	3,000	
Subtotal	$180,000		$157,000	$10,000			$12,000	$ 1,000	$ -0-	
Cash distributions:										
Outside creditors	(157,000)		(157,000)							
Partners' loans	(10,000)			(10,000)						
Partners' capital	(13,000)						(12,000)	(1,000)		
Postliquidation Balances, 7/31/X5	$ -0-		$ -0-	$ -0-			$ -0-	$ -0-		

[a]Denotes profit and loss sharing percentage.

A, $64,000; B, $32,000; C, $32,000; and D, $32,000. After exercising the right of setoff, partner A has a $6,000 capital balance; partner B has an $8,000 loan balance; and partners C and D have $7,000 and $24,000 capital deficits, respectively. At this point, the available $140,000 cash may be distributed to outside creditors. Assuming that partners C and D contribute funds to the partnership to eliminate their capital deficits, the $31,000 cash then may be distributed to outside creditors and partners A and B. The statement of realization and liquidation is prepared as shown in Illustration 30–6.

In this illustration, we assume that partners C and D made additional cash contributions to the partnership, thereby eliminating their capital deficits. Thus the partnership could make the remaining $17,000 payment to the outside creditors. Creditors occasionally take legal action against some or all of the partners as individuals when the creditors do not receive full satisfaction from the partnership. As a result, a partner personally may make payments to partnership creditors. Such payments should be reflected in the general ledger and on the statement of realization and liquidation as a reduction of partnership liabilities and an additional capital contribution by that partner. A partner's personal payments to creditors are in substance the equivalent of a cash contribution to the partnership that the partnership then distributes to the creditors.

ILLUSTRATION	**LOSS ON REALIZATION CREATES A DEFICIT BALANCE IN CERTAIN PARTNERS' CAPITAL ACCOUNTS: CERTAIN PARTNERS ARE PERSONALLY INSOLVENT**

Before illustrating in detail a situation in which a partnership is insolvent and certain of its partners are insolvent, we discuss the following legal questions raised in such circumstances:

1. If partnership creditors initiate legal proceedings against a partner who is personally insolvent, what is the legal status (priority of payment) of such claims in relation to the claims of that partner's personal creditors?

2. If a partner is personally insolvent and unable to eliminate the deficit balance in his or her capital account, thereby causing other partners to absorb that deficit balance (which is a breach of the partnership agreement entitling the wronged partners to legal recourse against the defaulting partner), what is the legal status of such claims in relation to the claims of that partner's personal creditors?

3. If a partner is personally insolvent, to what extent may such partner's personal creditors obtain payments from the partnership?

The answers to the first two questions are found in Section 40(i) of the UPA:

> Where a partner has become bankrupt or his estate is insolvent, the claims against his separate property shall rank in the following order:
> (I) Those owing to separate creditors.
> (II) Those owing to partnership creditors.
> (III) Those owing to partners by way of contribution.

The answer to the third question is found in Section 40(b) of the UPA, which specifies that partnership creditors have first claim on partnership assets. Consequently, these two sections of the UPA are consistent with the longstanding court procedure of **marshaling of assets,** which is summarized as follows: Partnership creditors have first priority as to partnership assets, and personal creditors of an insolvent partner have first priority as to such partner's personal assets. Under the **federal bankruptcy statutes,** however (which apply only in bankruptcy

ILLUSTRATION 30-6 Lump-Sum Liquidation: Partnership *Insolvent* and All Partners Personally *Solvent*

A, B, C, and D Partnership
Statement of Realization and Liquidation
July 19X5

	Assets		Outside Liabilities	Partners' Loans			Partners' Capital			
	Cash	Noncash		B	C	D	A(40%)[a]	B(20%)[a]	C(20%)[a]	D(20%)[a]
Preliquidation Balances, 6/30/X5	$ 10,000	$290,000	$157,000	$10,000	$5,000	$2,000	$70,000	$30,000	$ 20,000	$ 6,000
Realization of assets and allocation of loss	130,000	(290,000)					(64,000)	(32,000)	(32,000)	(32,000)
Subtotal	$140,000	$ -0-	$157,000	$10,000	$5,000	$2,000	$ 6,000	$ (2,000)	$(12,000)	$(26,000)
Exercise right of setoff				(2,000)	(5,000)	(2,000)		2,000	5,000	2,000
Subtotal	$140,000		$157,000	$ 8,000	$ -0-	$ -0-	$ 6,000	$ -0-	$ (7,000)	$(24,000)
Distribution to outside creditors	(140,000)		(140,000)							
Subtotal	$ -0-		$ 17,000	$ 8,000			$ 6,000		$ (7,000)	$(24,000)
Contributions by C and D ...	31,000								7,000	24,000
Subtotal	$ 31,000		$ 17,000	$ 8,000			$ 6,000		$ -0-	$ -0-
Cash distributions:										
Outside creditors	(17,000)		(17,000)							
Partners' loan	(8,000)			(8,000)						
Partners' capital	(6,000)						(6,000)			
Postliquidation Balances, 7/31/X5	$ -0-		$ -0-	$ -0-			$ -0-			

[a]Denotes profit and loss sharing percentage.

proceedings), partnership creditors share on a pro rata basis with personal creditors of an insolvent partner in the distribution of such partner's personal assets.

APPLICATION OF MARSHALING OF ASSETS   To illustrate the application of the marshaling of assets, assume the information in Illustration 30–6 with respect to partners' balances after (1) the realization loss of $160,000 is distributed, (2) the right of setoff is exercised, and (3) a $140,000 payment is made to outside creditors, leaving $17,000 owed to them. At this point, the partners' accounts are as follows:

Partner	Loan Balance	Capital Balance
A		$ 6,000
B	$8,000	
C		(7,000)
D		(24,000)

Assume that the personal status of each partner (exclusive of interest in or obligation to the partnership) is as follows:

Partner	Personal Assets	– Personal Liabilities	= Personal Net Worth (Deficit)
A	$50,000	$25,000	$25,000
B	4,000	15,000	(11,000)
C	16,000	6,000	10,000
D	20,000	33,000	(13,000)

1. Partner D has a capital deficit and is personally insolvent. Thus none of his personal assets is available for contribution to the partnership because his personal creditors are entitled to all of his personal assets. Consequently, partners A, B, and C must absorb his $24,000 capital deficit in their respective profit and loss sharing ratio, 4:2:2. Partner A's share is $12,000, partner B's is $6,000, and partner C's is $6,000.

2. Partner C had a $7,000 capital deficit, which increased to $13,000 when he absorbed his share of partner D's capital deficit. Partner C has a personal net worth of $10,000. Thus he can contribute $10,000 to the partnership, leaving a $3,000 deficit, which partners A and B must absorb in their respective profit and loss sharing ratio of 4:2. Partner A's share is $2,000 and partner B's share is $1,000.

3. Partner B had an $8,000 loan balance. His capital account, however, was charged with $6,000 when partner D's capital deficit was written off and $1,000 when partner C's capital deficit was written off. Thus $7,000 must be transferred from his loan account under the right of setoff to eliminate his capital deficit. This leaves $1,000 in his loan account, which, when distributed to him, is available to his personal creditors because he is personally insolvent.

4. Because partner A has the largest personal net worth, assume that partnership creditors took legal action against her (as opposed to proceeding against partner C, who is the only other personally solvent partner from whom they could collect anything). The creditors collected the $17,000 owed them from partner A personally. Partner A had a $6,000 capital balance, which was reduced by $12,000 for her share of partner D's capital deficit and $2,000 for her share of partner C's capital deficit. This gives her a capital deficit of $8,000. Her $17,000 payment to the partnership creditors, however, is the equivalent of a capital contribution. Thus, her capital account deficit is eliminated, and she now has a positive capital balance of $9,000.

5. This leaves the partnership with $10,000 cash, which is distributed to partner B ($1,000 in payment of his loan) and partner A ($9,000 in liquidation of her capital balance).

Illustration 30–7 summarizes the preceding sequence of events in a statement of realization and liquidation.

III INSTALLMENT LIQUIDATIONS

In an **installment liquidation,** the conversion of noncash assets into cash occurs over a period of time. As a result, the partnership realizes more proceeds than would be possible in a quick liquidation. Because of the lengthier conversion period, cash may become available for distribution to partners long before the last noncash asset is sold. In such situations, the partners usually want cash distributed as it becomes available.

THE TWO WORST-CASE ASSUMPTIONS

If capital accounts are not maintained in the profit and loss sharing ratio, cash may not be distributed to the partners on some arbitrary basis such as the profit and loss sharing ratio, the capital balances ratio, or personal needs. Such a distribution might result in later inequities to certain partners. For example, cash may be distributed to a partner who may not be able to return such cash to the partnership if a deficit balance subsequently is created in his or her capital account as a result of future losses on the conversion of noncash assets into cash. Such partner's deficit balance would have to be allocated to partners who have credit balances, and those partners would have to bear a larger portion of the loss than their profit and loss sharing percentages. To prevent this potential inequity, accountants use two worst-case assumptions to determine which partners should receive available cash at any particular time. These assumptions are as follows:

1. **First Worst-Case Assumption: All noncash assets are assumed to be completely worthless.** Thus a hypothetical loss equal to the carrying values of noncash assets is assumed to have occurred. On a worksheet, the hypothetical loss is allocated to the partners' capital account balances existing at that time.

2. **Second Worst-Case Assumption: Partners with deficit positions are assumed to be personally insolvent.** If, as a result of the first worst-case assumption, a partner's capital account is in a deficit position (on the worksheet only), we assume that **such partner is not able to make contributions to the partnership to eliminate the hypothetical deficit.** (This assumption is made regardless of the partner's personal financial status.) Accordingly, the hypothetical deficit balance is allocated to the partners who have credit balances, using their respective profit and loss sharing ratio. If, in turn, this process creates a hypothetical deficit balance in another partner's capital account, this hypothetical deficit balance is allocated (on the worksheet only) to the remaining partners who still have credit balances. This process is repeated until only partners with credit balances remain on the worksheet. Cash may then be distributed to the partners who have credit balances on the worksheet.

The result of these two assumptions is that cash is distributed only to the partners who have capital balances sufficient to absorb their share of (1) the maximum potential loss on noncash assets and (2) any capital deficiencies that may result to other partners as a result of a maximum loss on noncash assets. In other words, payments may be made safely to such partners with full assurance that the money

ILLUSTRATION 30–7 — Lump-Sum Liquidation: Partnership *Insolvent* and Some Partners Personally *Insolvent*

A, B, C, and D Partnership
Statement of Realization and Liquidation
July 19X5

	Assets		Outside Liabilities	Partners' Loans			Partners' Capital			
	Cash	Noncash		B	C	D	A(40%)[a]	B(20%)[a]	C(20%)[a]	D(20%)[a]
Preliquidation Balances, 6/30/X5	$ 10,000	$290,000	$157,000	$10,000	$5,000	$2,000	$70,000	$30,000	$ 20,000	$ 6,000
Realization of assets and allocation of loss	130,000	(290,000)					(64,000)	(32,000)	(32,000)	(32,000)
Subtotal	$140,000	$ –0–	$157,000	$10,000	$5,000	$2,000	$ 6,000	$(2,000)	$(12,000)	$(26,000)
Exercise right of setoff				(2,000)	(5,000)	(2,000)		2,000	5,000	2,000
Subtotal	$140,000		$157,000	$ 8,000	$ –0–	$ –0–	$ 6,000	$ –0–	$ (7,000)	$(24,000)
Distribution to outside creditors	(140,000)		(140,000)							
Subtotal	$ –0–		$ 17,000	$ 8,000			$ 6,000	$ 8,000	$ (7,000)	$(24,000)
Absorption of D's deficit							(12,000)	(6,000)	(6,000)	24,000
Subtotal	$ –0–		$ 17,000	$ 8,000			$ (6,000)	$ (6,000)	$(13,000)	$ –0–
Capital contribution by C	10,000								10,000	
Subtotal	$ 10,000		$ 17,000	$ 8,000			$ (6,000)	$ (6,000)	$ (3,000)	
Absorption of C's deficit							(2,000)	(1,000)	3,000	
Subtotal	$ 10,000		$ 17,000	$ 8,000			$ (8,000)	$ (7,000)	$ –0–	
Exercise right of setoff				(7,000)				7,000		
Subtotal	$ 10,000		$ 17,000	$ 1,000			$ (8,000)	$ –0–		
Capital contribution by A			(17,000)				17,000			
Subtotal	$ 10,000		$ –0–	$ 1,000			$ 9,000			
Cash distributions:										
Partners' loans	(1,000)			(1,000)						
Partners' capital	(9,000)						(9,000)			
Postliquidation Balances, 7/31/X5	$ –0–		$ –0–	$ –0–			$ –0–			

[a]Denotes profit and loss sharing percentage.

will not have to be returned to the partnership at some later date in the event of future realization losses.

Under this method of distributing cash to the partners, the capital accounts are brought into the profit and loss sharing ratio, usually only after several cash distributions have been made. Once the capital accounts have been brought into the profit and loss sharing ratio, cash distributions may be made using that ratio. The two worst-case assumptions need not be used for any future cash distributions because their use produces the same result as the profit and loss sharing ratio.

Applying the two worst-case assumptions shows that a partner's capital account (on the worksheet) is reduced for any loans the partnership has outstanding to the partner. Also, a partner's capital account (on the worksheet) is increased for any loan the partner may have outstanding to the partnership; this automatically provides for the hypothetical exercising of the right of setoff.

ILLUSTRATION	**LOSS ON REALIZATION CREATES A DEFICIT BALANCE IN CERTAIN PARTNERS' CAPITAL ACCOUNTS: ONE PARTNER IS PERSONALLY INSOLVENT**

To illustrate how these two worst-case assumptions apply to an installment liquidation, assume the following:

1. The partnership of A, B, C, and D has the same preliquidation balances as shown in Illustration 30–7.

2. The noncash assets of $290,000 are sold as follows:

Date Sold	Book Value	Proceeds	Loss
July 3, 19X5	$183,000	$168,000	$(15,000)
August 6, 19X5	70,000	25,000	(45,000)
September 9, 19X5	37,000	27,000	(10,000)
	$290,000	$220,000	$(70,000)

3. Cash was distributed to outside creditors and partners as it became available.

4. Partner D could contribute only $4,000 to the partnership during the liquidation proceedings. The other partners had to absorb his remaining $2,000 capital account deficit.

The statement of realization and liquidation is prepared as shown in Illustration 30–8. The cash distributions to partners were determined from the **schedule of safe payments** shown in Illustration 30–9, which is a supporting schedule to Illustration 30–8. The schedule of safe payments shows the cash distributions that may be made safely to individual partners concerning the objectives to minimize potential inequities and limit the accountant's legal exposure.

REVIEW POINTS FOR ILLUSTRATIONS 30–8 AND 30–9   Note the following:

1. The statement of realization and liquidation reflects only the historical transactions recorded in the general ledger. Although the statement covers the entire liquidation period, it was started when the liquidation process began and periodically updated as noncash assets were sold and cash distributions were made.

2. The schedule of safe payments to partners reflects the assumptions made at those dates when cash was available for distribution to partners. The purpose of the schedule is to determine which partners should receive the cash available at those dates.

A, B, C, and D Partnership
Statement of Realization and Liquidation
July 1, 19X5, through September 9, 19X5

	Assets		Outside Liabilities	Partners' Loans			Partners' Capital			
	Cash	Noncash		B	C	D	A(40%)[a]	B(20%)[a]	C(20%)[a]	D(20%)[a]
Preliquidation Balances, 7/1/X5	$ 10,000	$290,000	$157,000	$10,000	$5,000	$2,000	$70,000	$30,000	$20,000	$ 6,000
Realization of assets and allocation of loss, 7/3/X5	168,000	(183,000)					(6,000)	(3,000)	(3,000)	(3,000)
Subtotal	$178,000	$107,000	$157,000	$10,000	$5,000	$2,000	$64,000	$27,000	$17,000	$(3,000)
July Cash Distribution:										
Outside creditors	(157,000)		(157,000)							
Partners' loan	(10,000)[b]			(10,000)[b]						
Partners' capital	(11,000)[b]						(10,667)[b]	(333)[b]		
Subtotal	$ –0–	$107,000	$ –0–	$ –0–	$5,000	$2,000	$53,333	$26,667	$17,000	$ 3,000
Realization of assets and allocation of loss, 8/6/X5	25,000	(70,000)					(18,000)	(9,000)	(9,000)	(9,000)
Subtotal	$ 25,000	$ 37,000			$5,000	$2,000	$35,333	$17,667	$ 8,000	$(6,000)
Exercise right of setoff						(2,000)				2,000
Subtotal	$ 25,000	$ 37,000			$5,000	$ –0–	$35,333	$17,667	$ 8,000	$(4,000)
Cash contribution by D	4,000									4,000
Subtotal	$ 29,000	$ 37,000			$5,000		$35,333	$17,667	$ 8,000	$ –0–
August Cash Distribution										
Partners' loan	(3,750)[b]				(3,750)[b]					
Partners' capital	(25,250)[b]						(16,833)[b]	(8,417)[b]		
Subtotal	$ –0–	$ 37,000			$1,250		$18,500	$ 9,250	$ 8,000	
Realization of assets and allocation of losses, 9/9/X5	27,000	(37,000)					(4,000)	(2,000)	(2,000)	(2,000)
Subtotal	$ 27,000	$ –0–			$1,250		$14,500	$ 7,250	$ 6,000	$(2,000)
Write-off of D's deficit							(1,000)	(500)	(500)	2,000
Subtotal	$ 27,000				$1,250		$13,500	$ 6,750	$ 5,500	$ –0–
Final Cash Distribution										
Partners' loan	(1,250)				(1,250)					
Partners' capital	(25,750)						(13,500)	(6,750)	(5,500)	
Postliquidation Balances, 7/31/X5	$ –0–	$ –0–	$ –0–		$ –0–		$ –0–	$ –0–	$ –0–	$ –0–

[a]Denotes profit and loss sharing percentage.
[b]See supporting schedule in Illustration 30–9.

ILLUSTRATION 30–9	Supporting Schedule to Illustration 30–8

A, B, C, and D Partnership
Schedule of Safe Payments to Partners

	Partner			
	A(40%)[a]	B(20%)[a]	C(20%)[a]	D(20%)[a]
Computation to Determine How Available Cash on 7/3/X5 Should Be Distributed				
Capital and loan balances at cash distribution (from Illustration 30–8)				
Capital	$64,000	$27,000	$17,000	$ 3,000
Loan		10,000	5,000	2,000
Total	$64,000	$37,000	$22,000	$ 5,000
First worst-case assumption—Assume full				
loss on noncash assets of $107,000	(42,800)	(21,400)	(21,400)	(21,400)
Subtotal	$21,200	$15,600	$ 600	$(16,400)
Second worst-case assumption—Assume A, B, and C				
must absorb D's deficit	(8,200)	(4,100)	(4,100)	16,400
Subtotal	$13,000	$11,500	$ (3,500)	$ –0–
Repeat second worst-case assumption—				
Assume A and B must absorb C's deficit	(2,333)	(1,167)	3,500	
Cash to Be Distributed to Each Partner	$10,667	$10,333[b]	$ –0–	
Computation to Determine How Available Cash On 8/6/X5 Should Be Distributed				
Capital and loan balances at cash distribution (from Illustration 30–8)				
Capital	$35,333	$17,667	$ 8,000	
Loan			5,000	
Total	$35,333	$17,667	$13,000	$ –0–
First worst-case assumption—Assume full loss				
on noncash assets of $37,000	(14,800)	(7,400)	(7,400)	(7,400)
Subtotal	$20,533	$10,267	$ 5,600	$ (7,400)
Second worst-case assumption—Assume A, B, and C				
must absorb D's deficit	(3,700)	(1,850)	(1,850)	7,400
Cash to be distributed by each partner	$16,833	$ 8,417	$ 3,750[c]	$ –0–

[a]Denotes profit and loss sharing percentage.
[b]Of this amount, $10,000 is deemed a repayment of the loan.
[c]All of this amount is deemed a repayment of the loan.

3. The payments that may be made to partners, as shown on the schedule of safe payments, are first applied as a reduction of a partner's loan and then as a reduction of his or her capital in the statement of realization and liquidation.

4. After the first cash distribution to partners on July 3, 19X5, the capital accounts of partners A and B are in their respective profit and loss sharing ratio of 4:2. All future cash distributions to these two partners are in this 2:1 ratio.

5. After the second cash distribution to partners on August 6, 19X5, the capital accounts of partners A, B, and C (which includes partner C's loan account balance) are in their respective profit and loss sharing ratio of 4:2:2. All future cash distributions to these three partners are in this 4:2:2 ratio.

6. Obviously, the schedule of safe payments is prepared only after cash is available to distribute to partners. Thus it may be used only when the partnership is solvent.

CASH DISTRIBUTION PLAN

When cash is available to distribute to partners, a schedule of safe payments to partners must be prepared using the two worst-case assumptions (except for the final payment, of course). Distributing cash to partners in the sequence resulting from the use of the two worst-case assumptions brings the capital accounts into the profit and loss sharing ratio. (As determined earlier in the chapter, a partner's loan to the partnership is, in substance, part of that partner's capital investment.) Once the capital accounts are in this ratio, all future cash distributions to partners are made in the profit and loss sharing ratio.

By understanding the results of this process, we may analyze the relationship of the capital accounts at the beginning of liquidation to determine which partners receive cash as it becomes available. The analysis results in a **cash distribution plan.** A cash distribution plan has the advantage of informing partners at **the beginning of the liquidation process** when they will receive cash **in relation to the other partners.**

Understanding the methodology underlying the preparation of a cash distribution plan requires an intuitive understanding of the fact that when the capital accounts are not in the profit and loss sharing ratio, one or more partners have capital balances sufficient to absorb his, her, or their share of losses that exceed the partnership's net worth, whereas one or more other partners have capital balances sufficient to absorb only his, her, or their share of losses that are less than the partnership's net worth. To illustrate this fact, we present the following comparative analysis:

	Total	Partner			
		W(40%)	X(30%)	Y(20%)	Z(10%)
Actual preliquidation capital and loan balances	$100,000	$48,000	$33,000	$11,000	$ 8,000
Hypothetical capital and loan balances in the profit and loss sharing ratio of 4:3:2:1	$100,000	$40,000	$30,000	$20,000	$10,000
Percentage relationship of actual balances to hypothetical balances . .		120%	110%	55%	80%

Because their actual balances exceed the balances that would exist if they were kept in the profit and loss sharing ratio, only partners W and X could absorb their share of losses higher than the $100,000 partnership capital. On the other hand, because their actual balances are less than the balances that would exist if they were kept in the profit and loss sharing ratio, partners Y and Z could absorb only their share of losses that are less than the partnership capital of $100,000.

RANKING THE PARTNERS The percentage line of the preceding analysis ranks the partners in terms of which could absorb the largest loss to which could absorb the smallest loss. The ranking in this example is W, X, Z, and Y—that is, partner W (who has the highest percentage) can absorb the largest loss, and partner Y (who has the lowest percentage) can absorb the smallest loss. This ranking can be readily proved by calculating the exact loss needed to eliminate each partner's capital and loan balance. We divide each partner's capital and loan balance by his or her profit and loss sharing percentage. Continuing with our example, this calculation is as follows:

	Partner			
	W	**X**	**Y**	**Z**
Actual preliquidation capital balances	$ 48,000	$ 33,000	$11,000	$ 8,000
Profit and loss sharing percentage	40%	30%	20%	10%
Loss absorption potential	$120,000	$110,000	$55,000	$80,000
Ranking	1	2	4	3

Note that a $120,000 loss eliminates the capital and loan balance of partner W (the highest-ranking partner), whereas for partner Y (the lowest-ranking partner), a loss of only $55,000 eliminates his capital and loan balance.

Ranking the partners in this manner reveals the order in which cash should be distributed to them as it becomes available. Distributing cash in this order brings the capital balances into the profit and loss sharing ratio on a step-by-step basis, as follows:

1. **Distribution to highest-ranking partner.** Distribute sufficient cash to partner W so that his capital balance is brought into the profit and loss sharing ratio with the next highest-ranking partner (partner X).

2. **Distribution to two highest-ranking partners.** Distribute sufficient cash to partners W and X in their respective profit and loss sharing ratio of 4:3 so that their capital balances are brought into the profit and loss sharing ratio with the next highest-ranking partner (partner Z).

3. **Distribution to three highest-ranking partners.** Distribute sufficient cash to partners W, X, and Z in their respective profit and loss sharing ratio of 4:3:1 so that their capital balances are brought into the profit and loss sharing ratio with the next highest-ranking partner (partner Y).

Only the exact amount of cash distributed at each stage in this sequence needs to be determined. The calculations are shown in Illustration 30–10.

REVIEW POINTS FOR ILLUSTRATION 30–10 Note the following:

1. The cash distribution plan is operable only after outside creditors have been paid in full.

2. The schedule reflects only the order in which cash distributions to the partners will be made *if* cash is available to distribute to the partners.

3. The sequence of distributing cash in the cash distribution plan coincides with the sequence that would result if cash were distributed using the schedule of safe payments.

END-OF-CHAPTER REVIEW

SUMMARY OF KEY POINTS

1. Partners may greatly minimize the possibility of having to absorb another partner's deficit balance by specifying in the partnership agreement that capital balances are to be maintained in the profit and loss sharing ratio.

2. To the extent that a partner must absorb some or all of another partner's capital account deficit, the absorbing partner has **legal recourse** against the personal assets of the partner who could not make good the deficit balance through **setoff** or contribution.

3. In **lump-sum liquidations,** no distributions are made to the partners until the realization process is completed, when the full amount of the gain or loss on realization of the part-

ILLUSTRATION 30-10

W, X, Y, and Z Partnership
Schedule of Cash Distribution to Partners

	Partner			
	W	**X**	**Y**	**Z**
Preliquidation capital and loan balances	$48,000	$33,000	$11,000	$8,000
Ranking	1	2	4	3
Step 1: Cash to be distributed to W				
Balances, per above	$48,000	$33,000		
Balances in profit and loss ratio of 4:3 using				
X's actual balance as the base	44,000[a]	$33,000		
	$ 4,000			
Step 2: Cash to be distributed to W and X				
Balances, per above	$44,000	$33,000		$8,000
Balances in profit and loss ratio of 4:3:1 using				
Z's actual balance as the base	32,000[b]	24,000[c]		$8,000
	$12,000	$ 9,000		
Step 3: Cash to be distributed to W, X, and Z				
Balances, per above	$32,000	$24,000	$11,000	$8,000
Balances in profit and loss ratio of 4:3:2:1 using				
Y's actual balance as the base	22,000	16,500	$11,000	5,500
	$10,000	$ 7,500		$2,500

After this distribution, all capital accounts are in the profit and loss sharing ratio of 4:3:2:1. Accordingly, all future cash distributions are made in this ratio.

Sumary of Cash Distribution Plan

	W	**X**	**Y**	**Z**
First $4,000	$4,000			
Next $21,000 (4:3)	12,000	$9,000		
Next $20,000 (4:3:1)	10,000	7,500		$2,500
Any additional amounts (4:3:2:1)	40%	30%	20%	10%

[a]$33,000 × ⅘.
[b]$8,000 × ⁴⁄₁.
[c]$8,000 × ³⁄₁.

nership assets is known. In these cases, cash is distributed to the partners who have credit balances in their capital and loan accounts.

4. In **installment liquidations,** distributions are made to some or all of the partners as cash becomes available; thus, cash is distributed to partners before the full amount of the gain or loss on realization of the partnership assets is known. In these cases, cash distributions are made to partners in such a manner that the capital and loan balances of the individual partners are brought into line with the profit and loss sharing ratio.

5. The settlement of claims pursuant to legal recourse is governed by the **marshaling of assets principle.**

GLOSSARY OF NEW TERMS

Liquidation   The termination of a partnership's business activities.

Marshaling of assets   A legal doctrine whereby a partnership's creditors are given first claim on partnership assets, and personal creditors of an insolvent partner are given first claim on his or her personal assets.

Rule of setoff   The subtraction of a partner's deficit balance in his or her capital account from the balance of any loan outstanding to the partnership. Also, the subtraction of a partnership's loan to a partner from the partner's capital account.

SELF-STUDY QUESTIONS

(Answers are at the end of this chapter.)

1. Under the *rule of setoff*, which of these is *true*?
   a. A partnership's loan to a partner is deemed the equivalent of partnership capital.
   b. A deficit in a partner's capital account may be eliminated against his or her loan account to the partnership.
   c. Partnership assets must be set aside to pay off personal creditors of an insolvent partner before any cash distributions may be made to that partner.
   d. Partnership creditors have first priority against partnership assets.

2. In the *installment liquidation* of a partnership, how is cash distributed to partners?
   a. Equally
   b. In their normal profit and loss sharing ratio
   c. Using the ratio of the partners' capital balances
   d. Using the marshaling of assets procedure
   e. The ability to absorb losses

3. Under the *marshaling of assets* principle (and disregarding the federal bankruptcy laws), which is true?
   a. The capital and loan balances of the partners are combined.
   b. The two worst-case assumptions are used.
   c. A cash distribution plan is prepared.
   d. Cash is distributed to the partner having the highest capital balance.
   e. A distinction is made between personal liabilities and partnership liabilities.

4. The following condensed balance sheet is presented for the partnership of Acres, Farmer, and Tillman, who share profits and losses in the ratio of 3:2:1, respectively:

Cash	$ 60,000
Other assets	440,000
	$500,000
Liabilities	$200,000
Capital, Acres	30,000
Capital, Farmer	100,000
Capital, Tillman	170,000
	$500,000

The partners decided to liquidate the partnership and sell the other assets for $320,000. How should the available cash be distributed?
   a. Acres, –0–; Farmer, $40,000; Tillman, $140,000
   b. Acres, $60,000; Farmer, $60,000; Tillman, $60,000
   c. Acres, –0–; Farmer, $45,000; Tillman, $135,000
   d. Acres, –0–; Farmer, $53,333; Tillman, $127,667

5. The following condensed balance sheet is presented as of 7/1/X1 for the partnership of Rane, Waters, and Wells, who share profits and losses in the ratio of 5:3:2, respectively:

Cash	$ 20,000
Other assets	380,000
	$400,000
Liabilities	$100,000
Capital, Rane	210,000
Capital, Waters	43,000
Capital, Wells	47,000
	$400,000

The partners decided to liquidate the partnership. On 7/3/X1, the first cash sale of other assets with a $240,000 carrying amount realized $190,000. Safe installment payments to the partners were made on the same date. How should the available cash be distributed to the partners?
   a. Rane, $55,000; Waters, $33,000; Wells, $22,000

b. Rane, $108,000; Waters, –0–; Wells, $2,000
c. Rane, $105,000; Waters, –0–; Wells, $5,000
d. Rane, $115,000; Waters, –0–; Wells, $9,000

ASSIGNMENT MATERIAL

REVIEW QUESTIONS

1. How are *partnership* liquidations different from *corporate* liquidations?
2. What is the significance of maintaining partners' capital accounts in the profit and loss sharing ratio?
3. How is a *deficit* balance in a partner's capital account disposed of if that partner is unable to eliminate the deficit through setoff or contribution?
4. In what ratio should realization gains and losses during liquidation be shared among the partners? Why?
5. How is the *rule of setoff* applied?
6. What is the function of the *statement of realization and liquidation*?
7. In what order does the UPA specify that cash distributions are to be made to creditors and partners during liquidation?
8. Is the order in Question 7 strictly followed in all situations? Why or why not?
9. How does the marshaling of assets doctrine work?
10. Under what conditions may cash be distributed to partners on the *installment basis* rather than in a *lump sum*?
11. When a partnership is insolvent and some partners have positive capital account balances, but other partners have deficit balances, against which partners may creditors proceed personally to obtain full payment of their claims?
12. How is a partner's personal payment to partnership creditors treated on the partnership's books?

EXERCISES

E 30–1 **Lump-Sum Liquidation: Solvent Partnership Having Partners' Loans—All Partners Personally Solvent**   Partners Hall, Lane, and Tower share profits and losses in the ratio 3:2:1, respectively. The partners voted to liquidate the partnership when its assets, liabilities, and capital were as follows:

Cash	$ 2,000	Liabilities		$20,000
Noncash assets	78,000	Loans:		
		Hall		5,000
		Tower		10,000
		Capital:		
		Hall		20,000
		Lane		15,000
		Tower		10,000
	$80,000			$80,000

Assume that all the noncash assets were sold for $36,000, and all cash was distributed to outside creditors and partners.

Required   Prepare a statement of realization and liquidation.

E 30–2 **Lump-Sum Liquidation: Insolvent Partnership Having Loans to and from Partners—All Partners Personally Solvent**   Partners Bass, Singer, and Tennor share profits and losses equally. The partners voted to liquidate the partnership when its assets, liabilities, and capital were as follows:

Cash	$ 14,000	Liabilities	$ 80,000
Note receivable from Tennor	11,000	Loans:	
Other noncash assets	120,000	Bass	4,000
		Singer	16,000

(continued)

	Capital:	
	Bass	$ 15,000
	Singer	15,000
	Tennor	15,000
$145,000		$145,000

Additional Information
1. All the noncash assets of $120,000 were sold for $54,000.
2. Tennor instructed the partnership to write off the $11,000 he borrowed from the partnership because he has no liquid personal assets at this time (even though he is personally solvent).
3. All partners could eliminate any deficits in their capital accounts through setoff or contribution, or both.
4. All cash was distributed to outside creditors and partners.

Required   Prepare a statement of realization and liquidation.

E 30-3   **Lump-Sum Liquidation: Solvent Partnership Having Loans to and from Partners—Certain Partners Personally Insolvent**   Partners Criss, Kross, and Zigge share profits and losses in the ratio of 3:3:2, respectively. The partners voted to liquidate the partnership when its assets, liabilities, and capital were as follows:

Cash	$ 1,000	Liabilities	$34,000
Note receivable from Zigge	9,000	Loans:	
Other noncash assets	75,000	Kross	15,000
		Capital:	
		Criss	11,000
		Kross	10,000
		Zigge	15,000
	$85,000		$85,000

Additional Information
1. All the noncash assets of $75,000 were sold for $43,000.
2. Zigge was personally insolvent and unable to contribute any cash to the partnership.
3. Criss and Kross were both personally solvent and able to eliminate any deficits in their capital accounts through setoff or contribution.
4. All cash was distributed to outside creditors and partners.

Required   Prepare a statement of realization and liquidation.

E 30-4   **Lump-Sum Liquidation: Insolvent Partnership Having Loans from Partners—Certain Partners Personally Insolvent**   Partners Cattie, Deere, Fox, and O'Hare share profits and losses in the ratio of 5:2:2:1, respectively. The partners voted to liquidate the partnership when its assets and liabilities were as follows:

Cash	$ 15,000	Liabilities	$165,000
Noncash assets	235,000	Loans:	
		Deere	7,000
		Fox	5,000
		O'Hare	3,000
		Capital:	
		Cattie	40,000
		Deere	16,000
		Fox	10,000
		O'Hare	4,000
	$250,000		$250,000

Additional Information
1. All the noncash assets were sold for $135,000.
2. Cattie contributed $5,000 to the partnership after the noncash assets were sold. He has no additional funds beyond that needed to satisfy personal creditors.
3. All other partners were personally solvent and made capital contributions as necessary to eliminate deficits in their capital accounts.
4. All cash was distributed to outside creditors and partners.

Required   Prepare a statement of realization and liquidation.

E 30–5 **Insolvent Partnership and Insolvent Partners: Theory**   Q, R, S, and T are partners sharing profits and losses equally. The partnership is insolvent and is therefore being liquidated; its status and that of each partner follow:

Partner	Partnership Capital Balance	Personal Assets (exclusive of partnership interest)	Personal Liabilities (exclusive of partnership interest)
Q	$ 15,000	$100,000	$40,000
R	10,000	30,000	60,000
S	(20,000)	80,000	5,000
T	(30,000)	1,000	28,000
	$(25,000)		

Required   Select the correct response to the following:
Assuming that the UPA applies, the partnership creditors

1. Must first seek recovery against S because she is personally solvent and has a negative capital balance.
2. Will not be paid in full regardless of how they proceed legally because the partnership assets are less than its liabilities.
3. Must share R's interest in the partnership on a pro rata basis with R's personal creditors.
4. Have first claim to the partnership assets before any partner's personal creditors have rights to them.   (AICPA adapted)

E 30–6 **Installment Liquidation: Solvent Partnership Having Partner's Loan—First Cash Distribution to Partners**
Partners Deeds, Grant, and Trusty share profits and losses in the ratio 6:3:1, respectively. The partners voted to liquidate the partnership when its assets, liabilities, and capital were as follows:

Cash	$ 1,000	Liabilities	$35,000
Noncash assets	94,000	Loan:	
		Trusty	10,000
		Capital:	
		Deeds	30,000
		Grant	15,000
		Trusty	5,000
	$95,000		$95,000

Assume that noncash assets with a book value of $74,000 were sold for $54,000.

Required   Determine how the cash available *after* this sale should be distributed.

E 30–7 **Installment Liquidation: Solvent Partnership—First Cash Distribution to Partners**   Partners Springer, Sumner, and Winters share profits and losses in the ratio 5:3:2, respectively. The partners voted to liquidate the partnership when its assets, liabilities, and capital were as follows:

Cash	$ 40,000	
Other assets	210,000	
Liabilities		$ 60,000
Capital:		
Springer		48,000
Sumner		72,000
Winters		70,000
	$250,000	$250,000

The partnership will be liquidated over a long period of time. Cash is to be distributed to the partners as it becomes available. The *first* sale of noncash assets having a book value of $120,000 realized $90,000.

Required   Determine how the available cash should be distributed to the partners *after* this first sale.
(AICPA adapted)

E 30–8 **Installment Liquidation: Solvent Partnership With Partnership's and Partner's Loans—First Cash Distribution to Partners** Partners Castle, King, and Queen share profits and losses in the ratio 4:4:2, respectively. The partners voted to liquidate the partnership when its assets, liabilities, and capital were as follows:

Cash	$ 20,000	
Note receivable from Castle	10,000	
Other assets	170,000	
Liabilities		$ 50,000
Loan from King		30,000
Capital:		
Castle		37,000
King		15,000
Queen		68,000
	$200,000	$200,000

The partnership will be liquidated over a long period of time. Cash will be distributed to the partners as it becomes available. The *first* sale of noncash assets having a book value of $90,000 realized $50,000.

Required Determine how the available cash should be distributed to the partners *after* this first sale.

(AICPA adapted)

PROBLEMS

P 30–1* **Lump-Sum Liquidation: Solvent Partnership Having Partner's Loan—All Partners Personally Solvent** Partners Rockne and Stone share profits in the ratio 3:2, respectively. The partners agreed to liquidate the partnership when the assets, liabilities, and capital were as follows:

Cash	$ 6,000		Liabilities	$27,000
Noncash assets	44,000		Loan:	
			Stone	6,000
			Capital:	
			Rockne	14,000
			Stone	3,000
	$50,000			$50,000

Additional Information
1. Rockne agreed personally to take certain equipment having a $5,000 book value. (The partners estimated its current value at $6,500.)
2. Stone agreed personally to take certain office furniture having a book value of $3,000. (The partners estimated its current value at $2,000.)
3. All other noncash assets were sold for $25,000.
4. Liquidation expenses of $1,000 were incurred.
5. Cash was distributed to outside creditors and partners.

Required Prepare a statement of realization and liquidation.

P 30–2* **Lump-Sum Liquidation: Solvent Partnership Having Partners' Loans—Certain Partners Personally Insolvent** Partners Duke, Lord, Noble, and Prince share profits and losses in the ratio 4:3:2:1, respectively. The partners agreed to liquidate the partnership when it had assets, liabilities, and capital as follows:

Cash	$ 10,000		Liabilities	$ 78,000
Noncash assets	140,000		Loans:	
			Duke	4,000
			Lord	3,000

(continued)

---

*The financial statement information presented for problems accompanied by asterisks is also provided on MODEL 30 (filename: MODEL30) of the software disk that is available for use with the text, allowing the problem to be worked on the computer.

	Capital:	
	Duke	10,000
	Lord	10,000
	Noble	30,000
	Prince	15,000
$150,000		$150,000

Additional Information

1. The noncash assets were sold for $90,000.
2. Duke is personally insolvent.
3. Lord contributed $2,000 cash to the partnership; he had no other available funds in excess of amounts needed to satisfy personal creditors.
4. All cash was distributed to outside creditors and partners.

Required Prepare a statement of realization and liquidation.

P 30–3* **Lump-Sum Liquidation: Insolvent Partnership Having Partners' Loans—Certain Partners Personally Insolvent**
Partners Oates, Ryley, and Wheatman share profits and losses in the ratio 3:3:2, respectively. The partners agreed to liquidate the partnership when assets, liabilities, and capital were as follows:

Cash	$ 5,000	Liabilities	$48,000
Noncash assets	85,000	Loans:	
		Oates	10,000
		Ryley	3,000
		Capital:	
		Oates	11,000
		Ryley	10,000
		Wheatman	8,000
	$90,000		$90,000

Additional Information

1. The noncash assets were sold for $29,000.
2. Outside creditors of the partnership proceeded against Wheatman and collected from her $14,000 that the partnership was unable to pay.
3. The partnership incurred liquidation expenses of $4,000, which Ryley paid personally.
4. Oates is personally insolvent.
5. Ryley and Wheatman (who are both personally solvent) make a personal settlement between themselves.

Required Prepare a statement of realization and liquidation.

P 30–4 **Installment Liquidation: Schedule of Safe Payments—First Cash Distribution to Partners** On 1/1/X2, the partners of Allen, Brown, and Cox, who share profits and losses in the ratio of 5:3:2, respectively, decide to liquidate their partnership. The partnership trial balance at this date follows:

	Debit	Credit
Cash	$ 18,000	
Accounts receivable	66,000	
Inventory	52,000	
Machinery and equipment	249,000	
Accumulated depreciation		$ 60,000
Loan, Allen	30,000	
Accounts payable		53,000
Loan, Brown		20,000
Capital, Allen		118,000
Capital, Brown		90,000
Capital, Cox		74,000
	$415,000	$415,000

The partners plan a program of piecemeal conversion of assets to minimize liquidation losses. All available cash, less an amount retained to provide for future expenses, is to be distributed to the partners at the end of each month. The liquidation transactions for January 19X2 follow:

1. Accounts receivable of $51,000 was collected; the balance is uncollectible.
2. The amount of $38,000 was received for the entire inventory.
3. Liquidation expenses of $2,000 were paid.
4. Outside creditors were paid $50,000 after offset of a $3,000 credit memorandum received on 1/11/X2.
5. Cash of $10,000 was retained in the business at the end of the month for potential unrecorded liabilities and anticipated expenses.

Required   Prepare a schedule of safe payments showing how cash was distributed to the partners as of 1/31/X2.   (AICPA adapted)

P 30–5* **Installment Liquidation: Schedule of Safe Payments and Statement of Realization and Liquidation**   Partners Barley, Flax, and Rice share profits and losses in the ratio 6:3:1, respectively. The partners decided to liquidate the partnership on 6/30/X5, when its assets, liabilities, and capital were as follows:

Cash	$ 10,000	Liabilities	$ 42,000
Noncash assets	130,000	Loans:	
		Barley	4,000
		Flax	1,000
		Capital:	
		Barley	84,000
		Flax	5,000
		Rice	4,000
	$140,000		$140,000

Additional Information

1. On 7/1/X5, liquidation expenses were estimated at approximately $3,000. Actual liquidation expenses totaled only $2,500 and were paid as follows:

July 31, 19X5	$1,000
August 31, 19X5	1,000
September 30, 19X5	500
	$2,500

2. Noncash assets were sold as follows:

Date	Book Value	Proceeds
July 5, 19X5	$ 30,000	$ 36,000
August 7, 19X5	40,000	28,000
September 9, 19X5	60,000	44,000
	$130,000	$108,000

3. Partners were able to eliminate any deficits in their capital accounts through setoff or contribution as deficit balances occurred.
4. Cash was distributed to outside creditors and partners as it was available at the end of each month.

Required   Prepare a statement of realization and liquidation, including supporting schedules showing how cash was distributed to outside creditors and partners as it was available.

P 30–6 **Installment Liquidation: Schedule of Cash Distribution**   Partners Brickley, Glass, Steele, and Woods decide to dissolve their partnership. They plan to sell the assets gradually to minimize losses. They share profits and losses as follows: Brickley, 40%; Glass, 35%; Steele, 15%; and Woods, 10%. The partnership's trial balance as of 10/1/X1, the date on which liquidation begins, is shown below.

	Debit	Credit
Cash	$ 200	
Receivables	25,900	
Inventory, 10/1/X1	42,600	

(continued)

Equipment (net)	19,800	
Accounts payable		$ 3,000
Loan, Brickley		6,000
Loan, Glass		10,000
Capital, Brickley		20,000
Capital, Glass		21,500
Capital, Steele		18,000
Capital, Woods		10,000
	$88,500	$88,500

Required　**1.** Prepare a statement as of 10/1/X1 showing how cash will be distributed among partners by installments as it becomes available.

2. On 10/31/X1, $12,700 cash was available to the partners. How should it be distributed?

(AICPA adapted)

P 30–7　**Installment Liquidation: Schedule of Cash Distribution**　Partners Arbuckle, Beltmore, and Tanner want you to assist them in winding up the affairs of their partnership. You gather the following information:

1. The 6/30/X2 trial balance of the partnership is as follows:

	Debit	Credit
Cash	$ 6,000	
Accounts receivable	22,000	
Inventory	14,000	
Plant and equipment (net)	99,000	
Note receivable—Arbuckle	12,000	
Note receivable—Tanner	7,500	
Accounts payable		$ 17,000
Capital, Arbuckle		67,000
Capital, Beltmore		45,000
Capital, Tanner		31,500
	$160,500	$160,500

2. The partners share profits and losses as follows: Arbuckle, 50%; Beltmore, 30%; and Tanner, 20%.

The partners are considering a $100,000 offer for the accounts receivable inventory and for plant and equipment as of June 30. The $100,000 will be paid to the partners in installments, the number and amounts of which are to be negotiated.

Required　Prepare a cash distribution schedule as of 6/30/X2, showing how the $100,000 will be distributed as it is available.

(AICPA adapted)

P 30–8*　　**Installment Liquidation: Schedule of Cash Distribution and Statement of Realization and Liquidation**　Assume the facts in Problem 30–7, except that the partners decide to liquidate their partnership instead of accepting the $100,000 offer. Cash is distributed to the partners at the end of the month.

A summary of the liquidation transactions follows:

JULY

1. Collected $16,500 on accounts receivable; the balance is uncollectible.
2. Received $10,000 for the entire inventory.
3. Paid $1,000 liquidation expenses.
4. Retained $8,000 cash in the business at month-end.

AUGUST

1. Paid $1,500 liquidation expenses. As part payment of his capital, Tanner accepted a piece of special equipment that he developed that had a $4,000 book value. The partners agreed that a $10,000 value should be placed on the machine for liquidation purposes.
2. Retained $2,500 cash in the business at month-end.

SEPTEMBER

1. Received $75,000 on sale of remaining plant and equipment.
2. Paid $1,000 liquidation expenses.
3. No cash retained in the business.

Required   Prepare a statement of realization and liquidation.   (AICPA adapted)

✳ THINKING CRITICALLY ✳

✳ CASES ✳

C 30–1   **Manner of Sharing Realization Losses During Liquidation**   Jennings and Nelson recently formed a partnership under the following terms:

	Jennings	Nelson
Capital contributions	$80,000	$20,000
Time devoted to the business	100%	100%
Profit and loss sharing formula		
Interest rate on capital over $20,000	10%	10%
Residual profit and loss	50%	50%

You have been hired as the partnership's accountant. While closing the partnership books for the first month of operations, Jennings casually mentions to you that he believes that a "good and equitable" partnership agreement had been negotiated between himself and Nelson.

Required   How would you respond to this comment?

C 30–2   **Manner of Sharing Realization Losses During Liquidation**   Harper, McCord, and Stringer are attempting to form a partnership in which profits and losses are shared in the ratio 4:4:2, respectively. They *cannot* agree on terms of the partnership agreement relating to potential liquidation. Harper believes that it is a waste of time to have any provisions relating to liquidation because the prospective partners firmly believe that the business will be successful. McCord believes that in the event of liquidation, any realization losses should be shared in the ratio of the capital balances because this method allows each partner to absorb losses in relation to his or her capacity to do so. Stringer believes that any liquidation losses should be shared *equally* because if the business is *not* successful, it will most likely be the fault of each partner. As the accountant who will be keeping the partnership's books, you have been asked to settle this dispute.

Required   How would you respond to this request?

C 30–3   **Procedures for Distributing Available Cash to Partners**   The partnership of Dials and Winder is in the process of liquidation, which is expected to take several months. Dials, who is in need of cash, wants cash distributed to the partners as it is available. Winder believes that no cash should be distributed to either partner until all the assets are sold and the total realization gain or loss is known. Thus the partnership would *not* distribute cash to a partner and later request a capital contribution to absorb any capital deficits created by realization losses.

Required   Evaluate the positions of each partner.

C 30–4   **Procedures for Distributing Available Cash to Partners**   The partnership of Jurnell, Ledgley, and Post is in the process of being liquidated. The trial balance *immediately after* the sale of a portion of the non-cash assets and full payment to outside creditors is as follows:

Cash	$20,000	
Note receivable from Ledgley	14,000	
Other assets	36,000	
Loan, Jurnell		$ 5,000

(continued)

Capital:

Jurnell		11,000
Ledgley		20,000
Post		34,000
	$70,000	$70,000

Jurnell wants the available cash distributed to her to pay off her loan—she cites Section 40(b) of the UPA, which states that partners' loans have priority over partners' capital. Post wants the cash distributed to him because he has the largest capital investment. Ledgley believes that it should be distributed *equally*, which is how profits and losses are shared.

Required   1. Evaluate the positions of each partner.
2. Who should receive the $20,000 available cash?

ANSWERS TO SELF-STUDY QUESTIONS

1. b   2. e   3. e   4. a   5. c

ESTATES AND TRUSTS

The minute you read something that you can't understand, you can almost be sure it was drawn up by a lawyer.

WILL ROGERS

In this chapter, we consider the role accountants play in the administration of estates and trusts. Before proceeding into this subject, however, we discuss briefly the role accountants may play in estate planning, which takes place *before* an individual dies.

I THE ROLE ACCOUNTANTS PLAY IN ESTATE PLANNING

ESTATE PLANNING

People commonly make plans for the orderly transfer of their property upon their death to relatives, other persons, organizations, or trusts to be set up for the benefit of relatives. Such forethought is known as **estate planning** and is accomplished under the guidance of attorneys, often working closely with accountants. The *attorney's* role centers around preparing wills and, in many cases, trust agreements (discussed in detail later in the chapter). The *accountant's* role consists of suggesting planning techniques consistent with the objective of minimizing *transfer costs* (federal estate taxes, state inheritance taxes, and fees and expenses). In this capacity, an accountant often determines expected transfer costs under various options. An accountant may also play an important role in advising his or her client on accounting matters pertaining to trusts that are to be established.

Accountants' participation in estate planning is usually limited to cases in which individuals are wealthy or moderately wealthy. The Tax Reform Act of 1976 substantially overhauled the federal estate and gift tax laws, and an estimated 98% of all estates became exempt from estate and gift tax laws. However, inflation was lowering this percentage. Furthermore, certain inequities were perceived to exist still. To address these two areas, further changes were enacted in the Economic Recovery Tax Act of 1981, and an estimated 99.5% of all estates are now exempt from estate and gift tax laws. An accountant participating in estate planning must have substantial expertise in estate and gift taxes—a complex area of the tax laws. A detailed discussion of these laws and the use of planning techniques to minimize transfer costs is properly the subject matter of a tax course. A brief discussion of the estate and gift tax laws is included, however, later in the chapter.

THE TRUST FEATURE OF ESTATE PLANNING

Frequently, a will contains a provision for the establishment of a **trust**, whereby certain designated property of the decedent's estate is to be transferred to a **trustee** when the person dies. The trustee holds legal title to the property and administers it for the benefit of one or more other persons, who are called **beneficiaries.** Thus the trustee serves in a position of trust with respect to the beneficiaries. This is a fiduciary relationship, and the trustee is commonly referred to as a **fiduciary.** (Recall another type of fiduciary relationship discussed in Chapter 23 in connection with companies in bankruptcy proceedings.) The person creating the trust is referred to as the **trustor** (also known as the *grantor, donor, creator,* and *settlor*). The legal document creating the trust is the *trust agreement.* Trust beneficiaries are of the following two classes:

1. **Income beneficiary.** An income beneficiary is entitled to the income earned by the trust's assets, referred to as the *trust principal*, or *corpus.*
2. **Principal beneficiary.** A **principal beneficiary** is entitled to the principal, or *corpus*, of the trust, which is distributed according to the terms of the trust agree-

ment (usually at the specified termination date of the trust). A principal beneficiary is also known as a **residuary beneficiary** or **remainderman.**

The *income* and *principal* beneficiaries may or may not be the same person. A common arrangement is to name one's spouse as the *income* beneficiary for his or her remaining life and name one's children as the *principal* beneficiaries. Another common arrangement is to name one's minor children as both *income* and *principal* beneficiaries, with some or all of the income to be used for their support and the *principal* to be distributed to them when they reach a specified age.

THE BASIC ACCOUNTING PROBLEM

Regardless of whether the *income* or *principal* beneficiaries of a trust are the same person or persons, **it is necessary to account for the separate interests of each class.** Accomplishing this task is the subject of this chapter. The requirement of correct separate accounting for the interests of each class is the reason for the special theories and techniques for accounting for the administration of estates and trusts by fiduciaries. Otherwise, quite simple record-keeping procedures are adequate.

Accounting for the separate interests of each class of beneficiaries is even more difficult because a built-in clash of interests exists between the two classes. When the *principal* and *income* beneficiaries are *not* the same person or persons, the clash revolves around *who gets what.* When the *principal* and *income* beneficiaries *are* the same person or persons, the clash concerns the *timing of distributions.* Frequently, disputes between these interests lead to litigation.

Although a trust may be established by a transfer of property to the trustee during the transferor's lifetime (known as an **inter vivos trust**), we deal solely with trusts that are created by a gift made in the will of a decedent (known as a **testamentary trust**). Thus we must consider the administration of a decedent's estate in connection with the establishment of a trust.

RELATIONSHIP BETWEEN AN ESTATE AND A TESTAMENTARY TRUST

All states have enacted some form of legislation concerning the administration of trusts. State statutes pertaining to trusts are operative, in most cases, only to the extent that they do *not* conflict with the terms of a trust agreement. Twenty states have adopted the Revised Uniform Principal and Income Act (of 1962) either in its entirety or with modifications; accordingly, we base our discussion on this act. Under it, testamentary trusts are deemed to be created at the time of a person's death, even though the property to be placed in trust usually is *not* actually distributed to the trustee until some time *after* the person dies.[1] Property to be placed in trust becomes subject to the trust at the time of death; the rights of the *income beneficiary* are also established at the time of death. Therefore, the interests of the *income beneficiary* of the trust must be accounted for separately from the interests of the *principal beneficiary* of the trust **during the period of the estate administration,** as well as after the property is actually transferred to the trustee. (Some trust agreements simplify matters by specifying that the rights of the *income beneficiary* do *not* begin until the assets are *actually* transferred to the trustee.)

For accounting purposes, we treat the estate and the trust as separate accounting entities. (Conceptually, we view each of these entities as composing two accounting entities—a "principal entity" and an "income entity.") For tax-reporting purposes, estates and trusts both are treated as taxable entities. They are *not* legal entities, however, in the sense that corporations are legal entities.

---

[1]Revised Uniform Principal and Income Act, U.L.A. Volume 7A, Section 4 (St. Paul: West Publishing Co.).

II PRINCIPAL VERSUS INCOME

When a testamentary trust is established, every transaction must be analyzed to determine whether it relates to principal or income. An incorrect determination has important legal consequences to a fiduciary. If it is later determined that income has been overstated and the fiduciary cannot recover the amount of the overpayment from the income beneficiary, the fiduciary must make up the deficiency. In turn, if the error was made by the accountant or was based on the bad advice of the fiduciary's legal counsel, these persons may be professionally responsible to the fiduciary.

MANNER OF ANALYZING TRANSACTIONS

REFERENCE TO THE TRUST AGREEMENT   In determining whether a transaction pertains to principal or income, **GAAP is not the point of reference.** The trustor may create his or her own definition of income. In other words, the trustor may specify the receipts that are to be income and the receipts that are to be principal. Likewise, the trustor may specify disbursements to be treated as charges against income and disbursements to be treated as reductions of the principal. Accordingly, all transactions must be analyzed as to the decedent's intent.

Because the decedent is not available, the first step is to determine whether the decedent's intent is expressed in the trust agreement. Unfortunately, a common shortcoming of estate planning is that trust agreements usually do not explain in detail the treatment to be accorded specific types of receipts and disbursements. Many potential problems can be avoided if the decedent's personal accountant, who should have a knowledge of his or her client's properties, participates in the preparation of the trust agreement sections that pertain to accounting matters.

REFERENCE TO STATE LAW   If the treatment of an item *cannot* be resolved by referring to the trust agreement, the second step is to find out what the state law is on the subject. Again, GAAP is *not* the point of reference. The Revised Uniform Principal and Income Act specifically addresses the principal versus income treatment of several items. Much of the impetus for revising the original Uniform Principal and Income Act (of 1931) resulted from the development of new forms of investment property, the treatment of which was not specified in state statutes. The treatment accorded many items specifically dealt with in the act produces income results that would be obtained if GAAP is applied. For numerous other items, however, the treatment produces results that are quite contrary to GAAP. For example, the act provides that the following items be treated as increases and decreases, respectively, to the trust *principal* instead of to *income:*

1. Gains and losses on the sale of corporate securities.
2. Gains and losses on the sale of rental property.
3. Bond discounts (with certain exceptions) and bond premiums.

We present the general thrust of the act's accounting requirements later in the chapter. Section 5 of the act calls for income during the administration of an estate to be determined in the same manner that income is to be determined by a trustee in administering a trust. Thus the act applies to *estates* as well as *trusts.*

REFERENCE TO CASE LAW   If the treatment of an item is *not* covered in state law, the third step is to determine whether the courts have encountered and ruled on the same problem. If so, the answer is found in case law. If the answer cannot be found there, the fiduciary may petition the court for a determination.

THE ACCOUNTANT'S ROLE IN ANALYZING TRANSACTIONS   When the treatment to be accorded an item is *not* clearly set forth in the trust agreement or state statutes, the accountant does not determine whether an item pertains to principal or income. This is the function of the fiduciary, the fiduciary's legal counsel, or the courts. The accountant's role is expanded, of course, when the trust agreement specifies that income is to be determined in accordance with GAAP. Such cases are the exception, *not* the rule.

MANNER OF RECORD KEEPING

Because the interests of the principal beneficiary and the income beneficiary must be accounted for separately, it is necessary to identify the assets and transactions pertaining to *principal* and those pertaining to *income*. Conceptually, we may view the assets and transactions pertaining to *principal* as belonging to a separate accounting entity and do likewise for the assets and transactions pertaining to *income*. Thus a trust may be viewed as comprising *two* entities, each with a self-balancing set of books.

One method of record keeping is physically to maintain separate journals and general ledgers for each conceptual entity. An alternate method is to use *one* set of books for both entities but to use separately identified columns in the journals and separately identified accounts in the general ledger for principal and income. This technique allows separate trial balances to be prepared for each conceptual entity, as though two general ledgers were used. In practice, this technique is quite simple to work with, largely because cash is usually the only type of asset common to both *principal* and *income*. Regardless of which method is used, it is *not* necessary to use *one* bank account for cash pertaining to principal and another for cash pertaining to income, unless the trust agreement requires it. When only *one* set of books is used, the separation of the total cash balance is reflected in the general ledger through a Principal Cash ledger account and an Income Cash ledger account. *One* set of books is generally used in practice. We illustrate this manner of record keeping later in the chapter.

CASH BASIS VERSUS ACCRUAL BASIS

AT THE BEGINNING AND THE END OF THE INCOME BENEFICIARY'S RIGHTS   In most respects, the Revised Uniform Principal and Income Act provides for the use of the *accrual basis* in determining at the time of the person's death the assets to be treated as part of the trust principal. The purpose, of course, is to establish a reasonably fair and practical starting point to determine income for the income beneficiary. Specifically, the following items are to be included as part of the *trust principal* at the time of death:

1. Amounts due but *not* paid at the time of death (Section 4[a]).
2. Prorations of amounts not due at the time of death that pertain to periodic payments, including rents, interest, and annuities (Section 4[b]).
3. Corporate distributions declared for which the date of record precedes the person's death (Section 4[e]).

The *cash basis* is specified for all other items (Section 4[c]). In a somewhat parallel manner, the act provides in most respects for the use of the *accrual basis* on termination of an income interest to effect a reasonably fair and practical cutoff of the *income beneficiary's* interest (Sections 4[d] and [e]).

ACCOUNTING PERIODS BETWEEN THE BEGINNING AND THE END OF THE INCOME BENEFICIARY'S RIGHTS   For accounting periods between the beginning and the end of the *income beneficiary's* rights, the *accrual basis* in most respects does *not* fit in with the underlying objective of the fiduciary, which is to account for the

flow of assets in and out of his or her control. Accordingly, with one major exception, the *cash basis* is considered more appropriate for such accounting periods. The *accrual basis* offers much better measuring results, however, when determining the income of a business in which principal is invested.

AT THE END OF THE ESTATE ADMINISTRATION   When the income rights of the *income beneficiary* are established at the time of the person's death, the end of the estate administration is *not* relevant to the income and principal beneficiaries. Using the *accrual basis* is therefore unnecessary at the *end* of probate administration. Of course, if the trust agreement provides that income rights do not start until the *end* of the *estate administration*, accrual techniques are appropriate.

III   ACCOUNTING FOR ESTATES

PROBATE ADMINISTRATION

When a person dies, his or her property and liabilities (collectively referred to as the **estate**) must be administered, regardless of whether the person died with a will (referred to as having died **testate**) or without a will (referred to as having died **intestate**). Each state has laws concerning the affairs of decedents, commonly known as **probate law** or the **law of decedent estates.** A Uniform Probate Code exists, but only two states have adopted it. Accordingly, uniformity among the states in this area is negligible. The objectives of probate laws are to (1) discover and make effective the decedent's intent in the distribution of his or her property, (2) gather and preserve the decedent's property, and (3) provide for an efficient and orderly system of making payments of estate debts and distributions in the course of liquidating the estate. If the decedent does *not* have a will, property is distributed according to state inheritance tax laws.

Under the probate laws, decedent's affairs must be administered by fiduciaries who are subject to the control of the state **probate courts** (referred to in a few states as **surrogate** or **orphans' courts**). The following terms are used for estate fiduciaries:

1. An **executor** (if male) or **executrix** (if female) is named in the decedent's will as his or her personal representative in administering his or her estate and is appointed by the court to serve in that capacity.

2. An **administrator** (if male) or **administratrix** (if female) is appointed by the court when (a) a person dies intestate, (b) a person does *not* name anyone in his or her will, (c) the person named in the decedent's will refuses to serve as executor, or (d) the court refuses to appoint the person named in the will.

The title to a decedent's property is subject to the possession of the fiduciary and the control of the court, even though title passes at the time of death to the person or persons to whom the property is to be distributed. In short, the probate court serves as guardian of the estate. If a person dies testate, his or her will has no legal effect until it has been *probated*. **Probate** is the act by which the court determines whether the will submitted to it meets the statutory requirements concerning wills. If the court so determines, it issues a certificate or decree that enables the terms of the will to be carried out. The will is said to have been *admitted to probate.*

Basically, an estate fiduciary must (1) inventory the decedent's assets, (2) settle the claims of the decedent's creditors, (3) prepare and file the applicable income, estate, and inheritance tax returns, (4) distribute the remaining assets as gifts as the will provides, and (5) make the appropriate accountings to the court.

GIFT TERMINOLOGY

A gift of personal property by means of a will is called a **legacy.** The recipient of a legacy is called a **legatee.** Legacies are classified as follows:

1. A **specific legacy** is a gift of specified noncash items. For example, "my automobile to my son, Harvey."
2. A **demonstrative legacy** is a gift of cash for which a particular fund or source is designated from which payment is to be made. For example, "$1,000 to my sister, Christine, out of my savings account."
3. A **general legacy** is a gift of cash for which no particular fund or source is designated from which to make payment. For example, "$2,000 to my brother Chad."
4. A **residual legacy** is a gift of all personal property remaining after distribution of specific, demonstrative, and general legacies. For example, "the balance of my personal property to my wife, Ann Marie."

If the balance of the estate assets *after* payment of estate liabilities, taxes, and administrative expenses is insufficient to make good all of the various types of legacies, the legacies are deemed to be null and inoperative in the reverse of the order listed here (referred to as the process of **abatement**).

A gift of *real property* by means of a will is called a **devise.** The recipient of a devise is called a **devisee.** Devises are classified as specific, general, or residual. Estate assets to be transferred to a trustee pursuant to the establishment of a testamentary trust may be any type of legacy or devise. The most common type of legacy given to a trustee is a residual legacy, which we illustrate later in the chapter.

INVENTORY OF DECEDENT'S PROPERTY

The estate fiduciary's first major task in administering the estate is to inventory the decedent's property. Each item must then be valued at its current market value for federal estate and state inheritance tax purposes (using state inheritance tax or private appraisers, as required), and the appropriate tax forms must be filed. (We discuss these in more detail in the following section.) In addition, the estate fiduciary must submit to the probate court an inventory of the decedent's property subject to probate administration. Not all items included for estate tax and state inheritance tax purposes are subject to probate administration. Many states allow real property to pass *directly* to the beneficiaries (or to the trustee, in the case of real property placed in trust), *bypassing* probate administration. Likewise, many states allow certain types of personal property—such as personal effects, clothing, household items, and a limited amount of cash—to pass directly to beneficiaries outside of probate. State probate law must be consulted to determine which items are subject to probate administration; an attorney's services are usually used for this. Although required only by some states, a separate schedule should list the items *not* subject to probate administration, if only for the record.

In general, the following items are subject to probate administration:

1. Cash in checking and savings accounts, in a safety deposit box, and on hand.
2. Investments in stocks and bonds.
3. Interest accrued on bonds through the date of the person's death.
4. Dividends declared on stocks prior to the person's death.
5. Investments in businesses and partnerships.
6. Life insurance proceeds that name the estate as the beneficiary.
7. Notes and accounts receivable, including interest accrued through the date of the person's death.

8. Accrued rents and royalties receivable.

9. Advances to those named in the will as beneficiaries, including interest accrued through the date of death.

10. Unpaid wages, salaries, and commissions.

11. Valuables such as jewelry and coin collections.

12. Real estate *not* specifically exempted (the most common exemption is property held in joint tenancy, because all rights in such property immediately pass to the surviving tenant at the time of death).

Even though other items may be included for federal estate tax and state inheritance tax purposes, the fiduciary's accountability to the probate court comprises only the items subject to probate administration. The fiduciary must take control of these items for estate preservation purposes.

PAYMENT OF ESTATE LIABILITIES

The estate's liabilities must be paid before making any distributions to beneficiaries. Probate laws usually require the estate fiduciary to publish promptly notices in newspapers for a certain period calling for persons having claims against the decedent to file them within a specified period of time or be barred forever. The estate fiduciary is responsible for determining the validity of claims filed. If the estate assets are insufficient to pay all liabilities, payment must be made in accordance with the priority provided for in state law. This general order of priority follows:

1. Funeral expenses.

2. Estate administration expenses.

3. Allowances to support the decedent's spouse and dependent children for a specified period of time.

4. Expenses of the deceased's last illness.

5. Wages owed to the decedent's employees.

6. Debts owed to the federal, state, or local government that have priority under federal or state law.

7. Lien claims.

8. All other debts.

TAX MATTERS

The estate fiduciary is responsible for preparing and filing tax returns for the decedent and the decedent's estate.

DECEDENT'S FINAL INCOME TAX RETURN   A final income tax return must be filed for the decedent, covering the period from the date of the decedent's last income tax return to the date of death. Any taxes owed are paid from estate assets.

TAXATION OF ESTATE INCOME   An estate is a taxable entity, which comes into being at the time of the person's death. Estate income taxes must be filed annually on federal Form 1041 (U.S. Fiduciary Income Tax Return) until the estate is terminated upon discharge of the fiduciary by the probate court. The gross income of an estate is computed in the same manner as that of an individual. In addition to deductions for expenses relating to the generation of income, a deduction is allowed for net income currently distributable to beneficiaries. As a result, the estate is taxed only on the remaining net income not currently distributable. The beneficiaries, in turn, are taxed on the currently distributable net income. The tax rates that apply to estates are those that apply to trusts:

Taxable Income	Tax Rate
First $7,500	15.0%
Over $7,500	39.6%

The concept of estate income for tax-reporting purposes differs in many respects from the concept of estate income for fiduciary-reporting purposes. Accordingly, working paper adjustments to fiduciary book income amounts are usually necessary to determine gross income and deductions for income tax–reporting purposes.

STATE INHERITANCE TAXES   Most states impose an inheritance tax on the value of property to be distributed to each individual heir. This tax is based on the **right to receive or inherit** property; thus the burden of taxation falls on the recipient of the property. Although the taxes are paid to the state out of the estate assets, the estate fiduciary either seeks reimbursement from the individual heirs (when noncash assets are distributed) or reduces proportionately the amount to be distributed to each individual heir (when cash is distributed). The tax rates and allowable exemptions are based on the relationship of the heir to the decedent, with tax rates increasing and exemptions decreasing as the relationship becomes more distant. It is quite common, however, for wills to provide specifically that state inheritance taxes be paid out of the residue of the estate, so that the entire burden of taxation falls on the heirs who receive the residue.

FEDERAL ESTATE TAXES   Unlike state inheritance taxes, the federal estate tax is based on the **right to give** property. The burden of taxation, therefore, falls entirely on the estate, *not* on each individual heir. Of course, this merely reduces the amount of the residue of the estate that otherwise would be distributed to heirs. (Some state probate codes require the federal estate tax to be borne by each heir, as with the state inheritance taxes.) Assuming a decedent has made no gifts during his or her lifetime, estate taxes are calculated in the following manner:

1. The total value, or **gross estate,** of the decedent's property is determined at the time of death or, if the estate fiduciary elects, at a date six months after death. Property sold within six months of the person's death is valued at its selling price. (Recall that the gross estate for federal estate tax purposes is usually larger than the probate estate.)
2. The taxable estate is determined by deducting the following from the gross estate determined in step 1:
   a. Liabilities of the estate.
   b. Administrative expenses, including funeral expenses, court costs, and attorney fees.
   c. Casualty and theft losses during the administration of the estate.
   d. A **marital deduction** (a term used to describe **a transfer between spouses that is exempt from transfer taxes**). The marital deduction is unlimited; thus, any amount may be used.
   e. Charitable contributions.
3. The estate tax rates are then applied to the taxable estate to arrive at the **gross estate tax.** The estate tax rates are graduated from 18% on taxable estates in excess of $10,000 to a maximum of 55% on taxable estates in excess of $3,000,000.
4. Certain specified tax credits—such as state death taxes (with limitations) and the unified transfer tax credit—are subtracted from the gross estate tax to arrive at the **net estate tax.**

The *unified transfer tax credit* is the equivalent of an exemption. The following table shows the amount of the unified transfer tax credit and the related exemption equivalent:

Unified Transfer Tax Credit	Exemption Equivalent
$192,800	$600,000

Accordingly, a single individual may transfer a taxable estate of $600,000 and incur no federal estate tax.

Because a surviving spouse may take a marital deduction for any amount, all federal estate taxes otherwise payable can be deferred until the death of that surviving spouse. Thus the tax law treats a married couple as a single economic unit.

To use the unified credit fully, the marital deduction amount chosen generally is small enough to leave a taxable estate equal to the $600,000 exemption equivalent of the unified transfer tax credit. (The taxable estate of $600,000 is then placed in a trust for the decedent's children.) For example, assume that (1) Henry Steele passed away, (2) his gross estate is $3,700,000, and (3) all deductions other than the marital deduction are $100,000. With a marital deduction amount of $3,000,000, the taxable estate is $600,000, resulting in a gross estate tax of $192,800. Because of the unified transfer tax credit of $192,800, however, no net estate tax is payable. The unified transfer tax credit also can be used on the death of Steele's surviving spouse (who was transferred $3,000,000). Thus the exemption equivalent of $600,000 is really $1,200,000 for a married couple.

The calculation of estate taxes is substantially more complicated when the decedent has made gifts during his or her lifetime. One of the major changes in the Tax Reform Act of 1976 was to unify the previously separate estate and gift tax rate schedules into a combined transfer tax system, so that lifetime transfers and transfers at death are no longer taxed at different rates. The unified transfer tax credit is labeled as such because it also may be applied against gift taxes due on lifetime gifts. The amount of any unused credit is then applied against the gross estate tax.

THE OPENING ENTRY

Once an inventory of the decedent's property that is subject to probate administration has been compiled, the opening entry for the *principal entity* of the estate is made. The entry consists of debits to the various assets and a credit to an Estate Principal account. This account is merely a balancing account that facilitates the double-entry bookkeeping system. It does not reflect the *net worth* of the estate because the decedent's liabilities are not recorded as part of the opening entry. Liabilities are recorded in the books when they are paid, and such payments are eventually reflected as reductions to the Estate Principal account. This manner of accounting reflects the fiduciary's role, which is to **administer the decedent's assets** rather than attempting to establish and account for the net worth of the estate. As expected, no opening entry pertains to the *income entity*.

TRANSACTIONS PERTAINING TO PRINCIPAL

Transactions pertaining to principal are recorded by debiting or crediting the appropriate asset account and crediting or debiting, respectively, an account that is descriptive of the transaction. Transactions pertaining to principal may be grouped as follows:

1. **Transactions that increase principal:**
    a. Assets subsequently discovered.
    b. Gains on disposition of principal assets.
2. **Transactions that decrease principal:**
    a. Losses on disposition of principal assets.
    b. Payments of debts and certain taxes.

  c. Payment of funeral expenses.

  d. Payment of administrative expenses.

  e. Distributions of gifts.

3. Transactions that do not affect principal:

  a. Dispositions of principal assets at their carrying values.

  b. Receipts of amounts to be given to legatees (which are reflected as liabilities until paid), for example, interest on a bond.

  c. Disbursements of amounts held for legatees, as described in category (3)b.

  d. Payments of amounts chargeable to a beneficiary (which are reflected as receivables until collected).

The nonasset accounts debited or credited in categories 1 and 2 are *nominal* or *temporary* accounts that eventually are closed to the Estate Principal account. (Some finer points concerning *principal* transactions are discussed later in the chapter.)

TRANSACTIONS PERTAINING TO *INCOME*

The accounting techniques used for the principal entity also are used for the income entity. An income asset account is debited or credited, and the other half of the entry is to an account that substantively explains the transaction. Initially, the income entity has no assets. Revenues, expenses, and distributions to income beneficiaries are closed periodically to an Estate Income account, which accumulates undistributed earnings.

  A detailed discussion of the various types of income transactions and charges made against income is delayed until after the illustration of estate accounting. For simplicity, the illustration limits income transactions to interest on savings and bond investments, cash dividends on corporate stock investments, and interest on a partnership investment.

ILLUSTRATION | **THE OPENING ENTRY AND SUBSEQUENT TRANSACTIONS**

David Diamond died testate on March 27, 19X1, with the following provisions in his will:

1. The decedent's residence and household items are left to his wife, Krystal Diamond, who assumes the mortgage on the residence.
2. Cash of $150,000 is to be given to Krystal Diamond.
3. All the corporate stocks are to be given to the decedent's alma mater, Krebitsville University, for scholarships in accounting.
4. The decedent's automobile is to be given to Ruby Diamond, his sister.
5. The residual balance of the estate is to be placed in trust with the following terms:
  a. *Trustee:* Coral Point Bank
  b. *Income beneficiary:* Krystal Diamond, wife of the decedent, for the remainder of her natural life.
  c. *Principal beneficiaries:* Jade and Opal Diamond, the decedent's only two children. The principal is to be distributed at the later of (1) the date of death of Krystal Diamond or (2) when both Jade and Opal Diamond reach the age of 25. (If Krystal Diamond dies before both children reach the age of 25, they succeed her as income beneficiaries until they both reach age 25.)
  d. The *accrual basis* is to be used to determine principal at the time of death.
6. State inheritance taxes are to be paid out of the residue of the estate, *not* by the individual heirs, except for the case of the automobile given to Ruby Diamond.
7. The decedent's personal financial adviser, Jack Cass, is named executor of the estate.

David Diamond's estate consists of the following items, each listed at its current value:

Assets Subject to Probate Administration

Cash (including checking and savings accounts)	$	70,000
U.S. government and corporate bonds—face value,		
$350,000; cost, $341,000		337,000
Corporate stocks—cost, $38,000		63,000
Life insurance (payable to the estate)		100,000
Investment in partnership of Diamond, Ring, and Stone:		
Capital account balance at date of death,		
net of drawings $84,000		
Share of profits from close of preceding partnership		
accounting period to date of death 14,000		
Share of partnership goodwill deemed to exist at		
date of death (calculated according to the		
terms of the partnership agreement) 22,000		120,000
Accrued interest receivable on bonds		10,000
Accrued interest receivable on savings accounts		2,000
Dividends declared on corporate stocks		1,000
Automobile		7,000
Total	$	710,000

Assets *Not* Subject to Probate Administration

Residence and household items		240,000
Duplex rental unit (cost, $75,000) subject to		
secured loan of $55,000		110,000
Total Estate Assets		$1,060,000

Liabilities to Be Paid out of Probate Estate

Outstanding balance on credit cards	$	1,100
Medical expenses pertaining to illness		3,700
State and federal income taxes for the period 1/1/X1 to 3/27/X1....		5,500
Total	$	10,300

Liabilities *Not* to Be Paid out of Probate Estate

Mortgage on residence		30,000
Mortgage on duplex rental unit		55,000
Total Estate Liabilities	$	95,300

In reviewing the items making up the estate, note that we have assumed that the decedent's residence, household items, and the duplex rental unit are *not* subject to probate administration of the state probate law. Consequently, the residence and household items pass *immediately* to the decedent's surviving spouse *outside* probate, and the duplex rental unit passes *immediately* to the trustee *outside* of probate. None of these items is accounted for in the administration of the estate. Accounting for the depreciable assets of a trust (such as the duplex rental unit used in this illustration) is discussed and illustrated later in the chapter.

The opening entry in the estate books follows.

Principal Cash	70,000
Investment in Bonds	337,000
Investment in Stocks	63,000
Life Insurance Receivable	100,000
Investment in Partnership of Diamond, Ring, and Stone	120,000
Accrued Interest Receivable on Bonds	10,000
Accrued Interest Receivable on Savings Accounts	2,000

(continued)

Dividends Declared on Corporate Stocks	1,000	
Automobile	7,000	
Estate Principal		710,000

No liabilities are recorded because the accounting concerns the administration of estate assets.

Assumed transactions and related journal entries pertaining to activities completed by the executor during the administration of the estate from March 27, 19X1, to June 30, 19X2, are as follows:

Transaction	Entry		
1. Subsequent discovery of a checking account.	Principal Cash	700	
	Asset Subsequently Discovered		700
2. Receipt of life insurance proceeds.	Principal Cash	100,000	
	Life Insurance Receivable		100,000
3. Receipt of proceeds from liquidation of investment in partnership, along with interest to date of receipt.	Principal Cash	120,000	
	Income Cash	4,000	
	Investment in Partnership		120,000
	Interest Income		4,000
4. Receipt of interest on bonds.	Principal Cash	10,000	
	Income Cash	18,000	
	Accrued Bond Interest Receivable		10,000
	Interest Income		18,000
5. Receipt of interest on savings accounts.	Principal Cash	2,000	
	Income Cash	6,000	
	Accrued Interest Receivable on Savings Accounts		2,000
	Interest Income		6,000
6. Receipt of cash dividends on corporate stocks. (Receipts pertaining to dividends declared *during* the estate administration accrue to the legatee.)	Principal Cash	4,000	
	Accrued Dividends Receivable		1,000
	Liability to Krebitsville University		3,000
7. Payment of credit card, medical, and income tax liabilities.	Debts of Decedent	10,300	
	Principal Cash		10,300
8. Payment of funeral and administrative expenses.	Funeral and Administrative Expenses	11,000	
	Principal Cash		11,000
9. Payment of $49,300 inheritance taxes, $300 of which is to be borne by Ruby Diamond, who received the decedent's automobile.	Inheritance Taxes	49,000	
	Receivable from Legatee, Ruby Diamond	300	
	Principal Cash		49,300
10. Distribution of automobile as gift (a specific legacy) and collection of related inheritance taxes from legatee.	Principal Cash	300	
	Legacies Distributed	7,000	
	Receivable from Legatee, Ruby Diamond		300
	Automobile		7,000

(continued)

11. Distribution of corporate stocks as gift (specific legacy) to Krebitsville University, along with dividend receipts pertaining to dividends declared and received *during* the estate administration.	Legacies Distributed ....
	 Liability to Krebitsville University ....
	     Investment in Stocks ....
	     Principal Cash ....
		63,000
		 3,000
			
			 63,000
			 3,000

12. Sale of a portion of the bonds to raise cash. (Current value at Diamond's death was $9,600.)	Principal Cash ....
	     Investment in Bonds ....
	     Gain on Sale of Principal Asset ....
		9,800	
			 9,600
			 200

13. Distribution of cash (general legacy) to Krystal Diamond.	Legacies Distributed .... Principal Cash	150,000	 150,000
14. Payment of income taxes relating to estate income.	Estate Income Tax Expense .... Income Cash	4,600	 4,600
15. Payment of administration expenses pertaining to income.	Administration Expenses .... Income Cash	300	 300
16. Distributions to income beneficiary of trust.	Distributions to Income Beneficiary .... Income Cash	18,000	 18,000

We assume that no estate taxes are owed because of the use of the unlimited marital deduction. If estate taxes had been paid, the entry is as follows:

Estate Taxes	xxx	
Principal Cash		xxx

ILLUSTRATION   **CHARGE AND DISCHARGE STATEMENTS**

Continuing with our illustration, the only remaining task for the estate fiduciary is to submit an accounting to the probate court with a request to distribute the residual balance of the estate to the trustee, Coral Point Bank. Trial balances for the principal entity and the income entity as of June 30, 19X2, are presented in Illustration 31–1. Charge and discharge statements, which portray the activity of these entities through June 30, 19X2, are shown in Illustration 31–2. The charge and discharge statements are usually accompanied by supporting schedules—such as the detail of the decedent's debts paid and the detail of legacies distributed. Because they are quite simple, such schedules are not presented.

ILLUSTRATION   **CLOSING ENTRIES FOR THE ESTATE**

Assuming that the probate court authorizes the distribution of the residual Diamond estate assets to the trustee, the entries to record the distributions and close the estate books are as follows:

ILLUSTRATION 31–1

Estate of David Diamond
Trial Balance—Principal
June 30, 19X2

	Debit	Credit
Cash	$ 93,200	
Investments in bonds	327,400	
Estate principal		$710,000
Asset subsequently discovered		700
Gain on sale of principal asset		200
Debts of decedent	10,300	
Funeral and administrative expenses	11,000	
Inheritance taxes	49,000	
Legacies distributed	220,000	
Totals	$710,900	$710,900

Estate of David Diamond
Trial Balance—Income
June 30, 19X2

	Debit	Credit
Cash	$ 5,100	
Interest income		$28,000
Estate income tax expense	4,600	
Administrative expenses	300	
Distributions to income beneficiary	18,000	
Totals	$28,000	$28,000

Transaction	Entry		
1. Distribution of residual estate assets of principal entity to Coral Point Bank, trustee.	Legacies Distributed	420,600	
	Principal Cash		93,200
	Investment in Bonds		327,400
2. Distribution of residual estate assets of income entity to Coral Point Bank, trustee.	Distribution to Trustee for Income Beneficiary	5,100	
	Income Cash		5,100
3. Closing of *nominal* accounts of principal entity into estate principal.	Asset Subsequently Discovered	700	
	Gain on Sale of Principal Asset	200	
	Estate Principal	710,000	
	Debts of Decedent		10,300
	Funeral and Administrative Expenses		11,000
	Inheritance Taxes		49,000
	Legacies Distributed		640,600
4. Closing of *nominal* accounts of income entity.	Interest Income	28,000	
	Estate Income Tax Expense		4,600
	Administrative Expenses		300
	Distributions to Income Beneficiary		18,000
	Distribution to Trustee for Income Beneficiary		5,100

ILLUSTRATION 31–2

Estate of David Diamond
Jack Cass, Executor of the Estate
Charge and Discharge Statements
March 27, 19X1–June 30, 19X2

First, as to Principal:
  I charge myself as follows:

Assets per inventory	$710,000	
Assets discovered	700	
Gain on asset realization	200	$710,900

  I credit myself as follows:

Debts of decedent paid	$ 10,300	
Funeral and administrative expenses paid	11,000	
Inheritance taxes paid	49,000	
Legacies distributed	220,000	(290,300)

  Balance of the estate:

Principal cash	$ 93,200	
Investment in bonds	327,400	$420,600

Second, as to Income:
  I charge myself as follows:

Interest received on bonds	$ 18,000	
Interest received on savings accounts	6,000	
Interest received on partnership investment	4,000	$ 28,000

  I credit myself as follows:

Estate income taxes paid	$ 4,600	
Administrative expenses paid	300	
Distributions made to income beneficiary	18,000	(22,900)

  Balance of the estate:

Income Cash		$ 5,100

IV   ACCOUNTING FOR TRUSTS

Accounting for trusts is identical to accounting for estates, except that a Trust Principal account is used rather than Estate Principal for the principal entity, and a Trust Income account is used rather than Estate Income for the income entity to accumulate undistributed earnings. The nature of the transactions is also different. An estate fiduciary is concerned primarily with cleaning up a decedent's affairs and properly distributing estate property. A trustee, on the other hand, is concerned primarily with prudently managing a pool of assets in accordance with the powers granted to him or her by the trust agreement. This task usually involves buying and selling trust assets. Trustees must make periodic accountings to the principal and income beneficiaries and the probate court. A charge and discharge statement similar to the one illustrated for estates is used. Upon termination of the life of the trust, the trustee distributes the assets of the trust principal to the remainderman, makes a final accounting to the court, and requests to be discharged.

Using the illustration from the preceding section, the entries to record the receipt of the gifts from David Diamond's estate are as follows. This is the principal entity:

Principal Cash	93,200	
Investment in Bonds	327,400	
Trust Principal		420,600

This is the income entity:

Income Cash	....	5,100
Trust Income	....	5,100

TRANSACTIONS PERTAINING TO *PRINCIPAL*

Early in the chapter, we summarized the general thrust of the accounting requirements of the Revised Uniform Principal and Income Act regarding principal transactions. Some finer points of principal transactions follow:

1. The costs of investing and reinvesting principal assets are charged against principal.
2. The costs of preparing property for rental or sale are charged against principal.
3. Taxes levied on gains or profits allocated to principal are charged against principal.
4. The costs incurred in maintaining or defending any action to protect the trust or trust property or ensure title to any trust property are charged against principal.
5. Extraordinary repairs or costs incurred in making capital improvements paid for out of principal may be recouped from income through depreciation charges.
6. Trustee's fees and costs relating to the periodic accounting to the court of jurisdiction (court costs, attorney fees, and accounting fees, for example) are shared *equally* between principal and income.
7. Liquidating dividends are considered to be principal.
8. Stock dividends go to principal, not income.

TRANSACTIONS PERTAINING TO *INCOME*

As mentioned earlier, under the Revised Uniform Principal and Income Act, interest and cash dividends are considered *income* transactions. The act also includes the following as income: rents, loan repayment penalties, lease cancellation charges, lease renewal fees, and the net profits of any business in which principal is invested. Losses of any business in which principal is invested are charged to *principal,* because no provision exists for loss carryforward or carryback into any other calendar or fiscal year for purposes of calculating net income. Profits and losses of such businesses are to be determined using GAAP.

Among other things, the act includes as charges against *income* the interest expense on trust liabilities (such as a mortgage on a trust rental property), property taxes, insurance premiums, ordinary repairs, depreciation expenses (including depreciation charges pertaining to extraordinary repairs), income taxes attributable to trust income, a share of trustee fees and costs relating to periodic accounting to the court, and any other ordinary expense incurred in connection with the administration, management, or preservation of trust property. (Depreciation and unusual charges are discussed in detail in the following paragraphs because of the unique manner in which journal entries are recorded.)

DEPRECIATION   Under the act, depreciation is mandatory and results in preserving the estate principal for the principal beneficiaries. Under many state statutes, however, depreciation is provided at the discretion of the trustee. When depreciation is to be provided, a portion of the income entity's revenue flow must go to the principal entity. Because we view the trust as comprising two entities, the accounting entries to record depreciation produce results as if the *principal entity* had sent a bill to the *income entity* for the use or consumption of the depreciable asset. The entries are as follows:

1. To record depreciation:

	Income Entity	Principal Entity
Depreciation Expense	1,000	
Due to Principal	1,000	
Due from Income		1,000
Accumulated Depreciation		1,000

2. To record payment:

	Income Entity	Principal Entity
Due to Principal	1,000	
Income Cash	1,000	
Principal Cash		1,000
Due from Income		1,000

Whether or not to provide depreciation should be thoroughly explored in estate planning. Depreciation charges may deprive an *income beneficiary* of income necessary to maintain the standard of living intended by the decedent. Depreciation makes no sense if the properties are *appreciating* in value, as is the case with many rental properties. If depreciation is to be provided, it should be computed based on the *current value* of the property when it becomes subject to the trust.

UNUSUAL CHARGES AGAINST INCOME The Revised Principal and Income Act states:

> If charges against income are of unusual amount, the trustee may by means of reserves or other reasonable means charge them over a reasonable period of time and withhold from distribution sufficient sums to regularize distributions. [Section 13(b)]

The provision is somewhat ambiguous and open ended. Under the "by means of reserves" approach, the trustee must anticipate and estimate expected unusual charges *before* they are incurred. Charges are then made against income over a reasonable period of time *prior* to their incurrence, resulting in the buildup of a "reserve," or estimated liability. The cash distributable to the income beneficiary during these periods is limited; thus funds accumulate from which to make the expenditure when it actually arises. Under the "by other reasonable means" option, the trustee can have the *principal entity* make the expenditure when it arises but record the expenditure as a deferred charge, which is subsequently amortized against income.

The entries under each approach for an unusually large expenditure, such as painting an apartment building exterior, are as follows:

	Income Entity	Principal Entity
1. Accumulation Method:		
a. Periodic charge.		
Estimated Painting Expense	1,000	(no entry)
Estimated Future Liability	1,000	
b. Actual payment.		
Estimated Future Liability	5,000	(no entry)
Income cash	5,000	
2. Amortization Method:		
a. Actual payment.		
Painting of Building	(no entry)	5,000
Principal Cash		5,000

(continued)

b. Periodic amortization.

Painting Expense	1,000	
Due to Principal		1,000

Due from Income	1,000	
Painting of Building		1,000

END-OF-CHAPTER REVIEW

SUMMARY OF KEY POINTS

1. The fundamental function of estate and trust fiduciaries is to administer assets under their control rather than attempting to determine the net worth of an estate or trust. Accordingly, accounting for estates and trusts involves **accounting for assets** rather than **accounting for net worth.** As a result, special bookkeeping practices and accountability statements are used for estates and trusts that are quite unlike those found in commercial enterprises. Furthermore, the *cash basis* of accounting suffices in most instances.
2. Generally accepted accounting principles have virtually no application to estates and trusts. **Trust income** (including trust income during the administration of an estate) is determined according to the terms and provisions of the trust agreement. If the trust agreement is silent on the treatment to be accorded an item, **state statutes** control.
3. An accountant rendering services to a trust must recognize that his or her role is a passive one when it comes to determining the treatment to be accorded items that are not clearly set forth in the trust agreement or state statutes. Decisions on such matters should be referred to legal counsel or the courts. In most cases, an accountant rendering services to an estate or trust must also have expertise in estate, inheritance, and trust taxation.

GLOSSARY OF NEW TERMS

Administrator/Administratrix   A person appointed by the court to administer the affairs of a decedent when an executor is not appointed.

Bequest   Property received from a decedent's estate pursuant to terms in the decedent's last will and testament.

Demonstrative legacy   A gift of cash for which a particular fund or source is designated from which payment is to be made.

Devise   A gift of real property.

Devisee   The recipient of a devise.

Estate   The property of a decedent.

Estate planning   Making plans for the orderly transfer of one's property on death as desired, with a view toward minimizing transfer costs.

Executor/Executrix   A person who is named in a will to serve as the decedent's personal representative in administering the estate and who is appointed by the court to serve in that capacity.

General legacy   Gifts of cash for which no particular fund or source is designated.

Income beneficiary   The party to a trust who is entitled to the income earned on trust assets.

Inter vivos trust   A trust created during a person's life.

Intestate   A term used to refer to a person having died without a will.

Legacy   A gift of personal property.

Legatee   The recipient of a legacy.

Principal beneficiary   The party to a trust who is entitled to the trust principal.

Probate   The act by which a probate court determines whether a decedent's will meets the statutory requirements concerning wills.

Probate court   Courts in the state court system that have jurisdiction over the affairs of decedents.

Remainderman   The party to a trust who is entitled to the trust principal.

Residual legacy   A gift of all personal property remaining after distribution of specific, demonstrative, and general legacies.

Specific legacy   A gift of specified noncash items.

Testamentary trust   A trust that comes into being on a person's death, pursuant to provisions in the decedent's will.

Testate   A term used to refer to a person having died with a will.

Trust   An arrangement in which property is transferred to a person, called a *trustee,* who holds title to the property but administers it for the benefit of other parties, called the *beneficiaries.*

Trustee   That party to a trust who takes title to trust property and administers the property for the benefit of others.

Trustor   The party to a trust agreement who created the trust. (Also referred to as a *settlor, grantor, donor,* or *creator.*)

SELF-STUDY QUESTIONS

(Answers are at the end of this chapter.)

1. In determining whether a transaction pertains to principal or income, which of the following is *not* a point of reference, unless specified?
   a. Case law
   b. Generally accepted accounting principles
   c. State law
   d. The trust agreement
   e. None of the above
2. Under the Revised Uniform Principal and Income Act (of 1962), when are the rights of the income beneficiary established?
   a. At the time of death of the deceased person
   b. At the completion of the probate proceedings
   c. At the time the property is physically transferred to the trustee
   d. At the time the trust agreement is drawn up
   e. None of the above
3. Which of the following statements concerning tax matters is *false*?
   a. Federal estate tax is based on the right to give property.
   b. State inheritance taxes are based on the right to receive or inherit property.
   c. The marital deduction is unlimited in amount.
   d. The tax rates that apply to estate income are different from those that apply to trust income.
   e. None of the above.
4. Under the Revised Uniform Principal and Income Act (of 1962), which of the following is *false*?

   a. Gains on disposition of principal assets increase principal.
   b. Costs of investing and reinvesting principal assets are to be charged against principal.
   c. Depreciation is mandatory.
   d. Insurance premiums on principal assets are chargeable against income.
   e. None of the above.

ASSIGNMENT MATERIAL

REVIEW QUESTIONS

1. What role does GAAP play in determining trust income? Explain.
2. How do we determine whether a transaction pertains to *principal* or *income*?
3. What is the nature of the relationship between a trust *income* beneficiary and a trust *principal* beneficiary?
4. What are *legacies* and *devises*?

5. Are estate liabilities recorded in the opening entry for an estate? Explain why or why not.
6. An *estate fiduciary* may have to deal with what four types of taxes?
7. Under the Revised Uniform Principal and Income Act, when do the rights of *income* beneficiaries begin?
8. When is the *accrual method* used in accounting for estates and trusts?
9. What is the function of *probate administration*?
10. What are the major tasks of an *estate fiduciary*?
11. What is an accountant's role with respect to distinguishing between *principal* and *income* transactions?
12. Must assets and transactions pertaining to income be accounted for in separate general ledgers? Explain.

EXERCISES

E 31-1 **Estates: True or False** Indicate whether the following statements are true or false. Explain any false ones.

1. An estate is a taxable entity.
2. An estate is a legal entity.
3. The probate estate is usually smaller than the estate for federal tax purposes.
4. One function of an estate fiduciary is to account for the estate in a manner that continually reflects the estate's net worth.
5. Federal estate taxes are effectively borne by the residual beneficiaries of the estate.
6. State inheritance taxes are based on the right to give away one's property.
7. The Estate Principal account reflects the net worth of the estate at a given point in time.
8. Accounting for estates revolves around the administration of the decedent's assets.
9. The probate court essentially serves as the guardian of the estate.
10. A legacy is a gift of real property.

E 31-2 **Estates: Fill-in Statements** Fill in the missing words for the following items.

1. An estate fiduciary named in a decedent's will is called a(n) _____.
2. An estate fiduciary who is appointed by the probate court when no person is named in a decedent's will is called a(n) _____.
3. A gift of personal property is called a(n) _____.
4. A gift of real property is called a(n) _____.
5. The four types of legacies are _____, _____, _____, and _____.
6. A person who dies without a will is said to have died _____.
7. A person who dies with a will is said to have died _____.
8. State laws dealing with the affairs of decedents are commonly known as _____ _____.
9. Federal estate taxes are based on the right to _____ property.
10. State inheritance taxes are based on the right to _____ property.

E 31-3 **Trusts: True or False** Indicate whether the following statements are true or false. Explain any false ones.

1. When the income beneficiary and the principal beneficiary are the same person, no built-in clash of interests exists as in trusts in which these beneficiaries are not the same person.
2. An income beneficiary's rights begin when assets are actually transferred to the trustee.
3. In trust accounting matters, the terms of the trust agreement prevail over GAAP.
4. When the accounting treatment of an item is not clearly specified in the trust agreement, reference is made to GAAP.
5. The Revised Uniform Principal and Income Act of 1962 is somewhat outdated because it is based on GAAP in effect at that time.
6. When reference must be made to state laws to distinguish trust principal from trust income, the accountant's role is to interpret those laws concerning accounting matters.
7. The Revised Uniform Principal and Income Act specifies the use of the accrual basis for many items at the commencement of a trust.
8. Accounts and transactions pertaining to trust income must be accounted for in a separate ledger to prevent commingling of accounts and transactions with that of trust principal.
9. If the answer to an accounting question cannot be found by referring to the trust agreement, state law, or case law, reference is made to GAAP.

10. Trustors may specify their own definition of net income, even if this definition is contrary to state law pertaining to trust principal and income.

E 31–4   **Trusts: Fill-in Statements**   Fill in the missing words for the following items.

1. The person creating a trust is commonly called the _____.
2. Trusts established pursuant to the provisions of a will are called _____ trusts.
3. Trusts established during a person's life are called _____ trusts.
4. The party taking title to trust assets is called the _____.
5. The two classes of trust beneficiaries are the _____ beneficiaries and the _____ beneficiaries.
6. Another term for trust principal is trust _____.
7. The basis of accounting used in most respects when an income beneficiary's rights are established is the _____ basis.
8. Depreciation is _____ under the Revised Uniform Principal and Income Act.
9. When the accounting treatment of an item is in doubt, the first place to look is the _____ _____.
10. The _____ basis of accounting is used during the administration of a trust but *not* at the beginning and end of an income beneficiary's rights.

E 31–5   **Estates: Preparing Journal Entries**   Emory Feldspar died on 5/12/X1 with a provision in his will to establish a testamentary trust. His estate had the following assets subject to probate administration:

	Current Value
Cash in checking and savings accounts	$ 42,000
Investment in U.S. government bonds	387,000
Coin collection	11,000
Bond interest receivable	6,500
Total	$446,500

The estate fiduciary had the following receipts and disbursements from 5/12/X1 to 1/20/X2:

1. Personal liabilities totaling $2,200 were paid.
2. Funeral expenses of $1,800 were paid.
3. Federal estate taxes of $37,000 were paid.
4. State inheritance taxes of $14,000 were paid. Of this amount, $400 is to be borne by the legatee receiving the coin collection, and $1,100 is to be borne by the legatee (Children's Hospital) that is to receive $25,000 cash.
5. Administrative expenses of $3,300 were paid.
6. A note receivable of $2,000 was discovered in September 19X1.
7. The note receivable in item 6 was collected in December 19X1, along with $150 interest.
8. Interest on bonds totaling $22,000 was received.
9. Bonds having a current value of $60,500 at Feldspar's death were sold for $58,800.
10. The coin collection was distributed to the specified legatee, who reimbursed the estate for the inheritance taxes at that time.
11. Cash of $23,900 was distributed to Children's Hospital ($25,000 specified in the will – $1,100 state inheritance taxes).
12. Estate income taxes of $3,800 for the period 5/12/X1 to 12/31/X1 were paid.
13. Cash of $10,000 was distributed to the income beneficiary of the trust, Pearl Feldspar.

Required   1. Prepare the opening and subsequent transaction journal entries for the estate.
2. Prepare closing journal entries as of 1/20/X2.

E 31–6   **Trusts: Preparing Journal Entries**   Following are the 19X3 transactions of a trust that has investments in corporate bonds and an apartment house:

1. Rental receipts totaled $38,500.
2. Property taxes of $1,400 were paid.
3. Mortgage payments of $15,500 were made. Of this amount, $14,900 pertained to interest and $600 pertained to principal. (Assume that the mortgage liability is reflected as a liability in the trust general ledger only on a memorandum basis.)
4. Normal operating costs of the apartment totaling $7,300 were paid.

5. The exterior of the apartment building was painted in January 19X3 for $2,100, and payment was made at that time. The apartment exterior is painted approximately every seven years. (Assume that this qualifies as an "unusual amount," because that term is used in Section 13(b) of the Revised Uniform Principal and Income Act.)

6. The annual depreciation charge on the apartment is $4,500.

7. Bond investments having a face value of $50,000 matured during the year and were redeemed. (These bonds had a current value of $48,800 when they became subject to the trust.)

8. Federal trust income taxes of $450 pertaining to the prior year were paid.

9. Estimated federal trust income tax payments of $1,850 for the current year were paid.

10. The $2,200 trustee's fee for the year was paid.

11. Interest receipts on bond investments totaled $14,400.

12. Cash distributions of $9,000 were made to the income beneficiary.

Required
1. Prepare the trust transaction journal entries for the year.
2. Prepare the year-end closing entries.

PROBLEMS

P 31–1   **Estates: Preparing Charge and Discharge Statements**   The will of Elaine Ford, deceased, directed that her executor, Wayne Pilgrim, liquidate the entire estate within two years of the date of her death and pay the net proceeds and income, if any, to the Children's Town Orphanage. Ford, who never married, died 2/1/X4 after a brief illness.

An inventory of the decedent's property subject to probate administration was prepared, and the fair market value of each item was determined. The preliminary inventory, before the computation of any appropriate income accruals on inventory items, follows:

	Fair Market Value
Monument Valley Bank checking account	$ 6,000
$60,000 of 8% Bootville City school bonds, payable January 1 and July 1, maturity date of 7/1/X8	59,000
2,000 shares of Rider Corporation capital stock	220,000
Term life insurance, beneficiary—estate of Elaine Ford	20,000
Personal residence ($75,000) and furnishings ($15,000)	490,000

The following transactions occurred during 19X4:

1. The interest on the Bootville City bonds was collected. The bonds were sold on July 1 for $59,000, and the proceeds and interest were paid to the orphanage.

2. Rider Corporation paid cash dividends of $1 per share on March 1 and December 1, as well as a 10% stock dividend on July 1. All dividends were declared 45 days before each payment date and were payable to stockholders of record as of 40 days before each payment date. On September 2, Pilgrim sold 1,000 shares at $105 per share and paid the proceeds to the orphanage.

3. Because of a depressed real estate market, the personal residence was rented furnished at $300 per month commencing April 1. The rent is paid monthly, in advance. Real estate taxes of $900 for calendar year 19X4 were paid. The house and furnishings have estimated lives of 45 and 10 years, respectively. The part-time caretaker was paid four months' wages totaling $500 on April 30 for services performed and was released.

4. The Monument Valley Bank checking account was closed; the $6,000 balance was transferred to an estate bank account.

5. The term life insurance was paid on March 1 and deposited in the estate bank account.

6. The following disbursements were made:
   a. Funeral expenses, $2,000.
   b. Final illness expenses, $1,500.
   c. April 15 income tax remittance, $700.
   d. Attorney's and accountant's fees, $12,000.

7. On December 31, the balance of the undistributed income, except for $1,000, was paid to the orphanage. The balance of the cash on hand derived from the estate principal also was paid to the orphanage on December 31.

Required Prepare charge and discharge statements, separating principal and income, together with supporting schedules, on behalf of the executor for the period 2/1/X4 through 12/31/X4. The following supporting schedules should be included:

1. Original principal of estate.
2. Gain or Loss on Disposal of Estate Assets.
3. Funeral, Administration, and Other Expenses.
4. Debts of Decedent Paid.
5. Legacies Paid or Delivered.
6. Assets (Corpus) on Hand, 12/31/X4.
7. Income Collected.
8. Expenses Chargeable to Income.
9. Distributions of Income. (AICPA adapted)

P 31–2 **Estates: Preparing Charge and Discharge Statements** Ron Ho died in an accident on 5/31/X1. His will, dated 2/28/X0, provided that all just debts and expenses be paid and that his property be disposed of as follows:

1. Personal residence is devised to Donna Ho, widow. (Real property is *not* subject to probate administration in the state in which the deceased resided.)
2. U.S. Treasury bonds and Bubb Company stock are to be placed in trust. All income is to go to Donna Ho during her lifetime, with right of appointment on her death.
3. Happe Company mortgage notes are bequeathed to Lulu Ho Waters, daughter.
4. A bequest of $10,000 cash goes to Dave Ho, son.
5. Remainder of estate is to be divided equally between the two children.

The will further provided that during the administration period, Donna Ho was to be paid $800 a month out of estate income. Estate and inheritance taxes are to be borne by the residue. Dave Ho was named executor and trustee.

An inventory of the decedent's property was prepared. The fair market value of all items as of Ho's death was determined. The preliminary inventory, before computing any appropriate income accruals on inventory items, is as follows:

Personal residence property	$145,000
Jewelry—Diamond ring	9,600
Oahu Life Insurance Company—Term life insurance policy on life of Ron Ho; beneficiary, Donna Ho, widow	120,000
Marble Trust Company—8% savings account, Ron Ho, in trust for Lelani Waters (grandchild), interest credited January 1 and July 1; balance 5/31/X1	400
Hilo National Bank—Checking account; balance 5/31/X1	141,750
$200,000 U.S. Treasury bonds, 10%; interest payable March 1 and September 1	200,000
$10,000 Happe Company first mortgage notes, 12%, 19X5; interest payable June 30 and December 31	9,900
800 shares Bubb Company common stock	64,000
700 shares Maui Manufacturing Company common stock	70,000

The executor opened an estate bank account, to which he transferred the decedent's checking account balance. Other deposits, through 7/1/X2, follow:

Interest collected on bonds	
$200,000 U.S. Treasury	
7/1/X1	$10,000
3/1/X2	10,000
Dividends received on stock	
800 shares Bubb Company	
6/15/X1, declared 5/7/X1, payable to holders of record 5/27/X1	800
9/15/X1	800
12/15/X1	1,200

(continued)

3/15/X1	800
6/15/X1	800
Net proceeds of 6/19/X1 sale of 700 shares of Maui Manufacturing Company	68,810
Interest collected on Happe Company first mortgage notes, 6/30/X1	600

Payments were made from the estate's checking account through 7/1/X2 for the following items:

Funeral expenses	$ 2,000
Assessments for additional 19X0 federal and state income tax ($1,700)	
plus interests ($110) to 5/31/X1	1,810
19X1 income taxes of Ron Ho for the period 1/1/X1 through 5/31/X1	
in excess of estimated taxes paid by the decedent	9,100
Federal and state fiduciary income taxes, fiscal year ended 6/30/X1 ($75),	
and 6/30/X2 ($1,400)	1,475
State inheritance taxes	28,000
Monthly payments to Donna Ho: 13 payments of $800	10,400
Attorney's and accountant's fees	25,000
Payment of interest collected on Happe Company mortgage notes	
that accrues to legatee	600

The executor waived his commission; however, he wanted his father's diamond ring in lieu of the $10,000 specific legacy. All parties agreed to this in writing, and the court's approval was secured. All other specific legacies were delivered by 7/15/X1.

Required Prepare charge and discharge statements for principal and income, and supporting schedules to accompany the attorney's formal court accounting on behalf of the executor of the estate Ron Ho for the period 5/31/X1 through 7/1/X2. The following supporting schedules should be included:

1. Original Capital of Estate.
2. Gain on Disposal of Estate Assets.
3. Loss on Disposal of Estate Assets.
4. Funeral, Administration, and Other Expenses.
5. Debts of Decedent Paid.
6. Legacies Paid or Delivered.
7. Assets (Corpus) on Hand, 7/1/X2.
8. Proposed Plan of Distribution of Estate Assets.
9. Income Collected.
10. Distribution of Income.   (AICPA adapted)

P 31–3 **Trusts: Treatment of Disputed Items** A CPA firm has assigned you to work with the trustees of a large trust in the first annual accounting to the court. The income beneficiaries and the remaindermen cannot agree on the proper allocation of the following items on which the trust agreement is silent:

1. Costs incurred in expanding the garage facilities of an apartment house owned by the trust and held for rental income.
2. Real estate taxes on the apartment house.
3. Cost of casualty insurance premiums on the apartment house.
4. A 2-for-1 stock split of common stock held by the trust for investment.
5. Insurance proceeds received as the result of a partial destruction of an office building that the trust owned and held for rental income.
6. Costs incurred by the trust in the sale of a tract of land.
7. Costs incurred to defend title to real property held by the trust.

Required Locate a copy of the Revised Uniform Principal and Income Act in your library. Indicate the allocations between principal and income to be made for each item, using the act as the point of reference. Be sure to quote the applicable section of the act. (The purpose of this problem is to force you to search out items in the act, a task that is necessary in actual practice.)

P 31–4 **Trusts: Preparing Journal Entries and Charge and Discharge Statements** The postclosing combined trial balance for the principal entity and the income entity of a trust as of 12/31/X3 is as follows:

	Debit	Credit
Principal cash	$ 3,500	
Income cash	800	
Investments in bonds	123,400	
Investment in E & T Corporation common stock	86,200	
Duplex rental unit	95,000	
Accumulated depreciation on duplex rental unit		$ 12,000
Trust principal		296,100
Trust income		800
Totals	$308,900	$308,900

Following are the 19X4 trust transactions:

1. Rental receipts were $11,500.
2. Property taxes of $1,000 were paid.
3. Mortgage payments of $6,500 were made. Of this amount, $5,800 pertained to interest and $700 to principal. (The mortgage liability of $57,500 on the duplex at 12/31/X3 is recorded in the trust general ledger on a memorandum basis.)
4. Normal operating costs of the duplex rental unit totaling $600 were paid.
5. New carpeting was installed in both units of the duplex in January 19X4, at a cost of $1,800, with payment being made at that time. (New carpeting is installed approximately every 10 years.)
6. The annual depreciation charge on the duplex is $2,000. (Of the $95,000 value assigned to the duplex when it became subject to the trust, $15,000 was assigned to land, and $80,000 was assigned to the building, carpets, and drapes. The $80,000 is depreciated over 40 years.)
7. Bond investments having a face value of $25,000 matured during the year and were redeemed. (These bonds had a $25,500 current value when they became subject to the trust.)
8. Bonds having a face value of $20,000 were purchased in the open market for $19,000 on 7/1/X4. The maturity date of the bonds is 6/30/X9.
9. Interest receipts on bond investments totaled $9,800.
10. E & T Inc. declared a 10% stock dividend on 4/1/X4. The trust held 200 shares of E & T's common stock prior to this declaration. (The market price of common stock increased $30 per share during 19X4.)
11. Cash dividends of $3,300 on E & T's common stock were received.
12. The $1,500 trustee's fee for the year was paid.
13. Attorney's and accountant's fees for periodic judicial accounting totaling $1,200 were paid.
14. Cash distributions totaling $8,000 were made to the income beneficiary.
15. "Due to" and "due from" accounts are settled at year-end.

Required
1. Prepare the trust transaction journal entries for the year.
2. Prepare the year-end closing entries.
3. Prepare charge and discharge statements for the year for trust principal and trust income.

✳ THINKING CRITICALLY ✳

✳ CASES ✳

C 31–1   **Estate Planning**   Your client, Jan Landers, has asked your advice on accounting matters with respect to her attorney's preparation of a testamentary trust agreement. Jan wants all her residential property holdings placed in trust for the benefit of her husband (as income beneficiary) and her children (as principal beneficiaries).

Required   On what points should you advise your client? (Assume that you are located in a state that has adopted the Revised Uniform Principal and Income Act without modification.)

C 31–2   **Role of the Accountant**   An attorney who is your acquaintance has suggested that you attend a meeting that may lead to some work for you. At the meeting, you are informed that (1) Ken Dall died approximately one year ago, (2) the attorney is serving as the executor of the estate, (3) the residual balance of the estate is to be placed in trust, and (4) the trustee is Barbara Dall, Ken's widow. Barbara Dall describes the nature of the trust assets as bonds, residential rental properties, and the stock of a wholly owned corporation, which continues to operate. She requests that you become the accountant for the trust and, in that capacity, do the following:

1. Maintain the books and records.
2. Make all accounting decisions.
3. Prepare the fiduciary income tax returns.
4. Prepare the annual financial statements.

Required   How would you respond to this request? Elaborate on the points you should discuss with Barbara Dall.

ANSWERS TO SELF-STUDY QUESTIONS

1. b   **2.** a   **3.** d   **4.** e

CREDITS

Index

T

U

T

U

P 12-1 MODULES 1 and 2:
1. Parent's net income, $1,850,000;
Subsidiary's net income, $305,000
MODULE 3
1. Parent's net income, $1,745,000;
Subsidiary's net income, $305,000

P 12-2 1. $96,000 loss

P 12-3 1. $120,000 loss

P 12-4 1. $10,500 gain
4. Consolidated net income, $187,500;
Consolidated assets, $963,000

P 12-5 1. $20,000 loss
4. NCI in net income, $12,000;
CI in net income, $184,000;
Consolidated assets, $981,000

P 12-6 1. $19,000 gain
5. Investment balance—book value at 12/31/X3:
MOD 1, $274,400; MOD 2, $280,000;
MOD 3, $160,000
Investment balance—excess cost at 12/31/X3:
MOD 1, $48,000; MOD 2, $48,000;
MOD 3, $144,000
NCI in net income, $4,600;
CI in net income, $106,400

P 12-7 1. $31,500 gain;
2. $1,090,000
3. $72,000

P 12-8 1. $32,500 gain
2. $25,000 gain

Chapter 13

E 13-1 Debit APIC $21,000
E 13-2 Debit APIC $50,000
E 13-3 Ret. E. decrease of $160,000
E 13-4 No changes

P 13-1 Debit APIC $30,000
P 13-2 1. Decrease in parent's interest, $90,000
3. Debit APIC $63,000
P 13-3 1. Increase excess cost $27,000
2. Debit APIC $93,000
P 13-4 1. Decrease excess cost $48,000
2. Credit APIC $328,000
P 13-5 1. Decrease excess cost $54,000
2. Credit APIC $41,000
P 13-6 1. Parent's dilution, $225,000
P 13-7 1. Parent's accretion, $40,000
P 13-8 1. Investment balance at 12/31/X5:
MODULE 1; $701,000; MODULE 2, $705,000
5. NCI in net income, $71,000;
CI in net income, $848,000;
Consolidated assets, $2,446,000;
Consolidated Ret. E., $596,000;
NCI in net assets, $235,000
P 13-1A 1. NCI: At 12/31/X1, $134,000; At 12/31/X2, $136,000;
2. Debit NCI in Net Income $14,000 at 12/31/X1

Chapter 14

E 14-1 2. $38,000
E 14-2 2. $207,000
E 14-3 2. $31,000
E 14-4 1. $9,977,480
2. $1,132,520

E 14-5 1. $580,000 and $20,000
2. $567,391 and $32,609

P 14-1 1. $584,000
2. $30,000
P 14-2 1. $1,080,700
2. $21,800
P 14-3 1. $687,600
2. $21,400
P 14-4 1. $878,000 and $10,000
2. $868,352 and $19,648
P 14-5 1. $450,000 and $40,000
2. $430,851 and $59,149
3. Balances at 12/31/X1; CI, $1,157,533; NCI,
$205,447
P 14-6 2. $223,000

Chapter 15

E 15-1 Operating profit, $320,000
E 15-2 1. Segments A, B, D, and G
2. 75% test is *not* satisfied
E 15-3 S. America, Australia, Middle East
E 15-4 19X6 loss from discontinued operations, $150,000;
19X7 gain on disposal of discontinued oper., $78,000
E 15-5 Loss from *oper.*, $180,000; Loss on *disposal*, $750,000

P 15-1 1. Segments B, D, E and G
P 15-2 Consol. operating profit, $99,200
P 15-3 Segment A's operating profit, $290,000;
Consol. operating profit, $350,000
P 15-4 1. Consol. operating profit, $444,000;
Segment A's operating profit, $196,000
2. Consol. operating profit, $455,600;
Segment A's operating profit, $206,000
P 15-5 U.S. operating profit, $587,600;
Consol. operating profit, $717,600
P 15-6 Segment G, $200, $200, and $500
Segment H, $200, $100, and $200
P 15-7 Loss from discontinued operations, $(810,000);
Net income, $270,000

Chapter 16

E 16-1 1. Direct rate at 12/31/X1, 1 peso equals $.50
E 16-3 1. $78,000;
2. $5,000 FX loss
E 16-4 1. $210,000;
2. $20,000 FX loss

P 16-1 Vendor A: $400 FX loss at 7/10/X1, plus $2,400 FX
gain at 7/31/X1
Customer A: $100 FX loss at 7/20/X1, plus $200 FX
loss at 7/30/X1
P 16-2 Vendor A: $1,000 FX gain at 6/30/X1 and $2,000 FX
gain at 7/15/X1
Customer A: $1,400 FX loss at 6/30/X1 and $600 FX
loss at 7/10/X1
P 16-3 FX loss: 12/31/X1, $57 and $126; 1/5/X2, $156
and $66

E 16-1A 1. Expected rate at 12/31/X1: $.525
2. *Nominal* change $.075 (decrease); 3. *Real* change
$.015 (increase)

Chapter 17

E 17-1 2. Call, hedge; 5. Call, speculation; 7. Put, hedge
E 17-2 $.4864
E 17-3 1. Neither, sell, sell, neither, neither, sell
E 17-4 1. Buys, speculation; 4. Buys, hedge; 7. Sells, hedge
E 17-5 3. Exporting hedge; 6. Importing hedge
E 17-6 4. Recognize currently

P 17-1 $2,000 FX gain at 12/31/X1 on option
P 17-2 $10,000 FX gain at 12/31/X1 on option
P 17-3 2. $30,000 FX gain on at 12/31/X1 on option
P 17-4 1. 12/31/X1: Offsetting $2,400 FX gain and loss;
1/15/X2: Offsetting $400 FX gain and loss
P 17-5 1. 12/31/X1: Offsetting $2,400 FX gain and loss;
1/15/X2: Offsetting $400 FX gain and loss
P 17-6 1. 6/30/X1: Offsetting $1,500 FX gain and loss;
7/30/X1: Offsetting $500 FX gain and loss;
P 17-7 1. Capitalized cost of equipment, $480,000
P 17-8 1. FX Contract Value—Forward at 12/31/X1, $7,000 (favorable)
P 17-9 2. FX Contract Value—Forward at 12/31/X1, $12,000 (favorable)
4. Credit cash for $11,000
P 17-10 1. Intrinsic value, $10,000; Time value, $6,000
2. $80,000
3. $70,000 FX gain at 6/30/X1

Chapter 18

E 18-1 Debit Ret. E. for $60,000
E 18-2 Credit Ret. E. for $160,000
E 18-3 1. $(10,000)—Adverse
E 18-4 $(100,000)—Adverse
E 18-7 1a. $42,000; 1b. $13,000—Favorable
E 18-8 1. Parent records $9,000 loss
2. Subsidiary records 100,000 loss in LCUs
E 18-9 1. Dividend receivable, $2,700,000
2. FX Gain, $300,000

P 18-1 Credit Ret. E. $12,000
P 18-2 1. Translation adjustment, $(157,000)
2. Net income, $72,000
5. Loss on sale, $129,000
P 18-3 1. Translation adjustment, $195,000
2. Net income, $420,000
P 18-4 1. Parent records $200,000 loss
2. Subsidiary records 166,667 loss in pounds
3. $40,000
7. $2,000
P 18-5 1. $45,000 FX gain
P 18-6 1. Current year translation adjustment, $(79,000)
2. Ending Ret. E., $583,000
3. Parent records $22,000 FX loss
4. Defer $62,000 of intercompany profit
8. Consolidated net income, $1,436,000;
Consolidated assets, $5,007,000
P 18-7 1. Settle up at $54,000

Chapter 19

E 19-1 Brazil, Net *monetary liability* position;
Mexico, Net *monetary asset* position;
Belgium, Net *liability* position;
Ireland, Net *asset* position

E 19-2 1. $25,000—Favorable
2. $(10,000)—Adverse
E 19-3 1. $500,000—Favorable
2. $(100,000)—Adverse
E 19-6 2a. $30,000
2b. $63,000
E 19-7 a. $8,000; b. $(40,000)
E 19-8 1. $180,000; 2. $200,000
E 19-9 1 and 2. Sell, neither, neither, sell
3. Neither, buy, buy, neither

P 19-1 3. Decrease in cash of $100,000
P 19-2 1. Gain from remeasurement, $211,000
2. Net income, $195,000
P 19-3 1. FC transaction loss, $(286,000)
2. Net income, $329,000
P 19-4 1. Cash at 1/1/X3, 700,000 pesos
2. Net *decrease* in cash, $(148,000)
P 19-6 2. Credit deferred income taxes payable 2,500 LCUs

E 19-1A Debit investment in subsidiary $140,000
E 19-2A Credit deferred income taxes payable—foreign for $15,000

P 19-1A 1. Debit income tax expense for $48,000
2. $200,000
P 19-2A 1. Debit income tax expense for $50,000
P 19-3A 1. Debit income tax expense for $120,000
P 19-4A 1. Debit income tax expense for $30,000

Chapter 20

E 20-1 Correct economic reporting result: 3. $(20,000);
5. $20,000 *real* gain; 6. no effect
E 20-2 Correct economic reporting result: 1. $20,000 *nominal* gain; 4. $20,000 *nominal* gain; 5. no effect
E 20-3 Situation 2: favorable (a *real* gain)
Situation 4: unfavorable (an *imaginary* loss)
E 20-4 $943,000 for PPP approach
E 20-5 $.525

P 20-1 3. $2,000,000
P 20-2 Balance, 12/31/X2, $1,641,600
P 20-3 1. $634,000 increase in equity
2. $22,000 nominal gain
P 20-4 1. $617,000 increase in equity

Chapter 21

E 21-3 $60,000 each quarter
E 21-4 $1,100,000
E 21-5 Expense in second quarter

P 21-1 First quarter bonus expense, $16,000 or $10,000;
Second quarter bonus expense, $5,000 or $2,000
P 21-2 First quarter income tax expense, $200,000;
Second quarter income tax expense, $220,000
P 21-3 3. Revised estimated annual tax rate, 42.36%;
Second quarter income tax expense, $170,160

Chapter 22

There are no key figures for Chapter 22.

Continued on back endpapers

Continued from p. 1168

CHAPTER 23

E 23-1 1. No gain on restructuring
E 23-2 1. Gain on restructuring, $80,000
　　　　3. No gain on restructuring
E 23-3 1. No gain on restructuring
　　　　2. $92,000
　　　　3. 3%
E 23-4 1. Gain on restructuring, $40,000
E 23-5 1. Gain on restructuring, $75,000
E 23-6 Gain on restructuring, $7,000,000
E 23-7 Gain on restructuring, $2,500,000
E 23-8 $156,000 available to unsecured creditors

P 23-1 1. Gain on restructuring, $176,000
P 23-2 1. Gain on restructuring, $300,000
P 23-3 1. Gain on restructuring, $440,000
P 23-4 3a. Future interest expense, $–0–
　　　　3b. Future interest expense, $9,000,000
P 23-5 3a. Future interest expense, $323,000
　　　　4. Approx. effective interest rate, 5%
　　　　5. 19X1 interest expense, $163,850
P 23-6 2. Gain on restructuring, $375,000
　　　　3. Future interest expense, $150,000
P 23-7 1. Gain on debt discharge, $420,000
　　　　3. Debit APIC $130,000
P 23-8 1. Discount, $19,773,720;
　　　　　Gain on restructuring, $254,773,720
　　　　2. First-year interest expense, $42,033,942
P 23-9 1. Deficiency to unsecured creditors, $18,200
P 23-10 1. Deficiency to unsecured creditors, $41,000

CHAPTER 24

E 24-1 $775,000
E 24-2 Credit deferred revenues, $3,000
E 24-3 Credit revenues, $300,000
E 24-4 6. Credit Expenditures, $66,000
E 24-5 Fund Balance at 6/30/X2, $155,000
E 24-6 Credit Budgetary Fund Balance, $80,000
E 24-7 $4,000
E 24-8 $42,000 favorable variance
E 24-9 $10,000 favorable variance

P 24-1 2. Total expenditures, $899,000;
　　　　　Total revenues, $988,000
P 24-2 1. Revenues, $880,000; Expenditures, $830,000;
　　　　　Total Fund Balance at 6/30/X2, $260,000
　　　　2. Unreserved Fund Balance at 6/30/X2, $180,000
P 24-3 2. Credit Unreserved Fund Balance, $32,000
　　　　3. 6/30/X2 Fund Balance, $102,000
P 24-4 2. Credit Unreserved Fund Balance, $66,000
　　　　3. 6/30/X3 Fund Balance, $183,000
P 24-5 3. Credit Unreserved Fund Balance, $34,000
　　　　4. Total assets, $158,000; total Fund Balance, $142,000
P 24-6 3. Total expenditures, $832,000;
　　　　　6/30/X6 Fund Balance, $188,000
P 24-7 3. Excess of revenues over expenditures, $40,000;
　　　　　6/30/X5 Fund Balance, $260,000
P 24-8 5. 7/1/X6 Fund Balance (corrected retroactively),
　　　　　$80,000; 6/30/X7 Fund Balance (corrected), $88,000

CHAPTER 25

E 25-3 1. G, 2. K, 3. L, 4. L, 5. E, 6. J, 7. D, 8. A, 9. G, 10. A, B
E 25-4 1. B, 2. F, 3. D, 4. J, 5. B, 6. G, 7. A, 8. D, 9. I, 10. H

P 25-1 3. June 30, 19X3 Fund Balance, $3,020,000
P 25-2 Revenues (under) expenditures, $(1,076,000)
P 25-3 3. Fund Balance at June 30, l9X2: Capital Projects
　　　　　Fund, $–0–; Debt Service Fund, $8,000
　　　　4. Total assets and other debits (memorandum only),
　　　　　$158,000
P 25-4 3. Total other financing sources and uses: Capital
　　　　　Projects Fund, $550,000; Debt Service Fund, $27,000
　　　　4. Total assets and other debits (memorandum only),
　　　　　$1,121,000
P 25-5 2. June 30, 19X1 Ret. E., $600
P 25-7 Only 4 and 5 require entries
P 25-9 Debit Expenditures for $100,000 and Credit OFS-
　　　　Operating Transfer In, $100,000 in Debt Service Fund
P 25-10 Total Equity and other credits:
　　　　GF, $210,000; DS, $52,000; CP, $–0–; IS, $250,000;
　　　　T&AF, $330,000; GFA, $590,000; GLTD, $–0–

CHAPTER 26

E 26-1 D, A, B, B, D, A, A, F
E 26-2 B, D, D, D, E, D, B
E 26-3 I, I, D, A, A, A, B, H
E 26-4 G, G, A [E], C, B, A, G [E]

P 26-1 2. Unrestricted category, $292,000; Temporarily
　　　　　restricted category, $191,000
P 26-2 2. Unrestricted category, $414,000; Temporarily
　　　　　restricted category, $410,000
P 26-3 2. Unrestricted category, $883,000; Temporarily
　　　　　restricted category, $61,000
P 26-4 2. $80,000 unrealized gain **(UR)**
　　　　4. $44,000 loss **(UR)**
　　　　5. $55,000 loss **(PR)**

CHAPTER 27

E 27-1 E, A, C, A, A, D
E 27-2 Revenues, $6,400,000; Expenses $905,000
E 27-3 Credit other revenues
E 27-4 3. Credit fund balance $900,000
　　　　5. $500,000 in the PR column of Statement of Changes
　　　　　in Fund Balance

P 27-1 Total revenues, $33,300,000; Excess of expenses over
　　　　revenues and nonoperating income $(4,180,000)
P 27-2 2. Net increase in unrestricted Current Funds,
　　　　　$117,000
P 27-3 1. Transaction 5: Capital Projects Fund, credit other
　　　　　financing sources—bond proceeds, $5,000,000
P 27-4 3. Credit unrestricted fund balance $350,000
　　　　4. Credit net investment in plant $400,000
　　　　5. Credit unrestricted fund balance $500,000

CHAPTER 28

E 28-1 Divide equally
E 28-2 Monte, $89,000
E 28-3 1b. Bunn, $(2,800)
　　　　1c. Bunn, $(14,000)